Evidence

Cases and Materials

Fourth edition

J D Heydon MA, BCL
of Gray's Inn and the New South Wales Bar,
one of Her Majesty's Counsel

Mark Ockelton MA, BD
of Lincoln's Inn, Barrister,
Fellow (formerly Senior Lecturer) in the
Faculty of Law, University of Leeds,
an Adjudicator of Immigration Appeals

Butterworths
London, Charlottesville, Dublin, Durban, Edinburgh,
Kuala Lumpur, Singapore, Sydney, Toronto, Wellington
1996

CROYDON COLLEGE
LIBRARY

COPY 0290 7956

CLASS
347.06 HEY

United Kingdom	Butterworths, a Division of Reed Elsevier (UK) Ltd, Halsbury House, 35 Chancery Lane, LONDON WC2A 1EL and 4 Hill Street, EDINBURGH EH2 3JZ
Australia	Butterworths, SYDNEY, MELBOURNE, BRISBANE, ADELAIDE, PERTH, CANBERRA and HOBART
Canada	Butterworths Canada Ltd, TORONTO and VANCOUVER
Ireland	Butterworth (Ireland) Ltd, DUBLIN
Malaysia	Malayan Law Journal Sdn Bhd, KUALA LUMPUR
New Zealand	Butterworths of New Zealand Ltd, WELLINGTON and AUCKLAND
Singapore	Reed Elsevier (Singapore) Pte Ltd, SINGAPORE
South Africa	Butterworths Publishers (Pty) Ltd, DURBAN
USA	Michie, CHARLOTTESVILLE, Virginia

All rights reserved. No part of this publication may be reproduced in any material form (including photocopying or storing it in any medium by electronic means and whether or not transiently or incidentally to some other use of this publication) without the written permission of the copyright owner except in accordance with the provisions of the Copyright, Designs and Patents Act 1988 or under the terms of a licence issued by the Copyright Licensing Agency Ltd, 90 Tottenham Court Road, London, England W1P 9HE. Applications for the copyright owner's written permission to reproduce any part of this publication should be addressed to the publisher.

Warning: The doing of an unauthorised act in relation to a copyright work may result in both a civil claim for damages and criminal prosecution.

Any Crown copyright material is reproduced with the permission of the Controller of Her Majesty's Stationery Office.

© Reed Elsevier (UK) Ltd 1996

A CIP Catalogue record for this book is available from the British Library.

ISBN   0 406 08180 8

Set in Plantin by B & J Whitcombe, Nr Diss, Norfolk, IP22 2LP
Printed and bound in Great Britain by Redwood Books, Trowbridge, Wiltshire

Preface

This collection of cases and materials is intended to be suitable for use in all university courses on the law of evidence and in preparing for professional examinations. English cases and statutes form the basis for the book but American, Australian and Scots cases have been used where relevant. Other Commonwealth materials are occasionally mentioned, and leading American writers have often been relied on. In addition to the usual apparatus of questions, notes and suggestions for further reading, there is a very full commentary on the materials. For this reason, it is hoped that the book will serve as an independent guide to the subject, in any jurisdiction substantially based on English law, though it can equally be used as a supplement to a textbook.

Five years have passed since the manuscript of the last edition was prepared. The principal statutory changes in that time are to be found in the Criminal Justice and Public Order Act 1994. But the activities of the courts have called for a degree of revision, particularly in relation to similar fact evidence (*DPP v P* and *R v H*) and hearsay (*R v Kearley*).

The first-named author wishes to express his gratitude to the second-named author for his very considerable efforts in the preparation of this edition and particularly in taking on additional responsibility reflected on the title page.

The staff of Butterworths have been patient and very helpful. We owe thanks to Mrs S Flynn for her exemplary typing of the manuscript.

July 1996

J D H
M O

Acknowledgments

The publishers and authors make acknowledgment to the following for permission to quote copyright material:

The American Law Institute: E M Morgan, Introduction to the American Law Institute's *Model Code of Evidence*, 1942, pp 3–4 and 27.

Butterworths: *All England Law Reports*.

Butterworths of Australia: *The Australian Law Reports*.

Butterworth & Co (SA) Ltd: L H Hoffmann, *The South African Law of Evidence*, 2nd edn, 1970, pp 34, 38–9, 348, 353, 421 and 437–41.

Cambridge University Press: *The Pollock-Holmes Letters*, vol II, 1942, pp 284–5.

Canada Law Book Co Inc, 240 Edward St, Aurora, Ontario, L4G 3S9: *Dominion Law Reports*.

Carswell Co Ltd: Kaufman, *The Admissibility of Confessions*, 2nd edn, 1974, pp 16–17.

Collins & Sons & Co Ltd: S Bedford, *The Best We Can Do*, 1958, p 249.

Council of Law Reporting in Victoria: *Victorian Law Reports*; *Victorian Reports*.

David Higham Associates Ltd: C H Rolph, *Personal Identity*, Michael Joseph, 1957, pp 120–2.

Faculty of Advocates: *Session Cases and Justiciary Cases*.

W Green & Son Ltd: *Scots Law Times*.

Harvard Law Review Association: Sutherland, 79 Harv LR 21 (1965).

Her Majesty's Stationery Office: *11th Report of the Criminal Law Revision Committee*, Cmnd 4991, 1972; and Devlin Committee Report.

Incorporated Council of Law Reporting for England and Wales: *Law Reports* and *Weekly Law Reports*.

Incorporated Council of Law Reporting for Ireland: *Irish Reports*.

Incorporated Council of Law Reporting for Northern Ireland: *Northern Ireland Reports*.

John Wiley & Sons Inc: J H Skolnick, *Justice Without Trial*, 1966, p 217.

Law Book Co Ltd: *Australian Law Journal*; *Australian Law Journal Reports*; *Commonwealth Law Reports*; *NSW State Reports*; *South Australian State Reports*.

Little, Brown & Co: Maguire, *Evidence of Guilt*, 1959, para 3.062 n9; Wigmore, *A Treatise on Evidence*, 3rd edn, 1940, paras 822–3, 851, 857–8, 866–7, 924a, 1745, 1767, 2033, 2059, 2061, 2251.

Macmillan (London and Basingstoke): H R Trevor-Roper, *The European Witch Craze of the 17th and 18th Centuries*, Penguin edn, 1969, p 44.

J C Smith: *Criminal Evidence*, 1995, p 43.

Sweet & Maxwell Ltd: *Criminal Appeal Reports*; *Law Quarterly Review*; Cecil, *The English Judge*; Cross [1973] Crim LR at 332; Salmond, *Torts*, 16th edn, 1973, p 241; Williams [1973] Crim LR at 76–7.

Sweet & Maxwell Ltd and the author: Williams, *The Proof of Guilt*, 3rd edn, 1963, pp 88, 109–10, 113, 120–2.

West Publishing Co: *Atlantic Reporter*; *Federal Reporter*; W T Fryer (ed), *Selected Writings on the Law of Evidence and Trial*, 1957, p 846; McCormick, *Evidence*, 1st edn, 1954, para 109; *Federal Rules of Evidence*, Rules 801–806.

Williams & Wilkins & Co and Fred E Inbau: Inbau & Reid, *Criminal Interrogation and Confessions*, 2nd edn, 1967, contents page.

Yale Law Journal and Fred B Rothman & Co: Morgan, 31 Yale LJ 229.

Acknowledgment is also made of permission from the following to use material written by the authors:

Stevens & Sons Ltd and the Editors of the *Law Quarterly Review* and *Modern Law Review*: 87 LQR 214 (1971); 89 LQR 552 (1973); 37 MLR 601 (1974).

Sweet & Maxwell Ltd and the Editor of the *Criminal Law Review*: [1973] Crim LR 264 and 603; [1980] Crim LR 129.

Contents

Preface   v
Acknowledgments   vii
Abbreviations   xiii
Table of Statutes   xv
List of Cases   xxi

PART ONE   INTRODUCTION   1

Chapter 1   Introduction   3
1   The nature of the subject   3
2   Terminology   5
3   The function of judge and jury   8
4   Evidentiary ghosts   9
5   Special forms of evidence   9
6   Evidence not objected to   11
7   Arrangement   11

PART TWO   THE PROCESS OF PROOF   13

Chapter 2   The Burden of Proof   15
1   Introduction   15
2   How can the incidence of the two burdens of proof be determined?   16
3   The burden of proof of insanity   33
4   Shifting the burden   34

Chapter 3   Standard of Proof   37
1   Formulation of the standards   37
2   Justification   42
3   Past events and future events   43
4   How many standards?   50
5   Which standard?   52
6   Discharge of the evidential burden   56

Chapter 4   Presumptions   58
1   Introduction   58
2   The reasons for presumptions   60
3   Particular presumptions   62
4   Conflicting presumptions   76

Chapter 5   Corroboration or Support   79
1   Introduction   79
2   Identification evidence   83
3   Mandatory corroboration requirements   99
4   A warning from the judge   101
5   What is corroboration?   104

PART THREE   THE PROTECTION OF THE ACCUSED   115

Chapter 6   The Privilege against Self-incrimination   117
1   Introduction   117
2   The role of the judge   118
3   The importance of the privilege   124
4   Statutory restrictions on the privilege   129

Chapter 7   The Right to Silence   136
1   General   136
2   Inferences from out of court silence   145
3   Inferences from silence in court   150

Chapter 8   Confessions   153
1   The exclusionary rule   153
2   Evidence derived from inadmissible confessions   175
3   The conduct of investigations   180
4   American law   197
5   Other jurisdictions   206

Chapter 9   Unfair and Improperly Obtained Evidence   208
1   Unfairness to the accused: common law discretion   208
2   Unfairness of the proceedings: statutory discretion   212
3   Improperly obtained evidence in general   219

Chapter 10   The Accused's Character: Part I   253
1   Similar fact evidence   253
2   Other aspects of the accused's character   275

Chapter 11   The Accused's Character: Part II   277
1   When the section 1(*f*) prohibition applies: the relationship between
    section 1(*e*) and (*f*)   278
2   When the prohibition is lifted: the exceptions to section 1(*f*)   290
3   The consequences of lifting the prohibition   301

PART FOUR   HEARSAY   313

Chapter 12   Hearsay: the Exclusionary Rule   315
1   Rationale   315
2   The limits of the rule   317

Chapter 13   Hearsay Exceptions: Criminal Cases   339
1   Statements of deceased persons   339
2   Statements in public documents   342
3   Statutory exceptions   343
4   The value of hearsay evidence   350
5   Res gestae   350
6   Witnesses in previous cases   359
7   Further reform?   359

Chapter 14   Hearsay Exceptions: Civil Cases   361
1   Introduction   361
2   Hearsay in civil cases generally   361
3   Children   367
4   Other jurisdictions   369
5   The value of hearsay evidence   373

Chapter 15   Documentary Evidence   375
1   Proof of the contents of a document   375
2   Proof of execution of private documents   379
3   The parol evidence rule   383

Chapter 16   Opinion Evidence and Prior Proceedings   384
1   Opinion evidence   384
2   Evidence of prior findings in later proceedings   394

PART FIVE   WITNESSES   403

Chapter 17   Competence, Compellability and Oaths   405
1   Competence and compellability   405
2   Oath and affirmation   411

Chapter 18   Private Privilege   416
1   Legal professional privilege   416
2   Without prejudice statements   437
3   Miscellaneous   438

Chapter 19   Public Policy   440
1   State interest   440
2   Previous litigation   467

PART SIX   THE COURSE OF THE TRIAL   469

Chapter 20   The Course of the Trial   471
1   Civil cases   471
2   Criminal cases   488

PART SEVEN   MATTERS WHICH NEED NOT BE PROVED
                          BY EVIDENCE   497

Chapter 21   Judicial Notice   499
1   Introduction   499
2   Judicial notice at common law   502
3   Judicial notice: statutes   505
4   General   505

Index   509

Abbreviations

Baker – R W Baker, *The Hearsay Rule* (London, 1950).

Bentham – J Bentham, *A Rationale of Judicial Evidence* (*Works*, ed Bowring), Vols VI and VII.

Best – W M Best, *Principles of the Law of Evidence* (London, 1911, 11th edn).

Campbell and Waller – Enid Campbell and Louis Waller (eds), *Well and Truly Tried* (Sydney, 1982).

Carter – P B Carter, *Cases and Statutes on Evidence* (London, 1990, 2nd edn).

Cowan and Carter – Z Cowan and P B Carter, *Essays in the Law of Evidence* (Oxford, 1956).

CLRC – 11th Report of the Criminal Law Revision Committee, Evidence (General), Cmnd 4991.

Cross – Colin Tapper, *Cross & Tapper on Evidence* (London, 1995, 8th edn).

Devlin Committee – Report by Lord Devlin's Committee to the Secretary of State for the Home Department, April 1976.

Eggleston – Sir Richard Eggleston, *Evidence, Proof and Probability* (London, 1983, 2nd edn).

Glass – H H Glass (ed), *Seminars on Evidence* (Sydney, 1970).

Hoffmann – L H Hoffmann, *The South African Law of Evidence* (Durban, 1970, 2nd edn).

McCormick – C T McCormick, *Handbook of the Law of Evidence* (St Paul, Minn, 1954).

McCormick, 2nd edn – C T McCormick, *Handbook of the Law of Evidence* (St Paul, Minn, 1972, 2nd edn).

Maguire – Maguire, *Evidence: Common Sense and Common Law* (Chicago, 1947).

Nokes – G D Nokes, *An Introduction to the Law of Evidence* (London, 1967, 4th edn).

Phipson – S L Phipson, *Evidence* (London, 1990, 14th edn).

Tapper – C F Tapper (ed), *Crime, Proof and Punishment* (London, 1981).

Taylor – Pitt Taylor, *Treatise on the Law of Evidence* (London, 1931, 12th edn).

Thayer – J B Thayer, *Preliminary Treatise on Evidence at the Common Law* (Boston, 1898).

Wigmore – J H Wigmore, *Treatise on the Anglo-American System of Evidence in Trials at Common Law* (Boston, 1940, 3rd edn).

Williams – Glanville Williams, *The Proof of Guilt* (London, 1963, 3rd edn).

Zuckerman – A A S Zuckerman, *The Principles of Criminal Evidence* (Oxford, 1989).

Table of Statutes

References to *Statutes* are to Halsbury's Statutes of England (Fourth Edition) showing the volume and page at which the annotated text of the Act may be found. References in **bold** type indicate where the section of an Act is set out in part or in full.

	PAGE
Administration of Justice Act 1920 (22 *Statutes* 441)	
s 15	386
Administration of Justice Act 1985 (31 *Statutes* 931)	
s 33	438
Asylum and Immigration Appeals Act 1993 (31 *Statutes* 215)	
s 3(5)	186
Bankruptcy Law Consolidation Act 1849:	130
Bankers' Books Evidence Act 1879 (17 *Statutes* 115)	366
s 117	130
Bills of Exchange Act 1882 (5 *Statutes* 342):	157
Canada Act 1982	
Sch B	
Pt I (Charter of Rights and Freedoms):	178, 230
s 11(d)	229
24(2)	**228**, 229, 230
Cestui que Vie Act 1666 (37 *Statutes* 26):	65
Child Support Act 1991 (6 *Statutes* 638):	368
Children Act 1975	464
Children Act 1989 (6 *Statutes* 387):	48, 409, 427
s 1	48
7(1)	367, **368**
(2)–(5)	**368**
8(3)	51
31	43
(2)	**43**, 44, 45, 46, 47, 48
(a)	44, 45, 46, 47
(b)	44
(9)	43
38	46
Pt V (ss 43–52)	46
s 96	369
(1)	**409**, 411
(2)(a), (b)	363, **409**
(3)–(5)	361, **368**
(6), (7)	361
105	51
(1)	410

	PAGE
Children and Young Persons Act 1933 (6 *Statutes* 18)	
s 38(1)	408, **409**, 410
50	59
Children and Young Persons Act 1969 (6 *Statutes* 136)	457, 461
s 1	464
(1)	456
Civil Evidence Act 1968 (17 *Statutes* 168)	339, 346, 347, 365, 366, 367, 368, 374, 396, 416, 439, 465
Pt I (ss 1–10)	361, 475
s 1(1), (2)	**394**
(3), (4)	**395**
2	373, 374, 398
(1)	374
6(3)	**373**
(a)	374
9(1)	363
(2)(a)–(d)	363
(3)	364
(4)	364
(b)	341
(c)	340
11(1)	396, 399
(2)(a)	398, 399
(4)	395
12(1)–(5)	**395**
13	395
(1)–(3)	**400**
14(1)(a), (b)	117
16(1)(a)	117
(b)	438
(2)–(5)	438
Civil Evidence Act 1972 (17 *Statutes* 199)	393
s 4	386
Civil Evidence Act 1995	315, 339, 346, 361, 365, 369, 476
s 1	**366**, 367, **477**
(1)	**362**

PAGE

Civil Evidence Act 1995 – *contd*
s 1(2) **362**
   (a).................... 365, 367
   (3) **362**, 366
   (4) **362**
2 367
   (1)–(3) **362**
   (4) **362**, 365
3 .... **362**, 367
4 367
   (1) **362**
   (2) **362, 363**, 365
5 .... 366, 367
   (1), (2) **363**
6 .... 366, 367
   (1) **363**
   (2) **363**
     (b) 477
   (3) **363**, 479
   (4) **363**, 475
   (5) **363**
7 366
   (1) **363**
   (2) **363, 364**
   (3), (4) **364**
8 .... 366, 367, 379
   (1), (2) **364**
9 .... 335, 366, 367
   (1)–(5) **364**
11 .... **364**
13 .... **365**, 367
14 366
   (1)–(3) **365**
Civil Evidence (Scotland) Act 1988
s 7 335
Combinations of Workmen (1825) ... 130
s 6 130
Common Law Procedure Act 1854 (5
  Statutes 340)
s 27 381
Companies Act 1985 (8 *Statutes* 104): 133
s 434 197
Contempt of Court Act 1981 (11 *Statutes*
  185)
s 10 438
Copyright Act 1956 (11 *Statutes* 261)
s 9(8) 393
Copyright, Designs and Patents Act 1988
  (33 *Statutes* 273)
s 280, 284 438
Corrupt Practices (1858) 222, 223
County Courts Act 1984 (11 *Statutes* 603)
s 68 386
Courts and Legal Services Act 1990 (11
  Statutes 720)
s 119(1) 140
Criminal Appeal Act 1907 91

PAGE

Criminal Appeal Act 1968 (12 *Statutes*
  388)
s 2 8
Sch 2
  para 1A 343
Criminal Appeal Act 1995 8
Criminal Evidence Act 1898 (17 *Stat-*
  utes 130) 124, 137, 238, 284, 285,
          286, 293, 296, 297, 407
s 1 .... 287, **406**
   (a) **407**
   (b) **407**, 408
   (e) **124**, 127, 137, 164, **277**, 278,
       279, 282, 283, 287, 288,
           289, 290, 291
   (f) 123, 237, **277**, 278, 279, 280,
     281, 282, 283, 284, 285, 286,
     287, 288, 289, 290, 298,
     302, 304, 305, 306, 311
    (i) 278, 280, 281, 287, 290,
         291, 301, 302, 304
    (ii) 276, 280, 286, 290, 291,
       292, 293, 294, 297, 298,
      299, 301, 303, 304, 306,
       308, 309, 310, 311
    (iii) 280, 299, 300, 301, 303,
       308, 309, 310, 311, 407
Criminal Evidence Act 1965 ...... 320, 346
Criminal Justice Act 1925 (27 *Statutes*
  27) 348
s 13 .... 347, 349
Criminal Justice Act 1967 (12 *Statutes*
  358)
s 8 75
9 349
10 6
11 .... 76, 167, 496
Criminal Justice Act 1987 (12 *Statutes*
  1100) 197
s 4 .... 137, 139
6 .... 137, 139, 344
Criminal Justice Act 1988 (17 *Statutes*
  242)
Pt II (ss 23–28) 320, 345, 346
s 23 .... 347, 348, 349, 379
   (1) **343**
   (2) **343**, 346
   (3) **343**
    (b) 346
   (4) **343**
24 .... 346, 347, 348, 349, 379
   (1) **343**
    (ii) 347
   (3) **343**
   (4) **344**
25 347
   (1), (2) **344**

PAGE

Criminal Justice Act 1988 – *contd*
s 26 . . . . **344**, 347, 348
 (iii) 347
 27 . . . . **344**, **345**, 346, 366, 379
 28(1), (2) **345**
 30 . . . . 348, 393
 (1)–(5) **345**
 31 . . . . **345**, 348
 32(1), (2) 410
 32A 349, 411
 (3)(a) 411
 (c) 349
 33A 409
 (2A) **409**
 34(1) 409
 Schedule **345**, **346**
 Sch 13
 para 6 344
Criminal Justice Act 1991 (17 *Statutes* 268)
 s 52 . . . . 408, 412
 53 . . . . 138, 139
 54 . . . . 349, 411
 Sch 6
 para 5 . . . . 137, 139
Criminal Justice and Public Order Act
 1994 (32 *Statutes* 654)
 Pt III (ss 31–53) 191
 s 31 303
 32 80
 34 . . . . 111, 136, 140, 142, 166
 (1) **137**
 (2) **137**, **138**, 140
 (b) 140
 (3)–(5) **138**
 35 . . . . . . 136, 140, 141, 142, 152, 166
 (1) **138**, 140
 (2) **138**
 (3) 111, **138**, 140, 407
 (4) **138**, 140
 (5), (6) **138**
 36 . . . . . . 111, 136, 140, 142, 166, 191
 (1) **138**, **139**
 (2) **139**, 140
 (b) 140
 (3) **139**
 (4) **139**, 142
 (5), (6) **139**
 37 . . . 111, 136, 140, 142, 143, 166, 191
 (1) **139**
 (2) **139**, 140
 (3) **139**
 (4) **139**, 142
 (5) **139**
 38 136
 (1), (2) **140**
 (3) **140**, 141
 (4) 100, **140**
 (5) **140**
 (6) **140**, 142

PAGE

Criminal Justice and Public Order Act
 1994 – *contd*
 s 137(2) 186
 Sch 9
 para 33 409
Criminal Justice (Scotland) Act 1980
 (12 *Statutes* 745)
 s 2 206
Criminal Law Act 1967 (12 *Statutes* 328): 236
Criminal Law Act 1977 (12 *Statutes* 693)
 s 54 408
Criminal Procedure Act 1865 (17 *Stat-*
 utes 107)
 s 3 . . . . 363, **478**
 4, 5 . . . . 363, 478, **479**
 6 . . . . 304, 481
 8 . . . . 165, 381
Documentary Evidence Act 1868 (17
 Statutes 111)
 s 2 13
Documentary Evidence Act 1882 (17
 Statutes 120)
 s 2 365
European Communities Act 1972 (17
 Statutes 34) 118
Evidence Act 1845 (17 *Statutes* 92)
 s 2 505
Evidence Act 1938 (17 *Statutes* 140): 339
 s 3 382
 4 380
 30 381
Evidence (Colonial Statutes) Act 1907
 (17 *Statutes* 134)
 s 1 365
Evidence (Foreign, Dominion and Colonial Documents) Act 1933 (17
 Statutes 138)
 s 1 365
Factories Act 1961 (19 *Statutes* 646)
 s 29(1) **30**, **31**
Family Law Reform Act 1969 (17 *Stat-*
 utes 191)
 s 26 67
Finance Act 1946
 s 20(3) 132
Fugitive Offenders Act 1967
 s 4(1)(c) **49**, **50**
High Treason (1534)
 s 8 170
Homicide Act 1957 (12 *Statutes* 277)
 s 2(2) 18
Immigration Act 1971 (31 *Statutes* 52): 186
Imprisonment (Temporary Provisions)
 Act 1980 (34 *Statutes* 718) 186
Indecency with Children Act 1960 (12
 Statutes 297) 408
Indian Evidence Act 1872 . . . . 176, 206
 s 27 . . . . **179**
Insolvency Act 1986 (4 *Statutes* 717): 133

PAGE

Interpretation Act 1978 (41 *Statutes* 985)
  s 3   505
Intestates' Estates Act 1952 (17 *Statutes*
  359)
  s 1(4)   62
  Sch 1   62
Law of Property Act 1925 (37 *Statutes*
  72)
  s 184 . . . . 61, **62**, 66
Magistrates' Courts Act 1952
  s 81 . . . .   **19**
Magistrates' Courts Act 1980 (27 *Stat-
  utes* 143)
  s 43(4)   212
  101 . . . . 19, 30, 31
  144   345
Matrimonial Causes Act 1973 (27 *Stat-
  utes* 734)
  s 19   66
  48(1)   68
Mental Health Act 1959 (28 *Statutes*
  831)   101
Mental Health Act 1983 (28 *Statutes*
  846) 101, 186
  s 135, 136 . . . . 186, 188
Misuse of Drugs Act 1971 (28 *Statutes*
  687) 29, 32
  s 5(1), (4)   28
  7   28
Oaths Act 1838   414
Oaths Act 1961   414
Oaths Act 1978 (17 *Statutes* 213)
  s 4(2)   411
  5 . . . . 411, 413
Oaths and Evidence (Overseas Authorities
  and Countries) Act 1963 (17 *Statutes*
  163)
  s 5   365
Offences against the Person Act 1861 (12
  Statutes 87)   65
Perjury Act 1911 (12 *Statutes* 160)
  s 13   100
Police and Criminal Evidence Act 1984
  (12 *Statutes* 845) 79, 103, **157**, 159,
                                163, 175, 216,
                                217, 219, 439
  Pt II (ss 8–23)   428
  s 8–14   439
  10(2)   428
  Pt III (ss 24–33)   216
  Pt IV (ss 34–52)   216
  s 41   195
  Pt V (ss 53–65)   216
  s 56   212
  58 . . . . 103, 195, 212, 213
  60   196
  61   112
  62(10)   112
  63   112

PAGE

Police and Criminal Evidence Act 1984
  – *contd*
  Pt VI (ss 66–67)   213
  s 66 . . . . 97, 150, 154, 181, **184**
  67(1)–(8) **184**
  (9) **184**, 197
  (10) **184**
  (11) 180, **184**, 197
  68 . . . . 346, 366
  69 . . . . 343, 349, 360, 379
  (1) **348**
  (2)   348
  74(1)–(3) **399**, 400
  76 . . . . . . 104, 153, 154, 155, 156, 158,
              159, 160, 162, 164, 165, 166,
              182, 196, 215, 218, 243, 343
  (1) 153, **154**, 164, 166, 168
  (2) 122, **154**, 155, 160,
                        164, 165, 168, 178
  (a) 155, 156, 157, 158,
                        161, 162, 164
  (b) 157, 158, 159, 160,
                        161, 162, 164
  (3) **154**, 160, 165
  (4) 154, **178**, 180
  (5) 154, **178**, 180
  (6) 154, **178**, 180
  (7), (8) **154**
  77 . . . . 104, 174
  (1) **103**
  (2), (3) **104**
  78 . . . . 98, 142, 154, 155, 158, 160,
              163, 180, 208, 212, 213,
              214, 218, 219, 240,
              242, 243, 400
  (1) 7, **212**, 240, 243
  (2) **212**, 240
  79   489
  80(1) **407**
  (2)–(8) **408**
  (9) 416, 438
  81   393
  82   346
  (1) 153, **155**, 165, 166
  (3) 155, 208, **212**
  Sch 1
  para 5   439
  Sch 3
  para 8, 9   348
Police and Magistrates' Courts Act 1994
  s 37(9)   184
Prevention of Corruption Act 1916 (12
  Statutes 182)
  s 2   19
Prevention of Cruelty to, and protection
  of, Children Act 1889   464
Prevention of Terrorism (Temporary Provisions) Act 1989 (12 *Statutes* 1317)
  s 14   186

PAGE

Prevention of Terrorism (Temporary Provisions) Act 1989 – *contd*
Sch 5
para 6 186
Protection of Children Act 1978 (12 *Statutes* 732) 408
Purchase Tax Act 1963
s 24(6) 131, **132**, 134, 456
Rehabilitation of Offenders Act 1974 (12 *Statutes* 631) 275
s 4(1) 481
7(2) 481
Road Traffic Act 1988 (38 *Statutes* 823)
s 7 191
Road Traffic Offenders Act 1988 (38 *Statutes* 1056)
s 1, 2 197
Road Traffic Regulation Act 1984 (38 *Statutes* 507)
s 89(2) 100
Salmon Fisheries (Scotland) Act 1868: 221, 227
Sexual Offences Act 1956 (12 *Statutes* 239) 408
Sexual Offences Act 1967 (12 *Statutes* 351) 408
Sexual Offences (Amendment) Act 1976 (12 *Statutes* 685)
s 2 . . . . 294, 494
Summary Jurisdiction Act 1848 137
s 14 30
Summary Jurisdiction Act 1879
s 39(2) 30
Supreme Court Act 1981 (11 *Statutes* 966)
s 69(5) 386
72(1), (3) 122
Theft Act 1968 (12 *Statutes* 501)
s 25(3) 20
27(3) 275

Australia

New South Wales

Crimes Act 1900–74
s 413A, 413B 299
Evidence Act 1995
s 69(4) 335
Lie Detectors Act 1983 504

Victoria

Evidence Act 1928
s 141 211
Marriage Act 1928
s 80, 86 . . . . **54**

PAGE

Poisons Act 1962
Sch 4 . . . . 387, 388

Western Australia

Road Traffic Act 1974
s 66(1) 234
(2)(c) 234

Belize

Constitution 33
Criminal Code 33

Canada

Charter of Rights and Freedoms and Constitution Act 1982. *See* Canada Act 1982

Eire

Constitution 225
art 40(5) **226**

Jamaica

Constitution 227

Nigeria

Evidence Act 1958
s 29 . . . . **179**

USA

Constitution 125, 223, 245, 246, 248, 449
1st Amendment 128, 244
2nd, 3rd Amendment 244
4th Amendment **243**, 244, 245, 246, 248
5th Amendment 124, 128, 170, 198, 199, 244, 245, 246
6th Amendment 95, 198, 244
7th, 8th Amendment 244
14th Amendment 243, 244
18th Amendment 248
Bill of Rights 198, 228, 449
Federal Communications Act 1934
s 605 . . . . **244**, 245
National Prohibition Act 245
Omnibus Crime Control and Safe Streets Act 1968
s 701 205

List of Cases

Page references printed in **bold** type indicate where a case is set out.

PAGE

A

Abrath v North Eastern Rly Co (1883),
HL **20**
Adam v Fisher (1914), CA 461
Adami v R (1959), HC of A **380**
Adams v Lloyd (1858) 118, 120
Adams v New York (1904) 243
Adelaide Chemical and Fertilizer Co
Ltd v Carlyle (1940) 351, 354
Advocate (HM) v Hepper (1958) **223**
Advocate (HM) v M'Guigan (1936) .. 220
Advocate (HM) v McKay (1961) **224**
Advocate (HM) v Turnbull (1951): **221**, 223
Advocate's (Lord) Reference (No 1 of
1983) (1984) 206
Aher Raja Khima v Saurashtra (1956): 179
Air Canada v Secretary of State for
Trade (No 2) (1983), HL 451
Ajodha v The State (1981), PC 163
Albert, Re (1967) 66
Alderman v United States (1969) 244
Aldersey, Re, Gibson v Hall (1905) .. 66
Alderson v Clay (1816) 378
Alexander v R (1981) **92**, 337
Alexander v Rayson (1936), CA 471
Allied Pastoral Holdings Pty Ltd v
Comr of Taxation (1983) 473
Anchor Products Ltd v Hedges (1966): 69, 70
Anderson v Bank of British Columbia
(1876), CA 417, 422, 423
Anglo Czechoslovak and Prague Credit
Bank v Janssen (1943) 503
Annesley v Earl of Anglesea (1743): 417, 421
Argyll (Duchess of) v Duke of Argyll
(1967) 432
Arthur v Bezuidenhout and Mieny
(1962) 70
Ashburton (Lord) v Pape (1913),
CA **429**, 432
Asiatic Petroleum Co Ltd v Anglo
Persian Oil Co Ltd (1916), CA ... 440
A-G v Clough (1963) 461, 463
A-G v Cunard SS Co (1887) 121

PAGE

A-G v Foster (1963), CA 461, 463, 464
A-G v Good (1825) 318
A-G v Hitchcock (1847) 480
A-G v Mulholland (1963), CA ... 438, 461,
463, 464
A-G (NT) v Kearney (1985) 428
A-G (Rudely) v Kenny (1960) 385
A-G for Victoria v Riach (1978) 133
A-G for New South Wales v Martin
(1909) 168
A-G for The Northern Territory v
Maurice (1986)................427, 429
A-G's Reference (No 3 of 1979)
(1979), CA 475
Attwood v R (1960) 289
Auckland City Council v Brailey (1988): 92
Augustien v Challis (1847) **375**, 378
Australasian Meat Industry Employees
Union v Mudginberry Station Pty
Ltd (1986) 41
Australian Communist Party v
Commonwealth (1950) 504
Australian National Airlines
Commission v Commonwealth
of Australia (1975) 378, 451
Australian Oil Refining Pty Ltd v
Bourne (1980) 390
Aveson v Lord Kinnaird (1805) 359
Axon v Axon (1937) **64**, 68, 77
Aylesford Peerage (1885), HL 357

B

B v R (1992) 257
Backhouse v Jones (1839) 324
Bailey & Co Ltd v Clark, Son and
Morland (1938), HL 319
Baker v Campbell (1983): 427, 428, 429, 436
Balabel v Air-India (1988), CA 416
Balfour v Foreign and Commonwealth
Office (1994), CA 451
Ballard v North British Rly Co
(1923) 70
Bank of England v Riley (1992), CA: 133

PAGE

Bank of England v Vagliano Bros
(1891), HL 157
Bank of Nova Scotia v Hellenic Mutual
War Risks Association (Bermuda)
Ltd, The Good Luck (1992) 428
Bankers Trust Co v Shapira (1980), CA: 466
Barclays Bank plc v Eustice (1995), CA: 428
Barclays Bank plc v Taylor (1989), CA: 439
Barka v R (1974) 41
Barkway v South Wales Transport Co
Ltd (1949), CA; revsd (1950), HL: 69
Barnard v Sully (1931), DC 76
Basto v R (1954) 174
Bate, Re, Chillingworth v Bate (1947): 62
Bater v Bater (1951), CA 50, 54
Beese v Governor of Ashford Remand
Centre (1973), HL 197
Benjamin v The State (1915) 377
Benney v Dowling (1959) 168
Berger v Raymond & Son Ltd (1984): 254
Berkeley Peerage Case (1811), HL: 316, 317
Berry v Berry and Carpenter (1898): 494
Bessela v Stern (1877), CA 111, 148
Bevan Investments Ltd v Blackhall and
Struthers (No 2) (1978), CA 319
Bhimji v Chatwani (No 3) (1992) 118
Birmingham and Midland Motor Omni-
bus Co Ltd v London and North
Western Rly Co (1913), CA ... 422, 423
Bishopsgate Investment Management
Ltd (in provisional liquidation) v
Maxwell (1992), CA 133
Blackpool Corpn v Locker (1948), CA: 465
Blake v Albion Life Assurance Society
(1878) 274
Blake v DPP (1992) 466
Blatch v Archer (1774) 18, 152
Blunt v Park Lane Hotel Ltd (1942),
CA 117
Blyth v Blyth and Pugh (1966), HL: 68
Borowski v Quayle (1966) 387
Borthwick v Vickers (1973), DC 502
Bowen v Norman (1938) 67
Boyce v Chapman (1835) 53
Boyd v United States (1886) 246
Boyle v Wiseman (1855) 10 Exch
360 .... 123, 151
Boyle v Wiseman (1855) 11 Exch 647: 376
Bradford City Metropolitan Council v
K (1990) 365, 369
Brady (Inspector of Taxes) v Group
Lotus Car Companies plc (1987);
affd (1987), CA 34, 35, 36
Bram v US (1897) 170
Bramblevale Ltd, Re (1970), CA 41
Brandao v Barnett (1846), HL 504
Brannan v Peek (1948), DC 237, 240
Bratty v A-G for Northern Ireland
(1963), HL............. 17, 18, 22, 57

PAGE

Brebner v Perry (1961) **121**
Breen v R (1976) 494
Brewer v Williams (1977) 200
Brewster v Sewell (1820) 376
Briamore Manufacturing Ltd (in
liquidation), Re (1986) 436
Bridges v North London Rly Co
(1874), HL 56
Briginshaw v Briginshaw (1938):   39, 51, **54**
Brinegar v US (1949) **246**
Bristol Tramways etc Carriage Co Ltd
v Fiat Motors Ltd (1910), CA 157
British Coal Corpn v Dennis Rye Ltd
(No 2) (1988), CA 427
British Steel Corpn v Granada Television
Ltd (1981); on appeal (1981), CA;
affd (1981), HL 118, 119, 135, 438
Broad v Pitt (1828) 439
Broadhurst v R (1964), PC 8
Bromley v R (1986) 103
Brotherton v People (1878) 61
Brown v Brown (1947) 67
Brown v Mississippi (1926) 198
Brown v R (1913) 39, 351, 354, 356
Brown v Walker (1896) 124
Browne v Dunn (1893), HL 473
Browning v J W H Watson (Rochester)
Ltd (1953), DC 237, 239, 240
Brush, Re (1962) 62
Bryant v Foot (1868), Ex Ch 503
Bryce v Bryce (1933) 357, 358
Buccleuch (Duke) v Metropolitan
Board of Works (1872), HL 467
Buchanan v Moore [1963] NI 194, CA: 27
Bulk Materials (Coal Handling) Services
Pty Ltd v Coal and Allied
Operations Ltd (1988) 428
Bullard v R (1957), PC 17, 40
Bullivant v A-G for Victoria (1901),
HL...................... 419, 421
Bumper Development Corpn Ltd v
Metropolitan Police Comr (Union
of India, claimants) (1991), CA ... 387
Bunning v Cross (1978) 97, 212, **231**
Burdeau v McDowell (1921) 244
Burmah Oil Co Ltd v Bank of England
(1980), HL **446**
Burnes v R (1975) 164
Burns v Lipman (1974) 499
Butera v DPP (1987), (Aust HC) 9
Butler v Board of Trade (1971): **419, 430,** 433
Buttes Gas and Oil Co v Hammer
(No 3) (1981), CA; revsd
(1982), HL............ 427, 428, 450

C

Calcraft v Guest (1898), CA: 223, 425, **429,**
430, 431
Calderbank v Calderbank (1976), CA: 438

PAGE

Calley v Richards (1854) 426
Callis v Gunn (1964), DC . . . 227, 236, 242
Campbell v Tameside Metropolitan
   Borough Council (1982), CA: 456, 466
Carter v Cavenaugh (1848) 484
Carter v Northmore Hal Davey & Leake
   (managing partner) (1995) 426
Cavanagh v Nominal Defendant (1959): 318
Cavenett v Chambers (1968) 499
Chalmers v HM Advocate (1954): **177**, 206
Chamberlain v R (No 2) (1984) 41
Chambers v Mississippi (1973), US
   SC 340
Chandrasekera (alias Alisandiri) v R
   (1936), PC 321
Chan Wei-Keung v R (1967), PC 164
Chapman v Kirke (1948), DC 499
Chard v Chard (otherwise Northcott)
   (1956) **63**
Chastleton Corpn v Sinclair (1924) . . . 500
Cheney v R (1991) 257
Cheni (otherwise Rodriguez) v Cheni
   (1965) 68
Chic Fashions (West Wales) Ltd v
   Jones (1968), CA 431
Chinnaswamy Reddy v Andhra Pradesh
   (1962) 179
Clarke v Ryan (1960) 393
Cleland v R (1982) 163, 211, 212, 235
Cloyes v Thayer (1842) 118
Coffee, Re, Timbury v Coffee (1941): 504
Coffin v United States (1895) 58
Cole v Manning (1877), DC 107
Coleman v Southwick (1812) 316
Collins v R (1980) 165, 212
Collins v R (1987) **228**
Colvilles Ltd v Devine (1969), HL . . . 70
Comet Products UK Ltd v Hawkex
   Plastics Ltd (1971), CA 41
Commissioner for Railways (NSW) v
   Young (1962) **376**
Commissioners of Customs and Excise
   v Harz. See Customs and Excise
   Comrs v Harz
Commonwealth v A Juvenile (1974): 504
Commonwealth v Morrell (1868) 377
Commonwealth v Preece (1885) 164
Commonwealth Shipping Representa-
   tive v P and O Branch Service
   (1923), HL 503
Compagnie Financière et Commerciale
   du Pacifique v Peruvian Guano Co
   (1882), CA 447
Company Securities (Insider Dealing)
   Act 1985, Inquiry under the, Re
   (1988), HL 439
Constantine (Joseph) SS Line Ltd v
   Imperial Smelting Corpn Ltd,
   The Kingswood (1942), HL 17, **24**

PAGE

Controlled Consultants Pty Ltd v Comr
   for Corporate Affairs (1985) 135
Conway v Hotten (1976), DC 197
Conway v Rimmer [1968] 2 All ER
   304n, HL 441
Conway v Rimmer [1968] AC 910,
   HL . . . 422, **441**, 447, 448, 449, 450, 452,
         455, 458, 459, 460, 464, 465
Conwell v Tapfield (1981) 378
Cooper v Bech (No 2) (1975) 390
Cooper v McKenna, ex p Cooper (1960): 23
Cooper v R (1961) 254
Corporate Affairs Commission v
   Bradley (1974) 504
Corporate Affairs Comr v Green (1978): 56
Cox v Juncken (1947) 67
Cox v State (1879) 357
Cracknell v Smith (1960), DC 112, 151
Craig v R (1933) 84
Credland v Knowler (1951), DC . . . 109, 110
Crescent Farm (Sidcup) Sports Ltd v
   Sterling Offices Ltd (1972) 428
Cressy v Siward (1312) 81
Crompton (Alfred) Amusement Machines
   Ltd v Customs and Excise Comrs
   (No 2) (1974), HL: 422, 426, **455**, 457,
            459, 460, 462, 463
Crossland v DPP (1988) 100
Culcombe v Connecticut (1961) **202**
Customglass Boats Ltd v Salthouse
   Bros Ltd (1976) 319
Customs and Excise Comrs v Harz
   (1967), HL **131**, 174
Customs and Excise Comrs v Ingram
   (1948), CA 131
Cutts v Head (1984), CA 438

D

D (Infants), Re (1970), CA 459, 460,
                  464, 465
D (a minor), Re (1986) 366
D v National Society for the Prevention
   of Cruelty to Children (1978), CA;
   revsd (1978), HL 7, 433, 437, 439,
                 456, 462, 465
Daley v R (1994), PC 92
Danyluk v Danyluk (1964) 77
Daubert v Merrell Dow Pharmaceuticals
   Inc (1993) 386
Davey v Harrow Corpn (1958), CA: 504
Davidson v Quirke (1923) . . . 328, 329, 333
Davie v Edinburgh Magistrates (1953): 391
Davies v Fortior Ltd (1952) 358
Davies and Cody v R (1937) 92, 96, 98
Davis v Bunn (1936) 70
Davis v Davis (1950), CA 51
Davis v United States (1895), SC 33
Dawson v M'Kenzie (1908) 109
Dawson v R (1961) **40**, 296, 307

PAGE

De B v De B (1950) 494

De Clercq v R (1968) 164

Dellow's Will Trusts, Re, Lloyds Bank
  Ltd v Institute of Cancer Research
  (1964) 51

Demeter v R (1977) 339

Demirok v R (1977) 8, 405

Dennis v A J White & Co (1917), HL: 503

Derby & Co Ltd v Weldon (No 7) (1990): 428

Derby & Co Ltd v Weldon (No 8) (1990),
  CA 437

Derby & Co Ltd v Weldon (No 9) (1991): 378

Descoteaux v Mierzwinski (1982) 436

Dickins v Randerson (1901), DC 389

Dillon v R (1982), PC 74

Dingwall v J Wharton (Shipping) Ltd
  (1961), HL.................50, 112

DPP v A and BC Chewing Gum Ltd
  (1968) 390, 392

DPP v Beard (1920), HL 22

DPP v Billington (1988) 195

DPP v Blake (1989) 162

DPP v Boardman (1974), HL: 113, 259, 264,
                267, 269, 272, 274

DPP v Hester (1972), HL 101, 102

DPP v Jordan (1977), HL 390, 391

DPP v Kilbourne (1973), HL: 101, 102, 112

DPP v Morgan (1976), HL 15, 17, 34

DPP v Nieser (1959), DC 150

DPP v P (1991), HL 259, 261

DPP v Skinner (1989) 195

DPP v United Telecasters Ltd (1990): 32

Disher v Disher (1965) 472

Dixon's Estate, Re (1969) 66

Doe d Tatum v Catomore (1851) 382

Doe d Jenkins v Davies (1847) 8

Doe d West v Davis (1806) 379

Doe d Perry v Newton (1836) 381

Doe d Church and Phillips v Perkins
  (1790) 474

Doe d Mudd v Suckermore (1836): 380, 381

Doe d Devine v Wilson (1855), PC ... 381

Domican v R (1992) 92

Donnelly v United States (1913) 339

Donnini v R (1972) 303

Douglas, The (1882), CA 318

Dover v Maestaer (1803) 121

Doyle v Hofstader (1931) 126

Driscoll v R (1977) 211, 479

Dubai Bank Ltd v Galadari (1990), CA: 429

Duff Development Co Ltd v Kelantan
  Government (1924), HL........ 503

Dugdale v Kraft Foods Ltd (1977),
  EAT 502

Duncan, Re, Garfield v Fay (1968) ... 426

Duncan v Cammell Laird & Co Ltd
  (1942), HL.... 440, 441, 442, 444, 445,
                446, 447, 452, 464

Dwyer v Collins (1852) 375

PAGE

E

Eade v R (1924) 490, 494

Eagles v Orth (1976) 390

Earle v Castlemaine District Community Hospital (1974) 151, 152

Edwards v Brookes (Milk) Ltd (1963): 321

Elias v Pasmore (1934)...... 223, 250, 431

Elkins v United States (1960) 244

Engelke v Musmann (1928), HL 503

English Exporters (London) Ltd v
  Eldonwall Ltd (1973) 391

Environment Protection Authority v
  Caltex Refining Co Pty Ltd (1993): 135

Escobedo v Illinois (1964) ... 174, 175, 198

Ettenfield v Ettenfield (1940), CA ... 67

Everard v Opperman (1958) 18, 32

Everingham v Roundell (1838) 379

Ewer v Ambrose (1825) 478

F

Fagernes, The (1927), CA 503

Fairley v Fishmongers of London
  (1951) **221**, 223

Fanelli v United States Gypsum Co
  (1944) 476

Ferdinand Retzlaff, The (1972) **373**

Ferguson v R (1979), PC 37, 40

Feuerheerd v London General Omnibus
  Co (1918), CA 434

Fingleton v Lowen (1979) 329, 333

Firth, Re, ex p Schofield (1877), CA: 120

Fitzpatrick v Walter E Cooper Pty Ltd
  (1935) **70**

Fletcher, Re, Reading v Fletcher (1917),
  CA 358

Flight v Robinson (1844) 417

Forbes v Samuel (1913) 379

Fountain v Young (1807) 434

Fox v General Medical Council (1960),
  PC 477

Fredrichberg's Case. See Government
  Insurance Office of New South
  Wales v Fredrichberg

Freeman, ex p (1922) 111

Freeman v Cox (1878) 148

Fromhold v Fromhold (1952), CA ... 494

Frye v United States (1923) 386, 504

G

G (an infant) v Coltart (1967), DC: 257, 258

Gaio v R (1960) 321

Garcin v Amerindo Investment
  Advisors Ltd (1991) 367

Gardner, Re (1968) 321

Gartside v Outram (1856) 421

Gaskin v Liverpool City Council
  (1980), CA 466

Gatland v Metropolitan Police Comr
  (1968), DC 19

PAGE

General Accident Fire and Life
Assurance Corpn Ltd v Tanter,
The Zephyr (1984)   427
General Electric Co v General Electric
Co Ltd (1973), HL   319
Genese, Re, ex p Gilbert (1886), CA: 121
George v Coombe (1978)   122
George v Davies (1911)   504
Gerhardy v Brown (1985)   500
Gertz v Fitchberg RR (1884)   481
Ghani v Jones (1970), CA 250, 431
Gideon v Wainwright (1963)   198
Gilbey v Great Western Rly Co (1910),
CA. 358, 359
Glasgow Corpn v Central Land Board
(1956) 441, 444, 447, 449
Glendarroch, The (1894), CA   24
Global Funds Management (NSW)
Ltd v Rooney (1994)   426
Goddard v Nationwide Building
Society (1987), CA   436
Goldman v Hesper (1988), CA   427
Good Helmsman, The. See Harmony
Shipping Co SA v Davis,
The Good Helmsman
Good Luck, The. See Bank of Nova
Scotia v Hellenic Mutual War
Risks Association (Bermuda)
Ltd, The Good Luck
Goodman and Carr and Minister of
National Revenue, Re (1968)   421
Gosschalk v Rossouw (1966)   254
Government Insurance Office of New
South Wales v Fredrichberg
(1968) 70, 73
Government Transport Comr v
Adamcik (1961), HC of A   386
Grant v Downs (1976) 423, 424,
425, 500
Grant v R (1975), HC of A   41
Grant v Southwestern and County
Properties Ltd (1975)   378
Grazebrook (M and W) Ltd v Wallens
(1973), NIRC   426
Great Atlantic Insurance Co v Home
Insurance Co (1981), CA   427
Greenough v Eccles (1859)   478
Greenough v Gaskell (1833)   417
Grew v Cubitt (1951), DC   320
Grey v Australian Motorists and General
Insurance Co Pty Ltd (1976)   392
Griffith v R (1937)   270
Grismore v Consolidated Products Co
(1942)   392
Grofam Pty Ltd v Australia and New
Zealand Banking Group (1993) . . .   426
Guinness Peat Properties Ltd v Fitzroy
Robinson Partnership (a firm)
(1987), CA. 428, 436

PAGE

H

H (minors) (proof of abuse), Re (1995),
CA; on appeal sub nom H (minors)
(sexual abuse: standard of proof),
Re (1996), HL **43, 45, 51**
H v H (minor) (1990), CA 361, 368
H v Schering Chemicals Ltd (1983): 366, 386
Halbert v Mynar (1981)   66
Hale v Henkel (1906)   135
Hales v Kerr (1908)   257
Hall v Dunlop (1959)   32
Hall v R (1971), PC **146**
Hammond v Commonwealth of
Australia (1982) 133, 137
Hannan v Jennings (1969)   76
Harman v Secretary of State for the
Home Department (1983), HL . . .   466
Harmony Shipping Co SA v Davis,
The Good Helmsman (1979),
CA   391
Harmony Shipping Co SA v Saudi
Europe Line Ltd (1979), CA   426
Harris v DPP (1952), HL . . . 223, 227, 238,
240, **254**, 258,
259, 272, 306
Harris v New York (1971) . . . 204, 205, 244
Harris v Tippett (1811)   480
Harrison v Southcote and Moreland
(1751)   124
Hastie and Jenkerson (a firm) v
McMahon (1991), CA   378
Haw Tua Tau v Public Prosecutor
(1982), PC   56
Hawke's Bay Motor Co Ltd v Russell
(1972)   70
Hawkins v United States (1958)   500
Hay v HM Advocate (1968) **226**
Haynes v Doman (1899), CA **392**
Hayslep v Gymer (1834)   319
He Kow Teh v R (1985)   17
Hehir v Metropolitan Police Comr
(1982), CA   456
Henderson v Henry E Jenkins & Sons
and Evans (1970), HL   70
Hennessy v Wright (1888)   461
Hickman v Peacey (1945), HL   62
Hill v Baxter (1958) 21, 22, 23
Hill v R (1953)   310
Hinch v A-G (Vic) (1987)   41
Hinds v Sparks (1964)   400
Hindson v Monahan (1970)   378
Hine, Re (1897)   324
Hinton v Trotter (1931)   150
Hitchins v Eardley (1871)   8
Hoban's Glynde Pty Ltd v Firle Hotel
Pty Ltd (1973)   319
Hoch v R (1988)   263
Hocking v Ahlquist Bros Ltd (1944),
DC   377

PAGE

Hodgson, Re, Beckett v Ramsdale
  (1885), CA   80
Holcombe v Hewson (1810)   257
Holland v Jones (1917) 502, 506
Hollingham v Head (1858)   257
Hollington v F Hewthorn & Co Ltd
  (1943), CA 394, 396
Holloway v MacFeeters (1956) **332**
Holmes v DPP (1946), HL   22
Homes v Newman (1931)   350
Hooker Corpn Ltd v Darling Harbour
  Authority (1987) 436, 437
Hooley, Re, Rucker's Case (1898) . . .   463
Hope v Brash (1897), CA   461
Horman v Bingham (1972)   504
Hornal v Neuberger Products Ltd
  (1957), CA 51, **52**
Howe v R (1980), HC of A   41
Hubin v R (1927)   149
Hughes v National Trustees Executors
  and Agency Co of Australasia Ltd
  (1979) 11, 318
Hughes v Rogers (1841)   381
Hui Chi-ming v R (1992), PC   394
Humberside County Council v DPR
  (an infant), Re (1977)   336
Hunter v Chief Constable of West
  Midlands Police (1982), HL . . . 394, 399
Hunter v Mann (1974)   439
Hunter v State (1922)   350

I

ITC Film Distributors v Video
  Exchange Ltd (1982) 243, 435, 436
Ibrahim v R (1914), PC   210
Inglis v Inglis and Baxter (1968)   151
Ingram v Ingram (1956)   394
Ingram v Percival (1969), DC   502
Initial Services Ltd v Putterill (1968),
  CA   421
IRC v West-Walker (1954), (NZCA):   428
International Business Machines
  Corpn v Phoenix International
  (Computers) Ltd (1995)   426
Isaacs (M) & Sons Ltd v Cook (1925):   440
Istel (AT & T) Ltd v Tully (1993),
  HL 122, 126
Italia Express, The. See Ventouris v
  Mountain (No 2), The
  Italia Express

J

Jackson, Re, Jackson v Ward
  (1907)   66
Jackson v Williamson (1788)   467
Jayasena v R [1970] AC 618, (1970),
  PC 15, 29, 56
Jeffrey v Black (1978), DC 232, 236,
                                     239, 242

PAGE

Jelfs v Ballard (1799) 29, 30
Jensen v Ilka (1960)   112
John v Humphreys (1955), DC . . . 18, 27
Johnson v Lyford (1868)   75
Jones v DPP (1962), CCA; affd (1962),
  HL 278, **279**, 287, 288, 289,
                       291, 297, 303, 306
Jones v Dunkel (1959)   151
Jones v Metcalfe (1967), DC   320
Jones v National Coal Board (1957),
  CA   8
Jones v Owens (1870)   227
Jones v South Eastern and Chatham
  Rly Co's Managing Committee
  (1918), DC   494
Jones v Sutherland Shire Council
  (1979) 11, 333
Jones v Tarleton (1842)   377
Jones v Thomas (1934), DC   109
Jorgensen v News Media (Auckland)
  Ltd (1969)   394
Jozwiak v Sadek (1954)   358

K

K, Re. See Official Solicitor to the
  Supreme Court v K
Kaja v Secretary of State for the Home
  Department (1995)   50
Kajala v Noble (1982), CA   378
Katz v United States (1967)   245
Kavanagh v Chief Constable of Devon
  and Cornwall (1974), CA   336
Kawasaki Kisen Kabushiki Kaisha of
  Kobe v Bantham SS Co Ltd
  (No 2) (1939), CA   504
Kemp v R (1951)   257
Kennedy v HM Advocate (1944)   23
Kerr v Preston Corpn (1876)   431
Kerwood v R (1944) 295, 296
Khan v Khan (1982), CA   123
Khawaja v Secretary of State for the
  Home Department (1984), HL . . .   52
Kilby v R (1973), HC of A **489**
King v McLellan (1974)   122
King v R (1968), PC **226**
Kingston's (Duchess) Case (1776) . . .   463
Kingswood, The. See Constantine
  (Joseph) SS Line Ltd v Imperial
  Smelting Corpn Ltd,
  The Kingswood
Kite, The (1933)   70
Knight v R (1992)   41
Koscot Interplanetary (UK) Ltd, Re,
  Re Koscot AG (1972)   366
Kozul v R (1981)   6
Krell v Henry (1903), CA   25
Kuruma, Son of Kaniu v R (1955),
  PC **222**, 225, 227, 231, 236,
                       238, 239, 240, 252

PAGE

L

LB (Plastics) v Swish Products (1979);
 on appeal (1979), CA; revsd (1979),
 HL 393
Lafone v Griffin (1909) 379
Lal Chand Marwari v Mahant Ramrup
 Gir (1925), PC 64
Lamb v Evans (1893), CA 430
Lamb v Munster (1882) 122
Lamoureux v New York, New Haven
 Hartford Rly Co (1897) 485
Lancey (H R) Shipping Co Pty Ltd v
 Robson (1938) 254
Land Securities plc v Westminster City
 Council (1993) 396, 467
Lawrie v Muir (1950) **219**, 223, 225,
 231, 233
Leach (A B) & Co v Peirson (1927): 147
Lee v South West Thames Regional
 Health Authority (1985), CA 428
Lenthall v Mitchell (1933) 328
Leung Kam Kwok v R (1984), PC ... 166
Levene v Roxhan (1970), CA 401
Levitt (Jeffrey S) Ltd, Re (1992) 133
Lewis v James (1887) 463
Li Shu-ling v R (1989), PC 6
Lindop, Re, Lee-Barber v Reynolds
 (1942), CA 62
Lisenba v California (1941) 198
Lister v Smith (1863) 357
Lively Ltd v City of Munich (1977) ... 391
Lloyd v Mostyn (1842) 223, 429
Lloyd v Powell Duffryn Steam Coal
 Co Ltd (1914), HL **330**, 333
Lobban v R (1995), PC 477
London and County Securities Ltd v
 Nicholson (1980) 466
London and North Eastern Rly Co v
 Berriman (1946), HL 387
London United Investments plc, Re
 (1992), CA 133
Longthorn v British Transport
 Commission (1959) 422
Lonrho plc v Fayed (No 4) (1994), CA: 455
Loveden v Loveden (1810) 50
Lowery v R (1974), PC 274, 390, 488
Lubrizol Corpn v Esso Petroleum Co
 Ltd (1992) 429
Lucas v Williams & Sons (1892), CA: 377
Lui-Mei Lin v R (1989), PC: 168, 310, 407
Lyell v Kennedy (No 3) (1884), CA: 429, 436
Lyons (DF) Pty Ltd v Commonwealth
 Bank of Australia (1991) 254

M

McCulloch v Maryland 246
McDermott v R (1948) 174, 182, **210**
McDonald's System of Australia Pty Ltd v
 McWilliam's Wines Pty Ltd (1979): 319

PAGE

MacDonnell v Evans (1852) **375**
McGovern v HM Advocate (1950) ... **221**
McGowan v Carville (1960) 18, 32
McGreevy v DPP (1972), HL 37, 41
McGregor v Stokes (1952) ... 321, 328, 329
McGuiness v A-G of Victoria
 (1940) 438, 463
Mackowik v Kansas City (1906) 78
McNabb v United States (1943) 198
M'Naghten's Case. See R v
 McNaughton
MacPherson v R (1981) 163, 209
McQuaker v Goddard (1940), CA: 505, 506
McQueen v Great Western Rly Co
 (1875) **151**
McTaggart v McTaggart (1949),
 CA 437, 460
McVeigh v Beattie (1988) 112
Maeder (Frederic) Proprietary Ltd v
 Wellington City (1969) 70
Mahadervan v Mahadervan (1962) ... 68
Mahoney v Wright (1943) 107
Makin v A-G for New South Wales
 (1894), PC 254, 255, 259, 269,
 271, 282, 288
Malindi v R (1967), PC: 289, 291, 292, 297
Mallinson v Scottish Australian
 Investment Co Ltd (1920) 378
Mallory v United States (1957) 198
Manchester Brewery Co v Coombs
 (1901) 331
Mancini v DPP (1942), HL 17, 21, 22,
 33, 40
Mangano v Farleigh Nettheim (1965) . 499
Mansell v Clements (1874) 385
Mapp v Ohio (1961) 244
Marcoux and Solomon v R (1975),
 Can SC 122
Maritime National Fish Ltd v Ocean
 Trawlers Ltd (1935) 25
Marks v Beyfus (1890), CA 451, 457,
 461, 463
Mars v McMahon (1929) 148
Marshall v Watt (1953) 328, 333
Marshall v Wild Rose (Owners) (1910),
 HL 358
Mash v Darley (1914), CA 109, 110,
 112, 151
Mathewson v Police (1969) 328
Matthew v Flood (1938) 121
Matto v Crown Court at Wolverhampton
 (or DPP) (1987) 219, 243
Matusevich v R (1977), HC of A 311
Mawaz Khan v R and Amanat Khan
 (1967), PC 318
Mawson v Hartsink (1802) 486
Maxwell v DPP (1934), HL: 278, 280, 282,
 283, 284,
 301, 305

PAGE

Maxwell v Pressdram Ltd (1987),
  CA 438, 439
May v O'Sullivan (1955) 35, 56
Meath (Bishop) v Marquis of
  Winchester (1836), HL   380
Mechanical and General Inventions Co
  Ltd and Lehwess v Austin and Austin
  Motor Co Ltd (1935), HL   473
Medawar v Grand Hotel Co (1891), CA: 36
Merchant v R (1971)   233
Mezzo v R (1986), SC   92
Michelson v United States (1948): 483, 484,
                                        485
Miller v Minister of Pensions (1947):   **37**
Miller v Oregon (1907)   500
Mills v R (1995), PC 342, 358
Milne v Leisler (1862) 358, 359, 477
Milner and Atkins & Durbrow, Re
  (1968)   421
Minet v Morgan (1873)   425
Miranda v Arizona (1966) **167, 198**
Mole v Mole (1951), CA 437, 460
Monckton v Tarr (1930), CA 65, 77
Mood Music Publishing Co Ltd v De
  Wolfe Publishing Ltd (1976), CA: 253
Mooney v James (1949)   474
Moore v Hewitt (1947), DC   113
Moore v R Fox & Sons (1956), CA . . .   70
Moorov v HM Advocate (1930)   265
Moran v Burbine (1986)   205
Morgan v Morgan (1977)   406
Moriarty v London Chatham and
  Dover Rly Co (1870) **107**, 282, 367
Morison v Moat (1851); affd (1852):   430
Morris v London Iron and Steel Co
  Ltd (1988), CA   15
Motor Transport Comr v Collier-Moat
  Ltd (1960)   335
Mulbera, The (1937)   70
Mummery v Irvings Pty Ltd (1956) . . .   73
Murdoch v Taylor (1965), HL: 300, 303, 305,
                           308, 310, 473
Murphy v R (1976)   107
Murphy v R (1989), HC of A   392
Murphy v Waterfront Commission of
  New York Harbour (1964)   124
Murphy and Butt v R (1976)   106
Murray v DPP (1994), HL   143
Murray v United Kingdom (1994),
  ECtHR   141
Mutual Life Insurance Co v Hillmon
  (1892) 75, 358
Myers v DPP (1965), HL . . . 317, 319, 330,
                           340, 346, 365

N

NY v Quarles (1984)   204
Nardone v United States (1937)   244
Nardone v United States (No 2) (1939):   244

PAGE

Nash v Railways Comr (1963)   331
Nast v Nast and Walker (1972), CA . . .   438
National Mutual Holdings Pty Ltd v
  Sentry Corpn (1989)   387
National Trustees Executors and Agency
  Co of Australasia Ltd v A-G for State
  of Victoria (1973)   507
Nederlandse Reassurantie Groep
  Holding NV v Bacon &
  Woodrow (a firm) (1995)   416
Neill v North Antrim Magistrates'
  Court (1992), HL   358
Network Ten Ltd v Capital Television
  Holdings Ltd (1995)   428
Ng Ping On v Ng Choy Fung Kam
  (1963)   68
Nicholas v Penny (1950), DC   100
Nimmo v Alexander Cowan & Sons
  Ltd (1968)   30
Nixon v US (1974)   449
Nominal Defendant v Clements (1960):   477
Nominal Defendant v Haslbauer
  (1967)   70
Noor Mohamed v R (1949),
  PC 223, 227, 237, 238,
                        240, 255, 256, 306
Northumbria, The (1906), DC   24
Norwich Pharmacal Co v Customs and
  Excise Comrs (1974), HL **453**

O

Oakes v Uzzell (1932)   382
O'Brennan v Tully (1933)   463
O'Donnell v Reichard (1975)   152
Official Solicitor to the Supreme Court
  v K (1965), HL   368
Ogden v London Electric Rly Co
  (1933), CA 422, 423
O'Hara v Central Scottish Motor
  Traction Co (1941) . . . 70, 331, 352, 353
O'Hara v HM Advocate (1948) . . . 293, 297
O'Leary v R (1946) **273**, 352
Olmstead v United States (1928): 223, 233,
                             244, **245**
Omichund (or Omychund) v Barker
  (1745)   9
O'Reilly v Comr of State Bank of
  Victoria (1983)   427
Orme v Crockford (1824)   124
O'Rourke v Darbishire (1920), HL: **419**, 420,
                                        421
Orozco v Texas (1969)   204
Osmand, Re, Bennett v Booty (1906):   68
Overbury, Re, Sheppard v Matthews
  (1955) 67, 77
Owner v Bee Hive Spinning Co Ltd
  (1914), DC   376
Oxfordshire County Council v M
  (1994), CA   427

PAGE

P

P, Re (1991), CA 406
Pakala Narayana Swamy v Emperor
  (1939), PC 207
Palermo, The (1883), CA 429
Palko v Connecticut (1937) 244
Paric v John Holland (Construction)
  Pty Ltd (1985) 386
Parker v R (1912) 505
Parkes v R (1976), PC 147
Parkinson v Parkinson (1939) 66
Parry-Jones v Law Society (1969), CA: 427
Patel v Comptroller of Customs (1965): 320
Paterson v Martin (1966) 148
Payne v Harrison (1961), CA 472
Peach v Metropolitan Police Comr
  (1986), CA 456
Pearse v Pearse (1846) 231, 417
Peatling, Re (1969) 68, 78
Peete, Re, Peete v Crompton (1952): 68
People v Defore (1926) **245**
People v King (1968) 504
People v Lynch (1987) 179
People v Martin (1955) 244
People v Rodriguez (1862) 198
People v Spriggs (1964) 339
People, The v Bush (1921) 333
People, The v De Simone (1919) 354
People, The (A-G) v Casey (No 2)
  (1963) 92
People, The (A-G) v O'Brien
  (1965) 178, **225**, 227, 231, 233
Perkins v Vaughan (1842) 318
Perry v R (1982) 272
Pfennig v R (1995) 92, 260
Phené's Trusts, Re (1870), CA 64, 66
Piche v R (1970) **167**
Pickup v Thames and Mersey Marine
  Insurance Co Ltd (1878), CA 34
Piddington v Bennett and Wood
  Proprietary Ltd (1940) 480
Pidduck v Pidduck and Limbrick
  (1961) 151
Piening v Wanless (1968) 70
Piggott v Piggott (1938) 67
Pitman v Byrne (1926) 107, 109
Plato Films Ltd v Speidel (1961), HL: 483
Plomp v R (1963) 75
Plymouth Mutual Co-op and Industrial
  Society Ltd v Traders' Publishing
  Association Ltd (1906), CA 461
Police v Lavelle (1979) 240
Police v Machirus (1977) 328, 333
Police Service Board v Morris
  (1985) 117, 135
Polycarpou v Australian Wire Industries
  Pty Ltd (1995) 254
Popi M, The. See Rhesa Shipping Co
  SA v Edmunds, The Popi M

PAGE

Popovic v Derks (1961) **108**
Poricanin v Australian Consolidated
  Industries Ltd (1979) 34
Poriotis v Australian Iron and Steel Co
  Ltd (1963) 357
Potts v Miller (1940) 320
Povey v Povey (1972) 464
Power v State (1934) 113
Prabhoo v Uttar Pradesh (1963) 179
Practice Direction [1989] 1 WLR 631: 196
Practice Note [1962] 1 All ER 448,
  DC 56
Practice Note [1964] 1 All ER 237,
  CCA **181**
Practice Note [1975] 2 All ER 1072: 275
Practice Note (crown court: defendant's
  evidence) [1995] 2 All ER 499, CA: 142
Prasad v Ministry for Immigration
  (1991) 335
Preston-Jones v Preston-Jones (1951),
  HL 503
Prudential Assurance Co v Edmonds
  (1877), HL 66
Pyneboard Pty Ltd v Trade Practices
  Commission (1983)......... 134, 135

Q

Queen's Case (1820) 479

R

R v Abadom (1983), CA 335, 386, 391
R v Abbott (1955), CCA 489
R v Abraham (1973), CA 17
R v Absolam (1988), CA 196, 216
R v Acton Justices, ex p McMullen
  (1990) 348
R v Adair (1990), CA 301
R v Adams and Ross (1965) 493
R v Adamstein (1937) 484
R v Aiken (1925) 264
R v Alath Construction Ltd (1990), CA: 32
R v Alexander (1975) 474
R v All Saints, Worcester Inhabitants
  (1817) 117
R v Alladice (1988), CA 158, 162, 196,
                        213, 216, 217
R v Allen (1937) 266
R v Aloisio (1969) 494
R v Ameer and Lucas (1977), CA: 235, 240
R v Ananthanarayanan (1994), CA ... 264
R v Anderson (1972), CA........ 390, 392
R v Anderson (1988), CA.... 279, **286**, 290
R v Anderson (1993), CA 215
R v Andrews (1987), HL 351, **355**
R v Angeli (1978), CA 41, 165, 380
R v Apicella (1985), CA 243
R v Armstrong (1922), CCA...... 256, 274
R v Askew (1981), CA 107
R v Aspinall (1876), CA 507

PAGE

R v Attard (1958) 320
R v Austin (1912), CCA 342
R v Aves (1950), CCA 22
R v Aziz (1996), HL 257, 275, 303
R v Bagley (1926), CA 94, 97
R v Bailey (1924), CCA 259
R v Bainbridge (1960), CCA 397
R v Baldry (1852), CCR 174
R v Baldwin (1925), CCA 289
R v Ball (1911), HL 254, 258, 259, 266, **269**, 272
R v Barbery (1975), CA 477
R v Barker (1941), CCA 175, 238
R v Barnes (1921) 127
R v Barry (1991), CA 162
R v Bashir and Manzur (1969) 494
R v Baskerville (1916), CCA 79
R v Bath (1990), CA 91
R v Bathurst (1968), CA 140
R v Beattie (1989), CA 479
R v Beck (1982), CA 101, 102
R v Beckett (1913), CCA 385
R v Beckford (1991), CA 315
R v Bedingfield (1879) 331, 351, 353
R v Beere (1965) 178
R v Bell, ex p Lees (1980) 427
R v Bellamy (1985), CA 413
R v Bennett (1978), CA 17
R v Bentley (1991), CA 91
R v Benz (1989) 357
R v Bernadotti (1869) 342
R v Berriman (1854) **176**
R v Billings (1961) 295, 298
R v Birkett (1839) **105**
R v Birtles (1969), CA 241
R v Bishop (1975), CA 295
R v Black (1922), CCA 359
R v Black (1989) 178
R v Blastland (1985), HL ... 315, 326, 330, 331, 339
R v Bliss (1837) 357
R v Blithing (1983), CA 348
R v Boal (1965) 407
R v Bond (1906), CCR 265, 274
R v Bondy (1957) 111
R v Bonnor (1957) 66
R v Booth (1981), CA 478
R v Bottrill, ex p Kuechenmeister (1947), CA 503
R v Bouquet (1962) 94, 95
R v Boyes (1861) **119**
R v Bracewell (1978), CA 38, 275
R v Bradshaw (1985), CA 391
R v Braham and Mason (1976) 426
R v Brasier (1779), CCR 492
R v Britton (1987), CA 474
R v Britton and Richards (1989) 98
R v Britzman (1983), CA 295
R v Brophy (1982), HL 164

PAGE

R v Brown (1960), CCA 295, 306
R v Brown (1983), CA 42
R v Brown (1987), CA 466
R v Brown (1990), CA 197
R v Brown and Hedley (1867), CCR: 486
R v Browning (1991), CA 92
R v Bruce (1975), CA 300, 301
R v Buchan (1964), CCA 195
R v Buckland (1977) 152
R v Buckley (1873) 75, 358
R v Bundy (1910), CCA 98
R v Burchielli (1981) 92
R v Burdett (1820) **150**
R v Burgess (1968), CA 164
R v Burke (1858) 480
R v Burke (1985), CA 308
R v Burke (1990) 349
R v Burnett and Lee (1973) 240
R v Butterwasser (1948), CCA 276, 298
R v Byczko (No 2) (1977) 107
R v Calder and Boyars Ltd (1969), CA: 392
R v Cambridge (1994), CA 57
R v Camelleri (1922), CCA 493
R v Campbell (1956), CCA 268
R v Camplin (1978), HL 390
R v Canale (1990), CA 215, 219
R v Capner (1975) 240
R v Carey (1968), CA 298
R v Carr-Briant (1943), CCA 37
R v Cartwright (1914), CCA 98
R v Case (1991), CA 348
R v Central Criminal Court, ex p Francis & Francis (a firm) (1989), HL 428
R v Chandler (1956) 259
R v Chandler (1976), CA 147
R v Chandor (1959), CCA 268
R v Chapman (1911), CCA 98
R v Chapman (1969), CA 318
R v Charavanmuttu (1930), CCA 112
R v Chard (1971), CA 390
R v Cheltenham Justices, ex p Secretary of State for Trade (1977) 466
R v Chief Constable of West Midlands Police, ex p Wiley (1995), HL 451
R v Chin (1985) 496
R v Chitson (1909), CCA ...274, 278, 280, 281, 283, 284, 287, 290
R v Choney (1908) 434
R v Christie (1914), HL: **145**, 148, 149, 238, 240, 255, 305, 331, 337, 351, 353, 490
R v Clark (1955), CCA 292, 295
R v Clarke (1969), CA 17
R v Clewes (1830) 166
R v Coats (1932) 166
R v Cobbett (1831) 463
R v Cokar (1960), CCA 278, 291
R v Cole (1941), CCA 254

PAGE

R v Cole (1990), CA 347, **350**
R v Collier (1965), CCA 197
R v Collings (1976) 107, 337
R v Collins (1960), CCA 379
R v Condon (1980) 99
R v Conway (1990), CA 98
R v Cook (1918), CCA **181**
R v Cook (1959), CCA 292, 295, 298,
306, 307, 309
R v Cook (1987), CA 337, 476
R v Coote (1873), PC **123**, 131
R v Coroner, ex p Alexander (1982): 118
R v Cottle (1958) 23
R v Court (1962), CCA 224
R v Cowan (1995), CA **140**, 151, 152
R v Cox (1991), CA 164
R v Cox and Railton (1884),
CCR 121, 122, 419, 420
R v Cramp (1880); affd (1880) 110, 148
R v Crampton (1990), CA 161
R v Crawford (1965) 307
R v Crowhurst (1844) 282
R v Crown Court at Inner London
Sessions, ex p Baines & Baines
(a firm) (1988) 428
R v Crown Court at Manchester,
ex p Taylor (1988) 439
R v Curbishley (1963), CCA 295, 307
R v Curgerwen (1865) 33, 66
R v Daley (1987), CA 466
R v Dally (1990) 179
R v Da Silva (1990), CA 474, 475
R v Davidson and Tidd (1820) 105
R v Davies (1962) 385, 393
R v Davies (1963), CA 295
R v Davis (1975), CA 300
R v Davis (1979) 209
R v Davis (1990), CA 164
R v Davison (1988) 158
R v Deakin (1994), CA 8
R v De-Cressac (1985) 92
R v Deighton and Thornton (1954),
CCA 302
R v Delaney (1988), CA 158, 162, 216
R v Derby Magistrates' Court, ex p B
(1996), HL 426
R v Dickman (1910), CCA 98
R v Dillon (1983), CA 475
R v Director of Serious Fraud Office,
ex p Smith (1993), HL . . . 134, **136**, 197
R v Donohoe (1962) 342
R v Doolan (1988), CA 175, 216
R v Dossi (1918), CCA 107
R v Doughty (1965), CCA 254
R v Douglass (1989), CA 310
R v Dowley (1983), CA 107
R v Downey (1995), CA 261
R v Doyle (1967) 94, 95
R v Doyle (1987) 166

PAGE

R v Duffy (1979), CA 147
R v Dunbar (1958), CCA 18
R v Duncalf (1979), CA 303
R v Duncan (1981), CA 166, 477
R v Dunford (1990), CA 213
R v Dunkley (1927), CCA . . . 278, 285, 286,
297, 306
R v Dwyer (1925), CCA 93, 95
R v Edmunds (1833) 318
R v Edwards (1975), CA 18, **27**, 66
R v Eidinow (1932), CCA 289
R v Ellis (1910), CCA 289, 291
R v Ellis (1961), CCA 300, 309, 310
R v Ellwood (1908), CCA 75
R v Emmerson (1991), CA 196
R v Erdheim (1896), CCR 131
R v Eriswell Inhabitants (1790) 316
R v Evans (1950), CCA 274
R v Ewing (1983), CA 41, 165, 380
R v Fallon (1963), CCA 397
R v Fannon (1922) 94, 95
R v Farler (1837) **105**
R v Feigenbaum (1919), CCA 110, 147
R v Fenlon (1980), CA 494, 495
R v Ferguson (1909), CCA 291
R v Ferguson (1925), CCA 93, 95
R v Field, etc Justices, ex p White
(1895), DC 507
R v Fisher (1964) 295
R v Flack (1969), CA 258, **268**
R v Fletcher (1913), CCA 305
R v Flynn (1957), CCA 495, 496
R v Flynn (1963), CCA 306, 307
R v Foster (1834) 358
R v Foulder (1973) 240
R v Fox (1985), HL 243
R v Fox and Fisher (1953) 92
R v Francis (1874), CCR 274, 377
R v Freeman (1980) 107
R v Frost (1839), CCR 495
R v Fulling (1987), CA; affd (1987),
HL 153, **155**, 161, 243
R v Funderburk (1990), CA: 479, 481, 495
R v Galbraith (1981), CA 56, 92, 489
R v Gall (1989), CA 98
R v Gallagher (1974), CA 152
R v Gandfield (1846) 149, 358
R v Garbett (1847), Ex Ch . . . 122, 124, 130
R v Garner (1964) 274
R v Gaunt (1964), CCA 98
R v Gauthier (1943), CCA 23
R v Gaynor (1988) 98
R v Gazard (1838) 467
R v Geering (1849) 259
R v Gerard (1948), CCA 149
R v Gibson (1887), CCR 11, 331, 357
R v Gilbert (1977), CA 150
R v Gill (1963), CCA 17
R v Gill (1993), CA 214, 215

PAGE

R v Gilmore (1977) 390
R v Goldenberg (1988), CA **159**, 214
R v Golder (1960), CCA 479
R v Goode (1970) 92, 94, 95
R v Goodway (1993), CA 110, 479
R v Goss (1923), CCA 93, 95
R v Gould (1840) 179
R v Governor of Gloucester Prison,
   ex p Miller (1979), DC 474
R v Governor of Pentonville Prison,
   ex p Alves (1993), HL 479
R v Governor of Pentonville Prison,
   ex p Fernandez (1971), HL 49
R v Gray (1965) 163, 164
R v Gray (1973), CA 40
R v Gregg (1932), CCA 107
R v Grills (1910) **146**
R v Grills (1954) 259
R v Grout (1909), CCA 292, 298
R v Gunewardene (1951), CCA 486
R v Gunnell (1886), CCR 358
R v Guttridge (1840) 318
R v H (1995), HL 113, **261**
R v Hagan (1873) 358
R v Halford (1978), CA 197, 496
R v Hall (1952), CCA 274
R v Hall (1973), CA **359**
R v Hallett (1989) 216, 218
R v Hally (1962) 335
R v Halpin (1975), CA 340
R v Hamand (1985), CA 216, 218
R v Hammond (1941), CCA **163**
R v Hampshire County Council,
   ex p Ellerton (1985), CA 52
R v Hardy (1794) 10 State Tr 199:   474, 476
R v Hardy (1794) 10 State Tr 1076 . . . 276
R v Harris (1971) 92
R v Harrison-Owen (1951), CCA 274
R v Harry (1987), CA 329
R v Hartley (1941), CCA 113
R v Harvey (1800) 176
R v Harvey (1869) 381
R v Harvey (1988) 161
R v Haslam (1925), CCA 93, 95
R v Hatton (1976) 300
R v Hayden and Slattery (1959) 477
R v Hayes (1977), CA **411**, 413
R v Hennessey (1978), CA 451
R v Hepworth and Fearnley (1955),
   CCA 37, **38**
R v Hewitt (1991), CA 466
R v Heydon (1966) 308
R v Higgins (1829) 166
R v Hill (1851) 487
R v Hilton (1972), CA 473
R v Hinton (1961) 493
R v Hnedish (1958) 164
R v Holmes (1871), CCR 494
R v Holmes (1953), CCA 392

PAGE

R v Holy Trinity, Kingston-upon-Hull,
   Inhabitants (1827) 378
R v Hope (1909) 341
R v Horwood (1970), CA **266**
R v Houghton (1978), CA 209, 212
R v Hovell (1987) 348
R v Howick (1970), CA 98
R v Hudson (1912), CCA **292**, 295,
                                     305, 306
R v Hudson (1980), CA 208, 212
R v Hughes (1988), CA 196, 216
R v Hunt (1820), CCR 377
R v Hunt (1980), CA 499
R v Hunt (1987), HL **28**
R v Hunter (1969), CA 98
R v Ireland (1970), affd (1970) 231
R v Isequilla (1975), CA 209
R v Jackson (1953), CCA 112
R v Jarvis (1756) 19
R v Jarvis (1801) 27
R v Jeffries (1946) 183
R v Jenkins (1869), CCR 342
R v Jenkins (1945), CCA . . . 292, 295, 303,
                                 305, 306, 309
R v Jenkyns (1993) 10
R v Johannsen (1977), CA 113
R v John (1973), CA 98
R v Johnson (1864) **170**
R v Johnson (1961), CCA 17
R v Johnson (1989), CA 466
R v Johnson (1995), CA 219
R v Jones (1809) 285
R v Jones (1909), CCA 295
R v Jones (1923), CCA 292, 295, 306
R v Jones (1939), CCA 107
R v Jones (1969), CA 505
R v Junaid Khan (1987), CA 408
R v Justice of the Peace for Peterborough,
   ex p Hicks (1978) 426
R v Kane (1977), CA 495
R v Kansal (1993), CA 133
R v Keane (1977), CA 99
R v Kearley (1990), CA; revsd (1992),
   HL **324**, 330, 333, 360, 365
R v Keeling (1942), CCA 110, 147
R v Keenan (1989), CA: 163, 213, 214, **215**
R v Kelly (1988) 165
R v Kemble (1990), CA 411, 413
R v Kennaway (1917), CCA: 274, 278, 280,
                                 281, 283, 284,
                                     287, 290
R v Kenny (1992), CA 257
R v Kilner (1976) 209
R v King (1967), CA 110, 267
R v King (1983), CA 426
R v Kinglake (1870) 118
R v Kipali-Ikarum (1967) 342
R v Knight (1966), CCA 107
R v Krausz (1973), CA 294

PAGE

R v Kritz (1950), CCA 38
R v Kurasch (1915), CCA 278
R v Kuruwaru (1900) 342
R v Kwok Si Cheng (1976), CA 475
R v L (1994), CA 158
R v Ladlow, Moss, Green and Jackson
　(1989) 98
R v Lal Khan (1981), CA 405
R v Lawrence (1977) 494
R v Leatham (1861) 222
R v Lee (1950) **182**, 211
R v Lee (1976), CA 291, 297
R v Levy (1966), CCA 496
R v Lewes Justices, ex p Secretary of
　State for the Home Department
　(1972); on appeal sub nom
　Rogers v Secretary of State
　for the Home Department
　(1973), HL.... **451**, 457, 460, 461, 463
R v Lillyman (1896), CCR ... 490, 491, 493
R v Littleboy (1934), CCA 150
R v Liverpool Juvenile Court, ex p R
　(1988) 155, 165
R v Lobell (1957), CCA........ 17, 22, 23
R v Lockhart (1785) 176
R v Long (1973), CA............. 88
R v Lord George Gordon (1781) 318
R v Lord Stafford (1680) 486
R v Loughlin (1951), CCA 397
R v Loughlin (1982) 241
R v Lovegrove (1920), CCA 274
R v Lovett (1973), CA 310
R v Lucas (1981), CA 107, 110
R v Luffe (1807) 503
R v Lunnon (1988), CA 243, 400
R v Lupien (1970) 390
R v Lydon (1987), CA........... 321
R v McCay (1991), CA 197, 337, 357
R v McEvilly (1973), CA 236, 240
R v McFelin (1985) 10
R v McGuire (1975) 337
R v McGuire (1985), CA 340
R v McInnes (1989), CA 104
R v McKay (1967) 10
R v McKenna (1956) 112
R v MacKenney (1980) 390
R v McKenzie (Practice Note) (1992),
　CA 104
R v Mackintosh (1982), CA 212
R v McLean (1926), CCA 295, 304
R v McLean (1967), CA 320, 337
R v McLeod (1994), CA 303
R v McLernon (1990) 141
R v McNaughton (1843), HL 28
R v Madobi (1963) 341
R v Makanjuola (1995), CA 80
R v Male and Cooper (1893) 181
R v Manley (1962), CCA 295, 308
R v Maqsud Ali (1966), CCA 10, 337

PAGE

R v Marsh (1949), CCA 113
R v Martin (1967) 74
R v Martin (1988), CA 366
R v Martinez-Tobon (1994) 140, 407
R v Mason (1911), CCA 392
R v Mason (1987), CA..... 155, 162, 208,
　　　　　　　　　　214, **215**, 243
R v Mattey (1995), CA 348
R v Matthews (1989), CA 196
R v Matthews and Ford (1972).... 220, 378
R v Mayhew (1834) 100
R v Maynard (1979), CA 99
R v Mazzone (1985) 165
R v Mead (1824) 342
R v Mealey (1974), CA 236, 240
R v Meehan and Meehan (1978), CA: 302
R v Melany (1924), CCA 95
R v Merceron (1818) 130
R v Middleton (1975), CA 208
R v Miles (1943) 258
R v Miller (1952) 275, 278, 311
R v Miller (1986), CA **159**
R v Milliken (1969), CA 496
R v Mills (1978), CA 494
R v Minihane (1921), CCA 117
R v Minors (1989), CA 348, 349
R v Mir, Ahmed and Dalil (1989), CA: 301
R v Mitchell (1892) 148, 342
R v Mitchell (1952), CCA 112, 113
R v Morgan (1875) 342
R v Morin (1988) 41
R v Morris (1959), CCA 295
R v Morris (1969), CA 265
R v Morrison (1911), CCA...... 295, 303
R v Mortimer (1936), CCA 274
R v Mosey (1784) 176
R v Mosley (1825), CCR 342
R v Murphy (1965) 233, 237, 240
R v Murphy (1980), CA 390
R v Mutchke (1946) 321
R v Naidanovici (1962) 476
R v Naylor (1932), CCA 112
R v Neal (1947) 478
R v Neale (1977), CA 275
R v Nelson (1992), CA 405
R v Neshet (1990), CA 348
R v Ngahooro (1982) 337
R v Nichols (1967), CA 197
R v Nightingale (1977) 275
R v Nowaz (alias Karim) (1976), CA: 376
R v Nye (1977), CA 356
R v Oakley (1979), CA 390
R v O'Brien (1977) 339
R v O'Callaghan (1976) 390
R v O'Connor (1980), CA 100
R v O'Connor (1986), CA 243
R v Olbey (1971) 92
R v O'Leary (1988), CA..... 216, 240, 243
R v Oliva (1965), CCA 479

PAGE

R v Oliver (1944), CCA 27, 31
R v O'Loughlin and McLaughlin
   (1988) 218, 348, 366
R v O'Meally (No 2) (1953) 274
R v O'Neill (1950), CCA 165
R v Onufrejczyk (1955), CCA **38**
R v Orgles (1993), CA 467
R v Osborne (1905) 492, 493
R v Osbourne (or Osborne) (1973),
   CA 197, 337
R v O'Shannessy (1973) 240
R v Oxford City Justices, ex p Berry
   (1988) 155
R v Oyesiku (1971), CA 477, 479
R v Palmer (1983), CA 289
R v Paris (1992), CA 158, 165
R v Parker (1933), CCA 150
R v Parris (1988), CA 214, 216, 218
R v Patel (1981), CA 335
R v Patel (1992), CA 347
R v Patents Appeal Tribunal, ex p
   Baldwin and Francis Ltd (1959),
   CA; affd sub nom Baldwin and
   Francis Ltd v Patents Appeal
   Tribunal (1959), HL 388
R v Paul (1920), CCA 407
R v Payne (1872), CCA 406
R v Payne (1963), CCA: **224**, 235, 238, 239
R v Pearce (1979), CA 166
R v Pedrini (1964), CCA 488
R v Penny (1991), CA 40
R v Perera (1982) 107
R v Perkins (1840), CCR 341
R v Perry (1909), CCA 342
R v Petcherini (1855) 358
R v Pethig (1977) 240
R v Pettigrew (1980), CA 349
R v Phillips (1949) 209
R v Pieterson (1995), CA 10
R v Pike (1829) 341
R v Pike (1902), CCR 133
R v Pilcher (1974), CA 496
R v Pipe (1966), CA 406
R v Pitt (1982), CA 117, 405
R v Podola (1960), CCA 18
R v Pook (1871) 358
R v Powell (1986), CA 278, 304, 308
R v Power (1919), CCA 489
R v Power (1940) 148
R v Prager (1972), CA 158
R v Prefas (1986), CA 478
R v Preston (1909), CCA 295
R v Preston (1961) 92
R v Price (1969), CA 101
R v Prince (1990), CA 303
R v Putland and Sorrell (1946), CCA: . 31
R v Queeley (1995), CA 348
R v Quinn (1962), CCA 9
R v Quinn (1990), CA 98

PAGE

R v Quinn (1995), CA 98
R v Rampling (1987), CA 196
R v Rankine (1986), CA 466
R v Rappolt (1911), CCA 295, 306
R v Ratcliffe (1919), CCA 289
R v Rearden (1864) 274
R v Redd (1923), CCA 276, 291, 298
R v Redpath (1962), CCA 107
R v Reid (1994), CA 98
R v Reynolds (1950), CCA 8, 405
R v Rice (1963), CCA 319, 321
R v Richards (1965) 107
R v Richardson (1969), CA **482**
R v Richardson (1971), CA 475
R v Rider (1986), CA 100
R v Riley (1887), CCR 257, 494
R v Robb (1991), CA 386
R v Roberts (1936), CCA 289
R v Robertson (1968), CA 18
R v Robertson (1987), CA 400
R v Robinson (1994), CA 405
R v Rodley (1913), CCA 253
R v Rogan (1916) 258
R v Rogers (1950) 342
R v Rogers (1995), CA 315, 339
R v Rolfe (1952), CCA 107
R v Romeo (1982) 321
R v Rouse (1904), CCR 292, 294, 306
R v Rowson (1986), CA: 168, 310, 311, 407
R v Rowton (1865), CCR: 276, 285, 293, 296,
   297, 484, 486
R v Rudd (1948), CCA 405
R v Russell (1968), CA 101
R v Russell (1977), CA 93, 97
R v Ryan (1964), CCA 150
R v Ryder (1994), CA 264
R v Salahattin (1983) 147
R v Samuel (1956), CCA 291, 303
R v Samuel (1988), CA 196, 214, 215,
   216, 217, 243
R v Sang (1980), HL 37, 175, 208,
   212, **235**, 241
R v Sat-Bhambra (1988), CA: 155, 161, 162,
   166, 214
R v Savage (1970) 342
R v Scaife (1836) 342
R v Scott (1856), CCR 124, **130**
R v Scott (1921) 27
R v Sealby (1965) 320
R v Secretary of State for the Home
   Department, ex p Sivakumaran
   (1988), HL **49**
R v Seelig (1991), CA 133, 197
R v Seifert (1956) 320
R v Seiga (1961), CCA 93, 95
R v Sekhon (1986), CA 475, 477
R v Selvey. See Selvey v DPP
R v Setz-Dempsey and Richardson
   (1994), CA 347

PAGE

R v Seymour (1954), CCA 150, 397
R v Sharp (1988), HL 166, 315, 477
R v Sheean (1908) 292
R v Shellaker (1914), CCA 270
R v Shephard (1993), HL 348
R v Shone (1982), CA 335
R v Shrimpton (1851), CCR 276, 304
R v Sim (1987) 165
R v Simpson (1993), CA 264
R v Sims (1946), CCA 256, 267, 268
R v Slaney (1832) 118
R v Sloggett (1856), CCR 123
R v Smith (1845) 282
R v Smith (1915), CCA 255, 258, 259
R v Smith (1935), CCA 112
R v Smith (1968), CA 489
R v Smith (Percy) (1976), CA 337
R v Smith (1979), CA 390
R v Smith (1985), CA 112
R v Smith and Evans (1908), CCA . . . 98
R v Smurthwaite (1993), CA 214, 215
R v Smyth (1963) 17
R v Sparrow (1973), CA 166
R v Spencer (1987), HL 80, 101
R v Spiby (1990), CA 349
R v Spurge (1961), CCA 17, 18, 27
R v Squire (1990) 166
R v Staines (1974), CA 152
R v Stamford (1972), CA 390
R v Stannard (1965), CCA 300, 309
R v Stevenson (1971) 378
R v Stewart (1972) 209
R v Stone (1801) 27
R v Storey (1968), CA 477
R v Straffen (1952), CCA 259, **270**, 272,
                                      274, 281
R v Stronach (1988), CA 291, 292
R v Sullivan (1887) 103
R v Summers (1952), CCA 37, 38
R v Swensden (or Swanson) (1702) . . . 483
R v Sykes (1913), CCA 103
R v Tanner (1977), CA 295
R v Tate (1908), CCA 110
R v Taylor (1961) 354
R v Therens (1985) 230
R v Thompson (1893), CCR 223
R v Thompson (1966), CCA 291, 304
R v Thompson (1976), CA 477, 478
R v Thompson (1982), CA 359
R v Thomson (1912), CCA 358
R v Thorne (1981), CA 99
R v Threlfall (1914), CCA 100
R v Thynne (1977) 478
R v Tidd (1820) **105**
R v Tilley (1961), CCA 380
R v Tillott (1995) 10
R v Tomkins (1977), CA 436
R v Toner (1966) 164
R v Tragen (1956) 107

PAGE

R v Trigg (1963), CCA 107
R v Trim (1943) 17
R v Tripodi (1961); affd sub nom
  Tripodi v R (1961) 110
R v Trump (1979), CA 209
R v Tune (1944), CCA 150
R v Turnbull (1977), CA 79, **87**, 99
R v Turner (1816) 18, **26**, 27
R v Turner (1944), CCA 292, 294, 307
R v Turner [1975] QB 834, CA: 274, 275,
                                      386, 390
R v Turner (1975) 61 Cr App Rep 67,
  CA 315, 339, 406
R v Twaites (1990), CA 197
R v Twiss (1918), CCA 274
R v Tyrer (1989), CA 161
R v Uljee (1982) 436
R v Umoh (1986), CA 426
R v Unkles (1874) 103
R v Unsworth (1986) 291
R v Van Beelen (1972) 41
R v Varley (1982), CA **299**
R v Verelst (1813) 74
R v Vernon (1988) 196
R v Vickers (1972) 303, 304
R v Vincent, Frost and Edwards (1840):   358
R v Virgo (1978), CA 107, 474
R v Voisin (1918), CCA 168, 178, 208
R v Vye (1993), CA 275, 303
R v W (1994), CA 264
R v Wainwright (1875) 75, 358
R v Wainwright (1925), CCA 95
R v Waldman (1934), CCA 302
R v Wallwork (1958), CCA 410, 494
R v Walsh (1922) 94, 95
R v Walsh (1989), CA 213, 214
R v Warickshall (1783) **169, 176**
R v Waters (1989), CA 175
R v Watson (1817) 486
R v Watson (1913), CCA 237, 305
R v Watson (1980), CA 162
R v Wattam (1952), CCA 291
R v Watts (1983), CA 308
R v Weaver (1968), CA 165, 289
R v Weeder (1980), CA 92
R v Weighill (1945) 164
R v Weightman (1978) 406
R v Welsh (1983) 41
R v Westfall (1912), CCA 297
R v Weston-super-Mare Justices, ex p
  Townsend (1968), DC 307
R v Westwell (1976), CA 475
R v Wheater (1838), CCR 128
R v Wheeler (1967), CA 17
R v White (1786) 413
R v White (1865) 39
R v White (1964), CCA 197
R v Whitehead (1928), CCA 110, 147
R v Wickham (1971), CA 407

PAGE

R v Williams (1977), CA 196
R v Willis (1960), CCA 318
R v Willoughby (1988), CA 104
R v Willshire (1881), CCR 77
R v Wilmot (1988), CA 152
R v Winfield (1939), CCA 276, 278,
                               298, 304
R v Wink (1834) 494
R v Winsor (1865) 42
R v Wong Ah Wong (1957) 320
R v Wood (1877) 492
R v Wood (1911), CCA 150
R v Wood (1982) 337, 349
R v Woodcock (1789) **341**
R v Wray (1970) 209
R v Wright (1969) 164
R v Wright (1980) 390
R v Wright (1987), CA 410
R v Wylie (1804) 274
R v X, Y and Z (1989), CA 411, 412
R v Yacoob (1981), CA 19, 41, 405
R v Yap Chuan Ching (1976), CA ... 38
R v Z (1990), CA **409**
R v Zangoullas (1962), CCA 301
R (BM) v R (DN) (1978), CA 336
RI v Innis (1980) 205
Ramkishan Mithanlal Sharma v
   Bombay (1955) 179
Ramsay v Watson (1961) 391
Rank Film Distributors Ltd v Video
   Information Centre (a firm)
   (1982), HL 122
Raphael, Re, Raphael v D'Antin (1973): 396
Ratford v Northavon District Council
   (1987), CA 36
Ratten v R (1972), PC 324, 326, 329,
                          333, 351, **352**
Rattray v Rattray (1897) 223
Read v Bishop of Lincoln (1892) 504
Reid v Howard (1995), HC of A 122
Rejfek v McElroy (1965) 54
Rendell v Paul (1979) 507
Reynolds, Re, ex p Reynolds (1882),
   CA **119**
Reynolds v Llanelly Associated Tinplate
   Co Ltd (1948), CA 499, 501, 502
Rhesa Shipping Co SA v Edmunds,
   The Popi M (1985), HL 15, 40
Rice v Howard (1886), DC 477
Richardson v Schultz (1980) 389, 390
Riddick v Thames Board Mills Ltd
   (1977), CA 466
Rio Tinto Zinc Corpn v Westinghouse
   Electric Corpn. See Westinghouse
   Electric Corpn Uranium Contract
   Litigation MDL Docket No 235,
   Re (Nos 1 and 2)
Ritz Hotel Ltd v Charles of the Ritz Ltd
   (1988) 11, 319, 333

PAGE

Roberts v Allatt (1828) 121
Roberts v Humphreys (1873) 19
Robinson v South Australia State
   (No 2) (1931), PC: 444, 445, 447, 450
Rochfort v Trade Practices Comrs
   (1982) 135
Rochin v California (1952) 244
Rodgers v Rodgers (1964) 437
Rogers v Secretary of State for the
   Home Department. See R v Lewes
   Justices, ex p Secretary of State for
   the Home Department
Roper v Taylors Central Garages
   (Exeter) Ltd. See Taylors Central
   Garages (Exeter) Ltd v Roper
Rosher, Re, Rosher v Rosher (1884) ... 504
Rouch v Great Western Rly Co
   (1841) 357
Rowley v London and North Western
   Rly Co (1873) 389
Rumping v DPP (1964), HL 432
Rush & Tompkins Ltd v Greater
   London Council (1989), HL 437
Russell v A-G (1949) 68
Russell v Russell and Mayer (1924),
   HL 68

                 S

S v Becker (1968) 335
S v Letsoko (1964) 257
S v S (1972), HL 67
Salsbury v Woodland (1970), CA 6
Sankey v Whitlam (1978) 449, 450
Saul v Menon (1980) 507
Saull v Browne (1874) 431
Savings and Investment Bank Ltd v
   Gasco Investments (Netherlands)
   BV (1984) 366, 396
Scappaticci v A-G (1955) 357
Schneider v Leigh (1955), CA 426
Schwartz v Texas (1952) 245
Science Research Council v Nassé
   (1980), HL 451, 453, 466
Scott v Baker (1969) 76
Scott v London and St Katherine
   Docks Co (1865), Ex Ch 69
Scott v Numurkah Corpn (1954), HC
   of A 6
Scott v R (1989), PC 7, 348
Scott v Sampson (1882), DC 483
Scruples Imports Pty Ltd v Crabtree
   and Evelyn Pty Ltd (1983) 387
Seabrook v British Transport
   Commission (1959) 422
Secretary of State for Defence v Guardian
   Newspapers Ltd (1984), HL 438
Seeley (FF) Nominees Pty Ltd v El Ar
   Initiations (UK) Ltd (1990) 134
Sellen v Norman (1829) 76

PAGE

Selvey v DPP (1970), HL. . . . 237, 278, **292**,
    297, 298, 303,
    304, **305**, 308
Senat v Senat (1965) 474
Senior v Holdsworth, ex p Independent
    Television News Ltd (1975), CA: 378
Seyfang v G D Searle & Co (1973) . . . 391
Seymour v A-G for Commonwealth
    (1984) **211**
Shanahan, Re (1912) 123
Shaw v R (1952) 495
Shaw Savill and Albion Co Ltd v
    Commonwealth (1940) 503
Shearson Lehman Bros Inc v Maclaine
    Watson & Co Ltd (International
    Tin Council intervening) (No 2)
    (1988), HL 456
Shepherd v R (1990) 41
Sherrard v Jacob (1965) 385
Sherring (J H) & Co v Hinton (1932): 121
Silverman v United States (1961) 244
Silverthorne Lumber Co v United
    States (1920) 243
Simpson v Collinson (1964), CA 107
Sinclair v R (1947) **209**
Skandia Insurance Co Ltd v Skoljarer
    (1979) 34
Skinner & Co v Shew & Co (1894) 357
Slatterie v Pooley (1840) 376
Smith v Commonwealth Life Assurance
    Society Ltd (1935) 492
Sneddon v Stevenson (1967), DC . . . 237
Sociedade Nacional de Combustiveis
    de Angola UEE v Lundqvist
    (1991), CA 117, 119
Société Française Hoechst v Allied
    Colloids Ltd (1992) 426
Sodeman v R (1936), PC 18, **40, 42,** 54
Solosky v R (1979) 428
Sorby v Commonwealth of Australia
    (1983) 133, 134, 135
Spano v New York (1959) 171
Sparks v R (1964), PC: 315, 317, 490, 494
Spicer v Holt (1976), HL 232
Spieres v Parker (1786) 29
Standard Chartered Bank of Australia
    Ltd v Antico (1993) 427
Stark and Smith v HM Advocate (1938): 206
State v Di Vincenti (1957) 333
State v Graham (1959) 504
Statue of Liberty, The, Sapporo Maru
    M/S (Owners) v Steam Tanker
    Statue of Liberty (Owners)
    (1968) 10, 337, 349
Stauffner v Hanley (1978) 502
Stein v New York (1953) 198
Stirland v DPP (1944), HL: 278, 280, 283,
    284, 286, 302,
    304, 305

PAGE

Stobart v Dryden (1836) 323
Stone v Powell (1976) 245
Storey v Storey (1961), CA 471
Stupple v Royal Insurance Co Ltd
    (1971), CA **396**
Subramaniam v Public Prosecutor
    (1956), PC **317**
Sugden v Lord St Leonards (1876),
    CA 341
Sutton v R (1984) 259
Sutton v Sadler (1857) 60
Sutton v Sutton (1969) 395, 399
Swan v Salisbury Construction Co Ltd
    (1966), PC 70
Sweeny v Erving (1931) 70

T

Tate Access Floors Inc v Boswell (1990): 117
Taylor v Chief Constable of Cheshire
    (1986) 10, 337
Taylor v Ellis (1956) 19
Taylor v Taylor (Taylor intervening,
    Holmes cited) (1970), CA: 366, 367, 399
Taylor's Central Garages (Exeter) Ltd
    v Roper (1951) 499
Temple v Terrace Transfer Ltd (1966): 70
Teper v R (1952), PC **331**, 337, 351,
    353, 354, 357
Thain, Re, Thain v Taylor (1926), CA: 464
Thatcher v Charles (1961) 148
Theodoropoulas v Theodoropoulas
    (1964) 437, 460
Thomas v Connell (1838) 358
Thomas v Jones (1921), CA 107, 108,
    111, 147
Thomas v R (1960) **33, 39**
Thomas v R (1972) 41
Thomas v Thomas (1855) 26
Thompson v Manhattan Railway
    (1896) 332, 333
Thompson v R (1918), HL. . . 104, 258, **265**,
    267, 271,
    272, 274
Thompson v R (1968) 264
Thompson v Thompson (1956) 66
Thompson v Trevanion (1693) 353
Thorpe v Chief Constable of Greater
    Manchester Police (1989), CA . . . 253
Tickle v Tickle (1968) 359
Tomlin v Standard Telephones and
    Cables Ltd (1969), CA 437
Toohey v Metropolitan Police Comr
    (1965), HL. 390, **485**
Tracy Peerage Claim (1843), HL 384
Trade Practices Commission v Abbco
    Ice Works Pty Ltd (1994) 135
Transport Publishing Co Pty Ltd v
    Literature Board of Review (1956): 391
Trimbuk v Madhya Pradesh (1954) . . . 177

PAGE

Triplex Safety Glass Co Ltd v
Lancegaye Safety Glass
(1934) Ltd (1939), CA . . . 121, 122, 135
Truman (Frank) Export Ltd v Metro-
politan Police Comr (1977) 426
Tuckiar v R (1934) 425
Tunstall, Re, ex p Brown (1966) 450

U

Udai Bhan v Uttar Pradesh (1962) . . . 179
Ullmann v United States (1955) . . . 124, 126
Union Carbide Corpn v Naturin Ltd
(1987), CA 396
United States v Ash (1973) 95
United States v Feinberg (1944) 56
United States v Lopez (1971) 504
United States v Prout (1976) 56
United States v Reynolds (1952) 445
United States v Taylor (1972) 56
United States v White (1963) 483
United States v White (1971) 245

V

Van Beelen, Re (1974) 339
Van den Hoek v R (1986) 17
Varcoe v Lee (1919) 503
Vasquez v R (1994), PC 33
Vaughton v London and North
Western Rly Co (1874) 53
Vel v Chief Constable of North Wales
(or Owen) (1987) 214, 215
Ventouris v Mountain (No 2), The
Italia Express (1992), CA 346
Vetrovec v R (1982) **105**
Vocisano v Vocisano (1974) 356

W

Wakeley v R (1990) 473
Walder v United States (1954) 204, 244
Walker v Viney (1965) 168
Walker v Walker (1937) 376
Walters, Re (1987) 155
Walton v R (1989) 331, 333, 334, 358
Watkinson, Re (1952) 66
Watson v Cammell Laird & Co
(Shipbuilders and Engineers)
Ltd (1959), CA 429
Watson v Davidson (1966) 70
Watts v Indiana (1949) **202**
Waugh v British Railways Board
(1980), HL **421**, 436
Waugh v R (1950), PC 151, 342
Weal v Bottom (1966) 393
Webster v James Chapman & Co
(a firm) (1989) 436
Weeks v US (1914) 225, 243
Weld-Blundell v Stephens (1919), CA;
affd (1920), HL 421, 431, 433

PAGE

Wendo v R (1963) 165, 231
Wentworth v Lloyd (1864),
HL 118, 152, 425
Wentworth v Rogers (1984) 56
Wentworth v Rogers (No 10) (1987): 477
Westinghouse Electric Corpn Uranium
Contract Litigation MDL Docket
No 235, Re (1978), CA; revsd
sub nom Rio Tinto Zinc Corpn v
Westinghouse Electric Corpn
(1978), HL 117, 118, 122, 135
Westinghouse Electric Corpn Uranium
Contract Litigation MDL Docket
No 235 (No 2), Re (1978), CA;
revsd sub nom Rio Tinto Zinc
Corpn v Westinghouse Electric
Corpn (1978), HL 118, 121, 135
Wetherall v Harrison (1976), DC **500**
Wharam v Routledge (1805) 376
Wheeler v Le Marchant (1881), CA: **418**, 463
White v Bywater (1887), DC 389
Whitehouse v Jordan (1981), HL 385
Whitelocke v Musgrove (1833) 323
Wiedemann v Walpole (1891), CA . . . **111**
Wildman v R (1984) 315, 339
Williams v Home Office (1981) 451
Williams v Quebrada Railway, Land
and Copper Co (1895) 420
Willis v Bernard (1832) 358
Wilson v Buttery (1926) 56
Wilson v Kuhl (1979) 56
Witham v Holloway (1995) 41
Wolf v Colorado (1949) 244, 250
Wong Kam-Ming v R (1980), PC . . . 164
Wong Sun v US (1963) 198, 243
Woodhouse v Hall (1980), DC 318
Woods v Duncan (1946), HL 70
Woolmington v DPP (1935), HL . . . 16, **21**,
22, 23
Woon v R (1964) 149
Worley v Bentley (1976) 475
Worrall, Re, ex p Cossens (1820): 123, 124
Wright v Doe d Tatham (1837), Ex Ch;
affd (1838), HL **322**, 326, 329, 332

Y

Young v HM Advocate (1932) 407
Young v Masci (1932) 76
Young v Rank (1950) 471
Yuill v Corporate Affairs Commission
of New South Wales (1990) 429, 436

Z

Zanetti v Hill (1962), HC of A 56
Zephyr, The. See General Accident
Fire and Life Assurance Corpn
Ltd v Tanter, The Zephyr

PART ONE

Introduction

CHAPTER 1

Introduction

1 The nature of the subject

The Anglo-American law of evidence began to assume a modern form two centuries ago, though some of its rules are much older. Most of its principles reveal it as a child of our traditional system of adversary trial before a lay jury as opposed to inquisitorial trial by professional judges. These principles have survived into an age in which juries scarcely sit outside serious criminal cases.

The rules of evidence state what matters may be considered in proving facts and, to some extent, what weight they have. They are largely ununified and scattered, existing for disparate and sometimes conflicting reasons: they are a mixture of astonishing judicial achievements and sterile, inconvenient disasters. There is a law of contract, and perhaps to some extent a law of tort, but only a group of laws of evidence. Yet there is a concealed integration in the subject, and a change to one rule of evidence can have unforeseen consequences on the useful operation of others.

A large part of the subject consists of rules excluding relevant and often weighty information – rules based on 'calculated and supposedly helpful obstructionism' (Maguire, p 11). A small part of it consists of rules giving greater relevance and weight to facts than an initial reaction would always suggest. Now in ordinary life the only limitations on the matters taken into account in proving facts are those imposed by logic and common experience. Why does law differ in this respect from ordinary life? This question can be partly answered by surveying the character and main rules of the subject.

Much evidence is excluded because there is a risk of its being untrue or of unreliable inferences being drawn: hearsay evidence, confessions, the silence or misconduct of a party. Some evidence is excluded by reason of particular witnesses having a privilege not to speak in certain matters. Thus a lawyer's client is privileged not to reveal communications between himself and the lawyer, and the lawyer cannot reveal them without the client's consent; in this way full disclosure in the seeking of legal advice will be encouraged. A witness need not give answers which may incriminate him because there is a risk he will lie and will be induced not to testify at all. Certain statements made in the course of negotiation to settle disputes without prejudice are excluded to encourage recourse to frank negotiation rather than litigation.

Some evidence is excluded because it would be injurious to the public interest. The burden of proof rules state who must begin adducing evidence and

3

how much is necessary to prove certain points. Some facts are so notorious as not to require proof; the judge will take 'judicial notice' of them. Special rules govern the right and duty of different classes of person to testify. There are rules governing the course of the trial – the order in which evidence is admitted. The prior good or bad conduct and character of a party raises special problems of relevance and weight. Confessions and improperly obtained evidence are excluded partly to encourage a high standard of police behaviour.

Morgan: Introduction to the American Law Institute Model Code of Evidence (1942), pp 3–4

Thoughtful lawyers realise that a lawsuit is not, and cannot be made, a scientific investigation for the discovery of truth. The matter to be investigated is determined by the parties. They may eliminate many elements which a scientist would insist upon considering. The court has no machinery for discovering sources of information unknown to the parties or undisclosed by them. It must rely in the main upon data furnished by interested persons. The material event or condition may have been observed by only a few. The capacities and stimuli of each of these few for accurately observing and remembering will vary. The ability and desire to narrate truly may be slight or great. The trier of fact can get no more than the adversaries are able and willing to present. The rules governing the acceptable content of the data and the methods and forms of presenting them must be almost instantly applied in the heat and hurry of the trial. Prompt decision on the merits is imperative, for justice delayed is often justice denied. Sometimes a wrong decision quickly made is better than a right decision after undue procrastination. 'Some concession must be made to the shortness of human life.' The trier must assume that the data presented are complete, and the litigants must be satisfied with a determination of the preponderance of probability. If the data leave the mind of the trier in equilibrium, the decision must be against the party having the burden of persuasion. No scientist would think of basing a conclusion upon such data so presented. The court is not a scientific body. It is composed of one or more persons skilled in the law, skilled in the general art of investigation, but not necessarily skilled in the field which the dispute concerns, acting either alone or with a body of men not necessarily trained in investigation of any kind. Its final determination is binding only between the parties and their privies. It does not pronounce upon the facts for any purpose other than the adjustment of the controversy before it. Consequently there must be a recognition at the outset that nicely accurate results cannot be expected; that society and the litigants must be content with a rather rough approximation of what a scientist might demand. And it must never be forgotten that in the settlement of disputes in a court room, as in all other experiences of individuals in our society, the emotions of the persons involved – litigants, counsel, witnesses, judge and jurors – will play a part. A trial cannot be purely intellectual performance.

All this is not to say that the rules for conducting the investigation of the facts cannot be, or need not be, rational. Quite the contrary. In such a setting it is especially important that artificial barriers to logically persuasive data be removed. With such a tribunal acting in such circumstances the exercise of superlative psychological powers is not to be expected. Rules calling for nice intellectual discriminations and unusual intellectual and emotional controls are impossible of application. Speaking generally, the tribunal should hear and consider those data which reasonable men confronted with the necessity of acting in a matter of like importance in their everyday life would use in making up their minds what to do.

In England there are today comparatively very few points of evidence raised in civil cases; so the law of evidence has become to a large extent the law of criminal evidence. Its development tends to be skewed by the following considerations: (1) most serious cases are tried with a jury; (2) there is no appeal by the Crown from a jury acquittal, although there may be an Attorney-General's Reference on a point of law; (3) very few points of evidence have been the subject of Attorney-General's References; (4) few cases are the subject of appeals to the House of Lords. Thus (5) on the whole the law of evidence is developed by the Court of Appeal on appeals by those who claim to have been convicted wrongly: there is little or no parallel consideration of possible wrong acquittals. The result is that the rules tend to become slanted more and more to the protection of the accused, until such time as it is apparent that this process has gone too far, when, sometimes after enquiry by the Law Commission or a Royal Commission, the law is given what may be regarded as a push in the opposite direction. In recent years that reform has often taken the form of the replacement of a rule by a discretion: a clear example of the development and the reform is given by the history of the corroboration rules: see Chapter 5 of this and previous editions of this work, and Law Com No 202 (1991). There is perhaps a need for a body able to oversee the evolution of the law of evidence, able to guide it along the right lines rather than merely react to what has happened.

2 Terminology

A FACTS IN ISSUE AND COLLATERAL FACTS

The law of evidence governs the proof of 'facts in issue'. These are all the facts which the plaintiff or prosecutor and the defendant must prove to succeed. What they are in a given case is determined partly by whatever substantive rules of law apply and partly by reference to the charge and plea in criminal cases or the pleadings in civil cases. The substantive law and the pleadings in effect create a model or blueprint. The legal advisers of the parties seek to reconstruct, in conformity with that model, transactions or conditions that may once have happened or existed in the moving, buzzing confusion of the factual world. Facts in issue are distinguishable from 'subordinate' or 'collateral' facts. These are facts which affect the proof of facts in issue, either because they affect the credibility of a witness testifying to a fact in issue (eg proving his bias, bad eyesight or bad character) or because they affect the admissibility of an item of evidence tending to prove a fact in issue (eg police misconduct affecting the voluntariness of a confession).

B DIRECT TESTIMONY, HEARSAY, DOCUMENTS, REAL EVIDENCE AND CIRCUMSTANTIAL EVIDENCE

'Direct testimony' is the assertion of a witness about a fact of which he has direct knowledge offered as evidence of the truth of that which is asserted. 'Hearsay' or 'indirect testimony' is the assertion of a person, other than the witness who is testifying, offered as evidence of the truth of that which is asserted, rather than as evidence of the fact that the assertion was made (the latter being called 'original' evidence). There is a general rule against the admissibility of hearsay evidence which is now riddled with many common law and statutory exceptions (see ch 12, post). The contents of a document are admissible provided the original is produced; 'secondary evidence' by means of copies is admitted in many cases by way of exception (eg where the document is public, or lost, or impossible to produce; or where an opponent has failed to produce it after a notice to do so). 'Real evidence' is admitted when a court draws an inference from its own observation of some material object rather than relying on that of witnesses, eg the physical condition of a document or other physical object, the appearance of handwriting, photographs or films, the intonation of the voices on a tape recording, the appearance and demeanour of persons. Usually the admission of real evidence must be accompanied by the testimony of a witness to identify or explain it. In general neither views of the scene nor reconstructions of past events should be held without the consent and in the presence of the parties; but opinions differ on whether they are real evidence or merely an aid to the understanding of the evidence (cf *Salsbury v Woodland* [1970] 1 QB 324, [1969] 3 All ER 863, CA, with *Scott v Numurkah Corpn* (1954) 91 CLR 300, and see Solomon (1960) 34 ALJ 46). The latter case was relied on by analogy in *Kozul v R* (1981) 147 CLR 221, where it was held that juries are permitted to take exhibits into the jury room and conduct simple experiments but are not permitted to conduct experiments going beyond mere examination and evaluation in such a way as to lead to the creation of new evidentiary material. On the other hand, a film of an accused person re-enacting his crime may be received as a confession: *Li Shu-ling v R* [1989] AC 270, [1988] 3 All ER 138, PC. 'Circumstantial evidence' is any fact ('fact relevant to the issue') from which the existence of a fact in issue may be inferred. An item of circumstantial evidence may be proved by any other evidence, including circumstantial evidence. Circumstantial evidence is sometimes contrasted with other ('direct') evidence in that facts in issue are indirectly inferred rather than directly perceived. The inferences drawn from circumstantial evidence are often stated in presumptive form (see ch 4, post).

It should be noticed that the above forms of evidence need not always be relied on, for facts which are formally admitted or of which judicial notice is taken need not be proved. Formal admissions may be made in civil cases by a party (either in response to a notice to admit under RSC Ord 27, r 2, or otherwise) to save his opponent the trouble of proving them and to avoid the risk of having to pay his opponent's costs of so doing. Unlike informal admissions, admitted under an exception to the hearsay rule (see ch 14, post), they cannot be contradicted, they are only binding for purposes of the instant proceedings, they may be withdrawn or amended by leave, and they are made as part of the proceedings, not before them. Formal admissions may be made before the trial, but are commonly made during it if events so require. Formal admissions were permitted in criminal cases as well as civil by the Criminal Justice Act 1967, s 10. There is a dispute as to whether evidence in proof or disproof of a fact formally admitted is admissible.

C   RELEVANCE, ADMISSIBILITY, WEIGHT, DISCRETION

All evidence relevant to prove or disprove a fact in issue is admissible unless one of the exclusionary rules which make up so much of the law of evidence applies. What is admissible depends on rules of law which are supposed to be based on special considerations such as avoiding jury bias, deterring police misconduct, protecting state security and so forth. What is relevant is largely a matter of common experience (but see Eggleston in Glass, pp 53–89; Eggleston; L Jonathan Cohen, *The Probable and the Provable*; Glanville Williams [1979] Crim LR 297 and 340; and Cohen [1980] Crim LR 91). However, some presumptions based on circumstantial evidence are reminders of what is relevant, and some rules are reminders of what may not be relevant (eg proof of bad past conduct different from that with which the accused is charged). Prior decisions on relevance may sometimes be strongly persuasive from the viewpoint of later courts. Matters which are marginally relevant may be excluded because it would take too long to investigate them, or because they would distract the jury from the main issues, or because they raise the risk of further evidence on new issues being called, leading to decisions which may be unfair to parties not before the court. The difficulties of relevance usually arise acutely in the areas of similar fact and res gestae evidence (see chs 10 and 13, post).

It should be noted that evidence may be admissible for one purpose but not for another: a hearsay statement is admissible if the issue is whether it was made, but not if the issue is whether it is true. This rule of 'multiple admissibility' (Wigmore, para 13) may be dangerous, particularly in jury cases, but prevents too great a tension between paternalism and practical utility in the conduct of trials. A further notion is 'conditional admissibility'. Because evidence comes out by degrees at a trial, the relevance of some evidence may be conditional on later evidence which may or may not be given. If the earlier evidence is admitted, it is said to have been admitted conditionally or 'de bene esse'.

Like relevance, weight is a notion dependent on an appeal to common experience: our law has 'no orders for the reasoning faculty' (Thayer (1900) 14 Harv LR 139, p 141). Unlike admissibility, it is a question of fact for the jury.

Recently it has been recognised in a number of areas that the judge has a discretion at common law (hitherto little noticed outside criminal cases) to exclude relevant evidence if its probative force would be exceeded by its prejudicial effect. This applies to similar fact evidence (ch 10, post), evidence of the accused's bad record put to him in cross-examination (ch 11, post), statements made in the presence of the accused to which he gives no answer (ch 7, post) and illegally or improperly obtained evidence (ch 9, post; see generally Weinberg (1975) 21 McGill LJ 1). Probably the discretion is now quite general: *Scott v R* [1989] AC 1242, [1989] 2 All ER 305, PC. The court also has a statutory discretion in criminal proceedings to exclude prosecution evidence which would, if admitted, have such an adverse effect on the fairness of the proceedings that the court ought not to admit it: Police and Criminal Evidence Act 1984, s 78(1). A further kind of discretion applicable to both civil and criminal cases is a discretion to disallow hectoring questions in cross-examination and perhaps to absolve a witness from answering particular relevant questions even though no privilege exists (eg questions to a priest about a penitent's confession), though there are conflicting dicta on the subject in *D v National Society for the Prevention of Cruelty to Children* [1978] AC 171, [1977] 1 All ER 589, HL. But at common law there is no discretion to include relevant but inadmissible evidence.

3   The function of judge and jury

The division between the functions of judge and jury, and the merits and dangers of jury trial, have profoundly affected the modern law of evidence even as it applies in cases without a jury. Indeed, one of the most striking features of English law, which differentiates it from American, is the extent to which the judge controls the jury.

In general the judge decides issues of law, including admissibility of evidence, and directs the jury as to the meaning of the legal rules they must apply to the facts; the jury decides questions of fact. But the operation of formal admissions, estoppels, some presumptions and the evidence of judicial notice limits the jury's competence to find facts. Further, the judge decides whether there is any evidence fit to go to the jury on any fact in issue (see ch 3, post); what the ordinary meaning (but not any peculiar meaning) of words used by the parties is, save in defamation cases; what foreign law provides; whether the defendant in a malicious prosecution suit had reasonable and probable cause for prosecuting; whether a covenant in restraint of trade is unreasonable; whether facts precedent to the admissibility of items of evidence are proved. A 'trial within the trial' called the voir dire is used for this latter purpose, particularly in the case of confessions (see ch 8, post). Since it is often impossible to decide issues of admissibility without considering the evidence to be admitted, the jury is generally absent from the voir dire and from arguments about the admissibility of evidence. But the jury's absence during the voir dire may hamper them in determining the weight of later evidence, and they may think that the more often they are ordered out of the court the more likely the accused is to be guilty. Hence they should be present unless there is a risk of prejudice (*R v Reynolds* [1950] 1 KB 606, [1950] 1 All ER 335, CCA; contrast *Demirok v R* (1977) 137 CLR 20), or where the evidence in question is expert evidence going to the witness's capacity to tell the truth (*R v Deakin* [1994] 4 All ER 769, CA). Judges have differed on whether a full voir dire without the jury as well as the same testimony in the jury's presence should be permitted where the disputed fact preliminary to the admissibility of evidence is identical with the fact in issue (cf *Doe d Jenkins v Davies* (1847) 10 QB 314, with *Hitchins v Eardley* (1871) LR 2 P & D 248).

Judicial control over the jury in practice appears most strongly in the judge's summing up. It is usually undesirable for the judge simply to state the law without giving any guidance on how to apply it to the precise facts. Further he may give the jury, expressly or impliedly, his views on the credibility of witnesses and the evidence generally. However, it should be made clear to them that they are not bound by these views (*Broadhurst v R* [1964] AC 441, [1964] 1 All ER 111, PC). A conviction may be set aside on appeal as being 'unsafe' (s 2 of the Criminal Appeal Act 1968 as substituted by the Criminal Appeal Act 1995 following Runciman, paras 27-34) on a number of grounds including a wrong decision of law or a material irregularity in the course of the trial, either of which might involve a point of the law of evidence. The judge has wide discretionary powers in conducting the trial. However, these are controllable on appeal, particularly if he intervenes so much as to prevent parties or their counsel conducting the case properly (see *Jones v National Coal Board* [1957] 2 QB 55, [1957] 2 All ER 155, CA). The judge must act only on the evidence put before him by the parties, for each side has a right to deal with the other's evidence and neither can do this if the judge acts on secret information. New evidence may be received on appeal subject to the court's discretion, which in criminal cases is to be exercised after considering in particular whether the evidence is capable of being believed, whether it would afford grounds for allowing the appeal, and whether there is a reasonable explanation for not adducing it at the trial.

4 Evidentiary ghosts

There are two principles which once had, or were thought to have, much more importance in the law of evidence than they do now. It is important not to be misled by references to them.

Lord Hardwicke said: 'the judges and sages of the law have laid it down that there is but one general rule of evidence, *the best that the nature of the case will admit*' (*Omychund v Barker* (1745) 1 Atk 21 at 49). But it is not now true either that a party cannot introduce an item of evidence if better is available, or that he can introduce an item of evidence if, though it is defective, there is none better: much inadmissible hearsay would be admitted if the 'best evidence' rule were law. The rule that in general the original of a private document must be produced to prove its contents is usually said to be the sole survival of the rule (cf Thayer, ch 11), except that evidence which is not the best evidence may be ignored because it lacks weight and may even be excluded on this ground (eg *R v Quinn* [1962] 2 QB 245, [1961] 3 All ER 88, CCA).

Many of the rules of evidence are said to be justified by the maxim *res inter alios acta alteri nocere non debet*, which is intended to mean that a party to litigation should not be prejudiced by transactions between strangers. These include similar fact evidence (ch 10, post), hearsay evidence (ch 12, post) and judgments in earlier proceedings (ch 15, post). In truth these rules rest on other bases. Invocation of the maxim tends to beg questions as to the relevance and weight of evidence; its only real importance is in providing an historical explanation of some modern rules.

5 Special forms of evidence

Tape-recordings are sometimes admitted under exceptions to the hearsay rule if the words are relied on as evidence of their truth, sometimes as original evidence if the words are relied on simply as proof of the fact they were uttered, and sometimes as real evidence, where the intonation of the words is important.

A useful statement of the general principles, in *Butera v DPP (Vic)* (1987) 164 CLR 180, is as follows. A tape is not by itself admissible evidence of what is recorded on it, for by itself it is incapable of proving what is recorded on it. It is only admissible because it is capable of being used to prove what is recorded on it by being played on sound reproduction equipment: that produces evidence of the conversation or other sound recorded, and it is that evidence, aurally received, which is admissible to prove the relevant fact, namely the sounds recorded. The issues of what those sounds are should be proved by playing the tape in court if it be available, rather than by tendering evidence, written (eg a transcript of the tape) or oral, of what a witness heard when the tape was played over out of court. But if the tape is not available and its absence is accounted for satisfactorily, the evidence of its contents given by a witness who heard it being played over may be received as secondary evidence. Though the best evidence rule here excludes oral or written evidence of what a witness heard on the tape if the unavailability of the tape is not accounted for, it does not exclude evidence derived from the playing of a copy tape, provided the provenance of the original tape, the accuracy of the copying process and the provenance of the copy tape are satisfactorily proved. Where a tape is played, even though a transcript of it is not admissible as secondary evidence, the transcript may be admitted, not as independent evidence of the conversation or other sounds but as a means of assisting in the perception and understanding of the evidence tendered by the playing over of the tape (which may be indistinct or otherwise difficult to understand). The jury should be told this, and told that they cannot use the transcript as a substitute for the tape if they are not satisfied that the transcript correctly sets out what they heard on the tape. (See also *Taylor v Chief Constable of Cheshire* [1987] 1 All ER 225, [1986] 1 WLR 1479.)

These principles do not make admissible written translations of what was taped: the contents of a document written in a foreign language or an oral statement in a foreign language cannot be proved without a translation into English of what is written or spoken, and the translation must itself be given as evidence sworn to by the person who makes the translation. However, exceptionally the admission of transcripts in English of conversations in foreign languages recorded on tape are admitted where had this course not been adopted it would have been all but impossible for the jury to appreciate the cross-examination of the interpreters (*R v Maqsud Ali* [1966] 1 QB 688, [1965] 2 All ER 464, CCA).

Fingerprint evidence is very weighty circumstantial evidence; judicial notice is taken of the fact that each person's fingerprints are unique. Blood tests are real evidence (if the sole issue is the percentage of blood alcohol) or circumstantial evidence (eg if the issue is fitness to drive, or paternity). There are special statutory procedures for the sampling of blood (and breath and urine). Evidence of the behaviour of tracker dogs which follow a scent to the accused, may, if exceptionally reliable, be admissible circumstantial evidence: evidence is normally needed of the training, skill and habits of the particular dog and its handler (*R v Pieterson* [1995] 1 WLR 293, CA). Sufficiently reliable photographs and films of places and people, identified by a witness as such, are admissible; and a film of radar reception made without human intervention has been admitted (*The Statue of Liberty* [1968] 2 All ER 195, [1968] 1 WLR 739). Evidence of a person's behaviour under the influence of a truth drug is inadmissible for a number of technical reasons but principally because it is so unreliable (*R v McKay* [1967] NZLR 139). The same is true of lie detector evidence (in America as well as England, contrary to common belief). Hypnotically induced evidence may be admitted provided certain safeguards are complied with (*R v McFelin* [1985] 2 NZLR 750; *R v Jenkyns* (1993) 32 NSWLR 712). See also *R v Tillott* (1995) 38 NSWLR 1 (EMDR therapy).

6 Evidence not objected to

What is the evidentiary status of evidence to which objection could have been, but was not, taken? This interesting but difficult question usually arises in relation to hearsay evidence, but can arise elsewhere. The main authorities are Australian: see eg *Hughes v National Trustees Executors and Agency Co of Australasia Ltd* (1979) 143 CLR 134 at 153; *Jones v Sutherland Shire Council* [1979] 2 NSWLR 206 at 218–19; *Ritz Hotel Ltd v Charles of the Ritz Ltd* (1988) 15 NSWLR 158 at 170–1; see also *R v Gibson* (1887) 18 QBD 537, CCR. The law appears to be as follows.

(1) If evidence, admitted without objection, is legally admissible in proof of some issue in the case, its evidentiary use should be confined to that purpose.

(2) If one party by its conduct at the trial has led the other to believe that evidence, though hearsay, may be treated as evidence of the facts stated, and the other in reliance on that belief has refrained from adducing proper evidence, the former party may be precluded from objecting to the use of the evidence to prove the facts stated.

(3) If evidence, admitted without objection, is 'not legally admissible in proof of any issue', it may, once in, be used 'as proof to the extent of whatever rational persuasive power it may have': *Jones v Sutherland Shire Council* [1979] 2 NSWLR 206 at 219.

(4) Where a document is tendered by one party against the other without objection as an admission, the latter party and the court are entitled to rely on it against the tendering party to the extent to which it contains self-serving statements, though their weight is another question.

(5) In criminal cases, hearsay and other inadmissible evidence should be excluded by the court even if not objected to by the parties. On the other hand, there are authorities suggesting that in criminal cases as well as in civil, a doctrine of waiver operates, so that evidence admitted after a conscious decision not to object prevents any point being taken on appeal.

(6) The above principles do not apply to evidence which is irrelevant or excluded by an absolute rule of law (for example, the statutes excluding unstamped documents) but only to evidence in respect of which a party has a privilege or where there exists a rule of evidence which a party has an option to take advantage of or not as he chooses.

7 Arrangement

No two books on Evidence are laid out in the same way. The plan here adopted is rather like the subject in having no single basis. In the next part are discussed certain basic problems that pervade the entire law: on whom the burden of proof rests, what standard must be achieved, how certain presumptions operate, and how evidence is to be evaluated. Part II discusses those rules. Part III discusses those rules of evidence which, though they sometimes also arise outside criminal cases or serve other purposes, have as their principal aim the protection of the accused from wrong conviction or other forms of maltreatment by the state. These rules constitute perhaps the largest single part of the law of evidence in practice. Part IV discusses the rule against hearsay, which used to be the major technical rule of evidence in the sense that much of the law could be stated in terms of the rule and its exceptions; it has been the subject of extensive actual and proposed reforms. This part also deals with documentary evidence. Part V discusses who can testify as a witness, who can be forced to testify and which particular questions need not be answered by witnesses because of private or state privilege. Part VI discusses the rules governing the course of the trial. Finally, Part VII discusses matters which need not be proved by evidence in consequence of the doctrines of judicial notice. Doubts about whether estoppel is truly part of the law of evidence have led to its exclusion.

PART TWO

The Process of Proof

CHAPTER 2

The Burden of Proof

1 Introduction

The phrase 'burden of proof' has two senses to which a variety of different names are given. The first sense refers to the obligation of a party to persuade the trier of fact by the end of the case of the truth of certain propositions, failing which he will lose his case. What these propositions are depends on substantive rules of law and pleading. This first burden is variously called the 'legal burden', the 'persuasive burden', 'the burden of proof on the pleadings', 'the fixed burden of proof', 'the risk of non-persuasion' (Wigmore), 'the burden of proof' and the 'probative burden' (*DPP v Morgan* [1976] AC 182, [1975] 2 All ER 347). The courts are reluctant to decide cases merely in accordance with the burden of proof in this sense, but there are recent timely reminders that sometimes they must. Thus in *Rhesa Shipping Co SA v Edmunds* [1985] 2 All ER 712 at 718, [1985] 1 WLR 948 at 955–6, the House of Lords said, per Lord Brandon:

> 'the judge is not bound always to make a finding one way or the other with regard to the facts averred by the parties. He has open to him the third alternative of saying that the party on whom the burden of proof lies in relation to any averment made by him has failed to discharge that burden. No judge likes to decide cases on burden of proof if he can legitimately avoid having to do so. There are cases, however, in which, owing to the unsatisfactory state of the evidence or otherwise, deciding on the burden of proof is the only just course for him to take.'

See also *Morris v London Iron and Steel Co Ltd* [1988] QB 493 at 504, [1987] 2 All ER 496 at 503, CA.

The second sense of 'burden of proof' refers to one party's duty to produce sufficient evidence for a judge to call on the other party to answer. The incidence of this duty is determined by particular rules of evidence. This task of producing evidence fit to be considered by a jury is called the 'evidential burden', the 'burden of adducing evidence', or the duty 'of passing the judge'. As the Privy Council pointed out in *Jayasena v R* [1970] AC 618 at 624, [1970] 1 All ER 219 at 222, PC, it is misleading to call this a burden of proof when it is capable of discharge by evidence falling far short of proof. Failure to discharge the first burden will cause the trier of fact to decide against the proponent on that issue. Failure to discharge the second will cause the judge to decide against the proponent without calling on his opponent or letting the case go to the trier of fact at all.

A luxuriant terminology has characterised and caused confusion in the general area of burden of proof, and this part of it is no exception. Plainly, some of these names are better guides to meaning than others; but the case law is insufficiently settled to permit dogmatism. So long as the reasonably simple distinction stated is made clear, it matters little what names are used. The names 'legal' and 'evidential' burden will be used here.

The same evidence may serve both purposes. It is in fact misleading to suppose that some evidence is introduced to jump the 'evidential burden' hurdle and then other evidence to jump the 'legal burden' hurdle. On a given issue, the proponent will put in all his evidence. It will be for the judge to decide whether he has satisfied the evidential burden. The same evidence will, after the opponent has put his case, then be considered by the trier of fact, perhaps strengthened by the opponent's failure to answer it, or by the poor performance under examination-in-chief and cross-examination of the opponent or his witnesses. Even if the opponent says nothing and calls no evidence, the proponent may fail to satisfy the legal burden, for the judge may think he has made out a case to answer while the trier of fact finds his case not sufficiently weighty to satisfy the higher legal burden.

The evidential burden must be known when there is doubt as to who should or may begin calling evidence; and when there is a submission at the close of the proponent's case that he had not made out a case to answer. The legal burden must be known when the trier of fact is in doubt at the close of the evidence and when the judge is directing the trier of fact about this. A further occasion exists when either burden must be known: this is when an appellate court is hearing an appeal alleging some mistake respecting the first four occasions when the burden is relevant.

2   How can the incidence of the two burdens of proof be determined?

A common test for the incidence of the legal burden on a particular fact in issue is, 'Who would lose on that issue if the evidence is equally balanced at the end of the case?' A similar test for the evidential burden is 'Who would lose if no evidence at all were given?' But these questions merely restate the problem of working out which factors influence the formulation of the rules which answer the questions.

The general rules are that the evidential burden normally lies in the same place as the legal burden, and that the legal burden of proving facts lies on him who asserts them. These rules have the particular effect that, subject to the exceptions discussed below, the Crown bears the burdens of proof in criminal cases: *Woolmington v DPP* [1935] AC 462. The rule as to the legal burden exists because he who – whether as prosecutor or civil plaintiff – invokes the state's aid through its judicial system, with consequent trouble and expense to others, should justify his conduct by assuming the initial difficulty it entails. The rule tends to avoid harassing and vexatious litigation.

The rule as to the evidential burden exists in order to prevent a man being forced to justify his past conduct without a colourable case having been made against him. It protects the privacy of individuals against the state and their enemies or busybodies. It also partially controls capricious jury verdicts. Though these can be upset on appeal, they are better prevented by a directed verdict than cured retrospectively by the action of the appellate court. Another function arises in those criminal cases where an evidential burden is on the accused. Here the burden tends to force the accused to testify if he wishes to deny facts (particularly relating to a state of mind) which would be inferred from the prosecution's case. In these cases the rule also saves the prosecution from having to rebut a large number of defences, some of which may not in fact be relied on or have any basis. There are statutory exceptions to the above rule (see Williams, *Criminal Law: The General Part* (2nd edn), para 292, n 1). Further, the parties in a civil case may vary the burden of proof by agreement, express or implied; normally the agreement will be taken to relate to the legal burden of proof.

But the general rule may be qualified by the operation of numerous other factors.

One is the difficulty of proving a negative. The prosecution must sometimes prove a negative (eg absence of consent in rape); so must the proponent in a civil case (eg non-performance of a contract). But the fact that a negative might have to be proved by one party is sometimes a reason for placing the burden of proof on the other (*Joseph Constantine SS Line Ltd v Imperial Smelting Corpn Ltd, The Kingswood* [1942] AC 154, [1941] 2 All ER 165, HL).

Another exception to the general rule that the legal and evidential burdens are borne by the same party, ie he who asserts a fact, arises with certain defences in criminal cases. The Crown has the legal burden of proving murder and thus of negativing facts which justify or excuse homicide, but the accused bears the evidential burden of raising such issues as provocation (*Mancini v DPP* [1942] AC 1, [1941] 3 All ER 272, HL), self-defence (*R v Lobell* [1957] 1 QB 547, [1957] 1 All ER 734, CCA; *Bullard v R* [1957] AC 635, [1961] 3 All ER 470n, PC), sane automatism and drunkenness (*Bratty v A-G for Northern Ireland* [1963] AC 386, [1961] 3 All ER 523, HL). The same applies to mechanical defect on a charge of dangerous driving (*R v Spurge* [1961] 2 QB 205, [1961] 2 All ER 688, CCA); a reasonable excuse on a charge of failure to provide a specimen for a laboratory test in connection with possible traffic offences (*R v Clarke* [1969] 2 All ER 1008, [1969] 1 WLR 1109, CA); duress (*R v Gill* [1963] 2 All ER 688, [1963] 1 WLR 841, CCA; *R v Smyth* [1963] VR 737; *Van den Hoek v R* (1986) 161 CLR 158); necessity (*R v Trim* [1943] VLR 109); alibi (*R v Johnson* [1961] 3 All ER 969, [1961] 1 WLR 1478); the impossibility of carrying out a conspiracy (*R v Bennett* (1978) 68 Cr App Rep 168 at 177); honest and reasonable mistake (*He Kow Teh v R* (1985) 157 CLR 523); but not the prosecutrix's consent in rape (*DPP v Morgan* [1976] AC 182, [1975] 2 All ER 347). It is misleading to refer to these issues as 'defences', for this may suggest the accused bears a legal burden (*R v Wheeler* [1967] 3 All ER 829, [1967] 1 WLR 1531, CA; *R v Abraham* [1973] 3 All ER 694, [1973] 1 WLR 1270, CA). They should be put to the jury if there is some evidence of them whether or not the accused relies on them; defence counsel may have made a wrong choice of the issues on which to fight, or may think it tactically unwise to raise partly conflicting issues (*Mancini v DPP* [1942] AC 1, [1941] 3 All ER 272, HL; cf *R v Gill* [1963] 2 All ER 688, [1963] 1 WLR 841, CCA). An evidential burden may be discharged without the party bearing it having to give evidence, eg because of what the other side's witnesses say. This is an important practical point where the accused bears an evidential burden; the burden by no means completely undermines his right to silence.

It would be unfair for the Crown to have to rebut every possible fact which might be relied on by the defence. It would be difficult to do so without some understanding of what form the issue might take; it would lengthen the trial and confuse the jury with a multiplicity of irrelevant questions.

However, the legal burden of proving insanity (*Sodeman v R* [1936] 2 All ER 1138, PC) or insane automatism (*Bratty v A-G for Northern Ireland* [1963] AC 386, [1961] 3 All ER 532, HL) or unfitness to plead (*R v Podola* [1960] 1 QB 325, [1959] 3 All ER 418, CCA; *R v Robertson* [1968] 3 All ER 557, [1968] 1 WLR 1767, CA) or diminished responsibility (Homicide Act 1957, s 2(2); *R v Dunbar* [1958] 1 QB 1, [1957] 2 All ER 737, CCA) is on the accused on the balance of probabilities if he raises the issue; otherwise the Crown bears the legal burden of proving the defective mental state beyond reasonable doubt. The general rule that he who asserts a fact must prove it applies in this case because of the inherent unlikelihood of a defective mental state, because the accused knows far more about his state of mind than the prosecution, because such a state is very difficult to disprove 'in the air', without some evidence of it to be refuted and because it is desirable to prevent these defences being raised frivolously. Indeed, if the prosecution bore the burden, too many guilty accused persons might be acquitted.

Other relevant factors are that a fact is peculiarly within one party's knowledge, that it forms one of a number of possible excuses or qualifications, and that if the onus of proof rested on the other party he would have to prove a negative. If all three are present, the legal burden may be on the opponent of one who affirms (*R v Turner* (1816) 5 M & S 206, [1814–23] All ER Rep 713; p 26; post). The factor of peculiar knowledge alone is unlikely to alter the legal burden (*R v Spurge* [1961] 2 QB 205, [1961] 2 All ER 688, CCA); indeed its utility was attacked in *R v Edwards* [1975] QB 27, [1974] 2 All ER 1085, CA. However, it may be relevant in determining how much evidence discharges the evidential burden and the legal burden. In the latter connexion Lord Mansfield once remarked: 'It is certainly a maxim that all evidence is to be weighed according to the proof which it was in the power of one side to have produced, and in the power of the other to have contradicted' (*Blatch v Archer* (1774) 1 Cowp 63 at 65).

In England peculiar knowledge and the need to avoid making a party prove the negative have often been held, without express statutory words, to put an evidential burden on the accused: this commonly arises in crimes of carrying on some activity without a licence or certificate (eg *John v Humphreys* [1955] 1 All ER 793, [1955] 1 WLR 325; cf *McGowan v Carville* [1960] IR 330 and *Everard v Opperman* [1958] VLR 389). These authorities have now been extended so as to impose a persuasive burden in some circumstances: see *R v Edwards* [1975] QB 27, [1974] 2 All ER 1085, CA. It is justified by the triviality of these offences and the desirability of lightening the prosecution burden in respect of them. However, the cases constitute an anomalous exception to the general coincidence of legal and evidential burdens; indeed, since the weight of the two burdens in this area in practice tends to be the same, they virtually place the legal burden on the accused, which is very anomalous. Further, it is unclear that it is more onerous for the prosecution to produce a witness who says the accused did not on a former occasion produce his licence when asked, than for the witness to come to court to produce his licence or explain his failure to do so.

Another factor was enunciated by Lord Mansfield thus: 'It is a known distinction that what comes by way of proviso in a statute must be insisted on by way of defence by the party accused; but, where exceptions are in the enacting part of a law, it must appear in the charge that the defendant does not fall within any of them' (*R v Jarvis* (1756) 1 East 643n). This factor may be taken into account not only in statutes but also in agreements affecting the burden of proof. This test is a formalist one, for there is no logical difference between a class cut down by an exception and a smaller class which excludes crimes covered by the exception. There is no difference, as regards those not punished, between not punishing 'licensed persons' and punishing 'all mankind save those with a licence'. However, the test is justifiable if it genuinely does correspond with the intent of the legislator. This seems doubtful, because the test is not applied in any systematic way, and the cases reach different results on whether the legal burden as well as the evidential is affected. According to *R v Edwards*, supra, the common law was enacted in the Magistrates' Courts Act 1952, s 81, which provides that 'where the defendant to an information or complaint relies for his defence on any exception, exemption, proviso, excuse or qualification, . . . the burden of proving the exception, exemption, proviso, excuse or qualification shall be on him': see now the Magistrates' Courts Act 1980, s 101. It affects the legal burden (*R v Edwards*; see also *Roberts v Humphreys* (1873) LR 8 QB 483; *Taylor v Ellis* [1956] VLR 457; *Gatland v Metropolitan Police Comr* [1968] 2 QB 279 at 286, [1968] 2 All ER 100 at 103). Some other statutes, eg the Prevention of Corruption Act 1916, s 2, specifically place the burden by laying down that some fact shall be deemed to be the case unless the contrary is shown. See generally Chapter 4.

Another relevant factor is whether the fact alleged is common or uncommon; for if it is uncommon, it will be harder to prove, and he who alleges should prove; while if it is common, it is not unfair to expect that he who denies its existence should disprove it. This is one reason why the burden of proving insanity is on the accused. It also justifies the result in the *Constantine* case (p 24, post), which held that the burden of proving that frustration is self-induced rests on the party who denies frustration. In many frustration cases it is difficult to prove the cause, and in most (reported) cases frustration is not caused by the fault of the parties. The burden of proving a fact on which the admissibility of evidence depends rests on the party tendering the evidence: *R v Yacoob* (1981) 72 Cr App Rep 313.

In practice the incidence of the burden of proof is well settled in most cases. The particular rules are, as Wigmore says, based on 'broad reasons of expedience and fairness' (para 2486). The basic rule, that he who invokes the State's aid must prove his case, answers most questions; exceptions grow up in a piecemeal way which cannot be investigated in a detailed way here.

It might be noted that the Criminal Law Revision Committee recommended that, in general, statutory burdens placed on the accused should be evidential only, and that the same should be true of insanity (CLRC paras

137–42). The reasons were that such burdens frequently entail proof of a negative (ie proof of lack of blameworthy intent), and that they are anomalous exceptions to the general common law rule and the principle of such statutes as the Theft Act 1968, s 25(3) (which places only an evidential burden of proving that potential instruments of crime in the accused's possession were not for the purpose of committing certain crimes). The committee considered that any useful purpose behind the placing of any burden on the accused was sufficiently served by making it evidential only; and they felt that the need to direct the jury as to the difference between the burden on the prosecution of proving a matter beyond reasonable doubt and the burden on the accused of proving a matter on the balance of probabilities should be avoided. A less radical proposal of the Law Commission (Law Com 243 (1985)) favoured express drafting in instances where it was desired to cast a legal burden on the accused.

Abrath v North Eastern Rly Co   (1883) 11 QBD 440, [1881–5] All ER Rep 614, CA

This was an action for malicious prosecution in which an issue arose as to whether the burden of proving absence of reasonable and probable cause as well as the prosecution lay on the plaintiff. The Court of Appeal, in allowing an appeal from a Queen's Bench Divisional Court order for a new trial, decided that it did.

Bowen LJ: Whenever litigation exists, somebody must go on with it; the plaintiff is the first to begin; if he does nothing, he fails; if he makes a prima facie case, and nothing is done to answer it, the defendant fails. The test, therefore, as to the burden of proof or onus of proof, whichever term is used, is simply this: to ask oneself which party will be successful if no evidence is given, or if no more evidence is given than has been given at a particular point of the case, for it is obvious that as the controversy involved in the litigation travels on, the parties from moment to moment may reach points at which the onus of proof shifts, and at which the tribunal will have to say that if the case stops there, it must be decided in a particular manner. The test being such as I have stated, it is not a burden that goes on for ever resting on the shoulders of the person upon whom it is first cast. As soon as he brings evidence which, until it is answered, rebuts the evidence against which he is contending, then the balance descends on the other side, and the burden rolls over until again there is evidence which once more turns the scale. That being so, the question of onus of proof is only a rule for deciding on whom the obligation of going further, if he wishes to win, rests. It is not a rule to enable the jury to decide on the value of conflicting evidence. . . Now in an action for malicious prosecution the plaintiff has the burden throughout of establishing that the circumstances of the prosecution were such that a judge can see no reasonable or probable cause for instituting it. In one sense that is the assertion of a negative, and we have been pressed with the proposition that when a negative is to be made out the onus of proof shifts. That is not so. If the assertion of a negative is an essential part of the plaintiff's case, the proof of the assertion still rests upon the plaintiff. The terms 'negative' and 'affirmative' are after all relative and not absolute. In dealing with a question of negligence, that term may be considered either as negative or affirmative according to the definition adopted in measuring the duty which is neglected. Wherever a person asserts affirmatively as part of his case that a certain state of facts is present or is absent, or that a particular thing is insufficient for a particular purpose, that is an averment which he is bound to prove positively. It has been said that an exception exists in those cases where the facts lie peculiarly within the knowledge of the opposite party. The counsel for the plaintiff have not gone the length of contending that in all those cases the onus shifts, and that the person within whose knowledge the truth peculiarly lies is bound to prove or disprove the matter in dispute. I think a proposition of that kind cannot be maintained, and that the exceptions supposed to be found amongst cases relating to the game laws may be explained on special grounds.

. . . Who had to make good their point as to the proposition whether the defendants had taken reasonable and proper care to inform themselves of the true state of the case? The defendants were not bound to make good anything. It was the plaintiff's duty to shew the absence of reasonable care . . .

[Brett MR and Fry LJ concurred.]

Woolmington v Director of Public Prosecutions
[1935] AC 462, [1935] All ER Rep 1, HL

The accused was convicted of murder. His defence was accident. In his summing up to the jury Swift J said: 'Once it is shown to a jury that somebody has died through the act of another, that is presumed to be murder, unless the person who has been guilty of the act which causes the death can satisfy a jury that what happened was something less, something which might be alleviated, something which might be reduced to a charge of manslaughter, or something which was accidental, or something which could be justified.'

The accused appealed unsuccessfully to the Court of Appeal but successfully to the House of Lords.

Viscount Sankey LC: If at any period of a trial it was permissible for the judge to rule that the prosecution had established its case and that the onus was shifted on the prisoner to prove that he was not guilty and that unless he discharged that onus the prosecution was entitled to succeed, it would be enabling the judge in such a case to say that the jury must in law find the prisoner guilty and so make the judge decide the case and not the jury, which is not the common law . . . But while the prosecution must prove the guilt of the prisoner, there is no such burden laid on the prisoner to prove his innocence and it is sufficient for him to raise a doubt as to his guilt; he is not bound to satisfy the jury of his innocence.

. . . [W]here intent is an ingredient of a crime there is no onus on the defendant to prove that the act alleged was accidental. Throughout the web of the English Criminal Law one golden thread is always to be seen, that it is the duty of the prosecution to prove the prisoner's guilt subject to what I have already said as to the defence of insanity and subject also to any statutory exception. If, at the end of and on the whole of the case, there is a reasonable doubt, created by the evidence given by either the prosecution or the prisoner, as to whether the prisoner killed the deceased with a malicious intention, the prosecution has not made out the case and the prisoner is entitled to an acquittal. No matter what the charge or where the trial, the principle that the prosecution must prove the guilt of the prisoner is part of the common law of England and no attempt to whittle it down can be entertained. When dealing with a murder case the Crown must prove (a) death as the result of a voluntary act of the accused and (b) malice of the accused. It may prove malice either expressly or by implication. For malice may be implied where death occurs as the result of a voluntary act of the accused which is (i) intentional and (ii) unprovoked. When evidence of death and malice has been given (this is a question for the jury) the accused is entitled to show, by evidence or by examination of the circumstances adduced by the Crown that the act on his part which caused death was either unintentional or provoked. If the jury are either satisfied with his explanation or, upon a review of all the evidence, are left in reasonable doubt whether, even if his explanation be not accepted, the act was unintentional or provoked, the prisoner is entitled to the benefit of the doubt.

[These last five words were substituted by Lord Simon LC, with Viscount Sankey's consent, in *Mancini v DPP* [1942] AC 1 at 13, [1941] 3 All ER 272 at 280, HL, to cover the case of provocation, which does not entitle the accused to an acquittal but only to a conviction of manslaughter rather than murder.]

[Lords Atkin, Hewart CJ, Tomlin and Wright agreed.]

Hill v Baxter   [1958] 1 QB 277, [1958] 1 All ER 193, DC

The defendant pleaded that he became unconscious as a result of a sudden illness in answer to charges of dangerous driving. No evidence of this was produced. The magistrates acquitted him and the prosecutor successfully appealed to the Divisional Court.

Lord Goddard CJ: [U]ndoubtedly the onus of proving that he was in a state of automatism must be on him. This is not only akin to a defence of insanity, but it is a rule of the law of evidence that the onus of proving a fact which must be exclusively within the knowledge of a party lies on him who asserts it. This, no doubt, is subject to the qualification that where an onus is on the defendant in a criminal case the burden is not as high as it is on a prosecutor.

... I am content to rest my judgment on the ground that there was no evidence which justified the justices finding that he was not fully responsible in law for his actions ...

Devlin J: [in agreeing with the order proposed] I am satisfied that even in a case in which liability depended upon full proof of mens rea, it would not be open to the defence to rely upon automatism without providing some evidence of it. If it amounted to insanity in the legal sense, it is well established that the burden of proof would start with and remain throughout upon the defence. But there is also recognised in the criminal law a lighter burden which the accused discharges by producing some evidence, but which does not relieve the prosecution from having to prove in the end all the facts necessary to establish guilt. This principle has manifested itself in different forms; most of them relate to the accused's state of mind and put it upon him to give some evidence about it. Thus the fact that an accused is found in possession of property recently stolen does not of itself prove that he knew of the stealing. Nevertheless, it is not open to the accused at the end of the prosecution's case to submit that he has no case to answer; he must offer some explanation to account for his possession though he does not have to prove that the explanation is true: *R v Aves* [1950] 2 All ER 330, CCA. In a charge of murder it is for the prosecution to prove that the killing was intentional and unprovoked, and that burden is never shifted: *Woolmington v DPP* [1935] AC 462, [1935] All ER Rep 1, HL. But though the prosecution must in the end prove lack of provocation, the obligation arises only if there is some evidence of provocation fit to go to the jury: *Holmes v DPP* [1946] AC 588, [1946] 2 All ER 124, HL. The same rule applies in the case of self-defence: *R v Lobell* [1957] 1 QB 547, [1957] 1 All ER 734, CCA. In any crime involving mens rea the prosecution must prove guilty intent, but if the defence suggests drunkenness as negativing intention, they must offer evidence of it, if, indeed, they do not have to prove it: *DPP v Beard* [1920] AC 479 at 507, [1920] All ER Rep 21 at 31, HL. It would be quite unreasonable to allow the defence to submit at the end of the prosecution's case that the Crown had not proved affirmatively and beyond a reasonable doubt that the accused was at the time of the crime sober, or not sleepwalking or not in a trance or blackout. I am satisfied that such matters ought not to be considered at all until the defence has produced at least prima facie evidence. I should wish to reserve for future consideration when necessary the question of where the burden ultimately lies.

Pearson J: I agree with the judgment of the Lord Chief Justice subject to the reservation and explanations which Devlin J has made with regard to the burden of proof in a case such as this.

Bratty v A-G for Northern Ireland   [1963] AC 386, [1961] 3 All ER 523, HL

The accused was convicted of murdering an 18-year-old girl by strangulation. Two of his defences were insanity and insane automatism. An appeal to the Court of Criminal Appeal in Northern Ireland and the House of Lords against the judge's refusal to put the automatism defences to the jury failed. Some of their Lordships uttered dicta on the burden of proof of insane automatism.

Viscount Kilmuir LC: Where the defence succeeds in surmounting the initial hurdle (see *Mancini v DPP* [1942] AC 1, [1941] 3 All ER 272, HL), and satisfies the judge that there is evidence fit for the jury to consider, the question remains whether the proper direction is: (a) that the jury will acquit if, and only if, they are satisfied on the balance of probabilities that the accused acted in a state of automatism, or (b) that they should acquit if they are left in reasonable doubt on this point. In favour of the former direction it might be argued that, since a defence of automatism is (as Lord Goddard said in *Hill v Baxter* [1958] 1 QB 277 at 282, [1958] 1 All ER 193 at 195) very near a defence of insanity, it would be anomalous if there were any distinction between the onus in the one case and in the other. If this argument were to prevail it would follow that the defence would fail unless they established on a balance of probabilities that the prisoner's act was unconscious and involuntary in the same way as, under the M'Naghten Rules, they must establish on a balance of probabilities that the necessary requirements are satisfied.

Nevertheless, one must not lose sight of the overriding principle, laid down by this House in *Woolmington*'s case [1935] AC 462, [1935] All ER Rep 1, HL, that it is for the prosecution to prove every element of the offence charged. One of these elements is the accused's state of mind; normally the presumption of mental capacity is sufficient to prove that he acted consciously and voluntarily, and the prosecution need go no further. But if, after considering evidence properly left to them by the judge, the jury are left in real doubt whether or not the accused acted in a state of automatism, it seems to me that on principle they should acquit because the necessary mens rea – if indeed the actus reus – has not been proved beyond reasonable doubt.

Lord Denning: . . . [W]hilst the *ultimate* burden rests on the Crown of proving every element essential in the crime, nevertheless in order to prove that the act was a voluntary act, the Crown is entitled to rely on the *presumption* that every man has sufficient mental capacity to be responsible for his crimes: and that if the defence wish to displace the presumption they must give some evidence from which the contrary may reasonably be inferred. Thus a drunken man is presumed to have the capacity to form the specific intent necessary to constitute the crime, unless evidence is given from which it can reasonably be inferred that he was incapable of forming it, see the valuable judgment of the Court of Judiciary in *Kennedy v HM Advocate* 1944 JC 171 at 177, which was delivered by Lord Normand. So also it seems to me that a man's act is presumed to be a voluntary act unless there is evidence from which it can reasonably be inferred that it was involuntary. To use the words of Devlin J the defence of automatism 'ought not to be considered at all until the defence has produced at least prima facie evidence,' see *Hill v Baxter* [1958] 1 QB 227 at 285, [1958] 1 All ER 193 at 196; and the words of North J in New Zealand 'unless a proper foundation is laid', see *R v Cottle* [1958] NZLR 999 at 1025. The necessity of laying the proper foundation is on the defence: and if it is not so laid, the defence of automatism need not be left to the jury, any more than the defence of drunkenness (*Kennedy v HM Advocate* 1944 JC 171 at 177), provocation (*R v Gauthier* (1943) 29 Cr App Rep 113, CCA) or self-defence (*R v Lobell* [1957] 1 QB 547, [1957] 1 All ER 734, CCA) need be.

What, then, is a proper foundation? The presumption of mental capacity of which I have spoken is a provisional presumption only. It does not put the legal burden on the defence in the same way as the presumption of sanity does. It leaves the legal burden on the prosecution, but nevertheless, until it is displaced it enables the prosecution to discharge the ultimate burden of proving that the act was voluntary. Not because the presumption is evidence itself, but because it takes the place of evidence. In order to displace the presumption of mental capacity, the defence must give sufficient evidence from which it may reasonably be inferred that the act was involuntary. The evidence of the man himself will rarely be sufficient unless it is supported by medical evidence which points to the cause of the mental incapacity. It is not sufficient for a man to say 'I had a blackout': for 'blackout' as Stable J said in *Cooper v McKenna, ex p Cooper* [1960] Qd R 406 at 419, 'is one of the first refuges of a guilty conscience and a popular excuse'. The words of Devlin J in *Hill v Baxter* [1958] 1 QB 277 at 285, [1958] 1 All ER 193 at 197, should be remembered: 'I do not doubt that there are genuine cases of automatism and the like, but I do not see how the layman can safely attempt without the help of some medical or scientific evidence to distinguish the genuine from the fraudulent.' When the only cause that is assigned for an involuntary act is drunkenness, then it is only necessary to leave drunkenness to the jury, with the consequential directions, and not to leave automatism at all. When the only cause that is assigned for it is a disease of the mind, then it is only necessary to leave insanity to the jury, and not automatism. When the cause assigned is concussion or sleep-walking, there should be evidence from which it can reasonably be inferred before it should be left to the jury. If it is said to be due to concussion, there should be evidence of a severe blow shortly beforehand. If it is said to be sleep-walking, there should be some credible support for it. His mere assertion that he was asleep will not suffice.

Once a proper foundation is thus laid for automatism, the matter becomes at large and must be left to the jury. As the case proceeds, the evidence may weigh first to one side and then to the other: and so the burden may appear to shift to and fro. But at the end of the day the legal burden comes into play and requires that the jury should be satisfied beyond reasonable doubt that the act was a voluntary act.

Lord Morris of Borth-y-Gest: The 'golden rule' of the English criminal law that it is the duty of the prosecution to prove an accused person's guilt (subject to any statutory exception and subject to the special position which arises where it is given in evidence that an accused person is insane), does not involve that the prosecution must speculate as to and specifically anticipate every conceivable explanation that an accused person might offer.

[Lords Tucker and Hodson agreed with Viscount Kilmuir LC and Lord Morris.]

Joseph Constantine SS Line Ltd v Imperial Smelting Corpn Ltd, The Kingswood [1942] AC 154, [1941] 2 All ER 165, HL

Shipowners pleaded that an explosion on a ship, the cause of which was unascertained, had frustrated a charterparty for breach of which the charterers were claiming damages. Atkinson J held that the onus of proving that the frustration was induced by the shipowners' default was on the charterers. The Court of Appeal reversed him, and an appeal to the House of Lords against this decision succeeded.

Viscount Simon LC: . . . The question here is where the onus of proof lies; ie whether, when a supervening event has been proved which would, apart from the defendant's 'default', put an end to the contract, and when at the end of the case no inference of 'default' exists and the evidence is equally consistent with either view, the defence fails because the defendant has not established affirmatively that the supervening event was not due to his default.

I may observe, in the first place, that, if this were correct, there must be many cases in which, although in truth frustration is complete and unavoidable, the defendant will be held liable because of his inability to prove a negative – in some cases, indeed, a whole series of negatives. Suppose that a vessel while on the high seas disappears completely during a storm. Can it be that the defence of frustration of the adventure depends on the owner's ability to prove that all his servants on board were navigating the ship with adequate skill and that there was no 'default' which brought about the catastrophe? Suppose that a vessel in convoy is torpedoed by the enemy and sinks immediately with all hands. Does the application of the doctrine require that the owners should affirmatively prove that those on board were keeping a good look-out, were obscuring lights, were steering as directed, and so forth? There is no reported case which requires us so to hold. . . .

In this connection it is well to emphasise that when 'frustration' in the legal sense occurs, it does not merely provide one party with a defence in an action brought by the other. It kills the contract itself and discharges both parties automatically. The plaintiff sues for breach at a past date and the defendant pleads that at that date no contract existed. In this situation the plaintiff could only succeed if it were shown that the determination of the contract were due to the defendant's 'default', and it would be a strange result if the party alleging this were not the party required to prove it.

. . . Every case in this branch of the law can be stated as turning on the question whether from the express terms of the particular contract a further term should be implied which, when its conditions are fulfilled, put an end to the contract.

If the matter is regarded in this way, the question is as to the construction of a contract taking into consideration its express and implied terms. The implied term in the present case may well be – 'This contract is to cease to be binding if the vessel is disabled by an overpowering disaster, provided that disaster is not brought about by the default of either party.' This is very similar to an express exception of 'perils of the seas', as to which it is ancient law that by an implied term of the contract the shipowner cannot rely on the exception if its operation was brought about either (a) by negligence of his servants, or (b) by his breach of the implied warranty of seaworthiness. If a ship sails and is never heard of again the shipowner can claim protection for loss of the cargo under the express exception of perils of the seas. To establish that, must he go on to prove (a) that the perils were *not* caused by negligence of his servants, and (b) were not caused by any unseaworthiness? I think clearly not. He proves a prima facie case of loss by sea perils, and that he is within the exception. If the cargo owner wants to defeat that plea it is for him by rejoinder to allege and prove either negligence or unseaworthiness. The judgment of the Court of Appeal in *The Glendarroch* [1894] P 226, [1891–4] All ER Rep 484, CA, is plain authority for this.

. . . The decision in *The Northumbria* [1906] P 292, involves the same conclusion. Another example, from the law of bailment, confirms this view. Assume a bailment of goods to be kept in a named warehouse with an express exception of loss by fire. Proof of destruction by fire would prima facie excuse the bailee. The bailor could counter by alleging either (a) fire caused by the negligence of the bailee or (b) goods when burnt were not stored in the agreed warehouse. But it would be for the bailor not only to allege but to prove either (a) or (b), though he might rely on facts proved or admitted by the bailee as establishing his proposition.

Viscount Maugham: It is, however, to be noted that it is often a mere accident, for instance the condition of the market, which decides the question which of two parties will desire to rely on the doctrine of frustration. Yet it follows that, if the Court of Appeal is right, there are cases in which frustration would be held not to apply if the part setting up the principle was unable to discharge the onus of proof held to be on him, while a different result would follow if the other party were relying on frustration and he was able to discharge the onus.

. . . My Lords, if the principle of frustration is that the contract automatically comes to an end irrespective of the wishes of either party, provided only that the event is 'caused by something for which neither party was responsible' (see *Maritime National Fish Ltd v Owen Trawlers Ltd* [1935] AC 524 at 531, [1953] All ER Rep 86 at 90, PC), I can see no firm ground for the proposition that the party relying on frustration in an action or in arbitration proceedings must establish affirmatively that 'the cause was not brought into operation by his default'. (I am quoting from the judgment of Scott LJ in the present case.) Such a proposition seems to me to be equivalent to laying down that the determination of the contract by frustration is not the automatic result of the event, but is dependent on the option of the parties, for neither party can be compelled to call evidence to prove affirmatively that the cause was not due to his default. . . .

Other considerations seem to me to lead to the same conclusion. Frustration may occur, as I have already mentioned, in very different circumstances. First, in cases resembling the present where there has been the destruction of a specific thing necessary for the performance of the contract. Secondly, where performance becomes virtually impossible owing to a change in the law. Thirdly, where circumstances arise which make the performance of the contract impossible in the manner and at the time contemplated. Fourthly, where performance becomes impossible by reason of the death or incapacity of a party whose continued good health was essential to the carrying out of the contract. There may be other categories, and I have not forgotten the coronation and the review cases, of which *Krell v Henry* [1903] 2 KB 740, CA, is the leading example, but they do not come within the same principle of impossibility, and I do not desire to express any opinion about them. Taking the four groups which I have mentioned, a consideration of the many different kinds of events leading to the impossibility of performance leads, I think, to the view that it would be unreasonable, if not absurd, to lay on the person relying on frustration the onus of proof that he was not responsible for the event. In the first category we have the case of fire. Destruction of a building by fire is generally due to someone's fault or negligence. If the owner of a large building, in which he employs many persons, sets up the doctrine of frustration on the ground of the destruction of the building by fire, it may be quite impossible for him to prove affirmatively that one of his employees who has left his service was not guilty of default. If both the plaintiff and the defendant have had duties to perform in the building under the terms of the contract, the cause of the fire may be due to either of them. It would not be reasonable to throw this heavy onus on the party setting up frustration, since, having regard to the fourth proposition above stated, it may be mere accidental circumstances which cause one party rather than the other to rely on the doctrine. If the destruction of the thing is due to earthquake, volcanic action, flood, storm, lightning, restraint of princes, change in the law and so forth, it would seem to be absurd to apply the suggested doctrine of onus except in very unlikely circumstances. This shows, at any rate, that the rule stated by the Court of Appeal requires some qualification. Where the contract is for personal services, the performance of which by one party depends on his health and life, no one has ever yet suggested that, if the person promising the personal service is alive and sets up frustration, he must show that his illness was not due to some rash act on his part. Nor, if the promisor is dead, would it, I think, be reasonable to expect his legal personal representative to prove absence of some default leading to the disaster.

My Lords, I also agree with the view expressed by Atkinson J that the term or condition which might reasonably be implied in relation to the destruction of the vessel in this case, or in any case of true frustration, does not throw on the plaintiff or claimant the burden of proving something which it may be impossible in practice to prove. The term or condition is not for the benefit of one party rather than the other. As I have already indicated, it is usually impossible at the date of the contract to know, if frustration of the adventure takes place, which of the two parties will desire to rely on the doctrine. In these circumstances I cannot see why a court should decide that the parties ought to be presumed to have intended that the ordinary rules as to onus of proof ought not to apply.

... In general the rule which applies is '*Ei qui affirmat non ei qui negat incumbit probatio*'. It is an ancient rule founded on considerations of good sense and it should not be departed from without strong reasons.

Lord Wright: . . . The appeal can, I think, be decided according to the generally accepted view that frustration involves as one of its elements absence of fault, by applying the ordinary rules to onus of proof. If frustration is viewed (as I think it can be) as analogous to an exception, since it is generally relied on as a defence to a claim for failure to perform a contract, the same rule will properly be applied to it as to the ordinary type of exceptions. The defence may be rebutted by proof of fault, but the onus of proving fault will rest on the plaintiff. This is merely to apply the familiar rule which is applied, for instance, where a carrier by sea relies on the exception of perils of the seas. If the goods owner then desires to rebut that prima facie defence on the ground of negligence or other fault on the part of the shipowner, it rests on the goods owner to establish the negligence or fault.

Thus, on the view most favourable to the conclusion of the Court of Appeal I still reject it. In addition, the ordinary rule is that a man is not held guilty of fault unless fault is established and found by the court. This rule, which is sometimes described as the presumption of innocence, is no doubt peculiarly important in criminal cases or matters, but it is also true in civil disputes. Thus it was said in *Thomas v Thomas* (1855) 2 K & J 79, by Wood V-C 'possession is never considered adverse if it can be referred to a legal title'. I need not multiply citations for a principle familiar to lawyers. There is, for example, no presumption of fraud. It must be alleged and proved. So, also, of other wrongful acts or breaches of contract. If it is necessary, in order to defend a claim, to prove that it was a case of felo de se and not merely innocent suicide while of unsound mind, the full fact must be affirmatively proved. An illustration, perhaps germane, is afforded by the rules as to the onus of proof in cases of unseaworthiness. If at the end of the case it is not ascertainable on the evidence that the real cause of the loss was unseaworthiness, the defence must fail.

[Lords Russell of Killowen and Porter agreed.]

R v Turner   (1816) 5 M & S 206, [1814–23] All ER Rep 713

A statute of Anne made possession of game unlawful unless the accused brought himself within one of a number of qualifications listed in a statute of Charles II. An appeal against conviction on the ground that the prosecutor had not negatived the qualifications failed before the Court of King's Bench.

Lord Ellenborough CJ: The question is, upon whom the onus probandi lies; whether it lies upon the person who affirms a qualification, to prove the affirmative, or upon the informer, who denies any qualification to prove the negative. There are, I think, about ten different heads of qualification enumerated in the statute to which the proof may be applied; and, according to the argument of to-day, every person who lays an information of this sort is bound to give satisfactory evidence before the magistrates to negative the defendant's qualification upon each of those several heads. The argument really comes to this, that there would be a moral impossibility of ever convicting upon such an information. If the informer should establish the negative of any part of these different qualifications, that would be insufficient, because it would be said, non liquet, but that the defendant may be qualified under the other. And does not, then, common sense shew, that the burden of proof ought to be cast on the person, who, by establishing any one of the qualifications, will be well defended? Is not the Statute of Anne in effect a prohibition on every person to kill game, unless he brings himself within some one of the qualifications allowed by law; the proof of which is easy on the one side, but almost impossible on the other?

Bayley J: I am of the same opinion. I have always understood it to be a general rule, that if a negative averment be made by one party, which is peculiarly within the knowledge of the other, the party within whose knowledge it lies, and who asserts the affirmative is to prove it, and not he who avers the negative. And if we consider the reason of the thing in this particular case, we cannot but see that it is next to impossible that the witness for the prosecution should be prepared to give any evidence of the defendant's want of qualification. If, indeed, it is to be presumed, that he must be acquainted with the defendant, and with his situation or habits in life, then he might give general evidence what those were; but if, as it is more probable, he is unacquainted with any of these matters, how is he to form any judgment whether he is qualified or not, from his appearance only? Therefore, if the law were to require that the witness should depose negatively to these things, it seems to me, that it might lead to the encouragement of much hardihood of swearing. The witness would have to depose to a multitude of facts; he must swear that the defendant has not an estate in his own or his wife's right, of a certain value; that he is not the son and heir apparent of an esquire, etc; but how is it at all probable, that a witness should be likely to depose with truth to such minutiæ? On the other hand, there is no hardship in casting the burden of the affirmative proof on the defendant, because he must be presumed to know his own qualification, and to be able to prove it. If the defendant plead to the information, that he is a qualified person, and require time to substantiate his plea in evidence, it is a matter of course for the justices to postpone the hearing, in order to afford him time, and an opportunity of proving his qualifications. But if the onus of proving the negative is to lie on the other party, it seems to me, that it will be the cause of many offenders escaping conviction.

[Holroyd J agreed.]

R v Spurge   [1961] 2 QB 205, [1961] 2 All ER 688, CCA

The accused raised the defence of mechanical defect as a defence to a dangerous driving charge. His appeal against conviction failed because he was aware of the defect.

Salmon J: It has been suggested by counsel for the Crown that the onus of establishing any defence based on mechanical defect must be upon the accused because necessarily the facts relating to it are peculiarly within his own knowledge. The facts, however, relating a defence of provocation or self-defence to a charge of murder are often peculiarly within the knowledge of the accused since often the only persons present at the time of the killing are the accused and the deceased. Yet once there is any evidence to support these defences, the onus of disproving them undoubtedly rests upon the prosecution. There is no rule of law that where the facts are peculiarly within the knowledge of the accused, the burden of establishing any defence based on these facts shifts to the accused. No doubt there are a number of statutes where the onus of establishing a statutory defence is placed on the accused because the facts relating to it are peculiarly within his knowledge. But we are not here considering any statutory defence.

R v Edwards   [1975] QB 27, [1974] 2 All ER 1085, CA

The defendant was convicted of selling intoxicating liquor without a justices' licence. He appealed on the ground that since the prosecution had access to the register of licences in force it should have called evidence to show that no licence was in force.

Lord Widgery CJ, Lawton LJ and Ashworth J: [After referring to *R v Jarvis* (1801) 1 East 642; *R v Stone* (1801) 1 East 639; *R v Turner* (1816) 5 M & S 206; *R v Scott* (1921) 86 JP 69; *R v Oliver* [1944] KB 68, [1943] 2 All ER 800, CCA; *John v Humphreys* [1955] 1 All ER 793, [1955] 1 WLR 325 and *Buchanan v Moore* [1963] NI 194, among other cases:]
   In our judgment this line of authority establishes that over the centuries the common law, as a result of experience and the need to ensure that justice is done both to the community and to defendants, has evolved an exception to the fundamental rule of our criminal law that the prosecution must prove every element of the offence charged. This exception, like so much else in the common law, was hammered out on the anvil of pleading. It is limited to offences arising under enactments which prohibit the doing of an act save in specified circumstances or by persons of specified classes or with specified qualifications or with the licence or permission of specified authorities. Whenever the prosecution seeks to rely on this exception, the court must construe the enactment under which the charge is laid. If the true construction is that the enactment prohibits the doing of acts, subject to provisos, exemptions and the like, then the prosecution can rely upon the exception.

In our judgment its application does not depend upon either the fact, or the presumption, that the defendant has peculiar knowledge enabling him to prove the positive of any negative averment. As Wigmore pointed out in his great *Treatise on Evidence* (1905), vol 4, p 3525, this concept of peculiar knowledge furnishes no working rule. If it did, defendants would have to prove lack of intent. What does provide a working rule is what the common law evolved from a rule of pleading. We have striven to identify it in this judgment. Like nearly all rules it could be applied oppressively; but the courts have ample powers to curb and discourage oppressive prosecutors and do not hesitate to use them.

Two consequences follow from the view we have taken as to the evolution and nature of this exception. First, as it comes into operation upon an enactment being construed in a particular way, there is no need for the prosecution to prove a prima facie case of lack of excuse, qualification or the like; and secondly, what shifts is the onus: it is for the defendant to prove that he was entitled to do the prohibited act. What rests on him is the legal or, as it is sometimes called, the persuasive burden of proof. It is not the evidential burden.

When the exception as we have adjudged it to be is applied to this case it was for the defendant to prove that he was the holder of a justices' licence, not the prosecution.

R v Hunt   [1987] AC 352, [1987] 1 All ER 1, HL

Section 5(1) of the Misuse of Drugs Act 1971 makes it unlawful to possess a controlled drug, but subsection (4) gives a very limited defence to a person charged, if he proves that that defence is open to him. Section 7 gives power to make regulations exempting specified substances, or specified conduct, from the effect of s 5(1). Morphine is a controlled drug. The effect of the combination of ss 5(1) and 7 and the Misuse of Drugs Regulations 1973 is that it is in general terms an offence to possess morphine, but that it is not an offence to possess a preparation of morphine which contains 'not more than 0.2 per cent of morphine calculated as anhydrous morphine base' and meets certain other analytical conditions; and it is not an offence for a constable, a customs officer, or certain other persons to possess morphine in the course of their duties. The accused was charged with possession of morphine. At his trial the prosecution proved that he was in possession of a preparation containing morphine, but tendered no evidence of the proportion of morphine therein.

Lord Griffiths: The unchallenged evidence of the prosecution established that the appellant had had morphine in his possession, and in these circumstances the Court of Appeal held that if the appellant wished to escape conviction the burden lay upon him to prove on the balance of probability that the preparation of morphine fell within the relevant exception contained in the Regulations. As it was obvious that the appellant neither intended to nor could discharge this burden of proof, the Court of Appeal upheld the conviction. . . . The appellant challenges the decision of the Court of Appeal by two entirely distinct arguments. It is submitted that on the true construction of the Act and the Regulations the Court of Appeal were wrong to hold that the burden was upon the defendant to prove that the powder fell within Schedule 1 to the Regulations, an argument depending upon a close consideration of this particular legislation. But the appellant also raises an argument of far wider ranging significance based upon the decision of this House in *Woolmington v DPP* [supra] and involving the submission that the leading case of *R v Edwards* [supra] was wrongly decided by the Court of Appeal.

I propose first to consider the argument based upon *Woolmington v DPP*. The starting point is the celebrated passage in the speech of Viscount Sankey LC [supra].

The appellant submits that in using the phrase 'any statutory exception' Lord Sankey LC was referring to statutory exceptions in which Parliament had by the use of express words placed the burden of proof on the accused, in the same way as the judges in *M'Naghten's Case* (1843) 10 Cl & Fin 200 had expressly placed the burden of proving insanity upon the accused. There are, of course, many examples of such statutory drafting . . .

The appellant also relies upon a passage in the speech of Viscount Simon LC in *Mancini v DPP* [supra] in which he said, at p 11:

> '*Woolmington*'s case is concerned with explaining and reinforcing the rule that the prosecution must prove the charge it makes beyond reasonable doubt, and, consequently, that if, on the material before the jury, there is a reasonable doubt, the prisoner should have the benefit of it.

The rule is of general application in all charges under the criminal law. The only exceptions arise, as explained in *Woolmington*'s case, in the defence of insanity and in offences where onus of proof is specially dealt with by statute.'

It is submitted that the use of the word 'specially' indicates that Lord Simon LC considered that the reference in *Woolmington* was limited to express statutory burdens of proof.

From this premise, it is argued that as it is well settled that if a defendant raises any of the common law defences such as accident, self-defence, provocation or duress and there is evidence to support such a defence the judge must leave it to the jury with a direction that the burden is on the prosecution to negative that defence, so it must follow that if a defendant raises any statutory defence the same rule must apply, and provided there is evidence to support such a defence the burden lies on the prosecution to negative it, the only exceptions to this rule being those cases in which the statute has by express words placed the burden of proving the defence upon the defendant.

However, in *Woolmington* the House was not concerned to consider the nature of a statutory defence or upon whom the burden of proving it might lie. The House was considering a defence of accident to a charge of murder and were concerned to correct a special rule which appeared to have emerged in charges of murder whereby once it was proved that the defendant had killed the deceased a burden was held to lie upon the defendant to excuse himself by proving that it was the result of an accident or that he had been provoked to do so or had acted in self-defence. This in effect relieved the prosecution of the burden of proving an essential element in the crime of murder, namely the malicious intent, and placed the burden upon the accused to disprove it. It was this aberration that was so trenchantly corrected by Lord Sankey. In *Mancini* the House dealt with the duty of the judge to lay before the jury any line of defence which the facts might reasonably support and they also dealt with the particular nature of the defence of provocation. In neither appeal was the House concerned with a statutory defence and no argument was addressed on the nature or scope of statutory exceptions.

Before the decision in *Woolmington* there had been a number of cases in which in trials on indictment the courts had held that the burden of establishing a statutory defence fell upon the defendant although the statute did not expressly so provide: see for example *R v Turner* [supra]. ... I cannot accept that either Viscount Sankey or Lord Simon intended to cast doubt on these long-standing decisions without having had the benefit of any argument addressed to the House on the question of statutory exceptions. I am, therefore, unwilling to read the reference to 'any statutory exception' in *Woolmington*, at p 481, in the restricted sense in which the appellant invites us to read it. It is also to be observed that Lord Devlin in *Jayasena v R* [1970] AC 618, a decision of the Privy Council, commenting upon *Woolmington* said, at p 623:

'The House laid it down that, save in the case of insanity or of a statutory defence, there was no burden laid on the prisoner to prove his innocence and that it was sufficient for him to raise a doubt as to his guilt.'

Lord Devlin does not appear to restrict a statutory defence to one in which the burden of proof is expressly placed upon the defendant . . .

Mr Zucker [Counsel for the Appellant] in a most interesting argument has challenged the conclusion of *R v Edwards* and submitted that the common law rule . . . was that an exception contained in the same clause of the Act which created the offence had to be negatived by the prosecution but if the exception or proviso were in a subsequent clause of a statute or, although in the same section, were not incorporated with the enabling clause by words of reference it was a matter of defence. From this general rule Mr Zucker submits that there were but two exceptions, namely, the burden on a defendant under the gaming laws to show that he was qualified to keep guns, bows, dogs, etc, and, secondly, that where an act was prohibited unless done pursuant to a stipulated licence or authority the defendant had to prove that he possessed the necessary licence or authority.

The authorities certainly show that a rule of pleading had evolved by the beginning of the last century, and probably well before that, in the form of the general rule stated by Mr Zucker . . .

However, as Mr Zuckerman demonstrates in his learned article 'The Third Exception to the *Woolmington* Rule' (1976) 92 LQR 402 the judges did not always regard the rules of pleading and the rules as to the burden of proof as being the same. In *Spieres v Parker* (1786) 1 Durn & E 141 Lord Mansfield CJ said, at p 144, that the prosecutor must 'negative the exceptions in the enacting clause, though he threw the burden of proof upon the other side.' And in *Jelfs v Ballard*

(1799) 1 Bos & P 467, 468 Buller J said: 'The plaintiff must state in his scire facias everything that entitles him to recover; but it is a very different question what is to be proved by one party and what by the other.'

Sometimes, however, the judges do appear to have applied the old pleading rules to determine the burden of proof . . .

It seems likely that these cases played their part in leading Parliament to repeal section 14 of the Act of 1848 and to replace it by section 39(2) of the Summary Jurisdiction Act 1879 (42 & 43 Vict c 49) which was in substantially the same language as the present section 101 of the Magistrates' Courts Act 1980. As Lord Pearson pointed out in *Nimmo v Alexander Cowan & Sons Ltd* [1968] AC 107, Parliament was here emphasising that it was the substance and effect as well as the form of the enactment that mattered when considering upon whom it was intended that the burden of proof should lie under any particular Act.

It seems to me that the probabilities are that Parliament when it enacted section 14 of the Act of 1848 was intending to apply to summary trial that which they believed to be the rule relating to burden of proof evolved by the judges on trials on indictment. It seems unlikely that Parliament would have wished to introduce confusion by providing for different burdens of proof in summary trials as opposed to trials on indictment. Looking back over so many years this must, to some extent, be speculation and I bear in mind that whereas the defendant could give evidence on his own behalf in a summary trial it was not until 1898 that he was allowed to do so in a trial on indictment which might be a reason for placing a heavier burden of proof on the prosecution in trials on indictment.

However, my Lords, the common law adapts itself and evolves to meet the changing patterns and needs of society; it is not static. By the time the Act of 1879 was passed there were already many offences that were triable both summarily and on indictment. This list of offences has been growing steadily and the very crime with which we are concerned in this appeal is such an example. It is conceded that in the case of exceptions within the meaning of section 101 of the Act of 1980 the burden of proving the exception has been specifically placed upon the defendant. The law would have developed on absurd lines if in respect of the same offence the burden of proof today differed according to whether the case was heard by the magistrates or on indictment . . .

There have been a number of cases considered by the Court of Appeal since *Woolmington* concerning the burden of proof in licensing cases both on indictment and on summary trial. There is no indication in any of these cases that the court considered that there should be any difference of approach to the burden of proof according to whether the case was tried summarily or on indictment . . .

Whatever may have been its genesis I am satisfied that the modern rule was encapsulated by Lord Wilberforce in *Nimmo v Alexander Cowan & Sons Ltd*, when speaking of the Scottish section which was then the equivalent of the present section 101 of the Magistrates' Courts Act 1980:

'I would think, then, that the section merely states the orthodox principle (common to both the criminal and the civil law) that exceptions, etc, are to be set up by those who rely on them.'

I would summarise the position thus far by saying that *Woolmington* did not lay down a rule that the burden of proving a statutory defence only lay upon the defendant if the statute specifically so provided: that a statute can, on its true construction, place a burden of proof on the defendant although it does not do so expressly: that if a burden of proof is placed on the defendant it is the same burden whether the case be tried summarily or on indictment, namely, a burden that has to be discharged on the balance of probabilities.

The real difficulty in these cases lies in determining upon whom Parliament intended to place the burden of proof when the statute has not expressly so provided. It presents particularly difficult problems of construction when what might be regarded as a matter of defence appears in a clause creating the offence rather than in some subsequent proviso from which it may more readily be inferred that it was intended to provide for a separate defence which a defendant must set up and prove if he wishes to avail himself of it. This difficulty was acutely demonstrated in *Nimmo v Alexander Cowan & Sons Ltd*. Section 29(1) of the Factories Act 1961 provides:

'There shall, so far as is reasonably practicable, be provided and maintained safe means of access to every place at which any person has at any time to work, and every such place shall, so far as is reasonably practicable, be made and kept safe for any person working there.'

The question before the House was whether the burden of proving that it was not reasonably practicable to make the working place safe lay upon the defendant or the plaintiff in a civil action. However, as the section also created a summary offence the same question would have arisen in a prosecution. In the event, the House divided three to two on the construction of the section, Lord Reid and Lord Wilberforce holding that the section required the plaintiff or prosecution to prove that it was reasonably practicable to make the working place safe, the majority, Lord Guest, Lord Upjohn and Lord Pearson, holding that if the plaintiff or prosecution proved that the working place was not safe it was for the defendant to excuse himself by proving that it was not reasonably practicable to make it safe. However, their Lordships were in agreement that if the linguistic construction of the statute did not clearly indicate upon whom the burden should lie the court should look to other considerations to determine the intention of Parliament such as the mischief at which the Act was aimed and practical considerations affecting the burden of proof and, in particular, the ease or difficulty that the respective parties would encounter in discharging the burden. I regard this last consideration as one of great importance for surely Parliament can never lightly be taken to have intended to impose an onerous duty on a defendant to prove his innocence in a criminal case, and a court should be very slow to draw any such inference from the language of a statute.

When all the cases are analysed, those in which the courts have held that the burden lies on the defendant are cases in which the burden can be easily discharged. This point can be demonstrated by what, at first blush, appear to be two almost indistinguishable cases that arose under wartime regulations. In *R v Oliver* [1944] KB 68 the defendant was prosecuted for selling sugar without a licence. The material part of the Sugar (Control) Order . . . provided:

'Subject to any directions given or except under and in accordance with the terms of a licence permit or other authority granted by or on behalf of the Minister no . . . wholesaler shall by way of trade supply . . . any sugar.'

The Court of Criminal Appeal held that this placed the burden upon the defendant to prove that he had the necessary licence to sell sugar. In *R v Putland and Sorrell* [1946] 1 All ER 85, the defendant was charged with acquiring silk stockings without surrendering clothing coupons. The material part of the Consumer Rationing (Consolidation)Order 1944 . . . provided: 'A person shall not acquire rationed goods . . . without surrendering . . . coupons.' The Court of Criminal Appeal there held that the burden was upon the prosecution to prove that the clothing had been bought without the surrender of coupons. The real distinction between these two cases lies in the comparative difficulty which would face a defendant in discharging the burden of proof.

In *Oliver*'s case it would have been a simple matter for the defendant to prove that he had a licence if such was the case but in the case of purchase of casual articles of clothing it might, as the court pointed out in *Putland*'s case, be a matter of the utmost difficulty for a defendant to establish that he had given the appropriate number of coupons for them. It appears to me that it was this consideration that led the court to construe that particular regulation as imposing the burden of proving that coupons had not been surrendered upon the prosecution.

In *R v Edwards* the Court of Appeal expressed their conclusion in the form of an exception to what they said was the fundamental rule of our criminal law that the prosecution must prove every element of the offence charged. They said that the exception

'is limited to offences arising under enactments which prohibit the doing of an act save in specified circumstances or by persons of specified classes or with specified qualifications or with the licence or permission of specified authorities.'

I have little doubt that the occasions upon which a statute will be construed as imposing a burden of proof upon a defendant which do not fall within this formulation are likely to be exceedingly rare. But I find it difficult to fit *Nimmo v Alexander Cowan & Sons Ltd* into this formula, and I would prefer to adopt the formula as an excellent guide to construction rather than as an exception to a rule. In the final analysis each case must turn upon the construction of the particular legislation to determine whether the defence is an exception within the meaning of section 101 of the Act of 1980 which the Court of Appeal rightly decided reflects the rule for trials on indictment. With this one qualification I regard *R v Edwards* as rightly decided.

My Lords, I am, of course, well aware of the body of distinguished academic opinion that urges that wherever a burden of proof is placed upon a defendant by statute the burden should be an evidential burden and not a persuasive burden, and that it has the support of the distinguished signatories to the 11th Report of the Criminal Law Revision Committee, Evidence (General) (1972) (Cmnd 4991). My Lords, such a fundamental change is, in my view, a matter for Parliament and not a decision of your Lordships' House.

With these considerations in mind I turn now to the question of construction. The essence of the offence is having in one's possession a prohibited substance. In order to establish guilt the prosecution must therefore prove that the prohibited substance is in the possession of the defendant. As it is an offence to have morphine in one form but not an offence to have morphine in another form the prosecution must prove that the morphine is in the prohibited form for otherwise no offence is established . . .

I do not share the anxieties of the Court of Appeal that this may place an undue burden on the prosecution. It must be extremely rare for a prosecution to be brought under the Act of 1971 without the substance in question having been analysed. If it has been analysed there will be no difficulty in producing evidence to show that it does not fall within Schedule 1 to the Regulations. I pause here to observe that the analyst was in court during this trial and could, no doubt, have given this evidence if called upon to do so. In future the evidence can, of course, be included in the analyst's report. On the other hand if the burden of proof is placed upon the defendant he may be faced with very real practical difficulties in discharging it. The suspected substance is usually seized by the police for the purposes of analysis and there is no statutory provision entitling the defendant to a proportion of it. Often there is very little of the substance and if it has already been analysed by the prosecution it may have been destroyed in the process. In those cases, which I would surmise are very rare, in which it is intended to prosecute without an analyst's report there will have to be evidence from which the inference can be drawn that the substance was a prohibited drug and such evidence may well permit of the inference that it was not one of the relatively harmless types of compounds containing little more than traces of the drugs which are contained in Schedule 1 to the Regulations.

Finally, my Lords, as this question of construction is obviously one of real difficulty I have regard to the fact that offences involving the misuse of hard drugs are among the most serious in the criminal calendar and, subject to certain special defences the burden whereof is specifically placed upon the defendant, they are absolute. In these circumstances, it seems to me right to resolve any ambiguity in favour of the defendant and to place the burden of proving the nature of the substance involved in so serious an offence upon the prosecution.

[Lord Keith of Kinkel agreed with Lord Griffiths, and Lord Mackay of Clashfern and Lord Ackner delivered concurring judgments: Lord Templeman agreed in the result.]

COMMENT

1. Note that the courts of Eire (*McGowan v Carville* [1960] IR 330), Victoria (*Everard v Opperman* [1958] VLR 389) and New Zealand (*Hall v Dunlop* [1959] NZLR 1031 at 1036) differed from *R v Edwards*. See Zuckerman (1976) 92 LQR 401. But the principles of *R v Edwards* and *R v Hunt* were approved by the High Court of Australia in *DPP v United Telecasters Sydney Ltd* (1990) 168 CLR 594, and have been followed in England in *R v Alath Construction Ltd* [1990] 1 WLR 1255, CA (in which the trial judge, whose ruling was upheld by the Court of Appeal, was Mr Recorder Zucker QC).

2. *R v Hunt* has been welcomed in that it encourages a purposive construction in solving the question, rather than submission to the 'tyranny of verbal formulation', and criticised in that in departing from what is seen as the principle of *Woolmington* it potentially allows judges and considerations of policy, rather than Parliament and the words of the statute, to determine where the burden of proof lies. See Zuckerman (1987) 103 LQR 170; Mirfield [1988] Crim LR 19 and 233. Note that, as Tapper points out, (Cross, p 150), 'this was no mere incantation of high sounding theory, but was expressed in practical terms by reversing the Court of Appeal, and quashing the conviction on the basis of a very strict construction of the relevant provision, which could be taken to reduce to a minimum the number of cases in which a persuasive burden would be cast on the defence.' In *Vasquez v R* [1994] 3 All ER 674, [1994] 1 WLR 1304, PC, the Privy Council was concerned, inter alia, with the question whether in Belize a provision in the Criminal Code placing the burden of proving extreme provocation in order to reduce a charge of murder to manslaughter, was consistent with the Constitution, which established a presumption of innocence but authorised the placing of a burden of proving 'particular facts' on the accused. It was held that the absence of provocation was an essential part of the offence of murder, so that its presence could not be characterised as 'particular facts': the attempt to place the burden on the accused was unconstitutional.

QUESTIONS

1. How can *R v Edwards* be reconciled with *R v Curgerwen* (1865) LR 1 CCR 1?
2. Is the argument of *R v Edwards* and *R v Hunt* sufficient to show that this type of case was in truth contemplated by the House of Lords in *Woolmington* as a 'statutory exception'? Cf the passage from *Mancini v DPP* [1942] AC 1 at 11, [1941] 3 All ER 272 at 279, HL, to which Lord Griffiths refers in *R v Hunt*, supra.
3. What precisely is the justification for the rule that where, as in *R v Edwards*, a burden is placed on the accused, it is the legal and not merely the evidential burden?
4. Does the accused bear an evidential burden in respect of all defences which are more than mere denials of an allegation necessary to the prosecution's case? See Cross, pp 131–2; Glanville Williams (1978) 128 NLJ 182.

3   The burden of proof of insanity

There is some controversy over whether this should be properly placed on the accused, as English and Commonwealth courts have. American courts have differed sharply on the question and continue to do so.

Thomas v R   (1960) 102 CLR 584

Windeyer J: The 'golden thread that runs throughout the web of English criminal law' is broken by the defence of insanity. It is better to recognise this than to rationalise it. For there is really no logical answer to the rhetorical question of Harlan J, asked in the course of delivering the impressive judgment of the Supreme Court of the United States in *Davis v United States*, 'How, then, upon principle or consistently with humanity can a verdict of guilty be properly returned if the jury entertain a reasonable doubt as to the existence of a fact which is essential to guilt, namely, the capacity in law of the accused to commit that crime?' 160 US 469 at 488 (1895). Nevertheless, it is the firmly established rule of our law that when insanity is put forward as a defence to a criminal charge, it is for the defence to show that the accused was, in the relevant sense, insane.

Reference should be made to Williams, *Criminal Law: The General Part* (2nd edn), para 288. He argues that the legal burden of proving insanity can only rest on the accused where the issue is whether the accused knew that what he was doing was wrong. It cannot rest on him where the issue is whether the accused knew the nature and quality of his act, for if he does not, he lacks mens rea, and the burden of proving mens rea rests on the prosecution.

4   Shifting the burden

It is often said that during trial a 'shifting' of the burden of proof occurs. It is doubtful whether the phrase has much utility. It is used in four senses, of which the first and fourth are otiose and ambiguous, the second unnecessary, and the third wrong.

One function of the phrase is to describe the answer given by the court to the question whether the proponent on some issue has made out a case to answer. If there is a case to answer, the proponent has discharged the evidential burden; it has 'shifted'. In this sense the phrase is otiose since perfectly clear words already exist to make the point. It is also ambiguous. It may mean that the proponent's evidence has been weighty enough to entitle a reasonable man to decide in his favour, though not weighty enough to compel him to do so. The burden has shifted to the opponent in the sense that as a matter of prudence he should answer the case. If he fails to, he may, but will not necessarily, lose. The other sense of shifting the evidential burden applies where the proponent's evidence is so weighty as to compel a reasonable man to decide in the proponent's favour unless it is answered. The burden that has shifted forces the opponent to call evidence or lose (for an example of this usage see *Brady (Inspector of Taxes) v Group Lotus Car Companies plc* [1987] 2 All ER 674 at 686 per Sir Nicolas Browne-Wilkinson VC). Bridge calls the first kind of evidence 'prima facie' and the second 'presumptive' (12 MLR 273 at 277). Lord Denning would call the first burden 'provisional' (language adopted in *Poricanin v Australian Consolidated Industries Ltd* [1979] 2 NSWLR 419 at 425–6 and *DPP v Morgan* [1976] AC 182 at 217, [1975] 2 All ER 347 at 364, HL) and the second 'compelling' (61 LQR 379 at 380). The first shifting of the burden is 'tactical'; once it occurs it is important only to the parties. The second concerns more than a matter of tactics, and indicates failure or success in discharging the legal burden (Cross, pp 126-8). The difference, which is one of degree, may be illustrated by the case of a ship sinking. If unseaworthiness is alleged and the proponent proves that it sank six months after leaving port, the evidential burden would have shifted so as to put a provisional burden on the other side: he may, but will not necessarily, lose without further evidence. But if it is proved that the ship sank ten minutes after leaving its berth, the evidential burden would have so shifted as to put a compelling burden on the other side: the latter's silence will cause him to lose (*Pickup v Thames and Mersey Marine Insurance Co Ltd* (1878) 3 QBD 594, CA; *Skandia Insurance Co Ltd v Skoljarer* (1979) 142 CLR 375).

During a trial there can be no other shifting of any evidential burden that is relevant for the judge or trier of fact. A party may have to make all kinds of sudden decisions about either putting in new evidence which may improve or, if disbelieved, worsen his position, or adopting new lines of cross-examination depending on his estimate of the changing strength of his case; but this can have no legal significance because the evidential burden is relevant to the judge on two occasions: when he decides who has the right to begin and whether there is a case to answer. However, a second function of the phrase 'shifting the burden' is to state the truism that the state of convincing evidence on a given issue varies as the trial proceeds (an example of this usage is *Brady (Inspector of Taxes) v Group Lotus Car Companies plc* [1987] 3 All ER 1050 at 1059 per Mustill LJ: he calls this the 'evidentiary burden of proof'). The swinging back and forth of the evidential burden would only be legally significant if the trial was suddenly frozen at various stages. In fact the trial is only frozen at three points for particular purposes: the outset (who begins?), the end of the proponent's case (is there a case to answer?) and the end (who wins on that issue?). It is misleading to think of the trial as a tennis match and the evidential burden as a ball: 'there are no points to be gained merely by sending the evidential burden back across the net, and what is more, no one is keeping score . . . The shifting of the evidential burden during the trial is therefore . . . only part of a process of reasoning, sometimes convenient and sometimes dangerous, whereby the judge assesses the probabilities by dividing up the evidence into those facts which tend to support one party and those which his opponent has proved in reply' (Hoffmann, p 353).

A third sense in which the burden of proof is said to shift is when the legal burden is said to shift. However, this usage is probably not merely otiose or confusing, but wrong. Orthodoxy requires that the legal burden in fact never shifts (*May v O'Sullivan* (1955) 92 CLR 654). As Hoffmann says (p 348):

'If the impression of shifting is given, it will always be found that there is really more than one issue. For as a matter of ordinary logic, if the plaintiff proves a fact which places upon the defendant, in order to avoid an adverse judgment, the burden of disproving X, then what the plaintiff proved must have been something other than X. One cannot disprove a fact which is held to have been proved.'

The problem may be illustrated by the problem of proving a child's legitimacy. He who bears the legal burden must prove a valid marriage between the parents and birth in wedlock. Some say the legal burden of proving illegitimacy by non-access then shifts. The orthodox say there is not one issue of legitimacy but three – a valid marriage, birth in wedlock and access. The legal burden of the first two rests on one side, the legal burden of proving non-access on the other. There is no shifting of the burden. 'What shifts is the obligation; but it is an obligation to prove different facts' (Nokes, p 480). This reasoning is not affected by occasional difficulty in correctly isolating the issues. Admittedly it makes no practical difference which view is correct. The only functions of the legal burden are to determine who wins if the evidence is evenly balanced at the end of the case, and to suggest who should begin calling evidence (since the evidential burden and the legal burden usually lie in the same place). Orthodoxy and unorthodoxy produce the same result in both cases.

The discussion now leads to the fourth meaning of 'shifting the burden'. In a criminal case, the Crown has the legal burden of proving all issues but insanity. If it produces sufficient evidence to convict the accused, the 'ultimate burden' of proof can be said to have shifted to the accused, because he must prove insanity, adduce contradictory evidence or lose. There has been no shifting of any legal burden, for a new issue has arisen; but the ultimate burden of winning the case has shifted. (See also *Medawar v Grand Hotel Co* [1891] 2 QB 11, [1891–4] All ER Rep 571, CA; *Ratford v Northavon District Council* [1987] QB 357 at 370, [1986] 3 All ER 193 at 202, CA; *Brady (Inspector of Taxes) v Group Lotus Car Companies plc* [1987] 3 All ER 1050 at 1058 per Mustill LJ. 'Shifting the burden' in this sense is otiose language, for all it refers to is the necessity for a party to win on the case as a whole. It is also potentially confusing, for the ultimate burden may not be distinguished from the various legal burdens and may thus suggest there is only one legal burden, whereas in fact there is one legal burden for every issue in the case.

FURTHER READING

Adams, *Criminal Onus and Exculpations* (Wellington, NZ, 1968); Bridge 12 MLR 273; Denning (1945) 61 LQR 379; Kiralfy (ed), *The Burden of Proof* (London, 1987); Roberts [1995] Crim LR 783; Thayer, ch 9; Williams in Campbell and Waller.

CHAPTER 3

Standard of Proof

Miller v Minister of Pensions **[1947] 2 All ER 372**

Denning J: ... [T]he degree of cogency required in a criminal case before an accused person is found guilty ... is well settled. It need not reach certainty, but it must carry a high degree of probability. Proof beyond reasonable doubt does not mean proof beyond the shadow of a doubt. The law would fail to protect the community if it admitted fanciful possibilities to deflect the course of justice. If the evidence is so strong against a man as to leave only a remote possibility in his favour which can be dismissed with the sentence 'of course it is possible, but not in the least probable', the case is proved beyond reasonable doubt, but nothing short of that will suffice.

... [T]he degree of cogency ... required to discharge a burden in a civil case ... is well settled. It must carry a reasonable degree of probability, but not so high as is required in a criminal case. If the evidence is such that the tribunal can say: 'We think it more probable than not,' the burden is discharged, but, if the probabilities are equal, it is not.

1 Formulation of the standards

After some doubt, it is now settled that in civil cases the standard of proof is the balance of probabilities; in criminal cases the prosecution must attain a standard of proof beyond reasonable doubt, and the accused need attain only the lesser civil standard (*R v Carr-Briant* [1943] KB 607, [1943] 2 All ER 156, CCA). What remains doubtful is precisely how a standard should be explained to the jury. Appeals are often successful against judicial explanations, and in the 1950s the Court of Criminal Appeal strongly criticised the use of the time-honoured 'reasonable doubt' formula in criminal cases (*R v Summers* [1952] 1 All ER 1059, CCA). However, in ascending order of merit, it now seems permissible to say 'beyond reasonable doubt', or 'completely satisfied', or 'feel sure' (*R v Hepworth* [1955] 2 QB 600 at 603, [1955] 2 All ER 918, CCA) and the formula 'beyond reasonable doubt' is returning to favour in England: *McGreevy v DPP* [1973] 1 All ER 503, [1973] 1 WLR 276; *R v Sang* [1980] AC 402, [1979] 2 All ER 1222 at 1230 and 1237, HL; and *Ferguson v R* [1979] 1 All ER 877, [1979] 1 WLR 94, PC. It is not clear that attempts to improve on 'beyond reasonable doubt' can hope to succeed. Wigmore attacked the far wider range of American formulae as 'useless refinements', 'wordy quibbles' and 'maunderings', calculated only to confuse the jury and entrap the judge into forgetfulness of some detail or precedent. 'The truth is no one has yet invented or discovered a mode of measurement for the intensity of human belief. Hence there can be yet no successful method of communicating intelligibly to a jury a sound method of self-analysis for one's belief' (para 2497).

Scientific certainty is not required; a remote hypothesis may be set aside even if it cannot be scientifically disproved: *R v Bracewell* (1978) 68 Cr App Rep 44.

R v Hepworth and Fearnley   [1955] 2 QB 600, [1955] 2 All ER 918, CCA

The only indication given by the recorder in his summing up to the jury of the standard of proof was use of the word 'satisfied'. This was criticised by the Court of Criminal Appeal.

Lord Goddard CJ: It may be, especially considering the number of cases recently in which this question has arisen, that I misled courts because I said in *R v Summers* [1952] 1 All ER 1059, CCA – and I still adhere to it – that I thought that it was very unfortunate to talk to juries about 'reasonable doubt' because the explanations given as to what is and what is not a reasonable doubt are so very often extraordinarily difficult to follow and it is very difficult to tell a jury what is a reasonable doubt. To tell a jury that it must not be a fanciful doubt is something that is without any real guidance. To tell them that a reasonable doubt is such a doubt as to cause them to hesitate in their own affairs never seems to me to convey any particular standard; one member of the jury might say he would hesitate over something and another member might say that would not cause him to hesitate at all. I therefore suggested that it would be better to use some other expression, by which I meant to convey to the jury that they should only convict if they felt sure of the guilt of the accused. It may be that in some cases the word 'satisfied' is enough. Then, it is said that the jury in a civil case has to be satisfied and, therefore, one is only laying down the same standard of proof as in a civil case. I confess that I have had some difficulty in understanding how there is or there can be two standards; therefore, one would be on safe ground if one said in a criminal case to a jury: 'You must be satisfied beyond reasonable doubt' and one could also say: 'You, the jury must be completely satisfied,' or better still: 'You must feel sure of the prisoner's guilt.' But I desire to repeat what I said in *R v Kritz* [1950] 1 KB 82 at 89, [1949] 2 All ER 406 at 410: 'It is not the particular formula that matters: it is the effect of the summing-up. If the jury are made to understand that they have to be satisfied and must not return a verdict against a defendant unless they feel sure, and that the onus is all the time on the prosecution and not on the defence,' that is enough.

R v Onufrejczyk   [1955] 1 QB 388, [1955] 1 All ER 247, CCA

Oliver J said in summing up: 'the fact of death should be proved by such circumstances as render the commission of the crime morally certain and leave no ground for reasonable doubt'. The Court of Criminal Appeal criticised the use of the word 'morally'.

Lord Goddard CJ: It is always a pity, when dealing with evidence, to use epithets either to increase or decrease its value; and when cases in the books use expressions such as 'a high degree of certainty' or 'strong evidence' and so on, they really add nothing to what the law requires. The law requires a case to be proved, and a jury is warned and told that its members have to be satisfied on the evidence that the crime is proved, that the prisoner is guilty of the crime; and they should be told that if when they have heard the evidence they are not satisfied, and do not feel sure that the crime has been committed or that the prisoner has committed the crime, their verdict should be 'not guilty'. Let us leave out of account, if we can, any expression such as 'giving the prisoner the benefit of the doubt'. It is not a question of giving him the benefit of the doubt, for if the jury are left with any degree of doubt that the prisoner is guilty, the case has not been proved.

See also *R v Yap Chuan Ching* (1976) 63 Cr App Rep 7, CA.

Thomas v R (1960) 102 CLR 584

In the course of his summing up the trial judge said of the standard of proof: 'There is no particular magic about the way you've got to consider it, no special rules, you consider it in an ordinary common sense manner and in the way you would consider the more serious matters which come up for consideration and decision in your lives, and if considering it in that way . . . you come to a feeling of comfortable satisfaction that the accused is guilty, then you should find him so guilty.'

An appeal to the West Australian Court of Appeal failed but succeeded before the High Court of Australia.

McTiernan J: [T]here is a danger in venturing upon a novel elucidation of this principle of the criminal law. It is dubious advice to tell the jury that no particular magic is required to perform their duty. To assure them that they are not bound by any special rules is calculated to encourage them to believe they are chartered libertines. Surely they are bound to estimate the credit due to each witness and weigh the evidence and to deliberate in a judicial manner. The expression 'the more serious matters which come up for consideration' is vague. It would include a wide range of matters of various grades of seriousness. Experience of such matters is invaluable in the jury room but it is not right to tell the jury that they may decide whether the accused is guilty or not guilty in the same sort of fashion as they decide serious matters that arise for their decision out of court.

Fullager J: [W]hat is required to justify a conviction is proof beyond reasonable doubt; see generally *Brown v R* (1913) 17 CLR 570 at 584–6, 594–6. It should be noted that in this case Barton ACJ said: '. . . one embarks on a dangerous sea if he attempts to define with precision a term which is in ordinary and common use with relation to this subject matter, and which is usually stated to a jury without embellishment as a well understood expression' (at 584). Then 'comfortable satisfaction' has perhaps gained a certain currency, but even in civil cases it has little, in my opinion, to recommend it. It was used by Rich J in *Briginshaw v Briginshaw* (1938) 60 CLR 336 at 350, in relation to the standard of proof in cases where adultery is in issue. But his Honour was careful to distinguish the standard conveyed by that expression from the standard required in criminal cases and conveyed by the words 'proof beyond reasonable doubt'. In truth, to 'come to the feeling' referred to in his Honour's charge is by no means the same thing as being satisfied beyond reasonable doubt.

Kitto J: Whether a doubt is reasonable is for the jury to say; and the danger that invests an attempt to explain what 'reasonable' means is that the attempt not only may prove unhelpful but may obscure the vital point that the accused must be given the benefit of any doubt which the jury considers reasonable.

Windeyer J: [A]lthough the direction conveyed by the words taken as a whole and in relation to the rest of the charge must be said to be erroneous, I would point out that many of his Honour's phrases taken by themselves are not without precedent and approval. The reference to 'the more serious matters that come up for consideration and decision in your lives' is, however, somewhat weaker than Pollock CB's 'that degree of certainty with which you decide upon and conclude your own most important transactions in life'. And it is not without significance that the editors of Foster & Finlason's Report wrote in 1867 that that direction 'somewhat startled the profession' because it was a departure from 'the old, safe, well-established rule' that the jury should be satisfied beyond all reasonable doubt of the prisoner's guilt: see footnote to *R v White* (1865) 4 F & F 383. Attempts by paraphrase and embellishment to explain to juries what is meant by satisfaction beyond reasonable doubt are not always helpful. And explanation is not always necessary. Wigmore's observation on this point are filled with good sense (*Wigmore on Evidence* (3rd edn), vol IX para 2497, p 316). I would add, although it does not arise from any omission by the learned judge in this case, that, in my view, it is not desirable that the time-honoured expression 'satisfied beyond reasonable doubt' should be omitted and some substitute adopted. It is said that it was 'invented by the common-law judges for the very reason that it was capable of being understood and applied by men in the jury box' (quoted in *Wigmore on Evidence* (3rd edn), vol IX, para 2497, p 323). The expression 'proof beyond a doubt' conveys a meaning without lawyers' elaborations. Othello's meaning was clear enough: '. . . so prove it, that the probation bear no hinge nor loop to hang a doubt on'. For generations jurymen have been directed in terms of 'reasonable doubt', 'moral certainty' and 'the benefit of the doubt'. Now it has been suggested in England, mainly by Lord Goddard, that these phrases should be abandoned. With great respect for those whose great experience has led them to this view I think that it would be unfortunate if it were adopted in Australia. The House of Lords said in *Mancini v DPP* [1942] AC 1 at 13; [1941] 3 All ER 272 at 280, that a direction 'as to reasonable doubt' must be 'plainly given'.

The best and plainest way to give it is, I venture to think, to tell the jury that they must be satisfied beyond all reasonable doubt. In the same case it was said that there is 'no prescribed formula' – in *Bullard v R* it becomes 'no magic formula' [1957] AC 635 at 645, [1961] 3 All ER 470n, PC. But that no particular form of words is prescribed does not mean that an old and well-known expression is to be proscribed.

Of course, if the trial judge thinks that, influenced by advocacy or for some other reason, the jury may conjure up mere chimeras of doubt, he may well emphasise that for a doubt to stand in the way of a conviction of guilt it must be a real doubt and a reasonable doubt – a doubt which after a full and fair consideration of the evidence the jury really on reasonable grounds entertain.

[Taylor J agreed.]

See, in the same effect, *R v Gray* (1973) 58 Cr App Rep 177, CA; cf *Ferguson v R* [1979] 1 All ER 877, [1979] 1 WLR 94, PC.

Dawson v R   (1961) 106 CLR 1

Dixon CJ: [I]n my view it is a mistake to depart from the time-honoured formula. It is, I think, used by ordinary people and is understood well enough by the average man in the community. The attempts to substitute other expressions, of which there have been many examples not only here but in England, have never prospered. It is wise as well as proper to avoid such expressions.

Sodeman v R   (1936) 55 CLR 192

Starke J: English-speaking juries understand English words and phrases, as do most other English-speaking people, in their plain and ordinary significance. A phrase such as 'the preponderance of probabilities' is grandiloquent enough, but would probably be less understood by a jury than the common English words that they must be satisfied of the insanity of the accused.

According to *R v Penny* (1991) 94 Cr App Rep 345 at 350, CA, 'it is usually best to keep the direction on this important point short and clear'.

Fewer problems have arisen in formulating the civil standard, but the phrase 'balance of probabilities' does have its dangers. It may suggest that to satisfy the standard one need only introduce enough evidence to disturb a balanced pair of scales. But in fact if one party gives a little evidence and the other none, the former will not necessarily succeed. The former's contention may be inherently improbable; and failure to contradict an assertion does not necessarily make it credible. As Hoffmann says (p 365), 'What is being weighed in the "balance" is not quantities of evidence but the probabilities arising from that evidence and all the circumstances of the case.' In *Rhesa Shipping Co SA v Edmunds, The Popi M* [1985] 2 All ER 712 at 718, [1985] 1 WLR 948 at 956, HL, Lord Brandon said it was wrong for the trial judge to regard

'himself as compelled to choose between two theories, both of which he regarded as extremely improbable, or one of which he regarded as extremely improbable and the other of which he regarded as virtually impossible. He should have borne in mind, and considered carefully in his judgment, the third alternative which was open to him, namely that the evidence left him in doubt as to the cause of the aperture in the ship's hull, and that, in these circumstances, the ship owners had failed to discharge the burden of proof which was on them.'

In short, a specific level of probability must be attained, not a mere relative preponderance over the evidence of the opponent.

The standard of proof beyond reasonable doubt in criminal cases does not extend to facts relevant to sentence: *R v Welsh* [1983] 1 Qd R 592.

It is a misdirection to direct a jury about any presumption of innocence applying to witnesses, because that presumption is only relevant to the accused, and such a direction may lead the jury to the view that they should only reject the evidence of police officers if satisfied beyond reasonable doubt that they are lying: *Howe v R* (1980) 32 ALR 478.

The standard of proof of contempt of court, even civil contempt, is beyond reasonable doubt: *Re Bramblevale Ltd* [1970] Ch 128, [1969] 3 All ER 1062; *Comet Products UK Ltd v Hawkex Plastics Ltd* [1971] 2 QB 67 at 73, [1971] 1 All ER 1141 at 1144, per Lord Denning MR; *Australasian Meat Industry Employees Union v Mudginberry Station Pty Ltd* (1986) 161 CLR 98 at 106–9, per Gibbs CJ, Mason, Wilson and Deane JJ; *Hinch v A-G (Vic)* (1987) 164 CLR 15 at 50 and 86, per Deane J and Gaudron J; *Witham v Holloway* (1995) 69 ALJR 847.

The standard of proof resting on the prosecution of facts antecedent to admissibility is, it seems, the criminal standard: *R v Yacoob* (1981) 72 Cr App Rep 313; *R v Ewing* [1983] QB 1039, [1983] 2 All ER 645; cf *R v Angeli* [1978] 3 All ER 950, [1979] 1 WLR 26, CA. Apart from the special case of confessions, this approach may be questioned.

Where the case against the accused rests substantially on circumstantial evidence the jury should not convict unless the circumstances are inconsistent with any reasonable hypothesis other than guilt (*Grant v R* (1975) 11 ALR 503; *Barka v R* (1974) 133 CLR 82), but they need not receive an express direction to that effect as long as it is made plain they must be satisfied of guilt beyond reasonable doubt (*McGreevy v DPP* [1973] 1 All ER 503, [1973] 1 WLR 276; *Knight v R* (1992) 66 ALJR 860). See Glass (1981) 55 ALJ 842 at 852–3.

Is it wrong for the jury to consider each item of evidence separately and eliminate it from consideration unless satisfied beyond reasonable doubt? The authorities support a negative answer: see the High Court of Australia in *Chamberlain v R (No 2)* (1984) 153 CLR 521 at 534–9, 570, 599 and 626–7, and the Supreme Court of Canada in *R v Morin* (1988) 66 CR (3d) 1. Can the jury view a fact as a basis for an inference of guilt which is not itself, even at the end of the day when considered with other evidence, proved beyond reasonable doubt? The authorities favouring a negative answer are the majority in *Chamberlain's Case* (1984) 153 CLR 521 at 534–9, 570 and 599 (Deane J disagreeing at 626–7), and the minority in *Morin's Case*; see also *R v Van Beelen* [1972] 4 SASR 353 at 379; among those favouring a positive answer are the majority in *Morin's Case*, Eggleston, p 122, Glass (1981) 55 ALR 842 at 850–1. See also *Thomas v R* [1972] 2 NZLR 34, CA, and Wigmore, para 2497. In *Shepherd v R* (1990) 170 CLR 573 an intermediate position was expounded: it is not necessary that each individual item of evidence proffered as the basis of a

circumstantial inference should be proved beyond reasonable doubt, but intermediate facts constituting indispensable links in a chain of reasoning towards
an inference of guilt should be proved to the standard, and in some cases it
may be appropriate for the jury to be so directed.

J C Smith: Criminal Evidence (1995), p 43

Satisfying the jury is not necessarily the same as satisfying each individual juror. Take an
extreme case. D is charged with obtaining £1000 from P by deception and the indictment
alleges 12 separate false statements, each directed to obtaining the whole sum. It is sufficient for
the prosecution to prove that D made one of the statements dishonestly and thereby induced P
to pay the money. If the jury are all satisfied that he made statement no (1), knowing it to be
false, and thereby induced P to pay him £1000, this is enough. It is immaterial that they are not
satisfied, or disagree about, the remaining allegations; the verdict is guilty. Suppose, however,
that each juror is satisfied that one, and only one, of the 12 statements was made dishonestly;
but each juror is satisfied as to a different statement from every other juror. Each juror is satisfied that D is guilty of the offence of obtaining the money by deception because one operative
false statement is enough; but to say the jury is satisfied would be a travesty. Every allegation
made by the prosecution is disbelieved (or at least not believed) by 11 out of 12 jurors. . . . [The
author goes on to discuss *Brown* (1983) 79 Cr App Rep 115, CA.]

2   Justification

The formulation of the different standards of proof is one thing; their justification is another. The high modern criminal standard appears to have
originated at the end of the eighteenth century. Starkie adopted the test of
'moral certainty, to the exclusion of all reasonable doubt' in his treatise, published in 1824. The courts finally accepted the higher criminal standard in *R v
Winsor* (1865) 4 F & F 363. It is sometimes said that two standards are
impossible: either a thing is proved or it is not. It is also said that the criminal
standard makes it too difficult to convict the guilty. Both points are put only
by a small minority, and may be doubted.

Sodeman v R   (1936) 55 CLR 192

Dixon J: The difference between the two opposing degrees of persuasion cannot be regarded as
a matter of little or no importance. The daily experience of the administration of justice shows
the powerful effect produced by the high degree of certainty which the one demands. It also
illustrates how a sensible preponderance of evidence usually suffices to turn the scale when the
lower standard prevails.

Stephen: History of the Criminal Law, 1 pp 354, 438

If it be asked why an accused person is presumed to be innocent, I think the true answer is, not
that the presumption is probably true, but that society in the present day is so much stronger
than the individual, and is capable of inflicting so very much more harm on the individual than
the individual as a rule can inflict upon society, that it can afford to be generous. It is, however,
a question of degree, varying according to time and place, how far this generosity can or ought
to be carried . . .

[T]he saying that it is better that ten guilty men should escape than one innocent man should suffer [is] an observation which appears to me to be open to two decisive objections. In the first place, it assumes, in opposition to the fact, that modes of procedure likely to convict the guilty are equally likely to convict the innocent, and it thus resembles a suggestion that soldiers should be armed with bad guns because it is better that they should miss ten enemies than that they should hit one friend. In fact, the rule which acquits a guilty man is likely to convict an innocent one. Just as the gun which misses the object at which it is aimed is likely to hit an object at which it is not aimed. In the second place, it is by no means true that under all circumstances it is better that ten guilty men should escape than that one innocent man should suffer. Everything depends on what the guilty men have been doing, and something depends on the way in which the innocent man came to be suspected. I think it probable that the length to which this sentiment has been carried in our criminal courts is due to a considerable extent to the extreme severity of the old criminal law, and even more to the capriciousness of its severity and the element of chance which . . . was introduced into its administration.

QUESTION

Allen (*Legal Duties*, p 286) says: 'the acquittal of ten guilty persons is exactly ten times as great a failure to do *justice* as the conviction of one innocent person'. Do you agree? If so, is this relevant to the distinction between the criminal and civil standards of proof?

3 Past events and future events

Re H (Minors) (Sexual Abuse: Standard of Proof)
[1996] 1 All ER 1, [1996] 2 WLR 8, HL

Lord Nicholls: My Lords, the subject of this appeal is the care of children. Section 31 of the Children Act 1989 empowers the court to make an order placing a child in the care of a local authority or putting a child under the supervision of a local authority or a probation officer. Section 31(2) provides that a court may only make such an order:

'if it is satisfied (a) that the child concerned is suffering, or is likely to suffer, significant harm; and (b) that the harm, or likelihood of harm, is attributable to (i) the care given to the child, or likely to be given him if the order were not made, not being what it would be reasonable to expect a parent to give to him; or (ii) the child's being beyond parental control.'

In short, the court must be satisfied of the existence or likelihood of harm attributable either to the care the child is receiving or likely to receive or to the child being beyond parental control. Harm means ill-treatment or impairment of health or development: see section 31(9). This appeal concerns the need for the court to be 'satisfied' that the child is suffering significant harm or is 'likely' to do so.

The mother has four children, all girls. D1 and D2 were children of her marriage to Mr H in 1979. D1 was born in June 1978 and D2 in August 1981. Mr H and the mother then separated. In 1984 she commenced living with Mr R and they had two children: D3, born in March 1985, and D4, born in April 1992.

In September 1993, when she was 15, D1 made a statement to the police. She said she had been sexually abused by Mr R ever since she was 7 or 8 years old. She was then accommodated with foster-parents, and Mr R was charged with having raped her. In February 1994 the local authority applied for care orders in respect of the three younger girls. Interim care orders were made, followed by interim supervision orders.

In October 1994 Mr R was tried on an indictment containing four counts of rape of D1. D1 was the principal witness for the Crown. The jury acquitted Mr R on all counts after a very short retirement. Despite this the local authority proceeded with the applications for care orders in respect of D2, D3 and D4. These girls were then aged 13, 8 and 2 years. The local authority's case, and this is an important feature of these proceedings, was based solely on the alleged sexual abuse of D1 by Mr R. Relying on the different standard of proof applicable in civil and criminal matters, the local authority asked the Judge still to find that Mr R had sexually abused D1, or at least that there was a substantial risk he had done so, thereby, so it was said, satisfying the section 31(2) conditions for the making of a care order in respect of the three younger girls.

The applications were heard by Judge Davidson QC . . . He was not impressed by the evidence of Mr R or of the mother. Nevertheless he concluded he could not be sure 'to the requisite high standard of proof' that D1's allegations were true. He added:

> 'It must follow that the statutory criteria for the making of a care order are not made out. This is far from saying that I am satisfied the child's complaints are untrue. I do not brush them aside as the jury seem to have done. I am, at the least, more than a little suspicious . . . [and] would be prepared to hold that there is a real possibility that her statement and her evidence are true, nor has [Mr R] by his evidence and demeanour, not only throughout the hearing but the whole of this matter, done anything to dispel those suspicions, but this in the circumstances is nihil ad rem.'

By a majority comprising the President and Millett LJ, the Court of Appeal dismissed an appeal by the local authority. Kennedy LJ disagreed.

'Likely' to suffer harm

I shall consider first the meaning of 'likely' in the expression 'likely to suffer significant harm' in section 31 . . . In everyday usage one meaning of the word likely, perhaps its primary meaning, is probable, in the sense of more likely than not. This is not its only meaning. If I am going walking on Kinder Scout and ask whether it is likely to rain, I am using likely in a different sense. I am inquiring whether there is a real risk of rain, a risk that ought not to be ignored. In which sense is likely being used in this subsection?

In section 31(2) Parliament has stated the prerequisites which must exist before the court has power to make a care order. These prerequisites mark the boundary line drawn by Parliament between the differing interests. On one side are the interests of parents in caring for their own child, a course which prima facie is also in the interests of the child. On the other side there will be circumstances in which the interests of the child may dictate a need for his care to be entrusted to others. In section 31(2) Parliament has stated the minimum conditions which must be present before the court can look more widely at all the circumstances and decide whether the child's welfare requires that a local authority shall receive the child into their care and have parental responsibility for him. The court must be satisfied that the child is already suffering significant harm. Or the court must be satisfied that, looking ahead, although the child may not yet be suffering such harm, he or she is likely to do so in the future. The court may make a care order if, but only if, it is satisfied in one or other of these respects.

In this context Parliament cannot have been using 'likely' in the sense of more likely than not. If the word likely were given this meaning, it would have the effect of leaving outside the scope of care and supervision orders cases where the court is satisfied there is a real possibility of significant harm to the child in the future but that possibility falls short of being more likely than not. Strictly, if this were the correct reading of the Act, a care or supervision order would not be available even in a case where the risk of significant harm is as likely as not. Nothing would suffice short of proof that the child will probably suffer significant harm. The difficulty with this interpretation of section 31(2)(*a*) is that it would draw the boundary line at an altogether inapposite point. What is in issue is the prospect, or risk, of the child suffering significant harm. When exposed to this risk a child may need protection just as much when the risk is considered to be less than fifty-fifty as when the risk is of a higher order. Conversely, so far as the parents are concerned, there is no particular magic in a threshold test based on a probability of significant harm as distinct from a real possibility. It is otherwise if there is no real possibility. It is eminently understandable that Parliament should provide that where there is no real possibility of significant harm, parental responsibility should remain solely with the parents. That makes sense as a threshold in the interests of the parents and the child in a way that a higher threshold, based on probability, would not.

In my view, therefore, the context shows that in section 31(2)(*a*) 'likely' is being used in the sense of a real possibility, a possibility that cannot sensibly be ignored having regard to the nature and gravity of the feared harm in the particular case. Likely also bears a similar meaning, for a similar reason, in the requirement in section 31(2)(*b*) that the harm or likelihood of harm must be attributable to the care given to the child or 'likely' to be given him if the order were not made.

The burden of proof

The power of the court to make a care or supervision order only arises if the court is 'satisfied' that the criteria stated in section 31(2) exist. The expression 'if the court is satisfied,' here and elsewhere in the Act, envisages that the court must be judicially satisfied on proper material. There is also inherent in the expression an indication of the need for the subject matter to be affirmatively proved. If the court is left in a state of indecision the matter has not been established to the level, or standard, needed for the court to be 'satisfied . . .'

The standard of proof

[Extracted in section 4, infra.]

The threshold conditions

There is no difficulty in applying [the standard of the balance of probability] to the threshold conditions. The first limb of section 31(2)(a) predicates an existing state of affairs: that the child is suffering significant harm. The relevant time for this purpose is the date of the care order application. . . . Whether at that time the child was suffering significant harm is an issue to be decided by the court on the basis of the facts admitted or proved before it. The balance of probability standard applies to proof of the facts.

The same approach applies to the second limb of section 31(2)(a). This is concerned with evaluating the risk of something happening in the future: aye or no, is there a real possibility that the child will suffer significant harm? Having heard and considered the evidence, and decided any disputed questions of relevant fact upon the balance of probability, the court must reach a decision on how highly it evaluates the risk of significant harm befalling the child, always remembering upon whom the burden of proof rests.

Suspicion and the threshold conditions

This brings me to the most difficult part of the appeal. The problem is presented in stark form by the facts in this case. The local authority do not suggest that the first limb of section 31(2)(a) is satisfied in respect of D2, D3 or D4. They do not seek a finding that any of the three younger girls is suffering harm. Their case for the making of a care order is based exclusively on the second limb. In support of the allegation that D2, D3 and D4 are likely to suffer significant harm, the local authority rely solely upon the allegation that over many years D1 was subject to repeated sexual abuse by Mr R.

The judge held that the latter allegation was not made out. Mr R did not establish that abuse did not occur. The outcome on this disputed serious allegation of fact was that the local authority, upon whom the burden of proof rested, failed to establish that abuse did occur. However, the judge remained suspicious and, had it been relevant, he would have held there was a reasonable possibility that D1's allegations were true. The question arising from these conclusions can be expressed thus: when a local authority assert but fail to prove past misconduct, can the judge's suspicions or lingering doubts on that issue form the basis for concluding that the second limb of section 31(2)(a) has been established?

In many instances where misconduct is alleged but not proved this question will not arise. Other allegations may be proved. The matters proved may suffice to show a likelihood of future harm . . .

In the Court of Appeal in the present case [1995] 1 FLR 643 the President [said that since] the judge rejected the only allegation which gave rise to the applications for care orders, it was not then open to him to go on and consider the likelihood of harm to the children. Millett LJ agreed. He said:

'where the risk of harm depends on the truth of disputed allegations, the court must investigate them and determine whether they are true or false. Unless it finds that they are true, it cannot be satisfied that the child is likely to suffer significant harm if the order is not made.'

Kennedy LJ reached a different conclusion. To satisfy the second limb there must be acceptable evidence of a real risk that significant harm will be sustained, but he added:

'I . . . do not accept that if the evidence relates to alleged misconduct . . . that misconduct must itself be proved on a balance of probabilities before the evidence can be used to satisfy the threshold criteria in section 31(2)(a).'

A conclusion based on facts

The starting point here is that courts act on evidence. They reach their decisions on the basis of the evidence before them. When considering whether an applicant for a care order has shown that the child is suffering harm or is likely to do so, a court will have regard to the undisputed evidence. The judge will attach to that evidence such weight, or importance, as he considers appropriate. Likewise with regard to disputed evidence which the judge accepts as reliable. None of that is controversial. But the rejection of a disputed allegation as not proved on the balance of probability leaves scope for the possibility that the non-proven allegation may be true after all. There remains room for the judge to have doubts and suspicions on this score. This is the area of controversy.

In my view these unresolved judicial doubts and suspicions can no more form the basis of a conclusion that the second threshold condition in section 31(2)(a) has been established than they can form the basis of a conclusion that the first has been established. My reasons are as follows.

Evidence is the means whereby relevant facts are proved in court. What the evidence is required to establish depends upon the issue the court has to decide. At some interlocutory hearings, for instance, the issue will be whether the plaintiff has a good arguable case. The plaintiff may assert he is at risk of the defendant trespassing on his land or committing a breach of contract and that, in consequence, he will suffer serious damage. When deciding whether to grant an interlocutory injunction the court will not be concerned to resolve disputes raised by the parties' conflicting affidavit evidence.

At trials, however, the court normally has to resolve disputed issues of relevant fact before it can reach its conclusion on the issue it has to decide. This is a commonplace exercise, carried out daily by courts and tribunals throughout the country. This exercise applies as much where the issue is whether an event may happen in the future as where the issue is whether an event did or did not happen in the past. To decide whether a car was being driven negligently, the court will have to decide what was happening immediately before the accident and how the car was being driven and why. Its findings on these facts form the essential basis for its conclusion on the issue of whether the car was being driven with reasonable care. Likewise, if the issue before the court concerns the possibility of something happening in the future, such as whether the name or get-up under which goods are being sold is likely to deceive future buyers. To decide that issue the court must identify and, when disputed, decide the relevant facts about the way the goods are being sold and to whom and in what circumstances. Then, but only then, can the court reach a conclusion on the crucial issue. A decision by a court on the likelihood of a future happening must be founded on a basis of present facts and the inferences fairly to be drawn therefrom.

The same, familiar approach is applicable when a court is considering whether the threshold conditions in section 31(2)(a) are established. Here, as much as anywhere else, the court's conclusion must be founded on a factual base. The court must have before it facts on which its conclusion can properly be based. That is clearly so in the case of the first limb of section 31(2)(a). There must be facts, proved to the court's satisfaction if disputed, on which the court can properly conclude that the child is suffering harm. An alleged but non-proven fact is not a fact for this purpose. Similarly with the second limb: there must be facts from which the court can properly conclude there is a real possibility that the child will suffer harm in the future. Here also, if the facts are disputed, the court must resolve the dispute so far as necessary to reach a proper conclusion on the issue it has to decide.

There are several indications in the Act that when considering the threshold conditions the court is to apply the ordinary approach, of founding its conclusion on facts, and that nothing less will do. The first pointer is the difference in the statutory language when dealing with earlier stages in the procedures which may culminate in a care order. Under Part V of the Act a local authority are under a duty to investigate where they have 'reasonable cause to suspect' that a child is suffering or is likely to suffer harm. The court may make a child assessment order if satisfied that the applicant has 'reasonable cause to suspect' that the child is suffering or is likely to suffer harm. The police may take steps to remove or prevent the removal of a child where a constable has 'reasonable cause to believe' that the child would otherwise be likely to suffer harm. The court may make an emergency protection order only if satisfied there is 'reasonable cause to believe' that the child is likely to suffer harm in certain eventualities. Under section 38 the court may make an interim care order or an interim supervision order if satisfied there are 'reasonable grounds for believing' that the section 31(2) circumstances exist.

In marked contrast is the wording of section 31(2). The earlier stages are concerned with pre-liminary or interim steps or orders. Reasonable cause to believe or suspect provides the test. At those stages, as in my example of an application for an interlocutory injunction, there will usu-ally not have been a full court hearing. But when the stage is reached of making a care order, with the far-reaching consequences this may have for the child and the parents, Parliament pre-scribed a different and higher test: 'a court may only make a care order or supervision order if it is satisfied . . . that . . . the child . . . is suffering, or is likely to suffer, significant harm . . .'

This is the language of proof, not suspicion. At this stage more is required than suspicion, however reasonably based.

The next pointer is that the second threshold condition in paragraph (a) is cheek by jowl with the first. Take a case where a care order is sought in respect of a child on the ground that for some time his parents have been maltreating him. Having heard the evidence, the court finds the allegation is not proved. No maltreatment has been established. The evidence is rejected as insufficient. That being so, the first condition is not made out, because there is no factual basis from which the court could conclude that the child is suffering significant harm attributable to the care being given to him. Suspicion that there may have been maltreatment clearly will not do. It would be odd if, in respect of the selfsame non-proven allegations, the self-same insuffi-cient evidence could nonetheless be regarded as a sufficient factual basis for satisfying the court there is a real possibility of harm to the child in the future.

The third pointer is that if indeed this were the position, this would effectively reverse the bur-den of proof in an important respect. It would mean that once apparently credible evidence of misconduct has been given, those against whom the allegations are made must disprove them. Otherwise it would be open to a court to hold that, although the misconduct has not been proved, it has not been disproved and there is a real possibility that the misconduct did occur. Accordingly there is a real possibility that the child will suffer harm in the future and, hence, the threshold criteria are met. I do not believe Parliament intended that section 31(2) should work in this way.

Thus far I have concentrated on explaining that a court's conclusion that the threshold con-ditions are satisfied must have a factual base, and that an alleged but unproved fact, serious or trivial, is not a fact for this purpose. Nor is judicial suspicion, because that is no more than a judicial state of uncertainty about whether or not an event happened.

I must now put this into perspective by noting, and emphasising, the width of the range of facts which may be relevant when the court is considering the threshold conditions. The range of facts which may properly be taken into account is infinite. Facts include the history of mem-bers of the family, the state of relationships within a family, proposed changes within the membership of a family, parental attitudes, and omissions which might not reasonably have been expected, just as much as actual physical assaults. They include threats, and abnormal behaviour by a child, and unsatisfactory parental responses to complaints or allegations. And facts, which are minor or even trivial if considered in isolation, when taken together may suffice to satisfy the court of the likelihood of future harm. The court will attach to all the relevant facts the appropriate weight when coming to an overall conclusion on the crucial issue.

I must emphasise a further point. I have indicated that unproved allegations of maltreatment cannot form the basis for a finding by the court that either limb of section 31(2)(a) is estab-lished. It is, of course, open to a court to conclude there is a real possibility that the child will suffer harm in the future although harm in the past has not been established. There will be cases where, although the alleged maltreatment itself is not proved, the evidence does establish a com-bination of profoundly worrying features affecting the care of the child within the family. In such cases it would be open to a court in appropriate circumstances to find that, although not satis-fied the child is yet suffering significant harm, on the basis of such facts as are proved there is a likelihood that he will do so in the future.

That is not the present case. The three younger girls are not at risk unless D1 was abused by Mr R in the past. If she was not abused, there is no reason for thinking the others may be. This is not a case where Mr R has a history of abuse. Thus the one and only relevant fact is whether D1 was abused by Mr R as she says. The other surrounding facts, such as the fact that D1 made a complaint and the fact that her mother responded unsatisfactorily, lead nowhere relevant in this case if they do not lead to the conclusion that D1 was abused. To decide that the others are at risk because there is a possibility that D1 was abused would be to base the decision, not on fact, but on suspicion: the suspicion that D1 may have been abused. That would be to lower the threshold prescribed by Parliament.

Conclusion

I am very conscious of the difficulties confronting social workers and others in obtaining hard evidence, which will stand up when challenged in court, of the maltreatment meted out to children behind closed doors. Cruelty and physical abuse are notoriously difficult to prove . . .

I am also conscious of the difficulties facing judges when there is conflicting testimony on serious allegations. On some occasions judges are left deeply anxious at the end of a case. There may be an understandable inclination to 'play safe' in the interests of the child. Sometimes judges wish to safeguard a child whom they fear may be at risk without at the same time having to fasten a label of very serious misconduct on to one of the parents.

These are among the difficulties and considerations Parliament addressed in the Children Act 1989 when deciding how, to use the fashionable terminology, the balance should be struck between the various interests. As I read the Act, Parliament decided that the threshold for a care order should be that the child is suffering significant harm, or there is a real possibility that he will do so. In the latter regard the threshold is comparatively low. Therein lies the protection for children. But, as I read the Act, Parliament also decided that proof of the relevant facts is needed if this threshold is to be surmounted. Before the section 1 welfare test and the welfare 'checklist' can be applied, the threshold has to be crossed. Therein lies the protection for parents. They are not to be at risk of having their child taken from them and removed into the care of the local authority on the basis only of suspicions, whether of the judge or of the local authority or anyone else. A conclusion that the child is suffering or is likely to suffer harm must be based on facts, not just suspicion. . . . Sexual abuse not having been proved, there were no facts upon which the judge could properly conclude there was a likelihood of harm to the three younger girls.

[Lord Goff and Lord Mustill agreed.]

Lord Browne-Wilkinson: My Lords, I have the misfortune to disagree with the view reached by the majority of your Lordships. Although the area of disagreement is small, it is crucial both to the outcome of this appeal and to the extent to which children at risk can be protected by the courts.

I agree with my noble and learned friend, Lord Nicholls of Birkenhead, that the requirement in section 31(2) of the Children Act 1989, that the court must be satisfied that the child 'is likely to suffer significant harm' does not require the court to find that such harm is more likely than not: it is enough if the occurrence of such harm is a real possibility. I further agree with him that the burden of proving any relevant fact is on the applicant and that the standard of proof is the ordinary civil standard, ie balance of probabilities. The point on which I differ is how those principles fall to be applied by a judge faced with the decision whether he is 'satisfied' that the child is likely to suffer significant harm. Even on this point, I agree that the judge can only act on evidence and on facts which, so far as relevant, have been proved. He has to be satisfied by the evidence before him that there is a real possibility of serious harm to the child.

Where I part company is in thinking that the facts relevant to an assessment of risk ('is likely to suffer . . . harm') are not the same as the facts relevant to a decision that harm is in fact being suffered. In order to be satisfied that an event has occurred or is occurring the evidence has to show on balance of probabilities that such event did occur or is occurring. But in order to be satisfied that there is a risk of such an occurrence, the ambit of the relevant facts is in my view wider. The combined effect of a number of factors which suggest that a state of affairs, though not proved to exist, may well exist is the normal basis for the assessment of future risk. To be satisfied of the existence of a risk does not require proof of the occurrence of past historical events but proof of facts which are relevant to the making of a prognosis.

Let me give an example, albeit a dated one. Say that in 1940 those responsible for giving air-raid warnings had received five unconfirmed sightings of approaching aircraft which might be enemy bombers. They could not, on balance of probabilities, have reached a conclusion that any one of those sightings was of an enemy aircraft: nor could they logically have put together five non-proven sightings so as to be satisfied that enemy aircraft were in fact approaching. But their task was not simply to decide whether enemy aircraft were approaching but whether there was a risk of an air-raid. The facts relevant to the assessment of such risk were the reports that unconfirmed sightings had been made, not the truth of such reports. They could well, on the basis of those unconfirmed reports, have been satisfied that there was a real possibility of an air-raid and given warning accordingly.

So in the present case, the major issue was whether D1 had been sexually abused (the macro-fact). In the course of the hearing before the judge a number of other facts (the micro-facts) were established to the judge's satisfaction by the evidence. The judge in his careful judgment summarised these micro-facts: that D1 had been consistent in her story from the time of her first complaint; that her statement was full and detailed showing 'a classic unfolding revelation of progressively worse abuse'; that there were opportunities for such abuse by Mr R and that he had been lying in denying that he had ever been alone either with D1 or with any of the other children; that D2 had made statements which indicated that she had witnessed 'inappropriate' behaviour between Mr R and D1; that the mother (contrary to her evidence) also suspected that something had been going on between Mr R and D1 and had sought to dissuade D2 from saying anything to the social workers. The judge also found a number of micro-facts pointing the other way. Having summarised all these micro-facts pointing each way, he reached his conclusion on the macro-fact: 'I cannot be sure to the requisite high standard of proof that [D1's] allegations are true.' But he also made further findings (which he thought to be irrelevant in law) on the basis of the micro-facts . . .

[His] conclusion that there was a real possibility that the evidence of D1 was true was a finding based on evidence and the micro-facts that he had found. It was not a mere suspicion as to the risk that Mr R was an abuser: it was a finding of risk based on facts.

My Lords, I am anxious that the decision of the House in this case may establish the law in an unworkable form to the detriment of many children at risk. Child abuse, particularly sex abuse, is notoriously difficult to prove in a court of law. The relevant facts are extremely sensitive and emotive. They are often known only to the child and to the alleged abuser. If legal proof of actual abuse is a prerequisite to a finding that a child is at risk of abuse, the court will be powerless to intervene to protect children in relation to whom there are the gravest suspicions of actual abuse but the necessary evidence legally to prove such abuse is lacking. Take the present case. Say that the proceedings had related to D1, the complainant, herself. After a long hearing a judge has reached the conclusion on evidence that there is a 'real possibility' that her evidence is true, ie that she has in fact been gravely abused. Can Parliament really have intended that neither the court nor anyone else should have jurisdiction to intervene so as to protect D1 from any abuse which she may well have been enduring? I venture to think not.

R v Secretary of State for the Home Department, ex parte Sivakumaran
[1988] AC 958, [1988] 1 All ER 193, HL

The test for asylum under the 1951 United Nations Convention Relating to the Status of Refugees (as amended) is that the claimant show, inter alia, that he has a 'well-founded fear of persecution' if he is returned to his home country.

Lord Keith: . . . In my opinion the requirement that an applicant's fear of persecution be well-founded means that there has to be demonstrated a reasonable degree of likelihood that he will be persecuted . . . if returned to his own country. In *R v Governor of Pentonville Prison ex parte Fernandez* [1971] 1 WLR 987, this House had to construe section 4(1)(c) of the Fugitive Offenders Act 1967, which requires that a person shall not be returned under the Act if it appears

'that he might, if returned, be prejudiced at his trial or punished, detained or restricted in his personal liberty by reason of his race, religion, nationality or political opinions.'

Lord Diplock said, at p 994:

'My Lords, bearing in mind the relative gravity of the consequences of the court's expectation being falsified either in one way or in the other, I do not think that the test of the applicability of paragraph (c) is that the court must be satisfied that it is more likely than not that the fugitive will be detained or restricted if he is returned. A lesser degree of likelihood is, in my view, sufficient; and I would not quarrel with the way in which the test was stated by the magistrate or with the alternative way in which the test was stated by the divisional court. "A reasonable chance", "substantial grounds for thinking", "a serious possibility" – I see no significant difference between these various ways of describing the degree of likelihood of the detention or restriction of the fugitive on his return which justifies the court in giving effect to the provision of section 4(1)(c).'

I consider that this passage appropriately expresses the degree of likelihood to be satisfied in order that a fear of persecution may be well-founded.

QUESTION

Are the phrases adopted by their Lordships in *Re H, R v Governor of Pentonville Prison, ex p Fernandez,* and *R v Secretary of State for the Home Department, ex p Sivakumaran* merely linguistic consequences of the attempt to talk in probabilistic terms about present appreciation of future events? Or is it genuinely being said that the standard of proof is lower in these classes of case? See the next section and *Kaja v Secretary of State for the Home Department* [1995] Imm AR 1.

4   How many standards?

Is there any intermediate standard between the normal criminal and civil standard? For some purposes this is so in America, but not in England (*Dingwall v J Wharton (Shipping) Ltd* [1961] 2 Lloyd's Rep 213 at 216, HL per Lord Tucker). Certainly the existence of three standards would make jury direction even harder than the existence of two. However, depending on the issue, there may be within each standard variations in the amount of evidence required depending on the inherent likelihood or unlikelihood of the fact asserted.

Bater v Bater   [1951] P 35, [1950] 2 All ER 458, CA

A wife petitioned for divorce on grounds of cruelty. The commissioner said she had to prove her case beyond reasonable doubt. The Court of Appeal held that this was not a misdirection.
    Bucknill and Somervell LJJ held it was correct to apply the criminal standard of proof.

Denning LJ: The difference of opinion which has been evoked about the standard of proof in recent cases may well turn out to be more a matter of words than anything else. It is of course true that by our law a higher standard of proof is required in criminal cases than in civil cases. But this is subject to the qualification that there is no absolute standard in either case. In criminal cases the charge must be proved beyond reasonable doubt, but there may be degrees of proof within that standard.
    As Best CJ and many other great judges have said, 'in proportion as the crime is enormous, so ought the proof to be clear'. So also in civil cases, the case may be proved by a preponderance of probability, but there may be degrees of probability within that standard. The degree depends on the subject-matter. A civil court, when considering a charge of fraud, will naturally require for itself a higher degree of probability than that which it would require when asking if negligence is established. It does not adopt so high a degree as a criminal court, even when it is considering a charge of a criminal nature; but still it does require a degree of probability which is commensurate with the occasion. Likewise, a divorce court should require a degree of probability which is proportionate to the subject-matter.
    I do not think that the matter can be better put than it was by Lord Stowell in *Loveden v Loveden* (1810) 2 Hag Con 1 at 3. 'The only general rule that can be laid down upon the subject is, that the circumstances must be such as would lead the guarded discretion of a reasonable and

just man to the conclusion.' The degree of probability which a reasonable and just man would require to come to a conclusion – and likewise the degree of doubt which would prevent him coming to it – depends on the conclusion to which he is required to come. It would depend on whether it was a criminal case or a civil case, what the charge was, and what the consequences might be; and if he were left in real and substantial doubt on the particular matter, he would hold the charge not to be established: he would not be satisfied about it.

But what is a real and substantial doubt? It is only another way of saying a reasonable doubt; and a reasonable doubt is simply that degree of doubt which would prevent a reasonable and just man from coming to the conclusion. So the phrase 'reasonable doubt' takes the matter no further. It does not say that degree of probability must be as high as 99 per cent or as low as 51 per cent. The degree required must depend on the mind of the reasonable and just man who is considering the particular subject-matter. In some cases 51 per cent would be enough, but not in others. When this is realised, the phrase 'reasonable doubt' can be used just as aptly in a civil case or a divorce case as in a criminal case . . . The only difference is that, because of our high regard for the liberty of the individual, a doubt may be regarded as reasonable in the criminal courts, which would not be so in the civil courts. I agree therefore with my brothers that the use of the phrase 'reasonable doubt' by the commissioner in this case was not a misdirection any more than it was in *Briginshaw v Briginshaw* (1938) 60 CLR 336.

If, however, the commissioner had put the case higher and said that the case had to be proved with the same strictness as a crime is proved in a criminal court, then he would, I think, have misdirected himself, because that would be the very error which this court corrected in *Davis v Davis* [1950] P 125, [1950] 1 All ER 40, CA. It would be adopting too high a standard. The divorce court is a civil court, not a criminal court. I agree that the appeal should be dismissed.

Re H (Minors) (Sexual Abuse: Standard of Proof)
[1996] 1 All ER 1, [1996] 2 WLR 8, HL

[For the facts, see the extracts from this case in section 3, *supra*.]

Lord Nicholls: Where the matters in issue are facts the standard of proof required in non-criminal proceedings is the preponderance of probability, usually referred to as the balance of probability. This is the established general principle. There are exceptions such as contempt of court applications, but I can see no reason for thinking that family proceedings are, or should be, an exception. By family proceedings I mean proceedings so described in the Act of 1989, sections 105 and 8(3). Despite their special features, family proceedings remain essentially a form of civil proceedings. Family proceedings often raise very serious issues, but so do other forms of civil proceedings.

The balance of probability standard means that a court is satisfied an event occurred if the court considers that, on the evidence, the occurrence of the event was more likely than not. When assessing the probabilities the court will have in mind as a factor, to whatever extent is appropriate in the particular case, that the more serious the allegation the less likely it is that the event occurred and, hence, the stronger should be the evidence before the court concludes that the allegation is established on the balance of probability. Fraud is usually less likely than negligence. Deliberate physical injury is usually less likely than accidental physical injury. A step-father is usually less likely to have repeatedly raped and had non-consensual oral sex with his under age stepdaughter than on some occasion to have lost his temper and slapped her. Built into the preponderance of probability standard is a generous degree of flexibility in respect of the seriousness of the allegation.

Although the result is much the same, this does not mean that where a serious allegation is in issue the standard of proof required is higher. It means only that the inherent probability or improbability of an event is itself a matter to be taken into account when weighing the probabilities and deciding whether, on balance, the event occurred. The more improbable the event, the stronger must be the evidence that it did occur before, on the balance of probability, its occurrence will be established. Ungoed-Thomas J expressed this neatly in *In re Dellow's Will Trusts* [1964] 1 WLR 451, 455: 'The more serious the allegation the more cogent is the evidence required to overcome the unlikelihood of what is alleged and thus to prove it.'

This substantially accords with the approach adopted in authorities such as the well known judgment of Morris LJ in *Hornal v Neuberger Products Ltd* [1957] 1 QB 247, 266. This approach also provides a means by which the balance of probability standard can accommodate one's instinctive feeling that even in civil proceedings a court should be more sure before finding serious allegations proved than when deciding less serious or trivial matters.

No doubt it is this feeling which prompts judicial comment from time to time that grave issues call for proof to a standard higher than the preponderance of probability . . . The law looks for probability, not certainty. Certainty is seldom attainable. But probability is an unsatisfactorily vague criterion because there are degrees of probability. In establishing principles regarding the standard of proof, therefore, the law seeks to define the degree of probability appropriate for different types of proceedings. Proof beyond reasonable doubt, in whatever form of words expressed, is one standard. Proof on a preponderance of probability is another, a lower standard having the in-built flexibility already mentioned. If the balance of probability standard were departed from, and a third standard were substituted in some civil cases, it would be necessary to identify what the standard is and when it would apply. Herein lies a difficulty. If the standard were to be higher than the balance of probability but lower than the criminal standard of proof beyond reasonable doubt, what would it be? The only alternative which suggests itself is that the standard should be commensurate with the gravity of the allegation and the seriousness of the consequences. A formula to this effect has its attraction. But I doubt whether in practice it would add much to the present test in civil cases, and it would risk causing confusion and uncertainty. As at present advised I think it is better to stick to the existing, established law on this subject. I can see no compelling need for a change.

[Lord Goff and Lord Mustill agreed; Lord Browne-Wilkinson did not dissent on this point.]

The principle referred to by Denning LJ in *Bater v Bater*, supra, can also be illustrated by Lord Brougham's defence of Queen Caroline: 'The evidence before us is inadequate even to prove a debt – impotent to deprive of a civil right – ridiculous for convicting of the pettiest offence – scandalous if brought forward to support a charge of any grave character – monstrous if to ruin the honour of an English Queen' (*Speeches*, vol 1, p 227). The question is one of probability. The character of certain persons will make it unlikely they will commit certain conduct; and the character of certain forms of conduct makes it unlikely that they will be committed, eg because there are moral and legal sanctions against it. Though standards of proof do not vary from issue to issue, the quantum of evidence needed to meet the standard may vary, because more evidence will be needed to prove the occurrence of an improbable event than a likely one. In Hoffmann's words, 'To speak of variable standards of proof is . . . to confuse probabilities with the quantity of evidence needed to create them' (p 367).

The principle in question is often applied in disciplinary proceedings (*R v Hampshire County Council, ex p Ellerton* [1985] 1 All ER 599, [1985] 1 WLR 749, CA) and has been applied in connection with the exercise of executive discretion to interfere with liberty: *Khawaja v Secretary of State for the Home Department* [1984] AC 74, [1983] 1 All ER 765, HL.

5 Which standard?

If a crime is alleged in civil proceedings, the standard is the civil one, not the criminal.

Hornal v Neuberger Products Ltd   [1957] 1 QB 247, [1956] 3 All ER 970, CA

The plaintiff sued for damages for breach of warranty or alternatively for fraudulent misrepresentation. He alleged that the director of the defendant company had said a used capstan lathe had been reconditioned by certain toolmakers. The defendants denied this. The judge held that he was satisfied on the balance of probabilities, but not beyond reasonable doubt, that the statement had been made. The Court of Appeal held that the former was the correct standard.

Denning LJ: I must say that, if I was sitting as a judge alone, and I was satisfied that the statement was made, that would be enough for me, whether the claim was put in warranty or on fraud. I think it would bring the law into contempt if a judge were to say that on the issue of warranty he finds the statement was made, and that on the issue of fraud he finds it was not made.

Nevertheless, the judge having set the problem to himself, he answered it, I think, correctly; he reviewed all the cases and held rightly that the standard of proof depends on the nature of the issue. The more serious the allegation the higher the degree of probability that is required: but it need not, in a civil case, reach the very high standard required by the criminal law.

Hodson LJ: The comparative dearth of express authority on this topic is not surprising. No responsible counsel undertakes to prove a serious accusation without admitting that cogent evidence is required, and judges approach serious accusations in the same way without necessarily considering in every case whether or not there is a criminal issue involved. For example, in the ordinary case arising from a collision between two motor cars involving charges of negligence, I have never heard of a judge applying the criminal standard of proof, on the ground that his judgment might involve the finding of one of the parties guilty of a criminal offence.

The judge took great pains to consider the cases in which the question he posed had been considered. I do not propose to follow him in their review, agreeing as I do with his conclusion. I agree with him that in most civil cases, where the standard of proof in cases involving crime has been mentioned, there has been no argument, and the heavier burden of proof has been accepted by counsel or assumed as necessary by the judge. I also think that it is impossible to find a satisfactory explanation of all cases where divergent views have been taken. For example, it seems to have been taken for granted in what may be called the third party cases that the crime of a person not concerned in the action may be established on a balance of probabilities: see, for example, *Boyce v Chapman and Brown* (1835) 2 Bing NC 222, and *Vaughton v London and North Western Rly Co* (1874) LR 9 Exch 93. If the criminal standard were required in civil cases for the reason suggested in Taylor on Evidence (12th edn. vol 1, p 106), namely, that every man has a right to his character and not to have the presumption of innocence rebutted unless the strict standard were adopted, the third party cases would appear to be cases where the rule ought to be most strictly applied, since the third party may not even know of the charge which is being made against him in an action between two persons in whose dispute he is not interested, and even if he knows of it may have no opportunity of intervening in it.

Notwithstanding the existence of some cases where the point appears to have been argued and decided in a contrary sense, I think the true view, and that most strongly supported by authority, is that which the judge took, namely, that in a civil case the balance of probability standard is correct.

Morris LJ: He has said that if as to this he ought to be satisfied in the way in which a court or a jury would have to be satisfied before convicting in a criminal case, then in this case he was not so satisfied, but he was satisfied if he was entitled to decide the matter as issues in civil actions are decided, that is, according to the balance of probabilities. The precision of this revealed judicial heart-searching is impeccable from the point of view of its logical nicety. The question of fact which the judge had to decide was simply whether Mr Neuberger spoke the two words in question. If he did, the words might have been a warranty or they might have been a representation, which in this case would be actionable because fraudulent. It would be strange if different standards of proof as to the speaking of the two words could be applicable according as to what civil legal rights followed . . .

It is, I think, clear from the authorities that a difference of approach in civil cases has been recognised. Many judicial utterances show this. The phrase 'balance of probabilities' is often employed as a convenient phrase to express the basis upon which civil issues are decided. It may well be that no clear-cut logical reconciliation can be formulated in regard to the authorities on these topics. But perhaps they illustrate that 'the life of the law is not logic but experience'. In some criminal cases liberty may be involved; in some it may not. In some civil cases the issues may involve questions of reputation which can transcend in importance even questions of personal liberty. Good name in man or woman is 'the immediate jewel of their souls'.

But in truth no real mischief results from an acceptance of the fact that there is some difference of approach in civil actions. Particularly is this so if the words which are used to define that approach are the servants but not the masters of meaning. Though no court and no jury would give less careful attention to issues lacking gravity than to those marked by it, the very elements of gravity become a part of the whole range of circumstances which have to be weighed in the scale when deciding as to the balance of probabilities. This view was denoted by Denning LJ when in his judgment in *Bater v Bater* [1951] P 35 at 36–7, [1950] 2 All ER 458 at 459, CA, he spoke of a 'degree of probability which is commensurate with the occasion' and of 'a degree of probability which is proportionate to the subject-matter'.

In English law the citizen is regarded as being a free man of good repute. Issues may be raised in a civil action which affect character and reputation, and these will not be forgotten by judges and juries when considering the probabilities in regard to whatever misconduct is alleged. There will be reluctance to rob any man of his good name: there will also be reluctance to make any man pay what is not due or to make any man liable who is not or not liable who is. A court will not be deterred from a conclusion because of regret at its consequences: a court must arrive at such conclusion as is directed by the weight and preponderance of the evidence.

Rejfek v McElroy   (1965) 112 CLR 517

The action was for damages for fraudulent misrepresentation. The judge applied the criminal standard of proof. The High Court of Australia reversed him.

Barwick CJ, Kitto, Taylor, Menzies and Windeyer JJ: [T]he standard of proof to be applied in a case and the relationship between the degree of persuasion of the mind according to the balance of probabilities and the gravity or otherwise of the fact of whose existence the mind is to be persuaded are not to be confused. The difference between the criminal standard of proof and the civil standard of proof is no mere matter of words: it is a matter of critical substance. No matter how grave the fact which is to be found in a civil case, the mind has only to be reasonably satisfied and has not with respect to any matter in issue in such a proceeding to attain that degree of certainty which is indispensable to the support of a conviction upon a criminal charge.

A possible instance of a third standard of proof may be that applying in relation to a plea by the accused of insanity. In *Sodeman v R* [1936] 2 All ER 1138, 55 CLR 192 at 233 the Privy Council said the standard was 'not . . . higher' than the civil standard; does this mean it is lower? In the same case in the High Court of Australia Dixon J had stressed that the law knows only two standards, though his particular intention was apparently to challenge any notion that there was a standard intermediate between the criminal and the civil: pp 216–17.

Briginshaw v Briginshaw   (1938) 60 CLR 336

The Victorian Marriage Act 1928, s 80 provided: 'Upon any petition for dissolution of marriage, it shall be the duty of the court to satisfy itself, so far as it reasonably can, as to the facts alleged.' Section 86 provided: 'Subject to the provisions of this Act the court, if it is satisfied that the case of the petitioner is established, shall pronounce a decree nisi for dissolution of marriage.'

The High Court of Australia, on a divorce petition on the ground of adultery, held, contrary to the trial judge's view, that the Act did not require a standard of proof beyond reasonable doubt.

Latham CJ: There is no mathematical scale according to which degree of certainty of intellectual conviction can be computed or valued. But there are differences in degree of certainty, which are real, and which can be intelligently stated, although it is impossible to draw precise lines, as upon a diagram, and to assign each case to a particular subdivision of certainty. No court should act upon mere suspicion, surmise or guesswork in any case. In a civil case, fair inference may justify a finding upon the basis of preponderance of probability. The standard of proof required by a cautious and responsible tribunal will naturally vary in accordance with the seriousness or importance of the issue – see Wills: *Circumstantial Evidence* (5th edn), p 267, note *n*: 'Men will pronounce without hesitation that a person owes another a hundred pounds on evidence on which they certainly would not hang him, and yet all the rules of law applying to one case apply to the other and the processes are the same.'

I am not prepared to adopt the view, which was suggested in argument, that the difference between the criminal and civil standards of proof is really only a matter of words.

Rich J: The phrase 'satisfy itself, so far as it reasonably can' obviously reflects the influence of the common expression 'reasonable satisfaction'. In a serious matter like a charge of adultery the satisfaction of a just and prudent mind cannot be produced by slender and exiguous proofs or circumstances pointing with a wavering finger to an affirmative conclusion. The nature of the allegation requires as a matter of common sense and worldly wisdom the careful weighing of testimony, the close examination of facts proved as a basis of inference and a comfortable satisfaction that the tribunal has reached both a correct and just conclusion. But to say this is not to lay it down as a matter of law that such complete and absolute certainty must be reached as is ordinarily described in a criminal charge as 'satisfaction beyond reasonable doubt'. A petition for dissolution of marriage is not quasi-criminal, whatever the grounds . . .

Dixon J: The truth is that, when the law requires the proof of any fact, the tribunal must feel an actual persuasion of its occurrence or existence before it can be found. It cannot be found as a result of a mere mechanical comparison of probabilities independently of any belief in its reality. No doubt an opinion that a state of facts exists may be held according to indefinite gradations of certainty; and this has led to attempts to define exactly the certainty required by the law for various purposes. Fortunately, however, at common law no third standard of persuasion was definitely developed. Except upon criminal issues to be proved by the prosecution, it is enough that the affirmative of an allegation is made out to the reasonable satisfaction of the tribunal. But reasonable satisfaction is not a state of mind that is attained or established independently of the nature and consequence of the fact or facts to be proved. The seriousness of an allegation made, the inherent unlikelihood of an occurrence of a given description, or the gravity of the consequences flowing from a particular finding are considerations which must affect the answer to the question whether the issue has been proved to the reasonable satisfaction of the tribunal. In such matters 'reasonable satisfaction' should not be produced by inexact proofs, indefinite testimony, or indirect inferences. Everyone must feel that, when, for instance, the issue is on which of two dates an admitted occurrence took place, a satisfactory conclusion may be reached on materials of a kind that would not satisfy any sound and prudent judgment if the question was whether some act had been done involving grave moral delinquency . . . It is often said that such an issue as fraud must be proved 'clearly', 'unequivocally', 'strictly' or 'with certainty' . . . This does not mean that some standard of persuasion is fixed intermediate between the satisfaction beyond reasonable doubt required upon a criminal inquest and the reasonable satisfaction which in a civil issue may, not must, be based on a preponderance of probability. It means that the nature of the issue necessarily affects the process by which reasonable satisfaction is attained. When, in a civil proceeding, a question arises whether a crime has been committed, the standard of persuasion is, according to the better opinion, the same as upon other civil issues . . . But, consistently with this opinion, weight is given to the presumption of innocence and exactness of proof is expected.

. . . [I]t must very rarely happen that a tribunal of fact, upon a careful scrutiny and critical examination of the circumstances proved in evidence or of the testimony adduced, forms a definite opinion that adultery has been committed and yet retains a doubt, based upon reasonable grounds, of the correctness of the opinion. For the very practical reason that the decision of cases has not been found to depend upon the distinction the necessity has not arisen in England of attempting to define with precision the measure or standard of persuasion required before adultery is found in a matrimonial cause. At the same time, I think that the foregoing discussion of the authorities makes it clear that in England the high degree of persuasion exacted in the criminal jurisdiction has not been adopted as the standard where adultery is in issue in the matrimonial jurisdiction. It is a common experience that in criminal matters the great certainty demanded has a most important influence upon the result. The distinction between that and a lower standard of persuasion cannot be considered unreal.

[Starke and McTiernan JJ delivered concurring judgments.]

QUESTION

Does it follow from *Hornal's* Case and *Briginshaw's* Case
  (a) that one rendered paraplegic in a car accident bears a heavier burden of proving negligence than one who merely suffers abrasions in a car accident?
  (b) that the prosecution bears a heavier burden of proving armed robbery than it does of proving a theft of a small sum of money?

6   Discharge of the evidential burden

The test is generally thought to be: 'are there facts in evidence which if unanswered would justify men of ordinary reason and fairness in affirming the question which the plaintiff is bound to maintain?' (*Bridges v North London Rly Co* (1874) LR 7 HL 213 at 233, HL, per Brett J; and see *May v O'Sullivan* (1955) 92 CLR 654; and *Jayasena v R* [1970] AC 618 at 624, [1970] 1 All ER 219. In civil cases, the issue arises either in a non-suit application at the close of a beginning party's evidence or in an application for a verdict by direction either at that time or at the close of all the evidence. The evidence to be examined is confined to that which favours the beginning party. Similarly, in criminal cases where a submission of no case to answer is made, the judge should assume that the jury will accept the evidence and draw the inferences favouring the Crown; he should disregard all the evidence militating against the Crown case because the jury has authority to reject it: *R v Galbraith* [1981] 2 All ER 1060, [1981] 1 WLR 1039, CA. In *Haw Tua Tau v Public Prosecutor* [1982] AC 136 at 151, [1981] 3 All ER 14 at 19, the Privy Council stated one exception to the principle that the prosecution case should be taken at its highest: if the only prosecution evidence is 'so inherently incredible that no reasonable person could accept it as being true', the accused should be acquitted. There is doubt, in criminal cases, as to whether the standard of proof in judging the sufficiency of the prosecution evidence is civil (*United States v Feinberg* 104 F 2d 592 (1944) per Learned Hand J; *Wilson v Buttery* [1926] SASR 150; *Corporate Affairs Comr v Green* [1978] VR 505 at 513) or criminal (*United States v Taylor* 464 F 2d 240 (1972); *United States v Prout* 526 F 2d 380 (1976); *Wilson v Kuhl* [1979] VR 315 at 319; and, seemingly, *May v O'Sullivan* (1955) 92 CLR 654 and *Zanetti v Hill* (1962) 108 CLR 433). The latter view is supported by *Haw Tua Tau v Public Prosecutor* [1982] AC 136 at 151, [1981] 3 All ER 14 at 19, PC, and *Wentworth v Rogers* [1984] 2 NSWLR 422 at 429 and 436. The subject is penetratingly discussed by Glass (1981) 55 ALJ 842, who demonstrates that on principle the latter view is the better view.

> 'Where a no case application is being entertained, the question to be decided is "whether on the evidence as it stands the defendant could lawfully be convicted" (*May v O'Sullivan* (1955) 92 CLR 654 at 658) or "whether the evidence is such that a reasonable jury might convict" (*Practice Note* [1962] 1 All ER 448 sub nom *Practice Direction* [1962] 1 WLR 227). *Ex hypothesi* no person can lawfully be convicted unless his guilt is established beyond reasonable doubt. These pronouncements imply a conclusion that there is no case to answer unless the evidence adduced by the prosecution is capable of bringing satisfaction beyond reasonable doubt to the minds of a reasonable jury.
>   The legal necessity of applying a criminal standard of proof in determining whether there is

a case to answer can be demonstrated . . . by an argument of the *reductio ad absurdum* type. Suppose the trial judge rejects a no case submission on the grounds that the evidence, though not capable of proving guilt beyond reasonable doubt, can prove it to a lesser degree. Suppose the accused then calls no evidence and asks that the jury be directed to acquit. Since the application must by definition succeed, a judge is placed in the absurd position of having made two inconsistent rulings, namely, that on the same body of evidence the defendant could be and could not be lawfully convicted.'

Where an evidential burden rests on the accused, it is sufficient if he adduces evidence which might leave a jury in reasonable doubt on the issue: *Bratty v A-G for Northern Ireland* [1963] AC 386 at 419, HL, though in *R v Cambridge* [1994] 2 All ER 760, [1994] 1 WLR 971, CA, the Court of Appeal suggested obiter that the accused should have adduced evidence sufficient for a reasonable jury to find positively in his favour.

Similar principles apply in judging the sufficiency of evidence on appeal.

CHAPTER 4

Presumptions

1 Introduction

According to McCormick, pp 802–3, ' "presumption" is the slipperiest member of the family of legal terms, except its first cousin, "burden of proof" . . .'

Presumptions are of two kinds. First, a presumption is a conclusion which may or must be drawn until the contrary is proved; that is, the opponent of the presumption bears some burden of disproving it. In this sense presumptions are simply another way of stating the effect of rules as to the burden of proof. To say that 'an accused is *presumed* to be innocent' means only that the prosecution must prove his guilt; it is not a separate requirement; it is not in itself an item of evidence to put to the jury (cf the strange case of *Coffin v US* 156 US 432 (1895)). To say that the accused is presumed to be sane means only that he bears the burden of proving himself insane. The second kind of presumption is a conclusion (the 'presumed fact') which may or must be drawn if another fact (the 'basic fact') is first proved. If a child is born in wedlock, it is presumed legitimate. Indeed, both kinds of presumption can be classified in terms of what quantum of evidence will suffice to rebut them and on whom the onus of producing this quantum rests. Cross, for example, formerly stated four categories of presumption – conclusive, persuasive, evidential and provisional. These terms do not correspond with those of the courts; but no agreed classification exists, and the terms used by Cross usefully indicate the differences between presumptions. (See also Carter's analysis at pp 76–9.) With conclusive presumptions, no evidence can rebut the truth of the presumed fact. With persuasive presumptions, the presumed fact can be disbelieved by the tribunal if sufficient evidence is adduced to persuade the tribunal of the non-existence of the presumed fact on the balance of probability (or in some cases beyond reasonable doubt). If no evidence is offered to rebut an evidential presumption, the fact presumed must be taken to exist. (Thus if the accused gives no evidence of duress, he is taken to have acted without duress; he bears the evidential burden of proving duress and there is an evidential presumption that men do not normally act under duress.) An evidential presumption can be rebutted by evidence which if uncontradicted might persuade a reasonable tribunal of the non-existence of the presumed fact; the case will then be determined by the legal burden of proof in the light of all the evidence. In the case of provisional presumptions, a reasonable tribunal is entitled to disbelieve the presumed fact even if no rebutting evidence at all is adduced; however, in many circumstances failure to call rebutting evidence will cause the tribunal to hold the presumed fact to be true.

Conclusive presumptions (more traditionally called irrebuttable presumptions of law) are essentially not rules of evidence, since no evidence to rebut them is admissible; rather they are rules of substantive law misleadingly expressed in presumptive form. Hence it is a misnomer to call them 'presumptions'. An example is the presumption that everyone knows the law. Another is the presumption established by s 50 of the Children and Young Persons Act 1933 that children under ten cannot be guilty of any offence (a fact of which most of them are happily ignorant).

A persuasive presumption (traditionally called a presumption of law) imposes a legal burden of disproof on the other side. The standard is sometimes the balance of probabilities (eg the presumption that a person who has been absent and not heard of for seven years by those who would be likely to hear of him is dead). Sometimes the standard is beyond reasonable doubt, eg the presumption of legitimacy at common law on proof of birth in wedlock (though where the accused has to disprove legitimacy the burden on him would only be evidential because the only legal burden borne by the accused at common law is proving his insanity). That is, the tribunal *must* make a finding that the presumed fact is true if insufficient rebutting evidence is adduced, and it *must* find the presumed fact to be untrue if sufficient rebutting evidence is adduced. The probative force of persuasive presumptions sometimes corresponds with the common sense inferences from the facts, and sometimes exceeds them. Even if there were no presumption of legitimacy, it is easy as a matter of common sense to infer legitimacy from birth in wedlock in the absence of other facts. This may be compared with the different presumptions of death. Where a person has been absent for seven years unheard of by those who would be likely to hear of him, he is presumed to be dead in the absence of contrary evidence on a balance of probabilities. But if such a person is absent for a day less than seven years, there is (depending on the circumstances) only an evidential or provisional presumption of death. This extra probative value in certain circumstances is usually imposed for some special reason of policy such as convenience (seven years' absence is a convenient period after which to presume death for the purposes of distributing property). Such reasons also explain the differences in standard of proof required to rebut persuasive presumptions: the criminal standard was imposed for the common law presumption of legitimacy because children should not lightly be bastardised. But sometimes, no doubt, the criminal standard is imposed simply because of the strong probative force of the basic fact. It would seem that where presumptions have an artificially enhanced probative value less evidence is needed to rebut them than where the presumption is intrinsically probable.

Evidential presumptions are traditionally lumped together with persuasive presumptions as 'presumptions of law'. An evidential presumption imposes an evidential burden of proof on the other side: that is, it can be rebutted by evidence which is capable of persuading a reasonable tribunal of its untruth, though the tribunal would not necessarily be bound to draw that conclusion. If *no* rebutting evidence is adduced the tribunal must find that the presumed fact is true. If rebutting evidence of the kind indicated is adduced, the tribunal *may* find it untrue, but whether it does depends on its view of the facts as a whole. An example is the presumption of testamentary capacity. A claimant under a will bears a legal burden of proving its validity and hence the testator's sanity. But on proof of a duly executed will, it will be held valid (ie the testator will be presumed sane) unless the claimant's opponent can produce enough evidence of insanity to entitle a reasonable tribunal to hold the testator insane. If such evidence is produced, it is for the actual tribunal trying the case to decide whether it is convinced of sanity or insanity (*Sutton v Sadler* (1857) 3 CBNS 87). The evidence which destroys the evidential presumption of testamentary sanity that follows from due execution leaves the legal burden of proving sanity on the devisee; the tribunal then has to decide the matter on the facts without the aid of the evidential presumption.

Finally, there are provisional presumptions (traditionally called 'presumptions of fact'). These impose a 'tactical' burden of disproving their truth on the opponent. If he gives no rebutting evidence, he may win his case, because provisional presumptions are weak, and the tribunal may disbelieve them even without rebutting evidence. But he would be tactically wise to attempt to rebut any provisional presumption which may operate against him, because the court is entitled, though not bound, to find that the presumed fact is true; and sometimes it would be a perverse verdict if they did not. The leading examples of such presumptions are the inferences that can be drawn as a matter of common experience from circumstantial evidence, eg the presumption that personal habit or the ordinary course of business has been followed in a given case.

Since these presumptions are simply based on circumstantial evidence it is wrong to cite examples of them as binding authorities; circumstantial evidence which rightly has probative force in one case may not in another. Provisional presumptions are often in fact much weightier and more difficult to rebut than their name suggests. The categories just discussed do not constitute an iron hierarchy; presumptions are essentially guides to probability, and presumptions vary in this respect, both intrinsically and on the facts of particular cases. More evidence may be needed to rebut an improbable persuasive presumption than a highly probable provisional presumption. It is therefore more important for courts to remember this than to work out an accurate hierarchy of presumptions, which is perhaps one reason why no clear classification has been developed or accepted. The courts have been wise to avoid any misleading or tyrannical scheme, though some courts have achieved the worst of both worlds.

2   The reasons for presumptions

Why do presumptions exist?

First, presumptions often accord with the preponderance of probability and are thus simply short-hand ways of expressing conclusions that can be independently reached as a matter of common experience; or at least, the conclusion is so likely to be true that it ought to be reached in favour of one party unless the other disproves it. 'Sanity being the normal and usual condition of mankind, the law presumes that every individual is in that state': *Brotherton v People* 75 NY 159 at 162 (1878). But this explanation cannot account for all presumptions. Some of them do not state intrinsically likely propositions, eg the presumption of innocence. Another example is the commorientes presumption: where two or more persons die in circumstances making it uncertain which survived, the deaths are presumed for property purposes to have occurred in order of seniority (Law of Property Act 1925, s 184; p 62, post). But it is by no means likely on the balance of probability that the deaths occurred in that order.

Another reason why some presumptions exist is to save time at the trial. It would be both absurd and unduly onerous for the prosecution to have to prove in every case that the accused was sane; it is easier to put the burden on the defence.

Thirdly, it is often easier for one party to prove a fact than for his opponent to prove the contrary; for example where the knowledge of a fact is wholly with one party.

Fourthly, presumptions are useful in settling a problem where the ordinary rules of evidence lead to an impasse. If X and Y leave their property to each other provided the beneficiary survives the donor, but otherwise X leaves his to A and Y his to B, then if X and Y die in circumstances rendering it doubtful who died first, A and B each bear a legal burden of proving that they succeed. A will want to prove Y died first; B will want to prove X died first. Both would fail, and the next of kin would take, except for the fact that the Law of Property Act 1925, s 184, ensures that X is presumed to die first, if older than Y, so that all the property goes to B.

Fifthly, pressures of social policy have moulded some presumptions. It is undesirable that children be held illegitimate lightly, so there is a presumption of legitimacy; the stigma of illegitimacy retains some shock, even if the accusation of non-paternity against a man married to the mother of a child has more. Ownership is inferred from possession because stability of title is desirable. The driver of a car is presumed to be driving with the owner's consent in order to give anyone injured by the driver a better chance of recovery and also to encourage road safety by giving an inducement to owners to select careful drivers. Deaths are presumed to be due to accident rather than suicide partly so that life insurance contracts for the deceased's family will be performed rather than avoided by the insurer. The accused is presumed innocent because it is thought important not to convict men wrongly and this is one way of ensuring that the trier of fact takes care.

Sixthly, presumptions often operate to promote convenience. The presumption that a man unheard of by those who would be likely to do so is dead enables affairs of property to be wound up in a reasonable time.

Seventhly, evidential and provisional presumptions serve a variety of procedural purposes. They tend to force the accused to testify if he raises certain issues as to which he knows more than the prosecution or if suspicious circumstances have been proved against him like the possession of recently stolen property. They tend to prevent the jury's time being wasted by considering issues unsupported by evidence. They thus shorten the trial by dispensing with the evidence of one party if the other had adduced no evidence to support a finding in his favour. They prevent perverse verdicts. Thus the presumption of sanity saves the state the trouble of proving sanity in the vast number of cases where the question is not and could not successfully be raised by the accused.

3   Particular presumptions

There is Thayer's authority for the view that any comprehensive or detailed discussion of the hundreds of presumptions erected by the substantive law would be 'an unprofitable and monstrous task' (p 313). In particular, there is little point in discussing in detail what kinds of evidence can rebut presumptions, for these are essentially issues of fact and it is wrong to regard prior cases as establishing binding rules of law. But some points about a few presumptions should be made.

A   PERSUASIVE PRESUMPTIONS

(i)   Commorientes

Law of Property Act 1925, s 184

In all cases where . . . two or more persons have died in circumstances rendering it uncertain which of them survived the other or others, such deaths shall (subject to any order of the court), for all purposes affecting the title to property, be presumed to have occurred in the order of seniority. . . .

NOTES

1. This does not apply to deaths of husbands and wives intestate for the purpose of determining the benefits of spouses on intestacy: Intestates' Estates Act 1952, s 1(4) and 1st Schedule.
2. The relevant 'circumstances' are not limited to a common disaster: s 184 will apply if a husband dies at sea on an uncertain day and his wife dies about the same time in a nursing home (*Hickman v Peacey* [1945] AC 304 at 314–15, [1945] 2 All ER 215, HL, per Viscount Simon LC).
3. In *Hickman v Peacey* [1945] AC 304, [1945] 2 All ER 215, HL, the majority of the House of Lords held that s 184 applied even where the deaths might have been simultaneous because it is not possible to be sure who, if anyone, survived. The minority view would have narrowed s 184, for it would not be applied if the deaths were in fact consecutive. The minority view would also entail more litigation, to decide in each case whether the deaths were simultaneous or consecutive; and it would be difficult to formulate the test of simultaneity.
4. The standard of proof for rebutting the presumption is apparently the balance of probabilities, though the matter is a little obscure (*Re Bate, Chillingworth v Bate* [1947] 2 All ER 418).
5. The words in brackets do not entitle a court to apply or refuse to apply the presumption in its discretion (*Re Lindop, Lee-Barber v Reynolds* [1942] Ch 377, [1942] 2 All ER 46, CA; *Re Brush* [1962] VR 596).

(ii) Presumption of death

If a person is not heard of by those who would be likely to have done so, there is a provisional presumption (the strength of which depends on the circumstances) that he is dead. This presumption becomes persuasive if the person is unheard of for seven years.

Chard v Chard [1956] P 259, [1955] 3 All ER 721

A woman who married her husband in 1909 was last heard of in 1917. She was of normal health. In 1933 she would have been 44. Her husband was frequently in prison. It was impossible to find anyone who since 1917 would naturally have heard of her. No evidence of registration of her death could be found. In 1933 the husband remarried and in these proceedings he and his second wife sought decrees of nullity. Sachs J granted the decrees, holding that there was no evidence of the first wife's death.

Sachs J: On the basis, which I have adopted, that any presumption of continuance of life is simply one of fact, the various decisions cited to me and the dicta therein become reconciled. Further, due weight can thus be given in each case to the different circumstances of any given individual, eg whether a friendless orphan or a gregarious man in public life, whether in good or in bad health, and whether following a quiet or a dangerous occupation. . . .

My view is thus that in matters where no statute lays down an applicable rule, the issue of whether a person is, or is not to be presumed dead, is generally speaking one of fact and not subject to a presumption of law.

To that there is an exception which can be assumed without affecting the present case. By virtue of a long sequence of judicial statements, which either assert or assume such a rule, it appears accepted that there is a convenient presumption of law applicable to certain cases of seven years' absence where no statute applies. That presumption in its modern shape takes effect (without examining its terms too exactly) substantially as follows. Where as regards 'AB' there is no acceptable affirmative evidence that he was alive at some time during a continuous period of seven years or more, then if it can be proved first, that there are persons who would be likely to have heard of him over that period, secondly that those persons have not heard of him, and thirdly that all due inquiries have been made appropriate to the circumstances, 'AB' will be presumed to have died at some time within that period. (Such a presumption would, of course be one of law, and could not be one of fact, because there can hardly be a logical inference from any particular set of facts that a man had not died within 2,555 days but had died within 2,560.)

Mr Campbell has cogently argued that the greater regimentation and registration of our lives and deaths in 1955 now renders unrealistic any such general presumption, at any rate where a death certificate could be expected to be found but is not; and has suggested that as the dicta really originate from judgments of the first half of last century when the presumption of continuing life was also regarded as one of law, they too are now suspect. Further, it appears on examination that some of the above dicta derive either from some case . . . to which some statute applied, and that others . . . where there is no apparent trace of such an origin. . . . It is, however, not necessary for me to deal further with the questions raised by Mr Campbell because in the present case there is no one who has been shown to have been likely to have heard from the 1909 wife in the years 1917 to 1933 or, indeed, from 1933 to date and so such a rule could not operate.

The present case is thus one where there is no suggestion that in 1917 the 1909 wife was other than a woman of normal health, nor any evidence of any fact by reason of which her expectation of life could be regarded as greatly sub-normal. There are many factors which, as previously mentioned, might have led her not to wish to be heard of by the prisoner or his family, there is no one known who would naturally have heard of her, and there is no registration of a relevant death.

I accordingly approach the matter on the footing (1) that this is a case in which the court is put upon inquiry as to the validity of the 1933 marriage; (2) that once the husband was shown to have contracted the 1909 marriage it is for him (or his present wife) to prove facts from which a cessation before 18 May 1933 of the earlier marriage can be inferred before it can be said that the 1933 marriage is valid . . . (3) that there is in the present case no presumption of law either as to the continuance of life or as to death having supervened; (4) that this is thus one of the class of cases which has to be determined on its own facts.

Axon v Axon   (1937) 59 CLR 395

Mauro Herzich deserted his wife in 1923; she obtained a maintenance order against him. She heard no more of him, despite inquiries, and in 1932 she remarried. In these proceedings she sought maintenance against her second husband who pleaded that the marriage was void. At first instance this was granted, the court stating: 'strict proof is required of the existence of Herzich if the defence set up . . . is to succeed, and the defendant has failed to discharge the onus which lies upon him in this regard to the satisfaction of the court'. The husband's appeal to the Supreme Court of South Australia succeeded, and the High Court of Australia dismissed the appeal and remitted the matter to the magistrates for rehearing.

Dixon J: When it is proved that a human being exists at a specified time the proof will support the inference that he was alive at a later time to which, having regard to the circumstances, it is reasonably likely that in the ordinary course of affairs he would survive. It is not a rigid presumption of law. The greater the length of time the weaker the support for the inference. If it appears that there were circumstances of danger to the life in question, such as illness, enlistment for active service or participation in a perilous enterprise, the presumption will be overturned, at all events when reasonable inquiries have been made into the man's fate or whereabouts and without result. The presumption of life is but a deduction from probabilities and must always depend on the accompanying facts. 'In England it is only a general supposition of continuance, applicable to everything which has once been proved to exist – to an orange as well as a man; – a presumption which serves, in reasoning, to relieve from the necessity of constantly re-proving, from minute to minute, this once-proved fact of existence' (The late Professor J B Thayer, *Preliminary Treatise* on *Evidence at Common Law* (1898), p 348). As time increases, the inference of survivorship may become inadmissible, and after a period arbitrarily fixed at seven years, if certain conditions are fulfilled, a presumption of law arises under which a court must treat the life as having ended before the proceedings in which the question arises. If, at the time when the issue whether a man is alive or dead must be judicially determined, at least seven years have elapsed since he was last seen or heard of by those who in the circumstances of the case would according to the common course of affairs be likely to have received communications from him or to have learned of his whereabouts, were he living, then, in the absence of evidence to the contrary, it should be found that he is dead. But the presumption authorises no finding that he died at or before a given date. It is limited to a presumptive conclusion that at the time of the proceedings the man no longer lives. In *Lal Chand Marwari v Mahant Ramrup Gir* (1925) 42 TLR 159 at 160, Lord Blanesburgh, speaking for the Privy Council, said that there is only one presumption and that is that at the time when the suit was instituted the man there in question was no longer alive. 'There is no presumption at all as to when he died. That like any other fact is a matter of proof.' His Lordship observed as not a little remarkable that the contrary theory was still widely held, although so often shown to be mistaken. After stating how it reappeared in the case before the board, he continued: 'Searching for an explanation of this very persistent heresy their Lordships find it in words in which the rule both in India and in England is usually expressed. These words, taken originally from *Re Phené's Trusts* (1870) 5 Ch App 139, [1861–73] All ER Rep 514, run as follows: 'If a person has not been heard of for seven years, there is a presumption of law that he is dead; but at what time within that period he died is not a matter of presumption but of evidence and the onus of proving that the death took place at any particular time within the seven years lies upon the person who claims a right to the establishment of which that fact is essential.' Following these words, it is constantly assumed – not perhaps unnaturally – that where the period of disappearance exceeds seven years, death, which may not be presumed at any time during the period of seven years, may be presumed to have taken place at its close. This of course is not so. The presumption is the same if the period exceeds seven years. The period is one and continuous, though it may be divisible into three or four periods of seven years. Probably the true rule would be less liable to be missed, and would itself be stated more accurately, if, instead of speaking of a person who had not been heard of for seven years, it described the period of disappearance as one 'of not less than seven years'. It follows that in the present case the disappearance in 1923 of

Mauro Herzich gives rise to no presumption that he was dead on 6 January 1932. In fact the conditions were not fulfilled for presuming his death at the hearing before the court of summary jurisdiction when the order now in question was made. For, in the circumstances in which he left his wife, she was not a person with whom he would be likely to communicate or who would be likely to hear of his whereabouts. He was, in effect, a fugitive from her.

But the question is not whether a positive finding that he was dead on 6 January 1932 is justified by proof or legal presumption. It was for the respondent to overcome the presumption in favour of the marriage celebrated on that date between himself and the appellant. He failed to obtain from the court of summary jurisdiction an affirmative finding that Mauro Herzich was then alive, and unless such a finding is made the marriage must be treated as valid. Richards J, to whom *Monckton v Tarr* (1930) 23 BWCC 504 does not appear to have been cited, set aside the decision because he considered that the court had erroneously placed upon the alleged husband, the now respondent, the burden of proving that Mauro Herzich survived until 6 January 1932. But, in my opinion, it was not erroneous to place that onus upon him, and, if in the end the court of summary jurisdiction were not satisfied upon a balance of probabilities that her previous husband was alive on that day, the marriage with the now respondent, the celebration of which was proved by his alleged wife, the now appellant, must be upheld as valid.

At the same time, in considering whether the higher degree of probability was in favour of the inference that Mauro Herzich was then living, the court was bound to weigh with the other circumstances of the case the presumption arising from the fact that in 1923 he was thirty-nine years of age and, so far as appears, was in good health. He had already deserted his wife, and the order for maintenance would afford a powerful motive for his hiding his identity and suppressing his whereabouts from her. The husband attempted to prove that a man bearing the name Herzog was in fact Mauro Herzich, and the reasons of the court of summary jurisdiction contain the statement that, after a full consideration of the evidence, a substantial doubt remained in the minds of the court as to whether the man Herzog was in fact identical with Herzich. The reasons proceed to say that 'strict proof is required of the existence of Herzich'. These observations suggest that, in arriving at its conclusion, the court did not give consideration, or, at all events, full weight, to the presumption of life as affording, in the general circumstances of the case, presumptive proof of Mauro Herzich's existence on 6 January 1932 on which the court was at liberty to act if, on all the facts, a sufficient degree of probability arose to produce a reasonable satisfaction of his survival to that date. The question must be treated as one of fact, and the court demanded a stricter degree or heavier burden of proof than the law requires and treated the failure to prove to its complete satisfaction that Herzog and Herzich were one man and not two men as decisive against the husband.

[Latham CJ and Evatt J agreed in dismissing the appeal.]

NOTES

1. It is a question of fact whether a person is likely to have heard of the propositus. A husband who has been constantly in jail is not such a person (*Chard v Chard*, supra); similarly fugitives from the police or from creditors, or those who for some other reason have no wish to see their family, friends or neighbours again. In practice a person likely to have heard of the propositus is sought in the places he is known to have been in before ceasing to be heard from. It might be more logical to seek him in the places to which he went, but it would be more inconvenient, since such places may be unknown and even if they are known it may be hard to identify his likely circle.
2. The statutes referred to by Sachs J are as follows. The Cestui que Vie Act 1666 provides that if persons on whose lives estates depend remain beyond the seas or elsewhere absent themselves in this realm for the space of seven years they shall be accounted as naturally dead. The Offences against the Person Act 1861 defines bigamy and provides that nothing in the section shall extend to any person marrying a second time whose husband or wife shall

have been continually absent from such person for the space of seven years last past, and shall not have been known by that person to have been living within that time. The evidential burden of proving absence and lack of knowledge rests on the prosecution (*R v Curgerwen* (1865) LR 1 CCR 1; cf *R v Edwards* [1975] QB 27, [1974] 2 All ER 1085). *R v Bonnor* [1957] VLR 227 suggests by analogy that the legal burden of proving absence rests on the accused but this may be doubted.

The Matrimonial Causes Act 1973, s 19, permits the court, in proceedings brought by a married person, to make a decree presuming the death of the other spouse on reasonable grounds and dissolving the marriage. A rebuttable presumption of the propositus's death arises if he has been continually absent from the petitioner for seven years and the latter has no reason to believe that the propositus was living during that time. The reasons for believing in the continued existence of the propositus which prevent the presumption arising must be found in the seven-year period (*Thompson v Thompson* [1956] P 414, [1956] 1 All ER 603). The fact that the propositus would have been unlikely to get in touch with the petitioner during the seven-year period is immaterial, so that this is wider than the common law presumption of death (*Parkinson v Parkinson* [1939] P 346, [1939] 3 All ER 108).

3. Dixon J, in saying that the presumption of death after seven years does not entail any conclusion as to *when* death occurred other than that it occurred before the proceedings, is adopting the strict view of *Re Phené's Trusts* (1870) 5 Ch App 139, [1861–73] All ER Rep 514. That view is inconvenient in many instances where it is necessary not simply to prove that death has occurred (eg for life insurance purposes) but also to prove that it occurred before a certain time (eg a particular marriage). It has therefore not been followed in some cases, such as *Re Aldersey, Gibson v Hall* [1905] 2 Ch 181, [1904–7] All ER Rep 644, where for purposes of succession a child of the testator was presumed to have died seven years after he was last heard of. This lax view that death can be presumed after any seven-year period before proceedings, not simply the period ending in the date of proceedings, produces more convenient results. Where one person has died on a known date and another is presumed dead but his date of death is unknown, the equivalent of s 184 of the Law of Property Act 1925 has been applied to hold that the deaths occurred in order of seniority, since two persons have died in circumstances producing uncertainty as to which survived (*Re Watkinson* [1952] VLR 123; *In the Estate of Dixon* (1969) 90 WN (Pt 1) NSW 469). But absurd results have been shown to follow from this argument (*Re Albert* [1967] VR 875, which was followed in preference to *Dixon's* Case in *Halbert v Mynar* [1981] 2 NSWLR 659).

4. Is a person 'heard of' if the only information received about him is unreliable? See *Prudential Assurance Co v Edmonds* (1877) 2 App Cas 487, HL. If Sachs J in *Chard v Chard* is correct in demanding that due inquiry be made, is it sufficient if fruitless inquiries are made just before proceedings or need they be made persistently during the period of absence?

5. The court will conclude that a man presumed dead died unmarried or childless on the strength of very little evidence, though there is no formal presumption to this effect (*Re Jackson, Jackson v Ward* [1907] 2 Ch 354). The reverse is also true.

6. The amount of evidence which will rebut the presumption of death, both after less than seven and more than seven years, will vary depending on the circumstances. The fact that the seven-year presumption is usually stated as a persuasive presumption does not mean that in some cases it may not be easily rebutted.

7. The court may presume death after a short time if the circumstances in which the propositus disappeared warrant this, eg if he appeared to have committed suicide or accidentally drowned or perished in a snowstorm or died in battle. (Any motive the propositus has for feigning death will be considered.) In such cases there will rarely be any problem as to the time of death; if death is presumed at all, the time when it occurred will be indicated fairly exactly by the circumstances. The fact that the circumstances may allow death to be presumed quite soon after disappearance undermines the force of some of Wigmore's criticism of the rigidity of the seven-year rule (para 2531b).

FURTHER READING

Treitel (1954) 17 MLR 530.

(iii)   Presumption of legitimacy

A child is presumed legitimate on proof of birth or conception in lawful wedlock. Few problems remain. It is a persuasive presumption, now rebuttable on the balance of probabilities (Family Law Reform Act 1969, s 26; *S v S* [1972] AC 24, [1970] 3 All ER 107, HL). Its operation is unaffected by the fact that conception occurred before the relevant marriage was celebrated (*Cox v Juncken* (1947) 74 CLR 277) or birth after it was terminated (*Re Overbury, Sheppard v Matthews* [1955] Ch 122, [1954] 3 All ER 308). In the latter case the presumption is obviously easier to rebut than normal; but it is not rebutted simply by proof of remarriage before the child is born. The presumption does not apply where the husband and wife have been separated by judicial order, but it does apply where there is a maintenance order against the husband or the parties are living apart under a separation agreement or a decree nisi of divorce has been pronounced. These distinctions are artificial and ripe for review (see *Bowen v Norman* [1938] 1 KB 689, [1938] 2 All ER 776; *Ettenfield v Ettenfield* [1940] P 96, [1940] 1 All ER 293, CA; *Brown v Brown* (1947) 64 WNNSW 28).

The persuasive presumption of legitimacy should be distinguished from the provisional presumption that sexual intercourse between husband and wife is likely to have followed proved opportunities for it: the latter will generally be much weaker (see *Piggott v Piggott* (1938) 61 CLR 378 at 413, per Dixon J).

The presumption is rebuttable by such matters as the husband's impotence, his non-access, circumstances making it unlikely he would avail himself of access, blood group evidence, the colour or other features of the child, the conduct towards it of the wife and a putative natural father, or an admission by the latter. Proof of one or more acts of adultery will not necessarily rebut the presumption. A relevant factor may be the lapse of time between access and birth considered in relation to the maturity of the baby. Public reputation other than family reputation is inadmissible (*Re Osmand, Bennett v Booty* [1906] VLR 455 at 467). Either spouse may state whether intercourse occurred at any time during the marriage (Matrimonial Causes Act 1973, s 48(1), abolishing the rule in *Russell v Russell* [1924] AC 687 and the matrimonial intercourse privilege). The presumed unlikelihood of a wife committing adultery will be taken into account by the court.

PROBLEM

On 1 January H_1, who is married to W, dies. On 3 January W marries H_2. On 30 September a child is born. Discuss its legitimacy. (See Guttmann (1956) 5 ICLQ 217, at 222–7).

FURTHER READING

J J Bray in Campbell and Waller, pp 11–35.

(iv)   Presumption of formal validity of marriage

Where there is evidence of a ceremony of marriage which, on due compliance with the requisite formalities, is capable of producing a valid marriage by local law, the validity of the marriage will be presumed even though it cannot be proved that all the formalities were complied with. Indeed, the presumption arises whether the possible formal defects are trivial or extensive.

Whoever (other than an accused) attempts to rebut the presumption bears a legal burden, and there is authority for the standard being beyond reasonable doubt (*Mahadervan v Mahadervan* [1964] P 233, [1962] 3 All ER 1108). But in fact the standard is probably only the balance of probabilities, for this is the normal standard in matrimonial causes (*Blyth v Blyth* [1966] AC 643, [1966] 1 All ER 524, HL). 'It would be both tragic and chaotic' if the standard were lower (*Russell v A-G* [1949] P 391 at 394, per Barnard J).

There is also a presumption that the marriage is monogamous (*Ng Ping On v Ng Choy Fung Kam* [1963] SRNSW 782; *Cheni (otherwise Rodriguez) v Cheni* [1965] P 85 at 90, [1962] 3 All ER 873 at 877).

(v)   Essential validity

It is presumed that a formally valid marriage is essentially valid, ie that its parties were capable of marrying and consented to do so. It is unclear whether a legal or only an evidential burden rests on whoever attempts to rebut the presumption (cf *Axon v Axon* (1937) 59 CLR 395 at 407 and 415 with *Re Peete, Peete v Crompton* [1952] 2 All ER 599 and *Re Peatling* [1969] VR 214). However, it is submitted that the same burden should apply here as with the presumption of formal validity, legitimacy, and valid marriage arising from cohabitation and repute, namely a legal burden. The fact that those who perform marriage ceremonies take great care about matters of form but do not have to inquire as to capacity and consent does not affect the undesirability of questioning the validity of marriages without good reason. The standard of proof in rebuttal ought to be the balance of probabilities. It will often be met by proof of a prior marriage and the absence of any reason to suppose the death of the former spouse.

(vi)   Cohabitation and repute

There is a persuasive presumption that parties are validly married where they are proved to have lived together, holding themselves out as man and wife. It appears to be governed by the same rules as the presumption of formal validity; indeed the two often arise in the same case. It is difficult to rebut but may be rebutted by an admission.

(vii)   Res ipsa loquitur

The details of this subject are best studied in books on torts, but one evidential problem it raises should be outlined here.

In *Scott v London and St Katherine Docks Co* (1865) 3 H & C 596 at 601, [1861–73] All ER Rep 246 at 248, the majority of the Court of Exchequer Chamber said: 'There must be reasonable evidence of negligence . . . where the thing is shown to be under the management of the defendant or his servants, and the accident is such as, in the ordinary course of things, does not happen if those who have the management use proper care, it affords reasonable evidence, in the absence of explanation by the defendants, that the accident arose from want of care.' The later case law, however, has introduced complexity; the maxim res ipsa loquitur 'has not been allowed to speak for itself' (*Anchor Products Ltd v Hedges* (1966) 115 CLR 493 at 496, per Windeyer J).

It is clear that if the presumption applies the plaintiff is entitled to have his case left to the jury. Judges probably differ in their willingness to find proved the basic facts – a situation where the defendant has sole control and an accident which does not ordinarily happen if care is used; they also differ over what the res is which speaks, but the main controversy is about the effect of the presumption. There is authority for four views – that it is persuasive, or evidential, or provisional, or not a presumption at all. The bulk of English and some New Zealand authority favours one or other of the first two views; the bulk of authority elsewhere, particularly Australia, one or other of the latter two.

Barkway v South Wales Transport Co Ltd   [1949] 1 KB 54, [1948] 2 All ER 460, CA

Asquith LJ: . . . (i) If the defendants' omnibus leaves the road and falls down an embankment, and this without more is proved, then res ipsa loquitur, there is a presumption that the event is caused by negligence on the part of the defendants, and the plaintiff succeeds unless the defendants can rebut this presumption. (ii) It is no rebuttal for the defendants to show, again without more, that the immediate cause of the omnibus leaving the road is a tyre-burst, since a tyre-burst per se is a neutral event consistent, and equally consistent, with negligence or due diligence on the part of the defendants. When a balance has been tilted one way, you cannot redress it by adding an equal weight to each scale. The depressed scale will remain down . . . (iii) To displace the presumption, the defendants must go further and prove (or it must emerge from the evidence as a whole) either (a) that the burst itself was due to a specific cause which does not connote negligence on their part but points to its absence as more probable, or (b), if they can point to no such specific cause, that they used all reasonable care in and about the management of their tyres . . .

The above view seems now to have been adopted by the House of Lords (*Henderson v Henry E Jenkins & Sons* [1970] AC 282, [1969] 3 All ER 756, HL; and perhaps *Colvilles Ltd v Devine* [1969] 2 All ER 53, HL); the Privy Council (*Swan v Salisbury Construction Co Ltd* [1966] 2 All ER 138, PC); and the Court of Appeal (*Moore v R Fox & Sons* [1956] 1 QB 596, [1956] 1 All ER 182, CA; cf *Ballard v North British Rly Co* 1923 SC (HL) 43 at 54 and and 56, *The Kite* [1933] P 154, [1933] All ER Rep 234; *The Mulbera* [1937] P 82; *O'Hara v Central SMT Co Ltd* 1941 SC 363; *Woods v Duncan* [1946] AC 401 at 434, [1946] 1 All ER 420n, HL); the law of South Africa: *Arthur v Bezuidenhout and Mieny* 1962 (2) SA 566; the law of the United States: *Sweeny v Erving* 228 US 233 (1931) and the law of Canada: *Temple v Terrace Transfer Ltd* (1966) 57 DLR (2d) 631. In New Zealand, the decisions are divided: cf *Watson v Davidson* [1966] NZLR 853 at 856, and *Hawke's Bay Motor Co Ltd v Russell* [1972] NZLR 542 with *Frederic Maeder Pty Ltd (NZ) v Wellington City* [1969] NZLR 222.

Fitzpatrick v Walter E Cooper Pty Ltd   (1935) 54 CLR 200

Dixon J (in the High Court of Australia): When damage is caused by some unusual event which might reasonably be expected to happen only as the result of an omission to take ordinary precautions, or of a positive act of negligence, and it arises out of operations or the behaviour of inanimate things which are within the exclusive control of a party, no more is required to support an allegation of negligence against him unless and until some further facts appear which supply an explanation of the cause of the accident and displace the ground for inferring negligence. The circumstances may be so strong that a failure to be satisfied of negligence would be unreasonable. But, in my opinion, it is not the law that a legal presumption arises under which the burden of disproving negligence rests upon the party denying it, so that unless evidence is forthcoming reasonably sufficient to support a positive finding that negligence was absent, the party alleging negligence is entitled to a verdict as a matter of law. The distinction is clear between, on the one hand, a rule of law which, as soon as given facts appear, places the legal burden of proof upon the opposite party, and, on the other hand, a presumption of fact arising from circumstances, even if the presumption be so strong that, although the legal burden of proof is unchanged, a finding that the issue was not established would be set aside as unreasonable. In the first case, the court must direct a verdict if the party upon whom the legal burden of proof is thrown fails to adduce evidence sufficient to discharge it. For the sufficiency or insufficiency of evidence to prove a fact or the absence of a fact is always a question of law for the court. But, in the latter case, the court could never direct a verdict.

See also *Davis v Bunn* (1936) 56 CLR 246 at 254, 260 and 267–72; *Anchor Products Ltd v Hedges* (1966) 115 CLR 493; *Nominal Defendant v Haslbauer* (1967) 117 CLR 448; *Piening v Wanless* (1968) 117 CLR 498. But cf *Fitzpatrick's Case* at 207–8. In *Ballard v North British Rly Co* 1923 SC (HL) 43 at 56, Lord Shaw said of res ipsa loquitur, 'If that phrase had not been in Latin, nobody would have called it a principle.'

Government Insurance Office of New South Wales v Fredrichberg
(1968) 118 CLR 403

Barwick CJ (in the High Court of Australia): First, that the so-called 'doctrine' is no more than a process of logic by which an inference of negligence may be drawn from the circumstance of the occurrence itself where in the ordinary affairs of mankind, such an occurrence is not likely to occur without lack of care towards the plaintiff on the part of a person in the position of the defendant; or perhaps, as it might more accurately, in my opinion, be expressed, where, in the opinion of the judge, the jury would be entitled to think that such an occurrence was not likely to occur in the ordinary experience of mankind without such a want of due care on the part of such a person. Second, that a case in which this can properly be said should be allowed to go to the jury whether or not there is evidence of specific acts or occurrences which could be found to be negligent but that no presumption of any kind in favour of the plaintiff thereby arises. That the occurrence affords evidence of negligence does not merely not alter the onus which rests on the plaintiff to establish his case on the probabilities to the satisfaction of the jury, but does not give the plaintiff any entrenched or preferred position in relation to the decision by the jury of that question. I quite realise that it may be attractive to the mind to conclude that, because the jury is allowed to draw an inference of negligence from the occurrence for the reason that they are at liberty to think that it was not likely to occur without a want of care on the part of the defendant, the inference of negligence must be drawn by them if the ground upon which it may be drawn is not displaced by other evidence explaining the occurrence. That line of thought seems to me to have found favour with English courts and to have resulted in the creation by the decisions of those courts of a presumption of fact in favour of a plaintiff in such circumstances. But this court has been unable to accept such reasoning and the law is otherwise in Australia. In my opinion, the jury are not bound either to conclude that such an occurrence was unlikely to occur without negligence on the part of a person in the defendant's position or to draw the inference that it did in fact occur in the case before them because of the negligence of the defendant. All that has happened, in my opinion, at the point in the hearing of a case at which the judge rules that there is evidence of negligence on the part of the defendant furnished by the occurrence itself is that the judge is satisfied that a jury would be entitled to conclude that such an occurrence in the ordinary affairs of mankind is not likely to occur without negligence on the part of a person in the situation of the defendant. For the rest, it is a question for the jury whether they think the occurrence unlikely in this sense and, if so, whether in the particular case they will be satisfied that there was in fact relevant negligence.

We are not concerned in this case with the effect of any explanation of the occurrence which the defendant is able to give and as to the appropriate directions then to be given. What we are concerned with in this case is the question whether after it has been decided that there is evidence to go to the jury and there is no question of an explanation, the jury must be told not merely that on the evidence they may find against the defendant on the issue of liability without identifying any particular act of negligence but that because why they are at liberty so to find is because, in the ordinary affairs of mankind, the occurrence is not likely to occur without negligence on the part of the defendant. In my opinion, in general, the trial judge is not bound to explain to the jury the reason why he has ruled that there is evidence on which they may find a verdict for the plaintiff. To tell them that in the court's opinion such an occurrence is unlikely to occur without relevant negligence would be an error for it is their opinion of what is likely or unlikely which is of consequence at that stage of the trial. If it is a case where the occurrence itself provides the evidence of negligence, they will usually as men of the world recognise that the occurrence itself speaks of the likelihood of negligence if that is the fact. But of course there may be cases in which the nature of the occurrence, because of its complexity or of some other feature, makes it necessary for the jury to be given a direction such as I shall later mention. But the present is not a case of that kind. Here, there being neither complexity in the occurrence nor any attempted explanation of it, a direction that the jury can find for the plaintiff although they are not able to identify the particular act or acts of negligence which caused or contributed to the impact is, in my opinion, a sufficient direction.

But, in my opinion, there can be no objection to the judge informing the jury that they *may* take the view that the occurrence was not likely to have taken place without some negligence on the part of the defendant, provided he properly identifies for them what was relevantly the occurrence and the facts in relation to it of which they should be satisfied and makes it plain that though they may think that in the ordinary affairs of men such an occurrence is not likely to occur without negligence upon the part of a person in the place of the defendant, they must yet be satisfied in their minds that more probably than not the defendant was in fact negligent and that his negligence, even though they cannot identify the particular negligent act or omission, caused the plaintiff's injuries. As I have said, there may be cases in which these directions are not only permissible but, for the reasons above mentioned, necessary. I should mention in passing that my references to the defendant in the preceding paragraphs include, in cases where the defendant did not do the act or make the omission which is said to be in breach of duty, the person for whose acts or omissions the defendant is liable.

Thus there is, in my opinion, no room for counsel, as was claimed in this case, to discuss with the jury 'the doctrine of res ipsa and its effects'. Counsel can of course attempt to persuade the jury that, using their general knowledge of affairs, they should conclude that the occurrence because of its nature and circumstances was in all probability due to the defendant's negligence and in that connexion to urge that in point of fact they should take the view that the circumstances of the occurrence speak for themselves in that regard.

The English position has been explained as an accidental consequence of the virtual disappearance of civil juries in England. The judge has to decide both whether res ipsa loquitur applies and whether the plaintiff in the end succeeds in proving negligence. Once he decides that it does apply, ie that the facts suggest negligence, it is understandable that he requires persuasive proof in order to change his mind (Wright, *Cases on the Law of Torts* (4th edn, 1967), p 246.)

But whether this historical explanation be correct, the merits of the differing views are a separate issue.

Sometimes the debate is conducted as though res ipsa loquitur must always be a presumption of the same kind. From this point of view the English approach deserves support because it often works well. In circumstances where accidents are typically caused by negligence, in cases where no evidence can be found of the cause, less injustice will be caused by a persuasive presumption because the defendant is more likely than not to be negligent; any other rule would be harsh to more plaintiffs than the number of defendants who may be harshly treated by this rule. A more familiar justification for a persuasive presumption here is that in many modern cases, particularly those involving breakdowns in hospital or other institutional procedure, or defective machinery, or explosions during industrial processes, it will be far easier for the defendant to disprove negligence by proving, for example, the frequency of his inspection and maintenance and the quality of the methods used than for the plaintiff to prove the reverse. Further, the defendant is in a far better position to discover the precise cause of the accident than the plaintiff. The maxim also overcomes the problem common in medical cases where an inexpert plaintiff does not know what happened to him under an anaesthetic, and where there are several possible defendants who are reluctant to testify against each other. Thus a trend towards strict liability is disguised as negligence. Admittedly, in cases where these factors are not present the English view is defective in giving the plaintiff the benefit of the artificial weight attached to the presumption for no good reason.

But it is not necessary that res ipsa loquitur should always have the same effect; nor does it. Sometimes facts raising the presumption will be so weak that even if the defendant gives no evidence he may win and here the presumption will only be provisional. Sometimes the facts will be stronger; if the defendant gives no evidence the trier of fact would be perverse if the plaintiff lost, but the presumption is rebuttable by evidence less than that satisfying a legal burden on the defendant. Sometimes the presumption will be raised by facts so convincing that only proof which convinces the particular tribunal of its untruth will rebut it. Dixon J may be correct in *Fitzpatrick's Case* in saying that the court would have no power to direct a verdict; but the certainty of a successful appeal against a finding for a defendant who has not answered the facts raising the presumption means that on the assumed facts res ipsa loquitur operates as a persuasive presumption in the long run: the chances of ultimate success of the parties govern their trial tactics. There is no practical difference between a 'provisional' presumption which has the effect of a persuasive presumption, and a presumption which has the effect of a persuasive presumption, and a presumption technically called persuasive. In other words, the strength of the presumption will vary with the basic facts which bring it into play. The presumption here is different from that discussed in the preceding paragraph; it has no artificial weight superior to its natural weight. It is therefore inappropriate to label it as either persuasive, evidential or provisional except as the facts of particular cases suggest.

The High Court of Australia in *Mummery v Irvings Pty Ltd* (1956) 96 CLR 99 at 121 said that the presumption could not be persuasive because 'The rule . . . is merely descriptive of a method by which, in appropriate cases, a prima facie case of negligence may be made out and we can see no reason why a plaintiff, who is permitted to make out a prima facie case in such a way, should be regarded as in any different position from a plaintiff who makes out a prima facie case in any other way'. But if the inference is stronger than a prima facie one, as it may be on the facts, then the argument to that extent fails. Just as the English view is sometimes defective in giving too much weight to the presumption, so the Australian view is defective in giving too little: if it is constantly referred to as a presumption of fact, this obscures the possibility that it may be much stronger in the circumstances than such presumptions often are. Further, it is possible to imagine direct evidence which would have the effect of imposing a persuasive burden on the defendant, a witness who says 'The explosion occurred because the defendant's servant lit a cigarette near the petrol tank.' In these circumstances it will be hard for the defendant to succeed, though possible; and if he gives no evidence he will lose.

In *Mummery v Irvings Pty Ltd* (1956) 96 CLR 99, Dixon CJ said that where the plaintiff, instead of relying on mere proof of the occurrence, himself adduces evidence of the cause of the accident, the doctrine of res ipsa loquitur has no application, which is why it had no application when the defendant produced such evidence. But the doctrine will continue to apply, surely, if the evidence of the cause of the accident suggests negligence in the defendant. Such evidence would simply be part of the basic facts giving rise to the presumption. On the other hand, Barwick CJ's view (*Fredrichberg's Case* (1968) 118 CLR 403 at 413), that it is not a presumption at all but merely 'a process of logic by which an inference of negligence may be drawn' appears to overlook the fact that all provisional presumptions are of this kind, and that in particular cases a provisional presumption may be so convincing as to have the effect of an evidential or persuasive presumption.

The objection that res ipsa loquitur cannot shift the persuasive burden because that burden never shifts can be met in two ways. It might be said that the view that the persuasive burden never shifts is a useless dogma which can be ignored. A more orthodox reply would be that negligence is not the sole issue; in cases where the doctrine has the effect of shifting the persuasive burden there are really two issues. The plaintiff must prove facts which raise a persuasive inference of negligence; if he does, the defendant must prove non-negligence. The persuasive burden does not shift, but a different persuasive burden is imposed on the defendant after the plaintiff has discharged his.

Sometimes the English view produces a sensible result, and sometimes the Australian one does (*not* for converse reasons); but neither operating exclusively could do so in every case. Two kinds of res ipsa loquitur rule may be needed. One would be a persuasive presumption in cases where it is difficult for the plaintiff to discover how the accident occurred and in cases where the accident is more likely than not to be caused by negligence. The other would be a possible inference of negligence the strength of which is infinitely variable depending on the facts. The reasons for presumptions differ (pp 60–62, ante); the present law of res ipsa loquitur is a good example of the confusion that can be caused by failing to understand the different purposes a presumption may serve. Correspondence with reality is one aim; placing a burden on a defendant with means of knowledge is another; and the avoidance of injustice arising from a lack of evidence is a third. These aims cannot be achieved by a single verbally and substantively rigid rule. There is perhaps little point in calling the latter type of res ipsa loquitur principle a presumption because it would not add anything to the inferences which in any case arise outside the boundaries within which the maxim presently applies. Res ipsa loquitur would then simply cover those special cases where for some reason an artificial weight should be attributed to the basic fact, either to force the defendant to tell all he knows or because he is, on the law of averages, more likely to be negligent than not.

FURTHER READING

Atiyah (1972) 35 MLR 337; Lewis (1951) 11 CLJ 74; Morison in Glass (ed), ch 2; O'Connell [1954] CLJ 118; Prosser, *Handbook of the Law of Torts* (4th edn, 1971), paras 39–40; Eggleston, pp 110–13.

(viii)   Omnia praesumuntur rite esse acta

So far as appointments affecting the public at large are concerned, proof that someone acted in that capacity is evidence of his due appointment and capacity to act. This has been applied to state officials, companies and solicitors (though not in relation to any particular client). The presumption is probably persuasive, and so operates even against the accused (*R v Verelst* (1813) 3 Camp 432, cf *R v Martin* [1967] 2 NSWR 523 at 525). But it did not operate in *Dillon v R* [1982] AC 484, [1982] 1 All ER 1017, where the Privy Council said that the courts would not presume the existence of facts which are central to an offence, and that where the liberty of the subject was involved, there could be no presumption in favour of the Crown.

(ix)   Possession

There is a persuasive presumption that the possessor of property is its owner, and that the possessor of some land owns adjoining and similar land. This is sometimes called a presumption of lawful origin.

B   EVIDENTIAL AND PROVISIONAL PRESUMPTIONS

These two groups will be examined together because the major examples are circumstantial evidence, and the courts have not been careful to state what the precise effect of such evidence is. This is partly because its weight varies greatly according to the particular facts. It can be very misleading. Mark Twain has pointed out that when a woman sharpens a pencil one would think she did it with her teeth (*Puddnhead Wilson*, ch 20). The basic fact alone may prove the presumption beyond reasonable doubt or on the balance of probabilities, or may only shift an evidential or provisional burden. Hence nothing general can be said about these presumptions; no weight attaches to them other than their inherent probative value. First, it has been seen that a man's life is presumed to continue to exist (p 64, ante), and a similar *presumption of continuance* applies to the continued existence of a man's opinions, his partnership, his agency, his ownership, his car's speed.

Secondly, subject to questions of relevance and to the rule prohibiting the admission of similar fact evidence (ch 10, post), evidence of a man's *habits* may be admitted to prove that he followed them in a particular instance. The same is true of practices within a household or business, eg that immediately after being copied into a letter-book all letters were posted, or that letters handed to a servant were usually given to his master. The habit must be indulged often enough and in a sufficiently similar way to make the inference likely as a matter of common experience.

A third group concerns motive, plan, intention, capacity, opportunity. The presence or absence of motive to do an act is relevant to whether it was done; it is presumed that men act in accordance with their motives. This 'presumption', apart from being of even greater variation in terms of weight than normal, also often conflicts with the presumption of innocence. Further, 'there is a great difference between absence of proved motive and proved absence of motive' (*R v Ellwood* (1908) 1 Cr App Rep 181 at 182, CCA, per Channell J). But sometimes this presumption taken in conjunction with other circumstantial evidence has sufficed to prove guilt beyond reasonable doubt even though there is no evidence of any act of the accused causing the crime (*Plomp v R* (1963) 110 CLR 234). A similar presumption arises from acts of planning and preparation, and sometimes the doing of an act may be inferred from statements of intention to do it admitted as hearsay exceptions, subject to the possibility of a self-serving statement by a party or the intervention of some factor preventing the completion of the act. (Cf such cases as *Johnson v Lyford* (1868) LR 1 P & D 546; *R v Buckley* (1873) 13 Cox CC 293 and *Mutual Life Insurance v Hillmon* 145 US 285 (1892) with *R v Wainwright* (1875) 13 Cox CC 171.) Similarly the existence of an intention to do a thing may be inferred from the fact it was subsequently done, as long as there is no risk of manufacture. Further, there is the presumption that a man intends the natural consequences of his acts; since he is usually able to foresee the latter, it is often but not always reasonable to infer that he did foresee and intend them (see Criminal Justice Act 1967, s 8). Ability or inability to do a thing may raise a presumption that it was or was not done. The same is true of opportunity, particularly if the defence of alibi is not promptly raised so that the police cannot check it; indeed the alibi is inadmissible now under the

Criminal Justice Act 1967, s 11, in proceedings on indictment unless notice is given to the prosecution within seven days of the end of committal proceedings. The strength of the inference from opportunity varies, because it is much more likely that advantage will be taken of opportunities to commit some forms of conduct than others. The inference is strong in consensual sex cases. 'Clodius and Pompeia are found naked in bed together. A sufficient time for sexual relations to have taken place has elapsed. He has been in love with the girl for some time, and has written letters inviting her to have intercourse with him. Who would hesitate to condemn them both for adultery? Who is so lacking in common sense that he would be unaware of the usual consequences of night, wine, love, and a girl and boy together?' (Matthaeus, *De Criminibus Ad D* 48, 15, 6; see Hoffmann, p 369).

Fourthly, there is a presumption that the conduct and general practice of professional men or businessmen in one set of circumstances shows what objective standard should have been attained or what terms were accepted in the similar circumstances.

Fifthly, there is a presumption that mechanical devices are in working order. This applies to devices of a familiar and well-known kind like traffic lights, watches, speedometers, weighbridges, tyre pressure gauges, but not to strange ones, because if the machine is strange there is no basis for common sense and common experience to support the view that the machine normally works.

Sixthly, there is a presumption that the driver of a car is authorised to do so by the owner (*Barnard v Sully* (1931) 47 TLR 557; *Young v Masci* 289 US 253 at 259 (1932); *Hannan v Jennings* [1969] 1 NSWR 260). A similar principle that *what seems to be in order is in order* applies in a wide but uncertain way; it will be used only cautiously in cases where the accused challenges the fundamental procedural legality of the prosecution's conduct (*Scott v Baker* [1969] 1 QB 659, [1968] 2 All ER 993).

Seventhly, under the spoliation doctrine, inferences may be drawn from any lying, fraud, fabrication or suppression of evidence, flight or interference with the course of justice by a party. This conduct may be an implied admission of the weakness of his case.

Finally, a party's failure to give any satisfactory explanation in answer to an allegation made to him out of court may suggest it is well-founded, either because silence is assent, or because it shows a consciousness of guilt or liability, or because inferences from the material supporting the allegation, being unchallenged, are thereby strengthened. The presumption is the stronger where the facts are particularly within his knowledge. Hence silence is sometimes said to give rise to a provisional presumption. A similar presumption may arise from a party's delay in enforcing his rights (eg *Sellen v Norman* (1829) 4 C & P 80). In court, a party's failure to testify, to call a witness, or to produce a document ordinarily suggests that the absent evidence would not support him. Special problems arise with the silence of the accused (ch 7, post).

4   Conflicting presumptions

It is often said or assumed that though presumptions of different kinds cannot conflict, two presumptions of the same kind may do. The solution usually offered is to ignore them and decide the matter on the evidence as a whole, if necessary relying on an undischarged legal burden of proof. Thus in *Danyluk v Danyluk* [1964] WAR 124, W married H_1 in 1946 and H_2 in 1951, and alleged her first marriage was void because H_1 had married in 1937. There were persuasive presumptions that both the 1946 and the 1951 marriages were valid; but Hale J ignored these because they conflicted. He simply held that on the facts W was able to discharge the legal burden of proof resting on her that it was probable that H_1's spouse survived the war, with the assistance of the provisional presumption that life continues. The presumption of death after not being heard of did not arise because there was no evidence of inquiries about her. (See also *Monckton v Tarr* (1930) 23 BWCC 504, where the plaintiff widow failed to discharge the legal burden of proving that a husband of an earlier wife of her deceased spouse had survived until the marriage between the earlier wife and the plaintiff's husband, in spite of assistance from the provisional presumption of continuance. And see *R v Willshire* (1881) 6 QBD 366; *Re Overbury, Sheppard v Matthews* [1955] Ch 122, [1954] 3 All ER 308.)

This orthodox account of the problem seems wrong both in statement and solution. Presumptions may conflict, but this is not typical of, nor limited to, presumptions of the same kind. But even two presumptions of the same kind need not conflict, because a presumption merely directs that a conclusion should or may be drawn in the absence of a certain amount of contrary evidence. How much contrary evidence depends on the degree of probability associated with the presumption and all the circumstances of the case. A conflict between two presumptions of the validity of marriage is almost always illusory, because one in fact will be more probable than the other, and the general facts of the case will resolve any conflict between them, or at least will cause the case to be decided in accordance with the burden of proof. Further, presumptions of different kinds – a persuasive presumption and a provisional presumption – may or may not conflict; but this will not depend on the formal hierarchy but on the intrinsic weight of the presumptions on the facts. The persuasive presumption of innocence in theory outweighs the provisional or evidential presumption of theft based on the possession of stolen property; but if the accused does not testify he may very well be convicted. If H marries W_1 (aged 70) in 1900, W_2 (aged 20) in 1930, and W_3 in 1931, the persuasive presumption of the validity of the 1930 marriage does not conflict with the provisional presumption of continuance of W_1's life because the latter is so weak. On the other hand, the presumption of validity of the third marriage is much weaker than the presumption of the continuance of W_2's life.

Thus Dixon J in *Axon v Axon* (1937) 59 CLR 395 reasoned as follows. W, who claimed maintenance against H_2, bore the onus of proving that her marriage to him in 1932 was valid. She could rely on the presumption that her 1932 marriage was valid, thus placing a legal burden on H_2 of proving that H_1, whom W had married in 1911, survived until 1932. In the circumstances of the case, the presumption that H_1's life continued could be relied on by H_2 as being sufficient evidence in all the circumstances to discharge that burden. He held that the matter should be remitted to the justices because they appeared to hold erroneously that H_2 must prove H_1's survival beyond reasonable doubt rather than on the balance of probabilities. (The judgments of Latham CJ and Evatt J are obscure on this point and it is submitted they do not destroy the authority of Dixon J.)

To look briefly at the matter another way, when two witnesses differ on a point, the court does not regard them as cancelling each other out as in a mathematical equation: it attempts to discover which is the more credible. For presumptions no different process is adopted.

Whatever the correct approach to conflicting presumptions, it is thought that one recent solution is not likely to be helpful. In *Re Peatling* [1969] VR 214, McInerney J acted on a suggestion of Morgan's (44 Harv LR 906) that where presumptions conflict the solution depends on balancing the social policies underlying the presumptions. He held that in the case the presumption of validity of marriage and the presumption of innocence (ie against bigamy) should outweigh the presumption of continuance of life, because it was socially important that marriages be not lightly invalidated, and that persons be not lightly assumed guilty of bigamy. It is not clear that the same result could not have been reached simply by relying on the orthodox view that there was no conflict because the presumption of marriage is persuasive and the presumption of continuance on the facts only evidential or provisional; McInerney J rejected this because in his view, the presumption of marriage is not persuasive but only evidential. This is not the usual view and it is an odd one if the presumption is supported by such important social policies. The same result could also have been reached, if there is a conflict, by resorting to the legal burden of proof resting on the proponent of validity, which on the facts he might well have discharged. Further, the notion of balancing social policies is one which can only produce an uncertainty inappropriate in this area; if presumptions conflict it is better that parties fail for want of evidence than that they succeed after vague judicial speculation.

FURTHER READING

Bridge (1949) 12 MLR 273; Denning (1945) 61 LQR 379; Edwards (1969) Uni of WAL Rev 169; Eggleston (1963) 4 Melb ULR 180; Thayer, ch 8; Williams, *Criminal Law, The General Part* (2nd edn), ch 23.

QUESTIONS

1. 'Every presumption operates to satisfy the evidential burden' (Williams, *Criminal Law, The General Part* (2nd edn), p 877). Do you agree?

2. Prosser says (*Handbook of the Law of Torts* (4th edn, 1971), para 38): 'a presumption, as a rule of law applied in the absence of evidence, is not itself evidence, and can no more be balanced against evidence than two and a half pounds of sugar can be weighed against half-past two in the afternoon'. Do you agree?

Is Prosser's the same as the view that presumptions are 'bats of the law flitting in the twilight, but disappearing in the sunshine of actual facts' (*Mackowik v Kansas City, St J & CBR Co* 94 SW 256 at 262 (1906), per Lamm J)?

CHAPTER 5

Corroboration or Support

1 Introduction

It is very rare that a trial depends on only one piece of evidence, or even on evidence from a single source only. Normally the task of the trier of fact is to assess the combined effect of a number of items of evidence, noting in particular the effect which they have on one another. Evidence tending to confirm some fact of which other evidence is given is called 'corroboration' or 'support'. As a matter of common sense, the more corroboration is present the easier it is to prove a fact, and from this point of view a trier of fact will always look for corroboration. But there are two respects in which English law *requires* that attention be paid to this issue.

There are a few types of evidence which are regarded as being liable to incorrect assessment. The most common of these is identification evidence, which always needs special care. Sometimes the judge is obliged to withdraw from the jury a case based substantially on identification evidence, and he must always warn the jury of the dangers inherent in such evidence, and advise them to look for support (*R v Turnbull* [1977] QB 224, [1976] 3 All ER 549, CA); further, there are rules, both in the Police and Criminal Evidence Act 1984 Codes of Practice and elsewhere, which govern the process of obtaining identification evidence: see section 2 below. A few statutes specify a minimum evidential requirement: see section 3. Here corroboration is a requirement in the sense that no matter how convincing the evidence requiring corroboration is, the party relying on that evidence will fail unless he adduces corroboration.

Until very recently there were other categories of evidence in respect of which the trial judge was obliged to warn the jury against reliance without corroboration, and was obliged too to define corroboration (in the technical sense which it had acquired from the cases, particularly *R v Baskerville* [1916] 2 KB 658, [1916-17] All ER Rep 38, CCA) and to identify to the jury the items of evidence capable of being corroborative in this sense. The result was a particularly unwieldy direction: if the judge made a mistake in giving it, a successful appeal against conviction was almost inevitable; but it is extremely doubtful whether a jury could properly understand and act on a correct direction. There was a further difficulty: the requirement to give the 'full corroboration warning' in every case where these categories of evidence (one of which was the evidence of the complainant in a sexual case) occurred had meant that witnesses within those categories were effectively regarded as, in all circumstances, less credible than other witnesses. The Law Commission (Law Com 202, 1991) recommended the abolition of the rules requiring a 'full corroboration warning' so far as they survived (one had been abolished by statute in 1988): this has been achieved by s 32 of the Criminal Justice and Public Order Act 1994. Two questions arising from that legislation were the following. Given that the corroboration rules had become arcane and unsatisfactory, they were nevertheless based on sound judgments about the *possible* (rather than universal) dangers of such evidence. If, after s 32 came into effect, the judge was no longer obliged to give a corroboration warning, was the position that in the case of those types of evidence he should normally give such a warning in the exercise of his discretion? Secondly, if he said anything about corroboration, should he still use the full form of words hallowed by practice since *R v Baskerville*, supra? Both questions received a clear negative response in *R v Makanjuola* [1995] 1 WLR 1348, CA, where the Court of Appeal pointed out that to hold otherwise would nullify the effect of s 32. The judge has a discretion to give whatever warning, and in whatever terms, is appropriate. His exercise of that discretion is to be tailored to the individual circumstances of the case, untrammelled by the old law relating to the 'categories' of evidence requiring a 'full corroboration warning'. An appellate court will be disinclined to interfere with a trial judge's exercise of his discretion save in a case where that exercise is unreasonable in the *Wednesbury* sense. The judge's duty is merely to put the case to the jury fairly and adequately, making them fully aware of the difficulties or danger of the evidence in question. No particular form of words is necessary, and the judge need only refer specifically to potentially corroborative evidence if the circumstances of the case demand it (*R v Spencer* [1987] AC 128, [1986] 2 All ER 928, HL): see section 4.

Section 32 of the Criminal Justice and Public Order Act 1994, as applied in *R v Makanjuola*, supra, abrogates the law relating to what was capable of amounting to corroboration in the old, technical sense. Presumably, however, it does not affect previous decisions (which are strictly on matters of logic rather than law) about what evidence is, in this logical rather than legal sense, capable of offering support to other evidence: see section 5.

In civil cases there are no requirements relating to the number of witnesses, or to corroboration. Even in a claim against the estate of a deceased person, the requirement is of special care, rather than corroboration: *Re Hodgson* (1885) 31 Ch D 177, [1881-5] All ER Rep 931, CA.

Apart from perjury, the origins of corroboration requirements in English law are either statutory or very recent or both. In this respect the common law has traditionally differed from civil law systems; modern Scots law, for example, has at least a weak requirement that corroboration be looked for in every case. But the common law only set its face firmly against a general corroboration requirement in the seventeenth century; indeed the issue only arose on a substantial scale when the phenomenon of witnesses testifying in court in a characteristically modern way became widespread and the common law judges had to decide whether to follow the requirement of ecclesiastical and civilian systems of more than one witness. The triumphant view had to battle with a persistent medieval line of contrary opinion to the effect that 'the testimony of a single person is as the testimony of no one' (*Cressy v Siward* (1312) YB 5 Edw II, Selden Society vol 33 p 121 at 123; and see Wigmore, para 2032).

The historical reason why the common law judges eventually took the view that they did was that in the sixteenth century the jury were to some extent still regarded as witnesses themselves rather than open-minded triers of fact quite ignorant of the case before the trial. On this approach, any general demand for particular numerical requirements of witnesses would be considered otiose, because there were always twelve witnesses other than the one testifying. For the same reason, no judge could declare the evidence of any one witness insufficient. Apart from this historical reason, however, there is room for argument both about the sense of a general rule requiring or not requiring corroboration, and also about the justice of requiring corroboration in particular circumstances.

A number of points have traditionally been made in favour of a general corroboration requirement. First, such a rule prevents a man of honour being destroyed by the assertions of a single rogue. But rogues sometimes tell the truth and honourable men sometimes commit crimes; in any event, the right to undermine a rogue's credibility by attacking his character affords some solution to an honourable man accused of crime. Further, as Napoleon supposedly said when he abolished a two-witness rule in the Rhineland, 'one honourable man by his testimony could not prove a single rascal guilty; though two rascals by their testimony could prove an honourable man guilty' (Bonnier, *Traité des Preuves* (5th edn, 1888), para 293, cited in Wigmore, para 2033, n 3).

A second justification for a two-witness rule was advanced by Montesquieu: 'Reason requires two witnesses; because a witness who affirms, and a party accused who denies, make assertion against assertion, and it requires a third to turn the scale' (see Bentham, IX 6 c 1, para 1). The objection to this is that it is only a mechanical method of obtaining security, unrelated to the real forms and causes of unreliable testimony. In Bentham's words: '*Pondere, non numero*. From numbers (the particulars of the case out of the question) no just conclusion can be formed . . . In many cases, a single witness, by the simplicity and clearness of his narrative, by the probability and consistency of the incidents he relates, by their agreement with other matters of fact too notorious to stand in need of testimony, – a single witness (especially if situation and character be taken into account) will be enough to stamp conviction on the most reluctant mind. In other instances, a cloud of witnesses, though all were to the same fact, will be found wanting in the balance.' Further, the balance of opposed witnesses which supposedly has to be broken by an extra witness does not in fact generally exist. For example, the accused in a serious criminal charge has everything to gain and little to lose by lying, while a prosecution witness has much to lose and nothing to gain (except in special circumstances, as where he is an accomplice carrying out his side of a bargain by which the police will arrange for him to be leniently treated). It is more likely that the accused will lie than his accuser, and so Montesquieu's argument if anything suggests that the defence should always have to provide a plurality of witnesses.

A third point is that a general corroboration rule protects the innocent because 'it is hard for two or more so to agree upon all circumstances relating unto a lye, as not to thwart one another' (Algernon Sidney's *Apologia*, 9 How St Tr 916, at p 927). This is particularly so where the lies are detailed and the witnesses who tell them are subject to skilful cross-examination. But such a rule causes hardships which outweigh its benefits. First, it will lead to many crimes going unpunished and will in fact encourage crimes to be committed by persons aware of the difficulties of conviction. Bentham said that under a corroboration rule: 'those to whom, in consequence of the licence granted by this same rule, it might happen, and (if the rule were universally known) could not but happen, to suffer the same or worse punishment at the hands of malefactors, are altogether overlooked. The innocent who scarcely present themselves by so much as scores or dozens, engross the whole attention, and pass for the whole world. The innocent who ought to have presented themselves by millions, are overlooked, and left out of the account' (op cit). Secondly, a corroboration rule tends to increase the likelihood of perjury and subornation of perjury on the part of litigants attempting to comply with it, and a consequential decline in public respect for the entire legal system. Roger North noted of a Turkish law to this effect that an English merchant 'will directly hire a Turk to swear that fact of which he knows nothing; which the Turk doth out of faith he hath in the merchant's veracity; and the merchant is very safe in it, for, without two Turks to testify, he cannot be accused of the subornation. This is not, as here, accounted a villainous subornation, but an ease under an oppression, and a lawful means of coming into a just right' (Roger North, *Life of Sir Dudley North* (1744), p 46, quoted Wigmore, para 2033, n 3). Thirdly, as Best said, corroboration rules may 'produce a mischievous effect on the tribunal, by their natural tendency to react on the human mind; and they thus create a system of mechanical decision, dependent on the number of proofs, and regardless of their weight' (para 598).

In sum, to use Wigmore's words: 'The probative value of a witness' assertion is utterly incapable of being measured by arithmetic. All the considerations which operate to discredit testimony affect it in such varying ways for different witnesses that the net trustworthiness of each one's testimony is not to be estimated, either in itself or in reference to others' testimony, by any uniform numerical standard. Probative effects are too elusive and intangible for that. The personal element behind the assertion is the vital one, and is too multifarious to be measured by rule. "Testimony", as Boyle well said, "is like the shot of a long-bow, which owes its efficacy to the force of the shooter; argument [ie circumstantial inference] is like the shot of a cross-bow, equally forcible whether discharged by a giant or a dwarf" (quoted in 8 How St Tr 1041). The cross-bow notion of testimony – the notion that one man's shot is as forceful as any other man's – can find no defenders to-day' (para 2033).

These arguments suggest that any general corroboration requirement would be too wide. But experience has persuaded the legislature and the judges that sometimes corroboration should be looked for. This may be because of the *situation of the witness:* he may have a motive to lie, for example. Sometimes *the subject-matter of the case* carries dangers. Charges may be hard to disprove, or allegations may stir up prejudice against one party. Sometimes *the nature of what the testimony is about* carries dangers, for example, evidence of the speed of cars, or evidence of personal identification. Sometimes there is *some prudential reason unconnected with reliability* for requiring corroboration: the need for testimony of perjury to be corroborated is probably justified by the need to remove any factor which might prevent witnesses coming forward to testify; and this might occur were it possible to obtain a conviction for perjury on uncorroborated evidence.

It should be noted that even if no corroboration rule of any kind applies, the evidence of a single witness need not be acted upon even though it is uncontradicted. Stephen (*History of the Criminal Law of England*, vol 1, pp 400–1) noted disapprovingly that seventeenth century juries 'seem to have thought (as they very often still think) that a direct unqualified oath by an eye- or ear-witness has, so to speak, a mechanical value, and must be believed unless it is distinctly contradicted . . . [J]uries do attach extraordinary importance to the dead weight of an oath.' This approach was also attacked by Wigmore as a 'loose and futile but not uncommon heresy' (para 2034, n 3). The reasons why uncontradicted evidence should sometimes be ignored were stated thus by Stephen: 'The circumstances may be such that there is no check on the witness and no power to obtain any further evidence on the subject . . . [J]uries may very reasonably say we do not attach so much credit to the oath of a single person of whom we know nothing, as to be willing to destroy another person on the strength of it. This case arises where the fact deposed to is a passing occurrence – such as a verbal confession or a sexual crime – leaving no trace behind it, except in the memory of an eye- or ear-witness. . . . The justification for this is, that the power of lying is unlimited, the causes of lying and delusion are numerous, and many of them are unknown, and the means of detection are limited.'

2 Identification evidence

Hoffmann: The South African Law of Evidence, 2nd edn, pp 437–41

The accuracy of a witness's observation depends first, of course, upon his eyesight. Secondly, it will be affected by the circumstances in which he saw the person in question; the state of the light, how far away he was, whether he was able to see him from an advantageous position, how long he had him under observation. Thirdly, impressions of appearance may be distorted by the witness's prejudice and preconceptions. He may expect people who behave in a particular way or belong to a certain class to have some physical characteristic, which he will ascribe to such a person without having verified his belief by observation. Fourthly, his ability to form an accurate impression will be affected by his state of mind. Did he have any reason to take particular notice, or was his attention concentrated upon something else? Did he really see who was there, or did he think he was seeing the person whom he expected to be there? Was he in a state of mind to make a trustworthy observation of anything? . . . Fifthly, the distinctiveness of the person's appearance. The court will be able to observe whether the accused has any peculiar features, but some people look distinctive to one witness and not to another. Thus to a person of one race, everyone belonging to another race tends to look alike, and to a lesser extent the same is true of different age-groups. On the other hand, a person well known to the witness may register a distinctive impression even though the witness is unable to mention any peculiar features. . . .

[Recollection] depends, first, upon the strength of the witness's memory. Very young and very old people tend to forget more easily than others. Secondly, the nature of the original impression; for example, whether it was accompanied by any unusual incident which made it likely that the witness's impression would be preserved. Striking features are more likely to be remembered than ordinary ones, and if the person in question was known to the witness, he will be able to preserve the short-hand recollection 'I know X' better than he would remember X's individual features. The time lag is of course important, and perhaps most crucial of all is the extent to which the witness's original impression had been overlaid by subsequent suggestion and imagination. If a witness is shown a person who is alleged to have been the criminal, he is very likely to make a subconscious substitution of that person's features for those which he actually observed. The more he sees of the accused, the more certain he will become that he is the person whom he actually saw. The same process can happen if the witness is shown a photograph of the accused, or if it is suggested to him that the person whom he saw had certain features. It is because the possibility of suggestion seriously diminishes the value of identification evidence that the courts have insisted upon the holding of identification parades subject to stringent precautions. [Convictions may be set] aside because, instead of holding an identification parade, the police . . . simply [take] the accused to the sole identifying witness and [ask] him whether he was [is] the right man. Evidence of identification in such circumstances can have very little value. The same may be said of the usual question 'Do you see the man in court?' The witness would look very silly if he pointed to anywhere other than the dock.

. . . An identification witness should be asked to give a detailed description of the alleged criminal at the earliest possible moment. If there is a delay he is not only likely to forget but may have an opportunity to compare notes with other witnesses, which would diminish the value of his evidence. For the same reason, an identification parade should be held as soon as possible. . . .

The parade should consist of at least eight people who are similar to the accused in general appearance. In particular, the accused should not be dressed differently from the others or have any distinctive features which would inevitably attract attention . . . Care should be taken that the witness does not see the accused in custody before the parade, or while the parade is being formed. Courts have commented adversely upon witnesses being put into a room with a window through which they might have seen the parade. . . . The prosecution should also eliminate, as far as possible, the chance that someone may have told the witness which man to pick out. It is therefore undesirable that the officer investigating the case should also take charge of the parade, and the person who conducts the witness to the place where the parade is held should not have seen it being formed or know who the accused is.

If there are several witnesses, they should be segregated or kept under supervision before the parade to prevent them from comparing notes about the criminal's appearance, and a witness who has completed his identification should not be allowed to rejoin the others.

. . . [T]he witness may think that the police are unlikely to have held a parade unless it contains someone whom they suspect. Another possible solution is to hold a 'blank parade' before or after the one which includes the accused, the witness being told that more than one parade will be held.

If the witness fails to identify anyone, or picks out someone other than the accused, the prosecution should disclose this fact in evidence. . . .

Circumstantial evidence of identity may be provided by any characteristic which the person before the court and the person to be identified are shown to have in common. Traces left behind, such as fingerprints, footprints and palm prints are commonly used to provide circumstantial evidence of identification. . . .

History has taught the courts that identification evidence presents a special problem. They have been taught that lesson by actual *causes célèbres* involving wrong identifications – the Tichborne claimant, Beck and Slater, to mention only old examples. Experiments have often led to the same result. Why do these mistakes occur?

(a) Identification evidence is fragile and depends on complex reasoning. In *Craig v R* (1933) 49 CLR 429 at 446, Evatt and McTiernan JJ said:

'An honest witness who says "the prisoner is the man who drove the car", whilst appearing to affirm a simple, clear and impressive proposition, is really asserting: (1) that he observed the driver, (2) that the observation became impressed upon his mind, (3) that he still retains the original impression, (4) that such impression has not been affected, altered or replaced by published portraits of the prisoner, and (5) that the resemblance between the original impression and the prisoner is sufficient to base a judgment, not of resemblance, but of identity.'

(b) The witness may have had only a fleeting glimpse of the criminal's face, or seen it under bad conditions of light and weather for observation, or been too far away, or had his view impeded by passing traffic or a press of people. This difficulty weakens an identification even where the witness knows the person identified well.

(c) There are problems of defective memory. An identification may be defective if the witness had no special reason to remember the person identified. It may also be defective if there is a long interval between the time of observation and the time when the witness tells the police he is sure of the identification.

(d) A particular face may arouse a conventional attitude appropriate to the face of which it is a type.

(e) Another danger is that identification is a matter about which witnesses are most confident and dogmatic even where their grounds are slight, and in which personal pride, leading to stubbornness, becomes easily involved.

(f) Witnesses are prone to err in recognising outsiders – those of another race, or age, or class, or dress. To a white man, an old man, a rich man or a civilian, the black, the young, the poor, and the uniformed look alike.

(g) As Mason J said in *Alexander's* Case (see p 92, post), problems arise from 'the use by the police of methods of identification which, though well suited to the investigation and detection of crime, are not calculated to yield evidence of high probative value in a criminal trial'. Persons with criminal records are particularly open to the risk of being mistakenly identified. The police, in showing photographs of suspects to witnesses, will tend necessarily largely to use photographs of persons thought from their records possibly to be involved in the crime: it is a quick and convenient way, and often the only way, of getting eyewitnesses to draw the attention of the police to the likely suspects. Any identification by photograph of this kind may be difficult for the accused to attack in practice because of his fear of indirectly revealing his criminal record.

The value of the identification parade is usually overrated as a safeguard against that danger. According to the Devlin Committee Report, Table 1, in 1973 there were 2116 identification parades in England and Wales. In 944 the suspect was picked out, in 984 no one was, and in 188 some person other than the suspect was.

'It is the experience of the police that at the majority of such parades the witness picks out nobody or the "wrong" man. If a witness fails in this way, he may not be called at the trial, his evidence being useless. . . . It will be obvious that this fact seriously discounts the probative value of a positive identification. Quite apart from this, and even granting a reasonably good memory on the part of the witness, the danger of the identification parade is that the witness expects to find the guilty person present, and therefore points out the man who he thinks is most like the one he remembers. Thus all that an identification parade can really be said to establish is that the accused resembled the criminal much more closely than any other members of the public did, which is not saying very much': Williams, p 121.

Thus the procedure by which a witness picks out the accused from police photographs, identifies him in an identification parade, then identifies him at the trial, has pitfalls. There is a tendency, as was observed in

Alexander's Case (see p 92, post), to substitute a photograph image once seen for a hazy recollection of the person initially observed.

'When the witness is shown the photographs, he is likely to pick on the fact that best accords with his recollection of the culprit. Thereafter, his recollection of the culprit and recollection of the photograph are likely to be so merged that he can no longer separate them, even though in fact his identification was mistaken. Psychological tests show that if he thereafter sees the real criminal, he may no longer be able to recognise him as the person he saw previously, the sight of the photograph and efforts at recall having distorted the memory': Williams, p 122.

Further, it must be remembered that photographs can differ from nature: they are two-dimensional, static, often in black and white, and usually give a clear and well-lit view of the subject. Identification evidence is inherently capable of being influenced by suggestion; identification from police photographs or parades obviously carries that risk, to which should be added the unusual nature of this type of evidence in that it is artificially brought into existence, not naturally thrown up in the course of human affairs.

(h) The usual way of overcoming the risk of testimonial error is cross-examination. The value of identification evidence is very difficult to assess by that means. As the Devlin Committee said (paras 1.24 and 4.25):

'A witness says that he recognises the man, and that is that or almost that. There is no story to be dissected, just a simple assertion to be accepted or rejected. If a witness thinks that he has a good memory for faces when in fact he has a poor one, there is no way of detecting the failing.
. . . It is well known to legal practitioners as well as to forensic psychologists that eye-witnesses of an event can differ widely about the details of it. But normally when the court has to reach a conclusion about an incident or event, it does not have to make a finding on each detail; it is enough if out of the evidence as a whole there can be extracted as much of the story as it is necessary to know in order to determine the point at issue. But in identification evidence there is no story; the issue rests upon a single piece of observation. The state of the light, the point of observation and the distance from the object are useful if they can show that the witness must be using his imagination; but otherwise where there is a credible and confident assertion, they are of little use in evaluating it. Demeanour in general is quite useless. The capacity to memorise a face differs enormously from one man to another, but there is no way of finding out in the witness box how much of it the witness has got; no-one keeps a record of his successes and failures to submit to scrutiny.'

(i) Further, there is a tendency for repeated error to arise. Several identifying witnesses can each make the same mistake, so that the testimony of a second eyewitness may not offer much additional protection.

(j) A person may be over-ready to identify from motives of revenge or to find a scapegoat. And he may be prepared to support an identification made by another on the basis that though if his identification stood alone he would have doubts, they are resolved by the confidence of the other.

(k) A witness may be called upon to remember events and people of whom he was not taking particular notice.

(l) The process by which the features of a suspect are recollected and narrated may be affected by such special factors as the perusal of photographs or identikit pictures, staged confrontations with the accused, reading descriptions of the suspect and acceding to police suggestions as to the features of the guilty man.

A EVALUATION AT THE TRIAL

R v Turnbull   [1977] QB 224, [1976] 3 All ER 549, CA

Lord Widgery CJ, Roskill and Lawton LJJ, Cusack and May JJ: Each of these appeals raises problems relating to evidence of visual identification in criminal cases. Such evidence can bring about miscarriages of justice and has done so in a few cases in recent years. The number of such cases, although small compared with the number in which evidence of visual identification is known to be satisfactory, necessitates steps being taken by the courts, including this court, to reduce that number as far as is possible. In our judgment the danger of miscarriages of justice occurring can be much reduced if trial judges sum up to juries in the way indicated in this judgment.

First, whenever the case against an accused depends wholly or substantially on the correctness of one or more identifications of the accused which the defence alleges to be mistaken, the judge should warn the jury of the special need for caution before convicting the accused in reliance on the correctness of the identification or identifications. In addition he should instruct them as to the reason for the need for such a warning and should make some reference to the possibility that a mistaken witness can be a convincing one and that a number of such witnesses can all be mistaken. Provided this is done in clear terms the judge need not use any particular form of words.

Secondly, the judge should direct the jury to examine closely the circumstances in which the identification by each witness came to be made. How long did the witness have the accused under observation? At what distance? In what light? Was the observation impeded in any way, as for example by passing traffic or a press of people? Had the witness ever seen the accused before? How often? If only occasionally, had he any special reason for remembering the accused? How long elapsed between the original observation and the subsequent identification to the police? Was there any material discrepancy between the description of the accused given to the police by the witness when first seen by them and his actual appearance? If in any case, whether it is being dealt with summarily or on indictment, the prosecution have reason to believe that there is such material discrepancy they should supply the accused or his legal advisers with particulars of the description the police were first given. In all cases if the accused asks to be given particulars of such descriptions, the prosecution should supply them. Finally, he should remind the jury of any specific weaknesses which had appeared in the identification evidence.

Recognition may be more reliable than identification of a stranger, but even when the witness is purporting to recognise someone whom he knows, the jury should be reminded that mistakes in recognition of close relatives and friends are sometimes made.

All these matters go to the quality of the identification evidence. If the quality is good and remains good at the close of the accused's case the danger of a mistaken identification is lessened; but the poorer the quality, the greater the danger.

In our judgment when the quality is good, as for example when the identification is made after a long period of observation, or in satisfactory conditions by a relative, a neighbour, a close friend, a workmate and the like, the jury can safely be left to assess the value of the identifying evidence even though there is no other evidence to support it: provided always, however, that an adequate warning has been given about the special need for caution. Were the courts to adjudge otherwise, affronts to justice would frequently occur. A few examples, taken over the whole spectrum of criminal activity, will illustrate what the effects upon the maintenance of law and order would be if any law were enacted that no person could be convicted on evidence of visual identification alone.

Here are the examples. A had been kidnapped and held to ransom over many days. His captor stayed with him all the time. At last he was released but he did not know the identity of his kidnapper nor where he had been kept. Months later the police arrested X for robbery and as a result of what they had been told by an informer they suspected him of the kidnapping. They had no other evidence. They arranged for A to attend an identity parade. He picked out X without hesitation. At X's trial, is the trial judge to rule at the end of the prosecution's case that X must be acquitted?

This is another example. Over a period of a week two police officers, B and C, kept observation in turn on a house which was suspected of being a distribution centre for drugs. A suspected supplier, Y, visited it from time to time. On the last day of the observation B saw Y enter the house. He at once signalled to other waiting police officers, who had a search warrant to enter. They did so; but by the time they got in, Y had escaped by a back window. Six months later C saw Y in the street and arrested him. Y at once alleged that C had mistaken him for someone else. At an identity parade he was picked out by B. Would it really be right and in the interests of justice for a judge to direct Y's acquittal at the end of the prosecution's case?

A rule such as the one under consideration would gravely impede the police in their work and would make the conviction of street offenders such as pickpockets, car thieves and the disorderly very difficult. But it would not only be the police who might be aggrieved by such a rule. Take the case of a factory worker, D, who during the course of his work went to the locker room to get something from his jacket which he had forgotten. As he went in he saw a workmate, Z, whom he had known for years and who worked nearby him in the same shop, standing by D's open locker with his hand inside. He hailed the thief by name, Z turned round and faced D; he dropped D's wallet on the floor and ran out of the locker room by another door. D reported what he had seen to his chargehand. When the chargehand went to find Z, he saw him walking towards his machine. Z alleged that D had been mistaken. A directed acquittal might well be greatly resented not only by D but by many others in the same shop.

When, in the judgment of the trial judge, the quality of the identifying evidence is poor, as for example when it depends solely on a fleeting glance or on a longer observation made in difficult conditions, the situation is very different. The judge should then withdraw the case from the jury and direct an acquittal unless there is other evidence which goes to support the correctness of the identification. This may be corroboration in the sense lawyers use that word; but it need not be so if its effect is to make the jury sure that there has been no mistaken identification: for example, X sees the accused snatch a woman's handbag; he gets only a fleeting glance of the thief's face as he runs off but he does see him entering a nearby house. Later he picks out the accused on an identity parade. If there was no more evidence than this, the poor quality of the identification would require the judge to withdraw the case from the jury; but this would not be so if there was evidence that the house into which the accused was alleged by X to have run was his father's. Another example of supporting evidence not amounting to corroboration in a technical sense is to be found in *R v Long* (1973) 57 Cr App Rep 871. The accused, who was charged with robbery, had been identified by three witnesses in different places on different occasions but each had only a momentary opportunity for observation. Immediately after the robbery the accused had left his home and could not be found by the police. When later he was seen by them he claimed to know who had done the robbery and offered to help to find the robbers. At his trial he put forward an alibi which the jury rejected. It was an odd coincidence that the witnesses should have identified a man who had behaved in this way. In our judgment odd coincidences can, if unexplained, be supporting evidence.

The trial judge should identify to the jury the evidence which he adjudges is capable of supporting the evidence of identification. If there is any evidence or circumstances which the jury might think was supporting when it did not have this quality, the judge should say so. A jury, for example, might think support for identification evidence could be found in the fact that the accused had not given evidence before them. An accused's absence from the witness box cannot provide evidence of anything and the judge should tell the jury so. But he would be entitled to tell them that when assessing the quality of the identification evidence they could take into consideration the fact that it was uncontradicted by any evidence coming from the accused himself.

Care should be taken by the judge when directing the jury about the support for an identification which may be derived from the fact that they have rejected an alibi. False alibis may be put forward for many reasons; an accused, for example, who has only his own truthful evidence to rely on may stupidly fabricate an alibi and get lying witnesses to support it out of fear that his own evidence will not be enough. Further, alibi witnesses can make genuine mistakes about dates and occasions like any other witnesses can. It is only when the jury is satisfied that the sole reason for the fabrication was to deceive them and there is no other explanation for its being put forward can fabrication provide any support for identification evidence. The jury should be reminded that proving the accused has told lies about where he was at the material time does not by itself prove that he was where the identifying witness says he was.

In setting out these guidelines for trial judges, which involve only changes of practice, not law, we have tried to follow the recommendation set out in the Report which Lord Devlin's Committee made to the Secretary of State for the Home Department in April 1976. We have not followed that report in using the phrase 'exceptional circumstances' to describe situations in which the risk of mistaken identification is reduced. In our judgment the use of such a phrase is likely to result in the build up of case law as to what circumstances can properly be described as exceptional and what cannot. Case law of this kind is likely to be a fetter on the administration of justice when so much depends upon the quality of the evidence in each case. Quality is what matters in the end. In many cases the exceptional circumstances to which the report refers will provide evidence of good quality, but they may not; the converse is also true.

A failure to follow these guidelines is likely to result in a conviction being quashed and will do so if in the judgment of this court on all the evidence the verdict is either unsatisfactory or unsafe.

Patrick Devlin: The Judge (1979) pp 188–93, 197–8

There is a well-established precedent for handling this type of situation in which appearances are deceptive and in consequence the reliability of the witness is exceptionally difficult to assess. This is the rule that the jury must be warned that it is dangerous to act on such evidence unless it is corroborated. A type of case in which a warning is required is that in which a charge of a sexual offence is made by a woman; these are sometimes due to sexual neuroses which can produce phantasies in which the woman half or even wholly believes. There are not as yet any satisfactory forensic methods for the detection of make-believe in an honest witness.

But the Court of Criminal Appeal was born and had died (or more correctly had been assumed into the heaven where dwell the lords justices) before the appellate judges were ready to apply this palliative to cases of eye-witness identification. They said it should be left to each judge to decide whether or not the jury should be warned and they offered him no criteria to help him in his decision. In 1912 a man on a charge of murder was identified by no less than seventeen witnesses, but fortunately was able to establish an irrefutable alibi. In 1928 Oscar Slater, after he had spent nineteen years in prison and after a public agitation in which many distinguished people joined, had his conviction for murder quashed; he had been identified by fourteen witnesses. Nevertheless, cases continued to be left to the jury as if they raised only a simple issue between the identifier and the accused as to which was telling the truth. A submission that in such cases a warning should be given was rejected by the Court of Criminal Appeal in 1956. Six years later in 1962 the Supreme Court of the Republic of Ireland held that a warning should be given; the House of Lords, however, in a case from Northern Ireland indicated that it was better to leave such matters to 'the discerning guidance' of the trial judge. In 1966 the Donovan Committee recommended the widening of the powers of the Court of Appeal to quash convictions which they thought to be unsafe and unsatisfactory; the primary reason they gave for this was the danger of unsafe convictions in cases of disputed identity. In 1972 the Criminal Law Revision Committee under the chairmanship of Lord Edmund-Davies recommended that a warning to the jury should be required by statute. Also in 1972 there was another much publicised case of disputed identity in which George Ince was charged with murder; fortunately the jury at the first trial disagreed and at the second acquitted, for subsequently another man was convicted of the murder. All this left the judiciary unmoved. In *R v Long* in 1973 the Court of Appeal once again refused to require the trial judge to give a warning. They did, however, certify the question as a point of law of public importance for the House of Lords to consider, but the House refused leave to appeal.

In 1974 two shattering cases of mistaken identity came to light within four weeks of each other. In the first of them Mr Dougherty was convicted of shop-lifting, having been identified by two witnesses, at a time when he was on an excursion with some twenty other persons . . .

After he had served most of his sentence in prison and on a reference back to the Court of Appeal by the Home Secretary, Mr Dougherty got his alibi evidence before the Court and the prosecution threw up the sponge. Here was an opportunity to review the law and practice on a subject which the Lord Chief Justice was later to describe as 'perhaps the most serious chink in our armour'. But in conformity with the policy of giving decisions without reasons the court said no more than that the conviction was unsafe and that 'it disclosed a number of matters which we must look after in our own way and in our own time'. This type of answer is more common in administrative than in judicial circles.

This was on 14 March 1974. On 5 April the Home Secretary discharged with the grant of a free pardon a Mr Virag from the prison in which he had been for five years. As was conclusively proved in the subsequent inquiry, he had been wrongly identified by eight witnesses, four of them police officers, on six different occasions. The Home Secretary did me the honour of inviting me to be chairman of a committee which he set up on 1 May to consider the serious questions raised by these two cases about the law and procedure relating to identification.

The Committee's *Report* was published on 26 April 1976. Most of it was taken up with procedural questions, such as the conduct of identification parades, rather than the law . . . The Committee could not of course recommend the creation of case law; it was not within its province nor within that of the Home Secretary to advise the judges what to do, nor in the light of *R v Long* did there seem to be much likelihood that the judges would take any advice. So the recommendations had perforce to be for statutory enactment, though I for one would always have welcomed the use of case law instead. The first recommendation was for an absolute and unconditional rule that the jury should be directed or warned about the dangers of identification evidence. The second was for a general rule that the jury should not be allowed to convict on eye-witness evidence alone. This rule had to be general and not absolute because admittedly there would be exceptions, eg when the witness was identifying someone he knew well or who had been under frequent or prolonged observation. The Committee refused to codify a list of exceptions, holding that they were better left to be developed by case law; this was the case law whose introduction the Lord Chief Justice deplored. Thirdly, the Committee recommended that dock identifications should not be permitted save in circumstances in which the holding of a parade was impracticable or unnecessary, eg when the accused refused to attend or was already well known to the witness.

The Court of Appeal decided to forestall legislation by giving in July 1976 in three pending identification cases a comprehensive judgment laying down a new approach consisting of two sets of guide-lines. In the first the Court accepted at last the need for a warning and imposed the requirement in terms which make the description 'guide-line' sound rather mild. In the second the Court laid it down that cases in which the identification evidence was of poor quality should not, unless supported by other evidence, be left to the jury.

As to the first, for the moment I need say no more. As to the second, if it is true to say that to make law demands precision, it would appear to be equally true that to avoid making law demands obscurity. On the face of it what the Court is saying is only an unremarkable truism: it must be unsafe to convict on evidence of poor quality, whether it is evidence of identification or of any other sort. If the Court meant more than this, as I am sure that they must have done, one must search for a special meaning for 'quality'. Quality is not a word commonly used in legal language in relation to evidence. Reliability or weight are the expressions commonly used. Is 'quality' intended only to mean 'reliability'? In assessing reliability a jury is usually told to have regard to the reputation of the witness, his demeanour, the coherence and probability or otherwise of his story, and, where he is deposing to what he has seen, his opportunities for accurate observation, etc. This applies to evidence of every sort. The problem peculiar to evidence of visual identification is that this evidence, because of its type and not because of its quality, has a latent defect that may not be detected by the usual tests. The highly reputable, absolutely sincere, perfectly coherent, and apparently convincing witness may, as experience has quite often shown, be mistaken. Is then 'quality', when it is used in the judgment, referring to the character of a witness and to the way in which he gives his evidence, or to the nature of the evidence? The enquirer will find an indication both ways in the facts of the cases considered in the judgment. In one case the judgment refers to the quality as being 'meagre in the extreme' and follows this immediately with personal criticisms of a witness who 'had made up his mind'. In another case the court says:

'It is conceded that Miss Kennedy in particular was an impressive witness. But the quality of the identification was not good.'

But I think that the better view, although it involves a rather artificial and restricted use of the word, is that quality refers only to the circumstances in which identification is made, and that the key sentence in the judgment is:

'When, in the judgment of the trial judge, the quality of the identifying evidence is poor, as for example when it depends solely on a fleeting glance or on a longer observation made in difficult conditions . . . the judge should then withdraw the case from the jury and direct an acquittal unless there is other evidence which goes to support the correctness of the identification.'

This is the sentence on which trial judges are likely to fasten. They cannot really be expected to assess evidence as if it were a piece of cloth to be rubbed between finger and thumb and pronounced as shoddy or good stuff, and the results would vary widely if they did. They will take the two categories given as examples in the judgment, the 'fleeting glance' and 'the difficult conditions' (difficult in the ways suggested in the judgment, eg poor lighting or obstructed view), and disallow such cases. The adventurous may disallow some others, and so may the Court of Appeal. If the Court of Appeal gives reasons for the disallowance and the case is reported, a third category will be created. If the Court gives no reasons, there will be no addition to the categories. But quite likely zealous counsel will with the aid of the Registrar search among the transcripts for cases 'on all fours' with the one he is going to argue.

In short, while the rule proposed by the Committee is a general rule that unsupported evidence of identification should be left to the jury only in exceptional circumstances, such as repeated and prolonged observation, the *Turnbull* guide-lines will be operated as a general rule that such evidence should be left to the jury unless the identification was only a fleeting glimpse or was made under poor conditions. Recognition of familiar faces will be treated as a 'special category' common to both systems. The *Turnbull* rule imposes a lighter burden on the prosecution; an unsupported case, instead of being left to the jury as exceptional, will be left as one in which the evidence is not of poor quality. The object in both cases is the purely pragmatic one of devising a test which will result in the acquittal of as many as possible of the innocent and the conviction of as many as possible of the guilty. The *Turnbull* judges, who embody collectively much greater experience than the members of the Committee, may well be right in lightening the burden; time will show. But there is nothing to be gained by veiling the inevitable categorisation with nebulous distinctions between good and bad quality, *unless* – and to this I must return later – the Court of Appeal means to deliver empty judgments amounting only to declarations of good or bad quality.

The *Turnbull* judgment incorporated some general reflections intended to allay public disquiet about miscarriages of justice in identification cases. It did not refer in this connection to the beneficial effect of the warning to be given to the jury. The public, it seems, are to place their faith in the judges 'released from the limitations which the Criminal Appeal Act 1907 and the case law based upon it had put upon the old Court of Criminal Appeal'.

'We do not hesitate to use our extended jurisdiction whenever the evidence in a case justifies our doing so. In assessing a case, however, it is our duty to use our experience of the administration of justice. In every division of this Court that experience is likely to be extensive and helps us to detect the specious, the irrelevant and that which is intended to deceive . . .'

Long after everyone else had been convinced that identification evidence, and dock identification in particular, demanded special treatment and the imposition of a uniform rule, the judges persisted in thinking that it did not. When in 1976 they abandoned the position which they had affirmed only three years before in *R v Long*, they did not even trouble to overrule formally their earlier decision (this is the only case I know of an appellate court overruling one of its own decisions without mentioning it, except for the purpose of a complimentary reference to another aspect of it), let alone to explain to the public why they had changed their minds. Inevitably they left the public with the impression that they were yielding against their better judgment to the implied threat of a statutory rule which they would find even more irksome than case law. No doubt this is the sort of tactical misfortune that can occur in the development of any form of institutional life and it would not be sensible to suppose that the English judiciary is exempt from it. What marks it as an excess of complacency, is, first, that they should assume that an *ipse dixit* – a thing done in their own way and in their own time – says all that needs to be said; and secondly, their apparent belief that *R v Turnbull* was a case in which they could appropriately proclaim their own sagacity and their conviction that the future handling of a problem which they had ignored for so long could now be left exclusively in their hands. It is with this sort of utterance that the judiciary gives hostages to its critics.

COMMENTS

1. Experience with the *R v Turnbull* guidelines has shown that Lord Devlin's worries may have been justified. One example of the decision's being applied rather narrowly is *R v Bath* (1990) 154 JP 849, CA. *R v Turnbull* does not deal specifically with evidence of recognition; but the Court of Appeal has now held that a Turnbull warning is necessary in such cases too: *R v Bentley* (1991) 99 Cr App Rep 342, CA. Similar (but not identical) considerations apply to identification by senses other than sight, and to identification of things rather than persons. See *R v Browning* (1991) 94 Cr App Rep 109, CA; *Pfennig v R* (1995) 127 ALR 99.

2. The older Australian cases held that the identification warning was not compulsory, but need only be given where the circumstances warrant it: *Davies and Cody v R* (1937) 57 CLR 170; *R v Preston* [1961] VR 761, *R v Goode* [1970] SASR 69, *R v Harris* (1971) 1 SASR 447. The position was the same in New Zealand (*R v Fox and Fisher* [1953] NZLR 555) and Canada: eg *R v Olbey* (1971) 4 CCC (2d) 103. The *R v Turnbull* guidelines have now been adopted in Australia (*Domican v R* (1992) 173 CLR 555) (though not in all states, eg *R v De-Cressac* (1985) 1 NSWLR 381), New Zealand (*Auckland City Council v Brailey* [1988] 1 NZLR 103) and Canada (*Mezzo v R* [1986] 1 SCR 802, with criticism of the English Court of Appeal's failure to specify clearly the borderline between 'good quality' and 'poor quality' identification evidence). In Eire the warning is mandatory; *People (A-G) v Casey (No 2)* [1963] IR 33.

3. An identification by one witness may be used to constitute support for an identification by another provided the jury is warned that even a number of honest identification witnesses may be mistaken: *R v Weeder* (1980) 71 Cr App Rep 228, CA; cf *R v Burchielli* [1981] VR 611 at 616.

4. The requirement that the judge withdraw from the jury a case based on poor quality identification evidence standing alone is to be justified on the ground that the evidence is unreliable 'not because the judge considers that the witness is lying, but because the evidence even if taken to be honest has a base so slender that it is unreliable and therefore not sufficient to found a conviction: and indeed, as *R v Turnbull* itself emphasised, the fact that an honest witness may be mistaken on identification is itself a particular source of risk'. There is therefore no conflict with the *R v Galbraith* [1981] 2 All ER 1060, [1981] 1 WLR 1039, CA principle that, on a submission of no case, the judge must leave to the jury matters (such as the assessment of credibility) that are within their province: *Daley v R* [1994] AC 117, [1993] 4 All ER 86, PC.

B   GATHERING IDENTIFICATION EVIDENCE

Alexander v R   (1981) 145 CLR 395

Gibbs J: Evidence given by a witness identifying an accused as the person whom he saw at the scene of the crime, or in circumstances connected with the crime, will generally be of very little value if the witness has not seen the accused since the events in question and is asked to identify him for the first time in the dock, at least when the witness has not, by reason of previous knowledge or association, become familiar with the appearance of the accused. The reasons for this were explained in *Davies v R, Cody v R* (1937) 57 CLR 170 at 181–2. In particular, there is the danger that the witness will too readily come to believe, without any true recollection, that the man charged is the man whom he had previously seen, particularly if his own memory has become dim and there is some resemblance between the two men. The courts in England and Australia have long recognised the danger of acting upon evidence of identification made in those circumstances. It has accordingly become established practice for a witness to be asked to identify the accused at the earliest possible opportunity after the event, and for evidence to be given of that act of identification. Such evidence is, in practice, given not only by the person who made the identification but also by persons who saw it made.

In theory the manner in which an accused was identified out of court goes to the weight rather than to the admissibility of the evidence. However, the objections to the evidence of an identification made of an accused person when he is in the dock are almost equally open to evidence of the identification of an accused person which is given by a witness who has been shown the accused alone and as a suspect, and in *Davies v R, Cody v R* it was held that a conviction based on evidence of such a witness should be quashed as unsafe unless the identity of the accused was further proved by other evidence. The court went on to say, at 182: 'Where that further evidence consists in or includes other witnesses whose identification has been of the same kind, the number of witnesses, their opportunities of obtaining an impression or knowledge of the prisoner and other circumstances in the case must be taken into account by the court of criminal appeal for the purpose of deciding whether on the whole case the possibility of errors is so substantial as to make the conviction unsafe.'

The safest and most satisfactory way of ensuring that a witness makes an accurate identification is by arranging for the witness to pick out from a group the person whom he saw on the occasion relevant to the crime. If an identification parade is held for that purpose, it goes without saying that precautions must be taken to ensure that no prompting, suggestion or hint is given to the witness that any particular member of the group is the suspect. For example, it would be unfair and improper to show to a witness, before the identification parade was held, a simple photograph of a person who was said to be the suspect, and it would be unsafe to act on evidence of identification given in those circumstances: *R v Russell* [1977] 2 NZLR 20 at 27, CA. Indeed, where a suspect had been arrested, and it was intended to ask a witness to attempt to identify him at an identification parade, it would be unfair to show the witness, before the parade, a number of photographs including that of the suspect: *R v Goss* (1923) 17 Cr App Rep 196; *R v Haslam* (1925) 19 Cr App Rep 59, CCA. On the other hand it may be necessary for a police officer to show a number of photographs to a witness in an attempt to obtain information as to the identity of an offender; if such witness did identify the offender from a photograph, it would not necessarily be unfair for that witness later to be asked to select the offender from a group at an identification parade, but the fact that the witness had seen the photograph might affect the value of the later identification at the parade: see *R v Dwyer, R v Ferguson* [1925] 2 KB 799, CCA.

The value of holding an identification parade is not only that, if properly carried out, it provides the most reliable method of identification, but also that it is necessarily held in the presence of the accused, who is thereby enabled to observe, and later bring to light, any unfairness in the way in which the parade was conducted, or any weakness in the way in which the witness made the identification. However, as a matter of legal principle, it seems to me impossible to say that the admissibility of evidence of a prior act of identification depends on the fact that an identification parade was held. As a matter of law it would be equally admissible to prove that an identification was made by a witness who was shown a collection of photographs and selected one which he said was the photograph of the person concerned. There are, however, two grounds of objection to the proof of identification by means of police photographs. In the first place, the accused will of necessity be absent when the identification is made, and has no means of knowing whether there was any unfairness in the process or whether the witness was convincing in the way in which he made the identification. Secondly, the production in evidence at the trial of photographs coming from the possession of the police is very likely to suggest to the jury that the person photographed had a police record, probably for offences of the kind in question.

For these reasons, it is most undesirable that police officers who have arrested a person on a charge of having committed a crime should arrange for potential witnesses to identify that person except at a properly conducted identification parade. Similarly, speaking generally, an identification parade should, wherever possible, be held when it is desired that a witness should identify a person who is firmly suspected to be the offender. However, there is little support to be found in the authorities for the view that a conviction must necessarily be quashed if it is based on evidence that the accused was identified other than at an identification parade at a time when he had been charged or was definitely suspected, even though there was no valid reason why an identification parade could not have been arranged. The judgment of this court in *Davies v R, Cody v R*, supra, suggests that the proper approach is to consider whether the conviction can safely be sustained on the whole of the evidence.

In England, although the courts constantly insist on the importance of holding an identification parade, the Court of Criminal Appeal in *R v Seiga* (1961) 45 Cr App Rep 220, CCA dismissed an appeal against conviction in a case where photographs were used to identify the accused although he had been arrested and no reason was given why there should not have been an identification parade. In that case the witness who identified the accused in court had previously been shown, by a police officer, a group of photographs, including one of the accused. The Court of Criminal Appeal disapproved of the conduct of the police officer, but nevertheless sustained the conviction. In Australia, the question arose in *R v Bouquet* [1962] SRNSW 563 where the accused was identified by a witness who was shown a number of photographs after the accused had been arrested. An appeal against conviction was allowed on other grounds, but Sugerman J said, at 568, that the use of photographs instead of an identification parade goes to the weight and sufficiency of the evidence rather than its admissibility and may be specially significant when there is no other evidence identifying the accused. Wallace J, at 574, said that the procedure of holding an identification parade should be followed except in special circumstances. The other Australian cases were not so directly concerned with this question. In *R v Goode* [1970] SASR 69 the accused was identified from photographs before his arrest, and no parade was subsequently held; the court quashed the conviction because the warning given to the jury was insufficient. In *R v Fannon, R v Walsh* (1922) 22 SRNSW 427 and *R v Doyle* [1967] VR 698, and also in the New Zealand case *R v Russell*, supra, identification parades were held, but only after the identifying witness had identified the accused from a number of photographs produced by the police. In *R v Doyle* and *R v Russell* the photographs were shown to the witnesses during the investigation of the crime and before the arrest of the suspect; the report in *R v Fannon & Walsh* does not make it clear at what stage the photographs were shown. In all these cases the evidence of identification by means of the photographs was held admissible and the convictions were upheld. In *R v Russell*, Richmond P said, at 27: '. . . we respectfully agree with what was said in *R v Doyle* that evidence of identification by photograph is legally admissible and relevant. The real question in all cases is whether or not the trial judge ought to have exercised his discretion in favour of the accused to exclude admissible and relevant evidence on the ground that its prejudicial effect is out of proportion to its true evidential value, or on general grounds of "unfairness".'

Finally, reference should be made to the Canadian case *R v Bagley* [1926] 3 DLR 717. In that case, after the arrest of the accused, certain witnesses were shown a bundle of photographs, and later identified the accused at an identification parade. The conviction was affirmed, Macdonald CJA, in his dissenting judgment which is mentioned in *Davies and Cody v R* at 183, said, at 719, that he did not regard the question as one of admissibility of evidence but rather of weight, and that he would have sustained the verdict had the charge to the jury been sufficient.

The authorities support the conclusion that I have reached, which is that, as a matter of law, evidence of an identification made out of court by the use of photographs produced by the police is admissible. However, a trial judge has a discretion to exclude any evidence if the strict rules of admissibility operate unfairly against the accused. It would be right to exercise that discretion in any case in which the judge was of opinion that the evidence had little weight but was likely to be gravely prejudicial to the accused. In a case such as the present it seems to me proper for a trial judge, in deciding how he should exercise his discretion, to take into consideration that it is the duty of police officers investigating crime to take every precaution reasonably available to guard against the miscarriages of justice that can occur, and have in fact occurred, because of honest but mistaken evidence of identification, and that for this reason 'only in exceptional cases should photographs be used at a stage when some particular person is directly suspected by the police and they are able to arrange an identification parade or some other satisfactory alternative means whereby the witness can be asked directly to identify the suspected person': *R v Russell* at 28. If the trial judge admits the evidence, and the accused is convicted, the true question for the Court of Criminal Appeal is whether having regard to the whole of the evidence it would be so unsafe or unsatisfactory to allow the conviction to stand that to do so would amount to a miscarriage of justice. In considering that matter the Court of Criminal Appeal also will keep in mind the importance of ensuring that the most reliable evidence of identification is obtained in every case.

For the reasons I have given, I conclude that the evidence of the identifying witnesses in the present case was not inadmissible and that the learned trial judge was entitled to admit it in the exercise of his discretion. Once that evidence was admitted there was no reason to hold that the photographs themselves were inadmissible. There was no suggestion that there was anything objectionable about the photographs themselves – for example, they did not show the applicant wearing prison uniform or in handcuffs – and once evidence had been given that identification had been made by means of police photographs it does not seem to me to have been unfair to admit the photographs themselves, although again the trial judge had a discretion to exclude them if he considered that their prejudicial effect outweighed their probative value.

Mason J: The problems which afflict identification evidence have their origin in four principal sources: (a) the variable quality of the evidence much of which is inherently fragile; (b) the use by the police of methods of identification which, though well suited to the investigation and detection of crime are not calculated to yield evidence of high probative value in a criminal trial; (c) the consequential need to balance the interests of the accused in securing a fair trial against the interests of the state in the efficient investigation and detection of crime by the police; and (d) the difficulty of accommodating the reception of certain types of identification testimony to accepted principles of the law of evidence.

Identification is notoriously uncertain. It depends upon so many variables. They include the difficulty one has in recognising on a subsequent occasion a person observed, perhaps fleetingly, on a former occasion; the extent of the opportunity for observation in a variety of circumstances; the vagaries of human perception and recollection; and the tendency of the mind to respond to suggestions, notably the tendency to substitute a photographic image once seen for a hazy recollection of the person initially observed.

The use of photographs by police, especially photographs of known or suspected criminals, is an essential aid to the detection of persons who have committed crimes. Yet the use of such photographs before a jury may tend to suggest that the accused is known to the police as a criminal who has committed offences of the kind charged. And, as I have said, once a witness has seen a photograph which he links with the person seen, he tends to substitute the photographic image for his recollection.

Recognising these dangers the English courts have tended to draw a distinction between an identification made in the course of investigating a crime, when the police may request a potential witness to make an identification from photographs, and an identification made after the accused has been taken into custody, when the use of photographs is frowned upon and the arrangement of an identification parade is urged as the course to be preferred. In the second situation the purpose of the identification is purely evidentiary; it is designed to produce evidence for use at the trial.

Before I examine the questions which relate to the evidence of Beale and Williams there is another basic point to which I should refer, obvious though it is. Traditionally it has been accepted that a witness identifies the accused at the trial as the person whom he observed at the scene of, or in connection with, the crime. This 'in court' identification, sometimes described as primary evidence, is of little probative value when made by a witness who has no prior knowledge of the accused, because at the trial circumstances conspire to compel the witness to identify the accused in the dock. It has been the practice to reinforce this 'in court' identification by proving that the witness had earlier identified the accused out of court in a line-up or by selecting his photograph from a collection of photographs (*R v Fannon, R v Walsh* (1922) 22 SRNSW 427; *R v Bouquet* [1962] SRNSW 563; *R v Doyle* [1967] VR 698; see also *R v Goode* [1970] SASR 69; *Cross on Evidence*, 2nd Aust ed, p 54) though the propriety of proving the photographs has been challenged by the applicant . . .

The applicant relies heavily on *R v Wainwright* (1925) 19 Cr App Rep 52 to show that police photographs and identification of an accused by means of them are not receivable in evidence. There, Hewart LCJ said (at 54): '. . . it is unheard of that police photographs, and the identification of a defendant by means of them, should be put forward by the prosecution as part of its evidence in chief. It is manifest that this conviction cannot be supported.' It seems that the basis of the decision was that the effect of informing the jury that the accused was identified by the use of the police photographs was to tell them that the accused had a criminal record. Consequently the decision seems to proceed on the view that the prejudicial effect of the evidence is to outweigh its probative value.

This view underlies a number of English decisions, particularly those which draw a distinction between the use of police photographs during the investigation of an offence and their use after the accused has been taken into custody when identification should be made by a witness from a parade. Thus convictions based on identification made from police photographs shown to a witness after the accused has been taken into custody have been quashed (*R v Goss* (1923) 17 Cr App Rep 196; *R v Haslam* (1925) 19 Cr App Rep 59). See *R v Melaney* (1924) 18 Cr App Rep 2; *R v Dwyer, R v Ferguson* [1925] 2 KB 799 at 802–3; *R v Seiga* (1961) 45 Cr App Rep 220 at 224–5. See also the dissenting opinion of Brennan J in *United States v Ash* 413 US 300 (1973), a decision which turned on the Sixth Amendment. These cases favour the use of an identification parade as the appropriate mode of making an identification. They disapprove of photographic identification as a substitute for it, or as a preliminary to it after the accused has been taken into custody. They stress the prejudicial effect before a jury of identification from police photographs and impliedly, if not expressly, they suggest that the prejudicial effect outweighs the probative value of the evidence.

The reasons why an identification parade is to be preferred to identification from police photographs are expressed compellingly in the Devlin Report (para 5.21): 'The object of the parade is to surround the accused with a number of people bearing a sufficient resemblance to him. At the time when the photographs are shown there is no definite suspect or accused and so it is impossible to collect photographs resembling him; indeed the object at this stage is not to collect resemblances but to collect possible suspects so as to see if one can be picked out. Then the photographic album does not afford the full inspection that is given on parade. Whatever regulations were made for its conduct, there being no suspect, neither he nor his solicitor can be there to see that they are observed. Finally, the production of the album would be bound to arouse the suspicions of the jury as to how it came into existence and about the sort of men who found their way into it.'

Despite the shortcomings of identification from police photographs, the English decisions concede that evidence of such an identification is admissible and is properly received if it was made before the accused became a definite suspect or before he was taken into custody. The concession that the evidence is admissible and properly receivable in such circumstances acknowledges that it has probative value and that its probative value may outweigh its prejudicial effect. If identification evidence of this kind is acknowledged to have probative value which outweighs its prejudicial effect, when the identification is made before the accused is taken into custody or before he becomes a definite suspect, there is no strong reason for denying the same value to evidence of the same kind when the identification is made at a later stage. An element of unfairness in failing to arrange an identification parade may intrude, but the balance between probative value and prejudicial effect in the eye of the jury will remain unaltered.

Wainwright and the approach taken in the English cases is plainly at odds with the Australian decisions. In *Fannon and Walsh, Bouquet* and *Doyle*, evidence of the kind proscribed by *Wainwright* was admitted without adverse comment and the convictions were sustained. In *Doyle*, where *Fannon and Walsh* was applied, the Court of Criminal Appeal rightly observed that the evidence of identification from police photographs was admissible and relevant, though the trial judge none the less had a discretion to exclude it on the ground that its prejudicial effect outweighed its probative value. The court went on to observe that, though the evidence involved some possibility of prejudice to the accused, it might be considered by the jury to have had important probative value in showing that the witness was able to pick out one man from a large group of photographs as the man who committed the crime. The evidence was on this basis correctly admitted. In my opinion the Court of Criminal Appeal in *Doyle* was right in thinking that identification from police photographs may have an important probative value which will outweigh its prejudicial effect, more particularly if the jury are so instructed as to minimise the risk that they may take into account an adverse inference as to the accused's antecedents. In *Doyle*, the photographic identification was followed by identification at a parade. But this did not detract from the probative value of the photographic identification though, as the court remarked, the converse was not true.

On the other hand, in *Bouquet*, where the photographic identification was followed by identification in court, there being no parade, the majority held that identification by photograph only in the first instance was not a ground for excluding that evidence, but at most only went to its weight. It was pointed out that the question of its reliability might call for a special direction when there was no other evidence of identification.

In my opinion the Australian cases demonstrate that identification from police photographs is admissible evidence, that its probative value may be important, that the judge has a discretion to exclude it when he considers its prejudicial effect outweighs that value, and that directions may be given to ensure that unfair use is not made of the evidence. I follow them in preference to *Wainwright* and the other English cases. The approach taken in the Australian cases to which I have referred accords with what this court said in *Davies v R, Cody v R* (1937) 57 CLR 170 at 180–1, when it pointed out that 'in each case the question must be, not whether the identification has been conducted with propriety and fairness, but whether upon the whole evidence as it in fact existed when it came to be laid before the jury, and having full regard to the treatment of the matter at the trial, the actual verdict ought not to stand because a miscarriage of the kind described occurred.'

There is something to be said for the view that the admission and reception of identification evidence of the kind now in question should be governed by special rules. The evidence, whether it be based on photographs or on a parade, is artificial in the sense that it is brought into existence by the police for the purpose of providing evidence at a criminal trial, allowing for those cases in which the purpose is detection or investigation of crime. Because it is evidence which may be inherently fragile and it may be influenced by suggestion, considerations of fairness indicate that the police should, wherever possible, arrange for an identification parade, when the accused has greater opportunity of knowing the circumstances under which the identification comes to be made. Rules of admissibility based on fairness could readily be devised, as indeed they have been devised by the Devlin Committee. But in the end I have come to the conclusion that at this time we would be best advised to adhere to the approach which this court adopted in *Davies and Cody* by giving attention to the whole of the evidence and the treatment of the matter at the trial and deciding whether a miscarriage has occurred whereby the conviction cannot safely stand. In so doing we will best achieve a balance between the interests of the prosecution representing the State and the interests of the accused.

In my opinion, therefore, identification based on police photographs, as well as the photographs, is admissible in evidence, despite the suggestions made to the contrary in the English cases and in *R v Russell* [1977] 2 NZLR 20 at 28, CA. However, in some cases the circumstances may be such as to show that it would be unfair to receive them.

It is inherent in what I have already said that I reject the rigid proposition sought to be gleaned from the English cases that identification made from police photographs when the accused is in custody cannot be proved in evidence or ground a conviction. As *R v Bagley* [1926] 3 DLR 717 shows, there are some cases in which the police have little alternative but to resort to photographic identification after the accused has been taken into custody. And I should have thought it essential to the efficient investigation and detection of crime that the police should continue to be at liberty to ask a potential witness to make an identification from photographs, even though they have a particular suspect in mind. In case of serious crime it would unduly hamper police investigations if they were compelled to disclose to a suspect that he was under suspicion by requesting him to participate in an identification parade.

I acknowledge that in *Russell*, Richmond P said (at 28) that 'only in exceptional cases should photographs be used at a stage when some particular person is directly suspected by the police and they are able to arrange an identification parade or some other satisfactory alternative means whereby the witness can be asked directly to identify the suspected person'. This observation, as it seems to me, was not a statement of law. For my part, I have, for reasons already stated, difficulty in accepting a rigid rule which distinguishes between identification made before and after the accused was taken into custody. Certainly I would be unwilling to accept a rule which excluded the use of photographs in relation to a person who was under suspicion but had not been taken into custody.

The trial judge in the present case recognised that he had a discretion to exclude the evidence of Beale, and later that of Williams. He decided that the prejudicial effect of the evidence did not outweigh its probative value. The applicant, in attacking this exercise of discretion, relies, not only on the English decisions already mentioned, but also on the principle applied in *Bunning v Cross* [(1978) 141 CLR 54]. *Bunning v Cross* provides no support at all for the applicant. There, the evidence was illegally and irregularly obtained. None the less it was held that its cogency required that it should have been admitted. Reference to *Bunning v Cross* does not reveal the existence of a relevant factor omitted by the trial judge in exercising his discretion to admit the evidence.

[Aickin J agreed with Mason J; Stephen and Murphy JJ dissented.]

In England the conduct of investigations involving collecting and acting on identification evidence is covered by the misleadingly-entitled Code of Practice (Code D) for the Identification of Persons by Police Officers (Revised Edition Effective from 10 April 1995) made under s 66 of the Police and Criminal Evidence Act 1984. The Code provides (para 2.0) that a record be made of the description of a suspect as first given by a potential witness, and contains in Annexes A to E obligatory procedures for the subsequent conduct of identification parades, video identification, confrontation, showing photographs, and group identification. In a case involving disputed identification, an identification parade must be held if the suspect asks for one, unless specified circumstances apply (para 2.3). Failure to comply with the Code of

Practice has led trial judges to exclude evidence under s 78 of the Police and Criminal Evidence Act 1984 (*R v Britton and Richards* [1989] Crim LR 144; *R v Gaynor* [1988] Crim LR 242; *R v Ladlow, Moss, Green and Jackson* [1989] Crim LR 219), and the Court of Appeal has shown a tendency to approve (*R v Gall* (1989) 90 Cr App Rep 64, CA; cf *R v Quinn* [1990] Crim LR 581, CA) although it is not clear that this is a proper use of the discretion given by that section (see ch 9.2). If the evidence is not excluded, failures to comply with Code D should be drawn to the jury's attention: *R v Quinn* [1995] Crim LR 56, CA. In *R v Conway* (1990) 91 Cr App Rep 143, CA, it was held that the accused's conviction was unsafe, having been based on a dock identification obtained after a breach of the Code's requirement of an identification parade. Indeed, the general law on identification evidence is merely one aspect of the overriding discretion in a criminal trial judge to exclude any evidence if the strict rules of admissibility operate unfairly against the accused. It is commonly exercised where the judge considers the evidence to be of little weight but of considerable prejudicial effect. This position may arise because one of the following faulty procedures is adopted.

A conviction may be quashed if the witness is shown the accused alone after arrest: *R v Smith* (1908) 1 Cr App Rep 203; *R v Dickman* (1910) 5 Cr App Rep 135 at 142–3; *Davies and Cody v R* (1937) 57 CLR 170.

It is wrong for the suspect to be fully described to a witness who had only a very poor view of him: *R v Bundy* (1910) 5 Cr App Rep 270.

It is wrong to isolate the accused as suspect by indicating to the witness that the accused is suspected or charged: *R v Chapman* (1911) 7 Cr App Rep 53 at 55–6.

It is unsatisfactory to show the witness a photograph of the accused before the identification unless a range of photographs are offered. It may be noted that *Alexander's Case* was dismissed on appeal based on showing photographs to witnesses after suspicion had fastened on the accused; the majority denied that any strict rule should be centred on a distinction based on that point of time.

It is wrong for the accused to be first identified in the dock: *R v Cartwright* (1914) 10 Cr App Rep 219; *R v Gaunt* [1964] NSWR 864, CCA. If the identifying witness has no prior knowledge of the accused, his dock identification has no probative value: *R v Reid* [1994] Crim LR 442, CA. The reason is, as Mason J said in *Alexander's Case*, circumstances conspire to compel the witness to identify the accused in the dock. The court has a discretion to exclude such an identification: *R v Hunter* [1969] Crim LR 262, CA; *R v Howick* [1970] Crim LR 403; *R v John* [1973] Crim LR 113, CA.

The jury must not be told by the prosecution that before the witness identified the accused at an identification parade the witness had picked him out from police photographs, unless the defence has made it known that it will require the evidence or unless the prejudicial effect of the revelation is outweighed by its probative value.

Many regard a properly carried out identification parade as the most reliable means of identification. For one thing, it is inevitably held in the presence of the accused, who can observe and later relate any aspect of the parade weakening the reliability of the identification. For another, the parade is constructed on the basis of getting together people who look as similar to the suspect as possible; photographs collected to try to find the suspect cannot be collected with a view to getting persons as similar to the suspect as possible if there is none, and anyway a range of categories of appearance is needed to see if one can be picked out. But failure to hold a parade, even if one could have been held, is not a ground for automatically quashing a conviction: the proper approach is whether the conviction can safely be upheld on the whole of the evidence: *R v Maynard* (1979) 69 Cr App Rep 309. The accused does not have a right to bring a companion for inclusion in the identification parade: *R v Thorne* [1981] Crim LR 702. It seems to follow from *R v Condon* [1980] Crim LR 721, CA, that wherever a police officer is likely to be called as an identifying witness he should not be employed to arrest the suspected person or have any other dealing with him before an identification parade has been held, including sighting his photograph.

C ADMISSIBILITY OF ACTS OF PREVIOUS IDENTIFICATION

On the question of whether evidence may be given by a witness of his own or another's previous identification of the accused, see ch 12, pp 337–8, post.

FURTHER READING

Williams [1955] Crim LR 525 and *The Proof of Guilt*, pp 106–24; Williams and Hammelmann [1963] Crim LR 479, 545; 11th Report of the Criminal Law Revision Committee, paras 196–203; Best, pp 495–503; Rolph, *Personal Identity* (London, 1957), chs 3, 6, 7 and 8; Report to the Secretary of State for the Home Department of the Departmental Committee on Evidence of Identification in Criminal Cases, HC, 26 April 1976 (the Devlin Report); Williams [1976] Crim LR 407; Grayson [1977] Crim LR 509; Libling [1978] Crim LR 343; Jackson [1986] Crim LR 203.

QUESTIONS

1. If a man was picked out by more than one witness at an identification parade, how much more reliable would this make the conclusion that he was guilty?
2. Would you favour permitting the defence to call witnesses who failed to identify the accused?
3. Can the *Turnbull* guidelines fail to be satisfied even if there is corroboration? See *R v Keane* (1977) 65 Cr App Rep 247, CA, holding that a false alibi can only support an identification if the sole reason for it was to deceive the jury on the issue of identification.

3 Mandatory corroboration requirements

Corroboration is today *required* in English law in only a few cases, of which the following are the most important: identification evidence of poor quality (*R v Turnbull* [1977] QB 224, [1976] 3 All ER 549, CA; see previous section);

opinion evidence as to speeding in a motor vehicle (Road Traffic Regulation Act 1984, s 89(2)); and evidence as to the falsity of the statement (where that is relevant and not admitted by the accused) in prosecutions for perjury and kindred offences (Perjury Act 1911, s 13; *R v O'Connor* [1980] Crim LR 43, CA; *R v Rider* (1986) 83 Cr App Rep 207, CA). The obvious unreliability of a single witness's estimate of the speed of a car and the undesirability of prosecutions brought perhaps solely on the evidence of an offended householder or pedestrian who happened to see the number of a speeding car justifies the need for corroboration of this evidence: when there is in fact reliable evidence available the courts are inclined to take a generous view of the corroboration requirement (*Nicholas v Penny* [1950] 2 KB 466, [1950] 2 All ER 89, DC; *Crossland v DPP* [1988] 3 All ER 712, DC). Neither a conviction nor a prima facie case can be based solely on the accused's silence (Criminal Justice and Public Order Act 1994, s 38(4)).

Best: Principles of the Law of Evidence, 11th edn, para 607

The legislator dealing with the offence of perjury has to determine the relative weight of conflicting duties. Measured merely by its religious or moral enormity, perjury, always a grievous crime, would in many cases be the greatest of crimes, and as such be deserving of the severest punishment which the law could inflict. But when we consider the very peculiar nature of this offence, and that every person who appears as a witness in a court of justice is liable to be accused of it by those against whom his evidence tells, who are frequently the basest and most unprincipled of mankind; and when we remember how powerless are the best rules of municipal law without the co-operation of society to enforce them, – we shall see that the obligation of protecting witnesses from oppression, or annoyance, by charges, or threats of charges of having borne false testimony, is far paramount to that of giving even perjury its deserts. To repress that crime, prevention is better than cure; and the law of England relies, for this purpose, on the means provided for detecting and exposing the crime at the moment of commission, – such as publicity, cross-examination, the aid of a jury, etc; and on the infliction of a severe, though not excessive punishment, wherever the commission of the crime has been clearly proved. But in order to carry out the great objects above mentioned, our law gives witnesses the privilege of refusing to answer questions which tend to incriminate, or to expose them to penalty of forfeiture; it allows no action to be brought against a witness, for words written or spoken in the course of his evidence; and it throws every fence round a person accused of perjury. Besides, great precision is required in the indictment; the strictest proof is exacted of what the accused swore; and, lastly, the testimony of at least two witnesses must be forthcoming to prove its falsity. The result accordingly is that in England little difficulty, comparatively speaking, is found in obtaining voluntary evidence for the purposes of justice; and although many persons may escape the punishment awarded by law to perjury, instances of erroneous convictions for it are unknown, and the threat of an indictment for perjury is treated by honest and upright witnesses as a brutum fulmen.

NOTES

1. The 'two witnesses' referred to by Best are not always necessary, since the corroboration can be found in non-testimonial evidence: *R v Mayhew* (1834) 6 C & P 315; *R v Threlfall* (1914) 111 LT 168, CCA.
2. There are other illustrations apart from those given by Best of the general policy which encourages witnesses to come forward by protecting them; for example, it is a crime to intimidate witnesses.

4   A warning from the judge

A   IN GENERAL

The judge has an overriding duty to ensure that the jury are made aware of particular dangers in any evidence, so failure to give a proper warning where it is necessary on the facts of the case may lead to a conviction being quashed: see *R v Spencer* [1987] AC 128, [1986] 2 All ER 928, HL, below.

R v Spencer   [1987] AC 128, [1986] 2 All ER 928, HL

Lord Ackner: [T]he appellants in these consolidated appeals were members of the nursing staff at Rampton Hospital, which is a secure hospital catering for patients suffering from mental disorders. The majority of such patients have been sent to Rampton as the result of court orders made under the Mental Health Act 1959 or the Mental Health Act 1983, by reason of their having been convicted of serious crimes. A television programme was shown in 1979 which made a substantial number of allegations of ill-treatment to patients by the nursing staff over a period of some years. This led to police inquiries and resulted in separate trials at the Crown Court at Nottingham. In five of those trials, the defendants were convicted and your Lordships are concerned with two of such trials. . . .

In all the trials, the prosecution case against the nurses depended very largely on the uncorroborated evidence of a single patient. I say 'very largely' because there were apparently some alleged incidents of violence which were witnessed by patients who were themselves complainants to other incidents. . . . The Court of Appeal in *R v Beck* . . . observed ([1982] 1 All ER 807 at 813, [1982] 1 WLR 461 at 469):

'. . . [W]e in no way wish to detract from the obligation on a judge to advise a jury to proceed with caution where there is material to suggest that a witness's evidence may be tainted by an improper motive, and the strength of that advice must vary according to the facts of the case . . .'

It has been said, both in the Court of Appeal and in your Lordships' House, that the obligation to warn a jury does not involve some legalistic ritual to be automatically recited by the judge, or that some particular form of words or incantation has to be used and, if not used, the summing up is faulty and the conviction must be quashed (see *R v Russell* (1968) 52 Cr App Rep 147 at 150 per Diplock LJ). There is no magic formula which has to be used with regard to any warning which is given to juries (*R v Price* [1968] 2 All ER 282 at 285, [1969] 1 QB 541 at 546 per Sachs LJ). As this is no mere idle process it follows [even in cases requiring the 'full corroboration warning'] that there are no set words which must be adopted to express the warning. Rather must the good sense of the matter be expounded with clarity and in the setting of a particular case (see *DPP v Hester* [1972] 3 All ER 1056 at 1060, [1973] AC 296 at 309 per Lord Morris). The summing up should be tailored to suit the circumstances of the particular case (see *DPP v Kilbourne* [1973] 1 All ER 440 at 447, [1973] AC 729 at 741 per Lord Hailsham LC).

To my mind the question raised by these appeals is both simple to define and simple to answer. Given that it is common ground that a warning was required as to the way in which the jury should treat the evidence of the complainants, the question is: was that warning sufficient? Did it in clear terms bring home to the jury the danger of basing a conviction on the unconfirmed evidence of the complainants?

In [some] cases the potential unreliability of the sole or principal witness for the prosecution is obvious for all to see. These were such cases. The complainants were men of bad character. They had been sent to Rampton rather than to an ordinary prison, because they were mentally unbalanced. That they were anti-authoritarian, prone to lie or exaggerate and could well have old scores which they were seeking to pay off was not disputed. Notwithstanding that the possibility of their evidence being unreliable was patent, that it was clearly dangerous to prefer their evidence to that of the defendants, all men of good character on whose behalf witnesses had spoken in glowing terms, the judge nevertheless told the jury in the clearest possible terms, and repeated himself, that they must approach the evidence of the complainants with great caution. It is common ground that, having given that warning, he then identified the very dangers which justified the exercise of great caution. He gave three reasons: firstly, they were all persons of bad character; secondly, they were all persons suffering from some form of mental disorder; and, thirdly, they may have all conspired together to make false allegations. Thus the judge warned the jury of the dangers of relying on the complainants' testimony because, for the reasons which he gave, such testimony could well be unreliable. The judge, however, did not leave the matter there. As previously stated he pointed out, when dealing with each count, the details of the background of the complainant, his past criminal record, the nature of his mental disturbance and his history in the hospital and, perhaps most important of all, the hospital psychiatrist's view of the personality defects from which the patient suffered. . . . I agree with the Court of Appeal that he gave the emphatic warning which was required to meet the justice of the case.

The certified point of law is in these terms:

'In a case where the evidence for the Crown is solely that of a witness who is not in one of the accepted categories of suspect witnesses [previously requiring a "full corroboration warning"], but who, by reason of his particular mental condition and criminal connection, fulfilled the same criteria, must the judge warn the jury that it is dangerous to convict on his uncorroborated evidence.'

I would amend the question by substituting for the words 'the same criteria' 'analogous criteria'. I would then answer the question in the affirmative, adding, for the sake of clarity, that, while it may often be convenient to use the words 'danger' or 'dangerous', the use of such words is not essential to an adequate warning, so long as the jury are made fully aware of the dangers of convicting on such evidence. Again, for the sake of clarity I would further add that *R v Beck* [1982] 1 All ER 807, [1982] 1 WLR 461 was rightly decided and that . . . where there exists potential corroborative material the extent to which the trial judge should make reference to that material depends on the facts of each case. The overriding rule is that he must put the defence fairly and adequately.

Lord Hailsham (agreed and said): [In *DPP v Kilbourne* [1973] AC 729 at 740, [1973] 1 All ER 440 at 447] I added witnesses 'of admittedly bad character' to the number of cases where a warning of some kind was required as to the danger of convicting without corroboration. I was, of course, using the phrase in the technical sense of witnesses who have been shown to be not of a character to make them worthy to be believed on their oath. In this connection I must say that, even if there were not authority to support this view (and I believe there is plenty), I would regard it as a matter of sheer common sense that if a judge did not warn the jury of the possible danger of convicting an innocent man if they convicted solely on the disputed but uncorroborated testimony of such a person, his failure to do so would, apart from the proviso, make a verdict unsafe and unsatisfactory in the extreme . . .

The only other observation I would make on the certified question is that the modern cases, quite correctly in my view, are reluctant to insist on any magic formula or incantation, and stress instead the need that each summing up should be tailor-made to suit the requirements of the individual case; cf *DPP v Hester* [1972] 3 All ER 1056 at 1060, 1069, 1073, 1076, [1973] AC 296 at 309, 321, 325, 328 per Lord Morris, Lord Pearson and Lord Diplock. In particular, when, as here, it is agreed that no corroboration exists, a disquisition on what can or could amount to such if corroboration were needed is emphatically not required and greatly to be discouraged (see [1972] 3 All ER 1056 at 1076, [1973] AC 296 at 328 per Lord Diplock). Speaking for myself, I even dislike the expression 'categories' as applied to the cases. They are simply classes of cases where the experience of the courts has gradually hardened into rules of practice, owing, as my noble and learned friend points out, partly to the inherent dangers involved, and partly to the fact that the danger is not necessarily obvious to a lay mind. The less juries are confused by superfluous learning and the more their minds are directed to the particular issues relevant to the case before them, the more likely they are, in my view, to arrive at a just verdict.

[Lord Bridge, Lord Brandon and Lord Mackay agreed with Lord Ackner.]

NOTE

See also *Bromley v R* (1986) 161 CLR 315.

COMMENTS

1. For the meaning of the phrase 'full corroboration warning', see section 1 of this chapter.

2. As regards confessions, the present English position is that it is open to a jury to convict on an uncorroborated confession (see *R v Sullivan* (1887) 16 Cox CC 347, following *R v Unkles* (1874) IR 8 CL 50). However, circumstances may make a warning prudent. A case where the circumstances justified the warning which was in fact given is *R v Sykes* (1913) 8 Cr App Rep 233 at 237, CCA, where 'the murder was the talk of the countryside, and it might well be that a man under the influence of insanity or a morbid desire for notoriety would accuse himself of such a crime'. But it is probably only in an extreme case that an appeal for want of the warning would succeed; a case, in fact, where an appeal on the ground that the verdict was against the weight of the evidence would also succeed. In America there is a fixed rule that corroboration is necessary, but this extension seems mistaken. It is wrong to elevate the common sense consideration that in some circumstances an uncorroborated confession should be scrutinised cautiously into a rule of law requiring either actual corroboration or a universal corroboration warning. In practice it will be rare that the only evidence of guilt is a confession.

A number of recent English cases, however, have caused public concern. It has been felt that the police have been over-anxious to secure confessions to serious crimes, particularly terrorist offences. There have been successful appeals, sometimes after the accused had spent many years in prison (eg 'the Guildford four' and 'the Birmingham six'). It is often said that since the relevant convictions the law on confessions has changed so much as a result of the Police and Criminal Evidence Act 1984 (see ch 8) that errors of this sort are unlikely to occur again. But it must be remembered that terrorist offences are to some extent regarded as a separate category under the Act, particularly in s 58 (right of access to legal advice) and the Codes of Practice, particularly Code E (Tape Recording). See Pattenden (1991) 107 LQR 317.

B   BY STATUTE

Police and Criminal Evidence Act 1984

77   (1)   Without prejudice to the general duty of the court at a trial on indictment to direct the jury on any matter on which it appears to the court appropriate to do so, where at such a trial –
    (*a*)   the case against the accused depends wholly or substantially on a confession by him; and
    (*b*)   the court is satisfied –
        (i)   that he is mentally handicapped; and
        (ii)   that the confession was not made in the presence of an independent person, the court shall warn the jury that there is special need for caution before convicting the accused in reliance on the confession, and shall explain that the need arises because of the circumstances mentioned in paragraphs (*a*) and (*b*) above.

(2)   In any case where at the summary trial of a person for an offence it appears to the court that a warning under subsection (1) above would be required if the trial were on indictment, the court shall treat the case as one in which there is a special need for caution before convicting the accused on his confession.

(3)   In this section . . .

'mentally handicapped', in relation to a person, means that he is in a state of arrested or incomplete development of mind which includes significant impairment of intelligence and social functioning . . .

COMMENT

Note that this section makes no provision for those who are mentally *ill*; in appropriate circumstances, however, the effect of s 76 (see ch 8) may be that the case should be withdrawn from the jury: *R v McKenzie* (1992) 96 Cr App Rep 98, CA. For the question of the safety of convictions based solely on confession evidence to which s 77 does not apply, see comments to section 4A, above.

5   What is corroboration?

A   IN GENERAL

After the abolition of the obligatory corroboration warnings and the appended rules on what, in law could amount to corroboration, the remaining question will be whether the evidence relied upon as support does in truth add anything to the evidence to be supported. In all cases it is, however, important not to lose sight of the principle that what is being looked for is something which adds to or supports or confirms the doubtful evidence, not something which merely repeats it. So if W describes an assailant's facial characteristics and then at an identification parade picks out D, who has those characteristics, D's appearance does not support W's identification evidence, for at the identification parade W was merely acting out (ie repeating) his previous description (*R v Willoughby* (1988) 88 Cr App Rep 91, CA). It is otherwise if W describes some hidden characteristics (physical or psychological) of the assailant and D, who is picked out at the identification parade, turns out to have that characteristic (*R v McInnes* (1989) 90 Cr App Rep 99, CA; *Thompson v R* [1918] AC 221, HL). Similarly, facts equally consistent with the truth or falsity of the evidence to be corroborated cannot be corroboration, for they added nothing to its credibility.

Chief Baron Joy: Evidence of Accomplices, p 8 (Wigmore, para 2059)

The defect in the evidence is not in its *quantity*, but in its *quality*. The witness swearing directly to the prisoner's guilt, that guilt is established if the witness be credible. What, therefore, is required is to throw something, no matter of what nature, into the opposite scale, which will serve as a counterpoise to the impeachment of the witness' credit arising from the character in which he appears; something that will improve the *quality* of the proof which has been given by the accomplice; and *that* something may be anything which induces a rational belief in the mind of the jury that the narrative of the accomplice is in all respects a correct one.

R v Tidd **(1820) 33 State Tr 1483**

Garrow B: [I]t may not be unfit to observe . . . that the confirmation to be derived to an accomplice, is not a repetition by others of the whole story of the accomplice and a confirmation of every part of it, that would be either impossible or unnecessary and absurd. . . .

R v Farler **(1837) 8 C & P 106**

Lord Abinger CB: [C]orroboration ought to consist in some circumstance that affects the identity of the party accused. A man who has been guilty of a crime himself will always be able to relate the facts of the case, and if the confirmation be only on the truth of that history, without identifying the person, that is really no corroboration at all. If a man was to break open a house and put a knife to your throat, and steal your property, it would be no corroboration that he had stated all the facts correctly, that he had described how the person did put a knife to the throat and did steal the property. It would not at all tend to show that the party accused participated in it.

R v Birkett **(1839) 8 C & P 732**

The accused was charged with receiving a stolen sheep. One of the thieves testified that the other thief gave the sheep to the accused. Patteson J ruled that there was sufficient evidence of corroboration to be left to the jury.

Patteson J: If the confirmation had merely gone to the extent of confirming the accomplice as to matters connected with himself only, it would not have been sufficient. For example, the finding of the skins at the place at which the accomplice said they were would have been no sufficient confirmation of the evidence against the prisoner, because the witness might have put the skins there himself, but here we have a great deal more; we have a quantity of mutton found in the house in which the prisoner resides, and that I think is such a confirmation of the accomplice's evidence as I must leave to the jury.

Vetrovec v R **(1982) 136 DLR (3d) 89**

Dickson J (giving the judgment of the Supreme Court of Canada): The 'common sense' approach was originally followed in England. In *R v Davidson and Tidd* (1820) 33 State Tr 1338 at 1483, Baron Garrow instructed the jury as follows:

'. . . you are to look to the circumstances, to see whether there are such a number of important facts confirmed as to give you reason to be persuaded that the main body of the story is correct. . . . You are, each of you, to ask yourselves this question . . . Do I, upon the whole, feel convinced in my conscience, that this evidence is true, and such as I may safely act upon?'

This common sense approach to the matter was eventually discarded, however, in favour of the more technical view of Lord Reading in *Baskerville*. Corroboration became a certain sort of evidence, namely, evidence 'which confirms in some material particular not only the evidence that the crime has been committed, but also that the prisoner committed it'.

. . . With great respect, on principle Lord Reading's approach seems perhaps over-cautious. The reason for requiring corroboration is that we believe the witness has good reason to lie. We therefore want some other piece of evidence which tends to convince us that he is telling the truth. Evidence which implicates the accused does indeed serve to accomplish that purpose but it cannot be said that this is the only sort of evidence which will accredit the accomplice. This is because, as Wigmore said, the matter of credibility is an entire thing, not a separable one (ibid, p 424):

'. . . whatever restores our trust in him personally restores it as a whole; if we find that he is desiring and intending to tell a true story, we shall believe one part of his story as well as another, whenever, then, by any means, that trust is restored, our object is accomplished, and it cannot matter whether the efficient circumstance related to the accused's identity or to any other matter. The important thing is, not *how* our trust is restored, but whether it *is* restored at all.'

The point can be illustrated with the following simple example. The accomplice, 'A', testifies against the accused 'B' and 'C'. There is evidence implicating 'B' in the crime, but no evidence implicating 'C'. Nevertheless, since the supporting evidence relates to a vital issue in the case (the guilt of one of the accused) it bolsters the credibility of 'A' and increases the probability that he is telling the truth. We therefore believe his story and convict both 'B' and 'C'.

Such a situation arose in *Murphy and Butt v R* (1976) 70 DLR (3d) 42. The complainant alleged that she had been raped by the two appellants. Murphy admitted intercourse but alleged that it was with the complainant's consent, while Butt denied intercourse altogether. The principal issue was whether the complainant's distraught condition was corroboration of her testimony against Butt as well as against Murphy. The difficulty was that in and of itself, the hysterical condition merely tended to rebut the suggestion of intercourse with consent. This implicated the accused Murphy, who had admitted intercourse but alleged consent. But considered in isolation the hysterical condition did not directly implicate the accused Butt, who denied intercourse altogether. How, then, could the hysterical condition corroborate the complainant's testimony as against Butt?

The majority of the court emphasised that what was required was confirmation of a material particular of the evidence of the complainant. Once such confirmation was supplied, her testimony was rendered credible as a whole. Spence J, speaking for the majority, put the matter in this way (at 53):

> 'It is a material particular of that evidence which must be corroborated. There is no requirement that the whole of her evidence be corroborated. Were that the requirement, there would be no need for even the evidence of the complainant. The so-called corroborative evidence would be sufficient for a conviction.'

Spence J did not contend that the corroborative evidence implicated the accused Butt. Rather, in a carefully worded conclusion, Spence J noted that the corroborative evidence confirmed the complainant's story implicating each of the accused (at 54):

> 'It is all of that evidence plus the complainant's distraught condition upon which the Crown relies as corroboration of not only Murphy's but Butt's rape of the complainant. *The jury were entitled to consider all of that evidence and to come to the conclusion that that evidence . . . does corroborate the evidence of the complainant.* It was that evidence which the learned trial Judge left to the jury as evidence which they might find corroborative of the complainant's testimony.
> *In my view, the learned trial Judge was correct in his conclusion that that evidence was capable of corroborating the complainant's story implicating each of the accused.'* (Emphasis added.)

Spence J's approach was to look for evidence which confirmed the story of the complainant. Once the story was confirmed, the complainant could be believed and the accused convicted. Implicit in this approach, it seems to me, is a recognition of the inadequacy of the *Baskerville* definition of corroboration. Evidence implicating the accused is a possible but not a necessary element for corroboration. Here, even though there was no evidence implicating Butt, there was evidence confirming the story of the complainant and thus it was safe to convict. The important question, as Wigmore pointed out, is not how our trust is restored, but whether it is restored at all. . . .

B   EXAMPLES OF CORROBORATION OR SUPPORT

According to Wigmore (para 2059), decisions on the sufficiency of particular items of evidence as corroboration are 'mere useless chaff, ground out by the vain labour of able minds mistaking the true material for their energies'. But some questions of legal interest surround this issue.

(i)   To what extent can the person to be corroborated supply corroboration?

The logical requirement that corroboration be independent of the witness to be corroborated means that complaints, other prior statements (*R v Askew* [1981] Crim LR 398, CA) and documents used to refresh memory (*R v Virgo* (1978) 67 Cr App Rep 323, CA) cannot support the witness's own oral evidence. But the witness's physical condition may be relevant, eg a small child suffering from the same venereal disease as the accused (*R v Gregg* (1932) 24 Cr App Rep 13, CCA; *R v Jones* (1939) 27 Cr App Rep 33, CCA); the injuries suffered by a rape victim (*R v Trigg* [1963] 1 All ER 490, [1963] 1 WLR 305, CCA); or a distressed condition (*Murphy v R* (1976) 70 DLR (3d) 42), though particular care is necessary in case it be simulated (*R v Redpath* (1962) 46 Cr App Rep 319, CCA; *R v Knight* [1966] 1 All ER 647, [1966] 1 WLR 230, CCA) or be due to remorse, or simply be a consequence of rough handling during consensual intercourse (*R v Richards* [1965] Qd R 354); save in special circumstances, it probably has little weight: *R v Byczko (No 2)* (1977) 17 SASR 460; *R v Freeman* [1980] VR 1; cf *R v Dowley* [1983] Crim LR 168, CA; Oughton [1984] Crim LR 265. Serious bruises or wounds may support a sex victim's claim of non-consent; similarly if her clothes are blood-stained or badly torn. A medical examination for sperm traces and other signs may corroborate an allegation of intercourse if that is in issue.

(ii)   Admissions

The defendant's admissions, in court or outside it, may corroborate the case against him. His admission must go to some issue which is relevant to what has to be corroborated. In indecent assault cases, an admission of indecency short of assault suffices (*R v Rolfe* (1952) 36 Cr App Rep 4, CCA), but an admission of platonic handling does not (*R v Tragen* [1956] Crim LR 332, CCA; cf *R v Dossi* (1918) 87 LJKB 1024, CCA).

   In paternity cases admissions of sexual intercourse or other familiarity at other times may be corroboration (*Cole v Manning* (1877) 2 QBD 611; *Simpson v Collinson* [1964] 2 QB 80, [1964] 1 All ER 262, CA). Sometimes the admission is implied, as where a man agrees to support a woman's child (*Thomas v Jones* [1921] 1 KB 22 at 39, [1920] All ER Rep 462 at 470, CA).

(iii)   Lies

The fact that the accused has told lies may amount to corroboration of other evidence against him. No distinction is to be drawn between lies told out of court and lies told whilst giving evidence (*R v Lucas* [1981] QB 720, [1981] 2 All ER 1008, CA; *Pitman v Byrne* [1926] SASR 207; *R v Collings* [1976] 2 NZLR 104; *R v Perera* [1982] VR 901), and the same principles apply where the accused adopts lies told by others (*R v Perera*), or makes some other attempt to subvert the course of justice, eg by suborning witnesses (*Mahoney v Wright* [1943] SASR 61).

Moriarty v London, Chatham and Dover Rly Co   (1870) LR 5 QB 314

The plaintiff in a personal injury claim attempted to suborn false evidence. The Court of Queen's Bench held that evidence of his act was admissible.

Cockburn CJ: The conduct of a party to a cause may be of the highest importance in determining whether the cause of action in which he is plaintiff, or the ground of defence, if he is defendant, is honest and just; just as it is evidence against a prisoner that he has said one thing at one time and another at another, as shewing that the recourse to falsehood leads fairly to an inference of guilt. Anything from which such an inference can be drawn is cogent and important evidence with a view to the issue. So, if you can shew that a plaintiff has been suborning false testimony, and has endeavoured to have recourse to perjury, it is strong evidence that he knew perfectly well his cause was an unrighteous one. I do not say that it is conclusive; I fully agree that it should be put to the jury, with the intimation that it does not always follow, because a man, not sure he shall be able to succeed by righteous means, has recourse to means of a different character, that which he desires, namely, the gaining of the victory, is not his due, or that he has not good ground for believing that justice entitles him to it. It does not necessarily follow that he has not a good cause of action, any more than a prisoner's making a false statement to increase his appearance of innocence is necessarily a proof of his guilt, but it is always evidence which ought to be submitted to the consideration of the tribunal which has to judge of the facts; and therefore I think that the evidence was admissible, inasmuch as it went to shew that the plaintiff thought he had a bad case.

[Blackburn and Lush JJ agreed.]

Popovic v Derks   [1961] VLR 413

The alleged father falsely denied on oath in affiliation proceedings that he was a frequent visitor to the complainant's house and that he often took her out in his car. Sholl J in the Supreme Court of Victoria held that the lie was capable of being corroboration.

Sholl J: [C]orroboration is evidence rendering the factum probandum more probable by strengthening the proof of one or more facta probabilia. In an affiliation case the factum probandum is paternity. The most important factum probabile is intercourse at the material time. Corroboration may be of that factum probabile by evidence shewing that such intercourse was very likely, and thereby rendering more probable the complainant's evidence thereof.

In *Thomas v Jones* [1921] 1 KB 22, [1920] All ER Rep 462, CA, Scrutton LJ in a dissenting judgment, at 39–40, very clearly analysed the position. He said:

'What is meant by "corroboration in some material particular" that is, in a material fact? The vital fact to be proved in a bastardy case is that a child has been born to the applicant as the result of sexual connexion with the man. From the nature of the case it is almost inevitable that there never will be any direct corroboration of sexual connexion. The evidence in corroboration must always be circumstantial evidence of the main fact, that is to say, evidence from which it may be inferred that the main fact happened. For instance, the fact that the man has had connexion with the woman and a child has resulted is sometimes inferred from evidence of previous affection, that they had been seen together shewing affection to each other. Sometimes it is inferred from the fact of subsequent affection – that the man and woman are seen together shewing signs of affection. Sometimes it is inferred from the fact that the man has done acts which may be treated as recognising responsibility for the child as his child, statements that he will provide for the child, payments for the child, all facts from which as a matter of inference and probability it is more probable that the intercourse did take place than not. I quite agree with what Bankes LJ has said, that if the fact is such that the probabilities are equal one way or the other an inference cannot legitimately be drawn from it one way or the other. It must shew, even only slightly, more probability that intercourse took place than not, and if there is that balance of probability it is not for the court to say that it is so slight that it would not have acted upon it. If there is evidence on which the justices could have come to that view, it does not matter that the court would have come to a different view. It is similar to the question as to when there is evidence for the jury; if there is evidence it is for the jury to decide, and not for the judge.'

[I]ntercourse is merely a material circumstance or particular, – that is to say, material to the allegation of paternity, – and . . . corroboration is evidence tending to render more probable circumstantially the complainant's allegation of intercourse . . .

When an inference can be drawn that the defendant is falsely denying the circumstances because he fears that to admit them would appear inconsistent with his innocence, or throw suspicion upon himself, corroboration may be found. This is a kind of admission by conduct. That is to say, matters which otherwise might be ambiguous or colourless are rendered suspicious and corroborative by reason of the defendant's false denial – the inference open to the tribunal of fact being that, to him, the matter denied suggests guilt, so that, therefore, he is prepared falsely to deny it.

There is some analogy between this type of case and the case of flight rather than face interrogation or trial.

. . . In *Credland v Knowler* (1951) 35 Cr App Rep 48, Lord Goddard CJ at 54–5, when considering a false denial in a criminal case, said:

'Most of the argument and, no doubt, much of the case has dealt with the lie which the appellant told and the question whether the fact that the appellant told a lie is in itself corroboration. I should be very sorry to lay down, and I have no intention of laying down and I do not think any case has gone the length of laying down, that the mere fact that an accused person has told a lie can in itself amount to corroboration. It may, but it does not follow that it must. If a man tells a lie when he is spoken to about an alleged offence, the fact that he tells a lie at once throws great doubt upon his evidence, if he afterwards gives evidence, and it may be very good ground for rejecting his evidence, but the fact that his evidence ought to be rejected does not of itself amount to there being corroboration. In fact, I do not think we can put the proposition better than it was put by Lord Dunedin in *Dawson v M'Kenzie* 1908 SC 648, and the passage to which I am about to refer was approved by this Court in *Jones v Thomas* [1934] 1 KB 323, [1933] All ER Rep 535, DC.'

And his Lordship then went on to quote the passage already cited in this judgment from *Dawson v McKenzie*, supra. . . .

In *Pitman v Byrne* [1926] SASR 207 at 212–13, where a false denial was held to be capable of affording corroboration, the Full Court stated four principles which are relevant to the present problem; they were numbered (5) to (8) in that case:

'(5) The weight to be attributed to a deliberately false denial or to false evidence must therefore depend on the facts of the particular case. Where it is the denial of a proved opportunity, it is evidence from which the Court may, if it thinks fit, infer guilt in relation to that opportunity. But in a proper case it would seem that false evidence might conceivably be of such a character as to lead to an inference definitely inconsistent with the innocence of the defendant without any independent evidence of opportunity (*Mash v Darley* [1914] 3 KB 1226, CA). (6) It is a question of degree. The admission by conduct is in every case evidence which goes to the jury in support of the other evidence upon the whole case, but its weight varies. It depends upon the strength of the other evidence and the degree of deliberation and the enormity of conduct manifested. A false answer on the spur of the moment under cross-examination is a relatively slender peg on which to hang an inference of guilt. A fabricated charge of unchastity, as in *Mash v Darley*, supra, is stronger, but the subornation of perjured evidence to support a fabricated charge might afford an inference too strong to be reasonably explainable on any theory of innocence. . . .'

It seems clear from the above review of the authorities that a false denial of opportunity or other fact need not be suspicious in itself, since it is the very false denial which may be used by the tribunal of fact to confer on the opportunity or other fact the suspicious or sinister character which makes it corroborative, – for example, in an affiliation case, corroborative of the complainant's evidence of intercourse. I, therefore, think that Mr Shillito cannot be right in the present case, when he submits that the denials here relied on could not amount to corroboration, unless they were shewn to be denials of an opportunity independently proved to be suspicious. . . .

On the other hand, it cannot be right to say that a false denial of a fact is of not more significance than that fact would be if the respondent had, in the first instance, admitted it or not denied it; for there may be a world of difference between the effect of an admitted fact of a neutral character, such as the opportunity of intercourse, or presence at or near the scene of a crime at the material time, and the effect of that fact together with a false denial of it by the person alleged to be implicated. Dealing with this topic quite recently in *R v Tripodi* [1961] VR 186, (1961) 104 CLR 1 in relation to criminal matters, the Full Court has recently said at 193–4:

> 'It rests, we think, not so much on the denial itself of the accused, as on the conduct which it betokens. A verbal admission by the accused of the commission of the offence would not only be admissible evidence, but if believed the strongest evidence of its commission. Conduct of the accused too which tended to shew incriminatory incidents of the crime could also be, and often is, the subject of admissible evidence, for example, that he once possessed and had got rid of, or attempted to get rid of, the weapon with which the crime had been committed; that he had been seen running away from the scene of the crime just after it had been committed; that he had been apprehended and broken away and escaped; and there may be many others. It is his conduct which is put before the jury, and they may think that he lies from a consciousness that, if he tells the truth, the truth will convict him. The lying statement must, of course, relate to incriminatory features of the crime; for if it were otherwise, any lying statement by the accused might convict him of any crime in the calendar, and such a result has only to be stated to be at once rejected as the law. We think that this view may explain why the courts have not discriminated between statements made by the accused out of court and in his evidence in court. In the latter case the jury themselves observe his conduct in giving evidence and, if they think he is lying, draw their own conclusions as to why he is lying; and no doubt the prosecutor, in inviting the jury to reject the accused's denial, will suggest the reason.'

The rules governing the admissibility of lies as corroboration were set out in *R v Lucas* [1981] QB 720, [1981] 2 All ER 1008, CA; see also *R v Goodway* [1993] 4 All ER 894, CA. They are:

(a) The statement must be material, eg a false denial of association with the victim (*Credland v Knowler* (1951) 35 Cr App Rep 48) or witnesses, or an accomplice; a false alibi; false accusations of impropriety against other suspects or against the victim (*Mash v Darley* [1914] 3 KB 1226, CA).

(b) The statement must be false, without serious ambiguity.

(c) The statement must be deliberately false, and prompted not by fear of a wrong judgment but by fear of the truth. It must not be due to panic, accidental error, attempts to terminate inquiries quickly, shame, resentment at officious questioning, or a desire to avoid the discovery of other misconduct.

(d) The evidence of the falsity of the statement must proceed from some source independent of the witness to be corroborated. Thus in *R v King* [1967] 2 QB 338, [1967] 1 All ER 379, CCA, the accused may have uttered certain lies, but the only testimony that they were lies proceeded from two boys who complained of the accused's sexual misconduct. The boys could not corroborate themselves directly and they could not be allowed to do so by this indirect means.

(iv)   Silence out of court

The normal rule (ch 7, post) that silence can only exceptionally amount to assent to some proposition put to the accused means it will only exceptionally be corroboration, ie when a reply would be expected from an innocent man. This was so in *R v Cramp* (1880) 14 Cox CC 390 where a girl's father in effect accused the defendant of abetting her abortion and having in his possession material evidence of guilt. The normal rule is illustrated by *R v Tate* [1908] 2 KB 680, CCA; *R v Whitehead* [1929] 1 KB 99, [1928] All ER Rep 186, CCA; *R v Keeling* [1942] 1 All ER 507, CCA. *R v Feigenbaum* [1919] 1 KB 431, [1918–19] All ER Rep 489, CCA is wrong, and some other cases state the rule perhaps too widely, eg *Bessela v Stern* (1877) 2 CPD 265 at 272.

Sometimes silence coupled with flight is corroboration (*R v Bondy* (1957) 121 CCC 337). The failure of the defendant in affiliation proceedings to reply to a letter from the plaintiff's father (who was also the defendant's father-in-law) alleging paternity and stating that the matter would be put in a solicitor's hands if no reply were received was held to be corroboration in *Ex p Freeman* (1922) 39 WNNSW 73 at 75: 'One might ignore the accusation of a busy-body stranger, but this was a family affair in which the honour of accuser and accused were equally at stake.' Apart from cases where silence amounts to an admission, the only effect of silence will be to strengthen the opposing case and make the accused's denial less credible.

Silence in the face of questioning by those concerned with the investigation of offences may, subject to certain preconditions, entitle a trier of fact to draw 'such inferences as appear proper' under ss 34, 36 and 37 of the Criminal Justice and Public Order Act 1994: see ch 7, post.

Wiedemann v Walpole   [1891] 2 QB 534, CA

Lord Esher MR: Now there are cases – business and mercantile cases – in which the courts have taken notice that, in the ordinary course of business, if one man of business states in a letter to another that he has agreed to do certain things, the person who received that letter must answer it if he means to dispute the fact that he did so agree. So, where merchants are in dispute one with the other in the course of carrying on some business negotiations, and one writes to the other, 'but you promised me that you would do this or that', if the other does not answer the letter, but proceeds with the negotiations, he must be taken to admit the truth of the statement. But such cases as those are wholly unlike the case of a letter charging a man with some offence or meanness. Is it the ordinary habit of mankind, of which the courts will take notice, to answer such letters; and must it be taken, according to the ordinary practice of mankind, that if a man does not answer he admits the truth of the charge made against him? If it were so, life would be unbearable. A man might day by day write such letters, which, if they were not answered, would be brought forward as evidence of the truth of the charges made in them. The ordinary and wise practice is not to answer them – to take no notice of them. Unless it is made out to be the ordinary practice of mankind to answer, I cannot see that not answering is any evidence that the person who receives such letters admits the truth of the statements contained in them.

[Bowen and Kay LJJ agreed.]

Thomas v Jones   [1921] 1 KB 22, [1920] All ER Rep 462, CA

Scrutton LJ: The question of not immediately repudiating an accusation is one of very considerable difficulty, and is, in my view, entirely a question of degree. If a charge of outrageous conduct is made against a person in public, and he says nothing, I have always thought that a jury would be entitled to treat this silence as an admission, if it was the class of accusation in respect of which, and the people in the neighbourhood were the class of people from whom, a repudiation of an untrue charge would be expected. But I do not think the same principle applies to accusations made by private letter. Lunatics write all sorts of letters to all manner of people, and if the receiver of a letter from a lunatic making a charge were bound to write at once and deny it, the time of judges, at any rate, would be fully taken up by answering the letters. I quite agree with what was said in *Wiedemann v Walpole* [1891] 2 QB 534, CA.

(v)   Silence in court

Section 35(3) of the Criminal Justice and Public Order Act 1994 (see ch 7, post) provides that, where that section applies, the court may draw 'such inferences as appear proper' from the accused's silence in court. As suggested in ch 7, however, silence in court is not a separate item of evidence and, if relied upon, merely forms part of the framework against which the evidence is assessed by the trier of fact, and hence may strengthen the inferences to be drawn from the evidence against the accused. Accordingly, the following pre-1994 considerations appear to be relevant still.

The precise effect of silence is obscure. In *R v Jackson* [1953] 1 All ER 872 at 873, CCA, Lord Goddard CJ said, 'It is a matter which the jury could very properly take into account and very probably would,' but it was not corroboration. In *Cracknell v Smith* [1960] 3 All ER 569 at 571, DC, Lord Parker CJ said, 'If there is evidence against him, and some corroborative evidence, it may be that the justices are entitled to take into consideration the fact that he gave no evidence in considering the weight to be attached to the corroboration,' but silence was not itself corroboration. Lord Parker CJ's remark suggests silence strengthens the opposing case without being itself corroboration (*Jensen v Ilka* [1960] Qd R 274); it presumably also weakens the accused's own case, as with out of court silence. See also *R v Naylor* [1933] 1 KB 685, [1932] All ER Rep 152, CCA; *R v Smith* (1935) 25 Cr App Rep 119, CCA; *R v Charavanmuttu* (1930) 22 Cr App Rep 1, CCA. Thus the accused's silence may make it safe to convict without corroboration.

Failure to cross-examine does not corroborate evidence in chief (*Dingwall v J Wharton (Shipping) Ltd* [1961] 2 Lloyd's Rep 213 at 219, HL).

Silence is sometimes held corroborative when coupled with special circumstances. Thus when a putative father told one story to the justices but did not repeat it at the trial on assize, its falsity could be inferred and this was corroboration (*Mash v Darley* [1914] 3 KB 1226, CA). An unexplained absconding from bail has been held to be corroboration (*R v McKenna* (1956) 73 WNNSW 345). In these cases the court can imply an admission from conduct because there is something more than mere silence; hence these examples are not an exception to the general rule that silence alone is not corroboration.

(vi)   Failure to give samples

It has been held in *R v Smith* (1985) 81 Cr App Rep 286, CA, and *McVeigh v Beattie* [1988] Fam 69, [1988] 2 All ER 500, that refusal without proper cause to provide a bodily sample (a hair in the one case, a blood test in the other) was capable of affording corroboration. It is very difficult to reconcile these decisions with the general principle that there is no obligation to provide such samples. Under the Police and Criminal Evidence Act 1984, ss 61 and 63, however, fingerprints and non-intimate samples may be taken without the suspect's consent; by s 62(10) refusal to consent to the taking of an intimate sample may be treated as corroboration.

(vii)   Conduct on previous occasions

Let us assume the accused commits a series of crimes such that, under the similar fact evidence rules, evidence of one is admissible in respect to all the others because this is relevant to some issue (see ch 10, post). If the victims are different and independent, they may support one another (*DPP v Kilbourne* [1973] AC 729, [1973] 1 All ER 440, HL; *R v Mitchell* (1952) 36

Cr App Rep 79, CCA). The similar fact evidence itself can constitute corroboration, unless there is 'a real chance' that there has been collusion between the witnesses: *DPP v Kilbourne*, supra, at 750, 456; *DPP v Boardman* [1975] AC 421 at 444, 459, [1974] 3 All ER 887 at 897-8, 910, HL; *R v Johannsen* (1977) 65 Cr App Rep 101 at 105, CA; *R v H* [1995] 2 AC 596, [1995] 2 All ER 865, HL. If the victim is the same, any independent corroboration of one incident can constitute corroboration as to the others (eg *R v Hartley* [1941] 1 KB 5, CCA). Thus previous convictions of the accused for offences against the same victim may be corroboration (*R v Marsh* (1949) 33 Cr App Rep 185, CCA).

Hoffmann: The South African Law of Evidence, 2nd edn, p 421

Courts have sometimes found difficulty in holding that the evidence of witness A deposing to one offence could corroborate the evidence of witness B deposing to a different offence. On the other hand, the evidence of witness A will not be admissible under the similar fact rule unless it is sufficiently relevant to the question of whether the accused committed the other offence. If it is admissible at all, it must be on the ground that it confirms the evidence of witness B in a material particular affecting the accused. It should therefore be capable of corroborating his evidence.

(viii)   Mere opportunity

Mere opportunity is not corroboration without more. As one American judge gloomily remarked in a sex case, 'If proof of opportunity to commit a crime were alone sufficient to sustain a conviction, no man would be safe' (*Power v State* 30 P 2d 1059 at 1060 (1934) per Lockwood J). Repeated opportunities have often been held corroboration of intercourse, however, as has a period of close association, particularly if the association is exclusive (*Moore v Hewitt* [1947] KB 831, [1947] 2 All ER 270).

FURTHER READING

Anon (1972) 81 Yale LJ 1365; Bates (1973) 47 ALJ 178; (1974) 48 ALJ 85; Birch [1995] Crim LR 524; Coscowe (1960) 25 *Law and Contemporary Problems* 222; Dennis [1984] Crim LR 316; Jackson, 47 CLJ 428; Ligertwood (1976) 50 ALJ 158; Ludwig (1970) 36 Brooklyn LR 378; Mirfield, 107 LQR 450; [1995] Crim LR 448; Williams, ch 6.

PART THREE

The Protection of the Accused

CHAPTER 6

The Privilege against Self-Incrimination

1 Introduction

A witness when testifying must answer all relevant questions unless he can invoke some privilege to remain silent. The privilege against self-incrimination was stated by Goddard LJ in this way: 'no one is bound to answer any question if the answer thereto would, in the opinion of the judge, have a tendency to expose the deponent to any criminal charge, penalty or forfeiture which the judge regards as reasonably likely to be preferred or sued for' (*Blunt v Park Lane Hotel Ltd* [1942] 2 KB 253 at 257, [1942] 2 All ER 187 at 189, CA). The privilege also extends to the production of incriminating documents, including on discovery, and here it is controversial to a degree: *Sociedade Nacional de Combustiveis de Angola UEE v Lundqvist* [1991] 2 QB 310 at 338, [1990] 3 All ER 283 at 302, CA; *Tate Access Floors Inc v Boswell* [1991] Ch 512 at 532, [1990] 3 All ER 303 at 315. The privilege does not absolve a deponent from answers which tend to expose him to any other civil action; in particular, *Blunt's Case* decided that it did not apply where the answer might tend to establish the deponent's adultery. The 'penalty' referred to is a statutory penalty. It includes disciplinary offences under statutes regulating the police: *Police Service Board v Morris* (1985) 156 CLR 397. Further, in civil cases s 16(1)(*a*) of the Civil Evidence Act 1968 omits from the scope of the privilege answers which would tend to expose the witness to a forfeiture, and a similar change for criminal proceedings can only be a matter of time. The same may be said of other parts of the Civil Evidence Act resolving doubts in the common law for civil cases. The effect of these is that the privilege only applies to criminal offences and penalties under United Kingdom law, not foreign law (s 14(1)(*a*)) but it extends not only to questions tending to expose the witness to prosecution or the recovery of a penalty, but also to questions which have this effect on the witness's spouse (s 14(1)(*b*)). However, the privilege remains the witness's, and he can waive it even if the spouse objects. It is not clear whether the privilege in favour of spouses applies in criminal cases as well (*R v All Saints, Worcester Inhabitants* (1817) 6 M & S 194 at 200, 105 ER 1215 at 1218) but it is improbable that there is such a privilege (*Rio Tinto Zinc Corp v Westinghouse Electric Corpn* [1978] AC 547 at 637, [1978] 1 All ER 434 at 465 per Lord Diplock, HL and *R v Pitt* [1983] QB 25, [1982] All ER 63, CA) and there is certainly no further class of persons protected: *R v Minihane* (1921) 16 Cr App Rep 38, CCA. 'Penalty' is not limited to penalties in revenue cases but includes all penalties under United Kingdom law (*Rio Tinto Zinc Corpn v Westinghouse Electric Corpn* [1978] AC 547 at 564 and 569–70, [1977] 3 All ER 703 at 711 and 716, CA), including penalties for civil contempt (*Bhimji v Chatwani (No 3)* [1992] 4 All ER 912, [1992] 1 WLR 1158), and includes penalties imposable administratively without legal procedures such as fines under Articles 85, 189 and 192 of the European Economic Community Treaty: *Rio Tinto Zinc Corpn v Westinghouse Electric Corpn (No 2)* [1978] AC 547, [1978] 1 All ER 434, HL. Those penalties are provided for by United Kingdom law because they are recoverable under English law by virtue of the European Communities Act 1972. In criminal cases the common law privilege continues; it is undecided whether it is limited only to English law.

The privilege is in fact very personal. It is not analogous to Crown privilege, where the contents of a document are privileged in the sense that no one can give evidence of them (ch 19, post). If one who possesses a privilege against self-incrimination chooses to waive it, no litigant adversely affected can object. Indeed, if a litigant's witness makes a claim for privilege which is wrongly rejected, this is not a ground of appeal. The witness can by waiving his privilege give the evidence voluntarily: 'if instead of giving his evidence voluntarily he gives it under compulsion, what is the difference?' (*R v Kinglake* (1870) 22 LT 335 at 336, per Blackburn J). It is different if the court wrongly allows a claim of privilege, for here one party is improperly deprived of favourable evidence, whereas if the privilege is wrongly disallowed it simply results in the admission of relevant evidence (*Cloyes v Thayer* (1842) 3 Hill 564 at 566). No adverse inference should be drawn from the fact that the privilege is claimed since otherwise the privilege would be destroyed (*Wentworth v Lloyd* (1864) 10 HL Cas 589 at 590–2, HL), though it may be difficult to prevent the trier of fact (if the witness is a party to the case) or the prosecuting authorities (if he is not) from drawing such an inference. In this connexion it is worth noting that the privilege only prevents answers being given, it does not prevent questions being asked, even though the mere asking of the question will sometimes cause as much damage as the answer. Of course, to claim the privilege does not necessarily indicate guilt. Pollock CB once pointed out that 'a man may be placed under such circumstances with respect to the commission of a crime, that if he disclosed them he might be fixed upon by his hearers as a guilty person, so that the rule is not always the shield of the guilty, it is sometimes the protector of the innocent' (*Adams v Lloyd* (1858) 3 H & N 351 at 363). Irrelevant questions, as opposed to relevant though incriminating ones, may be objected to, but by the litigant affected rather than his witness.

2 The role of the judge

The privilege against self-incrimination applies not only to answers directly incriminating the witness but also answers that tend to do so indirectly. A number of such answers taken together or taken with other evidence might incriminate the witness in such a way that, if he is forced to answer, the dangers avoided by the privilege will occur (*R v Slaney* (1832) 5 C & P 213; *R v The Coroner, ex p Alexander* [1982] VR 731). In *British Steel Corpn v Granada*

Television Ltd [1981] AC 1096 at 1108, [1981] 1 All ER 417 at 425, CA, Megarry V-C said that the privilege did not extend so far as to permit the claimant to say: 'To answer this question might lead to a train of inquiry which, if pursued, might lead to some evidence which, if adduced, might tend to incriminate me.'; see also *Sociedade Nacional de Combustiveis de Angola UEE v Lundqvist* [1991] 2 QB 310 at 338, [1990] 3 All ER 283 at 292, CA. In any event, the witness's own view is not necessarily to be accepted: the court can override it.

R v Boyes   (1861) 1 B & S 311, [1861–73] All ER Rep 172

The witness invoking the privilege had been handed a pardon under the Great Seal. The effect of this was to prevent his prosecution for the offence, though not his impeachment, the latter being a very unlikely prospect. The Court of Queen's Bench (Cockburn CJ, Crompton, Hill and Blackburn JJ) denied his right to privilege.

[T]o entitle a party called as a witness to the privilege of silence, the court must see, from the circumstances of the case and the nature of the evidence which the witness is called to give, that there is reasonable ground to apprehend danger to the witness from his being compelled to answer. We indeed quite agree that, if the fact of the witness being in danger be once made to appear, great latitude should be allowed to him in judging for himself of the effect of any particular question: there being no doubt . . . that a question which might appear at first sight a very innocent one, might, by affording a link in a chain of evidence, become the means of bringing home an offence to the party answering. Subject to this reservation, a Judge is, in our opinion, bound to insist on a witness answering unless he is satisfied that the answer will tend to place the witness in peril.

Further than this, we are of opinion that the danger to be apprehended must be real and appreciable, with reference to the ordinary operation of law in the ordinary course of things – not a danger of an imaginary and unsubstantial character, having reference to some extraordinary and barely possible contingency, so improbable that no reasonable man would suffer it to influence his conduct. We think that a merely remote and naked possibility, out of the ordinary course of the law and such as no reasonable man would be affected by, should not be suffered to obstruct the administration of justice. The object of the law is to afford to a party, called upon to give evidence in a proceeding inter alios, protection against being brought by means of his own evidence within the penalties of the law. But it would be to convert a salutary protection into a means of abuse if it . . . were to be held that a mere imaginary possibility of danger, however remote and improbable, was sufficient to justify the withholding of evidence essential to the ends of justice.

Now, in the present case, no one seriously supposes that the witness runs the slightest risk of an impeachment by the House of Commons.

It appears to us, therefore, that the witness in this case was not, in a rational point of view, in the slightest real danger from the evidence he was called upon to give when protected by the pardon from all ordinary legal proceedings; and that it was therefore the duty of the presiding Judge to compel him to answer.

Re Reynolds, ex p Reynolds   (1882) 20 Ch D 294, [1881–5] All ER Rep 997, CA

Bacon CJ: What is the case before me? The witness is alleged to be a trustee of a settlement the validity of which the trustee in bankruptcy seeks to impeach. He is called as a witness, and the deed being produced, he is asked whether it is executed by him, and the answer is, 'I decline to answer because it might criminate me.' Am I not bound to exercise such portion of common sense as I possess, and to say whether an answer to that question can possibly criminate anybody? If a suit were instituted in the Court of Chancery against a trustee such a question would beyond all doubt, whether under the old practice or under the modern practice of interrogatories (the object of the court being that there should be no needless expense in proving the execution of the deed), be allowed, and it could not upon any conceivable ground have the effect of criminating the witness. It is the same, I think, with all the other questions. It is not suggested that the witness has done anything criminal. It could not be criminal to execute a deed. It could not be criminal to deal with the property comprised in the deed – if he did deal with it – I do not say that he did. It could not be criminal to charge him with having received a sum of £1000 and paid it unto his bankers. It cannot be said that any one of the questions put to the witness could ever form a link in any criminal action which might be brought against him. There is no doubt the principle is a very important one, I was going to say a sacred one, because the liberty of the subject is at all times a sacred matter, and if I saw there was any chance of the answer to the question whether he executed a deed or not forming a link in a chain, one end of which would be the accusation and the other the conviction of the witness, I should hesitate very much before I compelled him to answer; but as it stands no one who has listened to this examination can entertain any doubt that it comes clearly within the cases pointed out, where the court has been satisfied that the witness is trifling with the court, and is setting up excuses which have no kind of foundation. I do not hesitate to say that the witness is bound to answer the questions, and therefore he must submit to an examination before the Registrar. If he does not answer, I need not point out to him the consequence that would attend his refusal.

Court of Appeal

Jessel MR: There are two questions to be decided: one of general importance, the other confined to the circumstances of the particular case. The question of general importance is, whether, when a witness objects to answer a question put to him on the ground that the answer to it may tend to criminate him, the mere statement of his own belief that it will tend to criminate him is sufficient to excuse him from answering, or whether the Judge is entitled to decide, not merely accepting the witness's statement, whether the proposed question has really a tendency to criminate him, or may fairly be considered, under all the circumstances of the case, as having that tendency.

Now upon that, there are various dicta and one express decision in *R v Boyes*. I am quite aware that the decision of the Court of Queen's Bench in *R v Boyes* is not technically binding on this court, but at the same time it is a decision of the full Court of Queen's Bench, composed at that time of very eminent Judges, and I need not say that I should differ from them with very great hesitation.

That decision, as it appears to me, states the law correctly, and if it were necessary for the Court of Appeal to affirm it, we should, I think be doing well and wisely in saying that we do affirm it. It is unnecessary after it to refer to the prior authorities; they are all mere dicta. But, as regards the subsequent case of *Re Firth, ex p Schofield*, decided in 1877, I will say this, that I am not sure it is a mere dictum; I rather think it is a decision. There Lord Justice James said, with regard to an examination under this very 96th section ((1877) 6 Ch D 230 at 233): 'Of course when a witness objects on this ground to answer a question, the Judge will satisfy himself whether the objection is a genuine one.'

... [I]f you allowed the witness merely on his own statement of his belief that an answer to the question would tend to criminate him (for that is all, he is only bound to believe that) to refuse to answer, it would enable a friendly witness, who wished to assist one of the parties, to escape examination altogether, and to refuse to give his evidence. That would be an evil so great as far to overbear, as a question of public policy, the danger, if it is to be treated as a danger, of occasionally assisting to convict a guilty man out of his own mouth. Perhaps our law has gone even too far in the direction of protecting a witness from the chance of convicting himself. But without at all impugning the policy of the law, there must certainly be a larger policy which requires that a witness should answer when the Judge thinks that he is objecting to answer, not bona fide with the view of claiming privilege to protect himself, but in order to prevent other parties from getting that testimony which is necessary for the purposes of justice.

And even those Judges who have entertained the contrary opinion have made an exception in the case of mala fides. I need only refer for that to what was said by the late Lord Chief Baron Pollock in *Adams v Lloyd*, where, having stated the rule in favour of the protection of a witness on his own oath, he added ((1858) 3 H & N at 362): 'The only exception I know of is this, – where the Judge is perfectly certain that the witness is trifling with the authority of the court, and availing himself of the rule of law to keep back the truth, having in reality no ground whatever for claiming the privilege, then the Judge is right in insisting on his answering the question.'

Well now, this being so, the second question we have to consider is whether there is any reasonable ground for fearing that the questions, when answered, will tend to convict the witness of a criminal offence, or to criminate him in any way. Now, in order to decide that point the court must consider what the nature of the case is, and what the witness has said. When we look at the questions which the witness has refused to answer, the conviction, I think, must force itself upon the mind of any one that he refused to answer because he did not want to give the information, and that he was trifling with the court.

I do not for a moment think that the witness is under any bona fide belief that there will be any charge of conspiracy made against him, or that he had any idea of such a charge; in fact I think the notion of such an indictment could only present itself to the mind of someone who was very familiar indeed with the law of conspiracy. It appears to me that the witness did not wish to afford any assistance to the bankrupt's creditors in obtaining possession of the property which had been kept from them. I think that was the prevailing motive with him, and not any real fear of criminal proceedings.

[Cotton and Lindley LJJ gave judgments to the same effect.]

Brebner v Perry   [1961] SASR 177

The witness Seeley invoked the privilege against self-incrimination in criminal proceedings against Perry. Seeley had already made admission to the police implicating himself and Perry in the commission of the offence charged. The Supreme Court of South Australia disallowed the claim.

Mayo J: What is the general proposition in regard to the compulsion of a witness to answer where he objects? The matter was discussed and principles stated and elaborated in *J H Sherring & Co v Hinton* [1932] SASR 233, and in *Matthew v Flood* [1938] SASR 312. Where a witness who is on oath objects that the answer to a question put to him may incriminate him, and there is good reason to accept the objection as well founded he will be excused . . . Where the risk is removed by a pardon or by a lapse of time, certainly if there be a statutory limitation upon proceedings, the privilege of the witness no longer remains: *Roberts v Allatt* (1828) Mood & M 192; *Dover v Maestaer* (1803) 5 Esp 92 at 93; *A-G v Cunard Steamship Co* (1887) 4 TLR 177. The claim by the witness, although on oath, even if there be no doubt as to his credibility, is not sufficient. It must be shown to the court, from the circumstances, and the nature of the testimony that is sought to be educed, that there is reasonable ground he may be implicated in some offence by his answer. The fact that an offence (if any) would be of a trifling nature might be treated by the court as precluding reliance on privilege. On the other hand, the rarity of prosecutions of a nature that might be framed will not be regarded as an answer to an objection by the witness: *Triplex Safety Glass Co Ltd v Lancegaye Safety Glass (1934) Ltd* [1939] 2 KB 395, [1939] 2 All ER 613, CA [a case involving a risk of criminal prosecutions for libel].

A point that, at times, may have some importance is that any fact a witness is *wrongly* forced to disclose in answer to questions after he had objected to answer will be inadmissible if criminal proceedings are subsequently brought against him . . .

. . . Where a question concerns conduct that is in itself innocent, and will only involve risk to a witness as a link in chain of proof, he must satisfy the Court by facts that will, in that event, be outside the terms of the question that the answer would, or might tend to, incriminate him, eg *R v Cox and Railton* (1884) 14 QBD 153 at 175, [1881–5] All ER Rep 68 at 76. On the other hand questions can bear on their face sufficient indication of matter to which the witness will be exposed if he answer in a certain way: *Re Genese, ex p Gilbert* (1886) 3 Morr 223 at 226 . . .

Where an objection to answer is not bona fide for the protection of a witness himself, he will be compelled to answer . . .

Apply that aspect to the present matter. The witness had already, so far as it had been shown to the court, made himself liable to any prosecution that might have been laid. Can his objection to answer be treated as bona fide? I think not. He was not concerned with his own protection. His conduct was in the interest of the defendant.

The decision was apparently approved by Lord Denning MR in *Re Westinghouse Electric Corpn (No 2)* [1978] AC 547 at 574, [1977] 3 All ER 717 at 722.

The fact that an offence was committed many years ago may also cause the court to deny the claim to privilege. But the fact that a successful prosecution is unlikely through the soft-heartedness of prosecutor or jury does not destroy the privilege (*Triplex Safety Glass Co Ltd v Lancegaye Safety Glass (1934) Ltd* [1939] 2 KB 395, [1939] 2 All ER 613, CA).

One problem that stems from the rule that the witness's word as to the incriminating nature of what he is about to say is not enough is that 'The privilege must . . . be violated in order to ascertain whether it exists. The secret must be told in order to see whether it ought to be kept' (*R v Cox and Railton* (1884) 14 QBD 153 at 175, [1881–5] All ER Rep 68 at 76, per Stephen J). Often it will not be necessary for the entire secret to be told before the court has before it sufficient material to grant the privilege. But what if it is necessary to tell all, or even part, if the secret is incriminating? Cross suggested (3rd edn, p 247) that 'If difficulties were to arise in this regard they could no doubt be surmounted by allowing the witness to make his submission wholly or partially in camera, or under the protection of an understanding that no use could be made of his statements outside the proceedings in which they were given.' For examples of the practice, see Josling [1954] Crim L Rev 916 at 917, and [1971] Crim L Rev 13 at 33–4. Such undertakings are not binding as the law stands.

At common law, if a claim to privilege is wrongly rejected, anything the witness says will be treated as involuntary and inadmissible in subsequent proceedings (*R v Garbett* (1847) 1 Den 236). But s 76(2) of the Police and Criminal Evidence Act 1984 (ch 8.1), perhaps per incuriam, may have changed this result, unless the circumstances can be said to be those of 'oppression'.

The privilege does not operate so as to render immune from adverse inferences a suspect who refuses to take part in an identification parade: *Marcoux and Solomon v R* (1975) 60 DLR (3d) 119. Nor does it entitle a suspect to refuse to comply with a court order that his fingerprints be taken (*George v Coombe* [1978] Crim LR 47) or with a statutory duty to provide a sample of his breath: *King v McLellan* [1974] VR 773.

The necessary risk of prosecution is not sufficiently diminished to prevent the privilege applying by the undertaking of the person who gains the information to keep it secret: *Rank Film Distributors v Video Information Centre* [1982] AC 380, [1981] 2 All ER 76, HL. That decision has been reversed by s 72(1) of the Supreme Court Act 1981; the privilege is revoked in *Anton Piller* circumstances, but the answers given are inadmissible against the person answering and his spouse: s 72(3). In *Istel (AT & T) Ltd v Tully* [1993] AC 45, [1992] 3 All ER 523, HL, the risk of prosecution was held to have been sufficiently diminished by an agreement by the prosecuting authorities not to make use of the material divulged. See *Reid v Howard* (1995) 184 CLR 1.

In *Re Westinghouse* [1978] AC 547 at 573, [1977] 3 All ER 703 at 721, Lord Denning MR doubted whether the privilege was properly claimable in respect of a fear of prosecution for criminal libel, and doubted whether *Lamb v Munster* (1882) 10 QBD 110 and *Triplex Safety Glass Company Ltd v Lancegaye Safety Glass (1934) Ltd* [1939] 2 KB 395, [1939] 2 All ER 613, CA, would now be decided the same way; Roskill LJ spoke to the same effect at 580 and 726–7 and see Viscount Dilhorne at 627 and 427. The members of the Court of Appeal also offered various restatements, which in some circumstances may be helpful, of the *Boyes* test, eg 'can exposure to the risk of penalties . . . be regarded as so far beyond the bounds of reason as to be no more than a fanciful possibility?' (at 579 and 726). See also *Khan v Khan* [1982] 2 All ER 60, [1982] 1 WLR 513, CA.

The privilege must be expressly invoked by the witness (*Boyle v Wiseman* (1855) 10 Exch 647 at 653, per Pollock CB). In this respect it contrasts with the accused's rights not to be cross-examined about certain matters under s 1(*f*) of the Criminal Evidence Act 1898. If the witness could have claimed the privilege but fails to do so, the evidence will be admissible in the instant and in later proceedings (*R v Sloggett* (1856) Dears CC 656). It might be thought that the witness should be warned of his right and of how he can recognise it, but the judge is not required to give such a warning.

R v Coote   (1873) LR 4 PC 599, PC

Sir Robert Collier: The Chief Justice indeed suggests, that Coote may have been ignorant of the law enabling him to decline to answer criminating questions, and that if he had been acquainted with it he might have withheld some of the answers which he gave. As a matter of fact, it would appear that Coote was acquainted with so much of the law; but be this as it may, it is obvious, that to institute an inquiry in each case as to the extent of the prisoner's knowledge of law, and to speculate whether, if he had known more, he would or would not have refused to answer certain questions, would be to involve a plain rule in endless confusion. Their Lordships see no reason to introduce, with reference to this subject, an exception to the rule, recognised as essential to the administration of the Criminal Law, '*Ignorantia juris non excusat.*' With respect to the objection, that Coote when a witness should have been cautioned in the manner in which it is directed by statute, that persons accused before magistrates are to be cautioned (a question said by Mr Justice Badgley not to have been reserved, but which is treated as reserved by the Court), it is enough to say, that the caution is by the terms of the statutes applicable to accused persons only and has no application whatever to witnesses.

Wigmore: Treatise on the Anglo-American System of Evidence in Trials at Common Law, 3rd edn, para 2269

. . . [S]uch a warning would be an anomaly; it is not given for any other privilege; witnesses are in other respects supposed to know their rights; and why not here? . . . [I]n practical convenience, there is no demand for such a rule; witnesses are usually well enough advised beforehand by counsel as to their rights when such issues impend, and judges are too much concerned with other responsibilities to be burdened with the prevision of individual witness' knowledge; the risk of their being in ignorance should fall rather upon the party summoning than the party opposing.

Lord Eldon LC once said that giving such warnings was 'that, which every judge in the country used to do, though it is not so much in practice now as it was at that time' (*Re Worrall, ex p Cossens* (1820) Buck 531 at 544) and a warning is in fact still often given. The court probably has a discretion to exclude the evidence in a later trial if the privilege could have been but was not claimed (*Re Shanahan* (1912) 45 ILTR 254 at 258, per Holmes LJ).

It should be noted that a witness who fears he may be asked incriminating questions cannot refuse to be sworn at all. He must at least listen to each question and suffer any incriminating effect the question has by itself. If he wants to claim privilege he must do so in respect of each individual question. The old doctrine that once a witness chose to begin replying he had to answer every question relevant to the transaction in question was reversed in *R v Garbett* (1847) 1 Den 236.

Modern statutes setting up administrative tribunals often expressly preserve the privilege against self-incrimination in proceedings before them.

The Criminal Evidence Act 1898 enabled the accused to give evidence on his own behalf. But it was thought that if he retained the privilege against self-incrimination even in respect of the offence charged he would be too favourably placed, because he would be immune, if he so chose, from answering any questions in cross-examination. Section 1(e) therefore provides:

'A person charged and being a witness in pursuance of this Act may be asked any question in cross-examination notwithstanding that it would tend to incriminate him as to the offence charged.'

3   The importance of the privilege

The privilege has often been praised or justified. English judges have called it 'a most important right' (*Orme v Crockford* (1824) 13 Price 376 at 388, per Alexander LCB); 'most sacred' (*Re Worrall, ex p Cossens* (1820) Buck 531 at 540, per Lord Eldon LC); a 'general rule established with great justice and tenderness' (*Harrison v Southcote and Moreland* (1751) 2 Ves Sen 389 at 394, per Lord Hardwicke LC); 'a maxim of our law as settled, as important and as wise as almost any other in it' (*R v Scott* (1856) Dears & B 47 at 61, per Coleridge J). The American Founding Fathers inserted it into the Fifth Amendment to the Constitution as one of those 'principles of natural justice which had become permanently fixed in the jurisprudence of the mother country' (*Brown v Walker* 161 US 591 at 600 (1896)). There it is regarded as 'one of the great landmarks in man's struggle to make himself civilised . . . an expression of one of the fundamental decencies in this relation we have developed between government and man' (Erwin N Griswold, *The Fifth Amendment Today* (Cambridge, Mass, 1955) pp 7–8, partially quoted in *Ullman v US* 350 US 422 at 426 (1955), per Frankfurter J. See also *Murphy v Waterfront Commission of New York Harbour* 378 US 52 at 55–6 (1964), per Goldberg J).

The privilege against self-incrimination was worked out by the late Stuart judges (see Wigmore, para 2250). By the time of Blackstone it was settled law that, in his words, 'at the common law, *nemo tenebatur prodere se ipsum*: and his fault was not to be wrung out of himself, but rather to be discovered by other means and other men' (*Commentaries* (12th edn, London, 1795), IV, ch 22, p 296). For this there were historical reasons. In the early seventeenth century some prerogative courts indulged in unrestrained and wanton interrogation of suspects, often using torture. Selden reported that 'The rack is used nowhere as in England. In other countries 'tis used in judicature, when there is a *semiplena probatio*, a half-proof against a man, then to see if they can make it full, they rack him to try if he will confess. But here in England they take a man and rack him, I do not know why, nor when, not in time of judicature, but when somebody bids' (*Table Talk* (ed Pollock, London, 1927), p 133). By the late seventeenth century there was a strong judicial revulsion against this and against every feature of the prerogative courts. As Bentham said, 'what could be more natural than that, by a people infants as yet in reason, giants in passion, every distinguishable feature of a system of procedure directed to such ends should be condemned in the lump, should be involved in one undistinguishing mass of odium and abhorrence' (Bentham, IX, part IV, c iii, p 456). Bentham called this the 'argument by reference to unpopular institutions' (ibid, p 455).

A similar argument is the argument that since the privilege appears in the same part of the American constitution as the freedom of religion, of speech, and of the press, and provisions against unreasonable searches and seizures of the home, it is necessarily as important as these. The privilege has acquired 'a borrowed radiance from its close connection with these other rights which are genuine essentials of ordered liberty. It has gained a sort of sanctity by association' (McCormick, p 290).

Bentham is the principal opponent of the privilege.

Bentham: A Rationale of Judicial Evidence, Book IX, Pt 4, c iii

(a)   Pretences for exclusion [of the accused's testimony on compulsion] . . .

2.   The old woman's reason. The essence of this reason is contained in the word *hard*; 'tis hard upon a man to be obliged to criminate himself. Hard it is upon a man, it must be confessed, to be obliged to do anything that he does not like. That he should not much like to do what is meant by his criminating himself, is natural enough; for what it leads to, is, his being punished. What is no less hard upon him, is, that he should be punished: but did it ever yet occur to a man to propose a general abolition of all punishment, with this hardship for a reason for it? Whatever hardship there is in a man's being punished, that, and no more, is there in his thus being made to criminate himself . . .

Nor yet is all this plea of tenderness, – this double-distilled and treble-refined sentimentality, anything better than a pretence. From his own mouth you will not receive the evidence of the culprit against him; but in his own hand, or from the mouth of another, you receive it without scruple: so that at bottom, all this sentimentality resolves itself into neither more nor less than a predilection – a confirmed and most extensive predilection, for bad evidence . . .

3.   The fox-hunter's reason. This consists in introducing upon the carpet of legal procedure the idea of *fairness*, in the sense in which the word is used by sportsmen. The fox is to have a fair chance for his life: he must have (so close is the analogy) what is called *law* – leave to run a certain length of way for the express purpose of giving him a chance for escape. While under pursuit, he must not be shot: it would be as *unfair* as convicting him of burglary on a hen-roost in five minutes' time, in a court of conscience.

In the sporting code, these laws are rational, being obviously conducive to the professed end. Amusement is that end; a certain quantity of delay is essential to it: dispatch, a degree of dispatch reducing the quantity of delay below the allowed minimum, would be fatal to it . . . To different persons, both a fox and a criminal have their use; the use of a fox is to be hunted; the use of a criminal is to be tried . . .

Wigmore: Treatise on the Anglo-American System of Evidence in Trials at Common Law, 3rd edn, para 2251

The current judicial habit is . . . to laud it undiscriminatingly with false cant. A stranger from another legal sphere might imagine, in the perusal of our precedents, that the guilty criminal was the fond object of the court's doting tenderness, guiding him at every step in the path of unrectitude, and lifting up his feet lest he fall into the pits digged for him by justice. The judicial practice, now too common, of treating with warm and fostering respect every appeal to this privilege, and of amicably feigning each guilty invocator to be an unsullied victim hounded by the persecutions of a tyrant, is a mark of traditional sentimentality . . .

There ought to be an end of judicial cant towards crime. We have already had too much of what a wit has called 'justice tampered with mercy'.

. . . Courts should unite to keep the privilege strictly within the limits dictated by historic fact, cool reasoning, and sound policy.

A modern judicial sceptic is Lord Templeman, who pointed out in *Istel (AT & T) Ltd v Tully* [1993] AC 45 at 54, [1992] 3 All ER 523 at 530, that the purposes said to support the privilege had no application to documents or to some court orders: 'I regard the privilege against self-incrimination exercisable in civil proceedings as an archaic and unjustifiable survival from the past when the court directs the production of relevant documents and requires the defendant to specify his dealings with the plaintiff's property or money.' Lord Griffiths agreed (at 58 and 534).

The privilege admittedly has drawbacks. It generally favours the guilty. It may encourage authorities to use means of obtaining information more improper than questioning. It is less necessary in these days of a generally fair criminal procedure. But it will be suggested that it still serves some useful purposes. It ought not to be abolished or weakened merely because in particular cases its 'restraints are inconvenient or because the supposed malefactor may be a subject of public execration or because the disclosures of his wrong-doing will promote the public weal' (*Doyle v Hofstader* 177 NE 489 at 491 (1931), per Cardozo CJ). In Maguire's words, 'Liberty never comes free of charge' (*Evidence of Guilt* (Boston, 1959), para 2.02, n 6).

What are the useful purposes served by the privilege? First, if it did not exist, some witnesses would be faced with a painful trilemma. They would have a choice between punishment for silence when they have a duty to speak, punishment for perjury if they speak falsely, and punishment for their crimes if they speak the truth. This trilemma produces undesirable results. The privilege is thus said to protect the 'conscience and dignity of man' (*Ullmann v US* 350 US 422 at 446 (1955), per Black and Douglas JJ). Admittedly, as Bentham pointed out in the passage quoted above, such an argument is often said to be based on the sporting theory of justice: 'the use of a fox is to be hunted; the use of a criminal is to be tried' (Bentham, op cit, p 454). That is, just as it is poor fun if the fox has no chance to escape, so the criminal must not be unduly handicapped. Bentham also ridiculed it as 'the old woman's reason', imbued with a feeble sentimentalism which ought not to be displayed towards criminals. The sporting theory of justice may be ludicrous, and the notion of tenderness to criminals can be carried too far, but the privilege against self-incrimination does seem to be based on a deeply-felt public need. Public confidence in the administration of the law is an important value. 'Accustomed personal safeguards, fixed in men's minds by usage of decades and centuries, are not lightly to be destroyed' (Maguire, *Evidence of Guilt*, p 14).

Secondly, the privilege against self-incrimination is merely one rule among many which depend on the view that at least in theory the accused's guilt must be proved by the prosecution at an English criminal trial. Some have thought that this principle goes too far. The Canadian judge, Riddell J, once said: 'We have not yet arrived at the point that one accused of crime has so many and so high rights that the people have none. The administration of our law is not a game in which the cleverer and more astute is to win, but a serious proceeding by a people in earnest to discover the actual facts for the sake of public safety, the interest of the public generally. It is the duty of every citizen to tell all he knows for the sake of the people at large, their interest and security' (*R v Barnes* (1921) 61 DLR 623 at 638). There is of course no legal 'duty' of the kind suggested except as provided by statute. More importantly, there is something to be said in favour of weighting the scales in favour of the subject and against the state. The state has much better machinery for protecting its interests than its subjects; it should be made to rely on it. In Wigmore's words:

'. . . *any system of administration which permits the prosecution to trust habitually to compulsory self-disclosure as a source of proof must itself suffer thereby.* The inclination develops to rely mainly upon such evidence, and to be satisfied with an incomplete investigation of the other sources. The exercise of the power to extract answers begets a forgetfulness of the just limitations of that power . . . If there is a right to an answer, there soon seems to be a right to the expected answer' (para 2251).

Stephen's information as to why Indian policemen indulged in torture was that 'it is far pleasanter to sit comfortably in the shade rubbing red pepper into a poor devil's eyes than to go about in the sun hunting up evidence' (*History of the Criminal Law of England* (London, 1883), 1, p 442). This may be regarded as a very extreme form of the danger under consideration, but Parliament has often shared the view that there is a danger to be controlled. Thus in some cases where the privilege is completely abrogated by statute, safeguards are substituted. One is that only officials above a certain rank may extract answers under threat of lawful punishment. Another is that such a power should only be exercised with the approval of a high-ranking official. Thus sometimes when Parliament removes the privilege it feels the need of safeguards against the abuses that come from a lack of maturity, responsibility or sophistication. It is said that the argument cannot 'sustain the constant recognition of this privilege in purely civil proceedings where the government is not a factor' (Maguire, *Evidence: Common Sense and Common Law* (Chicago, 1947), p 106). But there too it would be undesirable to allow the government to rely on one civil litigant's power to force admissions of criminal conduct out of another.

Thirdly, the privilege removes one obstacle preventing witnesses coming forward. 'The witness-stand is today sufficiently a place of annoyance and dread. The reluctance to enter it must not be increased . . . To remove all limits of inquiry into the secrets of the persons who have no stake in the cause but can furnish help in its investigation, would be to add to the motives which now sufficiently dispose them to evade their duty' (Wigmore, para 2251). Maguire considers that this only 'affects an extremely small percentage of the total number of useful witnesses' (*Evidence of Guilt*, pp 13–14). But is this so? Parties to civil suits may invoke the privilege, though perhaps their interests may be set aside as deserving little sympathy. In England, the accused may invoke it, for though he is compelled to be present, and though he has no privilege against incriminating himself with respect to the offence charged (Criminal Evidence Act 1898, s 1(*e*)), he may wish to enter the box and claim the privilege with respect to other matters. There remain a large number of possible witnesses in civil and criminal cases whose reluctance to come forward and assist the interests of justice will be reduced if they know they have the privilege against self-incrimination. It is said that the privilege is not a real inducement to come forward because a claim of privilege will alert the police that the witness may have a criminal past (Meltzer (1951) 18 Univ of Ch LR 687 at 699). But the risks of embarrassment and of alerting the police will vary in gravity enormously from case to case, and do not destroy the overall value of the privilege.

Fourthly, because of the general terrors of appearing in court, a witness, it has been cogently argued, is 'under duress – his mind disturbed by the extraordinary situation in which he [finds] himself placed, and called on in the midst of these trying circumstances to weigh and consider the nature of each question, and the consequences of his answers; and if so, the law cannot estimate the exact degree of influence of the duress on the human mind' (*R v Wheater* (1838) 2 Mood CC 45 at 46–7, per Dundas arguendo). The point is that witnesses in a state of agitation are likely to perform poorly and possibly tell unconscious falsehoods; anything that reduces their fears makes their evidence more valuable.

Fifthly, the risk of perjury is reduced, because one important incentive to lie is absent if a claim to the privilege is upheld. The court can thus be more confident in the evidence it does hear from the witness. It has often been objected that the privilege involves an unacceptable sacrifice in the number of convictions. But it is questionable whether the problem is so serious. A successful claim of privilege does not completely absolve someone with a criminal past, for his objection will alert the investigating authorities to the fact that he has something to hide and they will thus increase their efforts to prove it by other evidence, if it exists. Another objection to the privilege is that it causes less evidence to be placed before the court, and this is unjust to those involved in the proceedings in that the truth is less likely to be discovered. However, if a witness's evidence really is important, it can be obtained by special devices such as a pardon, a promise by the authorities not to prosecute, or an immunity statute of the kind considered post, p 129. It is of course difficult to balance the beneficial effects of removing a general reason for not testifying from all potential witnesses against the detrimental effect of losing particular pieces of evidence in consequence of successful privilege claims proceeding from a small proportion of the total class of witnesses.

Finally, if a witness, in an attempt at self-preservation, simply refuses to answer and there is no privilege against self-incrimination to permit this, the courts may not be able to enforce their demands. The remedy for contempt may disrupt the orderly flow of the trial; it may destroy the appearance of judicial impartiality. The privilege thus reflects the unwillingness of the law to order the impossible.

One other commonly advanced argument should be noted. It is not a sound one as a matter of principle, but it explains the popularity of the privilege to some extent. The argument is that the privilege helps to frustrate bad laws and bad procedures. Sometimes the laws in question are those persecuting the holders of certain political beliefs. Thus in the United States during the 1950s the Fifth Amendment was praised for protecting certain freedoms of thought which were not then adequately protected by the First Amendment. The laws in question may be those proscribing conduct popular among large sections of the population – particular forms of gambling, liquor and drug consumption and sexual activity. The procedures which are felt to be bad are inquiries by administrative and legislative committees. The publicity they attract during and after their operation 'can have devastating effect upon people dragged into them. Their pronouncements or implications are not always controlled by practised habit of cautious and thorough inquiry' (Maguire, *Evidence of Guilt*, p 14). Here the privilege is praised because it helps to protect privacy.

Arguments of this last kind are commonly advanced against bad laws. But the problem is that if the privilege is too exclusive it tends to frustrate not only bad laws and improperly officious inquiries, but all laws and inquiries, good or bad. Further, the answer to bad laws is not to depend on other rules to frustrate them indirectly, but to repeal them directly. As Stephen said:

'In the old Ecclesiastical Courts and in the Star Chamber [the "ex officio" oath] was understood to be and was used as an oath to speak the truth on the matters objected against the defendant – an oath, in short, to accuse oneself. It was vehemently contended by those who found themselves pressed by this oath that it was against the law of God, and the law of nature, and that the maxim "*nemo tenetur prodere se ipsum*" was agreeable to the law of God, and part of the law of nature. In this, I think, as in most other discussions of the kind, the real truth was that those who disliked the oath had usually done the things of which they were accused, and which they regarded as meritorious actions, though their judges regarded them as crimes. People always protest with passionate eagerness against being deprived of technical defences against what they regard as bad law, and such complaints often give a spurious value to technicalities when the cruelty of the laws against which they have afforded protection has come to be commonly admitted' (*History of the Criminal Law* I, p 342).

It is thought that the privilege against self-incrimination is adequately supported without reliance on the 'bad laws' argument, however.

4 Statutory restrictions on the privilege

There are a large number of statutes which have removed the privilege against self-incrimination. They empower state officials to obtain information under the compulsion of punishment for failure to provide it satisfactorily. Sometimes these statutes make precise provision regarding the admissibility of the evidence in subsequent proceedings. Some statutes provide an 'immunity bath', as the American phrase has it, in which the risk of conviction is washed away if full disclosure is made. Another group of statutes provides that the information given shall not be admissible against the person providing it in any proceedings, civil or criminal, or in particular kinds of proceedings.

The real problem arises with statutes which make no provision for immunity or continued privilege but simply state that the information may be used in evidence against the informant or say nothing at all. It is a problem of some practical importance. These statutes relate to company officials in winding-up proceedings, officials investigating liability to taxation; the public examination of bankrupts, inquiries into election offences; police questioning with regard to certain offences; and many other areas.

The rule is that if the information has been lawfully obtained and the statute does not restrict the use to be made of it, it is admissible in subsequent proceedings. To that extent, then, the statutes in question have abolished the privilege against self-incrimination.

R v Scott   (1856) Dears & B 47

Lord Campbell CJ: The judgment which I will now read is concurred in by my Brothers Alderson, Willes, and Bramwell; my Brother Coleridge differs. We are of opinion that the defendant's examination before the Court of Bankruptcy was properly admitted in evidence by my Brother Willes, and that the conviction ought to be confirmed. This examination was taken in strict conformity with section 117 of 12 & 13 Vict c 106, which enacts that the bankrupt may be examined by the court 'touching all matters relating to his trade, dealings, or estate, or which may tend to disclose any secret grant, conveyance or concealment of his lands, tenements, goods, money or debts' . . . In *R v Garbett* ((1847) 1 Den 236), and in other cases, it has been held that where the defendant has been improperly compelled to answer questions tending to criminate himself, his answers cannot be given in evidence against him; but as the report of *R v Merceron* (1818) 2 Stark 366 was said by Lord Tenterden not to be correct, we have no decision to guide us as to the admissibility of this examination which was perfectly lawful. Being a genuine document signed by the defendant, prima facie it is admissible against him; and we will consider the several grounds on which the defendant's counsel has argued that it is not admissible . . . [One is that] the examination was compulsory. It is a trite maxim that the confession of a crime, to be admissible against the party confessing, must be voluntary; but this only means that it shall not be induced by improper threats or promises, because, under such circumstances, the party may have been influenced to say what is not true, and the supposed confession cannot be safely acted upon. Such an objection cannot apply to a lawful examination in the course of a judicial proceeding. Then the defendant's counsel objects that, in the course of this examination, threats were used; the alleged threats, however, were merely an explanation of the enactment of the Legislature upon the subject, and a warning to the defendant of the consequences which, in point of law, would arise from his refusing to give a true answer to the questions put to him. Finally, the defendant's counsel relies upon the great maxim of English law '*nemo tenetur se ipsum accusare*'. So undoubtedly says the common law of England. But Parliament may take away this privilege, and enact that a party may be bound to accuse himself; this is, that he must answer questions by answering which he may be criminated. This Act of Parliament, 12 & 13 Vict c 106, creates felonies and misdemeanours, and compels the bankrupt to answer questions which may show that he has been guilty of some of those felonies or misdemeanours. The maxim of the common law therefore has been overruled by the Legislature, and the defendant has been actually compelled to give and had given answers, shewing that he is guilty of the misdemeanour with which he is charged. The accusation of himself was an accomplished fact, and at the trial he was not called upon to accuse himself. The maxim relied upon applies to the time when the question is put, not to the use which the prosecutor seeks to make of the answer when the answer has been given. If the party has been unlawfully compelled to answer the question, he shall be protected against any prejudice from the answer thus illegally extorted; but a similar protection cannot be demanded where the question was lawful and the party examined was bound by law to answer it. At the trial the defendant's written examination, signed by himself, was in court, and the reading of it as evidence against him could be no violation of the maxim relied upon. The only argument, as we conceive, that can plausibly be put for the defendant is, that there is an implied proviso to be subjoined to the 117th section viz 'that the examination shall not be used as evidence against the bankrupt on any criminal charge'. To make it evidence there could be no necessity for any express enactment for that purpose, and an implied proviso appears all that can be contended for. But by this interpolation we may be more likely to defeat than to further the intention of the Legislature. Considering the enormous frauds practised by bankrupts upon their creditors, the object may have been, in an exceptional instance, to allow a procedure in England universally allowed in many highly civilised countries. Suppose section 117 had begun with a preamble reciting the frauds of bankrupts, and the importance of having these frauds detected and punished, it would be difficult to say that the Legislature intended that no use should be made of the examination except for civil purposes. When the legislature compels parties to give evidence accusing themselves, and means to protect them from the consequences of giving such evidence, the course of legislation has been to do so by express enactment, as in 6 Geo IV c 129, s 6, and the five other instances adduced in the argument in behalf of the prosecution. We therefore think we are bound to suppose that in this instance, in which no such protection is provided, it was the intention of the Legislature to compel the bankrupt to answer interrogatories respecting his dealings and conduct as a trader, although he might thereby accuse himself and to permit his answers to be used against him for criminal as well as civil purposes.

Coleridge J: I have the misfortune in this case to differ from the rest of the Court; and entertaining unfeignedly a great distrust of my own opinion I should gladly surrender it to theirs, if I could divest myself of the belief that the judgment, which I venture to think erroneous, goes also to impair a maxim of our law as settled, as important and as wise as almost any other in it; and, consequently, that it is a duty to enter my protest, however ineffectually, against it. The maxim to which I allude will, of course, be understood to be that which is familiar to all lawyers, – that no person can be compelled to criminate himself. It would be a wasting of time to support this maxim by authorities or to dwell upon its importance. The judgment from which I differ does not proceed upon a denial or disparagement of it; but on some such argument as this – every lawful examination of a party charged, conducted according to law, is admissible evidence against him; this examination was lawful by statute and has been lawfully conducted; therefore this examination is admissible evidence against the prisoner. Now I deny the major premise of this syllogism. I say that it is not true in the general and unqualified way in which it is stated. I say that an examination may be lawful for certain purposes and be lawfully conducted with these purposes in view; and yet not be admissible in evidence against the party charged when upon his trial on a criminal charge, even if that charge be founded on the matters before lawfully inquired into. We have here on the one hand an undisputed and indisputable maxim of the common law that no man shall be bound to accuse himself; on the other we have a statute not in terms professing to abrogate this maxim, but authorising commissioners of bankrupts to examine a bankrupt 'touching all matters relating to concealment of his lands, tenements, goods, money or debts'; and subjecting him to imprisonment indefinitely, without bail, if he refuse to answer. The same statute makes it a felony, punishable with transportation for life, for a bankrupt to conceal any part of his real or personal estate to the value of £10, with intent to defraud his creditors. How, then, upon general principles, are we to proceed in a seeming conflict between the common law and these provisions of the statute? Not, I apprehend, by assuming at once that there is a real conflict, and sacrificing the common law; but by carefully examining whether the two may not be reconciled, and full effect be given to both; and for this purpose it is most material to ascertain with what intent, and for what object, the bankrupt is compellable to undergo this examination, and to answer the questions put. If, for example, it should appear that he was to be examined with a view of procuring evidence against him on a criminal charge, instituted, or to be instituted, whatever one might think of the justice of such an enactment it would be idle to contend that it had not abrogated pro tanto the common law. If, on the other hand, it should be clear that the examination was authorised solely for the better discovery of the bankrupt's estate, and the bringing it into distribution amongst his creditors – that it would be unlawful to examine him for any other purpose – that he might lawfully refuse to answer any questions put merely for the purpose of extracting evidence against him on a criminal charge, then I conceive that you would be far advanced on your way to a conclusion which will prevent the statute from breaking in upon the common law.

Alderson B: I have nothing to say to what has fallen from my Brother Coleridge but this – that my judgment proceeds upon the ground, that if you make a thing lawful to be done, it is lawful in all its consequences; and one of its consequences is, that what may be stated by a person in a lawful examination, may be received in evidence against him. That is quite settled and comfortable to a most important maxim of English law.

This decision has been approved by the Privy Council (*R v Coote* (1873) LR 4 PC 599); the Court of Crown Cases Reserved (*R v Erdheim* [1896] 2 QB 260, [1895–9] All ER Rep 610); the Court of Appeal (*Customs and Excise Comrs v Ingram* [1948] 1 All ER 927, CA) and by dicta in the House of Lords in *Harz's Case*.

Commissioners of Customs and Excise v Harz
[1967] 1 AC 760, [1967] 1 All ER 177, HL

The defendants were accused of defrauding the Revenue of purchase tax; the main evidence against them consisted of statements obtained under threat of prosecution for infringing s 24(6) of the Purchase Tax Act 1963. The House of Lords stated that these statements would have been admissible if obtained in accordance with the statute.

Lord Reid: On 27 February, 1963, customs officers took possession of a number of Lee's books and began to question Harz and others. Harz said: 'We are not talking,' but the officers told him that he would be prosecuted if he did not answer. He gave certain answers on that occasion. On subsequent occasions, the last being in August, he and his solicitor, who was present, continued to believe that there was power to prosecute if he did not answer and in the course of long interrogations, one of which lasted more than three hours, he made certain incriminating admissions. I am of opinion that it must be held that this threat of prosecution was intended by the customs officers to apply and was thought by Harz to apply on all these occasions, and that this is a typical case of a suspected person being induced by a threat to make incriminating admissions. I think that it is clear that Harz would not have made these admissions if he had not been told that he must answer the officers' questions there and then and that if he refused he would be prosecuted.

In my opinion, the officers had no right to require Harz to submit to this prolonged interrogation and he could not have been prosecuted if he had refused to answer. The officers' power to interrogate was said to be derived from section 20(3) of the Finance Act, 1946 (now replaced by section 24(6) of the Purchase Tax 1963), which provides as follows:

'Every person concerned with the purchase or importation of goods, or with the application to goods of any process of manufacture, or with dealings with imported goods, shall furnish to the commissioners, within such time and in such form as they may require, information relating to the goods, or to the purchase or importation of them or to the application of any process of manufacture to them, or to dealings with them as they may specify, and shall, upon demand made by any officer or other person authorised in that behalf by the commissioners, produce any books or accounts or other documents of whatever nature relating thereto for inspection by that officer or person at such time and place as that officer or person may require.'

There is here a clear distinction between the right of an officer to demand production of documents and the right of the commissioners to require information to be furnished at such time and in such manner as they may require. The right of the officer is to require immediate production of documents and if the trader fails to produce documents in his possession of the kinds demanded he can be prosecuted. No doubt the officer can ask questions relating to documents of the kinds which he had demanded and the trader's answer or refusal to answer may be admissible in evidence. But the prosecution will not be for refusal to answer questions; it will be for refusal to produce documents, and I can see nothing to require the trader to give answers which may incriminate him.

The right of the commissioners to require information is quite different. If a demand for information is made in the proper manner, the trader is bound to answer the demand within the time and in the form required, whether or not the answer may tend to incriminate him, and, if he fails to comply with the demand, he can be prosecuted. If he answers falsely he can be prosecuted for that and if he answers in such a manner as to incriminate himself I can see no reason why his answer should not be used against him. Some statutes expressly provide that incriminating answers may be used against the person who gives them and some statutes expressly provide that they may not. Where, as here, there is no such express provision the question whether such answers are admissible evidence must depend on the proper construction of the particular statute. Although I need not decide the point, it seems to me to be reasonably clear that incriminating answers to a proper demand under this section must be admissible if the statutory provision is to achieve its obvious purpose.

If the admission with which the appeal is concerned had been obtained by a proper exercise of this power of the commissioners they might well have been admissible in evidence in this prosecution. It was argued in the first place that the officers who conducted the interrogation had not been properly authorised by the commissioners to exercise their powers. Probably they had not, but I need not pursue that because I think that the respondents succeed in their second argument. The trader is only bound to furnish information within such time and in such form as the commissioners require. The information will often be complicated and the commissioners can be relied on to fix a reasonable time. If the information required is simple and easily provided, the time required may be short. But I do not think that this entitles the commissioners to send a representative to confront the trader, put questions to him orally and demand oral answers on the spot. And I am certainly of opinion that it does not entitle them to send their representative to subject the trader to a prolonged interrogation in the nature of a cross-examination. This provision is in sharp contrast with provisions which expressly entitle officers to question persons with regard to particular matters, for example, to question passengers entering the country with regard to their luggage. When it is intended that officers shall obtain information by asking oral questions that is made plain in the statute. The Solicitor-General was asked whether he was aware of any other case in which a government department claimed the right to send a representative to interrogate a person for hours on end under the sanction that he would be prosecuted if he failed to answer any question and that any incriminating answer which he might give under threat of prosecution for failing to answer could be used in evidence against him. But he was unable to cite any parallel case. I am not to be taken as saying that every inquisitorial procedure is inherently objectionable: this case may indicate the contrary. But if any such procedure were introduced it would certainly contain safeguards which are absent from the procedure which the appellants support in this case.

[Lords Morris of Borth-y-Gest, Hodson, Pearce and Wilberforce agreed.]

Stress has been placed on the presumption that Parliament does not intend to abrogate the privilege: *Hammond v Commonwealth of Australia* (1982) 152 CLR 188 and *Sorby v Commonwealth of Australia* (1983) 152 CLR 281 at 289, 309, 311 and 316. At 293–5 of the latter case Gibbs CJ held that the fact that legislation provides that a statement made by a witness before a Royal Commission cannot be used in evidence against him does not abrogate the privilege; at 311–12 Murphy J spoke to the same effect; cf Brennan J at 322 and *A-G Victoria v Riach* [1978] VR 301. For examples of modern cases construing legislation as abrogating the privilege, see *Re Jeffrey S Levitt Ltd* [1992] Ch 457, [1992] 2 All ER 509; *Bishopsgate Investment Ltd v Maxwell* [1993] Ch 1, [1992] 2 All ER 856, CA; *R v Kansal* [1993] QB 244, [1992] 3 All ER 844, CA (all on provisions of the Insolvency Act 1986); *R v Seelig* [1991] 4 All ER 429, [1992] 1 WLR 148, CA; *Re London United Investments plc* [1992] Ch 578, [1992] 2 All ER 842, CA; *Bank of England v Riley* [1992] Ch 475, [1992] 1 All ER 769, CA (all on provisions of the Companies Act 1985).

There are several arguments put against the *R v Scott* doctrine, some of which are put by Coleridge J in his dissenting judgment. See also (1971) 87 LQR 214 and [1971] Crim L Rev 13 at 24–34. The principal objections are these.

A court's attempt to give effect to as many of a statute's possible aims as it can is foolish and self-stultifying, because these aims often conflict among themselves. If the purposes of questioning a taxpayer are to recover the taxes due, investigate tax evasion with a view to future prevention, discover leads to other criminals and punish the taxpayer's dishonesty, they cannot all be achieved by direct questioning. The fear of criminal prosecution for the evasion will induce a man to stay silent or to lie, and if he is successful, none of the aims of the investigation will be carried out. It is true that there are punishments for silence, but these will usually be less than for the crime of tax evasion which is concealed. Indeed the twin dangers of punishment for silence and punishment for tax evasion will force the taxpayer to lie (*R v Pike* [1902] 1 KB 552). He still runs a risk of punishment for lying, but it will often be a remote risk because *ex hypothesi* the Commissioners do not yet have enough independently acquired evidence to make a successful prosecution for tax evasion likely, and therefore will not have enough to prove that the taxpayer is lying.

The following general approach for the interpretation of statutes which provide for compulsory questioning is suggested. A statute will often have several possible purposes to be collected from a reading of it as a whole. Thus the information obtained by the Commissioners under the Purchase Tax Act 1963, s 24(6), could be used to claim the full tax owed by the individual questioned; it could be used to help the authorities understand the processes of tax evasion with a view to prevention of this by future legislation; it could be used to prosecute accomplices of the informant; and it could be used to prosecute the informant himself. Clearly the first three possible aims can only be carried out by forcing the taxpayer to answer all the questions, and to that extent the privilege against self-incrimination is abrogated, both because of the express words of s 24(6) ('shall furnish') and because any other conclusion would nullify those aims. But are his answers admissible at his later criminal trial? If so, the privilege against self-incrimination is completely destroyed. So severe a result can be avoided by regarding the aim of recovering tax as the statute's major purpose; the minor and obscure aim of helping to convict the taxpayer clashes with the clear purposes of the privilege against self-incrimination, and cannot in the absence of clear words be allowed to take effect. The other minor aims of preventing future tax evasion and prosecuting accomplices can take effect, because they do not conflict with the privilege. So although the taxpayer may have had to confess crimes at his interrogation, no purpose served by the privilege has been thwarted. Any later criminal prosecution will be based on independently obtained evidence. The state will not be tempted to relax in its efforts to obtain such evidence. The taxpayer's tendency to tell unconscious falsehoods through fear will be lessened because he knows no harm will come of the examination, and there will be no inducement to commit perjury out of fear of later criminal punishment. Of course, if the statutory aim is clearly to prevail over the purposes of the privilege it must be given full effect. What is suggested is that the privilege should not be held to be discarded lightly in a given case.

See generally *Pyneboard Pty Ltd v Trade Practices Commission* (1983) 152 CLR 328; *Sorby v Commonwealth of Australia* (1983) 152 CLR 281.

In *R v Director of the Serious Fraud Office, ex p Smith* [1993] AC 1 at 32, [1992] 3 All ER 456 at 465, HL, Lord Mustill, with whom the rest of the House concurred, said:

'Given the diversity of immunities and of the policies underlying them . . . it is not enough to ask simply whether Parliament can have intended to abolish a long-standing right of silence. Rather, an essential starting-point must be to identify what variety of this right is being invoked, and what are the reasons for believing that the right in question ought at all costs to be maintained.'

QUESTIONS

1. Is the limitation of the privilege in civil cases to crimes under United Kingdom law only sound? Would not any abuse of the privilege by appeal to possible incrimination under foreign systems be controlled by using the *R v Boyes* test of whether the danger is 'imaginary and unsubstantial'? See *F F Seeley Nominees Pty Ltd v El Ar Initiations (UK) Ltd* (1990) 96 ALR 468 at

472-3, analysing the English cases.

2. Should corporations be able to claim the privilege? Should unincorporated associations be able to? Compare *Triplex Safety Glass Company Ltd v Lancegaye Safety Glass (1934) Ltd* [1939] 2 KB 395, [1939] 2 All ER 613, CA; *British Steel Corpn v Granada Television Ltd* [1981] AC 1096 at 1178, [1981] 1 All ER 417 at 462, HL, with *Hale v Henkel* 201 US 43 (1906); *Environment Protection Authority v Caltex Refining Co Pty Ltd* (1993) 178 CLR 477; *Trade Practices Commission v Abbco Iceworks Pty Ltd* (1994) 123 ALR 503; Evidence Acts 1995 (Cth and NSW) s 187; *British Steel Corpn v Granada Television Ltd* [1981] AC 1096 at 1127, [1981] 1 All ER 417 at 439, HL.

3. Should the privilege extend to a refusal to reveal one's facial or other bodily features?

4. What are the similarities and differences between the privilege and the confession rule? (see ch 8, post, and Wigmore, para 2266.)

5. Should witnesses be warned of the fact that they have the privilege? If so, what consequences should follow a failure to give the warning?

6. What inferences against the witness can be legitimately drawn from a claim of privilege? How can the trier of fact be prevented from drawing others?

7. Does the law satisfactorily control inferences against a party by reason of the privilege being claimed by a non-party witness? Should cross-examination attempting to show why the witness is silent and whether it reflects on either party be permitted?

8. Would an answer not in itself incriminatory but which enables the police to derive evidence of the witness's guilt from other sources fall within the privilege?

9. Should a witness be entitled to answer questions in chief respecting a particular matter but claim the privilege as to other questions in cross-examination on that matter?

10. How convincing are the justifications offered for the privilege?

11. Was *R v Scott* rightly decided? Should the principle of the decision be followed in future?

12. Is the privilege limited to judicial proceedings? See *Sorby v Commonwealth of Australia* (1983) 152 CLR 281 at 315–22 per Brennan J; cf *Pyneboard Pty Ltd v Trade Practices Commission* (1983) 152 CLR 328 at 337–41 per Mason ACJ, Wilson and Dawson JJ; *Police Service Board v Morris* (1985) 156 CLR 397.

13. Do the directors of a company have a privilege against answering questions tending to incriminate it? See *Rio Tinto Zinc Corpn v Westinghouse Electric Corpn* [1978] AC 547 at 617, 623, 637–8 and 652, [1978] 1 All ER 434 at 449, 460, 465 and 476. The officer of an unincorporated association has no privilege against answering questions tending to incriminate the association: *Rochfort v Trade Practices Commission* (1982) 153 CLR 134 at 147 and 150.

14. The privilege protects a person from a requirement to produce or identify or reveal the whereabouts of or explain the contents of incriminating documents, but it does not prevent the seizure under warrant of incriminating documents; it is not a privilege against incrimination, but a privilege against self-incrimination: *Controlled Consultants Pty Ltd v Comr for Corporate Affairs* (1985) 156 CLR 385 at 393.

CHAPTER 7

The Right to Silence

1 General

Sections 34-38 of the Criminal Justice and Public Order Act 1994 do not abolish the right of silence. They merely provide that, under certain circumstances, the trier of fact may draw proper inferences from the accused's silence. There are stringent preconditions, but, even when they are met, there remains the question of precisely *what* inferences are justifiably drawn from silence.

R v Director of the Serious Fraud Office, ex parte Smith
[1993] AC 1, [1992] 3 All ER 456, HL

Lord Mustill: . . . I turn . . . to 'the right of silence'. This expression arouses strong but unfocused feelings. In truth it does not denote any single right, but rather refers to a disparate group of immunities, which differ in nature, origin, incidence and importance, and also as to the extent to which they have already been encroached upon by statute. Amongst these may be identified:
(1) A general immunity, possessed by all persons and bodies, from being compelled on pain of punishment to answer questions posed by other persons or bodies.
(2) A general immunity, possessed by all persons and bodies, from being compelled on pain of punishment to answer questions the answer to which may incriminate them.
(3) A specific immunity, possessed by all persons under suspicion of criminal responsibility whilst being interviewed by police officers or others in similar positions of authority, from being compelled on pain of punishment to answer questions of any kind.
(4) A specific immunity, possessed by persons undergoing trial, from being compelled to give evidence, and from being compelled to answer questions put to them in the dock.
(5) A specific immunity, possessed by persons who have been charged with a criminal offence, from having questions material to the offence addressed to them by police officers or persons in a similar position of authority.
(6) A specific immunity (at least in certain circumstances which it is unnecessary to explore), possessed by accused persons undergoing trial, from having adverse comment made on any failure (a) to answer questions before the trial, or (b) to give evidence at the trial.
Each of these immunities is of great importance, but the fact that they are all important and that they are all concerned with the protection of citizens against the abuse of powers by those investigating crimes makes it easy to assume that they are all different ways of expressing the same principle, whereas in fact they are not. In particular it is necessary to keep distinct the motives which have caused them to become embedded in English law; otherwise objections to the curtailment of one immunity may draw a spurious reinforcement from association with other, and different immunities commonly grouped under the title of a 'right to silence' . . .

We must look briefly at these various motives. The first is a simple reflection of the common view that one person should so far as possible be entitled to tell another person to mind his own business. All civilised states recognise this assertion of personal liberty and privacy. Equally, although there may be pronounced disagreements between states, and between individual citizens within states, about where the line should be drawn, few would dispute that some curtailment of the liberty is indispensable to the stability of society; and even in the United Kingdom today our lives are permeated by enforceable duties to provide information on demand, created by Parliament and tolerated by the majority, albeit in some cases with reluctance.

Secondly, there is a long history of reaction against abuses of judicial interrogation. The Star Chamber and the Council had the power to administer the oath and to punish recusants; and literally to press confessions out of those under interrogation. Even after the abuses of the Star Chamber had been curbed the magistrates, who in the absence of a modern police force had some of the functions of a modern juge d'instruction, had power to interrogate the accused before trial. It seems that the use of such powers to obtain a compulsory response to interrogation gradually faded away, and in practice were replaced by a caution, well before the caution became mandatory in 1848. Nevertheless, although the misuse of judicial interrogation is now only a distant history, it seems to have left its mark on public perceptions of the entire subject: and indeed not just public perceptions, for in the recent past there have been several authoritative and eloquent judicial reminders of the abuses of our former inquisitorial system and the need to guard against their revival. Amongst these are the oft-cited dicta of Murphy J in *Hammond v Commonwealth of Australia* (1982) 152 CLR 188. It may however be noted that the immunity against judicial interrogation is no longer as complete as it was, for the abolition by the Criminal Evidence Act 1898 of the rule that the accused was not even a competent witness at his own trial opened up the possibility that if he did give evidence he would expose himself to questioning by counsel for the prosecution and in appropriate circumstances by the judge himself; and his privilege against self-incrimination whilst giving evidence was expressly removed by section 1(e) of the Act of 1898.

Next there is the instinct that it is contrary to fair play to put the accused in a position where he is exposed to punishment whatever he does. If he answers, he may condemn himself out of his own mouth; if he refuses he may be punished for his refusal: see Williams, pp 52-3.

Finally there is the desire to minimise the risk that an accused will be convicted on the strength of an untrue extra-judicial confession, to which the law gives effect by refusing to admit confessions in evidence except upon proof that they are [admissible]. This motive, which became prominent when inquisitorial methods waned and extra-judicial confessions became an important, and in many instances by far the most important, weapon in the prosecution's armoury, was particularly weighty at a time when the accused could not rebut or explain away the confession by giving evidence on his own behalf. Even now, nearly 100 years after that disability has been removed, the imprint of the old law is still clearly to be seen . . .

[Lords Templeman, Bridge, Ackner and Lowry agreed.]

Criminal Justice and Public Order Act 1994

34 (1) Where, in any proceedings against a person for an offence, evidence is given that the accused –
   (a) at any time before he was charged with the offence, on being questioned under caution by a constable trying to discover whether or by whom the offence had been committed, failed to mention any fact relied on in his defence in those proceedings; or
   (b) on being charged with the offence or officially informed that he might be prosecuted for it, failed to mention any such fact,
being a fact which in the circumstances existing at the time the accused could reasonably have been expected to mention when so questioned, charged or informed, as the case may be, subsection (2) below applies.
   (2) Where this subsection applies –
   (a) a magistrates' court, in deciding whether to [commit the accused for trial];
   (b) a judge, in deciding whether to grant an application made by the accused under –
      (i) section 6 of the Criminal Justice Act 1987 (application for dismissal of charge of serious fraud in respect of which notice of transfer has been given under section 4 of that Act); or
      (ii) paragraph 5 of Schedule 6 to the Criminal Justice Act 1991 (application for dismissal

of charge of violent or sexual offence involving child in respect of which notice of transfer has been given under section 53 of that Act);

(c)   the court, in determining whether there is a case to answer; and

(d)   the court or jury, in determining whether the accused is guilty of the offence charged,

may draw such inferences from the failure as appear proper.

(3)   Subject to any directions by the court, evidence tending to establish the failure may be given before or after evidence tending to establish the fact which the accused is alleged to have failed to mention.

(4)   This section applies in relation to questioning by persons (other than constables) charged with the duty of investigating offences or charging offenders as it applies in relation to questioning by constables; and in subsection (1) above 'officially informed' means informed by a constable or any such person.

(5)   This section does not –

(a)   prejudice the admissibility in evidence of the silence or other reaction of the accused in the face of anything said in his presence relating to the conduct in respect of which he is charged, in so far as evidence thereof would be admissible apart from this section; or

(b)   preclude the drawing of any inference from any such silence or other reaction of the accused which could properly be drawn apart from this section.

. . .

35   (1)   At the trial of any person who has attained the age of fourteen years for an offence, subsections (2) and (3) below apply unless –

(a)   the accused's guilt is not in issue; or

(b)   it appears to the court that the physical or mental condition of the accused makes it undesirable for him to give evidence;

but subsection (2) below does not apply if, at the conclusion of the evidence for the prosecution, his legal representative informs the court that the accused will give evidence or, where he is unrepresented, the court ascertains from him that he will give evidence.

(2)   Where this subsection applies, the court shall, at the conclusion of the evidence for the prosecution, satisfy itself (in the case of proceedings on indictment, in the presence of the jury) that the accused is aware that the stage has been reached at which evidence can be given for the defence and that he can, if he wishes, give evidence and that, if he chooses not to give evidence, or having been sworn, without good cause refuses to answer any question, it will be permissible for the court or jury to draw such inferences as appear proper from his failure to give evidence or his refusal, without good cause, to answer any question.

(3)   Where this subsection applies, the court or jury, in determining whether the accused is guilty of the offence charged, may draw such inferences as appear proper from the failure of the accused to give evidence or his refusal, without good cause, to answer any question.

(4)   This section does not render the accused compellable to give evidence on his own behalf, and he shall accordingly not be guilty of contempt of court by reason of a failure to do so.

(5)   For the purposes of this section a person who, having been sworn, refuses to answer any question shall be taken to do so without good cause unless –

(a)   he is entitled to refuse to answer the question by virtue of any enactment, whenever passed or made, or on the ground of privilege; or

(b)   the court in the exercise of its general discretion excuses him from answering it.

(6)   Where the age of any person is material for the purposes of subsection (1) above, his age shall for those purposes be taken to be that which appears to the court to be his age.

. . .

36   (1)   Where –

(a)   a person is arrested by a constable, and there is –

(i)   on his person; or

(ii)   in or on his clothing or footwear; or

(iii)   otherwise in his possession; or

(iv)   in any place in which he is at the time of his arrest,

any object, substance or mark, or there is any mark on any such object; and

(b)   that or another constable investigating the case reasonably believes that the presence of the object, substance or mark may be attributable to the participation of the person arrested in the commission of an offence specified by the constable; and

(c)   the constable informs the person arrested that he so believes, and requests him to account for the presence of the object, substance or mark; and

(d)   the person fails or refuses to do so,

then if, in any proceedings against the person for the offence so specified, evidence of those matters is given, subsection (2) below applies.

(2)   Where this subsection applies –

(a)   a magistrates' court, in deciding whether to [commit the accused for trial];

(b)   a judge, in deciding whether to grant an application made by the accused under –

    (i)   section 6 of the Criminal Justice Act 1987 (application for dismissal of charge of serious fraud in respect of which notice of transfer has been given under section 4 of that Act); or

    (ii)   paragraph 5 of Schedule 6 to the Criminal Justice Act 1991 (application for dismissal of charge of violent or sexual offence involving child in respect of which notice of transfer has been given under section 53 of that Act);

(c)   the court, in determining whether there is a case to answer; and

(d)   the court or jury, in determining whether the accused is guilty of the offence charged, may draw such inferences from the failure or refusal as appear proper.

(3)   Subsections (1) and (2) above apply to the condition of clothing or footwear as they apply to a substance or mark thereon.

(4)   Subsections (1) and (2) above do not apply unless the accused was told in ordinary language by the constable when making the request mentioned in subsection (1)(c) above what the effect of this section would be if he failed or refused to comply with the request.

(5)   This section applies in relation to officers of customs and excise as it applies in relation to constables.

(6)   This section does not preclude the drawing of any inference from a failure or refusal of the accused to account for the presence of an object, substance or mark or from the condition of clothing or footwear which could properly be drawn apart from this section.

. . .

37   (1)   Where –

(a)   a person arrested by a constable was found by him at a place at or about the time the offence for which he was arrested is alleged to have been committed; and

(b)   that or another constable investigating the offence reasonably believes that the presence of the person at that place and at that time may be attributable to his participation in the commission of the offence; and

(c)   the constable informs the person that he so believes, and requests him to account for that presence; and

(d)   the person fails or refuses to do so,

then if, in any proceedings against the person for the offence, evidence of those matters is given, subsection (2) below applies.

(2)   Where this subsection applies –

(a)   a magistrates' court, in deciding whether to [commit the accused for trial];

(b)   a judge, in deciding whether to grant an application made by the accused under –

    (i)   section 6 of the Criminal Justice Act 1987 (application for dismissal of charge of serious fraud in respect of which notice of transfer has been given under section 4 of that Act);

    (ii)   paragraph 5 of Schedule 6 to the Criminal Justice Act 1991 (application for dismissal of charge of violent or sexual offence involving child in respect of which notice of transfer has been given under section 53 of that Act);

(c)   the court, in determining whether there is a case to answer; and

(d)   the court or jury, in determining whether the accused is guilty of the offence charged, may draw such inferences from the failure or refusal as appear proper.

(3)   Subsections (1) and (2) do not apply unless the accused was told in ordinary language by the constable when making the request mentioned in subsection (1)(c) above what the effect of this section would be if he failed or refused to comply with the request.

(4)   This section applies in relation to officers of customs and excise as it applies in relation to constables.

(5)   This section does not preclude the drawing of any inference from a failure or refusal of the accused to account for his presence at a place which could properly be drawn apart from this section.

. . .

38 (1)   In sections 34, 35, 36 and 37 of this Act –
'legal representative' means an authorised advocate or authorised litigator, as defined by section 119(1) of the Courts and Legal Services Act 1990; and 'place' includes any building or part of a building, any vehicle, vessel, aircraft or hovercraft and any other place whatsoever.

(2)   In sections 34(2), 35(3), 36(2) and 37(2), references to an offence charged include references to any other offence of which the accused could lawfully be convicted on that charge.

(3)   A person shall not have the proceedings against him transferred to the Crown Court for trial, have a case to answer or be convicted of an offence solely on an inference drawn from such a failure or refusal as is mentioned in section 34(2), 35(3), 36(2) or 37(2).

(4)   A judge shall not refuse to grant such an application as is mentioned in section 34(2)(*b*), 36(2)(*b*) and 37(2)(*b*) solely on an inference drawn from such a failure as is mentioned in section 34(2), 36(2) or 37(2).

(5)   Nothing in sections 34, 35, 36 or 37 prejudices the operation of a provision of any enactment which provides (in whatever words) that any answer or evidence given by a person in specified circumstances shall not be admissible in evidence against him or some other person in any proceedings or class of proceedings (however described, and whether civil or criminal).

In this subsection, the reference to giving evidence is a reference to giving evidence in any manner, whether by furnishing information, making discovery, producing documents or otherwise.

(6)   Nothing in sections 34, 35, 36 or 37 prejudices any power of a court, in any proceedings, to exclude evidence (whether by preventing questions being put or otherwise) at its discretion.

R v Cowan   [1996] QB 373, [1995] 4 All ER 939, CA

Lord Taylor CJ [giving the judgment of the court]: . . . [I]t is argued that section 35 either breaches or verges on breaching long established principles. Although, therefore, it is conceded that some effect must be given to the enactment, it should be applied only exceptionally and not in the general run of cases. [Counsel for the accused] submits that the section constitutes an infringement of the defendant's right of silence. By permitting a court or jury to draw an adverse inference should the defendant remain silent at trial, it is submitted that his free choice is inhibited.

It should be made clear that the right of silence remains. It is not abolished by the section; on the contrary, subsection (4) expressly preserves it. As to inhibitions affecting a defendant's decision to testify or not, some existed before the Act of 1994. On the one hand, a defendant whose case involved an attack on the character of a prosecution witness could well be inhibited from giving evidence by fear of cross-examination as to his own record. On the other hand, in certain cases, judges were entitled to comment on the defendant's failure to testify: *R v Martinez-Tobon* [1994] 2 All ER 90, [1994] 1 WLR 388, CA. Arguably, this put pressure on a defendant to give evidence. Even in a case calling only for the classic direction in *R v Bathurst* [1968] 2 QB 99, [1968] 1 All ER 1175, CA, a defendant might be inhibited from remaining silent for fear the jury would hold it against him that he chose to leave the prosecution evidence uncontradicted.

It is further argued that the section alters the burden of proof or 'waters it down' to use [counsel's] phrase. The requirement that the defendant give evidence on pain of an adverse inference being drawn is said to put a burden on him to testify if he wishes to avoid conviction.

In our view that argument is misconceived. First, the prosecution have to establish a prima facie case before any question of the defendant testifying is raised. Secondly, [there is] section 38(3) of the Act of 1994. . . . Thus the court or jury is prohibited from convicting solely because of an inference drawn from the defendant's silence. Thirdly, the burden of proving guilt to the required standard remains on the prosecution throughout. The effect of section 35 is that the court or jury may regard the inference from failure to testify as, in effect, a further evidential factor in support of the prosecution case. It cannot be the only factor to justify a conviction and the totality of the evidence must prove guilt beyond reasonable doubt . . .

[A]part from the mandatory exceptions in section 35(1), it will be open to a court to decline to draw an adverse inference from silence at trial and for a judge to direct or advise a jury against drawing such inference if the circumstances of the case justify such a course. But in our view there would need to be either some evidential basis for doing so or some exceptional factors in the case making that a fair course to take. It must be stressed that the inferences permitted by the section are only such 'as appear proper'. The use of that phrase was no doubt intended to leave a broad discretion to a trial judge to decide in all the circumstances whether any proper inference is capable of being drawn by the jury. If not he should tell them so; otherwise it is for the jury to decide whether in fact an inference should properly be drawn.

By way of guidance, a specimen direction has been suggested by the Judicial Studies Board in the following terms:

'The defendant has not given evidence. That is his right. But, as he has been told, the law is that you may draw such inferences as appear proper from his failure to do so. Failure to give evidence on its own cannot prove guilt but depending on the circumstances, you may hold his failure against him when deciding whether he is guilty. [There is evidence before you on the basis of which the defendant's advocate invites you not to hold it against the defendant that he has not given evidence before you namely . . . If you think that because of this evidence you should not hold it against the defendant that he has not given evidence, do not do so.] But if the evidence he relies on presents no adequate explanation for his absence from the witness box then you may hold his failure to give evidence against him. You do not have to do so. What proper inferences can you draw from the defendant's decision not to give evidence before you? If you conclude that there is a case for him to answer, you may think that the defendant would have gone into the witness box to give you an explanation for or an answer to the case against him. If the only sensible explanation for his decision not to give evidence is that he has no answer to the case against him, or none that could have stood up to cross-examination, then it would be open to you to hold against him his failure to give evidence. It is for you to decide whether it is fair to do so.' (The words in square brackets are to be used only where there is *evidence*.)

We consider that the specimen direction is in general terms a sound guide. It may be necessary to adapt or add to it in the particular circumstances of an individual case. But there are certain essentials which we would highlight. (1) The judge will have told the jury that the burden of proof remains upon the prosecution throughout and what the required standard is. (2) It is necessary for the judge to make clear to the jury that the defendant is entitled to remain silent. That is his right and his choice. The right of silence remains. (3) An inference from failure to give evidence cannot on its own prove guilt. That is expressly stated in section 38(3) of the Act. (4) Therefore, the jury must be satisfied that the prosecution have established a case to answer before drawing any inferences from silence. Of course, the judge must have thought so or the question whether the defendant was to give evidence would not have arisen. But the jury may not believe the witnesses whose evidence the judge considered sufficient to raise a prima facie case. It must therefore be made clear to them that they must find there to be a case to answer on the prosecution evidence before drawing an adverse inference from the defendant's silence. (5) If, despite any evidence relied upon to explain his silence or in the absence of any such evidence, the jury conclude the silence can only sensibly be attributed to the defendant's having no answer or none that would stand up to cross-examination, they may draw an adverse inference.

It is not possible to anticipate all the circumstances in which a judge might think it right to direct or advise a jury against drawing an adverse inference. Nor would it be wise even to give examples as each case must turn on its own facts. As Kelly LJ said in *R v McLernon* (1990) 10 NIJB 91 (a Northern Ireland case concerning provisions of article 4 of the Criminal Evidence (Northern Ireland) Order 1988 (SI No 1987 (NI20)), which are in terms similar to but stronger than those of section 35 of the Act of 1994), at p 102:

'the court has then a complete discretion as to whether inferences should be drawn or not. In these circumstances it is a matter for the court in any criminal case (1) to decide whether to draw inferences or not; and (2) if it decides to draw inferences what their nature, extent and degree of adversity, if any, may be. It would be improper and indeed quite unwise for any court to set out the bounds of either steps (1) or (2). Their application will depend on factors peculiar to the individual case.'

Kelly LJ was considering a trial without a jury, but we regard his remarks as applicable equally to the directions or advice a judge needs to give in his summing up to a jury.

We were referred to the opinion of the Commission of Human Rights in *Murray v United Kingdom* (1994) 18 EHRR CD 1. There, similar arguments to those advanced here were considered in relation to a 'judge alone' trial from Northern Ireland said to involve breaches of article 6 of the European Convention on Human Rights. We stress that decisions of the Commission and indeed those of the European Court of Human Rights itself are not binding upon this court. They are of assistance to resolve any ambiguity in our domestic law, but here we find no ambiguity in section 35. Nevertheless, the Commission's observations are of interest. Dealing with article 4 of the Northern Ireland Order of 1988, the Commission said, at p CD 9:

> 'Inferences from a failure to give explanations or evidence in court only become permissible under the Order when there is a prima facie case, ie the prosecution has submitted material which might lead to the conviction of the accused. It is apparent that, if the prosecution fails to make such a case to the court's satisfaction, the question of inferences will never arise. Moreover the commission is satisfied that the burden of proof remains on the prosecution throughout to prove an accused's guilt beyond a reasonable doubt. However, where a prima facie case has been presented to the court certain conclusions may always be drawn from the failure of the accused to rebut in defence the evidence against him. Further, the commission notes that a judge is not required to draw inferences and may only draw such inferences, and such degree of inferences, as may be proper.'

In a partially dissenting opinion, Mr. Nicholas Bratza sought, at p CD 16, to distinguish 'judge alone' cases where the judge's reasons for drawing inferences could be reviewed from jury cases where they could not. However, juries in criminal trials are required to draw inferences in numerous situations and provided that the judge gives them proper directions, we see no reason why the passage quoted from the Commission's opinion above should not apply equally to jury trials.

We wish to stress, moreover, that this court will not lightly interfere with a judge's exercise of discretion to direct or advise the jury as to the drawing of inferences from silence and as to the nature, extent and degree of such inferences. He is in the best position to have the feel of the case and so long as he gives the jury adequate directions of law as indicated above and leaves the decision to them, this court will be slow to substitute its view for his . . .

NOTES

1. Despite what Lord Taylor says in the passage extracted from *R v Cowan*, it is perhaps better to regard the silence (or failure to answer questions) itself not as evidence but as part of the matrix within which the other evidence in the case is assessed. Under ss 34, 36 and 37, however, there will need to be evidence that the accused was silent, which evidence is no doubt amenable to exclusion under s 78 of the Police and Criminal Evidence Act 1984: see s 38(6) and, generally, ch 9.2.

2. An appropriate form of words to be used by the judge on being informed by counsel that the accused does not intend to give evidence is set out in *Practice Note (Crown Court: Defendant's Evidence)* [1995] 2 All ER 499, [1995] 1 WLR 657, CA. The form there suggested was held in *R v Cowan* not to breach legal professional privilege.

3. The general caution used by those investigating offences has been reworded to include a warning about the possible consequences of silence. See Code C, para 10.4, in ch 8.3. Paragraphs 10.5A–C cover the procedure to be used in complying with ss 36(4) and 37(3), and require the interviewing officer to tell the suspect in ordinary language (a) what offence he is investigating; (b) what fact he is asking the suspect to account for; (c) that he believes this fact may be due to the suspect's taking part in the commission of the offence in question; (d) that a court may draw a proper inference if he fails or refuses to account for the fact about which he is being questioned; (e) that a record is being made of the interview and that it may be given in evidence if he is brought to trial. Even if this procedure is followed, there may be scope for investigation of whether the officer's belief was 'reasonable', before the court can be satisfied that the preconditions for drawing proper inferences have been met. Notice that the definition of 'place' for the purposes of s 37 in particular is very wide - wide enough for example to include a town. It is not a precondition under this section that the suspect be a trespasser in the place his presence in which he is required to explain.

4. For the Northern Ireland experience, see especially Jackson, 40 NILQ 105 (1989), [1991] Crim LR 404, 44 NILQ 103 (1993) and [1995] Crim LR 587, and *Murray v DPP* [1994] 1 WLR 1, HL.

Except as provided by certain statutes, there is no duty in English law to answer the out-of-court questions of the police or anyone else. Silence is not punishable: in this sense there is a right to silence. But silence may form the basis of certain inferences against a party. Three kinds of reasoning may be involved.

First, his silence may be taken as consent to whatever has been said to him; as an implied admission. This inference arises where a denial would be expected if the statement was false. Here silence operates rather like a nod; it is as if the party did not think it worth while wasting words in assenting to what he and the speaker know is obvious.

Secondly, silence may be taken, by itself or with other evidence, as a sign that the party is conscious of guilt or liability which he may be trying to hide. In this sense silence is a piece of conduct, like a lie or other interference with the course of justice, which operates as an implied admission that the party's case is bad. This is often confused with the first kind of implied admission but it is clearly different from it. The first kind of admission amounts to agreement with what is said; whereas the latter need not entail agreement with what is said, because the guilt evidenced may relate to some other crime. By the first kind of silence the party intends to convey agreement with what is said; by the second, he does not intend to convey agreement but shows a consciousness of guilt despite himself. Further, in the second case the statement made to the party may in fact not be strictly or even substantially true, but may remind the party of his guilt so that he then displays it. Hence the statement would not logically (as in the first case) be evidence of its truth, but would simply tend to prove that the party was guilty of some misconduct. If a man is accused of killing A and B and is silent, and in fact there is evidence that he killed A and C, his silence may amount to an assent to killing A and a sign that he is conscious of his guilt of killing C.

A slightly different form of this 'consciousness of guilt' reasoning may be used when the accused is silent in the face of an accusation but advances a defence at his trial. An inference is drawn from the belatedness of the defence to a consciousness at the time of the accusation that he has no true defence. In other words, though normally one may infer guilt from silence at the very moment of silence, sometimes the occurrence of later events permits the inference because they change the character of the silence.

The third inference takes a number of forms, but essentially it is that silence makes any defence advanced difficult to believe, so that the opposing case, being uncontradicted, becomes stronger. The difficulty of believing the defence may exist because the failure to disclose it until trial prevents any checking of it or because it has the appearance of being an afterthought, or because it is unsupported by the sworn evidence, tested in cross-examination, of one who is best able to support it. Plainly the distinction between this third inference and the first two, between using silence to weaken the defence case and *thus* strengthen the prosecution's, and using it directly to strengthen the prosecution's, is subtle, though real, and not easy to understand.

Sometimes the three inferences may all be drawn from a given set of facts; sometimes none can. Assume that a parent accuses a teacher of stealing money from a pupil's wallet at 6 pm on Monday, and that the teacher says nothing but bursts into tears. At the trial six weeks later he alleges for the first time that on Monday at 6 pm he was in a pub with friends. It may be possible legitimately to make the following inferences. The teacher admits guilt by not denying the outrageous charge at once as an innocent man would; the teacher's silent and ashamed demeanour indicates a consciousness of guilt of this and similar crimes; the alibi is unsupported because the friends cannot now remember whether on that day the accused drank with them as he sometimes did, and so the inferences from the prosecution's evidence become stronger. Changes in the facts will entail changes in the possible inferences.

The problem is that it is often dangerous to draw these inferences. Silence is quite unlike an express admission or even such an implied admission as a lie, or flight, or interference with the course of justice by destruction of evidence; silence is equivocal. A man may be silent in the face of an accusation for many reasons other than guilt. He may not have heard or understood what was said; he may not consider the charge to have been addressed to him; he may be silent because he is attempting to work out the meaning of an ambiguous statement. The accusation may be so sudden as to make him silent through confusion, as where he has just woken up. He may fear misreporting of any reply he makes; he may be shocked into silence by a false but serious charge; he may contemptuously consider it beneath his dignity to begin a debate about baseless and dishonourable accusations. He may not answer because he lacks knowledge of the matter in question. He may fear that to protest too much will be taken as a sign of guilt. He may believe he has a right of silence of which he wishes to avail himself, perhaps because he thinks an early disclosure of his defence will enable the other side to interfere with his witnesses. He may be silent because he wishes to protect others or to avoid disclosing discreditable but irrelevant facts about himself or others. Further, human reactions vary so much; the guilty may deny guilt strongly while the innocent stay silent. Shaw CJ once told a Massachusetts jury: 'Have you any experience that an innocent man, stunned under the mere imputation of such a charge though conscious of innocence, will always appear calm and collected? Or that a guilty man who, by knowledge of his danger, might be somewhat braced up for the consequences, would always appear agitated? Or the reverse? Judge you concerning it.' (*Webster's Trial*, Bemis' Rep 486; quoted by Wigmore, para 273.)

Another difficulty is determining how much of a statement a man approves by being silent – all or only part? If a man charged with murder pleads self-defence, and also denies that he has the mens rea for murder, what follows from his silence? Do we infer that he had mens rea and justification, or one, or the other? Common experience will often suggest inferences from silence, but will more often require extreme caution.

To what extent are inferences of the types discussed above justifiable? This is one of the most difficult questions in the law of evidence. What inferences can properly be drawn where a defendant's counsel raises a defence at the trial (which may or may not be supported by his sworn testimony) not mentioned by the defendant earlier? What inferences can properly be drawn from silence at the trial (whether or not the defendant was silent before the trial)?

2 Inferences from out of court silence

R v Christie   [1914] AC 545, [1914–15] All ER Rep 63, HL

A small boy said in the presence of the accused that the latter had indecently assaulted him. The accused said, 'I am innocent.'

The trial judge admitted this evidence. The Court of Criminal Appeal quashed the conviction on the ground that the evidence was wrongly admitted. The House of Lords, while dismissing the appeal on other grounds, held that the evidence was admissible.

Lord Atkinson: [T]he rule of law undoubtedly is that a statement made in the presence of an accused person, even upon an occasion which should be expected reasonably to call for some explanation or denial from him, is not evidence against him of the facts stated save so far as he accepts the statement, so as to make it, in effect, his own. If he accepts the statement in part only, then to that extent alone does it become his statement. He may accept the statement by word or conduct, action or demeanour, and it is the function of the jury which tries the case to determine whether his words, action, conduct, or demeanour at the time when a statement was made amounts to an acceptance of it in whole or in part. It by no means follows, I think, that a mere denial by the accused of the facts mentioned in the statement necessarily renders the statement inadmissible, because he may deny the statement in such a manner and under such circumstances as may lead a jury to disbelieve him, and constitute evidence from which an acknowledgment may be inferred by them.

Of course, if at the end of the case the presiding judge should be of opinion that no evidence has been given upon which the jury could reasonably find that the accused had accepted the statement so as to make it in whole or in part his own, the judge can instruct the jury to disregard the statement entirely. It is said that, despite this direction, grave injustice might be done to the accused, inasmuch as the jury, having once heard the statement, could not, or would not, rid their mind of it. It is, therefore, in the application of the rule that the difficulty arises. The question then is this: Is it to be taken as a rule of law that such a statement is not to be admitted in evidence until a foundation has been laid for its admission by proof of facts from which, in the opinion of the presiding judge, a jury might reasonably draw the inference that the accused had so accepted the statement as to make it in whole or in part his own, or is to be laid down that the prosecutor is entitled to give the statement in evidence in the first instance, leaving it to the presiding judge, in case no such evidence as the above mentioned should be ultimately produced, to tell the jury to disregard the statement altogether?

In my view the former is not a rule of law, but it is, I think, a rule which, in the interest of justice, it might be most prudent and proper to follow as a rule of practice.

Lord Moulton: . . . [T]he deciding question is whether the evidence of the whole occurrence is relevant or not. If the prisoner admits the charge the evidence is obviously relevant. If he denies it, it may or may not be relevant. For instance, if he is charged with a violent assault and denies that he committed it, that fact might be distinctly relevant if at the trial his defence was that he did commit the act, but that it was in self-defence. The evidential value of the occurrence depends entirely on the behaviour of the prisoner, for the fact that some one makes a statement to him subsequently to the commission of the crime cannot in itself have any value as evidence for or against him. The only evidence for or against him is his behaviour in response to the charge, but I can see no justification for laying down as a rule of law that any particular form of response, whether of a positive or negative character, is such that it cannot in some circumstances have an evidential value. I am, therefore, of opinion that there is no rule of law that evidence cannot be given of the accused being charged with the offence and of his behaviour on hearing such charge where that behaviour amounts to a denial of his guilt . . .

But while I am of opinion that there is no such rule of law, I am of opinion that the evidential value of the behaviour of the accused where he denies the charge is very small either for or against him, whereas the effect on the minds of the jury of his being publicly or repeatedly charged to his face with the crime might seriously prejudice the fairness of his trial.

Lord Reading: A statement made in the presence of one of the parties to a civil action may be given in evidence against him if it is relevant to any of the matters in issue. And equally such a statement made in the presence of the accused may be given in evidence against him at his trial.

In general, such evidence can have little or no value in its direct bearing on the case unless the accused, upon hearing the statement, by conduct and demeanour, or by the answer made by him, or in certain circumstances by the refraining from an answer, acknowledged the truth of the statement either in whole or in part, or did or said something from which the jury could infer such an acknowledgment, for if he acknowledged its truth, he accepted it as his own statement of the facts . . .

It might well be that the prosecution wished to give evidence of such a statement in order to prove the conduct and demeanour of the accused when hearing the statement as a relevant fact in the particular case, notwithstanding that it did not amount either to an acknowledgment or some evidence of an acknowledgment of any part of the truth of the statement. I think it impossible to lay down any general rule to be applied to all such cases, save the principle of strict law to which I have referred.

[Viscount Haldane LC and Lords Dunedin and Parker of Waddington concurred.]

R v Grills   (1910) 11 CLR 400

Isaacs J [in the High Court of Australia]: It is an elementary rule of law, going to the very foundation of justice, that no man shall be adjudged to be guilty of a crime upon evidence of another person's previous assertion. It matters not whether the assertion was made in the absence or the presence of the accused, as a mere assertion it cannot be regarded as any proof of the culpability of the accused or any confirmation of his accusers. But it is evident that upon such an assertion being made, and equally whether in the accused's absence or presence, he may admit its truth, and if he does, then it becomes evidence against him of his guilt, not because another has said it, but because of the admission. It is then equivalent to his own statement, and is receivable in that character. And it is further manifest that the acknowledgment of its correctness may be made in an infinite variety of ways. There may be an express and unqualified admission, or there may be a guarded admission, or there may be no direct but merely an implied acknowledgment, or there may be conduct, active or passive, positive or negative, from which, having regard to the ordinary workings of human nature, a total denial may be considered by reasonable men to be precluded, because, if innocence existed, an unequivocal or a qualified denial would in such a situation be expected.

Hall v R   [1971] 1 All ER 322, [1971] 1 WLR 298, PC

The accused was convicted of unlawful possession of ganja. A policeman told him after the search of his home which discovered the ganja that a co-accused had said the ganja belonged to him. He remained silent. He appealed to the Privy Council.

Lord Diplock: It is a clear and widely-known principle of the common law in Jamaica, as in England, that person is entitled to refrain from answering a question put to him for the purpose of discovering whether he had committed a criminal offence. A fortiori he is under no obligation to comment when he is informed that someone else has accused him of an offence. It may be that in very exceptional circumstances an inference may be drawn from a failure to give an explanation or a disclaimer, but in their Lordships' view silence alone on being informed by a police officer that someone else has made an accusation against him cannot give rise to an inference that the person to whom this information is communicated accepts the truth of the accusation. This is well established by many authorities such as *R v Whitehead* [1929] 1 KB 99, [1928] All ER Rep 186, CCA and *R v Keeling* [1942] 1 All ER 507, CCA. Counsel has sought to distinguish these cases on the ground that in them the accused had already been cautioned and told in terms that he was not obliged to reply. Reliance was placed on the earlier case of *R v Feigenbaum* [1919] 1 KB 431, [1918–19] All ER Rep 489, CCA, where the accused's silence when told of the accusation made against him by some children was held to be capable of amounting to corroboration of their evidence. It was submitted that the distinction between *R v Feigenbaum* and the later cases was that no caution had been administered at the time at which the accused was informed of the accusation. The correctness of the decision in *R v Feigenbaum* was doubted in *R v Keeling*. In their Lordships' view the distinction sought to be made is not a valid one and *R v Feigenbaum* ought not to be followed. The caution merely serves to remind the accused of a right which he already possesses at common law. The fact that in a particular case he has not been reminded of it is no ground for inferring that his silence was not in exercise of that right, but was an acknowledgement of the truth of the accusation.

See also *R v Salahattin* [1983] VR 521.

A   SILENCE AS CONSENT

Normally the trier of fact may draw the inference that the silence of the party in the face of the accusation is consent to it if this is open as a matter of fact, and the judge may give a direction to this effect. The exception to the rule is where the accusation is made in the presence of a policeman to an accused person; the Privy Council held in *Hall v R* (supra) that a blanket rule of prudence prevents the inference being drawn, whether or not the policeman cautioned the accused that he had a right to stay silent. Its justification is that in many cases innocent accused persons may fear the consequences of speaking and do not feel psychologically at liberty to do so. *Hall v R* was disapproved in *R v Chandler* [1976] 3 All ER 105, [1976] 1 WLR 585, CA, and distinguished by the Privy Council in *Parkes v R* [1976] 3 All ER 380, [1976] 1 WLR 1251, PC. *R v Chandler* was not favoured over *Hall v R* by the New Zealand Court of Appeal in *R v Duffy* [1979] 2 NZLR 432, CA.

In cases where the inference may be drawn, the test is whether a denial could reasonably be expected in the circumstances. The circumstances of a business relationship commonly permit the inference to be drawn; a defendant's silence in the face of correspondence becomes much more relevant in business cases than in affiliation cases. But in affiliation cases, in the absence of such special circumstances as a threat of legal action if there is no reply, or where the girl's father and the putative father are related, it is most unlikely that silence will prove paternity (*Thomas v Jones* [1921] 1 KB 22, [1920] All ER Rep 462, CA). It is much more natural to reply to accusations made publicly to one's face than to those in letters. There are many more reasons for not replying to letters than for silence – laziness, the time and money used, a dislike for or lack of facility in writing, the urgency of other affairs, a desire to discourage importunity. And there are reasons of policy against allowing evidence to be acquired in this way just as there are against 'inertia sellers'. Holmes J once said that a man can in this way 'no more impose a duty to answer a charge than he can impose a duty to pay by selling goods' (*AB Leach & Co v Peirson* 275 US 120 at 128 (1927)).

Regard must be paid to the status of the accuser. It is futile to argue with a madman, a drunk, a baby, or an hysterical mother whose child has just been run over (*Thatcher v Charles* (1961) 104 CLR 57). Where the accuser was on her deathbed the accused's silence was not evidence, partly because it was inappropriate to contradict her in such circumstances and partly because the accused was relying on the presence of his solicitor for protection (*R v Mitchell* (1892) 17 Cox CC 503). Accusations among relatives are often held to call for an answer because there are less likely to be inhibitions against speaking. If the party is in some respect superior to his accuser, silence may be due to contempt rather than consent, and officious busybodies who have little to do with the relevant events need not be answered.

Another factor is the situation of the party charged and the circumstances surrounding the charging. A man is not expected to speak after an accident if he is physically injured or shocked (*Thatcher v Charles* (1961) 104 CLR 57). Silence on being identified as a criminal is not an admission if the accused does not know what crime he is supposed to have committed, or the accusation does not relate to the appropriate issue. Windeyer J once said: 'A failure to answer an accusation "You drive too fast round here" could hardly be an admission by the appellant that he ought not to have backed his car where and when he did' (*Thatcher v Charles* (ibid), at 70). If the party's attempts to deny accusations are inhibited by the efforts of others present or by the need for decorum and orderly procedure in formal inquiries, silence is of no weight. A husband's failure to deny his wife's claim that marital relations had ceased would not be an admission; it is reasonable not to discuss intimate problems in public.

When will an indignant reply be expected? One test is the seriousness of an accusation, eg a charge of incest by a daughter to her father (*R v Power* [1940] QSR 111), or a breach of promise of marriage (*Bessela v Stern* (1877) 2 CPD 265, CA). Another is where there is more than a mere charge of crime, as in *R v Cramp*, where a father said to the accused: 'I have here those things which you gave my daughter to produce abortion' ((1880) 14 Cox CC 390). Another is the solemnity of the form of the accusation; so an executor's failure to dispute an affidavit alleging that he owes the estate money may be an admission (*Freeman v Cox* (1878) 8 ChD 148).

It is easier to infer an admission from silence to particular questions out of a large number than it is from a general refusal to answer any questions at all (*Paterson v Martin* (1966) 116 CLR 506 at 511).

It might be noted that implied admissions by silence often merge into implied admissions by vague and equivocal answers. An example is *Mars v McMahon* [1929] SASR 179 where the respondent in an affiliation case was addressed as follows: 'I understand that you do not deny having had connection with the girl [ten seconds' silence], but that others have also had connection with her.' The respondent replied: 'It's pretty rotten when she picks on me when I know that others have also been out with her.'

B   SILENCE EVIDENCING A CONSCIOUSNESS OF GUILT

In *R v Christie* [1914] AC 545 at 565–6, [1914–15] All ER Rep 63 at 71–2, HL, Lord Reading said that a statement made in the accused's presence was sometimes admissible 'in order to prove the conduct and demeanour of the accused when hearing the statement as a relevant fact in the particular case, notwithstanding that it did not amount . . . to an acknowledgment . . . of the truth of the statement'. The Criminal Law Revision Committee is technically correct in saying that this doctrine is not affected by the decision in *Hall v R* that silence in the presence of a policeman cannot be an admission of guilt, but it may be doubted whether *Hall v R* is substantially compatible with the application of the *R v Christie* doctrine to cases where a policeman is present. When a policeman is present, an inference that silence shows a consciousness of guilt is as dangerous as an inference that it shows consent to what was said.

The principle here is that normally the urge of self-preservation will induce a man to speak if charged with unlawful conduct; so silence shows that he is conscious of guilt.

Where silence is consent, a statement made to the party is admitted to prove the truth of its contents; the party has in effect adopted it. But the question may be whether 'the reaction of an accused person to the making of a statement in his presence may afford evidence of something other than the facts suggested in the statement'. This means that it may be difficult to discover what the party is impliedly admitting. If other evidence suggests the accused committed the crime charged, 'any conduct . . . demonstrative of guilt may go far to support a conclusion that the accused committed the very crime charged. But when there is no other evidence implicating the accused, an attitude of guilt, without more, may mean only that the accused was a participant in some wrongdoing, not that he committed the crime alleged, in manner and form alleged' (*Woon v R* (1964) 109 CLR 529 at 536, 542).

The inference of consciousness of guilt may be made from silence alone, but it is more commonly made from silence coupled with other conduct. The Supreme Court of Canada once drew the inference from silence followed by contradictory explanations (*Hubin v R* (1927) 48 CCC 172). Where the accused's reply was 'What I have to say I will say to the court', the judge legitimately remarked that the reply was an odd one when court proceedings had not yet been mentioned (*R v Gerard* [1948] 1 All ER 205, CCA).

There are many examples where a consciousness of guilt has been detected in silence. The failure of a victim of crime to complain speedily, eg the victim of rape, may be evidence of consent, unless there is some good reason for this such as fear of vengeance by the criminals (*R v Gandfield* (1846) 2 Cox CC 43). As with the case of silence as consent to a statement, a selective refusal to answer questions is more suspicious than a general refusal (*Woon v R* (1964) 109 CLR 529).

In *R v Christie* [1914] AC 545, [1914–15] All ER Rep 63, HL, the House of Lords decided that statements made in the presence of a party could be put to the jury before there was evidence of any admission from his conduct, though the contrary procedure was desirable. If there is no evidence of admission, injustice may be caused because the jury become so prejudiced by hearing the statements that they ignore any warning to put them aside. For this reason it is often necessary either to prevent the statement going before the jury or having a new trial.

Paragraph 16.4 of the Code of Practice for the Detention, Treatment and Questioning of Persons by Police Officers (Code C: revised edition 1995) made under the Police and Criminal Evidence Act 1984, s 66 ameliorates the position slightly by forbidding the police to tell the accused of a co-accused's statement, but permitting them to hand the accused a copy under caution.

C   SILENCE AS STRENGTHENING INFERENCES FROM THE OPPOSING CASE

The judge may warn the jury that they may give greater weight to the case against a silent party because of the absence of any credible defence; and this is so even if a warning of the right to silence has been given. A defence may not be credible because it was raised late (*R v Ryan* (1964) 50 Cr App Rep 144, CCA, the reasoning in which was criticised in *R v Gilbert* (1977) 66 Cr App Rep 237 at 244–5, CA), or because its lateness prevented the police checking it (*R v Parker* [1933] 1 KB 850, [1932] All ER Rep 718, CCA; *R v Littleboy* [1934] 2 KB 408, [1934] All ER Rep 434, CCA). In Napier J's phrase, 'a fishy story is all the worse for being stale' (*Hinton v Trotter* [1931] SASR 123 at 127).

Various examples of this reasoning may be noted. Silence strengthens the inference that a possessor of stolen goods is the thief or receiver of them (eg *R v Seymour* [1954] 1 All ER 1006, CCA). The inference arises because theft or receiving are by far the commonest ways of obtaining property unlawfully; so it is not open where the property was unlawfully obtained in some other way unless there are special circumstances, such as an association between the possessor and the person who originally obtained the goods (*DPP v Nieser* [1959] 1 QB 254 at 266–7, [1958] 3 All ER 662 at 669, DC). Silence strengthens the inference of breaking and entering with intent which can be drawn from illegal presence in another's house (*R v Wood* (1911) 7 Cr App Rep 56, CCA). Silence strengthens the inferences in favour of the plaintiff who proves facts to which the maxim res ipsa loquitur applies.

Though it should perhaps not be suggested that silence strengthens the inferences from other evidence if a policeman is present during questioning, that reasoning may be permitted if it is based not on silence alone but on the adequacy of an explanation which the accused had chosen to give for his silence. Thus in *R v Tune* (1944) 29 Cr App Rep 162, CCA, where the accused said he would prefer to have advice before explaining the matter in writing, the Court of Criminal Appeal upheld the judge's comment on the defence advanced: 'could not that have been said without legal advice?'

3   Inferences from silence in court

R v Burdett   (1820) 4 B & Ald 95 at 161–2

Abbott CJ: No person is to be required to explain or contradict, until enough has been proved to warrant a reasonable and just conclusion against him, in the absence of explanation or contradiction; but when such proof has been given, and the nature of the case is such as to admit of explanation or contradiction, if the conclusion to which the proof tends be untrue, and the accused offers no explanation or contradiction, can human reason do otherwise than adopt the conclusion to which the proof tends? [See also Best J and Holroyd J to the same effect at 121–2 and 140.]

McQueen v Great Western Rly Co (1875) LR 10 QB 569 at 574

Cockburn CJ: If a prima facie case is made out, capable of being displaced, and if the party against whom it is established might by calling particular witnesses and producing particular evidence to displace that prima facie case, and he omits to adduce that evidence, then the inference fairly arises, as a matter of inference for the jury and not as a matter of legal presumption, that the absence of the evidence is to be accounted for by the fact that even if it were adduced it would not disprove the prima facie case. But that always presupposes that a prima facie case has been established; and unless we can see our way clearly to the conclusion that a prima facie case has been established, the omission to call witnesses who might have been called on the part of the defendants amounts to nothing.

(See also *R v Cowan* [1996] QB 373, [1995] 4 All ER 939, CA.)

A   SILENCE AS AMOUNTING TO CONSENT

Where not every issue of fact is contested in a civil case, silence may be an admission. Failure to deny a charge of adultery is not always or by itself evidence of adultery, because there are many reasons for taking this course other than actually having committed adultery; eg the supposed adulterer may simply wish to end proceedings quickly and cheaply (*Inglis v Inglis and Baxter* [1968] P 639 at 646, [1967] 2 All ER 71 at 76). But failure to deny adultery may be evidence of it if damages are claimed against the co-respondent, since in such circumstances there is more incentive for an innocent man to deny the charge (*Pidduck v Pidduck* [1961] 3 All ER 481).

B   SILENCE EVIDENCING CONSCIOUSNESS OF GUILT

It is clear that the silence of an accused at the trial is not evidence of a consciousness of guilt (*Waugh v R* [1950] AC 203, PC). However, the silence of a party in a civil case may be (*Cracknell v Smith* [1960] 3 All ER 569). The reasons for the distinction probably turn on the importance of a finding of criminal guilt, the high criminal standard of proof, the risk of the accused convicting himself by a bad performance in the box, and the dangers of the accused exposing himself to cross-examination on his record. These points either do not apply in civil cases or are less important.

Silence may evidence guilt in this way: in *Mash v Darley* [1914] 3 KB 1226, CA, a putative father did not testify at the assizes that the mother was 'fast', though he had done so in earlier proceedings before the magistrates. From this it could be inferred that the statement was a lie and that it proceeded from a consciousness of guilt.

C   SILENCE STRENGTHENING INFERENCES FROM
OPPOSING EVIDENCE

A party's failure to testify or to produce evidence in a civil case 'gives colour to the evidence against him' (*Boyle v Wiseman* (1855) 10 Exch 647 at 651, per Alderson B). See *Jones v Dunkel* (1959) 101 CLR 298; *Earle v Castlemaine*

District Community Hospital [1974] VR 722; *R v Gallagher* [1974] 3 All ER 118, [1974] 1 WLR 1204, CA; *R v Staines* (1974) 60 Cr App Rep 160, CA; *O'Donnell v Reichard* [1975] VR 916. The same is true in criminal cases, both with respect to the accused not giving evidence and with respect to his not calling an available witness (as to which see *R v Gallagher* (supra)).

Several conditions must be satisfied before silence in court can be used to strengthen inferences from opposing evidence. First, there must be a case to answer. The trial may be stopped at the close of the proponent's case if it is too weak, and even if it continues on other issues a non-existent case cannot be strengthened by failure to answer it. The second condition is that the silent party must have been capable of answering the case against him. 'All evidence is to be weighed according to the proof which it was in the power of one side to have produced, and in the power of the other to have contradicted' (*Blatch v Archer* (1774) 1 Cowp 63 at 65, per Lord Mansfield CJ). Thirdly, there must be no apparent reason for silence other than inability to answer truthfully the case made. Such reasons include insanity, protection of others, and fear of disclosure of an accused's record. Another reason is the fact that the absent witness is the party's solicitor and the evidence not given would, if given, have led to a waiver of privilege. *Wentworth v Lloyd* (1864) 10 HL Cas 589, HL, which was not cited in the contrary decision of *R v Wilmot* (1988) 89 Cr App Rep 341, CA. Fourthly, in criminal cases care must be taken not to suggest that any onus which does not in fact rest on the accused rests on him: *R v Buckland* [1977] 2 NSWLR 452; *R v Cowan* [1996] QB 373, [1995] 4 All ER 939, CA. Fifthly, the Criminal Justice and Public Order Act 1994, s 35, requires certain preconditions before there is an inference from silence under that section.

FURTHER READING

Greer, 52 MLR 709 (1990); Mirfield [1995] Crim LR 612; Pattenden [1995] Crim LR 602.

CHAPTER 8

Confessions

Generally speaking, a confession is a statement by the accused in which he admits committing an offence, or admits some fact that goes to show he committed an offence. The common law developed, from the rules relating to admissions, a special one for confessions. A confession was only admissible against its maker if it was proved to be 'voluntary', which in due course developed a highly technical meaning: the confession must not have been obtained by inducement in the form of a fear of prejudice or hope of advantage excited or held out by a person in authority, or by oppression. The refinements of this definition were difficult to apply and often seemed to produce undesirable results; they were much criticised and proposals were made for their reform. In particular, the Criminal Law Revision Committee suggested that the law be rephrased so that confessions obtained by oppression continue to be excluded, but that in case of inducement the crucial question be whether the confession is reliable (CLRC 53–67). This proposal was in substance enacted in s 76 of the Police and Criminal Evidence Act 1984, which provided a new code for the admissibility of confessions, replacing the old law (*R v Fulling* [1987] QB 426, [1987] 2 All ER 65, CA). The Act also contains in s 82(1) a partial definition of 'confession', making it clear that the new law is to apply to all statements made by an accused and wholly or partially adverse to him, whether they would formerly have been classed as 'admissions' or 'confessions'.

The pre-1984 law remains of some incidental importance and interest because of references to it in the materials exploring the reasons for the development of a special rule for confessions (section 1G below) and in studying the rules in other jurisdictions, some of which have adopted the notion of 'voluntariness' from the English common law: sections 4 and 5 and ch 9.1 below.

1 The exclusionary rule

A THE STRUCTURE OF SECTION 76

The first subsection of s 76 makes any relevant confession (as defined in s 82(1)) admissible against its maker. This broad exception to the hearsay rule is then substantially modified by what follows. For if, as is usually the case, the confession is to be tendered by the prosecution, sub-ss (2) and (3) lay down a precondition to its admissibility. If (but only if) *either* it is represented to the court that certain vitiating factors may have been present, *or* the court of its own motion requires proof that they were not present, then the prosecution must prove the absence of those factors; failure to do so will render the confession inadmissible. The vitiating factors in question are causative oppression (partially defined in sub-s (8)) and potential unreliability. The section thus aims to protect the accused in two ways, sometimes called the disciplinary and the reliability principles. According to the first, evidence, including a confession, should not be admissible if it is obtained by misconduct on the part of the investigator: the courts, by refusing to hear the evidence, reinforce any other sanctions against the investigator, and by a constant practice of refusing to hear the evidence make it more unlikely that investigators will think it worth committing misconduct. According to the second, the basis for excluding some confessions is that they have been produced in such a way that they are or may be unreliable. The various rationales for the rules about the exclusion of confessions are considered further with the materials in section 1G of this chapter.

Section 76 requires careful analysis, but it cannot be understood in isolation. Even if a confession passes the tests imposed here it may be excluded by the court in its discretion either at common law or under s 78: see ch 9. And in considering questions of exclusion, whether obligatory or discretionary, the court may have regard to the extent to which there was compliance with the Codes of Practice made under s 66: see section 3 of this chapter.

Police and Criminal Evidence Act 1984

76 (1)   In any proceedings a confession made by an accused person may be given in evidence against him in so far as it is relevant to any matter in issue in the proceedings and is not excluded by the court in pursuance of this section.

(2)   If, in any proceedings where the prosecution proposes to give in evidence a confession made by an accused person, it is represented to the court that the confession was or may have been obtained –

(a)   by oppression of the person who made it; or

(b)   in consequence of anything said or done which was likely, in the circumstances existing at the time, to render unreliable any confession which might be made by him in consequence thereof, the court shall not allow the confession to be given in evidence against him except in so far as the prosecution proves to the court beyond reasonable doubt that the confession (notwithstanding that it may be true) was not obtained as aforesaid.

(3)   In any proceedings where the prosecution proposed to give in evidence a confession made by an accused person, the court may of its own motion require the prosecution, as a condition of allowing it to do so, to prove that the confession was not obtained as mentioned in subsection (2) above.

[Subsections (4)–(6) are concerned with evidence derived from inadmissible confessions: p 175, post.]

(7)   Nothing in Part VII of this Act [Documentary Evidence] shall prejudice the admissibility of a confession made by an accused person.

(8)   In this section 'oppression' includes torture, inhuman or degrading treatment, and the use or threat of violence (whether or not amounting to torture).

82 (1) In this Part of this Act –
'confession', includes any statement wholly or partly adverse to the person who made it, whether made to a person in authority or not and whether made in words or otherwise . . .

COMMENTS

✓**1.** Exclusion under s 76 is mandatory: if the prosecution are required to prove the admissibility of a confession and fail to do so, the confession is not admissible. No question of discretion arises. A confession which is not excluded by this section may however be excluded by the judge in the exercise of his discretion under s 78 or 82(3) (*R v Mason* [1987] 3 All ER 481 at 484, [1988] 1 WLR 139 at 143–4, CA; see generally ch 9).
2. The future tense of s 76(2) ('shall not allow') has two particular effects. First, the accused is entitled to have this matter determined before the confession is received in evidence. There will need to be a trial within a trial even in a magistrates' court (*R v Liverpool Juvenile Court, ex p R* [1988] QB 1, [1987] 2 All ER 668) and apparently also in extradition proceedings (*Re Walters* [1987] Crim LR 557). Likewise in committal proceedings where there is a disputed confession, the examining magistrates should determine its admissibility before allowing the prosecution to include it as part of their case. Otherwise the committal will be defective, though it seems that only in exceptional circumstances will it be quashed (*R v Oxford Justices, ex p Berry* [1988] QB 507, [1987] 1 All ER 1244). Secondly, once the confession has been admitted, rightly or wrongly, s 76(2) has no role to play. If the judge changes his mind and decides that the confession should not have been admitted he may exclude it only under the common law power preserved by s 82(3), for s 78 is similarly forward-looking (*R v Sat-Bhambra* (1988) 152 JP 365, 88 Cr App Rep 55, CA; again see ch 9 where the judicial discretion to exclude evidence is considered in detail).
3. A confession is admissible only against its maker, not another accused, save in the case of conspiracy before the common enterprise is at an end. But where two accused are tried together, a confession by one also implicating the other may be read out, in which case it is the judge's duty to warn the jury that it is evidence against its maker only.

B   OPPRESSION: SECTION 76(2)(a)

R v Fulling   [1987] QB 426, [1987] 2 All ER 65, CA

Lord Lane CJ: On 6 August 1986 in the Crown Court at Leeds before his Honour Judge Hurwitz and a jury the appellant was convicted by a majority verdict of ten to two of obtaining property by deception. . . .
The facts which gave rise to the charge were these. In September 1981 the appellant claimed some £5,665 from her insurers in respect of what she claimed was a burglary at her flat in Leeds. The insurance company in July 1982 paid her £5,212 in settlement of the claim.
Many months later a man called Turnpenny, an acknowledged criminal, gave to the police a mass of information about the activities of other criminals, which resulted in a large number of people being arrested, among them being the appellant. Turnpenny gave evidence that the appellant had told him that her 'burglary' was bogus, that a man called Maddon had committed

it and that she knew the whereabouts of the stolen property. She gave him to understand that the idea of the bogus burglary had been initiated by one Drewery, with whom the appellant had been living and with whom she was infatuated. Turnpenny conceded that he had good reasons for wishing to harm Drewery.

As a result of this information the appellant was arrested in the early hours of Friday, 12 July 1985. Drewery was arrested at the same time. She was interviewed twice on that day, but exercised her right to say nothing despite persistent questioning by the police. She was interviewed again on the following day, Saturday. The interview was split into two, with a break in between, according to the police of 50 minutes, according to her of about 5 or 10 minutes.

The police witnesses described how, after initially refusing to answer questions, her attitude started to change. One of the officers, Det Sgt Beech, said:

'*Q*. You've obviously got a lot on your mind, are you finding it difficult?   *A*. Yes.
Q. Would I be right in saying that you want to talk about this but every bone in your body is telling you that you shouldn't?   *A*. Something like that.'

Then came the break already described.

When the interview was resumed, in answer to questions from the officer she admitted a number of offences. Amongst them was the setting up of the bogus burglary: 'I approached a man in a pub because I was short of money and asked him if he would break in for me'. She admitted obtaining the money from her insurers. She said that she had spent some of it on a holiday for herself and Drewery. She expressed her sorrow at having committed the offences and said she felt relieved that she had confessed. She sought, it should be added, to exculpate Drewery.

Thus there were two legs to the prosecution case: Turnpenny's evidence and the police account of her confession. The only corroboration of the former was the latter. The prosecution conceded that if the confession goes, then the appeal should be allowed. They would not seek to rely on Turnpenny's uncorroborated evidence.

The only issue in the appeal is whether or not the confession was properly admitted.

A submission was made to the judge that the confession should be ruled inadmissible by virtue of the provisions of s 76 of the Police and Criminal Evidence Act 1984. . . .

It was represented to the judge that the confession was or might have been obtained by oppression of the appellant within the meaning of sub-s (2)(*a*).

The appellant's evidence on the voir dire as to her reason for making the confession was this. After the break in the final interview one of the police officers, Det Con Holliday, told her that Drewery, her lover, had been having for the last three years or so an affair with a woman called Christine Judge. Now Christine Judge was one of the many people who had been arrested as a result of Turnpenny's disclosures. She was in the next cell to the appellant and, said the appellant, Det Con Holliday told her so. These revelations, said the appellant, so distressed her that she 'just couldn't stand being in the cells any longer'. Then later in her evidence she said: 'As soon as the matter about Christine came out, Det Con Holliday left the room and my head was swimming. I felt numb and after a while I said to Det Sgt Beech, "Is it true?" and he said, "Ronnie shouldn't have said that, he gets a bit carried away. Look Ruth, why don't you make a statement?" '

She said that she knew Drewery had in 1982 had an affair with a woman called Christine. She had before the interview noticed that the cell next door to hers had the name Christine Judge on its door, but said she did not realise that this was the same Christine until the police told her. After she had made her confession she had shouted to Christine to ask her if what the police had told her was true. Up to that point she said she was not particularly expressing her distress, but once she had spoken to Christine she just cried and cried. Later in cross-examination she said, 'I agreed to a statement being taken, it was the only way I was going to be released from the cells', but she conceded that she was not suggesting that she had been offered bail in return for a statement. The officers denied that they had made to her any such revelation as she suggested.

The basis of the submission to the judge was that the information given to her by the police about Christine amounted to oppression, and that the confession was, or might have been, obtained thereby, and that the prosecution had failed to discharge the burden or proving beyond reasonable doubt that the confession was not so obtained.

In his ruling on the matter the judge declined to make any express finding of fact as to whether the appellant or the police were correct in their account of events. He was prepared to assume for the purposes of argument that the appellant's version of events was the true one and to judge the matter on that basis. That is the subject of criticism by counsel for the appellant, but we think he has no proper ground for complaint on that score.

The material part of the ruling runs as follows:

'Bearing in mind that whatever happens to a person who is arrested and questioned is by its very nature oppressive, I am quite satisfied that in s 76(2)(a) of the Police and Criminal Evidence Act 1984, the word oppression means something above and beyond that which is inherently oppressive in police custody and must import some impropriety, some oppression actively applied in an improper manner by the police. I do not find what was done in this case can be so defined and, in those circumstances, I am satisfied that oppression cannot be made out on the evidence I have heard in the context required by the statutory provision. I go on to add simply this, that I have not addressed my mind as to whether or not I believe the police or the defendant on this issue because my ruling is based exclusively on the basis that, even if I wholly believed the defendant, I do not regard oppression as having been made out. In those circumstances, her confession (if that is the proper term for it), the interview in which she confessed, I rule to be admissible.'

Counsel for the appellant has drawn our attention to a number of authorities on the meaning of 'oppression'. . . . [He] submits to us that on the strength of those decisions the basis of the judge's ruling was wrong, in particular when he held that the word 'oppression' means something above and beyond that which is inherently oppressive in police custody and must import some impropriety, some oppression actively applied in an improper manner by the police. It is submitted that that flies in the face of the opinions of their Lordships in *DDP v Ping Lin*.

The point is one of statutory construction. The wording of the 1984 Act does not follow the wording of earlier rules or decisions, nor is it expressed to be a consolidating Act, nor yet to be declaratory of the common law. The title runs as follows:

'An Act to make further provision in relation to the powers and duties of the police, persons in police detention, criminal evidence, police discipline and complaints against the police; to provide for arrangements for obtaining the views of the community on policing and for a rank of deputy chief constable; to amend the law relating to the Police Federations and Police Forces and Police Cadets in Scotland; and for connected purposes.'

It is a codifying Act, and therefore the principles set out in *Bank of England v Vagliano Bros* [1891] AC 107 at 144–5, [1891–4] All ER Rep 93 at 113 apply. Lord Herschell, having pointed out that the Bills of Exchange Act 1882 which was under consideration was intended to be a codifying Act, said:

'I think the proper course is in the first instance to examine the language of the statute and to ask what is its natural meaning, uninfluenced by any considerations derived from the previous state of the law, and not to start with inquiring how the law previously stood, and then, assuming that it was probably intended to leave it unaltered, to see if the words of the enactment will bear an interpretation in conformity with this view. If a statute, intended to embody in a code a particular branch of the law, is to be treated in this fashion, it appears to me that its utility will be almost entirely destroyed, and the very object with which it was enacted will be frustrated. The purpose of such a statute surely was that on any point specifically dealt with by it, the law should be ascertained by interpreting the language used instead of, as before, by roaming over a vast number of authorities in order to discover what the law was, extracting it by a minute examination of the prior decisions, dependent upon a knowledge of the exact effect even of an obsolete proceeding such as a demurrer to evidence.'

Similar observations are to be found in *Bristol Tramways Carriage Co Ltd v Fiat Motors Ltd* [1910] 2 KB 831 at 836 per Cozens-Hardy MR.

Section 76(2) of the 1984 Act distinguished between two different ways in which a confession may be rendered inadmissible: first, where it has been obtained by oppression (para (a)); second, where it had been made in consequence of anything said or done which was likely in the circumstances to render unreliable any confession which might be made by the defendant in consequence thereof (para (b)). Paragraph (b) is wider than the old formulation, namely that the confession must be shown to be voluntary in the sense that it was not obtained by fear of prejudice or hope of advantage, excited or held out by a person in authority. It is wide enough to cover some of the circumstances which under the earlier rule were embraced by what seems to be the artificially wide definition of oppression approved in *R v Prager* [1972] 1 All ER 1114, [1972] 1 WLR 260, CA.

This in turn leads us to believe that 'oppression' in s 76(2)(*a*) should be given its ordinary dictionary meaning. The Oxford English Dictionary as its third definition of the word runs as follows: 'Exercise of authority or power in a burdensome, harsh, or wrongful manner; unjust or cruel treatment of subjects, inferiors, etc; the imposition of unreasonable or unjust burdens.' One of the quotations given under that paragraph runs as follows: 'There is not a word in our language which expresses more detestable wickedness than *oppression.*'

We find it hard to envisage any circumstances in which such oppression would not entail some impropriety on the part of the interrogator. We do not think that the judge was wrong in using that test. What however is abundantly clear is that a confession may be invalidated under s 76(2)(*b*) where there is no suspicion of impropriety. No reliance was placed on the words of s 76(2)(*b*) either before the judge at trial or before this court. Even if there had been such reliance, we do not consider that the policeman's remark was likely to make unreliable any confession of the appellant's own criminal activities, and she expressly exonerated (or tried to exonerate) her unfaithful lover.

In those circumstances, in the judgment of this court, the judge was correct to reject the submission made to him under s 76 of the 1984 Act. The appeal is accordingly dismissed.

COMMENT

'Oppression' was a term of art in the pre-1984 law of confessions; the query laid to rest in *R v Fulling* is whether on its reappearance in the Act the word carries with it some or all of its incrustations of pre-1984 precedent.

The only major difficulty with this interpretation of 'oppression' appears to be that it may go too far. No doubt any breach, however slight, of the Code of Practice for the Detention, Treatment and Questioning of Persons by Police Officers (Code C: see section 3 below) would amount to 'exercise of power in a wrongful manner', which is the mildest meaning to be extracted from the Oxford English Dictionary definition used by the Court of Appeal. But the word 'oppression' seems to suggest conduct worse than merely not giving people all the privileges to which they are entitled, as indeed the illustrative quotation selected by the court confirms. Besides, the Court of Appeal has made it clear that not every breach of the Codes of Practice will lead to the inadmissibility of evidence obtained thereby (*R v Delaney* (1988) 88 Cr App Rep 338, CA), although deliberate malpractice may well lead to discretionary exclusion under s 78 (*R v Alladice* (1988) 87 Cr App Rep 380, CA). There is, however, reason (eg *R v Davison* [1988] Crim LR 442) to suppose that trial judges are occasionally misled by *R v Fulling* to stigmatise as oppressive conduct which cannot really bear that description.

Perhaps a more accurate flavour of the meaning of the word is that offered by the OED under 'oppressive':

'1. Of the nature of oppression or tyrannous treatment of subject, inferiors, etc; unjustly burdensome, harsh or merciless; tyrannical.'

It is clear that harsh, hectoring and bullying, or aggressive questioning may amount to oppression, or may not: it depends on the degree of pressure, the characteristics of the suspect and the motives of the questioner. See *R v Paris* (1992) 97 Cr App Rep 99, CA; *R v L* [1994] Crim LR 839, CA; *R v Miller, infra.* Motive may be important because the potential defect is that the confession was obtained '*by* oppression'.

R v Miller   [1986] 3 All ER 119, [1986] 1 WLR 1191, CA

The appellant was, as the interviewing officer knew, a paranoid schizophrenic. It was suggested that a long period of questioning had produced an episode of schizophrenic terror or delusion or both. One ground of appeal was that bringing about such an effect amounted to oppression. Although the case was decided well before the Police and Criminal Evidence Act 1984 came into effect, the Court of Appeal's judgment on this question proceeded almost entirely on the ordinary meaning of oppression.

Watkins LJ: . . . [Counsel for the appellant] contends that no matter what prompted the police officer to ask the offending questions, if the effect on them was to bring disorder into the mind when previously there was none, the defendant was by that oppressed. Only oppressive conduct could, it is argued, have produced that kind of oppressive state.

It is an ingenious argument, but it fails to convince us that the police officer's questions amounted to a form of oppression within the ordinary meaning of that word, and as was contemplated as oppressive conduct rendering a confession inadmissible in the cases cited on this subject both here and to the judge. We know of no other cases of assistance on this point. We think the judge was right when he said there was no basis for saying that the confession had been obtained by oppression, he earlier in his judgment having examined the whole process of interrogation in one interview after another.

It may well be, as the psychiatrist stated, that in all probability some of the questions triggered off hallucinations and flights of fancy, but that by itself is not, in our view, indicative of oppression. Whether questions skilfully and deliberately asked so as to produce that kind of disordered mind could amount to oppression is an altogether different matter. The judge did not find that such obviously wicked conduct had taken place. Had he done so, and been satisfied that the questions had the effect sought, we fail to see how he could have avoided ruling out the confession, whether this had to be considered on the basis of no discretion to do otherwise or as an exercise of discretion.

QUESTION

Would it have made any difference in *R v Fulling* if the appellant's story about what the police officer had said to her was true, but what the police officer had said to her was a deliberate lie?

C   POTENTIAL UNRELIABILITY: SECTION 76(2)(*b*)

R v Goldenberg   (1988) 88 Cr App Rep 285, CA

Neill LJ: The second ground of appeal concerned the interview which took place at Boreham Wood police station on 16 June 1987. At the trial counsel for the appellant sought to exclude evidence about this interview on the basis that it was unreliable. It was also argued at one stage that this evidence was not relevant and that its prejudicial effect outweighed its probative value.

The judge rejected these arguments in the following ruling:

'Mr Pownall relies in substance on the basis that the evidence may be unreliable under s 76 of the Police and Criminal Evidence Act. He submitted initially that such evidence was not relevant and that its prejudicial value in any event outweighed its probative value. He did not pursue that ultimately, and rightly so, as the evidence in my view is obviously relevant and highly probative. Its only prejudicial value is that that follows all admissions. I have to decide therefore the sole issues as to its reliability. Mr Pownall says that it may be unreliable because, on the face of it, the admissions in the interview are an attempt to get bail and, secondly, that as Mr Goldenberg was a heroin addict and as he had been in custody for some weeks, it might be expected that he would do or say anything, however false, to get bail, presumably thus to be able to feed his addiction. The earlier admissions by Mr Goldenberg seem to me highly relevant. He accepted in those earlier admissions following shortly after his arrest that in substance he had acquired heroin in order to sell that on through his co-defendants but at that early stage was not prepared to go into any further details. In these admissions he does go into some further detail but seems to limit those details, suggesting that he can only provide the fullness of them if and when granted bail. It seems to me, therefore, that this confession is perfectly consistent and follows on from his previous confessions. Bail may well have been in his mind, as indeed other motives may well have been, but there is nothing that I can see which suggests in any way that this confession is in any way unreliable. There is no evidence before me that he was suffering from heroin addiction at the time or shortly before 16 June but even if he had been, my view of the admissibility of this interview remains the same. I can see nothing, even in those circumstances, which would in any way render the admissions or the interview in any way unreliable. Of course, it is for the prosecution to satisfy me that the admissions in the interview are not unreliable and for the reasons that I have given they have done so. In my view, therefore, this interview (and the admissions contained in it) is admissible.'

In this court, though counsel did not abandon his submission that the evidence was more prejudicial than probative, the argument against the admissibility of evidence about the 16 June interview was put in two principal ways: (a) that the judge should have ruled against the admissibility of the evidence in accordance with s 76(2)(*b*) of the Police and Criminal Evidence Act 1984 (the 1984 Act) and (b) that, in the alternative, the Judge should have excluded the evidence in accordance with s 78 of the 1984 Act. . . .

The submission based on s 78 of the 1984 Act can be dealt with quite shortly. . . .

We turn therefore to the argument based on s 76 of the 1984 Act. Here, if the argument is well founded, the exclusion of the evidence is mandatory and in any event it is clear that the point was fully canvassed before the judge.

It was submitted on behalf of the appellant that the words 'said or done' in the phrase 'in consequence of anything said or done' could include what was said or done by the appellant himself.

He had requested the interview and his motive, it was said, was to obtain bail or alternatively, as one of the police officers said in the course of the trial, to obtain credit for helping the police. It was also submitted, though without great force, that the confession was unreliable because of the words used by Detective Sergeant Leader at the outset of the interview which might have led the appellant to think that anything he said would be 'off the record,' or at any rate would not be used against him in the present proceedings. It is to be noted that this alternative submission was not advanced at the trial.

It is important to remember that in the present case there was an application on behalf of the appellant that the evidence should not be admitted. The case therefore fell within s 76(2) of the 1984 Act rather than within s 76(3), under which the court may, of its own motion, require the prosecution to prove the reliability of a confession.

It follows therefore that if criticism is now to be made of the judge's ruling, it is necessary to bear in mind the arguments addressed to him at the trial. Thus the obligation on the court under s 76(2) arises where 'it is represented to the court that the confession was or may have been obtained in consequence of anything said or done which was likely, in the circumstances existing at the time, to render unreliable any confession which might be made by him in consequence thereof.'

In the present case it is clear that no reliance was placed at the trial on anything said or done by Detective Sergeant Leader at the start of the interview. The argument was based on what was said or done by the appellant himself and on his state of mind. It is in that context that the judge's ruling has to be considered. It is also to be noted that on the *voir dire* the appellant himself did not give evidence.

It was submitted on behalf of the appellant that in a case to which s 76(2)(*b*) of the 1984 Act applied, the court was concerned with the objective reliability of the confession and not merely with the conduct of any police officer or other person to whom the confession was made. Accordingly the court might have to look at what was said or done by the person making the confession, because the confession might have been made worse 'in consequence' of what he himself had said or done and his words or actions might indicate that this confession was or might be unreliable.

In our judgment the words 'said or done' in s 76(2)(*b*) of the 1984 Act do not extend so as to include anything said or done by the person making the confession. It is clear from the wording of the section and the use of the words 'in consequence' that a causal link must be shown between what was said or done and the subsequent confession.

In our view it necessarily follows that 'anything said or done' is limited to something external to the person making the confession and to something which is likely to have some influence on him.

In the circumstances of the present case we are satisfied that on the proper construction of s 76(2)(*b*) the judge's ruling as to the admissibility of evidence relating to the 16 June interview was correct.

COMMENTS

Three comments may be made on this unfortunate decision, which has been followed in *R v Crampton* (1990) 92 Cr App Rep 369, CA.

1. It is clear from the words of the section and from *R v Harvey* [1988] Crim LR 241 that the thing said or done does not have to be said or done by the interviewer; but the requirement that it be something external to the person making the confession is quite unwarranted by the statute. The court seems to base its reasoning on the words 'in consequence of', but this is very difficult to follow. 'Obtained by oppression' in s 76(2)(*a*) suggests that the 'obtainer' would need to be an agent of the 'oppressor', but the causal link expressed in s 76(2)(*b*) is substantially less personal. The court fails to give any value to this difference, or any reason for not doing so. The resultant test is likely to cause substantial anomalies. In *R v Sat-Bhambra* (1988) 88 Cr App Rep 55, CA, the judge excluded some statements by the accused under s 76 because, in the words of the report (at p 59), 'the police doctor gave the defendant valium to calm his nerves. There was evidence that the valium might have affected [him]'. On appeal the Court of Appeal, a few months before the decision in *R v Goldenberg*, expressly reserved its position on whether the voluntary regular ingestion by the defendant of another drug to control his diabetes could amount to 'something done', but appears to have had no objection to exclusion because of the valium. But was the valium not taken voluntarily by the accused? If the question is of potential unreliability, the source of the factor inducing unreliability should not matter. A person who is drunk may make a confession which in consequence of his drunkenness is likely to be unreliable; its admissibility should not depend on whether he got himself drunk voluntarily, or by having his drink 'spiked', or by having alcohol administered to him against his will. There is no requirement that bad faith on the part of anyone be shown (*R v Fulling* [1987] QB 426, [1987] 2 All ER 65, CA); the only requirement imposed by the statute is that the potential unreliability be in consequence of an event which can be described as 'anything said or done'.

2. The Court of Appeal's decision that 'a causal link must be shown' leads to the question 'by whom?' It should not be for the accused to show the link but for the prosecution to show its absence.

3. The trial judge's ruling seems to be dangerously nearly a decision that the confessions were not unreliable. But the question is different; it is whether the confession is *potentially* unreliable. The consistency of the confession is unlikely to be evidence of anything except its truth, which is at this stage irrelevant, as the section makes clear. (Cf *R v Tyrer* (1989) 90 Cr App Rep 446, CA.) On the other hand, if the prosecution show that, although the accused might not have made a confession at all if the circumstances had been different, nevertheless there is nothing likely to render unreliable the one he did make, it will not be excluded under s 76: *R v Alladice* (1988) 87 Cr App Rep 380, CA.

4. Things 'said or done' causing the exclusion of the confession have included an offer of bail (*R v Barry* (1991) 95 Cr App Rep 384, CA) an indication of a likely mild treatment by the court (*R v Delaney* (1988) 88 Cr App Rep 338, CA) and an untrue statement that the person being interviewed had already been identified as a participant in the offence (*DPP v Blake* [1989] 1 WLR 432, CA). It is, however, by no means clear why in these latter cases, the last in particular, there is any reason to suppose that the consequent confession was potentially unreliable. Cf *R v Mason* [1987] 3 All ER 481, [1988] 1 WLR 139, CA, and the three-stage reasoning process suggested in *R v Barry* (supra).

QUESTION

Both before the trial judge and on appeal *R v Fulling* (p 155, ante) was argued on the basis of s 76(2)(*a*). As regards s 76(2)(*b*) the Court of Appeal said

'we do not consider that the policeman's remark was likely to make unreliable any confession of the appellant's own criminal activities.'

Do you agree?

D   THE ROLES OF THE JUDGE AND JURY

If defence counsel wishes to object to the admissibility of a confession, he should inform the prosecution before the trial begins and counsel for the prosecution should not refer to that evidence in opening. At the time when the prosecution wishes to produce the confession, a procedure called the 'trial within the trial', or voir dire, begins. The jury is sent from the court, and the judge hears the evidence of the circumstances in which the confession was obtained, since the issue of admissibility is a question of law to be decided by him. Admissibility is the only issue at this stage; the truth of the confession is irrelevant. However, the method by which the confession was obtained has a bearing on its truth, since if it was obtained by violence, for example, it is less likely to be true than if given freely. And the question whether the confession is true is for the jury. So if the judge decides the confession is admissible, any witness who gave evidence on the voir dire may be called to give evidence again before the jury in an attempt to convince them it is untrue. If the judge decides on the voir dire that the confession is admissible, but later evidence in the main trial causes him to change his mind, he may direct the jury to disregard the confession; or direct the jury to acquit if there is no other substantial evidence against the accused; or direct a new trial: see *R v Watson* [1980] 2 All ER 293, [1980] 1 WLR 991, CA; *R v Sat-Bhambra* (1988) 88 Cr App Rep 55, CA.

The test of admissibility must be satisfied where the confession is signed but the accused denies authorship and alleges his signature was obtained by force: *Ajodha v The State* [1982] AC 204, [1981] 2 All ER 193, PC. The same case held that in those circumstances the judge must hold a voir dire and decide the question of authorship; if he admits the confession, the matter can be re-canvassed before the jury. See also *MacPherson v R* (1981) 37 ALR 81 at 88, where Gibbs CJ and Wilson J said that a voir dire is required where the accused denies making the confession but also alleges an inducement. But normally the question of whether a confession was made is for the jury, not the judge: that view was also asserted in *Ajodha's Case* at 222 and 202; cf *Cleland v R* (1982) 151 CLR 1 at 13 per Murphy J. So if the accused merely denies making the confession there is no scope for a voir dire. But after 1984 it will be a rare case where there is any question about whether the accused made a confession, except where there are also wholesale breaches of Code C; and it being the policy of the Police and Criminal Evidence Act 1984 to eliminate questions of this sort by ensuring that interviews with suspects are properly recorded, a confession whose very making is challenged may be excluded under s 78 (*R v Keenan* [1990] 2 QB 54, [1989] 3 All ER 598, CA; see ch 9.2).

R v Hammond   [1941] 3 All ER 318, CCA

On the voir dire the accused testified that his confession had been extracted by police violence, and in answer to a question 'Is it true?' said 'Yes'. The Court of Criminal Appeal held the question and answer admissible.

Humphreys J: This appeal is brought on the sole ground that the question which was put by counsel for the prosecution in cross-examination of the accused was inadmissible. In our view, it clearly was not admissible. It was a perfectly natural question to put to a person, and was relevant to the issue of whether the story which he was then telling of being attacked and ill-used by the police was true or false. It may be put as it was put by Viscount Caldecote LCJ in the early part of the argument of counsel for the appellant, that it surely must be admissible, and in our view is admissible, because it went to the credit of the person who was giving evidence. If a man says, 'I was forced to tell the story. I was made to say this, that and the other,' it must be relevant to know whether he was made to tell the truth, or whether he was made to say a number of things which were untrue. In other words, in our view, the contents of the statement which he admittedly made and signed were relevant to the question of how he came to make and sign that statement, and, therefore, the questions which were put were properly put.

This is a strange case. The accused's answer was as a matter of fact extraordinary and unexpected. The court's reasoning that the truth of the confession is relevant to the question whether the accused can be believed in saying it was extracted by violence is odd. If the confession is true this presumably shows that the accused tends to tell the truth, which suggests that he is telling the truth in saying the police were violent. Yet the court apparently thinks it tends to show him a liar on the basis that confessed criminals are likely to be liars, but if so his confession should be false. As a matter of policy, questions as to truth should not be permitted on the voir dire because they operate as an incitement to perjury and because the subsequent attitude of judge and counsel cannot remain unaffected by the accused's admission of guilt on the voir dire. Further, there is Queensland authority (*R v Gray*

[1965] Qd R 373; *R v Toner* [1966] QWN 44) for the view that the privilege against self-incrimination can be claimed by the accused on the voir dire, even though it cannot during the main trial (Criminal Evidence Act 1898, s 1(*e*)). There is South Australian authority for the view that, though they are admissible, the judge has a discretion to exclude the accused's admissions on the voir dire from the jury's consideration when the main trial resumes (*R v Wright* [1969] SASR 256). For these reasons there has been a division of opinion among Commonwealth courts as to whether *Hammond* should be followed (it was criticised in *R v Weighill* (1945) 2 DLR 471 and *R v Hnedish* (1958) 29 CR 347 but applied by the Supreme Court of Canada: *De Clercq v R* (1968) 70 DLR (2d) 530). See Neasey (1960) 34 ALJ 110. In *Wong Kam-Ming v R* [1980] AC 247, [1979] 1 All ER 939 the Privy Council held that *Hammond's Case* was wrong, that *Wright's Case* was wrong as to admissibility, that evidence as to the accused's testimony on the voir dire is inadmissible whether or not the confession is admissible, and that the accused may not be cross-examined in the main trial on what he said on the voir dire unless the impugned confession was admitted. *Wong Kam-Ming's Case* was applied in *R v Brophy* [1982] AC 476, [1981] 2 All ER 705, HL, which criticised *Wright's Case*. See also *Burnes v R* (1975) 132 CLR 248 at 263; Murphy [1979] Crim LR 364. But the matter is regrettably not settled: the doubts have been raised again by the wording of s 76. Subsection (1) effectively makes admissible any confession concerning which the prosecution are able to negative the factors in subs (2). It seems likely that in the case of an admission made in court on the voir dire it would be extremely easy to do so. As a matter of statutory construction, therefore, the view of the majority of the Privy Council in *Wong Kam-Ming v R* appears to have been overruled, at any rate so far as s 76(2)(*a*) is concerned. On the other hand, the Court of Appeal in *R v Davis* [1990] Crim LR 860 approved, in general terms, the majority view in *Wong Kam-Ming v R*. Section 76(2)*(b)* specifically makes the truth of the confession irrelevant (*R v Cox* [1991] Crim LR 276, CA), so the accused should presumably not be asked whether it is true. An admission made on the voir dire might be excluded by the judge in his discretion under s 78 on the ground that to let the jury hear it would make the proceedings unfair.

Another principle deriving from the orthodox division of functions between judge and jury is that, once the judge has decided the confession is admissible the jury must act on it if they believe it and have no right to reconsider the question of admissibility (*Chan Wei Keung v R* [1967] 2 AC 160, [1967] 1 All ER 948, PC; *R v Burgess* [1968] 2 QB 112, [1968] 2 All ER 54n, CA). Under s 76 this principle emerges from the fact that the question of admissibility falls to be considered only before the evidence is admitted. The contrary view was called in America the 'humane' rule because it gave the accused a double chance of having the confession excluded (*Commonwealth v Preece* (1885) 5 NE 494). But is it humane? Some judges may be reluctant to call the police liars and may resolve any doubt in favour of admissibility, relying on the jury's right of exclusion; that is, the second safeguard may make the judge lax, even though his experience and skill should make him the main safeguard. It is difficult to see any reason for departing from the orthodox division of functions by which admissibility is for the judge and weight for the jury. (See McKenna [1967] Crim LR 336.)

E BURDEN AND STANDARD OF PROOF

A number of questions that had arisen under the old law are dealt with by s 76. It is now clear that the burden of proof of admissibility is on the prosecution, that there is no evidential burden on the accused, and that the standard of proof under s 76(2) is beyond reasonable doubt: see *R v Paris* (1992) 97 Cr App Rep 99, CA. On this a different rule applies in Australia, where the courts favour proof on a balance of probabilities (*Wendo v R* (1963) 109 CLR 559; *Collins v R* (1980) 31 ALR 257; *R v Kelly* (1988) 78 ACTR 14). The merit of the English position is that since admitting a confession usually ensures the accused's conviction, great care should be taken before putting it to the jury. It falls into line with what appears to be the general rule in criminal cases that an issue tried on a voir dire should be decided in favour of the prosecution only on the criminal standard (*R v Angeli* [1978] 3 All ER 950, [1979] 1 WLR 26, CA; *R v Ewing* [1983] QB 1039, [1983] 2 All ER 645, CA; *R v Mazzone* (1985) 43 SASR 330; *R v Sim* [1987] 1 NZLR 356 – all on s 8 of the Criminal Procedure Act 1865 or its equivalent). The Australian position has advantages in the rare case where the judge is not satisfied as to the admissibility of a confession but the accused does not challenge it. The standard is not mentioned in s 76(3): according to Phipson (section 27–15, note 47) it is to be assumed to be the same, but it may be very difficult to attain a high standard of proof without the testing process of opposing evidence. Generally speaking the question of which test to apply probably makes no difference, at least in this area, since normally it will be a question simply of whether the judge believes the police or believes the accused.

It has been said that defence counsel should not allege involuntariness unless the accused is prepared to testify to that effect on oath (*R v O'Neill* (1950) 34 Cr App Rep 108). This, which is probably merely an example of a general principle about alleging improbable facts, is in practice unimportant since even though the burden of proof is on the prosecution, the accused's story is unlikely to be accepted in circumstances where the prosecution have made out some kind of case of voluntariness unless he testifies.

It is clear from s 76(2) that the accused does not have to adduce any evidence in order to put the prosecution to proof of the admissibility of the confession. The representation to the court must however be clearly made; it is not enough merely to hint at inadmissibility whilst cross-examining prosecution witness (*R v Liverpool Juvenile Court, ex p R* [1988] QB 1, [1987] 2 All ER 668).

F THE SCOPE OF THE CONFESSION RULE

The definition of 'confession' in s 82(1) covers any statement which is at least partly adverse to the person making it, and any such statement is therefore subject to the s 76 rules when tendered by the prosecution. Occasionally it may be right to edit a confession in order to exclude prejudicial material (*R v Weaver* [1968] 1 QB 353, [1967] 1 All ER 277); but normally the whole confession should be put in evidence, both the parts that tell against an accused and those in his favour, and the jury must consider it as a whole. Both the inculpatory and the exculpatory parts may be relied on as evidence of the facts stated: *R v Sharp* [1988] 1 All ER 65, [1988] 1 WLR 7, HL, approving the following statement by Lord Lane CJ in *R v Duncan* (1981) 73 Cr App Rep 359:

'Where a "mixed" statement is under consideration by the jury in a case where the defendant has not given evidence, it seems to us that the simplest, and, therefore, the method most likely to produce a just result, is for the jury to be told that the whole statement, both the incriminating parts and the excuses or explanations, must be considered by them in deciding where the truth lies. It is, to say the least, not helpful to try to explain to the jury that the exculpatory parts of the statement are something less than evidence of the facts they state. Equally, where appropriate, as it usually will be, the judge may, and should, point out that the incriminating parts are likely to be true (otherwise why say them?), whereas the excuses do not have the same weight. Nor is there any reason why, again where appropriate, the judge should not comment in relation to the exculpatory remarks upon the election of the accused not to give evidence.'

Previous respectable authority (*R v Sparrow* [1973] 1 WLR 488 at 496, CA; *R v Pearce* (1979) 69 Cr App Rep 365 at 369, CA; *Leung Kam-Kwok v R* (1984) 81 Cr App Rep 83 at 91, PC) had suggested that the jury were to be instructed to differentiate between the defendant's admission and his other statements and to treat only the former as evidence of the facts stated. Lord Lane's approach has much to commend it in the way of practicality, and is supported by old first instance practice (*R v Higgins* (1829) 3 C & P 603; *R v Clewes* (1830) 4 C & P 221) as well as by the Criminal Law Revision Committee (CLRC p 213). It is, however, not entirely satisfactory analytically that the exculpatory parts of a statement containing also some inculpatory parts are evidence of the facts stated, whereas the (exculpatory) parts of a wholly exculpatory statement are not (see below). Lord Havers's reference in *R v Sharp* to s 82(1) is hardly convincing, because the effect granted to admissible confessions by s 76(1) is that they may be given in evidence *against* the accused. There is no indication there that they may be used by the accused in his defence.

Sections 76 and 82(1) draw no distinction between statements confessing in full to the offence under investigation, and statements containing some lesser adverse admission, whether or not relevant to the present investigation. Presumably the accused's silence, if taken against him under the provisions of ss 34-37 of the Criminal Justice and Public Order Act 1994, cannot be a 'statement' within s 82(1); but a statement containing on its face *nothing* adverse to the person making it is also not a 'confession' within the definition and does not become one if subsequent investigation reveals that the accused was being less than frank with his interlocutor. 'A denial does not become an admission because it is inconsistent with another denial' (*R v Pearce* (1979) 69 Cr App Rep 365 at 370, per Lord Widgery CJ). Such a wholly exculpatory statement may, however, be of value to the prosecution in that its obvious untruth may help to undermine what the accused says in court. It is certainly not evidence of the facts stated – the exculpatory statements in it are not entitled to the status given by *R v Sharp* to exculpatory parts of confessions (*R v Squire* [1990] Crim LR 341) – but (as long as it is relevant) its admissibility is not subject to the restrictions imposed by the confession rules: *R v Sat-Bhambra* (1988) 88 Cr App Rep 55; *R v Coats* [1932] NZLR 401; *R v Doyle* [1987] 2 Qd R 732. North American jurisdictions have taken a different view, insisting that whenever the accused's own statements are used against him the prosecution must prove their admissibility as if they were confessions.

Miranda v Arizona   384 US 436 (1966)

Warren CJ (giving the majority judgment in the US Supreme Court): The warnings required and the waiver necessary in accordance with our opinion today are, in the absence of a fully effective equivalent, prerequisites to the admissibility of any statement made by a defendant. No distinction can be drawn between statements which are direct confessions and statements which amount to 'admissions' of part or all of an offense. The privilege against self-incrimination protects the individual from being compelled to incriminate himself in any manner; it does not distinguish degrees of incrimination. Similarly, for precisely the same reason, no distinction may be drawn between inculpatory statements and statements alleged to be merely 'exculpatory.' If a statement made were in fact truly exculpatory it would, of course, never be used by the prosecution. In fact, statements merely intended to be exculpatory by the defendant are often used to impeach his testimony at trial or to demonstrate untruths in the statement given under interrogation and thus to prove guilt by implication. These statements are incriminating in any meaningful sense of the word and may not be used without the full warnings and effective waiver required for any other statement.

Piche v R   (1970) 11 DLR (3d) 709

In the Supreme Court of Canada a majority held that no distinction is to be drawn between inculpatory and exculpatory statements.

Cartwright CJC: It appears to me to involve a strange method of reasoning to say that an involuntary statement harmful to the accused's defence shall be excluded because of the danger of its being untrue but that a harmful involuntary statement, of which there is not merely a danger of its being false but which the prosecution asserts to be false, should be admitted merely because, considered in isolation, it is on its face exculpatory.

If, on the other hand, one regards the rule against the admission of an involuntary statement as being based in part on the maxim *nemo tenetur se ipsum accusare*, the right of an accused to remain silent is equally violated whether, when he is coerced into making a statement against his will, what he says is on its face inculpatory or exculpatory.

Judson J (dissenting): At the trial, the accused gave evidence that she took the rifle from the rack with the intention of committing suicide, that it accidentally discharged, with the bullet striking the deceased, and that she then left the apartment.

I cannot accept the trial Judge's reasoning in this case that the statement was inculpatory because it went to the question of both opportunity and motive. This particular statement denied guilt. It was an assertion by the accused that she had not shot the man. A statement denying guilt cannot be a confession. As Wigmore said: 'This ought to be plain enough if legal terms are to have any meaning and if the spirit of the general principle is to be obeyed.'

The dissenting reasons in the Manitoba Court of Appeal in the present case refer to recent developments in the United States which indicate that there is no difference between a confession and an exculpatory statement. The matter seems to be summed up on this point in an article entitled 'Developments in the Law – Confessions' (1965–66) 79 Harv L Rev 1032–3.

The test which had led to this development seems to be that a confession must be the result of a free and reasoned choice, and that no distinctions among the categories of out-of-court statements can constitutionally be made, and that the test for admissibility must be the same for confessions, admissions and exculpatory statements.

The practical importance of the case under review is obvious. It is an essential part of work of the police to ask questions of suspects. It is only when the stage of confession is reached that the confession rules apply. If a person chooses to give the police an innocent explanation of his conduct and then at the trial goes into the witness-box and gives another innocent explanation inconsistent with the first, it is entirely appropriate for Crown counsel to cross-examine on this discrepancy and the reasons for it. This is particularly needed when an alibi is set up as a defence. There is no legislation in this country corresponding to the English legislation, s 11 of the Criminal Justice Act 1967 (UK), c 80, which requires the early and complete disclosure of the evidence in support of an alibi. There should be no recognition of any right on the part of an accused person to tell the police one innocent story and then tell another innocent story in the witness-box without the jury knowing anything about the conflict between the two.

Section 76(1) is made subject to the exclusion rules contained in that section, but they only affect evidence tendered on behalf of the prosecution. This subsection therefore in principle enables one defendant to use against his co-accused the latter's confession as evidence of the facts stated therein, without any of the safeguards imposed on confessions forming part of the prosecution case (CLRC para 53; [1989] Crim LR 603). Likewise, under the general law, an accused may cross-examine his co-accused as to credit on the basis of the latter's statement, even if it has been previously excluded; the only fetter is that the questions must be relevant: *R v James Rowson* [1986] QB 174, [1985] 2 All ER 539, CA; *Lui Mei-Lin v R* [1989] AC 288, [1989] 1 All ER 359, PC.

The confession rules do not apply to co-ordination tests performed by motorists (*Benney v Dowling* [1959] VR 237; *Walker v Viney* [1965] Tas SR 96). Nor do they apply to real evidence obtained from the accused, eg blood samples. Such matters are governed in England by the rules relating to illegally obtained evidence. Further, the confessions rules do not apply to the accused's non-testimonial conduct, ie to 'non-assertive' evidence.

In *R v Voisin* [1918] 1 KB 531, [1918–19] All ER Rep 491, CCA, the police were investigating the murder of a woman whose body was found in a parcel with a piece of paper containing the words 'Bladie Belgiam'. The accused was asked by them to write 'Bloody Belgian', and wrote 'Bladie Belgiam'. This evidence was held admissible because the accused's conduct was voluntary, but the question of voluntariness was really irrelevant since conduct is not confessional. A similar piece of evidence was important in the Lindbergh kidnapping in America. The kidnap notes always put the dollar sign after the number (eg 5$), and always transposed 'gh' to 'hg' (eg 'ouhgt'). Bruno Richard Hauptmann, who was executed for the crime, was given a test in which he made these errors (G Walker, *Kidnap* (Hamish Hamilton, London, 1961), p 237). There is obviously little danger of such non-testimonial 'confessions' being false, and it would seem that they are not in fact confessions but acts which identify the accused as much as his face or his other physical features like fingerprints.

FURTHER READING

Mirfield, *Confessions* (1985), ch 4; Elliot and Wakeham [1979] Crim LR 428.

QUESTIONS

In *A-G for New South Wales v Martin* (1909) 9 CLR 713, the accused had made two statements to the police after his arrest. In the first he denied killing the deceased and said he had seen nobody else near the scene of the crime. In the second, made the next day, he gave a full account of his own presence near the scene of the crime and described how his attention had been aroused by the sound of a gun and he had then seen a person, whom he also described, near the deceased. If these facts occurred in England today, would the prosecution need to satisfy the requirements of s 76(2) before adducing the accused's statements? *Should* they have to?

G   THE PURPOSES OF THE CONFESSION RULE

Why does the law make some confessions admissible? A number of reasons have been advanced over the last two hundred years, from the earliest appearance of the common law doctrine of the exclusion of confessions which were not 'voluntary'.

R v Warickshall   (1783) 1 Leach 263

Nares J and Eyre B: It is a mistaken notion that the evidence of confessions and facts which have been obtained from prisoners by promises or threats is to be rejected from a regard to public faith: no such rule ever prevailed . . . Confessions are received in evidence or rejected as inadmissible under a consideration whether they are or are not intitled to credit. A free and voluntary confession is deserving of the highest credit, because it is presumed to flow from the strongest sense of guilt, and therefore it is admitted as proof of the crime to which it refers; but a confession forced from the mind by the flattery of hope or the torture of fear comes in so questionable a shape when it is to be considered as evidence of guilt that no credit ought to be given to it, and therefore it is rejected.

Wigmore: Treatise on the American System of Evidence in Trials at Common Law, 3rd edn, paras 822, 823, 851, 866, 867

The law cannot attempt to weigh testimony before even listening to it. But it can take note of certain objective circumstances as leading with high probability to falsities. The circumstances which thus call for the rejection of a confession are usually described as involving either a *promise* or a *threat*. Thus, a promise, of certain pardon, when attached to a confession, may conceivably make a confession, irrespective of its truth, seem more desirable than silence with its contingencies; or a threat of instant hanging by a mob, unless a confession is forthcoming, may conceivably make the contingencies of a confession more desirable than the certain consequences of silence.

   . . . A confession is not excluded because of any *breach of confidence* or of good faith which may thereby be involved . . . Thus, so far as a promise, whether of secrecy, of favour, or of other action, or a misrepresentation of facts, has been the means of obtaining the confession, the exclusion that might ensue would in no way rest on the mere fact that a promise has been broken, a confidence violated, or a deception deliberately planned and carried out.

   . . . A confession is not excluded because of any *illegality* in the method of obtaining it or in the speaker's situation at the time of making it. The general principle – that the illegality of the source of evidence is no bar to its reception – is well established. . . .

   . . . [A] confession is not rejected because of any connection with the *privilege against self-crimination* . . . Thus, where a compulsory disclosure is offered, it may be admissible so far as the privilege against self-incrimination is concerned, and yet the question of its propriety as a confession may be raised. . . . The sum and substance of the difference is that the confession-rule aims to exclude self-incriminating statements which are *false*, while the privilege-rule gives the option of excluding those which are *true*. . . .

   . . . [E]very guilty person is almost always ready and desirous to confess, as soon as he is detected and arrested. This psychological truth, well known to all criminal trial judges, seems to be ignored by some Supreme Courts. The nervous pressure of guilt is enormous; the load of the deed done is heavy: the fear of detection fills the consciousness; and when detection comes the pressure is relieved; and the deep sense of relief makes confession a satisfaction. At that moment, he will tell all, and tell it truly. To forbid soliciting him, to seek to prevent this relief, is to fly in the face of human nature. It is natural and should be lawful, to take his confession at that moment – the best one. And this expedient, if sanctioned, saves the State a delay and expense in convicting him after he has reacted from his first sensations, has yielded to his friends' solicitations, and comes under the sway of the natural human instinct to struggle to save himself by the aid of all technicalities.

[Why do opinions differ sharply on the value of confessions?] We must separate (1) the confession as a proved fact, from (2) the process of proving an alleged confession.

(1) Now, assuming the making of a confession to be a completely proved fact – its authenticity beyond question and conceded – then it is certainly true that we have before us the highest sort of evidence. The confession of crime is usually as much against a man's permanent interests as anything well can be . . . [I]t carries a persuasion which nothing else does, because a fundamental instinct of human nature teaches each one of us its significance.

(2) But how do we get to believe in the fact of a confession having been made? Always and necessarily by somebody's testimony. And what is our experience of that sort of testimony on which we are asked to believe that a confession was made? A varying and sometimes discouraging experience. Paid informers, treacherous associates, angry victims and over-zealous officers of the law – these are the persons through whom an alleged confession is oftenest presented; and it is at this stage that our suspicions are aroused and our caution stimulated. . . . [S]uppose the accused denies absolutely the fact of confession; suppose the judge now begins to think to himself, 'Here is a confession which, if authentic, would make this man's guilt clear beyond doubt. But do you expect us to take it as authentic, against his denial, on the word of this man alone, who has such and such strong motives for inventing it for misinterpreting what was said? Must we not listen to him with the greatest doubt and suspicion?'

. . . [T]he only real danger and weakness in a confession – the danger of a false statement – is of a slender character, and the cases of that sort are of the rarest occurrence.

. . . [T]he notion that confessions should be guarded against and discouraged is not a benefit to the innocent, but a detriment. A full statement of the accused person's explanations, made at the earliest moment, is often the best means for him of securing a speedy vindication. The circumstances of suspicion may often be disposed of by a simple explanation, so clear and convincing that immediate release follows as a matter of course; while the clues which the innocent accused may be able to furnish will be equally serviceable in securing that evidence against the real culprit which a delay may frequently render unavailable. . . .

The policy of the future, then, should be to receive all well-proved confessions in evidence, and to leave them to the jury, subject to all discrediting circumstances, to receive such weight as may seem proper.

Foster: High Treason, C III, s 8

Hasty confessions, made to persons having no authority to examine, are the weakest and most suspicious of all evidence. Proof may be too easily procured; words are often misreported – whether through ignorance, inattention, or malice, it mattereth not to the defendant, he is equally affected in either case; and they are extremely liable to misconstruction; and withal, this evidence is not in the ordinary course of things to be disproved by that sort of negative evidence by which the proof of plain facts may be and often is confronted.

Bram v US   168 US 532 (1897)

White J: A brief consideration of the reasons which gave rise to the adoption of the Fifth Amendment, of the wrongs which it was intended to prevent, and of the safeguards which it was its purpose unalterably to secure, will make it clear that the generic language of the amendment was but a crystallisation of the doctrine as to confessions, well-settled when the amendment was adopted.

[Wigmore's comment is (para 823, n 5): 'no assertions could be more unfounded'.]

R v Johnson   (1864) Ir CL 60

Hayes J: [A] confession will be rejected if it appear to have been extracted by the presumed pressure and obligation of an oath, or by pestering interrogatories, or if it have been made by the party to rid himself of importunity, or if, by subtle and ensnaring questions, those which are framed so as to conceal their drift and object, he has been taken at a disadvantage and thus entrapped into a statement which, if left to himself, and in the full freedom of volition, he would not have made . . . [I]t is manifest to everyone's experience that, from the moment a person feels himself in custody on a criminal charge, his mental condition undergoes a very remarkable change, and he naturally becomes much more accessible to every influence that addresses itself either to his hopes or fears.

H R Trevor-Roper: The European Witch Craze of the Sixteenth and Seventeenth Centuries, Penguin 1969, pp 44–5

. . . [T]he Dark Ages knew no witch mania because they lacked judicial torture. . . . the decline and disappearance of witch-beliefs in the eighteenth century is due to the discredit and gradual abolition of torture in Europe.

. . . [W]itches' confessions became more detailed with the intensification of inquisitorial procedure . . . the identity of such confessions is more often to be explained by the identity of procedure than by any identity of experience. . . . Accused witches often admitted to their confessors that they had wrongly accused both themselves and others. . . . Some judges refused to allow testimony because they knew that it had been obtained by torture and was therefore unreliable. . . .

Spano v New York   360 US 315 (1959)

Warren CJ: The abhorrence of society to the use of involuntary confessions does not turn alone on their inherent untrustworthiness. It also turns on the deep-rooted feeling that the police must obey the law; that in the end life and liberty can be as much endangered from illegal methods used to convict those thought to be criminals as from the actual criminals themselves.

McCormick: Handbook of the Law of Evidence (1954), paras 109, 110

The possibility that the declarant's statement may be the product of an abnormal mind is an infirmity to which all testimony is susceptible. Is there a substantial *special* danger here in respect to confessions? Possibly, there may be. No adequate scientific study of the question seems to have been made, but the literature on psychiatry at the lawyer's level indicates that persons suffering with melancholia have a recognisable tendency towards self-accusation, which conceivably might be so exaggerated as to lead to a false confession of crime. Terror and excitement over an accusation may be so shocking as to cause a state of abnormal suggestibility and a delusion of guilt. . . . [A] brutal and notorious crime often brings an aftermath of false confessions by halfwits. . . . [But] these cases are much more often encountered by the doctors than by the police; and . . . when they do come before the police, they are usually, though not always, recognisable as abnormal by experienced officers. On the whole they can hardly be said to present a substantial special danger of untrustworthiness peculiar to confessions.

. . . [T]he subtlest and most laborious form of indirect pressure is the cumulative suggestive force of mere protracted questioning alone. Practically always the interrogation is conducted by a battery of questioners operating in relays, and usually the questioning is continuous, or nearly so, for such time as to deprive the victim of normal sleep . . . Prolonged and insistent questioning alone seems effective to shatter the resistance of at least the average casual suspect who is not a professional criminal. Obviously this form of pressure can usually be carried out by denying the prisoner his right to communicate with friends and counsel.

Best: Principles of the Law of Evidence, 11th edn, p 539

By artful questioning and working on their feelings, weak-minded individuals can be made to confess or impliedly admit almost anything; and to resist continued importunities to acknowledge even falsehood requires a mind of more than average firmness.

The common law of England . . . has . . . taken great care, perhaps too great care, to prevent suspected persons from being terrified, coaxed, cajoled, or entrapped into criminative statements, and it . . . prohibits judicial interrogation.

. . . It is sometimes impossible to ascertain the motive which has led to a confession indisputably false. In November, 1580, a man was convicted and executed, on his own confession, for the murder, near Paris, of a widow who was missing at the time but who two years afterwards returned to her home. And the celebrated case of Joan Parry and her two sons – who were executed in this country in the seventeenth century, for the murder of a man named Harrison who reappeared some years afterwards – affords another instance.

. . . Weak and timorous persons, confounded at finding themselves in the power of the law, or alarmed at the testimony of false witnesses, or the circumstantial evidence against them or distrustful of the honesty or capacity of their judges, hope by an avowal of guilt to obtain leniency at their hands.

Moreover, an innocent man, accused or suspected of a crime, may deem himself exposed to annoyance at the hands of some person, to whom his suffering as for that crime would be acceptable . . . [as] where the evidence necessary to establish the innocence of the confessionalist would be the means of disclosing transactions which it was the interest of many to conceal; or would bring before the world in the character of a criminal, some eminent individual, whose reward for a false acknowledgement of guilt would be great and whose vengeance for exposure might be terrible. Under circumstances like these, the accused is induced by threats or bribes to suppress the defence, and own himself the author of the crime imputed to him.

. . . [A] false confession of an offence may be made with the view of stifling inquiry unto other matters; as for instance, some more serious offence of which the confessionalist is as yet unsuspected.

The most fantastic shape of this anomaly springs from the state of mental unsoundness which is known by the name of taedium vitae. Several instances are to be found where persons tired of life have falsely accused themselves of *capital* crimes, which were either purely fictitious, or were committed by others.

. . . [Vanity may produce a confession.] False statements of this kind are sometimes the offspring of a morbid love of notoriety at any price. The motive that induces the adventurous youth to burn the temple of Ephesus would surely have been strong enough to induce him to declare himself, however innocent, the author of the mischief had it occurred accidentally.

Instances may be found of false confessions made with a view to some specific collateral end. . . . Soldiers engaged on foreign service not unfrequently declare themselves guilty of having committed crimes at home, in order that . . . they may escape from military duty. . . . And whether from such morbid love of notoriety, or mere weak-mindedness or a love of mischief, it is almost invariably the case that murders of a specially horrible kind – as for instance, the Whitechapel murders of prostitutes in 1888 and 1889 – are followed by a series of false confessions.

. . . [There are cases] where the person who makes the false confession is desirous of benefiting others; as, for instance, to save the life, fortune or reputation of, or to avert suffering from, a party whose interests are dearer to him than his own. . . .

The desire of *injuring* others has occasionally led to the like consequence. Persons reckless of their own fate have sought to work the ruin of their enemies by including false confessions of crimes and describing them as participators. We shall feel little surprise at this when we recollect how often persons have inflicted grievous wounds on themselves, and even in some instances, it is said, committed suicide, in order to bring down suspicion of intended or actual murder on detested individuals.

. . . [E]xtrajudicial, confessional statements . . . are subject to additional infirmative hypotheses, which are sometimes overlooked in practice. These are *mendacity* in the report, *misinterpretation* of the language used, and *incompleteness* of the statement.

1. '*Mendacity*' . . . [O]f all sorts of evidence, that which we are now considering is the most easy to fabricate, and however false the most difficult to confront and expose by any sort of counter-evidence . . .

2. '*Misinterpretation*' . . . [E]ntirely fallacious conclusions may be drawn from language uttered in jest, or by way of bravado. . . . [E]qually unfounded inferences are sometimes drawn from words . . . used with reference to an act not identical with the subject of accusation or suspicion; as where a man who has robbed or beaten another, learning that he has since died, utters an exclamation of regret for having ill-treated him. . . . [The greatest dangers arise from] the haste and eagerness of witnesses, and the love of the marvellous, so natural to the human mind, by

which people are frequently prompted to mistake expressions, as well as to imagine or exaggerate facts, especially where the crime is either very atrocious or very peculiar.

3. The remaining cause of error in confessorial evidence . . . is 'incompleteness'; ie where words, though not misunderstood in themselves, convey a false impression for want of some explanation which the speaker either neglected to give, or was prevented by interruption from giving, or which has been lost in consequence of the deafness or inattention of the hearers. 'Ill hearing makes ill rehearsing,' said our ancestors. Experience may have been forgotten or unheeded in consequence of witnesses not being aware of their importance, eg a man suspected of larceny acknowledges that he took the goods against the will of the owner, adding that he did so because he thought they were his own. Many a bystander, ignorant that this latter circumstance constitutes a legal defence, would remember only the first part of the statement.

. . . [I]t must never be forgotten that, in general . . . confessions constitute proof of a very satisfactory . . . character. Reason and the universal voice of mankind alike attest this, and legitimate use of the unhappy cases above recorded . . . is to put tribunals on their guard against attaching undue weight to this sort of evidence. The employing them as bugbears to terrify, or the converting them into excuses for indiscriminate scepticism or incredulity, is a perversion, if not a prostitution, of the human understanding.

Macaulay: History of England (Everyman edn), vol 1, ch 5, p 437

Words may easily be misunderstood by an honest man. They may easily be misconstrued by a knave. What was spoken metaphorically may be apprehended literally. What was spoken ludicrously may be apprehended seriously. A particle, a tense, a mood, an emphasis, may make the whole difference between guilt and innocence.

Hans Gross: Criminal Psychology (Trans Kallen, 1911), para 8, p 31 (quoted by Wigmore, Principles of Judicial Proof, 2nd edn (Boston, 1931), para 223

The confession is a very extraordinary psychological problem. In many cases the reasons for confession are very obvious. The criminal sees that the evidence is so complete that he is soon to be convicted and seeks a mitigation of the sentence by confession, or he hopes through a more honest narration of the crime to throw a great degree of the guilt on another. In addition there is a thread of vanity in confession – as among young peasants who confess to a greater share in a burglary than they actually had (easily discoverable by the magniloquent manner of describing their actual crime). Then there are confessions made for the sake of care and winter lodgings: the confession arising from 'firm conviction' (as among political criminals and others). There are even confessions arising from nobility, from the wish to save an intimate, and confessions intended to deceive, and such as occur especially in conspiracy and are made to gain time (either for the flight of the real criminal or for the destruction of compromising objects). Generally, in the latter case, guilt is admitted only until the plan for which it was made has succeeded; then the judge is surprised with a well-founded, regular, and successful establishment of an alibi. Not infrequently confession of small crimes is made to establish an alibi for a greater one . . .

Although this list of explicable confession types is long, it is in no way exhaustive. It is only a small portion of all the confessions that we receive; of these the greater part remain more or less unexplained . . . A number of cases may perhaps be explained through pressure of conscience, especially where there are involved hysterical or nervous persons who are plagued with vengeful images in which the ghost of their victim would appear, or in whose ear the unendurable clang of the stolen money never ceases, etc.

One justification for the confession rule suggested by Wigmore and by the judges in the influential early case of *R v Warickshall*, is that confessions which are not voluntary (in the technical sense) may well be false, whereas voluntary confessions are very likely to be true because they proceed from the promptings of remorse and the strain of continuously lying, and because of the unlikelihood of an innocent man acting so strongly against his self-interest as falsely to confess himself guilty. In an ideal world this basis for excluding confessions would demand an investigation of the accused's mind: was his motive for confessing such as to make it untrue? But motives being hard to investigate, the law has had to develop objective rules to exclude confessions. There are several possible sources of unreliability. One is the risk that the confession is fabricated, or misheard, or misreported. In England today this risk is much reduced in the case of confessions to police officers if they follow Code C or if a tape-recording is made: see section 3 of this chapter. Another problem is that the innocent may confess out of a desire for notoriety, or from shock, or suggestion, or hallucination. Another is that a suspect who is mentally incapable may make an untrue confession in order to please the investigator, without any conception of the consequences (see now Police and Criminal Evidence Act 1984, s 77: p 103, ante). Another is that the confessor may wish to protect another, or confess to a minor crime in order to avoid conviction for a major one, or obtain some other advantage from detention, eg protection or shelter. Thus the categories of voluntariness and truth are obviously not coincident; as the High Court of Australia remarked in *Basto v R* (1954) 91 CLR 628 at 640: 'A confessional statement may be voluntary and yet to act upon it might be quite unsafe; it may have no probative value. Or such a statement may be involuntary and yet carry with it the greatest assurance of its reliability or truth.' However, the vast bulk of confessions held inadmissible under the current rules are probably true, so that the reliability justification cannot support the width of the current law. Is a person likely to confess to what he has not done save in the face of the most grave pressure? Hence those who base the confession rule solely on reliability, as Wigmore did, may be strong critics of the current law.

It is difficult to estimate the effect of inducements on particular suspects; it is difficult to calculate the effect of inducements on particular suspects; it is difficult to calculate an individual's strengths and weaknesses, experience of the law and knowledge of his rights. So a wide rule excluding all confessions with an objective risk of untrustworthiness is defensible. However, there are some cases that are insupportable even on this basis.

A second rationale for the confession rule is that it is 'dangerous to leave such evidence to the jury' (*R v Baldry* (1852) 2 Den 430 at 442, per Pollock CB). A jury will too easily think a confession is decisive of guilt without paying attention to the other evidence. Confession evidence, which is so likely to result in a conviction if it is admitted, should be very carefully scrutinised.

Thirdly, as Lord Reid suggests in *Customs and Excise Comrs v Harz* [1967] 1 AC 760 at 820, [1967] 1 All ER 177 at 184, HL, there is a popular feeling that when a man is convicted solely on the basis of his own confession, the duty of the prosecution to prove him guilty has not been discharged. The prosecution should prove its own case, before a judge and jury in open court; it should not rely on men condemning themselves secretly under pressure in police stations, for there is a risk of agitated and frightened men lying even though innocent. This justification for the rule is like part of the rationale for the privilege against self-incrimination: the state should be made to rely on its powers of independent detection, not on confessions (see *McDermott v R* (1948) 76 CLR 501 at 513, per Dixon J; see also *Escobedo v Illinois* 378 US

478 (1964)). This is so even though Wigmore may be correct in asserting that there is no historical connexion between the two rules.

Fourthly, the special scrutiny of confessions tends to discourage undesirable police practices. The improprieties in question are of two kinds. One is a true prediction of an unlawful consequence ('Tell us the truth or we'll hit you'). The other is an untrue statement of law coupled with threats of criminal prosecution which, as the police know, will fail, eg the facts of *Harz's* case, involving threats to prosecute for failing to give information the police were not entitled to demand. This method of controlling impropriety is said to be indirect and clumsy – police misconduct should be controlled by disciplining the police. But at the moment the police discipline themselves. It is also said that the exclusion of confessions obtained by mild pressure, a very necessary form of evidence, may anger and frustrate the police so much that they become determined to use serious illegalities to bring the guilty to justice or at any rate destruction. Further, a confession may be used to obtain leads to other evidence even if not itself used in court. The issues here are similar to those respecting the exclusion of illegally obtained evidence.

However, in *R v Sang* [1980] AC 402 at 436, [1979] 2 All ER 1222 at 1230, HL, Lord Diplock denied that the law was based on any disciplinary principle, and as Cross pointed out (5th edition, p 539), 'It certainly strains language to say that it is "improper" for a police officer to give a perfectly correct answer to a question put to him by a suspect.' There is no doubt, however, that even after the Police and Criminal Evidence Act 1984 the confession rule is sometimes used to exclude confessions resulting from police misconduct short of oppression, though not in a very precise way: *R v Waters* [1989] Crim LR 62, CA; *R v Doolan* [1988] Crim LR 747, CA.

FURTHER READING

Birch [1989] Crim LR 95.

2 Evidence derived from inadmissible confessions

If the accused's confession is ruled inadmissible it may nevertheless be relevant in two quite independent ways. First, the inadmissible confession may show something about the accused's way of expressing himself, or familiarity with a particular language, or state of mind at the time the confession was made.

Secondly, the confession may have been acted upon in the sense that information contained in it may have enabled the police or other investigating authority to proceed in a particular way, for example recovering property from a place mentioned in the confession or interviewing a person named in the confession. In that case two questions arise. Is the subsequently discovered evidence admissible? If so, is the confession itself now admissible in whole or in part? Before 1984 the English law on this topic was difficult to discover and state. It was generally accepted that the subsequently discovered fact was admissible, the only authority to the contrary being the almost universally disapproved *R v Barker* [1941] 2 KB 381, [1941] 3 All ER 33. Some authorities (including those extracted below) clearly stated that there was to be no consequential admission of the confession. To allow the inadmissible confession to be heard would undercut the confession rules so far as they seek to control police misconduct, and to allow it even to be mentioned would be to tell the jury indirectly what they were forbidden to hear directly. Others, however, favoured a broader view. If part of a confession related directly to subsequently discovered fact, it would appear that that part of it at least is reliable and so should be admitted.

The majority of the Criminal Law Revision Committee took a middle line. They would have admitted the fact discovered, together with evidence that the discovery of this fact was made 'as a result of' a statement made by the accused. To allow more would cause difficulties of practice as well as policy (CLRC 68–9). This recommendation was not in the end adopted but is the rule in some other jurisdictions (see below).

R v Warickshall   (1783) 1 Leach 263

The accused was charged with receiving stolen property. It was found hidden in her bed in consequence of her improperly induced confession. The evidence of the finding was admitted.

Nares B (with whom Eyre B agreed): Confessions are received in evidence, or rejected as inadmissible, under a consideration whether they are not intitled to credit . . . This principle respecting confessions has no application whatever as to admission or rejection of facts . . . for a fact, if it exists at all, must exist invariably in the same manner, whether the confession from which it is derived be in other respects true or false. Facts thus obtained, however, must be fully and satisfactorily proved, without calling in the aid of any part of the confession from which they may have been derived . . . [T]he fact may be admitted on other evidence; for as no part of an improper confession can be heard, it can never be legally known whether the fact was derived through the means of such confession or no . . . [A]nd the consequences to public justice would be dangerous indeed; for if men were enabled to regain stolen property, and the evidence of attendant facts were to be suppressed, because they had regained it by means of an improper confession, it would be holding out an opportunity to compound felonies . . . It is true, that many able judges have conceived, that it would be an exceedingly hard case, that a man whose life is at stake, having been lulled into a notion of security by promises of favour, and in consequence of those promises has been induced to make a confession by the means of which the property is found, should afterwards find that the confession with regard to the property found is to operate against him. But this subject has more than once undergone the solemn consideration of the Twelve Judges; and a majority of them were clearly of opinion, that although confessions improperly obtained cannot be received in evidence, yet that any acts done afterwards might be given in evidence, notwithstanding that they were done in consequence of such confessions.

NOTE

R v Mosey (1784) 1 Leach 265n, and *R v Harvey* (1800) 2 East PC 658 are to the same effect, and *R v Lockhart* (1785) 1 Leach 386 extended the doctrine to permit the reception of the evidence whose identity had been discovered through the confession.

R v Berriman   (1854) 6 Cox CC 388

The accused was charged with concealment of the birth of her child. Erle J refused to admit a confession made to a magistrate.

Locke . . . [counsel for the prosecution] then proposed to put a witness a question, whether in consequence of the answer she had given to the magistrate, he had made a search in a particular spot, and had found a certain thing.

Erle J: No! *Not in consequence of what she said.* You may ask him what search was made, and what things were found, but under the circumstances, I cannot allow that proceeding to be connected with the prisoner.

The prisoner was acquitted.

Chalmers v HM Advocate   1954 JC 66

The accused made a confession which was inadmissible and then took police officers to a cornfield where he pointed out the purse of a murder victim. The High Court of Judiciary held that evidence of the pointing out had been wrongly admitted.

Lord Cooper LJ-G: I take next the episode of the cornfield. This is related to the interrogation in two ways. In point of time the visit to the cornfield followed immediately after the further interrogation which followed the taking of the 'statement'. Moreover it is admitted that during the further interrogation the appellant was asked what happened to the purse, and that it was 'in consequence of' his answer to that question that he was taken to the cornfield 'to facilitate any search'. I therefore regard the visit to the cornfield under the surveillance of the police as part and parcel of the same transaction as the interrogation, and, if the interrogation and the 'statement' which emerged from it are inadmissible as 'unfair', the same criticism must attach to the conducted visit to the cornfield. Next, I feel unable to accept the distinction drawn by the presiding Judge between statements and 'actings', and I suspect that a fallacy lurks in the words 'actings'. The actings of an accused, if unattended by such circumstances as are here presented, are normally competent evidence against him. For instance, if the police had kept watch on the accused and had seen him go to the cornfield to retrieve the purse, such evidence would have been perfectly competent. Again 'actings', in the sense of a gesture or sign, may be indistinguishable from a communication by word of mouth or by writing. The question here was – Where exactly is the purse? and this question might have been answered by an oral description of the place where it was, or by going to the place and silently pointing to that place. It seems to me to make no difference for present purposes which method of answering the question was adopted; from which it follows that, if, in the circumstances of this case, the 'statement' was inadmissible, the episode of the cornfield was equally inadmissible. The significance of the episode is plain, for it showed that the appellant knew where the purse was. If the police had simply produced and proved the finding of, the purse, that evidence would have carried them little or no distance in this case towards implication of the appellant. It was essential that the appellant should be linked up with the purse, either by oral confession or by its equivalent – tacit admission of knowledge of its whereabouts obtained as a sequel to the interrogation.

[Lord Thomson LJ-C and Lords Carmont, Patrick and Mackintosh concurred.]

COMMENT

As Lord Cooper LJ-G points out, the admission of the fact discovered and nothing more will sometimes incriminate the accused and sometimes not. It did not in *Chalmers' Case* or *Berriman's Case* or *Trimbuk v Madhya Pradesh* [1954] AIR SC 39 because there was no particular connexion, other than the inadmissible confession, between the accused and the public place where the thing was found. In *R v Warickshall* the fact discovered did incriminate the accused, because it was found in his bed, which of itself provided a link between him and it; similarly if the thing discovered bore fingerprints or other traces of the accused's dealing with it.

Police and Criminal Evidence Act 1984

76   . . .

(4)   The fact that a confession is wholly or partly excluded in pursuance of this section shall not affect the admissibility in evidence –

(a)   of any facts discovered as a result of the confession; or

(b)   where the confession is relevant as showing that the accused speaks, writes or expresses himself in a particular way, of so much of the confession as is necessary to show that he does so.

(5)   Evidence that a fact to which this subsection applies was discovered as a result of a statement made by an accused person shall not be admissible unless evidence of how it was discovered is given by him or on his behalf.

(6)   Subsection (5) above applies –

(a)   to any fact discovered as a result of a confession which is wholly excluded in pursuance of this section; and

(b)   to any fact discovered as a result of a confession which is partly so excluded, if that fact is discovered as a result of the excluded part of the confession.

COMMENTS

1. Subsection 4(*a*) enacts the narrow common law view, whilst sub-ss (5) and (6) follow the view of a minority in the Criminal Law Revision Committee. Section 76(2) (above, p 154) prevents the prosecution from using an excluded confession for any other hearsay or non-hearsay purposes other than those permitted by s 76(4)(*b*), so such a statement would not now be admissible to show, for example, the state of mind of its maker at the time he made it (see Andrews [1963] Crim LR 76). For the sort of thing which is envisaged by this paragraph, consider the facts of *R v Voisin* [1918] 1 KB 531, [1918–19] All ER Rep 491, CCA or the Lindbergh kidnapping case, both referred to in section 1F of this chapter. If the words 'Bladie Belgiam' or Hauptmann's misspellings had been contained in an inadmissible confession, s 76(4)(*b*) would now allow that part of the confession to be admitted.

2. The effect of sub-s (5) is that evidence that the fact was discovered as a result of the excluded confession may be given not only by the accused, but also by a co-accused or the prosecution if to amplify or contradict evidence already given by the accused. There is no provision making any part of the confession itself admissible in these circumstances.

OTHER JURISDICTIONS

A number of alternative approaches are possible. Which is chosen will depend largely on whether the local attitude to excluded confessions depends more on the disciplinary or the reliability principle. Thus in the United States of America, the 'fruit of the poisonous tree' doctrine, despite recent qualifications, has tended to prohibit the adduction in evidence of any facts discovered as a result of inadmissible confessions. *Chalmers v HM Advocate* has been followed by the Supreme Court of Queensland (Gibbs J) in *R v Beere* [1965] Qd R 370. Following the Charter of Rights and Freedoms, the position in Canada is now similar: *R v Black* (1989) 50 CCC (3d) 1. In Eire there is authority to the same effect (*People v O'Brien* [1965] IR 142 at 166,

SC), but it seems that if the evidence is obtained as a result of a deliberate contravention of constitutional rights it is absolutely inadmissible: *People v Lynch* [1987] IR 64 at 79, SC. But in countries to which the Indian Evidence Act applies the subsequently discovered fact is seen as confirming part of the confession and hence making that part admissible, and, as Wigmore pointed out, there are arguments for going further still. In New Zealand the High Court held in *R v Dally* [1990] 2 NZLR 184 that (although the subsequently discovered facts would apparently normally be admitted), there was no need to adopt an inflexible rule as to how much of the confirmed confession they made admissible. The matter should be dealt with by the judge in the exercise of his discretion.

Indian Evidence Act 1872

27 Provided that when any fact as deposed to is discovered in consequence of information received from a person accused of any offence, in the custody of a police officer, so much of such information, whether it amounts to a confession or not, as relates distinctly to the fact thereby discovered may be proved.

COMMENT

The previous section makes inadmissible most confessions made by persons in the custody of a police officer. There is a wealth of authority on the questions when the section applies (eg *Ramkishan Mithanlal Sharma v Bombay* [1955] AIR SC 104; *Aher Raja Khima v Saurashtra* [1956] AIR SC 217; *Prabhoo v Uttar Pradesh* [1963] AIR SC 1113) and precisely how much of the confession it makes admissible (eg *Udai Bhan v Uttar Pradesh* [1962] AIR SC 1116; *Chinnaswamy Reddy v Andhra Pradesh* [1962] AIR SC 1788) – which might tend to suggest that it is not a satisfactory compromise. It is based on the English authority of *R v Gould* (1840) 9 C & P 364; see Stephen, *Digest of the Law of Evidence* Art 22.

Evidence Act (Nigeria) 1958

29 Where information is received from a person who is accused of an offence, whether such person is in custody or not, and as a consequence of such information any fact is discovered, the discovery of that fact, together with evidence that such discovery was made in consequence of the information received from the accused, may be given in evidence where such information itself would not be admissible in evidence.

Wigmore: Treatise on the Anglo-American System of Evidence in Trials at Common Law, 3rd edn, para 858

No principle ever appears to have been offered to justify or explain this [position] . . .
    There is, however, apparently an explanation for it. In the case of a confession of stealing goods and their subsequent discovery as described (almost the only situation over which this question arises), there is just one hypothesis on which the jury may stop short of believing the confession after this confirmation, namely, the accused may know of the stealing and of the

place of hiding, but he may still *not* be the thief. Now we may determine to ignore the improbability of the latter consequence, but we cannot ignore the former. That his confession of stealing is true may be hard to avoid, but that he knew where the stolen goods were . . . is impossible to avoid. We shall admit, then, what as rational beings we are obliged to admit, but we shall stubbornly draw the line there; that seems to be the rationale of the above distinction. The result is, that so far as the discovery shows that the person knew where the stolen goods were, we are about to hear about it, but we are to hear nothing more.

Now, in thus accepting whatever bears on his knowledge, the line becomes hard to draw. There may be several places to draw it. (1) The law may admit merely the fact that the discovery was made, and that it was made in consequence of a statement by that person. Or (2) it may go further and admit the details of the accused's conduct in that he went to the place and pointed out the goods. Or (3) it may go still further and admit the words of his statement describing the property and the place, exhibiting as they do a detailed knowledge on his part, and yet falling short of confession of the stealing. All these show knowledge and only knowledge.

The distinction, then, while it is artificial and against common sense, has at least a certain intelligibility beneath it.

The drawbacks of this rule are that it undercuts the confession rule so far as the rule seeks to deprive the police of the benefits of misconduct, and, as Wigmore points out (below), that problems may arise in determining how much should be admitted apart from the consequential fact.

Wigmore: Treatise on the Anglo-American System of Evidence in Trials at Common Law, 3rd edn, para 857

[A] confirmation on material points produces ample persuasion of the trustworthiness of the whole. It can hardly be supposed that at certain parts the possible fiction stopped and the truth began, and that by a marvellous coincidence the truthful parts are exactly those which a subsequent search (more or less controlled by chance) happened to confirm . . . If we are to cease distrusting any part, we should cease distrusting all.

FURTHER READING

Cowen and Carter, ch 2; Gotlieb, 72 LQR 209.

QUESTION

Is the use allowed to be made of confessions by s 76(4)–(6) compatible with the rationale of the rules relating to the exclusion of confessions?

3   The conduct of investigations

The subject-matter of this section and the next chapter are closely related, for the terms of s 67(11) of the Police and Criminal Evidence Act 1984 (below) taken with s 78 (ch 9.2) lead to the possibility of the exclusion of evidence at the trial because it has not been gathered in accordance with the rules for the conduct of investigations. However, it is convenient to consider the rules and the consequences of their breach separately.

During the nineteenth century the judges began developing ideas independently of the confession rule on how police interrogation should be
conducted. As has been noted earlier, there was substantial judicial suspicion
of the police. Some judges thought the police should ask no questions of a
man in custody, because the accused was incompetent and could not explain
away admissions. In *R v Male* (1893) 17 Cox CC 689 at 690, Cave J said:
'The law does not allow the judge or the jury to put questions in open court
to prisoners; and it would be monstrous if the law permitted a police officer to
go, without anyone being present to see how the matter was conducted, and
put a prisoner through an examination, and then produce the effects of that
examination against him.' More succinctly, 'a policeman should keep his
mouth shut and his ears open'. Others thought that questioning was permissible, provided the suspect was cautioned – told he was not obliged to say
anything. The purpose of the caution was to remove any thought in the
accused's mind that he *must* talk. Some judges thought it to be necessary in all
cases, others thought its absence was merely prima facie evidence of involuntariness. To clear up doubts the police requested assistance: thus Hawkins J in
1882 wrote a foreword to the Police Code containing many points similar to
the later Judges' Rules. But doubts persisted. In 1906, at the Birmingham
Assizes, one policeman was judicially criticised for using the caution, and
another for not using it. In 1912 a code called the Judges' Rules was issued.
Their spirit was that police questioning must be permitted but controlled.
The Judges' Rules have been superseded in England by the Code of Practice
(Code C) made under s 66 of the Police and Criminal Evidence Act 1984,
but the introduction to their last revision in 1964 remains an accurate state-
ment of principle.

R v Cook   (1918) 34 TLR 515, CCA

Darling J: It would be a lamentable thing if the police were not allowed to make enquiries, and
if statements made by prisoners were excluded because of a shadowy notion that if the prisoners
were left to themselves they would not have made them.

Practice Note (Judges' Rules)   [1964] 1 All ER 237, [1964] 1 WLR 152, CCA

Lord Parker CJ: The origin of the Judges' Rules is probably to be found in a letter dated
October 26, 1906, which the then Lord Chief Justice, Lord Alverstone, wrote to the Chief
Constable of Birmingham in answer to a request for advice in consequence of the fact that on the
same circuit one judge had censured a member of his force for having cautioned a prisoner, while
another judge had censured a constable for having omitted to do so. The first four of the present
rules were formulated and approved by the judges of the King's Bench Division in 1912; the
remaining five in 1918. They have been much criticised, inter alia, for alleged lack of clarity and
of efficacy for the protection of persons who are questioned by police officers; on the other hand
it has been maintained that their application unduly hampers the detection and punishment of
crime. A committee of judges has devoted considerable time and attention to producing, after
consideration of representative views, a new set of rules which has been approved by a meeting of
all the Queen's Bench Judges.

The judges control the conduct of trials and the admission of evidence against persons on trial
before them: they do not control or in any way initiate or supervise police activities or conduct.
As stated in paragraph (e) of the introduction to the new rules, it is the law that answers and
statements made are only admissible in evidence if they have been voluntary in the sense that

they have not been obtained by fear of prejudice or hope of advantage, exercised or held out by a person in authority, or by oppression. The new rules do not purport, any more than the old rules, to envisage or deal with the many varieties of conduct which might render answers and statements involuntary and therefore inadmissible. The rules merely deal with particular aspects of the matter. Other matters such as affording reasonably comfortable conditions, adequate breaks for rest and refreshment, special procedures in the case of persons unfamiliar with the English language or of immature age or feeble understanding are proper subjects for administrative directions to the police.

These rules do not affect the principles:

(a) That citizens have a duty to help a police officer to discover and apprehend offenders;

(b) That police officers, otherwise than by arrest, cannot compel any person against his will to come to or remain in any police station;

(c) That every person at any stage of an investigation should be able to communicate and to consult privately with a solicitor. This is so even if he is in custody provided that in such a case no unreasonable delay or hindrance is caused to the processes of investigation or the administration of justice by his doing so;

(d) That when a police officer who is making inquiries of any person about an offence has enough evidence to prefer a charge against that person for the offence, he should without delay cause the person to be charged or informed that he may be prosecuted for the offence;

(e) That it is a fundamental condition of the admissibility in evidence against any person, equally of any oral answer given by that person to a question put by a police officer and of any statement made by that person, that it shall have been voluntary . . .

NOTE

Principle (e) should now be read in the light of the Police and Criminal Evidence Act 1984, s 76, which replaces the concept of 'voluntariness' as a precondition of admissibility for confessions.

R v Lee   (1950) 82 CLR 133

After three hours' questioning one accused confessed and on being confronted with the confession the other two did so as well. Their appeals to the High Court of Australia against admitting the evidence failed.

Latham CJ, McTiernan, Webb, Fullager and Kitto JJ: There seems to be really one rule, the rule that a statement must be voluntary in order to be admissible. Any one of a variety of elements, including a threat or promise by a person in authority, will suffice to deprive it of a voluntary character. It is implicit in the statement of the rule, and it is now well settled, that the Crown has the burden of satisfying the trial judge in every case as to the voluntary character of a statement before it becomes admissible . . .

No question of discretion can arise unless the statement in question is a voluntary statement in the common law sense. If it is non-voluntary it is . . . legally inadmissible. If it is voluntary, circumstances may be proved which call for an exercise of discretion. The only circumstance which has been suggested as calling for an exercise of the discretion is the use of 'improper' or 'unfair' methods by police officers in interrogating suspected persons or persons in custody (*McDermott v R* (1948) 76 CLR 501 at 506–7 and 513). What is impropriety in police methods and what would be unfairness in admitting in evidence against an accused person a statement obtained by improper methods must depend upon the circumstances of each particular case, and no attempt should be made to define and thereby to limit the extent of the application of these concepts . . .

. . . The placing of an onus on the Crown in connexion with the exercise of a discretion to reject evidence of the kind in question represents in our opinion a new departure, and we do not think that there is any justification for it. The discretion rule represents an exception to a rule of law, and we think that it is for the accused to bring himself within the exception. We have called attention to the great breadth of the common law rule that a statement is not admissible unless it is proved to be voluntary. If it is proved to be voluntary then it is *prima facie* admissible. It is admissible as a matter of law unless reason is shown for rejecting it in the exercise of discretion.

. . . Surely, if the judge thought that 'impropriety' was calculated to cause an untrue admission to be made, that would be a very strong reason for exercising his discretion against admitting the statement in question. If, on the other hand, he thought that it was not likely to result in an untrue admission being made, that would be a good reason, though not a conclusive reason, for allowing the evidence to be given . . .

With regard to the Chief Commissioner's Standing Orders, which correspond in Victoria to the Judges' Rules in England, they are not rules of law, and the mere fact that one or more of them have been broken does not of itself mean that the accused has been so treated that it would be unfair to admit his statement. Nor does proof of a breach throw any burden on the Crown of showing some affirmative reason why the statement in question should be admitted. As has already been pointed out, the protection afforded by the rule that a statement must be voluntary goes so far that it is only reasonable to require that some substantial reason should be shown to justify a discretionary rejection of a voluntary admission. The rules may be regarded in a general way as prescribing a standard of propriety, and it is in this sense that what may be called the spirit of the rules should be regarded. But it cannot be denied that they do not in every respect afford a very satisfactory standard. Their language is in some cases imperative and in others merely advisory: sometimes the word 'must' is used: sometimes the word 'should', and the tendency to take them as a standard can easily develop into a tendency to apply rejection of evidence as in some sort a sanction for a failure by a police officer to obey the rules of his own organisation, a matter which is of course entirely for the executive. It is indeed, we think, a mistake to approach the matter by asking as separate questions, first, whether the police officer concerned has acted improperly, and if he has, then whether it would be unfair to reject the accused's statement. It is better to ask whether, having regard to the conduct of the police and all the circumstances of the case, it would be unfair to use his own statement against the accused. We know of no better exposition of the whole matter than that which is to be found in the two passages from the judgment of Street J . . . *R v Jeffries* (1946) 47 SRNSW 284 at 312 . . . His Honour said:

'It is a question of degree in each case, and it is for the presiding Judge to determine, in the light of all the circumstances, whether the statements or admissions of the accused have been extracted from him under conditions which render it unjust to allow his own words to be given in evidence against him.'

His Honour then proceeded to refer to the account of the trial of Jones and Hulton published in the *Old Bailey Trial Series*. 'It was conceded,' he said, that in that case 'the examination demonstrably transgressed the limits permitted under the Judges' Rules'. It appeared, however, that the accused was in a condition properly to answer to the 'gruelling questioning' which had been administered to him, and the learned trial judge admitted the evidence. An appeal was dismissed by the Court of Criminal Appeal. His Honour then concludes:

'The obligation resting upon police officers is to put all questions fairly and to refrain from anything in the nature of a threat, or any attempt to extort an admission. But it is in the interests of the community that all crimes should be fully investigated with the object of bringing malefactors to justice, and such investigations must not be unduly hampered. They must be aimed at the ascertainment of the truth, and must not be carried out with the idea of manufacturing evidence or extorting some admission and thereby securing a conviction. Upon the particular circumstances of each case depends the answer to the question as to the admissibility of such evidence'.

But in any case an invitation to explain established facts can hardly be called cross-examination in any relevant sense. It is cross-examination in the sense of breaking down the will and extorting admissions by persons who are being questioned by the police that is to be reprehended. Rule 8 was not applicable to any material time.

. . . It is, of course, of the most vital importance that detectives should be scrupulously careful and fair. The uneducated – perhaps semi-literate – man who has a 'record' and is suspected of some offence may be practically helpless in the hands of an over-zealous police officer. The latter may be honest and sincere, but his position of superiority is so great and so over-powering that a 'statement' may be 'taken' which seems very damning but which is really very unreliable. The case against an accused person in such a case sometimes depends entirely on the 'statement' made to police. In such a case it may well be that his statement, if admitted, would prejudice him very unfairly. Such persons stand often in grave need of that protection which only an extremely vigilant court can give them. They provide the real justification for the Judges' Rules in England and the Chief Commissioner's Standing Orders in Victoria, and they provide (if we are to assume that the requirement of voluntariness is not enough to ensure justice) a justification for the existence of an ultimate discretion as to the admission of confessional evidence. The duty of police officers to be scrupulously careful and fair is not, of course, confined to such cases. But, where intelligent persons are being questioned with regard to a murder, the position cannot properly be approached from quite the same point of view. A minuteness of scrutiny, which in the case may be entirely appropriate, may in another be entirely misplaced and tend only to a perversion of justice. Each case must, of course, depend upon its own circumstances considered in their entirety. No better guidance is, we think, to be found than in the passages from the judgment of Street J in *R v Jeffries* which we have quoted above.

Police and Criminal Evidence Act 1984

66   The Secretary of State shall issue codes of practice in connection with –
　(a)　the exercise by police officers of statutory powers –
　　　(i)　to search a person without first arresting him; or
　　　(ii)　to search a vehicle without making an arrest;
　(b)　the detention, treatment, questioning and identification of persons by police officers;
　(c)　searches of premises by police officers; and
　(d)　the seizure of property found by police officers on persons or premises.

67   (1)   When the Secretary of State proposes to issue a code of practice to which this section applies, he shall prepare and publish a draft of that code, shall consider any representations made to him about the draft and may modify the draft accordingly.
　(2)   This section applies to a code of practice under section 60 or 66 above.
　(3)   The Secretary of State shall lay before both Houses of Parliament a draft of any code of practice prepared by him under this section.
　(4)   When the Secretary of State has laid the draft of a code before Parliament, he may bring the code into operation by order made by statutory instrument.
　(5)   No order under subsection (4) above shall have effect until approved by a resolution of each House of Parliament.
　(6)   An order bringing a code of practice into operation may contain such transitional provisions or savings as appear to the Secretary of State to be necessary or expedient in connection with the code of practice thereby brought into operation.
　(7)   The Secretary of State may from time to time revise the whole or any part of a code of practice to which this section applies and issue that revised code; and the foregoing provisions of this section shall apply (with appropriate modifications) to such a revised code as they apply to the first issue of a code.
　(8)   [Repealed by Police and Magistrates' Courts Act 1994, s 37(9)]
　(9)   Persons other than police officers who are charged with the duty of investigating offences or charging offenders shall in the discharge of that duty have regard to any relevant provision of such a code.
　(10)   A failure on the part –
　(a)　of a police officer to comply with any provision of such a code; or
　(b)　of any person other than a police officer who is charged with the duty of investigating offences or charging offenders to have regard to any relevant provision of such a code in the discharge of that duty;
shall not of itself render him liable to any criminal or civil proceedings.
　(11)   In all criminal and civil proceedings any such code shall be admissible in evidence; and if any provision of such a code appears to the court or tribunal conducting the proceedings to be relevant to any question arising in the proceedings it shall be taken into account in determining that question . . .

NOTE

Five Codes have been issued, of which revised editions of the first four came into effect on 1 April 1991, and newly revised versions of all five on 10 April 1995. The five are as follows:
- Code of Practice for the Exercise of Police Officers of Statutory Powers of Stop and Search (Code A);
- Code of Practice for the Searching of Premises by Police Officers and the Seizure of Property found by Police Officers on Persons or Premises (Code B);
- Code of Practice for the Detention, Treatment and Questioning of Persons by Police Officers (Code C);
- Code of Practice for the Identification of Persons by Police Officers (Code D);
- Code of Practice on Tape Recording (Code E).

The following extracts from Code C give a fair idea of its content, tone and concerns.

Code C: Code of Practice for the Detention, Treatment and Questioning of Persons by Police Officers (Revised 1995)

1 General

1.1 All persons in custody must be dealt with expeditiously, and released as soon as the need for detention has ceased to apply.

1.1A A custody officer is required to perform the functions specified in this code as soon as is practicable. A custody officer shall not be in breach of this code in the event of delay provided that the delay is justifiable and that every reasonable step is taken to prevent unnecessary delay. the custody record shall indicate where a delay has occurred and the reason why. [*See Note 1H*]

1.2 This code of practice must be readily available at all police stations for consultation by police officers, detained persons and members of the public.

1.3 The notes for guidance included are not provisions of this code, but are guidance to police officers and others about its application and interpretation. Provisions in the annexes to this code are provisions of this code.

1.4 If an officer has any suspicion, or is told in good faith, that a person of any age may be mentally disordered or mentally handicapped, or mentally incapable of understanding the significance of questions put to him or his replies, then that person shall be treated as a mentally disordered or mentally handicapped person for the purposes of this code.

1.5 If anyone appears to be under the age of 17 then he shall be treated as a juvenile for the purposes of this code in the absence of clear evidence to show that he is older.

1.6 If a person appears to be blind or seriously visually handicapped, deaf, unable to read, unable to speak or has difficulty orally because of a speech impediment, he should be treated as such for the purposes of this code in the absence of clear evidence to the contrary.

1.7 In this code 'the appropriate adult' means:

(a) in the case of a juvenile:

(i) his parent or guardian (or, if he is in care, the care authority or voluntary organisation);

(ii)   a social worker; or

(iii) failing either of the above, another responsible adult aged 18 or over who is not a police officer or employed by the police.

(b)   in the case of a person who is mentally disordered or mentally handicapped:

(i)   a relative, guardian or other person responsible for his care or custody;

(ii) someone who has experience of dealing with mentally disordered or mentally handicapped persons but is not a police officer or employed by the police (such as an approved social worker as defined by the Mental Health Act 1983 or a specialist social worker); or

(iii) failing either of the above, some other responsible adult aged 18 or over who is not a police officer or employed by the police.

1.8   Whenever this code requires a person to be given certain information he does not have to be given it if he is incapable at the time of understanding what is said to him or is violent or likely to become violent or is in urgent need of medical attention, but he must be given it as soon as practicable.

1.9   Any reference to a custody officer in this code includes an officer who is performing the functions of a custody officer.

1.10   This code applies to persons who are in custody at police stations whether or not they have been arrested for an offence and to those who have been removed to a police station as a place of safety under sections 135 and 136 of the Mental Health Act 1983.

1.11   Persons in police detention include persons taken to a police station after being arrested under section 14 of the Prevention of Terrorism (Temporary Provisions) Act 1989 or under paragraph 6 of Schedule 5 to that Act by an examining officer who is a constable.

1.12.   This code does not apply to the following groups of people in custody:

(i)   people who have been arrested by officers from a police force in Scotland exercising their powers of detention under section 137(2) of the Criminal Justice and Public Order Act 1994 (Cross Border Powers of Arrest etc);

(ii) people arrested under section 3(5) of the Asylum and Immigration Appeals Act 1993 for the purpose of having their fingerprints taken;

(iii) people who have been served a notice advising them of their detention under powers contained in the Immigration Act 1971;

(iv) convicted or remanded prisoners held in police cells on behalf of the Prison Service under the Imprisonment (Temporary Provisions) Act 1980;

but the provisions on conditions of detention and treatment in sections 8 and 89 of this code must be considered as the minimum standards of treatment for such detainees.

Notes for Guidance

1A   Although certain sections of this code (eg, section 9 – treatment of detained persons) apply specifically to persons in custody at police stations, those there voluntarily to assist with an investigation should be treated with no less consideration (eg, offered refreshments at appropriate times) and enjoy an absolute right to obtain legal advice or communicate with anyone outside the police station.

1B   This code does not affect the principle that all citizens have a duty to help police officers to prevent crime and discover offenders. This is a civic rather than a legal duty; but when a police officer is trying to discover whether, or by whom, an offence has been committed he is entitled to question any person from whom he thinks useful information can be obtained, subject to the restrictions imposed by this code. A person's declaration that he is unwilling to reply does not alter this entitlement.

1C The parent or guardian of a juvenile should be the appropriate adult unless he is suspected of involvement in the offence, is the victim, is a witness, is involved in the investigation or has received admissions. In such circumstances it will be desirable for the appropriate adult to be some other person. If the parent of a juvenile is estranged from the juvenile, he should not be asked to act as the appropriate adult if the juvenile expressly and specifically objects to his presence.

1H Paragraph 1.1A is intended to cover the kinds of delays which may occur in the processing of detained persons because, for example, a large number of suspects are brought into the police station simultaneously to be placed in custody, or interview rooms are all being used, or where there are difficulties in contacting the appropriate adult, solicitor or interpreter.

. . .

2 Custody records

2.1   A separate custody record must be opened as soon as practicable for each person who is brought to a police station under arrest or is arrested at the police station having attended there voluntarily. All information which has to be recorded under this code must be recorded as soon as practicable, in the custody record unless otherwise specified.

. . .

[The recording and authentication of nearly every step taken in connexion with a person's detention and questioning is a major concern of the Code. The provisions requiring such records have not, on the whole, been extracted here.]

3 Initial action

(a) Detained persons: normal procedure

3.1   When a person is brought to a police station under arrest or is arrested at the police station having attended there voluntarily the custody officer must tell him clearly of the following rights and of the fact that they are continuing rights which may be exercised at any stage during the period in custody.

    (i)   the right to have someone informed of his arrest in accordance with section 5 below;

    (ii)   the right to consult privately with a solicitor in accordance with section 6 below, and the fact that independent legal advice is available free of charge; and

    (iii)   the right to consult this and the other codes of practice.

3.2   In addition the custody officer must give the person a written notice setting out the above three rights, the right to a copy of the custody record in accordance with paragraph 2.4 above and the caution in the terms prescribed in section 10 below. The notice must also explain the arrangements for obtaining legal advice. The custody officer must also give the person an additional written notice briefly setting out his entitlements while in custody. The custody officer shall ask the person to sign the custody record to acknowledge receipt of these notices and any refusal to sign must be recorded on the custody record.

3.3   A citizen of an independent commonwealth country or a national of a foreign country (including the Republic of Ireland) must be informed as soon as practicable of his rights of communication with his High Commission, Embassy or Consulate.

3.4   The custody officer shall note on the custody record any comment the person may make in relation to the arresting officer's account but shall not invite comment. If the custody officer authorises a person's detention he must inform him of the grounds as soon as practicable and in any case before that person is questioned about any offence. The custody officer shall note any comment the person may make in respect of the decision to detain him but, again, shall not invite comment. The custody officer shall not put specific questions to the person regarding his involvement in any offence, nor in respect of any comments he may make in response to the arresting officer's account or the decision to place him in detention. Such an exchange is likely to constitute an interview as defined by paragraph 11.1A and would require the associated safeguards included in section 11.

3.5   The custody officer shall ask the detained person whether at this time he would like legal advice.

. . .

(b)   Detained persons: special groups

. . .

(c)   Persons attending a police station voluntarily

3.15   Any person attending a police station voluntarily for the purpose of assisting with an investigation may leave at will unless placed under arrest. If it is decided that he should not be allowed to do so then he must be informed at once that he is under arrest and brought before the custody officer, who is responsible for ensuring that he is notified of his rights in the same way as other detained persons. If he is not placed under arrest but is cautioned in accordance with section 10 below, the officer who gives the caution must at the same time inform him that he is not under arrest, that he is not obliged to remain at the police station but that if he remains at the police station he may obtain free legal advice if he wishes. The officer shall point out that the right to legal advice includes the right to speak with a solicitor on the telephone and ask him if he wishes to do so.

3.16   If a person who is attending the police station voluntarily (in accordance with paragraph 3.15) asks about his entitlement to legal advice, he should be given a copy of the notice explaining the arrangements for obtaining legal advice.

. . .

4   Detained persons' property

4.1   The custody officer is responsible for:

(a)   ascertaining:

(i)   what property a detained person has with him when he comes to the police station (whether on arrest, re-detention on answering to bail, commitment to prison custody on the order or sentence of a court, lodgement at the police station with a view to his production in court from such custody, arrival at a police station on transfer from detention at another station or from hospital or on detention under section 135 or 136 of the Mental Health Act 1983);

(ii)   what property he might have acquired for a unlawful or harmful purpose while in custody.

(b)   the safekeeping of any property which is taken from him and which remains at the police station.

To these ends the custody officer may search him or authorise his being searched to the extent that he considers necessary (provided that a search of intimate parts of the body or involving the removal of more than outer clothing may be made in accordance with Annex A to this code). A search may only be carried out by an officer of the same sex as the person searched.

. . .

5 Right not to be held incommunicado

5.1   Any person arrested and held in custody at a police station or other premises may on request have one person known to him or who is likely to take an interest in his welfare informed at public expense as soon as practicable of his whereabouts. If the person cannot be contacted the person who has made the request may choose up to two alternatives. If they too cannot be contacted the person in charge of detention or of the investigation has discretion to allow further attempts until the information has been conveyed.

5.2   The exercise of the above right in respect of each of the persons nominated may be delayed only in accordance with Annex B to this code.

. . .

6 Right to legal advice

(a) Action

6.1   Subject to the provisos in Annex B all people in police detention must be informed that they may at any time consult and communicate privately, whether in person, in writing or on the telephone with a solicitor, and that independent legal advice is available from the duty solicitor.

6.3   A poster advertising the right to have legal advice must be prominently displayed in the charging area of every police station.

6.4   No police officer shall at any time do or say anything with the intention of dissuading a person in detention from obtaining legal advice.

6.5   The exercise of the right of access to legal advice may be delayed only in accordance with Annex B to this code. Whenever legal advice is requested (and unless Annex B applies) the custody officer must act without delay to secure the provision of such advice to the person concerned. If, on being informed or reminded of the right to legal advice, the person declines to speak to a solicitor in person, the officer shall point out that the right to legal advice includes the right to speak with a solicitor on the telephone and ask him if he wishes to do so. If the person continues to waive his right to legal advice the officer shall ask him the reasons for doing so, and the reasons shall be recorded on the custody record or the interview record as appropriate. . . . Once it is clear that a person neither wishes to speak to a solicitor in person or by telephone he should cease to be asked his reasons.

6.6   A person who wants legal advice may not be interviewed or continue to be interviewed until he has received it unless:

(a)   Annex B applies; or

(b)   an officer of the rank of superintendent or above has reasonable grounds for believing that:

   (i)   delay will involve an immediate risk of harm to persons or serious loss of, or damage to, property; or

   (ii)   where a solicitor, including a duty solicitor, has been contacted and has agreed to attend, awaiting his arrival would cause unreasonable delay to the process of investigation; or

(c)   the solicitor nominated by the person, or selected by him from a list:

   (i)   cannot be contacted; or

   (ii)   has previously indicated that he does not wish to be contacted; or

   (iii) having been contacted, has declined to attend;

and the person has been advised of the Duty Solicitor Scheme (where one is in operation) but has declined to ask for the duty solicitor, or the duty solicitor is unavailable. (In these circumstances the interview may be started or continued without further delay provided that an officer of the rank of Inspector or above has given agreement for the interview to proceed in those circumstances.)

(d) The person who wanted legal advice changes his mind. In these circumstances the interview may be started or continued without further delay provided that the person has given his agreement in writing or on tape to being interviewed without receiving legal advice and that an officer of the rank of Inspector or above has given agreement for the interview to proceed in those circumstances.

6.7   Where 6.6(b)(i) applies, once sufficient information to avert the risk has been obtained, questioning must cease until the person has received legal advice or 6.6(a), (b)(ii), (c) or (d) apply.

6.8   Where a person has been permitted to consult a solicitor and the solicitor is available (ie present at the station or on his way to the station or easily contactable by telephone) at the time the interview begins or is in progress, he must be allowed to have his solicitor present while he is interviewed.

6.9   The solicitor may only be required to leave the interview if his conduct is such that the investigation officer is unable properly to put questions to the suspect.

. . .

7   Citizens of independent Commonwealth countries or foreign nationals

. . .

8   Conditions of Detention

. . .

9   Treatment of Detained Persons

. . .

10   Cautions

(a)   When a caution must be given

10.1   A person whom there are grounds to suspect of an offence must be cautioned before any questions about it (or further questions if it is his answers to previous questions that provide grounds for suspicion) are put to him regarding his involvement or suspected involvement in that offence if his answers or his silence (ie failure or refusal to answer a question or to answer satisfactorily) may be given in evidence to a court in a prosecution. He therefore need not be cautioned if questions are put for other purposes, for example, solely to establish his identity or his ownership of any vehicle or to obtain information in accordance with any relevant statutory requirement or in furtherance of the proper and effective conduct of a search.

10.2   Whenever a person who is not under arrest is initially cautioned before or during an interview he must at the same time be told that he is not under arrest and is not obliged to remain with the officer (see paragraph 3.15).

10.3   A person must be cautioned upon arrest for an offence unless:

(a) it is impracticable to do so by reason of his condition or behaviour at the time; or

(b) he has already been cautioned immediately prior to arrest in accordance with paragraph 10.1 above.

(b)   Action: general

10.4   The caution shall be in the following terms:

'You do not have to say anything. But it may harm your defence if you do not mention when questioned something which you later rely on in court. Anything you do say may be given in evidence.'

Minor deviations do not constitute a breach of this requirement provided that the sense of the caution is preserved.

10.5   When there is a break in questioning under caution the interviewing officer must ensure that the person being questioned is aware that he remains under caution. If there is any doubt the caution should be given again in full when the interview resumes.

Special warnings under sections 36 and 37 of the Criminal Justice and Public Order Act 1994

. . .

11   Interviews: general

(a)   Action

11.1   Following a decision to arrest a suspect he must not be interviewed about the relevant offence except at a police station (or other authorised place of detention) unless the consequent delay would be likely:

(a)   to lead to interference with or harm to evidence connected with an offence or interference with or physical harm to other persons; or

(b)   to lead to the alerting of other persons suspected of having committed an offence but not yet arrested for it; or

(c)   to hinder the recovery of property obtained in consequence of the commission of a offence.

Interviewing in any of these circumstances shall cease once the relevant risk has been averted or the necessary questions have been put in order to attempt to avert that risk.

11.1A An interview is the questioning of a person regarding his involvement or suspected involvement in a criminal offence or offences which, by virtue of paragraph 10.1 of Code C, is required to be carried out under caution. Procedures undertaken under section 7 of the Road Traffic Act 1988 do not constitute interviewing for the purposes of this code.

11.2   Immediately prior to the commencement or re-commencement of any interview at a police station or other authorised place of detention, the interviewing officer shall remind the suspect of his entitlement to free legal advice and that the interview can be delayed for him to obtain legal advice. It is the responsibility of the interviewing officer to ensure that all such reminders are noted in the record of interview.

11.2A At the beginning of an interview carried out in a police station, the interviewing officer, after cautioning the suspect, shall put to him any significant statement or silence which occurred before his arrival at the police station, and shall ask him whether he confirms or denies that earlier statement or silence and whether he wishes to add anything. A 'significant' statement or silence is one which appears capable of being used against the suspect, in particular a direct admission of guilt, or failure or refusal to answer a question, or to answer it satisfactorily, which might give rise to an inference under Part III of the Criminal Justice and Public Order Act 1994.

11.3   No police officer may try to obtain answers to questions or to elicit a statement by the use of oppression or shall indicate, except in answer to a direct question, what action will be taken on the part of the police if the person being interviewed answers questions, makes a statement or refuses to do either. If the person asks the officer directly what action will be taken in the event of his answering questions, making a statement or refusing to do either, then the officer may inform the person what action the police propose to take in that event provided that that action is itself proper and warranted.

11.4   As soon as a police officer who is making enquiries of any person about an offence believes that a prosecution should be brought against him and that there is sufficient evidence for it to succeed, he should ask the person if he has anything further to say. If the person indicates that he has nothing more to say the officer shall without delay cease to question him about that offence.

. . .

(b)   Interview records

11.5   (a)   An accurate record must be made of each interview with a person suspected of an offence, whether or not the interview takes place at a police station.

(b)   The record must state the place of the interview, the time it begins and ends, the time the record is made (if different), any breaks in the interview and the names of all those present; and must be made on the forms provided for this purpose or in the officer's pocket-book or in accordance with the code of practice for the tape-recording of police interviews with suspects.

(c)   The record must be made during the course of the interview, unless in the investigating officer's view this would not be practicable or would interfere with the conduct of the interview, and must constitute either a verbatim record of what has been said or, failing this, an account of the interview which adequately and accurately summarises.

11.7   If an interview record is not made during the course of the interview it must be made as soon as practicable after its completion.

11.8   Written interview records must be timed and signed by the maker.

11.9   If an interview record is not completed in the course of the interview the reason must be recorded in the officer's pocket book.

11.10   Unless it is impracticable the person interviewed shall be given the opportunity to read the interview record and to sign it as correct or to indicate the respects in which he considers it inaccurate. If the interview is tape-recorded the arrangements set out in the relevant code of practice apply. If the person concerned cannot read or refuses to read the record or to sign it, the senior police officer present shall read it over to him and ask him whether he would like to sign it as correct (or make his mark) or to indicate the respects in which he considers it inaccurate. The police officer shall then certify on the interview record itself what has occurred.

11.11   If the appropriate adult or the person's solicitor is present during the interview, he should also be given an opportunity to read and sign the interview record (or any written statement taken down by a police officer).

11.12   Any refusal by a person to sign an interview record when asked to do so in accordance with the provisions of the code must itself be recorded.

11.13   A written record should also be made of any comments made by a suspected person, including unsolicited comments, which are outside the context of an interview but which might be relevant to the offence. Any such record must be timed and signed by the maker. Where practicable the person shall be given the opportunity to read that record and to sign it as correct or to indicate the respects in which he considers it inaccurate. Any refusal to sign should be recorded.

(c) Juveniles, the mentally disordered and the mentally handicapped

11.14 A juvenile or a person who is mentally disordered or mentally handicapped, whether suspected or not, must not be interviewed or asked to provide or sign a written statement in the absence of the appropriate adult unless Annex C [urgent interviews] applies.

11.16 Where the appropriate adult is present at an interview, he should be informed that he is not expected to act simply as an observer; and also that the purposes of his presence are, first, to advise the person being questioned and to observe whether or not the interview is being conducted properly and fairly, and secondly, to facilitate communication with the person being interviewed.

Notes for Guidance

11A An interview is the questioning of a person regarding his involvement or suspected involvement in a criminal offence or offences. Questioning a person only to obtain information or his explanation of the facts or in the ordinary course of the officer's duties does not constitute an interview for the purpose of this code. Neither does questioning which is confined to the proper and effective conduct of a search.

12 Interviews in police stations

12.1 If a police officer wishes to interview, or conduct enquiries which require the presence of, a detained person the custody officer is responsible for deciding whether to deliver him into his custody.

12.2 In any period of 24 hours a detained person must be allowed a continuous period of at least 8 hours for rest, free from questioning, travel or any interruption arising out of the investigation concerned. This period should normally be at night. The period of rest may not be interrupted or delayed unless there are reasonable grounds for believing that it would:

(i)   involve a risk of harm to persons or serious loss of, or damage to, property;

(ii) delay unnecessarily the person's release from custody; or

(iii) otherwise prejudice the outcome of the investigation.

If a person is arrested at a police station after going there voluntarily, the period of 24 hours runs from the time of his arrest and not the time of arrival at the police station.

12.3 A detained person may not be supplied with intoxicating liquor except on medical directions. No person who is unfit through drink or drugs to the extent that he is unable to appreciate the significance of questions put to him and his answers may be questioned about an alleged offence in that condition except in accordance with Annex C [urgent interviews].

Notes for Guidance

12A If the interview has been contemporaneously recorded and the record signed by the person interviewed in accordance with paragraph 11.10 above, or has been tape recorded, it is normally unnecessary to ask for a written statement. Statements under caution should normally be taken in these circumstances only at the person's express wish. An officer may, however, ask him whether or not he wants to make such a statement.

. . .

13 Interpreters

. . .

14 Questioning: special restrictions

. . .

15   Reviews and extensions of detention

. . .

16   Charging of detained persons

16.1   When an officer considers that there is sufficient evidence to prosecute a detained person, and that there is sufficient evidence for a prosecution to succeed, and that the person has said all that he wishes to say about the offence, he should without delay (and subject to the following qualification) bring him before the custody officer who shall then be responsible for considering whether or not he should be charged. When a person is detained in respect of more than one offence it is permissible to delay bringing him before the custody officer until the above conditions are satisfied in respect of all the offences (but see paragraph 11.4). Any resulting action should be taken in the presence of the appropriate adult if the person is a juvenile or mentally disordered or mentally handicapped.

16.2   When a detained person is charged with or informed that he may be prosecuted for an offence he shall be cautioned [in the terms of paragraph 10.4].

16.3   At the time a person is charged he shall be given a written notice showing particulars of the offence with which he is charged and including the name of the officer in the case (in terrorist cases, the officer's warrant number instead), his police station and the reference number for the case. So far as possible the particulars of the charge shall be stated in simple terms, but they shall also show the precise offence in law with which he is charged. The notice shall begin with the following words:

'You are charged with the offence(s) shown below. You do not have to say anything. but it may harm your defence if you do not mention now something which you later rely on in court. Anything you do say may be given in evidence.'

If the person is a juvenile or is mentally disordered or mentally handicapped the notice shall be given to the appropriate adult.

16.4   If at any time after a person has been charged with or informed he may be prosecuted for an offence a police officer wishes to bring to the notice of that person any written statement made by another person or the content of an interview with another person, he shall hand to that person a true copy of any such written statement or bring to his attention the content of the interview record, but shall say or do nothing to invite any reply or comment save to caution him in the terms of paragraph 10.4 above. If the person cannot read then the officer may read it to him. If the person is a juvenile or mentally disordered or mentally handicapped the copy shall also be given to, or the interview record brought to the attention of, the appropriate adult.

16.5   Questions relating to an offence may not be put to a person after he has been charged with that offence, or informed that he may be prosecuted for it, unless they are necessary for the purpose of preventing or minimising harm or loss to some other person or to the public or for clearing up an ambiguity in a previous answer or statement, or where it is in the interests of justice that the person should have put to him and have an opportunity to comment on information concerning the offence which has come to light since he was charged or informed that he might be prosecuted. Before any such questions are put he shall be cautioned in the terms of paragraph 10.4 above.

. . .

Annex B: DELAY IN NOTIFYING ARREST OR ALLOWING ACCESS TO LEGAL ADVICE

1.   The rights set out in sections 5 or 6 of the code or both may be delayed if the person is in police detention in connection with a serious arrestable offence, has not yet been charged with an offence and an officer of superintendent or above has reasonable grounds for believing that the exercise of either right:

(i)   will lead to interference with or harm to evidence connected with a serious arrestable offence or interference with or physical injury to other persons; or

(ii)   will lead to the alerting of other persons suspected of having committed such an offence but not yet arrested for it; or

(iii) will hinder the recovery of property obtained as a result of such an offence.

3.   Access to a solicitor may not be delayed on the grounds that he might advise the person not to answer any questions or that the solicitor was initially asked to attend the police station by someone else, provided that the person himself then wishes to see the solicitor. In the latter case the detained person must be told that the solicitor has come to the police station at another person's request, and must be asked to sign the custody record to signify whether or not he wishes to see the solicitor.

4.   These rights may be delayed only for as long as is necessary and, subject to paragraph 9 below, in no case beyond 36 hours after the relevant time as defined in section 41 of the Police and Criminal Evidence Act 1984. If the above grounds cease to apply within this time, the person must as soon as practicable be asked if he wishes to exercise either right, the custody record must be noted accordingly, and action must be taken in accordance with the relevant section of the code.

5.   A detained person must be permitted to consult a solicitor for a reasonable time before any court hearing.

Criminal Law Revision Committee: 11th Report, 1972 (Cmnd 4991), para 43

It is of no help to an innocent person to caution him to the effect that he is not obliged to make a statement. Indeed, it might deter him from saying something which might exculpate him. On the other hand the caution often assists the guilty by providing an excuse for keeping back a false story until it becomes difficult to expose its falsity . . . In any event practised criminals have little respect for the caution.

 . . . [T]he first caution . . . has been objected to on the ground that it interrupts the natural course of interrogation and unduly hampers the police, as there may be a good deal more information which they wish to get, perhaps involving other offences and persons, after the stage when they have 'evidence which would afford reasonable grounds for suspecting that [the person being questioned] has committed an offence' . . .

NOTES

1. Technical breaches of the Code of Practice do not affect admissibility: the judge has a discretion to exclude the resulting evidence (see ch 9). As will be seen, this makes English law in practice substantially different from American.
2. Arresting persons on one charge and questioning them on another is permitted. There should be no questioning, after the accused is charged, respecting the offence charged (para 16.5), but this may occur respecting other offences (*R v Buchan* [1964] 1 All ER 502, [1964] 1 WLR 365, CCA).
3. The right to consult the Codes (para 3.1) does not thereby permit an arrested motorist to delay giving a breath specimen until he has read them (*DPP v Skinner* (1989) 153 JP 605, [1990] RTR 254, DC). Nor does the right to consult a solicitor (Police and Criminal Evidence Act 1984, s 58 and Code C para 6) permit a similar delay (*DPP v Billington* [1988] 1 All ER 435, [1988] RTR 231, DC). See Tucker [1990] Crim LR 177 and para 11.1A.
4. The right to consult a solicitor is a 'fundamental right of a citizen' and can only be delayed under s 58 and Annex B by reference to the circumstances of the specific case; a vague fear about alerting accomplices cannot be the ground

for refusing access to *any* solicitor (*R v Samuel* [1988] QB 615, [1988] 2 All ER 135, CA). There is no power to delay access to a solicitor after a suspect has been charged with an offence (ibid). But where a person is wrongly refused access to a solicitor as a result of a mistake rather than misconduct, a confession will not necessarily be excluded (unless, of course, it is inadmissible under s 76): *R v Alladice* (1988) 87 Cr App Rep 380, CA. So a person who agrees to be interviewed without a solicitor after being told, because of a mistake, that no duty solicitor is available, cannot expect to have the resulting confession excluded (*R v Hughes* [1988] Crim LR 519, CA; cf *R v Vernon* [1988] Crim LR 445).

5. The question what constitutes an 'interview' for the purposes of the Code (and therefore whether a record should have been made) has caused some difficulty. The Court of Appeal has tended to give a wide interpretation to the word (*R v Absolam* (1988) 88 Cr App Rep 332; *R v Matthews* (1989) 91 Cr App Rep 43). The 1991 edition of Code C was intended to clarify some of the problems raised in the cases, but was not satisfactory (Runciman, para 10). The 1995 definition is clearer: 'interview' is now defined in para 11.1A and para 11.13 makes it clear that a suspect's comments should be recorded even if they are not made in the context of an interview. Even if the exact words are taken down in accordance with para 11.5, there are dangers because the tone of voice is lost; the dangers are greater where a statement obtained by question and answer is reduced to a continuous narrative. The qualifying context of what is said will be changed by the omission of the questions and by the juxtaposition of answers that may not have originally appeared together. Section 60 of the Police and Criminal Evidence Act 1984, supplemented by Code E and a *Practice Direction* [1989] 1 WLR 631, 89 Cr App Rep 132, provides for interviews to be tape-recorded, a policy proposed only by a minority in the Criminal Law Revision Committee (CRLC para 52) and viewed without enthusiasm by the Royal Commission on Criminal Procedure, though many initial worries have been removed by the operation of the practice. Tape-recording of interviews became compulsory on 1 January 1992. At present it applies only to offences, other than terrorist offences (para 3.2), triable on indictment: there are no proposals to extend it to offences triable only summarily (though there have been some recordings of interviews with terrorist suspects, and some video recordings, on an experimental basis). Where a tape-recording is available it may itself be evidence in the case; the jury may hear it, and may take it with them when they retire; they may be provided with a summary or a transcript (*R v Rampling* [1987] Crim LR 823, CA; *R v Emmerson* [1991] Crim LR 194, CA). The fact that times of questioning must be noted in a written record is designed to help determine whether a neat and well-constructed statement in fact accords with what occurred. If 200 words took five hours to obtain, this suggests that the statement should be carefully scrutinised. See *R v Williams* (1977) 67 Cr App Rep 10, CA.

6. As regards the caution, the Criminal Law Revision Committee's first point has some force, even now that the words 'against you' have been dropped from older forms of caution. But in reply to the second objection it may be said that the accused has a right to silence; he must be told of it, otherwise the law will be protecting only hardened criminals who know their rights; the form of caution has been changed in consequence of the modification of the right to silence: see ch 7.

7. The 'evidence' mentioned in paras 11.4 and 16.1 must be evidence admissible in court; so the police can question a man without cautioning him on the basis of a hearsay underworld tip-off (*R v White* [1964] Crim LR 270, CCA; *R v Osbourne* [1973] QB 678, [1973] 1 All ER 649, CA). It is not necessary when the police are taking preliminary statements from a number of persons in a case such as an affray for them to check every person individually to see if they have sufficient evidence so as to make it necessary to administer a caution: *R v Halford* (1978) 67 CR App Rep 318, CA.

8. For the purposes of paras 16.2 and 16.4 'charged' means that the accused must be formally charged at a police station, not merely be told why he is being arrested. 'Informed that he may be prosecuted' covers cases where the suspect has not been arrested but where in the course of questioning a time comes when the police contemplate that a summons may be issued (*R v Collier* [1965] 3 All ER 136, [1965] 1 WLR 1470, CCA). The implication is that since more evidence is needed to support a charge than to support an arrest, it is possible to question persons in custody. A person who is told he will be charged with certain offences is 'charged' for the purposes of the restrictions in para 16: *Conway v Hotten* [1976] 2 All ER 213. Service of notice of intended prosecution (Road Traffic Offenders Act 1988, ss 1, 2) does not amount to informing a person that he may be prosecuted for an offence for these purposes.

9. Section 67(9) extends the Code beyond the police to those who have a legal duty to investigate offences (*R v Twaites and Brown* (1990) 92 Cr App Rep 235, CA, [1990] Crim LR 863 and commentary). The Code may be taken to apply by analogy to professional investigators who are likely to know the caution but not ordinary citizens who by chance find themselves in a position where they happen to be interrogating suspects (*R v Nichols* (1967) 51 Cr App Rep 233, CA). Thus it applies to shop detectives but not a shop manager questioning a suspected shoplifter. It does not apply to DTI inspectors making investigations under s 434 of the Companies Act 1985 (*R v Seelig and Spens* (1991) 94 Cr App Rep 17, CA), nor (probably) to foreign detectives seeking extradition of a suspect (*Beese v Governor of Ashford Remand Centre* [1973] 3 All ER 689 at 693, HL). As regards officials of the Serious Fraud Office, the provisions of the Code are superseded by the specific procedure laid down in the Criminal Justice Act 1987: *R v Director of the Serious Fraud Office, ex p Smith* [1993] AC 1, [1992] 3 All ER 456, HL.

10. Astonishingly, the Court of Appeal held in *R v McCay* [1991] 1 All ER 232, [1990] 1 WLR 645, CA, that the effect of s 67(11) was to make admissible any evidence obtained by following the Code procedures, regardless of the exclusionary effect of the hearsay rule. See commentary at [1990] Crim LR 340.

4 American law

The relevant American law can be divided into three groups: the *McNabb-Mallory* rule, the due process requirement, and the *Escobedo-Miranda* doctrine.

The *McNabb-Mallory* rule requires federal courts to exclude even voluntary confessions obtained during a period of illegal detention, ie during a period when the accused should have been brought before a committing magistrate.

The rule is not binding on state courts because it does not proceed from the Bill of Rights but rather the US Supreme Court's supervisory powers over inferior federal courts (*McNabb v US* 318 US 332 (1943); *Mallory v US* 354 US 449 (1957)). Most of the states have declined to follow it.

The rules worked out by the Supreme Court regarding breach of the due process clauses of the Bill of Rights do bind the states. It is clear that due process is infringed by a confession extorted by physical torture (*Brown v Mississippi* 297 US 278 (1926)). What of interrogation? It is not 'inherently coercive' as is physical violence. Interrogation does have social value in solving a crime, as physical force does not. The limits in any case depend upon a weighing of the circumstances of pressure against the power of resistance of the person confessing (*Stein v New York* 346 US 156 at 184–5 (1953)). Confessions have been excluded on grounds of frightening interrogation practices such as moving prisoners from jail to jail; questioning unclothed, standing, sleepless or very hungry prisoners; very long relay questioning; questioning during lengthy incommunicado detention; the excessive use of pretended sympathy with the prisoner; particularly when these methods are used against very young, or ignorant, or timid, or mentally or physically ill prisoners, or prisoners whose race puts them at a social disadvantage. The balancing process used means that a strong-minded man can suffer a lot of unpleasantness and his confession will not be excluded (eg *Lisenba v California* 314 US 219 (1941)). The due process requirement has thus led to an expansion of the voluntariness requirement. Further, a confession obtained as the result of an illegal search and seizure is inadmissible (*Wong Sun v US* 83 S Ct 407 (1963); *People v Rodriguez* 182 NE 2d 651 (1862)).

Finally, there is the *Escobedo-Miranda* doctrine. Defendants have a right to be warned of their right to silence and of their right to counsel (*Escobedo v Illinois* 378 US 478 (1964)) at public expense (*Gideon v Wainwright* 372 US 335 (1963)). A long interrogation will be treated as evidence of the accused not having waived these rights even if the police testify that he has. This case law is based on the Fifth Amendment ('No person shall be compelled in any criminal case to be a witness against himself') and the Sixth ('the accused shall . . . have the Assistance of Counsel'). The doctrine was most fully formulated in *Miranda*.

Miranda v Arizona   384 US 436 (1966)

The accused made a confession of kidnapping and rape after two hours' questioning. He had not been warned of his right to have a lawyer present during the interrogation. The US Supreme Court held the confession inadmissible.

Warren CJ: Our holding will be spelled out with some specificity in the pages which follow but briefly stated it is this: the prosecution may not use statements, whether exculpatory or inculpatory, stemming from custodial interrogation of the defendant unless it demonstrates the use of procedural safeguards effective to secure the privilege against self-incrimination. By custodial interrogation, we mean questioning initiated by law enforcement officers after a person has been taken into custody or otherwise deprived of his freedom of action in any significant way. As for the procedural safeguards to be employed, unless other fully effective means are devised to inform accused persons of their right of silence and to assure a continuous opportunity to exercise it, the following measures are required. Prior to any questioning, the person must be warned that he has a right to remain silent, that any statement he does make may be used as evidence against him, and that he has a right to the presence of an attorney, either retained or appointed. The defendant may waive effectuation of these rights, provided the waiver is made voluntarily, knowingly and intelligently. If, however, he indicates in any manner and at any stage of the process that he wishes to consult with an attorney before speaking there can be no questioning. Likewise, if the individual is alone and indicates in any manner that he does not wish to be interrogated, the police may not question him. The mere fact that he may have answered some questions or volunteered some statements on his own does not deprive him of the right to refrain from answering any further inquiries until he has consulted with an attorney and thereafter consents to be questioned . . .

[These cases] share salient features – incommunicado interrogation of individuals in a police-dominated atmosphere, resulting in self-incriminating statements without full warnings of constitutional rights . . .

Again we stress that the modern practice of in-custody interrogation is psychologically rather than physically oriented . . . Interrogation still takes place in privacy. Privacy results in secrecy and this in turn results in a gap in our knowledge as to what in fact goes on in the interrogation rooms. A valuable source of information about present police practices, however, may be found in various police manuals and texts which document procedures employed with success in the past, and which recommend various other effective tactics . . .

. . . The current practice of incommunicado interrogation is at odds with one of our Nation's most cherished principles – that the individual may not be compelled to incriminate himself. Unless adequate protective devices are employed to dispel the compulsion inherent in custodial surroundings, no statement obtained from the defendant can truly be the product of his free choice.

The question in these cases is whether the privilege [against self-incrimination] is fully applicable during a period of custodial interrogation . . . We are satisfied that all the principles embodied in the privilege apply to informal compulsion exerted by law-enforcement officers during in-custody questioning. An individual swept from familiar surroundings into police custody, surrounded by antagonistic forces, and subjected to the techniques of persuasion described above cannot be otherwise than under compulsion to speak. As a practical matter, the compulsion to speak in the isolated setting of the police station may well be greater than in courts or other official investigations, where there are often impartial observers to guard against intimidation or trickery . . .

. . . The entire thrust of police interrogation . . . in all the cases today, was to put the defendant in such an emotional state as to impair his capacity for rational judgment. The abdication of the constitutional privilege – the choice on his part to speak to the police – was not knowingly or competently because of the failure to apprise him of his rights; the compelling atmosphere of the in-custody interrogation, and not an independent decision on his part, caused the defendant to speak.

The Fifth Amendment privilege is so fundamental to our system of constitutional rule and the expedient of giving an adequate warning as to the availability of the privilege so simple, we will not pause to inquire in individual cases whether the defendant was aware of his rights without a warning being given. Assessments of the knowledge the defendant possessed, based on information as to age, education, intelligence, or prior contact with authorities, can never be more than speculation; a warning is a clearcut fact. More important, whatever the background of the person interrogated, a warning at the time of the interrogation is indispensable to overcome its pressures and to insure that the individual knows he is free to exercise the privilege at that point in time.

The warning of the right to remain silent must be accompanied by the explanation that anything said can and will be used against the individual in court. This warning is needed in order to make him aware not only of the privilege, but also of the consequences of forgoing it. It is only through an awareness of these consequences that there can be any assurance of real understanding and intelligent exercise of the privilege. Moreover, this warning may serve to make the individual more acutely aware that he is faced with a phase of the adversary system – that he is not in the presence of persons acting solely in his interest.

The circumstances surrounding in-custody interrogation can operate very quickly to overbear the will of one merely made aware of his privilege by his interrogators. Therefore, the right to have counsel present at the interrogation is indispensable to the protection of the Fifth Amendment privilege under the system we delineate today. Our aim is to assure that the individual's right to choose between silence and speech remains unfettered through the interrogation process.

The presence of counsel at the interrogation may serve several significant subsidiary functions as well. If the accused decides to talk to his interrogators, the assistance of counsel can mitigate the dangers of untrustworthiness. With a lawyer present the likelihood that the police will practice coercion is reduced, and if coercion is nevertheless exercised the lawyer can testify to it in court. The presence of a lawyer can also help to guarantee that the accused gives a fully accurate statement to the police and that the statement is rightly reported by the prosecution at trial.

If an individual indicates that he wishes the assistance of counsel before any interrogation occurs, the authorities cannot rationally ignore or deny his request on the basis that the individual does not have or cannot afford a retained attorney. The financial ability of the individual has no relationship to the scope of the rights involved here. The privilege against self-incrimination secured by the Constitution applies to all individuals. The need for counsel in order to protect the privilege exists for the indigent as well as the affluent. In fact, were we to limit these constitutional rights to those who can retain an attorney, our decisions today would be of little significance. The cases before us as well as the vast majority of confession cases with which we have dealt in the past involve those unable to retain counsel. While authorities are not required to relieve the accused of his poverty, they have the obligation not to take advantage of indigence in the administration of justice.

The Court's new rules aim to offset these minor pressures and disadvantages intrinsic to any kind of police interrogation. The rules do not serve due process interests in preventing blatant coercion since, as I noted earlier, they do nothing to contain the policeman who is prepared to lie from the start. The rules work for reliability in confessions almost only in the Pickwickian sense that they can prevent some from being given at all . . .

Harlan J (whom Stewart and White JJ joined) dissenting: What the court largely ignores is that its rules impair, if they will not eventually serve wholly to frustrate, an instrument of law enforcement that has long and quite reasonably been thought worth the price for it. There can be little doubt that the court's new code would markedly decrease the number of confessions. To warn the suspect that he may remain silent and remind him that his confession may be used in court are minor obstructions. To require also an express waiver by the suspect and an end to questioning whenever he demurs must heavily handicap questioning. And to suggest or provide counsel for the suspect simply invites the end of the interrogation . . .

How much harm this decision will inflict on law enforcement cannot fairly be predicted with accuracy . . . We do know that some crimes cannot be solved without confessions, that ample expert testimony attests to their importance in crime control and that the court is taking a real risk with society's welfare in imposing its new regime on the country. The social costs of crime are too great to call the new rules anything but a hazardous experimentation. While passing over the costs and risks of its experiment, the court portrays the evils of normal police questioning in terms which I think are exaggerated. Albeit stringently confined by the due process standards interrogation is no doubt often inconvenient and unpleasant for the suspect. However, it is no less so for a man to be arrested and jailed, to have his house searched, or to stand trial in court, yet all this may properly happen to the most innocent given probable cause, a warrant, or an indictment. Society has always paid a stiff price for law and order, and peaceful interrogation is not one of the dark moments of the law.

[Clark J dissented.]

See *Brewer v Williams* 97 S Ct 1232 (1977).

The debate on the American position is represented by the following. Inbau and Reid's *Criminal Interrogation and Confessions* (Baltimore, 1967, 2nd edn) is one of a group of interrogation manuals widely used among the American police. The practices described in its 1st edition were one factor in the Supreme Court's decision in cases like *Miranda* to extend its protection of suspects, and in that sense it defeated its own ends. Its fascinating mixture of commonsense and oppressive methods, presented with a solemnity at times hilarious, is adequately represented by part of its table of contents.

THE INTERROGATION OF SUSPECTS

Tactics and Techniques for the Interrogation of Suspects whose Guilt is Definite or Reasonably Certain

A. Display an Air of Confidence in the Subject's Guilt
B. Point out Some, but by No Means All, of the Circumstantial Evidence Indicative of a Subject's Guilt
C. Call Attention to the Subject's Physiological and Psychological Evidence Symptoms of Guilt
D. Sympathize with the Subject by Telling Him That Anyone Else under Similar Conditions or Circumstances Might Have Done the Same Thing
E. Reduce the Subject's Guilt Feeling by Minimizing the Moral Seriousness of the Offense
F. Suggest a Less Revolting and More Morally Acceptable Motivation or Reason for the Offense Than That Which Is Known or Presumed
G. Sympathise with the Subject by (1) Condemning His Victim, (2) Condemning His Accomplice, or (3) Condemning Anyone Else Upon Whom Some Degree of Moral Responsibility Might Conceivably Be Placed for the Commission of the Crime in Question
H. Utilize Displays of Understanding and Sympathy in Urging the Subject to Tell the Truth
I. Point Out the Possibility of Exaggeration on the Part of the Accuser or Victim or Exaggerate the Nature and Seriousness of the Offense Itself
J. Have the Subject Place Himself at the Scene of the Crime or in Some Sort of Contact with the Victim or the Occurrence
K. Seek an Admission of Lying about Some Incidental Aspect of the Occurrence
L. Appeal to the Subject's Pride by Well-Selected Flattery or by a Challenge to His Honor
M. Point out to the Subject the Grave Consequences and Futility of a Continuation of His Criminal Behaviour
O. Rather Than Seek a General Admission of Guilt, First Ask the Subject a Question as to Some Detail of the Offense, or Inquire as to the Reason for Its Commission
P. When Co-Offenders Are Being Interrogated and the Previously Described Techniques Have Been Ineffective, 'Play One Against the Other'

Tactics and Techniques for the Interrogation of Suspects Whose Guilt is Uncertain

Q. Ask the Subject if He Knows Why He is Being Questioned
R. Ask the Subject to Relate All He Knows about the Occurrence, the Victim, and Possible Suspects
S. Obtain from the Subject Detailed Information about His Activities before, at the Time of, and after the Occurrence in Question
T. Where Certain Facts Suggestive of the Subject's Guilt are Known, Ask Him about Them Rather Casually and as Though the Real Facts Were Not Already Known
U. At Various Intervals Ask the Subject Certain Pertinent Questions in a Manner which Implies that the Correct Answers Are Already Known
V. Refer to Some Non-Existing Incriminating Evidence to Determine whether the Subject Will Attempt to Explain It Away; if He Does, That Fact is Suggestive of His Guilt
W. Ask the Subject whether He Ever 'Thought' about Committing the Offense in Question or One Similar to It
X. In Theft Cases, if a Suspect Offers to Make Restitution, That Fact Is Indicative of Guilt
Y. Ask the Subject whether He Is Willing to Take a Lie-Detector Test. The Innocent Person Will Almost Always Steadfastly Agree to Take Practically Any Test to Prove His Innocence, whereas the Guilty Person is More Prone to Refuse to Take the Test or to Find Excuses for not Taking It, or for Backing Out of His Commitment to Take It
Z. A Subject Who Tells the Interrogator, 'All Right, I'll Tell You What You Want, but I didn't Do it,' Is, in All Probability, Guilty

GENERAL SUGGESTIONS REGARDING THE INTERROGATION OF CRIMINAL SUSPECTS

1. Interview the Victim, the Accuser, or the Discover of the Crime before Interrogating the Suspect Himself
2. Be Patient
3. Make No Promises When Asked, 'What Will Happen to Me if I tell the Truth?'

4.   View with Skepticism the So-called 'Conscience-Stricken' Confession
5.   When a Subject Has Made Repeated Denials of Guilt to Previous Interrogators, First Question Him, Whenever Circumstances Permit, about Some Other, Unrelated Offense of a Similar Nature of Which He Is Also Considered to be Guilty
6.   An Unintelligent, Uneducated Criminal Suspect, with a Low Cultural Background, Should Be Interrogated on a Psychological Level Comparable to That Usually Employed in the Questioning of a Child Respecting an Act of Wrongdoing

THE INTERROGATION OF WITNESSES AND OTHER PROSPECTIVE INFORMANTS

1.   Assure the Willing but Fearful Witness or Other Prospective Informant That He Will Not Be Harmed by the Offender or His Relatives or Friends, and That He will Receive Police Protection in the Event Such Protection Becomes Necessary
2.   Whenever a Witness or Other Prospective Informant Refuses to Cooperate Because He Is Deliberately Protecting the Offender's Interests, or Because He Is Anti-Social or Anti-Police in His Attitude, Seek to Break the Bond of Loyalty between the Subject and the Offender, or Accuse Him of the Offense and Proceed to Interrogate Him as Though He Were Actually Considered to Be the Offender Himself

NOTE

Many of these techniques are calculated to produce an untrue confession in that they entail asking for the accused's assent to a relatively innocuous version of what he has done. In court this may deliberately or by a misunderstanding be presented as a confession to a much more serious crime. The oppressive and fatiguing nature of the above kind of questioning may have the same tendency.

Watts v Indiana   338 US 49 (1949)

Jackson J (in the US Supreme Court): . . . The suspect neither had nor was advised of his right to get counsel. This presents a real dilemma in a free society. To subject one without counsel to questioning which may and is intended to convict him, is a real peril to individual freedom. To bring in a lawyer means a real peril to solution of the crime because, under our adversary system, he deems that his sole duty is to protect his client – guilty or innocent – and that in such a capacity he owes no duty whatever to help society with its crime problem. Under this conception of criminal procedure, any lawyer worth his salt will tell the suspect in no uncertain terms to make no statement to police under any circumstances.

Culcombe v Connecticut   367 US 568 (1961)

Frankfurter J (US Supreme Court majority opinion): Despite modern advances in the technology of crime detection, offences frequently occur about which things cannot be made to speak. And where there cannot be found innocent human witnesses to such offences, nothing remains – if police investigation is not to be balked before it has fairly begun – but to seek out possibly guilty witnesses and ask them questions, witnesses, that is, who are suspected of knowing something about the offence precisely because they are suspected of implication in it . . .

But persons who are suspected of crime will not always be unreluctant to answer questions put by the police. Since under the procedures of Anglo-American criminal justice they cannot be constrained by legal process to give answers which incriminate them, the police have resorted to other means to unbend their reluctance, lest criminal investigation founder. Kindness, cajolery, entreaty, deception, persistent cross-questioning, even physical brutality have been used to this end. In the United States, 'interrogation' has become a police technique, and detention for purposes of interrogation is a common, although generally unlawful practice. Crime detection officials, finding that if their suspects are kept under tight police control during questioning they are less likely to be distracted, less likely to be recalcitrant and, of course, less likely to make off and escape entirely, not infrequently take such suspects into custody for 'investigation'.

This practice has its manifest evils and dangers. Persons subjected to it are torn from the reliances of their daily existence and held at the mercy of those whose job it is – if such persons have committed crime, as it is supposed they have – to convict them for it. They are deprived of freedom without a proper judicial tribunal having found them guilty, without a proper judicial tribunal having found even that there is probable cause to believe that they may be guilty. What actually happens to them behind the closed door of the interrogation room is difficult if not impossible to ascertain. Certainly, if through excess of zeal or aggressive impatience or flaring up of temper in the face of obstinate silence, a prisoner is abused, he is faced with the task of overcoming, by his lone testimony, solemn official denials. The prisoner knows this – knows that no friendly or disinterested witness is present – and the knowledge may itself induce fear. But, in any case, the risk is great that the police will accomplish behind their closed door precisely what the demands of our legal order forbid: make a suspect the unwilling collaborator in establishing his guilt. This they may accomplish not only with ropes and a rubber hose, not only by relaying questioning persistently, insistently subjugating a tired mind, but by subtler devices.

In the police station a prisoner is surrounded by known hostile forces. He is disoriented from the world he knows and in which he finds support. He is subject to coercing impingements, undermining even if not obvious pressures of every variety. In such an atmosphere questioning that is long continued – even if it is only repeated at intervals, never protracted to the point of physical exhaustion – inevitably suggests that the questioner has a right to, and expects, an answer. This is so, certainly, when the prisoner has never been told that he need not answer and when, because his commitment to custody seems to be at the will of his questioners, he has every reason to believe that he will be held and interrogated until he speaks.

. . . But if it is once admitted that questioning of suspects is permissible, whatever reasonable means are needed to make the questioning effective must also be conceded to the police. Often prolongation of the interrogation period will be essential, so that a suspect's story can be checked and, if it proves untrue, he can be confronted with the lie; if true, released without charge. Often the place of questioning will have to be a police interrogation room, both because it is important to assure the proper atmosphere of privacy and non-distraction if questioning is to be made productive, and because, where a suspect is questioned but not taken into custody, he – and in some cases his associates – may take prompt warning and flee the premises. Legal counsel for the suspect will generally prove a thorough obstruction to the investigation. Indeed, even to inform the suspect of his legal right to keep silent will prove an obstruction. Whatever fortifies the suspect or seconds him in his capacity to keep his mouth closed is a potential obstacle to the solution of crime.

Arthur E Sutherland Jr   (1965) 75 Harv LR 21

Suppose a well-to-do testatrix says she intends to will her property to Elizabeth. John and James want her to bequeath it to them instead. They capture the testatrix, put her in a carefully designed room, out of touch with everyone but themselves and their convenient 'witnesses', keep her secluded there for hours while they make insistent demands, weary her with contradictions of her assertions that she wants to leave her money to Elizabeth, and finally induce her to execute the will in their favour. Assume that John and James are deeply and correctly convinced that Elizabeth is unworthy and will make base use of the property if she gets her hands on it, whereas John and James have the noblest and most righteous intentions . . .

At once one will hear the response that the testatrix is not a criminal; that obtaining a surrender of rights from a criminal is different; that the interest of the state demands that criminals should not be coddled. That is to say we are told that a man with his life at stake should be able to surrender an ancient constitutional right to remain silent, under compulsions which in a surrender of a little property would obviously make the transaction void.

Reardon J   (1969) 43 ALJ 508

The broad discretion to exclude evidence improperly obtained is perhaps best employed by the judge who is a true professional judge, who is appointed for life, and who is removed from all intrinsic pressures. This can be said of but a few of the judges in [the United States]. We have . . . some 3,600 *nisis prius* jury trial judges in the fifty states and only a very small percentage of those are appointed for life as are the members of our Federal judiciary . . . [T]hey may serve as judges for six years, sometimes be defeated, return to practice and then run again, the net effect being that . . . continuity of service . . . is too seldom found . . . This has something to do with the endeavours which Chief Justice Warren made in the *Miranda* case to set down in precise terms the tests for admission or non-admission of confessions.

Jerome H Skolnick: Justice without Trial, New York 1966, p 219

Arguments about legal standards are usually unrealistic, whether they come from civil liberties advocates or law enforcement spokesmen. Each group assumes the behavioural efficacy of legally formulated restraints. The civil libertarian typically feels that tighter strictures ought to be placed on police, and that if they were, police would feel obliged to conform. The law enforcement spokesman makes a matching behavioural assumption when he argues that restraints on police behaviour are already too severe. My observations suggest, in contrast to both these positions, that norms located within police organisation are more powerful than court decisions in shaping police behaviour, and that actually the process of interaction between the two accounts ultimately for how police behave.

NOTES

1. *Orozco v Texas* 394 US 324 (1969) holds that *Miranda* applies when a suspect is questioned *in his own home* at 4 am, not merely in a police station. The case illustrates the harshness of the doctrine, as is revealed by White J's dissent. The suspect was awake when police entered. They asked his name, whether he had been at a certain restaurant that night, whether he owned a pistol and where his was. He answered the first three questions quickly, and the fourth was then repeated. He then showed them the pistol hidden in a nearby washing machine. This was not the long drawn-out psychological questioning aimed at by *Miranda*. Had he stayed in bed he could have been arrested, his house searched and his gun found, quite legally.

Miranda warnings may be abridged, omitted or delayed if public safety demands quick action: *NY v Quarles* 467 US 649 (1984) (locating loaded gun left in a place to which the public had access).

A rather questionable limitation of the *Miranda* doctrine was devised in *Harris v NY* 401 US 222 (1971). The Supreme Court there held that a confession inadmissible in the prosecution's case in chief for violating *Miranda* could be used to impeach the credibility of the defendant's testimony at the trial if its trustworthiness were adequate. Cross's comment is 'could any decision make the law look more of a hypocrite?' ([1973] Crim LR 329, at 330). The Court purported to follow *Walder v US* 347 US 62 (1954), but there illegally obtained real evidence was used to impeach the accused's testimony not on matters directly related to the case against him but on matters collateral to the crime charged. The accused not only denied the charges but said he never dealt in or possessed drugs, and the evidence was to rebut the latter claim and to challenge credibility. As Brennan J said, dissenting in *Harris*, 'The Court

today tells the police that they may freely interrogate an accused incommunicado and without counsel and know that although any statement they obtain in
violation of *Miranda* cannot be used on the State's direct case, it may be introduced if the defendant has the temerity to testify in his own defence' (401 US
222 at 232). Further qualifications have tended to show that *Miranda* has a
rather limited role in preventing deceptive police practices. In *RI v Innis* 446
US 291 (1980) the investigating officers fulfilled the *Miranda* requirements but
then held a conversation about the case in the suspect's hearing. He intervened
with a damaging admission. In *Moran v Burbine* 475 US 412 (1986) a lawyer,
retained for the suspect without his knowledge, had been promised that he
would not be further interviewed that day. He was, and after being read his
Miranda warnings, confessed. In both cases the Supreme Court refused to
exclude the evidence.

2. American judge-made confessions law has changed, first from sole reliance
on the common law to the common law rule combined with an investigation
of the particular circumstances of a defendant to see if he could stand up to
the treatment given him (the due process requirement). There has been
superadded a stricter and more objective test of whether certain warnings
have been given (*Miranda*). The legislature has dictated a return to the second
position in the Omnibus Crime Control and Safe Streets Act 1968, s 701.

3. The differences between English and American law on police procedure
are sometimes attributed to differences in social composition, public trust for
the police and for the judges who administer the very discretionary English
rules, and public respect for the criminal law generally. See p 248, post.

4. Kalven and Zeisel (op cit p 142) present some evidence of the importance
of confessions to the prosecution. A confession was offered in 19 per cent of
cases investigated overall; 43 per cent of homicides, 16 per cent assaults, 27
per cent rape, 30 per cent burglary, 1 per cent drunken driving and 3 per cent
narcotics offences. It must be remembered that confessions are often very useful to the police even if they are not introduced at the trial because they
provide leads to other evidences or incriminating real evidence; or because
they cause the accused to plead guilty. (See (1966) 79 Harv LR 935 at 942–3.)

5. A study of the operation of the confession rule in New Haven, Connecticut ((1967) 76 Yale LJ 1519) suggests there have been more confessions
since *Miranda*, not less. Though about one quarter of suspects were not
warned of their rights at all, and a majority were not given the full *Miranda*
warnings, more of those who were warned confessed than those who were not
warned. This may be because detectives always warned those they thought
were on the point of confessing, to ensure the admissibility of the confession.
The full *Miranda* warnings tended to be given in cases where the police had
enough evidence to go to trial, but not enough for a conviction. If there was a
lot of evidence against the accused they did not bother. A further reason for
the fact that warnings did not reduce the likelihood of a confession was that
'on several occasions we noted that a suspect seemed to be thrown off guard
by the warning. He apparently thought that if the police could give these
warnings they must have him' (p 1573). The study also cast light on a number of other *Miranda* issues. The decision was bad for police morale, since
they regarded it as insulting. Suspects often failed to understand or grasp the
significance of the warnings, perhaps because of the bored police manner of

giving them. The study shows that interrogation is less necessary than is sometimes thought, because in most cases where it was used the police had enough evidence to convict the suspect without interrogation. Interrogation was used simply to confirm the case or discover accomplices. Indeed, 'unless the criminal is caught red-handed or unless witnesses are available, the police with their limited resources for scientific investigation cannot amass even enough evidence to arrest a suspect. And since such evidence when available is all but conclusive, by the time the police have a suspect . . . interrogation is unnecessary' (p 1613). Finally, the study indicated that police methods are less harsh than Inbau and Reid suggest.

QUESTION

Compare the extracts from Code C (p 185, ante) with the contents list of Inbau and Reid (p 201, ante). To what extent are the differences in attitude explicable on the basis of a difference in the exclusionary rule between England and America?

5   Other jurisdictions

In Scotland, after 'the retreat from *Chalmers*' (*Chalmers v Lord Advocate* 1954 JC 66) the only test of admissibility is fairness, and there is a prima facie presumption in favour of admitting in evidence a suspect's answers to lawful questioning, so as to leave the final decision to the jury (*Lord Advocate's Reference (No 1 of 1983)* 1984 JC 52). Detention of suspects for up to six hours without arrest or charge is allowed under the Criminal Justice (Scotland) Act 1980, s 2; during detention a suspect may be questioned, and in the case of a serious offence a tape-recorder will be used. The position changes entirely once a suspect has been arrested or charged: the duty then is to bring him before a court as soon as possible. Further police questioning about the answers is not admissible (*Stark and Smith v HM Advocate* 1938 JC 170). Truly spontaneous remarks are admissible, however.

The police may and do ask the accused further questions about matters irrelevant to the actual charge (eg the whereabouts of stolen property or the accused's accomplices), but these matters are not intended to be put in evidence, nor could they be. The position is thus much more pro-accused than in England, where the practical effect of the Code is weaker. Corroboration of the accused's implication in the crime (not merely that the crime was committed) is necessary.

It is sometimes suggested that the Indian Evidence Act system (drafted by Sir James Fitzjames Stephen and in force in India and parts of Africa) be enforced generally. It provides for confessions made to the police being generally inadmissible, unless they are made before a magistrate. But it would not necessarily restrict coercion, which could equally occur before the accused is brought before the magistrate. Secondly, the public reputation for impartiality of the judiciary might suffer were they brought into the investigatory process. Thirdly, the effect of the strict exclusionary rule has been to produce a narrow interpretation of what is a 'confession': *Pakala Narayana Swamy v Emperor* [1939] AIR 47, PC.

In France the accused may not be interrogated by the police, but he may be questioned by the examining magistrate (*juge d'instruction*), who can depute a policeman to make inquiries.

The great variety of practices and panaceas shows the difficulty of the problem of confessions.

FURTHER READING

Anon (1966) 79 Harv LR 935; Baker, *The Hearsay Rule* (1950) pp 53–63; Birch [1989] Crim LR 95; Brownie [1967] Crim LR 75; Burtt, *Legal Psychology* (New York, 1931); Lord MacDermott (1968) 21 CLP 1; Mirfield, *Confessions* (1985); Neasey (1969) 43 ALJ 482; Pattenden (1983) 32 ICLQ 812; Sutherland (1965) 79 Harv LR 21; Zuckerman, ch 15.

CHAPTER 9

Unfair and Improperly Obtained Evidence

Throughout the common-law world, the courts have faced the question whether evidence, otherwise admissible, should be excluded, either because of the way in which it was obtained, or because its admission would be unfair to the accused. The judicial discretions evolved in England and elsewhere, discussed in sections 1 and 3 of this chapter, undoubtedly still exist in England and may well form the basis of future development. for the present, however, the English courts have focussed on the possibilities offered by the vague wording of s 78 of the Police and Criminal Evidence Act 1984: see section 2 of this chapter.

1 Unfairness to the accused: common law discretion

The judge, in the exercise of his power to control the trial, has a discretion to exclude evidence obtained from the accused after the commission of the offence, despite the fact that it may be formally admissible. (If it is inadmissible, of course, no question of discretion arises.) This discretion applies to confessions as it does to other forms of evidence, and breach of the Codes of Practice is merely one example of the grounds on which it may be exercised. It is a common law discretion (*R v Voisin* [1918] 1 KB 531, [1918–19] All ER Rep 491, CCA; *R v Hudson* (1980) 72 Cr App Rep 163, CA; and see the introduction to the 1964 revision of the Judges' Rules, p 181, ante). Despite the obscurity of its precise content, the Criminal Law Revision Committee recommended its retention (CLRC para 278). It was expressly preserved in *R v Sang* [1980] AC 402 at 437, [1979] 2 All ER 1222 at 1231, HL, per Lord Diplock; see also *R v Middleton* [1975] QB 191 at 197–8, [1974] 2 All ER 1190 at 1195, CA; *R v Mason* [1987] 3 All ER 481 at 484, [1988] 1 WLR 139 at 144, CA. It is therefore also preserved by s 82(3) of the Police and Criminal Evidence Act 1984. It has usually been known as the 'unfairness' jurisdiction, though this is a misnomer as well as inviting confusion with the statutory discretion under the Police and Criminal Evidence Act 1984, s 78. The jurisdiction depends not on fairness but on such issues as reliability and police standards. There is little specific judicial authority as to its width because in practice the Judges' Rules and the Codes of Practice tend to cover most of the field, and because in recent years in England there has been a tendency to appeal (rightly or wrongly) to the s 78 discretion rather than this one. One reason for excluding evidence is where its probative value is small in relation to its prejudicial effect on the accused. This reason is acted on throughout the law of evidence in criminal cases (eg illegally obtained evidence, cross-examination on the accused's record, similar fact evidence), but it has been applied here so as to exclude the confession of an adult whose mental age did not exceed five and one half years in *R v Stewart* (1972) 56 Cr App Rep 272. The judge, relying on *Sinclair v R* (1947) 73 CLR 316, said that 'the circumstances must be very special to warrant exclusion' but that they existed in the case before him. (See also *R v Phillips* [1949] NZLR 316 at 347; *R v Isequilla* [1975] 1 All ER 77, [1975] 1 WLR 316; *R v Kilner* [1976] Crim LR 740; *R v Davis* [1979] Crim LR 167 and cf *R v Wray* (1970) 11 DLR (3d) 673, adopting a narrow view of the doctrine.)

However, the discretion to exclude on grounds of unfairness extends beyond unreliability. For example, it would apply to serious police misconduct falling outside the Code: *R v Trump* (1979) 70 Cr App Rep 300 at 303, CA.

The discretion was exercised against an experienced well-educated criminal who confessed, not because of stress caused by loneliness but because he believed he had obtained immunity by assisting the police: *R v Houghton* (1978) 68 Cr App Rep 197, CA. The burden of proof of unfairness is on the accused: *MacPherson v R* (1981) 37 ALR 81 at 86.

Sinclair v R (1947) 73 CLR 316

An argument that the accused's confession should have been excluded because he was at that time mentally unsound was rejected by the High Court of Australia.

Dixon J: The tendency in more recent times has been against the exclusion of relevant evidence for reasons founded on the supposition that the medium of proof is untrustworthy, in the case of a witness, because of his situation and, in the case of evidentiary material, because of its source. The days are gone when witnesses were incompetent to testify because they were parties to or married to a party, because of interest, because of their religious beliefs or want of them or because of crime or infamy. We now call the evidence and treat the factors which formerly excluded it as matters for comment to the tribunal of fact, whose duty it is to weigh the evidence. It must be remembered that the rules relating to the presumptive involuntariness of confessions were developed at a time when the incompetency of witnesses on such grounds was a matter of daily inquiry and, moreover, when the prisoner could not testify. These are all considerations against extending the principle upon which confessions resulting from intimidation or from a threat made or promise given in reference to the charge by a person in authority are excluded as involuntary to cases of insanity where the will may be affected or there may be a liability to confuse the data of experience with those of imagination, so that such factors without more would be enough to exclude a confession.

It is hardly necessary to say that, where there has been pressure or other inducement, the mental condition of a person purporting to confess invalidates his confession as evidence. That objection, in my opinion, cannot be sustained unless a description or degree of derangement is shown much more destructive of the possibility of safely using the confession as a circumstance tending to prove the criminal acts.

Boyd Sinclair's mental state did not disable him from observing, appreciating, recollecting and recounting real occurrences, events of experiences. The fact that his mind, in its schizophrenic state, may have been stored with imaginary episodes and with the memory of unreal dramatic situations would, of course, make it impossible to place reliance upon his confessional statements as intrinsically likely to be true. The tendency of his mental disorder to dramatic and histrionic assertion formed another difficulty in attaching an inherent value to what he said. But it is to be noticed that his condition did no more than make it possible that the source of any confessional statement made lay in these tendencies. His was not a case in which it could be said that the higher probability was in favour of his confession of such a crime being the product of imagination. Reason suggests that in such circumstances it is for the tribunal of fact to ascertain or verify the factual basis of the statements of a man in such a mental condition by comparing their contents with the independent proofs of the circumstances and occurrences to which they relate. It happens that external facts independently proved do supply many reasons for supposing that the confessional statements made by Boyd Sinclair were substantially correct. Though this consideration is not relevant to the question of the legal admissibility of such statements, it provides an example of the inconvenience or undesirability of a rule of rigid exclusion.

It may be conceded that a confession may in fact be made by a person whose unsoundness of mind is such that no account ought to be taken of his self-incriminating statements for any evidentiary purpose as proof of the criminal acts alleged against him. In such a case it might properly be rejected. It is enough in the present case to say that I do not think that Boyd Sinclair's derangement was such as to place his confessional statements in that category. His mental condition was not shown to be inconsistent with any standard of criterion we should adopt as the test of admissibility in evidence upon a criminal trial because it appears that the prisoner making it was at the time of unsound mind and, by reason of his mental condition, exposed to the liability of confusing the products of his disordered imagination or fancy with fact.

[Latham CJ and Rich, Starke and McTiernan JJ agreed.]

McDermott v R   (1948) 76 CLR 501

The accused made a confession while under arrest and after being cautioned but before being charged. He had been questioned for one hour, and the trial judge found that there had been no insistence or pressure by the police. An appeal to the High Court of Australia failed.

Dixon J: The application for special leave is based upon the view that the learned judge possessed a discretion to exclude the statements and that he erroneously exercised this discretion in deciding to admit them. The view that a judge presiding at a criminal trial possesses a discretion to exclude evidence of confessional statements is of comparatively recent growth. To some extent the course of its development is traced by Lord Sumner in *Ibrahim's Case*, [1914] AC 599 at 611–14, [1914–15] All ER Rep 874, PC. In part perhaps it may be a consequence of a failure to perceive how far the settled rule of the common law goes in excluding statements that are not the outcome of an accused person's free choice to speak. In part the development may be due to the fact that the judges in 1912 framed or approved of rules for the guidance of the police in their inquiries . . . and not unnaturally have sought to insist on their observance. In part too it may be due to the existence of the jurisdiction of the Court of Criminal Appeal to quash a conviction if the court is of opinion that on any ground whatsoever there was a miscarriage of justice. But whatever may be the cause, there has arisen almost in our own time a practice in England of excluding confessional statements made to officers of police if it is considered upon a review of all the circumstances that they have been obtained in an improper manner. The abuse of the power of arrest by using the detection of an accused person as an occasion for securing from him evidence by admission is treated as an impropriety justifying the exclusion of the evidence. So is insistence upon questions or an attempt to break down or qualify the effect of an accused person's statement so far as it may be exculpatory. The practice of excluding statements so obtained is supported by the Court of Criminal Appeal in England, which will quash convictions where evidence has been received which in the opinion of that Court has been obtained improperly, that is, in some such manner.

It is acknowledged that the rules drawn up by the judges at the request of the Home Secretary as guides for police officers have no binding force upon the courts . . . Nevertheless the tendency among English judges appears to be strong to treat them as standard of propriety for the purpose of deciding whether confessional statements should be received.

It is apparent that a rule of practice has arisen, deriving almost certainly from the strong feeling for the wisdom and justice of the traditional English principle expressed in the precept *nemo tenetur se ipsum accusare*. It may be regarded as an extension of the common law rule excluding voluntary statements. In referring the decision of the question whether a confessional statement should be rejected to the discretion of the judge, all that seems to be intended is that he should form a judgment upon the propriety of the means by which the statement was obtained by reviewing all the circumstances and considering the fairness of the use made by the police of their position in relation to the accused. The growth of rules of practice and their hardening so that they look like rules of law is a process that is not unfamiliar . . .

. . . Here as well as in England the law may now be taken to be, apart from the effect of such special statutory provisions as s 141 of the Evidence Act 1928 (Vict), that a judge at the trial should exclude confessional statements if in all the circumstances he thinks that they have been improperly procured by officers of police, even although he does not consider that the strict rules of law, common law and statutory, require the rejection of the evidence. The Court of Criminal Appeal may review his decision and if it considers that a miscarriage has occurred it will allow an appeal from the conviction.

But the facts of the present case do not bring it within any rule established in Australia which requires the rejection of the confessional statements complained of. The fact that the police intended to arrest the prisoner, that they virtually held him in custody and delayed for an hour making the charge, and that they asked him questions are not in themselves enough to require that the statements the prisoner made to them should be excluded. The character of the questions, the absence of any insistence or pressure in putting them, the fact that no questions were put directed to breaking down or destroying the prisoner's answers or statements and the fact that there was no attempt to entrap, mislead or persuade him into answering the questions, still less into answering them in any particular way, these are all matters which negative such a degree of impropriety as to require the exclusion of the testimony as to the prisoner's admissions.

[Latham CJ and Williams J agreed.]

Seymour v Attorney-General (Commonwealth) (1984) 53 ALR 513

Fitzgerald J: Fairness is an indefinable concept which depends upon all the circumstances of each particular case. Although the question raised by the special discretion to exclude confessional evidence is whether the reception of the confession would be unfair to the accused, the fairness with which he was treated when the confession was obtained will be of relevance on that question. Considerations personal to the accused, including age, race, intellect, education, and literacy will bear upon whether he has been fairly treated. The lawfulness and propriety of the conduct of those by whom the confession was obtained may similarly affect whether it is fair to use the confession against the accused; that consideration is associated with the second of the general discretions referred to above, but it also is material to the special discretion to exclude confessional evidence on the ground of unfairness. It is not presently necessary to consider whether *R v Lee* (1950) 82 CLR 133 at 150–1 is authority for the proposition that a consideration of fairness is confined to the means by which the confession was obtained or other circumstances surrounding the making of the confession. However, there is no obvious justification for an attempt to catalogue exhaustively or to limit what matters are or may be relevant to the special discretion to exclude confessional evidence as unfair. For example, considerations personal to the accused may be of significance to the reliability of the confession, even if the accused was not treated unfairly, improperly, or illegally. Further, there seems no reason why the factor with which the first of the general discretions referred to above is concerned, namely the balance between the prejudicial effect and the inculpatory value of evidence, may not also be relevant to the fairness of admitting confessional evidence: see *Cleland v R* (1982) 151 CLR 1 at 15, per Murphy J. As Deane J pointed out in that case at 18, 'the question is not whether the accused was treated unfairly; it is whether the reception of the confession would be unfair to him'. It seems unrealistic to attempt to compartmentalise the various considerations which may bear upon unfairness and to permit some only to be considered in relation to each different area of discretion.

In *Driscoll v R* (1977) 137 CLR 517 the High Court of Australia held that in all cases where an unsigned written confession is tendered, the judge should carefully consider whether to exclude it; while the oral evidence of the confession will remain admissible, the jury may regard the writing as somehow strengthening the oral evidence and it may have a disproportionate influence when taken into a jury room.

The Magistrates' Courts Act 1980, s 43(4), requires a person in custody to be brought before a magistrate as soon as possible. Failure to comply may lead to exclusion of any confession: *R v Houghton* (1978) 68 Cr App Rep 197, CA, and *R v Mackintosh* (1982) 76 Cr App Rep 177, CA, though in those cases the confession was admitted; it was excluded in *R v Hudson* (1980) 72 Cr App Rep 163. A like piece of legislation is s 56 of the Police and Criminal Evidence Act 1984, which entitles a person in custody not to be held incommunicado; and under s 58 of the same Act a person in police detention is entitled to have access to legal advice. One would have expected these rights to give rise to an exercise of the 'unfairness' jurisdiction on their breach; but in practice applications have been made under, and granted or refused on the basis of, the statutory discretion contained in s 78; though, as will be seen, it is sometimes difficult to see how that section can have been applicable.

It should be noted that in Australia (unlike England since *R v Sang* [1980] AC 402, [1979] 2 All ER 1222, HL) a confession which is legally admissible, and the use of which would not be unfair, may nevertheless be excluded by the exercise of the *Bunning v Cross* (1978) 141 CLR 54 discretion to exclude unlawfully obtained evidence (see p 231): *Cleland v R* (1982) 151 CLR 1. That case thus decides that the discretion to reject illegally obtained evidence is not limited to real evidence. In that case different views were enunciated on the frequency with which in the circumstances the discretion would be exercised in favour of rejection: Gibbs CJ (with whom Wilson J agreed) said rejection on that ground would be most exceptional (at 9; see also *Collins v R* (1980) 31 ALR 257 at 317); Murphy J said at 16 that if that ground were present the evidence should generally be excluded; Deane J at 27 said that where a confession was procured during a period of unlawful imprisonment, special circumstances, such as the slightness of the illegality, would have to exist before the confession was admitted; Dawson J at 35 took a similar view. What, it may be asked, is the difference between the unfairness discretion and the *Bunning v Cross* discretion? The former depends on fairness to the accused, while the latter depends not on the position of the particular accused individual but on whether the illegal conduct complained of is sufficiently serious or frequent in occurrence to warrant sacrificing a possible conviction in order to express disapproval of and discourage unacceptable police methods.

2   Unfairness of the proceedings: statutory discretion

Police and Criminal Evidence Act 1984

78   (1)   In any [criminal] proceedings the court may refuse to allow evidence on which the prosecution proposes to rely to be given if it appears to the court that, having regard to all the circumstances, including the circumstances in which the evidence was obtained, the admission of the evidence would have such an adverse effect on the fairness of the proceedings that the court ought not to admit it.

(2)   Nothing in this section shall prejudice any rule of law requiring a court to exclude evidence.

82   . . .

(3)   Nothing in this Part of this Act shall prejudice any power of a court to exclude evidence (whether by preventing questions from being put or otherwise) at its discretion.

NOTES

1. The parliamentary history of this section is of some interest. It had no equivalent in early drafts of the Bill. At Committee stage in the House of Lords, Lord Scarman moved an amendment in the terms indicated below. The government responded with an amendment in the same words as the present s 78, except that the exclusionary discretion was limited to evidence 'obtained from an accused person'. Lord Scarman's amendment won the day in the Lords, but in the House of Commons was replaced by s 78 as it now stands. Lord Scarman's proposed clause was as follows (Hansard, HL Deb, Vol 455, cols 427–8):

'(1)   If it appears to the court in any [criminal] proceedings that any evidence (other than a confession) proposed to be given by the prosecution may have been obtained improperly, the court shall not allow the evidence to be given unless –

    (a)   the prosecution proves to the court beyond reasonable doubt that it was obtained lawfully and in accordance with a code of practice (where applicable) issued, approved, and in force, under Part VI of this Act; or

    (b)   the court is satisfied that anything improperly done in obtaining it was of no material significance in all the circumstances of the case and ought, therefore, to be disregarded; or

    (c)   the court is satisfied that the probative value of the evidence, the gravity of the offence charged, and the circumstances in which the evidence was obtained are such that the public interest in the fair administration of the criminal law requires the evidence to be given, notwithstanding that it was obtained improperly.

(2)   For the purposes of this section, evidence shall be treated as having been obtained improperly if it was obtained –

    (a)   in breach of any provision of this Act or of any other enactment or rule of law; or

    (b)   in excess of any power conferred by or obtained under this Act or any other enactment; or

    (c)   in breach of any provision of a code of practice issued, approved, and in force under Part VI of this Act; or

    (d)   as a result of any material deception in obtaining or exercising any power under this Act or any other enactment.'

It will be observed that this proposal would have given rise to an expectation that evidence would be excluded if it was obtained by improper *treatment* of the accused. Section 78, however, says nothing of this: it is limited to circumstances where the accused's *trial* will be unfair. In view of the section's history, it is reasonable to assume that this difference is intentional, although it has not been clearly observed by the courts: *R v Alladice* (1988) 87 Cr App Rep 380 at 385, CA; *R v Walsh* (1989) 91 Cr App Rep 161, CA; *R v Dunford* (1990) 91 Cr App Rep 150, CA; see Birch [1989] Crim LR 95; commentary on *R v Walsh* [1989] Crim LR 822. The wording of s 78 suggests that many of the 'flood' (*R v Keenan* [1989] 3 All ER 598 at 601, CA) of cases claiming that the statutory exclusionary discretion should be exercised on the grounds of a breach of the Codes of Practice or even of the procedural provisions of the Act should more properly have been argued, with perhaps greater benefit to the accused, on the basis of the unfairness discretion. This observation applies particularly to the cases where the debate has centred on the right to legal advice (Police and Criminal Evidence Act 1984, s 58; Code C passim; *R v Alladice* (1988) 87 Cr App Rep 380). The denial of access to a solicitor may well amount to improper treatment, but it is difficult to see how it prevents the defendant having a fair trial. The same may be said of agent provocateur or entrapment evidence, to which in principle s 78 is applicable (*R v Smurthwaite and Gill* [1994] 1 All ER 898, CA, setting out guidelines but holding the particular evidence in question not inadmissible). It follows that many purported exercises of the s 78 discretion (there is a list of reported instances up to June 1995 in Zander, *The Police and Criminal Evidence Act 1984*, 3rd edition, 1995, pp 238–43) were probably wrong as a matter of the strict interpretation of the statute. The courts appear to be exercising a discretion which, while nominally derived from s 78, is concerned generally with the exclusion of unfair evidence. As, however, this jurisdiction is based neither on the common law (the pre-1984 cases and the Commonwealth authorities have rarely been cited when s 78 has been invoked) nor on the formulation approved by Parliament, the result is far from satisfactory analytically, philosophically or practically. 'Section 78 has become established and accepted as a means for the courts to determine what breaches of the rules or improper conduct are acceptable on a case by case basis without any clearly articulated theory' (Zander, op cit, p 237).

2. The power is to exclude 'evidence on which the prosecution proposes to rely'. This includes confessions (*R v Mason* [1987] 3 All ER 481, [1988] 1 WLR 139, CA); it would also include a statement obtained by, for example, oppression from a witness other than the accused. It is not limited to evidence fairly, or unfairly obtained, and it is not limited to evidence proposed to be tendered by the prosecution.

3. The power is to 'refuse to allow evidence . . . to be given', so it can only be exercised before the evidence is given: *R v Sat-Bhambra* (1988) 88 Cr App Rep 55. In *Vel v Owen* (1987) 151 JP 510, [1987] Crim LR 496 the Divisional Court held that an accused was not entitled in the magistrates' court to have the question of whether evidence should be excluded under s 78 determined at a trial within the trial, but it is difficult to reconcile this decision with either the words of the section or *R v Sat-Bhambra*. The trial judge normally has the difficult task of weighing up the question of fairness during the prosecution case, possibly before he knows what the defence will be (*R v Keenan* [1990] 2 QB 54, [1989] 3 All ER 598, CA). On appeal, the Court of Appeal in examining the exercise of the discretion is restricted to looking at the case as it appeared to the judge at that time, and cannot take into account matters which developed later in the trial (*R v Parris* (1988) 89 Cr App Rep 68, CA; *R v Goldenberg* (1988) 152 JP 557, 88 Cr App Rep 285). The Court of Appeal may intervene if the judge failed to exercise his discretion at all (perhaps because he wrongly thought he did not have one: *R v Samuel* [1988] QB 615, [1988] 2 All ER 135, CA) or failed to exercise it properly (perhaps by considering the wrong issue or failing to consider the right one: *R v Mason* [1987] 3 All ER 481, [1988] 1 WLR 139, CA) but otherwise will not generally substitute its own discretion for that of the trial judge.

4. The phrase 'such an adverse effect' indicates that it is not every adverse effect on the fairness of the proceedings which will cause the evidence to be excluded: *R v Walsh* (1989) 91 Cr App Rep 161, CA.

5. On principle, the accused must bear the burden of persuading the court that the discretion should be exercised in his favour (*Vel v Owen* (1987) 151 JP

510). There may, however, be circumstances in which the state of the prosecution evidence is such that the accused will be able to discharge this burden without any defence evidence: *R v Keenan* [1990] 2 QB 54, [1989] 3 All ER 598, CA. In *R v Canale* (1990) 91 Cr App Rep 1 at 5, CA there is an indication that the burden is to be equated with that under s 76. Cf *R v Anderson* [1993] Crim LR 447, CA.

6. 'The provision is cast in terms of such vagueness and generality as to furnish little guidance to the court' (Cross, p 483). The Court of Appeal has responded by indicating that it is undesirable to lay down general guidance for trial judges (*R v Samuel* [1988] QB 615 at 630, [1988] 2 All ER 135 at 146, CA, though particular circumstances may give rise to such guidelines, as for example in *R v Smurthwaite and Gill* [1994] 1 All ER 898, CA). The cases below are therefore only to be regarded as indications of the circumstances in which the discretion will be exercised.

R v Mason   [1987] 3 All ER 481, [1988] 1 WLR 139, CA

The appellant and his solicitor were both told by the police that the appellant's fingerprint had been found in damning circumstances. The solicitor advised the appellant accordingly, and he made a full confession. At the trial the police officers admitted that what they had said about the fingerprint was a deliberate lie. The trial judge refused to exclude the confession under s 78.

Watkins LJ: It is obvious from the undisputed evidence that the police practised a deceit not only on the appellant, which is bad enough, but also on the solicitor whose duty it was to advise him. In effect, they hoodwinked both solicitor and client. That was a most reprehensible thing to do. It is not however because we regard as misbehaviour of a serious kind conduct of that nature that we have come to the decision soon to be made plain. This is not the place to discipline the police. That has been made clear here on a number of previous occasions. We are concerned with the application of the proper law. The law is, as I have already said, that a trial judge has a discretion to be exercised, of course on right principles, to reject admissible evidence in the interests of a defendant having a fair trial. The judge in the present case appreciated that, as . . . his ruling shows. So the only question to be answered by this court is whether, having regard to the way the police behaved, the judge exercised that discretion correctly. In our judgment he did not. He omitted a vital factor from his consideration, namely the deceit practised on the appellant's solicitor. If he had included that in his consideration of the matter we have not the slightest doubt that he would have been driven to an opposite conclusion, namely that the confession be ruled out and the jury not permitted therefore to hear of it. If that had been done, an acquittal would have followed for there was no other evidence in the possession of the prosecution.

For those reasons we have no alternative but to quash this conviction.

Before parting with this case, despite what I have said about the role of the court in relation to disciplining the police, we think we ought to say that we hope never again to hear of deceit such as this being practised on an accused person, and more particularly possibly on a solicitor whose duty it is to advise him, unfettered by false information from the police.

R v Keenan   [1990] 2 QB 54, [1989] 3 All ER 598, CA

At the appellant's trial for possession of an offensive weapon the prosecution sought to rely on statements made by the appellant to the police in which he admitted possession, but denied ownership, of the weapon. No record was made of the interviews containing those statements. At a voir dire the trial judge ruled that the statements were admissible and that any breach of the Code of Practice could be cured by the appellant's giving evidence of his version of the events. As it turned out (unknown to the judge at that early stage of the trial) the appellant's case was that the interviews had never taken place at all.

Hodgson J: [A] matter of immediate concern arises from the transcript of these officers' evidence. Time and again when counsel for the appellant put the relevant provisions of Code C to the officers, they said not only that they had not known of the provisions at the time but that they still did not know of them. Indeed in respect of two paragraphs Pc Edwards said he knew of none of his colleagues who were aware of them. If that statement is correct, such a degree of ignorance some 18 months after the 1984 Act came into force (1 January 1986) is appalling, particularly on the part of officers in the Metropolitan Force, which force, as this court knows, conducted a 'trial run' of the Act's provisions for many months before the Act came into force . . .

[Counsel for the appellant] made in effect two main submissions. The first was that, having been denied the opportunity of indicating at the time whether he agreed or disagreed with what was recorded, the appellant was now at a disadvantage compared with the police officers many months later. That submission addressed the possibility that the appellant's case, when revealed, might be that the interview in fact took place but was inaccurately recorded.

Second, she submitted that, by the improper obtaining of evidence, the appellant had been denied the choice he otherwise might have had of not giving evidence and of relying on the jury rejecting the much weaker case the prosecution would then have had.

The third possibility (and the one that in the end turned out to be the case advanced) was that the interview never took place at all. Counsel cannot be blamed for not uncovering this contention at that stage. She was not asked what her case was and she was not obliged to disclose it.

Towards the end of the argument counsel for the prosecution adverted to a problem which is also bound to arise in these cases. Having dealt with the limited extent of the admissions allegedly made and the fact that they had not yet been challenged either whether they were in fact made or, if made, were true, he said, 'I cannot, therefore, judge at present, frankly whether it is fair or unfair to the conduct of the defence of this case'.

After hearing further argument the assistant recorder, without giving reasons, ruled against the submission . . .

In our consideration of this case we have been referred to, or have referred to the following cases: *R v Samuel* [1988] 2 All ER 135, [1988] QB 615, *R v Alladice* (1988) 87 Cr App R 380, *R v O'Leary* (1988) 87 Cr App R 387, *R v Delaney* (1988) 88 Cr App R 338, *R v Absolam* (1988) 88 Cr App R 332, *R v Doolan* [1988] Crim LR 747, *R v Hughes* (28 April 1988, unreported), *R v Hallett* (7 March 1989, unreported), *R v Parris* (1988) 89 Cr App R 68 and *R v Hamand* (1985) 82 Cr App R 65. We have endeavoured in what follows to give full weight to everything said in these cases.

Code C, in extension of the provisions of Pt III (arrest), Pt IV (detention) and Pt V (questioning and treatment of persons by police), addresses two main concerns. First, it provides safeguards for detained persons and provides for their proper treatment with the object of ensuring that they are not subjected to undue pressure or oppression. Equally importantly, these code provisions are designed to make it difficult for a detained person to make unfounded allegations against the police which might otherwise appear credible. Second, it provides safeguards against the police inaccurately recording or inventing the words used in questioning a detained person. These practices are compendiously described by the slang 'to verbal' and 'the verbals'.

Again, equally importantly, the provisions, if complied with, are designed to make it very much more difficult for a defendant to make unfounded allegations that he has been 'verballed' which appear credible. (It is to be hoped that the general introduction of tape recording will make it even more difficult.)

In *R v Delaney* (1988) 88 Cr App R 338 this court adverted to something else which makes it desirable that the code provisions as to verballing should be strictly complied with. *R v Delaney* was a case where the appellant had been interviewed at length, but no contemporaneous record was made and it was not until the following day that a note was made by the interviewing officer. In giving the judgment of this court Lord Lane CJ said (at 341–2):

'By failing to make a contemporaneous note, or indeed any note, as soon as practicable, the officers deprived the court of what was, in all likelihood, the most cogent evidence as to what did indeed happen during these interviews and what did induce the appellant to confess. To use the words of [counsel for the appellant] to the court this morning, the judge and the prosecution were pro tanto disabled by the omission of the officers to act in accordance with the Codes of Practice, disabled from having the full knowledge upon which the judge could base his decision.'

When the defence seek to exclude evidence obtained by or in circumstances alleged to amount to breaches of the 1984 Act or the codes, there are a number of different situations which may face the judge. (a) One or more breaches of the code may be apparent in the custody record itself or from the witness statements. Examples of the first situation might be where an order has been made by an officer of insufficiently high rank or no meal has been offered at the proper time (para 8.6). This case affords an example of the second. It was almost certain, on the evidence of the witness statements themselves, that there had been a breach of para 11.3(*b*)(ii), and a glance at the officers' notebooks would have revealed breaches of the other two paragraphs. (b) There may be a prima facie breach which, if objection is taken, must be justified by evidence adduced by the prosecution. An order refusing access to a solicitor can only be justified by compelling evidence from the senior police officer who made the order: see *R v Samuel* [1988] 2 All ER 135, [1988] QB 615. (c) There may be alleged breaches which can probably only be established by the evidence of the defendant himself, eg cases of alleged oppression or in relation to para 13 of the code (persons at risk).

Clearly the procedure appropriate in each case may vary. In (a) it may be that all that will be necessary will be an admission by the prosecution, followed by argument. However, in cases like the instant one, we do not think that the prosecution will often be content to take this course in cases where they wish to persuade the judge to allow them to adduce their evidence despite the breaches.

We have in mind what this court said in *R v Delaney* in a passage from the judgment immediately following the one already cited. Lord Lane CJ said (at 342):

'The judge of course is entitled to ask himself why the officers broke the rules. Was it mere laziness or was it something more devious? Was it perhaps a desire to conceal from the court the full truth of the suggestions they had held out to the defendant? These are matters which may well tip the scales in favour of the defendant in these circumstances and make it impossible for the judge to say that he is satisfied beyond reasonable doubt, and so require him to reject the evidence.'

In (b) the prosecution will clearly have to call evidence to justify the order made. In such cases the defence may wish to call evidence from, for example, the solicitor to whom the defendant sought to have access. On occasion the defence may feel it desirable to call the defendant himself, as was done with disastrous results in *R v Alladice* (1988) 87 Cr App R 380 . . .

We think it unlikely that in situations (a) and (b) the defendant will usually be called to give evidence at the stage of the proceedings when the Act and codes are under consideration.

Cases such as we have envisaged under (c) above are likely to be rare. The whole structure of the legislation, which has at its heart placing control in the hands of a uniformed station officer independent of the investigating officers, is aimed at preventing any abuse of powers by the police.

In this case we are concerned with the provisions of the code aimed at preventing verballing and the credible allegation of verballing. In such cases evidence from the defendant at the stage where admissibility is in issue is most unlikely to be needed by the defence. If the proper procedures have, on the face of the record, been observed, then the defendant's contentions, eg that the apparently properly conducted and contemporaneously recorded interviews were inaccurate or did not happen, might possibly succeed with a jury but would be most unlikely to succeed before a judge alone.

But where, as in the instant case, the breaches are obvious a different situation inevitably arises. The trial judge has no means of knowing what will ensue after he has made his ruling. If he rules against admissibility, it may be that where, as here, the other evidence is not strong the defendant will exercise his right not to give evidence. To permit the evidence of the interview to be given may therefore effectively deprive the defendant of a right he would otherwise have had. And, if the evidence is admitted, the judge does not know what the response to it will be. Clear possibilities are, first, that the defendant will give evidence that the interview never took place at all or that, although it took place, the questions and answers were fabricated, second, he may say that the interview took place but that the questions and answers were inaccurately recorded or, third, he might accept the fact that the interview took place and the accuracy of the record.

Even more obviously the judge has no means at that stage of deciding what the truth of the matter is. If he admits the evidence, that task will fall to the jury, not to him. If he rules against admitting the evidence, there will never be a decision . . .

It is clear from the authorities to which we have referred that there have been a number of different ways in which the courts have approached the problems which arise when objection is taken to admissibility on the ground that there have been breaches of the codes of practice.

Additionally the situations in which the cases have reached this court have varied. Apart from the main difference between cases where a judge has erroneously ruled that there has been no breach and cases where he has correctly found a breach but exercised his discretion to permit the evidence to be given, the way in which the voir dire has been conducted by the judge and counsel has varied widely. Sometimes counsel has called the defendant, sometimes not. Sometimes he has revealed to the judge, whether in cross-examination or submission, what the eventual response to the evidence will be, or may be, if it is admitted; sometimes, as here, he has not.

A difficulty perceived by the judge and counsel in this case was that, at the stage when objection was taken, the trial judge was not apprised of all the facts. In such cases he cannot know what will happen if he admits the evidence, nor what will happen if he excludes it (will the defendant then go into the witness box?).

At first sight it seems unjust that evidence, otherwise admissible, should be excluded under s 78 when, if all the facts, and particularly what the defence's response is going to be, were known, it would be clear that admission of the evidence would not have 'an adverse effect on the fairness of the proceedings'.

We have given this problem anxious consideration but, within the confines of our present rules of criminal procedure, we can see no way in which this difficulty can be avoided. The decision has to be made at a stage when the judge does not know the full facts. In *R v Parris* (1988) 89 Cr App R 68 at trial, when the interview evidence had been admitted, the defence contended that it was fabricated. In giving the judgment of the court Lord Lane CJ, referring to that contention, said (at 73): 'This was his case when he later gave evidence on oath, a fact which is irrelevant for our purposes, since we must judge matters as at the time the submission was made.' . . .

We think that in cases where there have been 'significant and substantial' breaches of the 'verballing' provisions of the code, the evidence so obtained will frequently be excluded. We do not think that any injustice will be caused by this. It is clear that not every breach or combination of breaches of the code will justify the exclusion of interview evidence under s 76 or s 78: see *R v Hallett* (7 March 1989, unreported). They must be significant and substantial. If this were not the case, the courts would be undertaking a task which is no part of their duty; as Lord Lane CJ said in *R v Delaney* (at 341): 'It is no part of the duty of the court to rule a statement inadmissible simply in order to punish the police for failure to observe the codes of practice.'

But if the breaches are 'significant and substantial' we think it makes good sense to exclude them. At the voir dire stage a judge can foresee that a number of different situations may arise which the 'verballing' provisions are specifically designed to prevent. If the rest of the evidence is strong, then it may make no difference to the eventual result if he excludes the evidence. In cases when the rest of the evidence is weak or non-existent, that is just the situation where the temptation to do what the provisions are aimed to prevent is greatest, and the protection of the rules most needed.

As we have said before, this case was tried at a time when Bench and Bar were struggling to understand and properly apply new and complicated provisions, and it is entirely understandable if the assistant recorder got it wrong. We think he did. He was wrong to assume that any unfairness could be cured by the appellant going into the witness box. If the appellant intended not to give evidence if the officers' evidence was excluded, then admitting it unfairly robbed him of his right to remain silent: see *R v Hamand* (1985) 82 Cr App R 65. If the defence case was to be (as it turned out to be in fact) that the evidence was concocted, then it was unfair to admit it, because by doing so the appellant was not only forced to give evidence but also, by attacking the police, to put his character in issue. If the defence was to be that the interview was inaccurately recorded, then it was plainly unfair to admit it, because it placed the appellant at a substantial disadvantage in that he had been given no contemporaneous opportunity to correct any inaccuracies nor would he have his own contemporaneous note of what he had said.

COMMENT

Both cases indicate ways in which a defect in the investigative process can produce unfairness at the trial, by having the effect of depriving the accused of an essential procedural right (independent legal advice or the right of silence). See also *R v O'Loughlin and McLaughlin* [1988] 3 All ER 431, 85 Cr App Rep 157, CCC (prosecution case based on written evidence alone). There is, one may say, a basic model English criminal trial, and too great a deviation from that model produces unfairness. The Police and Criminal Evidence Act 1984 develops the model by provisions which, if complied with, will ensure that certain matters are not realistically subject to challenge at the trial. Some breaches of the Police and Criminal Evidence Act 1984 or the Codes of Practice will result in so great a deviation from the Act's model that, again, there is unfairness, as shown by the effect of the lack of a record in *R v Keenan*. See also *R v Canale* [1990] 2 All ER 187, 91 Cr App Rep 1, CA. The discretion to exclude evidence whose prejudicial effect outweighs its probative value is closely linked to the fairness of the proceedings themselves, so giving rise to proper exclusion under s 78 too: *R v Johnson* [1995] Crim LR 53, CA. Possibly there is a fourth class of case properly dealt with under s 78, where the prosecution evidence is so badly tainted by illegality that any ensuing trial is bound to be unfair. An example is perhaps *Matto v DPP* [1987] RTR 337, [1987] Crim LR 641, DC. But the circumstances would surely have to be extreme to have an effect on the fairness of the proceedings themselves. Otherwise, however, the evidence should perhaps be excluded by exercise of the unfairness jurisdiction (section 1 of this chapter) rather than s 78.

FURTHER READING

Birch [1989] Crim LR 95; Gelowitz (1990) 106 LQR 327; Hunter [1995] Crim LR 558.

3 Improperly obtained evidence in general

What about other kinds of improperly obtained evidence? Is evidence obtained by a crime, tort, breach of contract or confidence, invasion of privacy, trick or agent provocateur admissible? The answer of most common law jurisdictions outside America is that such evidence is admissible but may be excluded in the discretion of the court. The law is theoretically very similar in Scotland, but in practice the Scottish and latterly the Australian courts are more ready to exercise their discretion in favour of exclusion and to some extent they have worked out consistent principles to govern the discretion. As the following cases illustrate, the same cannot be said of other jurisdictions. In England the restrictive decision of the House of Lords in *R v Sang* (p 235, post) has led the lower courts to concentrate almost entirely on developing the statutory discretion discussed in the preceding section of this chapter.

A   THE COMMONWEALTH AND EIRE

Lawrie v Muir   1950 SLT 37

The defendant was convicted of using milk bottles without the consent of the true owners. The Scottish Milk Bottle Exchange Ltd carried on the business of collecting and restoring bottles to their true owners. It was approved by the Scottish Milk Marketing Board; all contracts between the Board and producers and distributors of milk provided that the company's inspectors might inspect the premises of any producer or distributor in contractual relations with the Board to examine bottles in their possession. Two inspectors displayed their warrant cards to the defendant who was entitled to refuse them permission to inspect because she was not in contractual relations with the Board. But she did not do so and the inspectors found the bottles. The High Court of Justiciary held that the evidence had been wrongly admitted.

Lord Cooper LJ-G: From the standpoint of principle it seems to me that the law must strive to reconcile two highly important interests which are liable to come into conflict – (a) the interest of the citizen to be protected from illegal or irregular invasions of his liberties by the authorities, and (b) the interest of the State to secure that evidence bearing upon the commission of crime and necessary to enable justice to be done shall not be withheld from courts of law on any merely formal or technical ground. Neither of these objects can be insisted upon to the uttermost. The protection of the citizen is primarily protection for the innocent citizen against unwarranted, wrongful and perhaps high-handed interference, and the common sanction is an action of damages. The protection is not intended as a protection for the guilty citizen against the efforts of the public prosecutor to vindicate the law. On the other hand, the interest of the State cannot be magnified to the point of causing all the safeguards for the protection of the citizen to vanish, and of offering a positive inducement to the authorities to proceed by irregular methods. It is obvious that excessively rigid rules as to the exclusion of evidence bearing upon the commission of a crime might conceivably operate to the detriment and not the advantage of the accused, and might even lead to the conviction of the innocent; and extreme cases can easily be figured in which the exclusion of a vital piece of evidence from the knowledge of a jury because of some technical flaw in the conduct of the police would be an outrage upon common sense and a defiance of elementary justice. For these reasons . . . I adopt as a first approximation to the true rule the statement of Lord Justice Clerk Aitchison [in *HM Advocate v M'Guigan* 1936 JC 16] that 'an irregularity in the obtaining of evidence does not *necessarily* make that evidence inadmissible'.

. . . Lord Aitchison seems to me to have indicated that there was in his view no absolute rule and that the question was one of circumstances. I respectfully agree. It would greatly facilitate the task of judges were it possible to imprison the principle within the framework of a simple and unqualified maxim, but I do not think that it is feasible to do so . . . Irregularities require to be excused, and infringements of the formalities of the law in relation to these matters are not lightly to be condoned. Whether any given irregularity ought to be excused depends upon the nature of the irregularity and the circumstances under which it was committed. In particular, the case may bring into play the discretionary principle of fairness to the accused which has been developed so fully in our law in relation to the admission in evidence of confessions or admissions by a person suspected or charged with a crime. That principle would obviously require consideration in any case in which the departure from the strict procedure had been adopted deliberately with a view to securing the admission of evidence obtained by an unfair trick. Again, there are many statutory offences in relation to which Parliament has prescribed in detail in the interests of fairness a special procedure to be followed in obtaining evidence; and in such cases . . . it is very easy to see why a departure from the strict rules has often been held to be fatal to the prosecution's case. On the other hand, to take an extreme instance figured in argument, it would usually be wrong to exclude some highly incriminating production in a murder trial merely because it was found by a police officer in the course of a search authorised for a different purpose or before a proper warrant had been obtained.

. . . I am unable to accept the suggestion that a distinction should be drawn between the statutory offence, the malum prohibitum, and the common law crime, the malum in se, for the interests of the State are as much involved in offences against penal statutes as in offences against the common law, and the former category has greatly expanded in recent times . . . It is specially to be noted that the two inspectors who in this instance exceeded their authority were not police officers enjoying a large residuum of common law discretionary powers, but the employees of a limited company acting in association with the Milk Marketing Board, whose only powers are derived from contracts between the Board and certain milk producers and distributors, of whom the appellant is not one. Though the matter is narrow I am inclined to regard this last point as sufficient to tilt the balance against the prosecution, upon the view that persons in the special position of these inspectors ought to know the precise limits of their authority and should be held to exceed these limits at their peril. It is found that the inspectors acted in good faith, but it is incontrovertible that they obtained the assent of the appellant to the search of her shop by means of a positive misrepresentation made to her.

[Cf *R v Matthews and Ford* [1972] VR 3.]

M'Govern v HM Advocate   1950 SLT 133

The accused was suspected of blowing open a safe with explosives. Before arresting and charging him the police scraped his fingernails for traces of explosives, which chemical analysis subsequently revealed to be present. This conduct amounted to assault, since there was no right to search without warrant before arrest. The High Court of Justiciary held that the evidence had been wrongly admitted.

Lord Cooper LJ-G: [I]rregularities of this kind always require to be 'excused' or condoned, if they can be excused or condoned, whether by the existence of urgency, the relative triviality of the irregularity or other circumstances. This is not a case where I feel disposed to 'excuse' the conduct of the police. The proper procedure for search of the appellant's house by obtaining a search warrant was duly followed out, and it would have been very simple for the police to have adopted the appropriate procedure in relation to a search of his person. Why they did not do so, we do not yet know. Exactly the same information was available to them when they scraped the appellant's fingernails as when they charged and apprehended him shortly afterwards; and, if the charge and apprehension were justified, these should have preceded and not followed the examination of his person.

. . . [T]here is no option but to quash this conviction because, unless the principles under which police investigations are carried out are adhered to with reasonable strictness, the anchor of the entire system for the protection of the public will very soon begin to drag.

Fairley v Fishmongers of London   1951 SLT 54

An inspector employed by the respondents reported his opinion that the appellant was in unlawful possession of salmon in breach of the Salmon Fisheries (Scotland) Act 1868 to the Ministry of Food, who had a duty to investigate breaches of the salmon laws. A Ministry of Food official with an official warrant helped the respondent's inspector to search local cold stores, from one of which salmon owned by the appellant was removed by the respondent's inspector, who had no search warrant under the 1868 Act. The evidence was held by the High Court of Justiciary to have been rightly admitted.

Lord Cooper LJ-G: The respondent's inspector could have applied for a search warrant . . . and I have little doubt that, if he had, he would have got one. He did not. Moreover, while the Ministry enforcement officer was, I think, entitled to enter the store in search of evidence bearing upon any contravention of the food regulations or of the Order dealing with salmon, he had no concern with infringements of the Salmon Fisheries (Scotland) Acts though it would have been quite in order for him to have reported to the proper authorities any evidence incidentally obtained by him and bearing upon such an infringement. It follows that the procedure whereby the incriminating evidence was obtained was not strictly in accordance with any statutory or other authority. On the other hand . . . [i]n the words of finding, 'The said inspectors acted in good faith, in a mistaken belief as to their powers and in an endeavour in the public interest to vindicate the law in relation to an offence which constituted a considerable evil and was difficult to detect'. The approach to the Ministry of Food was not improper in view of their possible interest in the matter. I can find nothing to suggest that any departure from the strict procedure was deliberately adopted with a view to securing the admission of evidence obtained by an unfair trick . . . [I]n the present instance the irregularity ought to be 'excused' . . .

[Lords Carmont and Keith agreed.]

HM Advocate v Turnbull   1951 SLT 409

A warrant was granted to search for documents in the possession of the accused, an accountant. It was limited to documents relating to a particular client of the accused, but other documents were seized, and it was held that the latter were not admissible in evidence because they had been obtained by an illegal search or seizure. Lord Guthrie in the High Court of Justiciary excluded the evidence.

Lord Guthrie: In the present case there were, first, no circumstances of urgency. Second, the retention and use over a period of six months of the documents bearing to relate [sic] to other matters than that mentioned in the petition show that the actions complained of were deliberate. The police officers did not accidentally stumble upon evidence of a plainly incriminating character in the course of a search for a different purpose. If the documents are incriminating, their incriminating character is only exposed by careful consideration of their contents. Third, if information was in the hands of the criminal authorities implicating the accused in other crimes, these could have been mentioned in the petition containing the warrant under which the search was authorised. If they had no such information, the examination of private papers in the hope of finding incriminating material was interference with the rights of a citizen. Therefore to hold that evidence so obtained was admissible would, as I have said, tend to nullify the protection afforded to a citizen by the requirements of a magistrate's warrant, and would offer a positive inducement to the authorities to proceed by irregular methods. Fourth, when I consider the matter in the light of the principle of fairness to the accused, it appears to me that the evidence so irregularly and deliberately obtained is intended to be the basis of a comparison between the figures actually submitted to the Inspector of Taxes and the information in the possession of the accused. If such important evidence upon a number of charges is tainted by the method by which it was deliberately secured, I am of opinion that a fair trial upon these charges is rendered impossible.

NOTE

A striking feature of this case was that it could be seen at once that the retention of the documents was not justified by the warrant, but it required six months' examination to discover fraudulent matter in them. The illegality on the officers' part was thus deliberate.

Kuruma, Son of Kaniu v R   [1955] AC 197, [1955] 1 All ER 236, PC

The accused, a Kenyan African, while travelling to his reserve, passed along a road on which he knew there would be a road block. He could have gone by another route on which there was no road block. He was stopped and searched illegally in that the searchers were not of the rank of assistant inspector or above. The police alleged that they found two rounds of ammunition and a pocket knife. The accused was convicted of unlawful possession of ammunition, and appealed to the Privy Council, who held the evidence admissible.

Lord Goddard: It is only right to say that the two rounds of ammunition differed from those which the police officers then had as part of their equipment. The prisoner all along denied that he was carrying these rounds, and at the trial also denied that he had a pocket knife on him. The police said they had returned the knife to him after he was in custody. No explanation was given of this remarkable action on their part, nor was the knife produced at the trial nor any reason given for its absence. It is also to be observed that three other persons, two police officers and one civilian, were said to have been present when the prisoner was searched, one of them indeed was said to have actually picked up the two rounds after they had fallen from the prisoner's shorts. Their Lordships think it was most unfortunate, considering the grave character of the offence charged, which carries a capital penalty, that these important witnesses were not called by the prosecution: it was not suggested that they were not available. The assessors were all in favour of an acquittal, but the magistrate overruled them and convicted the appellant . . .

In their Lordships' opinion the test to be applied in considering whether evidence is admissible is whether it is relevant to the matters in issue. If it is, it is admissible and the court is not concerned with how the evidence was obtained. While this proposition may not have been stated in so many words in any English case there are decisions which support it, and in their Lordships' opinion it is plainly right in principle. In *R v Leatham* (1861) 8 Cox CC 498, an information for penalties under the Corrupt Practices Act, objection was taken to the production of a letter written by the defendant because its existence only became known by answers he had given to the commissioners who held the inquiry under the Act, which provided that answers before that tribunal should not be admissible in evidence against him. The Court of Queen's Bench held that though his answers could not be used against the defendant, yet if a clue was thereby given to other evidence, in that case the letter, which would prove the case it was admissible. Crompton J said: [at 501] 'It matters not how you get it; if you steal it even, it would be admissible.' *Lloyd v Mostyn* (1842) 10 M & W 478 was an action on a bond. The person in whose possession it was objected to produce it on the ground of privilege. The plaintiff's attorney, however, had got a copy of it and notice to produce the original being proved the court admitted the copy as secondary evidence. To the same effect was *Calcraft v Guest* [1898] 1 QB 759, [1895–9] All ER Rep 346. There can be no difference in principle for this purpose between a civil and a criminal case. No doubt in a criminal case the judge always has a discretion to disallow evidence if the strict rules of admissibility would operate unfairly against an accused. This was emphasised in the case before this Board of *Noor Mohamed v R* [1949] AC 182, [1949] 1 All ER 365, PC, and in the recent case in the House of Lords, *Harris v DPP* [1952] AC 694, [1952] 1 All ER 1044, HL. If, for instance, some admission of some piece of evidence, eg a document, had been obtained from a defendant by a trick, no doubt the judge might properly rule it out. It was this discretion that lay at the root of the ruling of Lord Guthrie in *HM Advocate v Turnbull* 1951 JC 96. The other cases from Scotland to which their Lordships' attention was drawn, *Rattray v Rattray* 1897 25 R (Ct of Sess) 315; *Lawrie v Muir* 1950 JC 19 and *Fairley v Fishmongers of London* 1951 JC 14, all support the view that if the evidence is relevant it is admissible and the court is not concerned with how it is obtained. No doubt their Lordships in the Court of Justiciary appear at least to some extent to consider the question from the point of view whether the alleged illegality in the obtaining of the evidence could properly be excused, and it is true that Horridge J in *Elias v Pasmore* [1934] 2 KB 164, [1934] All ER Rep 380, used that expression. It is to be observed, however, that what the judge was there concerned with was an action of trespass, and he held that the trespass was excused. In their Lordships' opinion, when it is a question of the admission of evidence strictly it is not whether the method by which it was obtained is tortuous but excusable but whether what has been obtained is relevant to the issue being tried. Their Lordships are not now concerned with whether an action for assault would lie against the police officers and express no opinion on that point. Certain decisions of the Supreme Court of the United States of America were also cited in argument. Their Lordships do not think it necessary to examine them in detail. Suffice it to say that there appears to be considerable difference of opinion among the judges both in the State and Federal courts as to whether or not the rejection of evidence obtained by illegal means depends on certain articles in the American Constitution. At any rate, in *Olmstead v United States* (1928) 277 US 438 the majority of the Supreme Court were clearly of the opinion that the common law did not reject relevant evidence on that ground. It is right, however, that it should be stated that the rule with regard to the admission of confessions, whether it be regarded as an exception to the general rule or not, is a rule of law which their Lordships are not qualifying in any degree whatsoever. The rule is that a confession can only be admitted if it is voluntary, and therefore one obtained by threats or promises held out by a person in authority is not to be admitted. It is only necessary to refer to *R v Thompson* [1893] 2 QB 12; [1891–4] All ER Rep 376 where the law was fully reviewed by the Court for Crown Cases Reserved.

As they announced at the conclusion of the arguments, their Lordships have no doubt that the evidence to which objection has been taken was properly admitted.

HM Advocate v Hepper   1958 JC 39

Police officers investigating a particular offence called at the accused's house and were given permission by him to search it. They removed an attaché case unconnected with the matter being investigated but relevant to a later charge of theft. Lord Guthrie in the High Court of Justiciary held the evidence admissible.

Lord Guthrie: [T]he problem is always to reconcile the interest of society in the detection of crime with the requirement of fairness to an accused person . . . In *Turnbull* [p 221, ante] at 103, I distinguished that case, in which I excluded evidence as to the documents taken possession of by police officers searching the accused's premises under a search warrant which clearly did not cover these documents, from a case in which police officers accidentally stumbled upon evidence of a plainly incriminating character in the course of a search for a different purpose . . . It may be that the article which the police officers stumbled upon in their search of the accused's house was not an article of a plainly incriminating character, but it was at least an article of a very suspicious character, since it was an attaché case which contained within it the name and address of another person. In the circumstances, I do not think that the police officers acted in any way improperly in taking away that article in order to make further inquiries about it. If they had not done so, it might have disappeared . . . But even if it cannot be put so highly, and if it be thought that their action was irregular, I am still of opinion that the evidence, even if irregularly obtained, is admissible in view of the interest of society in the detection of crime.

HM Advocate v M'Kay   1961 JC 47

An objection was made to the admission at a trial in Scotland of documents seized during a search of the accused's house in Dublin by the Dublin police under an Eire warrant; the documents seized were not in the accused's name. Lord Wheatley in the High Court of Justiciary admitted the evidence.

Lord Wheatley: [E]ven if . . . there was irregularity here, the two tests of fairness and urgency fall to be applied. It is suggested that, since the warrant to search merely referred to authority to search for cash to the amount of £35,000, it would be unfair to the accused to allow evidence of other documents recovered to be admitted on the authority of such a warrant, because, while the accused and his wife had taken no objection to a search for money under that warrant, that did not mean that they might not have taken objection to a search for other documents . . . [B]ut it would seem reasonable to suppose that they accepted [the warrant] as authority to search the house for money or for some trace of it.

[The court therefore held that there was no unfairness. The matter was urgent since the documents might be lost or deliberately destroyed, the accused had escaped from Scottish prison custody pending the charge and had been living under a false name in Eire. The documents were accordingly admitted.]

R v Payne   [1963] 1 All ER 848, [1963] 1 WLR 637, CCA

Lord Parker CJ: This appellant was convicted on 27 July 1962, at London Sessions of driving a car whilst unfit through drink and of being in charge of a car while unfit . . . It is against those two convictions that he now appeals . . .

The short point here is almost identical with the point which was taken in the case of *R v Court* [1962] Crim LR 697, CCA, which came before this court on the very day when London Sessions were dealing with the present appellant, namely, 27 July 1962. In both *R v Court* and this case the appellants were asked when they went to the police station whether they were willing to be examined by a doctor, and it was made clear to them in each case that the purpose of that was that the doctor should see whether the appellant was suffering from any illness or disability. In each case the respective appellant was told that it was no part of the doctor's duty to examine him in order to give an opinion as to his unfitness to drive. Those statements to the appellants were made at that time pursuant to a definite policy, which was that the doctor called would not examine a defendant in order to ascertain whether he was unfit to drive, but would examine him merely in order to see whether he was suffering from any other illness or physical disability and in particular whether he was fit to leave the police station.

In the present case the doctor was a Dr Henry. He was in fact called as a witness for the prosecution and, having been called he proceeded to give evidence, and strong evidence, in regard to the extent to which the appellant was under the influence of drink. The chairman said in his summing-up:

> 'At the end the doctor came to the conclusion, having examined him very thoroughly, you may think – he did not complete it for about half an hour – that the accused was under the influence of drink to such an extent as to be unfit to have proper control of a car.'

In *R v Court*, this court pointed out that while such evidence from the doctor in circumstances such as these was clearly admissible, nevertheless the chairman in the exercise of his discretion ought to have refused to allow that evidence to be given on the basis that if the accused realised that the doctor would give evidence on that matter he might refuse to subject himself to examination.

The present case is, in the opinion of this court, on all fours with *R v Court*, and in those circumstances the court is constrained to quash the convictions on counts one and three, and the order for disqualification.

People v O'Brien   [1965] IR 142

Premises to be searched were inadvertently misdescribed in the warrant as '118 Cashel Road, Crumlin' instead of '118 Captain's Road, Crumlin'. The search led to the discovery of stolen goods which were the subject of the charge, but it was technically a trespass in consequence of the misaddressing. The evidence was held by the Eire Supreme Court to have been correctly admitted.

Kingsmill Moore J (with whom Lavery and Budd JJ agreed): Three answers are possible. First, that if evidence is relevant it cannot be excluded on the ground that it was obtained as a result of illegal action: second, that if it was obtained as a result of illegal action it is never admissible: third, that where it was obtained by illegal action it is a matter for the trial judge to decide, in his discretion, whether to admit it or not, subject, in cases where the evidence has been admitted, to review by an appellate court.

It seems to me that neither the first nor the second answer is sustainable. The first answer represents the earlier portion of Lord Goddard's judgment in *Kuruma's Case* [1955] AC 197, [1955] 1 All ER 236, PC, but even Lord Goddard found it necessary to allow exceptions to the rule, namely where the strict rules of admissibility would operate unfairly against the accused, instancing the obtaining of a document by a trick. Courts in both England and Ireland have frequently refused to admit evidence which was undoubtedly relevant where the probative value of the evidence would be slight and its prejudicial effect would be great . . . Moreover, the Attorney-General has refused to argue for this rule in its unqualified form, conceding that evidence obtained by methods of gross personal violence or other methods offending against the essential dignity of the human person should not be received . . .

The second answer would open up equal difficulties. The exclusionary rule laid down in *Weeks v US* 232 US 383 (1914) was not accepted in many of the State courts. An absolute exclusionary rule prevents the admission of relevant and vital facts where unintentional or trivial illegalities have been committed in the course of ascertaining them. Fairness does not require such a rule and common sense rejects it.

Some intermediate solution must be found . . . [I]n every case a determination has to be made by the trial judge as to whether the public interest is best served by the admission or by the exclusion of evidence of facts ascertained as a result of, and by means of, illegal actions, and that the answer to the question depends on a consideration of all the circumstances. On the one hand, the nature and extent of the illegality have to be taken into account. Was the illegal action intentional or unintentional, and, if intentional, was it the result of an *ad hoc* decision or does it represent a settled or deliberate policy? Was the illegality one of a trivial or technical nature or was it a serious invasion of important rights the recurrence of which would involve a real danger to necessary freedoms? Were there circumstances of urgency or emergency which provide some excuse for the action? Lord Goddard in *Kuruma's Case* [1955] AC 197, [1955] 1 All ER 236, PC, mentions as a ground for excluding relevant evidence that it has been obtained by a 'trick' and the Lord Justice-General in *Lawrie's Case* 1950 SLT 37 refers to an 'unfair trick'. These seem to me to be more dubious grounds for exclusion. The police in the investigation of crime are not bound to show their hand too openly, provided they act legally. I am disposed to lay emphasis not so much on alleged fairness to the accused as on the public interest that the law should be observed even in the investigation of crime. The nature of the crime which is being investigated may also have to be taken into account . . .

. . . [Here] the mistake was a pure oversight and it has not been shown that the oversight was noticed by anyone before the premises were searched. I can find no evidence of deliberate treachery, imposition, deceit or illegality; no policy to disregard the provisions of the Constitution or to conduct searches without a warrant; nothing except the existence of an unintentional and accidental illegality to set against the public interest of having crime detected and punished.

. . . I do not think that the necessity of a collateral inquiry is an adequate reason for establishing a general rule that all relevant evidence is admissible notwithstanding the illegality of the means used to prove it.

Walsh J (with whom O'Dalaigh CJ agreed): [I]n this country the practice in modern times has been to exclude every part of a confession which had been improperly obtained or induced irrespective of whether part of it at least could be shown by subsequent facts to have been true. It is also true to say that the practice has always been to admit in evidence facts, if they were relevant, which had been derived from the inadmissible statement or confession . . . Every Judge in our courts is bound to uphold the laws and while he cannot condone or even ignore illegalities which come to his notice, his first duty is to determine the issue before him in accordance with law and not to be diverted from it or permit it to be wrongly decided for the sake of frustrating a police illegality, or drawing public attention to it . . .

In my judgment the law in this country has been that the evidence in this particular case is not rendered inadmissible and that there is no discretion to rule it out by reason only of the fact that it was obtained by means of an illegal as distinct from an unconstitutional seizure . . . If a stage should be reached where this court was compelled to come to the conclusion that the ordinary law and police disciplinary measures have failed to secure compliance by the police with law, then it would be preferable that a rule of absolute exclusion should be formulated rather than that every trial judge, when the occasion arises, should also be asked to adjudicate upon the question of whether the public good requires the accused should go free without full trial rather than that the police should be permitted the fruits of the success of their lawless ventures. Apart from the anomalies which might be produced by the many varying ways in which that discretion could be exercised by individual judges, the lamentable state of affairs which would call for such a change in the existing law of evidence would certainly justify absolute exclusion rather than a rule which might appear to lend itself to expediency rather than to principle.

[Art 40, para 5 of the Constitution provides: 'The dwelling of every citizen is inviolable and shall not be forcibly entered save in accordance with law.'] The courts in exercising the judicial powers of government of the state must recognise the paramount position of constitutional rights and must uphold the objection of an accused person to the admissibility at his trial of evidence obtained or procured by the state or its servants or agents as a result of a deliberate and conscious violation of the constitutional rights of the accused person where no extraordinary excusing circumstances exist, such as the imminent destruction of vital evidence or the need to rescue a victim in peril. A suspect has no constitutional right to destroy or dispose of evidence or to imperil the victim. I would also place in the excusable category evidence obtained by a search incidental to and contemporaneous with a lawful arrest although made without a valid search warrant. [Here the violation was not deliberate and hence the evidence was admissible.]

Hay v HM Advocate   1968 SLT 334

A warrant was granted to two police doctors to examine the accused's teeth to see if they corresponded with marks on the body of a murdered girl. The High Court of Justiciary held that even if the warrant was not legal, the medical evidence had been properly admitted because 'there was in this case an element of urgency, since a visit to the dentist or an injury to the accused's teeth could have destroyed the evidence'.

King v R   [1969] 1 AC 304, [1968] 2 All ER 610, PC

Lord Hodson: On 11 January, Sergeant Isaacs, Acting Corporal Gayle, Acting Corporal Linton and other police went to 20 Ladd Lane to search for ganja under the Dangerous Drugs Law. The warrant was read by Sergeant Isaacs on the premises. It was read to a woman on the premises and not apparently directly to the appellant but the appellant and another man, who was also searched, were told that the police were there to carry out a search for ganja. Corporal Gayle searched the appellant and found the ganja in one of his trouser pockets and arrested him.

The ganja was subsequently analysed by the government analyst and a certificate obtained on analysis put in evidence.

Although the search was not authorised by the Dangerous Drugs Law or the Constabulary Force Law there was no evidence that the appellant was wilfully misled by the police officers or any of them into thinking that there was such authorisation.

Corporal Gayle admitted at the trial that he knew the warrant was to search the premises of Joyce Cohen and that it referred to the search of no-one else. He suspected that the appellant might have had ganja on him and did not offer him the opportunity of being searched in front of a justice of the peace although he knew of that right of a citizen.

It can therefore be said that he should have had the advantage of a search before a magistrate and the choice of this was never offered to him.

The substantial argument on behalf of the appellant was that, in the discretion of the court, the evidence produced as a result of the search, which was the whole of the evidence against him, ought, though admissible, to have been excluded as unfair to him.

Before referring to *Kuruma, Son of Kaniu v R* [1955] AC 197, [1955] 1 All ER 236, PC, it is convenient to refer to some earlier decisions. *Jones v Owens* (1870) 34 JP 759 was a decision of the Divisional Court of the King's Bench Division. There a constable who had no right to search the person of the appellant did so and finding 25 young salmon in his pocket summoned him under the Salmon Fishery Acts for illegally having these in his possession. The appellant was convicted by the justices and on appeal it was said by Mellor J (at 760) (Lush J concurring):

'I think it would be a dangerous obstacle to the administration of justice if we were to hold, because evidence was obtained by illegal means it could not be used against a party charged with an offence. The justices rightly convicted the appellant.'

This matter has been discussed in a number of Scottish cases which were reviewed in *Kuruma, Son of Kaniu v R* [1955] AC 197, [1955] 1 All ER 236, PC.

It should be prefaced that in the Scottish cases to which reference will be made the court is directing its mind to the admissibility of evidence and in this connexion to a discretion to be exercised whether or not to admit evidence in cases where it could be said to be unfair to the accused to do so.

In the English cases the evidence under consideration is admissible in law (whether illegally obtained or not) and the exercise of discretion is called for in order to decide whether, even though admissible, it should be excluded in fairness to the accused. The same end is reached in both jurisdictions though by a slightly different route . . .

The discretion in criminal cases to disallow evidence if the strict rules of admissibility would operate unfairly against an accused has been emphasised before this Board in *Noor Mohamed v R* [1949] AC 182, [1949] 1 All ER 365, PC, and in the House of Lords in *Harris v DPP* [1952] AC 694, [1952] 1 All ER 1044, HL, as was pointed out by Lord Goddard in *Kuruma, Son of Kaniu v R* [1955] AC 197, [1955] 1 All ER 236, PC . . .

Callis v Gunn [1964] 1 QB 495, [1963] 3 All ER 677, DC, is another case where *Kuruma, Son of Kaniu v R* was considered. It was held that evidence of fingerprints was relevant and admissible. It had been excluded by magistrates and on appeal by the prosecutor, which was allowed, it was held by the Divisional Court that, while the court had an overriding discretion to disallow evidence if its admission would operate unfairly against a defendant, there were no representations by the police officer who took the fingerprints and nothing to justify the justices in excluding the evidence.

Lord Parker CJ in referring to the discretion said (p 502) that as he understood it,

'. . . it would certainly be exercised by excluding the evidence if there was any suggestion of it having been obtained oppressively, by false representations, by a trick, by threats, by bribes, anything of that sort . . .'

The appellant relied in support of his submission that the evidence illegally obtained against him should be excluded on the argument that it was obtained in violation of his constitutional rights, and reference was made to an Irish case of *The People v O'Brien* [1965] IR 142 where the point was discussed by the Supreme Court of Eire. The provision of the Jamaican Constitution scheduled to the Jamaica Order in Council, No 1550 of 1962 (para 19) gives protection to persons against search of persons or property without consent.

This constitutional right may or may not be enshrined in a written constitution, but it seems to their Lordships that it matters not whether it depends on such enshrinement or simply upon the common law as it would do in this country. In either event the discretion of the court must be exercised and has not been taken away by the declaration of the right in written form.

Having considered the evidence and the submissions advanced, their Lordships hold that there is no ground for interfering with the way in which the discretion has been exercised in this case.

This is not in their opinion a case in which evidence has been obtained by conduct of which the Crown ought not to take advantage. If they had thought otherwise they would have excluded the evidence even though tendered for the suppression of crime.

NOTE

The Canadian Constitution now provides (Constitution Act 1982, s 24(2)):

'Where . . . a court concludes that evidence was obtained in a manner that infringed or denied any rightful freedoms guaranteed by this charter, the evidence shall be excluded if it is established that, having regard to all the circumstances, the admission of it in the proceedings will bring the administration of justice into disrepute.'

This has led to abandonment of a narrow discretion and the commencement of a flood of litigation relating to what circumstances are relevant to the exercise of the exclusionary power.

Collins v R   (1987) 38 DLR (4th) 508

The accused was tried on a charge of possessing heroin for the purpose of trafficking. Police officers had the accused under observation in a pub. One person who joined the accused and then left the pub was found by the officers to have heroin in his car. The officers returned to the pub and approached the accused. One of them grabbed her by the throat to prevent her swallowing any evidence. Her mouth was empty, but the officer observed she was holding something which turned out to be a balloon containing heroin. The trial judge held that the search was unreasonable but that the evidence was admissible. An appeal by her against conviction was dismissed by the British Columbia Court of Appeal, but a further appeal was allowed by the Supreme Court of Canada.

Lamer J: On the record as it now stands, the appellant has established that the search was unreasonable and violated her rights under 8 of the Charter. As Seaton JA pointed out in the Court of Appeal, s 24(2) has adopted an intermediate position with respect to the exclusion of evidence obtained in violation of the Charter. It rejected the American rule excluding all evidence obtained in violation of the *Bill of Rights* and the common law rule that all relevant evidence was admissible regardless of the means by which it was obtained. Section 24(2) requires the exclusion of the evidence, 'if it is established that, having regard to all the circumstances, the admission of it in the proceedings would bring the administration of justice into disrepute'.

At the outset, it should be noted that the use of the phrase 'if it is established that' places the burden of persuasion on the applicant, for it is the position which he maintains which must be established. Again, the standard of persuasion required can only be the civil standard of the balance of probabilities. Thus, the applicant must make it more probable than not that the admission of the evidence would bring the administration of justice into disrepute.

It is whether *the admission of the evidence* would bring the administration of justice into disrepute that is the applicable test. Misconduct by the police in the investigatory process often has some effect on the repute of the administration of justice, but s 24(2) is not a remedy for police misconduct, requiring the exclusion of the evidence if, because of this misconduct, the administration of justice was brought into disrepute. Section 24(2) could well have been drafted in that way, but it was not. Rather, the drafts of the Charter decided to focus on the admission of the evidence in the proceedings, and the purpose of s 24(2) is to prevent having the administration of justice brought into *further disrepute* by the admission of the evidence in the proceedings. This further disrepute will result from the admission of evidence that would deprive the accused of a fair hearing, or from judicial condonation of unacceptable conduct by the investigatory and prosecutorial agencies. It will also be necessary to consider any disrepute that may result from the exclusion of the evidence. It would be inconsistent with the purpose of s 24(2) to exclude evidence if its exclusion would bring the administration of justice into greater disrepute than would its admission. Finally, it must be emphasised that even though the inquiry under s 24(2) will necessarily focus on the specific prosecution, it is the long-term consequences of regular admission or exclusion of this type of evidence on the repute of the administration of justice which must be considered . . .

The concept of disrepute necessarily involves some element of community views, and the determination of disrepute thus requires the judge to refer to what he conceives to be the views of the community at large. This does not mean that evidence of the public's perception of the repute of the administration of justice . . . will be determinative of the issue . . . Members of the public generally become conscious of the importance of protecting the rights and freedoms of accused only when they are in some way brought closer to the system either personally or through the experience of friends or family . . .

The Charter is designed to protect the accused from the majority, so the enforcement of the Charter must not be left to that majority.

The approach I adopt may be put figuratively in terms of the reasonable person test proposed by Professor Yves-Marie Morissette in his article, 'The Exclusion of Evidence under the Canadian Charter of Rights and Freedoms: What to Do and What Not to Do', 29 McGill LJ 521 at p 588 (1984). In applying s 24(2), he suggested that the relevant question is: 'Would the admission of the evidence bring the administration of justice into disrepute in the eyes of the reasonable man, dispassionate and fully apprised of the circumstances of the case?' The reasonable person is usually the average person in the community, but only when that community's current mood is reasonable.

The decision is thus not left to the untrammelled discretion of the judge. In practice, as Professor Morissette wrote, the reasonable person test is there to require of judges that they 'concentrate on what they do best: finding within themselves, with cautiousness and impartiality, a basis for their own decisions, articulating their reasons carefully and accepting review by a higher court where it occurs.' It serves as a reminder to each individual judge that his discretion is grounded in community values, and, in particular, long-term community values. He should not render a decision that would be unacceptable to the community when that community is not being wrought with passion or otherwise under passing stress due to current events. In effect, the judge will have met this test if the judges of the Court of Appeal will decline to interfere with his decision, even though they might have decided the matter differently, using the well-known statement that they are of the view that the decision was not unreasonable.

In determining whether the admission of evidence would bring the administration of justice into disrepute, the judge is directed by s 24(2) to consider 'all the circumstances'. The factors which are to be considered and balanced have been listed by many courts in the country . . . The factors that the courts have most frequently considered include:
- what kind of evidence was obtained?
- what Charter right was infringed?
- was the Charter violation serious or was it of a merely technical nature?
- was it deliberate, wilful or flagrant, or was it inadvertent or committed in good faith?
- did it occur in circumstances of urgency or necessity?
- were there other investigatory techniques available?
- would the evidence have been obtained in any event?
- is the offence serious?
- is the evidence essential to substantiate the charge?
- are other remedies available?

I do not wish to be seen as approving this as an exhaustive list of the relevant factors, and I would like to make some general comments as regards these factors.

As a matter of personal preference, I find it useful to group the factors according to the way in which they affect the repute of the administration of justice. Certain of the factors listed are relevant in determining the effect of the admission of the evidence on the fairness of the trial. The trial is a key part of the administration of justice, and the fairness of Canadian trials is a major source of the repute of the system and is now a right guaranteed by s 11(*d*) of the Charter. If the admission of the evidence in some way affects the fairness of the trial, then the admission of the evidence would *tend* to bring the administration of justice into disrepute and, subject to a consideration of the other factors, the evidence gradually should be excluded.

It is clear to me, that the factors relevant to this determination will include the nature of the evidence obtained as a result of the violation and the nature of the right violated and not so much the manner in which the right was violated. Real evidence that was obtained in a manner that violated the Charter will rarely operate unfairly for that reason alone. The real evidence existed irrespective of the violation of the Charter and its use does not render the trial unfair. However, the situation is very different with respect to cases where, after a violation of the Charter, the accused is conscripted against himself through a confession, or other evidence emanating from him. The use of such evidence would render the trial unfair, for it did not exist prior to the violation and it strikes at one of the fundamental tenets of a fair trial, the right against self-incrimination. Such evidence will generally arise in the context of an infringement of the right to counsel . . . The use of self-incriminating evidence obtained following a denial of the right to counsel will, generally, go to the very fairness of the trial and should generally be excluded. It may also be relevant, in certain circumstances, that the evidence would have been obtained in any event without the violation of the Charter.

There are other factors which are relevant to the seriousness of the Charter violation and thus to the disrepute that will result from judicial acceptance of evidence obtained through that violation. As Le Dain J wrote in [*R v Therens* (1985) 18 DLR (4th) 655 at 686]:

'The relative seriousness of the constitutional violation has been assessed in the light of whether it was committed in good faith, or was inadvertent or of a merely technical nature, or whether it was deliberate, wilful or flagrant. Another relevant consideration is whether the action which constituted the constitutional violation was motivated by urgency or necessity to prevent the loss or destruction of the evidence.'

I should add, that the availability of other investigatory techniques and the fact that the evidence could have been obtained without the violation of the Charter tend to render the Charter violation more serious. We are considering the actual conduct of the authorities and the evidence must not be admitted on the basis that they could have proceeded otherwise and obtained the evidence properly. In fact, their failure to proceed properly when that option was open to them tends to indicate a blatant disregard for the Charter, which is a factor supporting the exclusion of the evidence.

The final relevant group of factors consists of those that relate to the effect of excluding the evidence. The question under s 24(2) is whether the system's repute will be better served by the admission or the exclusion of the evidence, and it is thus necessary to consider any disrepute that may result from the exclusion of the evidence. In my view, the administration of justice would be brought into disrepute by the exclusion of evidence essential to substantiate the charge, and thus the acquittal of the accused, because of a trivial breach of the Charter. Such disrepute would be greater if the offence was more serious. I would thus agree with Professor Morissette that evidence is more likely to be excluded if the offence is less serious (supra, pp 529–31). I hasten to add, however, that if the admission of the evidence would result in an unfair trial, the seriousness of the offence could not render that evidence admissible. If any relevance is to be given to the seriousness of the offence in the context of the fairness of the trial, it operates in the opposite sense: the more serious the offence, the more damaging to the system's repute would be an unfair trial.

Finally, a factor which, in my view, is irrelevant is the availability of other remedies. Once it has been decided that the administration of justice would be brought into disrepute by the admission of the evidence, the disrepute will not be lessened by the existence of some ancillary remedy . . .

I still am of the view, that the resort to tricks that are not in the least unlawful let alone in violation of the Charter to obtain a statement should not result in the exclusion of a free and voluntary statement unless the trick resorted to is a dirty trick, one that shocks the community. That is a very high threshold, higher, in my view, than that to be attained to bring the administration of justice into disrepute in the context of a violation of the Charter . . .

The evidence obtained as a result of the search was real evidence, and, while prejudicial to the accused as evidence tendered by the Crown usually is, there is nothing to suggest that its use at the trial would render the trial unfair. In addition, it is true that the cost of excluding the evidence would be high: someone who was found guilty at trial of a relatively serious offence will evade conviction. Such a result could bring the administration of justice into disrepute. However, the administration of justice would be brought into greater disrepute, at least in my respectful view, if this court did not exclude the evidence and dissociate itself from the conduct of the police in this case which, always on the assumption that the officer merely had suspicions, was a flagrant and serious violation of the rights of an individual. Indeed, we cannot accept that police officers take flying tackles at people and seize them by the throat when they do not have reasonable and probable grounds to believe that those people are either dangerous or handlers of drugs. Of course, matters might well be clarified in this case if and when the police officer is offered at a new trial an opportunity to explain the grounds, if any, that he had for doing what he did. But if the police officer does not then disclose additional grounds for his behaviour, the evidence must be excluded.

[Dickson LCJ, Wilson and La Forest JJ concurred. Le Dain J concurred generally, while reserving his opinion on the significance of the effect of admitting the evidence on the fairness of the trial. McIntyre J dissented.]

Bunning v Cross   (1978) 141 CLR 54

Stephen and Aickin JJ: The Chief Justice said in *R v Ireland* ((1970) 126 CLR 321 at 335, [1970] ALR 727 at 735):

'Whenever such unlawfulness or unfairness appears, the judge has a discretion to reject the evidence. He must consider its exercise. In the exercise of it, the competing public requirements must be considered and weighed against each other. On the one hand there is the public need to bring to conviction those who commit criminal offences. On the other hand is the public interest in the protection of the individual from unlawful and unfair treatment. Convictions obtained by the aid of unlawful or unfair acts may be obtained at too high a price. Hence the judicial discretion.'

The statement represents the law in Australia; it was concurred in by all other members of the Court in *R v Ireland* and has since been applied in a number of Australian cases. Its concluding words echo the sentiments expressed long ago by Knight Bruce VC when, in a different yet relevant context, he said:

'The discovery and vindication and establishment of truth are main purposes certainly of the existence of courts of justice; still, for the obtaining of these objects, which however valuable and important, cannot be usefully pursued without moderation, cannot be either usefully or creditably pursued unfairly or gained by unfair means, not every channel is or ought to be open to them. The practical inefficacy of torture is not, I suppose, the most weighty objection to that mode of examination . . . Truth, like all other good things, may be loved unwisely – may be pursued too keenly – may cost too much': *Pearse v Pearse* (1846) 1 De G & Sm 12.

The statement of principle in *Ireland's* case differs from some statements of principle overseas but reflects much of what was said by Zelling J when Ireland's appeal was before the Full Court of the Supreme Court of South Australia (*R v Ireland* [1970] SASR 416 at 444–8). That judgment of Zelling J in turn cites extensively from the judgment of Kingsmill Moore J in *The People v O'Brien* [1965] IR 142, where a far-reaching survey of authority is undertaken.

There exists a marked contrast between, on the one hand, the approach manifest in *Ireland's* case and also in cases decided in the Irish and Scottish courts, of which the judgment of the Lord Justice-General, speaking for seven members of the High Court of Justiciary, in *Lawrie v Muir* 1950 SLT 37 is among the most explicit as to the principles involved, and on the other hand that of English and Canadian courts and of their Lordships in the Judicial Committee. In *Kuruma, Son of Kaniu v R* [1955] AC 197, [1955] 1 All ER 236, PC, Lord Goddard CJ, speaking for their Lordships in the Judicial Committee, appears to acknowledge as the only basis for exclusion of evidence illegally obtained that familiar discretion, applicable in all criminal trials, to disallow evidence if the strict rules of admissibility would operate unfairly against an accused. It was of this discretion that Lavan SPJ spoke in the present case. In *Wendo v R* (1963) 109 CLR 559 at 562, [1964] ALR 292 at 293, Dixon CJ said that he did not believe that *Kuruma's* case had put at rest 'the controversial question whether evidence which is relevant should be rejected on the ground that it is come by unlawfully or otherwise improperly'. That it had not been put at rest is apparent from what is now the Australian law on the subject, founded upon the passage which we have cited from Barwick CJ in *Ireland's* case.

As we understand it, the law in Australia now differs somewhat from that in England. What Lord Goddard CJ, speaking for their Lordships, said in *Kuruma's* case reflects the latter. Whatever may initially have been the authority of *Ireland's* case in the light of the earlier decision of their Lordships in *Kuruma* we have no hesitation in following the principles established in *Ireland's* case, and this for the reasons which we later discuss.

According to *Kuruma* the decision to be exercised when real evidence is sought to be tendered in a criminal trial is no different from, is indeed but an instance of, that general discretion which always exists to exclude admissible evidence when to admit it will be unfair to the accused. Perhaps the most common instance of such a discretion arising is when the evidence in question is of relatively slight probative value but is highly prejudicial to the accused. *Kuruma* treats the case of real evidence unlawfully obtained as merely a further instance which opens the way to the exercise of this same discretion. Quite recently Lord Edmund-Davies, in recounting the arguments of counsel, spoke, we think without any disapproval, of the case of unlawfully obtained real evidence, in that case a breathalyser test result, as depending on 'the application of the ordinary principles of the common law illustrated by such cases as *Kuruma v R* . . .': *Spicer v Holt* [1976] 3 All ER 71 at 82, [1976] 3 WLR 398 at 409, HL. More recently still in *Jeffrey v Black* [1978] QB 490, [1978] 1 All ER 555, Lord Widgery CJ, in a case involving evidence procured by an unlawful search, applied *Kuruma's* case on the admissibility of the evidence and went on to describe the relevant discretion as no more than that general discretion 'which every judge has all the time in respect of all the evidence which is tendered by the prosecution'. It was a discretion to be exercised when it would be 'unfair or oppressive' to allow particular evidence to be called by the prosecution but was applicable only to 'very exceptional situations' (All ER at 559, WLR at 900).

The contrast between these statements of principle and that enunciated in *Ireland's* case becomes apparent as soon as the objects sought to be attained by the exercise of the discretion, as stated in the judgment of Barwick CJ in *Ireland's* case, are examined. What *Ireland* involves is no simple question of ensuring fairness to an accused but instead the weighing against each other of two competing requirements of public policy, thereby seeking to resolve the apparent conflict between the desirable goal of bringing to conviction the wrongdoer and the undesirable effect of curial approval, or even encouragement, being given to the unlawful conduct of those whose task it is to enforce the law. This being the aim of the discretionary process called for by *Ireland* it follows that it by no means takes as its central point the question of unfairness to the accused. It is, on the contrary, concerned with broader questions of high public policy, unfairness to the accused being only one factor which, if present, will play its part in the whole process of consideration.

Since it is with these matters of public policy that the discretionary process called for in *Ireland* is concerned it follows that it will have a more limited sphere of application than has that general discretion to which Lord Widgery refers, which applies in all criminal cases. It applies only when the evidence is the product of unfair or unlawful conduct on the part of the authorities (or, as Dixon CJ put it in *Wendo's* case, unlawful or improper conduct). Moreover, it does not entrench upon the quite special rules which apply to the case of confessional evidence. Its principal area of operation will be in relation to what might loosely be called 'real evidence', such as articles found by search, recordings of conversations, the result of breathalyser tests, fingerprint evidence and so on.

The relevance of the competing policy considerations to which we have referred becomes of especial importance in an age of sophisticated crime and crime detection when law enforcement increasingly depends upon electronic surveillance and eavesdropping, the unannounced search of premises or of the person and upon scientific methods, whether of identification, by fingerprints or voiceprints, or of ascertainment of bodily states, as by blood alcohol tests and the like. In many such cases the question of fairness does not play any part. 'Fair' or 'unfair' is largely meaningless when considering fingerprint evidence obtained by force or a trick or even the evidence of possession of, say, explosives or weapons obtained by an unlawful search of body or baggage, aided by electronic scanners. There is no initial presumption that the State, by its law enforcement agencies, will in the use of such measures of crime detection observe some given code of good sportsmanship or of chivalry. It is not fair play that is called in question in such cases but rather society's right to insist that those who enforce the law themselves respect it, so that a citizen's precious right to immunity from arbitrary and unlawful intrusion into the daily affairs of private life may remain unimpaired. A discretion exercisable according to the principles in *Ireland's* case serves this end, whereas one concerned with fairness may often have little relevance to the question.

Several passages from earlier cases exemplify the principle which finds expression in *Ireland's* case. [They quoted from *People v O'Brien* [1965] IR 142 at 160 and *Lawrie v Muir* 1950 JC 19, 1950 SLT 37.]

In *King v R* their Lordships do indeed, while applying *Kuruma*, so enlarge the matters to be considered under the rubric of unfairness to the accused, a concept which they observe to be 'not susceptible of close definition', that it closely approaches what was said in *Ireland's* case. Their Lordships agreed with Lord MacDermott CJ who had said, in *R v Murphy* [1965] NI 138 at 149, that unfairness to the accused was to be judged 'in the light of all the material facts and findings and all the surrounding circumstances. The position of the accused, the nature of the investigations and the gravity or otherwise of the suspected offence may all be relevant.' Their Lordships concluded by a phrase which perhaps savours more of the *Ireland* approach than that of *Kuruma*: they spoke of 'conduct of which the Crown ought not to take advantage'.

If, then, for Australia the law on this topic is as stated in *Ireland's* case and affirmed in *Merchant v R* (1971) 126 CLR 414 at 417–8, [1971] ALR 736 at 738, and if, accordingly, it is by reference to large matters of public policy rather than solely to considerations of fairness to the accused that the discretion here in question is to be exercised, it becomes necessary to state, with such precision as the subject will allow, criteria upon which this discretion is to be exercised. This cannot, we think, be done in the abstract but only by reference to the case in hand. Otherwise the exercise of judicial discretion may become fettered by rules, seemingly apt enough when first conceived but inappropriate to all the varied circumstances with which courts will be confronted in the future.

We have already summarised his Worship's reasons for his particular exercise of discretion. In our view that exercise miscarried because of misconcepts about the matters which should be taken into account and, perhaps, an excessive concern with 'unfairness', which appears to us to play no part in this case.

His Worship in his reasons refers to an 'unconscious trick' and appears throughout to be largely concerned with the concept of fairness to the accused. We would agree with those members of the Full Court who were unable to discern anything unfair in what occurred; to our minds unfairness does not enter into this case, any more than it should in a case of the unlawful search of person or premises. If a 'breathalyser' test, properly performed and with all attendant safeguards observed, discloses an excessive level of alcohol in a motorist's blood it is in no sense 'unfair' to use it in the conviction of the motorist, just as it is surely not 'unfair' to use, against a person accused of having in his possession weapons or explosives, evidence obtained by means of an unlawful body search so long, once again, as that search is so conducted as to provide all proper safeguards against weapons or explosives being 'planted' on the accused in the course of the search.

These are cases into which unfairness does not enter at all. They are, however, cases in which the considerations referred to in *Ireland's* case may be of the greatest relevance. The liberty of the subject is in increasing need of protection as governments, in response to the demand for more active regulatory intervention in the affairs of their citizens, enact a continuing flood of measures affecting day-to-day conduct, much of it hedged about with safeguards for the individual. These safeguards the executive, and, of course, the police forces, should not be free to disregard. Were there to occur wholesale and deliberate disregard of these safeguards its toleration by the courts would result in the effective abrogation of the legislature's safeguards of individual liberties, subordinating it to the executive arm. This would not be excusable, however desirable might be the immediate end in view, that of convicting the guilty. In appropriate cases it may be 'a less evil that some criminals should escape than that the Government should play an ignoble part': per Holmes J in *Olmstead v United States* 277 US 438 at 470 (1928). Moreover, the courts should not be seen to be acquiescent in the face of the unlawful conduct of those whose task it is to enforce the law. On the other hand it may be quite inappropriate to treat isolated and merely accidental non-compliance with statutory safeguards as leading to inadmissibility of the resultant evidence when, of their very nature, they involve no overt defiance of the will of the legislature or calculated disregard of the common law and when the reception of the evidence thus provided does not demean the court as a tribunal whose concern is in upholding the law.

The first material fact in the present case, once the unlawfulness involved in the obtaining of the 'breathalyser' test results is noted, is that there is here no suggestion that the unlawfulness was other than the result of a mistaken belief on the part of police officers that, without resort to an 'on the spot' 'alcotest', what they had observed of the appellant entitled them to do what they did. The magistrate himself described what occurred as an *unconscious* trick, a phrase which, whatever its precise meaning, is at least inconsistent with any conscious appreciation by the police that they were acting unlawfully. This impression is consistent with the evidence as a whole; no deliberate disregard of the law appears to have been involved. The police officers' erroneous conclusion that the appellant's behaviour demonstrated an incapacity to exercise proper control of his car may well have been much influenced by what they observed of his staggering gait. Unlike the magistrate, they were unaware that the appellant suffered from a chronic condition of his knee joints which could, apparently, affect his gait. If the unlawfulness was merely the result of perhaps understandably mistaken assessment by the police of the inferences to be drawn from what they observed of the appellant's conduct this must be of significance in any exercise of discretion. Although such errors are not to be encouraged by the courts they are relatively remote from the real evil, a deliberate or reckless disregard of the law by those whose duty it is to enforce it.

The second matter to be noted is that the nature of the illegality does not in this case affect the cogency of the evidence so obtained. Indeed the situation is unusual in that the evidence, if admitted, is conclusive not of what it demonstrates itself but of guilt of the statutory offence of driving while under the influence of alcohol to an extent rendering him incapable of having proper control of his vehicle.

To treat cogency of evidence as a factor favouring admission, where the illegality in obtaining it has been either deliberate or reckless, may serve to foster the quite erroneous view that if such evidence be but damning enough that will of itself suffice to atone for the illegality involved in procuring it. For this reason cogency should, generally, be allowed to play no part in the exercise of discretion where the illegality involved in procuring it is intentional or reckless. To this there will no doubt be exceptions: for example where the evidence is both vital to conviction and is of a perishable or evanescent nature, so that if there be any delay in securing it, it will have ceased to exist.

Where, as here, the illegality arises only from mistake, and is neither deliberate nor reckless, cogency is one of the factors to which regard should be had. It bears upon one of the competing policy considerations, the desirability of bringing wrongdoers to conviction. If other equally cogent evidence, untainted by any illegality, is available to the prosecution at the trial the case for the admission of evidence illegally obtained will be the weaker. This is not such a case, due to the mistaken reliance of the police, when they first intercepted the applicant, upon what they thought to be their powers founded upon s 66(2)(c) of the Act.

A third consideration may in some cases arise, namely the ease with which the law might have been complied with in procuring the evidence in question. A deliberate 'cutting of corners' would tend against the admissibility of evidence illegally obtained. However, in the circumstances of the present case, the fact that the appellant was unlawfully required to do what the police could easily have lawfully required him to do, had they troubled to administer an 'alcotest' at the roadside, has little significance. There seems no doubt that such a test would have proved positive, thus entitling them to take the appellant to a police station and there undergo a 'breathalyser' test. Although ease of compliance with the law may sometimes be a point against admission of evidence obtained in disregard of the law, the foregoing, together with the fact that the course taken by the police may well have been the result of their understandably mistaken assessment of the condition of the applicant, leads us to conclude that it is here a wholly equivocal factor.

A fourth and important factor is the nature of the offence charged. While it is not one of the most serious crimes it is one with which Australian legislatures have been much concerned in recent years and the commission of which may place in jeopardy the lives of other users of the highway who quite innocently use it for their lawful purposes. Some examination of the comparative seriousness of the offence and of the unlawful conduct of the law enforcement authority is an element in the process required by *Ireland's* case.

Finally, it is no doubt a consideration that an examination of the legislation suggests that there was a quite deliberate intent on the part of the legislature narrowly to restrict the police in their power to require a motorist to attend a police station and there undergo a 'breathalyser' test. This last factor is, of course, one favouring rejection of the evidence. However, it is to be noted that by the terms of s 66(1) the legislation places relatively little restraint upon 'on the spot' breath testing of motorists by means of an 'alcotest' machine. It is essentially the interference with personal liberty involved in being required to attend a police station for breath testing, rather than the breath testing itself (albeit by means of a more sophisticated appliance), that must here enter into the discretionary scales.

The magistrate does not appear to have considered some of the above criteria. He seems to have much relied upon what he regarded, we think erroneously, as the 'inherent unfairness' of what occurred and to have stressed the prejudicial nature of the evidence, which was only prejudicial in the sense that it was by statute made conclusive of the guilt of the appellant. He also does not seem directly to have accorded any weight to the public interest in bringing to conviction those who commit criminal offences.

In the end we believe that the balance of considerations must come down in favour of the admission of the evidence.

[Barwick CJ agreed with the above reasoning and that the evidence was admissible; Jacobs J held that the evidence had been lawfully obtained; Murphy J held that the evidence was inadmissible.]

NOTE

The statement that the discretionary rule does not entrench upon the rules applying to confessions must be read in the light of *Cleland v R* (1982) 151 CLR 1; confessions obtained by illegal or improper means may be excluded.

R v Sang [1980] AC 402, [1979] 2 All ER 1222, HL

The issue was whether evidence obtained by means of incitement by an agent provocateur should be excluded.

Lord Diplock: [It was] submitted that if the judge were satisfied at a 'trial within a trial' that the offence was instigated by an agent provocateur acting on the instructions of the police and, but for this, would not have been committed by the accused, the judge had a discretion to refuse to allow the prosecution to prove its case by evidence.

In support of this submission counsel was able to cite a number of dicta from impressive sources which, on the face of them, suggest that judges have a very wide discretion in criminal cases to exclude evidence tendered by the prosecution on the ground that it has been unfairly obtained. In addition there is one actual decision of the Court of Criminal Appeal in *R v Payne* [1963] 1 All ER 848, [1963] 1 WLR 637, where a conviction was quashed upon the ground that the judge ought to have exercised his discretion to exclude admissible evidence upon that ground – though this was not a case of entrapment. Moreover there had also been a recent decision at the Central Criminal Court (*R v Ameer and Lucas* [1977] Crim LR 104, CA) in a case which did involve an agent provocateur where Judge Gillis, after a lengthy trial within a trial, had exercised his discretion by refusing to allow the prosecution to call any evidence to prove the commission of the offence by the accused.

In order to avoid what promised to be a lengthy 'trial within a trial, ' which would be fruitless if Judge Buzzard were to rule as a matter of law that he had no discretion to exclude relevant evidence tendered by the prosecution to prove the commission of the offence, even though it had been instigated by an agent provocateur and was one which the accused would never have committed but for such inducement, the judge first heard legal submissions on this question. He ruled that even upon that assumption he had no discretion to exclude the prosecution's evidence. In consequence of this ruling the appellant withdrew his plea of not guilty and pleaded guilty.

It is only fair to the police to point out that there never was a trial within a trial. The judge's ruling made it unnecessary to go into the facts relating to the appellant's claim that he was induced by a police informer to commit a crime of a kind which but for such persuasion he would never have committed: so no evidence was ever called to prove that there had been any improper conduct on the part of the police or of the prosecution.

The appeal to the Criminal Division of the Court of Appeal (Roskill and Ormrod LJJ and Park J) was dismissed. Their judgment which was delivered by Roskill LJ includes a helpful and wide-ranging review of the previous cases, embracing not only those in which agents provocateurs had been involved but also those in which the existence of a wide discretion in the judge to exclude any evidence tendered by the prosecution which he considered had been unfairly obtained, had been acknowledged in obiter dicta by courts of high authority. As a result of their examination of these authorities they certified as the point of law of general importance involved in their discretion, a much wiser question than is involved in the use of agents provocateurs. It is:

'Does a trial judge have a discretion to refuse to allow evidence – being evidence other than evidence of admission – to be given in any circumstances in which such evidence is relevant and of more than minimal probative value.'

I understand this question as inquiring what are the circumstances, if there be any, in which such a discretion arises; and as not being confined to trials by jury. That the discretion, whatever be its limits, extended to whoever presides in a judicial capacity over a criminal trial, whether it be held in the Crown Court or in a magistrates' court, was expressly stated by Lord Widgery CJ in *Jeffrey v Black* [1978] QB 490, [1978] 1 All ER 555, an appeal by the prosecution to a Divisional Court by way of case stated from magistrates who had exercised their discretion to exclude evidence of possession of drugs that had been obtained by an illegal search of the accused's room by the police. The Divisional Court held that the magistrates had exercised their discretion wrongly in the particular case; but Lord Widgery CJ, while stressing that the occasions on which the discretion ought to be exercised in favour of excluding admissible evidence would be exceptional, nevertheless referred to it as applying to 'all the evidence which is tendered by the prosecution' and described its ambit in the widest terms, at 498:

'. . . if the case is such that not only have the police officers entered without authority, but they have been guilty of trickery or they have misled someone, or they have been oppressive or they have been unfair, or in other respects they have behaved in a manner which is morally reprehensible, then it is open to the justices to apply their discretion and decline to allow the particular evidence to be let in as part of the trial.'

One or other of the various dyslogistic terms which Lord Widgery uses to describe the kind of conduct on the part of the police that gives rise to judicial discretion to exclude particular pieces of evidence tendered by the prosecution can be found in earlier pronouncements by his predecessor Lord Parker CJ, notably in *Callis v Gunn* [1964] 1 QB 495, 502, where he adds to them false representations, threats and bribes; while unfairness and trickery are referred to in dicta to be found in a judgment of the Privy Council in *Kuruma, Son of Kaniu v R* [1955] AC 197, 204, the case which is generally regarded as having first suggested the existence of a wide judicial discretion of this kind. What is unfair, what is trickery in the context of the detection and prevention of crime, are questions which are liable to attract highly subjective answers. It will not have come as any great surprise to your Lordships to learn that those who preside over or appear as advocates in criminal trials are anxious for guidance as to whether the discretion really is so wide as these imprecise expressions would seem to suggest and, if not, what are its limits. So, although it may not be strictly necessary to answer the certified question in its full breadth in order to dispose of the instant appeal I think that your Lordships should endeavour to do so.

Before turning to that wider question however, I will deal with the narrower point of law upon which this appeal actually turns. I can do so briefly. The decisions in *R v McEvilly* (1973) 60 Cr App Rep 150 and *R v Mealey* (1974) 60 Cr App Rep 59 that there is no defence of 'entrapment' known to English law are clearly right. Many crimes are committed by one person at the instigation of others. From earliest times at common law those who counsel and procure the commission of the offence by the person by whom the actus reus itself is done have been guilty themselves of an offence, and since the abolition by the Criminal Law Act 1967 of the distinction between felonies and misdemeanours, can be tried, indicted and punished as principal offenders. The fact that the counsellor and procurer is a policeman or a police informer, although it may be of relevance in mitigation of penalty for the offence, cannot affect the guilt of the principal offender; both the physical element (actus reus) and the mental element (mens rea) of the offence with which he is charged are present in his case.

My Lords, this being the substantive law upon the matter, the suggestion that it can be evaded by the procedural device of preventing the prosecution from adducing evidence of the commission of the offence does not bear examination. Let me take first the summary offence prosecuted before magistrates where there is no practical distinction between a trial and a 'trial within a trial.' There are three examples of these in the books, *Brannan v Peek* [1948] 1 KB 68, [1947] 2 All ER 572; *Browning v JWH Watson (Rochester) Ltd* [1953] 2 All ER 775, [1953] 1 WLR 1172; *Sneddon v Stevenson* [1967] 2 All ER 1277, [1967] 1 WLR 1051. Here the magistrates in order to decide whether the crime had in fact been instigated by an agent provocateur acting upon police instructions would first have to hear evidence which ex hypothesi would involve proving that the crime had been committed by the accused. If they decided that it had been so instigated, then, despite the fact that they had already heard evidence which satisfied them that it had been committed, they would have a discretion to prevent the prosecution from relying on that evidence as proof of its commission. How does this differ from recognising entrapment as a defence – but a defence available only at the discretion of the magistrates?

Where the accused is charged upon indictment and there is a practical distinction between the trial and a 'trial within a trial, ' the position, as it seems to me, would be even more anomalous if the judge were to have a discretion to prevent the prosecution from adducing evidence before the jury to prove the commission of the offence by the accused. If he exercised the discretion in favour of the accused he would then have to direct the jury to acquit. How does this differ from recognising entrapment as a defence – but a defence for which the necessary factual foundation is to be found not by the jury but by the judge and even where the factual foundation is so found, the defence is available only at the judge's discretion.

My Lords, this submission goes far beyond a claim to a judicial discretion to exclude *evidence* that has been obtained unfairly or by trickery; nor in any of the English cases on agents provocateurs that have come before appellate courts has it been suggested that it exists. What it really involves is a claim to a judicial discretion to acquit an accused of any offences in connection with which the conduct of the police incurs the disapproval of the judge. The conduct of the police where it has involved the use of an agent provocateur may well be a matter to be taken into consideration in mitigation of sentence; but under the English system of criminal justice, it does not give rise to any discretion on the part of the judge himself to acquit the accused or to direct the jury to do so, notwithstanding that he is guilty of the offence. Nevertheless the existence of such a discretion to exclude the evidence of an agent provocateur does appear to have been acknowledged by the Courts-Martial Appeal Court of Northern Ireland in *R v Murphy* [1965] NI 138. That was before the rejection of 'entrapment' as a defence by the Court of Appeal in England; and Lord MacDermott CJ in delivering the judgment of the court relied upon the dicta as to the existence of a wide discretion which appeared in cases that did not involve an agent provocateur. In the result he held that the court-martial had been right in exercising its discretion in such a way as to admit the evidence.

I understand your Lordships to be agreed that whatever be the ambit of the judicial discretion to exclude admissible evidence it does not extend to excluding evidence of a crime because the crime was instigated by an agent provocateur. In so far as *R v Murphy* suggests the contrary it should no longer be regarded as good law.

I turn now to the wider question that has been certified. It does not purport to be concerned with self incriminatory admissions made by the accused himself after commission of the crime though in dealing with the question I will find it necessary to say something about these. What the question is concerned with is the discretion of the trial judge to exclude all other kinds of evidence that are of more than minimal probative value.

Recognition that there may be circumstances in which in a jury trial the judge has a discretion to prevent particular kinds of evidence that is admissible from being adduced before the jury, has grown up piecemeal. It appears first in cases arising under proviso (*f*) of section 1 of the Criminal Evidence Act 1898, which sets out the circumstances in which an accused may be cross-examined as to his previous convictions or bad character. The relevant cases starting in 1913 with *R v Watson* (1913) 109 LT 335 are conveniently cited in the speech of Lord Hodson in *R v Selvey* [1970] AC 304, a case in which this House accepted that in such cases the trial judge had a discretion to prevent such cross-examination, notwithstanding that it was strictly admissible under the statute, if he was of opinion that its prejudicial effect upon the jury was likely to outweigh its probative value.

Next the existence of a judicial discretion to exclude evidence of 'similar facts,' even where it was technically admissible, was recognised by Lord du Parcq, delivering the opinion of the Privy Council in *Noor Mohamed v R* [1949] AC 182, 192. He put the grounds which justified its exercise rather more narrowly than they had been put in the 'previous conviction' cases to which I have been referring; but in *Harris v DPP* [1952] AC 694 at 707, Viscount Simon, with whose speech the other members of this House agreed, said that the discretion to exclude 'similar facts' evidence should be exercised where the 'probable effect' (sc prejudicial to the accused) 'would be out of proportion to its true evidential value.'

That phrase was borrowed from the speech of Lord Moulton in *R v Christie* [1914] AC 545 at 559. That was neither a 'previous conviction' nor a 'similar facts' case, but was one involving evidence of an accusation made in the presence of the accused by the child victim of an alleged indecent assault and the accused's failure to answer it, from which the prosecution sought to infer an admission by the accused that it was true. Lord Moulton's statement was not confined to evidence of inferential confessions but was general in its scope and has frequently been cited as applicable in cases of cross-examination as to bad character or previous convictions under the Criminal Evidence Act 1898 and in 'similar facts' cases. So I would hold that there has now developed a general rule of practice whereby in a trial by jury the judge has a discretion to exclude evidence which, though technically admissible, would probably have a prejudicial influence on the minds of the jury, which would be out of proportion to its true evidential value.

Ought your Lordships to go further and to hold that the discretion extends more widely than this, as the comparatively recent dicta to which I have already referred suggest? What has been regarded as the fountain head of all subsequent dicta on this topic is the statement by Lord Goddard delivering advice of the Privy Council in *Kuruma v R* [1955] AC 197, [1955] 1 All ER 236. That was a case in which the evidence of unlawful possession of ammunition by the accused was obtained as a result of an illegal search of his person. The Board held that this evidence was admissible and had rightly been admitted; but Lord Goddard although he had earlier said at 203 that if evidence is admissible 'the court is not concerned with how the evidence was obtained, ' nevertheless went on to say, at 204:

'No doubt in a criminal case the judge always has a discretion to disallow evidence if the strict rules of admissibility would operate unfairly against an accused. This was emphasised in the case before this Board of *Noor Mohamed v R* [1949] AC 182, [1949] 1 All ER 365, and in the recent case in the House of Lords, *Harris v DPP* [1952] AC 694, [1952] 1 All ER 1044. *If, for instance, some admission of some piece of evidence, eg a document, had been obtained from a defendant by a trick, no doubt the judge might properly rule it out.*'

Up to the sentence that I have italicised there is nothing in this passage to suggest that when Lord Goddard spoke of admissible evidence operating 'unfairly' against the accused he intended to refer to any wider aspect of unfairness than the probable prejudicial effect of the evidence upon the minds of the jury outweighing its true evidential value; though he no doubt also had in mind the discretion that had long been exercised in England under the Judges' Rules to refuse to admit confessions by the accused made after the crime even though strictly they may be admissible. The instance given in the passage I have italicised appears to me to deal with a case which falls within the latter category since the document 'obtained from a defendant by a trick' is clearly analogous to a confession which the defendant has been unfairly induced to make and had, indeed, been so treated in *R v Barker* [1941] 2 KB 381, [1941] 3 All ER 33 where an incriminating document obtained from the defendant by a promise of favours was held to be inadmissible.

It is interesting in this connection to observe that the only case that has been brought to your Lordships' attention in which an appellate court has actually excluded evidence on the ground that it had been unfairly obtained (*R v Payne* [1963] 1 All ER 848, [1963] 1 WLR 637) would appear to fall into this category. The defendant, charged with drunken driving, had been induced to submit himself to examination by a doctor to see if he was suffering from any illness or disability, upon the understanding that the doctor would not examine him for the purpose of seeing whether he were fit to drive. The doctor in fact gave evidence of the defendant's unfitness to drive based upon his symptoms and behaviour in the course of that examination. The Court of Criminal Appeal quashed the conviction on the ground that the trial judge ought to have exercised his discretion to exclude the doctor's evidence. This again, as it seems to me, is analogous to unfairly inducing a defendant to confess to an offence, and the short judgment of the Court of Criminal Appeal is clearly based upon the maxim *nemo debet prodere se ipsum*.

In no other case to which your Lordships' attention has been drawn has either the Court of Criminal Appeal or the Court of Appeal allowed an appeal upon the ground that either magistrates in summary proceedings or the judge in a trial upon indictment ought to have exercised a discretion to exclude admissible evidence upon the ground that it had been obtained unfairly or by trickery or in some other way that is morally reprehensible; though they cover a wide gamut of apparent improprieties from illegal searches, as in *Kuruma v R* itself and in *Jeffrey v Black* [1978] QB 490, [1978] 1 All ER 555 (which must be the high water mark of this kind of illegality) to the clearest cases of evidence obtained by the use of agents provocateur. Of the later an outstanding example is to be found in *Browning v JWH Watson (Rochester) Ltd* [1953] 2 All ER 775, [1953] 1 WLR 1172 where Lord Goddard CJ remitted the case to the magistrates *with a direction that the offence had been proved*, but pointedly reminded them that it was open to them to give the defendant an absolute discharge and to award no costs to the prosecution.

Nevertheless it has to be recognised that there is an unbroken series of dicta in judgments of appellate courts to the effect that there is a judicial discretion to exclude admissible evidence which has been 'obtained' unfairly or by trickery or oppressively, although except in *R v Payne* [1963] 1 All ER 848, [1963] 1 WLR 637, there never has been a case in which those courts have come across conduct so unfair, so tricky or so oppressive as to justify them in holding that the discretion ought to have been exercised in favour of exclusion. In every one of the cases to which your Lordships have been referred where such dicta appear, the source from which the evidence sought to be excluded had been obtained has been the defendant himself or (in some of the search cases) premises occupied by him; and the dicta can be traced to a common ancestor in Lord Goddard's statement in *Kuruma v R* [1955] AC 197 which I have already cited. That statement was not, in my view, ever intended to acknowledge the existence of any wider discretion than to exclude (1) admissible evidence which would probably have a prejudicial influence upon the minds of the jury that would be out of proportion to its true evidential value; and (2) evidence tantamount to a self-incriminatory admission which was obtained from the defendant, after the offence had been committed, by means which would justify a judge in excluding an actual confession which had the like self-incriminating effect. As a matter of language, although not as a matter of application, the subsequent dicta go much further than this; but in so far as they do so they have never yet been considered by this House.

My Lords, I propose to exclude, as the certified question does, detailed consideration of the role of the trial judge in relation to confessions and evidence obtained from the defendant after commission of the offence that is tantamount to a confession. It has a long history dating back to the days before the existence of a disciplined police force, when a prisoner on a charge of felony could not be represented by counsel and was not entitled to give evidence in his own defence either to deny that he had made the confession, which was generally oral, or to deny that its contents where true. The underlying rationale of this branch of the criminal law, though it may originally have been based upon ensuring the reliability of confessions is, in my view, now to be found in the maxim *nemo debet prodere se ipsum*, no one can be required to be his own betrayer or in its popular English mistranslation 'the right to silence.' That is why there is no discretion to exclude evidence discovered as the result of an illegal search but there is discretion to exclude evidence which the accused has been induced to produce voluntarily if the method of inducement was unfair.

Outside this limited field in which for historical reasons the function of the trial judge extended to imposing sanctions for improper conduct on the part of the prosecution before the commencement of the proceedings in inducing the accused by threats, favour or trickery to provide evidence against himself, your Lordships should, I think, make it clear that the function of the judge at a criminal trial as respects the admission of evidence is to ensure that the accused has a fair trial according to law. It is no part of a judge's function to exercise disciplinary powers over the police or prosecution as respects the way in which evidence to be used at the trial is obtained by them. If it was obtained illegally there will be a remedy in civil law; if it was obtained legally but in breach of the rules of conduct for the police, this is a matter for the appropriate disciplinary authority to deal with. What the judge at the trial is concerned with is not how the evidence sought to be adduced by the prosecution has been obtained, but with how it is used by the prosecution at the trial.

A fair trial according to law involves, in the case of a trial upon indictment, that it should take place before a judge and a jury; that the case against the accused should be proved to the satisfaction of the jury beyond all reasonable doubt upon evidence that is admissible in law; and, as a corollary to this, that there should be excluded from the jury information about the accused which is likely to have an influence on their minds prejudicial to the accused which is out of proportion to the true probative value of admissible evidence conveying that information. If these conditions are fulfilled and the jury receive correct instructions from the judge as to the law applicable to the case, the requirement that the accused should have a fair trial according to law is, in my view, satisfied; for the fairness of a trial according to law is not all one-sided; it requires that those who are undoubtedly guilty should be convicted as well as that those about whose guilt there is any reasonable doubt should be acquitted. However much the judge may dislike the way in which a particular piece of evidence was obtained before proceedings were commenced, if it is admissible evidence probative of the accused's guilt it is no part of his judicial function to exclude it for this reason. If your Lordships so hold you will be reverting to the law as it was laid down by Lord Moulton in *R v Christie* [1914] AC 545, Lord du Parcq in *Noor Mohamed v R* [1949] AC 182, [1949] 1 All ER 365 and Viscount Simon in *Harris v DPP* [1952] AC 694, [1952] 1 All ER 1044 before the growth of what I believe to have been a misunderstanding of Lord Goddard's dictum in *Kuruma v R* [1955] AC 197, [1955] 1 All ER 236.

I would accordingly answer the question certified in terms which have been suggested by my noble and learned friend, Viscount Dilhorne, in the course of our deliberations on this case. (1) A trial judge in a criminal trial has always a discretion to refuse to admit evidence if in his opinion its prejudicial effect outweighs its probative value. (2) Save with regard to admissions and confessions and generally with regard to evidence obtained from the accused after commission of the offence, he has no discretion to refuse to admit relevant admissible evidence on the ground that it was obtained by improper or unfair means. The court is not concerned with how it was obtained. It is no ground for the exercise of discretion to exclude that the evidence was obtained as the result of the activities of an agent provocateur. I would dismiss this appeal.

[Viscount Dilhorne, Lords Salmon, Fraser and Scarman agreed with the answer proposed.]

NOTES

1. The discretion to exclude improperly obtained evidence is often stated but rarely acted on outside Scotland, Eire, Australia, and, more recently, Canada.
2. Compare the quite detailed range of factors isolated by the Scots, Eire and Australian courts as being relevant to the discretion with the very vague position in the rest of the Commonwealth. The difficulty of codifying the relevant factors may be one reason why the Criminal Law Revision Committee recommended no change in the law (para 68). *R v Sang* may have then narrowed the discretion; if so, it has probably been widened again, but without precision, by s 78(1) of the Police and Criminal Evidence Act 1984 (p 212, ante). Section 78(2) provides that nothing in s 78 is to prejudice any rule of law requiring a court to exclude evidence (eg on the ground that its prejudicial effect exceeds its probative value: *R v O'Leary* (1988) 153 JP 69, 87 Cr App Rep 387, CA).
3. Before *R v Sang*, the question whether the court had a discretion to exclude evidence gained as a result of entrapment received conflicting answers. In favour of the discretion were several English and New Zealand decisions. The English cases are single judge decisions: *R v Foulder* [1973] Crim LR 45; *R v Burnett and Lee* [1973] Crim LR 748; *R v Ameer and Lucas* [1977] Crim LR 104, CA. The New Zealand cases are *R v O'Shannessy* (1973) unreported: see [1975] NZLR at 414, and Barlow [1976] NZLR 304; *R v Capner* [1975] 1 NZLR 411; *R v Pethig* [1977] 1 NZLR 448; *Police v Lavelle* [1979] 1 NZLR 45. To the same effect were dicta by Lord McDermott CJ sitting in the Courts-Martial Appeal Court of Northern Ireland: *R v Murphy* [1965] NI 138. But there were English cases against it: *R v McEvilly* (1973) 60 Cr App Rep 150; *R v Mealey* (1974) 60 Cr App Rep 59. There are also English cases which suggest the discretion does not exist, because the police conduct was strongly criticised but the evidence was admitted: eg *Brannan v Peek* [1948] 1 KB 68, [1947] 2 All ER 572; *Browning v JWH Watson (Rochester) Ltd* [1953] 2 All ER 775, [1953] 1 WLR 1172; *R v*

Birtles [1969] 2 All ER 1131n, [1969] 1 WLR 1047, CA. The House of Lords unanimously rejected the cases favouring the discretion. The main justification for doing so was based on the undesirability of evading the non-existence of entrapment as a substantive doctrine by the evidential device of exclusion: see [1980] AC 402 at 432–3, 441, 443 and 454, and [1979] 2 All ER 1222 at 1227, 1234, 1235–6 and 1245. Lord Salmon said to recognise the discretion 'would amount to giving the judge the power of changing or disregarding the law': at 443 and 1236.

This way of approaching the matter expands the scope of the discretion in order to show its danger by exaggerating the harm it will cause. The issue is not whether, if entrapment exists, the court should have a discretion to exclude *all* otherwise admissible evidence. The issue is simply whether to exclude evidence which proceeds directly from the entrapment. If D commits a crime (eg selling heroin) at E's instigation, the discretion would be to exclude E's evidence, but not that of O, an observer who witnessed sales; or P1, a police officer who finds traces of heroin on D's premises and discovers that large sums of money are paid to D; or P2, a police officer to whom D confessed his guilt. Admittedly, often the only prosecution evidence would be E's, but this would not by any means always be so. It follows that the problem appears to have been characterised wrongly. The same comment may be made on Lord Fraser's view that:

'the present case does not truly raise a question of evidence at all. On the assumed facts here, the evidence against the accused would not have been obtained improperly and would not be open to any objection as evidence. The objection to admitting it would be that the accused had been unfairly induced to commit the offence which the evidence tended to prove, and that would be in effect letting in the defence of entrapment': at 446 and 1238.

Evidence gained *by the entrapper* would be improperly obtained; other evidence would not be, it is suggested.

But whatever may be thought of the reasoning leading to the denial of a discretion to reject evidence obtained by entrapment (which has not been accepted in New Zealand: *R v Loughlin* [1982] NZLR 236 at 238); there is no doubting the clarity and decisiveness of that unanimous denial. The same cannot be said of those parts of the speeches dealing with the general discretion to exclude improperly obtained evidence.

The court's general discretion to exclude evidence

In *R v Sang* [1980] AC 402, [1979] 2 All ER 1222, HL, Lord Diplock and Viscount Dilhorne answered the question before the House as follows (see pp 437 and 442, and 1231 and 1235):

'(1) A trial judge in a criminal trial has always a discretion to refuse to admit evidence if in his opinion its prejudicial effect outweighs its probative value.
(2) Save with regard to admissions and confessions and generally with regard to evidence obtained from the accused after commission of the offence, he has no discretion to refuse to admit relevant admissible evidence on the ground that it was obtained by improper or unfair means.'

But though all purported to agree with the answer thus given, the three remaining judges did not really agree. Lord Salmon (at 445 and 1237) only agreed with this answer on the understanding that the judge's duty to secure a fair trial was not confined to the instances listed; this view appears, however, to conflict with the answer. Lord Fraser (at 450 and 1241) did not accept that the discretion to exclude was limited to cases where the prejudicial effect of the evidence exceeded its probative value but said any wider discretion applied only to evidence and documents obtained from the accused person on premises occupied by him. Lord Fraser considered his view was caught by Lord Diplock's language, presumably the words 'evidence obtained from the accused after the commission of the offence'. Lord Scarman (at 456 and 1247) was prepared to exclude evidence on grounds other than that its prejudicial effect exceeded its probative value provided the evidence was obtained from the accused. The view of Lord Diplock and Viscount Dilhorne is rather narrower than that of the other three members of the House. The question put to the House (and the answer to it) was much wider than the facts of the case necessitated. The unanimity of the answer, ambiguous though it is, confirms what a review of the authorities indicates, that the English discretion to exclude illegally and improperly obtained evidence is narrow – much narrower than in Scotland and Ireland, and narrower than that recognised as proper by the High Court of Australia. Why is the discretion narrow? Let us first examine the views of Lord Diplock and Viscount Dilhorne.

First, Lord Diplock points to the need for certainty in administering the criminal law, so that judges and advocates may run criminal proceedings with more assurance. 'What is unfair, what is trickery in the context of the detection and prevention of crime are questions which are liable to attract highly subjective answers.' The point has force so far as trickery, misleading conduct, oppression, unfairness, morally reprehensible conduct (*Jeffrey v Black* [1978] QB 490, [1978] 1 All ER 555), false representations, threats, or bribes (*Callis v Gunn* [1964] 1 QB 495 at 502 per Lord Parker CJ) are concerned. But has it so much force where actual illegality has occurred – an unlawful search, a trespass, an assault? Indeed, has it force when the chief prosecution witness is guilty of the crime of inciting the accused to commit the crime charged?

Secondly, Lord Diplock said (at 434 and 1228) that the Privy Council in its decision in *Kuruma v R* did not intend to extend the discretion to exclude improperly obtained evidence beyond the discretion to exclude evidence, the prejudicial effect of which exceeds its probative value. This is probably correct.

To the extent that the Privy Council intended anything more, it was only intended that evidence be excluded if an analogy could be drawn with a confession which the accused had then been unfairly induced to make. Lord Diplock said that the numerous wide statements of the discretion since *Kuruma's Case* had to be read in the light of the fact that in all the cases cited the source of the evidence was the accused himself or premises occupied by him.

This approach has the merit, apart from the likelihood of guilty persons being punished, of bringing greater certainty into preparation for trial. It avoids the mushiness and unpredictability of a general doctrine of exclusion for 'unfairness', now found in statutory form in s 78 of the Police and Criminal Evidence Act 1984.

The division in the House is seen by the fact that while Lord Diplock and Viscount Dilhorne disapproved certain wide dicta in *Callis v Gunn* and *Jeffrey v Black*, Lord Salmon did not comment on them and Lords Fraser and Scarman approved them, at least up to a point. But does it give adequate weight to the factor stressed in *Bunning v Cross*, namely the importance of insisting on obedience to the law by those who enforce it? For authorities after *R v Sang*, see *R v Fox* [1986] AC 281, [1985] 3 All ER 392, HL; *R v Apicella* (1985) 82 Cr App Rep 295, CA.

At least in theory, there are now two possible bodies of law to consider in England: the traditional discretion (which in civil cases may have been affected by what the House of Lords said about criminal cases in *R v Sang*) and the new statutory discretion in criminal cases conferred by s 78(1) of the Police and Criminal Evidence Act 1984: see section 2 of this chapter. Exclusion is rare in civil cases, but material obtained by a contempt of court was not admitted in *ITC Film Distributors v Video Exchange Ltd* [1982] Ch 431, [1982] 2 All ER 241. In *Matto v Crown Court at Wolverhampton* [1987] RTR 337, [1987] Crim LR 641, DC, it was held that the statutory discretion was no narrower than the common law. In *R v Mason* [1987] 3 All ER 481 at 484, [1988] 1 WLR 139 at 144, CA, Watkins LJ said (surely incorrectly; cf also *R v Fulling* [1987] QB 426, [1987] 2 All ER 65, CA) that s 78(1) only restated the common law; the court also held that s 78(1) extended to all evidence, including confessions, even though they were dealt with specifically in s 76; see also *R v Samuel* [1988] QB 615, [1988] 2 All ER 135, CA (confession after refusal of access to solicitor). And in *R v O'Leary* (1988) 153 JP 69, 87 Cr App Rep 387, CA, it was held that s 78 extended beyond circumstances of impropriety. See also *R v O'Connor* (1986) 85 Cr App Rep 298, CA, and *R v Lunnon* (1988) 88 Cr App Rep 71, CA.

B AMERICA

Before 1914 the position was that improperly obtained evidence was always admissible (*Adams v NY* 192 US 585 (1904)). Since then the law has changed through judicial construction of two amendments to the Constitution, the Fourth and Fourteenth. The Fourth provides: 'The right of the people to be secure in their persons, houses, papers, and effects, against unreasonable searches and seizures, shall not be violated, and no warrants shall issue but upon probable cause, supported by oath or affirmation, and particularly describing the place to be searched, and the persons or things to be seized.' In 1914 the Supreme Court decided in *Weeks v US* that evidence obtained in violation of the Fourth Amendment was inadmissible in Federal criminal trials, because if it could be used, 'the protection of the Fourth Amendment . . . [would be] of no value and . . . might as well be stricken from the Constitution' (232 US 383 at 393 (1914), per Day J). This exclusionary doctrine was extended to 'the fruit of the poisonous tree' – evidence indirectly derived from a breach of the Fourth Amendment, such as leads suggested by the results of the search and seizure (*Silverthorne Lumber Co v US* 251 US 385 (1920)). The doctrine applies not only to real evidence, but oral evidence, eg statements overheard by driving a spike mike into the wall of a house during an unlawful search of the accused's house (*Wong Sun v US* 371 US 471 (1963)).

The issue raised by the Fourteenth Amendment is whether the 'liberties' guaranteed by the first eight amendments are liberties within the Fourteenth Amendment's guarantee that a State shall not 'deprive any person of life, liberty or property, without due process of law'. In 1937 the Supreme Court decided that only rights 'implicit in the concept of ordered liberty' fell within the Fourteenth Amendment (*Palko v Connecticut* 302 US 319 at 325 (1937), per Cardozo J). In 1949, in *Wolf v Colorado*, the whole Fourth Amendment was held to guarantee such rights, and was therefore binding on the States as well as the Federal Government. But the Supreme Court refused to hold that the exclusionary doctrine by which Federal courts were bound also applied to State courts, because the States were entitled to rely on other effective methods of enforcing the Fourth Amendment if they wished, and many of them did not operate the exclusionary rule (338 US 25 (1949)). In *Rochin v California* another aspect of the due process requirements of the Fourteenth Amendment was revealed when it was held that the forcible stomach pumping of the accused, which showed that he had swallowed drugs, infringed this Amendment because it shocked the conscience (342 US 165 (1952)). The next step was *Elkins v US* 364 US 206 (1960), where the Supreme Court abandoned the 'silver platter' doctrine which had permitted the admission of evidence in Federal courts if unconstitutionally obtained by a State officer and handed over to the Federal prosecutor. This foreshadowed the decision in *Mapp v Ohio* 367 US 643 (1961), that the exclusionary doctrine should be applied to State courts as well as Federal: *Wolf's* Case was reversed, it was said, because the majority of the States now favoured the exclusionary rule, and alternative methods of vindicating the Fourth Amendment had proved their inadequacy. Three limitations on the exclusionary rule should be noted. An accused person has no standing to invoke the rule if the evidence was obtained through an invasion of *another's* rights (*Alderman v US* 394 US 165 (1969); cf *People v Martin* 290 P 2d 855 (1955), where the Californian Supreme Court in bank took the opposite view). Secondly, the rule does not apply if the evidence was obtained by a private individual other than a state official (*Burdeau v McDowell* 256 US 465 (1921)). Thirdly, the rule does not apply where the evidence is admitted not on the issue of the accused's guilt but on some collateral issue (*Walder v US* 347 US 62 (1954); *Harris v NY* 401 US 222 (1971)).

The related issues of eavesdropping and wiretapping have been treated as follows. In *Olmstead v US* wiretapping from outside the accused's premises was held not to be a search and seizure and therefore not to infringe the Fourth Amendment; the fact that it infringed state legislation did not make it inadmissible (277 US 438 (1928)). The Fourth Amendment was for many years held only to apply to evidence obtained by electronic devices which penetrated into premises (*Silverman v US* 365 US 505 (1961)) though s 605 of the Federal Communications Act 1934 provided that 'no person not being authorised by the sender shall intercept any communication and divulge or publish the existence, contents, substance, purport, effect or meaning of such intercepted communication to any person'. This was held to prohibit the use of evidence thus obtained by a federal officer in court (*Nardone v US* 302 US 379 (1937)) or to obtain leads to other evidence used in court (*Nardone v US (No 2)* 308 US 338 (1939)). Now, however, it has been held that *Olmstead* is wrong and that the Fourth Amendment applies to wiretapping and eavesdropping, the test being whether the government's activities 'violated the privacy upon which [the accused] justifiably relied' (*Katz v US* 389 US 347 (1967); *US v White* 401 US 745 (1971)). State courts will be bound in accordance with the *Mapp* doctrine. (Thus the effect of *Schwartz v Texas* 344 US 199 (1952), holding that the rule excluding evidence obtained in violation of s 605 did not apply to state courts, is reversed.)

These developments are controversial. A recent check to them has been effected in *Stone v Powell* 428 US 465 (1976) and later cases: see Stuntz [1989] Crim LR 117.

People v Defore   150 NE 585 (1926)

The New York Court of Appeals refused to exclude illegally obtained evidence.

Cardozo J: We are confirmed in this conclusion when we reflect how far-reaching in its effect upon society the new consequences would be. The pettiest peace officer would have it in his power, through overzeal or indiscretion, to confer immunity upon an offender for crimes the most flagitious. A room is searched against the law, and the body of a murdered man is found. If the place of discovery may not be proved, the other circumstances may be insufficient to connect the defendant with the crime. The privacy of the home has been infringed, and the murderer goes free ... We may not subject society to these dangers until the Legislature has spoken with a clearer voice.

Olmstead v US   277 US 438 (1928)

The majority of the United States Supreme Court held that the use in evidence of private telephone conversations obtained by wiretapping did not infringe the Fourth and Fifth Amendments.

Holmes J (dissenting): I think, as Mr Justice Brandeis says, that apart from the Constitution the Government ought not to use evidence obtained and only obtainable by a criminal act. There is no body of precedents by which we are bound, and which confines us to logical deduction from established rules. Therefore we must consider the two objects of desire, both of which we cannot have, and make up our minds which to choose. It is desirable that criminals should be detected, and to that end that all available evidence should be used. It also is desirable that the Government should not itself foster and pay for other crimes, when they are the means by which the evidence is to be obtained. If it pays its officers for having got evidence by crime I do not see why it may not as well pay them for getting it in the same way, and I can attach no importance to protestations of disapproval if it knowingly accepts and pays and announces that in the future it will pay for the fruits. We have to choose, and for my part I think it a less evil that some criminals should escape than that the Government should play an ignoble part.

For those who agree with me, no distinction can be taken between the Government as prosecutor and the Government as judge. If the existing code does not permit district attorneys to have a hand in such dirty business it does not permit the judge to allow such iniquities to succeed.

Brandeis J (dissenting): The defendants were convicted of conspiring to violate the National Prohibition Act. Before any of the persons now charged had been arrested or indicted, the telephone by means of which they habitually communicate with one another and with others had been tapped by federal officers. To this end, a lineman of long experience in wire-tapping was employed, on behalf of the Government and at its expense. He tapped eight telephones, some in the homes of the persons charged, some in their offices. Acting on behalf of the Government and in their official capacity, at least six other prohibition agents listened over the tapped wires and reported the messages taken. Their operations extended over a period of nearly five months. The typewritten record of the notes of conversations overheard occupies 775 typewritten pages ...

The Government makes no attempt to defend the methods employed by its officers. Indeed, it concedes that if wire-tapping can be deemed a search and seizure within the Fourth Amendment, such wire-tapping as was practised in the case at bar was an unreasonable search and seizure, and that the evidence thus obtained was inadmissible. But it relies on the language of the Amendment; and it claims that the protection given thereby cannot properly be held to include a telephone conversation.

'We must never forget', said Mr Chief Justice Marshall in *McCulloch v Maryland* 4 Wheat 316 at 407, 'that it is a constitution we are expounding.' Since then, this Court has repeatedly sustained the exercise of power by Congress, under various clauses of that instrument, over objects of which the Fathers could not have dreamed . . .

When the Fourth and Fifth Amendments were adopted, 'the form that evil had theretofore taken', had been necessarily simple. Force and violence were then the only means known to man by which a Government could directly effect self-incrimination. It could compel the individual to testify – a compulsion effected, if need be, by torture. It could secure possession of his papers and other articles incident to his private life – a seizure effected, if need be, by breaking and entry. Protection against such invasion of 'the sanctities of a man's home and the privacies of life' was provided in the Fourth and Fifth Amendments by specific language. *Boyd v United States* 116 US 616 at 630 (1886). But 'time works changes, brings into existence new conditions and purposes'. Subtler and more far-reaching means of invading privacy have become available to the Government. Discovery and investigation have made it possible for the Government, by means far more effective than stretching upon the rack, to obtain disclosure in court of what is whispered in the closet.

Moreover, 'in the application of a constitution, our contemplation cannot be only of what has been but of what may be'. The progress of science in furnishing the Government with means of espionage is not likely to stop with wire-tapping. Ways may some day be developed by which the Government, without removing papers from secret drawers, can reproduce them in court, and by which it will be enabled to expose to a jury the most intimate occurrences of the home. Advances in the psychic and related sciences may bring means of exploring unexpressed beliefs, thoughts and emotions. 'That places the liberty of every man in the hands of every petty officer' was said by James Otis of much lesser intrusions than these. To Lord Camden, a far slighter intrusion seemed 'subversive of all the comforts of society'. Can it be that the Constitution affords no protection against such invasions of individual security? . . .

The protection guaranteed by the Amendments is much broader in scope. The makers of our Constitution undertook to secure conditions favourable to the pursuit of happiness. They recognised the significance of man's spiritual nature, of his feelings and of his intellect. They knew that only a part of the pain, pleasure and satisfactions of life are to be found in material things. They sought to protect Americans in their beliefs, their thoughts, their emotions and their sensations. They conferred, as against the Government, the right to be let alone – the most comprehensive of rights and the right most valued by civilised men. To protect that right, every unjustifiable intrusion by the Government upon the privacy of the individual, whatever the means employed, must be deemed a violation of the Fourth Amendment. And the use, as evidence in a criminal proceeding, of facts ascertained by such intrusion must be deemed a violation of the Fifth.

Applying to the Fourth and Fifth Amendments the established rule of construction, the defendants' objections to the evidence obtained by wire-tapping must, in my opinion, be sustained. It is, of course, immaterial where the physical connection with the telephone wires leading into the defendants' premises was made. And it is also immaterial that the intrusion was in aid of law enforcement. Experience should teach us to be most on our guard to protect liberty when the Government's purposes are beneficent. Men born to freedom are naturally alert to repel invasion of their liberty by evil-minded rulers. The greatest dangers to liberty lurk in insidious encroachment by men of zeal, well-meaning but without understanding.

Independently of the constitutional question, I am of opinion that the judgment should be reversed. By the laws of Washington, wire-tapping is a crime.

[Stone J concurred with Holmes and Brandeis JJ.]

Brinegar v US   338 US 160 (1949)

Jackson J (dissenting in the US Supreme Court): Uncontrolled search and seizure is one of the first and most effective weapons in the arsenal of every arbitrary government. And one need only briefly to have dwelt and worked among a people possessed of many admirable qualities but deprived of these rights to know that the human personality deteriorates and dignity and self-reliance disappear where homes, persons and possessions are subject at any hour to unheralded search and seizure by the police.

But the right to be secure against searches and seizures is one of the most difficult to protect. Since the officers are themselves the chief invaders, there is no enforcement outside of court.

Only occasional and more flagrant abuses come to the attention of the courts, and then only those where the search and seizure yields incriminating evidence and the defendant is at least sufficiently compromised to be indicted . . . There may be, and I am convinced that there are, many unlawful searches of homes and automobiles of innocent people which turn up nothing incriminating, in which no arrest is made, about which courts do nothing, and about which we never hear.

Courts can protect the innocent against such invasion only indirectly and through the medium of excluding evidence obtained against those who frequently are guilty . . .

We must remember that the extent of any privilege of search and seizure without warrant which we sustain, the officers interpret and apply themselves and will push to the limit. We must remember, too, that freedom from unreasonable search differs from some of the other rights of the Constitution in that there is no way in which the innocent citizen can invoke advance protection. For example, any effective interference with freedom of the press, or free speech, or religion, usually requires a course of suppressions against which the citizen can and often does go to the court and obtain an injunction. Other rights, such as that to an impartial jury or the aid of counsel, are within the supervisory power of the courts themselves. Such a right as just compensation for the taking of private property may be vindicated after the act in terms of money.

But an illegal search and seizure usually is a single incident, perpetrated by surprise, conducted in haste, kept purposely beyond the court's supervision and limited only by the judgment and moderation of officers whose own interests and records are often at stake in the search. There is no opportunity for injunction or appeal to disinterested intervention. The citizen's choice is quietly to submit to whatever the officers undertake or to resist at risk of arrest or immediate violence.

And we must remember that the authority which we concede to conduct searches and seizures without warrant may be exercised by the most unfit and ruthless officers as well as by the fit and responsible, and resorted to in case of petty misdemeanours as well as in the case of the gravest felonies.

Wigmore: Treatise on the Anglo-American System of Evidence in Trials at Common Law, 3rd edn, paras 2183–4

Necessity does not require, and the spirit of our law does forbid, the attempt to do justice incidentally and to enforce penalties by indirect methods. An employer may perhaps suitably interrupt the course of his business to deliver a homily to his office-boy on the evils of gambling or the rewards of industry. But a judge does not hold court in a street-car to do summary justice upon a fellow-passenger who fraudulently evades payment of his fare; and, upon the same principle, he does not attempt, in the course of a specific litigation, to investigate and punish all offences which incidentally cross the path of that litigation. Such a practice might be consistent with the primitive system of justice under an Arabian sheikh; but it does not comport with our own system of law. It offends, in the first place, by trying a violation of law without that due complaint and process which are indispensable for its correct investigation in hand, for the sake of a matter which is not a part of it. It offends further, in that it does this unnecessarily and gratuitously; for since the persons injured by the supposed offence have not chosen to seek redress or punishment directly and immediately, at the right time and by the proper process, there is clearly no call to attend to their complaints in this indirect and tardy manner. The judicial rules of Evidence were never meant to be an indirect process of punishment. It is not only anomalous to distort them to that end, but it is improper (in the absence of express statute) to enlarge the fixed penalty of the law, that of fine or imprisonment, by adding to it the forfeiture of some civil right through loss of the means of proving it. The illegality is by no means condoned; it is merely ignored . . .

[The spread of the *Weeks* doctrine is due] to the temporary recrudescence of individualistic sentimentality for freedom of speech and conscience, stimulated by the stern repressive war-measures against treason, disloyalty and sedition, in the years 1917–1919. In a certain type of mind, it was impossible to realise the vital necessity of temporarily subordinating the exercise of ordinary civic freedom during a bloody struggle for national safety and existence. In resistance to these war-measures, it was natural for the misguided pacifists or semi-pro-German interests to invoke the protection of the Fourth Amendment. Thus invoked and made prominent, all its ancient prestige was revived and sentimentally misapplied. In such a situation, the always watchful forces of criminality, fraud, anarchy and law-evasion perceived the advantage and made vigorous use of it. After the enactment of the Eighteenth Amendment and its auxiliary legislation, prohibiting the sale of intoxicating liquors, a new and popular occasion was afforded for the misplaced invocation of this principle; and the judicial excesses of many Courts in sanctioning its use give an impression of easy complaisance which would be ludicrous if it were not so dangerous to the general respect for law and order in the community . . .

. . . For the sake of indirectly and contingently protecting the Fourth Amendment, this view appears indifferent to the direct and immediate result, viz, of making Justice inefficient, and of coddling the law-evading classes of the population. It puts Supreme Courts in the position of assisting to undermine the foundations of the very institutions they are set there to protect. It regards the over-zealous officer of the law as a greater danger to the community than the unpunished murderer or embezzler or panderer . . .

The doctrine of *Weeks v US* also exemplifies a trait of our Anglo-American judiciary peculiar to the mechanical and unnatural type of justice. The natural way to do justice here would be to enforce the healthy principle of the Fourth Amendment directly, ie by sending for the highhanded, over-zealous marshall who had searched without a warrant, imposing a thirty-day imprisonment for his contempt of the Constitution, and then proceeding to affirm the sentence of the convicted criminal. But the proposed indirect and unnatural method is as follows:

'Titus, you have been found guilty of conducting a lottery; Flavius, you have confessedly violated the Constitution. Titus ought to suffer imprisonment for crime, and Flavius for contempt. But no! We shall let you *both* go free. We shall not punish Flavius directly, but shall do so by reversing Titus' conviction . . . Our way of upholding the Constitution is not to strike at the man who breaks it, but to let off somebody else who broke something else.'

C   CONCLUSION

The debate on the merits of a rule of general inclusion as opposed to one of general exclusion turns on the following principal points.

(i) The first is based on certain supposed differences between the societies and legal systems of England and America. It is said that though the American rule may be necessary there, it serves no useful purpose in English conditions. No strict exclusionary rule is needed to deter British police from excesses, for they are trustworthy, their methods are basically proper, and they face much less serious problems than American police forces. Hence 'England, with a generally homogeneous society, has been able to afford the luxury of thinking that civil liberties somehow take care of themselves' (Karlen, *Anglo-American Criminal Justice* (London, 1967), p 98). Another point is that most conduct branded as criminal in England is popularly felt to be rightly so stigmatised and to merit punishment, so that trivial police illegalities can be tolerated in the prosecution of what are felt to be serious crimes. Search and seizure problems in England mainly concern the recovery of stolen goods and the obtaining of breath and blood samples in connexion with drunken driving charges. But most American cases concern gambling and the illicit possession of liquor and drugs. These are popularly felt not to be blameworthy. A seizure of real evidence is usually necessary for their successful prosecution. At common law searches must be incidental to a lawful arrest, or they require the obtaining of consent or a warrant; these powers are inadequate because they allow time for the destruction of evidence. In other words, illegal means are inevitable if these unpopular victimless crimes are to be prosecuted; a strict exclusionary rule is needed to control the resulting widespread lawlessness in law enforcement, and this is feasible since the powers of American courts to order a retrial are much wider than those of English courts. In America, unlike England, the disproportion between a trivial unpopular crime and a serious police illegality can be stark. Finally, since the English judiciary is much smaller and more homogeneous than the American, it is said to be safer to leave a discretion to admit illegally obtained evidence in their hands, since it is much more likely to be uniformly exercised.

These arguments are less convincing than they were forty years ago. Whether justifiably or not, the public reputation of the police has declined; and some British cities are moving towards the American mixture of minorities, unemployment and poverty which is said to make the crime problem so intractable. An increasing part of the public takes the same attitude today to drug offences as in America. And there are now a very large number of High Court and Crown Court judges exercising the *Kuruma* discretion, not to mention many thousands of magistrates; it is too much to hope for a uniformly administered discretion in these circumstances.

(ii) Another argument for the English position is that the American law involves the sacrifice of reliable evidence for the sake of deterring the police from misconduct, thus favouring only the guilty and causing two wrongs to occur instead of only one.

Pursuit of this collateral inquiry delays and confuses the accused's trial. The sole purpose of such a trial is to discover the truth and make a correct finding as to the accused's guilt or innocence. It is not a game in which the prosecution's hands are to be tied so that it can only act 'fairly'. The impropriety of the police conduct in no way disables the court from giving a fair and impartial judgment. The wrong-doing policeman should not be punished by exclusion of the evidence, which injures only the public at large and not the policeman, but by the pursuit of other remedies. The accused might launch a private prosecution, or sue in tort. The policeman's superiors may criticise or discipline him, or prevent his promotion, or even prosecute him. Well-publicised judicial criticism and the consequential arousing of public opinion will deter the police better than the exclusion of the evidence; and if it does not, there is probably something wrong with the police too deep-rooted to be cured by the law of evidence. In any event, the exclusionary rule is not to obtain evidence in court but to harass criminals unpunishable in other ways, and the exclusionary rule accentuates these tendencies. It is difficult for the police to understand technically worded, often unreasoned rulings which may appear inconsistent with each other and which may change in future. Finally, reliance on the exclusionary rule may sap the eagerness of officials to pursue alternative ways of controlling the police.

These arguments are vulnerable at a number of points. It is not necessarily true that the exclusionary rule protects only the guilty: its deterrent effect ensures that in future both guilty *and innocent* persons will be protected from illegal investigation. Nor is it necessarily true that illegally obtained real evidence is reliable: for as *Kuruma v R* shows, there will sometimes be a doubt whether the evidence is in fact connected with the accused.

It is true that the exclusionary rule involves a collateral inquiry in a criminal trial, but it does at least vindicate the accused's rights at once; he need not start new proceedings in another court to obtain redress, thus incurring more expense. Further, the English rule involves even more of a collateral inquiry, for not only must there be an investigation of whether illegality has occurred, but also an inquiry into whether fairness demands exclusion. Then the remedies other than exclusion, more direct though they may be, are unsatisfactory. Criminal prosecution may fail because of the sympathy of jury and magistrates for the accused. Police solidarity means that the state is unlikely to undertake them. As an American judge put it, 'Self-scrutiny is a lofty ideal, but its exaltation reaches new heights if we expect a District Attorney to prosecute himself or his associates for well-meaning violations of the search and seizure clause during a raid the District Attorney or his associates have ordered' (*Wolf v Colorado* 338 US 25 at 42 (1949), per Murphy J dissenting). Police leaders will be sympathetic to the illegal conduct of their inferiors as long as the latter remain within the unwritten traditions, codes and norms of the force as opposed to the law of the land. There may be no independent civilian body to prosecute or investigate the police. The poor and uneducated who comprise the bulk of criminals and the bulk of innocent police victims are unlikely to know how to prosecute the police, or to be able to do so, particularly if they are in prison as a result of the admission of the evidence illegally obtained. Even the innocent victim of criminal police conduct may be reluctant to prosecute because he will not wish it to be known he was under suspicion.

Civil actions for trespass, assault, false arrest and damage to property may be unsatisfactory in several ways. The individual policeman may not be thought to be worth suing. In any event he will not be deterred by the fear of such actions because of the convention that the local police authority indemnifies him. The victim may fear the further loss of privacy entailed in a suit, or subsequent police victimisation. Substantial damages are only recoverable in the event of actual loss or malice; they may be mitigated by the plaintiff's bad reputation, which will also affect his credibility and increase the chance of a finding of reasonable cause for arrest. Aggravated damages may be awarded in respect of oppressive, arbitrary or unconstitutional conduct by State servants, but juries are unlikely so to punish an officer whose efforts, albeit illegal, uncovered crime. In *Elias v Pasmore* [1934] 2 KB 164 at 173, [1934] All ER Rep 380 at 384, Horridge J held that no action would lie if the evidence seized is subsequently used in a criminal prosecution; this doctrine was cut down in *Ghani v Jones* [1970] 1 QB 693, [1969] 3 All ER 1700, CA, by the Court of Appeal so as to permit seizure only where the police have reasonable grounds for believing that a serious offence has been committed, that the evidence is material, and that the person in possession of it is party to the crime. Despite this narrowing, there remains a substantial area of immunity which will tempt the police to act even when the conditions in which it arises do not exist. Often there will be no remedy either because the police conduct has not been unlawful at all (eg non-trespassory invasions of privacy) or because even though their conduct is criminal no civil action lies.

As for the deterrent effect of the exclusionary rule, though this will operate more respecting police conduct designed to produce evidence in court than other conduct, American research indicates that the rule has some effect in improving police training in civil liberties matters. It has also led to more compliance with the law in relation to searches for gambling apparatus and stolen goods, though not drugs and weapon offences (Oaks (1970) 37 U of Chi LR 665). Accordingly, though the exclusion of illegally obtained evidence would be unnecessary if there were a well-established statutory civil action against the state coupled with the establishment of an independent authority to prosecute the individuals responsible for illegality, at the moment there seems to be some case for the exclusion of illegally obtained evidence.

(iii) The exclusionary rule is said to place too big a burden on the police in an age of rising crime rates in that some crimes can only be prosecuted by relying on illegally obtained real evidence. Criminals are not restricted in their choice of weapons; nor should the police be. An exclusionary rule will injure police morale; it will cause them to perjure themselves about such matters as whether the requirements for lawful arrest were satisfied; it will cause them, in their search for evidence, to commit serious illegalities which they hope will not be discovered, on the principle that they may as well run the risk of being hanged for a sheep as for a lamb; and will lead them to harass those they cannot convict. Trivial police blunders should not lead to the exclusion of evidence, for this destroys respect for the law by letting the guilty go free on what the police and the public thing are mere technicalities. Further, the rule gives corrupt policemen the power to immunise criminals from conviction by collusively making what appear to be illegal searches, thus satisfying, in a sham way, public pressure for law enforcement.

The contrary view is that it is not so much the exclusionary rule of evidence which hampers the police, but the substantive rules governing warrants, arrest, search and so forth. It may be that these rules, largely formed before the appearance of modern police forces and modern crimes and criminals, require modification, but this should be done directly, not by admitting evidence obtained in breach of them. It may be easier to convict criminals by admitting such evidence; it does not follow that it is impossible to convict them without it. To permit its use on any large scale encourages laziness and inefficiency, for the police may come to rely on improperly obtained evidence instead of more normal detective methods. In so far as some crimes are very difficult to prosecute without real evidence, the burden should be borne by the prosecution as is normal, not the defence. The causes of the modern crime wave are various, but exclusionary rules of evidence are unlikely to be among them to any significant degree. Respect for the law may be weakened by the spectacle of criminals escaping conviction on technicalities; it will be even more weakened if the police get convictions from serious misconduct. It is wrong for the state to participate in and condone illegal conduct by individual policemen, and thus profit from its own wrong; the judicial process must not be contaminated.

The government's behaviour should be a model for that of private citizens. Though perhaps blunders should be condoned, persistent and deliberate misconduct should not be. Finally, the immunising of the guilty by corrupt policemen does not seem a grave danger. If a policeman is corrupt, he has many other methods of helping criminals without going to these lengths. In any case, if other police misconduct is controlled by internal police discipline, why not this form of it?

FURTHER READING

Andrews [1963] Crim LR 15; JTC [1969] Jur Rev 55; Cowen and Carter, ch 3; Gray [1966] Jur Rev 89; Pattenden, *Judicial Discretion and Criminal Litigation* (1990) ch 7; Robertson [1995] Crim LR 805; Weinberg (1975) 21 McGill LJ; Williams [1955] Crim LR 339; Zuckerman, ch 16.

QUESTIONS

1. How satisfactory is the Privy Council's handling of American law in *Kuruma, Son of Kaniu v R* [1955] AC 197, [1955] 1 All ER 236, PC? How satisfactory was its handling of Scots law?
2. Ought distinctions to be drawn between evidence obtained by illegal means depending on whether the illegality arises by a rule of the common law, or a statutory rule, or a constitutional rule, or a rule entrenched in a written constitution?
3. Should a distinction be drawn between illegally and unfairly obtained evidence?
4. It has been suggested that illegally obtained evidence should be excluded more readily than unfairly obtained evidence, because illegal acts usually affect both guilty and innocent adversely, but tricks do not. For example, if a car driver is persuaded by the police to take a medical examination after an accident, supposedly to see if he has concussion but in fact to see if he is drunk enough to be prosecuted, this will benefit the innocent and injure only the guilty (see JTC [1969] Jur Rev 55 at 69). Is this argument sound?

CHAPTER 10

The Accused's Character: Part I

1 Similar fact evidence

A THE COMMON LAW RULE

(i) General

Three rules govern the admissibility of past bad behaviour offered as evidence that a particular act was done. First, the bad behaviour must be relevant to the alleged act: it must tend to prove it. Evidence that a boy stole apples in 1913 is not relevant to whether in 1943 he robbed a bank. Evidence of consensual intercourse is irrelevant to an earlier charge of rape (*R v Rodley* [1913] 3 KB 468, [1911–13] All ER Rep 688, CCA).

Secondly, even if it is relevant, the past bad behaviour is inadmissible if its only relevance is to show that the actor has a bad disposition, and his disposition is not highly relevant to some issue at the trial. Evidence of a man's convictions for robbing banks would be admissible if his explanation for possessing money stolen from a bank in 1943 was that he found it in the street: for his disposition would be highly relevant to his supposedly innocent state of mind. But such evidence would be inadmissible if he said that at the time of the robbery he was in another country robbing a bank: his disposition would not then be relevant to any issue at the trial. However, evidence that he broke into a bank on Tuesday and was found removing clothing discovered by bank officials after a robbery on Monday would be admissible because it has a relevance other than proving bad disposition: it shows actual participation in the Monday crime. In civil cases such evidence is more readily received: it suffices that it is relevant, and not oppressive or unfair to the other side, and that the other side has fair notice of it: *Mood Music Publishing Co Ltd v De Wolfe Ltd* [1976] Ch 119, [1976] 1 All ER 763, CA. In *Thorpe v Chief Constable of the Greater Manchester Police* [1989] 2 All ER 827 at 831, [1989] 1 WLR 665 at 670, CA, Dillon LJ limited the view that the evidence was more readily received in civil cases to non-jury cases.

Thirdly, in criminal cases, even though evidence of bad behaviour is technically admissible under the first two rules, it may be excluded because its prejudicial effect exceeds its probative value. Thus if evidence of a man's prior bank robberies proceeded only from a paid police informer known to have a grudge against the accused, the evidence might well be excluded.

Because relevance is an issue of degree on which minds can differ, some cases cited under the second rule may be examples of the first, and vice versa (eg *Harris v DPP* [1952] AC 694, [1952] 1 All ER 1044, HL). A fairly clear example of the first rule is *HR Lancey Shipping Co Pty Ltd v Robson* [1938] ALR 429. There a man was injured by the breaking of a ship's block shackle; evidence of a later fall of the mast was excluded because there was no proof of any common cause. Another is *Cooper v R* (1961) 105 CLR 177: the fact that the accused was a Communist atheist hostile to missionaries was irrelevant to whether he was likely to publish seditious words. There is little authority on the third rule, for detailed consideration of it is of recent origin and depends very much on a discretion governed only by the particular facts. Matters such as unreliability or staleness (*R v Cole* (1941) 165 LT 125) would be relevant to the discretion; also the fact that it is unclear whether the conduct is criminal (*R v Doughty* [1965] 1 All ER 560; [1965] 1 WLR 331, CCA). There is a doubt as to whether the discretion applies in civil cases: *Polycarpou v Australian Wire Industries Pty Ltd* (1995) 36 NSWLR 49; *Gosschalk v Rossouw* 1966 (2) SA 476. *Berger v Raymond & Son Ltd* [1984] 1 WLR 625 purported to apply an exclusionary discretion, but it seems that in substance the language was only a loose characterisation of the second rule discussed above. There may be another discretion applicable in a civil case, namely, to exclude evidence which, though relevant, is only remotely relevant or has small probative value compared to the additional issues which it would raise and the additional time required for their investigation, or which might tend to confuse the trier of fact as to the real issues: *DF Lyons Pty Ltd v Commonwealth Bank of Australia* (1991) 28 FCR 597 at 604 and 607.

This chapter is mainly concerned with the second rule, but, first, *Harris v DPP* shows how hard it sometimes is to distinguish the first two rules.

Harris v Director of Public Prosecution   [1952] AC 694, [1952] 1 All ER 1044, HL

The accused was charged with eight larcenies of money committed in May, June and July 1951 from a certain office in an enclosed market at times when most of the gates were shut and the accused, a police officer, might have been on solitary duty there. In each case the same means of access were used and only part of the amount which might have been taken was taken. No thefts occurred while the accused was on leave. The accused was found by two detectives in the immediate vicinity of the office at the time of the last larceny. Though they were well-known to him he avoided them for a period sufficient to hide marked money taken from the office till and found in a coal bin near where he was first seen. The accused was convicted on only the eighth count. He appealed against conviction to the Court of Criminal Appeal unsuccessfully and to the House of Lords successfully on the ground that evidence of the first seven thefts was irrelevant to the eighth.

Viscount Simon: In my opinion, the principle laid down by Lord Herschell LC in *Makin v A-G for New South Wales* [1894] AC 57, [1891–4] All ER Rep 24, PC remains the proper principle to apply, and I see no reason for modifying it. *Makin's* case was a decision of the Judicial Committee of the Privy Council, but it was unanimously approved by the House of Lords in *R v Ball* [1911] AC 47, HL; and has been constantly relied on ever since. It is, I think, an error to attempt to draw up a closed list of the sort of cases in which the principle operates: such a list only provides instances of its general application, whereas what really matters is the principle itself and its proper application to the particular circumstances of the charge that is being tried. It is the application that may sometimes be difficult, and the particular case now before the

House illustrates that difficulty.

The principle as laid down by the then Lord Chancellor is as follows ([1894] AC 57 at 65; [1891–4] All ER Rep 24 at 25–6, PC):

'It is undoubtedly not competent for the prosecution to adduce evidence tending to show that the accused has been guilty of criminal acts other than those covered by the indictment, for the purpose of leading to the conclusion that the accused is a person likely from his criminal conduct or character to have committed the offence for which he is being tried. On the other hand, the mere fact that the evidence adduced tends to show the commission of other crimes does not render it inadmissible if it be relevant to an issue before the jury, and it may be so relevant if it bears upon the question whether the acts alleged to constitute the crime charged in the indictment were designed or accidental, or to rebut a defence which would otherwise be open to the accused.' . . .

There is a second proposition which ought to be added under this head. It is not a rule of law governing the admissibility of evidence, but a rule of judicial practice followed by a judge who is trying a charge of crime when he thinks that the application of the practice is called for. Lord du Parcq referred to it in *Noor Mohamed v R* [1949] AC 182 at 192, [1949] 1 All ER 365 at 370, PC, immediately after the passage above quoted, when he said that

'in all such cases the judge ought to consider whether the evidence which it is proposed to adduce is sufficiently substantial, having regard to the purpose to which it is professedly directed, to make it desirable in the interest of justice that it should be admitted. If, so far as that purpose is concerned, it can in the circumstances of the case have only trifling weight, the judge will be right to exclude it. To say this is not to confuse weight with admissibility. The distinction is plain, but cases must occur in which it would be unjust to admit evidence of a character gravely prejudicial to the accused even though there may be some tenuous ground for holding it technically admissible. The decision must then be left to the discretion and the sense of fairness of the judge.'

This second proposition flows from the duty of the judge when trying a charge of crime to set the essentials of justice above the technical rule if the strict application of the latter would operate unfairly against the accused. If such a case arose, the judge may intimate to the prosecution that evidence of 'similar facts' affecting the accused, though admissible, should not be pressed because its probable effect 'would be out of proportion to its true evidential value' (per Lord Moulton in *R v Christie* [1914] AC 545 at 559; [1914–15] All ER Rep 63 at 69, HL). Such an intimation rests entirely within the discretion of the judge.

It is, of course, clear that evidence of 'similar facts' cannot in any case be admissible to support an accusation against the accused unless they are connected in some relevant way with the accused and with his participation in the crime . . . But evidence of other occurrences which merely tend to deepen suspicion does not go to prove guilt. This is the ground, as it seems to me, on which the Judicial Committee of the Privy Council allowed the appeal in *Noor Mohamed v R* [1949] AC 182; [1949] 1 All ER 365, PC. The Board there took the view that the evidence as to the previous death of the accused's wife was not relevant to prove the charge against him of murdering another woman, and if it was not relevant it was at the same time highly prejudicial . . .

It remains to examine certain reported cases dealing with admissibility of evidence of 'similar acts' decided since *Makin's Case* [1894] AC 57, PC, to which the Attorney-General referred us. Rightly understood, these cases do not seem to me to involve any enlargement of the area within which evidence of 'similar facts' might be admitted.

In *R v Smith* (1915) 84 LJ KB 2153; [1914–15] All ER Rep 262, CCA, the accused was charged with murdering a woman, immediately after going through a form of marriage with her, by drowning her in a bath in the lodging where they were staying. Evidence was held to be rightly admitted of very similar circumstances which connected the accused with the deaths at a later date of two other women who were drowned in their baths after the accused had gone through a form of marriage with each of them in turn. In all three cases it was shown that the accused benefited by the death. In all three cases the prisoner urged the woman to take a bath and was on the premises when she prepared to do so. The ground on which the evidence of the two later occurrences was admissible was that the occurrences were so alike and the part taken by the accused in arranging what the woman would do was so similar in each case as to get rid of any suggestion of accident. The decision . . . therefore involved no extension of the principle laid down in *Makin's Case*. The challenged evidence was admissible both to show that what happened in the case of the first woman was not an accident and also to show what was the intention with which the accused did what he did.

In *R v Armstrong* [1922] 2 KB 555 at 566; [1922] All ER Rep 153 at 155, CCA, the accused was indicted for the murder of his wife by administering arsenic to her. The wife was shown to have died from arsenical poisoning, but the defence urged that it was not shown that the husband had administered the poison to her, but that she had committed suicide. The accused had purchased a quantity of arsenic and made it up into a number of small packets, each containing what would constitute a fatal dose, but offered the explanation that he had purchased the poison merely to use it as a weed-killer in his garden. The prosecution called evidence to show that, eight months after the death of his wife, he secretly administered arsenic to another person. The Court of Criminal Appeal held that this evidence was admissible because it went to disprove the suggestion that he had purchased and kept arsenic for an innocent purpose. The decision . . . appears to me to involve no enlargement of the principle in *Makin's Case*. Lord Hewart CJ rightly observed [1922] 2 KB 555 at 566, [1922] All ER Rep 153 at 155, CCA:

> 'The fact that he was subsequently found not merely in possession of but actually using for a similar deadly purpose the very kind of poison that caused the death of his wife was evidence from which the jury might infer that that poison was not in his possession at the earlier date for an innocent purpose.' . . .

In *R v Sims* [1946] KB 531 at 539, [1946] 1 All ER 697 at 701, CCA, there is a passage in the judgment of Lord Goddard CJ which appears to have raised doubts in some quarters as to whether the principle in *Makin's* case was being extended. The Lord Chief Justice there observed that one method of approaching the relevant problem is to start with the general proposition that all evidence that is 'logically probative' is admissible unless excluded by established rules, and that it would follow that evidence for the prosecution 'is admissible irrespective of the issues raised by the defence'. It is the words 'logically probative' which have raised doubts in some minds. Such a phrase may seem to invite philosophic discussion which would be ill-suited to the practical business of applying the criminal law with justice to all concerned. But I do not understand the Lord Chief Justice by the use of such a phrase to be enlarging the ambit of the principle in *Makin's Case* at all or to be disregarding the restrictions which Lord Herschell indicated. In one sense, evidence of previous bad conduct or hearsay evidence might be regarded as having, logically, a probative value, but, of course, the judgment in *Sims' Case* is not opening the door to that. I understand the passage quoted to mean no more than what I have already formulated, viz, that the prosecution may advance proper evidence to prove its case without waiting to ascertain what is the line adopted by the defence. Lord du Parcq, in *Noor Mohamed v R* [1949] AC 182 at 194–6, [1949] 1 All ER 365 at 371–2, PC, points out the possibility of misunderstanding the Lord Chief Justice's words and proceeds to put his own construction upon them. In substance, I agree with his interpretation. There is, however, this to be added. The proper working of the criminal law in this connexion depends on the due observance of both the propositions which I have endeavoured to expound in this judgment . . . A criminal trial in this country is conducted for the purpose of deciding whether the prosecution has proved that the accused is guilty of the particular crime charged, and evidence of 'similar facts' should be excluded unless such evidence has a really material bearing on the issues to be decided . . . With this explanation, I see no reason to differ from the conclusion in *R v Sims*.

[Lords Porter, Morton of Henryton and Tucker agreed.]

Lord Oaksey (dissenting): I do not understand your Lordships to hold that the evidence of what happened in July was inadmissible or should have been excluded on any of the counts 1 to 7 and, if that is so, it could, in my opinion, only be because of the same similarities in the evidence, from which it might be inferred that the accused stole the money on the first occasions although there was no direct evidence that he was in fact present when the money was stolen on any one of those occasions. The question may be tested in this way: can it be said that no jury could reasonably find that one person committed all eight thefts? In my opinion, the same similarity must be equally relevant whether it is adduced on one count or on the others.

RATIONALE

The law is wary of admitting similar fact evidence for the following reasons. First, the effect of this evidence may be unduly prejudicial even on a trained tribunal; before a completely untrained jury it may have an effect entirely disproportionate to its actual probative value. Sometimes its probative value is great; sometimes it is small because it is stale, or not similar enough, or of infrequent occurrence. The jury may too easily hang a dog because he has a bad name. They may be unwilling to entertain the possibility that a bad man had reformed. 'The more revolting the suggestion, the more a jury may be likely to lose sight of the fact that it may not be true' (Cowen and Carter, p 146). And even if they are not fully convinced he is guilty of this charge, they may feel compelled to punish him for his past behaviour. Secondly, similar fact evidence raises many collateral issues which it may be too distracting, expensive and time consuming to investigate in the light of the main issues of the case. Thirdly, it may take the person against whom it is tendered by surprise unless he is prepared to defend himself with respect to all the bad acts of his life. Fourthly, if similar fact evidence is too freely admissible it may encourage the police not to search for the real criminal but instead to discover someone with a possible opportunity and a record. In the same way it may be possible for the criminal to cover his tracks by committing the crime in circumstances where another man with a record may be suspected.

LIMITS

Similar fact evidence is usually introduced by the prosecution against the accused; but it could be introduced by the accused against the prosecution, eg to show that certain policemen habitually induce involuntary confessions (*S v Letsoko* 1964 (4) SA 768) or to point to a person other than the accused as the guilty party (*Cheney v R* (1991) 99 ALR 360 at 368-9, suggesting that the criteria of admissibility may be lower when the accused is tendering the evidence, since the accused need only raise a reasonable doubt as to guilt). Evidence of prior intercourse between the accused and a woman complaining of rape is admissible as relevant to consent (*R v Riley* (1887) 18 QBD 481). Similar fact evidence is also introduced in civil cases (eg *Hales v Kerr* [1908] 2 KB 601, DC). In civil cases the special need to avoid prejudicing the accused is absent, and trial is not usually by jury. There seems no reason why a party should not introduce relevant evidence of his own bad character provided he understands what he is doing: *B v R* (1992) 175 CLR 599; *R v Kenney* [1992] Crim LR 800, CA.

Evidence of prior good conduct is often rejected for want of relevance or weight, or because it would raise too many collateral issues (*Holcombe v Hewson* (1810) 2 Camp 391; *Hollingham v Head* (1858) 4 CBNS 388). However, the accused may raise his good character as evidence of innocence as well as supporting credibility: *R v Aziz* [1996] 1 AC 41, [1995] 3 All ER 149, HL.

Conduct in respect of which the accused was acquitted cannot normally be relied on as similar act evidence (*Kemp v R* (1951) 83 CLR 341; *G v Coltart*

[1967] 1 QB 432, [1967] 1 All ER 271, DC; cf *R v Miles* (1943) 44 SRNSW 198).

The defence which similar fact evidence rebuts must be 'raised in substance if not in so many words . . . The mere theory that a plea of not guilty puts everything material in issue is not enough for this purpose. The prosecution cannot credit the accused with fancy defences in order to rebut them at the outset with some damning piece of prejudice' (*Thompson v R* [1918] AC 221 at 232, [1918–19] All ER Rep 521 at 526, HL, per Lord Sumner). Of course, if the prosecution had always to wait for a defence to be raised expressly, the accused might often succeed unfairly in a submission that there is no case to answer despite the availability of admissible and weighty similar fact evidence: so the prosecution may rebut defences reasonably likely to be run by the accused on the facts (*Harris v DPP* [1952] AC 694 at 706–7, [1952] 1 All ER 1044 at 1047, HL). An admission of the fact which the prejudicial evidence is meant to prove will prevent it being admitted (*R v Rogan* [1916] NZLR 265 at 304). But a mere plea of not guilty is not enough to prevent similar fact evidence being admitted, for defences fairly attributable to the accused can be rebutted. (See Gooderson [1959] CLJ 210 at 224–8.)

BASIS OF ADMISSION

The admissibility of similar fact evidence depends on its relevance in the light of an appeal to the unlikelihood of coincidence.

In particular, admissibility depends not only on strong similarity between the similar fact evidence and the main evidence, but on an appeal to a strong dissimilarity between all the events and what might ordinarily be expected to happen. In *Thompson v R* [1918] AC 221, [1918–19] All ER Rep 521, HL, the appeal is 'Wouldn't it be odd if two boys wrongly identified as a man who interfered with them an innocent man who was in fact a practising homosexual?' In *R v Ball* [1911] AC 47, HL, it is: 'Wouldn't it be odd if a brother and sister who had committed incest frequently in the past now lived together as man and wife, sleeping in the same bed, without committing incest?' A simple example is *R v Smith* (1915) 84 LJ KB 2153, [1914–15] All ER Rep 262, CCA. Smith was charged with murdering his wife in her bath by drowning. There was no direct evidence of this other than opportunity. But two other wives had been drowned in the same way. 'No reasonable man would believe it possible that Smith had successively married three women, persuaded them to make wills in his favour, bought three suitable baths, placed them in rooms which could not be locked, taken each wife to a doctor and suggested to him that she suffered from epileptic fits, and had then been so unlucky that each of the three had had some kind of fit in the bath and been drowned' (per Lord Maugham, quoted by Williams, p 230). It follows that attention must be paid both to the issues in the case and the facts as a whole.

The precise issues must be identified because, for example, the disposition of the accused will make his innocence a much stranger coincidence if he admits the actus reus but denies some part of the mens rea than if he denies the actus reus (see *R v Flack* [1969] 2 All ER 784, [1969] 1 WLR 937, CA). The actus reus may nevertheless be proved by sufficiently strong similar fact evidence: *Makin v A-G for New South Wales* [1894] AC 57, [1891–4] All ER Rep 24, PC; *R v Ball* [1911] AC 47, HL. Probably the similarities in the evidence must be greater when the actus reus is in question.

The evidence as a whole must be borne in mind. The similar fact evidence must be taken together with the other evidence: *DPP v Boardman* [1975] AC 421 at 457, [1974] 3 All ER 887 at 909; *Sutton v R* (1984) 152 CLR 528 at 532. A very clearly proved disposition to commit a particular crime may be inadmissible if there is nothing to connect the accused with the crime charged. A very slight connexion, such as possible opportunity, may suffice, however (*R v Straffen* [1952] 2 QB 911, [1952] 2 All ER 657, CCA). And the accused may even be convicted though there is no directly proved connexion other than possible opportunity between him and the similar facts, eg cases of poisoning in a household (*R v Geering* (1849) 18 LJMC 215; *R v Grills* (1954) 73 WNNSW 303; and see *R v Chandler* (1956) 56 SRNSW 335). This is why *Harris v DPP* [1952] AC 694, [1952] 1 All ER 1044, HL, is so controversial. Further, relatively weak evidence of disposition may be admissible if the other evidence is very strong (eg *R v Ball* [1911] AC 47, HL).

But the difficulties of this reasoning should be remembered. In Lord Hewart CJ's words: 'The risk, the danger, the logical fallacy is indeed quite manifest to those who are in the habit of thinking about such matters. It is so easy to derive from a series of unsatisfactory accusations, if there are enough of them, an accusation which at least appears satisfactory. It is so easy to collect from a mass of ingredients, not one of which is sufficient, a totality which will appear to contain what is missing' (*R v Bailey* [1924] 2 KB 300 at 305, [1924] All ER Rep 466 at 467).

Director of Public Prosecutions v P [1991] 2 AC 447, [1991] 3 All ER 337, HL

Lord Mackay of Clashfern LC: The Court of Appeal . . . certified the following questions for this House:

'1. Where a father or stepfather is charged with sexually abusing a young daughter of the family, is evidence that he also similarly abused other young children of the family admissible (assuming there to be no collusion) in support of such charge in the absence of any other "striking similarities"?

2. Where a defendant is charged with sexual offences against more than one child or young person, is it necessary in the absence of "striking similarities" for the charges to be tried separately?'

. . . As this matter has been left in *R v Boardman* I am of opinion that it is not appropriate to single out 'striking similarity' as an essential element in every case in allowing evidence of an offence against one victim to be heard in connection with an offence against another. Obviously, in cases where the identity of the offender is in issue, evidence of a character sufficiently special reasonably to identify the perpetrator is required . . .

From all that was said by the House in *R v Boardman* I would deduce the essential feature of evidence which is to be admitted is that its probative force in support of the allegation that an accused person committed a crime is sufficiently great to make it just to admit the evidence, notwithstanding that it is prejudicial to the accused in tending to show that he was guilty of another crime. Such probative force may be derived from striking similarities in the evidence about the manner in which the crime was committed and the authorities provide illustrations of that of which *R v Straffen* [1952] 2 QB 911, [1952] 2 All ER 657, CCA, and *R v Smith* (1915) 11 Cr App Rep 229, [1914-15] All ER Rep 262, CCA, provide notable examples. But restricting the circumstances in which there is sufficient probative force to overcome prejudice of evidence relating to another crime to cases in which there is some striking similarity between them is to restrict the operation of the principle in a way which gives too much effect to a particular manner of stating it, and is not justified in principle. Hume on Crimes, 3rd ed (1844), vol II, p 384, said long ago:

'the aptitude and coherence of the several circumstances often as fully confirm the truth of the story, as if all the witnesses were deponing to the same facts.'

Once the principle is recognised, that what has to be assessed is the probative force of the evidence in question, the infinite variety of circumstances in which the question arises, demonstrates that there is no single manner in which this can be achieved. Whether the evidence has sufficient probative value to outweigh its prejudicial effect must in each case be a question of degree.

The view that some feature of similarity beyond what has been described as the paederast's or the incestuous father's stock in trade before one victim's evidence can be properly admitted upon the trial of another [rests on decisions which] fall to be overruled.

In the present case the evidence of both girls describes a prolonged course of conduct in relation to each of them. In relation to each of them force was used. There was a general domination of the girls with threats against them unless they observed silence and a domination of the wife which inhibited her intervention. The defendant seemed to have an obsession for keeping the girls to himself, for himself. The younger took on the role of the elder daughter when the elder daughter left home. There was also evidence that the defendant was involved in regard to payment for the abortions in respect of both girls. In my view these circumstances taken together gave strong probative force to the evidence of each of the girls in relation to the incidents involving the other, and was certainly sufficient to make it just to admit the evidence, notwithstanding its prejudicial effect. This was clearly the view taken by the Court of Appeal and they would have given effect to it were it not for the line of authority in the Court of Appeal to which I have referred . . .

When a question of the kind raised in this case arises I consider that the judge must first decide whether there is material upon which the jury would be entitled to conclude that the evidence of one victim, about what occurred to that victim, is so related to the evidence given by another victim, about what happened to that other victim, that the evidence of the first victim provided strong enough support for the evidence of the second victim to make it just to admit it notwithstanding the prejudicial effect of admitting the evidence. This relationship, from which support is derived, may take many forms and while these forms may include 'striking similarity' in the manner in which the crime is committed, consisting of unusual characteristics in its execution, the necessary relationship is by no means confined to such circumstances. Relationships in time and circumstances other than these may well be important relationships in this connection. Where the identity of the perpetrator is in issue, and evidence of this kind is important in that connection, obviously something in the nature of what has been called in the course of the argument a signature or other special feature will be necessary. To transpose this requirement to other situations where the question is whether a crime has been committed, rather than who did commit it, is to impose an unnecessary and improper restriction upon the application of the principle . . .

I would answer the first question posed by the Court of Appeal by saying that the evidence referred to is admissible if the similarity is sufficiently strong, or there is other sufficient relationship between the events described in the evidence of the other young children of the family, and the abuse charged, that the evidence if accepted, would so strongly support the truth of that charge that it is fair to admit it notwithstanding its prejudicial effect. It follows that the answer to the second question is no, provided there is a relationship between the offences of the kind I have just described.

[Lords Keith of Kinkel, Emslie, Templeman and Ackner concurred.]

NOTES

The High Court of Australia has said that *DPP v P* represents the law in Australia, New Zealand and Canada: *Pfennig v R* (1995) 182 CLR 461 at 478-84 per Mason CJ, Deane and Dawson JJ.

The 'striking similarity' test continues to be applied where identification is in issue: eg *R v Downey* [1995] 1 Cr App Rep 547, CA.

R v H [1995] 2 AC 596, [1995] 2 All ER 865, HL

[What follows deals with similar fact evidence, but not corroboration]

Lord Mackay of Clashfern LC: The Court of Appeal . . . certified that a point of law of general public importance was involved in the decision to dismiss the appeal. This was:

'How should the trial judge deal with a similar fact case (*Director of Public Prosecutions v P* [1991] 2 AC 447) where the Crown proposes to call more than one complainant and to rely on each as corroborating the evidence of the other or others, and the defence demonstrates that there is a risk that the evidence is contaminated by collusion or by other factors?'

[There is a] possibility that in some circumstances the probative force required for evidence to be similar fact evidence might be affected by circumstances such as collusion between the witness or other contamination of their evidence. In any event it is in my opinion clear that it is not correct to regard independence as a condition precedent that evidence should be admitted as similar fact evidence.

There is a further consideration that to the extent to which evidence proposed to be adduced as similar fact evidence is undermined in its aspect of probative force by circumstances affecting its weight and reliability, these circumstances will also have a bearing on its prejudicial effect. Indeed it may well be important in order that the reliability of the evidence is tested fully that circumstances pointing to collusion or other contamination affecting the weight and the reliability of the evidence are before a jury, even if there is severance of the relevant counts in the indictment.

Although there was no question of collusion or other contamination of the evidence raised in *Director of Public Prosecutions v P* . . . I think it is important to notice that the test of necessary relationship was put upon the basis that the evidence is accepted. I consider this an essential for a test of the kind set out in *Director of Public Prosecutions v P* to be workable since it is obvious that if the evidence is not accepted it will have no probative force at all. By admitting evidence as similar fact evidence the judge is not to be held as having accepted that the evidence is true. That is properly a matter for the jury if the judge decides that the evidence should properly be admissible before them. In the present case I have no doubt that the evidence was properly admitted as similar fact evidence . . .

[E]vidence of collusion on the face of the documents may be an aspect of the decision whether or not to admit evidence as similar fact evidence in some circumstances and . . . there may be circumstances in which a voir dire might be necessary to determine whether evidence proffered as similar fact evidence should be admitted as such having regard to the circumstances pointing to collusion. This House held in *Director of Public Prosecutions v P* that the test involves a comparison of the probative force of the evidence with the prejudicial effect of it on the basis that the evidence is accepted as true, accordingly the circumstances in which collusion could play a part at this stage I cannot myself envisage but since it is not possible to envisage every circumstance that may arise I am not prepared to rule it out completely.

. . . I would return as the answer to the question of law posed in the present case:

Where there is an application to exclude evidence on the ground that it does not qualify as similar fact evidence and the submission raises a question of collusion (not only deliberate but including unconscious influence of one witness by another) the judge should approach the question of admissibility on the basis that the similar facts alleged are true and apply the test set out by this House in *Director of Public Prosecutions v P* . . . accordingly. It follows that generally collusion is not relevant at this stage.

Secondly, if a submission is made raising a question of collusion in such a way as to cause the judge difficulty in applying the test referred to he may be compelled to hold a voir dire. The situations in which collusion is relevant in the consideration of admissibility would arise only in a very exceptional case of which no illustration was afforded in the argument on this appeal but I regard it as right to include this as a possibility since it is difficult to foresee all the circumstances that might arise. The present is certainly not a case in which the risk of collusion affects the application of the test.

Lord Mustill: [I]t is important to note the ambiguity of the word 'collusion'. In its more limited sense this may denote a wicked conspiracy in which the complainants put their heads together to tell lies about the defendant, making up things which never happened. It is however clear that the argument for the appellant, and the authorities on which it is based, give the word a much wider meaning; wide enough to embrace any communications between witnesses, even without malign intent, which may lead to the transfer of recollections between them, and hence to an unconscious elision of the differences between the stories which each would independently have told ... It may well be that the logic of the appellant's propositions, if sound, applies to both situations alike, but in terms of their practical consequences the two are worlds apart.

For convenience, the two situations may be labelled 'conspiracy' and 'innocent infection'. Dealing first with 'conspiracy', the deliberate and malicious fabrication of untrue stories whose details chime because that is what they are designed to do, I find it hard to envisage that where the committal papers are so frank or artless that they disclose on their face a real risk of fabrication the matter will ever be brought to trial. If there are such cases, they must surely be a small minority, by comparison with those where the witness statements show no more than the opportunity (although not necessarily the reality) of 'innocent infection'. Such an opportunity is commonplace. For example, where the offender is a stepfather or other male living with the mother, or an uncle, each child may be silent in fear of attracting the mother's displeasure or of breaking up the family unit until a confidence made to a boyfriend or teacher opens up the story, and all the siblings feel free to speak. At this point there is bound to be an exchange of recollection. Again, in those distressing cases where a dominant male abuses each young member of the family successively the children will often be hesitant to speak outside the family circle; and yet it would be absurd to take for granted that there has been no discussion at all amongst them. In all these cases there is the opportunity for innocent infection, and the possibility that one account has unintentionally drawn upon another cannot be evaluated a priori. It must follow from the appellant's argument that in every such case the prosecution is required to prove beyond reasonable doubt that in fact the risk has not materialised, before the evidence of one complainant can be placed before the jury for testing and evaluation in the usual way, at least so far as it is relied upon in relation to the offences said to have been committed against the other complainant.

The practical implications of this proposition were not fully explored in argument, nor can I find that they are faced up to in the impressive body of authority cited in support. It seems to be assumed that at least in some cases the task can be performed simply by oral submissions in the absence of the jury. I cannot accept this. How can a risk whose potential is ever-present be negatived upon the scrutiny of papers which, ex hypothesi, say nothing about it? In practice, the only reliable way of finding out whether the complainants have unintentionally embroidered their stories is by asking them, and seeing how they respond: ie by holding what in the authorities and in argument was called a 'voir dire'. It follows, if the argument for the appellant was right, that the judge will be required in almost every case to hold a preliminary trial at which the complainants will be subjected to the ordeal of a first inquisition about whether their stories have been compromised by borrowing (an inquisition which they will have to undergo again in the presence of the jury if their evidence is, against all the odds, admitted) solely in order to see whether the prosecution have proved a negative which will often be unprovable. This is more than I am willing to accept. The possibility of innocent infection is one amongst many factors which the jury will have to take into account; but to treat it as a unique 'threshold issue' loads the scales unfairly against the prosecution, and hence against the interests of those who cannot protect themselves. The risk to an innocent defendant of false inferences drawn from multiple allegations must never be underestimated, but a sense of proportion is essential. For my part, unless the logic of the rule which permits the reception of evidence of similar facts inexorably so demands, I would not be willing to impose a practice which would in many cases make the just prosecution of these offences impossible.

There is a further consequence, not so far as I am aware tackled by the English authorities. It requires a little elaboration, and for ease of discussion I will take a hypothetical case, where the two sisters are named Mary and Jane; each complains that their natural father has committed a sexual assault whilst she was alone in her own bedroom: the assaults are charged on the same indictment as counts 1 and 2 respectively: and there is a single trial on the two indictments. (The names and relationships are not those of the present case).

I will approach this by first varying the facts a little. It is undeniable that in each of the following situations the evidence of Mary is admissible, even if there are reasons to suspect that she and Jane have put their heads together to concoct it. 1. Where there is a single count charging an offence against Mary herself: 'Dad did these things to me in my bedroom.' 2. Where the evidence of Mary is led in support of a count relating to Jane: 'I went into Jane's bedroom and saw Dad doing things to her.' 3. Where the evidence of Mary is directly relevant to charges concerning both sisters: 'I went into Jane's bedroom where Dad did these things to me and then I saw him doing the same things to Jane.'

It could not, I believe, be suggested that in any one of these cases the judge has the right, far less the duty, to convene a 'pre-trial trial' for the purpose of deciding whether the evidence of Mary is so compromised by the risk of collusion between herself and Jane that the jury cannot safely be allowed to hear it. Why then should the position be different in the example given, where the evidence of Mary about what happened in her own bedroom is adduced in support of the count relating to Jane? There is of course the obvious difference that, even if believed, Mary's evidence in the latter case will be admissible only if it relates to 'similar facts' to those of which Jane will speak. Nevertheless, there is no obvious reason why this feature should call for a special treatment of conspiracy which, as in the other cases instanced, goes to the weight which the jury will attach to the evidence, not to the permissibility of allowing it to be given at all. Obviously, if the suspicion of conspiracy leads the jury to discount the evidence it will be worthless as evidence of similar facts, just as it is worthless as evidence of everything else. But this is for the jury, not for a preliminary investigation and ruling by the judge.

Moreover, the practical consequences of adopting this procedure would be strange. Imagine that the judge does hold a voir dire and concludes that the possibility of conspiracy cannot be excluded beyond reasonable doubt. According to the appellant's argument he must withdraw from the jury the possibility of reliance on Mary's evidence about what happened in her own bedroom, as capable of shedding light on what may have happened in Jane's bedroom on the occasion covered by count 2; and vice versa as regards the evidence of Jane so far as it bears indirectly on the allegations made by Mary under count 1. But this still leaves Mary's direct evidence on count 1 when she is the complainant, and Jane's kindred evidence on count 2. What is to happen to this? It plainly cannot be inadmissible, however overshadowed its veracity may be by the possibility of conspiracy. Nor, under any current theory could the judge invoke a discretion to rule it out in advance, simply because he is not sure that it is true. So it would appear that having heard the complainants in the absence of the jury, and decided that there is a real risk that the evidence may be untrue and that the apparently similar facts are not facts at all, he is still required to leave to the jury in relation to the individual counts the possibility of finding as proved beyond reasonable doubt, on precisely the same evidence, that the events described by the sisters really did happen. I can make no sense of this. The only escape would be to lay down that in every such case the counts relating to different complainants must be tried separately. There are indications in the Australian authorities that this consequence may indeed have been accepted, and I would for my part have wished to give close attention to an account of the way in which the doctrines prevailing in that jurisdiction since *Hoch v R* (1988) 165 CLR 292 are working in practice. In the event, no such account has been given, and in its absence I can only say that to require the jury to be left in ignorance when trying the offence against Jane that there is admissible evidence that the same defendant has done a similar thing to Mary is so much at variance with the long-standing practice of courts in England and (it would seem to me) so much at variance with the demands of justice for the complainants, that I would not be willing to endorse it unless the logic of the doctrine of similar facts so demands. It may be that the root of the problem lies, not so much in the law of evidence, but in the intellectual basis of the decision on whether or not to order severance of counts, a decision which has hitherto been consistently regarded as a matter for the experience and acumen of the trial judge. No such analysis of the problem has been enterprised in the present case, and the argument for the appellant must be taken as it stands.

Lord Lloyd of Berwick: . . . Rather than choose a particular formulation, it therefore seems better to say that where a risk of collusion or contamination is apparent on the face of the documents, it will always be an element, and exceptionally a decisive element, in deciding whether the probative force of the similar fact evidence is sufficiently strong to justify admitting the evidence, notwithstanding its prejudicial effect.

[Lords Griffiths and Nicholls of Birkenhead concurred in dismissing the appeal.]

NOTE

This case was argued after discordant decisions of the Court of Appeal had been given, principally *R v Ananthanarayanan* [1994] 2 All ER 847, [1994] 1 WLR 788; *R v Ryder* [1994] 2 All ER 859 and *R v W* [1994] 2 All ER 872, [1994] 1 WLR 800.

QUESTIONS

1. In *R v Simpson* (1993) 99 Cr App Rep 48 at 53, prosecuting counsel 'acknowledged the difficulty of defining the extent to which *DPP v P* extended the limits of admissibility'. What is that difficulty?

2. Is it appropriate, in applying *R v H*, to recognise exceptions for:

(a)   Cases where the identity of the accused is in issue?

(b)   Cases where the opportunity of the accused to commit the offences is in issue?

(c)   Cases where the alleged conduct which is the subject of the similar fact evidence is not the subject of any charge in the proceedings?

(d)   Cases where the defence is something other than the simple denial of the conduct alleged?

The strength of the appeal to the unlikelihood of coincidence often depends on the high degree of similarity of similar fact evidence. It tends to limit the number of persons likely to commit the crime. Sometimes so much similarity has been demanded that the court has placed 'too high a premium on versatility and too heavy a penalty on dullness' (DWL, 54 LQR 335 at 336 (1938)). But in general it is right that where the means of committing a crime 'might have been adopted in either case by anyone of an indefinite number of persons and where no other connexion . . . is shown to have existed' the evidence is inadmissible (*R v Aiken* [1925] VLR 265 at 268). Similarly, the possession of material suitable for safebreaking is inadmissible on a charge of housebreaking: *Thompson v R* (1968) 42 ALJR 16. Similarity narrows the gap between proving the accused was a wrongdoer in general and proving he did this particular wrong. The similarity must often be so marked as to suggest a special system or technique identifying the accused as the criminal; but the use of terms like 'system' or 'technique' obscures the fact that the basic test is a high degree of relevance, and this depends on all the evidence. The need for some special connexion proved through similarity used as the basis for an appeal to coincidence means that similar fact evidence is more readily admitted in unusual crimes than common ones: eg poisoning, incest, unnatural sexual cases, perverted murders. If crimes are common, others may have done them. If crimes are rare, most people are inhibited from committing them, and proof of lack of inhibition is very relevant. Lord Wilberforce has warned that: 'It is for the judge to keep close to current mores. What is striking in one age is normal in another; the perversions of yesterday may be the routine or the fashion of tomorrow': *DPP v Boardman* [1975] AC 421 at 444, [1974] 3 All ER 887 at 898, HL.

Further, the amount of proximity in time to be looked for depends partly on the crimes involved. 'A man whose course of conduct is to buy houses, insure them, and burn them down, or to acquire ships, insure them, and scuttle them, or to purport to marry women, defraud and desert them, cannot repeat the offence every month, or even perhaps every six months' (*Moorov v HM Advocate* 1930 JC 68 at 89 per Lord Sands).

The similarity of admissible similar facts may vary; so may their number. One previous abortion was enough in *R v Bond* [1906] 2 KB 389, [1904–7] All ER Rep 24; many previous burglaries might not be enough. If a man has aborted one servant girl pregnant by him, he would do well not to conduct a medical examination of another one: the suggestion of systematic misconduct is strong. But a convicted burglar cannot help walking near houses. If he were found in a house, or some marked similarity of method were proved, fewer similar facts would need to be proved (Williams, p 232).

Reported similar fact cases, of which there are vast numbers, are notorious for disputes and doubts about rules of law, though most of them are probably rightly decided. Opinions differ as to which are rightly decided largely because the question is one of relevance and therefore of degree. Not too much weight should be placed on seemingly identical prior authorities: like modern negligence cases, these are decisions of fact dressed up as decisions of law. They have very little binding effect on later courts. Dicta or even decisions in one case may be inapplicable to later cases because they are based on unexplained assumptions about which issues are relevant and how striking similarities are (eg this is especially so when indecent photographs are inspected: see *R v Morris* (1969) 54 Cr App Rep 69, CA; Eggleston in Glass (ed) p 87). The main principles can be observed in the following cases.

Thompson v R [1918] AC 221, [1918–19] All ER Rep 521, HL

The accused was charged with committing acts of gross indecency on two boys on 16 March. They said that on that day he arranged to meet them again on 19 March near a public toilet. On that date he told them to go away, gave them money and said that the tall man nearby was a policeman. He was then arrested. The accused's defence was an alibi. He said that he had never seen the boys before 19 March, and only gave the boys money to buy soap to get their faces washed, to make them stop staring at him and to go away. Two powder puffs found on the accused when arrested and several photographs of naked boys discovered at his lodgings were admitted. The accused's appeals against conviction to the Court of Criminal Appeal and House of Lords failed.

Lord Atkinson: . . . It would be strange, indeed, if one man should commit with the boys the offence charged on the 16th, and make an assignation with them to commit it again upon the 19th, that another man should, with an intent to do the same, take up and fulfil the first man's engagement, personate him as it were, and keep the appointment the first had made. It would appear to me that evidence which goes to prove that the prisoner had in his transactions with these boys on the 19th an intent or desire to commit an indecent offence with them, if circumstances should permit, becomes evidence to identify him as the person who actually committed on the 16th the offence for which he was indicted . . . For what purpose could the prisoner carry upon him on this day the powder puffs? He could not, by them, promote the cause of charity or cleanliness. He could not have carried them for such a purpose – the time had not arrived for their use; but can it be reasonably doubted that they were carried to be used when needed? The possession of them is in my opinion admissible in evidence to show, when taken in connexion with the facts proved, that the prisoner harboured on that day an intent to commit an act of indecency with these boys should occasion offer. Well, if these photographs of naked boys, some when apparently approaching adolescence, all I think indecent in their attitude, and some apparently depraved in suggestion, had been found on the person of the accused I do not see how any distinction could well have been drawn between them and the powder puffs. They too are, it is stated, implements for carrying out the same design. I do not know, and it is not stated, whether they are used to stimulate the depraved lusts of those given to such practices, or to corrupt the mind of those whose assistance or sufferance such people seek; but this I think is clear, that they could not be needed for the work of a hygienic enthusiast so devoted to youthful cleanliness that he gave to two boys he had never met before, and who had teased him by staring at him, two shillings to get their dirty faces washed. The fact that they were found in the prisoner's drawer and not on his person may make them less cogent evidence of a criminal intent towards these boys than if they had been found upon his person; but still, in my view, the possession of them is some evidence of the existence of a criminal intent towards these boys on March 19, and, if so, some evidence of the identity of the person harbouring that intent with the person who had committed the crime charged upon March 16.

[Lords Finlay LC, Parker of Waddington, Sumner and Parmour agreed.]

NOTES

1. The case depends on an appeal to the unlikelihood of an innocent man identified on the 19th having the same characteristic as the guilty man of the 16th – homosexuality. 'That common characteristic might have been a cauliflower ear or an Old Etonian tie: it happened to be a propensity' (Cowen and Carter, p 119). The appeal weakens as the characteristic becomes more common, and the likelihood of homosexuals assembling near public toilets must be considered. If the place was not a frequent resort of homosexuals, or not at that time, the appeal grows stronger. It weakens, however, as the strength of the evidence of practising homosexuality declines. This evidence, based on the powder puffs, was strong in *Thompson v R*. This case was subsequently misinterpreted to permit evidence of homosexual tendencies in all homosexual cases. General homosexual tendencies will only be admissible in exceptional circumstances; prior homosexual conduct is much more likely to be admissible to prove its repetition with the same person. The same is true of other sexual relations (eg *R v Ball* [1911] AC 47, HL, and see the lengthy review of the case law in *R v Allen* [1937] St R Qd 32).

2. The courts have since become more alert to the dangers of both children's evidence and identification evidence. Despite this and other points, it is not suggested that *Thompson v R* is wrong as a decision on the identity issue on its own facts, however much it was later misunderstood.

R v Horwood   [1970] 1 QB 133, [1969] 3 All ER 1156, CA

The accused was convicted of attempting to procure the commission with himself of an act of gross indecency by a fourteen year old boy. The accused gave the boy a lift along a country road. The boy said they got out to look for rabbits when the accused made the proposal and he ran away. The accused said he got out to urinate and on returning to the car found the boy had gone. At a police interview the accused was asked: 'Are you a homosexual?' He replied, 'I used to be: I'm cured now. The doctor's given me some pills to take when the urge comes on. I go out with girls now like anyone else.' The question and answer were admitted. The Court of Appeal held this to be wrong.

O'Connor J: In *R v King* [1967] 2 QB 338, [1967] 1 All ER 379, CA, two boys alleged that the defendant met them in a public lavatory in the afternoon and committed acts of indecency; and that by arrangement he met them again in the evening, took them to his flat for the night and committed acts of indecency. The defendant denied the afternoon meeting, admitted the evening meeting, admitted that he took the boys home, admitted that he slept in the same bed as one of the boys but denied any act of indecency. In cross-examination he was asked: 'Are you a homosexual?' He answered: 'Yes.' The court held that the question and answer were properly admitted.

[Lord Parker CJ said:] 'It is no different to put to a man the question: "Are you a homosexual?", than to put to him certain indecent photographs of a homosexual nature found in his possession and say to him: "Are these yours?" In the judgment of the court, following the case of *Thompson* [1918] AC 221, [1918–19] All ER Rep 521, HL, that question was prima facie perfectly legitimate. In passing, it is to be observed that the principle laid down by Lord Sumner is not one of completely general application, but must be limited to certain particular crimes, and the common one to which it has been applied is sexual cases.'

In *Thompson v R* the only issue was the identity of the accused, and it is clear that, in that case, evidence of the possession of the photographs was admitted in proof of identity and for no other purpose. In *R v King* there was an issue of identity as to the afternoon incidents spoken to by the boys, the subject of counts in the indictment. No doubt that fact was in this court's mind when applying *Thompson v R*. Having said that, we are satisfied that the real ground for admitting the evidence in that case was to rebut the defence of innocent association . . .

Assuming that the expression 'I am a homosexual' does not necessarily convey that the accused has committed homosexual offences, it must be only in very exceptional circumstances that evidence of this nature can be admitted to rebut innocent association. *R v King* was an exceptional case; the admitted facts were such that the admission that the accused was a homosexual could properly be said to be relevant to the issue before the jury. In our judgment, that decision cannot be taken as authority for the proposition that in all cases where a man is charged with a homosexual offence he may be asked either by the police or in the witness box the question: 'Are you a homosexual?' In cases where identity is not in issue, the occasions on which such evidence can properly be admitted must be very rare. In the present case, the nature of the admitted association, namely, the appellant taking the boy for a drive in his motor car in broad daylight, can be contrasted with that in *R v King* taking the boy home and getting into bed with him. In the present case, the real dispute was whether the opportunity for committing the offence had ever arisen, for there was no suggestion of indecency in the motor car.

NOTE

This affirms the so-called 'narrow view' of *R v Sims* [1946] KB 531, [1946] 1 All ER 697, to the effect that evidence of homosexual disposition is only admissible where, as in that case, there was a strikingly similar technique or where as in *Thompson v R* [1918] AC 221, [1918–19] All ER Rep 521, HL, the appeal to the unlikelihood of coincidence on the facts is very strong for some other reason. It rejected the 'broad view' that evidence of homosexuality is always admissible on homosexual charges. On principle the broad view seems wrong. It would be a wide exception to the general rule against similar fact evidence; it assumes too readily that homosexuals may not change their habits; it increases the power of policemen and blackmailers unduly; and in any event, a tendency to homosexuality does not necessarily entail promiscuity. See now *DPP v Boardman* [1975] AC 421, [1974] 3 All ER 887, which made it plain that no special rule applies to homosexual or other sexual cases: at 441, 443, 445–6 and 458, and at 895, 897–8, 907 and 909.

R v Flack   [1969] 2 All ER 784, [1969] 1 WLR 937, CA

The accused was charged with committing incest with his three sisters. The trial judge stated that the evidence on any one count was admissible against the accused on the others. The Court of Appeal held this to be wrong.

Salmon LJ: The passage in *R v Sims* [1946] KB 531 at 540, [1946] 1 All ER 697 at 701, CCA, relied on by the Crown read as follows:

'The probative force of all the acts together is much greater than one alone; for, whereas the jury might think one man might be telling an untruth, three or four are hardly likely to tell the same untruth unless they were conspiring together. If there is nothing to suggest a conspiracy their evidence would seem to be overwhelming. Whilst it would no doubt be in the interests of the prisoner that each case should be considered separately without the evidence of the others, we think that the interests of justice require that on each case the evidence of the others should be considered, and that even apart from the defence raised by him, the evidence would be admissible.'

The passage in *R v Campbell* [1956] 2 QB 432 at 439, [1956] 2 All ER 272 at 276, CCA relied on by the Crown is shorter, but to much the same effect, and reads as follows:

'At the same time we think a jury may be told that a succession of these cases may help them to determine the truth of the matter provided they are satisfied that there is no collaboration between the children to put up a false story.'

These passages seem to suggest that, whenever a man is charged with a sexual offence against A, evidence may always be adduced by the Crown in support of that charge of similar alleged offences by the accused against B, C and D. This court does not think that those passages were ever intended to be so understood. If, however, this is their true meaning, they go much further than was necessary for the purpose of the decisions, and cannot, in the view of this court, be accepted as correctly stating the law.

In *R v Sims* the accused had admitted that he invited each of the men to his house. He said he had done so solely for the purpose of conversation and playing cards. Each man said he had been invited to the house for the purpose of buggery. The question was whether this was a guilty or an innocent association. As Lord Goddard CJ said ([1946] KB 531 at 540, [1946] 1 All ER 697 at 701, CCA):

'. . . the visits of the men to the prisoner's house were either for a guilty or innocent purpose; that they all speak to the commission of the same class of acts upon them tends to show that in each case the visits were for the former and not the latter purpose.'

This was plainly right, and the correctness of the decision in *R v Sims* has never been doubted. The evidence of B, C and D was clearly admissible against A to negative the defence of innocent association.

In *R v Campbell*, the passage to which reference has been made was unnecessary for the decision which turned on the extent to which the evidence of one child could corroborate that of another. The correctness of the decision itself in *R v Campbell* has never been questioned. It is only the passage to which reference has already been made about which any criticism is possible. In *R v Chandor* Lord Parker CJ, referring to the passage from *R v Campbell* which has been read, said ([1959] 1 QB 545 at 549–50, [1959] 1 All ER 702 at 704, CCA):

'Unqualified it would appear to cover a case where the accused was saying that the incident in question never took place at all. To take an incident in the present case, the accused said that in respect of an alleged offence with a boy . . . at View Point – he . . . had never met the boy at View Point at all. Yet, if this passage in *R v Campbell* is unqualified it would apply to just such a case. We do not think that the passage in *R v Campbell* was ever intended to cover that. Indeed, so far as we know the authorities have never gone so far as that, nor do we see how they could . . . There are of course, many cases in which evidence of a succession of incidents may properly be admissible to help to determine the truth of any one incident, for instance, to provide identity, intent, guilty knowledge or to rebut a defence of innocent association. On such issues evidence of a succession of incidents may be very relevant, but we cannot say that they have any relevance to determine whether a particular incident ever occurred at all.'

This court respectfully agrees with every word of Lord Parker CJ's judgment in *R v Chandor*.

In the present case, the defence consisted of a complete denial that any such incident as that to which the appellant's sisters spoke had ever occurred. No question of identity, intent, system, guilty knowledge, or of rebutting a defence of innocent association ever arose. That was plain at any rate at the conclusion of the evidence, whatever may have been the position when the application for separate trials was originally made. Accordingly, the evidence of an alleged offence against one sister could not be evidence of the alleged offences against the others.

In *Boardman's* Case [1975] AC 421 at 452, [1974] 3 All ER 887 at 905, Lord Hailsham denied that there was any distinction between innocent association cases and cases of complete denials. See also Lord Cross at 458 and 909–10. *Boardman's* Case is also significant in approving *Sim's* Case, at least in its ratio.

R v Ball [1911] AC 47, CCA and HL

The accused, a brother and sister, were convicted of incest committed during certain periods in 1910. The main prosecution evidence was that the accused, who held themselves out as married, were seen together at night in a house which had only one furnished bedroom, containing a double bed showing signs of occupation by two persons. The brother had been seen coming from the bedroom in a half-dressed state while the woman was in nightdress. The similar fact evidence admitted by Scrutton J was that three years earlier, before incest was made criminal, the accused had lived together as man and wife sharing a bed, and that a baby had been born, the accused being registered as its parents.

Scrutton J: I am of opinion that evidence of previous acts would be admissible to explain the relation in which two parties are found which has to be interpreted by the jury. I do not like to use the word 'scheme', although that word is used; but I think relation is the word which best expresses the principle which I wish to convey.

I only wish further to say that as I understand the case of *Makin v A-G for New South Wales* [1894] AC 57, [1891–4] All ER Rep 24, PC, it does involve very much the same principle. In that case the prisoner was being tried for the murder of a child, and what was proved was that he had received the child from the mother for a very small sum, and that its skeleton was found in his back garden. Now those facts are in themselves consistent with death by an ordinary disease and irregular burial, or they are consistent with murder to get rid of the child and to take advantage of the sum received for its maintenance. It was proposed to tender evidence that a number of other skeletons had been found in the back garden of a previous residence of the prisoners, and that a number of other children had been entrusted to the prisoner also for inadequate sums, and that all those children had disappeared. I do not think that that evidence was given to show intent, because the first thing to show was not intent, but that the prisoners had done the act at all, that they had actually killed the child; it was not till they killed the child that the question of the intent with which they did it arose, and I think that that evidence must have been given to enable the jury to draw the proper inference as to the sort of business or transaction that the prisoners were carrying on, of which the disappearance of this particular child was one incident. From proving the sort of business carried on to proving the relation to the parties seems to me a very small step.

[The accused's appeal to the Court of Criminal Appeal succeeded.]

Darling J: If on the facts of this case an act of intercourse was proved, no question could arise as to the mens rea with which the act was done, for the statute forbids the act as in itself criminal. If without the admission of the disputed evidence the fact of the two accused persons occupying the same bed on the date or dates charged with insufficient proof that intercourse took place between them on that date or those dates, then the fact that intercourse took place between them on former occasion could only be tendered to show that they were persons likely to have intercourse on the particular dates – a ground on which evidence is not receivable.

[The prosecutor's appeal to the House of Lords succeeded.]

Lord Atkinson (in argument): . . . Surely in an ordinary prosecution for murder you can prove previous acts or words of the accused to show he entertained feelings of enmity towards the deceased, and that is evidence not merely of the malicious mind with which he killed the deceased, but of the fact that he killed him. You can give in evidence the enmity of the accused towards the deceased to prove that the accused took the deceased's life. Evidence of motive necessarily goes to prove the fact of the homicide by the accused, as well as his 'malice afore-thought', inasmuch as it is more probable that men are killed by those who have some motive for killing them than by those who have not.

Lord Loreburn LC: . . . I consider that this evidence was clearly admissible on the issue that this crime was committed – not to prove the mens rea, as Darling J considered, but to establish the guilty relations between the parties and the existence of a sexual passion between them as elements in proving that they had illicit connexion in fact on or between the dates charged. Their passion for each other was as much evidence as was their presence together in bed of the fact that when there they had guilty relations with each other.

My Lords, I agree that Courts ought to be very careful to preserve the time-honoured law of England, that you cannot convict a man of one crime by proving that he had committed some other crime; that, and all other safeguards of our criminal law, will be jealously guarded; but here I think the evidence went directly to prove the actual crime for which these parties were indicted.

[The Earl of Halsbury and Lords Ashbourne, Alverstone CJ, Atkinson, Gorell, Shaw of Dunfermline, Mersey and Robson agreed.]

QUESTION

Would the similar fact evidence have been admissible if the accused had shared a house but slept in different bedrooms?

NOTES

1. The case shows that the previous misconduct need not be a criminal or civil wrong. See also *R v Shellaker* [1914] 1 KB 414, CCA and *Griffith v R* (1937) 58 CLR 185.
2. The similar fact evidence might be thought weak in two respects: the events were not very recent, and the statute making incest a crime would be a new deterrent to its commission. But this was compensated for by the strength of the other evidence.

R v Straffen   **[1952] 2 QB 911, [1952] 2 All ER 657, CCA**

The accused was charged with strangling a young girl, Linda Bowyer. The death occurred in a quiet country area at a time when the accused was in the area having escaped for a short time from Broadmoor, an institution for the criminally insane. The accused said to the police: 'I did not kill her' at a time when neither the police nor the newspapers had referred to the death of a girl. Cassels J admitted evidence of two previous murders of young girls committed by the accused. The Court of Criminal Appeal upheld his decision.

Slade J: . . . The grounds on which the admissibility of the evidence was urged by the Solicitor-General in the court below was the similarity of the deaths and of the circumstances surrounding them in the case of the two murders at Bath, on the one hand, with the circumstances of the murder at Little Farley, on the other. He stated the similarities to be, first that each of the victims was a young girl; secondly, that each of the young girls was killed by manual strangulation; thirdly, that in each case there was no attempt at sexual interference or any apparent motive for the crime; fourthly, that in none of the three cases was there any evidence of a struggle; and, fifthly, that in none of the three cases was any attempt made to conceal the body although the body could have been easily concealed. Those similarities were fortified by the medical evidence . . .

. . . In the opinion of the court, [the] evidence was rightly admitted, not to show, to use the words of counsel for the appellant, that the appellant was a professional strangler but to show that he strangled Linda Bowyer – in other words, to identify the murderer of Linda Bowyer as being the same person as the person who had murdered the other two little girls in precisely the same way. I see no distinction in principle between this case and *Thompson v R* [1918] AC 221, [1918–19] All ER Rep 521, HL, and, indeed, I think one cannot distinguish abnormal propensities from identification. Abnormal propensity is a means of identification.

. . . [There it was] the abnormal propensity of homosexuality. In the present case it is an abnormal propensity to strangle young girls without any apparent motive, without any attempt at sexual interference, and to leave their dead bodies where they can be seen and where presumably their deaths would be rapidly detected.

QUESTION

Would the similar fact evidence have been admitted if (a) Straffen had not shown knowledge of the death of a girl in his statement to the police; or (b) someone else who had a record of murdering old women had escaped from Broadmoor about the same time; or (c) the murder was committed in central London?

(ii)   Formulation

The formulation of the similar fact rule has sometimes caused controversy. The most commonly cited is Lord Herschell's in *Makin v A-G for New South Wales* [1894] AC 57 at 65, [1891–4] All ER Rep 24 at 25–26 (p 255, ante); but others should be noted.

Cross on Evidence, 4th edn, p 310

Evidence of the misconduct of a party on other occasions (including his possession of incriminating material) must not be given if the only reason why it is substantially relevant is that it shows a disposition towards wrongdoing in general, or the commission of the particular crime or civil wrong with which such party is charged . . . [But] if the argument can be rendered more specific, and made to support a suggestion that the accused is disposed towards a particular method, as opposed to a particular kind, of wrongdoing, evidence of his misconduct on other occasions may become admissible.

Cross on Evidence, 5th edn, p 355

Evidence of the misconduct of the accused on other occasions (including his possession of incriminating material) must not be given unless it goes beyond showing a general disposition towards wrongdoing, or the commission of a particular kind of crime, and has specific probative value in relation to the charge before the court, due regard being paid to the other evidence in the case, and to defences which may reasonably be supposed to call for rebuttal.

Hoffmann: The South African Law of Evidence, 2nd edn, pp 34 and 38–9

The prosecution may not adduce evidence of improper conduct by the accused on other occasions if its only relevance is to show that the accused is a person of bad disposition, and his disposition is not highly relevant to an issue raised at the trial . . . [S]imilar fact evidence will be admissible *either* (i) if it has a relevance in addition to showing the accused's disposition *or* (ii) if it shows only the accused's disposition but this is highly relevant to the issue of guilt. Under the first head, similar fact evidence may be technically admissible even though its relevance is very slight. The courts have therefore emphasised the judge's discretion to exclude such evidence in cases where its prejudicial content is so out of proportion to its true evidential value that it would be unfair to the accused to admit it. Under the second head, this problem cannot arise.

There has been a sterile debate about whether Lord Herschell was stating a general exclusionary rule subject to a list of specific exceptions, or whether he was stating a general rule excluding evidence for some purposes and a general rule including the same evidence for others. For what it is worth, the latter view is now generally thought to be the sounder (*Harris v DPP* [1952] AC 694 at 705, [1952] 1 All ER 1044 at 1046, HL), though as a matter of convenience lists of exceptional areas where similar fact evidence is likely to be admitted are made.

Lord Herschell suggests that the similar fact evidence to be admitted must be relevant in some way different in kind from proof of disposition; see also *Boardman's* Case [1975] AC 421 at 452–3, [1974] 3 All ER 887 at 904–5. But this is not always so (see Murphy J in *Perry v R* (1982) 150 CLR 580 at 593). In *R v Straffen* [1952] 2 QB 911, [1952] 2 All ER 657, CCA, the only relevance of the similar fact evidence was to prove Straffen's disposition; given his disposition, the killing must have been done by him. In *R v Ball* [1911] AC 47, HL, the only relevance of the prior incest was to prove a disposition to commit incest; it supported an inference that the accused took advantage of the many opportunities to commit incest afforded by sharing a bed. (See also *Thompson v R* [1918] AC 221, [1918–19] All ER Rep 521, HL.) On the other hand, the evidence in *Makin's* Case was introduced to show all the babies had been murdered: it was unlikely that so many would die of natural causes. That conclusion achieved, it followed that the accused had murdered them because they had the best opportunities and motives. The relevance of the evidence was to prove the fact of the crime, not the disposition of the accused.

In substance the views of Cross and Hoffmann are the same, but Hoffmann's formulation is perhaps to be preferred. The difference is that the former suggests evidence proving a particular method of acting on a disposition is admissible, while the latter says that evidence of disposition is admissible if highly relevant to the issue. Similar fact evidence is often thought of as rebutting particular defences associated with want of mens rea, but it can also rebut denials by the accused that he had anything to do with the actus reus and that there was any actus reus at all.

Similar fact evidence is also thought of as requiring a high degree of similarity with the crime charged, and Cross's first definition expresses this. This overlooks the fact that the admissibility of similar fact evidence must always be considered in the light of the main evidence in the case: hence the second definition.

(iii)   Examples of similar fact evidence

Facts which are part of the same transaction

Two groups of cases which are often said to illustrate similar fact evidence are those concerning offences of a continuing nature and those involving proof of discreditable incidents as part of the particular crime charged. These are only examples in a limited sense because they do not involve the use of past misconduct to prove a present crime; they simply involve proof of particular matters all of which are part of one crime. Further, they are not true examples because often the misconduct proved is not similar to that charged.

Offences of a continuing nature render admissible past misconduct by virtue of the definition of the offence. Committing a public nuisance by making a highway dangerous, or permitting premises to be used as a brothel are not crimes which depend on certain single acts at a particular moment; a single crime is committed over a period, and particular incidents during it may be proved.

If a crime occurs at a particular time but events before or after are so closely connected with it in time, place or other circumstance as properly to be part of the same transaction, then evidence of those events is admissible.

O'Leary v R   (1946) 73 CLR 566

The employees of a timber camp went on a drunken orgy lasting several hours. One was found near death next morning, having been struck eight or nine times on the head with a bottle; kerosene had been poured on him and his clothes ignited. Several circumstances connected the accused with the crime. The High Court of Australia held that evidence of violent assaults by the accused on other employees, including the deceased, during the orgy, all of which were brutal blows to the head, was admissible, not as similar fact evidence but because it disclosed a connected series of events to be considered as one transaction.

Dixon J: The evidence disclosed that, under the influence of the beer and wine he had drunk and continued to drink, he engaged in repeated acts of violence which might be regarded as amounting to a connected course of conduct. Without evidence of what, during that time, was done by those men who took any significant part in the matter and especially evidence of the behaviour of the prisoner, the transaction of which the alleged murder formed an integral part could not be truly understood and, isolated from it, could only be presented as an unreal and not very intelligible event. The prisoner's generally violent and hostile conduct might well serve to explain his mind and attitude and, therefore, to implicate him in the resulting homicide . . . In my opinion, for the reasons given, evidence of his conduct was admissible for the purpose stated.

In the charge to the jury the evidence was not presented exactly in this way. It was put rather that the crime, in its circumstances, was of a description which showed that it must have been committed by a man of a particular disposition, that such a disposition amounted to a specific means of connecting or identifying the culprit and that the prisoner's conduct earlier in the period might be considered to show that, for the time being, he possessed that disposition. I do not think that this is an accurate way of treating the purpose for which the conduct of the prisoner was admissible. I am unable to see in the mere brutality of the crime or the fact that the assailant concentrated his attack on the head of the deceased any such specific connexion with the prior acts of the prisoner as to afford, so to speak, an identifying mark of the sort referred to in the decisions which appear to have been in the learned judge's contemplation.

[Latham CJ, Rich J and William J agreed. Starke J held the evidence admissible as similar fact evidence but not on the majority ground. McTiernan J dissented.]

Other examples of this doctrine include: a series of events showing a background of hostility between the parties (*R v Garner* [1964] NSWR 1131); a series of crimes committed under the influence of a continuing threat (*R v Rearden* (1864) 4 F & F 76); other crimes confessed by the accused to his victim as part of his criminal plan (eg *R v Chitson* [1909] 2 KB 945, CCA), other crimes which confirm the stories of accomplices of the accused (*R v Kennaway* [1917] 1 KB 25, [1916–17] All ER Rep 651, CCA); other crimes which explain the conduct of the victim of the main crime (*R v Lovegrove* [1920] 3 KB 643, CCA); crimes which confirm parts of a confession to other crimes (*R v Evans* [1950] 1 All ER 610, CCA); and where the accused commits three burglaries in one night, stealing a shirt at one place and leaving it at another: *R v Wylie* (1804) 1 Bos & PNR 92 at 94; *R v O'Meally (No 2)* [1953] VLR 30.

Rebutting defences

The usual way of setting out the law of similar fact evidence is to list defences which are rebuttable by such evidence. This is convenient and not harmful as long as it is remembered that the list is not closed and that the overriding questions are those of relevance and weight. If the list approach is used more strictly, it falls foul of the strictures enunciated in *Boardman's* Case [1975] AC 421 at 442–3, 452–3, 456 and 458–9, [1974] 3 All ER 887 at 896, 905, 908 and 909–10 per Lords Wilberforce, Hailsham and Cross. Admissibility depends on probative force in the particular case. Many of the cases cited above involve the use of similar fact evidence to rebut denial of the actus reus, or denial that it was caused voluntarily (cf *R v Harrison-Owen* [1951] 2 All ER 726, CCA) or intentionally (*R v Mortimer* (1936) 25 Cr App Rep 150, CCA). 'That the same accident should repeatedly occur to the same person is unusual, especially so when it confers a benefit on him' (*R v Bond* [1906] 2 KB 389 at 420–1, [1904–7] All ER Rep 24 at 41, per AT Lawrence J).

Other defences rebuttable by similar fact evidence are mistake (eg *R v Francis* (1874) LR 2 CCR 128); innocent motive (eg the use of instruments for a medical examination rather than to procure abortion: *R v Bond* [1906] 2 KB 389, [1904–7] All ER Rep 24 at 41, or possessing arsenic to kill weeds rather than unwanted wives and professional rivals: *R v Armstrong* [1922] 2 KB 555, [1922] All ER Rep 153, CCA); and innocent association (*R v Hall* [1952] 1 KB 302, [1952] 1 All ER 66, CCA). The defence of mistaken identity may be rebutted by appealing to the unlikelihood of a mistakenly identified innocent man having the accused's disposition, the latter being proved either by past bad acts (*R v Straffen* [1952] 2 QB 911; [1952] 2 All ER 657, CCA) or possession of the instruments of the crime charged (*Thompson v R* [1918] AC 221, [1918–19] All ER Rep 521, HL; *R v Twiss* [1918] 2 KB 853, CCA). Many frauds would be incapable of proof without similar fact evidence (*Blake v Albion Life Assurance Society* (1878) 4 CPD 94 at 101).

Attacking a co-accused

In *Lowery v R* [1974] AC 85, [1973] 3 All ER 662 the Privy Council held admissible psychiatric evidence tendered by one co-accused person to show that the other was more likely to be guilty. In *R v Turner* [1975] QB 834,

[1975] 1 All ER 70 the Court of Appeal said the decision should be limited to its own facts, and in *R v Bracewell* (1978) 68 Cr App Rep 44, CA, it was distinguished. If opinion evidence of D2's propensity is admissible, as *Lowery's* Case suggests, why is not similar fact evidence of D2's propensity? In *R v Neale* (1977) 65 Cr App Rep 304, CA, similar fact evidence of that kind was held inadmissible, but it was not directly relevant to the defence of the party tendering it. See also *R v Nightingale* [1977] Crim LR 744. Compare *R v Miller* [1952] 2 All ER 667, where similar fact evidence was admitted.

FURTHER READING

Brett, 6 Res Judicatae 471 (1954); Cowen and Carter, ch 4; Cross, 75 LQR 333 (1959); [1973] Crim LR 400; Eggleston in Glass, pp 53–89; Elliott [1983] Crim LR 284; Gooderson [1959] CLJ 210; Hoffmann, pp 34–58; Stone, 46 Harv LR 954 (1933); Tapper (1973) 36 MLR 56; Williams, pp 229–38; Cross [1975] Crim LR 62; Hoffmann (1975) 91 LQR 193; Piragoff, *Similar Fact Evidence*; Sklar (1977) 23 McGill LJ 60; Tapper in Campbell and Waller; Weinberg in Campbell and Waller; Carter (1985) 48 MLR 29; Forbes, *Similar Facts*; Zuckerman, ch 12.

B STATUTORY RULES

A number of statutes permit the introduction of the accused's record. For example, the Theft Act 1968, s 27(3), provides that on a charge of handling stolen goods, evidence of handling goods stolen within the previous twelve months, or of convictions for theft or handling within the previous five years shall be admissible to prove the accused's knowledge or belief that the goods were stolen. This and similar provisions exist because of the frequent difficulty of proving mens rea. (See Cross, pp 409–10; Phipson, paras 17–64.)

It may be noted that where reference to convictions which are 'spent' by reason of the Rehabilitation of Offenders Act 1974 can be reasonably avoided it should be; reference in open court requires the authority of the judge, only to be given if the interests of justice require it: *Practice Note* [1975] 2 All ER 1072, [1975] 1 WLR 1065.

2 Other aspects of the accused's character

Evidence of the accused's good character may be introduced by his own testimony, examination of defence witnesses, or cross-examination of prosecution witnesses. The evidence is admissible to show the unlikelihood of him committing the offence charged and to enhance his credibility, and appropriate jury directions to this effect must be given: *R v Vye* [1993] 3 All ER 241, [1993] 1 WLR 471, CA; *R v Aziz* [1996] 1 AC 41, [1995] 3 All ER 149, HL. This can be regarded as a generous exception to the rule prohibiting evidence of disposition so far as the first purpose is concerned, and a generous exception to the normal rule against accrediting witnesses so far as the second is concerned. If the evidence is introduced for the first purpose it must be relevant to the crime charged. '[S]uppose a man is charged with an unnatural crime; would it be any evidence at all to that man's character that he paid his bills regularly . . . ?' (Erskine, arguendo, *R v Hardy* (1794) 24 State Tr 1076). The position is less clear if character evidence is introduced solely to enhance credibility. The normal rule is that the credibility of witnesses may be impeached by any conviction: is any evidence of good character admissible to prove the likelihood of truth-telling? Character here strictly means 'reputation' (*R v Rowton* (1865) Le & Ca 520, [1861–73] All ER Rep 549). It does not include a witness's opinions of the accused's disposition, though in practice the accused's past good acts are often referred to. This is certainly so when the accused himself is testifying to his good character: one can hardly testify to one's own reputation with any confidence, for a man's reputation is what people say about him when he is not there (Hoffmann, p 32). This development does something to temper a rather irrational rule (see Wigmore, para 1986).

If the accused testifies to his good character, he may be cross-examined as to his record under the Criminal Evidence Act 1898, s 1(*f*)(ii)(ch 11, post). If the accused's witnesses testify to his good character, the prosecution may cross-examine them about their credibility, and about their knowledge of the accused's reputation; his convictions are admissible to rebut his good character (*R v Redd* [1923] 1 KB 104 at 107, [1922] All ER Rep 435 at 436, CCA; *R v Winfield* [1939] 4 All ER 164, CCA); and the prosecution may call witnesses to the accused's bad character. If prosecution witnesses under cross-examination admit that the accused has a good character, the prosecution may contradict it by evidence of his bad reputation and convictions. It seems that the proof of the accused's bad character by means of his convictions is permissible despite their irrelevance either to his guilt of the crime charged or his credibility (*R v Winfield* [1939] 4 All ER 164, CCA; cf *R v Shrimpton* (1851) 2 Den 319 at 322). If the accused has testified, this follows from the general rule that any witness's credit may be destroyed by proving his convictions; if the accused has not testified, the anomaly has an independent existence (Gooderson, 11 CLJ 377).

Apart from the above instances and the law of similar fact evidence, the accused's bad character is inadmissible unless it is a fact in issue (*R v Butterwasser* [1948] 1 KB 4, [1947] 2 All ER 415, CCA).

But in fact one of the above instances – cross-examination as to character of an accused who puts his good character in issue – is common in practice. It is part of the general question, one of the most difficult in the law of evidence, of cross-examining the accused on his record. This is the subject of the next chapter.

CHAPTER 11

The Accused's Character: Part II

Criminal Evidence Act 1898 (as amended)

1 ...

    (*e*) A person charged and being a witness in pursuance of this Act may be asked any question in cross-examination notwithstanding that it would tend to criminate him as to the offence charged.

    (*f*) A person charged and called as a witness in pursuance of this Act shall not be asked, and if asked shall not be required to answer, any question tending to show that he has committed or been convicted of or been charged with any offence other than that wherewith he is then charged, or is of bad character, unless –

        (i) the proof that he has committed or been convicted of such other offence is admissible evidence to show that he is guilty of the offence wherewith he is then charged; or

        (ii) he has personally or by his advocate asked questions of the witnesses for the prosecution with a view to establish his own good character, or has given evidence of his good character, or the nature or conduct of the defence is such as to involve imputations on the character of the prosecutor or the witnesses for the prosecution; or the deceased victim of the alleged crime; or

        (iii) he has given evidence against any other person charged in the same proceedings.

Section 1(*f*) was enacted to make special provision for the accused when his common law incapacity to testify was abolished. Had he been given complete immunity from cross-examination as to character, he would have been much better off than other witnesses. He would have had a licence to smear his accusers without any sanction other than punishment for perjury, which is little feared by one already being tried for another and perhaps more serious crime. He would have been free to attack his co-accused, which might have resulted in his own unjust acquittal or the co-accused's unjust conviction. He would have been free to allege his own good character without the risk of embarrassing cross-examination. And admissible similar fact evidence could not have been put to him. On the other hand, had he been treated as an ordinary witness, he would have been liable to cross-examination on all his past convictions to show his lack of *credibility*, and these might have been misused by the jury to prove his *guilt* of the crime charged. In this way a possibly innocent man with a record would have been deterred from doing his case justice by telling his story on oath; the great gift of the right to testify would have been denied to the bulk of accused persons.

The legislation is thus a compromise. The accused is shielded from disclosure of his record until he 'throws away his shield' either by raising his own

277

good character or by casting imputations on the prosecution, or by casting imputations on his co-accused. He can be cross-examined on admissible similar fact evidence under s 1(*f*)(i) independently of the way he conducts his case. This compromise has often been admired and it is perhaps better than either of the extremes it seeks to avoid. The structure of provisos (*e*) and (*f*) is in principle clear and simple. Section 1(*e*) permits some questions; s 1(*f*) prohibits others, save that in certain circumstances that prohibition is lifted. In detail, however, the interpretation of the Act has caused a number of difficulties. These relate, firstly, to the relationship between the provisos 1(*e*) and 1(*f*), that is to say to the question whether the general permission of 1(*e*) or the general prohibition of 1(*f*) applies to the case in question; and, secondly, to the meaning of the paragraphs of s 1(*f*), that is to say whether the general prohibition is in force or is lifted in the case in question.

1   When the section 1(*f*) prohibition applies: the relationship between section 1(*e*) and (*f*)

On one view s 1(*e*) permits questions directly criminating the accused as to the offence charged, while s 1(*f*) prohibits questions indirectly criminating the accused by eliciting and suggesting inferences from his record or which impugn his credibility (*Maxwell v DPP* [1935] AC 309 at 318, [1934] All ER Rep 168 at 172–3, HL, per Viscount Sankey LC; *R v Cokar* [1960] 2 QB 207, [1960] 2 All ER 175, CCA). The other view is that s 1(*e*) permits questions which tend to criminate the accused as to the offence charged directly or indirectly, while s 1(*f*) merely prohibits cross-examination as to credit (see *R v Chitson* [1909] 2 KB 945, CCA; *R v Kurasch* [1915] 2 KB 749, CCA; *R v Kennaway* [1917] 1 KB 25, [1916–17] All ER Rep 651, CCA; *R v Miller* [1952] 2 All ER 667. The first view is difficult to accommodate to the words of the statute, but the second would seem to render s 1(*f*)(i) otiose.

In *Jones v DPP* [1962] AC 635, [1962] 1 All ER 569, HL, a majority of the House of Lords upheld the first view, and the cases supporting the second can only be regarded as correct on some other ground. The first view has a tendency to give the prohibition on cross-examination of the accused in s 1(*f*) a wide operation, but the beneficial effects of this tendency for the accused are greatly limited by the conjunction of three other considerations. First, the prohibition on questions 'tending to show' a bad record or character refers to questions tending to reveal it for the first time to the jury (ibid); secondly, 'character' throughout s 1(*f*) includes both record and reputation (ibid per Lord Denning at 671, 580, contra, Lord Devlin at 699, 598); *Stirland v DPP* [1944] AC 315 at 325, [1944] 2 All ER 13 at 17, HL; *Selvey v DPP* [1970] AC 304, [1968] 2 All ER 497, HL; *R v Dunkley* [1927] 1 KB 323, [1926] All ER Rep 187, CCA); thirdly, an accused's character is in general indivisible (cf *Stirland v DPP* [1944] AC 315 at 327, [1944] 2 All ER 13 at 18, HL; *R v Winfield* [1939] 4 All ER 164, 27 Cr App Rep 139, CCA; *R v Powell* [1986] 1 All ER 193, [1985] 1 WLR 1364, CA). Thus if the jury already know anything against an accused's 'character' in this wide sense, he is at risk of being questioned about the whole of it: the s 1(*f*) prohibition does not apply,

because the questions will not 'show' his character to the jury: *R v Anderson* [1988] QB 678, [1988] 2 All ER 549, CA. His only hope is that the judge will exercise in his favour the discretion to disallow questions.

Jones v Director of Public Prosecutions   [1962] AC 635, [1962] 1 All ER 569, HL

The accused was charged with murdering a girl guide. Before the trial the accused set up a false alibi; in his evidence he alleged instead that he had spent the night in question with a prostitute and testified to his wife's angry reaction to his late return. This testimony was strikingly similar to that given by him at an earlier trial during which he was convicted of raping a girl guide. The prosecution obtained leave to cross-examine the accused to show that the similarities were so close as to make the defence incredible, and did so in a way which, though vague, 'must have created the impression in the minds of the jury that the appellant had shortly before the murder of [the girl guide] either committed or been charged with some offence on a Friday night which was reported in a newspaper on the following Sunday' ([1962] AC 635 at 643, [1961] 3 All ER 668 at 672-3, CCA). In his own evidence in chief the accused admitted having been 'in trouble' with the police before, and his counsel had put before the jury a similar admission contained in a statement of the accused's to the police.

The Court of Criminal Appeal and the House of Lords (by a 3-2 majority) dismissed appeals against conviction on the ground that the cross-examination did not 'tend to show' the accused's bad record or character: 'tend to show' meant 'tend to reveal to the jury for the first time' rather than 'tend to prove'.

Lord Reid (with whom Viscount Simonds agreed): It is well established that the 1898 Act has no application to evidence given by any person other than the accused: where it was competent before that Act for a witness to prove or refer to a previous conviction of the accused, that is still competent. What the Act does is to alter the old rules as regards the accused. It might merely have provided that the accused should be a competent witness; then the ordinary rules would have applied to him. But it goes on to afford to him protection which the ordinary rules would not give him: it expressly prohibits certain kinds of question being put to him. That must mean questions which would be competent and relevant under the ordinary rules, because there was no need to prohibit any question which would in any event have been excluded by the ordinary rules. So what must now be considered is what kinds of question, which would have been competent and relevant under the ordinary rules of evidence, does the Act prohibit . . .

This raises at once the question what is the proper construction of the words in proviso (*e*), 'tend to criminate him as to the offence charged'. Those words could mean 'tend to convince or persuade the jury that he is guilty', or they could have the narrower meaning – 'tend to connect him with the commission of the offence charged'. If they have the former meaning, there is at once an insoluble conflict between provisos (*e*) and (*f*). No line of questioning could be relevant unless it (or the answers to it) might tend to persuade the jury of the guilt of the accused. It is only permissible to bring in previous convictions or bad character if they are so relevant, so, unless proviso (*f*) is to be deprived of all content, it must prohibit some questions which would tend to criminate the accused of the offence charged if those words are used in the wider sense. But if they have the narrower meaning, there is no such conflict. So the structure of the Act shows that they must have the narrower meaning.

So I turn to consider proviso (*f*). It is absolute prohibition of certain questions unless one or other of the three conditions is satisfied. It says the accused 'shall not be asked, and if asked shall not be required to answer' certain questions. It was suggested that this applies to examination in chief as well as to cross-examination. I do not think so. The words 'shall not be required to answer' are quite inappropriate for examination in chief. The proviso is obviously intended to protect the accused. It does not prevent him from volunteering evidence, and does not in my view prevent his counsel from asking questions leading to disclosure of a previous conviction or bad character if such disclosure is thought to assist in his defence.

The questions prohibited are those which 'tend to show' certain things. Does this mean tend to prove or tend to suggest? Here I cannot accept the argument of the Attorney-General; what matters is the effect of the questions on the jury. A veiled suggestion of a previous offence may be just as damaging as a definite statement. In my judgment, 'tends to show' means tends to

suggest to the jury. But the crucial point in the present case is whether the questions are to be considered in isolation or whether they are to be considered in the light of all that had gone before them at the trial. If the questions or line of questioning has to be considered in isolation I think that the questions with which this appeal is concerned would tend to show at least that the accused had previously been charged with an offence. The jury would be likely to jump to that conclusion, if this was the first they had heard of this matter. But I do not think that the questions ought to be considered in isolation. If the test is the effect the questions would be likely to have on the minds of the jury that necessarily implies that one must have regard to what the jury had already heard. If the jury already knew that the accused had been charged with an offence, a question inferring that he had been charged would add nothing and it would be absurd to prohibit it. If the obvious purpose of this proviso is to protect the accused from possible prejudice, as I think it is, then 'show' must mean 'reveal', because it is only a revelation of something new which could cause such prejudice.

I shall not detain your Lordships by analysing the questions to which objection is taken to see whether they contained any material revelation of anything which the jury were unlikely to infer from the evidence already given by the accused in chief. I need only refer to the speech about to be delivered by my noble and learned friend, Lord Morris of Borth-y-Gest, and to the judgment of the Court of Criminal Appeal. For the reasons which they give, I am of opinion that this appeal should be dismissed on the ground that these questions were not prohibited because they did not 'tend to show' any of the matters specified in proviso (f).

But, in case it should be thought that some of the views which I have expressed are not in accord with what was said by Lord Simon in *Stirland v DPP* [1944] AC 315, [1944] 2 All ER 13, HL. I must say something about that case. That was a case where the accused had put his character in issue and the questions which it was held ought not to have been put to him in cross-examination dealt with an occasion when a former employer had questioned him about a suspected forgery. But the case did not turn on proviso (f) because the second exception in the proviso was satisfied by the accused having given evidence of his good character and therefore the proviso was excluded.

Lord Simon did, however, state six rules which should govern cross-examination to credit of an accused person. First he set out proviso (f). Then comes the rule which gives rise to the difficulty ([1944] AC 315 at 326, [1944] 2 All ER 13 at 18, HL):

> '2. He may, however, be cross-examined as to any of the evidence he has given in chief, including statements concerning his good record, with a view to testing his veracity or accuracy or to showing that he is not to be believed on his oath.'

Applied to a case where the accused has put his character in issue I think that is correct, because then proviso (f) does not apply. But I do not think that Lord Simon can have meant it to apply in its general form to a case where proviso (f) does operate, because earlier in his speech he said ([1944] AC 315 at 322, [1944] 2 All ER 13 at 16, HL):

> 'This House has laid it down in *Maxwell v DPP* [1935] AC 309, [1934] All ER Rep 168, HL that, while paragraph (f) of this section absolutely prohibits any question of the kind there indicated being put to the accused in the witness box unless one or other of the conditions (i), (ii) or (iii) is satisfied, it does not follow that such questions are in all circumstances justified whenever one or other of the conditions is fulfilled.'

Thus he recognised the absolute character of the prohibition except where one or other of the conditions is satisfied, so he cannot have intended to say that there is another case, not covered by the conditions, where the proviso also does not apply, namely, where questions are put with a view to testing the veracity of the accused's evidence in chief. But if he did mean that it was certainly obiter and I would not agree with it. It would in effect be legislating by adding a fourth condition to proviso (f). The Attorney-General refused to take this point and I think he was perfectly right.

It is said that the views which I have expressed involve overruling two decisions of the Court of Criminal Appeal, *R v Chitson* [1909] 2 KB 945, CCA and *R v Kennaway* [1917] 1 KB 25, [1916–17] All ER Rep 651, CCA. I do not think so. I think the decisions were right but the reasons given for them were not. In the former case the accused was charged with having had carnal knowledge of a girl aged 14. Giving evidence, she said that the accused told her that he had previously done the same thing to another girl, who, she said, was under 16. No objection

was taken to this evidence, I assume rightly. So before the accused gave evidence the jury already knew that he was alleged to have committed another offence. If the views which I have already expressed are right, cross-examining the accused about this matter disclosed nothing new to them and therefore did not offend against the prohibition in proviso (f). But the judgment of the court was not based on that ground: it was said that although the questions tended to prove that the accused was of bad character they also tended to show that he was guilty of the offence with which he was charged. For the reasons which I have given I do not think that that is sufficient to avoid the prohibition in proviso (f).

R v Kennaway [1917] 1 KB 25, [1916–17] All ER Rep 651, CCA, was a prosecution for forgery. Accomplices giving evidence for the prosecution described the fraudulent scheme of which the forgery was a part and related a conversation with the accused in which he stated to them that some years earlier he had forged another will in pursuance of a similar scheme. Then in cross-examination the accused was asked a number of questions about this other forgery. Those questions were held to have been properly put to him. Here, again, these questions disclosed nothing new to the jury and I can see no valid objection to them. But again that was not the ground of the court's decision. Their ground of decision was similar to that in *Chitson's Case* [1909] 2 KB 945, CCA and I need not repeat what I have said about that case.

Lord Denning: My Lords, much of the discussion before your Lordships was directed to the effect of 1(f) of the Criminal Evidence Act 1898: and, if that were the sole paragraph for consideration, I should have thought that counsel for the Crown ought not to have asked the questions he did. My reasons are these:

First: The questions *tended* to show that Jones had been charged with an offence, even though he had himself brought out the fact that he had previously been charged in a court of law with another offence. True it is that they did not point definitely to that conclusion, but they conveyed that impression, and that is enough. Counsel may not have intended it, but that does not matter. What matters is the impression the questions would have on a jury. The Attorney-General said that, if the questions left the matter evenly balanced, so that there was some other conclusion that could equally well be drawn, as, for instance, that Jones had not been 'charged' in a court of law but had only been interrogated in a police station, there was no bar to the questions being asked. I cannot agree. If the questions asked by the Crown are capable of conveying two impressions – one objectionable and the other not – then they 'tend to show' each of them: and the questions must be excluded, lest the jury adopt the worse of the two impressions. I do not think that it is open to the prosecution to throw out prejudicial hints and insinuations – from which a jury might infer that the man had been charged before – and then escape censure under the cloak of ambiguity.

Second: I think that the questions tended to *show* that Jones had been 'in trouble' before. It is one thing to confess to having been in trouble before. It is quite another to have it emphasised against you with devastating detail. Before these questions were asked by the Crown, all that the jury knew was that at some unspecified time in the near or distant past, this man had been in trouble with the police. After the questions were asked, the jury knew, in addition, that he had been very recently in trouble for an offence on a Friday night which was of so sensational a character that it featured in a newspaper on the following Sunday – in these respects closely similar to the present offence – and that he had been charged in a court of law with that very offence. It seems to me that questions which tend to reveal an offence, thus particularised, are directly within the prohibition in s 1(f) and are not rendered admissible by his own vague disclosure of some other offence. I do not believe that the mere fact that he said he had been in trouble before with the police – referring as he did to an entirely different matter many years past – let in this very damaging cross-examination as to recent events.

Third: The questions do not come within the exception (i) to s 1(f). There was no evidence before the court of any 'other offence' which would be admissible evidence to show that he had been guilty of this murder. If the prosecution had given evidence of the previous rape with its attendant circumstances, there might have been such similarities as to render the proof of that offence admissible to prove identity, see *R v Straffen* [1952] 2 QB 911, [1952] 2 All ER 657, CCA: but in the absence of such evidence, I do not see how these questions could be justified in cross-examination under exception (i). Before any cross-examination is permissible under exception (i), the prosecution must lay a proper foundation for it by showing some 'other offence which is admissible evidence to show that he is guilty'. The prosecution should normally do it by giving evidence in the course of their case; though there may be cases in which they might, with the leave of the judge, do it for the first time in cross-examination. No such foundation was laid here.

If the case rested solely on s 1(*f*), I would therefore have held that these questions were inadmissible. But I do not think it rests on s 1(*f*). In my judgment, the questions were admissible under s 1(*e*) which says that a person charged

'may be asked any question in cross-examination notwithstanding that it would tend to criminate him as to the offence charged.'

As to this subsection, Viscount Sankey LC, speaking for all in this House in *Maxwell's Case* [1935] AC 309 at 318, [1934] All ER Rep 168 at 172–3, HL said that under s 1(*e*)

'a witness may be cross-examined in respect of the offence charged, and cannot refuse to answer questions directly relevant to the offence on the ground that they tend to incriminate him: thus if he denies the offence, he may be cross-examined to refute the denial.'

I would add that, if he gives an explanation in an attempt to exculpate himself he may be cross-examined to refute his explanation. And none the less so because it tends incidentally to show that he had previously been charged with another offence.

Let me first say why I think in this case the questions were directly relevant to the offence charged. They were directly relevant because they tended to refute an explanation which the accused man had given. He had given a detailed explanation of his movements on the crucial weekend, and so forth, all in an attempt to exculpate himself. The prosecution sought to show that this explanation was false: and I think it was of direct relevance for them to do so. From the very earliest times, long before an accused man could give evidence on his own behalf, the law has recognised that, in considering whether a man is guilty of the crime charged against him, one of the most relevant matters is this: What explanation did he give when he was asked about it? Was that explanation true or not? If he gives a true explanation, it tells in his favour. If he gives a false explanation, it tells against him. The prosecution have, therefore, always been entitled, as part of their own case, to give evidence of any explanation given by the accused and of its truth of falsity. Thus if a man, who is found in possession of a stolen watch, tells a policeman that he bought it for £5 from a tradesman, whom he names, the prosecution can call that tradesman, as part of their case, to say whether that was true or not. If true, it is an end of the case against the accused. If false, it goes a long way to prove his guilt, see *R v Crowhurst* (1844) 1 Car & Kir 370 by Alderson B, *R v Smith* (1845) 2 Car & Kir 207 by Lord Denman CJ. So also if a man, who is charged with murder at a specified time and place, tells a policeman that he was at the house of his sister-in-law at the time, as Jones did here, the prosecution can call the sister-in-law, as part of their case, to say it was false and that he was not at her house at all. So also if he tries, as Jones did, to get his sister-in-law to say that he was at her house at that time, contrary to the fact, the prosecution can call the sister-in-law to say that he tried to suborn her to give false testimony: for the simple reason that 'the recourse to falsehood leads fairly to an inference of guilt', see *Moriarty v London, Chatham and Dover Rly Co* (1870) LR 5 QB 314 at 319, by Cockburn CJ. In this very case Jones's sister-in-law, Mrs Eldridge, gave such evidence for the prosecution without any objection being taken to it, even though it tended to show that he was guilty of another offence, namely, the offence of attempting to pervert the course of justice.

Now, suppose the man does this further thing which Jones did here. He discards the story that he went to his sister-in-law's house and puts forwards a different story. He says that he went up to London and was with a prostitute, but he does not identify her. So the prostitute cannot be called to falsify his story. Nevertheless the prosecution can falsify it by other evidence, if they have it available. They can call such evidence as part of their own case, even though it tends incidentally to show that he was guilty of another offence. For instance, they could prove that his finger-prints were on the window of a house that was broken into at Yateley that night. '. . . the mere fact that the evidence adduced tends to show the commission of other crimes does not render it inadmissible if it be relevant to an issue before the jury,' see *Makin v A-G of New South Wales* [1894] AC 57 at 65, [1891–4] All ER Rep 24 at 26, PC. Evidence that he had committed burglary would not be admissible to prove that he had committed murder: but evidence that he was at Yateley would be admissible to prove that he was in the vicinity and had recourse to falsehood to explain his whereabouts. The prosecution would be entitled to call this evidence, even though it tended to show that he was guilty of burglary.

Such is the law as it is, and always has been, as to the evidence which can be called for the prosecution. They can, in the first place, give evidence of any explanation given by the accused of his movements and they can, in the second place, give evidence that his explanation is false,

even though it tends incidentally to show the commission by him of some other offence. Now, when Parliament in 1898 enabled an accused man to give evidence on his own behalf, they did not cut down evidence of this kind for the prosecution. And when the prosecution gives such evidence, it must be open to the accused man himself to answer it. He must be able to give evidence about it and to be cross-examined upon it. He can be cross-examined as to any explanation he has given and as to its truth or falsity: and he can be cross-examined upon it none the less because incidentally it may tend to show that he has been guilty of some other offence.

No one, surely, can doubt the validity of *R v Chitson* [1909] 2 KB 945, CCA, and *R v Kennaway* [1917] 1 KB 25, [1916–17] All ER Rep 651, CCA, at least to this extent, that when the prosecution have legitimately given in evidence any explanation or statement made by the accused relative to the offence charged, he can be cross-examined as to the truth or falsity of it, even though incidentally it may tend to show that he has been guilty of some other offence or is of bad character.

Now, the only difference is that, whereas in those cases the accused man made his explanation or statement *before* the trial, in the present case he made his explanation (about his conversations with his wife, and so forth) for the first time *at* the trial when he went into the witness box to give evidence on his own behalf. But this cannot give him any protection from a cross-examination to which he would otherwise be exposed. His explanation is not made sacrosanct, it is not made incapable of challenge, simply because he gives it at the trial instead of at an earlier stage. The prosecution are entitled to expose its falsity, no matter whether he gives it at the trial or beforehand. And they are not precluded from doing so merely because the exposure of it tends to show that he has been guilty of some other offence or is of bad character. The situation is precisely covered by the second proposition in *Stirland's Case* [1944] AC 315 at 326, [1944] 2 All ER 13 at 18, HL, where Viscount Simon LC in this House, with the assent of all present, said that, notwithstanding the prohibition in section 1(*f*), the accused man

'may, however, be cross-examined as to any of the evidence he has given in-chief, including statements concerning his good record,'

and including, I would add, any explanation offered by him 'with a view to testing his veracity or accuracy or to showing that he is not to be believed on his oath'.

It is noteworthy that everyone at the trial of Jones acted on this view of the law. No one suggested that the questions were absolutely prohibited. All that was suggested was that it was a matter of discretion. And that is, I think, the true position. The judge was entitled in his discretion to exclude them if he thought they were so prejudicial as to outweigh their probative value. It was his discretion, not that of the prosecution. He did not exclude them but permitted them to be asked. They were, therefore, properly put.

In conclusion I would say that I view with concern the suggestion that the reasoning in *R v Chitson* [1909] 2 KB 945, CCA, and *R v Kennaway* [1917] 1 KB 25, [1916–17] All ER Rep 651, CCA was wrong and that what Viscount Simon LC said in *Stirland's Case* [1944] AC 315, [1944] 2 All ER 13, HL, is no longer a safe guide. Those cases have governed the practice in our criminal courts for years: and the result has been wholly beneficial. It is not, in my opinion right to resort now to a literal reading of the Act so as to displace them.

Lord Morris of Borth-y-Gest: . . . My Lords, it seems to me that the clearest guidance as to provisos (*e*) and (*f*) was given in *Maxwell's Case*. In his speech, [1935] AC 309 at 318–19, [1934] All ER Rep 168 at 172–3, HL Viscount Sankey LC said:

'In section 1, proviso (*e*), it has been enacted that a witness may be cross-examined in respect of the offence charged, and cannot refuse to answer questions directly relevant to the offence on the ground that they tend to incriminate him: thus if he denies the offence, he may be cross-examined to refute the denial. These are matters directly relevant to the charge on which he is being tried. Proviso (*f*), however, is dealing with matters outside, and not directly relevant to, the particular offence charged; such matters, to be admissible at all, must in general fall under two main classes: one is the class of evidence which goes to show not that the prisoner did the acts charged, but that, if he did these acts, he did them as part of a system or intentionally, so as to refute a defence that if he did them he did them innocently or inadvertently . . .

The other main class is where it is sought to show that the prisoner is not a person to be believed on his oath, which is generally attempted by what is called cross-examination to credit. Closely allied with this latter type of question is the rule that, if the prisoner by himself or his witnesses seeks to give evidence of his own good character, for the purpose of showing that it is unlikely that he committed the offence charged, he raises by way of defence an issue as to his good character, so that he may fairly be cross-examined to show the contrary. All these matters are dealt with in proviso (f) . . .'

In his speech in *Stirland v DPP* [1944] AC 315 at 324, [1944] 2 All ER 13 at 17, HL Viscount Simon LC said that he was disposed to think that in (f), where the word 'character' occurs four times, there is a combination of the conceptions of general reputation and of actual moral disposition.

Having regard to what has been laid down in *Maxwell's Case* and in *Stirland's Case*, I do not find it necessary to embark upon 'a close study and comparison' of earlier cases such as *R v Chitson* [1909] 2 KB 945, CCA and *R v Kennaway* [1917] 1 KB 25, [1916–17] All ER Rep 651, CCA. If the results reached in those cases can be supported it must not be on any line of reasoning that runs counter to what has been laid down in *Maxwell's Case* and in *Stirland's Case*.

Lord Devlin: My Lords, I would dismiss this appeal on the short ground that the questions objected to were relevant to an issue in the case upon which the appellant had testified in chief. It is not disputed that the issue to which the questions related was a relevant one. It concerned the identification of the appellant as being at the material time at the scene of the crime. He testified that at the material time he was with a prostitute in the West End and he supported this alibi by giving evidence of a conversation which he had with his wife about it a day or two later. The purpose of the questions objected to was to obtain from the appellant an admission (which was given) that when he was being questioned about his movements in relation to another incident some weeks earlier he had set up the same alibi and had supported it with an account of a conversation with his wife in almost identical terms; the prosecution suggested that these similarities showed the whole story of the alibi to be an invented one. In order to make good his point by means of cross-examination it was necessary for Mr Griffith-Jones for the prosecution to identify to some extent the occasion on which the previous questioning had taken place and to refer to a newspaper report which had entered into the conversation between the appellant and his wife. On this the Court of Criminal Appeal has said:

'In our view this part of the cross-examination of the appellant, taken as a whole, must have created the impression in the minds of the jury that the appellant had shortly before the murder of Brenda Nash either committed or been charged with some offence on a Friday night which was reported in a newspaper on the following Sunday.'

The Attorney-General has argued that the questions do not go as far as the Court of Criminal Appeal thought. This is a difficult point, but I do not think it has to be considered in the bare form in which it was put. If the questions are relevant to an issue, they are, in my view, admissible, notwithstanding that incidentally they suggest that the appellant has committed an offence. If they are not relevant to an issue, the prosecution had no business to introduce the matter at all. They were suggestive and damaging questions and objectionable as such; and it is unnecessary to determine whether the objection is more securely based on the terms of the Act of 1898 or upon the ground that it was irrelevant matter 'tending to lead the minds of the jury astray into false issues'; *Maxwell v DPP* [1935] AC 309, [1934] All ER Rep 168, HL. But the concession of relevance supplies in my opinion the short and simple answer to the whole case . . .

I turn now to consider an alternative construction of the Act that avoids these difficulties. Hitherto, I have been using the word 'character' in the sense in which it was used in the argument, that is, as meaning the quality or disposition of the man. But in the law of evidence 'character' normally means 'reputation'. Strictly speaking, it is not permissible to give evidence of particular acts done by the prisoner, unconnected with the offence charged, in order to show his disposition, whether his general character is in issue or not; for a man's character in the eyes of the law depends not on his disposition but on his reputation. This interpretation explains a feature of the proviso that puzzled the Court of Criminal Appeal in this case, namely, why a distinction is drawn in it between evidence showing previous offences and evidence showing bad character; the two overlap unless the latter is construed, as the court thought it ought to be, as evidence showing 'that the accused is otherwise (that is, apart from any offence within the first part) of bad character'. The true answer, I think, is that the Act is dealing with two entirely different categories of evidence. Evidence of previous offences would not strictly under the old rule have been allowed as evidence of bad character; that must be spoken to by persons who know of the reputation which the prisoner actually enjoyed, whether deserved or not. Evidence of bad reputation would, of course, have been inadmissible to prove the commission of a specific offence. This interpretation of 'character' explains also why evidence of discreditable acts falling short of an offence is not, where relevant, exempted from the prohibition, while evidence showing a previous offence is, where relevant, so exempted. Discreditable acts falling short of an offence are not within the terms of the prohibition at all. That does not mean that such evidence, because not specifically prohibited, is admissible; under the ordinary law of evidence it is excluded unless it is relevant to an issue. All reference to bad character is therefore naturally excluded from the first exception; there are no circumstances in which reputation can be admissible on the issue; evidence of reputation is admissible only if the accused introduces character under the second and third exceptions.

My Lords, I find it impossible to believe that the framers of the Act of 1898 did not intend 'character' to have the meaning of 'reputation'. Although the merits of the rule had frequently been questioned, it was firmly settled in the eighteenth century. A vigorous attempt to dislodge it was made in 1865 and was unsuccessful. In *R v Rowton* (1865) Le & Ca 520, [1861–73] All ER Rep 549 it was authoritatively laid down by eleven out of the thirteen judges sitting in the Court of Crown Cases Reserved that evidence of the prisoner's character must not be evidence of particular facts but evidence of general reputation only. Even the two dissenting judges, though they were prepared to interpret character as including actual moral disposition, did not consider that evidence could be given of concrete examples of conduct. Not all the judges liked the rule. But Cockburn CJ said (1965) Le & Ca 520 at 532, [1861–73] All ER Rep 549 at 552:

'I take my stand on this: I find it uniformly laid down in the books of authority that the evidence to character must be evidence of general character in the sense of reputation . . .'

On the first proposition I have already referred to *R v Rowton* (1865) Le & Ca 520, [1861–73] All ER Rep 549 and have indicated that the rule which that case laid down was never popular with practitioners. As early as 1809 Lord Ellenborough CJ said in *R v Jones* (1809) 2 Camp 131, 31 State Tr 251 at 310:

'. . . it is very remarkable, but there is no branch of evidence so little attended to.'

It appears that under the Act of 1898 character was almost invariably treated as including moral disposition. In *R v Dunkley* [1927] 1 KB 323, [1926] All ER Rep 187, CCA, counsel for the defence cross-examined the principal witness for the prosecution and suggested that her story was fabricated because she thought she had a grievance against the prisoner; and the prisoner in his evidence in chief said that the witness's story was untrue and was due to malice. On this the prisoner was cross-examined about his own character. In the Court of Criminal Appeal one of the arguments advanced for the appellant was that the reputation of the witness had not been attacked. On this argument Lord Hewart CJ after reciting the proviso, spoke as follows, at 329, 190:

'It is apparent that within the space of a very few lines the word "character" is used in this part of this section no fewer than four times. It is also apparent that the imputations which are spoken of in the closing words of the passage I have read are described, not as imputations on the prosecutor or the witnesses for the prosecution, but as imputations on the character of the prosecutor or the witnesses for the prosecution. In those circumstances it is not difficult to suppose that a formidable argument might have been raised on the phrasing of this statute, that the character which is spoken of is the character which is so well known in the vocabulary of the criminal law – namely, the general reputation of the person referred to; in other words, that "character" in that context and in every part of it, in the last part no less than in the first, in the third part no less than in the second, bears the meaning which the term "character" was held to bear, for example, in the case of *R v Rowton* (1865) Le & Ca 520, [1861–73] All ER Rep 549 . . . Nevertheless, when one looks at the long line of cases beginning very shortly after the passing of the Criminal Evidence Act 1898, it does not appear that that argument has ever been so much as formulated. It was formulated yesterday. One can only say that it is now much too late in the day even to consider that argument, because that argument could not now prevail without the revision, and indeed to a great extent the overthrow, of a very long series of decisions.'

In *Stirland v DPP* [1944] AC 315 at 326, [1944] 2 All ER 13 at 17, HL, Lord Simon LC referred to this case and said that he was disposed to think that in the word 'character' in proviso (*f*) both conceptions were combined . . .

If *R v Dunkley* [1927] 1 KB 323, [1926] All ER Rep 187, CCA, is not to be upheld and character means 'reputation', it follows, for the reasons I have already given, that the prohibition in proviso (*f*) was not infringed by the questioning objected to in this case. Undoubtedly the questions tended to show that the accused had done something discreditable which had brought him into trouble with the police, but they did not present him as a man of generally bad reputation. If, as may well be argued, they went further than that and tended to show that he had committed some offence, nevertheless they were not prohibited because the evidence about that offence was an essential part for which he was being tried.

If *R v Dunkley* [1927] 1 KB 323, [1926] All ER Rep 187, CCA, is to be upheld, it can in my opinion be upheld only on the reasoning on which the judgment is itself based, namely, that it is too late to argue – at any rate in relation to the Act of 1898 – that 'character' should bear the meaning of reputation only. Indeed, I cannot see any other ground on which the decision could be defended. To take only one point, is it possible to argue that when Parliament in proviso (*f*)(ii) referred to the accused as giving 'evidence of his good character', it contemplated that he might give evidence to show that he was a man of good moral disposition when 30 years before the court which was then of final appeal had in one of the most fully considered judgments in its history decided that that was precisely what he could not do? . . .

The difficulty and danger inherent in the approach adopted by the Court of Criminal Appeal is that it sets no clear limits to the extent of the cross-examination. If cross-examination is permitted because it goes to an issue raised by the defence, the judge knows where he is: he will permit cross-examination that is relevant to that issue and no more. Thus, in the present case counsel could have asked about the nature of the 'trouble' because, if it were shown to be quite trivial, it would be an inadequate excuse for manufacturing a false alibi. If the issue were different, it might be relevant to show the gravity of the trouble instead of its triviality. In other cases, it might be improper to go into the nature of the trouble at all. Relevance affords a clear guide as to what the limit should be: revelation does not. If it means no more than that the accused can be asked to repeat himself, it is at best otiose and at worst objectionable. It would, for example, be objectionable if it were done merely for the purpose of 'rubbing it in'. If the accused can be asked to do more than repeat himself, how much more? When the accused puts his whole character in issue, the door is thrown wide open; but when he puts only a part of it in issue, I can see no satisfactory way of defining a limit except by the test of relevance. I do not think that some vague rule which enables the prosecution to ask what it likes so long as it does not make out the accused's character to be substantially worse than he himself had suggested would be at all a safe guide. If, for instance, in this case the questions had not been relevant to the second alibi, I think it would have been quite wrong, just because the prisoner had mentioned a previous record and trouble with the police, to refer to an incident in the newspaper, thus running the risk that the jury might feel that they ought to pay attention to the newspaper publicity in connexion with the earlier offence.

R v Anderson   [1988] QB 678, [1988] 2 All ER 549, CA

The appellant was charged with conspiracy to cause a number of explosions, including that at the Grand Hotel, Brighton, during the Conservative Party Conference in September 1984. In the course of her evidence in chief she sought to explain the evidence against her on the basis that it was evidence not of the conspiracy charged, but of another conspiracy: a conspiracy to smuggle escaping prisoners from Ireland through Scotland to the continent of Europe, as part of which she was to accompany individual men to try to give the impression of an innocent couple on holiday, so hoodwinking immigration officers. The prosecution, who had no previous indication of this defence, sought to cross-examine her to elicit the fact that she was 'wanted' by the police in Northern Ireland. The purpose was to undermine her defence: it would surely be surprising if a person who had already attracted police notice were chosen to assist escaping prisoners in this way, because if both the couple were 'wanted' (albeit for different matters) the chances of discovery would be doubled.

Lord Lane CJ: The way in which the problem can be put is this. A defendant is faced with prosecution evidence which prima facie incriminates her of the offence charged. She puts forward in evidence an explanation of that prosecution case which is consistent with her innocence of the offence charged. The prosecution wish to cross-examine her about that explanation. Cross-examination necessarily involves questions which tend to show that she, the defendant, has committed a criminal offence, the nature of which the prosecution neither require nor intend to reveal. Are they allowed, by the terms of s 1 of the Criminal Evidence Act 1898, to ask those questions? I have no doubt the immediate reaction of the practitioner would be, 'Of course they are allowed to ask the questions. If not it would be giving the dishonest defendant an unjust and ludicrous advantage.' The same practitioner would no doubt add, 'in any event, the judge has an overriding discretion to reject the submission and disallow the questions if he thinks that they are going to produce unfairness to the defendant in the particular circumstances.'

Counsel for Anderson will not mind us saying that it seems to have been his initial reaction, and indeed was the initial reaction of the court of first instance in a number of the reported cases, that this was a matter solely of discretion. To take one or two examples, *R v Kennaway* [1917] 1 KB 25, [1916–17] All ER Rep 651 and *R v Chitson* [1909] 2 KB 945. Perhaps most surprisingly of all, also *Jones v DPP* [1962] 1 All ER 569, [1962] AC 635, which we shall have to examine in more detail in a moment. In that case, in the court at first instance, the trial judge being Sachs J, the problem of the Criminal Evidence Act 1898 hardly raised its head, if at all. It was only later when the matter came to be examined on appeal that the difficulties started to arise. This is, indeed, one of those situations where the criminal law in practice functions quite satisfactorily until one starts to subject the relevant statute to a minute scrutiny.

Section 1 of the 1898 Act is a nightmare of construction. No doubt the reasons for its difficulty may be found in its parliamentary history, but we are not allowed nor do we wish to embark on that sort of research. There is no need for me to read all the terms of the Act. Those have already been read to us and we can take them as read, but this appeal is yet another example of the perennial problem caused by the wording. Section 1(*e*) allows the accused person to be asked 'any question in cross-examination notwithstanding that it would tend to criminate him as to the offence charged'. Section 1(*f*), however, provides that he shall not be asked 'any question tending to show that he has committed or been convicted of or charged with any offence' subject to certain exceptions. Those two provisions are mutually contradictory, at least on the face of them, as has been said more than once by courts over the last 90 years. The reason for that is this: a question which tends to incriminate the defendant as to the offence charged, and so is relevant and admissible under para (*e*), may very well tend to show, and often does, that the defendant has committed another offence and so is inadmissible under para (*f*). This problem has been the subject of differing views and those differing views are exemplified by the opinions in five of their Lordships in *Jones v DPP* [1962] 1 All ER 569, [1962] AC 635.

The facts in that case are, very briefly, that Jones was charged with the murder of a young girl guide. He put forward an account of his movements which, to all intents and purposes, was the same, almost word for word, as an account he had put forward some three months earlier when he was charged with an offence of rape committed on another young girl guide. Not surprisingly the prosecution wished to cross-examine Jones about this remarkable coincidence with a view to showing that his account was false. The question obviously indicated that he had committed another offence. The Court of Criminal Appeal held that the judge was correct to have allowed the questions because they said that Jones had, in his evidence-in-chief, said that he had 'been in trouble with the police'. Since the words 'tending to show' meant 'revealing', the question asked of the defendant did not 'tend to show' the commission of a crime, because that crime had already been revealed to the jury. In other words, if the revelation regarding a previous conviction has already been made to the jury, the prohibition does not apply.

This was the basis on which the majority in the House of Lords (Viscount Simonds, Lord Reid and Lord Morris, Lord Denning and Lord Devlin dissenting) dismissed the appeal. Their Lordships, however, did not leave the matter there. They ventured on a discussion of the difficulties raised by the section, a discussion which is relevant to the present case. The majority supported the view that para (*e*) is subordinate to and governed by para (*f*)(i). Lord Reid's view was that the words of para (*e*) have two possible interpretations (see [1962] 1 All ER 569 at 575, [1962] AC 635 at 663). They could, first of all, mean 'tend to convince or persuade a jury that he [the defendant] is guilty' or, second, 'tend to connect him [the defendant] with the commission of the offence charged'. If they have the first meaning, the broader meaning, that, in Lord Reid's view, produces the insoluble conflict with para (*f*) which we mentioned a moment or two ago. If, on the other hand, they have the second meaning, the narrower meaning, there is no such conflict because para (*f*) could then apply to questions which tend to persuade a jury that the defendant is guilty. That, of course, leaves the residual problem which is not easy to answer, namely how close the connection must be with the offence to bring it within the narrower meaning of para (*e*).

Lord Denning and Lord Devlin were in the minority and we do not feel it necessary to refer to their speeches save to say that they are interesting interpretations of the 1898 Act. Lord Reid seems to have thought that it was open to the House at some time or other to reconsider the matter if it should be directly raised (see [1962] 1 All ER 569 at 577, [1962] AC 635 at 666).

In the present case there was, in the question, a clear tendency to show that Martina Anderson had committed an offence other than that with which she was charged; obviously so because otherwise she would not be 'wanted' by the police. So in the light of the decision in *Jones v DPP* the question would be admissible in any of the following circumstances, that is applying the reasoning which we have attempted to set out as explained by the House of Lords: first of all, if there was no tendency to reveal the commission of an offence as in *Jones v DPP*, for example, because the commission of an offence had already (properly) been made known to the jury; second, if the proof of the commission tended to connect the defendant with the offence charged; and, third, if the defendant had given evidence of her own good character.

The third matter can be dealt with very shortly. Counsel for Anderson did persuade the prosecution to concede that the appellant was of good character, apart from being 'wanted' by the police, but that concession was only made after the judge had ruled on the submission and consequently that would not, we are prepared to assume, be a ground for admitting the evidence under s 1(*f*) of the 1898 Act.

As to the tendency to reveal, Anderson had already revealed that it was likely that she had committed a number of offences in respect of any one of which she might well have been 'wanted' by the police. There was probably a conspiracy to assist the escape of a prisoner, probably forgery of documents, probably conspiracy to forge, possession of firearms and so on, as already set out when we detailed the evidence which she gave before the jury. Thus it was already revealed that she had committed offences, although it might be that she was not yet 'wanted' by the police in respect of them. The jury already knew, therefore, that she had committed a number of offences, and the fact that she was 'wanted' by the police in respect of an unspecified offence, and therefore was probably guilty of committing an unspecified offence, was not, on the reasoning in *Jones v DPP*, in the view of this court, a revelation to the jury.

As to the second point: does evidence which tends to destroy the defendant's innocent explanation of prima facie damning circumstances, connect the defendant with the crime so as to come within Lord Reid's analysis of the meaning of para (*e*)? We are inclined to think that it may, but we prefer to base our conclusion primarily on the fact that the appellant had already revealed that she had committed crimes.

There is however a different approach which is perhaps less artificial than the reasoning in *Jones v DPP*, if we may say so.

Section 1 of the 1898 Act did nothing to alter the pre-existing law regarding what evidence the prosecution were entitled to adduce in order to prove their case. As Lord Reid said in *Jones v DPP* [1962] 1 All ER 569 at 574, [1962] AC 635 at 662:

'These words of s 1 of the Act of 1898 have no application to evidence given by any person other than the accused: where it was competent before that Act for a witness to prove or refer to a previous conviction of the accused, that is still competent. What the Act does is to alter the old rules as regards the accused.'

The extent of that pre-existing law had been examined only four years previously in *Makin v A-G for New South Wales* [1894] AC 57, [1891–4] All ER Rep 24. Lord Herschell LC said ([1894] AC 57 at 65, [1891–4] All ER Rep 24 at 25–6):

'It is undoubtedly not competent for the prosecution to adduce evidence tending to show that the accused has been guilty of criminal acts other than those covered by the indictment for the purpose of leading to the conclusion that the accused is a person likely from his criminal conduct or character to have committed the offence for which he is being tried. On the other hand, the mere fact that the evidence adduced tends to show the commission of other crimes does not render it inadmissible if it be relevant to an issue before the jury, and it may be so relevant if it bears upon the question whether the acts alleged to constitute the crime charged in the indictment were designed or accidental, or to rebut a defence which would otherwise be open to the accused.'

Thus, if the prosecution know that a particular defence is going to be advanced, they may (subject to the judge's discretion) call evidence to rebut it as part of their own substantive case even if that tends to show the commission of other crimes. The defendant can plainly then be cross-examined about the matter. If the prosecution do not know of the defence in advance, then they may call evidence to rebut it and the defendant can then be recalled, if that is desired, to deal with the rebutting evidence. The judge in the present case, wisely, the evidence not being in dispute, allowed that somewhat laborious process to be short-circuited. The result however was just as much in accordance with authority and the 1898 Act as if the procedure had been carried out in extenso.

These considerations strengthen our view that the judge's decision in the present case was correct. There only remains to deal with the question of discretion. We take the view that there is ample authority that the judge could exercise his discretion in the way that he did. Obviously he examined the matter very closely and we, in our judgment, feel he was not only entitled to exercise his discretion as he did, but was correct in doing so.

COMMENTS

1. The minority view of the relationship between s 1(*e*) and s 1(*f*) appears to have been adopted in the construction of similar legislation in the High Court of Australia (*Attwood v R* (1960) 102 CLR 353 at 361–2, acknowledging the difficulty about the function of s 1(*f*)(i) if this interpretation is adopted) and in South Africa (Hoffmann, p 62). It was also recommended by the Criminal Law Revision Committee (CLRC para 117).
2. The Privy Council in *Malindi v R* [1967] 1 AC 439, [1966] 3 All ER 285, PC, supported the view that 'character' included disposition. It was held that where the accused was charged with conspiring for political ends to commit arson, cross-examination on passages in his notebooks stating that violence was politically necessary infringed s 1(*f*) because it suggested bad character in the sense of a disposition to resort to violence. In *R v Anderson* 'character' is clearly taken as embracing both individual criminal acts (those claimed by the defendant) and reputation (the being 'wanted'), even though the former, being previously unsuspected, can have no connexion with the latter.
3. Section 1(*f*) depends on the effect, not the motive, of the questioning: the Act does not say 'with a view to show' but 'tending to show' (*R v Ellis* [1910] 2 KB 746 at 757, [1908–10] All ER Rep 488 at 491, CCA). Counsel must not drive or trap the accused into throwing away his shield (*R v Baldwin* [1925] All ER Rep 402, CCA; *R v Eidinow* (1932) 23 Cr App Rep 145, CCA). The prohibition in s 1(*f*) applies to questions by not only prosecution counsel, but also the judge (*R v Ratcliffe* (1919) 89 LJKB 135, CCA) and counsel for a co-accused (*R v Roberts* [1936] 1 All ER 23, CCA). Further, questions falling within the prohibition may not be put unless the exceptions apply, even though on other grounds they would be permissible (*Jones v DPP* [1962] AC 635, [1962] 1 All ER 569, HL). But the proviso does not prevent the accused tendering his own record (ibid at 663, 575, per Lord Reid). When inadmissible evidence accidentally gets before the jury the judge has three choices. He can discharge the jury and recommence the trial; he can direct the jury to take no account of the evidence (*R v Palmer* [1983] Crim LR 252, CA); or, if he thinks the first course too drastic and the second too likely to concentrate the jury's minds on the evidence which they may have forgotten, he can say nothing (see *R v Weaver* [1968] 1 QB 353, [1967] 1 All ER 277, CA).

4. In *Jones v DPP* and *R v Anderson* the initial evidence showing bad character was put in by the defence. It has the same effect if given by prosecution
witnesses, provided it is validly admitted. The evidence of the prosecutrix in *R
v Chitson* [1909] 2 KB 945, CCA, and of the accomplices testifying for the
prosecution in *R v Kennaway* [1917] 1 KB 25, [1916–17] All ER Rep 651,
CCA, was held to permit cross-examination on the accused's bad character
thus revealed, because it tended to reveal nothing new; and in *R v Anderson*
the fact that the prosecution *could* have tendered evidence of the accused's
bad character to rebut her defence was adduced as an alternative reason for
the decision: [1988] QB 678 at 689, [1988] 2 All ER 549 at 556, CA. It is
this inclusion of prior or potential *prosecution* evidence which really minimises
the benefit for the defendant of the *Jones* majority's narrow interpretation of
s 1(*e*) and broad interpretation of s 1(*f*). The Criminal Law Revision Committee recommended that the doubt about the meaning of 'tending to show'
be resolved by a statutory amendment adopting the majority view: CLRC
para 117.

FURTHER READING

McNamara, 9 Adel LR 290 (1983); [1988] Crim LR 298; Tapper, 51 MLR
785; Munday [1990] Crim LR 92.

QUESTIONS

1. Evaluate the arguments for the views of the majority and of the minority in
Jones v DPP on the relationship between s 1(*e*) and s 1(*f*).
2. Consider the views of the majority and the minority in *Jones* on the meaning of 'tending to show', and in particular, (a) whether, given the words of the
statute, the words could have been interpreted so as to refer only to revelations
made as part of the defence case (cf Comment 3 above); (b) whether, given
the words of the statute and the binding authority of *Jones v DPP* the Court of
Appeal in *R v Anderson* could have held the cross-examination to be prohibited
by s 1(*f*); (c) whether the decision in *R v Anderson* gives any cause for concern.

2   When the prohibition is lifted: the exceptions to section 1(*f*)

In effect there are four classes of exception in the three paragraphs of s 1(*f*),
for s 1(*f*)(ii) comprises two distinct 'limbs'.

SECTION 1(*f*)(i)

This paragraph covers principally cross-examination on admissible 'similar
fact' evidence, but also convictions proved under special statutory exceptions
(see ch 10, ante). Had it not been enacted, the similar fact rule, so far as it is a

rule of inclusion, would have been largely abolished by the main part of s 1(*f*). Cross-examination under s 1(*f*)(i) is permissible whether or not the Crown has first adduced evidence in chief to prove that the accused committed the other crime. Section 1(*f*)(i) requires only that the evidence be 'admissible', not that it 'has been admitted' (*Jones v DPP* [1962] AC 635 at 685, [1962] 1 All ER 569 at 589, HL). 'Nevertheless we think it might in general be undesirable that such matter should be first adduced in cross-examination; in a case, unlike the present, in which the accused desired to dispute or explain the alleged similarity of circumstances or pattern of the two offences he would thereby both be deprived of any opportunity to cross-examine prosecution witnesses and be exposed to the gravely prejudicial effect of suggestive questions to which his negative answers might be of no avail' (*Jones v DPP* [1962] AC 635 at 646, [1961] 3 All ER 668 at 675, CCA; see also Lord Denning at 668 and [1962] 1 All ER 569 at 578, and Lord Morris at 685 and [1962] 1 All ER 569 at 589).

The paragraph refers only to cases where 'the proof that he has committed or been convicted of such other offence is admissible evidence to show that he is guilty'. So even if it is logically relevant to show that he was *acquitted* on the previous occasion, he cannot be cross-examined under this paragraph: *R v Cokar* [1960] 2 QB 207, [1960] 2 All ER 175, CCA. Unless the questions are directly relevant to guilt (s 1(*e*) as interpreted in *Jones v DPP*) or the jury know the accused is of bad character (so that s 1(*f*) does not apply) he therefore cannot be asked about his previous *successful* defences. (Cf *R v Unsworth* [1986] Tas R 173.)

THE FIRST LIMB OF SECTION 1(*f*)(ii)

What is usually called 'the first limb of s 1(*f*)(ii)' permits cross-examination on the accused's record if he seeks to establish 'his good character'. The paragraph applies when the accused gives evidence of his previous law-abiding conduct, eg returning lost property to its owner (*R v Samuel* (1956) 40 Cr App Rep 8, CCA) or regular religious observance (*R v Ferguson* (1909) 2 Cr App Rep 250, CCA). But whether a statement amounts to an assertion of the accused's good character must in general be a matter of degree for the judge (*R v Stronach* [1988] Crim LR 48, CA). To attack the character of a person not called as a prosecution witness is not to assert one's own good character: *R v Lee* [1976] 1 All ER 570, [1976] 1 WLR 71. The paragraph does not apply when a defence witness praises the accused's character without being asked to (*R v Redd* [1923] 1 KB 104, [1922] All ER Rep 435, CCA), nor when the accused asserts that the circumstances surrounding the crime show him to be innocent (*R v Ellis* [1910] 2 KB 746, [1908–10] All ER Rep 488, CCA; *Malindi v R* [1967] 1 AC 439 at 543, [1966] 3 All ER 285 at 293, PC). It was held not to apply when the accused said he had once been fined in order to show that he feared being arrested for not paying the fine and had therefore run away from a policeman: he did not mean to suggest that this was his only conviction (*R v Thompson* [1966] 1 All ER 505, CCA; and see *R v Wattam* (1952) 36 Cr App Rep 72 at 78, CCA). The wording of the paragraph limits in several ways the circumstances in which the shield will be lost.

It does not apply where the evidence of good character is given in chief by prosecution witnesses, or in cross-examination by defence witnesses, nor where it is merely incidental to some other matter (*Malindi v R* [1967] 1 AC 439, [1966] 3 All ER 285, PC; *R v Stronach* [1988] Crim LR 48, CA).

THE SECOND LIMB OF SECTION 1(*f*)(ii)

R v Hudson   [1912] 2 KB 464, CCA

Lord Alverstone CJ (giving the judgment of a full court): We think that the words of the section, 'unless the nature or conduct of the defence is such as to involve imputations,' &c, must receive their ordinary and natural interpretation, and that it is not legitimate to qualify them by adding or inserting the words 'unnecessarily', or 'unjustifiably', or 'for purposes other than that of developing the defence', or other similar words.

Selvey v Director of Public Prosecutions   [1970] AC 304, [1968] 2 All ER 497, HL

The accused was charged with committing buggery on a young man. The prosecution evidence included, apart from the complainant's testimony, medical evidence that the complainant had been sexually interfered with and indecent photographs found in the accused's room. The accused denied the charge; denied knowledge of the photographs and alleged that they had been planted; and said that the complainant had told him in the accused's room on the afternoon of the relevant day that he was 'prepared to go on the bed' and that already that day he had permitted an act of buggery on himself for £1 and would do the same again for money. Stable J asked the accused whether he was inviting the jury to disbelieve the complainant because he was 'that sort of young man'; the accused said: 'Yes.' Stable J then permitted cross-examination on the accused's record; he warned the jury that the only relevance of the record was to prove lack of credibility. The accused's appeals against conviction failed before the Court of Criminal Appeal and the House of Lords.

Viscount Dilhorne: The cases to which I have referred, some of which it is not possible to reconcile, in my opinion finally establish the following propositions:

(1) The words of the statute must be given their ordinary natural meaning (*R v Hudson* [1912] 2 KB 464, CCA; *R v Jenkins* (1945) 114 LJKB 425, CCA; *R v Cook* [1959] 2 QB 340, [1959] 2 All ER 97, CCA).

(2) The section permits cross-examination of the accused as to character both when imputations on the character of the prosecutor and his witness are cast to show their unreliability as witnesses independently of the evidence given by them and also when the casting of such imputations is necessary to enable the accused to establish his defence (*R v Hudson; R v Jenkins; R v Cook*).

(3) In rape cases the accused can allege consent without placing himself in peril of such cross-examination (*R v Sheean* (1908) 21 Cox CC 561; *R v Turner* [1944] KB 463, [1944] 1 All ER 599, CCA). This may be because such cases are sui generis (per Devlin J in *R v Cook* [1959] 2 QB 340 at 347, [1959] 2 All ER 97 at 101), or on the ground that the issue is one raised by the prosecution.

(4) If what is said amounts in reality to no more than a denial of the charge, expressed, it may be, in emphatic language, it should not be regarded as coming within the section (*R v Rouse* [1904] 1 KB 184; *R v Grout* (1909) 74 JP 30, CCA; *R v Jones* (1923) 87 JP 147, CCA; *R v Clark* [1955] 2 QB 469, [1955] 3 All ER 29, CCA).

Applying these propositions to this case, it is in my opinion clear beyond all doubt that the cross-examination of the accused was permissible under the statute.

Lord Pearce (agreed and said): My Lords, ever since the Criminal Evidence Act 1898 came into force there has been difficulty and argument about the application of the words in section 1(*f*)(ii) 'the nature of conduct of the defence is such as to involve imputations on the character of the prosecutor or the witnesses for the prosecution.'

Two main views have been put forward. One view adopts the literal meaning of the words. The prosecutor is cross-examined to show that he has fabricated the charge for improper reasons. That involves imputations on his character. Therefore, it lets in the previous convictions of the accused. The practical justification for this view is the 'tit for tat' argument. If the accused is seeking to cast discredit on the prosecution, then the prosecution should be allowed to do likewise. If the accused is seeking to persuade the jury that the prosecutor behaved like a knave, then the jury should know the character of the man who makes these accusations, so that it may judge fairly between them instead of being in the dark as to one of them.

The other view would limit the literal meaning of the words. For it cannot, it is said, have been intended by Parliament to make a man liable to have his previous convictions revealed whenever the essence of his defence necessitates imputations on the character of the prosecutor. This revelation is always damaging and often fatal to a defence. The high-water mark of this argument is the ordinary case of rape. In this the vital issue (as a rule) is whether the woman consented. Consent (as a rule) involves imputations on her character. Therefore, in the ordinary case of rape, the accused cannot defend himself without letting in his previous convictions. The same argument extends in varying lesser degrees to many cases.

The argument in favour of a construction more liberal to the accused is supported in two ways.

First, it is said that character is used in the sense in which it was used in *R v Rowton* (1865) Le & Ca 520, where the full court ruled that evidence of good character must be limited solely to general reputation and not to a man's actual disposition . . .

. . . [I]t might be justifiable to consider whether 'character' means in the context solely general reputation, if a reassessment could lead to any clarification of the problem. But in my opinion it leads nowhere. For I cannot accept the proposition that to accuse a person of a particular knavery does not involve imputations on his general reputation. The words 'involve' and 'imputations' are wide. It would be playing with words to say that the allegation of really discreditable matters does not involve imputations on his general reputation, if only as showing how erroneous that reputation must be. The argument is, however, a valuable reminder that the Act is intending serious and not trivial imputations.

The second part of the argument in favour of a construction more liberal to the accused is concerned with the words 'the conduct or nature of the defence'. One should, it can be argued, read conduct or nature as something superimposed on the essence of the defence itself. In *O'Hara v HM Advocate* 1948 JC 90 at 98 the learned Lord Justice-Clerk (Lord Thomson), after a careful review of the English cases, construed 'conduct' as meaning the actual handling of the case by the accused or his advocate. He found difficulty with 'nature' but said:

'But the more general considerations which I have mentioned persuade me to the view that "nature" is to be read, not as meaning something which is inherent in the defence, but as referable to the mechanism of the defence; nature being the strategy of the defence and conduct the tactics.'

This argument has obvious force, particularly in a case of rape, where the allegation of consent is in truth no more than a mere traverse of the essential ingredient which the Crown have to prove, namely, want of consent. But the argument does not, and I think cannot, fairly stop short of contending that *all* matters which are relevant to the crime, that is, of which rebutting evidence could be proved, are excluded from the words 'conduct or nature of the defence'.

To take the present case as an example, the evidence having established physical signs on the victim of the alleged offence, his admission that he had previously committed it with somebody else was relevant. So, too, was his admission that he had been paid £1 for it, since, when the conversation was relevant, it could not be right to bowdlerise it. And, therefore, it is said, the putting of the allegation in cross-examination and the evidence given by the accused was an essentially relevant part of the defence and therefore was not within the words 'the nature or conduct of the defence'. If Mr Jeremy Hutchison's forceful argument on the proper construction of the subsection is right, the story told by the accused did not let in the convictions.

So large a gloss upon the words is not easy to justify, even if one were convinced that it necessarily produced a fair and proper result which Parliament intended. But there are two sides to the matter. So liberal a shield for an accused is in many cases unfair to a prosecution.

[Lord Guest, Lord Hodson and Lord Wilberforce agreed.]

COMMENTS

1. The harshness of the *R v Hudson* doctrine as approved in *Selvey v DPP* is qualified by two glosses on the meaning of 'imputation' and (possibly) one on the meaning of 'the nature or conduct of the defence'.

(a) In *R v Turner* a full Court of Criminal Appeal held that for the accused in a rape case to allege consent on the part of a complainant was not an imputation despite the suggestion that the complainant was a dangerous liar and possibly promiscuous. The court said, in defiance of *R v Hudson*, that 'some limitation must be placed on the words of the section, since to decide otherwise would be to do grave injustice never intended by Parliament'. Indeed the case was a strong one, involving an allegation not only that the victim consented but that she initiated intercourse by an act of gross indecency on the accused ([1944] KB 463, [1944] 1 All ER 599, CCA). The merit of the *R v Turner* doctrine is thus that the accused can advance his entire defence – his view of all the events – with impunity. It was approved in *Selvey v DPP*. If the accused wishes to support his defence of consent by reference to the complainant's sexual experience with others, he will need the judge's leave (Sexual Offences (Amendment) Act 1976, s 2), but if the result is that the complainant is shown to be generally of loose morals s 1(*f*)(ii) still apparently does not come into play (*R v Krausz* (1973) 57 Cr App Rep 466, CA; cf Phipson, pp 18–40). Three possible bases of the *R v Turner* doctrine have been advanced. One is that it is an exception to the *R v Hudson* doctrine which is sui generis because of the peculiar harshness of applying *R v Hudson* to rape. But if the basis of *R v Hudson* is that the courts must obey the clearly expressed rule of Parliament, despite any hardships this causes, the same should apply to rape; and if it is legitimate to temper the statutory words in rape cases it must be legitimate to do so elsewhere. The injustice of not being able to run a proper defence to rape is no greater than not being able to run a proper defence to any other crime. A second basis of *R v Turner* is that since in rape the prosecution must prove non-consent, the accused in alleging consent is doing no more than denying the charge. But why should the accused's right to conduct his defence properly depend on whether his defence raises an issue on which the prosecution bears some burden of proof rather than he? The third basis of *R v Turner* is that rape is an area where the court's discretion to prevent cross-examination on the record will always be exercised in the accused's favour; but a discretion always exercised the same way can scarcely be called a discretion. Despite these problems, the existence of the *R v Turner* qualification is now beyond doubt.

(b) The other major limitation on the *R v Hudson* doctrine was first clearly stated in *R v Rouse*. The accused said of the chief prosecution witness's evidence: 'It is a lie and he is a liar.' This was held not to be an imputation because it was 'a plea of not guilty put in forcible language such as would not be unnatural in a person in the defendant's rank in life' ([1904] 1 KB 184 at 186). It is thus possible to plead not guilty, and to deny particular facts alleged by the prosecution. It is even possible to make express attacks on the prosecution that do not elaborate too greatly the inferences often to be drawn from contradicting the prosecution, mainly that their witnesses are lying. To suggest a reason for a prosecution witness's lie is not an imputation unless the reason itself imputes bad character: to say that a witness lied because he wanted his wife to be out of contact with the accused is not an imputation because to be unhappily married is not a sign of bad character (*R v Manley* (1962) 126 JP 316, CCA). The more elaborate and explicit the attack, the more likely it is that an imputation has been made. It is not an imputation to call a man a liar, but it is to say 'his brother won't speak to him because he is a horrible liar' (*R v Rappolt* (1911) 6 Cr App Rep 156, CCA). Examples of imputations include statements that a prosecution witness is promiscuous (eg *R v Jenkins* (1945) 114 LJKB 425, CCA); a homosexual (*R v Bishop* [1975] QB 274, [1974] 2 All ER 1206, CA); in charge of a disorderly house (*R v Morrison* (1911) 6 Cr App Rep 159, CCA); a thief (*R v Morris* (1959) 43 Cr App Rep 206, CCA); a police agent (and hence biased) (*R v Fisher* [1964] NZLR 1063); motivated by spite, revenge or self-interest (eg *R v McLean* (1926) 19 Cr App Rep 104); and party to the offence (*R v Hudson* [1912] 2 KB 464, CCA). To deny making a confession is one thing, because it may simply imply that the police mistook what was said; but it is an imputation to say that the police induced confessions (eg *R v Cook* [1959] 2 QB 340, [1959] 2 All ER 97, CCA); or fabricated them by dictating them and making the accused sign (*R v Clark* [1955] 2 QB 469, [1955] 3 All ER 29, CCA); or obtained remands in order to fabricate evidence (*R v Jones* (1923) 87 JP 147, CCA); or suppressed evidence favouring the defence (*R v Billings* [1961] VR 127); or conspired in advance to concoct a story (*R v Davies* [1963] Crim LR 192, CCA); or to plant evidence on the accused (*R v Curbishley* [1963] Crim LR 778, CCA). See also *R v Tanner* (1977) 66 Cr App Rep 56, CA. The attribution to the prosecutor of drunken and incompetent driving and the abuse of other drivers is an imputation (*R v Brown* (1960) 124 JP 391, CCA). So though the *Rouse* doctrine permits one to deny allegations, it does not permit the raising of the details which might make that denial credible. In particular, as Latham CJ has pointed out, it must tempt the police to extract confessions by violence from persons of bad character who cannot set up the violence at their trial for fear of exposing their records (*Kerwood v R* (1944) 69 CLR 561 at 577). In *R v Britzman* [1983] 1 All ER 369 at 373, [1983] 1 WLR 350 at 355, CA, the Court of Appeal said that cross-examination should not be allowed if there is merely a denial, however emphatic or offensively made, of an act or even a short series of acts amounting to one incident or in what was said to have been a short interview. But if the accused denies a long interview or the evidence of a long period of observation he is almost by necessity implying that the police evidence is fabricated and so casting imputations on the prosecution witnesses.

(c) Some courts have acted on the view that the words 'nature or conduct of the defence' require them not to act on remarks of the accused which are 'incidental' to the defence. In a way this is the reverse of the doctrine denied in *R v Hudson*. The 'necessity' doctrine is that a remark necessary to the defence is not an imputation; this doctrine is that a remark *unnecessary* to the defence is not an imputation. The English authorities are all old (*R v Preston* [1909] 1 KB 568, CCA; *R v Jones* (1909) 3 Cr App Rep 67, CCA) and it is doubtful whether they can stand with *Selvey v DPP*. It is probable that today an English court would deal with an incidental loss of the accused's shield by exercising its discretion to disallow cross-examination: section 3C, post.

2. The literal reading of the paragraph approved in *Selvey v DPP* is often thought to be unduly narrow, because it makes it very difficult for the accused with a record to raise a defence in any detail where he contradicts the prosecution rather than explaining away facts which the prosecution allege against him. Whatever the drawbacks of the literal interpretation or the merits of rival arguments the former is undoubtedly the law in England since *Selvey v DPP*. In other jurisdictions there are two main lines of argument sometimes leading to a different result.

   (a) The *Dawson v R* (1961) 106 CLR 1 doctrine (often called the *Kerwood v R* (1944) 69 CLR 561 doctrine, but this is a misnomer, for the doctrine was first stated in *Dawson's* Case and has never been repeated) is that no imputation exists where the accused states expressly what would follow implicitly from his evidence denying the Crown case and the evidence supporting it. 'The question is not one depending on forms of expression, the use of phrases, the stating explicitly what is implicit.' An imputation depends on 'the use of matter which will have a particular or specific tendency to destroy, impair or reflect upon the character of the prosecutor or witnesses called for the prosecution, quite independently of the possibility that such matter, were it true, would in itself provide a defence' (1961) 106 CLR 1 at 9–10 and 13–14, per Dixon CJ). The merit of these views is that they advance to the full logical extent of the position taken up in *R v Rouse*. They deny the relevance of any distinction between inferring fabrication or lying and expressly stating it. *R v Rouse* represents a practical watering down of the strictest *R v Hudson* position but involves an illogical distinction between inferences from denials and (except in the case of assertions about lies) express statements of impropriety. Dixon CJ would have destroyed that illogically. Thus in *Dawson v R* itself the accused denied guilt, denied confessing to the police and alleged that the police had invented most of the questions and answers in his record of interview. Dixon CJ considered the latter remark not to be an imputation because it said no more than could be inferred from the accused's other denials. The majority of the High Court of Australia disagreed.

   (b) The 'necessity' argument is that any attack on the prosecution which the accused has to make in putting up his defence should be permissible: see Runciman, para 8.31. A number of different avenues have been used to reach this destination, and the precise destination sometimes varies accordingly.

   One avenue is frankly expediency. The section would be entirely harsh and unworkable unless something is done to moderate the strictness of the words. The Parliamentary legislation will cause injustice unless it is amended by judicial legislation. It is unwise to rely solely on the use of the judge's discretion for this will vary in its operation from judge to judge. In any event there was no general discretion to exclude evidence in 1898, so that Parliament must have intended the Act to be made workable in some other way.

   A second avenue turns on the view that 'character' means 'general reputation' rather than disposition or conduct. To say a policeman induced a confession is not an attack on his reputation – on what the world thinks of him – it merely asserts bad behaviour. In 1898 it was very likely that this was the meaning of 'character' because the Court for Crown Cases Reserved, with thirteen judges sitting and two dissenting, had decided in *R v Rowton* that evidence of the accused's 'character' must be confined to evidence of reputation

((1865) Le & Ca 520, [1861–73] All ER Rep 549). Parliament must have thought that the prosecutor's 'character' would have the same meaning; a legislator of 1898 would have seen no point in being more precise. This argument is historically strong, but though it has some followers still (notably Lord Devlin in *Jones v DPP* [1962] AC 635 at 710–11, [1962] 1 All ER 569 at 605, HL) and has been considered intrinsically 'formidable', it has been ignored by too large a mass of inconsistent authority since *R v Dunkley* [1927] 1 KB 323 at 329, [1926] All ER Rep 187 at 190.

A third avenue has been relied on in Scotland. Just as the accused cannot raise his own good character independently of the issues in the case without throwing away his shield under the first limb of s 1(*f*)(ii), so he cannot make a general attack on a prosecution witness's good character under the second limb. 'But it is one thing to attack the character of a witness generally and another to do so inferentially by asking questions which are relevant to the defence and, indeed, without which the true facts cannot be ascertained' (*O'Hara v HM Advocate* 1948 JC 90 at 98). This is essentially the distinction between cross-examining to the issue and cross-examining to credit.

A fourth avenue depends on the argument that the 'nature or conduct of the defence' must refer to 'something superimposed on the essence of the defence itself' (*Selvey v DPP* [1970] AC 304 at 354, [1968] 2 All ER 497 at 522, HL per Lord Pearce).

Fifthly, Lanham has pointed out ((1972) 5 NZULR 21 at 34) that under the first limb of s 1(*f*)(ii), the shield is not lost if the accused gives evidence of good character relevant to his defence. In *Malindi v R* [1967] 1 AC 439, [1966] 3 All ER 285, PC the accused, charged with conspiracy to commit arson, was held by the Privy Council not to have thrown away his shield by giving evidence that at certain meetings he disagreed with and disapproved of violence. If evidence of the accused's good character necessary for the development of his defence can be admitted without loss of the shield under the first limb of s 1(*f*)(ii), why cannot evidence of a prosecution witness's bad character be admitted under the second? The answer may lie in the difference between the words 'with a view to' in the first limb of s 1(*f*)(ii) and 'is such as to' in the second.

The final test, of which little has been made, is one of proportionality. An attack should not be an imputation unless it is serious enough to justify the accused being subjected to the dangerous consequences of losing his shield (*R v Westfall* (1912) 7 Cr App Rep 176 at 179). This approach has sometimes been used in connexion with the court's exercise of its discretion to prevent cross-examination after the shield has been thrown away. But it seems too uncertain to use as a rule of construction; and it is hard to see why the admissibility of the record should be controlled by what the defence is. '[I]f the conduct of the interviewer was criminal, the defendant must impute criminality . . . [T]he defendant does not choose what conduct he will have the police officer adopt in questioning him' (Lanham (1972) 5 NZULR 21 at 35).

3. Section 1(*f*)(ii) as a whole does not cause the defendant to lose his shield if he attacks the character of a person not called as a prosecution witness (*R v Lee* [1976] 1 All ER 570, [1976] 1 WLR 71, CA), unless that person is the deceased victim of the alleged offence. Nor does it apply if the prosecution deliberately trap the accused into making statements which would cause him to lose his shield: *R v Grout* (1909) 3 Cr App Rep 64, CCA. If he attacks the prosecution's witnesses without himself testifying, his record cannot be admitted under s 1(*f*), which refers only to questions asked in cross-examination (*R v Butterwasser* [1948] 1 KB 4, [1947] 2 All ER 415, CCA). But if he calls witnesses who testify to his good character, his record can be put to them in rebuttal: *R v Redd* [1923] 1 KB 104, CCA; *R v Winfield* [1939] 4 All ER 164.

The judge should warn the defence when the shield is about to be lost, at any rate under the second limb: *R v Cook* [1959] 2 QB 340, [1959] 2 All ER 97, CCA, though failure to do so will not necessarily cause a conviction to be quashed (*Selvey v DPP* [1970] AC 304 at 342, [1968] 2 All ER 497 at 510, HL).

4. Even when the defendant has thrown away his shield, the right to cross-examine him under s 1(*f*)(ii) is subject to the judge's discretion to disallow questions: see section 3C, post. The recognition of this discretion is relatively recent in this as in other areas of the law of evidence. But the use of judicial discretion to overcome the problems of the section should be regarded as at most an ancillary aid for the following reasons. It leads to uncertainty in practice and differences from judge to judge: the accused's counsel will therefore never know how far the defence can safely go. Reliance on discretion to solve evidentiary problems tends to confuse settled rules of law and to cause loss of contact with fundamental principle; and it tends towards the reversal of established rules without express recognition of or adequate reason for the change. (See Livesey [1968] CLJ 290 at 302–9.)

5. What should be done about the second limb of s 1(*f*)(ii)? The rule in *Selvey's* Case tends to prevent an accused with a record proving misconduct in the prosecutor or impropriety in the making of a confession which is necessary to the accused's defence. It shares with the 'necessity' doctrine the difficulty that the accused is deterred from attacking the prosecution's general credibility when this is, because of an undoubtedly bad record, highly suspect, particularly since the judge has no duty to acquaint the jury with a prosecution witness's record if defence counsel has chosen not to (*R v Carey* (1968) 52 Cr App Rep 305, CA). There is no equivalent rule deterring the prosecution from attacking defence witnesses. The prosecution may reveal the bad character of their own witness to the jury, but the accused ought not to have to rely on the prosecution's discretion (Humphreys [1955] Crim LR 739 at 742). The rule is itself an exception, against the accused, to the normal rules encouraging full freedom of speech in court, and its limitations are anomalous. Admittedly one effect of the rule is to ensure fairness to the impugned witness. 'A respectable man who was obliged to give evidence against his assailant or traducer may well feel a deep sense of injustice if he is subjected to a series of unfounded accusations by someone whom practically everyone except the jury before whom the farce is enacted knows to be a man with a criminal record' (Cross (1969) 6 Syd LR 173 at p 181). This may make respectable people unwilling to complain of crime and act as witnesses. But this problem is probably better handled in some other way. The judge has power to stop defence counsel offending in this way (*R v Billings* [1961] VR 127 at 136–7). Cross suggests that it might be desirable for the jury which tried the case to be reconvened to decide the further question of whether the accused committed perjury, or for

the court to take irresponsibility in conducting the defence into account in determining the sentence (op cit, p 181). But to rely on loss of the shield as a disincentive to perjury is unsatisfactory.

Some members of the Criminal Law Revision Committee were not persuaded by these arguments and indeed would have preferred the accused to be treated in every respect as an ordinary witness. The majority were against this for the above reasons and on the additional ground that such a change would, as in Canada and the United States, induce the accused with a record not to testify and thus reduce the value of the trial as a means of determining the truth. Another minority favoured the complete repeal of the second limb of s 1(*f*)(ii). But the majority favoured amendment so that the accused would only throw away his shield by asking questions of which 'the main purpose . . . was to raise an issue as to the witness's credibility'. If the shield is thrown away, the cross-examination of the accused must be relevant only to his *credibility*, which may be intended to suggest that for this purpose his character is to be divisible, so that only lying or dishonest conduct can be put to him. The final suggested change is that imputations on the *prosecutor*, as opposed to a prosecution witness, should no longer throw away the shield (11th Report, para 128). These changes were in substance enacted in New South Wales in 1974: see Crimes Act 1900–74, ss 413A and 413B.

QUESTIONS

1. X, an accused person, (*a*) denies on oath making and signing a long detailed confession of assault; (*b*) says it was fabricated by the police; and (*c*) says that his defence is that he had to resist violently the victim's improper advances. Would (*a*), (*b*) or (*c*) have the effect of the accused's shield being lost under (i) the law stated in *Selvey v DPP*; (ii) the law stated by Dixon CJ in *Dawson v R*; (iii) the 'necessity' doctrine?
2. Would it be desirable to allow the accused to indulge in normal cross-examination of prosecution witnesses as to credit?

FURTHER READING

Griew [1961] Crim LR 142, 213; Lanham, 5 NZULR 21; Heydon, 7 Syd LR 166.

SECTION 1(*f*)(iii)

R v Varley   [1982] 2 All ER 519, CA

Varley and Dibble were jointly charged with robbery. Dibble said in evidence that they had both participated in the robbery, but that he had acted under duress from Varley. Varley said that Dibble's evidence was untrue and that he, Varley, had not taken any part in the robbery. The trial judge allowed Dibble's counsel to cross-examine Varley on his previous convictions under s 1(*f*)(iii).

Kilner Brown J: . . . The operation of this particular part of the proviso seems to have given rise to no difficulty and no detailed analysis for well over 60 years. No doubt, as Lord Pearce indicated in his speech in *Murdoch v Taylor* [1965] 1 All ER 406 at 411, [1965] AC 574 at 586, 'the practice and the general view of bench and bar alike was that a judge had a discretion whether to give leave to cross-examine under s 1(*f*)(iii)' and, in difficult cases where it was not easy to determine whether the evidence could be categorised as 'against' or where such questioning could well be unduly prejudicial, a judge would decline to rule that the proposed questions could be put. But this discretionary power was removed from trial judges by the Court of Criminal Appeal in *R v Ellis* [1961] 2 All ER 928, [1961] 1 WLR 1064, when it was decided that cross-examination of a co-defendant who have given evidence against a person jointly charged with him was a matter of right and not of discretion.

The decision was approved by four of the Lords of Appeal (Lord Pearce dissenting) in *Murdoch's* case [1965] 1 All ER 406, [1965] AC 574. This decision created difficult problems in practice because either to establish or to destroy this right involved, in many cases, an acute analysis of whether or not the evidence which had been given was 'against' the other party charged. It sparked off a whole series of cases which have come before this court and at least the one (*Murdoch's* case) in the House of Lords. The instant case is a very good example of the additional burden placed on the trial judge. The application and the resistance to it occupied many hours of judicial time and took up no less than 57 pages of recorded transcript.

Although the judgment of the Court of Criminal Appeal in *R v Stannard* [1964] 1 All ER 34, [1965] 2 QB 1 was undoubtedly meant to have been of assistance to trial judges in their consideration of whether evidence was 'against' or not, in practice, it has in fact added to their burden and it has caused considerable anxiety to other divisions of this court as it did to Lord Reid and was tacitly ignored by Lord Morris in *Murdoch's* case. What was the nature of the guidance in *R v Stannard* [1964] 1 All ER 34, [1965] 2 QB 1? It was this, approved and amended by Lord Donovan in *Murdoch's* case [1965] 1 All ER 406 at 416, [1965] AC 574 at 592: ' . . . "evidence against" means evidence which supports the prosecution's case in a material respect or which undermines the defence of the co-accused.' There are three reported cases in the Court of Appeal, Criminal Division, in which this interpretation has been considered and to which we were referred. They are *R v Davis (Alan Douglas)* [1975] 1 All ER 233, [1975] 1 WLR 345, *R v Bruce* [1975] 3 All ER 277, [1975] 1 WLR 1252 and *R v Hatton* (1976) 64 Cr App R 88. Now, putting all the reported cases together, are there established principles which might serve as guidance to trial judges when called on to give rulings in this very difficult area of the law? We venture to think that they are these and, if they are borne in mind, it may not be necessary to investigate all the relevant authorities. (1) If it is established that a person jointly charged has given evidence against the co-defendant that defendant has a right to cross-examine the other as to previous convictions and the trial judge has no discretion to refuse an application. (2) Such evidence may be given either in chief or during cross-examination. (3) It has to be objectively decided whether the evidence either supports the prosecution case in a material respect or undermines the defence of the co-accused. A hostile intent is irrelevant. (4) If consideration has to be given to the undermining of the other's defence care must be taken to see that the evidence clearly undermines the defence. Inconvenience to or inconsistency with the other's defence is not of itself sufficient. (5) Mere denial of participation in a joint venture is not of itself sufficient to rank as evidence against the co-defendant. For the proviso to apply, such denial must lead to the conclusion that if the witness did not participate then it must have been the other who did. (6) Where the one defendant asserts or in due course would assert one view of the joint venture which is directly contradicted by the other such contradiction may be evidence against the co-defendant.

We apply these principles to the facts of this case and particularly the latter two. Here was Dibble going to say, as he did, that he took part in the joint venture because he was forced to do so by Varley. The appellant, Varley, was saying that he was not a participant and had not gone with Dibble and had not forced Dibble to go. His evidence therefore was against Dibble because it amounted to saying that not only was Dibble telling lies but that Dibble would be left as a participant on his own and not acting under duress. In our view, the judge was right to rule that cross-examination as to previous convictions was permissible.

COMMENTS

1. Evidence by an accused which, if believed, would lead to the acquittal of the co-accused is not evidence 'against' the latter, even if it is inconsistent with

the latter's defence: *R v Zangoullas* [1962] Crim LR 544, CCA; *R v Bruce* [1975] 3 All ER 277, [1975] 1 WLR 1252, CA. The question is whether the effect of the accused's evidence on his co-accused is to 'have dropped him completely in it' (*R v Adair* [1990] Crim LR 571, CA, per Ward J).

2. The fact that the co-accused's case is hopeless does not mean that the accused cannot undermine it and so bring s 1(*f*)(iii) into play: *R v Mir, Ahmed and Dalil* [1989] Crim LR 894, CA.

FURTHER READING

Dennis [1983] CLP 177.

3 The consequences of lifting the prohibition

A RELEVANCE

Maxwell v Director of Public Prosecutions   [1935] AC 309, [1934] All ER Rep 168, HL

The accused was charged with manslaughter of a woman in the course of procuring an abortion. He gave evidence of his good character and was asked in cross-examination about a previous acquittal on the same charge. The House of Lords quashed his conviction.

Viscount Sankey LC: The substantive part of that proviso is negative in form and as such is universal and is absolute unless the exceptions come into play. Then come the three exceptions: but it does not follow that when the absolute prohibition is superseded by a permission, that the permission is as absolute as the prohibition. When it is sought to justify a question it must not only be brought within the terms of the permission, but also must be capable of justification according to the general rules of evidence and in particular must satisfy the test of relevance. Exception (i) deals with the former of the two main classes of evidence referred to above, that is, evidence falling within the rule that where issues of intention or design are involved in the charge or defence, the prisoner may be asked questions relevant to these matters, even though he has himself raised no question of his good character. Exceptions (ii) and (iii) come into play where the prisoner by himself or his witnesses has put his character in issue, or has attacked the character of others. Dealing with exceptions (i) and (ii), it is clear that the test of relevance is wider in (ii) than in (i); in the latter, proof that the prisoner has committed or been convicted of some other offence can only be admitted if it goes to show that he was guilty of the offence charged. In the former (exception (ii)), the questions permissible must be relevant to the issue of his own good character and if not so relevant cannot be admissible. But it seems clear that the mere fact of a charge cannot in general be evidence of bad character or be regarded otherwise than as a misfortune. It seemed to be contended on behalf of the respondent that a charge was per se such evidence that the man charged, even though acquitted, must therefore remain under a cloud, however innocent. I find it impossible to accept any such view. The mere fact that a man has been charged with an offence is no proof that he committed the offence. Such a fact is, therefore, irrelevant; it neither goes to show that the prisoner did the acts for which he is actually being tried nor does it go to his credibility as a witness. Such questions must, therefore, be excluded on the principle which is fundamental in the law of evidence as conceived in this country, especially in criminal cases, because, if allowed, they are likely to lead the minds of the jury astray into false issues; not merely do they tend to introduce suspicion as if it were evidence, but they tend to distract the jury from the true issue – namely, whether the prisoner in fact committed the offence on which he is actually standing his trial. It is of the utmost importance for a fair trial that the evidence should be prima facie limited to matters relating to the transaction which forms the subject of the indictment and that any departure from these matters should be strictly confined.

It does not result from this conclusion that the word 'charged' in proviso (*f*) is otiose: it is clearly not so as regards the prohibition; and when the exceptions come into play there may still be cases in which a prisoner may be asked about a charge as a step in cross-examination leading to a question whether he was convicted on the charge, or in order to elicit some evidence as to statements made or evidence given by the prisoner in the course of the trial on a charge which failed, which tend to throw doubt on the evidence which he is actually giving, though cases of this last class must be rare and the cross-examination permissible only with great safeguards.

Again, a man charged with an offence against the person may perhaps be asked whether he had uttered threats against the person attacked because he was angry with him for bringing a charge which turned out to be unfounded. Other probabilities may be imagined. Thus, if a prisoner has been acquitted on the plea of autrefois convict such an acquittal might be relevant to his credit, though it would seem that what was in truth relevant to his credit was the previous conviction and not the fact that he was erroneously again charged with the same offence; again, it may be, though it is perhaps a remote supposition, that an acquittal of a prisoner charged with rape on the plea of consent may possibly be relevant to a prisoner's credit.

But these instances all involve the crucial test of relevance. And in general no question whether a prisoner has been convicted or charged or acquitted should be asked or, if asked, allowed by the judge, who has a discretion under proviso (*f*), unless it helps to elucidate the particular issue which the jury is investigating, or goes to credibility, that is, tends to show that he is not to be believed on his oath; indeed the question whether a man has been convicted, charged or acquitted ought not to be admitted, even if it goes to credibility, if there is any risk of the jury being misled into thinking that it goes not to credibility but to the probability of his having committed the offence of which he is charged. I think that it is impossible in the present case to say that the fact that the prisoner had been acquitted on a previous charge of murder or manslaughter, was relevant, or that it tended in the present case to destroy his credibility as a witness.

[Lords Blanesburgh, Atkin, Thankerton and Wright concurred.]

COMMENTS

1. In *Stirland v DPP* [1944] AC 315, [1944] 2 All ER 13, HL, Lord Simon said that despite the prohibition on questions about charges, the accused may be asked about them if he has denied them under oath, for he may be asked about any of his statements to test veracity. But the House of Lords held that the word 'charged' meant 'charged in court' so that an accused who had been taxed by his employer with some criminal act was not lying in saying that he had never been charged.

2. The prohibition of questions on irrelevant matters entails a general prohibition of questions about acquittals, even where (as in *Maxwell v DPP*) the accused has thrown away his shield; and in *R v Meehan* [1978] Crim LR 690, CA, the prohibition appears to have been extended to a previous charge allowed to lie on the file. There is an exception to this general rule whenever an acquittal or mere charge is relevant. To the examples given by Lord Sankey in *Maxwell v DPP* may be added *R v Waldman* (1934) 24 Cr App Rep 204, CCA; *R v Deighton* [1954] Crim LR 208, CCA. When the accused has *not* thrown away his shield the prohibition on questions about acquittals and mere charges flows from the wording of s 1(*f*)(i): section 2, ante.

B   PURPOSE

When cross-examination of the accused is permitted under s 1(*f*)(i) it is because proof of the other offence is admissible 'to show that he is guilty'. It follows that the admissibility granted by this paragraph is confined to questions directed to guilt, and does not extend to questions seeking only to attack the accused's credit or credibility (*Jones v DPP* [1962] AC 635 at 663, [1962] 1 All ER 569 at 575, HL).

When the accused tenders evidence of his good character he is generally entitled to have the jury told that his character makes it more unlikely both that he committed the crime charged and that he is lying on oath (*R v Vye* [1993] 3 All ER 241, [1993] 1 WLR 471, CA; *R v Aziz* [1996] AC 41, [1995] 3 All ER 149, HL). So the purpose of cross-examination under the first limb of s 1(*f*)(ii) is likewise both to prove guilt and to challenge credibility (*R v Samuel* (1956) 40 Cr App Rep 8, CCA; cf *Donnini v R* (1972) 128 CLR 114 at 123, per Barwick CJ).

The purpose of cross-examination under the second limb of s 1(*f*)(ii) is tit for tat (*R v Jenkins* (1945) 31 Cr App Rep 1 at 15, CCA; *Selvey v DPP* [1970] AC 304 at 353, [1968] 2 All ER 497 at 521, per Lord Pearce): the accused has thrown away his shield and should therefore be treated like any other witness, whose record and character can be used to show his evidence is not to be believed. In the case of an ordinary witness the damage can rarely go further, for the witness himself is not on trial. When, however, the witness whose character has been revealed is the defendant himself, there is an obvious danger that the jury will infer from it that he committed the offences charged, particularly if he has a record of offences of a similar nature. The trial judge should give the jury a clear direction that the knowledge they have about the accused's character is to be used for this purpose only, and that they must not use it against him on the direct question of his guilt. In, eg *R v Vickers* [1972] Crim LR 101, CA; *R v Prince* [1990] Crim LR 49, CA, the accused's convictions were quashed because such a direction had not been given; and a model direction was approved in *R v Morrison* (1911) 6 Cr App Rep 159, CCA, although the direction apparently given to the jury by Darling J in that case (see *The Trial of Steinie Morrison*, ed H Fletcher Moulton (1922), pp 277–8) surely went too far, by suggesting that the defendant's career as a burglar would make it easy for him to fake the alibi on which he relied.

This rule is well established despite its practical difficulties; *R v Duncalf* [1979] 2 All ER 1116, 69 Cr App Rep 206, CA, which appears to be against it, may be misreported: cf [1979] 1 WLR 918 and see Pattenden [1982] Crim LR 707 at 714–8 and *R v McLeod* (infra). Its rationale has, however, been somewhat dented by the addition, by s 31 of the Criminal Justice and Public Order Act 1994, of the reference to the deceased victim as a person, an attack on whose character causes the shield to be lost; for it cannot now be said that the situation envisaged by the second limb of s 1(*f*)(ii) is that the trier of fact needs to balance the credit of *witnesses* against one another. As to how much of the detail of previous offences may be brought out, see *R v McLeod* [1994] 3 All ER 254, [1994] 1 WLR 1500, CA, and critique in Cross, pp 442-5. Even here the Court of Appeal asserted that the purpose is to show that the accused is not worthy of belief, not that he has a particular disposition; though the fact that otherwise admissible questions will tend also to show disposition does not render them inadmissible.

Cross-examination under s 1(*f*)(iii) is intended only to attack the accused's credit: *Murdoch v Taylor* [1965] AC 574 at 584, 593, [1965] 1 All ER 406 at 409, 416, HL. As to the extent to which one accused can cross-examine the other with the intention of showing that it was that other, and not he, who committed the offence, see Pattenden, op cit, at p 719–20.

Although the purpose of the cross-examination is limited in the ways set out above, the benefits to the accused are somewhat illusory, because of the general principle that the character of the accused is indivisible, and because of the practical difficulty of getting a jury to use what they know against a defendant for one purpose rather than another. The principle of indivisibility of character means that if his character is in issue the jury may know the total-ity of the accused's character, including his reputation and his convictions, and that he therefore has no right that the judge exercise his discretion in any particular way to disallow certain questions, eg because the answer will reveal a fact that the jury are likely to use for the wrong purpose (*R v Winfield* [1939] 4 All ER 164, CCA; *Stirland v DPP* [1944] AC 315 at 324, [1944] 2 All ER 13 at 18, HL; *R v Powell* [1986] 1 All ER 193, [1985] 1 WLR 1364, CA; cf *R v Shrimpton* (1851) 2 Den 319 at 322). So far as the record is intro-duced to shake credibility, this unfortunate result follows not from any fault in s 1(*f*) but from the general rule that any conviction of a witness can be put to him to shake his credibility under the Criminal Procedure Act 1865, s 6. The practical difficulty becomes particularly acute where the defence amounts to a denial, so that the jury must be instructed that the defendant's character may induce them to disbelieve his denial, but may not independently lead them to believe he is guilty. 'The jury must not infer that the accused is guilty because he is the kind of man who would do the kind of thing charged, but they may disregard his protestations of innocence because he is the kind of man who would make false imputations against others' (Cross (1969) 6 Syd LR 173 at 182; and see *R v Vickers* [1972] Crim LR 101, CA). It is strange that the law's decision about which evidence should be excluded because it is too dan-gerous for a jury should be reversed merely because the accused attacks the prosecution.

FURTHER READING

Pattenden [1982] Crim LR 707; Munday [1986] Crim LR 511; Seabrooke [1987] Crim LR 231.

C   THE JUDGE'S DISCRETION

The judge's approval should be obtained before questions infringing the main part of s 1(*f*) are asked: as much harm could be caused by the question as by the answer (*R v McLean* (1926) 134 LT 640, CCA). If the application for approval is made under s 1(*f*)(i) the judge has to decide whether the questions should be allowed on 'similar fact' principles: see ch 10. If the accused has thrown away his shield under s 1(*f*)(ii) the judge has a discretion to allow or disallow questions that have become admissible under the first limb (*R v Thompson* [1966] 1 All ER 505, [1966] 1 WLR 405, CA) or the second (*Selvey v DPP* [1970] AC 304, [1968] 2 All ER 497, HL). If the accused has given evidence against a co-accused, the latter has an absolute right to cross-examine, but the prosecution and (probably) other co-accused may only do so subject to the judge's discretion: *Murdoch v Taylor* [1965] AC 574, [1965] 1 All ER 406, HL.

Selvey v DPP   [1970] AC 304, [1968] 2 All ER 497, HL

[For the facts, see p 292].

Viscount Dilhorne: I now turn to the question whether a judge has discretion to refuse to permit such cross-examination of the accused even when it is permissible under the section. Mr Caulfield submitted that there was no such discretion and contended that a judge at a criminal trial had no power to exclude evidence which was admissible. He submitted that the position was correctly stated by Bankes J in *R v Fletcher* (1913) 9 Cr App Rep 53 at 56, when he said:

> 'Where the judge entertains a doubt as to the admissibility of evidence, he may suggest to the prosecution that they should not press it, but he cannot exclude evidence which he holds to be admissible.'

Since that case it has been said in many cases that a judge has such a discretion. In *R v Christie* [1914] AC 545, [1914–15] All ER Rep 63, HL, where the question was as to the admissibility of a statement made in the presence and hearing of the accused, Lord Moulton said at 559 and 69:

> 'Now, in a civil action evidence may always be given of any statement or communication made to the opposite party, provided it is relevant to the issues. The same is true of any act or behaviour of the party. The sole limitation is that the matter thus given in evidence must be relevant. I am of opinion that, as a strict matter of law, there is no difference in this respect between the rules of evidence in our civil and in our criminal procedure. But there is a great difference in the practice. The law is so much on its guard against the accused being prejudiced by evidence which, though admissible, would probably have a prejudicial influence on the minds of the jury which would be out of proportion to its true evidential value, that there has grown up a practice of a very salutary nature, under which the judge intimates to the counsel for the prosecution that he should not press for the admission of evidence which would be open to this objection and such an intimation from the tribunal trying the case is usually sufficient to prevent the evidence being pressed in all cases where the scruples of the tribunal in this respect are reasonable. Under the influence of this practice, which is based on an anxiety to secure for everyone a fair trial, there has grown up a custom of not admitting certain kinds of evidence which is so constantly followed that it almost amounts to a rule of procedure.'

In *R v Watson* (1912) 8 Cr App Rep 249 at 254, CCA, the first case when the exercise of discretion in relation to cases coming within the section was mentioned, Pickford J said:

> 'It has been pointed out that to apply the rule [in *R v Hudson* [1912] 2 KB 464, CCA] strictly is to put a hardship on a prisoner with a bad character. That may be so, but it does not follow that a judge necessarily allows the prisoner to be cross-examined to character, he has a discretion not to allow it, and the prisoner has that protection.'

In *Maxwell v DPP* [1935] AC 309, [1934] All ER Rep 168, HL and in *Stirland v DPP* [1944] AC 315, [1944] 2 All ER 13, HL it was said in this House that a judge has that discretion. In *R v Jenkins* (1945) 31 Cr App Rep 1 at 15, CCA, Singleton J said:

> 'If and when such a situation arises [the question whether the accused should be cross-examined as to character] it is open to counsel to apply to the presiding judge that he may be allowed to take the course indicated . . . Such an application will not always be granted, for the judge has a discretion in the matter. He may feel that even though the position is established in law, still the putting of such questions as to the character of the accused person may be fraught with results which immeasurably outweigh the result of questions put by the defence and which make a fair trial of the accused person almost impossible. On the other hand, in the ordinary and normal

case he may feel that if the credit of the prosecutor or his witnesses has been attacked, it is only fair that the jury should have before them material on which they can form their judgment whether the accused person is any more worthy to be believed than those he attacked. It is obviously unfair that the jury should be left in the dark about an accused person's character if the conduct of his defence has attacked the character of the prosecutor or the witness for the prosecution within the meaning of the section. The essential thing is a fair trial and that the legislature sought to ensure by s 1, sub-s(*f*).'

Similar views were expressed in *Noor Mohamed v R* [1949] AC 182, [1949] 1 All ER 365, PC by Lord du Parcq; in *Harris v DPP* [1952] AC 694, [1952] 1 All ER 1044, HL; in *R v Cook* [1959] 2 QB 340, [1959] 2 All ER 97, CCA; in *Jones v DDP* [1962] AC 635, [1962] 1 All ER 569, HL, and in other cases.

In the light of what was said in all these cases by judges of great eminence, one is tempted to say, as Lord Hewart said in *Dunkley* [1927] 1 KB 323, [1926] All ER Rep 187, CCA, that it is far too late in the day even to consider the argument that a judge has no such discretion. Let it suffice for me to say that in my opinion the existence of such a discretion is now clearly established.

Mr Caulfield posed the question, on what principles should such a discretion be exercised. In *R v Flynn* [1963] 1 QB 729 at 737, [1961] 3 All ER 58 at 63, CCA, the court said:

'. . . where . . . the very nature of the defence necessarily involves an imputation, against a prosecution witness or witnesses, the discretion should, in the opinion of this court, be as a general rule exercised in favour of the accused, that is to say, evidence as to his bad character or criminal record should be excluded. If it were otherwise, it comes to this, that the Act of 1898, the very Act which gave the charter, so to speak, to an accused person to give evidence on oath in the witness box, would be a mere trap because he would be unable to put forward any defence, no matter how true, which involved an imputation on the character of the prosecutor or any of his witnesses, without running the risk, if he had the misfortune to have a record, of his previous convictions being brought up in court while being tried on a wholly different matter.'

No authority is given for this supposed general rule, in my opinion, the court was wrong in thinking that there was any such rule. If there was any such general rule, it would amount under the guise of the exercise of discretion, to the insertion of a proviso to the statute of the very kind that was said in *R v Hudson* [1912] 2 KB 464, CCA, not to be legitimate.

I do not think it possible to improve upon the guidance given by Singleton J in the passage quoted above from *R v Jenkins* (1945) 31 Cr App Rep 1 at 15, CCA by Lord du Parcq in *Noor Mohamed v R* [1949] AC 182, [1949] 1 All ER 365, PC or by Devlin J in *R v Cook* [1959] 2 QB 340, [1959] 2 All ER 97, CCA as to the matters which should be borne in mind in relation to the exercise of the discretion. It is now so well established that on a charge of rape the allegation that the woman consented, although involving an imputation on her character, should not expose an accused to cross-examination as to character, that it is possible to say, if the refusal to allow it is a matter of discretion, that there is a general rule that the discretion should be so exercised. Apart from this, there is not, I think, any general rule as to the exercise of discretion. It must depend on the circumstances of each case and the overriding duty of the judge to ensure that a trial is fair.

It is desirable that a warning should be given when it becomes apparent that the defence is taking a course which may expose the accused to such cross-examination. That was not given in this case but the failure to give such a warning would not, in my opinion, justify in this case the allowing of the appeal.

Lord Guest (agreed and said): If I had thought that there was no discretion in English law for a judge to disallow admissible evidence, as counsel for the Crown argued, I should have striven hard and long to give a benevolent construction to s 1(*f*)(ii), which would exclude such cases as *R v Rouse* [1904] 1 KB 184, 'liar', *R v Rappolt* (1911) 6 Cr App Rep 156, CCA, 'horrible liar', *R v Jones* (1923) 87 JP 147, 17 Cr App Rep 117, CCA, rape and other sexual offences, *R v Brown* (1960) 44 Cr App Rep 181, CCA 'self defence'. I cannot believe that Parliament can have intended that in such cases an accused could only put forward such a defence at peril of having his character put before the jury. This would be to defeat the benevolent purposes of the 1898 Act which was for the first time to allow the accused to give evidence on his own behalf in all criminal cases. This would deprive the accused of the advantage of the Act. But I am not persuaded by the Crown's argument and I am satisfied upon a review of all the authorities that in

English law such a discretion does exist . . .

I find it unnecessary to say much more on the principles upon which discretion should be exercised. The guiding star should be fairness to the accused. This idea is best expressed by Devlin J in *R v Cook* [1959] 2 QB 340, [1959] 2 All ER 97, CCA. In following this star the fact that the imputation was a necessary part of the accused's defence is a consideration which will no doubt be taken into account by the trial judge. If, however, the accused or his counsel goes beyond developing his defence in order to blacken the character of a prosecution witness, this no doubt will be another factor to be taken into account. If it is suggested that the exercise of this discretion may be whimsical and depend on the individual idiosyncrasies of the judge, this is inevitable where it is a question of discretion; but I am satisfied that this is a lesser risk than attempting to shackle the judge's power within a straitjacket.

[Lord Pearce, Lord Hodson and Lord Wilberforce agreed.]

COMMENTS

In *R v Flynn* [1963] 1 QB 729, [1961] 3 All ER 58, CCA, it was said that the court should refuse to admit the record if the imputation is a necessary part of the defence. But in *Selvey*, the House of Lords said that this could only be regarded as one factor in the exercise of the discretion, not an overriding one. It was also said in *Flynn* that if there was nothing exceptional in the case the discretion should be exercised in the accused's favour. Though this was not disapproved in *Selvey* it seems to be little acted on. It seems to be agreed that the discretion should be exercised in the accused's favour in the following circumstances. One is where the damage caused by the defence attack is trivial and the accused's record is bad (*R v Turner* [1944] KB 463 at 470–1, [1944] 1 All ER 599 at 602, CCA), particularly if the record contains convictions of crimes similar to that now charged, since the jury may wrongly use them as evidence of guilt; for this reason the judge ought to inform himself of the extent and gravity of the record before it is admitted (*R v Crawford* [1965] VR 586). The thinness of the main case should be remembered, as well as the weakness of the evidence contradicting the accused's attack (*Dawson v R* (1961) 106 CLR 1 at 16). In *R v Cook* [1959] 2 QB 340, [1959] 2 All ER 97, CCA, it was said that a discretion should be exercised in the accused's favour if he is not represented, or if the attack is not directly on the witness but on the police generally or the charge is not deliberate or elaborated, or if no warning to the accused or his counsel has been given by judge or prosecution counsel, or if a mere mistake rather than serious impropriety is alleged against the prosecution witnesses. Obviously the warning to the accused should not be given in open court (*R v Weston-Super-Mare Justices, ex p Townsend* [1968] 3 All ER 225n). If the accused is charged on several counts and he makes an imputation against a witness on one count only, the record should not be admitted because it would prejudice him on all counts (*R v Curbishley* [1963] Crim LR 778, CCA). On the other hand, 'if there is a real issue about the conduct of an important witness which the jury will inevitably have to settle in order to arrive at their verdict, then . . . the jury is entitled to know the credit of the man on whose word the witness's character is being impugned' (*R v Cook* [1959] 2 QB 340 at 348, [1959] 2 All ER 97 at 101, CCA). The discretion should also be exercised against the accused if he alleges that a prosecution witness is an accomplice in an attempt to gain the advantage of the rule requiring that the jury be warned of the danger of convicting on accomplice evidence without corroboration (*R v Manley* (1962) 126 JP 316, CCA). It has been said that the record is more likely to be admitted the more it consists of crimes of dishonesty rather than violence, because the former are more relevant to credibility (*R v Heydon* [1966] 1 NSWR 708 at 733 and 735).

In England, however, the accused's expectation of having discretion exercised in his favour remains uncertain, for the Court of Appeal have more or less consistently (cf *R v Watts* [1983] 3 All ER 101, CA) reasserted the doctrine of the indivisibility of the accused's character. In *R v Powell* [1986] 1 All ER 193, [1985] 1 WLR 1364, CA, Lord Lane CJ, after approving the analysis of the authorities and 'cardinal principles' set out by Ackner LJ in *R v Burke* (1985) 82 Cr App Rep 156, CA, said: 'The fact that the defendant's convictions are not for offences of dishonesty, the fact that they are for offences bearing a close resemblance to the offences charged, are matters for the judge to take into consideration when exercising his discretion, but they certainly do not oblige the judge to disallow the proposed cross-examination'. And it should be remembered that in *Selvey v DPP* [1970] AC 304, [1968] 2 All ER 497, HL, the trial judge allowed the accused's previous convictions for homosexual offences to be put to him, but not those for dishonesty, a course of action that passed muster in the House of Lords.

FURTHER READING

Gooderson, 11 CLJ 377; Livesey [1968] CLJ 291; Pattenden, *Judicial Discretion and Criminal Litigation* (1990) pp 250–9.

Murdoch v Taylor   [1965] AC 574, [1965] 1 All ER 406, HL

Murdoch, who had a criminal record, was jointly tried with Lynch, who did not, for receiving stolen cameras. Lynch gave evidence implicating Murdoch; Murdoch gave evidence alleging that Lynch alone had control and possession of a box containing the stolen cameras. He was then cross-examined on his record by Lynch's counsel. The Court of Criminal Appeal and the House of Lords dismissed Murdoch's appeal, holding that Murdoch had given evidence 'against' Lynch.

Lord Donovan: On the question of discretion, I agree with the Court of Criminal Appeal that a trial judge has no discretion whether to allow an accused person to be cross-examined as to his past criminal offences once he has given evidence against his co-accused. Proviso (*f*)(iii) in terms confers no such discretion and, in my opinion, none can be implied. It is true that in relation to proviso (*f*)(ii) such a discretion does exist; that is to say, in the cases where the accused has attempted to establish his own good character or where the nature and conduct of the defence is such as to involve imputations on the character of the prosecutor or of a witness for the prosecution.

But in these cases it will normally, if not invariably, be the prosecution which will want to bring out the accused's bad character – not some co-accused; and in such cases it seems to me quite proper that the court should retain some control of the matter. For its duty is to secure a fair trial and the prejudicial value of evidence establishing the accused's bad character may at times wholly outweigh the value of such evidence as tending to show that he was guilty of the crime alleged.

These considerations lead me to the view that if, in any given case (which I think would be rare), the prosecution sought to avail itself of the provisions of proviso (*f*)(iii) then here, again, the court should keep control of the matter in the like way. Otherwise, if two accused gave evidence one against the other, but neither wished to cross-examine as to character, the prosecution could step in as of right and reveal the criminal records of both, if both possessed them. I cannot think that Parliament in the Act of 1898 ever intended such an unfair procedure. So far as concerns the prosecution, therefore, the matter should be one for the exercise of the judge's discretion, as it is in the case of proviso (*f*)(ii). But when it is the co-accused who seeks to exercise the right conferred by proviso (*f*)(iii) different considerations come into play. He seeks to defend himself; to say to the jury that the man who is giving evidence against him is unworthy of belief; and to support that assertion by proof of bad character. The right to do this cannot, in my opinion, be fettered in any way.

Finally, it is said that the decision in *Stannard* [1965] 2 QB 1, [1964] 1 All ER 34, CCA, if upheld, will make it impossible for a person to defend himself at all effectively if he has a criminal record and is charged jointly with some other person. If he knows that the other person is guilty, and if in the witness box he speaks the truth, then he is liable to have his criminal past disclosed with fatal results.

This would, indeed, be a melancholy result, but I do not think the prospect is so gloomy. To test the matter, let me assume the case of two accused each charged with the same offence – No 1 in fact being guilty but having no criminal record, No 2 being in fact innocent but having such a record. No 1 has nothing to lose by going into the witness box and accusing No 2 of the crime; No 2 quite truthfully in his evidence accuses No 1, whereupon the past criminal record of No 2 is disclosed to the jury by or on behalf of No 1. It is said that No 2 would have practically no hope of avoiding a conviction – hence the argument for an over-riding discretion in the judge, although this would not necessarily cure the situation.

But in the case supposed, what would be the position in practice? In the first place, if No 2 were in fact innocent, it would be in the highest degree unlikely that he would be found relying simply on his own denial. There would almost invariably be some evidence to support his defence. In the second place, his counsel or the judge or both would explain to the jury just how it was that accused No 1 was able to force the revelation of No 2's record. The judge would probably go on to exhort the jury not to let that revelation sway their minds and to consider the case against No 2 primarily on the basis of the other evidence. The assistant recorder in the present case indeed went further and told the jury to ignore Murdoch's past altogether. It would be a very unusual jury which, in these circumstances, did not require cogent proof of guilt before convicting. Indeed, the effect of the disclosure of No 2's past might have the result of causing the jury to give consideration to the case surpassing in carefulness even their usual high standard.

[Lord Reid, Lord Evershed and Lord Morris of Borth-y-Gest agreed with Lord Donovan on this point.]

Lord Pearce (dissenting on the existence of the discretion): It is common ground that, until the case of *R v Ellis* [1961] 2 All ER 928, CCA, decided briefly to the contrary, the practice and the general view of bench and bar alike was that a judge had a discretion whether to give leave to cross-examine under s 1(*f*)(iii). Moreover, it has long been established practice and law that the right to cross-examine under s 1(*f*)(ii) is subject to the judge's discretion (see the cases of *R v Jenkins* (1945) 114 LJKB 425, CCA, and *R v Cook* [1959] 2 QB 340, [1959] 2 All ER 97, CCA). Therefore, the right under s 1(*f*)(iii) would also seem, prima facie at least, to be subject to the judge's discretion. For there is nothing in the words of the Act which justifies any discrimination between the two subsections on the point in issue.

Admittedly the situation arising under s 1(*f*)(ii) differs from that arising under s 1(*f*)(iii). Under the former, an exercise of discretion could only deprive the prosecution of a right which they would otherwise have had; and the courts have always been ready to do that when fairness seemed to demand it. Under s 1(*f*)(iii), however, the judge, in using a discretion to refuse the introduction of a defendant's bad record, could only do so at the expense of a co-defendant. And how, it is argued, can he properly do this?

It is certainly not an easy problem. But the difficult burden of holding the scales fairly, not only as between the prosecution and defendants, but also as between the defendants themselves, and of doing his best thereby to secure a fair trial for all concerned, falls inevitably on the trial judge and is generally achieved in practice with considerable success. The use of a judicial discretion under s 1(*f*)(iii) as between co-defendants would be but an addition to the judge's existing burden.

The exercise of such a discretion would be within fairly narrow limits and the prima facie right could only be withheld for good judicial reasons. Two obvious examples occur to one of situations in which the judge ought to use a discretion to refuse a defendant's request to introduce a co-defendant's bad character. The first is where that defendant's counsel has deliberately led a co-defendant into the trap, or has, for the purpose of bringing in his bad record, put questions to him in cross-examination which will compel him, for the sake of his own innocence, to give answers that will clash with the story of the other defendant, or compel him to bring to the fore-front implications which would otherwise have been unnoticed or immaterial. The second type of situation is where the clash between the two stories is both inevitable and trivial, and yet the damage by the introduction of a bad record (perhaps many years previous) will in the circum-stances be unfairly prejudicial. Any attempt to deal with such a situation by means of the maxim de minimis is really to import some sort of discretion in disguise. For if a defendant is entitled to an absolute right, he can claim it on any technical ground that exists, whether it be large or small, fair or unfair; and however unfair or technical the ground may be, the right will be equally valuable to a defendant who can make his escape over the (perhaps innocent) body of a co-defendant.

In such a difficult matter which may not infrequently arise in borderline cases, the judge, who sees the general run of the case as it unfolds before him, can produce a fairer result by the exer-cise of a judicial discretion than by the strict and fettered application of an arbitrary rule of law.

In *Hill v R* [1953] Tas SR 54 the Court of Criminal Appeal in Tasmania . . . made it clear that in their opinion a discretion existed . . .

In my view, there should not be denied to the judges the discretion which in practice they exercised for so many years before the decision in the case of *Ellis* [1961] 2 All ER 928, CCA took it out of their capable hands.

COMMENTS

1. In *Murdoch v Taylor* the co-accused allowed to cross-examine was the co-accused against whom evidence had been given. The argument for allowing a third accused, neither attacker nor attacked, to join in and cross-examine without the judge having any discretion to prevent it are, to say the least, less compelling: *R v Lovett* [1973] 1 All ER 744, [1973] 1 WLR 241. The Court of Appeal has, however, extended the rule in *Murdoch v Taylor* to this effect in *R v Rowson* [1986] QB 174, [1985] 2 All ER 539, holding that a judicial dis-cretion can never be exercised in favour of an accused where to do so would prevent a co-accused from putting before the jury evidence otherwise admiss-ible. See also *Lui Mei Lin v R* [1989] AC 288, [1989] 1 All ER 359, PC; *R v Douglass* (1989) 89 Cr App Rep 264 at 271, CA.

2. The court can refuse leave to the prosecution to cross-examine under s 1(*f*)(iii) but cannot refuse it to a co-accused; however, it can probably refuse leave to a co-accused under s 1(*f*)(ii). See *R v Lovett* [1973] 1 All ER 744 at 749, where the Court of Appeal said: 'A and B are jointly charged with the same offence; A (who has a criminal record) gives no evidence against B, but he does make imputations against a Crown witness. On the other hand B (with a clean record) has it in mind to throw all the blame upon A and, for this purpose, it would obviously be helpful to him if he could discredit A by cross-examining him on his bad record. In such circumstances, the Crown themselves may or may not have it in mind to cross-examine A on these lines, but in either case they unquestionably must first seek and obtain the court's permission. Then ought B, against whom A has alleged nothing, to be in a position to cross-examine A *as of right* on these matters? We think that justice demands a negative answer . . .' In *R v Rowson* (above) this view was described as 'exceptional' and its present status is unclear.

3. Probably a co-accused may cross-examine his co-accused as of right on matters other than his record (*Murdoch v Taylor* [1965] AC 574 at 584, [1965] 1 All ER 406 at 409, HL; see Carvell, [1965] Crim LR 419) including

a statement which if tendered by the prosecution would be an inadmissible confession (*R v Rowson* [1986] QB 174, [1985] 2 All ER 539, CA); and also on his convictions and prior offences under s 1(*f*)(i) (*R v Miller* [1952] 2 All ER 667).

4. The slightly differently worded Victorian equivalent to s 1(*f*) (there is a reference to leave in sub-para (ii)) caused division in *Matusevich v R* (1977) 137 CLR 633 so far as sub-para (iii) was concerned. Stephen and Murphy JJ held that it did not permit the prosecutor to cross-examine; Gibbs, Mason and Aickin JJ held that it did, but only with the leave of the court.

QUESTION

The Criminal Law Revision Committee did not recommend any change in the rule that the court has no discretion to prevent the co-accused cross-examining under s 1(*f*)(iii). It said: 'there might be a case for giving a discretion to the court in order to enable it to do justice, as far as possible, in a case where A has, say, only one relevant conviction and B has twenty. Suppose A has given evidence that B committed the offence. B cross-examines A in order to show that A committed the offence and puts A's single conviction to him. B may then refuse to give evidence himself . . . but may call witnesses to say that A committed the offence. A cannot put B's record to him, and it might be thought fairer that the court should be able to redress the balance by forbidding B to question A about his conviction. But the majority think that the present rule should be preserved as the lesser of two evils . . . In particular . . . [there might be] too much difference in the way in which [any] discretion was exercised. For different judges might take different views on the general question which of the two evils mentioned was the lesser one' (CLRC, para 132). Do you agree?

FURTHER READING

CLRC, paras 114–32 (reviewed, Tapper, 36 MLR 56, 167); Stone, 51 LQR 443, 58 LQR 369; Munday [1985] CLJ 62.

PART FOUR

Hearsay

CHAPTER 12

Hearsay: the Exclusionary Rule

There are many formulations of the rule against hearsay, which vary slightly in detail. It could be put thus: 'express or implied assertions which are not made at the trial by the witness who is testifying, and assertions in documents produced to the court when no witness is testifying, are inadmissible as evidence of the truth of that which was asserted' (see Cross, 3rd edn, p 387; Cowen and Carter, p 1; *R v Sharp* [1988] 1 All ER 65 at 68, [1988] 1 WLR 7 at 11, HL). In essence, witnesses must only be allowed to testify from personal knowledge. The only really controversial aspect of this definition is the inclusion of implied assertions (see p 321, post). The prior consistent or inconsistent statements of witnesses do not generally fall within the hearsay ban at common law because such statements are not evidence of the truth of what they assert but merely go to credibility (pp 476 and 479, post).

The rule against hearsay is applied against the accused as well as in his favour (*Sparks v R* [1964] AC 964, [1964] 1 All ER 727, PC (statement by victim exculpating accused); *R v Turner* (1975) 61 Cr App Rep 67 at 87, CA; and *R v Blastland* [1986] AC 41, [1985] 2 All ER 1095, HL (statement by third party admitting offence); cf *Wildman v R* (1984) 12 DLR (4th) 641). See Carter (1987) 103 LQR 107. However, in *R v Beckford* [1991] Crim LR 833, CA, a conviction of one co-accused was set aside as unsafe and unsatisfactory where the other co-accused had made a confession excluded as being inadmissible and had not entered the witness-box. This case was described as turning on its own special facts in *R v Rogers* [1995] 1 Cr App Rep 374 at 381, CA.

There is a difficulty – perhaps only a temporary one – in discussing the rule against hearsay. In criminal cases, the common law rule with its many common law and statutory exception holds sway. In civil cases, the Civil Evidence Act 1995 has enacted a new regime. This chapter discusses certain general problems which are either common to both systems or a necessary preliminary to understanding both. A discussion of the rule in criminal cases in its main aspects and a separate discussion of the civil rule will follow in Chapters 13 and 14.

1 Rationale

Several reasons are commonly given to justify the rule. First, hearsay statements when related to the court emanate originally from persons not under oath nor subject to cross-examination, 'the greatest legal engine ever invented for the discovery of truth' (Wigmore, para 1367). Hence they are unreliable. The maker's lack of veracity, or his defective powers of memory, perception and narration, cannot be tested by detailed questions; his demeanour cannot be observed. 'Whoever has attended to the examination, the cross-examination, and the re-examination of witnesses . . . has observed what a very different shape their story appears to take in each of these stages . . .' (*Berkeley Peerage Case* (1811) 4 Camp 401 at 405, per Bayley J). 'A person who relates a hearsay is not obliged to enter into any particulars, to answer any questions, to solve any difficulties, to reconcile any contradictions, to explain any obscurities, to remove any ambiguities; he entrenches himself on the simple assertion that he was told so, and leaves the burden entirely on his dead or absent author': *Coleman v Southwick* (1812) 9 Johns 150, per Chancellor Kent. There also seems to be a tendency for light and ill-considered statements to be made more readily out of court and behind a person's back than in court or to his face. There are certainly dangers springing from the absence of cross-examination, but perhaps the unreliability is not so great as to justify an all-embracing exclusionary rule. The lack of an oath is not so important; for statements on oath not made in the instant proceeding are hearsay: *R v Eriswell (Inhabitants)* (1790) 3 Term Rep 707.

Secondly, it is said to be desirable that the best evidence be given: direct evidence should be given in preference to hearsay. But if the maker of the statement is dead or unobtainable, a hearsay report of the statement is the best evidence and should, on this reasoning, be admitted. Further, an out-of-court statement made soon after an event may be much more valuable than one made in court years later: it is less stale and may be unaffected by interest and the heat of litigation.

Thirdly, there is a danger of inaccuracy through repetition. If A tells the court what B told him C said, or did, there are two sources of possible error: B may have misheard C or misunderstood what he was doing, and A may have misheard B. As Baker says (p 19): 'Everyone is familiar with the ease and rapidity with which a story grows. As it is passed from mouth to mouth some additional fact is added; perhaps, too, a little colour to make it a better tale. With each handing on of the story, the further away from the truth it becomes; detail is added to detail as the story grows and in the end the accumulated mass swamps the core of truth at its centre. Misunderstanding, faulty memory, and misreporting make the story increasingly inaccurate and unreliable.' This is a sounder argument in the case of oral hearsay than written. And the danger is ignored or the risk is run in connexion with statements introduced to prove that they were made rather than to prove the truth of what they assert, for these fall outside the hearsay ban (p 317, post).

Fourthly, it is said that if the rule were relaxed the courts would be swamped with a proliferation of evidence (some of it raising collateral issues which might protract the trial) directed to establishing a particular fact, ie, both direct evidence and hearsay. This ought to be, though it may not be, an unreal danger; expense and common sense ought to ensure that the parties will in fact only put forward their strongest evidence. And though hearsay may raise collateral issues which lengthen the trial, it may equally be so convincing as to shorten it.

Fifthly, there is a fear that juries will attach undue weight to hearsay evidence without realising its weaknesses: 'no man can tell what effect it may have upon their minds' (*Berkeley Peerage Case* (1811) 4 Camp 401 at 415, per Mansfield CJ). But some (though not all) think that the weaknesses of hearsay evidence are normally obvious as a matter of common sense to the better-educated modern jury and that any difficult cases can be dealt with by explicit judicial directions. On the other hand, modern education may not be particularly helpful in weighing hearsay; indeed, the property qualifications of earlier times may have helped to ensure that there were hard-headed men in the jury box.

Critics of the present law in criminal cases contend that it has many disadvantages. The rule can operate unjustly where it excludes hearsay evidence of a person who is dead, or unavailable, or unidentifiable. It means that a case may be decided without taking into account all the available evidence, imperfect though some of it may be. The need to call direct rather than hearsay evidence adds to the cost of proving facts which are not really in dispute. The rule tends to confuse witnesses by preventing them from telling their story in a natural way. The present law is very complicated; the many exceptions to the main exclusionary rule require much space to state. Finally, the evidence excluded is often highly reliable and would be thought convincing by ordinary men in their everyday affairs: see *Myers v DPP* [1965] AC 1001, [1964] 2 All ER 881, HL. The rule may operate harshly in preventing the accused from clearing himself in reliance on hearsay (*Sparks v R* [1964] AC 964, [1964] 1 All ER 727, PC).

2 The limits of the rule

A ORIGINAL EVIDENCE

Subramaniam v Public Prosecutor [1956] 1 WLR 965, PC

The accused was charged with unlawful possession of ammunition. His defence was that he had been captured by terrorists and was acting under duress. The trial judge held that evidence of his conversations with terrorists were inadmissible unless the terrorists testified. The Privy Council allowed the appeal.

Mr LMD De Silva: In ruling out peremptorily the evidence of conversation between the terrorists and the appellant the trial judge was in error. Evidence of a statement made to a witness by a person who is not himself called as a witness may or may not be hearsay. It is hearsay and inadmissible when the object of the evidence is to establish the truth of what is contained in the statement. It is not hearsay and is admissible when it is proposed to establish by the evidence, not the truth of the statement, but the fact that it was made. The fact that the statement was made, quite apart from its truth, is frequently relevant in considering the mental state and conduct thereafter of the witness or of some other person in whose presence the statement was made. In the case before their Lordships statements could have been made to the appellant by the terrorists, which, whether true or not, if they had been believed by the appellant, might reasonably have induced in him an apprehension of instant death if he failed to conform to their wishes.

In the rest of the evidence given by the appellant statements made to him by the terrorists appear now and again to have been permitted, probably inadvertently, to go in. But, a complete, or substantially complete, version according to the appellant of what was said to him by the terrorists and by him to them has been shut out. This version, if believed, could and might have afforded cogent evidence of duress brought to bear upon the appellant. Its admission would also have meant that the complete story of the appellant would have been before the trial judge and assessors and enabled them more effectively to have come to a correct conclusion as to the truth or otherwise of the appellant's story.

Charles Dickens: Pickwick Papers, Chapter 34

'I believe you are in the service of Mr Pickwick, the defendant in this case. Speak up, if you please, Mr Weller.'

'I mean to speak up, sir,' replied Sam. 'I am in the service o' that 'ere gen'l'man, and a wery good service it is.'

'Little to do, and plenty to get, I suppose?' said Sergeant Buzfuz, with jocularity.

'Oh, quite enough to get, sir, as the soldier said ven they ordered him three hundred lashes,' replied Sam.

'You must not tell us what the soldier, or any other man, said, sir,' interposed the judge, 'it's not evidence.'

'Wery good, my lord', replied Sam.

Subramaniam's Case reveals the fallacy in what the judge said to Sam Weller. The evidence held admissible in *Subramaniam's* Case is often called 'original' evidence as opposed to 'hearsay'. The actual facts of the case concern proof of statements made to a person, not to show the truth of what was said in them, but to show the hearer's state of mind (see also *R v Willis* [1960] 1 All ER 331, [1960] 1 WLR 55). There are numerous other illustrations of it. Statements constituting defamation, injurious falsehood, passing off, or intimidation are admitted simply to prove that they were made. So too words of discharge to an employee. Statements to an accused are admissible to prove motive even though their truth is not in issue (*R v Edmunds* (1833) 6 C & P 164). The shouts of a mob are admissible to prove that the mob was likely to frighten bystanders (*R v Lord Gordon* (1781) 21 State Tr 485). Where a road accident victim had to prove that she had made due inquiry and search for the identity of the car that struck her, her report that the police told her they could not find it was admissible: the issue was not the truth of the police statements but the fact that they were made (*Cavanagh v Nominal Defendant* (1959) 100 CLR 375); see also *Perkins v Vaughan* (1842) 4 Man & G 988; *The Douglas* (1882) 7 PD 151. Statements by a person may be relevant independently of their truth in several ways. Ludicrous statements may prove insanity. False statements may prove a consciousness of guilt (*A-G v Good* (1825) M'Cle & Yo 286; *Mawaz Khan v R* [1967] 1 AC 454, [1967] 1 All ER 80, PC). Demands for money by the complainant of rape may prove consent (*R v Guttridge* (1840) 9 C & P 471). Proof of failure of a doctor to object to a breath test being given to a driver is not hearsay if the only issue is whether he objected rather than whether a lack of objection was well founded (*R v Chapman* [1969] 2 QB 436, [1969] 2 All ER 321, CA). Statements by a testator as to why he made his will as he did are admissible in testator's family maintenance proceedings to prove why he disposed of his estate as he did, but not to prove that the contents of the statements are true: *Hughes v National Trustees, Executors and Agency Co of Australasia Ltd* (1979) 143 CLR 134 at 150.

One group of illustrations of original evidence are 'operative words', eg words of gift or words of contractual or other offer: a recent example is *Woodhouse v Hall* (1980) 72 Cr App Rep 39. Assertive statements may also be admitted without infringing the hearsay rule if they are put forward to qualify some act done, eg statements that money being handed to an executor was given to the declarant by the deceased. The statement is not evidence of the gift but it does prevent an inference that the declarant, by handing the money over, admits having no right to it: *Hayslep v Gymer* (1834) 1 Ad & El 162. Proof of market research surveys has been admitted on the ground that a survey is not hearsay, as merely showing the opinion of the public; thus in *Customglass Boats Ltd v Salthouse Bros Ltd* [1976] 1 NZLR 36 a survey was admitted in a passing-off case to show what opinions, rightly or wrongly, persons in yachting circles held as to the reputation attaching to a particular name. See also *Bevan Investments Ltd v Blackhall and Struthers (No 2)* [1978] 2 NZLR 97. Cf *McDonald's System of Australia Pty Ltd v McWilliam's Wines Pty Ltd* (1979) 28 ALR 236 at 252–4; *Hoban's Glynde Pty Ltd v Firle Hotel Pty Ltd* (1973) 4 SASR 503. The basis on which such evidence may be tendered remains controversial. See *Ritz Hotel Ltd v Charles of the Ritz Ltd* (1988) 15 NSWLR 158; *A Bailey & Co Ltd v Clark, Son & Moreland* [1938] AC 557, [1938] 2 All ER 377, HL; and *General Electric Co v General Electric Co Ltd* [1972] 2 All ER 507, [1972] 1 WLR 729, HL.

Another possible ground of admission of such evidence, if it is hearsay, is that it is a collection of statements concerning the makers' state of mind: see below.

B   THE EXCLUSION OF RELIABLE EVIDENCE

There is evidence which, though plainly reliable, is excluded under the hearsay rule. The rule is based on the need to avoid unreliability, but in its operation it is a technical rule, independent of any reliability or unreliability existing on the particular facts. For English courts this was finally settled by *Myers v DPP* [1965] AC 1001, [1964] 2 All ER 881, HL.

The accused were charged with conspiracy. They bought wrecked cars with their logbooks. They stole other cars and disguised them so as to make them conform to the wrecked cars' logbooks. The stolen cars were then sold as renovated wrecks. To prove that the cars sold were stolen, the prosecution called an officer in charge of the records made by the manufacturers of the stolen cars. He produced microfilms of the cards filled in by workmen showing the numbers moulded into secret parts of the stolen cars' cylinder blocks. These numbers coincided with the cylinder block numbers of the cars sold. In effect this was evidence of what the officer had said the workmen had written. The trial judge admitted it. The Court of Criminal Appeal upheld his decision; they said the evidence was not hearsay because 'its probative value does not depend on the credit of an unidentified person but rather on the circumstances in which the record is maintained and the inherent probability that it will be correct rather than incorrect' ([1965] AC 1001 at 1008, [1965] 1 All ER 881 at 886–7, following *R v Rice* [1963] 1 QB 857, [1963] 1 All ER 832, CCA). The House of Lords allowed the appeal by a bare majority, holding that it was hearsay, that no existing hearsay exception applied, and that in the interests of certainty the creation of new hearsay exceptions was for Parliament, not the courts. It was hearsay because the officer was reporting the workmen's account of the numbers as evidence of the truth of what they said. It was true that the evidence was highly reliable, but the admissibility of evidence depended not on reliability but on technical satisfaction of the above test. There was no discretion to admit reliable evidence which infringed an exclusionary rule. The judicial refusal to change the law despite its faults has some force, but so has Lord Pearce's dissenting judgment. He said that the anonymity and reliability of modern records of mass production was a new social fact and the law should change to take account of it. Such evidence might be vital to an accused's defence, and it would be strange if so irrational and technical a rule could be permitted to lead to a wrong conviction. There was no reason to suppose that the courts had lost their nineteenth century power to create new exceptions; the law was already so untidy that it could hardly be made worse by new exceptions (and see *Potts v Miller* (1940) 64 CLR 282 at 292, 302–4; see also *R v Seifert* (1956) 73 WNNSW 358).

The actual result of *Myers v DPP* was reversed by legislation (Criminal Evidence Act 1965; see now Part II of the Criminal Justice Act 1988, discussed in ch 13.3, post), but its reasoning has been relied on by other courts. Some courts have used somewhat questionable reasoning to evade the consequences of the *Myers v DPP* approach. It would seem desirable to apply *Myers v DPP* or to recognise frankly some new hearsay exception, but not to misapply the technical definition of hearsay discussed in *Myers v DPP*. One sound application of the *Myers* reasoning was *Jones v Metcalfe* [1967] 3 All ER 205, [1967] 1 WLR 1286. A collision caused by a lorry occurred. A witness took the lorry's number and reported it to the police. At the trial the witness said he had forgotten the number but had given it to the policeman. The policeman's evidence as to the number was held to be inadmissible hearsay. Any attempt to justify admissibility by arguing that the policeman was not advancing what was told to him as evidence of its truth, but simply revealing the result of the instruction to him to write the number down, must founder on the fact that the court is asked to act on the statement not because it was made, but because what it contains is true. The technicality of the result is demonstrated by the fact that if the policeman had been seen recording the witness's statement of the number, the latter could have refreshed his memory from the record and the number would have been admitted. (See also *Grew v Cubitt* [1951] 2 TLR 305; *R v McLean* (1967) 52 Cr App Rep 80, CA, criticised by Libling [1977] Crim LR 268 at 276–8, and defended by Smith [1978] Crim LR 58–9.) A statement on goods that they were manufactured in a particular place is hearsay (*Patel v Customs Comptroller* [1966] AC 356, [1965] 3 All ER 593, PC). A car's logbook is inadmissible evidence of the engine number (*R v Sealby* [1965] 1 All ER 701). If a policeman interrogates a suspect whose language he does not understand through an interpreter, then the suspect's translated answers cannot be admitted unless the interpreter is called as a witness and either states that he remembers the original answer and his translations, or refreshes his memory from notes. What the interpreter said to the policeman is proffered as evidence of its truth (*R v Wong Ah Wong* [1957] SRNSW 582; *R v Attard* (1958) 43 Cr App Rep 90). The interpreter cannot be regarded as the suspect's agent to make any admission; nor can the interpreter merely be regarded as a telephone or conduit-pipe, for telephones merely transmit sounds, but interpreters can make mistakes. In South Africa and Australia it has been held that the evidence is admissible as not being hearsay (*R v Mutchke* [1946] AD 874; *Gaio v R* (1960) 104 CLR 419). Since some interpreters in these jurisdictions may forget the conversation and may be too illiterate to take notes, this view ensures that the criminal justice system does not break down; but it would seem better in principle to erect a new exception to the hearsay rule rather than juggle with the definition of hearsay. The interpreter's statements of what the suspect said are hearsay because the policeman has no personal knowledge of their accuracy.

There has been much debate about the accuracy of certain decisions on the scope of hearsay. In *R v Rice* [1963] 1 QB 857, [1963] 1 All ER 832, CCA, it was held that an air ticket made out in the name of Rice was admissible evidence that Rice had travelled on the appropriate flight. Yet this would seem to be hearsay. The ticket in effect contains the booking clerk's report of what someone else said to him when booking the ticket, and is designed to prove the truth of what is said. The result has some sense, but is technically wrong (see *Re Gardner* (1968) 13 FLR 345; *R v Romeo* (1982) 30 SASR 243 at 264; *R v Lydon* (1987) 85 Cr App Rep 221 at 224, CA. Cf Hoffmann, p 92, n 15). The same may be said of *Edwards v Brookes (Milk) Ltd* [1963] 3 All ER 62, [1963] 1 WLR 795, DC, where statements made by persons not called as witnesses who said they were agents of the accused were admitted. The evidence that the 'agents' were agents came from them only and was reported to the court by others.

C   IMPLIED ASSERTIONS

(i)   General

It is clear that the hearsay rule extends to express assertions. Express assertions are normally statements intended to be assertive. But the phrase also includes conduct intended to be assertive, eg nods, gestures and signs. (See *Chandrasekera v R* [1937] AC 220, [1936] 3 All ER 865, PC.) It is also clear that the rule does not extend to non-assertive behaviour, eg the leaving of fingerprints or footprints. But does the rule extend to implied assertions – statements or conduct not intended to be assertive but which rest on some assumption of fact believed by the maker of the statement or the doer of the act which can be inferred by the court? This is a difficult question and, so far as it has been considered, a controversial one.

The problem arises in a number of areas where evidence is generally held admissible, but it is unclear whether in the courts' view such evidence is not assertive, or whether it is an implied assertion falling outside the hearsay rule, or an implied assertion admitted as an exception to the hearsay rule. A learned writer, who has analysed the problem with exemplary clarity, divides the cases into six groups (Weinberg (1973) 9 Melb ULR 268). One concerns illegal gambling, where a policeman picks up a ringing telephone at premises suspected of being used for illicit gambling, and hears a caller attempting to make a bet: he is impliedly asserting a belief that he is speaking to a betting house (cf *McGregor v Stokes* [1952] VLR 347, where the calls were said not to be assertive at all). A second is where one suspected of misconduct flees, for this indicates a consciousness of guilt: he is impliedly asserting a belief in his own guilt. (The problem of admissibility is rarely discussed here because even if the flight is an implied assertion subject to the hearsay rule it will usually be admissible within the admissions exception.) Into this category might also be placed lies, interference with witnesses, and destruction of real evidence. Thirdly, the problem arises where a doctor is seen to treat a patient in a particular way: this is an implied assertion that the patient is ill. Fourthly, treatment by one person of another in an affectionate, or violent, or jeering, or paternal way is an implied assertion that the first is married to, or hates, or regards as mad, or regards as his child, the second. Such treatment is admissible evidence of relationship, but the question whether this is non-hearsay or an exception to hearsay is rarely discussed. Fifthly, silence in the face of an accusation or after receiving goods is an implied assent to the accusation or approval of the goods. The inference of assent will often be a dangerous one, however, making cross-examination particularly desirable. Finally, a statement by one person identifying another – 'Hello, X!' – is an implied assertion that the second person is X.

In these cases the usual hearsay dangers are less strongly present than normal: the maker of the assertion is less likely to be lying. 'People do not say "Hello X" in order to deceive passers-by into thinking that X is there, and doctors do not place bodies on mortuary vans unless they have good reason to believe the bodies to be corpses' (Cross, 5th edn, p 470). This would be an unnecessarily elaborate kind of lie.

Wright v Doe d Tatham   (1837) 7 Ad & El 313

The issue was whether John Marsden had sufficient mental capacity to make a valid will. The following evidence of incompetency was received without objection: treatment with disrespect by his steward; treatment as a child by his menial servants and residents of his village; the fact that he was called 'Silly Jack' and 'Silly Marsden' by local residents; the fact that boys shouted at him 'There goes crazy Marsden', threw dirt at him and persuaded a passer by to see him home. As evidence of competency, three letters addressed to Marsden were proffered, but were held inadmissible by the Court of Exchequer Chamber and the House of Lords. Parke B discussed the problem of implied assertions in detail, and some remarks of Bosanquet J should be noted.

Parke B: . . . [You] have no right to use in evidence the fact of writing and sending a letter to a third person containing a statement of competence, on the ground that it affords an inference that such an act would not have been done unless the statement was true, or believed to be true, although such an inference no doubt would be raised in the conduct of the ordinary affairs of life, if the statement were made by a man of veracity. But it cannot be raised in a judicial inquiry; and, if such an argument were admissible, it would lead to the indiscriminate admission of hearsay evidence of all manner of facts.

Further, it is clear that an acting to a much greater extent and degree upon such statements to a third person would not make the statements admissible. For example, if a wager to a large amount had been made as to the matter in issue by two third persons, the payment of that wager, however large the sum, would not be admissible to prove the truth of the matter in issue. You would not have had any right to present it to the jury as raising an inference of the truth of the fact, on the ground that otherwise the bet would not have been paid. It is, after all, nothing but the mere statement of that fact, with strong evidence of the belief of it by the party making it. Could it make any difference that the wager was between the third person and one of the parties to the suit? Certainly not. The payment by other underwriters on the same policy to the plaintiff could not be given in evidence to prove that the subject insured had been lost. Yet there is an act done, a payment strongly attesting the truth of the statement, which it implies, that there had been a loss. To illustrate this point still further, let us suppose a third person had bet-ted a wager with Mr Marsden that he could not solve some mathematical problem, the solution of which required a high degree of capacity; would payment of that wager to Mr Marsden's banker be admissible evidence that he possessed that capacity? The answer is certain; it would not. It would be evidence of the fact of competence given by a third party not upon oath.

Let us suppose the parties who wrote these letters to have stated the matter therein contained, that is, their knowledge of his personal qualities and capacity for business, on oath before a magistrate, or in some judicial proceedings to which the plaintiff and defendant were not parties. No one could contend that such statement would be admissible on this issue; and yet there would have been an act done on the faith of the statement being true, and a very solemn one, which would raise in the ordinary conduct of affairs a strong belief in the truth of the statement, if the writers were faith-worthy. The acting in this case is of much less importance, and certainly is not equal to the sanction of an extra-judicial oath.

Many other instances of a similar nature, by way of illustration, were suggested by the learned counsel for the defendant in error, which, on the most cursory consideration, any one would at once declare to be inadmissible in evidence. Others were supposed on the part of the plaintiff in error, which, at first sight, have the appearance of being mere facts, and therefore admissible, though on further consideration they are open to precisely the same objection. Of the first description are the supposed cases of a letter by a third person to any one demanding a debt, which may be said to be a treatment of him as a debtor, being offered as proof that the debt was really due; a note, congratulating him on his high state of bodily vigour, being proposed as evidence of his being in good health; both of which are manifestly at first sight objectionable. To the latter class belong the supposed conduct of the family or relations of a testator, taking the same precautions in his absence as if he were a lunatic; his election, in his absence, to some high and responsible office; the conduct of a physician who permitted a will to be executed by a sick testator; the conduct of a deceased captain on a question of seaworthiness, who, after examining every part of the vessel, embarked in it with his family; all these, when deliberately considered, are, with reference to the matter in issue in each case, mere instances of hearsay evidence, mere statements, not on oath, but implied in or vouched by the actual conduct of persons by whose acts the litigant parties are not to be bound.

Bosanquet J: . . . It is obvious that the contents of letters may be dictated by various motives, according to the dispositions and circumstances of the writers. Language of affection, of respect, of rational or amusing information, may be addressed from the best of motives to persons in a state of considerable imbecility, or labouring under the strangest delusions. The habitual treatment of deranged persons as rational is one mode of promoting their recovery. A tone of insult or derision may be employed in a moment of irritation in writing to a person in full possession of his reason; what judgment can be formed of the intention of the writers, without an endless examination into the circumstances which may have influenced them? And what opinion can be collected of the capacity of the receiver without ascertaining how he acted when he read the language addressed to him? To me it appears that the admission in proof of capacity of letters unaccompanied by other circumstances than such as are stated in this record would establish an entirely new precedent in a Court of Common Law, from which very great inconvenience might result upon trials of sanity, as well of the living as of the dead . . .

COMMENT

In *Stobart v Dryden* (1836) 1 M & W 615 Parke B said that the signature of the attesting witness on a deed was admissible evidence of its due execution; it was a fact showing that he did what in the ordinary course of business he would have done had he seen the deed executed (cf *Whitelocke v Musgrove* (1833) 1 Cr & M 511). Yet on his reasoning in *Wright* it would seem to be an implied assertion. Cross (5th edn, p 471) therefore suggests that Parke B was prepared to admit implied assertions which did not raise side issues. This does not correspond with Parke B's language.

QUESTIONS

1. What view would Parke B take of the evidence of incompetency admitted without objection in *Wright?* (Cf *Re Hine* 37 A 384 (1897).)
2. In *Backhouse v Jones* (1839) 6 Bing NC 65, the acts of creditors in returning goods to a bankrupt were held not to be admissible as evidence of the creditors' belief as to their entitlement to keep possession, any more than their express declarations would be.

R v Kearley   [1992] 2 AC 228, [1992] 2 All ER 345, HL

Lord Oliver of Aylmerton: The circumstances giving rise to this appeal are these. After raiding the premises and after the appellant had been arrested, police officers remained on the premises for several hours. During that period some 15 telephone calls from a variety of callers were made to the premises and were intercepted by police officers either in the absence of the appellant or at any rate without his hearing their content. In 10 of these the caller asked for 'Chippie', a nickname by which the appellant was known, and asked for drugs. During the same period nine visitors, some at least being apparently persons who had earlier telephoned, came to the door of the premises seeking 'Chippie'. Seven of these callers indicated that they wanted to purchase drugs and some at least were carrying cash in their hands. None of these persons, with the exception of a Mr Fry, who was named specifically in connection with count 5 upon which the appellant was convicted and who gave evidence in connection with that count, was called as a witness. The prosecution, however, proposed to call the police officers who had intercepted the telephone calls or had received the callers at the house to give evidence of the facts of the telephone calls or personal calls and of the contents of the conversations which they then had with those persons. That evidence was objected to on the ground that it was inadmissible as hearsay, since it was to be adduced not simply as evidence of the fact that calls were made but for the purposes of showing (a) that drugs were being supplied at the premises on a commercial scale and (b) that it was the appellant who was supplying them. After considerable argument in the absence of the jury, the objection was overruled and the officers' testimony was received . . . [The] Court of Appeal (Criminal Division) . . . certified the following question as one of general public importance:

'Whether evidence may be adduced at a trial of words spoken (namely a request for drugs to be supplied by the defendant), not spoken in the presence or hearing of the defendant, by a person not called as a witness, for the purpose not of establishing the truth of any fact narrated by the words, but of inviting the jury to draw an inference from the fact that the words were spoken (namely that the defendant was a supplier of drugs).'

. . . The distinction between utterance as relevant fact and utterance as evidence of the accuracy of what is uttered is neatly expressed in the opinion of the Board of the Privy Council delivered by Lord Wilberforce in *Ratten v R* [1972] AC 378, 387, [1971] 3 All ER 801, 805:

'The mere fact that evidence of a witness includes evidence as to words spoken by another person who is not called, is no objection to its admissibility. Words spoken are facts just as much as any other action by a human being. If the speaking of the words is a relevant fact, a witness may give evidence that they were spoken. A question of hearsay only arises when the words spoken are relied on "testimonially", ie, as establishing some fact narrated by the words.'

Thus, in that case, a telephone call from the wife of the accused, who had been shot dead by him, as he claimed accidentally, and in which she asked for the police, was held to be rightly admitted as evidence simply of a telephone call made by a lady in a distressed state made at a time when the accused denied that any call was made and in the context of his contention that the shooting was accidental. It is to be noted, however, that in so far as it was admissible as evidence from which the jury could be invited to infer that the caller was being attacked by her husband, the Board found it admissible only as part of the res gestae, ie as an exception to the hearsay rule.

Thus the question which presents itself in the instant appeal can be expressed thus: was the evidence of the police officers being tendered simply as evidence of the fact of the conversation or was it introduced 'testimonially' in order to demonstrate the truth either of something that was said or of something that was implicit in or to be inferred from something that was said? . . .

My Lords, to any ordinary layman asked to consider the matter, one might think that the resort of a large number of persons to 11, Perth Close all asking for 'Chippie', all carrying sums of cash and all asking to be supplied with drugs, would be as clear an indication as he could reasonably expect to have that 11, Perth Close, was a place at which drugs were available; and if he were to be asked whether or not this showed also that 'Chippie' was dealing in drugs, I cannot help feeling that his answer would be 'Of course it does.' But so simple – perhaps, one might say, so attractively common sense – a layman's approach is not necessarily a reliable guide to criminal trial . . .

Indeed, even accepting the layman's immediate impression, if one goes on to ask 'Why do you say, "Of course?"' the matter becomes a little more complex. The answer to that question has to be 'because, of course, they would not go and ask for drugs unless they expected to get them.' But then if one asks, 'Well, why did they expect to get them?' even the layman is compelled into an area of speculation. They expected to get them either because they had got them before or because they had been told, rightly or wrongly, or had heard or thought or guessed that there was somebody called 'Chippie' at 11, Perth Close who supplied drugs. So, straight away, even the layman is, on analysis, compelled to accept that his instinctive 'of course' rests upon a process of deductive reasoning which starts from an assumption about the state of mind or belief of a number of previously unknown individuals of whom the only known facts are that they telephoned or called at 11, Perth Close and made offers to purchase drugs . . . The first inquiry must be, 'Is it relevant evidence?' for nothing that is not relevant is admissible . . . [A] fact to be relevant must be probative, and if one asks whether the fact that a large number of persons called at the premises seeking to purchase from 'Chippie' renders probable the existence of a person at the premises called 'Chippie' who is willing to supply drugs, the answer can, I think, only be in the affirmative. But the difficulty here is that it is only the combination of the facts (a) that persons called, (b) that they asked for 'Chippie' and (c) that they requested drugs, which renders the evidence relevant. The mere fact that people telephoned or called, in itself, is irrelevant for it neither proves nor renders probable any other fact. In order to render evidence of the calls relevant and therefore admissible there has to be added the additional element of what the callers said, and it is here that the difficulty arises. What was said – in each case a request for drugs – is, of course, probative of the state of mind of the caller. But the state of mind of the caller is not the fact in issue and is, in itself, irrelevant, for it is not probative of anything other than its own existence. It becomes relevant only if and so far as the existence of other facts can be inferred from it. So far as concerns anything in issue at the trial, what the caller said and the state of mind which that fact evinces, become relevant and probative of the fact in issue (namely, the intent of the appellant) only if, or because, (i) what was said amounts to a statement, by necessary implication, that the appellant has in the past supplied drugs to the speaker (as in two cases in which requests were made for 'the usual') or (ii) it imports the belief or opinion of the speaker that the appellant has drugs and is willing to supply them. And here, as it seems to me, we are directly up against the hearsay rule . . . Clearly if, at the trial, the prosecution had sought to adduce evidence from a witness to the effect that the appellant had, in the past, supplied him with quantities of drugs, that evidence would have been both relevant and admissible; but equally clearly, if it had been sought to introduce the evidence of a police constable to the effect that a person not called as a witness had told him, in a conversation in a public house, that the appellant had supplied drugs, that would have been inadmissible hearsay evidence and so objectionable. It cannot, it is cogently argued, make any difference that exactly the same evidence is introduced in an indirect way by way of evidence from a witness that he had overheard a request by some other person for 'the usual', from which the jury is to be asked to infer that which cannot be proved by evidence of that other person's direct assertion. Equally if, at the trial, the prosecution had sought to adduce evidence from a witness not that drugs had been supplied but that it was his opinion or belief that drugs had been or would be supplied, that evidence would be inadmissible as amounting to no more than a statement of belief or opinion unsupported by facts upon which the belief is grounded. A fortiori, it is argued, that same inadmissible belief or opinion cannot be introduced by inference from the reported statement of someone who is not even called as a witness. Thus, it is said, in seeking to introduce the evidence of the police officers of what callers said, the Crown faces the difficulty that it has to contend that by combining two inadmissible items of evidence – that is to say, the evidence of the calls (which are, standing alone, inadmissible because irrelevant) and the evidence of what was said by the callers (which might be relevant but is inadmissible because hearsay) – it can produce a single item of admissible evidence.

The impermissibility of such a course rests upon a well established principle expounded in the context of civil proceedings some 150 years ago in *Wright v Doe d Tatham* (1837) 7 Ad & El 313 . . .

Now certainly the rigour with which hearsay evidence is excluded has been considerably modified by statute, but the general soundness of the views expressed by the Court of Exchequer Chamber in *Wright v Doe d Tatham* (1837) 7 Ad & El 313, outwith the statutory and common law exceptions, has not, so far as I am aware, been challenged in or affected by subsequent authority during the past 150 years . . .

I do not, moreover, think that the admission of the evidence of the police officers in the present case can be justified by seeking to equiparate it with the evidence of the telephone call which was held to have been rightly admitted in *Ratten v R* [1972] AC 378, [1971] 3 All ER 801, for there, as already mentioned, the evidence had a double relevance. The fact that a call was made by a woman who was both frightened and hysterical, was clearly material to the jury's determination of the likelihood or unlikelihood of the accused's claim that the shooting took place accidentally while he was engaged in the innocuous process of cleaning his gun. That is a long way from the instant case where the conversation is relied upon not as a circumstance surrounding an act of the accused but as indicative of the speaker's view of the accused's intentions. In so far as it was considered permissible in *Ratten* to draw from the contents of the call the inference that the deceased was saying that she was under attack from her husband and that that was true, that could be justified only by treating the contents as part of the res gestae. It has not been contended that the calls in the present case, made after the arrest of the appellant, can come into that category.

A more modern example of the impermissibility of drawing inferences from hearsay assertions is provided by *R v Blastland* [1986] AC 41, [1985] 2 All ER 1095, where the accused, who was charged with murder, attempted to call witnesses to testify that a third person, not called as a witness, had stated, before the body was found, that a young boy had been murdered. That evidence was tendered for the purpose of enabling an inference to be drawn, from the knowledge of the maker of the statement of the boy's death, that he had been responsible for it, although it was accepted that evidence of a confession of guilt by the same persons was rightly excluded as inadmissible hearsay. In the course of his speech, my noble and learned friend, Lord Bridge of Harwich quoted and approved the following words of the trial judge (Bush J), at 53 and 1099:

'The real purpose and relevance of calling the evidence as to the state of mind is to say that in effect that was an implied admission of the knowledge of the crime, which is an implied admission of the crime itself and that too I regard as hearsay evidence and inadmissible.'

Lord Bridge went on to observe, at 53-54 and 1099:

'Hearsay evidence is not excluded because it has no logically probative value. Given that the subject matter of the hearsay is relevant to some issue in the trial, it may clearly be potentially probative. The rationale of excluding it as inadmissible, rooted as it is in the system of trial by jury, is a recognition of the great difficulty, even more acute for a juror than for a trained judicial mind, of assessing what, if any, weight can properly be given to a statement by a person whom the jury have not seen or heard and which has not been subject to any test of reliability by cross-examination . . . It is, of course, elementary that statements made to a witness by a third party are not excluded by the hearsay rule when they are put in evidence solely to prove that state of mind either of the maker of the statement or the person to whom it was made. What a person said or heard said may well be the best and most direct evidence of that person's state of mind. This principle can only apply, however, when the state of mind evidenced by the statement is either itself directly in issue at the trial or of direct and immediate relevance to an issue which arises at the trial. It is at this point, as it seems to me, that the argument for the appellant breaks down.'

If we now apply that to the facts of the instant case, what is in issue is the state of mind of the appellant: did he or did he not have an intent to deal in drugs? Is the existence of that state of mind in the appellant proved or rendered more probable by the fact that a third person, not even proved to have been known to him, has called at the premises where he and two other persons live and has asked a police officer to supply drugs? I find it very difficult to see how it can be except by treating it as an assertion by the caller to the police officer that the appellant is a supplier of drugs, an assertion clearly inadmissible as hearsay because tendered as evidence of fact. To put it another way, the circumstance of the call and the request in combination becomes relevant only by virtue of the latter's very inadmissibility. So one is faced with a circular and self defeating process. The requests of the callers cannot establish or, without more, render probable the existence of that state of mind in the appellant. They establish only what was the state of mind or belief of the callers, which was never in issue and which can be relevant to the issue only if there exists and can be proved the state of mind of the appellant, which is the very thing that they are tendered to establish . . .

I have had the advantage of reading in draft the speeches prepared by my noble and learned friends, Lord Griffiths and Lord Browne-Wilkinson. Whilst I share their unease at the rejection of what any layman would regard as a tolerably plain indication that the appellant had been engaged in trading in drugs, I have not felt able to accept their analysis of the relevance and admissibility of the evidence tendered. The pith of the argument – and I hope that I do not misstate it – is that the acts of callers in going or telephoning to the premises, explained by their states of mind as revealed by their contemporaneous words, is some evidence which a jury could properly take into account in deciding whether the appellant had an intention to supply because it demonstrates that there was an established potential market, ie a pool of willing purchasers, which the accused had the opportunity of supplying. It is the relevance of this in relation to the only issue in the case – the intention of the accused to supply that market – that I have not felt able to accept. 'Some evidence which a jury could take into account' means no more than that the evidence is probative. But then, one asks, of what is it probative? What is it about the existence of a potential customer or of a body of customers, whether substantial or not, that tends to render it more or less likely that a given individual intends to supply their requirements? Can one, for instance, legitimately infer an intention to make a gift to charity from evidence of calls made by collectors seeking donations?

Clearly the existence of a body of potential customers provides the opportunity to the accused (and, indeed, to anyone else who knows of their existence) to supply their requirements if he has the wish or intention to do so. But in what way does it establish that intention? The fact that potential customers make statements indicative of their existence as potential customers demonstrates no more than their desire to be supplied by anyone minded to supply them, which would, on this analysis, include also the police officers who intercepted calls. The general proposition that any statement indicating that the maker of the statement is a potential customer of an accused person for the purpose of purchasing drugs is admissible as evidence of the accused's intent to supply is manifestly insupportable. But it is said, following the Australasian cases to which I will refer later, that what renders such evidence admissible in the instant case is that the statements were made on the occasion of visits to or calls at the premises where the accused lived. The visits or calls, irrelevant in themselves, were invested with a relevance as 'acts' of the persons concerned by the contemporaneous words which, though inadmissible as hearsay if they stood alone as proof of the veracity of the belief which they indicate, are nevertheless admissible as 'explaining' the state of mind of the caller in performing the act of making the call or visiting the premises. From that combination of words and acts it is said that it is permissible to infer that the accused had dealt in and was dealing in drugs, that is to say that he was known to the callers as a drug dealer, which is what I take to be intended in the reference to 'an established market'. To my mind, this reasoning is fallacious in that it mistakes the real purpose of the evidence by investing the acts of the callers in calling or visiting the premises with an entirely false significance, so that they become merely a peg on which to hang the statement. The issue to which the evidence is directed is not, as it was in the Australian cases, the use which was being made of the accused's house. It is the intention or state of mind of the accused and it is, on analysis, the content of the statement and that alone from which the jury are invited to infer that intention. The fact that it was made in the course of a telephone call or at the front door of the house – the circumstance which, it is said, the statement is admissible to 'explain' – adds nothing at all. One can illustrate this with a simple example. Suppose that the evidence of a police officer was that he was in a café in the neighbourhood of the accused's house when he overheard a number of conversations in which the speakers indicated that they had assembled there with the intention of going on to visit the accused in order to buy drugs from him. Such statements would no doubt explain the 'acts' of the speakers in being present at the café, but I can see no possible basis upon which they could be admitted as evidence of the accused's intention except by reliance upon the manifestly insupportable proposition to which I have referred. How can it make any difference that the words were spoken not at a nearby café but at the front door of the house? In neither case does the place where the words were spoken or the means by which they were communicated have any significance at all apart from the words themselves. To say that they are admitted in order to 'explain' an act which is, in itself, without any significance is merely to conceal the true purpose of their admission. Their significance lies not in where or how they were spoken but in the fact that they were spoken at all.

The critical point of divergence – and I agree that it is a narrow point – is perhaps most clearly encapsulated in the proposition that if the callers had themselves been called to give evidence at the trial and if their evidence had consisted solely and exclusively of a statement that, on the relevant day, they had called at the house and asked to be supplied with drugs, that evidence must have been admitted. I have not felt able to accept this, for I cannot see how that evidence, standing alone, could have any possible relevance to any issue at the trial. It neither supports nor detracts from the existence of the intention which is in issue. It can do so only if and to the extent that it is treated as a demonstration not merely of the caller's hope, but of his belief or opinion, that 'Chippie' is a supplier of drugs. Introduced for that purpose it would, in my view, be manifestly inadmissible and the judge would, it seems to me, be bound to direct the jury to ignore it.

Accordingly, I for my part feel compelled to answer the certified question in the negative.

That question, however, has been framed in such a way as to relate to a request made by a single caller. Can it make any difference that in fact the evidence submitted related to a large number of callers and requests made within a matter of a few hours? To put it another way, can a substantial number of items of evidence, each inadmissible individually, acquire by association with one another a quality of cumulative admissibility which they do not possess individually? I find it impossible to see how they can. If, as I believe is the correct analysis, the evidence relating to each caller demonstrates no more than that caller's individual and inadmissible belief, the cumulative beliefs of a number of callers could demonstrate no more than the existence of a common reputation which, in any event, would be inadmissible in evidence save on an issue of pedigree or of public right.

The Crown relies, however, on a number of Commonwealth decisions concerned with illegal gaming in which not dissimilar evidence has been admitted. The issue in these cases was whether the accused, as the occupier of certain premises, was using them for the purpose of betting. As I have understood the judgments, the reception of evidence of calls by persons (mostly unidentified) who were not called as witnesses was justified on the ground that an attempt by a third person to place a bet although not communicated to or received by the accused, was, because unlikely to be accidental, logically probative of the conduct of the accused on the premises and thus admissible to prove the use to which the premises were being put by him. Of these cases the editor of *Cross on Evidence*, 7th edn, said at 525:

'A defensible line can be drawn between evidence of a call explicitly asserting premises to be used for betting, which is hearsay and admissible neither directly as evidence of the nature of the premises, nor circumstantially as evidence of the belief of such callers; and evidence of the receipt of calls ostensibly placing bets which is admissible directly to show that such calls were made, and circumstantially to show the beliefs of their makers.'

I confess that I find difficulty in seeing a logically defensible distinction between an inference to be drawn from an express assertion (viz that that which is asserted is true) (impermissible) and an inference to be drawn from precisely the same assertion made by implication (permissible). That calls are made to premises is, by itself, irrelevant, for it is probative of nothing but the fact that the calls have been made. They have no independent relevance of their own but become relevant only by virtue of the caller's purpose in making them based in turn upon the caller's belief that bets will be accepted, which in turn is relevant only as an assertion by the callers that the premises are used for betting . . . [He discussed *Davidson v Quirke* [1923] NZLR 552, *Lenthall v Mitchell* [1933] SASR 231, *McGregor v Stokes* [1952] VLR 347 and *Marshall v Watt* [1953] Tas SR 1.]

All these cases were prosecutions for the statutory offence of using premises for the purpose of betting and the evidence was tendered as probative of the use being made of the premises. In *Mathewson v Police* [1969] NZLR 218 and in *Police v Machirus* [1977] 1 NZLR 288, however, similar evidence was admitted in support of a charge not relating to the user of premises but simply that the accused had acted as a bookmaker contrary to a statutory prohibition. It may be said to be a point of distinction that in all these cases, with the exception of the two New

Zealand cases last referred to, the charges related specifically to the use being made of premises so that calls at or to the premises might be said to have some special and independent relevance. For myself, I do not, however, find this a convincing ground of distinction. What one looks for in vain in all cases is some convincing analysis of how the proven acts and intentions of other people can be relevant to the acts and intentions of the accused person beyond the assertion that they demonstrated some sort of prior agreement – an assertion which has to rest on the belief or opinion of persons not called to give evidence. In *Fingleton v Lowen* (1979) 20 SASR 312, Zelling J, whilst accepting that such evidence was admissible to show the use or character of premises, declined to follow the two last-mentioned New Zealand cases on the ground that the purpose for which the evidence was there tendered, namely to show the caller's purpose to make a bet specifically with the accused, rendered it a clear infringement of the hearsay rule. He said at 318:

'The substance of the message was inadmissible because that involved a statement of the truth of the assertion that they were seeking to bet with [the appellant]. The truth of that statement could not be proved by hearsay evidence, but it would seem to have been necessary if the appellant was, as he was, to be convicted of carrying on the business of a bookmaker, because it was his business and his identity that had to be proved.'

The distinction is a fine one, the logic of which is, I confess, not immediately apparent to me. The use or character of the premises was relevant only to the charge that the defendant was using them for the purpose of betting; and evidence that persons had attempted to place bets was relevant only as establishing either a past experience or a present belief that their bets would be accepted. If this was admissible in order to identify the purpose for which the premises were being used, I find it difficult to see why it should not equally be admissible for identifying the person who was using them. The basis of its admissibility has to rest upon the assumption expressed by Salmond J in *Davidson v Quirke* [1923] NZLR 552, 555:

'Such a practice does not arise by accident or mistake, and points logically to the inference that such use of the telephone by outsiders has its source in the agreement and purpose of the occupier himself.'

That, if it is permissible reasoning, applies as much to identify the occupant as it does to establishing the use which he makes of the premises.

But is it permissible reasoning having regard to *Wright v Doe d Tatham* (1837) 7 Ad & El 313, *R v Harry* (1987) 86 Cr App Rep 105 and the authorities in this House which have already been referred to? I have to say, though I do so with a little reluctance, that I do not think that it is. I cannot think that Salmond J would have sought to defend the introduction of testimony of a single betting call as evidence of the agreement or purpose of the occupier of the premises to which that call was made. The feature which appears to have persuaded him that the evidence was admissible was that it related to a multiplicity of calls from which it could be inferred that there was a 'practice', leading in turn to an inference of an agreement between the occupier and the callers. That inference, however, must on analysis rest upon the supposition that the callers would not have sought to place bets unless they believed that their bets would be accepted. Such a belief in a number of people does not normally arise by accident and therefore the fact that it is held by a number of people is evidence of its truth. In other words, that which would be inadmissible as evidence of the truth of the belief of a single caller is nevertheless admissible as evidence of the truth of a more general belief. The rationale of that can only be that whilst it is credible that one person may harbour and act upon a mistaken belief, it is less credible that two or three or more persons would do so. Thus the existence of the cumulative belief is admissible as evidence of its truth.

If that was indeed the reasoning it cannot in my judgment be reconciled with the English authorities. The multiplicity of calls can go only to indicating that a shared belief is more likely to be true than a belief held by a single person or a few people. That, however, goes to weight or reliability, not to admissibility and it cannot in itself make admissible that which is inadmissible . . .

McGregor v Stokes [1952] VLR 347 (and, referentially, the remarks of Salmond J in *Davidson v Quirke* [1923] NZLR 552) were referred to and accepted in *Ratten v R* [1972] AC 378, [1971] 3 All ER 801, as support for the proposition that a telephone call is a composite act consisting of the making of the call and the words spoken. The cases were not subjected to any analysis in the opinion of the Board and, like my noble and learned friend Lord Bridge of Harwich, I do not consider that this reference can properly be treated as expressing the Board's general approbation of these cases, the correctness of which does not, from the report of the argument of counsel for the appellant, appear to have been challenged.

The Court of Appeal [(Criminal Division), (1990) 93 Cr App Rep 222] in the instant case followed *Davidson v Quirke* and *McGregor v Stokes* as representing not only the law of New Zealand and Victoria but also the law of England. For the reasons which I have sought to explain, I do not think that they do. Nor does it seem to me that, however desirable it may seem in the instant case, it would be right for this House to adopt a new rule which would let in implied assertions where express assertions would be excluded. I cannot, for my part, see any logical difference between evidence of a positive assertion and evidence of an assertion expressed as a question from which the positive assertion is to be inferred. In both cases the opinion or belief of the maker is unsworn and untested by cross-examination and is equally prejudicial. To admit such statements as evidence of the fact would, in my opinion, not only entail a radical departure from the underlying reasoning in *R v Blastland* [1986] AC 41, [1985] 2 All ER 1095 and *Myers v Director of Public Prosecutions* [1965] AC 1001, [1964] 2 All ER 881, and the over-ruling of a case of high authority which has stood unchallenged for a century and a half but would involve embarking upon a process of judicial legislation.

[Lords Bridge of Harwich and Ackner delivered concurring speeches. Lords Griffiths and Browne-Wilkinson delivered dissenting speeches.]

Lloyd v Powell Duffryn Steam Coal Co Ltd   [1914] AC 733, HL

The issue was whether a child was the son of a man killed by an accident arising out of and in the course of his employment with the respondents. The deceased, knowing the child's mother was pregnant, had promised to marry her; he had also told his landlady and a friend that he was going to marry her because of the pregnancy. The Court of Appeal held that these statements were declarations against interest, and hence admissible as a hearsay exception. The House of Lords held the statements admissible but not as an exception to the hearsay rule.

Lord Atkinson: . . . To treat the statements made by the deceased as statements made by a deceased person against his pecuniary interest, and therefore, though hearsay, proof of the facts stated, is wholly to mistake their true character and significance. This significance consists in the improbability that any man would make these statements, true or false, unless he believed himself to be the father of the child of whom Alice Lloyd was pregnant.

Lord Moulton: It can scarcely be contested that the state of mind of the putative father and his intentions with regard to the child are matters relevant to the issue, whether there was a reasonable anticipation that he would support the child when born. It may be that an intention on his part so to do might be implied from the fact of his paternity and his recognition of it. But whether this be so or not, the attitude of mind of the putative father is that from which alone one can draw conclusions as to the greater or less probability of his supporting the child when born, and therefore evidence to prove that attitude of mind must be admissible if it be the proper evidence to establish such a fact. Now, it is well established in English jurisprudence, in accordance with the dictates of common sense, that the words and acts of a person are admissible as evidence of his state of mind. Indeed, they are the only possible evidence on such an issue. It was urged at the Bar that although the acts of the deceased might be put in evidence, his words might not. I fail to understand the distinction. Speaking is as much an act as doing.

It must be borne in mind that there is nothing in the admission of such evidence which clashes with the rooted objection in our jurisprudence to the admission of hearsay evidence. The testimony of the witnesses is to the act, ie to the deceased speaking these words, and it is the speaking of the words which is the matter that is put in evidence and which possesses evidential value. The evidence, is, therefore, not in any respect open to the objection that it is secondary or hearsay evidence.

[Earl Loreburn and Lord Shaw of Dunfermline gave concurring judgments.]

NOTE

1. This was followed in *Nash v Railways Comr* [1963] SRNSW 357. Conduct as evidence of the badness of beer was admitted in *Manchester Brewery Co Ltd v Coombs* [1901] 2 Ch 608.
2. The last two sentences of Lord Moulton's speech as quoted above were approved in *R v Blastland* [1986] AC 41 at 56–7, [1985] 2 All ER 1095 at 1101 and apparently in *Walton v R* (1989) 166 CLR 283 at 288–9.

QUESTION

Do you agree with the House of Lords' view in *Lloyd's* Case?

Teper v R [1952] AC 480, [1952] 2 All ER 447, PC

The accused was convicted of arson. A policeman named Cato testified that at 2 am, at least twenty-six minutes after the fire started and more than a furlong away from it, he heard a woman shouting, 'Your place burning and you going away from the fire.' He then noticed a black car containing a fair man resembling the accused. The woman was not called. The Privy Council held that the evidence was inadmissible; it did not fall within the res gestae exception to the hearsay rule.

Lord Normand: [The res gestae exception] appears to rest ultimately on two propositions – that human utterance is both a fact and a means of communication, and that human action may be so interwoven with words that the significance of the action cannot be understood without the correlative words and the dissociation of the words from the action would impede the discovery of truth. But the judicial applications of these two propositions, which do not always combine harmoniously, have never been precisely formulated in a general principle. Their Lordships will not attempt to arrive at a general formula, nor is it necessary to review all of the considerable number of cases cited in the argument. This, at least, may be said, that it is essential that the words sought to be proved by hearsay should be, if not absolutely contemporaneous with the action or event, at least so clearly associated with it, in time, place and circumstance, that they are part of the thing being done, and so an item or part of real evidence and not merely a reported statement: *R v Bedingfield* (1879) 14 Cox CC 341; *O'Hara v Central Scottish Motor Traction Co Ltd* 1941 SC 363. How slight a separation of time and place may suffice to make hearsay evidence of the words spoken incompetent is well illustrated by the two cases cited. In *Bedingfield's* case a woman rushed with her throat cut out of a room in which the injury had been inflicted into another room where she said something to persons who saw her enter. Their evidence about what she said was ruled inadmissible by Cockburn CJ. In *O'Hara's* case, a civil action, the event was an injury to a passenger brought about by the sudden swerve of the omnibus in which she was travelling. The driver of the omnibus said in his evidence that he was forced to swerve by a pedestrian who hurried across his path. Hearsay evidence of what was said by a man on the pavement at the scene of the accident as soon as the injured party had been attended to was held to be admissible in corroboration of the driver's evidence. But what was said twelve minutes later and away from the scene by the same man was held not part of the res gestae. In *R v Christie* [1914] AC 545, [1914–15] All ER Rep 63, HL, the principle of the decision in *Bedingfield's* case was approved by Lord Reading with whom Lord Dunedin concurred, and no criticism of it is to be found in the speeches of the other noble and learned Lords who sat with them. In *R v Gibson* (1887) 18 QBD 537, the prosecutor gave evidence in a criminal trial that, immediately after he was struck by a stone, a woman going past, pointing to the prisoner's door, said: 'The person who threw the stone went in there.' This evidence was not objected to at the trial, but it was admitted by counsel for the prosecution in a Case Reserved that the evidence was incompetent. The conviction was quashed, and from their judgments it is clear that the learned judges who took part in the decision were far from questioning the correctness of counsel's admission. In *Gibson's* case the words were closely associated in time and place with the event, the assault. But they were not directly connected with that event itself. They were not words spontaneously forced from the woman by the sight of the assault, but were prompted by the sight of a man quitting the scene of the assault and they were spoken for the purpose of helping to bring him to justice.

The special danger of allowing hearsay evidence for the purpose of identification requires that it shall only be allowed if it satisfies the strictest test of close association with the event in time, place and circumstances . . .

There is yet another proposition which can be affirmed, viz that for identification purposes in a criminal trial the event with which the words sought to be proved must be so connected as to form part of the res gestae is the commission of the crime itself – the throwing of the stone, the striking of the blow, the setting fire to the building, or whatever the criminal act may be. Counsel for the Crown submitted that any relevant event or action may be accompanied by words which may have to be proved in order to bring out its true significance. There is a limited sense in which this is true, but it is not always true, and much depends on the use to be made of the evidence. In *Christie's* case hearsay evidence of certain words uttered by a child, the victim of indecent assault, in the presence and hearing of the accused were held to be admissible in explanation of the demeanour of the accused in response to them. But the evidence was held inadmissible for the purpose of showing that the child identified the accused as his assailant. In the present case identification is the purpose for which the hearsay was introduced, and its admission goes far beyond anything that has been authorised by any reported case.

NOTE

The probative value of the evidence depended on two identifications – the woman's and Cato's – of a man of another race at night. It depended on Cato's attention being directed to a particular person in a crowd when any other member of the crowd might have been meant. The innuendo in the statement was not unambiguously clear: on one view the evidence was irrelevant to the issue of who caused the fire. There was thus ample reason for excluding the evidence apart from the Privy Council's assumption that it was hearsay and their decision that it fell outside the res gestae exception.

Holloway v MacFeeters   (1956) 94 CLR 470

After a car struck a pedestrian the driver ran away. In the High Court of Australia Dixon CJ and Kitto J said that this fact was inadmissible evidence of his negligence as an admission, and hence they were prepared to assume it was hearsay.

Dixon CJ: [O'Bryan J in the court below said] that the jury might infer that the driver knew that he had run down the man and severely injured him and had yet left him where he lay. The jury might regard this behaviour as implying a consciousness of guilt and as being of the nature of an admission. As to the view that it is tantamount to an admission by conduct, the difficulty is that the driver is not a party to the proceedings nor is the nominal defendant sued on his behalf. The admissions of the driver would not, as such, be receivable in evidence against the nominal defendant.

NOTE

What position is desirable?

One view is that all implied assertions are hearsay and inadmissible unless they fall within an existing exception (eg Baker, p 6; *Wright v Doe d Tatham* (1837) 7 Ad & El 313 at 388, per Parke B; *Thompson v Manhattan Rly Co* 42

NY Sup 896 (1896); *People v Bush* 133 NE 201 (1921); *Marshall v Watt* [1953] Tas SR 1 at 7, per Gibson J; *State v Di Vincenti* 93 S (2d) 676 (1957); *Ratten v R* [1972] AC 378, [1971] 3 All ER 801, PC; *R v Kearley* [1992] 2 AC 228; [1992] 2 All ER 345, HL). Advocates of this extreme view, while admitting that implied assertions are usually free from the risk of manufacture, feel they may be unreliable because of defects in the powers of perception, memory, or expression of the maker of the assertion.

Another is that all implied assertions are hearsay, but new exceptions should be created to take account of special guarantees of reliability associated with some of this kind of evidence. Thus if the matters to be inferred from the actor's conduct are within his knowledge and his conduct was detrimental to him, it should be admitted (Morgan (1935) 48 Harv LR 1138 at 1158–60). An example might be Parke B's losing gambler. Another test is to give the court a discretion to admit the evidence if on the facts it seemed reliable, eg because the actor has based important decisions on the belief which he is impliedly asserting. An example might be Parke B's sea captain who after testing a vessel embarks on it with his family. Two examples of different forms of adherence to this second view are to be found in the respective reasons for judgment of Mason CJ and Deane J in *Walton v R* (1989) 166 CLR 283 at 293–4, 295–6 and 308.

A third view is that non-assertive statements are hearsay but not non-assertive conduct. (See *Davidson v Quirke* [1923] NZLR 552, where the acts of phoning a gaming house were admitted as not being hearsay, and details of what the callers said were admissible under the hearsay exception for statements explaining the purpose of acts (p 357, post).) See also *Police v Machirus* [1977] 1 NZLR 288. These two cases were disapproved in *Fingleton v Lowen* (1979) 20 SASR 312. This was Cross's view. He drew the distinction for three main reasons. One is that deeds speak louder than words. Another is that if conduct were hearsay the scope of the rule would be tremendously extended. Thirdly, the real reason for excluding much impliedly assertive conduct is not unreliability but the risk of a multiplicity of side-issues. Where there are few side-issues the evidence is admissible (Cross, 5th edn, at p 472 and (1969) 7 U of Melb LR 1 at 12–13). Nothing was said in *R v Kearley* [1992] 2 AC 228, [1992] 2 All ER 345, HL, which concerned assertions implied from words rather than from conduct, as to this possible distinction.

If no hearsay reform were likely, there would be much to be said for this view. But ours is a reforming age, and new exceptions could be created if the hearsay rule were widened. Further, Cross's view is illogical. 'What rationale can there be for treating "Hello X" as hearsay, but not the non-assertive conduct of a soldier seen saluting another person as evidence that the person concerned was an officer?' (Weinberg, op cit, p 285). It is not in fact clear that deeds always do speak louder than words. What speaks loudly is a deed or a statement based on serious motives.

A fourth view is that no implied assertion is hearsay (eg *American Law Institute Model Code* (1942) r 501(1); *Jones v Sutherland Shire Council* [1979] 2 NSWLR 206 at 229–33; *Ritz Hotel Ltd v Charles of the Ritz Ltd* (1988) 15 NSWLR 158 at 172, and perhaps *Lloyd v Powell Duffryn Steam Coal Co Ltd* [1914] AC 733). But it is irrational to distinguish express assertions from implied, particularly since the dangers of inaccurate observation, memory and narration exist just as strongly without the safeguard of cross-examination in both cases.

A fifth view is that statements not intended to be assertive are inadmissible hearsay unless the assertion impliedly made is about something the declarant himself has or has not done: in such cases the chance of error is very small.

A sixth view may be detectable in the majority reasoning in *Walton v R* (1989) 166 CLR 283 at 302–4: a statement or non-verbal conduct containing an implied assertion is admissible if it has probative value other than as an assertion, but inadmissible if it has no probative value other than as an assertion.

On this view, even though a statement or non-verbal conduct which contains an assertion on the truth of which the court is asked to rely may be said to have a hearsay element, it is admissible if tendered as a relevant fact or a fact relevant to a fact in issue; on the other hand, a statement or non-verbal conduct which has no probative value other than as an assertion is not admissible. They gave as an example of the former the tender of statements by a testatrix as to her son's misconduct to prove her state of mind but not to prove that the misconduct actually occurred. They gave as an example of the latter statements by a deceased person that she was going to meet the accused at a particular place, the relevance of this being that 'it might be inferred that she acted in accordance with her intention'. Such statements would only have probative value if they are truthful and accurate and to rely upon them is to rely to some extent upon the truth of any assertion or implied assertion contained in them. To that extent an element of hearsay may be said to be present.

But the element of hearsay need not necessarily preclude evidence of that kind being treated as conduct from which an inference can be drawn rather than as an assertion which is put forward to prove the truth of the facts asserted.

In principle, this approach frankly acknowledges the force of the considerations underlying the first view, but seeks to side-step them by characterising the conduct in question as having a circumstantial as well as a testimonial character, and by precluding the trier of fact from taking account of the testimonial character. Yet the probative value of the circumstantial conduct might be thought in many instances to rest on its testimonial character.

Some American writers have tried to solve the implied assertions problem by asking if cross-examination of the maker of the assertion would assist in judging his veracity, memory, observation or narrative powers.

Thus Maguire (p 16) puts these examples. (*a*) The issue is A's deafness. As he read a book aloud a mechanical buzzer was operated at different levels. A's tone of voice never changed, and expert testimony is that this could not have been maintained if the buzzing had been audible to A. (*b*) The issue is B's deafness. B was blindfolded and a tuning fork was moved towards and away from him. He stated its movements accurately. (*c*) The issue is whether C's leg is paralysed. A doctor testifies that when he thrust a needle into the leg in different places, C gave no sign of pain. (*d*) A man is shot dead in the middle of a crowd. D, an enemy of the victim, runs away. Maguire says that (*a*) is a case where cross-examination of A could not destroy our belief in his deafness. However, (*b*) involves B's manifestation of belief, and there may be something fraudulent about the test which could be exposed by cross-examining B. But only veracity arises, not powers of memory, observation or narrative. If it is thought the risk of fraud is slight enough, the evidence might be admitted as not being a case where cross-examination could make any difference. In (c) the risk of fraud is greater. In (d) problems about D's sincerity and motives arise – because he may wish to distract attention from the real killer. Problems akin to narration arise – what did D mean by running away? It may be due to a consciousness of guilt, or to a fear of becoming mixed up in a discreditable affair. Problems akin to observation arise – D may mistakenly think he killed the man. Maguire concludes: 'the decisions have not made us sure whether the rule may be invoked when only testimonial qualities *other than sincerity* could be dissected by the cross-examiner. This uncertainty is very bad indeed for practical administration of the rule' (p 23). His analysis does reveal a possible line of division between hearsay and non-hearsay which would coincide with Parke B's if it is drawn at the point when cross-examination begins to have some value on any aspect of sincerity, observation, memory or narration. If the line is drawn in a less exclusionary place it would not.

(ii) Negative hearsay

Does the common law rule apply to 'negative hearsay'? Assume the issue is whether the accused purported to make payments to employees of his firm who in fact did not exist, and that there is a practice in the firm of making out a file on each employee. Is an accountant's evidence that he searched for the files of the employees allegedly paid but did not find them admissible? Such evidence was admitted in *S v Becker* 1968 (1) SA 18. Yet an out of court statement 'The accused employs only A, B and C, but not D' would be hearsay with respect to D's non-employment. The same must be so of a statement 'The accused employs only A, B and C'. If the hearsay rule extends to implied assertions by conduct, proof of a practice of making files on all employees and only finding files on A, B and C must also be hearsay. The NSW Law Reform Commission on Evidence (Business Records) (LRC 17, 1973) made a recommendation (since enacted as s 69(4) of the Evidence Act 1995 (Cwth and NSW); see also Civil Evidence (Scotland) Act 1988, s 7 and Civil Evidence Act 1995, s 9) that negative hearsay be admissible, which assumes it is hearsay, not admissible at common law (and see *R v Hally* [1962] Qd R 214).

But in *R v Abadom* [1983] 1 All ER 364, [1983] 1 WLR 126, CA; *R v Shone* (1982) 76 Cr App Rep 72, CA, and *R v Patel* [1981] 3 All ER 94 at 96, CA, the Court of Appeal indicated that negative hearsay based on business records was admissible. See also *Motor Transport Comr v Collier-Moat Ltd* [1960] SRNSW 238; *Prasad v Minister for Immigration, Local Government and Ethnic Affairs* (1991) 101 ALR 109 at 122.

FURTHER READING

Ashworth and Pattenden (1986) 102 LQR 292; Baker, *The Hearsay Rule* (London, 1950); Carter (1993) 109 LQR 573; Cross (1956) 72 LQR 91, 7 U of Melb LR 1 (1969); Finman (1962) 14 Stanford LR 682; Guest (1985) 101

LQR 385; [1988] CLP 33; Harrison (1955) 7 Res Judicatae 58; Hutchins and Slesinger (1928) 28 Col LR 432 and (1929) 38 Yale LJ 283; Jefferson (1944) 58 Harv LR 1; McCormick (1930) 39 Yale LJ 489; Maguire (1961) 14 Vanderbilt LR 741; Morgan (1921) 30 Yale LJ 355; (1922) 31 Yale LJ 229; (1927) 40 Harv LR 712; (1929) 42 Harv LR 461; (1935) 48 Harv LR 1138; (1948) 62 Harv LR 177; (1952) 5 Vanderbilt LR 451; Sorenson and Sorenson (1953) 28 NYULR 1213; Tribe (1974) 87 Harv LR 957; Weinberg (1973) 9 U of Melb LR 268; Zuckerman ch 11.

(iii)   Other cases

There are some, and if the day-to-day decisions of trial courts were analysed with care, probably many, instances where the rule does not apply. Examples are: (probably) the court's inherent paternal and lunacy jurisdictions, custody matters (*R(BM) v R(DN)* [1978] 2 All ER 33, [1977] 1 WLR 1256, CA), non-adversary proceedings such as those turning on whether a child is in need of care and control (*Humberside County Council v DPR (an infant)* [1977] 3 All ER 964, [1977] 1 WLR 1251, DC), and traditional administrative juris-dictions (*Kavanagh v Chief Constable of Devon and Cornwall* [1974] QB 624, [1973] 3 All ER 697, CA). There are of course many tribunals where the hearsay rule does not apply by statute.

QUESTIONS

1. Guy Burgess is being tried for espionage. Three issues in the case are: (i) did Burgess post a letter just outside the Russian Embassy on 1 March? (ii) is Burgess a habitual drunkard? and (iii) what is the age of Burgess's chauffeur?

Is any of the following evidence admissible on issue (i): (*a*) the fact that the envelope of the letter allegedly posted near the Embassy is postmarked '1 March' by a post office near the Embassy; (*b*) the evidence of a passer-by that on 1 March he heard Kim Philby (who cannot be found to testify) say to someone outside the Embassy 'Goodbye, Guy'; (*c*) on 1 March an Old Etonian tie marked 'GB' is found near the Embassy; (*d*) as in (*c*), but a wit-ness testifies that earlier that day he saw Burgess wearing such a tie?

Is any of the following evidence admissible on issue (ii): (*d*) the evidence of Donald McLean's butler that he always found empty whisky bottles in Burgess's room after his visits; (*e*) the evidence of a passer-by that he heard McLean say to Burgess, 'You've been shaking very badly lately, Guy'; (*f*) the evidence of a steward at the Reform Club, of which Burgess was a member, that the Secretary often told him to lock up the whisky if Burgess was left alone in the bar?

Is any of the following admissible on issue (iii): (*g*) the testimony of Burgess's chauffeur that his own age was twenty-four; (*h*) Burgess's testimony that the chauffeur was thirty-four? Could the jury be told to form their own view of the chauffeur's age by drawing inferences from his appearance?

2. Leopold and Loeb go into an isolated cottage with a small boy. The boy is killed shortly before the police arrive. Leopold runs away and cannot sub-sequently be found. Is Leopold's flight admissible evidence in favour of Loeb at Loeb's trial for murdering the boy?

3. W claims to have seen D committing a crime. At her direction a police officer makes a sketch of D. Can the sketch be tendered at D's trial? See *R v Smith* [1976] Crim LR 511, CA.

4. (a) Is a photograph tendered by a person who did not take it admissible?

(b) Is a drawing or 'photofit' picture of a person admissible? Does it matter whether or not the person who gave the instructions to the maker is called? See *R v Cook* [1987] QB 417, [1987] 1 All ER 1049, CA.

5. In what circumstances is the hearsay rule an obstruction to the admission of calculations or measurements done by such machines or devices as computers, slide rules, X-ray spectrometers and weighing machines? See *R v Wood* [1982] Crim LR 667, CA.

6. To what extent is the hearsay rule an obstruction to the admission of films of radar tracers, tape-recordings and video films of offences being committed? See *The Statue of Liberty* [1968] 2 All ER 195, [1968] 1 WLR 739; *R v Maqsud Ali* [1966] 1 QB 688, [1965] 2 All ER 464, CCA; *Taylor v Chief Constable of Cheshire* [1987] 1 All ER 225, [1986] 1 WLR 1479, DC.

7. On the extremely difficult inter-relationship of the rule against hearsay, the rule against prior consistent statements, and proof of identity, see Gooderson [1968] CLJ 74; Libling [1977] Crim LR 268; Weinberg (1980) 12 MULR 532; *R v Christie* [1914] AC 545, [1914–15] All ER Rep 63; *Alexander v R* (1981) 145 CLR 395; *R v McGuire* [1975] 4 WWR 124; *R v Osbourne* [1973] QB 678, [1973] 1 All ER 649, CA; *R v Collings* [1976] 2 NZLR 104; *R v Ngahooro* [1982] 2 NZLR 203; *Teper v R* [1952] AC 480, [1952] 2 All ER 447, PC; *R v McLean* (1967) 52 Cr App Rep 80, CA; *R v McCay* [1991] 1 All ER 232, [1990] 1 WLR 645 and comment at [1990] Crim LR 340.

(a) W1 identifies the accused outside the court; can he prove that identification in court? Does admissibility turn on whether he also identifies the accused in court?

(b) W1 makes an out of court identification witnessed by W2. Can W2 prove it in court? Does admissibility depend on W1 making an in court identification and testifying to his out of court identification?

(c) Is W2's evidence of W1's prior identification admissible if W1 identifies the accused in court, but does not testify to his out of court identification?

(d) If W1 says in court that the accused is not the person who committed the offence, and denies previously identifying the accused as the offender, can W2 prove that W1 did previously identify the offender?

(e) W1 gives evidence but does not identify the accused in the dock as the offender – a peculiar factual circumstance which might be legitimately explained by a change in the appearance of the accused, for example as a result of growing a beard or suffering facial burns. W2 says that W1 made an out of court identification of the accused. Is the evidence of W1 that previously he identified the accused admissible? Is the evidence of W2 admissible?

(f) If W1 cannot make an in court identification and is unable to recollect making an out of court identification, can W2 give evidence of an out of court identification by W1?

(g) W1 cannot make an in court identification. He does testify that he previously identified the offender, that he believed that identification was accurate, but is unable to say that he identified the accused. Can W2 say that W1 identified the accused on the earlier occasion?

(h)   W1 cannot make an in court identification, and cannot swear to making an accurate out of court identification, but refreshes his memory from a document prepared by him or under his supervision. No actual recollection is revived, but he is prepared to swear that the contents of the document are true. Is his evidence admissible? Can W2 give evidence of what W1 said so as to fill in gaps in W1's testimony?

CHAPTER 13

Hearsay Exceptions: Criminal Cases

At common law the hearsay rule became riddled with exceptions. A major piece of reform was undertaken in civil cases in the Evidence Act 1938, and still more fundamental reforms in the Acts of 1968 and 1995. While reform in criminal cases has taken place in stages since 1965, the process has not gone as far as in civil cases. The following discussion does not propose to be complete, but seeks to mention briefly certain hearsay exceptions which have one or more of the following qualities: a continued importance even after reforms similar to the Civil Evidence Act 1968; present practical importance in criminal cases; and intrinsic interest.

1 Statements of deceased persons

A   DECLARATIONS AGAINST INTEREST

The oral or written statement by a deceased person of a fact which he knew to be against his pecuniary or proprietary interest at the time he made it is admissible as evidence of the fact and all collateral facts mentioned provided the declarant had personal knowledge of them. The basis of admissibility is that truth is guaranteed by the unlikelihood of a man lying against his own interests. This exception arose in civil cases involving contract, property or status much more than in criminal cases, because the declarations had to tend to impose pecuniary or proprietary, but not criminal, liabilities, but it was discussed in *R v Rogers* [1995] 1 Cr App Rep 374, CA. The result of the rule is that the accused cannot tender a confession by a third party that he was guilty: *Re Van Beelen's Petition* (1974) 9 SASR 163; *R v Turner* (1975) 61 Cr App Rep 67 at 88, CA; *R v Blastland* [1986] AC 41, [1985] 2 All ER 1095, HL; cf *Demeter v R* (1977) 75 DLR (3d) 251; *R v O'Brien* (1977) 76 DLR (3d) 513; *Wildman v R* (1984) 12 DLR (4th) 641. The traditional rule was affirmed by the United States Supreme Court in *Donnelly v United States* (228 US 243 (1913)). Holmes J dissented on the ground that 'no other statement is so much against interest as a confession of murder, it is far more calculated to convince than dying declarations, which would be let in to hang a man' (p 278). Some American courts have extended the exception to statements against penal interest made by living persons: *People v Spriggs* 389 P 2d 377

(1964); *Chambers v Mississippi* 410 US 295 (1973). As the court in *Van Beelen's* Case stressed, many declarations against penal interest are likely to be deliberately false.

B   DECLARATIONS IN THE COURSE OF DUTY

The oral or written statement by a deceased person made under a duty to record or report his acts is admissible evidence of the truth of such parts of the statement as it was his duty to record or report, provided the record or report was made roughly contemporaneously with the act done, and provided the declarant had no motive to lie. The reasons for the exception are, first, necessity: there might be no other evidence of what an employee did; and secondly, that the likelihood of dismissal for incompetent recording or reporting guarantees reliability. This exception too largely arose in civil cases.

There is no requirement that the recorder have personal knowledge: a record was admitted where one official had knowledge of the matter and the statutory duty to record it and forward it to another official who had the duty to preserve it and show it to members of the public (*R v Halpin* [1975] QB 907, [1975] 2 All ER 1124, CA (a case illustrating the capacity of the courts to create new hearsay exceptions, even if not explicitly, even after *Myers v DPP* [1965] AC 1001, [1964] 2 All ER 881, HL)). The rule applies only to statements of facts, not opinions: *R v McGuire* (1985) 81 Cr App Rep 323, CA.

C   DECLARATIONS AS TO PUBLIC OR GENERAL RIGHTS

An oral or written statement by a deceased person concerning the reputed existence of a public or general right is admissible as evidence of its existence provided the declaration was made before a dispute had arisen, and in the case of general rights, provided the declarant had competent knowledge. Public rights affect the entire population, general rights affect particular classes of person. The exception exists because other evidence is usually unavailable; and because most neighbours know about local matters affecting the community, and are likely to discuss them in public, so that false statements will be contradicted. The exception is an extreme example of the admission of multiple hearsay – hearsay on hearsay. It has little modern application, but was preserved for civil cases by the Civil Evidence Act 1968, s 9(4)(c). It has virtually no application in practice to criminal cases.

D   PEDIGREE DECLARATIONS

Oral or written statements of a deceased person, or statements to be implied from family conduct, are admissible as evidence of pedigree provided the declarant was a blood relation or the spouse of a blood relation of the person whose pedigree is in issue, and provided the declaration was made before the dispute arose. The exception is based on necessity and on the fact that it is natural for people to talk of their family in a truthful way if there is no interest to be served. It can have scarcely any application to criminal cases, except possibly incest; it was preserved in civil cases by the Civil Evidence Act 1968, s 9(4)(*b*).

E   TESTATORS' DECLARATIONS ABOUT THEIR WILLS

The oral or written statement of a deceased testator after the execution of his will is admissible evidence of the contents, but not the execution, of the will. The exception is based on the testator's unique means of knowledge and his general lack of reason to lie. It is noteworthy as the last hearsay exception explicitly created by the English courts (*Sugden v Lord St Leonards* (1876) 1 PD 154, [1874–80] All ER Rep 21, CA). It can have virtually no practical application in criminal cases.

F   DYING DECLARATIONS

The oral or written statement of a deceased person is admissible evidence of the cause of his death at a trial for his murder or manslaughter provided that when the statement was made the declarant would have been a competent witness and was under a settled hopeless expectation of death.

R v Woodcock   (1789) 1 Leach 500

The accused was charged with murdering his wife. She made a statement implicating him at a time when her death was inevitable as a result of eight head wounds. She died forty-eight hours later. She remained coherent until death but never expressed any realisation of dying. Eyre CB left the issue of whether she was under a settled hopeless expectation of death to the jury, who convicted the accused.

Eyre CB: [T]he general principle on which this species of evidence is admitted is, that they are declarations made in extremity, when the party is at the point of death, and when every hope of this world is gone: when every motive to falsehood is silenced, and the mind is induced by the most powerful considerations to speak the truth; a situation so solemn, and so awful, is considered by the law as creating an obligation equal to that which is imposed by a positive oath administered in a Court of Justice . . . [I]nasmuch as she was mortally wounded, and was in a condition which rendered almost immediate death inevitable; as she was thought by every person about her to be dying . . . her declarations . . . ought to be considered by a jury as being made under the impression of her approaching dissolution; for resigned as she appeared to be, she must have felt the hand of death, and must have considered herself as a dying woman.

NOTES

1. The same point about the basis of admissibility is made in *R v Hope* [1909] VLR 149. Normally no inquiry into the declarant's religious beliefs is made; but a four-year-old's declaration was excluded in *R v Pike* (1829) 3 C & P 598 and that of a ten-year-old admitted after enquiry in *R v Perkins* (1840) 9 C & P 395. In *R v Madobi* (1963) 6 FLR 1 the dying declaration exception was not applied to the statement of an indigenous Papuan, whose

community believed that the future life would be spent pleasantly on a nearby island (not followed in *R v Kipali-Ikarum* [1967–8] P & NGLR 119 and *R v Savage* [1970] Tas SR 137). In India and Pakistan dying declarations, though admissible, are treated with suspicion, because of a practice of a dying man revenging himself on all his enemies by blaming them for his death. But in *R v Kuruwaru* (1900) 10 QLJ 139 the dying declaration of a Mohammedan was admitted; Griffith CJ seemed to consider that it was enough that the declarant had a religious belief. Nor is any special inquiry undertaken in South Africa (Hoffmann, pp 121–4). The exception now probably operates quite independently of Eyre CB's rationale (47 ALJ 92).

2. The condition of extremity that on one view helps guarantee veracity on another is a possible source of errors of memory, and narration. (The danger of having to rely on leading questions, for example, is considerable: *R v Mitchell* (1892) 17 Cox CC 503; and incomplete dying declarations are inadmissible: *Waugh v R* [1950] AC 203, PC.) The jury should be told that the declaration is not subject to cross-examination (ibid).

3. There need not be a settled hopeless expectation of immediate death: *R v Perry* [1909] 2 KB 697, CCA. Quite long periods have elapsed, eg eleven days (*R v Mosley* (1825) 1 Mood CC 97); three weeks (*R v Bernadotti* (1869) 11 Cox CC 316).

4. Despite *R v Woodcock*, the courts have been reluctant to infer a settled hopeless expectation of death (eg *R v Jenkins* (1869) LR 1 CCR 187), though subsequent hopes of recovery do not affect the admissibility of a declaration made under such expectation (*R v Austin* (1912) 8 Cr App Rep 27, CCA). In particular, there has been reluctance to make an inference from the severity of wounds (eg *R v Morgan* (1875) 14 Cox CC 341; cf *R v Donohoe* [1962] NSWR 1144). See *R v Rogers* [1950] SASR 102.

5. The statement is admissible for the accused as well as against him (*R v Scaife* (1936) 2 Lew CC 150).

6. In *Mills v R* [1995] 3 All ER 865 at 875-6, [1995] 1 WLR 511 at 521-2, PC, the Privy Council declined to reject the dying declaration exception, while accepting that on a suitable occasion an inquiry might be usefully conducted into whether the requirements for the reception of such a declaration could be re-stated in a more flexible form.

QUESTION

Is there any reason for limiting admissibility to murder and manslaughter prosecutions, as settled in *R v Mead* (1824) 2 B & C 605?

2   Statements in public documents

A public document coming from the proper place or a certified copy of it is evidence of every fact stated in it. A public document must be made under a strict duty to inquire into all the circumstances recorded, must be concerned with a public matter, must be intended to be retained, and must be meant for public inspection. Examples are registers of births, deaths and marriages, and public surveys, reports and returns. The exception is justified by necessity and by the reliability of public records. It usually arises in civil cases but has some application to criminal ones.

3 Statutory exceptions

A STATEMENTS IN DOCUMENTS

Criminal Justice Act 1988

23 (1) Subject –
   (a) to subsection (4) below;
   (b) to paragraph 1A of Schedule 2 to the Criminal Appeal Act 1968 (evidence given orally at original trial to be given orally at retrial); and
   (c) to section 69 of the Police and Criminal Evidence Act 1984 (evidence from computer records),
a statement made by a person in a document shall be admissible in criminal proceedings as evidence of any fact of which direct oral evidence by him would be admissible if –
   (i) the requirements of one of the paragraphs of subsection (2) below are satisfied; or
   (ii) the requirements of subsection (3) below are satisfied.
   (2) The requirements mentioned in subsection (1)(i) above are –
   (a) that the person who made the statement is dead or by reason of his bodily or mental condition unfit to attend as a witness;
   (b) that –
      (i) the person who made the statement is outside the United Kingdom; and
      (ii) it is not reasonably practicable to secure his attendance; or
   (c) that all reasonable steps have been taken to find the person who made the statement, but that he cannot be found.
   (3) The requirements mentioned in subsection (1)(ii) above are –
   (a) that the statement was made to a police officer or some other person charged with the duty of investigating offences or charging offenders; and
   (b) that the person who made it does not give oral evidence through fear or because he is kept out of the way.
   (4) Subsection (1) above does not render admissible a confession made by an accused person that would not be admissible under section 76 of the Police and Criminal Evidence Act 1984.

24 (1) Subject –
   (a) to subsections (3) and (4) below;
   (b) to paragraph 1A of Schedule 2 to the Criminal Appeal Act 1968; and
   (c) to section 69 of the Police and Criminal Evidence Act 1984,
a statement in a document shall be admissible in criminal proceedings as evidence of any fact of which direct oral evidence would be admissible, if the following conditions are satisfied –
   (i) the document was created or received by a person in the course of a trade, business, profession or other occupation, or as the holder of a paid or unpaid office; and
   (ii) the information contained in the document was supplied by a person (whether or not the maker of the statement) who had, or may reasonably be supposed to have had, personal knowledge of the matters dealt with.
   (2) Subsection (1) above applies whether the information contained in the document was supplied directly or indirectly but, if it was supplied indirectly, only if each person through whom it was supplied received it –
   (a) in the course of a trade, business, profession or other occupation; or
   (b) as the holder of a paid or unpaid office.
   (3) Subsection (1) above does not render admissible a confession made by an accused person that would not be admissible under section 76 of the Police and Criminal Evidence Act 1984.

(4)   A statement prepared otherwise than in accordance with section 29 below or an order under paragraph 6 of Schedule 13 to this Act or [letters of request] or under section 30 or 31 below for the purposes –

    (*a*)   of pending or contemplated criminal proceedings; or

    (*b*)   of a criminal investigation,

shall not be admissible by virtue of subsection (1) above unless –

      (i)   the requirements of one of the paragraphs of subsection (2) of section 23 above are satisfied; or

     (ii)   the requirements of subsection (3) of that section are satisfied; or

    (iii)   the person who made the statement cannot reasonably be expected (having regard to the time which has elapsed since he made the statement and to all the circumstances) to have any recollection of the matters dealt with in the statement.

25   (1)   If, having regard to all the circumstances –

    (*a*)   the Crown Court –

      (i)   on a trial on indictment;

     (ii)   on an appeal from a magistrates' court; or

    (iii)   on the hearing of an application under section 6 of the Criminal Justice Act 1987 (applications for dismissal of charges of fraud transferred from magistrates' court to Crown Court); or

    (*b*)   the criminal division of the Court of Appeal; or

    (*c*)   a magistrates' court on a trial of an information,

is of the opinion that in the interest of justice a statement which is admissible by virtue of section 23 or 24 above nevertheless ought not to be admitted, it may direct that the statement shall not be admitted.

(2)   Without prejudice to the generality of subsection (1) above, it shall be the duty of the court to have regard –

    (*a*)   to the nature and source of the document containing the statement and to whether or not, having regard to its nature and source and to any other circumstances that appear to the court to be relevant, it is likely that the document is authentic;

    (*b*)   to the extent to which the statement appears to supply evidence which would otherwise not be readily available;

    (*c*)   to the relevance of the evidence that it appears to supply to any issue which is likely to have to be determined in the proceedings; and

    (*d*)   to any risk, having regard in particular to whether it is likely to be possible to controvert the statement if the person making it does not attend to give oral evidence in the proceedings, that its admission or exclusion will result in unfairness to the accused or, if there is more than one, to any of them.

26   Where a statement which is admissible in criminal proceedings by virtue of section 23 or 24 above appears to the court to have been prepared, otherwise than in accordance with section 29 below or an order under paragraph 6 of Schedule 13 to this Act or under section 30 or 31 below, for the purposes –

    (*a*)   of pending or contemplated criminal proceedings; or

    (*b*)   of a criminal investigation,

the statement shall not be given in evidence in any criminal proceedings without the leave of the court, and the court shall not give leave unless it is of the opinion that the statement ought to be admitted in the interests of justice; and in considering whether its admission would be in the interests of justice, it shall be the duty of the court to have regard –

      (i)   to the contents of the statement;

     (ii)   to any risk, having regard in particular to whether it is likely to be possible to controvert the statement if the person making it does not attend to give oral evidence in the proceedings, that its admission or exclusion will result in unfairness to the accused or, if there is more than one, to any of them; and

    (iii)   to any other circumstances that appear to the court to be relevant.

27   Where a statement contained in a document is admissible as evidence in criminal proceedings, it may be proved –

    (*a*)   by the production of that document; or

    (*b*)   (whether or not that document is still in existence) by the production of a copy of that document, or of the material part of it, authenticated in such manner as the court may approve; and it is immaterial for the purposes of this subsection how many removes there are between a copy and the original.

28 (1) Nothing in this Part of this Act shall prejudice –
  (*a*) the admissibility of a statement not made by a person while giving oral evidence in court which is admissible otherwise than by virtue of this Part of this Act; or
  (*b*) any power of a court to exclude at its discretion a statement admissible by virtue of this Part of this Act.
  (2) Schedule 2 to this Act shall have effect for the purpose of supplementing this Part of this Act.

30 (1) An expert report shall be admissible as evidence in criminal proceedings, whether or not the person making it attends to give oral evidence in those proceedings.
  (2) If it is proposed that the person making the report shall not give oral evidence, the report shall only be admissible with the leave of the court.
  (3) For the purpose of determining whether to give leave the court shall have regard –
  (*a*) to the contents of the report;
  (*b*) to the reasons why it is proposed that the person making the report shall not give oral evidence;
  (*c*) to any risk, having regard in particular to whether it is likely to be possible to controvert statements in the report if the person making it does not attend to give oral evidence in the proceedings, that its admission or exclusion will result in unfairness to the accused or, if there is more than one, to any of them; and
  (*d*) to any other circumstances that appear to the court to be relevant.
  (4) An expert report, when admitted, shall be evidence of any fact or opinion of which the person making it could have given oral evidence.
  (5) In this section 'expert report' means a written report by a person dealing wholly or mainly with matters on which he is (or would if living be) qualified to give expert evidence.

31 For the purpose of helping members of juries to understand complicated issues of fact or technical terms Crown Court Rules may make provision –
  (*a*) as to the furnishing of evidence in any form, notwithstanding the existence of admissible material from which the evidence to be given in that form would be derived; and
  (*b*) as to the furnishing of glossaries for such purposes as may be specified;
in any case where the court gives leave for, or requires, evidence or a glossary to be so furnished.

SCHEDULE

1. Where a statement is admitted as evidence in criminal proceedings by virtue of Part II [ss23–28] of this Act –
  (*a*) any evidence which, if the person making the statement had been called as a witness, would have been admissible as relevant to his credibility as a witness shall be admissible for that purpose in those proceedings;
  (*b*) evidence may, with the leave of the court, be given of any matter which, if that person had been called as a witness, could have been put to him in cross-examination as relevant to his credibility as a witness but of which evidence could not have been adduced by the cross-examining party; and
  (*c*) evidence tending to prove that that person, whether before or after making the statement, made (whether orally or not) some other statement which is inconsistent with it shall be admissible for the purpose of showing that he contradicted himself.
2. A statement which is given in evidence by virtue of Part II of this Act shall not be capable of corroborating evidence given by the person making it.
3. In estimating the weight, if any, to be attached to such a statement regard shall be had to all the circumstances from which any inference can reasonably be drawn as to its accuracy or otherwise.
4. Without prejudice to the generality of any enactment conferring power to make them –
  (*a*) Crown Court Rules
  (*b*) Criminal Appeal Rules; and
  (*c*) rules under section 144 of the Magistrates' Courts Act 1980,
may make such provision as appears to the authority making any of them to be necessary or may

make such provision as appears to the authority making any of them to be necessary or expedient for the purposes of Part II of this Act.

5.   (1)   In Part II of this Act –
    'document' means anything in which information of any description is recorded;
    'copy', in relation to a document, means anything onto which information recorded in the document has been copied, by whatever means and whether directly or indirectly; and
    'statement' means any representation of fact, however made.

    (2)   For the purposes of Part II of this Act evidence which, by reason of a defect of speech or hearing, a person called as a witness gives in writing or by signs shall be treated as given orally.

6.   In Part II of this Act 'confession' has the meaning assigned to it by section 82 of the Police and Criminal Evidence Act 1984.

COMMENTS

The problem caused by the application of the exclusionary hearsay rule to statements in almost certainly reliable business documents, where nobody could remember the transaction but the maker of the document had every reason to make it accurate, came to a head in *Myers v DPP* [1965] AC 1001, [1964] 2 All ER 881, HL; see ch 12.2B, ante. The immediate result of that decision was the Criminal Evidence Act 1965, which was in due course replaced by the Police and Criminal Evidence Act 1984, s 68 (now also repealed). Meanwhile, the Fraud Trials Committee Report (1986) under the chairmanship of Lord Roskill recognised that in fraud trials similar difficulties arise because of the often convoluted nature of transactions which, again, nobody (other than perhaps the defendant) can be expected to remember, so that unless documentary evidence is admitted unmeritorious acquittals will ensue. Lord Roskill's recommendation was that the judge should have a discretion to admit otherwise inadmissible documentary evidence, where there could be no serious challenge to its reliability (paras 5.26 ff). The recommendation was limited to fraud trials because of the terms of reference of the Committee, and has not been acted upon, but provided the impetus for reform. The present law deals separately with four types of documentary hearsay.

1. If the hearsay statement was originally made by a person in a document, then the document itself, or a copy of it – see s 27 – is admissible under s 23 to prove the fact stated if the person is unavailable for one of the reasons in s 23(2), or (if the statement was made to a police officer, etc) for one of the reasons in s 23(3)(*b*). Admissibility is subject to the court's exclusionary discretion under s 25. The opportunity has been taken to tidy up the drafting of the reasons for the witness's unavailability, so as to avoid some of the difficulties which had arisen with similar wording in the Civil Evidence Act 1968. The definition of 'document' has been brought into line with that in the Civil Evidence Act 1995, but the ambiguous phrase 'made . . . in a document' remains(for which see *Ventouris v Mountain (No 2)* [1992] 3 All ER 414, [1992] 1 WLR 887,CA).

2. If the hearsay statement is contained in a document created or received by a person in the course of his job, the document, or a copy of it – see s 27 – is admissible under s 24 to prove the fact stated provided that the person who supplied the information in question did so from his own personal knowledge.

Admissibility is subject to the court's exclusionary discretion under s 25. Unlike s 23, there is no requirement of unavailability, and there is no requirement that the document produced to the court contains the very statement of the person with personal knowledge: 'second-hand' hearsay (ie third-hand information) is admissible under s 24. But in that case every person through whom the information was passed must have received it in the course of his job. The link with a job (here widely defined to avoid problems which had arisen under the previous legislation and the unclear notion of 'duty' which appeared in the Civil Evidence Act 1968) is supposed to ensure trustworthiness: most people try to do their various jobs accurately; many documents produced in the course of a job form part of a system which allows cross-checking; and the regular performance of a task promotes reliability. It is, however, very doubtful whether s 24 gives any assurance of accuracy to the documents it makes admissible. For the arguments in favour of the link with a job apply only where the document is created, or information in it has been passed on, by a person doing his job. Similar reasoning does not apply when a document however created, is, after its creation, *received* by a person as part of his job. Sections 23 and 24 have the remarkable result that if (not as part of my job) I make a statement in writing, the writing may be admissible if I am unavailable (s 23); but if ever the writing is put in the post, or handed to a solicitor preparing a case for trial, it becomes admissible (regardless of my availability) under s 24. Indeed it is difficult to see how the writing could be put in evidence without at some stage being 'received by a person . . . as the holder of a paid or unpaid office' because handing the document to the court usher would seem to be accurately described by those words. It is, however, unlikely that Parliament intended s 23 to be completely without effect. There are other signs of inadequate drafting in s 24. Who is 'the maker of the statement' in s 24(1)(ii)? If it is *not* the person who supplied the information, what is the meaning of 'whether or not' in s 24(1)(ii)?

3. If the hearsay statement is contained in a document which appears to have been prepared for the purposes of a criminal investigation or proceedings, it will not be admissible under ss 23–25 unless an inclusionary discretion is exercised in its favour: s 26. The purpose of this provision is to preserve the general rule requiring oral evidence in criminal trials and because it has been felt that documents of this sort are particularly prone to the danger of fabrication. As regards the exercise of the discretion, in *R v Cole* [1990] 2 All ER 108, [1990] 1 WLR 866, CA, the Court of Appeal held that in considering whether 'it is likely to be possible to controvert the statement' (s 26(iii)) the court is not required to take into account the right of the defendant not to give evidence or call witnesses: even if the admission of the statement would practically compel him to call evidence to contradict it, that is not a factor against admission. On the other hand, the lack of opportunity to test the statement, by investigation or cross-examination, is a powerful factor weighing against the inclusionary discretion, whether the evidence is tendered by the accused (*R v Patel* (1992) 97 Cr App Rep 294, CA) or the Crown (*R v Setz-Dempsey* (1994) 98 Cr App Rep 23, CA). The 1988 Act does not repeal s 13 of the Criminal Justice Act 1925, which remains in force and which it overlaps; but in *R v Cole* (above) the court took the view that in cases of overlap the test in the 1988 Act is appropriate, subject to all other powers to exclude. For the application of the 1925 Act, see *R v Blithing* (1983) 77 Cr App Rep 86, CA; *Scott v R* [1989] AC 1242, [1989] 2 All ER 305, PC, holding that the discretion to exclude should be exercised 'with great restraint'. It has been suggested (McEwan [1989] Crim LR 629) that, in view of the almost complete failure of the Pigot Report (section C, post) to deal with vulnerable witnesses other than children, the documentary hearsay provisions might be used to fill the gap. The main considerations then should be the centrality of the question dealt with by the evidence, compared with the document's apparent reliability in the context of the other evidence in the case: *R v O'Loughlin* [1988] 3 All ER 431; *R v Neshet* [1990] Crim LR 578, CA; cf *R v Hovell* [1987] 1 NZLR 610.

4. Sections 30 and 31 (which are not subject to s 26) make useful provision for making complicated evidence more intelligible.

5. Where the prosecution seek to have statements admitted under s 23 or 24 they must be proved admissible to the criminal standard (*R v Acton Justices, ex p McMullen* (1990) 92 Cr App Rep 98, DC; *R v Minors* [1989] 2 All ER 208, [1989] 1 WLR 441, CA) by admissible evidence, not using the hearsay contained in the documents: *R v Case* [1991] Crim LR 192. If the statements are introduced by the defence, the standard is the balance of probabilities: *R v Mattey and Queeley* [1995] Crim LR 308, CA.

B   STATEMENTS PRODUCED BY COMPUTER

Police and Criminal Evidence Act 1984

69 (1) In any [criminal] proceedings, a statement in a document produced by a computer shall not be admissible as evidence of any fact stated therein unless it is shown –
  (a) that there are no reasonable grounds for believing that the statement is inaccurate because of improper use of the computer;
  (b) that at all material times the computer was operating properly, or if not, that any respect in which it was not operating properly or was out of operation was not such as to affect the production of the document or the accuracy of its contents; and
  (c) that any relevant conditions specified in rules of court under subsection (2) below are satisfied.

COMMENTS

1. No rules have been made under s 69(2), but paras 8 and 9 of Sch 3 to the Act provide that evidence identifying the document, establishing that it was produced by a computer and that the computer was functioning sufficiently well may be given by producing a certificate signed by a person occupying a responsible position in relation to the operation of the computer, subject to the court's discretion to require oral evidence of these matters. In any event, however, there needs to be affirmative evidence that the computer was working properly: *R v Shephard* [1993] AC 380, [1993] 1 All ER 225, HL. It is not sufficient to rely on the presumption of the proper functioning of machines.

2. The phraseology of s 69 is exclusionary: it admits nothing but provides that certain documents may not be received unless they pass the tests it imposes. Thus, if a computer printout incorporates a hearsay statement, it

must comply with s 23 (eg a statement made by a person typing it into his word-processor) or s 24 of the Criminal Justice Act 1988 or fall within some other exception to the hearsay rule; it must also comply with s 69: *R v Minors* [1989] 2 All ER 208, [1989] 1 WLR 441, CA. When a computer printout contains a statement which is not hearsay, because the machine is being used to collect, process and record information automatically without inputting facts from human minds, no hearsay exception need be established (*The Statue of Liberty* [1968] 2 All ER 195, [1968] 1 WLR 739; *R v Wood* (1982) 76 Cr App Rep 23, CA) but s 69 must still be complied with. The only case where the contents of a computer printout will be admissible in evidence apart from s 69 is where what is relied on is not a statement: 'If the question is whether a bank account has been credited with £100, the entry '£100' in the credit column is the crediting of the account, not a statement that the account has been credited . . . If the account is kept on a computer, the printout is either the fact or a copy of the fact, not evidence of any fact stated therein' (JCS commenting on *R v Minors* (above) in [1989] Crim LR 360). The interpretation of the statutory provisions relating to evidence produced by computers has been hampered by what appears to be widespread misunderstanding of the hearsay issues involved: see eg *R v Pettigrew* (1980) 71 Cr App Rep 39, CA; *R v Spiby* (1990) 91 Cr App Rep 186, CA; *R v Burke* [1990] Crim LR 401; Road Traffic Review Report (the North Report) (1988) paras 3.17–26; Smith [1981] Crim LR 387; Ockelton, 5 Road Law 95. The decision of the House of Lords in *R v Shephard* (supra) has now provided authoritative clarification of these matters.

C CHILDREN

Section 54 of the Criminal Justice Act 1991 inserts a new s 32A into the Criminal Justice Act 1988. The new section provides for a video-recording of an interview with a child witness (other than a defendant) to be used in the Crown Court or a youth court as that witness's examination-in-chief. Admission is to be subject to the leave of the court, but will normally be allowed after investigation of the circumstances in which the recording was made, unless 'in the interests of justice the recording ought not to be admitted' (s 32A(3)(c)). It will, however, always be necessary for the party tendering the recording also to call the child so that he is available for the cross-examination. This provision, implementing some of the recommendations of the *Report of the Advisory Group on Video Evidence* (1989) (The Pigot Report), forms another statutory exception to the hearsay rule in criminal cases. See further, ch 17.1C, post.

D OTHER

The Criminal Justice Act 1967, s 9 provides for agreed statements of facts to be admitted. There are numerous instances other than s 13 of the Criminal Justice Act 1925 where dispositions of an absent deponent may be proved in criminal cases. (See Phipson, paras 10–15 to 10–26, 10–28.) Confessions are covered in ch 8, ante.

FURTHER READING

Birch [1989] Crim LR 15; Jackson, 40 NILQ 105; McEvoy [1993] Crim LR 480, [1994] Crim LR 430; Smith [1994] Crim LR 426; Spencer [1994] Crim LR 628.

4 The value of hearsay evidence

R v Cole   [1990] 2 All ER 108, [1990] 1 WLR 866, CA

Ralph Gibson LJ: It was rightly acknowledged . . . that if the statement was properly admitted the judge's direction with reference to it was correct and fair. The judge said:

> 'As far as Mr Luff's statement is concerned, you have heard it read out. It has these obvious limitations: when someone's statement is read out you do not have the opportunity of seeing that person in the witness box and sometimes when you see someone in the witness box you get a very much clearer opinion of whether or not that person is sincere and honest and accurate. Furthermore, when that evidence is tested under cross-examination you may get an even clearer view. Sometimes cross-examination takes away very much from a witness's reliability, sometimes it adds to it so you can say, "despite the testing I am absolutely certain he is right", but that process cannot happen in the present case because Mr Luff is dead so I would suggest to you that you cannot possibly pay as much attention to Mr Luff's evidence as anybody else but for what it is worth let me summarise it.'

5 Res gestae

'Res gestae' means 'the transaction'. Evidence relevant to a 'transaction' and arising contemporaneously with it may be admissible. The res gestae label has never been very popular.

'If you wish to tender inadmissible evidence, say it is part of the res gestae' (Lord Blackburn, quoted by Cross, 5th edn, p 43, n 13). The rules are 'huddled confusedly with a lot of rag-tag-and-bobtail material under the damnably unhelpful label "res gestae"' (Maguire, p 148). It is 'a phrase adopted to provide a respectable legal cloak for a variety of cases to which no formula of precision can be applied' (*Homes v Newman* [1931] 2 Ch 112 at 120, per Lord Tomlin). Pollock once wrote to Holmes that 'I am reporting, with some reluctance, a case on the damnable pretended doctrine of res gestae, and wishing some high legal authority would prick that bubble of verbiage: the unmeaning term merely fudges the truth that there is no universal formula for all the kinds of relevancy' (*Pollock-Holmes Letters*, 23 April 1931 (Cambridge, 1942), vol 2 pp 284–5). '[T]here are few problems in the law of evidence more unsolved than what things are to be embraced in those occurrences that are designated in the law as the "res gestae"' (*Hunter v State* (1922) 40 NJL 536, quoted by Wigmore, para 1745). 'This . . . collection of fact situations . . . is so confusing in its scope as almost to demand that a reader cease thinking before he go mad' (Wright, 20 Can B Rev 714 at 716). 'The marvellous capacity of a Latin phrase to serve as a substitute for reasoning, and the confusion of thought inevitably accompanying the use of inaccurate terminology are nowhere better illustrated than in the decisions dealing with the admissibility of evidence as "res gestae". It is probable that this troublesome expression owes its existence and persistence in our law of evidence to an inclination of judges and lawyers to avoid the toilsome exertion of exact analysis and precise thinking' (Morgan (1922) 31 Yale LJ 229).

As usual, Wigmore's comments are the fullest and strongest.

'There has been such a confounding of ideas, and such a profuse and indiscriminate use of the shibboleth "res gestae", that it is difficult to disentangle the real basis of principle involved. On the one hand, to repeat without comment the often meaningless and unhelpful language of the courts is to shirk the duty of the expositor of the law as it is. On the other hand, to discriminate between the principles genuinely involved is to risk the reproach of representing as law that which the courts do not concede . . .

. . . It ought wholly to be repudiated, as a vicious element in our legal phraseology . . . [A]ny name would be preferable to an empty phrase so encouraging to looseness of thinking and uncertainty of decision' (paras 1745, 1767).

A PRELIMINARY PROBLEMS

One problem can be briefly stated. The rules as to what res gestae evidence is admissible are extraordinarily hard to formulate with precision, because they essentially depend on a high degree of relevance.

Another problem is whether res gestae evidence is original or hearsay. Some have considered that such evidence can only be admitted as original evidence and not evidence of the truth of what it asserts under a hearsay exception (eg *R v Christie* [1914] AC 545 at 553, [1914–15] All ER Rep 63 at 66, HL, per Lord Atkinson, *Adelaide Chemical and Fertilizer Co Ltd v Carlyle* (1940) 64 CLR 514, at 530–3, per Dixon J). But this is not the modern view (*Carlyle's* Case, at 526, per Starke J; *Ratten v R* [1972] AC 378, [1971] 3 All ER 801, PC, p 352, post). Sometimes res gestae evidence is admitted as original evidence and sometimes under an exception to the hearsay rule.

A third problem is that there are two views of the basis of admissibility as a hearsay exception. The traditional view depends heavily on the notion that the statement is part of the event comprised by independently proved facts in issue. For this reason a principal requirements is contemporaneity between the statement and the fact in issue, for the lack of time to reflect will reduce the chance of invention. Another factor looked for is any difference in location between event and utterance. Some English cases and almost all decisions of the High Court of Australia have interpreted these requirements very strictly. In *R v Bedingfield* (1879) 14 Cox CC 341 the deceased whose throat had just been cut walked out of a room in which the accused was and said 'Oh dear, Aunt, see what Bedingfield has done to me!' or something similar. This was excluded because it was said 'after the act was completed'. In *R v Andrews* [1987] AC 281 at 300, [1987] 1 All ER 513 at 520, HL, the House of Lords held that *R v Bedingfield* would not be so decided today. In *Brown v R* (1913) 17 CLR 570 the deceased's statements were excluded because they were uttered while he was walking away from where he had been attacked: his motive was not to avoid another attack but to obtain medical aid. *Teper v R* [1952] AC 480, [1952] 2 All ER 447, PC (ch 12, ante) is a sound application of this rule; the statement charging the accused with flight and implicitly with arson was made twenty-five minutes after the fire, which was the relevant event, not his flight. (The general unreliability of the evidence is discussed, ch 12, ante.)

A liberal approach is seen in *O'Hara v Central Scottish Motor Traction Co* 1941 SC 363, where a statement by a pedestrian some minutes after a motor accident was admitted because the 'accident must still have left a vivid impression on the minds of all who took part in the incident . . . [T]he incident was so clearly bound up with the happening of the accident that without it the history of the accident as offered to the Court in evidence would not be complete' (at 382, per Lord Normand).

But this is rather exceptional. The narrowness with which the traditional rule is generally interpreted seems mistaken. Morgan has pointed out that the evidence is admissible because the shortness of time ensures that there can be no unreliability caused by the declarant's defective memory or carefully worked out lie; and the hearer of the declaration will have opportunities to check the truth of what is said ((1922) 31 Yale LJ 229 at 236–9). Attention should be paid to these issues rather than to mechanical tests of the identity of the transaction or whether narration is occurring or whether strict contemporaneity exists.

However, the Privy Council has advanced what seems to be a new view which depends on reliability. Sometimes the guarantee of reliability will be found in a spontaneous response to an unusual event; sometimes in involvement in an event. It is similar to one developed by Wigmore (para 1747). It may offer the courts a chance to reduce the exclusionary effect of the hearsay rule.

Ratten v R   [1972] AC 378, [1971] 3 All ER 801, PC

About the time the accused's wife was shot by the discharge of his gun, which he asserted to be accidental, the telephonist at the local exchange received a call from the accused's house. The voice, which was hysterical and sobbing, said 'Get me the police please'. The telephonist's testimony was admitted at the trial and appeals to the Victorian Full Court and the Privy Council failed. The latter held that if the words were hearsay they were admissible under the res gestae exception, but that they were not hearsay.

Lord Wilberforce: Their Lordships, as already stated, do not consider that there is any hearsay element in the evidence, nor in their opinion was it so presented by the trial judge, but they think it right to deal with the appellant's submission on the assumption that there is, ie that the words said to have been used involve an assertion of the truth of some facts stated in them and that they have been so understood by the jury. The Crown defended the admissibility of the words as part of the res gestae a contention which led to the citation of numerous authorities.

The expression res gestae, like many Latin phrases, is often used to cover situations insufficiently analysed in clear English terms. In the context of the law of evidence it may be used in at least three different ways:

1. When a situation of fact (eg a killing) is being considered, the question may arise when does it end. It may be arbitrary and artificial to confine the evidence to the firing of the gun or the insertion of the knife without knowing, in a broader sense, what was happening. Thus in *O'Leary v R* evidence was admitted of assaults, prior to a killing committed by the accused during what was said to be a continuous orgy. As Dixon J said ((1946) 73 CLR 566 at 577):

'Without evidence of what, during that time, was done by those men who took any significant part in the matter and specially evidence of the behaviour of the prisoner, the transaction of which the alleged murder formed an integral part could not be truly understood and, isolated from it, could only be presented as an unreal and not very intelligible event.'

2. The evidence may be concerned with spoken words as such (apart from the truth of what they convey). The words are then themselves the res gestae or part of the res gestae, ie are the relevant facts or part of them.

3. A hearsay statement is made either by the victim of an attack or by a bystander – indicating directly or indirectly the identity of the attacker. The admissibility of the statement is then said to depend on whether it was made as part of the res gestae. A classical instance of this is the much debated case of *R v Bedingfield* (1879) 14 Cox CC 341, and there are other instances of its application in reported cases. These tend to apply different standards, and some of them carry less than conviction. The reason why this is so is that concentration tends to be focused on the opaque or at least imprecise Latin phrase rather than on the basic reason for excluding the type of evidence which this group of cases is concerned with. There is no doubt what this reason is: it is twofold. The first is that there may be uncertainty as to the exact words used because of their transmission through the evidence of another person than the speaker. The second is because of the risk of concoction of false evidence by persons who have been the victim of assault or accident.

The first matter goes to weight. The person testifying to the words used is liable to cross-examination: the accused person (as he could not at the time when earlier reported cases were decided) can give his own account if different. There is no such difference in kind or substance between evidence of what was said and evidence of what was done (for example between evidence of what the victim said as to an attack and evidence that he (or she) was seen in a terrified state or was heard to shriek) as to require a total rejection of one and admission of the other.

The possibility of concoction, or fabrication, where it exists, is on the other hand an entirely valid reason for exclusion, and is probably the real test which judges in fact apply. In their Lordships' opinion this should be recognised and applied directly as the relevant test: the test should be not the uncertain one whether the making of the statement was in some sense part of the event or transaction. This may often be difficult to establish: such external matters as the time which elapses between the events and the speaking of the words (or vice versa), and differences in location being relevant factors but not, taken by themselves, decisive criteria. As regards statements made after the event it must be for the judge, by preliminary ruling, to satisfy himself that the statement was so clearly made in circumstances of spontaneity or involvement in the event that the possibility of concoction can be disregarded. Conversely, if he considers that the statement was made by way of narrative of a detached prior event so that the speaker was so disengaged from it as to be able to construct or adapt his account, he should exclude it. And the same must in principle be true of statements made before the event. The test should be not the uncertain one, whether the making of the statement should be regarded as part of the event or transaction. This may often be difficult to show. But if the drama, leading up to the climax, has commenced and assumed such intensity and pressure that the utterance can safely be regarded as a true reflection of what was unrolling or actually happening, it ought to be received. The expression res gestae may conveniently sum up these criteria, but the reality of them must always be kept in mind: it is this that lies behind the best reasoned of the judges' rulings.

A few illustrations may be given. One of the earliest, and as often happens also the clearest, is that of Holt CJ at nisi prius in *Thompson v Trevanion* (1693) Skin 402. He allowed that 'what the wife said immediate upon the hurt received, and before that she had time to devise or contrive anything for her own advantage' might be given in evidence, a statement often quoted and approved. *R v Bedingfield* (1879) 14 Cox CC 341 is more useful as a focus for discussion, than for the decision on the facts. Their Lordships understand later indications of approval (*R v Christie* [1914] AC 545, [1914–15] All ER Rep 63, HL; and *Teper v R* [1952] AC 480, [1952] 2 All ER 447, PC) to relate to the principle established, for, although in a historical sense the emergence of the victim could be described as a different res from the cutting of her throat, there could hardly be a case where the words uttered carried more clearly the mark of spontaneity and intense involvement.

In a lower key the evidence of the words of the careless pedestrian in *O'Hara v Central SMT Co* 1941 SC 363 was admitted on the principle of spontaneity. The Lord President (Lord Normand) said (at 381) that there must be close association: the words should be at least de recenti and not after an interval which would allow time for reflection and concocting a story. Lord Fleming said (at 386):

'Obviously statements made after there has been time for deliberation are not likely to be entirely spontaneous, and may, indeed, be made for the express purpose of concealing the truth', and Lord Moncrieff (at 389–90) refers to the 'share in the event' which is taken by the person reported to have made the statement. He contrasts an exclamation 'forced out of a witness by the motion generated by an event' with a subsequent narrative. The Lord President reaffirmed the principle stated in this case in an appeal to this Board in *Teper v R* [1952] AC 480, [1952] 2 All ER 447, PC, stressing the necessity for close association in time, place and circumstances between the statement and the crucial events.

In Australia, a leading authority is *Adelaide Chemical and Fertilizer Co Ltd v Carlyle* (1940) 64 CLR 514 in which the High Court considered the admissibility of a statement made soon after the breaking of a sulphuric acid jar over his legs by the injured man. This question was not decisive to the decision, but was discussed by Starke and Dixon JJ with numerous citations. Both emphasise and illustrate the uncertainty of decided cases and legal writers on the question of admissibility of statements of this type and on the question what they may be admitted to prove. Dixon J with some caution reaches the conclusion that although English law, in the general view of lawyers, admits statements only as parts or details of a transaction not yet complete, while in America, greater recognition is given to the guarantee of truth provided by spontaneity and the lack of time to devise or contrive, yet English decisions do show some reliance on the greater trustworthiness of statements made at once without reflection. In an earlier case in the High Court (*Brown v R* (1913) 17 CLR 570) where evidence was excluded, Isaacs and Powers JJ in their joint judgment (at 597) put the exclusion on the ground that it was a mere narration respecting a concluded event, a narration not naturally or spontaneously emanating from or growing out of the main narration but arising as an independent and additional transaction.

In *People v De Simone* 121 NE 761 (1919), the Court of Appeals of New York admitted evidence that a passer-by immediately after a shooting had shouted 'He ran over Houston Street'. Collin J referred to deeds and acts which are –

'forced or brought into utterance or existence by and in the evolution of the transaction itself, and which stand in immediate causal relation to it.'

The evidence was, expressly, not admitted as part of the res gestae, because it was not so interwoven or connected with the principal event (ie the shooting which the person did not see) as to be regarded as part of it.

These authorities show that there is ample support for the principle that hearsay evidence may be admitted if the statement providing it is made in such conditions (always being those of approximate but not exact contemporaneity) of involvement or pressure as to exclude the possibility of concoction or distortion to the advantage of the maker or the disadvantage of the accused.

Before applying it to the facts of the present case, there is one other matter to be considered, namely the nature of the proof required to establish the involvement of the speaker in the pressure of the drama, or the concatenation of events leading up to the crisis. On principle it would not appear right that the necessary association should be shown only by the statement itself, otherwise the statement would be lifting itself into the area of admissibility. There is little authority on this point. In *R v Taylor* 1961 (3) SA 616 where witnesses said they had heard scuffles and thuds during which the deceased cried out 'John, please don't hit me any more. You will kill me', Fannin AJ said that it would be unrealistic to require the examination of the question (sc of close relationship) without reference to the terms of the statement sought to be proved (at 619).

'Often the only evidence as to how near in time the making of the statement was to the act it relates to, and the actual relationship between the two, will be contained in the statement itself.'

Facts differ so greatly that it is impossible to lay down any precise general rule: it is difficult to imagine a case where there is no evidence at all of connexion between statement and principal event other than the statement itself, but whether this is sufficiently shown must be a matter for the trial judge. Their Lordships would be disposed to agree that, amongst other things, he may take the statement itself into account.

In the present case, in their Lordships' judgment, there was ample evidence of the close and intimate connexion between the statement ascribed to the deceased and the shooting which occurred very shortly afterwards. They were closely associated in place and in time. The way in which the statement came to be made (in a call for the police) and the tone of voice used, showed intrinsically that the statement was being forced from the deceased by an overwhelming pressure of contemporary event. It carried its own stamp of spontaneity and this was endorsed by the proved time sequence and the proved proximity of the deceased to the appellant with his gun. Even on the assumption that there was an element of hearsay in the words used, they were safely admitted. The jury was, additionally, directed with great care as to the use to which they might be put. On all counts, therefore, their Lordships can find no error in law in the admission of the evidence. They should add that they see no reason why the judge should have excluded it as prejudicial in the exercise of discretion.

R v Andrews   [1987] AC 281, [1987] 1 All ER 513, HL

Lord Ackner: My Lords, may I therefore summarise the position which confronts the trial judge when faced in a criminal case with an application under the res gestae doctrine to admit evidence of statements, with a view to establishing the truth of some fact thus narrated, such evidence being truly categorised as 'hearsay evidence'. (1) The primary question which the judge must ask himself is: can the possibility of concoction or distortion be disregarded? (2) To answer that question the judge must first consider the circumstances in which the particular statement was made, in order to satisfy himself that the event was so unusual or startling or dramatic as to dominate the thoughts of the victim, so that his utterance was an instinctive reaction to that event, thus giving no real opportunity for reasoned reflection. In such a situation the judge would be entitled to conclude that the involvement or the pressure of the event would exclude the possibility of concoction or distortion, providing that the statement was made in conditions of approximate but not exact contemporaneity. (3) In order for the statement to be sufficiently 'spontaneous' it must be so closely associated with the event which has excited the statement that it can be fairly stated that the mind of the declarant was still dominated by the event. Thus the judge must be satisfied that the event which provided the trigger mechanism for the statement was still operative. The fact that the statement was made in answer to a question is but one factor to consider under this heading. (4) Quite apart from the time factor, there may be special features in the case, which relate to the possibility of concoction or distortion. In the instant appeal the defence relied on evidence to support the contention that the deceased had a motive of his own to fabricate or concoct, namely a malice which resided in him against O'Neill and the appellant because, so he believed, O'Neill had attacked and damaged his house and was accompanied by the appellant, who ran away, on a previous occasion. The judge must be satisfied that the circumstances were such that, having regard to the special feature of malice, there was no possibility of any concoction or distortion to the advantage of the maker or the disadvantage of the accused. (5) As to the possibility of error in the facts narrated in the statement, if only the ordinary fallibility of human recollection is relied on, this goes to the weight to be attached to and not to the admissibility of the statement and is therefore a matter for the jury. However, here again there may be special features that may give rise to the possibility of error. In the instant case there was evidence that the deceased had drunk to excess, well over double the permitted limit for driving a motor car. Another example would be where the identification was made in circumstances of particular difficulty or where the declarant suffered from defective eyesight. In such circumstances the trial judge must consider whether he can exclude the possibility of error.

Croom-Johnson LJ in giving the judgment of the Court of Appeal, Criminal Division dismissing the appeal stated, in my respectful view quite correctly, that the Common Serjeant had directed himself impeccably in his approach to the evidence that he had heard. It is perhaps helpful to set out verbatim how the judge stated his conclusions:

'I am satisfied that soon after receiving very serious stab wounds the deceased went downstairs for help unassisted and received some assistance. He was able to talk for a few minutes before he became unconscious. I am satisfied on the evidence, and not only the primary evidence but the inference of fact to which I am irresistibly driven, that the deceased only sustained the injuries a few minutes before the police arrived and subsequently, of course, the ambulance took him to hospital. Even if the period were longer than a few minutes, I am satisfied that there was no possibility in the circumstances of any concoction or fabrication of identification. I think that the injuries which the deceased sustained were of such a nature that it would drive out of his mind any possibility of him being activated by malice and I cannot overlook as far as the identification was concerned, he was right over Mr O'Neill who was a former co-defendant with the accused.'

Where the trial judge has properly directed himself as to the correct approach to the evidence and there is material to entitle him to reach the conclusions which he did reach, then his decision is final, in the sense that it will not be interfered with on appeal. Of course, having ruled the statement admissible the judge must, as the Common Sergeant most certainly did, make it clear to the jury that it is for them to decide what was said and to be sure that the witnesses were not mistaken in what they believed had been said to them. Further, they must be satisfied that the declarant did not concoct or distort to his advantage or the disadvantage of the accused the statement relied on and where there is material to raise the issue, that he was not activated by any malice or ill-will. Further, where there are special features that bear on the possibility of mistake then the jury's attention must be invited to those matters.

[Lords Bridge of Harwick, Brandon of Oakbrook, Griffiths and Mackay of Clashfern agreed.]

QUESTIONS

1. Is Lord Wilberforce's test any more certain than the traditional one?
2. Much res gestae evidence has been admitted in the past without some exciting event occurring. Is Lord Wilberforce's view limited to such events? He says the statement must be made 'in circumstances of spontaneity or *involvement in the event* [so] that the possibility of concoction can be disregarded'. Do the italicised words meet the problem?
3. Is the absence of a possibility of concoction merely an assumed and hoped-for consequence of other requirements or an independent requirement of admissibility? *R v Andrews*, which approved the *Ratten v R* approach, suggested the latter. Cf *Vocisano v Vocisano* (1974) 130 CLR 267. In *R v Nye* (1977) 66 Cr App Rep 252, CA, the court suggested as a further requirement that there be no possibility of error, but this appears to be wrong, except where there are 'special features' giving rise to this possibility: *R v Andrews*.
4. It is worth noting that in *Brown v R* (1913) 17 CLR 570 at 597 a statement was excluded because it was 'not naturally or spontaneously emanating from or growing out of the main transaction, but arising as an independent and additional transaction' (per Isaacs and Powers JJ). This has some similarity with the *Ratten v R* test. It may show, however, that that test can be interpreted just as narrowly as the traditional tests.
5. McCormick says: 'Psychologists would probably concede that excitement stills the voice of reflective self-interest but they might question whether this factor of reliability is not over-borne by the distorting effect which shock and excitement might have on observation and judgment. But they might well conclude that contemporaneous statements both excited and unexcited are so valuable for the accurate reconstruction of the facts that the need is not to narrow the use of excited statements but to widen the exception to embrace as well unexcited declarations of observers near the time of the happening' (p 579). Do you agree?

NOTE

Lord Wilberforce lists the three main ways in which so-called res gestae evidence is used. The second – as original evidence – is discussed in ch 12, ante. The third – as a hearsay exception – is under discussion here. The first was considered in ch 10, ante, as a quasi-exception to the general ban on similar fact evidence. To avoid confusion it might be best to confine the term res gestae to evidence admitted as an exception to the hearsay rule because of its high degree of relevance to a fact in issue in time, place or some other way.

B EXAMPLES

An American judge once said: 'The difficulty of formulating a description of the res gestae which will serve for all cases seems insurmountable. To make the attempt is something like trying to execute a portrait which shall enable the possessor to recognise every member of a numerous family' (*Cox v State* 64 Ga 374 at 410 (1879), quoted by Wigmore, para 1745).

However, Cross (5th edn, pp 575–91) has usefully divided the cases of admissible res gestae evidence into four partly overlapping and probably non-exhaustive categories. In traditional doctrine they all shared the requirement of contemporaneity, which turns on difficult questions of degree and which will not be pursued further.

(i) Statements accompanying and explaining relevant acts

The statement must be made by the actor and it must relate to the act it accompanies (*R v Bliss* (1837) 7 Ad & El 550, [1835–42] All ER Rep 372).

He knows more about his motives than anyone else; the requirement of contemporaneity to some extent helps guarantee sincerity. The evidence is admissible to prove the actor's intention in acting and his reason for acting, but not to prove the existence of any fact mentioned in his statement of reasons (*Skinner & Co v Shew & Co* [1894] 2 Ch 581). Examples are: a bankrupt's statements as to his intentions in going or remaining abroad (*Rouch v Great Western Rly Co* (1841) 1 QB 51); a statement of intention to remain in a certain country or a statement of reasons for going there (*Bryce v Bryce* [1933] P 83, [1932] All ER Rep 788; *Scappaticci v A-G* [1955] P 47, [1955] 1 All ER 193n); a wife's statement as to why she was leaving her husband (*Aylesford Peerage* (1885) 11 App Cas 1 at 3, HL, per Lord Blackburn); a testator's statements of a non-testamentary intention at the time of executing a codicil (*Lister v Smith* (1863) 3 Sw & Tr 282); a statement accompanying the act of being present at a particular place (*R v Benz* (1989) 168 CLR 110); a statement accompanying the act of recognition of a suspect at an identification parade (*R v McCay* [1991] 1 All ER 232, [1990] 1 WLR 645, CA).

(ii) Statements concerning an event in issue

It is to this category that *Ratten v R* principally relates. The relation between statement and event must be direct, and care must be devoted to the definition of 'event'. If the accused is charged with assault, the relevant event is the accused's act of assault, not his subsequent flight, so that an exclamation provoked by his flight is not part of the res gestae (*Teper v R* [1952] AC 480 at 488, [1952] 2 All ER 447 at 450, PC, discussing *R v Gibson* (1887) 18 QBD 537). The maker of the statement must usually have witnessed the event in issue (*Poriotis v Australian Iron & Steel Ltd* [1963] SRNSW 991). For examples, see *R v Foster* (1834) 6 C & P 325; *Milne v Leisler* (1862) 7 H & N 786 at 796; *Davies v Fortior Ltd* [1952] 1 All ER 1359n; *Mills v R* [1995] 3 All ER 865, [1995] 1 WLR 511, PC.

(iii) Statements about the maker's mental or emotional state

The evidence is only admissible to prove what the maker's mental or emotional state was, but not to prove the existence of any fact he said he knew or believed (*Thomas v Connell* (1838) 4 M & W 267; *R v Gunnell* (1886) 16 Cox CC 154).

By this means may be proved such matters as political or religious opinion; anger; a person's belief that libellous remarks refer to the plaintiff (*Jozwiak v Sadek* [1954] 1 All ER 3); marital affection (*Willis v Bernard* (1832) 8 Bing 376); dislike of a child (*R v Hagan* (1873) 12 Cox CC 357); and fear (*R v Vincent, Frost and Edwards* (1840) 9 C & P 275; *R v Gandfield* (1846) 2 Cox CC 43). Statements reported in market surveys may be admissible under this head: see ch 12, ante. In *Neill v North Antrim Magistrates' Court* [1992] 4 All ER 846 at 854, [1992] 1 WLR 1220 at 1229, HL, it was said that the statement 'I am afraid' was not admissible directly to show that the speaker was afraid, but rather to prove that the words were said, coupled with any consistency of demeanour, with a view to the court's drawing an inference that the speaker was afraid. In that event the statement was being admitted as original evidence, not under an exception to the hearsay rule.

If a man's intention is proved by his hearsay statements to exist at one time, the question then arises whether the continuance or prior existence of the intention can be inferred, and whether the doing of an act can be inferred from the statement of an intention to do it.

What is sometimes called the presumption of continuance will permit the first inference to be drawn provided there is, in the circumstances, not too long an interval between the time of the statement and the time at which the intention must be proved to exist (eg *Re Fletcher, Reading v Fletcher* [1917] 1 Ch 339 at 342). However, the self-serving statements of a party will not support such an inference unless made at the same time as a relevant act (*R v Petcherini* (1855) 7 Cox CC 79; *Bryce v Bryce* [1933] P 83, [1932] All ER Rep 788).

The authorities conflict on whether the doing of an act can be inferred from a statement of an intention to do it (cf *R v Buckley* (1873) 13 Cox CC 293; and *Marshall v SS Wild Rose (Owners)* [1910] AC 486, HL, with *R v Pook* (1871) 13 Cox CC 172n; *R v Wainwright* (1875) 13 Cox CC 171 and *R v Thomson* [1912] 3 KB 19, CCA; and see generally *Walton v R* (1989) 166 CLR 283). A controversial decision of the United States Supreme Court held that a statement of intention to meet a man could be admitted to prove that its maker did meet the man (*Mutual Life Insurance Co v Hillmon* 145 US 285 (1892)). In this case the inference of the happening of a bilateral act such as a meeting is harder to draw than the inference of an act which the speaker could perform by himself, without the reciprocal action of another. But in suitable circumstances there would seem to be no danger of unreliability in drawing the inference.

(iv) Statements of physical sensation

A man's statements of his contemporaneous physical sensation, but not its possible causes, are admissible as evidence of that fact (*Gilbey v Great Western*

Rly Co (1910) 102 LT 202). But if a patient's beliefs as to his physical condition are in issue, a doctor's statements to him are admissible as evidence of that belief, though not as evidence of the truth of what the doctor said (*Tickle v Tickle* [1968] 2 All ER 154). Contemporaneity seems to be more laxly interpreted here than in other res gestae cases (*Aveson v Lord Kinnaird* (1805) 6 East 188; *R v Black* (1922) 16 Cr App Rep 118 at 119).

(v) Original evidence

It is perhaps worth noting again that all the above cases are instances of res gestae evidence admitted as an exception to the hearsay rule. Depending on the issues, res gestae evidence may be original evidence (eg as a prior consistent statement made at the same time as an event in issue to support the witness's consistency: *Milne v Leisler* (1862) 7 H & N 786, post).

FURTHER READING

Gooderson [1956] CLJ 199, [1957] CLJ 55; Hutchins and Slesinger (1929) 38 Yale LJ 283; Maguire (1925) 38 Harv LR 709; Morgan (1922) 31 Yale LJ 229; Nokes (1954) 70 LQR 370; Stone (1939) 55 LQR 66; Wells, *Evidence and Advocacy*, ch 9 and Appendix.

6   Witnesses in previous cases

R v Hall   [1973] QB 496, [1973] 1 All ER 1, CA

Forbes J: [W]e think it plain that a deposition properly taken before a magistrate on oath in the presence of the accused and where the accused has had the opportunity of cross-examination was always admissible at common law in criminal cases if the deponent was dead, despite the absence of opportunity to observe the demeanour of the witness. The only difference between such a deposition and the transcript of evidence given at a previous trial is that the transcript is not signed by the witness. Provided it is authenticated in some appropriate way, as by calling the shorthand writer who took the original note, there seems no reason to think that such a transcript should not be equally receivable in evidence.

In *R v Thompson* [1982] QB 647, [1982] 1 All ER 907, CA, it was held that a transcript of evidence was admissible on a retrial on the same charge if the witness was unable to attend the retrial through death or illness or incapacity to be called.

7   Further reform?

The Law Commission (WP No 138, *Hearsay and Related Topics*) notes that the hearsay rule is arcane and complex, but that it can form an important factor in the protection of the accused against a miscarriage of justice. Its provisional proposals, offered for discussion, are that hearsay should in principle remain inadmissible in criminal cases, but that there should be new general exceptions for first-hand hearsay and for cases where the maker of the statement is unavailable or refuses to give evidence. The existing statutory exceptions should be preserved, and should be supplemented by a limited inclusionary discretion. Section 69 of the Police and Criminal Evidence Act 1984 should be repealed, and the hearsay rule should be defined so as to reverse the effect of *R v Kearley* [1992] 2 AC 228, [1992] 2 All ER 345, HL.

CHAPTER 14

Hearsay Exceptions: Civil Cases

1 Introduction

There are several broad possibilities for reforming the rule against hearsay. One is to adopt the technique of s 96(3)–(7) of the Children Act 1989; that is, to enact statutes on a piecemeal basis to destroy particular anomalies forced on the courts by the common law rule (eg *H v H* [1990] Fam 86, [1989] 3 All ER 740, CA): section 3 below. Another is to enact a hearsay code containing a broad hearsay rule with numerous clearly stated exceptions, as has been done in some jurisdictions of the United States of America: section 4 below. A third is to abolish the ban on hearsay completely; the judge would exclude evidence of too little weight to form the basis of a finding of fact, but apart from that the weight of all the evidence, hearsay or not, would be a matter for the trier of fact. This was the intended effect of the Civil Evidence Act 1995, but, as explained in the comments in section 2 below, that result is not quite achieved.

2 Hearsay in civil cases generally

In civil proceedings, after the decline in jury trials, the hearsay rule was found to be unduly restrictive. Judges sitting in civil cases built up a body of expertise in the evaluation of evidence, and could be trusted to attribute appropriate weight to evidence that came to them indirectly. Following recommendations of the Law Reform Committee, Thirteenth Report, *Hearsay Evidence in Civil Proceedings*, Cmnd 2964 (1966), Parliament enacted the Civil Evidence Act 1968. Part I of that Act made all statements (whether hearsay or not) admissible, but restricted the mode of proof of multiple oral hearsay, with the result that statements made in documents, and first-hand oral hearsay ('A told me that X happened') became admissible. Second-hand hearsay ('A told me that B told him that X happened') or multiple hearsay ('A told me that B told him that C told her . . .') might be admissible if it formed part of a business record. There were complex procedural rules, and there were provisions dealing with computerised records, which inevitably became quickly outdated. The 1968 Act was far from comprehensive in its abolition of the hearsay rule, and was never extended to magistrates' courts. The Act was a combination of the first and second methods described above, with overtones of the third. The difficulties in applying some of its provisions together with the fact that the procedural rules were more often acknowledged in the breach than the observance, and an increasing feeling that finding facts should, where possible, be based on a review of all relevant evidence, rather than being unbalanced by rules of exclusion, led to a further review by the Law Commission (Law Com No 216) who proposed the Bill that has become the Civil Evidence Act 1995.

Civil Evidence Act 1995

1   (1)   In civil proceedings evidence shall not be excluded on the ground that it is hearsay.
    (2)   In this Act –
    (*a*)   'hearsay' means a statement made otherwise than by a person while giving oral evidence in the proceedings which is tendered as evidence of the matters stated; and
    (*b*)   references to hearsay include hearsay of whatever degree.
    (3)   Nothing in this Act affects the admissibility of evidence admissible apart from this section.
    (4)   The provisions of sections 2 to 6 (safeguards and supplementary provisions relating to hearsay evidence) do not apply in relation to hearsay evidence admissible apart from this section, notwithstanding that it may also be admissible by virtue of this section.

2   (1)   A party proposing to adduce hearsay evidence in civil proceedings shall, subject to the following provisions of this section, give to the other party or parties to the proceedings –
    (*a*)   such notice (if any) of that fact, and
    (*b*)   on request, such particulars of or relating to the evidence,
as is reasonable and practicable in the circumstances for the purpose of enabling him or them to deal with any matters arising from its being hearsay.
    (2)   Provision may be made by rules of court –
    (*a*)   specifying classes of proceedings or evidence in relation to which subsection (1) does not apply, and
    (*b*)   as to the manner in which (including the time within which) the duties imposed by that subsection are to be complied with in the cases where it does apply.
    (3)   Subsection (1) may also be excluded by agreement of the parties; and compliance with the duty to give notice may in any case be waived by the person to whom notice is required to be given.
    (4)   A failure to comply with subsection (1), or with rules under subsection (2)(*b*), does not affect the admissibility of the evidence but may be taken into account by the court –
    (*a*)   in considering the exercise of its powers with respect to the course of proceedings and costs, and
    (*b*)   as a matter adversely affecting the weight to be given to the evidence in accordance with section 4.

3   Rules of court may provide that where a party to civil proceedings adduces hearsay evidence of a statement made by a person and does not call that person as a witness, any other party to the proceedings may, with the leave of the court, call that person as a witness and cross-examine him on the statement as if he had been called by the first-mentioned party and as if the hearsay statement were his evidence in chief.

4   (1)   In estimating the weight (if any) to be given to hearsay evidence in civil proceedings the court shall have regard to any circumstances from which any inference can reasonably be drawn as to the reliability or otherwise of the evidence.
    (2)   Regard may be had, in particular, to the following –
    (*a*)   whether it would have been reasonable and practicable for the party by whom the evidence was adduced to have produced the maker of the original statement as a witness;
    (*b*)   whether the original statement was made contemporaneously with the occurrence or existence of the matters stated;
    (*c*)   whether the evidence involves multiple hearsay;

(d) whether any person involved had any motive to conceal or misrepresent matters;
(e) whether the original statement was an edited account, or was made in collaboration with another or for a particular purpose;
(f) whether the circumstances in which the evidence is adduced as hearsay are such as to suggest an attempt to prevent proper evaluation of its weight.

5 (1) Hearsay evidence shall not be admitted in civil proceedings if or to the extent that it is shown to consist of, or to be proved by means of, a statement made by a person who at the time he made the statement was not competent as a witness.

For this purpose 'not competent as a witness' means suffering from such mental or physical infirmity, or lack of understanding, as would render a person incompetent as a witness in civil proceedings; but a child shall be treated as competent as a witness if he satisfies the requirements of section 96(2)(a) and (b) of the Children Act 1989 (conditions for reception of unsworn evidence of child).

(2) Where in civil proceedings hearsay evidence is adduced and the maker of the original statement, or of any statement relied upon to prove another statement, is not called as a witness –
(a) evidence which if he had been so called would be admissible for the purpose of attacking or supporting his credibility as a witness is admissible for that purpose in the proceedings; and
(b) evidence tending to prove that, whether before or after he made the statement, he made any other statement inconsistent with it is admissible for the purpose of showing that he had contradicted himself.

Provided that evidence may not be given of any matter of which, if he had been called as a witness and had denied that matter in cross-examination, evidence could not have been adduced by the cross-examining party.

6 (1) Subject as follows, the provisions of this Act as to hearsay evidence in civil proceedings apply equally (but with any necessary modifications) in relation to a previous statement made by a person called as a witness in the proceedings.

(2) A party who has called or intends to call a person as a witness in civil proceedings may not in those proceedings adduce evidence of a previous statement made by that person, except –
(a) with the leave of the court, or
(b) for the purpose of rebutting a suggestion that his evidence has been fabricated.

This shall not be construed as preventing a witness statement (that is, a written statement of oral evidence which a party to the proceedings intends to lead) from being adopted by a witness in giving evidence or treated as his evidence.

(3) Where in the case of civil proceedings section 3, 4 or 5 of the Criminal Procedure Act 1865 applies, which make provision as to –
(a) how far a witness may be discredited by the party producing him,
(b) the proof of contradictory statements made by a witness, and
(c) cross-examination as to previous statements in writing,

this Act does not authorise the adducing of evidence of a previous inconsistent or contradictory statement otherwise than in accordance with those sections.

This is without prejudice to any provision made by rules of court under section 3 above (power to call witness for cross-examination on hearsay statement).

(4) Nothing in this Act affects any of the rules of law as to the circumstances in which, where a person called as a witness in civil proceedings is cross-examined on a document used by him to refresh his memory, that document may be made evidence in the proceedings.

(5) Nothing in this section shall be construed as preventing a statement of any description referred to above from being admissible by virtue of section 1 as evidence of the matters stated.

7 (1) The common law rule effectively preserved by section 9(1) and(2)(a) of the Civil Evidence Act 1968 (admissibility of admissions adverse to a party) is superseded by the provisions of this Act.

(2) The common law rules effectively preserved by section 9(1) and (2)(b) to (d) of the Civil Evidence Act 1968, that is, any rule of law whereby in civil proceedings –
(a) published works dealing with matters of a public nature (for example, histories, scientific works, dictionaries and maps) are admissible as evidence of facts of a public nature stated in them,

    (*b*)   public documents (for example, public registers, and returns made under public authority with respect to matters of public interest) are admissible as evidence of facts stated in them, or

    (*c*)   records (for example, the records of certain courts, treaties, Crown grants, pardons and commissions) are admissible as evidence of facts stated in them,

shall continue to have effect.

    (3)   The common law rules effectively preserved by section 9(3) and (4) of the Civil Evidence Act 1968, that is, any rule of law whereby in civil proceedings –

    (*a*)   evidence of a person's reputation is admissible for the purpose of proving his good or bad character, or

    (*b*)   evidence of reputation or family tradition is admissible –

        (i)   for the purpose of proving or disproving pedigree or the existence of a marriage, or

        (ii)   for the purpose of proving or disproving the existence of any public or general right or of identifying any person or thing,

shall continue to have effect in so far as they authorise the court to treat such evidence as proving or disproving that matter.

    Where any such rule applies, reputation or family tradition shall be treated for the purposes of this Act as a fact and not as a statement or multiplicity of statements about the matter in question.

    (4)   The words in which a rule of law mentioned in this section is described are intended only to identify the rule and shall not be construed as altering it in any way.

8   (1)   Where a statement contained in a document is admissible as evidence in civil proceedings, it may be proved –

    (*a*)   by the production of that document, or

    (*b*)   whether or not that document is still in existence, by the production of a copy of that document or of the material part of it,

authenticated in such manner as the court may approve.

    (2)   It is immaterial for this purpose how many removes there are between a copy and the original.

9   (1)   A document which is shown to form part of the records of a business or public authority may be received in evidence in civil proceedings without further proof.

    (2)   A document shall be taken to form part of the records of a business or public authority if there is produced to the court a certificate to that effect signed by an officer of the business or authority to which the records belong.

    For this purpose –

    (*a*)   a document purporting to be a certificate signed by an officer of a business or public authority shall be deemed to have been duly given by such an officer and signed by him; and

    (*b*)   a certificate shall be treated as signed by a person if it purports to bear a facsimile of his signature.

    (3)   The absence of an entry in the records of a business or public authority may be proved in civil proceedings by affidavit of an officer of the business or authority to which the records belong.

    (4)   In this section –

'records' means records in whatever form;

'business' includes any activity regularly carried on over a period of time, whether for profit or not, by any body (whether corporate or not) or by an individual;

'officer' includes any person occupying a responsible position in relation to the relevant activities of the business or public authority or in relation to its records; and

'public authority' includes any public or statutory undertaking, any government department and any person holding office under Her Majesty.

    (5)   The court may, having regard to the circumstances of the case, direct that all or any of the above provisions of this section do not apply in relation to a particular document or record, or description of documents or records.

11   In this Act 'civil proceedings' means civil proceedings, before any tribunal, in relation to which the strict rules of evidence apply, whether as a matter of law or by agreement of the parties.

    References to 'the court' and 'rules of court' shall be construed accordingly.

13 In this Act –

. . .

'document' means anything in which information of any description is recorded, and 'copy', in relation to a document, means anything onto which information recorded in the document has been copied, by whatever means and whether directly or indirectly;

'hearsay' shall be construed in accordance with section 1(2);

'oral evidence' includes evidence which, by reason of a defect of speech or hearing, a person called as a witness gives in writing or by signs;

'the original statement', in relation to hearsay evidence, means the underlying statement (if any) by –

    (a)   in the case of evidence of fact, a person having personal knowledge of that fact, or

    (b)   in the case of evidence of opinion, the person whose opinion it is; and

'statement' means any representation of fact or opinion, however made.

14 (1)   Nothing in this Act affects the exclusion of evidence on grounds other than that it is hearsay. This applies whether the evidence falls to be excluded in pursuance of any enactment or rule of law, for failure to comply with rules of court or an order of the court, or otherwise.

    (2)   Nothing in this Act affects the proof of documents by means other than those specified in section 8 or 9.

    (3)   Nothing in this Act affects the operation of the following enactments –

    (a)   section 2 of the Documentary Evidence Act 1868 (mode of proving certain official documents);

    (b)   section 2 of the Documentary Evidence Act 1882 (documents printed under the superintendence of Stationery Office);

    (c)   section 1 of the Evidence (Colonial Statutes) Act 1907 (proof of statutes of certain legislatures);

    (d)   section 1 of the Evidence (Foreign, Dominion and Colonial Documents) Act 1933 (proof and effect of registers and official certificates of certain countries);

    (e)   section 5 of the Oaths and Evidence (Overseas Authorities and Countries) Act 1963 (provision in respect of public registers of other countries).

COMMENTS

The legislative trend has been towards abolition of the hearsay rule, but judicial development of the hearsay rule has taken a contrary direction, with courts insisting on its strict application in the absence of established exceptions (*Myers v DPP* [1965] AC 1001, [1964] 2 All ER 881, HL; *Bradford City Metropolitan Council v K* [1990] Fam 140, CA) and confirming that the rule excludes conduct as well as statements (*R v Kearley* [1992] 2 AC 228, [1992] 2 All ER 345, HL): see ch 12. The 1995 Act applies only to hearsay as defined in s 1(2)(a), and so not to hearsay in the wider sense recognised in *R v Kearley*, supra. This is a surprising and unfortunate feature of the Act, which, as a result, makes admissible the more unreliable and leaves inadmissible the more reliable hearsay evidence. There is, unlike in the 1968 Act (which is repealed), no power under the 1995 Act to admit hearsay by agreement: hearsay not made admissible by the Act is, following the principle in *Bradford City Metropolitan Council v K*, supra, inadmissible. Subject to this considerable reservation and to the other provisions of the 1995 Act, all hearsay, of whatever degree, is admissible, and remains admissible even if adduced without observing the procedural rules: s 2(4). Such failure, together with other matters listed in s 4, is to be taken into account by the trier of fact in assessing the weight to be attributed to the evidence. The list of factors in s 4(2) is clearly not exclusive, and the enactment of such a list carries some danger; but it was thought advisable, particularly as the Act (unlike its predecessor) is to apply in magistrates' courts.

Section 5 ensures that an out-of-court statement will not be admissible as hearsay if it was made by a person who, for reasons of incompetence, could not have given oral evidence to the same effect, and extends, to any person upon whose accuracy the court must depend if minded to rely on the hearsay statement, the common-law rules by which the credibility of a witness may be impeached or supported.

Section 6 makes provision for previous statements of persons called as witnesses in the present proceedings.

Sections 7 and 14 preserve a few common-law exceptions to the hearsay rule. It is important to notice in addition that, as provided by s 1(3) the admissibility (as distinct from the mode of proof) of evidence admissible apart from s 1 is unaffected by the Act. Thus, where there is already in place a régime for the admission of hearsay evidence, as there is in the case of cases related to children (section 3 of this chapter) or under the Bankers' Books Evidence Act 1879, it is not replaced by the 1995 Act. The old rules relating to admissions are supposed to have been superseded by s 1; for a remaining problem see 'Question' infra.

Section 8 makes provision for the proof of statements contained in documents. It is modelled on s 27 of the Criminal Justice Act 1988 and, like that section, has no general application to the proof of documents themselves, or to their contents other than statements. Many documents which are relevant in civil proceedings are relied upon not for statements in them but because of their legal effect: for example, cheques, wills, conveyances, licences, Land Registry documentation. This section has no application to such documents, for which see generally ch 15.

Section 9 provides a 'fast-track' procedure for proof of documents which are part of the records of a business (as very widely defined) or public authority. This section *is* about documents, rather than the statement in them; but it is unfortunate that the draftsman did not take the opportunity to provide a proper definition of 'record', which had caused a certain amount of difficulty in the 1968 Act and in other related legislation. See *Re Koscot Interplanetary (UK) Ltd, Re Koscot AG* [1972] 3 All ER 829. In *H v Schering Chemicals Ltd* [1983] 1 All ER 849, [1983] 1 WLR 143, Bingham J held that 'record' meant any document which could be regarded as an original or primary source of information in the sense that it either gave effect to a transaction or contained a contemporaneous register of information supplied by those with direct knowledge of the facts: it did not extend to digests or analyses of primary sources. This dictum has been approved and applied perhaps unnecessarily stringently to exclude the reports of inspectors of companies appointed by the Trade Secretary (not primary: *Savings and Investment Bank v Gasco BV* [1984] 1 All ER 296, [1984] 1 WLR 271) and notes taken by a solicitor of his interview with a witness (selective, and intended to remind, not record: *Re D (a minor)* (1986) 2 FLR 189). In criminal proceedings the same word in s 68 of the Police and Criminal Evidence Act 1984 (now repealed) was held not to include depositions because statements in proceedings are made to the tribunal, not to its scribe: *R v O'Loughlin and McLaughlin* [1988] 3 All ER 431, 85 Cr App Rep 157; *R v Martin* [1988] 3 All ER 440, [1988] 1 WLR 655, CA. There seems to be no justification for this last restriction of 'record', which would be precluded in civil cases by the contrary decision in *Taylor v*

Taylor [1970] 2 All ER 609, [1970] 1 WLR 1148, CA, where a transcript of prior legal proceedings was held admissible under s 4(1) as a record compiled by a shorthand writer. As the Law Commission points out (op cit, para 4.42), 'business and other records have long been treated as belonging to a class of evidence which can be regarded as likely to be reliable'. Their reliability stems from a combination of various factors: pride in one's job and fear of losing it; regularity of practice leading to efficiency and accuracy; the possibility of cross-checks, balancing and audit, drawing attention to any inaccuracies. Section 1 of the 1995 Act removes the need for special treatment of *statements in* business documents, because all statements in documents are admissible in all proceedings to which the act applies. As a result, this Act is able to go further than its predecessor, and recognise the special reliability of business documents by making them easy to prove, whether or not they contain statements. The result is as follows. If a business document is relied on *other than for any statement in it*, it can be received in evidence under the provisions of s 9. If, however, a party seeks to persuade the court to rely on a *statement in* a business document, the provisions of this section would appear to replace (or fulfil) the authentication requirements of s 8, but the statements are still subject to the notice and guidance requirements of ss 2-6. This is nearly, but not quite, what was intended by the Law Commission: op cit, para 4.38 reads '. . . business and other records will be admitted under [s 1]. We intend that the court's approach to the reliability of the records should be governed by the same considerations as will apply to all other forms of hearsay evidence, namely the weighing provisions contained in [s 4].' The Act does not quite achieve that intention, because although it makes statements in business records subject to the same régime as all other statements, that régime only applies to statements, not to documentary evidence in general. The difficulty arises from the apparent assumption, in the passage cited, that records are a 'form of hearsay evidence'. 'Hearsay' is confined by s 1(2)(*a*) of this Act to statements: records may be (or include) statements, or they may not - in which case ss 1-6 and 8 do not apply to them. The definition of 'document' in the 1968 Act, which was similar to that in s 13 of the 1995 Act, was held wide enough to allow evidence by video link in *Garcin v Amerindo Investment Advisors Ltd* [1991] 4 All ER 655, [1991] 1 WLR 1140.

QUESTION

A machine injures an employee. The employer has it fenced more securely. What evidential value does the employer's act have? (See *Moriarty v London Chatham and Dover Rly Co* (1870) LR 5 QB 314.)

3 Children

Children Act 1989

7   (1)   A court considering any question with respect to a child under this Act may –
     (*a*)   ask a probation officer; or
     (*b*)   ask a local authority to arrange for –
        (i)   an officer of the authority; or

(ii)   such other person (other than a probation officer) as the authority considers appropriate,

to report to the court on such matters relating to the welfare of that child as are required to be dealt with in the report.

(2)   The Lord Chancellor may make regulations specifying matters which, unless the court orders otherwise, must be dealt with in any report under this section.

(3)   The report may be made in writing, or orally, as the court requires.

(4)   Regardless of any enactment or rule of law which would otherwise prevent it from doing so, the court may take account of –

(*a*)   any statement contained in the report; and

(*b*)   any evidence given in respect of the matters referred to in the report,

in so far as the statement or evidence is, in the opinion of the court, relevant to the question which it is considering.

(5)   It shall be the duty of the authority or probation officer to comply with any request for a report under this section.

96   (3)   The Lord Chancellor may by order make provision for the admissibility of evidence which would otherwise be inadmissible under any rule of law relating to hearsay.

(4)   An order under subsection (3) may only be made with respect to –

(*a*)   civil proceedings in general or such civil proceedings, or class of civil proceedings, as may be prescribed; and

(*b*)   evidence in connection with the upbringing, maintenance or welfare of a child.

(5)   An order under subsection (3) –

(*a*)   may, in particular, provide for the admissibility of statements which are made orally or in a prescribed form or which are recorded by any prescribed method of recording;

(*b*)   may make different provision for different purposes and in relation to different descriptions of court; and

(*c*)   may make such amendments and repeals in any enactment relating to evidence (other than in this Act) as the Lord Chancellor considers necessary or expedient in consequence of the provision made by the order . . .

Children (Admissibility of Hearsay Evidence) Order 1993 (SI 1993 No 621)

. . .

2   In –

(*a*)   civil proceedings before the High Court or a county court; and

(*b*)   (i)   family proceedings, and

(ii)   civil proceedings under the Child Support Act 1991 in a magistrates' court,

evidence given in connection with the upbringing, maintenance or welfare of a child shall be admissible notwithstanding any rule of law relating to hearsay.

COMMENT

Hearsay evidence of children's statements of their experiences had been admitted quite generally in proceedings relating to the welfare of the children until the Court of Appeal drew attention in *H v H* [1990] Fam 86, [1989] 3 All ER 740, CA to the strict rules: in most civil proceedings in the High Court hearsay evidence was admissible under the Civil Evidence Act 1968 and not otherwise. Wardship proceedings are an exception, for the court's role in them is 'parental and administrative'; they are not subject to the rules of evidence, in particular the hearsay rule: *Re K* [1965] AC 201, [1963] 3 All ER 191, HL. In care proceedings in the juvenile court there was no power to admit hearsay except under common law exceptions to the rule: *Bradford City*

Metropolitan Council v K [1990] Fam 140, [1990] 2 WLR 532. The immediate effect of the Court of Appeal's decision in *H v H* was the addition of s 96 to the Children Bill then before Parliament. This exemption from the hearsay rule is more liberal than that extended to all civil proceedings by the Civil Evidence Act 1995, because it is not subject to the notice and weighing provisions of that Act.

4   Other jurisdictions

United States Federal Rules of Evidence

Rule 801
Definitions

The following definitions apply under this article:

(a)   **Statement.** A 'statement' is (1) an oral or written assertion of (2) nonverbal conduct of a person, if it is intended by him as an assertion.

(b)   **Declarant.** A 'declarant' is a person who makes a statement.

(c)   **Hearsay.** 'Hearsay' is a statement, other than one made by the declarant while testifying at the trial or hearing, offered in evidence to prove the truth of the matter asserted.

(d)   **Statements which are not hearsay.** A statement is not hearsay if –

(1)   **Prior statement by witness.** The declarant testifies at the trial or hearing and is subject to cross-examination concerning the statement, and the statement is (A) inconsistent with his testimony, and was given under oath subject to the penalty of perjury at a trial, hearing, or other proceeding, or in a deposition, or (B) consistent with his testimony and is offered to rebut an express or implied charge against him of recent fabrication or improper influence or motive, or (C) one of identification of a person made after perceiving him; or

(2)   **Admission by party-opponent.** The statement is offered against a party and is (A) his own statement, in either his individual or a representative capacity or (B) a statement of which he has manifested his adoption or belief in its truth, or (C) a statement by a person authorised by him to make a statement concerning the subject, or (D) a statement by his agent or servant concerning a matter within the scope of his agency or employment, made during the existence of the relationship, or (E) a statement by a co-conspirator of a party during the course and in furtherance of the conspiracy.

Rule 802
Hearsay Rule

Hearsay is not admissible except as provided by these rules or by other rules prescribed by the Supreme Court pursuant to statutory authority or by Act of Congress.

Rule 803
Hearsay exceptions; availability of declarant immaterial

The following are not excluded by the hearsay rule, even though the declarant is available as a witness:

(1)   **Present sense impression.** A statement describing or explaining an event or condition made while the declarant was perceiving the event or condition, or immediately thereafter.

(2)   **Excited utterance.** A statement relating to a startling event or condition made while the declarant was under the stress of excitement caused by the event or condition.

(3)   **Then existing mental, emotional, or physical condition.** A statement of the declarant's then existing state of mind, emotion, sensation, or physical condition (such as intent, plan, motive, design, mental feeling, pain, and bodily health), but not including a statement of memory or belief to prove the fact remembered or believed unless it relates to the execution, revocation, identification, or terms of the declarant's will.

(4)   Statements for purposes of medical diagnosis or treatment. Statements made for purposes of medical diagnosis or treatment and describing medical history, or past or present symptoms, pain, or sensations, or the inception or general character of the cause or external source thereof insofar as reasonably pertinent to diagnosis or treatment.

(5)   Recorded recollection. A memorandum or record concerning a matter about which a witness once had knowledge but now has insufficient recollection to enable him to testify fully and accurately, shown to have been made or adopted by the witness when the matter was fresh in his memory and to reflect that knowledge correctly. If admitted, the memorandum or record may be read into evidence but may not itself be received as an exhibit unless offered by an adverse party.

(6)   Records of regularly conducted activity. A memorandum, report, record, or data compilation, in any form, of acts, events, conditions, opinions, or diagnoses, made at or near the time by, or from information transmitted by, a person with knowledge, if kept in the course of a regularly conducted business activity, and if it was the regular practice of that business activity to make the memorandum, report, record, or data compilation, all as shown by the testimony of the custodian or other qualified witness, unless the source of information or the method or circumstances of preparation indicate lack of trustworthiness. The term 'business' as used in this paragraph includes business, institution, association, profession, occupation, and calling of every kind, whether or not conducted for profit.

(7)   Absence of entry in records kept in accordance with the provisions of paragraph (6). Evidence that a matter is not included in the memoranda reports, records, or data compilations, in any form, kept in accordance with the provisions of paragraph (6), to prove the nonoccurrence or nonexistence of the matter, if the matter was of a kind of which a memorandum, report, record, or data compilation was regularly made and preserved, unless the sources of information or other circumstances indicate lack of trustworthiness.

(8)   Public records and reports. Records, reports, statements, or data compilations, in any form, of public offices or agencies, setting forth (A) the activities of the office or agency, or (B) matters observed pursuant to duty imposed by law as to which matters there was a duty to report, excluding, however, in criminal cases matters observed by police officers and other law enforcement personnel, or (C) in civil actions and proceedings and against the Government in criminal cases, factual findings resulting from an investigation made pursuant to authority granted by law, unless the sources of information or other circumstances indicate lack of trustworthiness.

(9)   Records of vital statistics. Records or data compilations, in any form, of births, fetal deaths, deaths, or marriages, if the report thereof was made to a public office pursuant to requirements of law.

(10)   Absence of public record or entry. To prove the absence of a record, report, statement, or data compilation, in any form, or the nonoccurrence or nonexistence of a matter of which a record, report, statement, or data compilation, in any form, was regularly made and preserved by a public office or agency, evidence in the form of a certification in accordance with rule 902, or testimony, that diligent search failed to disclose the record, report, statement, or data compilation, or entry.

(11)   Records of religious organisations. Statements of births, marriages, divorces, deaths, legitimacy, ancestry, relationship by blood or marriage, or other similar facts of personal or family history, contained in a regularly kept record of a religious organisation.

(12)   Marriage, baptismal, and similar certificates. Statements of fact contained in a certificate that the maker performed a marriage or other ceremony or administered a sacrament, made by a clergyman, public official, or other person authorised by the rules or practices of a religious organisation or by law to perform the act certified, and purporting to have been issued at the time of the act or within a reasonable time thereafter.

(13)   Family records. Statements of fact concerning personal or family history contained in family bibles, genealogies, charts, engravings or rings, inscriptions on family portraits, engravings on urns, crypts, or tombstones, or the like.

(14)   Records of documents affecting an interest in property. The record of a document purporting to establish or affect an interest in property, as proof of the content of the original recorded document and its execution and delivery by each person by whom it purports to have been executed, if the record is a record of a public office and an applicable statute authorises the recording of documents of that kind in that office.

(15)   Statements in documents affecting an interest in property. A statement contained in a document purporting to establish or affect an interest in property if the matter stated was relevant to the purpose of the document, unless dealings with the property since the document was made have been inconsistent with the truth of the statement or the purport of the document.

(16) **Statements in ancient documents.** Statements in a document in existence twenty years or more the authenticity of which is established.

(17) **Market reports, commercial publications.** Market quotations, tabulations, lists, directories, or other published compilations, generally used and relied upon by the public or by persons in particular occupations.

(18) **Learned treatises.** To the extent called to the attention of an expert witness upon cross-examination or relied upon by him in direct examination, statements contained in published treatises, periodicals, or pamphlets on a subject of history, medicine, or other science or art, established as a reliable authority by the testimony or admission of the witness or by other expert testimony or by judicial notice. If admitted, the statements may be read into evidence but may not be received as exhibits.

(19) **Reputation concerning personal or family history.** Reputation among members of his family by blood, adoption, or marriage, or among his associates, or in the community, concerning a person's birth, adoption, marriage, divorce, death, legitimacy, relationship by blood, adoption, or marriage, ancestry, or other similar fact of his personal or family history.

(20) **Reputation concerning boundaries or general history.** Reputation in a community, arising before the controversy, as to boundaries of or customs affecting lands in the community, and reputation as to events of general history important to the community or State or nation in which located.

(21) **Reputation as to character.** Reputation of a person's character among his associates or in the community.

(22) **Judgment of previous conviction.** Evidence of a final judgment, entered after a trial or upon a plea of guilty (but not upon a plea of nolo contendere), adjudging a person guilty of a crime punishable by death or imprisonment in excess of one year, to prove any fact essential to sustain the judgment, but not including, when offered by the Government in a criminal prosecution for purposes other than impeachment, judgments against persons other than the accused. The pendency of an appeal may be shown but does not affect admissibility.

(23) **Judgment as to personal, family, or general history, or boundaries.** Judgments as proof of matters of personal, family or general history, or boundaries, essential to the judgment, if the same would be provable by evidence of reputation.

(24) **Other exceptions.** A statement not specifically covered by any of the foregoing exceptions but having equivalent circumstantial guarantees of trustworthiness, if the court determines that (A) the statement is offered as evidence of a material fact; (B) the statement is more probative on the point for which it is offered than any other evidence which the proponent can procure through reasonable efforts; and (C) the general purposes of these rules and the interests of justice will best be served by admission of the statement into evidence. However, a statement may not be admitted under this exception unless the proponent of it makes known to the adverse party sufficiently in advance of the trial or hearing to provide the adverse party with fair opportunity to prepare to meet it, his intention to offer the statement and the particulars of it, including the name and address of the declarant.

Rule 804
Hearsay exceptions; declarant unavailable:

(a) **Definition of unavailability.** 'Unavailability as a witness' includes situations in which the declarant –
(1) is exempted by ruling of the court on the ground of privilege from testifying concerning the subject matter of his statement; or
(2) persists in refusing to testify concerning the subject matter of his statement despite an order of the court to do so; or
(3) testifies to a lack of memory of the subject matter of his statement; or
(4) is unable to be present or to testify at the hearing because of death or then existing physical or mental illness or infirmity; or
(5) is absent from the hearing and the proponent of his statement has been unable to procure his attendance (or in the case of a hearsay exception under subdivision (b)(2), (3) or (4), his attendance or testimony) by process or other reasonable means.

A declarant is not unavailable as a witness if his exemption, refusal, claim of lack of memory, inability, or absence is due to the procurement or wrongdoing of the proponent of his statement for the purpose of preventing the witness from attending or testifying.

(b)   **Hearsay exception.** The following are not excluded by the hearsay rule if the declarant is unavailable as a witness:

(1)   **Former testimony.** Testimony given as a witness at another hearing of the same or a different proceeding, or in a deposition taken in compliance with law in the course of the same or another proceeding, if the party against whom the testimony is now offered, or, in a civil action or proceeding, a predecessor in interest, had an opportunity and similar motive to develop the testimony by direct, cross, or redirect examination.

(2)   **Statement under belief of impending death.** In a prosecution for homicide or in a civil action or proceeding, a statement made by a declarant while believing that his death was imminent, concerning the cause of circumstances of what he believed to be his impending death.

(3)   **Statement against interest.** A statement which was at the time of its making so far contrary to the declarant's pecuniary or proprietary interest, or so far tended to subject him to civil or criminal liability, or to render invalid a claim by him against another, that a reasonable man in his position would not have made the statement unless he believed it to be true. A statement tending to expose the declarant to criminal liability and offered to exculpate the accused is not admissible unless corroborating circumstances clearly indicate the trustworthiness of the statement.

(4)   **Statement of personal or family history.** (A) A statement concerning the declarant's own birth, adoption, marriage, divorce, legitimacy, relationship by blood, adoption, or marriage, ancestry, or other similar fact of personal or family history, even though the declarant had no means of acquiring personal knowledge of the matter stated; or (B) a statement concerning the foregoing matters, and death also, of another person, if the declarant was related to the other by blood, adoption, or marriage or was so intimately associated with the other's family as to be likely to have accurate information concerning the matter declared.

(5)   **Other exceptions.** A statement not specifically covered by any of the foregoing exceptions but having equivalent circumstantial guarantees of trustworthiness, if the court determines that (A) the statement is offered as evidence of a material fact; (B) the statement is more probative on the point for which it is offered than any other evidence which the proponent can procure through reasonable efforts; and (C) the general purposes of these rules and the interests of justice will best be served by admission of the statement into evidence. However, a statement may not be admitted under this exception unless the proponent of it makes known to the adverse party sufficiently in advance of the trial or hearing to provide the adverse party with a fair opportunity to prepare to meet it, his intention to offer the statement and the particulars of it, including the name and address of the declarant.

Rule 805
Hearsay within hearsay

Hearsay included within hearsay is not excluded under the hearsay rule if each part of the combined statement conforms with an exception to the hearsay rule provided in these rules.

Rule 806
Attacking and supporting credibility of declarant

When a hearsay statement, or a statement defined in Rule 801(d)(2), (C), (D), or (E), has been admitted in evidence, the credibility of the declarant may be attacked, and if attacked may be supported, by any evidence which would be admissible for those purposes if the declarant had testified as a witness. Evidence of a statement or conduct by the declarant at any time, inconsistent with his hearsay statement, is not subject to any requirement that he may have been afforded an opportunity to deny or explain. If the party against whom a hearsay statement has been admitted calls the declarant as a witness, the party is entitled to examine him on the statement as if under cross-examination.

COMMENT

The Federal Rules govern proceedings in both civil and criminal proceedings in the Federal jurisdiction of the United States of America. In addition, about half the states have adopted codes based on the Federal Rules to cover proceedings in state courts.

American Law Institute Model Code of Evidence

Rule 503

Evidence of a hearsay declaration is admissible if the judge finds that the declarant
  (a) is unavailable as a witness, or
  (b) is present and subject to cross-examination.

COMMENT

Rule 503 forms part of a comprehensive code which basically permits only 'first-hand' hearsay; allows the trial judge to exclude hearsay evidence on the ground of its being not sufficiently probative; and preserves the traditional exceptions to the hearsay rule. The radical change of attitude to hearsay required by Rule 503 is often thought to be one of the main reasons why the Model Code was not adopted in any jurisdiction.

5 The value of hearsay evidence

The Ferdinand Retzlaff [1972] 2 Lloyd's Rep 120

After a maritime collision in the English Channel in 1965, the plaintiff's ship was taken to North Shields, where the necessary repairs were executed, together with regular repairs and servicing, which would have been due shortly afterwards. The plaintiffs claimed against the defendants for loss of time caused by the need to make the collision repairs. The defendants argued that not all the time lost was due to the collision because the time spent in repairs had been increased by doing the regular repairs as well: they tendered evidence of the time which it would have taken to do the collision repairs alone at the nearest possible place, Bremen. The defendants were successful before the Admiralty Registrar.

Brandon J: The plaintiffs challenge the Registrar's finding on this point, their main contention being that the nature of the evidence adduced by the defendants on the matter was so unsatisfactory that the Registrar should not have accepted it at all, or at any rate should not have accepted it at anything like its face value . . .
  The evidence adduced by the defendants consisted in the main of letters exchanged between the Association of Bremen Underwriters and A-G Weser in April and July, 1970. The letters contained questions put to A-G Weser at the request of the defendants' solicitors for the purpose of the reference, and A-G Weser's answers to those questions . . .
  On the footing that the letters were properly admitted, the question remains what weight should be given to them. As to this, s 6(3) of the Act of 1968 provides:
    In estimating the weight, if any, to be attached to a statement admissible in evidence by virtue of section 2 . . . of this Act regard shall be had to all the circumstances from which any inference can reasonably be drawn as to the accuracy or otherwise of the statement and,

in particular –

(a) in the case of a statement falling within section 2(1) . . . of this Act, to the question whether or not the statement was made contemporaneously with the occurrence or existence of the facts stated . . .

In the present case there are, in my view, a number of circumstances to which regard should be had in judging the weight to be attached to the statements in the letters. First, the letters were written in response to letters from representatives of the defendants' insurers, which made it clear that answers to the questions raised were to be given without obligation and were to be used solely for the purpose of contesting the plaintiffs' allegedly unjustified claim. Second, the questions to which answers were given in the letters related to what might have happened, but did not happen, five years earlier. The statements in the letters, therefore, related to hypothetical facts only, and were about as uncontemporaneous with the existence of those facts (if hypothetical facts can have an existence) as they could have been. Third, as I said when discussing admissibility, it was not shown to what extent, if at all, the writers or writer of the letters could speak from their or his own knowledge about the matters concerned. Fourth, the only material furnished to A-G Weser for the purpose of answering the questions was the repair account from Smith's dock. They had no shell expansion plan or other details of the plating which had to be repaired.

Apart from these matters, it is necessary, in the case of any unsworn statement put in evidence under s 2 of the Act of 1968 the maker of which is not called, to take account of the fact that the evidence is unsworn and cannot be tested by cross-examination. The latter point is, in my view, particularly important where the evidence relates, as here, to hypothetical rather than actual facts.

The Registrar appears to have accepted the statements made in those letters at their face value. There is nothing in his reasons for decision to indicate that, in estimating the weight to be attached to them, he had any, or any sufficient regard to the various matters which I have mentioned as relevant. Indeed I feel bound to infer from the fact that he accepted the statements at their face value, that he cannot have done so. In these circumstances I consider that I am entitled, indeed bound, to make my own evaluation of the evidence.

My view is quite simply that matters of this importance, in a case of this kind, should be proved by oral evidence, and that letters obtained at the time and in the way that these were obtained should have little weight attached to them. I cannot think that the Civil Evidence Act, 1968, was intended, in general, to change the long-established system by which seriously disputed central issues in civil cases are tried on oral evidence, given on oath and capable of being tested by cross-examination, and to substitute for it a system of trial on unsworn documents brought into existence by parties to the proceedings *post litem motam*, and I do not think the Act should be used, or rather abused, so as to produce such a result.

CHAPTER 15

Documentary Evidence

If a document is to be proved, the original will often have to be tendered, and the document tendered will have to be 'authenticated': its due execution will have to be proved. Even if those requirements are satisfied, the admissibility of statements in the document will depend on the other rules of evidence, principally the hearsay rule.

1 Proof of the contents of a document

MacDonnell v Evans (1852) 11 CB 930

Maule J: If you want to get at the contents of a written document, the proper way is to produce it, if you can. That is a rule in which the common sense of mankind concurs.

Augustien v Challis (1847) 1 Exch 279

Parke B: The moment it appears that there is a lease, you cannot speak about its contents without producing it.

Hence a party who wishes to rely on the words used in a document for any purpose other than that of identifying it must adduce primary evidence of its contents by tendering the original unless an exception applies. The principal non-statutory exceptions are as follows:
(a) The original is in the possession or control (in the sense that the opponent can procure it as of right) of the opponent of the party wishing to rely on the document and the opponent fails to do so either after receiving a notice to produce it pursuant to RSC Ord 24, r 10 or otherwise, or where the document is itself a notice, or where the nature of the proceedings themselves informs a party he must produce the original (eg a prosecution for driving without being properly insured). While at common law the notice to produce need not be complied with, it excludes the objection that not all reasonable steps have been taken to procure the original. It gives the opposing party the chance to produce the document if he pleases and thereby to secure the best evidence of its contents if he wishes: *Dwyer v Collins* (1852) 7 Exch 639. A party who serves a notice

and calls for the documents it identifies must tender them if required to by the recipient of the notice, even if they would be inadmissible had they been tendered by the latter: *Walker v Walker* (1937) 57 CLR 630. Hence a notice to produce cannot be used as a means of gaining a right of inspecting a document without using it if it is unfavourable: *Wharam v Routledge* (1805) 5 Esp 235.

(b) The document is in the possession of a stranger who lawfully refuses to produce it after service of a subpoena duces tecum (eg because privilege has been claimed, or because the recipient lawfully claims diplomatic privilege: *R v Nowaz* [1976] 3 All ER 5, [1976] 1 WLR 830, CA). But secondary evidence is inadmissible where a third party has unlawfully failed to produce a document on subpoena. The purpose of these rules is to prevent unreliable secondary evidence being admitted against one party by collusion between his opponent and the stranger to a litigation.

(c) The original cannot be found after due search. What is 'due' search depends on the value of the document, so that secondary evidence of non-valuable documents is more easily tendered than it is of valuable ones. 'The presumption of law is, that a man will keep all those papers which are valuable to himself, and which may, with any degree of probability, be of any future use to him. The presumption on the contrary is, that a man will not keep those papers which have entirely discharged their duty, and which are never likely to be required for any purpose whatsoever': *Brewster v Sewell* (1820) 3 B & Ald 296 at 300, per Bayley J.

(d) The production of the original is in practice impossible, eg because it is written on a tombstone, a wall or a banner, or because by law it may not be moved (eg a licence required to remain continuously on a factory wall: *Owner v Bee Hive Spinning Co Ltd* [1914] 1 KB 105).

(e) The production of the original would be highly inconvenient owing to the public nature of the document, or because it is an entry in a banker's book or a book of accounts.

(f) The opponent orally admits the contents of the document: *Slatterie v Pooley* (1840) 6 M & W 664.

See also RSC Ord 27, r 4(3): the effect of service of a list of documents in the High Court is that a party who has served a list of documents by way of discovery is deemed to have received a notice to produce those of them in his possession, custody or power.

Commissioner for Railways (NSW) v Young
(1962) 106 CLR 535, High Court of Australia

An issue arose as to whether, though a jar containing a sample of blood taken from a deceased person was not produced, oral evidence of the writing on the label could be admitted.

Windeyer J: There is probably no rule of evidence that is better known than that secondary evidence of the contents of written documents is, in general, not receivable. 'The contents of every written paper are, according to the ordinary and well-established rules of evidence, to be proved by the paper itself, and by that alone, if the paper be in existence' is the way in which the judges stated it in the Full Court. In cases of this sort the writing is not relied upon for its meaning, but only as an identification mark. Its meaning is of no significance. The distinction is adverted to in the judgment of Martin B in *Boyle v Wiseman* (1855) 11 Exch 360 at 367. And it has been expressly made in some American cases, especially *Commonwealth v Morrell* 99 Mass 542 (1868) and *Benjamin v The State* 67 So 792 (1915) where parol evidence of the writing on tags and price tickets was admitted to identify articles stolen, on the basis that it was matter of description and identity only. But at the time when the witness McDonald was asked what was written on the label his answer would not have identified the vessel he had with that containing blood of the deceased, for there was then no evidence of what had been on its label. True it is that, when a question is whether B saw the same thing as A had seen, it may often be immaterial whether A or B be first called to describe what he had seen. But Doctor Sheldon had already been asked what he had written and had not answered. In the circumstances the learned judge was not required to admit evidence from McDonald, no foundation for it having been laid. It appeared that the defendant's counsel was really trying to get what was on the label before the jury as itself evidence of what was in the bottle. This it was not. What is written on the label on a bottle, or other container, may in some cases be some evidence of what the contents are. Whether or not in a particular case that is so, and how cogent such evidence is, depends upon the circumstances. As the evidence stood in this case what was written on the label could not establish what was in the bottle even if the bottle had been produced. Counsel for the appellant argued that McDonald could have been permitted to say what was written on the bottle the contents of which he examined if only Doctor Sheldon had been permitted to say what had been written on the bottle into which he had put blood of the deceased. That, I have no doubt, is so. If the writings corresponded the jury might, in the circumstances, infer that the blood that McDonald examined was the sample that had been labelled and sealed at the autopsy. I do not agree that to enable the jury to infer identity any greater description of the bottle was required or any exact tracing of its movements and whereabouts from the time it left the morgue till the time McDonald got it. The question was simply: was it the sample of blood? That would have been for the jury to say, if there were any evidence before them. It was not something that had to be proved beyond reasonable doubt, nor was it necessary that every possibility that it was not the same blood should have been eliminated. The respondent's attitude on this aspect seemed to me quite mistaken.

For these reasons, if when Doctor Sheldon was asked what he had written on the label on the bottle, the question had been pressed and it had been made clear to the learned judge that the purpose was merely to describe an identifying mark, it seems probable that the question would have been allowed and properly allowed.

Dixon CJ: '[T]here is no case whatever deciding that, when the issue is as to the state of a chattel, eg the soundness of a horse, or the equality of the bulk of the goods to the sample, the production of the chattel is primary evidence and that no other evidence can be given until the chattel is produced in court for the inspection of the jury': per Lord Coleridge CJ for the Court of Crown Cases Reserved in *R v Francis* (1874) LR 2 CCR 128 at p 133. This is true of a picture where the question is whether a photograph is a copy: *Lucas v Williams & Son* [1892] 2 QB 113. It is true of an article of clothing where the question is as to its manufactured condition: *Hocking v Ahlquist Bros Ltd* [1944] KB 120, [1943] 2 All ER 722. It has been held too, that upon the trial of an indictment containing counts for an unlawful assembly, seditious combinations and the like, production was unnecessary of flags, banners and placards bearing seditious inscriptions and devices. Abbott CJ for the Court of Queen's Bench said: 'With respect to the last point, the reception of the evidence as to the inscriptions on the flags or banners, I think it was not necessary either to produce the flags or give notice to the defendants to produce them. The cases requiring the production of a writing itself will be found to apply to writings of a very different character. There is no authority to show that in a criminal case ensigns, banners, or other things exhibited to public view, and of which the effect depends upon such public exhibition, must be produced or accounted for on the part either of the prosecutor or of the defendants. And in many instances the proof of such matters from eye-witnesses, speaking to what they saw on the occasion, has been received, and its competency was never, to my knowledge, called in question until the present time. Inscriptions used on such occasions are the public expression of the sentiments of those who bear and adopt them, and have rather the character of speeches than of writings. If we were to hold that words inscribed on a banner so exhibited could not be proved without the production of the banner, I know not upon what reason a witness should be allowed to mention the colour of the banner, or even to say that he saw a banner displayed, for the banner itself may be said to be the best possible evidence of its existence and its colour': *R v Hunt* (1820) 3 B & Ald 566 at 574, 575. The decision is not considered sound by *Wigmore* (loc cit) and is treated by Parke B in *Jones v Tarleton* (1842) 9 M & W 675 at 676, as meaning that the evidence of the inscriptions is received as part of the *res gestae*; but it illustrates the distinction between physical things bearing written inscriptions and documents the written contents of which amount to what may be called an instrument or writing which, because of the significance of what it expresses, has some legal or evidentiary operation or effect material to the case. In the present case the purpose of offering the evidence was simply to prove that the sealed jar leaving the hands of Dr Stratford Sheldon was the same sealed jar that came to the hands of Mr McDonald. The proof depended upon the identity of the character and condition of the jar in all respects and most particularly its label. The statement upon the label that it contained the blood of the deceased, if that was what it stated, could not be used as evidence of that fact. But the identity of the writing on the jar in Dr Stratford Sheldon's hand with what Dr Stratford Sheldon stated that he wrote was an admissible evidentiary fact forming part of the description. It seems clear enough, on reading the evidence closely, that the label was pasted on the vessel as so to form part of its then condition and was not a mere detachable ticket. In other words, the vessel was an 'inscribed chattel' of which the correct view is that the full description was admissible by oral proof for the purpose of identification.

It follows that the evidence was wrongly rejected.

COMMENTS

1. The primary evidence rule applies only to documents, not physical objects. Tape-recordings have for this purpose been classified as objects, not documents: *Kajala v Noble* (1982) 75 Cr App Rep 149; *R v Matthews* [1972] VR 3; cf *R v Stevenson* [1971] 1 All ER 678, [1971] 1 WLR 1 and *Conwell v Tapfield* [1981] 1 NSWLR 595. See also *Hindson v Monahan* [1970] VR 84. On the other hand, for the purposes of discovery, courts in England, Canada and Australia have applied a wider definition, including a tape (*Australian National Airlines Commission v Commonwealth* (1975) 132 CLR 582, following *Grant v Southwestern and County Properties Ltd* [1975] Ch 185, [1974] 2 All ER 465), a 'fax' (*Hastie and Jenkerson v McMahon* [1991] 1 All ER 255, [1990] 1 WLR 1575) and an entry on a computer disk (*Derby v Weldon (No 9)* [1991] 2 All ER 901, [1991] 1 WLR 652). In *Senior v Holdsworth, ex p Independent Television News* [1976] QB 23, [1975] 2 All ER 1009 there was a division in the Court of Appeal as to whether a film was a 'document' within the meaning of Ord 20, r 8(1) of the County Court Rules giving power to require production of documents by summons. The rule does not apply to identifying marks such as a monogram on clothing, the number on a car, or the words and figures on breathalysing instruments.

2. The rule prevents reference being made to a document to prove its contents, but not to identify it, or to establish its bare existence.

3. The rule applies only if reliance is placed on the precise words of the document. The exact amount of rent cannot be proved without tendering the original of the lease: *Augustien v Challis* (1847) 1 Exch 279. But other means can be used to prove the fact of tenancy (*R v Holy Trinity, Kingston-upon-Hull (Inhabitants)* (1827) 7 B & C 611); or partnership (*Alderson v Clay* (1816) 1 Stark 405; *Mallinson v Scottish Australian Investment Co Ltd* (1920) 28 CLR 66). In McCormick's terminology (para 234) this excepts 'collateral writings' from the rule. Any narration by a witness is likely to include many references to writings without direct reliance on their precise terms. Trials would become intolerably clogged if this exception or qualification did not exist.

4. There is much technical learning on what the original of a document is, and the purpose of the tender affects the question. If a telegram is tendered

against the receiver, the original is what he received; if it is tendered against the sender, it is what he sent. A counterpart lease executed only by the lessee is the original when it is tendered against him; the other part of the original as against the lessor: *Doe d West v Davis* (1806) 7 East 363. Duplicates of a deed executed by all parties are all originals: *Forbes v Samuel* [1913] 3 KB 706.

5. In general, there are no degrees of secondary evidence. If the rule does not apply or an exception to it does, oral evidence of the document may be given without accounting for the lack of copies, and there is no compulsion to tender 'better' rather than less good copies. A copy of a copy is admissible: *Lafone v Griffin* (1909) 25 TLR 308; *R v Collins* (1960) 44 Cr App Rep 170; cf *Everingham v Roundell* (1838) 2 Mood & R 138.

6. The rule has several justifications. First, it helps prevent fraud, which may not be detectable from a copy. Secondly, the exact words of a document may be crucial in determining rights. Non-mechanically reproduced documents are prone to contain error, and oral evidence of the contents of a document is more prone to error than other oral evidence. Thirdly, the rule helps prevent error arising by reason of passages being taken out of context. The problems which the rule seeks to meet are partially overcome by pre-trial discovery procedures, which have the result in practice that a great many copies of documents are tendered by consent.

NOTE

Both s 27 of the Criminal Justice Act 1988 and s 8 of the Civil Evidence Act 1995 contain provisions allowing the use of copies of documents rather than the original. These sections are, however, of rather restricted scope. They apply respectively to civil and criminal proceedings in general, but are limited to situations where 'a statement contained in a document is admissible as evidence'. The provisions are not restricted to hearsay and would therefore apply in criminal cases to all documents to which s 69 of the Police and Criminal Evidence Act 1984 applies as well as to documentary hearsay made admissible by s 23 or 24 of the 1988 Act. They would not, however, apply to the terms of a contract, which are promises, not statements. Further, neither of these provisions in terms allows oral evidence of the contents of a document.

2 Proof of execution of private documents

Documents must be authenticated before they can be admitted. In ordinary life if one receives a letter purporting to be signed by X one assumes it is signed by X. But in theory X's signature may have been forged. There is a general rule that, to avoid fraud or mistaken attributions of authorship, proof of authenticity must be offered. In strictness that rule is a necessary one; in practice it is rarely necessary and compliance can be time consuming and expensive. This has produced two results: the creation of exceptions of wide scope, and the frequent tendering of evidence in defiance of the rule by consent.

Proof of the 'due execution' of a private document is proof that it was signed by the person by whom it purports to have been signed and, if it has to be attested, that it was attested. Proof of the due execution of a document is necessary where the document is private. If the document is more than 20 years old and comes from proper custody there is a presumption of formal validity: Evidence Act 1938, s 4. 'Proper custody' is that which is reasonable and natural in the particular circumstances, not necessarily that which is the 'best and most proper place of deposit': *Bishop of Meath v Marquis of Winchester* (1836) 3 Bing NC 183.

The necessity of that rule is based on the fact that the older a document the harder it will be to call persons who witnessed it, or saw it made, or know the handwriting of the author. The sense of the rule is that commonly the older a document the stronger will be the inferences as to its authenticity to be drawn from the circumstances. 'Facts which may be suggested as indicative of genuineness include unsuspicious appearance, emergence from natural custody, prompt recording, and, in the case of a deed or will, possession taken under the instrument. Age itself may be viewed as giving rise to some inference of genuineness in that an instrument is unlikely to be forged for fruition at a time in the distant future': McCormick, 2nd edn, para 223.

If a document is in the possession of an opposing party who has refused to produce it after receiving a notice to do so, proof of due execution is not required.

Proof of a signature or handwriting may be effected directly, through the testimony (or admissible hearsay assertion) of the person who signed or of a person who observed the signing. It may be effected indirectly, by means of opinion evidence emanating from a person who did not see the document signed, but who is acquainted with the handwriting of the person in question, either by having seen him write on other occasions, or by having corresponded with and participated in transactions with him 'upon the faith that letters purporting to have been written or signed by him have been so signed or written': *Doe d Mudd v Suckermore* (1836) 5 Ad & El 703 at 705, per Coleridge J. A signature may also be proved indirectly by comparison: a disputed document is compared with a document which is proved to have been written or signed by the person whose signature is in issue. Normally, particularly in criminal cases, the comparison is and ought to be carried out by a handwriting expert, rather than merely by a layman or by the court: *R v Tilley* [1961] 3 All ER 406, [1961] 1 WLR 1309; cf *Adami's* Case. In criminal cases the court must be satisfied beyond reasonable doubt that the specimen handwriting with which the disputed document is compared is that of the person whose writing is in issue: *R v Ewing* [1983] QB 1039, [1983] 2 All ER 645, CA, reversing *R v Angeli* [1978] 3 All ER 950, [1979] 1 WLR 26, CA.

Adami v R   (1959) 108 CLR 605, High Court of Australia

The accused was charged with having forged two savings bank withdrawal forms. Three other withdrawal forms in respect of the same bank account were admitted in evidence. The applicant had been asked to write on a piece of paper some words and figures, and that document was tendered with a piece of his genuine handwriting forming a standard of comparison, and was marked exhibit N.

Dixon CJ, McTiernan, Fullagar, Kitto and Menzies JJ: The first position taken up by his counsel in support of this application is that the jury may well have used the three forms of withdrawal dated 3, 4 and 17 December 1958 against the prisoner in support of the conclusion that the two withdrawal forms the subject of the information were forged, and yet neither upon the question of medium of proof nor upon that of relevancy was there any proper ruling or any proper direction to the jury.

At the conclusion of the Crown case it was, one may think, open to the learned judge to hold that so far as medium of proof might go as distinguished from relevancy, a foundation had been laid for treating the document as admissible against the prisoner. Section 30 of the *Evidence Act, 1929–1957*, which is founded on s 8 of '*Denman's Act*', ie *Criminal Procedure Act*, 1865 (28 and 29 Vict c 18) and on s 27 of the *Common Law Procedure Act* 1854 (17 and 18 Vict c 125) provides that a comparison of a disputed writing with any writing proved to the satisfaction of the judge to be genuine shall be permitted to be made by witnesses and such writings and the evidence of the witnesses respecting that same may be submitted to the Court as evidence of the genuineness or otherwise of the writing in dispute. *Blackburn J* seems at one time to have considered that the provision could not be used without the assistance of witnesses, expert or otherwise, as to the handwriting (*R v Harvey* (1869) 11 Cox CC 546) but this is not now regarded as correct. What the provision made possible was the use of a writing inadmissible in evidence except for the sole purpose of providing a standard of comparison of handwriting. That formerly could not be done. See *Doe d Mudd v Suckermore* (1836) 5 Ad & El 703; *Doe d Perry v Newton* (1836) 5 Ad & El 514; *Hughes v Rogers* (1841) 8 M & W 123; *Doe d Devine v Wilson* (1855) 10 Moo PCC 502 at 530. But after the adoption of these provisions, in a case of a disputed writing or writings, a writing not otherwise relevant to the issue became admissible for the purpose of providing a standard of comparison of handwriting. It was necessary that the writing so to be used as a standard should be properly proved to the satisfaction of the judge to be the handwriting of the party concerned. Clearly enough Exhibit N was admissible under the section as a standard of comparison for the purpose of determining whether the writing upon the two forms in respect of which the prisoner was charged was or was not his. So much was not disputed. It was, however, suggested that the three additional forms were not writings in dispute within the rule expressed by the provision and their authorship could not be established by comparison with Exhibit N; still less could a comparison be instituted between the five documents. But it is an error to treat the three additional documents as not writing in dispute. The prisoner by no means admitted them to be his and indeed he expressly denied that he had signed the name of Giovanni Cazzaro to any withdrawal form. As to the comparison of the five forms one with another, that would establish nothing against the prisoner if each and every one of the five were not brought into comparison with Exhibit N. A careful comparison of the three withdrawal forms of 3, 4 and 17 December respectively with Exhibit N, the document admitted as the genuine writing of the prisoner and for the purpose of supplying a standard of comparison suggests that it is a reasonable conclusion that they are all in the same handwriting. But that comparison the learned presiding judge never made for the purpose of admitting them in evidence against the prisoner. Suppose, however, that his Honour had made this comparison and had decided that he was warranted in treating the documents as sufficiently appearing to be connected with the prisoner to enable him to admit them in evidence against him, leaving it to the jury to decide the question whether they came from the prisoner. On that assumption, on what grounds of relevance were they admissible against the prisoner? The admission of the evidence as relevant is not dependent necessarily upon its probative force on the central issue, namely the issue whether the prisoner was the man who wrote and presented the two withdrawal forms dated 5 December and 10 December respectively, those the subject of the counts in the information. But it is plain that on the assumption that Cazzaro's denial that he withdrew the money was accepted, and obviously the jury did accept it, the crimes charged in the information formed two steps in a course of conduct on the part of the guilty person which could only be understood properly if the connected steps by which the transaction was made up were laid before the jury. Those steps were the theft of a pass book and passport and the withdrawal of the amount at deposit by the use of the passbook and withdrawal slips covering the whole amount. The withdrawals all took place between 3 and 17 December 1958 and comprised the whole sum deposited. That means that the withdrawals covering the amount in credit within a period of fourteen days were obviously interconnected. Assuming that it was open to the judge to treat all five withdrawal forms as presumptively attributable to the prisoner because of the learned judge's view of the similarity of all five withdrawal forms or perhaps more precisely of the three the admissibility of which is now in question, it seems to have been open to the learned judge to admit them in evidence on this footing and submit them to the jury. The difficulty is, however, that it is not the way the matter was dealt with at the trial by his Honour. Of the logical hypotheses by which the five withdrawals might be explained, no doubt one is that Cazzaro himself was the man who made them and it would seem that it is this hypothesis that struck his Honour's mind as a real possibility and led him to present the case to the jury as he did in his charge to them. The hypothesis which the jury found to be the truth was simply that the identification of Wood was correct and the person was the prisoner. There were of course other hypotheses open, as for example that it was some other denizen of Nos 14 and 16 Shannon Place or someone who did not reside there but knew all about those who did. Looking at the documents and comparing them with Exhibit N it does seem that the comparison affords prima facie reason for admitting them in evidence against the prisoner, it being for the jury to decide on the whole evidence whether their authorship should be ascribed to him. But except to give coherence and intelligence to what really was an entire transaction in relation to Cazzaro's bank account the additional three withdrawals were not really of probative strength in showing that he was the man.

When the whole circumstances are considered it appears that they might properly have been admitted in evidence and it does not seem that the course actually taken at the trial, irregular as it apparently was, is a sufficient reason for this Court intervening and reversing the conviction.

COMMENTS

1. When a will has to be proved in other than common form, its attestation must be proved. Attestation is proved by calling one of the attesting witnesses if any are available. Other evidence is inadmissible unless all the attesting witnesses are dead, insane, beyond the jurisdiction or untraceable. If none of the attesting witnesses can be called, steps must be taken to prove the handwriting of one of them, this being 'secondary evidence of attestation'. If that is impossible, persons who, though not attesting witnesses, witnessed the execution can prove it, and such witnesses are treated as having been called by the court so that they may be cross-examined by the party seeking to prove execution: *Oakes v Uzzell* [1932] P 19. Section 3 of the Evidence Act 1938 provides that in any proceedings, whether civil or criminal, an instrument to the validity of which attestation is requisite (testamentary documents apart) may be proved in the manner in which it might be proved if no attesting witness were alive.

2. A document is presumed to have been executed on the date which it bears.

3. An alteration to a deed is presumed to have been made before execution, for that favours validity; an alteration to a will is presumed to have been made after execution, for that is not inconsistent with validity: *Doe d Tatum v Catomore* (1851) 16 QB 745.

4. A party on whom a list of documents is served by way of discovery is deemed to admit that a document described as an original or a true copy is an original or a true copy respectively, unless authenticity is challenged in the pleadings or by notice: RSC Ord 27, r 4.

5. The difficulty in complying with strict authentication requirements is also alleviated by RSC Ord 27, r 5, providing for the service of a notice to admit authenticity: if authenticity is disputed by a counter notice but later proved, the party against whom it is proved will have to pay the costs of proof.

6. Finally, it may be noted that in civil (but not criminal) proceedings documents which ought to have been stamped for the purposes of stamp duty are inadmissible. This is not a rule which the parties can waive. The objection must be taken by the court, which here acts in aid of the revenue. In practice the problem is overcome by the undertaking to the court of the solicitor of the party tendering the document to stamp it and pay the duty; he then obtains indemnity from his client. That undertaking is a serious one, and the even course of litigation can often be suddenly upset in practice by the necessity to reflect on whether the fruits of possible victory are equivalent to what will have to be paid in stamp duty. If the original cannot be found or is not produced after due notice to do so, it will be presumed to have been stamped.

3 The parol evidence rule

The rule that oral evidence may not be admitted to alter, vary or add to the terms of a written instrument is contiguous to, if not over the border of, the substantive law of contract. It is best left to works on that subject: see for example Treitel, *The Law of Contract* (9th edn, 1995), pp 176–85

FURTHER READING

Phipson, chs 35 and 36; Cross, ch 18, Thayer, ch 11; McCormick, 3rd edn, chs 22 and 23, Brown, *Documentary Evidence in Australia* (1988).

CHAPTER 16

Opinion Evidence and Prior Proceedings

1 Opinion evidence

The orthodox doctrine is that a witness may not give his opinion unless (a) he is an expert testifying on a matter calling for the expertise he possesses: or (b) it is extremely difficult to separate opinions from facts, and the witness's opinion will help the court. There is a further rule or principle, of diminishing scope, that as far as possible the witness should not give his opinion on the ultimate issue – the very issue the court has to decide.

An opinion is an inference from observed facts. Since most human discourse is largely made up of opinions, an insistence that no statements of opinion be made would be unworkable. Expert opinions are necessary to point out to laymen the inferences they cannot themselves draw, and non-expert opinions must be admitted where this is convenient in the interests of a reasonably normal prose during the giving of testimony. But in practice English courts have applied the rule even more loosely so that technical difficulties have been tempered. This is partly because of the lack of theoretical attention devoted to the subject and the paucity of leading cases.

Non-expert opinion evidence on matters requiring expertise is excluded because it is irrelevant or insufficiently weighty: such evidence on matters not requiring expertise which would not assist the court is superfluous. The rule against evidence on the ultimate issue depends on a fear of a witness usurping jury functions. There is a general feeling also that expert witnesses are selected to prove a case and are often close to being professional liars: 'it is often quite surprising to see with what facility, and to what an extent, their view can be made to correspond with the wishes or the interests of the parties who call them. They do not, indeed, wilfully misrepresent what they think, but their judgments become so warped by regarding the subject in one point of view, that, even when conscientiously disposed, they are incapable of forming an independent opinion. Being zealous partisans, their Belief becomes synonymous with faith as defined by the Apostle, and it too often is but "the substance of things *hoped for*, the evidence of things *not* seen"' (Taylor, p 59). Lord Campbell put it more harshly: 'hardly any weight is to be given to the evidence of what are called scientific witnesses; they come with a bias on their minds to support the cause in which they are embarked' (*Tracy Peerage Claim* (1843) 10 Cl & Fin 154 at 191). And Best says: 'there can be no doubt that testimony is daily received in our courts as "scientific evidence" to which it is almost profanation to apply the term; as being revolting to common sense, and inconsistent with the commonest honesty on the part of those by whom it is given' (p 491). That concern was recently reflected by Lords Wilberforce and Fraser in warning that expert evidence should be independent of influence by legal advisers, 'uninfluenced as to form or content by the exigencies of litigation' (save presumably so far as formal rules of admissibility of evidence are concerned): *Whitehouse v Jordan* [1981] 1 All ER 267 at 281 and 284, [1981] 1 WLR 246 at 256–7 and 268.

A   NON-EXPERT OPINION EVIDENCE AT COMMON LAW

A non-expert may give his opinion if the facts on which it was based were too fleeting to be noticed or remembered, or if it would disturb the flow of his narrative too much to state them. He may give a compendious account of what he observed by stating an opinion. Questions about identity are very clear illustrations of both points. When one recognises a particular old man, one does not consciously notice his white hair, his shortness, his pipe and so on; even if one did, one might not remember all the features that help one to recognise him; and even if one remembered, it would make the giving and hearing of testimony intolerable if witnesses identifying the man listed all his physical traits and left it to the court to draw an inference. Other examples apart from identity of persons, things and handwriting are age; speed; temperature; weather; light; the passing of time; sanity; the condition of objects – new, shabby, worn; emotional and bodily states; and intoxication. The hostility of the law to opinion evidence is partly supported by the fact that these are all cases where it is very easy for witnesses to make mistakes.

There has been some tendency to expand the admissibility of non-expert opinion evidence of this kind.

It is often said that courts are hostile to non-experts expressing their opinions on the ultimate issue, but the rule is often evaded and sometimes broken, as in the cases of estimates of value (*R v Beckett* (1913) 8 Cr App Rep 204, CCA); and opinions as to whether an act would have been done had some circumstance been different (*Mansell v Clements* (1874) LR 9 CP 139).

The English and Irish courts differ on the question of unfitness to drive through drink, the Irish considering that a non-expert can testify to this (*A-G (Rudely) v Kenny* (1960) 94 ILTR 185), the English considering that the witness's opinion on drunkenness alone can be admitted (*R v Davies* [1962] 3 All ER 97). This is perhaps open to criticism, for 'as in the case of the inference that a person is under the influence of drink, the inference that the same person was incapable of having proper control may depend on the whole picture, on the conjoint effect of numerous facts and circumstances which lead to a sound conclusion but cannot be faithfully or completely reproduced in evidence' (*Sherrard v Jacob* [1965] NI 151 at 163, per Lord MacDermott).

B   EXPERT OPINION EVIDENCE AT COMMON LAW

Before giving his opinion, the expert must show himself to be properly qualified in the matter he is about to give his opinion of. The expertise – a developed body of knowledge or skill outside the experience of the jury – may be acquired by training or experience.

The matter must be one calling for expertise, and this varies from time to time as common knowledge changes. In the United States the test for admissibility was for a long time stated in *Frye v United States* 293 F 1013 at 1014 (1923): the learning 'from which the deduction is made must be sufficiently established to have gained a general acceptance in the particular field to which it belongs'. Since *Daubert v Merrell-Dow Pharmaceuticals* 125 L Ed 2d 469 (1993) the test has been whether the theory relied on is falsifiable, what the known or potential error rate of applying it is, whether the findings have been subjected to peer review and publication, and its general acceptance. The latter approach has not yet been taken up outside the United States. Numerous cases outside the United States have operated consistently with the former approach, but it is questionable whether general acceptance is necessary. Thus evidence was not rejected where an unproven theory not supported by the weight of scientific opinion was advanced (*Government Transport Comr v Adamcik* (1961) 106 CLR 292), but the expertise alleged must rise above that of an opinion given by 'a quack, a charlatan or an enthusiastic amateur' (*R v Robb* (1991) 93 Cr App Rep 161 at 166, CA).

The usual examples include scientific, architectural, engineering and technical issues, problems of tool marks and ballistics, blood tests, the provisions of foreign law, the identity of hand-writing and fingerprints, questions of artistic taste, economic comment and prediction in restrictive trade practices cases, and issues of business practice and market value. There is some overlap with matters on which non-expert evidence is given. Normally the facts with reference to which the opinion was given are not proved by the expert; they must be separately proved and he must give an opinion on them put to him in hypothetical questions which properly identified them: *R v Turner* [1975] QB 834 at 840, [1975] 1 All ER 70, CA. If the facts ultimately found by the court do not accord with the hypotheses, the opinion loses corresponding weight. It remains admissible until a point is reached at which there is non-correspondence in an important, not merely a trifling, respect: *Paric v John Holland (Constructions) Pty Ltd* (1985) 62 ALR 85. He may, however, testify to the facts if he observed them. Once the primary facts are found, an expert is entitled to draw on the work of others in his field of expertise (including unpublished works) in arriving at his conclusion, but this material should be referred to so that the cogency of the conclusion can be tested: *R v Abadom* [1983] 1 All ER 364, [1983] 1 WLR 126, CA. If an expert refers to the results of research published by a reputable authority in a reputable journal, the court will ordinarily regard those results as supporting any inferences fairly to be drawn from them unless or until a different approach is shown to be proper: *H v Schering Chemicals Ltd* [1983] 1 All ER 849, [1983] 1 WLR 143.

On proof of foreign law, see Civil Evidence Act 1972, s 4; Administration of Justice Act 1920, s 15; Supreme Court Act 1981, s 69(5); County Courts Act 1984, s 68. The existence, the nature and the scope of the rules and principles of the law of a foreign jurisdiction are issues of fact to be decided by the judge, then, on which evidence is receivable; on the other hand, the effect of the application of those rules and principles, as so ascertained, to the particular facts and circumstances of the case before the court is a question of law for the court of the forum, on which evidence is not receivable. Where the relevant rules and principles of foreign law are so framed as to confer discretions on the courts which administer them, evidence is receivable as to the manner in which those discretions are exercised, with reference to any pattern or course of decision: *National Mutual Holdings Pty Ltd v Sentry Corpn* (1989) 87 ALR 539 at 556 per Gummow J. See also *Scruples Imports Pty Ltd v Crabtree and Evelyn Pty Ltd* (1983) 1 IPR 315 at 325.

The court is not entitled to reject the evidence of expert witnesses if they agree as to the effect of the foreign law and instead conduct its own researches into that law by recourse to text books and foreign law reports: the court must base its findings on the effect of that law on the evidence given by the expert witnesses. There is no rule that the local courts will take the exposition of foreign law by the Supreme Court of the foreign jurisdiction as wholly authoritative and as an opinion to be preferred to that of any witness (*Bumper Development Corpn Ltd v Metropolitan Police Comr* [1991] 4 All ER 638, [1991] 1 WLR 1362, CA).

Borowski v Quayle   [1966] VR 382, Supreme Court of Victoria

Gowans J: The informant, having given evidence of the defendant's admission that he had purchased one dozen 'Evacillin' 9,000,000 units from Drug Houses of Australia Ltd, Shepparton Branch, proceeded to say ' "Evacillin" is a form of penicillin'. He was stopped on an objection of counsel for the defendant that this was hearsay evidence and inadmissible even if the informant gave evidence to establish his qualifications as an expert pharmaceutical chemist, because the fact of the physical nature of the substance 'Evacillin' was a matter which could only be established by analysis either by the witness or some other person. The prosecution proposed to adduce evidence of the witness's qualifications as an expert and as to what he had learned in the past from books, lectures, discussions and research to justify the assertion by him that 'Evacillin' was an antibiotic.

After considering the submissions the magistrate announced that he assumed that the witness's qualifications as an expert 'would be proved in due course' (by which I take him to mean that they could be proved) and with this in mind he would uphold the objection that the evidence sought to be given was hearsay evidence.

The ruling appears to have assumed a number of things – that expert evidence cannot travel beyond the statement of an opinion: that an expert cannot give evidence to establish any fact unless it be within his own knowledge: that in so far as his evidence is directed to a question of scientific fact and is based upon books, lectures, discussions and the research of others, it is hearsay and inadmissible on that ground.

These assumptions involve misconceptions of law. The area of admissible evidence by experts is not confined within such limits.

It is appropriate to discuss the subject in its relation to the considerations which were involved in the present proceedings. By a process of reference the relevant reg 31A was concerned with the item in Schedule Four of the Poisons Act 1962 described as 'antibiotic substances however derived'. The term 'antibiotic substance' is a technical one. But a court cannot treat such a term in a statute as having no meaning for it. If not assisted by evidence it may itself have resort to technical dictionaries of authority. The *British Medical Dictionary* conveys the import of the word in terms of the function it describes and names penicillin as the first drug to which the term was applied. But in the absence of such aid evidence may be given as to the meaning and denotation of the technical term. Thus in *London Rly Co v Berriman* [1946] AC 278 at 294, [1946] 1 All ER 255, Lord Macmillan said: 'I recognise that when parliament employs technical terms without definition in a statute dealing with a particular art or industry courts of law are entitled to have the assistant of skilled persons in the interpretation of such terms and indeed the present statute and rules contain numerous technical terms as to whose meaning in railway parlance evidence would be almost indispensable.' And Lord Porter at (AC) 306, said: 'The class whose understanding is to be taken into consideration includes all those conversant with the industry concerned.' And Lord Simonds, at (AC) 310, said: 'It is only by reference to the industry that the meaning can be ascertained . . . it remains a question of evidence what the words mean in the industry. They are a term of art and it is by those skilled in the art that I must be instructed.'

There is also a long passage dealing with the matter in the judgment given by Parker, LJ (as he then was), in the Court of Appeal in *R v Patents Appeal Tribunal, ex p Baldwin & Francis Ltd* [1959] 1 QB 105, [1958] 2 All ER 368. A witness conversant with the area of knowledge concerned with drugs could thus give evidence as to what is meant by 'antibiotic substances' and what drugs were known by that term, and in particular that penicillin is an antibiotic substance. The informant has said in his affidavit before me that but for the ruling he would have said in his evidence: 'Penicillin is an antibiotic substance included in Schedule Four of the Poisons Act 1962.' That he could by evidence have qualified himself to say this is beyond doubt, because, after the ruling, he was permitted without objection to give his qualifications by reference to his being a registered pharmaceutical chemist, his holding of various lectureships and offices and his experience in retail pharmacy. He has also sworn that he could have amplified this narration in a way which associated his experience and learning with antibiotic substances and penicillin, and that he could have supported his statement by reference to works of authority in pharmaceutical practice. In spite of a submission to the contrary, I consider this evidence would have been ample for the purpose. This evidence would have been directed to matter travelling outside opinion and dependent to a degree upon knowledge based upon hearsay. But this is an area where the hearsay rule does not apply and the matter dealt with in the evidence would clearly have been admissible. In *Wigmore on Evidence*, 3rd ed, vol 2, pp 784–5, para 665(b), it is said: 'The data of every science are enormous in scope and variety. No one professional man can know from personal observation more than a minute fraction of the data which he must every day treat as working truths. Hence a reliance on the *reported data of fellow-scientists*, learned by perusing their reports in books and journals. The law must and does accept this kind of knowledge from scientific men. On the one hand, a mere layman, who comes to court and alleges a fact which he has learned only by reading a medical or a mathematical book, cannot be heard. But, on the other hand, to reject a professional physician or mathematician because the fact or some facts to which he testifies are known to him only upon the authority of others would be to ignore the accepted methods of professional work and to insist on finical and impossible standards. Yet it is not easy to express in usable form that element of professional competency which distinguishes the latter case from the former. In general, the considerations which define the latter are (a) a professional experience, giving the witness a knowledge of the trustworthy authorities and the proper source of information, (b) an extent of personal observation in the general subject, enabling him to estimate the general plausibility, or probability of soundness, of the views expressed, and (c) the impossibility of obtaining information on the particular technical detail except through reported data in part or entirely. The true solution must be to trust the discretion of the trial judge, exercised in the light of the nature of the subject and the witness's equipments. The decisions show in general a liberal attitude in receiving technical testimony based on professional reading.'

But this evidence of the meaning and denotation of the technical term 'antibiotic' would have been incomplete and inconclusive without the further evidence tendered through the witness that ' "Evacillin" is a form of penicillin'. It was this which evoked the objection and to which the magistrate's attention was directed. That the witness could have qualified himself as having some familiarity with the preparation known as 'Evacillin' is again beyond doubt, because after the ruling he was led to say without objection that he was familiar with it and had dispensed it and that stocks of it were held by chemists, veterinary surgeons and sometimes doctors and that it was commonly sold in vials and under the name 'Evacillin'. He says also in his affidavit before me that he could have gone on to say that its appearance, preparation and packaging was characteristic of penicillin. But this might reasonably have been regarded as falling short of sufficient evidence of identification.

The evidence that would have qualified the witness to make the identification, it was said, and which he could have given according to his affidavit, was to this effect (a) that for seven or eight years he was an employee of Imperial Chemical Industries of Australia and New Zealand who were at the time the only importers into Australia of penicillin and who were supplying it to numerous formulating companies in Australia, including Glaxo Laboratories, which were packing it for Evans Medical (Australia) Pty Ltd for sale by the latter company as 'Evacillin'; (b) that he had been consulted by Evans Medical (Australia) Pty Ltd as to the wording of the labels on the product Evacillin which it manufactured, and on those labels and in the literature accompanying it the product was referred to as a form of procaine penicillin, the term 'procaine' identifying the kind of salt used with the penicillin and the duration of its effect; and (c) that in a commonly used guide required by law to be kept in every pharmacy and entitled 'Prescription Proprietaries Guide' published by the Australasian Pharmaceutical Publishing Co Ltd, 'Evacillin' is referred to as being a form of procaine penicillin.

I would regard the statement in (a) that Glaxo Laboratories packed penicillin for Evans Medical (Australia) Pty Ltd for sale by it as 'Evacillin' as inadmissible by a valid application of the hearsay rule and as not related in point of time with the circumstances operating at the relevant time.

But (b) and (c) fall into a different category. They amount to a statement by a witness shown or assumed to be conversant with the industry, trade or calling of retail pharmacy that sources commonly relied upon in retail pharmacy identify 'Evacillin' as a form of penicillin. It is not a sufficient answer to say that this amounts to hearsay from the manufacturers or from the publishers of the Guide. There is a further element stated explicitly or implicitly that it is information commonly relied upon in the calling of pharmacy. Records and materials of that kind may be the basis of evidence by one who is qualified as familiar with the business activity or calling in question. Thus an accountant (not an actuary) who stated that he had personal experience as to the mode in which insurance business was conducted could give evidence as to the average duration of life of two persons of given ages by reference to certain tables which he said were used by insurance officers, called the 'Carlisle Tables': see *Rowley v London and North Western Rly Co* (1873) LR 8 Exch 221. The average duration of life of two persons of the given ages was a fact and the source was hearsay. Nevertheless the evidence was admissible. The illustration is supported by the cases in which drug standards have been proved by reference to the *British Pharmacopoeia*, *White v Bywater* (1887) 19 QBD 582; *Dickins v Randerson* [1901] 1 KB 437. The principle is treated in *Wigmore*, 3rd ed, vol 6, pp 22–3, s 1702, in this way:

'In a few narrow and usually well defined classes of cases, a recognition has been given, by way of exception to the Hearsay rule, to certain commercial and professional lists, registers, and reports. Their admissibility in some instances is placed upon judicial principle, in others it arises solely from statutory innovation; but in most of the classes a statute has carried out hints originally given judicially. The Necessity . . . in all of these cases lies partly in the usual inaccessibility of the authors, compilers, or publishers in other jurisdictions; but chiefly in the great practical inconvenience that would be caused if the law required the summoning of each individual whose personal knowledge has gone to make up the final result. The necessity therefore is of the sort that is recognised in the preceding two Exceptions, ie a practical inconvenience existing generally for the statements as a class: and hence it is not required that the death, insanity, absence from the jurisdiction, or the like, of the author shall be shown before the statement can be used. The Circumstantial Probability of Trustworthiness . . . is found in the consideration that these lists, registers, reports, etc, are prepared for the use of the trade or profession and are therefore habitually made with such care and accuracy as will lead them to be relied upon for commercial and professional purposes. There is a subjective test of trustworthiness, in that the author knows beforehand that his work will have no commercial or professional market unless it is found to have usual accuracy and that its inaccuracies will probably be discovered; and further in that there is ordinarily no motive to deceive. There is an objective test, in that the habitual use of the work by the trade or profession has tested its usual and practical accuracy and has sanctioned its trustworthiness. Thus the chief considerations which are recognised as the source of trustworthiness for the other Exceptions . . . are found to exist here also. Upon some such reasons may easily be justified the admission of standard price-lists, of printed reports, of judicial decisions, of deed-abstracts and of sundry publications such as speed-registers, pedigree-registers and the like, now to be considered.'

I am, therefore, of opinion that assuming the appropriate qualifying evidence had been given (and this was assumed in the ruling) the evidence that 'Evacillin' is a form of penicillin was admissible, and was relevant to establish a link in a chain tending to establish that 'Evacillin' was an antibiotic substance.

NOTES

Recent examples of the recognition of new fields of expertise include studies of the effects of wearing car seatbelts in accidents (*Richardson v Schultz* (1980)

25 SASR 1; cf *Eagles v Orth* [1976] Qd R 313); car accident investigation (*R v Oakley* (1979) 70 Cr App Rep 7, CA; *R v Murphy* [1980] QB 434, [1980] 2 All ER 325, CA; cf *Cooper v Bech (No 2)* (1975) 12 SASR 151); spectrographic analysis (*R v Gilmore* [1977] 2 NSWLR 935); the views of a stockbroker and merchant banker as to the likelihood of a certain statement raising share prices (*R v Wright* [1980] VR 593). But conclusions as to the slipperiness of an oil platform covered with water are not within a field of expertise (*Australian Oil Refining Pty Ltd v Bourne* (1980) 28 ALR 529).

Recent problems have arisen in relation to the evidence of psychiatrists and psychologists. Such evidence is not admissible to prove lack of intent by the accused to commit the crime, but is admissible to show his lack of capacity to form intent: *R v Lupien* (1970) 9 DLR (3d) 1. A psychologist was not permitted to say that an accused person was unlikely to have made stylistically different confessions: *R v O'Callaghan* [1976] VR 441. The Privy Council held that expert psychiatric evidence was admissible at the instance of one co-accused person to show that the other co-accused person had the more aggressive personality and was more likely to have committed the crime: *Lowery v R* [1974] AC 85, [1973] 3 All ER 662. On the other hand, in *R v Turner* [1975] QB 834 at 840–1, [1975] 1 All ER 70 at 75, CA, the Court of Appeal rejected psychiatric evidence as to the effect on the accused, who was not mentally ill, of a confession of infidelity by his girlfriend, this being a matter the ordinary experience and knowledge of the jury entitled them to deal with: 'the fact that an expert witness has impressive scientific qualifications does not by that fact alone make his opinion on matters of human nature and behaviour within the limits of normality any more helpful than that of the jurors themselves: but there is a danger that they may think it does'. See also *R v Chard* (1971) 56 Cr App Rep 268, CA; *R v Smith* [1979] 3 All ER 605, [1979] 1 WLR 1445; *DPP v Camplin* [1978] AC 705 at 727, [1978] 2 All ER 168 at 182–3, HL, per Lord Simon of Glaisdale, rejecting the view that expert evidence was inadmissible as to how a person of reasonable self-control would be likely to react. Hence while psychiatric evidence may be called to show that a witness suffering from a mental disability is incapable of giving reliable evidence (see *Toohey v Metropolitan Police Comrs* [1965] AC 595, [1965] 1 All ER 506, HL: see p 485, post), it has been held that psychiatric evidence may not be called in order to warn a jury about a witness who is capable of giving reliable evidence but who may well not be doing so, for if a witness is capable of giving reliable evidence it is for the jury to decide whether or not he is (*R v MacKenney* (1980) 72 Cr App Rep 78): but what if the likelihood of the evidence being reliable turns on issues of mental disease? Expert evidence on the affect of obscene material on very young children has been held admissible (*DPP v A and BC Chewing Gum Ltd* [1968] 1 QB 159, [1967] 2 All ER 504), but it is not admissible in other obscenity prosecutions (*R v Anderson* [1972] 1 QB 304, [1971] 3 All ER 1152, CA; *R v Stamford* [1972] 2 QB 391, [1972] 2 All ER 427, CA; *DPP v Jordan* [1977] AC 699, [1976] 3 All ER 775, HL). This is because 'ordinary human nature, that of people at large, is not a subject of proof by evidence, whether supposedly expert or not. But particular descriptions of persons may conceivably form the subject of study and special knowledge. This may be because they are abnormal in mentality or abnormal in behaviour as a result of circumstances peculiar to their history or situation . . . But before opinion evidence may be given upon the characteristics, responses or behaviour of any special category of persons, it must be shown that they form a subject of special study or experience and only the opinions of one qualified by special training or experience may be received. Evidence of his opinion must be confined to matters which are the subject of his special study or experience': *Transport Publishing Co Pty Ltd v Literature Board of Review* (1956) 99 CLR 111 at 118–19, per Dixon CJ, Kitto and Taylor JJ, approved in *DPP v Jordan* [1977] AC 699, [1976] 3 All ER 775, HL.

As a general rule the courts will not require an expert to give expert evidence against his wishes in a case where he had no connection with the facts or the history of the matter in issue, and hence will set aside a subpoena on him (*Seyfang v GD Searle & Co* [1973] QB 148, [1973] 1 All ER 290; *Lively Ltd v City of Munich* [1977] 1 Lloyd's Rep 420). The general rule was not applied in *Harmony Shipping Co SA v Davis* [1979] 3 All ER 177, [1979] 1 WLR 1380, CA, but there it was not the expert, but one party, who sought to set aside the subpoena, and the field of expertise, handwriting, was one in which there are few experts.

In strict orthodoxy, he must be careful not to mix up hearsay evidence with his opinion. Thus the High Court of Australia has held that a doctor may not say what a patient told him about his past symptoms as evidence of the existence of those symptoms; but he may say what the patient told him so as to explain the grounds for his opinion of the patient's condition (*Ramsay v Watson* (1961) 108 CLR 642: *R v Bradshaw* (1985) 82 Cr App Rep 79, CA). Yet this rule is often not observed, particularly in valuation cases.

A valuer will often base his estimate of value on what others have told him of comparable jobs. Indeed, the opinion evidence of a valuer sometimes conflicts with another orthodox rule – that experts should reveal the facts on which their opinion is based. 'Thus a valuer may be unable to recall all the details of all the sales on which he bases his opinion, yet he may be closer to the mark than a less experienced practitioner who has made an exhaustive examination of comparable sales . . . [I]t is permissible to qualify a valuer, ask his opinion as to value, and leave the opposition to cross-examine as to the material on which the opinion is founded' (Eggleston, in Glass (ed), p 70). In *English Exporters (London) Ltd v Eldonwall* [1973] Ch 415, [1973] 1 All ER 726, Megarry J confirmed this view in holding that an expert valuer could express his opinion on values even though substantial contributions to the formation of those opinions were made by hearsay; but he could not give hearsay evidence as to the facts of transactions lying outside his personal knowledge. See also *R v Abadom* [1983] 1 All ER 364, [1983] 1 WLR 126, CA.

Further, in the course of testifying experts have a 'duty to furnish the judge or jury with the necessary scientific criteria for testing the accuracy of their conclusions, so as to enable the judge or jury to form their own independent judgment by the application of these criteria to the facts proved in evidence' (*Davie v Edinburgh Magistrates* 1953 SC 34 at 40). The aim is to avoid the court being led into accepting an opinion based on false premises. This aim may be more difficult to achieve the more technical the criteria involved.

If expert evidence conflicts the court must choose between the experts. This difficult task is perhaps only to be accomplished by comparing their qualifications, their experience and their general credibility.

The orthodox view is that experts may not testify on the ultimate issue, particularly if this is an issue of law.

Haynes v Doman [1899] 2 Ch 13, CA

The case concerned the validity of a covenant against competition contained in a contract for the employment of a hardware manufacturer's servant.

Lindley MR: [T]here are affidavits from persons in the trade, stating their views of the reasonableness of the restrictive clause on which this case turns. The introduction of this class of evidence is a novelty. In my opinion it is inadmissible, and ought not to be attended to. Evidence from persons in the trade is admissible to inform the court of its nature, and of what is customary in it, and of anything requiring attention in the mode of conducting it, and of any particular dangers requiring precautions, and what precautions are required in order to protect a person carrying on the business from injury by a person leaving his service. But the reasonableness of a contract depends on its true construction and legal effect, and is consequently a question for the court, and on such a question the opinion of witnesses is out of place.

But there is an increasing tendency to permit testimony on the ultimate issue (*R v Mason* (1911) 76 JP 184, CCA; *R v Holmes* [1953] 2 All ER 324, [1953] 1 WLR 686; *Murphy v R* (1989) 167 CLR 94 at 110–11 and 126–7). In *DPP v A and BC Chewing Gum Ltd* [1968] 1 QB 159 at 164, Lord Parker CJ said:

'I cannot help feeling that with the advance of science more and more inroads have been made into the old common law principles. Those who practice in the criminal courts see every day cases of experts being called on the question of diminished responsibility, and although technically the final question "Do you think he was suffering from diminished responsibility?" is strictly inadmissible, it is allowed time and time again without any objection.'

See *R v Calder & Boyars Ltd* [1969] 1 QB 151, [1968] 3 All ER 644, CA; *R v Anderson* [1972] 1 QB 304, [1971] 3 All ER 1152, CA; also *Grismore v Consolidated Product Co* 5 NW (2d) 646 (1942); *Grey v Australian Motorists and General Insurance Co Pty Ltd* [1976] 1 NSWLR 669 at 675–6. Neither experts nor anyone else may testify on an ultimate issue where that is a question of law or a mixed question of law or fact. At 663 the court in *Grismore's* Case said:

'When a standard, or a measure, or a capacity has been fixed by law, no witness whether expert or non-expert, nor however qualified, is permitted to express an opinion as to whether or not the person or the conduct in question measures up to that standard. On that question the court must instruct the jury as to the law, and the jury must draw its own conclusion from the evidence. However courts have permitted both scientific and practical experts to express their opinion whether a certain method used, or course of conduct, was a proper one.'

As the Criminal Law Revision Committee say (para 268), 'This is natural, because it would often be artificial for the witness to avoid, or pretend to avoid, giving his opinion on a matter merely because it is the ultimate issue in the case and because his opinion on the ultimate issue may be obvious from the opinions which he has already expressed.' It may also be said that an expert is far more likely to be right on an ultimate issue requiring expertise to determine than a lay judge or jury (at least if no issue of law is directly involved). The same might be said of valuation cases. It is certainly true that opinion evidence on the ultimate issue is more freely allowed for experts than for non-experts, eg the issue of unfitness to drive through drink (*R v Davies* [1962] 3 All ER 97, [1962] 1 WLR 1111).

The law of expert opinion evidence involves a constant tension between orthodoxy and admissibility in which the latter is beginning to triumph both at common law and by legislation. The process may be traced in the High Court of Australia in the retreat from *Clarke v Ryan* (1960) 103 CLR 486. That case adopted strict tests of expertise, depending on qualifications rather than experience; of the division between fact and inferences; of the corresponding division between expert witness functions and jury functions. It may have been unduly influenced by the unsatisfactoriness of the 'expert' testimony received. However that may be, later decisions have gone close to reversing it, though Menzies J remained an adherent. (See eg *Weal v Bottom* (1966) 40 ALJR 436.)

Advance notice must be given of the intention to adduce expert evidence in criminal proceedings: Police and Criminal Evidence Act 1984, s 81; Crown Court (Advance Notice of Expert Evidence) Rules 1987. In default, the evidence is inadmissible without the leave of the court.

C STATUTORY REFORM

The Civil Evidence Act 1972 and RSC Ord 38, rr 35–44 (see Phipson, paras 27–17 to 27–30) amend the law in civil cases, and the Criminal Law Revision Committee made proposals to the same effect for criminal cases (CLRC paras 266–71). Some changes were made by the Criminal Justice Act 1988, s 30: ch 13.3, ante. Hearsay statements of opinion are admissible in the same way as hearsay statements of fact. A witness may give his opinion on the ultimate issue; but a non-expert may not be asked for his opinion on the ultimate issue, though he may give it in the form of a statement 'made as a way of conveying relevant facts personally perceived by him'. Statute may make particular kinds of non-expert evidence admissible, eg in relation to three-dimensional reproductions of two-dimensional works: see Copyright Act 1956, s 9(8); *LB (Plastics) Ltd v Swish Products Ltd* [1979] RPC 551 at 630.

A witness may give evidence of foreign law whether or not he is entitled to practise in the relevant jurisdiction. A finding by an English court on a question of foreign law will be prima facie evidence of that law; this will avoid the need for the point to be proved in later proceedings. There is power for the judge to sit with assessors – experts appointed by the court other than the parties – in Admiralty actions, but no extension of this was recommended by the Law Reform Committee, Cmnd 4889, paras 14–16.

QUESTION

Can an expert give opinion evidence which is based on disclosures to him which are privileged?

FURTHER READING

Law Reform Committee, 17th Report, Evidence of Opinion and Expert Evidence 1970, Cmnd 4489; Cowen and Carter, ch 5; Hammelmann (1947) 10 MLR 32; Jackson [1984] Crim LR 75; Learned Hand (1901) 15 Harv L Rev 40; Maguire, pp 23–31; Samuels in Glass; Basten (1977) 40 MLR 184; Zuckerman, ch 5.

2   Evidence of prior findings in later proceedings

⸌A   PERSUASIVE PRESUMPTIONS

The rule stated in *Hollington v F Hewthorn & Co Ltd* [1943] KB 587, [1943] 2 All ER 35, CA, was that convictions and judgments are not evidence in later proceedings of the facts on which they were founded. The rule was based partly on the view that the later court should not be bound by the earlier's opinion. There were exceptions to the rule: the proof of convictions in cross-examination as to credit, judgments as evidence of public rights, judgments as facts in issue or relevant facts (*Ingram v Ingram* [1956] P 390, [1956] 1 All ER 785). In certain respects it operated sensibly. Plainly acquittals in criminal cases should not be taken as evidence of innocence in later civil cases, because of the higher standards of proof in criminal cases. Nor is an acquittal of a principal offender of murder, and his conviction of manslaughter, admissible at the trial of an accessory (*Hu Chi-Ming v R* [1992] 1 AC 34, [1991] 3 All ER 897, PC). But for many reasons the rule was found unsatisfactory and has been much criticised (the most damaging salvoes were fired by the New Zealand Court of Appeal in *Jorgensen v News Media (Auckland) Ltd* [1969] NZLR 961 and by Cowen and Carter, ch 6). See also *Hunter v Chief Constable of West Midlands Police* [1982] AC 529 at 543; [1981] 3 All ER 727 at 734, HL.

Civil Evidence Act 1968

1   (1)   In any civil proceedings the fact that a person has been convicted of an offence by or before any court in the United Kingdom or by a court-martial there or elsewhere shall (subject to subsection (3) below) be admissible in evidence for the purpose of proving, where to do so is relevant to any issue in those proceedings, that he committed that offence, whether he was so convicted upon a plea of guilty or otherwise and whether or not he is a party to the civil proceedings; but no conviction other than a subsisting one shall be admissible in evidence by virtue of this section.

(2)   In any civil proceedings in which by virtue of this section a person is proved to have been convicted of an offence by or before any court in the United Kingdom or by a court-martial there or elsewhere –

(a)   he shall be taken to have committed that offence unless the contrary is proved: and

(b)   without prejudice to the reception of any other admissible evidence for the purpose of identifying the facts on which the conviction was based, the contents of any document which is admissible as evidence of the conviction, and the contents of the information, complaint, indictment or charge-sheet on which the person in question was convicted, shall be admissible in evidence for that purpose.

(3) Nothing in this section shall prejudice the operation of section 13 of this Act or any other enactment whereby a conviction or a finding of fact in any criminal proceedings is for the purposes of any other proceedings made conclusive evidence of any fact.

(4) Where in any civil proceedings the contents of any document are admissible in evidence by virtue of subsection (2) above, a copy of that document, or of the material part thereof, purporting to be certified or otherwise authenticated by or on behalf of the court or authority having custody of that document shall be admissible in evidence and shall be taken to be a true copy of that document or part unless the contrary is shown.

12 (1) In any civil proceedings –
    (a) the fact that a person has been found guilty of adultery in any matrimonial proceedings; and
    (b) the fact that a person has been found to be the father of a child in relevant proceedings before any court in England and Wales or has been adjudged to be the father of a child in affiliation proceedings before any court in the United Kingdom,
shall (subject to subsection (3) below) be admissible in evidence for the purpose of proving, where to do so is relevant to any issue in those civil proceedings, that he committed the adultery to which the finding relates or, as the case may be, is (or was) the father of that child, whether or not he offered any defence to the allegation of adultery or paternity and whether or not he is a party to the civil proceedings; but no finding or adjudication other than a subsisting one shall be admissible in evidence by virtue of this section.

(2) In any civil proceedings in which by virtue of this section a person is proved to have been found guilty of adultery as mentioned in subsection (1)(a) above or to have been found or adjudged to be the father of a child as mentioned in subsection (1)(b) above –
    (a) he shall be taken to have committed the adultery to which the finding relates or, as the case may be, to be (or have been) the father of that child, unless the contrary is proved; and
    (b) without prejudice to the reception of any other admissible evidence for the purpose of identifying the facts on which the finding or adjudication was based, the contents of any document which was before the court, or which contains any pronouncement of the court, in the other proceedings in question shall be admissible in evidence for that purpose.

(3) Nothing in this section shall prejudice the operation of any enactment whereby a finding of fact in any matrimonial or affiliation proceedings is for the purposes of any other proceedings made conclusive evidence of any fact.

(4) Subsection (4) of section 11 of this Act shall apply for the purposes of this section as if the reference to subsection (2) were a reference to subsection (2) of this section.

(5) In this section –
'matrimonial proceedings' means any matrimonial cause in the High Court or a county court in England and Wales or in the High Court in Northern Ireland, any consistorial action in Scotland, or any appeal arising out of any such cause of action . . .
'affiliation proceedings' means, in relation to Scotland, any action of affiliation and aliment;
and in this subsection 'consistorial action' does not include an action of aliment only between husband and wife raised in the Court of Sessions or an action of interim aliment raised in the sheriff court.

NOTES

1. Under s 11, the court in the second case will require proof of the prior conviction; it may be necessary to identify the convicted person with the person against whom that conduct is alleged, and a witness of the incident may be needed for this purpose. Under s 12 the process of identification may be carried out by reference to the pleadings, decree and transcript of judgment in the earlier case: *Sutton v Sutton* [1969] 3 All ER 1348, [1970] 1 WLR 183.
2. Where the defendant seeks to argue that a prior conviction or finding of adultery or paternity was wrong, the court, in considering exercise of its discretion to admit the statements of witnesses in the prior proceedings under

RSC Ord 38, r 28 will be more likely to admit the statements at the instance of the plaintiff. This will avoid the plaintiff having to call the witnesses and the defendant being able to cross-examine them. If the defendant denies the relevance of the conviction, finding of adultery or paternity, the position may be different, for the burden of proof of relevancy lies on the plaintiff. The statements might only be admissible on terms that the witnesses are called at the second trial.

3. The presumption under s 11 does not arise in the case of convictions subject to appeal: though they are 'subsisting' it would be wrong for the civil court to act on a conviction which was liable to be quashed. The correct course is to adjourn the civil trial (*Re Raphael* [1973] 3 All ER 19, [1973] 1 WLR 998).

4. Section 11(1) has been held not to apply to convictions in a French court; *Union Carbide Corpn v Naturin Ltd* [1987] FSR 538, CA.

5. The Act does not, and the rule in *Hollington v F Hewthorn & Co Ltd* thus continues to, apply to the findings of arbitrators (*Land Securities plc v Westminster City Council* [1993] 4 All ER 124, [1993] 1 WLR 286, a case in which Hoffman J revealed an unfashionable and significant affection for the rule). It also applies to reports of company inspectors (*Savings and Investment Bank Ltd v Gasco Investments (Netherlands) BV* [1984] 1 All ER 296, [1984] 1 WLR 271).

Stupple v Royal Insurance Co Ltd   [1971] 1 QB 50, [1970] 3 All ER 230, CA

The plaintiff was convicted of armed robbery of a bullion van owned by a bank. The main evidence against him was the finding of some stolen money in his flat. In these proceedings the plaintiff and his wife claimed the money from the insurance company who had paid off the bank. Stupple sought to show he was not guilty of the robbery. Paull J gave judgment for the defendants. The Court of Appeal dismissed the plaintiff's appeals.

Lord Denning MR: Mr Hawser, for Mr Stupple, submitted that the only effect of the Act was to shift the burden of proof. He said that, whereas previously the conviction was not admissible in evidence at all, now it was admissible in evidence, but the effect was simply to put on the man the burden of showing, on the balance of probabilities, that he was innocent. He claimed that Mr Stupple had done so.

I do not accept Mr Hawser's submission. I think that the conviction does not merely shift the burden of proof. It is a weighty piece of evidence of itself. For instance, if a man is convicted of careless driving on the evidence of a witness, but that witness dies before the civil action is heard (as in *Hollington v F Hewthorn & Co Ltd* [1943] KB 587, [1943] 2 All ER 35, CA), then the conviction tells in the scale in the civil action. It speaks as clearly as the witness himself would have done, had he lived. It does not merely reverse the burden of proof. If that was all it did, the defendant might well give his own evidence negativing want of care, and say: 'I have discharged the burden. I have given my evidence and it has not been contradicted.' In answer to the defendant's evidence, the plaintiff can say to him: 'But your evidence is contradicted. It is contradicted by the very fact of your conviction.'

In addition, Mr Hawser sought, as far as he could, to minimise the effect of shifting the burden. In this, too, he did not succeed. The Act does not merely shift the evidential burden, as it is called. It shifts the *legal* burden of proof. I explained the difference long ago, in 1945, in an article in the Law Quarterly Review 61 LQR 379. Take a running-down case where a plaintiff claims damages for negligent driving by the defendant. If the defendant has not been convicted, the legal burden is on the plaintiff throughout. But if the defendant has been convicted of careless driving, the legal burden is shifted. It is on the defendant himself. At the end of the day, if the judge is left in doubt the defendant fails because the defendant has not discharged the legal burden which is upon him. The burden is, no doubt, the civil burden. He must show, on the balance of probabilities, that he was not negligent . . . But he must show it nevertheless. Otherwise he loses by the very force of the conviction.

How can a man who has been convicted in a criminal trial, prove his innocence in a subsequent civil action? He can, of course, call his previous witnesses and hope that the judge will believe them now, even if they were disbelieved before. He can also call any fresh witnesses whom he thinks will help his case. In addition, I think he can show the witnesses against him in the criminal trial were mistaken. For instance, in a traffic accident he could prove that a witness who claimed to have seen it was miles away and committed perjury. This would not, of course, prove his innocence directly, but it would do so indirectly by destroying the evidence of which he was convicted. So in this case Mr Stupple could prove that Mr Ford was mistaken.

In any case, what weight is to be given to the criminal conviction? This must depend on the circumstances. Take a plea of guilty. Sometimes a defendant pleads guilty in error: or in a minor offence he may plead guilty to save time and expense, or to avoid some embarrassing fact coming out. Afterwards, in the civil action, he can, I think, explain how he came to plead guilty.

Take next a case in the magistrates' court when a man is convicted and bound over or fined a trifling sum, but had a good ground of appeal, and did not exercise it because it was not worth while. Can he not explain this in a civil court? I think he can. He can offer any explanation in his effort to show that the conviction was erroneous: and it is for the judge at the civil trial to say how far he has succeeded.

In my opinion, therefore, the weight to be given to a previous conviction is essentially for the judge at the civil trial. Just as he has to evaluate the oral evidence of a witness, so he should evaluate the probative force of a conviction.

If the defendant should succeed in throwing doubt on the conviction, the plaintiff can rely, in answer, on the conviction itself; and he can supplement it, if he thinks it desirable, by producing (under the hearsay sections) the evidence given by the prosecution witness in the criminal trial, or, if he wishes, he can call them again. At the end of the civil case, the judge must ask himself whether the defendant has succeeded in overthrowing the conviction. If not, the conviction stands and proves the case.

Such being the principles, I turn to apply them to the present case. We have the conviction of Stupple for armed robbery. We have the circumstances from which it arises. They were: – (1) the fact that a bullion van was ambushed on 27 September 1963, and £87,000 in notes were stolen from it; (2) the fact that four days later Stupple was found in possession of nearly £1,000 of the stolen notes; (3) the fact that he gave no acceptable explanation of how he came by them; (4) the fact that he put forward an alibi which was not acceptable.

On those facts it was open to the jury, at the criminal trial, to find that he was guilty, not merely of receiving but of the robbery itself. I remember well that at one time it was thought that recent possession of stolen goods, without more, justified only a conviction for receiving and not for the theft itself. But Lord Goddard CJ scotched that fallacy in *R v Loughlin* (1951) 35 Cr App Rep 69 and *R v Seymour* [1954] 1 All ER 1006, [1954] 1 WLR 678. It is open to the jury to convict of the theft itself. And in this regard recent possession of stolen *money* bears a stronger colour than recent possession of stolen *goods*. 'Hot money' travels fast: but usually into the hands of those who have helped to get it. Phillimore J put it thus to a jury in a robbery case:

'When it comes to money, what is the natural view, the ordinary view, where somebody has got £100, the proceeds of a robbery, within a few hours of the robbery? I suppose it is possible that a thief may have come to him and said: "This is hot money, and if you give me £20 for it, I will give you £100." But the natural thing would be, you may think, that a man who has got proceeds in the shape of money, when it is a money snatch, was probably involved in the actual robbery . . .' See *R v Fallon* (1963) 47 Cr App Rep 160 at 165, CCA.

He may not have been present at the robbery itself but he may have been the brains behind it, he may have helped organise it, or he may have provided the tools with which to do it. It matters not which. The money gets to him as his share. In any of those cases he would be an accessory before the fact and as much guilty of robbery as if he had been at the scene itself: see *R v Bainbridge* [1960] 1 QB 129, [1959] 3 All ER 200, CCA.

I regard the conviction of Stupple in these circumstances, after a four and a half weeks trial, by a jury who were unanimous, as entitled to great weight in this civil action. It is not conclusive. It can be rebutted. But how does Stupple seek to prove that he was innocent of the robbery? He adduces some fresh material. In particular, evidence to show that Mr Ford may have been mistaken in his identification of the notes; and evidence of the other convicted men, who say that Stupple was not present at the robbery and had nothing to do with it. Otherwise the evidence was little more than a repetition of the evidence at the criminal trial, plus Mr Allpress and Mr Cappuccini, who did not count for much. All of this fell far short of discharging the burden on Stupple to prove that he was innocent of the robbery. The conviction stands firm.

Winn LJ: I do not myself think that it was any requisite, or, indeed, any proper, part of the function of the judge to consider what view he himself might have taken of the case had he sat on it either as juryman or judge: nor was it on a correct view relevant to his decision whether there had been an unsuccessful application to the Court of Appeal for leave to appeal against the conviction.

Buckley LJ: There remains . . . the problem of what weight, if any, should be accorded to the proved fact of conviction in deciding whether any other evidence adduced is sufficient to discharge the onus resting on B. In my judgment no weight is in this respect to be given to the mere fact of conviction.

If, as seems to be the case, I differ from Lord Denning MR in this respect, I do so with the greatest diffidence.

The effect of the bare proof of conviction is, I think, spent in bringing section 11(2)(a) into play. But very much weight may have to be given to such circumstances of the criminal proceedings as are brought out in the evidence in the civil action. Witnesses called in the civil proceedings may give different evidence from that which they gave in the criminal proceedings. Witnesses may be called in the civil proceedings who might have been but were not called in the criminal proceedings, or vice versa. The judge may feel that he should take account of the fact that the judge or jury in the criminal proceedings disbelieved a witness who is called in the civil proceedings, or that the defendant pleaded guilty or not guilty, as the case may be. Many examples could be suggested of ways in which what occurred or did not occur in the criminal proceedings may have a bearing on the judge's decision in the civil proceedings: but the judge's duty in the civil proceedings is still to decide that case on the evidence adduced to him. He is not concerned with the evidence in the criminal proceedings except so far as it is reproduced in the evidence called before him, or is made evidence in the civil proceedings under the Civil Evidence Act, 1968, section 2, or is established before him in cross-examination. He is not concerned with the propriety of the conviction except so far as his view of the evidence before him may lead him incidentally to the conclusion that the conviction was justified or is open to criticism; but even if it does so, this must be a consequence of his decision and cannot be a reason for it. The propriety or otherwise of the conviction is irrelevant to the steps leading to his decision.

It was suggested in argument that so to view section 11 would result in the issues in the criminal proceedings being retried in the civil proceedings, and that this would be contrary to an intention on the part of the legislature to avoid this sort of duplication.

I do not myself think that this would be the result in most cases, and I do not discern any such general intention in the section. If the fact of conviction were meant to carry some weight in determining whether the convicted man has successfully discharged the onus under section 11(2)(a) of proving that he did not commit the offence, what weight should it carry? I cannot discover any measure of the weight which the unexplored fact of conviction should carry. Although the section has made proof of conviction admissible and has given proof of conviction a particular statutory effect under section 11(2)(a), it remains, I think, as true today as before the Act that mere proof of conviction proves nothing relevant to the plaintiff's claim, and it clearly cannot be intended to shut out or, I think, to mitigate the effect of any evidence tending to show that the convicted person did not commit the offence. In my judgment, proof of conviction under this section gives rise to the statutory presumption laid down in section 11(2)(a), which, like any other presumption, will give way to evidence establishing the contrary on the balance of probability, without itself affording any evidential weight to be taken into account in determining whether that onus has been discharged.

With respect to the judge, I think that he was unnecessarily alarmed at the possibility of his reaching a different conclusion from the conclusion reached at the criminal trial, where both the burden of proof and the standard of proof differed from those in the action, and by the Court of Criminal Appeal.

NOTES

1. The standard of proof is the balance of probabilities: see also *Sutton v Sutton* [1969] 3 All ER 1348, [1970] 1 WLR 183.

2. In *Taylor v Taylor* [1970] 2 All ER 609, [1970] 1 WLR 1148, CA, Davies LJ appeared to share Lord Denning MR's view.

Zuckerman, (1971) 87 LQR 21, has argued that both Lord Denning MR and Buckley LJ were wrong. His view is that s 11 permits the convicted person to prevent the presumption of guilt based on the conviction from applying by attacking the propriety of the conviction. Its propriety could be attacked either by introducing new evidence or by showing some defect in the proceedings or faulty reasoning. 'A distinction should be drawn between proving that a conviction is not justifiable, on the one hand, and between positively proving that the convicted person did not, in reality, commit the offence for which he has been convicted, on the other hand. For proving that a conviction is unjustified it would be sufficient to show that the proceedings leading to it were improper, or that the conclusion of guilt does not follow from the evidence produced, or that the witnesses committed perjury. But this is to say nothing about the question of guilt or innocence' (p 24). He concludes from this view that the conviction therefore has no intrinsic weight. But the premise, though arguable, seems false; for s 11(1) refers to 'subsisting' convictions, not 'justifiable' ones, and s 11(2)(*a*) refers to 'a person . . . proved to have been convicted' not 'properly convicted'. Further, the conclusion does not seem to follow from the premise. The idea of the conviction having weight may be wrong as a matter of statutory interpretation but it is given some support by the fact that jury decisions in favour of guilt are very likely to be correct. If a conviction were improper, it would have less weight; but it must be proved to be improper. It seems that in order to rebut the presumption it is not necessary to show that the conviction was obtained by fraud or collusion or to adduce fresh evidence not reasonably obtainable before: *Hunter v Chief Constable of West Midlands Police* [1982] AC 529 at p 544, [1981] 3 All ER 727 at 735–6, HL.

Police and Criminal Evidence Act 1984

74 (1) In any proceedings the fact that a person other than the accused has been convicted of an offence by or before any court in the United Kingdom or by a Service court outside the United Kingdom shall be admissible in evidence for the purpose of proving, where to do so is relevant to any issue in those proceedings, that the person committed that offence, whether or not any other evidence of his having committed that offence is given.

(2) In any proceedings in which by virtue of this section a person other than the accused is proved to have been convicted of an offence by or before any court in the United Kingdom or by a Service court outside the United Kingdom, he shall be taken to have committed that offence unless the contrary is proved.

(3) In any proceedings where evidence is admissible of the fact that the accused has committed an offence, in so far as that evidence is relevant to any matter in issue in the proceedings for a reason other than a tendency to show in the accused a disposition to commit the kind of offence with which he is charged, if the accused is proved to have been convicted of the offence –

(*a*) by or before any court in the United Kingdom; or

(*b*) by a Service court outside the United Kingdom,

he shall be taken to have committed that offence unless the contrary is proved.

COMMENT

'Issue' refers not only to essential ingredients of the offence charged, but evidential issues: *R v Robertson* [1987] QB 920, [1987] 3 All ER 231, CA. The court in that case said that s 74 was a provision which should be sparingly used. There would be occasions where, although the evidence might be technically admissible, its effect was likely to be so slight that it would be wiser not to adduce it. This would be particularly so where there was any danger of a contravention of s 78, which gives the court power to exclude the admission of evidence which would have such an adverse effect on the fairness or proceedings that the court ought not to admit it. There was nothing to be gained by adducing evidence of doubtful value at the risk of having the conviction quashed because the admission of that evidence rendered the conviction unsafe or unsatisfactory. Plainly, the court pointed out that where the evidence was admitted, the judge should be careful to explain to the jury the effect of the evidence and its limitations. See also Munday [1990] Crim LR 236; *R v Lunnon* (1988) 88 Cr App Rep 71, CA.

B   A CONCLUSIVE PRESUMPTION

Civil Evidence Act 1968

13 (1)   In an action for libel or slander in which the question whether a person did or did not commit a criminal offence is relevant to an issue arising in the action, proof that, at the time when that issue falls to be determined, that person stands convicted of that offence shall be conclusive evidence that he committed that offence; and his conviction thereof shall be admissible in evidence accordingly.

(2)   In any such action as aforesaid in which by virtue of this section a person is proved to have been convicted of an offence, the contents of any document which is admissible as evidence of the conviction, and the contents of the information, complaint, indictment or charge-sheet on which that person was convicted, shall, without prejudice to the reception of any other admissible evidence for the purpose of identifying the facts on which the conviction was based, be admissible in evidence for the purpose of identifying those facts.

(3)   For the purposes of this section a person shall be taken to stand convicted of an offence if but only if there subsists against him a conviction of that offence by or before a court in the United Kingdom or by a court-martial there or elsewhere.

COMMENTS

This prevents convicted persons using defamation actions in a gold-digging manner; cases such as *Hinds v Sparks* [1964] Crim LR 717 cannot recur. It also prevents convicted persons proving that they were unjustly convicted, but there are other methods of doing that. It does not apply to acquittals, contrary to the recommendation of the Law Reform Committee's 15th Report, para 29.

A statement of claim for defamation alleging that the plaintiff was not properly convicted may not be struck out as an abuse of the process of the court if defamatory matter other than that relating to the convictions is alleged, even though the effect on the plaintiff's reputation of his convictions may be such as to destroy his chance of recovering more than nominal damages (*Levene v Roxhan* [1970] 3 All ER 683, [1970] 1 WLR 1322, CA). Normally the statement of claim would be struck out to prevent the plaintiff using the terror of protracted litigation to get some settlement from the defendant even though he would not succeed at the final hearing.

PART FIVE

Witnesses

CHAPTER 17

Competence, Compellability and Oaths

1 Competence and compellability

If a person is a competent witness, he may give evidence at the instance of the party calling him if he wishes. If he is a compellable witness, he must give evidence. A witness who is competent but not compellable should be told this before he gives evidence (*R v Nelson* [1992] Crim LR 653, CA); but if he chooses to give evidence he has waived his non-compellability and is treated like any other witness. He cannot refuse to answer particular questions except on some other basis: *R v Pitt* [1983] QB 25, [1982] 3 All ER 63, CA.

The evidence of a competent witness is evidence in the case for all purposes, and may be expressly relied upon even by a party at whose instance the witness was not competent, or not compellable: *R v Rudd* (1948) 32 Cr App Rep 138.

The onus of proving that a witness is competent is on the party calling him, at any rate where that is the prosecution (*R v Yacoob* (1981) 72 Cr App Rep 313), and in that case the standard of proof is beyond reasonable doubt (ibid). The question is determined by the judge on inquiry by him. The jury should be present in court, so that they hear the questions and see the witness's demeanour, in order to form their conclusions as to the weight to be attached to the evidence if it is, in the end, admitted: 'If the judge cannot make up his mind whether the witness is competent or not without hearing evidence, the jury cannot be expected to decide whether she is credible or not without hearing the same evidence' (JCS commenting on *R v Robinson* [1994] Crim LR 356 at 357; see also *R v Reynolds* [1950] 1 KB 606, [1950] 1 All ER 335, CCA; *R v Lal Khan* (1981) 73 Cr App Rep 190, CA). In *Demirok v R* (1977) 137 CLR 20, however, the majority of the High Court of Australia agreed with Gibbs J's view at 31 that as the question of admissibility is solely for the judge to consider there is no reason why the jury should be present when evidence is being given on it. If the questions, or the answers to them, are relevant on some other issue the evidence should be given again. But in England the only possible exception to the *Reynolds* rule appears to be when the proposed witness's competence is to be determined without making inquiry of him, when 'the best procedure' is for a decision to be taken 'at the beginning of the trial', presumably by voir dire in the absence of the jury (*R v Yacoob* (1981) 72 Cr App Rep 313, CA).

A   CIVIL CASES

The general rule in civil cases is that all persons are competent and compellable witnesses.

To the general rule there are some exceptions. Persons who have sovereign or diplomatic immunity are competent but not compellable. A mentally diseased person is not competent or compellable unless he understands the nature and consequences of an oath. For the special position of children see section 1C of this chapter.

The court in civil cases has a discretion with relation to compellability and can override the general rule when it would be oppressive to compel a particular witness to give evidence, even if his evidence would be likely to be both admissible and relevant: *Morgan v Morgan* [1977] Fam 122, [1977] 2 All ER 515; *Re P* (1991) Times, 24 January, CA.

B   CRIMINAL CASES

The general rule is the same as in civil cases, and is subject to the same exceptions, with different special rules for children, and with the addition of the following.

The accused is not a competent prosecution witness, so one co-accused cannot be called by the prosecution to give evidence against another (*R v Payne* (1872) LR 1 CCR 349). There are various courses open to the prosecution for rendering competent persons who might be caught by this rule. The prosecution might file a nolle prosequi (an undertaking by the Attorney-General to stay proceedings against an accused person, which is not binding but is in practice kept). A particeps criminis may simply not be prosecuted. A co-accused may be acquitted after a decision not to offer evidence against him. A co-accused may plead guilty, so that his case is no longer an issue for the jury and he can testify for the prosecution; in general he should be sentenced before testifying, so that he will not be tempted to give false evidence in the hope of a lighter sentence. The prosecution may have two accused tried separately so that one can testify at the other's trial. In *R v Pipe* (1966) 51 Cr App Rep 17, CA, it was held to be irregular to call the witness until proceedings against him had been completed.

In *R v Turner* (1975) 61 Cr App Rep 67 the Court of Appeal rejected an argument that the evidence of an accomplice who might be influenced by continuing inducements as to immunity should be rejected as a matter of practice, though if very powerful inducements to lie were present the judge might exercise his discretion against permitting the evidence. See also *R v Weightman* [1978] 1 NZLR 79.

The competence of the accused as a witness for himself or for a co-defendant, and the competence and compellability of the spouse of an accused, are governed by statute.

Criminal Evidence Act 1898

1   Every person charged with an offence shall be a competent witness for the defence at every stage of the proceedings, whether the person so charged is charged solely or jointly with any

other person. Provided as follows
  (a) A person so charged shall not be called as a witness in pursuance of this Act except upon his own application.

COMMENTS

1. The accused is competent for the defence, but he is not compellable even for a co-defendant: proviso (*a*). However, if one co-accused does give evidence against another, he exposes himself to cross-examination on his record under the Criminal Evidence Act 1898, s 1 (*f*)(iii), by the co-accused and the prosecution. Further the prosecution may cross-examine a co-accused and his testimony under cross-examination is evidence against his co-accused. The judge has a discretion to limit the cross-examination, but opinions differ on its scope: cf *R v Paul* [1920] 2 KB 183, CCA and *Young v HM Advocate* 1932 JC 63 at 74, where it was said: 'a prosecutor is not entitled, under the cloak of cross-examination, to examine an accused upon matters irrelevant to the question of his own guilt, and extraneous to any evidence he has given, in order to make him an additional witness against his co-accused.' It may be difficult to draw the distinction at the time. (See Gooderson (1953) 11 CLJ 209, [1971] Crim LR 13 at 14–20.)

2. An accused who has pleaded guilty is not a 'person charged' and has therefore ceased to be a co-prisoner within the Criminal Evidence Act 1898; he is therefore competent and compellable for a co-accused (*R v Boal* [1965] 1 QB 402 at 415, [1964] 3 All ER 269 at 275, CCA).

3. The reality of the accused's non-compellability was previously secured to some extent by proviso (*b*), which read as follows: 'the failure of any person charged with an offence to give evidence shall not be made the subject of any comment by the prosecution', but that security had been gradually eroded before the repeal of the proviso by s 35(3) of the Criminal Justice and Public Order Act 1994. For the present position see ch 7. The judge himself may comment on an accused's failure to give evidence. The principles involved were restated by the Court of Appeal in *R v Martinez-Tobon* [1994] 2 All ER 90 at 98, just before the 1994 Act came into effect. The essentials are that the accused is under no obligation to give evidence, and the jury should not assume he is guilty simply because he has not given evidence. In clear cases a stronger comment may be appropriate. Again, for details see ch 7. The right of one co-accused to comment on the failure of another to give evidence is completely untrammelled (*R v Wickham* (1971) 55 Cr App Rep 199, CA), and more recent dicta of the Privy Council (*Lui-Mei Lin v R* [1989] AC 288 at 297, [1989] 1 All ER 359 at 363, PC) and the Court of Appeal (*R v Rowson* [1986] QB 174, [1985] 2 All ER 539, CA) suggest that this will remain the rule.

Police and Criminal Evidence Act 1984

80 (1) In any proceedings the wife or husband of the accused shall be competent to give evidence –
  (a) subject to subsection (4) below, for the prosecution; and
  (b) on behalf of the accused or any person jointly charged with the accused.

(2)   In any proceedings the wife or husband of the accused shall, subject to subsection (4) below, be compellable to give evidence on behalf of the accused.

(3)   In any proceedings the wife or husband of the accused shall, subject to subsection (4) below, be compellable to give evidence for the prosecution or on behalf of any person jointly charged with the accused if and only if –

(a)   the offence charged involves an assault on, or injury or a threat of injury to, the wife or husband of the accused or a person who was at the material time under the age of sixteen; or

(b)   the offence charged is a sexual offence alleged to have been committed in respect of a person who was at the material time under that age; or

(c)   the offence charged consists of attempting or conspiring to commit, or of aiding, abetting, counselling, procuring or inciting the commission of, an offence falling within paragraph (a) or (b) above.

(4)   Where a husband and wife are jointly charged with an offence neither spouse shall at the trial be competent or compellable by virtue of subsection (1)(a), (2) or (3) above to give evidence in respect of that offence unless that spouse is not, or is no longer, liable to be convicted of that offence at the trial as a result of pleading guilty or for any other reason.

(5)   In any proceedings a person who has been but is no longer married to the accused shall be competent and compellable to give evidence as if that person and the accused had never been married.

(6)   Where in any proceedings the age of any person at any time is material for the purposes of subsection (3) above, his age at the material time shall for the purposes of that provision be deemed to be or to have been that which appears to the court to be or to have been his age at that time.

(7)   In subsection (3)(b) above 'sexual offence' means an offence under the Sexual Offences Act 1956, the Indecency with Children Act 1960, the Sexual Offences Act 1967, section 54 of the Criminal Law Act 1977 or the Protection of Children Act 1978.

(8)   The failure of the wife or husband of the accused to give evidence shall not be made the subject of any comment by the prosecution.

(9)   . . .

COMMENTS

The effect is that, unless she too is a defendant, the accused's wife is always competent, is always compellable for her husband, but is compellable for the prosecution or her husband's co-defendant only in cases of the three types listed in sub-s (3). If she is a defendant herself, her status as a defendant takes precedence: s 80(4). For comments and discussion of some difficulties caused by the wording of s 80, see Creighton [1990] Crim LR 34.

Despite the phrasing of the above paragraph, the rules apply in the same way to the husband or an accused woman as they do to the wife of an accused man. But an unmarried partner has no special status, nor does the partner in a polygamous second marriage (*R v Junaid Khan* (1987) 84 Cr App Rep 44, CA).

Note that, contrary to the recommendations of CLRC, para 154, and despite the repeal of proviso (b) to s 1 of the Criminal Evidence Act 1898, comment, by the prosecution, on the failure of an accused's spouse to testify is still prohibited: s 80(8).

C   CHILDREN

A power to take unsworn evidence from a child of tender years in criminal cases only was granted by s 38(1) of the Children and Young Persons Act 1933 (below). A similar rule for civil cases followed in 1989. Section 52 of the

Criminal Justice Act 1991 inserts a new s 33A into the Criminal Justice Act 1988, which provides that a witness who has not reached the age of 14 shall in criminal proceedings give evidence unsworn, and declares that s 38(1) of the 1933 Act 'shall cease to have effect'. A further addition was made by Sch 9, para 33 of the Criminal Justice and Public Order Act 1994, which inserts into s 33A sub-s 2A:

'A child's evidence shall be received unless it appears to the court that the child is incapable of giving intelligible testimony.'

Thus there is now no incompetence on the ground of infancy alone, and a presumption in favour of competence, but it is by no means clear that the new provision achieves its intended effect, which was to abolish altogether any need for pre-testimonial examination.

In civil proceedings, however, the special test contained in the 1989 Act will for the present continue to be applicable; and no doubt it will be applied according to the authorities on the very similar test in the repealed s 38(1).

Children and Young Persons Act 1933 *(Repealed)*

38 (1)   Where, in any proceedings against any person for any offence, any child of tender years called as a witness does not in the opinion of the court understand the nature of the oath, his evidence may be received, though not given upon oath, if, in the opinion of the court, he is possessed of sufficient intelligence to justify the reception of the evidence, and understands the duty of speaking the truth . . . [proviso requiring corroboration repealed by Criminal Justice Act 1988, s 34(1)].

Children Act 1989

96 (1)   Subsection (2) applies where a child who is called as a witness in any civil proceedings does not, in the opinion of the court, understand the nature of an oath.
(2)   The child's evidence may be heard by the court if, in its opinion –
(*a*)   he understands that it is his duty to speak the truth; and
(*b*)   he has sufficient understanding to justify his evidence being heard.

R v Z   **[1990] 2 QB 355, [1990] 2 All ER 971, CA**

In a trial for incest, the chief prosecution witness was the accused's daughter, aged five at the time of the offence and six at the time of the trial. After questioning her by video link the judge decided she was competent to give unsworn evidence.

Lord Lane CJ: The question in each case which the court must decide is whether the child is possessed of sufficient intelligence to justify the reception of the evidence, and understands the duty of speaking the truth.

Those criteria will inevitably vary widely from child to child and may indeed vary according to the circumstances of the case, the nature of the case, and the nature of the evidence which the child is called on to give. Obviously the younger the child the more care the judge must take before he allows the evidence to be received. But the statute lays down no minimum age, and the matter accordingly remains in the discretion of the judge in each case. It may be very rarely that a five-year-old will satisfy the requirements of s 38(1). But nevertheless the discretion remains to be exercised judicially by the judge according to the well-known criteria for the exercise of judicial discretion.

I put the matter that way in the light of the fact that we have been referred to a decision of this court in *R v Wallwork* (1958) 42 Cr App Rep 153. That was a case where the appellant was charged with incest with his daughter aged five. Lord Goddard CJ, delivering the judgment of the court, said (at 160–1):

'We now come to the point which has given the court considerable difficulty. The child was called as a witness, but said nothing. The court deprecates the calling of a child of this age as a witness. Although the learned judge had the court cleared as far as it can be cleared, it seems to us to be unfortunate that she was called and, with all respect to the learned judge, I am surprised that he allowed her to be called. The jury could not attach any value to the evidence of a child of five; it is ridiculous to suppose that they could. Of course, the child could not be sworn . . . but in any circumstances to call a little child of the age of five seems to us to be most undesirable, and I hope it will not occur again.'

The other more recent case to which we have been referred is *R v Wright* (1987) 90 Cr App Rep 91 . . .

So far as *R v Wallwork* is concerned, that decision, some considerable number of years ago in 1958, has really been overtaken by events. First of all, it will be seen from the words of Lord Goddard CJ that part of the concern which he expressed was concern over the position of the child itself in court, when he mentions the fact the court was cleared so far as it was possible to have it cleared. That particular problem has now to a great extent been cured by the system of video links, which of course in Lord Goddard's days were not even imagined . . .

It seems to us that Parliament, by repealing the proviso to s 38(1), was indicating a change of attitude by Parliament, reflecting in its turn a change of attitude by the public in general to the acceptability of the evidence of young children and of increasing belief that the testimony of young children, when all precautions have been taken, may be just as reliable as that of their elders.

For those reasons we would be reluctant in any way to fetter the discretion of the judge set out in s 38(1), save to say, which scarcely needs saying, as already expressed the younger the child the more care must be taken before admitting the child's evidence . . .

The next submission was that the judge should have withdrawn the case from the jury, first of all, it was submitted, at the close of the prosecution case . . .

It is suggested by counsel for the applicant that [certain] answers really indicated that the child was either not reliable or did not understand what was going on, and in any event cast such a doubt, goes the submission, on her evidence that the judge should have withdrawn the case from the jury at the close of the prosecution evidence.

The answer to that, in the judgment of this court, is simple. The jury had heard what this little girl had said in chief . . . The fact that she may have given answers which cast some doubt on that at a later stage was something eminently for the jury to decide. That is what they were there for, to decide whether the little girl was to be relied on as being accurate and truthful or not. It would have been quite improper for the judge to have usurped that function of the jury, and to have taken it on himself to decide at that stage whether the little girl was to be relied upon or not.

COMMENTS

1. As regards the upper age for a child to give unsworn evidence, 'child' for the purposes of the Children Act 1989 means a person who has not reached the age of 18 (s 105(1)).

2. A witness under the age of 14 in a trial on indictment may with the leave of the court give evidence (sworn or unsworn) through a live television link under the Criminal Justice Act 1988, s 32(1), if the offence is one listed in s 32(2). The same section allows a witness of any age who is outside the United Kingdom, with the leave of the court, to give evidence by live television link in any trial on indictment. The latter provision is simply to avoid needless travel, but the former is intended to protect the child from the rigours of appearing in the courtroom and particularly from having to confront her alleged attacker or molester. An alternative procedure, sanctioned in *R v X, Y and Z* (1989) 91 Cr App Rep 36, CA, is to erect a screen to prevent the children seeing the dock. These provisions have to some extent, and for some proceedings, been superseded by s 32A (inserted by s 54 of the Criminal Justice Act 1988). This section provides for the use of a video-recording of an interview of a child witness as that witness's evidence in chief, subject to the judge's discretion to exclude it or part of it. One of the matters to be taken into account in deciding whether to exclude is that 'it appears that the child witness will not be available for cross-examination' (s 32A(3)(*a*)), but such availability is not a prerequisite to the admission of the tape.

3. '[T]he test ... whether the child "understands the duty of speaking the truth" seems inadequate; for even very young children understand this duty in a general way without necessarily understanding the particular importance of telling the truth in the proceedings. Some judges feel that the inquiry which they have to make sometimes verges on farce ... We recommend that ... the new test should be whether in the opinion of the court the child "is possessed of sufficient intelligence to justify the reception of his evidence and understands the importance of telling the truth in [the] proceedings".' (CLRC paras 205–6.) This recommendation was not implemented by the draftsman of the 1989 Act. Is it a valid point? If so, would the proposed amendment be practicable?

FURTHER READING

Spencer and Flin, *The Evidence of Children* (2nd edn, 1993).

2 Oath and affirmation

In general, oral evidence is given by witnesses who have sworn a religious oath to tell the truth (for forms of oath, see Phipson, pp 157–60). An oath administered in a form which a witness accepts without objection or declares to be binding on him is valid even if in fact he has no religious belief: Oaths Act 1978, s 4(2). The same applies if the theology of his religious belief specifically inhibits a religious obligation arising from the oath in the form in which he has taken it: *R v Kemble* [1990] 3 All ER 116, [1990] 1 WLR 1111, CA (Muslim witness sworn on New Testament). A witness may object to taking an oath, or the form he prefers may not be practicable, and in that case he may be permitted or required to make a solemn affirmation instead of taking an oath (Oaths Act 1978, s 5). Where a child of tender years is to give evidence in a criminal case the pre-1991 test for whether he should be sworn is set out in *R v Hayes* [1977] 2 All ER 288, [1977] 1 WLR 234, CA (below), and, subject to the comments following the extract, presumably the same test applies to a child giving evidence in a civil case: see Children Act 1989, s 96(1).

R v Hayes [1977] 2 All ER 288, [1977] 1 WLR 234, CA

Bridge LJ: The transcript does read rather surprisingly considering this was a boy of 12 at the time he was called to give evidence ... He was asked if he had religious instruction at school, and shook his head. Then the judge said: 'You don't? Do they teach you about the Bible? Have they told you about God or Jesus?' and he answered, 'No'.

'*Q*. Do you know what I mean by God? Have you heard of God?   *A*. No.'

Later, there follows this series of questions and answers:

'*Q*. Do you think there is a God?   *A*. Yes . . .
'*Q*. You know what it means to tell the truth don't you?   *A*. Yes.
'*Q*. You know it's important to tell the truth?   *A*. Yes.
'*Q*. Not to tell lies. You understand that it is important particularly today when you are here? *A*. Yes.
'*Q*. Will you promise before God that you will tell the truth?   *A*. Yes.
'*Q*. And you will stick to that?   *A*. Yes [and then the boy was permitted to take the oath].'

If the series of questions and answers started with the question, 'Do you think there is a God?' and the answer, 'Yes', there would really be no substance in counsel's complaints, but the fact that the earlier questions and answers, on their face, reveal the boy declaring that he is wholly ignorant of the existence of God does lend some force to the submission that if the essence of the sanction of the oath is a divine sanction, and if it is an awareness of that divine sanction which the court is looking for in a child of tender years, then here was a case where, on the face of it, that awareness was absent. The court is not convinced that that is really the essence of the court's duty in the difficult situation where the court has to determine whether a young person can or cannot properly be permitted to take an oath before giving evidence. It is unrealistic not to recognise that, in the present state of society, amongst the adult population the divine sanction of an oath is probably not generally recognised. The important consideration, we think, when a judge has to decide whether a child should properly be sworn, is whether the child has a sufficient appreciation of the solemnity of the occasion, and the added responsibility to tell the truth, which is involved in taking an oath, over and above the duty to tell the truth which is an ordinary duty of normal social conduct.

Against the background of those general considerations of principle, we think it right also to approach the matter on the footing that this is very much a matter within the discretion of the trial judge and we think that this court, although having jurisdiction to interfere if clearly satisfied that the trial judge's discretion was wrongly exercised, should hesitate long before doing so . . .

Counsel for the applicant very frankly concedes that the watershed dividing children who are normally considered old enough to take the oath and children normally considered too young to take the oath, probably falls between the ages of eight and ten. Both boys here were over the age of ten . . . In all the circumstances we are not satisfied . . . that there was any failure on the part of the judge to investigate the fitness of these two boys to take the oath, or that, in his decision that they should be permitted to do so, he erred in any way.

COMMENTS

1. Before statutory reforms in 1988 and 1989 the *unsworn* evidence of a child in criminal cases had to be corroborated before a conviction could depend on it, and unsworn evidence could not be given in civil cases at all. There was therefore considerable pressure to administer the oath to children as young as possible, in order to validate their evidence. The requirements having changed, the pressure no longer exists, and it is to be hoped that trial judges will show a greater tendency to allow children to give their evidence unsworn. In *R v X, Y and Z* (1990) 91 Cr App Rep 36, CA, however, the Court of Appeal made no adverse comment on the fact that a child of eight-and-a-half was sworn.

2. The Criminal Law Revision Committee recommended that children under 14 should give unsworn, and others sworn evidence: CLRC para 206. This recommendation is implemented with respect to criminal proceedings by s 52 of the Criminal Justice Act 1991: see section 1C of this chapter. Therefore, although the reported cases on whether a child witness should be sworn are all criminal cases, the discussion is now only relevant to civil proceedings.

3. If a proposed witness is found competent to be sworn, he should take the oath, even if he has no detectable religious knowledge or belief. The option of affirming is available only in the circumstances set out in Oaths Act 1978, s 5, ie normally if the witness himself requests it; so it cannot be imposed by the judge: *R v Bellamy* (1985) 82 Cr App Rep 222, CA.

REFORM?

The decisions in *R v Hayes* [1977] 2 All ER 288, [1977] 1 WLR 234, CA; *R v Bellamy* (1985) 82 Cr App Rep 222, CA; and *R v Kemble* [1990] 3 All ER 116, [1991] 1 WLR 1111, CA, illustrate the modern tendency of the courts, perhaps in line with social trends, to treat the oath as of formal and secular significance only and devoid of any religious import. It would seem to follow that the oath should be abolished for most purposes, since if it is to be treated in this way the form of words is either meaningless or a blasphemy. It could be replaced as the 'default option' by an affirmation, but remain as an alternative for a witness who wished to take it. This reform has been often suggested, but progress has been prevented by the fact that oaths are used in all legal proceedings and in a number of other circumstances as well. No law reform body with limited terms of reference has therefore felt able to make recommendations. Some of the arguments were set out by the Criminal Law Revision Committee.

Criminal Law Revision Committee, 11th Report, 1972, paras 280–1

280. The reasons why the majority consider that the oath should be replaced by an undertaking to tell the truth are given below:
(i) The oath is a primitive institution which ought not to be preserved unless there is a good reason for preserving it. Its use has been traced back to times when man believed that a verbal formula could itself produce desired results, as in the case of the curse. Curses were operative magic performances, and the oath was a conditional self-curse. With the growth of religious belief it was thought that God was the executor of man's oath. He was believed to respond to its magic. The oath was an imprecation to heaven calling upon the supernatural powers to bring disaster on the speaker if he uttered falsehood. This was the basis of the Anglo-Saxon system of compurgation, which rested on the belief that the taking of a false oath brought automatic supernatural punishment. This view of the oath lasted for a surprisingly long time. A judicial expression of the traditional view of the oath is to be found as late as 1786 in *R v White* (1 Leach 430), where at a trial at the Old Bailey for horse-stealing a man was rejected as a witness because he 'acknowledged that he had never learned the catechism, was altogether ignorant of the obligations of an oath, a future state of reward and punishment, the existence of another world, or what became of wicked people after death'. The court said 'that an oath is a religious asseveration, by which a person renounces the mercy, and imprecates the vengeance of heaven, if he do not speak the truth; and therefore a person who has no idea of the sanction which this appeal to heaven creates, ought not to be sworn as a witness in any court of justice'. However, in 1817 Bentham attacked the traditional view with his usual vigour. He pointed to the 'absurdity, than which nothing can be greater', of the supposition that 'by man, over the Almighty, *power* should be exercised or exercisable; man the legislator and judge, God the sheriff and executioner; man the despot, God his slave' (*Swear Not at All*, pp 3–4).

(ii) It might be said that, although the original purpose of the oath is no longer relevant, it nevertheless has value now in that it serves to call the attention of a witness who believes in God to the fact that, if he tells a lie, he will incur the divine displeasure. But if this is its justification, it is curious that it is only in the case of lying in certain official proceedings that the citizen has his attention called to his assumed belief in divine retribution. We do not draw attention to this possibility for any other purpose of law enforcement.

(iii) There have already been large inroads into the practice of taking the oath. Originally, non-believers were prevented from taking the oath because this would have involved practising a kind of deception on the state. Eventually, however, concern for the promotion of trade brought about a change of attitude and infidels were allowed to take the oath and so to testify in legal proceedings. The Oaths Act 1838 (c 105) for the first time allowed persons other than Christians and Jews to be sworn in such form as the witness might declare to be binding on him. In effect this involved an abandonment for these persons of an inquiry into their beliefs as to the hereafter . . . The last stage has been the Oaths Act 1961 (c 21) which empowers the court to require a witness to affirm instead of taking the oath if it would not be 'reasonably practicable without inconvenience or delay' to administer the oath to him in the way appropriate to his religion. In passing this Act Parliament recognised that there is nothing wrong in requiring a person to give evidence without being sworn even though he has a religious belief and it is not contrary to this to take an oath. It seems difficult, therefore, to see why this should not apply to all witnesses.

(iv) To many people it is incongruous that the Bible should be used, and the Deity invoked, in giving evidence of such matters as, for example, a common motoring offence. In evaluating evidence, little attention is paid to the mere fact that it has been given on oath. In any case it is probable that many witnesses who in fact have no religious belief take the oath because they do not wish to call attention to themselves or because they fear that the impact of their evidence will be weakened if they depart from the customary oath.

(v) If it is right to regard it as incongruous to require ordinary witnesses to take the oath, this is specially inappropriate in the case of the accused. The accused, if guilty (and sometimes even if not), is under an obvious temptation to lie. Our proposals involve putting pressure on him to give evidence, and it may seem to many excessive to require him to take a religious oath as well.

(vi) There would be a good case for keeping the oath if there were a real probability that it increases the amount of truth told. The majority do not think that it does this very much. For a person who has a firm religious belief, it is unlikely that taking the oath will act as any additional incentive to tell the truth. For a person without any religious belief, by hypothesis the oath can make no difference. There is value in having a witness 'solemnly and sincerely' promise that he will tell the truth, and from this point of view the words of the affirmation are to many at least more impressive than the customary oath. The oath has not prevented an enormous amount of perjury in the courts. A witness who wishes to lie and who feels that the oath may be an impediment can easily say that taking an oath is contrary to his religious belief.

We need hardly say that we have no wish to offend any religious feelings, nor do we see why anything said above should do so. Moreover, the replacement of the oath by some form of declaration has been advocated several times recently in legal periodicals and in two of the observations sent to us, and the arguments in the periodicals do not seem to have provoked any arguments to the contrary. In 1968 the Magistrates' Association at their annual meeting voted by a narrow majority (140–130) that the oath sworn in magistrates' courts should be replaced by a simple promise to tell the truth, *The Times*, 12 October 1968. In July 1970 the Memorandum of the Council of the Law Society on Oaths, Affirmations and Statutory Declarations recommended that 'the present forms of oaths, affirmations and statutory declarations should be abolished and replaced by a single, non-religious form of promise or declaration for use on all occasions where formality is required'. In any event, whether the oath is kept or replaced, we hope that steps will be taken to ensure greater solemnity when a witness swears or makes the declaration. In our opinion it may be desirable that the oath or declaration should always be administered by the judge or presiding magistrate, as is the practice in Scotland. If it is decided to abolish the witness's oath, the question of the jurors' oath will require consideration; for if the jurors took the oath and the witnesses made a declaration, this might suggest that the witnesses' duty was less important than the jurors'. We express no opinion as to the abolition or preservation of other oaths.

281. The minority are strongly opposed to the replacement of the witness's oath by a declaration. They recognise that there is force in the arguments for this as set out in the previous paragraph; but they do not find any of them convincing. In their opinion there are many persons to whom the oath, administered properly and in complete silence, serves to bring home most strongly the solemnity of their obligation to tell the truth and to be careful about what they say in giving their evidence.

Henry Cecil: The English Judge (1970), pp 102–5

The average witness has never been in a courtroom before and is pretty terrified at the thought, let alone the reality. He comes into court where he sees a bewigged and robed judge on a dais and counsel in wigs and gowns and an usher in a gown. It is the daily round for the legal profession. It is a nightmare for the witness. His name is called and he goes to the witness-box. The usher tells him to take the Bible in his right hand and repeat the words on the card. Perhaps he has not got the right glasses with him or in his nervousness cannot find them in his pocket. Eventually he succeeds in finding them and, wondering if he has committed an offence by being so slow, he looks at the card . . .

Finally he completes the ordeal and takes an oath which, if he or anyone else thought about it, he has little chance of being allowed to keep. As all lawyers know, it runs as follows:

'I swear by Almighty God that the evidence I shall give shall be the truth, the whole truth and nothing but the truth.'

Or, alternatively, if there is an affirmation:

'I, John Jones, do solemnly and sincerely and truly declare and affirm that . . .' etc.

The words 'so help me God,' which used to appear at the end of the oath, are no longer used. In consequence, a person is made to swear that the evidence he gives will be true when, if he is a reasonably intelligent and honest man, he knows perfectly well that it may not be true, particularly if the events about which he is to speak took place about a year previously. If he believes in God, why should he be compelled to swear by God that he will do something which he knows he may not be able to do? If he asked leave to say, 'I swear that I will do my best to tell the truth' he would be refused such leave. Next he is required to swear that his evidence will contain the whole truth. In many cases the laws of evidence will not permit him to tell the whole truth . . . Why should a witness be compelled to swear by his Maker that he will do something that he won't be allowed to do? Finally, witnesses have to swear that their evidence will contain nothing but the truth. An honest and intelligent man knows perfectly well that something which is untrue may creep into his evidence. He may believe it to be true but it may be completely false.

It is right that the solemnity of the occasion should be impressed upon the witness and upon those in court. But there would be no difficulty in doing this and providing an oath which the witness could really keep. In Scotland the judge administers the oath himself and stands up to do so. What could be the objection to the Scottish practice in that respect being adopted in England and to the judge rising and saying to the witness: 'Do you swear by Almighty God' (or, if the witness wishes to affirm, 'Do you promise') 'that you will do your best to tell the truth?' That could be done with dignity and solemnity.

It would mean something and it would be far less difficult for the witness than having to undergo the present ordeal. He would simply answer 'yes' or 'I do' and the judge could ensure by the way in which he looked at the witness and said the words that it was a very important occasion . . .

A suggestion made to me was that the oath should be abolished and that instead the judge should ask the witness some such question as this: 'Do you know that the law requires you on pain of heavy penalties to give full and honest evidence to the best of your recollection?' and then wait for the witness to say 'Yes.'

FURTHER READING

Weinberg, 3 Mon LR 26.

CHAPTER 18

Private Privilege

The type of privilege discussed in this chapter arises when a person can choose to prevent a witness from answering particular questions or to prevent a person producing particular documents. It is distinct from the non-competence or non-compellability of a witness; these expressions refer to the incapacity of a witness or his right to refuse to testify at all. And it is distinct from the privilege against self-incrimination, which is personal to the witness.

Private privilege may be waived by its possessor; the matters it relates to may be proved by other evidence; no adverse inference should be drawn from a claim to it; and the wrongful refusal of a claim by a witness is not a ground of appeal by the party who called that witness, for the privilege is personal to the witness.

The modern tendency is to restrict existing privileges and only reluctantly to create new ones. The privilege against self-incrimination (ch 6, ante) was narrowed by the Civil Evidence Act 1968, a statute which abolished several other privileges in civil cases and which has been followed for criminal cases by s 80(9) of the Police and Criminal Evidence Act 1984. There are in fact only two private privileges of major importance apart from the privilege against self-incrimination.

1 Legal professional privilege

Communications between a lawyer and his client made in confidence for the purpose of pending litigation or for the purpose of obtaining professional advice may not be disclosed without the client's authority (actual or ostensible). Hence the privilege does not extend beyond communications seeking or conveying legal advice to everything that passes between solicitor and client within the ordinary business of a solicitor: *Balabel v Air-India* [1988] Ch 317, [1988] 2 All ER 246, CA. It has been suggested to extend beyond legal advice to advice on 'the commercial wisdom of entering into a given transaction in relation to which legal advice is also sought' (*Nederlandse Reassurantie Groep Holding NV v Bacon & Woodrow* [1995] 1 All ER 976 at 983): this is heterodox. The privilege also extends to communications between lawyer or client and a third party for the purposes of litigation.

416

A RATIONALE

The privilege is usually said to exist for the following reasons. Human affairs and the legal rules governing them are complex. Men are unequal in wealth, power, intelligence and capacity to handle their problems. To remove this inequality and to permit disputes to be resolved in accordance with the strength of the parties' cases, lawyers are necessary, and the privilege is required to encourage resort to them and to ensure that *all* the relevant facts will be put before them, not merely those the client thinks favour him. If lawyers are only told some of the facts, clients will be advised that their cases are better than they actually are, and will litigate instead of compromising and settling. Lawyer–client relations would be full of 'reserve and dissimulation, uneasiness, and suspicion and fear' without the privilege; the confidant might at any time have to betray confidences. (See *Pearse v Pearse* (1846) 1 De G & Sm 12 at 28, per Knight Bruce VC. See also *Annesley v Earl of Anglesea* (1743) 17 State Tr 1139 at 1225–40; *Greenough v Gaskell* (1833) 1 My & K 98 at 103, [1824–34] All ER Rep 767 at 770; *Anderson v Bank of British Columbia* (1876) 2 Ch D 644 at 649, and C, 'On the Production of Cases prepared for the Opinion of Counsel' (1837) 17 Law Magazine 51 at 68.) Bentham, consistently with his general policy of removing obstacles to the discovery of truth, used two main arguments against the privilege. One was that its abolition would enhance professional standards by removing any power to hide the accused's guilt. But surely professional standards are not influenced so much by the law of evidence as by prevailing moral standards and the operation of internal professional discipline and criminal punishment? Secondly, Bentham argued that if abolition meant that clients repose less confidence in their lawyers 'wherein will consist the mischief? The man by the supposition is guilty; if not, by the supposition there is nothing to betray' (Book IX, Pt IV, c 5); and see *Flight v Robinson* (1844) 8 Beav 22 at 36. But both sides in civil cases will tend to have strong points and weak: 'a person who has a partly good cause would often be deterred from consultation by virtue of the bad part or the part that might possibly (to his notion) be bad' (Wigmore, para 2291). Further, even if in a criminal case the client is wholly guilty, it is wrong to allow the prosecution to use his admissions to his lawyer, for the police might come to rely as far as possible on this kind of evidence to the exclusion of independently obtained evidence. If there were no privilege, the accused would stay silent: the prosecution would gain nothing and the accused would lose in that what he thinks incriminating may not be so in fact. Another argument sometimes put against the privilege is that it increases unfounded claims: 'It is common knowledge in the profession that a potential litigant will consult lawyer A and ascertain that he has no cause of action because a certain fact was X instead of Y, and that the same litigant later brings action through lawyer B when he has assumed that the certain fact was Y and not X' (Morgan, Foreword, American Law Institute Model Code of Evidence (1942), p 27). But if the danger exists at all, it is outweighed by the likelihood of bad advice being given because of lack of information. And in civil cases the parties are compellable; in criminal cases the accused often enters the box. Clients will avoid deliberate lying which if revealed in cross-examination may cause defeat and result in a perjury prosecution. For similar reasons the privilege may be thought to cause very little harm in modern conditions, since so far as the client is skilfully cross-examined and does not lie, he will have to tell the court anything relevant he told his lawyer. Admittedly these conditions may be regarded by some as over-optimistic, and the capacity of one party to cross-examine the opposing party depends on the latter giving evidence in his own case, which he cannot normally be compelled to do.

B   SCOPE

Wheeler v Le Marchant   (1881) 17 Ch D 675, CA

This was an action for specific performance of a building contract to lease building land from the defendants. The defendants claimed privilege for letters passing between their solicitors and their surveyors. The Court of Appeal refused to grant privilege except so far as they were prepared after the dispute arose and with reference to existing or contemplated litigation.

Jessel MR: . . . What they contended for was that documents communicated to the solicitors of the Defendants by third parties, though not communicated by such third parties as agents of the clients seeking advice, should be protected, because those documents contained information required or asked for by the solicitors, for the purpose of enabling them the better to advise the clients. The cases, no doubt, establish that such documents are protected where they have come into existence after litigation commenced or in contemplation, and when they have been made with a view to such litigation, either for the purpose of obtaining advice as to such litigation, or of obtaining evidence to be used in such litigation, or of obtaining information which might lead to the obtaining of such evidence, but it has never hitherto been decided that documents are protected merely because they are produced by a third person in answer to an inquiry made by the solicitor. It does not appear to me to be necessary, either as a result of the principle which regulates this privilege or for the convenience of mankind, so to extend the rule. In the first place, the principle protecting confidential communications is of a very limited character. It does not protect all confidential communications which a man must necessarily make in order to obtain advice, even when needed for the protection of his life, or of his honour, or of his fortune. There are many communications which, though absolutely necessary because without them the ordinary business of life cannot be carried on, still are not privileged. The communications made to a medical man whose advice is sought by a patient with respect to the probable origin of the disease as to which he is consulted, and which must necessarily be made in order to enable the medical man to advise or to prescribe for the patient, are not protected. Communications made to a priest in the confessional on matters perhaps considered by the penitent to be more important even than his life or his fortune, are not protected. Communications made to a friend with respect to matters of the most delicate nature, on which advice is sought with respect to a man's honour or reputation, are not protected. Therefore it must not be supposed that there is any principle which says that every confidential communication which it is necessary to make in order to carry on the ordinary business of life is protected. The protection is of a very limited character, and in this country is restricted to the obtaining the assistance of lawyers, as regards the conduct of litigation or the rights to property. It has never gone beyond the obtaining of legal advice and assistance, and all things reasonably necessary in the shape of communication to the legal advisers are protected from production or discovery in order that that legal advice may be obtained safely and sufficiently.

Now, keeping that in view, what has been done is this: The actual communication to the solicitor by the client is of course protected, and it is equally protected whether it is made by the client in person or is made by an agent on behalf of the client, and whether it is made to the solicitor in person or to a clerk or subordinate of the solicitor who acts in his place and under his direction. Again, the evidence obtained by the solicitor, or by his direction, or at his instance, even if obtained by the client, is protected if obtained after litigation has been commenced or threatened, or with a view to the defence or prosecution of such litigation. So, again, a communication with a solicitor for the purpose of obtaining legal advice is protected though it relates to a dealing which is not the subject of litigation, provided it be a communication made to the solicitor in that character and for that purpose. But what we are asked to protect here is this. The solicitor, being consulted in a matter as to which no dispute has arisen, thinks he would like to know some further facts before giving his advice, and applies to a surveyor to tell him what the state of a given property is, and it is said that the information given ought to be protected because it is desired or required by the solicitor in order to enable him the better to give legal advice. It appears to me that to give such protection would not only extend the rule beyond what has been previously laid down, but beyond what necessity warrants. The idea that documents like these require protection has been stated, if I may say so, for the first time to-day, and I think the best proof that the necessities of mankind have not been supposed to require this protection is that it has never heretofore been asked. It seems to me we ought not to carry the rule any further than it has been carried. It is a rule established and maintained solely for the purpose of enabling a man to obtain legal advice with safety. That rule does not, in my opinion, require to be carried further.

[Brett and Cotton LJJ delivered concurring judgments.]

O'Rourke v Darbishire   [1920] AC 581, [1920] All ER Rep 1, HL

Lord Sumner: No one doubts that the claim for professional privilege does not apply to documents which have been brought into existence in the course of or in furtherance of a fraud to which both solicitor and client are parties. To consult a solicitor about an intended course of action, in order to be advised whether it is legitimate or not, or to lay before a solicitor the facts relating to a charge of fraud, actually made or anticipated, and make a clean breast of it with the object of being advised about the best way in which to meet it, is a very different thing from consulting him in order to learn how to plan, execute, or stifle an actual fraud. No one doubts again that you can neither try out the issue in the action on a mere interlocutory proceeding, nor require the claimant to carry the issue raised to a successful trial before he can obtain production of documents which are only relevant to that issue and only sought for the purpose of proving it. I am, however, sure that it is equally clear in principle that no mere allegation of a fraud, even though made in the most approved form of pleading, will suffice in itself to overcome a claim of professional privilege, properly formulated.

Butler v Board of Trade   [1971] Ch 680, [1970] 3 All ER 593

The defendants began a prosecution against the plaintiff. The plaintiff claimed privilege for a copy of a letter written by his solicitor to him. The defendants' argument that any privilege was lost because the letter was in preparation for a criminal design by the plaintiff was rejected by Goff J.

Goff J: It is submitted on behalf of the defendants, however, that as the plaintiff is charged with criminal offences, and the letter is relevant hereto, which it undoubtedly is, the privilege does not apply. Now, it is clear that a sufficient charge of crime or fraud will in certain circumstances destroy the privilege, but there is a dispute between the parties about what it is necessary to show for that purpose. The defendants say that relevance is alone sufficient, and the position is in effect so stated in the Supreme Court Practice 1970, vol 1 p 377, para 24/5/9. The plaintiff submits, however, that it is necessary to go further and to show that the professional advice was in furtherance of the crime or fraud, as is said in Phipson on Evidence, 11th edn, p 251, para 590, and 36 Halsbury's Laws (3rd edn) p 51, para 72, or in preparation for it: see *R v Cox and Railton* (1884) 14 QBD 153 at 165, [1881–5] All ER Rep 68 at 70; see per the Earl of Halsbury LC in *Bullivant v A-G for Victoria* [1901] AC 196, at 201, [1900–3] All ER Rep 812 at 814, HL, and see also 10 Halsbury's Laws (3rd edn) p 479, para 877.

As questions of this nature have to be determined on a prima facie basis, often without seeing the documents or knowing what was orally communicated, the two tests will, I think, in many and probably most cases be found in practice to produce the same result because in most cases of relevance the proper prima facie inference will be that the communication was made in preparation for or in furtherance or as part of the criminal or fraudulent purpose. However, the two tests are not the same and in the present case cannot, I think, possibly produce the same result. On the information before me, the letter was nothing but a warning volunteered, no doubt wisely, but still volunteered by the solicitor that if her client did not take care he might incur serious consequences, which she described. I cannot regard that on any showing as being in preparation for, or in furtherance or as part of, any criminal designs on the part of the plaintiff. I must, therefore, decide which test is correct, and I prefer the narrower view.

First, that appears to me to be the true effect of *R v Cox and Railton*. Counsel for the defendants argued to the contrary and he relied on the passage where Stephen J said (1884) 14 QBD 153 at 165, [1881–5] All ER Rep 68 at 70:

'We must take it, after the verdict of the jury, that so far as the two defendants, Railton and Cox, were concerned, their communication with Mr Goodman was a step preparatory to the commission of a criminal offence, namely, a conspiracy to defraud.'

That passage, he argues, cannot mean that the criminal trial disclosed that they went to see Mr Goodman with an already-formed criminal intention, for that the verdict did not show, and, therefore, the true explanation must be, that the evidence was held rightly admitted because it was relevant to the criminal offence subsequently proved to have been committed. I do not so read it. The court by then knew that a criminal offence had been committed and the evidence which had been admitted showed that criminal purpose existed in the minds of Cox and Railton when they saw Mr Goodman, since ((1884) 14 QBD 153 at 156, (1881–5) All ER Rep 68 at 70): 'It was expressly arranged that the partnership should be kept secret'. As I see it, the court having to decide ex post facto whether the evidence has been rightly admitted, inferred that the advice was preparatory to the crime proved, and it will be observed that immediately after the passage in question Stephen J went on to say ((1884) 14 QBD 153 at 165, [1881–5] All Rep 68 at 70):

'The question, therefore is, whether, if a client applies to a legal adviser for advice intended to facilitate or to guide the client in the commission of a crime or fraud, the legal adviser being ignorant of the purpose for which his advice is wanted, the communication between the two is privileged? We expressed our opinion at the end of the argument that no such privilege existed.'

If relevance alone is the test, it follows that privilege could never be claimed in cases of crime or fraud, except as to communications in connexion with the defence. That, in my judgment, is too narrow, and inconsistent with the whole tenor of *R v Cox and Railton*. Stephen J said that they would first state the principle on which the present case must be decided, then set out in the forefront the nature of the privilege itself and then draw the exception to it in these terms ((1884) 14 QBD 153 at 166–7, [1881–5] All ER Rep 68 at 76):

'The reason on which the rule is said to rest cannot include the case of communications, criminal in themselves, or intended to further any criminal purpose, for the protection of such communications cannot possibly be otherwise than injurious to the interests of justice, and to those of the administration of justice. Nor do such communications fall within the terms of the rule. A communication in furtherance of a criminal purpose does not "come into the ordinary scope of professional employment".'

Further, the relevance test is in my judgment negatived by the conclusions of the court (ibid) and in particular the words:

'We are far from saying that the question whether the advice was taken before or after the offence will always be decisive as to the admissibility of such evidence.'

Secondly, in my judgment all the members of the House of Lords in *O'Rourke v Darbishire* [1920] AC 581, [1920] All ER Rep 1, HL, with the possible exception of Lord Wrenbury, clearly adopted the narrower test, and that is binding on me. Counsel for the defendants relied very strongly on the decision of Kekewich J in *Williams v Quebrada Rly, Land and Copper Co*. That learned judge appears [1895] 2 Ch 751, at 756, to have construed *R v Cox and Railton* as laying down the relevance test, but if he did I respectfully beg leave to disagree, and in any case this was long before *O'Rourke v Darbishire*. The actual decision, can, I think, be supported on either test since where, as also in *R v Cox and Railton*, the alleged criminal or fraudulent purpose consists in endeavouring to defeat another's rights by unlawful means, advice as to the nature and extent of those rights and the limits of one's own lawful powers may well be regarded when considered on a prima facie basis as at least in preparation for that unlawful purpose.

Counsel for the defendants also relied on the Canadian cases of *Re Goodman and Carr and Minister of National Revenue* (1968) 70 DLR (2d) 670 and *Re Milner* (1968) 70 DLR (2d) 429. *Re Goodman* does not really assist because the court there found that there was no prima facie case of fraud, but it is to be noted that the judge cited passages which support the limited view of the exception, and in particular (1968) 70 DLR (2d) 670 at 673 the headnote in *R v Cox and Railton*. In *Re Milner* it was assumed that relevance was the basis of the exception, but there was no argument or decision as to the ambit of the exception. The only question before the court was whether there was a sufficient prima facie case of fraud. I do not, therefore, find anything in these cases to deflect me from the decision which I have otherwise reached. In my judgment, therefore, on the limited facts before me, the original letter is privileged and the copy confidential.

. . . It thus becomes unnecessary for me to decide the further question which was canvassed, whether in any case the charge of crime is for the purposes of the question in this special case sufficiently averred, in accordance with the principles laid down by Lord Halsbury LC in *Bullivant's Case* [1901] AC 196 at 201, [1900–3] All ER Rep 812 at 814, HL and by Lord Sumner in *O'Rourke v Darbishire* [1920] AC 581 at 613–14, [1920] All ER Rep 1 at 11, HL, although in my view the answer would be in the negative on the assumed facts because I think that it comes back to the original question. If one rejects the bare relevance test, as I have done, then what has to be shown prima facie is not merely that there is a bona fide and reasonably tenable charge of crime or fraud but a prima facie case that the communications in question were made in preparation for or in furtherance or as part of it.

It was then argued that the copy letter having left the care of the solicitor and come into the hands of the defendants, so that one is no longer in the realm of privilege but of confidence, there can be no equity which the plaintiff can set up because of the principle succinctly summed up by Wood V-C in *Gartside v Outram* (1856) 26 LJ Ch 113 at 114 in the phrase, 'there is no confidence as to the disclosure of iniquity'. Lord Denning MR cited that in *Initial Services Ltd v Putterill* [1968] 1 QB 396 at 405, [1967] 3 All ER 145 at 148, CA and then said:

'In *Weld-Blundell v Stephens* [1919] 1 KB 520 at 527, Bankes LJ rather suggested that the exception was limited to the proposed or contemplated commission of a crime or a civil wrong; but I should have thought that that was too limited. The exception should extend to crimes, frauds and misdeeds, both those actually committed as well as those in contemplation, provided always – and this is essential – that the disclosure is justified in the public interest. The reason is because "no private obligations can dispense with that universal one which lies on every member of the society to discover every design which may be formed, contrary to the laws of the society, to destroy the public welfare". See *Annesley v Earl of Anglesea* (1743) 17 State Tr 1139 at 1223–46. The disclosure must, I should think, be to one who has a proper interest to receive the information.'

In my judgment, however, that does not apply to the present case. At the trial, the defendants may or may not prove the criminal offences with which the plaintiff is charged, and the letter if received in evidence may or may not help them to do so; but although, if more were known of the facts, one might find some communication falling within this exception, I cannot see in this bare warning any element of vice which the umbrella of confidence may not in general cover.

Waugh v British Railways Board   [1980] AC 521, [1979] 2 All ER 1169, HL

The plaintiff's husband was employed by the defendant railways board. In a collision between locomotives, he received injuries from which he died. The practice of the board when an accident occurred was that on the day of the accident a brief report was made to the railway inspectorate, soon afterwards a joint internal report ('the joint inquiry report') was prepared incorporating statements of witnesses, which was also sent to the inspectorate, and in due course a report was made by the inspectorate for the Department of the Environment. The heading of the joint inquiry report stated that it had finally to be sent to the board's solicitor for the purpose of enabling him to advise the board.

Lord Wilberforce: Whatever [the] heading may say, the affidavit makes it clear that the report was prepared for a dual purpose; for what may be called railway operation and safety purposes and for the purpose of obtaining legal advice in anticipation of litigation, the first being more immediate than the second, but both being described as of equal rank or weight. So the question arises whether this is enough to support a claim of privilege, or whether, in order to do so, the second purpose must be the sole purpose, or the dominant or main purpose. If either of the latter is correct, the claim of privilege in this case must fall.

My Lords, before I consider the authorities, I think it desirable to attempt to discern the reason why what is (inaccurately) called legal professional privilege exists. It is sometimes ascribed to the exigencies of the adversary system of litigation under which a litigant is entitled within limits to refuse to disclose the nature of his case until the trial. Thus one side may not ask to see the proofs of the other side's witnesses or the opponent's brief or even know what witnesses will be called: he must wait until the card is played and cannot try to see it in the hand. This argument cannot be denied some validity even where the defendant is a public corporation whose duty it is, so it might be thought, while taking all proper steps to protect its revenues, to place all the facts before the public and to pay proper compensation to those it has injured. A more powerful argument to my mind is that everything should be done in order to encourage anyone who knows the facts to state them fully and candidly – as Sir George Jessel MR said, to bare his breast to his lawyer: *Anderson v Bank of British Columbia* (1876) 2 Ch D 644 at 699. This he may not do unless he knows that his communication is privileged.

But the preparation of a case for litigation is not the only interest which calls for candour. In accident cases '. . . the safety of the public may well depend on the candour and completeness of reports made by subordinates whose duty it is to draw attention to defects': *Conway v Rimmer* [1968] AC 910 at 914 per Lord Reid. This however does not by itself justify a claim to privilege since, as Lord Reid continues:

> '. . . no one has ever suggested that public safety has been endangered by the candour or completeness of such reports having been inhibited by the fact that they may have to be produced if the interests of the due administration of justice should ever require production at any time.'

So one may deduce from this the principle that while privilege may be required in order to induce candour in statements made for the purposes of litigation it is not required in relation to statements whose purpose is different – for example to enable a railway to operate safely.

It is clear that the due administration of justice strongly requires disclosure and production of this report: it was contemporary; it contained statements by witnesses on the spot; it would be not merely relevant evidence, but almost certainly the best evidence as to the cause of the accident. If one accepts that this important public interest can be overridden in order that the defendant may properly prepare his case, how close must the connection be between the preparation of the document and the anticipation of litigation? On principle I would think that the purpose of preparing for litigation ought to be either the sole purpose or at least the dominant purpose of it: to carry the protection further into cases where that purpose was secondary or equal with another purpose would seem to be excessive, and unnecessary in the interest of encouraging truthful revelation. At the lowest such desirability of protection as might exist in such cases is not strong enough to outweigh the need for all relevant documents to be made available.

There are numerous cases in which this kind of privilege has been considered. A very useful review of them is to be found in the judgment of Havers J in *Seabrook v British Transport Commission* [1959] 2 All ER 15, [1959] 1 WLR 509 which I shall not repeat. It is not easy to extract a coherent principle from them. The two dominant authorities at the present time are *Birmingham and Midland Motor Omnibus Co Ltd v London and North Western Rly Co* [1913] 3 KB 850 and *Ogden v London Electric Rly Co* (1933) 49 TLR 542, both decisions of the Court of Appeal. These cases were taken by the majority of the Court of Appeal in the present case to require the granting of privilege in cases where one purpose of preparing the document(s) in question was to enable the defendants' case to be prepared whether or not they were to be used for another substantial purpose. Whether in fact they compel such a conclusion may be doubtful – in particular I do not understand the *Birmingham* case to be one of dual purposes at all: but it is enough that they have been taken so to require. What is clear is that, though loyally followed, they do not now enjoy rational acceptance; in *Longthorn v British Transport Commission* [1959] 2 All ER 32, [1959] 1 WLR 530 the manner in which Diplock J managed to escape from them, and the tenor of his judgment, shows him to have been unenthusiastic as to their merits. And in *Alfred Crompton Amusement Machines Ltd v Customs and Excise Comrs (No 2)* [1974] AC 405 at 432 Lord Cross of Chelsea pointedly left their correctness open, while Lord Kilbrandon stated, at 435, that he found the judgment of Scrutton LJ in *Ogden v London Electric Rly Co* (1933) 49

TLR 542 at 543–544, 'hard to accept'. Only Viscount Dilhorne (dissenting) felt able to follow them in holding it to be enough if one purpose was the use by solicitors when litigation was anticipated.

The whole question came to be considered by the High Court of Australia in 1976: *Grant v Downs* (1976) 135 CLR 674. This case involved reports which had 'as one of the material purposes for their preparation' submission to legal advisers in the event of litigation. It was held that privilege could not be claimed. In the joint judgment of Stephen, Mason and Murphy JJ, in which the English cases I have mentioned were discussed and analysed, it was held that 'legal professional privilege' must be confined to documents brought into existence for the sole purpose of submission to legal advisers for advice or use in legal proceedings. Jacobs J put the test in the form of a question, at 692: '. . . does the purpose' – in the sense of intention, the intended use – 'of supplying the material to the legal adviser account for the existence of the material?' Barwick CJ stated it in terms of 'dominant' purpose. This is closely in line with the opinion of Lord Denning MR in the present case that the privilege extends only to material prepared 'wholly or mainly for the purpose of preparing [the defendant's] case.' The High Court of Australia and Lord Denning MR agree in refusing to follow *Birmingham and Midland Motor Omnibus Co Ltd v London and North Western Rly Co* [1913] 3 KB 850 and *Ogden v London Electric Rly Co* (1933) 49 TLR 542, as generally understood.

My Lords, for the reasons I have given, when discussing the case in principle, I too would refuse to follow those cases. It appears to me that unless the purpose of submission to the legal adviser in view of litigation is at least the dominant purpose for which the relevant document was prepared, the reasons which require privilege to be extended to it cannot apply. On the other hand to hold that the purpose, as above, must be the sole purpose would, apart from difficulties of proof, in my opinion, be too strict a requirement, and would confine the privilege too narrowly: as to this I agree with Barwick CJ in *Grant v Downs* (1976) 135 CLR 674, and in substance with Lord Denning MR. While fully respecting the necessity for the Lords Justices to follow previous decisions of their court, I find myself in the result in agreement with Lord Denning's judgment. I would allow the appeal and order disclosure of the joint report.

Lord Edmund-Davies: Referring to 'the rule which protects confidential communications from discovery as regards the other side,' Sir George Jessel MR said in *Anderson v Bank of British Columbia* (1876) 2 Ch D 644 at 649:

'The object and meaning of the rule is this: that as, by reason of the complexity and difficulty of our law, litigation can only be properly conducted by professional men, it is absolutely necessary that a man, in order to prosecute his rights or to defend himself from an improper claim, should have recourse to the assistance of professional lawyers, and it being so absolutely necessary, it is equally necessary, to use a vulgar phrase, that he should be able to make a clean breast of it to the gentleman whom he consults with a view to the prosecution of his claim, or the substantiating his defence against the claim of others; that he should be able to place unrestricted and unbounded confidence in the professional agent, and that the communications he so makes to him should be kept secret, unless with his consent (for it is his privilege, and not the privilege of the confidential agent), that he should be enabled properly to conduct his litigation. That is the meaning of the rule.'

And in the Court of Appeal James LJ summed up the position, at 656, by speaking succinctly of

'. . . an intelligible principle, that as you have no right to see your adversary's brief, you have no right to see that which comes into existence merely as the materials for the brief.'

Preparation with a view to litigation – pending or anticipated – being thus the essential purpose which protects a communication from disclosure in such cases as the present, what in the last resort is the touchstone of the privilege? It is sufficient that the prospect of litigation be merely one of the several purposes leading to the communication coming into being? And is that sufficient (as Eveleigh LJ in the present case held) despite the fact that there is also 'another . . . and even more important purpose'? Is it enough that the prospect of litigation is a *substantial* purpose, though there may be others equally substantial? Is an *appreciable* purpose sufficient? Or does it have to *be the main* purpose? Or *one* of its *main* purposes (as in *Ogden v London Electric Rly Co* (1933) 49 TLR 542)? Ought your Lordships to declare that privilege attaches only to material which (in the words of Lord Denning MR) 'comes within the words "wholly or mainly" for the purpose of litigation'? Or should this House adopt the majority decision of the High Court of Australia in *Grant v Downs* (1976) 135 CLR 674, that legal professional privilege must be confined to documents brought into existence for the *sole* purpose of submission to legal advisers for advice or for use in legal proceedings?

An affirmative answer to each of the foregoing questions can be supported by one or more of the many reported decisions. And so can a negative answer. But no decision is binding upon this House, and your Lordships are accordingly in the fortunate position of being free to choose and declare what is the proper test. And in my judgment we should start from the basis that the public interest is, on balance, best served by rigidly confining within narrow limits the case where material relevant to litigation may be lawfully withheld. Justice is better served by candour than by suppression. For, as it was put in the *Grant v Downs* majority judgment, at 686: '. . . the privilege . . . detracts from the fairness of the trial by denying a party access to relevant documents or at least subjecting him to surprise.'

Adopting that approach, I would certainly deny a claim to privilege when litigation was merely one of several purposes of equal or similar importance intended to be served by the material sought to be withheld from disclosure, and a fortiori where it was merely a minor purpose. On the other hand, I consider that it would be going too far to adopt the '*sole* purpose' test applied by the majority in *Grant v Downs*, which has been adopted in no United Kingdom decision nor, as far as we are aware, elsewhere in the Commonwealth. Its adoption would deny privilege even to material whose outstanding purpose is to serve litigation, simply because another and very minor purpose was also being served. But, inasmuch as the *only* basis of the claim to privilege in such cases as the present one is that the material in question was brought into existence for use in legal proceedings, it is surely right to insist that, before the claim is conceded or upheld, such a purpose must be shown to have played a paramount part. Which phrase or epithet should be selected to designate this is a matter of individual judgment. Lord Denning MR, as we have seen, favoured adoption of the phrase employed in the Law Reform Committee's Sixteenth Report, viz, 'material which came into existence . . . *wholly or mainly*' for the purpose of litigation (para 17). 'Wholly' I personally would reject for the same reason as I dislike 'solely,' but 'mainly' is nearer what I regard as the preferable test. Even so, it lacks the element of clear paramountcy which should, as I think, be the touchstone. After considerable deliberation, I have finally come down in favour of the test propounded by Barwick CJ in *Grant v Downs* (1976) 135 CLR 674, in the following words, at 677:

> 'Having considered the decisions, the writings and the various aspects of the public interest which claim attention, I have come to the conclusion that the court should state the relevant principle as follows: a document which was produced or brought into existence either with the *dominant* purpose of its author, or of the person or authority under whose direction, whether particular or general, it was produced or brought into existence, of using it or its contents in order to obtain legal advice or to conduct or aid in the conduct of litigation, at the time of its production in reasonable prospect, should be privileged and excluded from inspection.' (Italics added.)

Dominant purpose, then, in my judgment, should now be declared by this House to be the touchstone. It is less stringent a test than 'sole' purpose, for, as Barwick CJ added, 135 CLR 674, 677:

> '. . . the fact that the person . . . had in mind other uses of the document will not preclude that document being accorded privilege, if it were produced with the requisite dominant purpose.'

Applying such test to the facts of the present case, we have already seen that privilege was claimed in Mr Hastings's affidavit on several grounds. Thus, the report of 6 May 1976, was produced in accordance with the long-standing practice of the board regarding 'accidents occurring on or about any railway . . . in order to assist in establishing the causes of such accidents,' and this whether or not (so your Lordships were informed) any personal injuries were sustained and even where there was no prospect of litigation ensuing. This particular report was called for in accordance with such practice and:

> '*One of the principal purposes* for so doing was so that they could be passed to the board's chief solicitor to enable him to advise the board on its legal liability and if necessary conduct its defence to these proceedings.' (Italics added.)

Were the 'sole purpose' test adopted and applied, on the board's own showing their claim to privilege must fail. Then what of the 'dominant purpose' test which I favour? Dominance again is not claimed by the board, but merely that use in litigation was 'one of the principal purposes'. Such moderation is only to be expected in the face of a claim arising out of a fatal accident. Indeed, the claims of humanity must surely make the dominant purpose of any report upon an accident (particularly where personal injuries have been sustained) that of discovering what happened and why it happened, so that measures to prevent its recurrence could be discussed and, if possible, devised. And, although Barwick CJ in *Grant v Downs* (1976) 135 CLR 674, observed, at 677, that

'. . . the circumstance that the document is a "routine document" will not be definitive. The dominant purpose of its production may none the less qualify it for professional privilege,'

the test of dominance will, as I think, be difficult to satisfy when inquiries are instituted and reports produced automatically whenever any mishap occurs, whatever its nature, its gravity, or even its triviality.

My Lords, if, as I hold, '*dominant* purpose' be the right test of privilege from disclosure, it follows that the board's claim to privilege must be disallowed, and the same applies if the '*sole* purpose' test be applied. I would therefore allow this appeal and restore the order of Master Bickford Smith in favour of disclosure.

Lord Russell of Killowen: My Lords, it has already been demonstrated by my noble and learned friend Lord Wilberforce that if, in order to attract privilege from its production, it is necessary that the joint internal report should owe its genesis to either the sole or the dominant purpose that it should be used for the purpose of obtaining legal advice in possible or probable litigation, the evidence in this case falls short of both those standards. At the conclusion of the arguments in this appeal I was minded, while agreeing that anything less than the standard of the dominant purpose would not suffice to support a claim for privilege from production, to prefer the higher standard of the sole purpose, in line with as I understand them the judgments of the majority in the High Court of Australia in *Grant v Downs* (1976) 135 CLR 674. It appeared to me that such a standard had the merit of greater simplicity in a decision on a claim for privilege from production, as being a line easier to draw and to apply to the facts of a particular case. However on reflection I am persuaded that the standard of sole purpose would be in most, if not all, cases impossible to attain, and that to impose it would tilt the balance of policy in this field too sharply against the possible defendant. Moreover to select the standard of dominant purpose is not to impose a definition too difficult of measurement. It is to be met with in other fields of the law, of which I need instance only the question in bankruptcy law whether there has been a fraudulent preference of a creditor.

In summary, therefore, my Lords, I am in agreement with the speech of my noble and learned friend Lord Wilberforce, and would allow this appeal and order the production to plaintiff of the joint internal report.

[Lords Simon and Keith agreed.]

NOTES

The client's privilege survives any particular piece of litigation; it runs on to his successors in title (*Minet v Morgan* (1873) 8 Ch App 361; *Calcraft v Guest* [1898] 1 QB 759, [1895–9] All ER Rep 346, CA). There may be problems over divided title and compulsory acquisition.

The privilege is not to be destroyed by counsel simply because he thinks his client has no case (*Tuckiar v R* (1934) 52 CLR 335).

No adverse inference should be drawn from the claim of the privilege: *Wentworth v Lloyd* (1864) 10 HL Cas 589, HL. In practice it may prove hard for human nature to avoid this.

The privilege applies even in respect of a foreign legal adviser and in respect of proceedings contemplated in a foreign court (*Re Duncan, Garfield v Fay* [1968] P 306, [1968] 2 All ER 395). It also applies where foreign lawyers advise on the strategy to be adopted in English proceedings by reference to English Law (*International Business Machines Corp v Phoenix International (Computers) Ltd* [1995] 1 All ER 413) and where an English patent attorney advises in relation to foreign proceedings (*Société Française Hoechst v Allied Colloids Ltd* [1992] FSR 66).

A genuine belief by a client that a person was entitled to give legal advice is sufficient to render that person a 'lawyer' for the purpose of creating the privilege (*Calley v Richards* (1854) 19 Beav 401; *Grofam Pty Ltd v Australia & New Zealand Banking Group Ltd* (1993) 45 FCR 445; *Global Funds Management (NSW) Ltd v Rooney* (1994) 36 NSWLR 122).

The privilege only protects communications made, not facts learnt, eg the client's handwriting.

The communication must be confidential: if it takes place in the presence of strangers it will not be protected, unless it was intended to be protected or it was made in the presence of the third party as a matter of necessity: *R v Braham* [1976] VR 547.

The privilege applies as between the heads of a government department and their internal legal advisers: *Alfred Crompton Amusement Machines Ltd v Customs and Excise Comrs (No 2)* [1974] AC 405, [1973] 2 All ER 1169, HL. The same is doubtless true of private business. The privilege has been extended to communications passing between non-lawyers and their clients before industrial tribunals: *M & W Grazebrook Ltd v Wallens* [1973] 2 All ER 868 at 871. It has not been extended to non-lawyers acting as legal aid officers assisting prisoners, though recognition of a 'public agreement' privilege in these circumstances was said to be 'desirable': *R v Umoh* (1986) 84 Cr App Rep 138 at 143, CA.

The privilege will not arise unless the lawyer and client either are in fact in a lawyer–client relationship or contemplate it.

The privilege belongs to the client; it does not protect the maker of any report to the client or the lawyer if the client does not object to production (*Schneider v Leigh* [1955] 2 QB 195, [1955] 2 All ER 173, CA).

The accused has no right to the production of documents protected by legal professional privilege (*R v Derby Magistrates' Court, ex p B* [1996] AC 487, [1995] 4 All ER 526, HL; *Carter v Managing Partner, Northmore Hal Davey & Leake* (1995) 183 CLR 121).

In both civil and criminal proceedings, legal professional privilege attaches to confidential communications between a solicitor and an expert, but not to the expert's opinion, or the chattels or documents on which he bases his opinion. Hence in a criminal trial the Crown is entitled to subpoena as a witness a handwriting expert whom the defence has consulted but does not wish to call as a witness, and is entitled to production of documents sent to the expert by the defence for examination and on which the expert has based his opinion: *R v King* [1983] 1 All ER 929, [1983] 1 WLR 411, CA, following *R v Justice of the Peace for Peterborough, ex p Hicks* [1978] 1 All ER 225, [1977] 1 WLR 1371, and *Harmony Shipping Co SA v Saudi Europe Line Ltd* [1979] 1 WLR 1380, cf *Frank Truman Export Ltd v Metropolitan Police Comr* [1977] QB 952 at 961 and 963, [1977] 3 All ER 431 at 439 and 440–1. As Dunn LJ said in *King's* Case at 931 and 414, 'it would be strange if a forger could hide behind a claim of legal professional privilege by the simple device of sending all the incriminating documents in his possession to his solicitors to be examined by an expert'. A document not privileged in a client's hands is not privileged in his solicitor's hands.

The privilege does not extend to information (including the address of the solicitor's client) which will enable the court to discover the whereabouts of a ward of court (or child the subject of a custody order) where residence is being concealed from it: *R v Bell, ex p Lees* (1980) 146 CLR 141. It is not clear, nor perhaps does it matter, whether this rule is independently based or is merely part of the general exception relating to the furtherance of illegality. It may depend on the protection of children, since there is power to override legal professional privilege in an unfavourable expert's report obtained for proceedings under the Children Act 1989 (*Oxfordshire County Council v M* [1994] Fam 151, [1994] 2 All ER 269, CA).

The privilege may be lost by waiver. Waiver can occur in consequence of mistakes made by the client's advisers and even against the client's interests or wishes, because the legal adviser of a client has ostensible authority in the conduct of litigation: *Great Atlantic Insurance Co v Home Insurance Co* [1981] 2 All ER 485 at 494, [1981] 1 WLR 529 at 539, CA. If a party, whether before or during the trial, and whether intentionally or not, discloses to the other party a privileged document or part of one, it will be held to have waived privilege with respect to everything else in the document or documents on that subject matter; a waiver of privilege will be held to have occurred by imputation or implication or association in respect of material which it would be unfair or misleading for the waiving party to hold back in view of what has been disclosed. See *General Accident Fire and Life Assurance Corpn Ltd v Tanter, The Zephyr* [1984] 1 All ER 35, [1984] 1 WLR 100 and cases there cited; *A-G for the Northern Territory v Maurice* (1986) 161 CLR 475. A reference to a document in pleadings or an affidavit may well not be a waiver; to set it or part of it out probably will be: *Buttes Gas and Oil Co v Hammer (No 3)* [1981] QB 223, [1980] 3 All ER 475, CA. The above discussion has assumed that there has been a partial waiver: whether waiver has in fact occurred in circumstances of inadvertence can be a difficult issue and is discussed at p 436, post. Waiver can be made for specific proceedings only or a specific part of the proceedings only: *Goldman v Hesper* [1988] 3 All ER 97, [1988] 1 WLR 1238, CA; *British Coal Corpn v Dennis Rye Ltd (No 2)* [1988] 3 All ER 816, [1988] 1 WLR 1113, CA. If a party, by pleadings or evidence, expressly or impliedly makes an assertion about the content of confidential communications between that party and a legal adviser, fairness to the other party may require that the assertion be treated as a waiver of privilege: *Standard Chartered Bank of Australia Ltd v Antico* (1993) 36 NSWLR 87 at 94-5.

Authority is divided on the question of whether the doctrine of legal professional privilege applies only in judicial and quasi-judicial proceedings. In favour of the view that it is so limited is *Parry-Jones v Law Society* [1969] 1 Ch 1, [1968] 1 All ER 177, CA. In favour of the view that it applies more widely, so as, for example, to prevent a police constable carrying out an otherwise lawful search, are the High Court of Australia (*Baker v Campbell* (1983) 153 CLR 52), in which the court by a bare majority reversed its own decision in *O'Reilly v Comr of State Bank of Victoria* (1983) 153 CLR 1, the New Zealand

Court of Appeal (*IRC v West-Walker* [1954] NZLR 191) and the Supreme
Court of Canada (*Solosky v R* (1979) 105 DLR (3d) 745).

In England special provisions are made in relation to searches for privileged
material: Police and Criminal Evidence Act 1984, Part II.

Communications are not privileged if made in furtherance of crime or
fraud (it is otherwise in the case of, eg, the torts of interference with contract
and conspiracy: *Crescent Farm (Sidcup) Sports Ltd v Sterling Offices Ltd*
[1972] Ch 553, [1971] 3 All ER 1192). This conclusion is supported by the
terms of s 10(2) of the Police and Criminal Evidence Act 1984 ('intention of
furthering a criminal purpose'), which has been said to enact the common
law: *R v Central Criminal Court, ex p Francis & Francis (a firm)* [1989] AC
346 at 382–5 and 395, [1988] 3 All ER 775 at 788–91 and 799 per Lords
Griffiths and Goff of Chieveley. Cf *Baker v Campbell* (1983) 153 CLR 52 at
86 per Murphy J. Impermissible purposes include prejudicing the interests of
creditors (*Barclays Bank plc v Eustice* [1995] 4 All ER 511, [1995] 1 WLR
1238, CA) and deliberate abuse of statutory power (*A-G (NT) v Kearney*
(1985) 158 CLR 500). It is not necessary that there be sufficient evidence to
establish fraud on the balance of probabilities; the policy considerations
underlying the privilege must be weighed with the gravity of the charge of
fraud made (*Derby & Co Ltd v Weldon (No 7)* [1990] 3 All ER 161, [1990] 1
WLR 1156).

Does legal professional privilege attach to documents which are the means
of carrying out, or are evidence of, transactions which are not themselves for
the giving or receiving of advice or part of the conduct of actual or anticipated
litigation? The cases suggest a negative answer: see *R v Crown Court at Inner
London Sessions, ex p Baines & Baines (a firm)* [1988] QB 579, [1987] 3 All
ER 1025, an authority on s 10 of the Police and Criminal Evidence Act 1984,
but relevant to the common law since s 10 has been said to enact the common law (see above; see also *Baker v Campbell* (1983) 153 CLR 52 at 122–3
per Dawson J).

If two parties with a common interest and a common solicitor exchange
information for the dominant purpose of informing each other of the facts,
or issues, or advice received, or of obtaining legal advice in respect of contemplated or pending litigation, the document or copies containing that
information are privileged from production in the hands of each: *Buttes Gas
and Oil Co v Hammer (No 3)* [1981] QB 223, [1980] 3 All ER 475, CA.
One such party could not waive privilege without the other's consent: *Lee v
South West Thames Regional Health Authority* [1985] 2 All ER 385, [1985] 1
WLR 845, CA. The common interest may be that of insured and insurer
(*Guinness Peat Properties Ltd v Fitzroy Robinson Partnership* [1987] 2 All ER
716 at 725, [1987] 1 WLR 1027 at 1038-9, CA) and potential underwriter
and insured (*Bulk Materials (Coal Handling) Services Pty Ltd v Coal and
Allied Operations Ltd* (1988) 13 NSWLR 689). It is not necessary that the
parties have a common solicitor; but must the identity of interest between
the parties be so close that they could have used the same lawyer? Compare
*Bank of Nova Scotia v Hellenic Mutual War Risks Association (Bermuda) Ltd
(The Good Luck)* [1992] 2 Lloyd's Rep 540 at 542 and *Network Ten Ltd v
Capital Television Holdings Ltd* (1995) 36 NSWLR 289.

To what extent does privilege attach where an original document is created for purposes other than litigation or legal advice, and copies are made for those purposes? The latest English authority suggests that in the case of individual documents, the making of a copy for the purpose of litigation or advice of an unprivileged original does not cause privilege to arise for the copy (*Dubai Bank v Galadari* [1990] Ch 98, [1989] 3 All ER 769, CA), but accepts the correctness of earlier decisions granting privilege to a copy made by a lawyer of a document in the hands of a third party (*The Palermo* (1883) 9 PD 6, CA; *Watson v Cammell Laird & Co (Shipbuilders and Engineers) Ltd* [1959] 2 All ER 757, [1959] 1 WLR 702, CA), and to a collection, resulting from the lawyer's professional knowledge, research and skill, of unprivileged documents (*Lyell v Kennedy (No 3)*) (1884) 27 Ch D 1, CA). See also *Lubrizol Corpn v Esso Petroleum Co Ltd* [1992] 1 WLR 957.

The general rule that a statute will not be construed to take away a common law right unless a legislative intent to do so clearly emerges by express words or necessary implication applies to legislation which arguably abolishes legal professional privilege in particular circumstances: eg *Baker v Campbell* (1983) 153 CLR 52 at 96–7, 116–17 and 123 per Wilson J, Deane J and Dawson J; *A-G for the Northern Territory v Maurice* (1986) 161 CLR 475 at 490–1 per Deane J. In practice, given the importance now often assigned to the privilege, this can be quite a high hurdle for the legislature: eg *Yuill v Corporate Affairs Commission of New South Wales* (1990) 20 NSWLR 386.

C   LOSS OF THE PRIVILEGE

Calcraft v Guest   [1898] 1 QB 759, [1895–9] All ER Rep 346, CA

Certain documents in respect of which the plaintiff could claim legal professional privilege by accident fell into the defendant's hands. The Court of Appeal held the defendant entitled to give secondary evidence of the documents.

Lindley MR: It appears that the appellant has obtained copies of some of these documents, and is in a position to give secondary evidence of them; and the question is whether he is entitled to do that. That appears to me to be covered by the authority of *Lloyd v Mostyn* (1842) 10 M & W 478 . . . That was an action on a bond which was said to be privileged from production on the ground of its having come into the hands of the solicitor in confidence . . . The plaintiff then tendered in evidence a copy of the bond . . . Parke B said: '. . . Where an attorney entrusted confidentially with a document communicates the contents of it, or suffers another to take a copy, surely the secondary evidence so obtained may be produced. Suppose the instrument were even stolen, and a correct copy taken, would it not be reasonable to admit it?' The matter dropped there; but the other members of the Court (Lord Abinger, Gurney B, and Rolfe B) all concurred in that, which I take it is a distinct authority that secondary evidence in a case of this kind may be received.

[Rigby and Vaughan Williams JJ concurred.]

Lord Ashburton v Pape   [1913] 2 Ch 469, CA

The defendant improperly obtained certain letters written by the plaintiff to his solicitor. The Court of Appeal upheld the grant of an injunction to restrain the defendant from disclosing certain privileged letters or making copies of them, and an exception to the injunction inserted by Neville J permitting use of the documents in certain pending bankruptcy proceedings.

Cozens-Hardy MR: Neville J . . . made an order that Pape do forthwith hand over to Nocton all original letters from the plaintiff to Nocton or his firm in Pape's possession or control. Pape naturally said 'I do not object to that; I will deliver up the originals, because I have got copies.' Then the order goes on in this way: 'And it is ordered that the defendants Edward James Pape, Charles William Langford and Thomas Howard Redfern their servants and agents be restrained until judgment or further order from publishing or making use of any of the copies of such letters or any information contained therein except for the purpose of the pending proceedings in the defendant Edward James Pape's bankruptcy and subject to the direction of the Bankruptcy Court.' Now, the question is raised that that exception is wrong, and that the injunction ought to go to the full extent until the trial of the action, namely, from publishing or making use of any of the copies of letters or information contained therein. In my opinion the contention of the appellant is right. Nocton's clerk, of course, had no right whatever to hand over the originals to Pape nor to make any copies of any sort or kind, and Pape, who was really a party to this transaction, was quite clearly under the same obligation, and liable to precisely the same jurisdiction as has long been exercised by this Court. I do not go back to *Morison v Moat* (1851) 9 Hare 241, which, although not the first, is probably the leading authority on the point, but one passage from *Lamb v Evans* [1893] 1 Ch 218 at 235, CA, in a judgment of Kay LJ, states briefly and, I think, with perfect accuracy what the true law is upon this subject. He says referring to *Morison v Moat*: 'Then the judgment goes on to give several instances, and many of them are of cases where a man, being in the employment of another, has discovered the secrets of the manufacture of that other person, or has surreptitiously copied something which came under his hands while he was in the possession of that trust and confidence, and he has been restrained from communicating that secret to anybody else, and anybody who has obtained that secret from him has also been restrained from using it.' Apart, therefore, from these pending or threatened proceedings in bankruptcy, it seems to me to be perfectly clear that the plaintiff can obtain the unqualified injunction which he asks for. Now, can it make any difference that Pape says 'I want, by means of these copies, to give secondary evidence in the bankruptcy proceedings?' In my opinion that is no ground for making any distinction. The rule of evidence as explained in *Calcraft v Guest* [1898] 1 QB 759, [1895–9] All ER Rep 346, CA, merely amounts to this, that if a litigant wants to prove a particular document which by reason of privilege or some circumstance he cannot furnish by the production of the original, he may produce a copy as secondary evidence although that copy has been obtained by improper means, and even, it may be, by criminal means. The Court in such an action is not really trying the circumstances under which the document was produced. That is not an issue in the case and the Court simply says, 'Here is a copy of a document which cannot be produced; it may have been stolen, it may have been picked up in the street, it may have improperly got into the possession of the person who proposes to produce it, but that is not a matter which the Court in the trial of the action can go into.' But that does not seem to me to have any bearing upon a case where the whole subject-matter of the action is the right to retain the originals or copies of certain documents which are privileged. It seems to me that, although Pape has had the good luck to obtain a copy of these documents which he can produce without a breach of this injunction, there is no ground whatever in principle why we should decline to give the plaintiff the protection which in my view is his right as between him and Pape, and that there is no reason whatever why we should not say to Pape in pending or future proceedings, 'You shall not produce these documents which you have acquired from the plaintiff surreptitiously, or from his solicitor, who plainly stood to him in a confidential relation.' For these reasons I think the appeal ought to be allowed so far as it asks, and only so far as it asks, to strike out the exception.

[Kennedy and Swinfen Eady LJJ gave concurring judgments.]

Butler v Board of Trade   [1971] Ch 680, [1970] 3 All ER 593

The plaintiff sought a declaration that the defendants were not entitled to produce a copy of a letter written to him by his solicitor in evidence at a prosecution being brought against him by the defendants. Goff J refused the declaration.

Goff J: There remains, however, the final question whether the law or equity as to breach of confidence operates in the terms of para 14 of the special case to give the plaintiff 'any equity to prevent the defendants from tendering a copy of the letter in evidence in any of the said criminal proceedings'

where, if tendered it would, as I see it, clearly be admissible: see *Calcraft v Guest* [1898] 1 QB 759 at 764, subject of course to the overriding discretion of the trial court to reject it if it thought its use unfair. The plaintiff relies on the decision of the Court of Appeal in *Lord Ashburton v Pape*, where, a party to certain bankruptcy proceedings having by a trick obtained a copy of a privileged letter, Neville J granted an injunction restraining him and his solicitors from publishing or making use of it, save for the purposes of those proceedings, and the Court of Appeal varied the order by striking out the exception, so that the injunction was unqualified.

Before I consider that further, I can dispose briefly of the argument advanced by counsel for the defendants that the plaintiff cannot be entitled to any relief in equity, because he does not come with clean hands. That seems to me to beg the question. If the letter was part of a criminal project then the copy is not protected anyhow. If, however, it was not such a part then the mere fact, if it be so, that it may help the defendants prove their case on the criminal charge does not soil the hands of the plaintiff with respect to his proprietary interests in the copy.

I turn back to *Ashburton v Pape*. In the present case there was no impropriety on the part of the defendants in the way in which they received the copy, but that, in my judgment, is irrelevant because an innocent recipient of information conveyed in breach of confidence is liable to be restrained. I wish to make it clear that there is no suggestion of any kind of moral obliquity on the part of the solicitors, but the disclosure was in law a breach of confidence. Nevertheless, that case does differ from the present in an important particular, namely that the defendants are a department of the Crown and intend to use the copy letter in a public prosecution brought by them. As far as I am aware, there is no case directly in point on the question whether that is merely an immaterial difference of fact or a valid distinction, but in my judgment it is the latter because in such a case there are two conflicting principles, the private right of the individual and the interest of the State to apprehend and prosecute criminals: see per Lord Denning MR in *Chic Fashions (West Wales) Ltd v Jones* [1968] 2 QB 299 at 313, [1968] 1 All ER 229 at 236, CA and in *Ghani v Jones* [1970] 1 QB 693 at 708, [1969] 3 All ER 1700 at 1704, CA.

In my judgment it would not be a right or permissible exercise of the equitable jurisdiction in confidence to make a declaration at the suit of the accused in a public prosecution in effect restraining the Crown from adducing admissible evidence relevant to the crime with which he is charged. It is not necessary for me to decide whether the same result would obtain in the case of a private prosecution, and I expressly leave that point open.

My reasons for the conclusion I have reached are as follows: first, it is clear that if the copy letter were in the hands of a third party I would in restraining him have to except the power of the trial court to subpoena him to produce the latter and his obligation to comply with that order: see per Bankes LJ in *Weld-Blundell v Stephens* [1919] 1 KB 520 at 527, CA. It would be strange if the defendants could subpoena a witness to produce this document yet, having it themselves, not be allowed to tender it in evidence. Secondly, and even more compelling, is the effect of the conflict between the two principles to which I have already referred. In *Elias v Pasmore* [1934] 2 KB 164 at 173, [1934] All ER Rep 380 at 384, it was held accordingly by Horridge J that the police were justified in retaining and using at the trial of Hetherington, documents belonging to Elias which they had seized irregularly when entering the premises to arrest Hetherington. True it is that in *Ghani v Jones* Lord Denning MR criticised the dictum of Horridge J as being too wide, in that he gave the police a right to use the documents in the trial of any person, but with that qualification Lord Denning MR accepted what Horridge J had said. Thus *Elias v Pasmore* is authority for the proposition that the right and duty of the police to prosecute offenders prevails over the accused's right of ownership. He cannot demand his own goods back. By analogy it seems to me that the interest and duty of the defendants as a department of the State to prosecute offenders under the Companies Act 1948 must prevail over the offender's limited proprietary right in equity to restrain a breach of confidence, and here, of course, the doubt suggested by Lord Denning MR does not arise because the accused and the person entitled to the benefit of the confidence are one and the same. This view of the matter is further supported by *Ghani v Jones* itself and the statement by Lord Denning MR of the relevant principles, and particularly the second and third, guiding the right of the police to retain and use articles where no man has been arrested or charged, and a fortiori where, as here, a criminal prosecution is actually pending. I find some further support for this conclusion in the cases of *Saull v Browne* (1874) 9 Ch App 364 and *Kerr v Preston Corpn* (1876) 6 Ch D 463, which say that in general a court of equity will not interfere with a criminal prosecution, although the question there was one of restraining it altogether. For these reasons, in my judgment, the answer to the question propounded in para 14 of the special case is in the negative and the action must be dismissed.

Before parting with the case, however, I should perhaps comment on the speech of Viscount Radcliffe in *Rumping v DPP* [1964] AC 814 at 845, [1962] 3 All ER 256 at 266–7, HL. Counsel for the plaintiff, rightly observing that Lord Radcliffe differed from the rest of the House because they held that there was no rule of public policy rendering marital communications inadmissible, relied on Lord Radcliffe's observation in support of his claim that the copy letter was confidential, there being legal professional privilege for the original. As I have said, in my judgment that follows and counsel had no need to support himself with his dissenting judgment or with *Margaret, Duchess of Argyll v Duke of Argyll* [1967] Ch 302, [1965] 1 All ER 611, on which he also relied. Lord Radcliffe did, however, say this in *Rumping's* Case [1964] AC 814 at 845, [1962] 3 All ER 256 at 266–7, HL:

'Ought the law to apply a different rule merely because the letter has miscarried and has come into the hands of the police? Considering the history and the nature of the principle that lies behind the special rules governing testimony of husband and wife in criminal trials, I do not think that it should. If it does, we must recognise the implications that, personally, I find overwhelmingly distasteful. A husband may gasp or mutter to his wife some agonised self-incrimination, intended for no ear in the world but hers: yet the law will receive and proceed on the evidence of the successful eavesdropper, professional, amateur or accidental. It is free, I suppose, to entertain the testimony of the listening device, if properly proved. An incriminating letter may be intercepted by any means: it may be snatched from the wife's hand after receipt, taken into custody if she has mislaid it accidentally, withdrawn from her possession by one means or another: in all these cases, it is said, the trophy may be carried into court by the prosecution and, given proof that the prisoner is its author, the law has no rule that excludes it from weighing against him as a confession.'

It might be thought at first sight that this is inconsistent with my judgment, but it is not, because there Lord Radcliffe held that communications between husband and wife were not only privileged from disclosure but inadmissible, and therefore his observations about the police intercepting the letter and so forth have no relevance to the question whether they may retain and use in evidence a copy which is admissible but which was supplied to them in breach of confidence.

NOTES

1. Reference should be made to a valuable note by Tapper (1972) 35 MLR 83 and see (1974) 37 MLR 601, Andrews (1989) 105 LQR 608, Newbold (1991) 107 LQR 99. The cases are puzzling. One oddity is that Cozens-Hardy MR, who led for the successful defendant in *Calcraft v Guest*, was a party to *Ashburton v Pape*. His reconciliation of the decisions at a technical level can be regarded as a success only at that level. There is obscurity in the sentence: 'It seems to me that, although Pape has had the good luck to obtain a copy of these documents which he can produce without a breach of this injunction, there is no ground whatever in principle why we should decline to give the plaintiff the protection which in my view is his right as between him and Pape.' This appears to contradict what has gone before in suggesting that the copies can be used in later litigation. The problem may be solved by taking 'this injunction' to refer to Neville J's limited injunction (in contrast to the wide injunction granted by the Court of Appeal). Further, other reports remove the contradiction from what Cozens-Hardy MR says, eg 'although, if Pape has the good luck to obtain a copy of these documents which he can produce without a breach of this injunction . . .' (82 LJ Ch 527 at 529; see Tapper, op cit, at p 86).

2. Goff J in *Butler v Board of Trade* [1971] Ch 680 at 690–1 appears to misunderstand *Ashburton v Pape* in saying: 'if the copy letter were in the hands of a third party I would in restraining him have to except the power of the trial court to subpoena him to produce the letter and his obligations to comply with that order: see per Bankes LJ in *Weld-Blundell v Stephens* [1919] 1 KB 520 at 527.' Bankes LJ there says: 'No contract would be implied as between a professional man and his client not to disclose communications if required by process of law to do so, whereas a contract might well be implied not to disclose the same communications voluntarily.' As Tapper says (op cit, at p 87), this is inconclusive since it 'envisages the confidence arising out of the supposed obligation not to disclose, and not independently of it'. That is, it does not refer to a confidence arising from legal professional privilege or from the duty, enforceable by injunction, not to make copies of privileged documents within the *Ashburton v Pape* doctrine.

3. Whether or not *Calcraft v Guest* and *Ashburton v Pape* are reconcilable at a technical level, they seem to be fundamentally in conflict. If the *Calcraft* doctrine is sound on the basis that it causes more relevant evidence to be put before the court, it is odd that its result can be thwarted by obtaining an injunction in separate proceedings. Alternatively, if the *Ashburton* doctrine is sound in holding that an injunction is obtainable in separate proceedings, why should not the client be entitled to rely on it in the main proceedings to which it is relevant and which he might lose if he cannot? The client's success should not depend on the date at which he found out that he was the victim of a wrongdoer; it should not depend on the chance of whether there is time to institute independent proceedings. It is hard to see that the principal proceedings would be much delayed by determining the issue, admittedly a collateral one, of whether the original was privileged.

4. It should be noted that dicta in *Butler v Board of Trade* substantially extend *Ashburton v Pape* in that Goff J purports to protect all confidential information: 'an innocent recipient of information conveyed in breach of confidence is liable to be restrained' ([1971] Ch 680 at 690). If this were correct, it would mean that the long debate about whether priests, doctors, journalists and other professional men should have a privilege similar to that of lawyers has been pointless, since they were already covered as recipients of confidential information; and *D v National Society for the Prevention of Cruelty to Children* [1978] AC 171, [1977] 1 All ER 589, HL, suggests that it is not correct. The dicta in *Butler's* Case should therefore be confined to the particular context: confidential relationships arising out of information gained by a third party to the lawyer–client relationship. Indeed it would be less likely to cause confusion not to say that an original document is privileged and a copy confidential, but to say that both are privileged.

5. The 'third party exception' to legal professional privilege seems unjust in several ways. The exception arose in an age when eavesdropping and the purloining and intercepting of communications was difficult, rare and unfavoured. Similarly, the Law Reform Committee felt that though the exception was bad there was no urgent need to change it, because 'the circumstances envisaged seldom occur in practice, and in civil proceedings professional etiquette would militate against unfair advantage being taken of them' (16th Report on Privilege in Civil Proceedings, Cmnd 3472 (1967), para 33). Both points are now suspect. For example, though formerly eavesdropping could be guarded against by a proper choice of meeting place and a simple inspection of it, there are now a variety of very efficient mechanical eavesdropping devices. It is not enough to say that the client should take reasonable precautions against disclosure (Wigmore, paras 2325–6), because even if he does he will not be safe. The increased use of these devices may have made them respectable, so that the operation of professional etiquette is unlikely to be a safeguard. A related point is that the client is almost certain to be ignorant of the possibility of losing his privilege. His lawyer will doubtless encourage him to speak by telling him of the privilege, but he is unlikely to tell the client of how it can be lost. If the client knows the exception he may be reluctant to speak for fear of eavesdropping, particularly in prison cells, so that the exception conflicts with the policy of the privilege. If he does not know the exception, it is unfair for his admissions to be held against him since he will not have realised that he was in fact putting himself at risk at the very moment when he sought help. Further, as the Law Reform Committee said, it seems wrong that a party should obtain a procedural advantage as a result of his own or another's wilful misconduct (Cmnd 3472, para 32). Ordered legal procedure seeks to overcome the ill-effects of self-help; to permit one litigant to win his case by stealing documents is regressive.

The exception seems out of step with the policy of legal professional privilege from another point of view. The policy demands that privilege attaches to an interview with a person whom the client mistakenly thinks to be a legal adviser, whether the mistake arises as a result of deceit or innocently (*Feuerheerd v London General Omnibus Co Ltd* [1918] 2 KB 565; cf *Fountain v Young* (1807) 6 Esp 113). Now if the privilege exists when the client mistakenly trusts in a man whom he thinks to be a lawyer, why should it not exist when the client mistakenly trusts in the confidentiality of communications with the lawyer learnt by a third party? A Canadian case provokes further thought on these lines. In *R v Choney* a police agent entered the cell of the accused who could speak only Ruthenian, and represented himself to be an interpreter working for the accused's solicitor and mandated by the latter to get the accused to tell him everything about the case. The accused's incriminating admissions were taken down by two persons concealed behind his cell. Perdue JA and the Manitoba Court of Appeal excluded the evidence of both the interpreter and the eavesdroppers. Several reasons were given for the latter decision. First, had the interviewer been a real lawyer or his agent, he might have taken precautions against eavesdropping ((1908) 13 CCC 289 at 293, per Perdue JA). This point is sound, though neutral on the question of whether the *Calcraft* exception is correct. Secondly, Phippen JA said 'we must treat the whole as an interview with several persons who had fraudulently adopted the character of solicitor's representatives' (ibid, at 296; Richards JA agreed at 295). This is fictitious; the accused never believed there was more than one representative. Thirdly, the interpreter's evidence was excluded because it was gained by a trick, and 'as part of the trick the listeners were placed where they could overhear what passed' (ibid, at 296, per Phippen JA). This is more convincing, and suggests that all breaches of the privilege should result in exclusion of the evidence.

A further respect in which English law on this point is at odds with its underlying justification is this. The English rule is that the privilege is lost even if the disclosure is made voluntarily by the lawyer in bad faith. The evidence is admissible whether the client's privilege is violated by his lawyer or a third party. The client is only protected against a faithless lawyer if the latter attempts to violate the privilege while in court. This makes the privilege easily capable of being evaded. American decisions have overcome this weakness by a compromise: the privilege continues if a breach of confidence occurs as a result of the lawyer's voluntary conduct (Wigmore, para 2325, n 1). As a practical matter this is a step in the right direction, though it lacks the internal consistency of the English position. But it provokes the question: if the privilege survives the lawyer's bad faith why should it not survive the opponent's bad faith?

6. How does the rule under consideration relate to the rule that illegally or improperly obtained evidence is admissible, subject to the discretion of the judge in a criminal trial to exclude evidence the admission of which would operate unfairly against the accused? Now whatever the merits of admitting the ordinary kind of improperly obtained evidence, there are surely stronger arguments against admitting evidence seized in violation of legal privilege. This involves a double impropriety: the client is the victim of wrongful conduct at the very moment when he thought he was safest against it. In any event, there are strong arguments against the English common law rule admitting illegally obtained evidence, see ch 9.3. The courts in Scotland, Eire and Australia tend to permit admission only if it is required in connexion with crimes which cannot be prosecuted without it, or if it was obtained by accidental or trivial illegality, or in circumstances requiring urgent action. Such a rule has the drawback of uncertainty of operation; any exception to legal privilege, operating in a much narrower area, can be governed by simpler and more clear-cut rules. One compromise might be the Law Reform Committee's proposal that only evidence obtained by crimes or deliberate torts should remain privileged. But in the interests of maintaining the integrity of the policies underlying the legal privilege, and remembering that the privilege will cause little evidence to be lost to the court in cases where the client goes into the witness-box, it may be thought desirable to continue the privilege no matter how the third party came to learn of the privileged information.

7. It is instructive to observe the changes over the last thirty years in American law reform proposals. In 1942 the American Law Institute's Model Code of Evidence, r 210(c)(iii), provided that the privilege only continued when the third person learnt of the confidential communication 'as a result of an intentional breach of the lawyer's duty of non-disclosure by the lawyer or his agent or servant'. In 1953 the Uniform Rules of Evidence, r 26(1)(c), went further in providing that the client could prevent third parties disclosing a privileged communication 'if it came to the knowledge of such witness (i) in the course of its transmittal between the client and the lawyer, or (ii) in a manner not reasonably to be anticipated by the client, or (iii) as a result of breach of the lawyer–client relationship'. The 1971 version of the proposed Federal Rules of Evidence, r 503(b), made the client's right to prevent third parties testifying unqualified (though in the event the final version of the rules left matters of privilege in general to the common law).

In *ITC Film Distributors Ltd v Video Exchange Ltd* [1982] Ch 431, [1982] 2

All ER 241, Warner J refused to extend *Calcraft v Guest* to documents obtained by a trick practised in the courtroom. *R v Uljee* [1982] 1 NZLR 561 went further. The New Zealand Court of Appeal excluded evidence by a police constable as to what passed between the accused and his solicitor. The case is a strong one, for the constable was there not to eavesdrop but in case someone attempted to leave the premises. Cooke J asserted the following general rule: 'A third party who has overheard [a communication subject to legal professional privilege], if oral, or come into possession of it or a copy of it, if written, should not be allowed to give evidence of it unless the client waives the privilege'; communications for criminal or unlawful purposes remain unprotected.

While *R v Uljee* is the furthest point to which any court has gone, *Calcraft v Guest* has been described as 'rather remarkable' by Gibbs CJ in *Baker v Campbell* (1983) 153 CLR 52 at 67, as perhaps requiring 'some qualification' by Mason J in the same case at 80, as arguable by Deane J in the same case at 112, and as an authority not to be followed in Australia by Brennan J in the same case at 110. In *Goddard v Nationwide Building Society* [1987] QB 670 at 686, [1986] 3 All ER 264 at 272, CA, Nourse LJ said the 'spirit' of *Lord Ashburton v Pape* ought to be supreme; and in that case at 683 and 270 May LJ said that the law was not 'logically satisfactory'. On the other hand, the rule in *Calcraft v Guest* has been said 'probably' to be the law by Lord Simon of Glaisdale in *Waugh v British Railways Board* [1980] AC 521 at 536, [1979] 2 All ER 1169 at 1177, and as authority in *Goddard v Nationwide Building Society* [1987] QB 670 at 683, [1986] 3 All ER 264 at 270 and 271, CA. It was followed in *R v Tomkins* (1977) 67 Cr App Rep 181, CA, and by the Supreme Court of Canada in *Descoteaux v Mierzwinski* (1982) 141 DLR (3d) 590. See also *Guinness Peat Properties Ltd v Fitzroy Robinson Partnership (a firm)* [1987] 2 All ER 716, [1987] 1 WLR 1027, CA; *Re Briamore Manufacturing Ltd (in liq)* [1986] 3 All ER 132, [1986] 1 WLR 1429; *Webster v James Chapman & Co* [1989] 3 All ER 939 and *Hooker Corpn Ltd v Darling Harbour Authority* (1987) 9 NSWLR 538. In view of the state of the authorities, it is hard to disagree with Mahoney JA's view that the question may be ripe for re-examination by appropriate appellate courts: *Yuill v Corporate Affairs Commission of New South Wales* (1990) 20 NSWLR 386 at 412.

8. The subject just discussed intersects with problems of waiver in the not uncommon circumstance of accidental disclosure in the course of discovery of privileged material. The Court of Appeal has recently stated the principles as follows in *Guinness Peat Properties Ltd v Fitzroy Robinson Partnership (a firm)* [1987] 2 All ER 716, [1987] 1 WLR 1027, CA. First, where a solicitor for one party mistakenly includes a document for which privilege could properly have been claimed in a list of documents without claiming privilege, the court will permit the list to be amended before inspection has occurred. (Indeed, probably a mere reference of that kind is not a waiver even of a limited sort: *Lyell v Kennedy (No 3)* (1884) 27 Ch D 1 at 24. Certainly it has been held not to be in circumstances of accelerated discovery: *Hooker Corpn Ltd v Darling Harbour Authority* (1987) 9 NSWLR 538.) Secondly, in general where the document has been inspected by the other party, it is too late for the party claiming privilege to attempt to correct the mistake by applying for a *Lord Ashburton v Pape* injunction. Thirdly, exceptions exist to that general rule where inspection has been procured by fraud or where the inspecting party has been permitted to see the document only as the result of an obvious mistake: a *Lord Ashburton v Pape* injunction would ordinarily be granted in the absence of some vitiating factor such as inordinate delay (*Derby & Co Ltd v Weldon (No 8)* [1990] 3 All ER 762, [1991] 1 WLR 79, CA). The Court of Appeal recognised the possibility of other exceptions, and *Hooker Corpn Ltd v Darling Harbour Authority* (1987) 9 NSWLR 538 is an example in circumstances of accelerated discovery in a commercial cause.

2 Without prejudice statements

If a party to litigation has previously made an offer to compromise it, there may be circumstances in which the offer constitutes an admission because it reveals a consciousness of the unsoundness of his case. However, any offer of a compromise made without prejudice to the maker's rights cannot be admitted into evidence, and is not liable to inspection on discovery, without the consent of both maker and receiver; these principles apply also against third parties as well against the parties to the negotiations: *Rush & Tompkins Ltd v Greater London Council* [1989] AC 1280, [1988] 3 All ER 737, HL. The purpose of the privilege is to reduce litigation by encouraging the settlement and compromising of disputes. See Vaver (1974) 9 UBCL Rev 85.

Whether letters are without prejudice depends not on whether they are so headed but on the intentions of the parties.

Statements made to a mediator by estranged spouses may not be disclosed by him without the consent of the parties (*McTaggart v McTaggart* [1949] P 94, [1948] 2 All ER 754, CA); this is so when only one of the parties has approached a mediator (*Mole v Mole* [1951] P 21, [1950] 2 All ER 328, CA). Mediators would include doctors, clergymen, solicitors, marriage guidance counsellors, probation officers and children's welfare officers. The privilege is joint in the sense that it cannot be waived without the consent of both spouses (*Theodoropoulas v Theodoropoulas* [1964] P 311, [1963] 2 All ER 772). The statements made may concern reconciliation, the custody of children, or financial arrangements (*Rodgers v Rodgers* (1964) 114 CLR 608). This type of privilege is analysed as a 'public interest' exception to admissibility in *D v National Society for the Prevention of Cruelty to Children* [1978] AC 171, [1977] 1 All ER 589, HL; see p 456, post.

As a general rule, even if an agreement is reached as a result of without prejudice negotiations the privilege does not cease to apply: *Rush & Tompkins Ltd v Greater London Council* [1989] AC 1280, [1988] 3 All ER 737, HL. However, without prejudice communications may be examined to decide whether an agreement has in fact been reached (*Tomlin v Standard Telephones and Cables Ltd* [1969] 3 All ER 201, [1969] 1 WLR 1378, CA).

Without prejudice communications to which this privilege applies may be admitted merely to prove that certain statements were made, eg as libels, acts of bankruptcy, or threats to sue for patent infringement, or to prove the dates on which they were made in order to establish or rebut defences turning on delay.

A common modern technique is a making of offers 'without prejudice save as to costs'; the offer is inadmissible on liability, but may be admitted on the question of costs to show the unreasonableness of the behaviour of the party who did not accept the offer in the light of the ultimate outcome of the case: *Cutts v Head* [1984] Ch 290, [1984] 1 All ER 597; *Calderbank v Calderbank* [1976] Fam 93, [1975] 3 All ER 333, CA; RSC Ord 22, r 14.

3 Miscellaneous

A ABOLITION

The Civil Evidence Act 1968, s 16, and the Police and Criminal Evidence Act 1984, s 80(9), abolished a number of privileges. One was the rule that a party cannot be compelled to produce any document relating solely to his own case and not tending to impeach that case or support his opponent's (s 16(2) of the 1968 Act). This had no application to criminal cases. Another was the rule that a person other than a party could not be compelled to produce any document relating to his title to land (s 16(1)(*b*)). This has virtually no practical application in criminal proceedings. Thirdly, a witness in any proceedings instituted in consequence of adultery, whether party or not, could refuse to answer questions tending to show his or her adultery (s 16(5), see *Nast v Nast* [1972] Fam 142, [1972] 1 All ER 1171, CA). This never existed in criminal cases. Fourthly, spouses had a privilege not to give evidence of whether marital intercourse did or did not occur during any period; it was abolished in civil cases by s 16(4) of the Civil Evidence Act 1968 and in criminal cases by s 80(9) of the Police and Criminal Evidence Act 1984. Fifthly, a husband or wife had a privilege not to disclose any communication made to him or her by the other spouse during the marriage. It was abolished in civil cases by s 16(3) of the Civil Evidence Act 1968 and in criminal cases by s 80(9) of the Police and Criminal Evidence Act 1984.

B CREATION OF NEW PRIVILEGES

There is a statutory privilege co-extensive with legal professional privileges for communications between a person and his patent agent: see now s 280 of the Copyright, Designs and Patents Act 1988. A similar privilege was created for communications with trade mark agents by s 284, and for communications with licensed conveyancers by s 33 of the Administration of Justice Act 1985. There is strong authority against journalists having a privilege respecting their sources of information (*McGuiness v A-G of Victoria* (1940) 63 CLR 73; *A-G v Mulholland* [1963] 2 QB 477, [1963] 1 All ER 767, CA; *British Steel Corpn v Granada Television Ltd* [1981] AC 1096, [1981] 1 All ER 417). A limited statutory privilege has been created by s 10 of the Contempt of Court Act 1981, but it does not apply where the party seeking disclosure establishes that 'disclosure is necessary in the interests of justice or national security or for the prevention of disorder or crime' unless the court exercises its discretion in favour of non-disclosure: *Secretary of State for Defence v Guardian Newspapers Ltd* [1985] AC 339, [1984] 3 All ER 601, HL; *Maxwell v Pressdram Ltd* [1987]

1 All ER 656, [1987] 1 WLR 298, CA; *Re An Inquiry under the Company Securities (Insider Dealing) Act 1985* [1988] AC 660, [1988] 1 All ER 203, HL.

The Civil Evidence Act 1968 and the Police and Criminal Evidence Act 1984 did not grant any new privileges, eg to ministers of religion or medical practitioners; and the Criminal Law Revision Committee had recommended no change (CLRC paras 273–6). Part II (ss 8–14) of the Police and Criminal Evidence Act 1984 does aim to provide a certain amount of protection for 'excluded material' (chiefly medical and psychological records and journalistic material: s 11) and 'special procedure material' (including material, other than that to which the legal professional privilege applies, acquired in the course of a trade, profession or occupation, and held subject to a duty of confidence: s 14). In order to obtain such material, an application must be made inter partes to a Circuit Judge according to the procedure laid down in Sch 1 to the Act. This protection, however, is somewhat illusory. It can only apply to material which has a physical existence (eg as a document, including information stored in a computer: Sch 1, para 5). It does not amount to a privilege, and nothing in the Act prevents the holder of the information being called as a witness and questioned about it. A further disadvantage for the confidant is that he has no locus standi in the proceedings before the Circuit Judge, and may indeed not know that the application has been made (*R v Crown Court at Manchester, ex p Taylor* [1988] 2 All ER 769, [1988] 1 WLR 705, DC; *Barclays Bank plc v Taylor* [1989] 3 All ER 563, [1989] 1 WLR 1066, CA; Zuckerman [1990] Crim LR 472).

In the absence of privilege, the court has a discretion to disallow questions which unduly embarrass the witness (*Hunter v Mann* [1974] QB 767, [1974] 2 All ER 414, DC, but there was division on this point in the House of Lords in *D v National Society for the Prevention of Cruelty to Children* [1978] AC 171, [1977] 1 All ER 589; and see *Broad v Pitt* (1828) 3 C & P 518). Most jurisdictions other than England recognise a privilege at common law or by statute for a range of confidential communications outside lawyer–client or similar relationships.

CHAPTER 19

Public Policy

1 State interest

Evidence may be excluded on grounds of 'public policy' or 'Crown privilege'. The latter title, though commonly used, is really a misnomer, because the essence of a privilege is that it can be waived by its holder, whereas if a claim to Crown privilege is not taken by the Crown or one of the parties, it must be taken by the court. The relevant rules are usually applied to the disclosure of documents, but extend also to oral evidence.

The court may uphold a claim to the privilege if the contents of a document should not be revealed in the public interest, eg because they would assist the nation's enemies in wartime to understand the design of a new submarine: *Duncan v Cammell Laird & Co Ltd* [1942] AC 624, [1942] 1 All ER 587, HL. Other examples are military plans (*Asiatic Petroleum Co Ltd v Anglo-Persian Oil Co Ltd* [1916] 1 KB 822, [1916–17] All ER Rep 637, CA) and diplomatic despatches (*M Isaacs & Sons Ltd v Cook* [1925] 2 KB 391). This is usually referred to as a 'contents' claim. The court may also uphold a 'class' claim, namely that a document should not be disclosed because, though its own contents are innocuous, it belongs to a class of documents which should not be produced. Class claims are usually based on the argument that the success of the claim is necessary for the proper functioning of the public service in that if it were not upheld civil servants would communicate with each other less candidly.

The usual method of claiming the privilege is for the Minister or permanent head of the relevant department to swear an affidavit or certify that each document to be excluded should be excluded on either class or contents grounds. The Minister or permanent head must himself inspect the documents for which he claims privilege and personally judge whether or not it should be disclosed. The judge has a discretionary power to inspect the documents and judge for himself whether the interests of the administration of justice in full disclosure outweigh the injurious effects of disclosure on the interests of the State. If the former consideration prevails, the judge may order disclosure.

On a number of these points there were differences between the English courts on the one hand and the rest of the common law world and Scotland on the other between 1942 and 1968. This culminated in many critical dicta in the Court of Appeal in the middle 1960s. The differences were resolved by the House of Lords in *Conway v Rimmer*.

Conway v Rimmer   [1968] AC 910, [1968] 1 All ER 874, HL

A probationer police constable was prosecuted for theft by a superintendent. The jury stopped the case. In subsequent proceedings for malicious prosecution brought by the constable against the superintendent the Home Secretary claimed privilege for three probationary reports and a report by a District Police Training Centre on the plaintiff, as well as a report leading to his prosecution. The House of Lords held that the courts had jurisdiction to inspect the document and order production. (Subsequently production was ordered: [1968] AC 910 at 996–7, [1968] 2 All ER 304n.)

Lord Reid: The question whether such a statement by a Minister of the Crown should be accepted as conclusively preventing any court from ordering production of any of the documents to which it applies is one of very great importance in the administration of justice. If the commonly accepted interpretation of the decision of this house in *Duncan v Cammell Laird & Co Ltd* [1942] AC 624, [1942] 1 All ER 587, HL, is to remain authoritative the question admits of only one answer – the Minister's statement is final and conclusive. Normally I would be very slow to question the authority of a unanimous decision of this House only twenty-five years old which was carefully considered and obviously intended to lay down a general rule. But this decision has several abnormal features. Viscount Simon LC thought that on this matter the law in Scotland was the same as the law in England, and he clearly intended to lay down a rule applicable to the whole of the United Kingdom. In *Glasgow Corpn v Central Land Board* 1956 SC (HL) 1, however, this House held that that was not so, with the result that today on this question the law is different in the two countries. There are many chapters of the law where for historical and other reasons it is quite proper that the law should be different in the two countries; but here we are dealing purely with public policy – with the proper relation between the powers of the executive and the powers of the courts – and I can see no rational justification for the law on this matter being different in the two countries. Secondly, events have proved that the rule supposed to have been laid down in *Duncan's* case is far from satisfactory. In the large number of cases in England and elsewhere which have been cited in argument much dissatisfaction has been expressed, and I have not observed even one expression of whole-hearted approval. Moreover, a statement made by Viscount Kilmuir, LC in 1956 on behalf of the government, to which I shall return later, makes it clear that that government did not regard it as consonant with public policy to maintain the rule to the full extent which existing authorities had held to be justifiable.

I have no doubt that the case of *Duncan v Cammell Laird & Co Ltd* was rightly decided. The plaintiff sought discovery of documents relating to the submarine. That is including a contract for the hull and machinery and plans and specifications. The First Lord of the Admiralty had stated that 'it would be injurious to the public interest that any of the said documents should be disclosed to any person'. Any of these documents might well have given valuable information, or at least clues, to the skilled eye of an agent of a foreign power; but Lord Simon took the opportunity to deal with the whole question of the right of the Crown to prevent production of documents in a litigation. Yet a study of his speech leaves me with the strong impression that throughout he had primarily in mind cases where discovery or disclosure would involve a danger of real prejudice to the national interest. I find it difficult to believe that his speech would have been the same if the case had related, as the present case does, to discovery of routine reports on a probationer constable . . . [S]umming up towards the end, he said ([1942] AC 624 at 642, [1942] 1 All ER 587 at 595, HL):

> 'The rule that the interest of the State must not be put in jeopardy by producing documents which would injure it is a principle to be observed in administering justice, quite unconnected with the interests or claims of the particular parties in litigation . . .'

Surely it would be grotesque to speak of the interest of the State being put in jeopardy by disclosure of a routine report on a probationer. Lord Simon did not say very much about objections ([1942] AC 624 at 635, [1942] 1 All ER 587 at 592, HL)

> '. . . based upon the view that the public interest requires a particular class of communications with, or within, a public department to be protected from production on the ground that the candour and completeness of such communications might be prejudiced if they were ever liable to be disclosed in subsequent litigation rather than upon the contents of the particular document itself.'

At the end he said that a Minister ([1942] AC 624 at 642, [1942] 1 All ER 587 at 595, HL)

'. . . ought not to take the responsibility of withholding production except in cases where the public interest would otherwise be damnified, eg where disclosure would be injurious to national defence, or to good diplomatic relations, or where the practice of keeping a class of documents secret is necessary for the proper functioning of the public service.'

I find it difficult to believe that he would have put these three examples on the same level if he had intended the third to cover such minor matters as a routine report by a relatively junior officer. My impression is strengthened by the passage at the very end of the speech ([1942] AC 642 at 643, [1942] 1 All ER 587 at 595–6, HL):

'. . . The public interest is also the interest of every subject of the realm, and while, in these exceptional cases, the private citizen may seem to be denied what is to his immediate advantage, he, like the rest of us, would suffer if the needs of protecting the interests of the country as a whole were not ranked as a prior obligation.'

Would he have spoken of 'these exceptional cases' or of 'the needs of protecting the interests of the country as a whole' if he had intended to include all manner of routine communications? Did he really mean that the protection of such communications is a 'prior obligation' in a case where a man's reputation or fortune is at stake and withholding the document makes it impossible for justice to be done?

It is universally recognised that here there are two kinds of public interest which may clash. There is the public interest that harm shall not be done to the nation or the public service by disclosure of certain documents, and there is the public interest that the administration of justice shall not be frustrated by the withholding of documents which must be produced if justice is to be done. There are many cases where the nature of the injury which would or might be done to the nation or the public service is of so grave a character that no other interest, public or private, can be allowed to prevail over it. With regard to such cases it would be proper to say, as Lord Simon did, that to order production of the document in question would put the interest of the state in jeopardy; but there are many other cases where the possible injury to the public service is much less and there one would think that it would be proper to balance the public interests involved. I do not believe that Lord Simon really meant that the smallest probability of injury to the public service must always outweigh the gravest frustration of the administration of justice.

It is to be observed that, in a passage which I have already quoted, Lord Simon referred to the practice of keeping a class of documents secret being '*necessary* (my italics) for the proper functioning of the public interest'. But the certificate of the Home Secretary in the present case does not go nearly so far as that. It merely says that the production of a document of the classes to which it refers would be 'injurious to the public service': it does not say what degree of injury is to be apprehended. It may be advantageous to the functioning of the public service that reports of this kind should be kept secret – that is the view of the Home Secretary – but I would be very surprised if anyone said that that was necessary.

There are now many large public bodies, such as British Railways, and the National Coal Board, the proper and efficient functioning of which is very necessary for many reasons, including the safety of the public. The Attorney-General made it clear that Crown privilege is not and cannot be invoked to prevent disclosure of similar documents made by them or their servants, even if it were said that this is required for the proper and efficient functioning of that public service. I find it difficult to see why it should be *necessary* to withhold whole classes of routine 'communications with or within a public department', but quite unnecessary to withhold similar communications with or within a public corporation. There the safety of the public may well depend on the candour and completeness of reports made by subordinates, whose duty it is to draw attention to defects. So far as I know, however, no one has ever suggested that public safety has been endangered by the candour or completeness of such reports having been inhibited by the fact that they may have to be produced if the interests of the due administration of justice should ever require production at any time.

I must turn now to a statement made by Viscount Kilmuir LC in this House on 6 June 1956. When counsel proposed to read this statement your Lordships had doubts, which I shared, as to its admissibility; but we did permit it to be read, and, as the argument proceeded, its importance emerged. With a minor amendment made on 8 March 1962, it appears still to operate as a direction to, or at least a guide for, Ministers who swear affidavits. So we may assume that in the present case the Home Secretary acted in accordance with the views expressed in Lord Kilmuir's statement. The statement sets out the grounds on which Crown privilege is to be claimed. Having set out the first ground that disclosure of the contents of the particular document would injure the public interest, it proceeds:

'The second ground is that the document falls within a class which the public interest requires to be withheld from production, and Lord Simon particularised this head of public interest as "the proper functioning of the public service".'

There is no reference to Lord Simon's exhortation, which I have already quoted, that a Minister ought not to take the responsibility of withholding production of a class of documents except where the practice of keeping a class of documents secret is necessary for the proper functioning of the public service. Then the statement proceeds:

'The reason why the law sanctions the claiming of Crown privilege on the "class" ground is the need to secure freedom and candour of communications with and within the public service, so that government decisions can be taken on the best advice and with the fullest information. In order to secure this it is necessary that the class of documents to which privilege applies should be clearly settled, so that the person giving advice or information should know that he is doing so in confidence. Any system whereby a document falling within the class might, as a result of a later decision, be required to be produced in evidence, would destroy that confidence and undermine the whole basis of class privilege, because there would be no certainty at the time of writing that the document would not be disclosed.'

But later in the statement, the position taken is very different. A number of cases are set out in which Crown privilege should not be claimed. The most important for present purposes is:

'We propose that if medical documents, or indeed other documents, are relevant to the defence in criminal proceedings, Crown privilege should not be claimed.'

The only exception specifically mentioned is statements by informers. That is a very wide-ranging exception, for the Attorney-General stated that it applied at least to all manner of routine communications and even to prosecutions for minor offences. Thus it can no longer be said that the writer of such communications has any 'certainty at the time of writing that the document would not be disclosed'. So we have the curious result that 'freedom and candour of communication' is supposed not to be inhibited by knowledge of the writer that his report may be disclosed in a criminal case, but would still be supposed to be inhibited if he thought that his report might be disclosed in a civil case.

The Attorney-General did not deny that, even where the full contents of a report have already been made public in a criminal case, Crown privilege is still claimed for that report in a later civil case; and he was quite candid about the reason for that. Crown privilege is claimed in the civil case not to protect the document – its contents are already public property – but to protect the writer from civil liability should he be sued for libel or other tort. No doubt the government have weighed the danger that knowledge of such protection might encourage malicious writers against the advantage that honest reporters shall not be subjected to vexatious actions, and have come to the conclusion that it is an advantage to the public service to afford this protection; but it seems very far removed from the original purpose of Crown privilege.

The statement, as it has been explained to us, makes clear another point. The Minister who withholds production of a 'class' document has no duty to consider the degree of public interest involved in a particular case by frustrating in that way the due administration of justice. If it is in the public interest in his view to withhold documents of that class, then it matters not whether the result of withholding a document is merely to deprive a litigant of some evidence on a minor issue in a case of little importance, or on the other hand is to make it impossible to do justice at all in a case of the greatest importance. I cannot think that it is satisfactory that there should be no means at all of weighing, in any civil case, the public interest involved in withholding the document against the public interest that it should be produced. So it appears to me that the present position is so unsatisfactory that this House must re-examine the whole question in light of the authorities.

Two questions will arise: first, whether the court is to have any right to question the finality of a Minister's certificate and, secondly, if it has such a right, how and in what circumstances that right is to exercised and made effective.

A Minister's certificate may be given on one or other of two grounds: either because it would be against the public interest to disclose the contents of the particular document or documents in question, or because the document belongs to a class of documents which ought to be withheld whether or not there is anything in the particular document in question disclosure of which would be against the public interest. It does not appear that any serious difficulties have arisen or are likely to arise with regard to the first class. However wide the power of the court may be held to be, cases would be very rare in which it could be proper to question the view of the responsible Minister that it would be contrary to the public interest to make public the contents of a particular document. A question might arise whether it would be possible to separate those parts of a document of which disclosure would be innocuous from those parts which ought not to be made public, but I need not pursue that question now. In the present case your Lordships are directly concerned with the second class of documents.

[Lord Reid discussed the earlier authorities and continued:] The last important case before *Duncan's Case* was *Robinson v South Australia State (No 2)*. The state government had assumed the function of acquiring and marketing all wheat grown in the state and distributing the proceeds to the growers. A number of actions was brought alleging negligence in carrying out this function. The Australian courts had upheld objections by the state to discovery of a mass of documents in their possession. For reasons into which I need not enter, the Privy Council could not finally decide the matter. What they did was ([1931] AC 704 at 723, [1931] All ER Rep 333 at 341, PC):

'. . . to remit the case to the Supreme Court of South Australia with a direction that it is a proper one for the exercise by that court of its power of itself inspecting the documents for which privilege is set up in order to see whether the claim is justified. Their lordships have already given reasons for their conclusion that the court is possessed of such a power.'

This case was of course dealt with in *Duncan's* case, but not, I venture to think, in a very satisfactory way. Lord Simon said that ([1942] AC 624 at 641, [1942] 1 All ER 587 at 595, HL): 'Their Lordships' conclusion was partly based on their interpretation of a rule of court . . .' In fact it was not. The passage which I have quoted occurs in the judgment before there is any reference to the rule of court. Beyond that Lord Simon said no more than 'I cannot agree with this view'. So he thought that, even where discovery is sought in an action against the State arising out of what was in effect a commercial transaction, the view of the Minister is conclusive. Lord Kilmuir's statement, however, promised a considerable relaxation in contract cases.

I shall not examine the earlier Scottish authorities in detail because the position in Scotland has now been made clear in the *Glasgow Corpn* case, where the earlier authorities were fully considered. Viscount Simonds said (1956 SC (HL) 1 at p 11):

'In the course of the present appeal we have had the advantage of an exhaustive examination of the relevant law from the earliest times, and it has left me in no doubt that there always has been and is now in the law of Scotland an inherent power of the court to override the Crown's objection to produce documents on the ground that it would injure the public interest to do so.'

Now I must examine the English cases since 1942 . . .

These cases open up a new field which must be kept in view when considering whether a Minister's certificate is to be regarded as conclusive. I do not doubt that it is proper to prevent the use of any document, wherever it comes from, if disclosure of its contents would really injure the national interest, and I do not doubt that it is proper to prevent any witness, whoever he may be, from disclosing facts which in the national interest ought not to be disclosed. Moreover, it is the duty of the court to do this without the intervention of any Minister if possible serious injury to the national interest is readily apparent. In this field, however, it is more than ever necessary that in a doubtful case the alleged public interest in concealment should be balanced against the public interest that the administration of justice should not be frustrated. If the Minister, who has no duty to balance these conflicting public interests, says no more than that in his opinion the public interest requires concealment, and if that is to be accepted as conclusive in this field as well as with regard to documents in his possession, it seems to me not only that very serious injustice may be done to the parties, but also that the due administration of justice may be gravely impaired for quite inadequate reasons.

It cannot be said that there would be any constitutional impropriety in enabling the court to overrule a Minister's objection. That is already the law in Scotland. In Commonwealth jurisdictions from which there is an appeal to the Privy Council the courts generally follow *Robinson's* case [1931] AC 704, [1931] All ER Rep 333, PC, and, where they do not, they follow *Duncan's* case [1942] AC 624, [1942] 1 All ER 587, HL, with reluctance; and a limited citation of authority from the United States seems to indicate the same trend. I observe that in *United States v Reynolds*, Vinson CJ in delivering the opinion of the Supreme Court said (345 US 1 at 9–10 (1952)):

'Regardless of how it is articulated, some like formula of compromise must be applied here. Judicial control over the evidence in a case cannot be abdicated to the caprice of executive officers. Yet we will not go so far as to say that the court may automatically require a complete disclosure to the judge before the claim of privilege will be accepted in any case. It may be possible to satisfy the court, from all the circumstances of the case, that there is a reasonable danger that compulsion of the evidence will expose military matters which, in the interest of national security, should not be divulged. When this is the case, the occasion for the privilege is appropriate, and the court should not jeopardise the security which the privilege is meant to protect by insisting upon an examination of the evidence, even by the judge alone in chambers.'

Lord Simon did not say that courts in England have no power to overrule the executive. He said in *Duncan's* case [1942] AC 624 at 642, [1942] 1 All ER 587 at 599, HL:

'The decision ruling out such documents is the decision of the judge . . . It is the judge who is in control of the trial, not the executive, but the proper ruling for the judge to give is as above expressed.'

that is, to accept the Minister's view in every case. In my judgment, in considering what it is 'proper' for a court to do we must have regard to the need, shown by twenty-five years' experience since *Duncan's* case, that the courts should balance the public interest in the proper administration of justice against the public interest in withholding any evidence which a Minister considers ought to be withheld.

I would therefore propose that the House ought now to decide that courts have and are entitled to exercise a power and duty to hold a balance between the public interest, as expressed by a Minister, to withhold certain documents or other evidence, and the public interest in ensuring the proper administration of justice. That does not mean that a court would reject a Minister's view: full weight must be given to it in every case, and if the Minister's reasons are of a character which judicial experience is not competent to weigh then the Minister's view must prevail; but experience has shown that reasons given for withholding whole classes of documents are often not of that character. For example a court is perfectly well able to assess the likelihood that, if the writer of a certain class of document knew that there was a chance that his report might be produced in legal proceedings, he would make a less full and candid report than he would otherwise have done.

I do not doubt that there are certain classes of documents which ought not to be disclosed whatever their content may be. Virtually everyone agrees that cabinet minutes and the like ought not to be disclosed until such time as they are only of historical interest; but I do not think that many people would give as the reason that premature disclosure would prevent candour in the cabinet. To my mind the most important reason is that such disclosure would create or fan ill-informed or captious public or political criticism. The business of government is difficult enough as it is, and no government could contemplate with equanimity the inner workings of the government machine being exposed to the gaze of those ready to criticise without adequate knowledge of the background and perhaps with some axe to grind. That must in my view also apply to all documents concerned with policy making within departments including it may be minutes and the like by quite junior officials and correspondence with outside bodies. Further, it may be that deliberations about a particular case require protection as much as deliberations about policy. I do not think that it is possible to limit such documents by any definition; but there seems to me to be a wide difference between such documents and routine reports. There may be special reasons for withholding some kinds of routine documents, but I think that the proper test to be applied is to ask, in the language of Lord Simon in *Duncan's* case, whether the withholding of a document because it belongs to a particular class is really 'necessary for the proper functioning of the public service'.

It appears to me that, if the Minister's reasons are such that a judge can properly weigh them, he must on the other hand consider what is the probable importance in the case before him of the documents or other evidence sought to be withheld. If he decides that on balance the documents probably ought to be produced, I think that it would generally be best that he should see them before ordering production and, if he thinks that the Minister's reasons are not clearly expressed, he will have to see the documents before ordering production. I can see nothing wrong in the judge seeing documents without their being shown to the parties. Lord Simon said in *Duncan's* case [1942] AC 624 at 640, [1942] 1 All ER 587 at 594, HL, that, where the Crown is a party, this would amount to communicating with one party to the exclusion of the other. I do not agree. The parties see the Minister's reasons. Where a document has not been prepared for the information of the judge, it seems to me a misuse of language to say that the judge 'communicates with' the holder of the document by reading it. If on reading the document he still thinks that it ought to be produced, he will order its production.

It is important, however, that the Minister should have a right to appeal before the document is produced. This matter was not fully investigated in the argument before your lordships; but it does appear that in one way or another there can be an appeal if the document is in the custody of a servant of the Crown or of a person who is willing to co-operate with the Minister. There may be difficulty if it is in the hands of a person who wishes to produce it. That difficulty, however, could occur today if a witness wishes to give some evidence which the Minister unsuccessfully urges the court to prevent from being given. It may be that this is a matter which deserves further investigation by the Crown authorities.

The documents in this case are in the possession of a police force. The position of the police is peculiar. They are not servants of the Crown and they do not take orders from the government. But they are carrying out an essential function of government, and various Crown rights, privileges and exemptions have been held to apply to them . . . It has never been denied that they are entitled to Crown privilege with regard to documents, and it is essential that they should have it.

The police are carrying on an unending war with criminals many of whom are today highly intelligent. So it is essential that there should be no disclosure of anything which might give any useful information to those who organise criminal activities; and it would generally be wrong to require disclosure in a civil case of anything which might be material in a pending prosecution, but after a verdict has been given, or it has been decided to take no proceedings, there is not the same need for secrecy. With regard to other documents there seems to be no greater need for protection than in the case of departments of government.

It appears to me to be most improbable that any harm would be done by disclosure of the probationary reports on the appellant or of the report from the Police Training Centre. With regard to the report which the respondent made to his chief constable with a view to the prosecution of the appellant there could be more doubt, although no suggestion was made in argument that disclosure of its contents would be harmful now that the appellant has been acquitted. As I have said, these documents may prove to be of vital importance in this litigation.

In my judgment this appeal should be allowed and these documents ought now to be required to be produced for inspection. If it is then found that disclosure would not, in your lordships' view, be prejudicial to the public interest, or that any possibility of such prejudice is, in the case of each of the documents, insufficient to justify its being withheld, then disclosure should be ordered.

[Lords Morris of Borth-y-Gest, Hodson, Pearce and Upjohn delivered concurring judgments.]

Burmah Oil Company Limited v Bank of England
[1980] AC 1090, [1979] 3 All ER 700, HL

An agreement was made between the appellant oil company and the Bank of England acting under the direction of the government with a view to rescuing the company from financial difficulties. One term of the agreement was a sale to the bank of shares in British Petroleum. The company commenced proceedings to set aside the sale. Crown privilege was claimed for some of the bank's documents.

Lord Scarman: It is said – and this view commended itself to the majority of the Court of Appeal – that the bank has given very full discovery of the documents directly relevant to the critical issue in the action, namely, the conduct by the bank of the negotiations with Burmah: that Burmah knows as much about this issue as does the bank: and that it can be fully investigated and decided upon the documents disclosed and the evidence available to Burmah without recourse to documents noting or recording the private discussions between the bank and the government. Upon this view, Burmah's attempt to see these documents is no more than a fishing expedition.

I totally reject this view of the case. First, as a matter of law, the documents for which immunity is claimed relate to the issues in the action and, according to the *Peruvian Guano* formulation, 11 QBD 55, may well assist towards a fair disposal of the case. It is unthinkable that in the absence of a public immunity objection and without a judicial inspection of the documents disclosure would have been refused. Secondly, common sense must be allowed to creep into the picture. Burmah's case is not merely that the bank exerted pressure: it is that the bank acted unreasonably, abusing its power and taking an unconscionable advantage of the weakness of Burmah. Upon these questions the withheld documents may be very revealing. This is not 'pure speculation.' The government was creating the pressure: the bank was exerting it upon the government's instructions. Is a court to assume that such documents will not assist towards an understanding of the nature of the pressure exerted? The assumption seems to me as unreal as the proverbial folly of attempting to understand Hamlet without reference to his position as the Prince of Denmark. I do not understand how a court could properly reach the judge's conclusion without inspecting the documents: and this he refused to do. The judge in my opinion wrongly exercised his discretion when he refused to inspect unless public policy (of which public interest immunity is a manifestation) required him to refuse.

It becomes necessary, therefore, to analyse closely the public interest immunity objection made by the minister and to determine the correct approach of the court to a situation in which there may be a clash of two interests – that of the public service and that of justice.

In *Conway v Rimmer* [1968] AC 910 this House had to consider two questions. They were formulated by Lord Reid in these terms, at 943:

> '. . . first, whether the court is to have any right to question the finality of a minister's certificate and, secondly, if it has such a right, how and in what circumstances that right is to be exercised and made effective.'

The House answered the first question, but did not, in my judgment, provide, nor was it required to provide, a complete answer to the second.

As I read the speeches in *Conway v Rimmer* the House answered the first question by establishing the principle of judicial review. The minister's certificate is not final. The immunity is a rule of law: its scope is a question of law: and its applicability to the facts of a particular case is for the court, not the minister, to determine. The statement of Lord Kilmuir LC of 6 June, 1956 (all that is relevant is quoted in *Conway v Rimmer* at 922) that: 'The minister's certificate on affidavit setting out the ground of the claim must in England be accepted by the court . . .' is no longer a correct statement of the law. Whether *Conway v Rimmer* be seen as a development of or a departure from previous English case law is a matter of no importance. What is important is that it aligned English law with the law of Scotland and of the Commonwealth. It is the heir apparent not of *Duncan v Cammell Laird & Co Ltd* [1942] AC 624 but of *Robinson v State of South Australia (No 2)* [1931] AC 704 and of *Glasgow Corpn v Central Land Board* 1956 SC (HL) 1.

Having established the principle of judicial review, the House had in *Conway v Rimmer* [1968] AC 910 a simple case on the facts to decide. The question was whether routine reports, albeit of a confidential character, upon a former probationary police constable should in the interests of justice be disclosed in an action brought by him against his former superintendent in which he claimed damages for alleged malicious prosecution. There was a public interest in the confidentiality of such reports, but the Home Secretary, in his affidavit objecting to production on the ground of injury to the public interest, did not go so far as to say that it was necessary for the proper functioning of the public service to withhold production. On the other hand, the reports might be of critical importance in the litigation. Granted the existence of judicial review, here was a justiciable issue of no great difficulty. The House decided itself to inspect the documents, and, having done so, ordered production.

In reaching its decision the House did indicate what it considered to be the correct approach to the clash of interests which arises whenever there is a question of public interest immunity. The approach is to be found stated in two passages of Lord Reid's speech: pp 940C–F and 952C–G. The essence of the matter is a weighing, on balance, of the two public interests, that of the nation or the public service in non-disclosure and that of justice in the production of the documents. A good working, but not logically perfect, distinction is recognised between the contents and the classes of documents. If a minister of the Crown asserts that to disclose the contents of a document would, or might, do the nation or the public service a grave injury, the court will be slow to question his opinion or to allow any interest, even that of justice, to prevail over it. Unless there can be shown to exist some factor suggesting either a lack of good faith (which is not likely) or an error of judgment or an error of law on the minister's part, the court should not (the House held) even go so far as itself to inspect the document. In this sense, the minister's assertion may be said to be conclusive. It is, however, for the judge to determine whether the minister's opinion is to be treated as conclusive. I do not understand the House to have denied that even in 'contents' cases the court retains its power to inspect or to balance the injury to the public service against the risk of injustice, before reaching its decision.

In 'class' cases the House clearly considered the minister's certificate to be more likely to be open to challenge. Undoubtedly, however, the House thought that there were certain classes of documents, which ought not to be disclosed however harmless the disclosure of their contents might be, and however important their disclosure might be in the interest of justice. Cabinet minutes were cited as an example. But the point did not arise for decision. For the documents in *Conway v Rimmer* [1968] AC 910, though confidential, were 'routine,' in no way concerned with the inner working of the government at a high level; and their production might well be indispensable to the doing of justice in the litigation.

The point does arise in the present case. The documents are 'high level'. They are concerned with the formulation of policy. They are part of the inner working of the government machine. They contain information which the court knows does relate to matters in issue in the action, and which may, on inspection, prove to be highly material. In such circumstances the minister may well be right in his view that the public service would be injured by disclosure. But is the court bound by his view that it is *necessary* for the proper functioning of the public service that they be withheld from production? And, if non-disclosure is necessary for that purpose, is the court bound to hold that the interest in the proper functioning of the public service is to prevail over the requirements of justice?

If the answer to these two questions is to be in the affirmative as Lord Reid appears to suggest in *Conway v Rimmer*, I think the law reverts to the statement of Lord Kilmuir. A properly drawn minister's certificate, which is a bona fide expression of his opinion, becomes final. But the advance made in the law by *Conway v Rimmer* was that the certificate is not final. I think, therefore, that it would now be inconsistent with principle to hold that the court may not – even in a case like the present – review the certificate and balance the public interest of government to which alone it refers, against the public interest of justice, which is the concern of the court.

I do not therefore accept that there are any classes of document which, however harmless their contents and however strong the requirement of justice, may never be disclosed until they are only of historical interest. In this respect I think there may well be a difference between a 'class' objection and a 'contents' objection – though the residual power to inspect and to order disclosure must remain in both instances. A Cabinet minute, it is said, must be withheld from production. Documents relating to the formulation of policy at a high level are also to be withheld. But is the secrecy of the 'inner workings of the government machine' so vital a public interest that it must prevail over even the most imperative demands of justice? If the contents of a document concern the national safety, affect diplomatic relations or relate to some state secret of high importance, I can understand an affirmative answer. But if they do not (and it is not claimed in this case that they do), what is so important about secret government that it must be protected even at the price of injustice in our courts?

The reasons given for protecting the secrecy of government at the level of policy-making are two. The first is the need for candour in the advice offered to ministers: the second is that disclosure 'would create or fan ill-informed or captious public or political criticism.' Lord Reid in *Conway v Rimmer* [1968] AC 910, 952, thought the second 'the most important reason.' Indeed, he was inclined to discount the candour argument.

I think both reasons are factors legitimately to be put into the balance which has to be struck between the public interest in the proper functioning of the public service (ie, the executive arm of government) and the public interest in the administration of justice. Sometimes the public service reasons will be decisive of the issue: but they should never prevent the court from weighing them against the injury which would be suffered in the administration of justice if the document was not to be disclosed. And the likely injury to the cause of justice must also be assessed and weighed. Its weight will vary according to the nature of the proceedings in which disclosure is sought, the relevance of the documents, and the degree of likelihood that the document will be of importance in the litigation. In striking the balance, the court may always, if it thinks it necessary, itself inspect the documents.

Inspection by the court is, I accept, a power to be exercised only if the court is in doubt, after considering the certificate, the issues in the case and the relevance of the documents whose disclosure is sought. Where documents are relevant (as in this case they are), I would think a pure 'class' objection would by itself seldom quieten judicial doubts – particularly if, as here, a substantial case can be made out for saying that disclosure is needed in the interest of justice.

I am fortified in the opinion which I have expressed by the trend towards inspection and disclosure to be found both in the United States and in Commonwealth countries. Of course, the United States have a written constitution and a Bill of Rights. Nevertheless both derive from the common law and British political philosophy. Mutatis mutandis, I would adopt the principle accepted by the Supreme Court in *Nixon v United States* 418 US 683 which is summarised in 41 L Ed 2d 1039, 1046:

'Neither the doctrine of separation of powers, nor the need for confidentiality of high level communications, without more, can sustain an absolute unqualified presidential privilege of immunity from judicial process under all circumstances; although the President's need for complete candour and objectivity from advisers calls for great deference from the courts, nevertheless when the privilege depends solely on the broad, undifferentiated claim of public interest in the confidentiality of such conversations, a confrontation with other values arises; absent a claim of need to protect military, diplomatic or sensitive national security secrets, it is difficult to accept the argument that even the very important interest in confidentiality of Presidential communications is significantly diminished by production of such material for in camera inspection with all the protection that a United States District Court will be obliged to provide.'

In Australia the High Court had to consider the problem in a recent case where the facts were, admittedly, exceptional. In *Sankey v Whitlam* 53 ALJR 11 the plaintiff sought declarations that certain papers and documents, to which the magistrate in criminal proceedings instituted by the plaintiff against the defendants had accorded privilege, should be produced. The offences alleged against Mr Whitlam, a former Prime Minister, and others were serious – conspiracies to act unlawfully in the conduct of official business. Gibbs ACJ dealt with the issue of Crown privilege as follows at 23:

'For these reasons I consider that although there is a class of documents whose members are entitled to protection from disclosure irrespective of their contents, the protection is not absolute, and it does not endure for ever. The fundamental and governing principle is that documents in the class may be withheld from production only when this is necessary in the public interest. In a particular case the court must balance the general desirability that documents of that kind should not be disclosed against the need to produce them in the interests of justice. The court will of course examine the question with especial care, giving full weight to the reasons for preserving the secrecy of documents of this class, but it will not treat all such documents as entitled to the same measure of protection – the extent of protection required will depend to some extent on the general subject matter with which the documents are concerned. If a strong case has been made out for the production of the documents, and the court concludes that their disclosure would not really be detrimental to the public interest, an order for production will be made. In view of the danger to which the indiscriminate disclosure of documents of this class might give rise, it is desirable that the government concerned, Commonwealth or State, should have an opportunity to intervene and be heard before any order for disclosure is made. Moreover no such order should be enforced until the government concerned has had an opportunity to appeal against it, or test its correctness by some other process, if it wishes to do so (cf *Conway v Rimmer* [1968] AC 910, 953).'

Both *Nixon's* case 418 US 683 and *Sankey v Whitlam* 53 ALJR 11 are far closer to the Scottish and Commonwealth stream of authority than to the English. In the *Glasgow Corpn* case 1956 SC (HL) 1, Viscount Simonds said at 11:

'that there always has been and is now in the law of Scotland an inherent power of the court to override the Crown's objection to produce documents on the ground that it would injure the public interest to do so.'

In *Robinson v State of South Australia (No 2)* [1931] AC 704 the Privy Council reminded the Supreme Court of South Australia of the existence of this power. The power must be exercised judicially, and all due weight must be given to the objections of the Crown: that is all.

Something was made in argument about the risk to the nation or the public service of an error at first instance. Injury to the public interest – perhaps even very serious injury – could be done by production of documents which should be immune from disclosure before an appellate court could correct the error. This risk is inherent in the principle of judicial review. The House in *Conway v Rimmer* [1968] AC 910 recognised its existence, but, nevertheless, established the principle as part of our law. Gibbs J also mentioned it in *Sankey v Whitlam* 53 ALJR 11. I would respectfully agree with Lord Reid's observations on the point in *Conway v Rimmer* [1968] AC 910, 953D: '. . . it is important that the minister should have a right to appeal before the document is produced.'

In cases where the Crown is not a party – as in the present case – the court should ensure that the Attorney-General has the opportunity to intervene before disclosure is ordered.

For these reasons I was one of a majority of your Lordships who thought it necessary to inspect the 10 documents. Having done so, I have no doubt that they are relevant and, but for the immunity claim, would have to be disclosed, but their significance is not such as to override the public service objections to their production. Burmah will not suffer injustice by their non-disclosure, while their disclosure would be, in the opinion of the responsible minister, injurious to the public service. I would, therefore, dismiss the appeal.

By way of tail-piece I mention the strange affair of the edited documents. The bank, claiming immunity for part, but not the whole, of certain documents, covered up the parts to the disclosure of which it objected. Burmah's advisers were able to penetrate the cover and read their contents. They did not tell their client what they had seen. Should they now be disclosed, the cover having been blown? The issue evaporated because it became clear in argument that Burmah were ultimately fighting to see only the 10 documents, which a majority of your Lordships has now inspected. But the accident of an insufficient cover cannot weaken the objection of public interest immunity. Even if the parties allow discovery, the court must take the objection of its own motion: and this may have to be done even before the Crown intervenes.

[Lords Salmon, Edmund-Davies and Keith agreed that the documents should be inspected; Lord Wilberforce dissented on that issue. The majority agreed that the claim for privilege was good.]

QUESTIONS

1. Did the House of Lords in *Conway v Rimmer* distinguish or overrule *Duncan's* Case?

2. What is the difference between reasons 'which judicial experience is not competent to weigh' and others?

3. How strong is the candour argument? Do you agree with Lord Pearce's words: 'What policeman *could* be deterred from candour by the thought that a judge might read his notes? One imagines that he would rather be put on his mettle to make sure that his observations were sound and accurate, and be stimulated by the thought that he might prove to be the one impartial recorder on whom justice between the parties might ultimately turn' ([1968] AC 910 at 985, [1968] 1 All ER 874 at 910)?

NOTES

1. Claims to privilege in criminal cases are unlikely to be made or to succeed: *Re Tunstall, ex p Brown* (1966) 67 SRNSW 1.

2. In *Buttes Gas and Oil Co v Hammer (No 3)* [1981] QB 223, [1980] 3 All

ER 475, CA, the Court of Appeal held that foreign state privilege is unknown to English law, but Donaldson and Brightman LJJ said there is a United Kingdom public interest, permitting exclusion from evidence in the court's discretion, in withholding from production without the consent of a foreign sovereign the contents of confidential documents passed to or issued by that sovereign or concerning the interests of his State in connection with an international dispute.

3. See generally *Williams v Home Office* [1981] 1 All ER 1151; *Air Canada v Secretary of State for Trade (No 2)* [1983] 2 AC 394, [1983] 1 All ER 910, HL.

4. In *Australian National Airlines Commission v Commonwealth of Australia* (1975) 132 CLR 582 Mason J refused to uphold a claim of Crown privilege based on the risk of industrial action; cf *Science Research Council v Nassé* [1980] AC 1028, [1979] 3 All ER 673, HL.

5. In *R v Chief Constable of the West Midlands, ex p Wiley* [1995] 1 AC 274, [1994] 3 All ER 420, HL, a class claim to documents coming into existence in consequence of the investigation of a complaint against police was denied.

6. The court has power to inspect documents which are the subject of 'contents' claims – even documents as sensitive as Cabinet minutes (*Air Canada v Secretary of State for Trade (No 2)* [1983] 2 AC 394 at 432, [1983] 1 All ER 910 at 915), but it has been said that once there is an actual or potential risk to national security demonstrated by an appropriate certificate the court would not exercise its right to inspect (*Balfour v Foreign and Colonial Office* [1994] 2 All ER 588, [1994] 1 WLR 681, CA).

7. Normally the privilege only applies to communications within government departments, but there is one traditional instance of its application to communications from outsiders. In public prosecutions, provided no injustice is caused to the accused, a witness cannot be asked to give answers which would reveal the names of informants: *Marks v Beyfus* (1890) 25 QBD 494, CA (though in some cases the need to protect the liberty of the subject may prevail over the need to protect informers: *R v Hennessey* (1978) 68 Cr App Rep 419, CA). It now seems the informer's exception is not isolated.

Rogers v Secretary of State for the Home Department
[1973] AC 388, [1972] 2 All ER 1057, HL

A company of which Rogers was a director sought the Gaming Board's consent to the grant of licences in respect of bingo halls to be managed by Rogers. The Board was obliged to take into account Rogers's character. They made inquiries of the Sussex Police, and in reply the Assistant Chief Constable of Sussex wrote a letter to the Board, which later refused the consent sought. Rogers began proceedings for criminal libel regarding the contents of the letter. The Home Secretary claimed privilege in respect of the letter and a copy. The House of Lords upheld the claims.

Lord Reid: The ground put forward has been said to be Crown privilege. I think that that expression is wrong and may be misleading. There is no question of any privilege in the ordinary sense of the word. The real question is whether the public interest requires that the letter shall not be produced and whether the public interest is so strong as to override the ordinary right and interest of a litigant that he shall be able to lay before a court of justice all relevant evidence. A Minister of the Crown is always an appropriate and often the most appropriate person to assert this public interest, and the evidence or advice which he gives to the court is always valuable and may sometimes be indispensable. But in my view it must always be open to any person interested to raise the question and there may be cases where the trial judge should himself raise the question if no one else has done so. In the present case the question of public interest was raised by both the Attorney-General and the board. In my judgment both were entitled to raise the matter. Indeed I think that in the circumstances it was the duty of the board to do as they have done.

The claim in the present case is not based on the nature of the contents of this particular letter. It is based on the fact that the board cannot adequately perform their statutory duty unless they can preserve the confidentiality of all communications to them regarding the character, reputation or antecedents of applicants for their consent.

Claims for 'class privilege' were fully considered by this House in *Conway v Rimmer*. It was made clear that there is a heavy burden of proof on any authority which makes such a claim. But the possibility of establishing such a claim was not ruled out. I venture to quote what I said in that case ([1968] AC 910 at 952, [1968] 1 All ER 874 at 888, HL):

> 'There may be special reasons for withholding some kinds of routine documents, but I think that the proper test to be applied is to ask, in the language of Lord Simon in *Duncan's* case, whether the withholding of a document because it belongs to a particular class is really "necessary for the proper functioning of the public service"' ([1942] AC 624 at 642, [1942] 1 All ER 587 at 595, HL).

I do not think that 'the public service' should be construed narrowly. Here the question is whether the withholding of this class of documents is really necessary to enable the board adequately to perform its statutory duties. If it is then we are enabling the will of Parliament to be carried out.

There are very unusual features about this case. The board require the fullest information they can get in order to identify and exclude persons of dubious character and reputation from the privilege of obtaining a licence to conduct a gaming establishment. There is no obligation on anyone to give any information to the board. No doubt many law abiding citizens would tell what they know even if there was some risk of their identity becoming known, although many perfectly honourable people do not want to be thought to be mixed up in such affairs. But it is obvious that the best source of information about dubious characters must often be persons of dubious character themselves. It has long been recognised that the identity of police informers must in the public interest be kept secret and the same considerations must apply to those who volunteer information to the board. Indeed it is in evidence that many refuse to speak unless assured of absolute secrecy.

The letter called for in this case came from the police. I feel sure that they would not be deterred from giving full information by any fear of consequences to themselves if there were any disclosure. But much of the information which they can give must come from sources which must be protected and they would rightly take this into account. Even if information were given without naming the source, the very nature of the information might, if it were communicated to the person concerned, at least give him a very shrewd idea from whom it had come.

It is possible that some documents coming to the board could be disclosed without fear of such consequences. But I would think it quite impracticable for the board or the court to be sure of this. So it appears to me that, if there is not to be very serious danger of the board being deprived of information essential for the proper performance of their difficult task, there must be a general rule that they are not bound to produce any document which gives information to them about an applicant.

We must then balance that fact against the public interest that the course of justice should not be impeded by the withholding of evidence. We must, I think, take into account that these documents only came into existence because the applicant is asking for a privilege and is submitting his character and reputation to scrutiny. The documents are not used to deprive him of any legal right. The board have a wide discretion. Not only can they refuse his application on the ground of bad reputation although he may say that he has not deserved that reputation; it is not denied that the board can also take into account any unfavourable impression which he has made during an interview with the board. Natural justice requires that the board should act in good faith and that they should so far as possible tell him the gist of any grounds on which they propose to refuse his application so that he may show such grounds to be unfounded in fact. But the board must be trusted to do that; we have been referred to their practice in this matter and I see nothing wrong in it.

In the present case the board told Mr Rogers nothing about the contents of this letter because they say that they had sufficient grounds for refusing his application without any need to rely on anything in the letter. Their good faith in this matter is not subject to any substantial challenge.

If Mr Rogers had not by someone's wrongful act obtained a copy of the letter there was no reason why he should ever have known anything about it.

In my judgment on balance the public interest clearly requires that documents of this kind should not be disclosed, and that public interest is not affected by the fact that by some wrongful means a copy of such a document had been obtained and published by some person.

Lord Pearson: It seems to me that the proper procedure is that which has been followed, I think consistently, in recent times. The objection to disclosure of the document or information is taken by the Attorney-General or his representative on behalf of the appropriate Minister, that is to say, the political head of the government department within whose sphere of responsibility the matter arises, and the objection is expressed in or supported by a certificate from the appropriate Minister. This procedure has several advantages: (1) the question whether or not the disclosure of the document or information would be detrimental to the public interest on the administrative or executive side is considered at a high level; (2) the court has the assistance of a carefully considered and authoritative opinion on that question; (3) the Attorney-General is consulted and has opportunities of promoting uniformity both in the decision of such questions and in the formulation of the grounds on which the objections are taken. The court has to balance the detriment to the public interest on the administrative or executive side, which would result from the disclosure of the document or information, against the detriment to the public interest on the judicial side, which would result from non-disclosure of a document or information which is relevant to an issue in legal proceedings. Therefore the court, although naturally giving great weight to the opinion of the appropriate Minister conveyed through the Attorney-General or his representative, must have the final responsibility of deciding whether or not the document or information is to be disclosed.

Although that established procedure is the proper procedure, it is not essential as a matter of law. It is not always practicable. If the appropriate Minister is not available, some other Minister or some highly-placed official must act in his stead. If it becomes evident in the course of a trial or in interlocutory proceedings that perhaps some document or information ought in the public interest to be protected from disclosure, it must be open to the party or witness concerned or the court itself to raise the question. If such a situation arises in the course of a trial, the court can adjourn the trial for the appropriate Minister or the Attorney-General to be consulted, but the court will be reluctant to adjourn the trial unless it is really necessary to do so, and in some cases that will be unnecessary because the court is able to give an immediate answer.

The expression 'Crown privilege' is not accurate, although sometimes convenient. The Crown has no privilege in the matter. The appropriate Minister has the function of deciding, with the assistance of the Attorney-General, whether or not the public interest on the administrative or executive side requires that he should object to the disclosure of the document or information, but a negative decision cannot properly be described as a waiver of a privilege.

[Lords Morris of Borth-y-Gest, Simon of Glaisdale and Salmon delivered concurring judgments.]

NOTE

The phrase 'Crown privilege' was attacked by every member of the House except Lord Morris: 'public policy' was preferred, but in *Science Research Council v Nassé* [1980] AC 1028 at 1087, [1979] 3 All ER 673, HL, Lord Scarman expressed a preference for 'Crown privilege' because it 'at least emphasised the very restricted area of public interest immunity'.

Norwich Pharmacal Co v Customs and Excise Commissioners
[1974] AC 133, [1973] 2 All ER 943, HL

The appellants were owners and licensees of a patent for a chemical called furazolidone. The patent was being infringed by illegal imports of the substance. The appellants instituted proceedings against the Commissioners to obtain the names and addresses of the importers. The

Commissioners made a claim for privilege in an affidavit sworn by Sir Louis Petch, the Chairman of the Commissioners. It was denied by Graham J, upheld by the Court of Appeal, but denied by the House of Lords.

Lord Reid: [W]e have to weigh the requirements of justice to the appellants against the considerations put forward by the respondents as justifying non-disclosure. They are twofold. First it is said that to make such disclosures would or might impair or hamper the efficient conduct of their important statutory duties. And secondly, it is said that such disclosure would or might be prejudicial to those whose identity would be disclosed.

There is nothing secret or confidential in the information sought or in the documents which came into the hands of the respondents containing that information. Those documents are ordinary commercial documents which pass through many different hands. But it is said that those who do not wish to have their names disclosed might concoct false documents and thereby hamper the work of the Customs. That would require at least a conspiracy between the foreign consignor and the importer and it seems to me to be in the highest degree improbable. It appears that there are already arrangements in operation by the respondents restricting the disclosure of certain matters if the importers do not wish them to be disclosed. It may be that the knowledge that a court might order discovery in certain cases would cause somewhat greater use to be made of these arrangements. But it was not suggested in argument that that is a matter of any vital importance. The only other point was that such disclosure might cause resentment and impair good relations with other traders: but I find it impossible to believe that honest traders would resent failure to protect wrongdoers.

Protection of traders from having their names disclosed is a more difficult matter. If we could be sure that those whose names are sought are all tortfeasors, they do not deserve any protection. In the present case the possibility that any are not is so remote that I think it can be neglected. The only possible way in which any of these imports could be legitimate and not an infringement would seem to be that someone might have exported some furazolidone from this country and then whoever owned it abroad might have sent it back here. Then there would be no infringement. But again that seems most unlikely.

But there may be other cases where there is much more doubt. The validity of the patent may be doubtful and there could well be other doubts. If the respondents have any doubts in any future case about the propriety of making disclosure they are well entitled to require the matter to be submitted to the court at the expense of the person seeking the disclosure. The court will then only order discovery if satisfied that there is no substantial chance of injustice being done.

I would therefore allow this appeal.

Viscount Dilhorne: I do not accept the proposition that all information given to a government department is to be treated as confidential and protected from disclosure, but I agree that information of a personal character obtained in the exercise of statutory powers, information of such a character that the giver of it would not expect to be used for any purpose other than that for which it is given, or disclosed to any person not concerned with that purpose, is to be regarded as protected from disclosure, even though there is no statutory prohibition of its disclosure. But not all information given to a government department, whether voluntarily or under compulsion is of this confidential character and the question is whether the names of the importers of the furazolidone were given in confidence. I do not think that that is established. The names and addresses of the importers had to be given to the master of the ship and made known to all those taking part in securing the transit of the chemicals. Presumably the parcels of furazolidone had on them the names and addresses of the consignees for all to see, though they may, I do not know, have not disclosed that the contents of the parcels were furazolidone. The documents completed for the transit of the chemicals and for Customs which show the names of the consignees and the contents of the parcels do not seem to me more confidential than consignment notes completed for British Railways and British Road Services.

I must confess that I am not in the least impressed by the 'candour' argument. I really cannot conceive it to be realistic to suggest that the vast majority of importers who do not infringe patents or do other wrongs, will be in the least deterred from giving proper information to Customs by the knowledge that pursuant to an order of the court the names of the wrongdoers are disclosed by Customs.

Lord Cross of Chelsea: Sir Louis says that he is afraid that the good relations and mutual confidence which usually exist between the officers of the Customs and traders would be seriously impaired if it became known that any information of a confidential character obtained from traders under statutory powers might have to be disclosed by the commissioners otherwise than under the provisions of a statute enabling them to disclose it. The traders whose good relations with the Customs Sir Louis is anxious to maintain are, presumably, honest traders. Any honest trader who was disturbed at the thought that a court could order the disclosure of importers' names in circumstances such as exist here would be a most unreasonable man and I cannot believe that there would be many such. No doubt dishonest traders might be disturbed by the knowledge that such disclosure could be ordered, and Sir Louis gives it as a further ground for the claim of privilege that dishonest traders who now tell the Customs the truth with regard to the character of the goods and the identity of the importers may be driven to giving false information. An argument that one should not try to stop one form of wrongdoing out of fear that some of the wrongdoers may take to committing yet further offences in order to be able to maintain their original course of wrongdoing is not very attractive. But in any case I think that Sir Louis's fears on this head are exaggerated. On the question of public interest I agree with Graham J and disagree with the Court of Appeal.

[Lords Morris of Borth-y-Gest and Kilbrandon delivered concurring judgments.]

NOTES

1. Had the documents been relevant to litigation between two private parties, neither could have claimed any private privilege.
2. In *Conway v Rimmer* [1968] AC 910 at 946, [1968] 1 All ER 874 at 884, HL, Lord Reid said: 'If the State insists on a man disclosing his private affairs for a particular purpose, it requires a very strong case to justify that disclosure being used for other purposes.' Hence public interest immunity attaches to documents in the hands of the Inland Revenue relating to a taxpayer's affairs, but not to documents in the taxpayer's own possession: *Lonrho plc v Fayed (No 4)* [1994] QB 775, [1994] 1 All ER 870, CA.

Alfred Crompton Amusements Machines Ltd v Customs and Excise Commissioners (No 2)   [1974] AC 405, [1973] 2 All ER 1169, HL

An issue arose between the company and the Commissioners as to the correct assessment for purchase tax on certain machines made by the company. The Commissioners, in an affidavit sworn by their Chairman, Sir Louis Petch, claimed privilege for certain documents containing information supplied by third parties. The House of Lords upheld the claim.

Lord Cross of Chelsea: 'Confidentiality' is not a separate head of privilege, but it may be a very material consideration to bear in mind when privilege is claimed on the ground of public interest. What the court has to do is to weigh on the one hand the considerations which suggest that it is in the public interest that the documents in question should be disclosed and on the other hand those which suggest that it is in the public interest that they should not be disclosed and to balance one against the other. Plainly there is much to be said in favour of disclosure. The documents in question constitute an important part of the material on which the commissioners based their conclusion that the appellants sell to retailers. That is shown by the reply which the commissioners made to the request for particulars under paragraph 5(*b*) of the defence. Yet if the claim to privilege made by the commissioners is upheld this information will be withheld from the arbitrator. No doubt it will form part of the brief delivered to counsel for the commissioners and may help to probe the appellants' evidence in cross-examination; but counsel will not be able to use it as evidence to controvert anything which the appellants' witnesses may say. It is said, of course, that the appellants cannot reasonably complain if the commissioners think it right to tie their own hands in this way. But if the arbitrator should decide against them the appellants may feel – however wrongly – that the arbitrator was unconsciously influenced by the fact that the commissioners stated in their pleadings that they had this further evidence in support of their view which they did not disclose and which the appellants had no opportunity to controvert. Moreover, whoever wins it is desirable that the arbitrator should have all the relevant material before him. On the other hand, there is much to be said against disclosure. The case is not, indeed, as strong as the case against disclosing the name of an informer – for the result of doing that would be that the source of information would dry up whereas here the commissioners will continue to have their powers under section 24(6) [of the Purchase Tax Act 1963]. Nevertheless, the case against disclosure is, to my mind, far stronger than it was in the *Norwich Pharmacal* case. There it was probable that all the importers whose names were disclosed were wrongdoers and the disclosure of the names of any, if there were any, who were innocent would not be likely to do them any harm at all. Here, on the other hand, one can well see that the third parties who have supplied this information to the commissioners because of the existence of their statutory powers would very much resent its disclosure by the commissioners to the appellants and that it is not at all fanciful for Sir Louis to say that the knowledge that the commissioners cannot keep such information secret may be harmful to the efficient working of the Act. In a case where the considerations for and against disclosure appear to be fairly evenly balanced the courts should I think uphold a claim to privilege on the ground of public interest and trust to the head of the department concerned to do whatever he can to mitigate the ill-effects of non-disclosure. Forbes J was so impressed by those possible ill-effects that he failed to appreciate how reasonable Sir Louis's objections to disclosure were and dismissed them with the remark. 'We are not living in the early days of the Tudor administration'. I do not regard Sir Louis as a modern Cardinal Morton. His objections to disclosure were taken in the interests of the third parties concerned as much as in the interests of the commissioners and if any of them is in fact willing to give evidence, privilege in respect of any documents or information obtained from him will be waived.

[Lords Reid, Morris of Borth-y-Gest and Kilbrandon and Viscount Dilhorne agreed.]

QUESTIONS

1. How can Lord Cross's last sentence be reconciled with the view that the right and duty to object to disclosure on public interest grounds is not a privilege and cannot be waived? See also *Peach v Metropolitan Police Comr* [1986] QB 1064 at 1071, [1986] 2 All ER 129 at 131, CA. Does the answer depend on whether there is ever a public interest in keeping secret information which those interested in secrecy do not wish to remain secret (*Hehir v Metropolitan Police Comr* [1982] 2 All ER 335 at 341, [1982] 1 WLR 715 at 723) or have published (*Shearson Lehman Bros Inc v Maclaine Watson Co Ltd (International Tin Council intervening) (No 2)* [1988] 1 All ER 116, [1988] 1 WLR 16, HL)? Does it depend on a distinction between 'contents' claims and 'class claims' (*Campbell v Tameside Metropolitan Borough Council* [1982] QB 1065 at 1073, [1982] 2 All ER 791 at 795, CA)?
2. Do these decisions unduly exalt state interests above those of persons who make confidential communications to priests and doctors?
3. What differences are there between the *Norwich Pharmacal* and *Alfred Crompton* cases which compelled a different result?

D v National Society for the Prevention of Cruelty to Children
[1978] AC 171, [1977] 1 All ER 589, HL

The National Society for the Prevention of Cruelty to Children ('NSPCC') received and investigated complaints from members of the public about cases of ill-treatment or neglect of children under an express pledge of confidentiality and was authorised under s 1(1) of the Children and Young Persons Act 1969 to bring care proceedings in respect of children. The society received a complaint from an informant about the treatment of a 14-month-old girl, and an inspector of the society called at the parents' home. The mother subsequently brought an action against the society for damages for personal injuries alleged to have resulted from the society's negligence. The society applied for an order that there should be no discovery or inspection ordered under RSC Ord 24, r 2(1), of any documents which revealed or might reveal the identity of the complainant, on the grounds, inter alia, that the proper performance by the society of its duties under its charter and the Act of 1969 required that the absolute confidentiality of information given in confidence should be preserved, that if disclosure were ordered in the mother's action its sources of information would dry up and that that would be contrary to the public interest.

Lord Diplock: The fact that information has been communicated by one person to another in confidence . . . is not of itself a sufficient ground for protection from disclosure in a court of law the nature of the information or the identity of the informant if either of these matters would assist the court to ascertain facts which are relevant to an issue upon which it is adjudicating: *Alfred Crompton Amusement Machines Ltd v Customs and Excise Comrs (No 2)* [1974] AC 405, 433–4. The private promise of confidentiality must yield to the general public interest that in the administration of justice truth will out, unless by reason of the character of the information or the relationship of the recipient of the information to the informant a more important public interest is served by protecting the information or the identity of the informant from disclosure in a court of law.

The public interest which the NSPCC relies upon as obliging it to withhold from the plaintiff and from the court itself material that could disclose the identity of the society's informant is analogous to the public interest that is protected by the well established rule of law that the identity of police informers may not be disclosed in a civil action, whether by the process of discovery or by oral evidence at the trial: *Marks v Beyfus* (1890) 25 QBD 494.

The rationale of the rule as it applies to police informers is plain. If their identity were liable to be disclosed in a court of law, these sources of information would dry up and the police would be hindered in their duty of preventing and detecting crime. So the public interest in preserving the anonymity of police informers had to be weighed against the public interest that information which might assist a judicial tribunal to ascertain facts relevant to an issue upon which it is required to adjudicate should be withheld from that tribunal. By the uniform practice of the judges which by the time of *Marks v Beyfus* 25 QBD 494 had already hardened into a rule of law, the balance has fallen upon the side of non-disclosure except where upon the trial of a defendant for a criminal offence disclosure of the identity of the informer could help to show that the defendant was innocent of the offence. In that case, and in that case only, the balance falls upon the side of disclosure.

My Lords, in *R v Lewes Justices, ex p Secretary of State for the Home Department* [1973] AC 388 this House did not hesitate to extend to persons from whom the Gaming Board received information for the purposes of the exercise of their statutory functions under the Gaming Act 1968 immunity from disclosure of their identity analogous to that which the law had previously accorded to police informers. Your Lordships' sense of values might well be open to reproach if this House were to treat the confidentiality of information given to those who are authorised by statute to institute proceedings for the protection of neglected or ill-treated children as entitled to less favourable treatment in a court of law than information given to the Gaming Board so that gaming may be kept clean. There are three categories of persons authorised to bring care proceedings in respect of neglected or ill-treated children: local authorities, constables and the NSPCC. The anonymity of those who tell the police of their suspicions of neglect or ill-treatment of a child would be preserved without any extension of the existing law. To draw a distinction in this respect between information given to the police and that passed on directly to a local authority or to the NSPCC would seem much too irrational a consequence to have been within the contemplation of Parliament when enacting the Children and Young Persons Act 1969. The local authority is under an express statutory duty to bring care proceedings in cases where this is necessary if neither the police nor the NSPCC have started them, while, as respects the NSPCC, the evidence shows that, presumably because it is not associated in the public mind with officialdom, the public are readier to bring information to it than to the police or the welfare services of the local authority itself.

Upon the summons by the NSPCC for an order withholding discovery of documents to the extent that they were capable of revealing the identity of the society's informant, it was for the judge to weigh the competing public interests involved in disclosure and non-disclosure and to form his opinion as to the side on which the balance fell. In a careful judgment in which he reviewed the relevant authorities Croom-Johnson J ordered that disclosure should not be given. Upon an interlocutory summons relating to discovery this was a matter upon which the judge had a discretion with which an appellate court would not lightly interfere, but the reasoning by which his decision was supported is of wider application. It would also rule out any attempt to ascertain the identity of the NSPCC's informant by questions put to witnesses at the trial and would dispose of the plaintiff's claim to disclosure of the informant's identity as part, and perhaps to her the most important part, of the substantive relief she seeks. The interlocutory judgment thus raises matters of principle fit for the consideration of this House.

For my part I would uphold the decision of Croom-Johnson J and reverse that of the Court of Appeal. I would do so upon what in argument has been referred to as the 'narrow' submission made on behalf of the NSPCC. I would extend to those who give information about neglect or ill-treatment of children to a local authority or the NSPCC a similar immunity from disclosure of their identity in legal proceedings to that which the law accords to police informers. The public interest served by preserving the anonymity of both classes of informants are analogous; they are of no less weight in the case of the former than in that of the latter class, and in my judgment are of greater weight than in the case of informers of the Gaming Board to whom immunity from disclosure of their identity has recently been extended by this House.

In the Court of Appeal, as in this House, counsel for the NSPCC advanced, as well as what I have referred to as the narrow submission, a broad submission that wherever a party to legal proceedings claims that there is a public interest to be served by withholding documents or information from disclosure in those proceedings it is the duty of the court to weigh that interest against the countervailing public interest in the administration of justice in the particular case and to refuse disclosure if the balance tilts that way. This broad submission, or something rather like it confined to information imparted in confidence, was adopted in his dissenting judgment by Lord Denning MR, but as I have already indicated there is the authority of this House that confidentiality of itself does not provide a ground of non-disclosure; nor am I able to accept the proposition that the basis of all privilege from disclosure of documents or information in legal proceedings is to prevent the breaking of a confidence. For my part, I think this House would be unwise to base its decision in the instant case upon a proposition so much broader than is necessary to resolve the issue between the parties.

The majority of the Court of Appeal rejected both the broad and narrow submissions. In essence their ground for doing so was that 'public interest' as a ground for withholding disclosure of documents or information was but another term for what had before *Conway v Rimmer* [1968] AC 910 been called 'Crown privilege' and was available only where the public interest involved was the effective functioning of departments or other organs of central government. 'Crown privilege' they regarded as having always been so confined; *Conway v Rimmer* [1968] AC 910 did not extend the ambit of Crown privilege: all it did was to decide that a claim by a minister of the Crown that documents were of a class which in the public interest ought not to be disclosed was not conclusive but that it was for the court itself to decide whether the public interest which would be protected by non-disclosure outweighed the public interest in making available to the court information that might assist it in doing justice between the litigants in the particular case.

This narrow view as to the scope of public interest as a ground for protecting documents and information from disclosure was supported in argument before this House by copious citations of passages taken from judgments in previous cases in the course of which documents for which a claim to non-disclosure had been described as relating to essential functions of government, to the performance of statutory duties, to the public service or to the interests of the state. From this your Lordships were invited to infer that the document in question would not have been entitled to protection from disclosure unless it fell within the description used in the particular case.

My Lords, the maxim expressio unius, exclusio alterius is not a canon of construction that is applicable to judgments. To construe a judgment as if its function were to lay down a code of law is a common error into which the English reliance upon precedent makes it easy to fall. A cautious judge expresses a proposition of law in terms that are wide enough to cover the issue in the case under consideration; the fact that they are not also wide enough to cover an issue that may arise in some subsequent case does not make his judgment an authority against any wider proposition.

I see no reason and I know of no authority for confining public interest as a ground for non-disclosure of documents or information to the effective functioning of departments or organs of central government. In *Conway v Rimmer* [1968] AC 910 the public interest to be protected was the effective functioning of a county police force; in *Re D (Infants)* [1970] 1 WLR 599 the interest to be protected was the effective functioning of a local authority in relation to the welfare of boarded-out children. In the instant case the public interest to be protected is the effective functioning of an organisation authorised under an Act of Parliament to bring legal proceedings for the welfare of children. I agree with Croom-Johnson J that this is a public interest which the court is entitled to take into consideration in deciding whether the identity of the NSPCC's informants ought to be disclosed. I also agree that the balance of public interest falls on the side of non-disclosure.

I would allow this appeal.

Lord Hailsham of St Marylebone: The appellant society argued, in effect, for a general extension in range of the nature of the exceptions to the rule in favour of disclosure. This, it was suggested, could be summarised in a number of broad propositions, all in support of the view that, where an identifiable public interest in non-disclosure can be established, either there is a firm rule against disclosure (for example, legal professional privilege or state secrets) or the court has a discretion whether or not to order disclosure, and that this discretion must be exercised against disclosure in all cases where, after balancing the relevant considerations, the court decides that the public interest in non-disclosure outweighs the ordinary public interest in disclosure. The appellants contended that new cases will arise from time to time calling for a protection from disclosure in classes of case to which it was not previously extended, and that the courts had in practice shown great flexibility in adapting these principles to new situations as and when these arise. The appellants contended that some of those entitled to the benefits of protection had, and some had not, been subject to statutory or common law duties or been clothed with government authority or been answerable to Parliament or the executive. This contention was aimed at the majority judgments in the Court of Appeal which in substance disallowed the appellant's claim to immunity on the grounds that they are a private society clothed arguably with authority to fulfil a function but not a duty which they are compelled to perform, and that they are not in any sense either an organ of central government or part of the public service. The appellants noted that the dissenting judgment of Lord Denning MR, which was in their favour, largely relied on the confidentiality which the appellants had pledged to potential informants. Their own contention was that, while the mere fact that a communication was made in confidence did not of itself justify non-disclosure, the fact of confidentiality was relevant to reinforce the view that disclosure would be against the public interest. In this connection the appellants cited *Alfred Crompton Amusement Machines Ltd v Customs and Excise Comrs (No 2)* [1974] AC 405. Lastly the appellants contended that there was no reported case in which the court, once it had identified a public interest in non-disclosure, had ever regarded itself as debarred from taking it into consideration or from weighing its importance against the damage to be apprehended from excluding relevant evidence.

These contentions have at least the merit of propounding a lucid and coherent system. Nevertheless, I am compelled to say that, in the breadth and generality with which they were put forward, I do not find them acceptable.

They seem to me to give far too little weight to the general importance of the principle that, in all cases before them, the courts should insist on parties and witnesses disclosing the truth, the whole truth, and nothing but the truth, where this would assist the decision of the matters in dispute. In the second place, I consider that the acceptance of these principles would lead both to uncertainty and to inconsistency in the administration of justice. If they were to be accepted, we should remember that we should be laying down a large innovation not merely in the law of discovery but equally in the law of evidence, which has to be administered not merely in the High Court, but in the Crown Courts, the county courts and the magistrates' courts throughout the land. What is the public interest to be identified? On what principles can it be defined? On what principles is the weighing-up process to proceed? To what extent, if at all, can the right to non-disclosure be waived? Can secondary or extraneous evidence of the facts not disclosed be permitted? To what extent should the Crown be notified of the fact that the issue has been raised? These questions are all manageable if the categories of privilege from disclosure and public interest are considered to be limited. Indeed, reported authority, which is voluminous, shows that largely they have been solved. But to yield to the appellants' argument on this part of the case would be to set the whole question once more at large, not merely over the admitted categories and the existing field but over a much wider, indeed over an undefined, field.

Thirdly, and perhaps more important, the invitation of the appellants seems to me to run counter to the general tradition of the development of doctrine preferred by the English courts. This proceeds through evolution by extension or analogy of recognised principles and reported precedents. Bold statements of general principle based on a review of the total field are more appropriate to legislation by Parliament which has as its command techniques of inquiry, sources of information and a width of worldly-wise experience far less restricted than those available to the courts in the course of contested litigation between adversaries.

On the other hand, I find equally unattractive the more restricted and even, occasionally, pedantic view of the authorities advanced on behalf of the respondent. This was based on a rigid distinction, for some purposes valuable, between privilege and public interest, and an insistence on a narrow view of the nature of the interest of the public, reflected in the reasoning of the majority in the Court of Appeal, which would virtually have restricted the public interest cases to the narrower interests of the central organs of the state, or what might be strictly called the public service. The effect of the argument would not merely limit the ambit of possible categories of exception to the general rule. In my view, it would virtually ensure that the categories would now have to be regarded as effectively closed. In her printed case the respondent contended that:

'No party is protected from his obligation to disclose documents on the grounds of public interest unless there is some connection between the claim of protection and the functions of central government or the public service of the state . . . The expression 'Crown privilege' has been criticised but . . . it accurately reflects the basic requirement that there must be a connection with the Crown or public service of the state.'

In support of this contention the respondent referred inter alia to *Conway v Rimmer* [1968] AC 910, to *R v Lewes Justices, ex p Secretary of State for the Home Department* [1973] AC 388 and to *Alfred Crompton Amusement Machines Ltd v Customs and Excise Comrs (No 2)* [1974] AC 405. There is, of course, a sense, which will become apparent as I proceed, in which the appellant's claim can be brought squarely within the respondent's principle. But the principle is itself, as I shall show, open to criticism. In particular the argument was based on what was described as a fundamental principle that the exceptions to the general rule requiring disclosure all come within one or the other of two rigidly confined categories, one described as privilege, when secondary evidence could be given or the privilege could be waived, and the other as 'public interest' where these possible escapes were excluded. But this, it was contended, was virtually restricted to the category formerly, but inaccurately, referred to as 'Crown privilege'.

The result of this is that I approach the problem with a caution greater than that contended for the appellants, but with a willingness to extend established principles by analogy and legitimate extrapolation more flexible than was admitted by the respondent.

I am emboldened to do so by the reflection that, quite apart from legislation like the Civil Evidence Act 1968, the law of evidence has steadily developed since my own practice at the Bar began in 1932. This can be seen by a consideration of cases like *McTaggart v McTaggart* [1949] P 94, *Mole v Mole* [1951] P 21, *Theodoropoulas v Theodoropoulas* [1964] P 311, which undoubtedly developed from the long recognised category of 'without prejudice' negotiations but which in my opinion has now developed into a new category of a public interest exception based on the public interest in the stability of marriage. I think the case, widely canvassed in argument, of *R v Lewes Justices, ex p Secretary of State for the Home Department* [1973] AC 388 was a clear extension of the previous 'Crown privilege' type of case by which, for the first time, communications to the Gaming Board were recognised as a suitable object of such 'privilege.' Possibly *Re D (infants)* [1970] 1 WLR 599 is another example, for it decided, I think, for the first time, that local authority records of child care investigations were immune from disclosure in wardship proceedings to which they would otherwise be relevant. I believe that traces of similar evolution, for instance in the field of legal professional privilege, can be found in the 19th century authorities.

I find it also interesting to note that the report (Law Reform Committee Sixteenth Report (Privilege in Civil Proceedings) (1967) (Cmnd 3472)) to which judges of every Division of the High Court were signatories, which was referred to extensively by counsel for both sides, shows a definite development in the law and practice in the precise field now under discussion from what it was generally considered to be when I entered the profession in 1932.

According to paragraph 1 of that report, which is before us, but which represents no more than contemporary textbook authority:

'Privilege in the main is the creation of the common law whose policy, pragmatic as always, has been to limit to a minimum the categories of privileges' (sic) 'which a person has an absolute right to claim, *but to accord to the judge a wide discretion to permit a witness, whether a party to the proceedings or not, to refuse to disclose information where disclosure would be a breach of some ethical or social value and non-disclosure would be unlikely to result in serious injustice in the particular case in which it is claimed'* (emphasis mine).

This doctrine was not merely an incidental statement at the beginning of the report. It runs right through it, and forms the basis of some of the most notable conclusions (see, for example, paragraph 3, paragraph 7, paragraphs 36, 37, paragraphs 41, 43, paragraphs 48–52).

Counsel for the respondent, who was himself, as he candidly confessed, signatory to the report, was constrained to argue that the report, the authors of which included Lords Pearson and Diplock, Winn and Buckley LJJ, Orr J and the present Vice-Chancellor (Megarry V-C), was an inaccurate representation of the then existing state of the law, and that the two cases (*A-G v Clough* [1963] 1 QB 773 and *A-G v Mulholland; A-G v Foster* [1963] 2 QB 477) cited in the report to support the proposition did not in truth do so, were wrong if they did and, being modern, departed from legal principle. Speaking for myself, I am sure that the law has in fact developed in this field during my lifetime, and I find it incredible that paragraph 1 of the report cited, bearing the weight of judicial authority I have described, does not represent the current practice of the courts in 1967, although in fact it goes plainly beyond the current practice of my youth.

For these reasons, I feel convinced that I am entitled to proceed more boldly than counsel for the respondent argued, though more timidly than the robust counsels of the appellant's counsel urged.

The authorities, therefore, seem to me to establish beyond doubt that the courts have developed their doctrine in this field of evidence. An example of this is seen in the privilege extended to editors of newspapers in the 19th century, before the present Ord 82, r 6 was passed, to refuse to answer interrogatories in defamation cases where the issue was malice and the plaintiff desired to discover their sources (cf *Hope v Brash* [1897] 2 QB 188; *Hennessy v Wright* (1888) 21 QBD 509; *Plymouth Mutual Co-operative and Industrial Society Ltd v Traders' Publishing Association Ltd* [1906] 1 KB 403). This practice, robustly developed by the judges of the Queen's Bench Division (in contrast with the contemporary Chancery Division practice even after 1873), can only have been based on public policy. It has been stressed that these cases relate to discovery and not to questions to witnesses at the trial. This may well be so, at least at present, but certainly they illustrate the use by the court of a discretion, and its sensitiveness to public policy where discretion exists. Until the introduction of the new rules it is within my recollection that interrogatories and discovery on the lines disallowed in the newspaper cases were frequently allowed in other defamation cases where malice was in issue, although it was pointed out in argument that the newspaper principle was, at least once, applied, rather strangely, to MPs in *Adam v Fisher* (1914) 30 TLR 288.

In all this argument, however, two facts stand out unmistakably as true beyond dispute. The first is that the welfare of children, particularly of young children at risk of maltreatment by adults, has been, from the earliest days, a concern of the Crown as parens patriae, an object of legal charities and in latter years the subject of a whole series of Acts of Parliament, of which the Act of 1969 is only an example, and that not the latest. The second is that the information given by informants to the police or to the Director of Public Prosecutions, and now, since *R v Lewes Justices, ex p Secretary of State for the Home Department* [1973] AC 388, to the Gaming Board, is protected from disclosure in exactly the manner demanded by the appellants. The question, and it is I believe the only question, necessary to be decided in this appeal, is whether an extension of this established principle to information relating to possible child abuse supplied to the appellants is a legitimate extension of a known category of exception or not. For this purpose it is necessary to consider the position of the appellants in relation to the enforcement provisions of the Children and Young Persons Act 1969 . . .

Of the three classes with locus standi to initiate care proceedings, it is common ground that information given to the police is protected to the extent demanded by the society. This is clear from many cases including *Marks v Beyfus* (1890) 25 QBD 494 (which applied the principle to the Director of Public Prosecutions), and many of the recent cases in your Lordships' House. The rule relating to the immunity accorded to police informants is in truth much older, so old and so well established, in fact, that it was not and could not be challenged in the instant case before your Lordships. Once, however, it is accepted that information given to the police in the instant case would have been protected, it becomes, in my judgment, manifestly absurd that it should not be accorded equally to the same information if given by the same informant to the local authority (who would have been under a duty to act on it) or to the appellant society, to whom, according to the undisputed evidence, ordinary informants more readily resort.

The last point seems to have been realised, at least to some extent, by Sir John Pennycuick . . . [See [1978] AC at 203B–D.] But I cannot see the sense of allowing the immunity where care proceedings actually result, but not in cases where the society or the local authority, after sifting the information, and assessing the credentials of the informants, decide in the event upon an alternative course. It is not for the informant to predict what course the recipient of the information may take, nor does his (or her) right to anonymity depend upon the outcome. The public interest is that the parties with locus standi to bring care proceedings should receive information under a cloak of confidentiality. It may well be that neither the police, nor the local authority, nor the society, can given an absolute guarantee. The informant may in some cases have to give evidence under subpoena. In other cases their identity may come to light in other ways. But the police, the local authority and the society stand on the same footing. The public interest is identical in relation to each. The guarantee of confidentiality has the same and not different values in relation to each. It follows that the society is entitled to succeed upon the appeal.

Lord Denning MR in his dissenting judgment, places his own reasoning on the pledge of confidentiality given by the society, and seeks to found the immunity upon this pledge. I do not think that confidentiality by itself gives any ground for immunity (cf for example per Lord Cross of Chelsea in *Alfred Crompton Amusement Machines Ltd v Customs and Excise Comrs (No 2)* [1974] AC 405, 433). Confidentiality is not a separate head of immunity. There are, however, cases when confidentiality is itself a public interest and one of these is where information is given to an authority charged with the enforcement and administration of the law by the initiation of court proceedings. This is one of those cases, whether the recipient of the information be the police, the local authority or the NSPCC. Whether there be other cases, and what these may be, must fall to be decided in the future. The categories of public interest are not closed, and must alter from time to time whether by restriction or extension as social conditions and social legislation develop.

The result is that this appeal must be allowed, and an order made in the terms formulated by Croom-Johnson J.

Lord Simon of Glaisdale: There have been three attempts to impose a comprehensive and coherent pattern on this branch of the law: I have great sympathy with the object, though I feel bound to express reservations in the case of each. They are that of Lord Denning MR in the instant case, that of the Law Reform Committee in their Sixteenth Report, and that of counsel for the appellants in his main argument. The solution of Lord Denning MR was to suggest confidentiality of a communication (or in the relationship of the parties) as the criterion for exclusion. The Law Reform Committee found a common factor in (paragraph 1):

'a wide discretion [in the court] to permit a witness, whether a party to the proceedings or not, to refuse to disclose information where disclosure would be a breach of some ethical or social value and non-disclosure would be unlikely to result in serious injustice in the particular case in which it is claimed.'

Counsel for the appellants, while relying on much in the Law Reform Committee's report, put his case with slightly different emphasis. He argued that in each case (save those governed by an existing rule against disclosure) the court will weigh any public interest in the withholding of information against the public interest that all relevant evidence should be adduced to the court, and if the former is preponderant the evidence will be excluded.

I do not think that the confidentiality of the communication provides in itself a satisfactory basis for testing whether relevant evidence should be withheld. First, it does not sufficiently reflect the true basis on which any evidence is excluded – namely, the public interest. Even *Wigmore (Evidence*, 1st ed, vol IV (1905), sec 2285; 3rd ed (1940), vol VIII, sec 2285), who stipulates for a principle of confidentiality as a condition of testimonial privilege (and I emphasise that he is dealing only with privilege), states (sec 2286):

'In general, then, *the mere fact that a communication was made in express confidence*, or in the implied confidence of a *confidential relation*, does not create a privilege. This [3rd ed: 'common law'] rule is questioned today.' (His italics.)

In the words of *Wigmore*, for the privilege to attach, the relationship between the parties to the communication: 'must be one which in the opinion of the community ought to be sedulously *fostered'* (sec 2285; his italics).

Secondly, a juridical basis of confidentiality does not explain why, in relation to certain classes of excluded evidence, there can be no waiver of the immunity. Thirdly, certain evidence is excluded not because it is confidential (even in the sense of being secret) but because it relates to affairs of state. For example, it was on that ground and not irrelevance that Cobbett was precluded in his trial for seditious libel from asking a witness whether it would not be wise to follow his (Cobbett's) advice as to how to deal with current civil disturbance (*R v Cobbett* (1831) 2 State Tr NS 789, 877). Fourthly, the law would operate erratically and capriciously according to whether or not a particular communication was made confidentially: Delane, the great 19th century editor of 'The Times,' always refused to receive information under the seal of secrecy, because sooner rather than later he would get the same information from a source he could use. Fifthly, it is undesirable that exclusion should be conferred by confidentiality irrespective of the public interest: after all, an attempt to bribe is generally made confidentially (cf *Lewis v James* (1887) 3 TLR 527; *Re Hooley, Rucker's Case* (1898) 79 LT 306; *McGuiness v A-G of Victoria* (1940) 63 CLR 73). Sixthly, confidentiality was in fact the original and far-reaching ground of exclusion. A man of honour would not betray a confidence, and the judges as men of honour themselves would not require him to. Thus originally legal professional privilege was that of the legal adviser, not the client. (For the foregoing, see *Wigmore, Evidence*, secs 2286, 2290.) But, with the decline in the ethos engendering the rule, the law moved decisively away from it. The turning point was the *Duchess of Kingston's Case* (1776) 20 State Tr 355, 386–91, where both the duchess's surgeon and a personal friend, Lord Barrington, were compelled to give evidence in breach of confidence. Seventhly, there is massive authority in addition to *Wigmore, Evidence* and the *Duchess of Kingston's Case* against confidentiality by itself conferring exclusion: Sir George Jessel MR in *Wheeler v Le Marchant* (1881) 17 Ch D 675, 681; Lord Parker of Waddington CJ in *A-G v Clough* [1963] 1 QB 773, 787; Lord Denning MR in *A-G v Mulholland*; *A-G v Foster* [1963] 2 QB 477, 489, Donovan LJ and Danckwerts LJ agreeing; Lord Salmon in *R v Lewes Justices, ex p Secretary of State for the Home Department* [1973] AC 388, 411H–412A; Lord Cross of Chelsea in *Alfred Crompton Amusement Machines Ltd v Customs and Excise Comrs (No 2)* [1974] AC 405, 433H; *O'Brennan v Tully* (1933) 69 ILTR 115 (cited with approval in *A-G v Mulholland*; *A-G v Foster* at 491); *McGuiness v A-G of Victoria* 63 CLR 73, which contains a judgment of characteristic authority by Dixon J dealing with the plea of confidentiality (cited with approval in *A-G v Clough* at 790–1 and in *A-G v Mulholland*; *A-G v Foster* at 491): see also *Bray on Discovery* (1885) at 303. I think the true rule is expressed in *Wigmore, Evidence* and in the passage referred to in the speech of Lord Cross of Chelsea in *Alfred Crompton Amusement Machines Ltd v Customs and Excise Comrs (No 2)* [1974] AC 405, 433:

'"Confidentiality" is not a separate head of privilege, but it may be a very material consideration to bear in mind when privilege is claimed on the ground of public interest.'

(It is only right to say that counsel for the appellants did not rely on confidentiality pur sang as a criterion of exclusion, but rather on the way it was put by Lord Cross.) For the reasons I have given I do not myself think that confidentiality in itself establishes any public interest in the exclusion of relevant evidence, but rather that it may indirectly be significant where a public interest extrinsically established (for example, provision of professional legal advice or effective policing) can only be vindicated if its communications have immunity from forensic investigation.

I naturally feel the same temerity in approaching the report of the powerful Law Reform Committee as I do in approaching the judgment of the learned Master of the Rolls. But since counsel for the appellants relied greatly on the report for his wide general proposition, I feel bound to express my reservations. I would start by pointing out that the committee was concerned only with civil proceedings, and within them only with 'privilege' from disclosure. Even though the rules of criminal evidence may differ in some respects from civil, any wide judicial discretion to admit or reject evidence should, I think, at least be tested against what would be acceptable in a criminal trial. Secondly, I do not think that *A-G v Clough* [1963] 1 QB 773 or *A-G v Mulholland*; *A-G v Foster* [1963] 2 QB 477 really supports the existence of such a wide discretionary power as the committee considered to vest in the court (except for the judgment of Donovan LJ in the latter case, at 492). Thirdly, the massive authority I referred to in the preceding paragraph of this speech must at least be weighed in the other scale: see also *Marks v Beyfus* (1890) 25 QBD 494, per Lord Esher MR at 498, Bowen LJ at 500 – not a matter of discretion, but a rule of law. Fourthly, I think that the true position is that the judge may not only rule as a matter of law or practice on the admissibility of evidence, but can also exercise a considerable moral authority on the course of a trial. For example, in the situations envisaged the judge is likely to say to counsel: 'You see that the witness feels that he ought not in conscience to answer that question. Do you really press it in the circumstances?' Such moral pressure will vary according to the circumstances – on the one hand, the relevance of the evidence; on the other, the nature of the ethical or professional inhibition. Often indeed such a witness will merely require a little gentle guidance from the judge to overcome his reluctance. I have never myself known this procedure to fail to resolve the situations acceptably. But it is far from the exercise of a formal discretion. And if it comes to the forensic crunch, as it did in many of the cases I have referred to (to which can be added the Parnell Inquiry Commission, 103rd day: see footnote to *Wigmore, Evidence*, sec 2286; also another passage cited in *A-G v Mulholland*; *A-G v Foster* [1963] 2 QB 477, 490–1), it must be law, not discretion, which is in command. It may be that the members of the Law Reform Committee considered that a consistent use of moral persuasion had resulted in a rule of practice emerging; cf *Povey v Povey* [1972] Fam 40, 48–9 (although I am not convinced myself that it has). Lastly, many of the practical objections voiced by my noble and learned friend, Lord Hailsham of St Marylebone, to the main and wider proposition advanced on behalf of the appellants seem to me to apply equally to the proposition of the Law Reform Committee. But it may be that some of the relationships will need re-examination as matters of practice or law; and it is to be borne in mind that it has been found expedient in some jurisdictions to modify the common law rule of disclosure by giving statutory immunity to, for example, doctors or priests.

My Lords, I have dwelt on this matter because, as I said, counsel for the appellants relied considerably on the report for his wide proposition – a general discretion in the court to weigh conflicting public interests in the adduction or exclusion of evidence. He also, of course, relied on *Conway v Rimmer* [1968] AC 910, where conflicting public interests were indeed weighed. But your Lordships' House was really there concerned with the validity of claims by the Crown (based on *Duncan v Cammell Laird & Co Ltd* [1942] AC 624) that the executive could procure the exclusion of evidence by a conclusive ministerial certificate that the evidence belonged to a class the disclosure of any part of which would be detrimental to the public interest. Your Lordships' House overruled *Duncan v Cammell Laird & Co Ltd* in this respect and further laid down that if in doubt the court could itself look at a document in the light of any ministerial certificate in order to ascertain whether its forensic publication could really affect the public interest adversely. I do not think that *Conway v Rimmer* provides any real foundation for the appellants' wide proposition.

That proposition does, on the other hand, reflect the general principles underlying this branch of the law, as I endeavoured to state them near the outset of this speech. Nevertheless, your Lordships are here concerned with public policy, with all the circumspection which such concern enjoins.

The first question on such a circumspect approach is not so much to canvass general principle as to ascertain whether the law has recognised an existing head of public policy which is relevant to this case. Of that there can be no doubt. The need of continuity in society; the legal application to children of the traditional role of the Crown as parens patriae; its exercise in the Court of Chancery in such a way as to make the welfare of a child the first and paramount consideration in matters of custody and guardianship (*Re Thain (An Infant)* [1926] Ch 676); a vast code of legislation starting with the Prevention of Cruelty to Children Act 1889 and culminating in the Children Act 1975; *Re D (Infants)* [1970] 1 WLR 599, decided in this very branch of the law – all this attests beyond question a public interest in the protection of children from neglect or ill-usage.

The patria potestas in respect of children in need of help has been largely devolved on local authorities. But the appellants, not only by royal charter but also by statutory recognition, have an important role to play. Apart from the police and the local authority, they are the only persons authorised to take care proceedings in respect of a child or young person (Children and Young Persons Act 1969, section 1; Children and Young Persons Act 1969 (Authorisation for the purposes of Section 1) Order 1970). They have, of course, other important functions for the protection of children from neglect or ill-usage . . .

. . . Is protection of their sources of information necessary for the proper performance of their functions by the appellants? As to this there is uncontradicted and entirely plausible evidence. The answer is 'yes.' This satisfies *Wigmore's* second test: the element of confidentiality is 'essential to the full and satisfactory maintenance of the relation between' the appellants and their informants (sec 2285). And the answers to this and the preceding question together meet *Wigmore's* third criterion: the relation is 'one which in the opinion of the community ought to be sedulously fostered' (sec 2285).

The final question, my Lords, is whether the appellants' sources of information can be withheld from forensic investigation by extending on strict analogy an established rule of law. I have already cited long-standing and approved authority to the effect that sources of police information are not subject to forensic investigations. This is because liability to general disclosure would cause those sources of information to dry up, so that police protection of the community would be impaired. Exactly the same argument applies in the instant case if for 'police' you read 'NSPCC' and for 'community' you read 'that part of the community which consists of children who may be in peril.' There can be no material distinction between police and/or local authorities on the one hand and the appellants on the other as regards protection of children. It follows that, on the strictest analogical approach and as a matter of legal rule, the appellants are bound to refuse to disclose their sources of information.

I would therefore allow the appeal.

Lord Edmund-Davies: In the result, I believe that the law applicable to all civil actions like the present one may be thus stated:

(I) In civil proceedings a judge has no discretion, simply because what is contemplated is the disclosure of information which has passed between persons in a confidential relationship (other than that of lawyer and client), to direct a party to that relationship that he need not disclose that information even though its disclosure is (a) relevant to and (b) necessary for the attainment of justice in the particular case. If (a) and (b) are established, the doctor or the priest must be directed to answer if, despite the strong dissuasion of the judge, the advocate persists in seeking disclosure. This is also true of all other confidential relationships in the absence of a special statutory provision, such as the Civil Evidence Act 1968, regarding communications between patent agents and their clients.

(II) But where (i) a confidential relationship exists (other than that of lawyer and client) *and* (ii) disclosure would be in breach of some ethical or social value involving the public interest, the court has a discretion to uphold a refusal to disclose relevant evidence provided it considers that, on balance, the public interest would be better served by excluding such evidence.

(III) In conducting the necessary balancing operation between competing aspects of public interest, the presence (or absence) of involvement of the central government in the matter of disclosure is *not* conclusive either way, though in practice it may affect the cogency of the argument against disclosure. It is true that in *Blackpool Corpn v Locker* [1948] 1 KB 349, [1948] 1 All ER 85 the Court of Appeal dismissed a local authority's claim to exclude their interdepartmental communications in the public interest, Scott LJ saying, at 380: 'No such privilege has yet, so far as I know, been conceded by the courts to any local government officer when his employing authority is in litigation.' But it is worthy of note that he went on to observe that, although

'Public interest is, from the point of view of English justice, a regrettable and sometimes dangerous form of privilege, though at times unavoidable . . . *no such ground was put forward in the plaintiffs' affidavit.*' (The italics are mine.)

We therefore cannot be sure how that case would otherwise have been decided, but we do know from *Conway v Rimmer* [1968] AC 910 and *Re D (Infants)* [1970] 1 WLR 599 that an organ of central government does not now necessarily have to be involved before a claim for non-disclosure can succeed. In my judgment, Scarman LJ therefore went too far in asserting in the Court of Appeal in the present case [1976] 3 WLR 124, 139 that '. . . state interest alone can justify the withholding of relevant documents . . .' So to assert is, in the wise words of one commentator,

'. . . to place too high a value on the arbitrary factor of the status of the possessor of the information. It also assumes that organisations can be classified into those which have the status of a "central organ of government" . . . and those which do not. Such a classification is surely impracticable.' (Joseph Jacob, 'Discovery and Public Interest' [1976] PL 134, 138.)

(IV) The sole touchstone is the public interest, and not whether the party from whom disclosure is sought was acting under a 'duty' – as opposed to merely exercising 'powers.' A party who acted under some duty may find it easier to establish that public interest was involved than one merely exercising powers, but that is another matter.

(V) The mere fact that relevant information was communicated in confidence does not necessarily mean that it need not be disclosed. But where the subject matter is clearly of public interest, the *additional* fact (if such it be) that to break the seal of confidentiality would endanger that interest will in most (if not all) cases probably lead to the conclusion that disclosure should be withheld. And it is difficult to conceive of *any* judicial discretion to exclude relevant and necessary evidence save in respect of confidential information communicated in a confidential relationship.

(VI) The disclosure of all evidence relevant to the trial of an issue being at all times a matter of considerable public interest, the question to be determined is whether it is clearly demonstrated that in the particular case the public interest would nevertheless be better served by excluding evidence despite its relevance. If, on balance, the matter is left in doubt, disclosure should be ordered.

[Lord Kilbrandon agreed that the appeal should be allowed.]

NOTES

1. Is *D's* Case based on
(a) an analogy with informer cases, or
(b) a general doctrine of public interest?
Later cases appear to invoke reasoning of the latter kind. Cf *R v Cheltenham Justices, ex p Secretary of State for Trade* [1977] 1 All ER 460, [1977] 1 WLR 95; *Science Research Council v Nassé* [1980] AC 1028, [1979] 3 All ER 673, HL; *London and County Securities Ltd v Nicholson* [1980] 3 All ER 861, [1980] 1 WLR 948; *Bankers Trust Co v Shapira* [1980] 3 All ER 353, [1980] 1 WLR 1274, CA; *Gaskin v Liverpool City Council* [1980] 1 WLR 1549, CA; *Campbell v Tameside Metropolitan Borough Council* [1982] QB 1065, [1982] 2 All ER 791, CA. Is there any relevant distinction between a doctrine appropriate to the scope of inspection of discovered documents (with which several of the above cases are concerned) and a doctrine to regulate the admissibility of evidence?
2. Does *D's* Case suggest that *Conway v Rimmer* is too wide, and that the law has in practice been pushed towards that stated in *Duncan's* Case?
3. Apart from the uncertain and potentially wide doctrine of exclusion of evidence in the public interest which has arisen in the wake of, though perhaps without being justified by the language of, *D's* Case, the court has powers operating on the borderland of public and private privilege which tended to prevent the free disclosure of unprivileged materials. Thus a litigant who obtains inspection of a discovered document in one set of proceedings is only permitted to use it for the purposes of those proceedings, and not in relation to new claims against the defendant (*Riddick v Thames Board Mills Ltd* [1977] QB 881, [1977] 3 All ER 677, CA), nor for distribution to a journalist, even if it has been read in open court (*Harman v Secretary of State for the Home Department* [1983] 1 AC 280, [1982] 1 All ER 532, HL).
4. The rule protecting the identity of an informer entails rules preventing the identification of the owner or occupier of the premises used for surveillance and preventing the identification of the premises themselves; the latter rules exist only for the fulfilment of the informer rule and not as separate rules in their own right: *R v Rankine* [1986] QB 861 at 867, [1986] 2 All ER 566 at 570, CA; *R v Brown and Daley* (1987) 87 Cr App Rep 52, CA; *R v Johnson* [1989] 1 All ER 121, [1988] 1 WLR 1377, CA. Cf *R v Hewitt* (1991) 95 Cr App Rep 81, CA; *Blake v DPP* (1992) 97 Cr App Rep 169, DC.

FURTHER READING

Andrews (1988) 104 LQR 410; Clark (1969) 32 MLR 142; Tapper (1974) 37 MLR 92; Tapper (1978) 41 MLR 192; Zuckerman in Tapper.

2 Previous litigation

It should be noted that on grounds of public policy judges of inferior courts cannot be compelled to testify about the cases they have heard: *R v Gazard* (1838) 8 C & P 595. Arbitrators can be compelled to testify but not to give reasons for their award (*Duke of Buccleuch v Metropolitan Board of Works* (1872) LR 5 HL 418, HL) unless the award does not constitute a res judicata between the parties, being relied on as evidence in other proceedings between strangers (*Land Securities plc v Westminster City Council* [1993] 4 All ER 124, [1993] 1 WLR 286). Evidence will not be received from jurors as to their discussions: *Jackson v Williamson* (1788) 2 Term Rep 281. It may, however, be taken as part of an inquiry as to whether the jury should be discharged (*R v Orgles* [1993] 4 All ER 533, [1994] 1 WLR 108, CA). There is little authority on advocates.

PART SIX

The Course of the Trial

CHAPTER 20

The Course of the Trial

Some of the subjects now to be discussed are among the most obscure and misunderstood in the law. The rules often have to be teased out of ancient authorities operating against a different statutory background. The rules also are often waived, by consent or ignorance, in practice. What follows attempts to concentrate on the main principles rather than the mass of detail which has become encrusted on them by the case law.

1 Civil cases

A ORDER

The 'right to begin' is the right to make a speech to the court explaining the issues. The right depends on who has the right to begin calling evidence, and this will be the plaintiff if he has the evidential burden on any issue raised by the pleadings, as he almost always does and is henceforth assumed. After he addresses the court, he begins calling witnesses. After he examines them ('examination-in-chief') the defendant may cross-examine them and the plaintiff may re-examine them. The plaintiff will make a closing speech if the defendant does not call witnesses; the defendant will then have a right to reply. If the defendant calls witnesses (who may be cross-examined by the plaintiff) the procedure will be: plaintiff's opening, plaintiff's witnesses, defendant's opening, defendant's witnesses, defendant's final speech, plaintiff's reply. In particular proceedings or for special reasons the order may be varied. The 'orality' of the trial is not absolute: there is an increasing trend towards the giving of evidence in chief by written statement or affidavit.

This procedure may be interrupted by arguments about the admissibility of evidence or other points of law. At the close of the plaintiff's case the defendant may submit that there is no case to answer. If this is done before a judge with a jury, the judge must put the maker of the submission to an election; if he adheres to the submission he must not call evidence (*Alexander v Rayson* [1936] 1 KB 169, CA; *Storey v Storey* [1961] P 63, [1960] 3 All ER 279, CA). However, the judge has a discretion not to compel an election in civil cases tried by jury. In *Young v Rank* [1950] 2 KB 510 at 515, [1950] 2 All ER

166 at 169 Devlin J offered this explanation:

'[I]n a case tried by judge alone the Court of Appeal has a complete power of rehearing, and if evidence for the defendant has not been taken and the court disagrees with the ruling of the trial judge, it is, in effect, prevented from exercising its power of rehearing and has no alternative but to send the case back for retrial, which will result in additional costs to the parties. In cases of trial by jury, the Court of Appeal has no power of rehearing, and, if the verdict of the jury is set aside for any reason, the court has no power except to send it back for re-trial.'

The judge may delay taking his decision on a submission of no case to answer until after the jury's verdict; this avoids the need for a new trial if an appeal against his decision to uphold the submission succeeds. It does produce a slightly unattractive appearance of judicial overruling of juries. An appeal may be dismissed even though the appellate court thinks the submission should have been upheld if subsequent evidence is against the party making it (*Payne v Harrison* [1961] 2 QB 403, [1961] 2 All ER 873, CA). In making his decision on a 'no case' submission, the judge should take the plaintiff's case at its highest: see ch 3, ante. If the judge decides against the submission the case continues; but even if the defendant gives no evidence the trier of fact may decide against the plaintiff. This may arise because of the difference between the evidential burden of proof and the legal burden; or because the credibility of the witnesses is such that in truth the plaintiff's case is not, at the end of the trial, capable of being taken at its highest.

In proceedings before magistrates the doctrine of election applies. If the magistrates hold there is a case to answer, the maker of the submission should be given a further opportunity to address them (*Disher v Disher* [1965] P 31, [1963] 3 All ER 933).

B   KINDS OF EXAMINATION

(i)   Examination-in-chief

The purpose of questions put to a witness in chief is to obtain evidence supporting the case of the party calling the witness. In various respects examination-in-chief is more restricted than cross-examination. Leading questions can be used less freely; and though an unfavourable witness may be contradicted by other evidence he cannot be discredited unless he proves hostile.

(ii)   Cross-examination

The purpose of cross-examination is to destroy those parts of the witness's testimony which tell in favour of the party calling him and to obtain testimony favourable to the cross-examiner. Both aims are achieved by cross-examination to the issue; only the first aim is achieved by cross-examination which seeks to destroy the witness's credit. The normal rules of admissibility apply, but the cross-examiner has greater freedom than the examiner-in-chief. He may use leading questions, he may ask about previous inconsistent statements and prove them if they are denied, he may ask questions about bad character, previous convictions, unreliability or bias, and prove the convictions, the physical or mental causes of unreliability, or the bias if they are denied. A witness may probably be cross-examined by any party (*Murdoch v Taylor* [1965] AC 574 at 584, [1965] 1 All ER 406 at 409, HL, per Lord Morris of Borth-y-Gest; *R v Hilton* [1972] 1 QB 421, [1971] 3 All ER 541, CA). It may be noted that any question relevant to the issues in the case may be asked even though the witness gave no evidence about the matter in chief. Some American jurisdictions took the narrower course, and a further refinement rejected by English law is to permit questions by the cross-examiner about all relevant matters save matters relating to the cross-examiner's affirmative case.

However, the witness is to some extent protected even under cross-examination. If it is proposed to contradict him by subsequent evidence on any point, that point must be put to him so that he can explain any misunderstanding, unless the witness and the party calling him are on notice that his version is in contest. This is the rule in *Browne v Dunn* (1893) 6 R 67, HL, exhaustively explained in *Allied Pastoral Holdings Pty Ltd v Comr of Taxation* [1983] 1 NSWLR 1. If this is not done the cross-examiner may be taken to accept the evidence. The judge has a discretion to disallow improper or aggressive questions. It must be conducted with courtesy, which is not inconsistent with effectiveness: *Mechanical and General Inventions Co Ltd and Lehwess v Austin and Austin Motor Co Ltd* [1935] AC 346, HL. The judge has a discretion to terminate unduly lengthy cross-examination: *Wakeley v R* (1990) 93 ALR 79.

(iii) Re-examination

The purpose of re-examination is to rehabilitate the witness's testimony from the effects of cross-examination, if this is necessary. It is generally subject to the same rules as examination-in-chief. Further, re-examination must be confined to matters arising out of the cross-examination, and new material cannot be introduced without the judge's leave. This avoids the danger of the other side being unable to examine the witness on the material.

C SPECIAL PROBLEMS

(i) Leading questions

A leading question is one which 'leads' the witness by suggesting the answer desired or assuming the existence of disputed facts. In examination-in-chief or re-examination such questions are frowned on. Questions assuming the existence of disputed facts are not generally permitted in cross-examination either. Leading questions of the first kind encourage and make too easy the coaching of witnesses, and they pander to human laziness or produce misleading results when put to a witness too polite to correct what he may regard as an unimportant inaccuracy. The assumption of disputed facts may improperly influence the jury and may be unfair to the witness if he cannot answer directly but has to enter upon a seemingly evasive explanation. The first (and sometimes the second) kind of leading question is, however, permitted for introductory, formal or undisputed matters, for questioning about identity, and to bring a witness's attention to some special point. The judge has considerable discretion as to how many leading questions may be asked, for they do save time and enable testimony to be given naturally. They are widely permitted in cross-examination so as to focus the attention of witness and court on the points on which his testimony is being challenged and tested; see *Mooney v James* [1949] VLR 22 at 28, per Barry J:

> 'The basis of the rule that leading questions may be put in cross-examination is the assumption that the witness's partisanship, conscious or unconscious, in combination with the circumstance that he is being questioned by an adversary will produce the state of mind that will protect him against suggestibility. But if the court is satisfied there is no ground for the assumption, the rule has no application, and the judge may forbid cross-examination by questions which go to the length of putting into the witness's mouth the very words he is to echo back again. (Cf *R v Hardy* (1794) 24 State Tr 199 at 755, per Buller J.) Answers given in such circumstances usually would not assist the court in its investigation because they would be valueless, and in the exercise of his power to control and regulate the proceedings the Judge may properly require counsel to abandon a worthless method of examination.'

Isolated answers to leading questions have little value: a witness's credibility can be seen better in his answers to non-leading questions.

(ii) Refreshing memory

A witness may 'refresh his memory' by referring to documentary records of the facts in issue. The document need not itself be admissible. The document must have been made about the time of the facts being testified to; as always, this is a vague question of degree. (In *R v Governor of Gloucester Prison, ex p Miller* [1979] 2 All ER 1103, [1979] 1 WLR 537, DC, this was rather surprisingly said to be a rule of practice but not of law.) Thus the 'proper foundation' for an application that the witness be permitted to refresh his memory (albeit through a leading question) is to ask whether the events were fresh in his mind when the document was made: *R v Da Silva* [1990] 1 All ER 29, [1990] 1 WLR 31, CA. The document must have been made by or under the supervision of the witness. The document must be handed to the opponent for inspection to enable cross-examination to occur on its contents; the trier of fact has a right to see it. The original must be produced (at least if the opponent requires it: *R v Alexander* [1975] VR 741) if the document does not actually revive the witness's memory of what he swears to, but instead simply makes him confident as to the truth of what he recorded. (This will often arise with policemen and doctors who record many very similar events that may culminate in litigation; they cannot be expected to remember them in detail but they can swear to the truth of their record.) However, if the document actually causes him to remember the fact, the original need not be produced (*Doe d Church and Phillips v Perkins* (1790) 3 Term Rep 749). Using the document to refresh memory does not make it evidence of the truth of its contents: *R v Virgo* (1978) 67 Cr App Rep 323, CA. Nor is it made evidence by the opponent inspecting it and cross-examining on the parts used to refresh memory (*Senat v Senat* [1965] P 172, [1965] 2 All ER 505). But more extensive cross-examination or reliance on the parts of the document makes it evidence at the insistence of the party calling the witness (*R v Britton* [1987] 2 All ER 412, [1987] 1 WLR 539, CA), and is equivalent to calling a witness for the purposes of the order of speeches. If it is admitted in this way, it goes only to credibility, as an exception to the rule against the reception of previous statements, not to the issue: *R v Virgo* (1978) 67 Cr App Rep 323, CA.

Further, the document may be tendered, though not as evidence of the truth of its contents, nor even as going to credibility, where it is difficult for the trier of fact to follow the cross-examination of the witness who has refreshed his memory, or where it is a useful aide mémoire to the witness's evidence if it is long and involved: *R v Sekhon* (1986) 85 Cr App Rep 19, CA. And it has been held that a document used to refresh memory on which there has been cross-examination may be tendered in re-examination if inspection of it would assist the trier of fact to determine whether it is bogus or not: *R v Dillon* (1983) 85 Cr App Rep 29n, CA. A witness may refresh his memory from a statement or transcription of notes where the statement or transcription is substantially the same as the original note, but if it is not the judge has a discretion to prevent refreshment: *R v Kwok Si Cheng* (1976) 63 Cr App Rep 20, CA. Memory may also be refreshed from a full note made some time after the composition of brief jottings contemporaneously with the relevant facts: *A-G's Reference (No 3 of 1979)* (1979) 69 Cr App Rep 411, CA.

There is no general rule that prospective witnesses cannot, before giving evidence, see the statements they made at or near the time of the relevant event; on the other hand, they have no right to do so: *R v Westwell* [1976] 2 All ER 812, CA. If a prosecution witness does so refresh his memory, it is desirable (though not a rule of procedure) that the defence be so informed: *Worley v Bentley* [1976] 2 All ER 449.

It has been held that the above rules apply only to the refreshing of memory in court: *R v Richardson* [1971] 2 QB 484, [1971] 2 All ER 773, CA; but this decision has been doubted: Howard [1972] Crim LR 351.

A recent extension of the law on refreshment of memory was effected in *R v Da Silva* [1990] 1 All ER 29, [1990] 1 WLR 31, CA. In that case the Court of Appeal held that the judge had a discretion to permit a witness who has begun to give evidence to refresh his memory from a statement made near the time of the events in issue, even if it was not contemporaneous, provided he is satisfied:

'(1) That the witness indicates that he cannot now recall the details of events because of the lapse of time since they took place;
(2) That he made a statement much nearer the time of the events and that the contents of the statement represented his recollection at the time he made it;
(3) That he had not read the statement before coming into the witness-box;
(4) That he wished to have an opportunity to read the statement before he continued to give evidence.

We do not think that it matters whether the witness withdraws from the witness-box and reads his statement, as he would do if he had had the opportunity before entering the witness-box, or whether he reads it in the witness-box. What is important is that if the former course is adopted, no communication must be had with the witness, other than to see that he can read the statement in peace. Moreover, if either course is adopted, the statement must be removed from him when he comes to give his evidence, and he should not be permitted to refer to it again, unlike a contemporaneous statement which may be used to refresh memory while giving evidence.'

The law relating to refreshing memory has been made of much less practical importance in civil cases by the Civil Evidence Act 1995. While that Act abolishes the rule against hearsay and thereby renders documents used to refresh memory admissible in chief, s 6(4) provides that it does not affect any of the rules of law as to the circumstances in which, where a witness is cross-examined on a document used by him to refresh memory, that document may be made evidence: p 363, ante.

QUESTIONS

1. What is the significance of the distinction between genuine and non-genuine revival of recollection? Save on the witness's own statement, how is it to be determined whether recollection has been genuinely revived or not?

2. Where there is no revival of present recollection, is the rule that the document which is used to refresh memory is not evidence of the facts asserted and need not comply with other rules of admissibility realistic? See *R v Naidanovici* [1962] NZLR 334.

3. '[M]emory of things long past can be accurately restored in all sorts of ways. The creaking of a hinge, the whistling of a tune, the smell of seaweed, the sight of an old photograph, the taste of nutmeg, the touch of a piece of canvas, may bring vividly to the foreground of consciousness the recollection of events that happened years ago and which would otherwise have been forgotten. If a recollection thus awakened be then set down on paper, why should not that paper properly serve in the courtroom, as it does in everyday life, to prod the memory at still a later date?': *Fanelli v United States Gypsum Co* 141 F 2d 216 at 217 (1944) per Frank J. Does this justify an abandonment of the present rules as to refreshment of memory?

(iii)   Previous consistent statements

There used to be a general rule that a witness might not be asked in chief whether he has made a prior statement consistent with his present testimony, nor might other witnesses prove it. The rule existed to prevent the manufacture of self-serving evidence by party-witnesses: 'The presumption . . . is . . . that every man, if he was in a difficulty, or in the view to any difficulty, would make declarations for himself': *R v Hardy* (1794) 24 State Tr 199 at 1093. The rule also prevents the introduction of collateral issues and superfluous testimony. It proceeds on the assumption that a witness ought prima facie to be regarded as giving truthful evidence so that there is no need for the bolstering of his credibility. It had the substantial drawback of preventing witnesses telling their stories in a natural way, ie by stating facts observed and statements made about them to others. It is also doubtful whether it might not have been better to admit statements made near the time of the facts in issue rather than be limited to those made years later at the trial. In civil cases the rule has been substantially eroded by the Civil Evidence Act 1995: see ch 14, ante.

A sketch or 'photofit' made by a police officer under the instructions of a witness has been held not to be within the rule against prior consistent statements on the ground that it is not a statement, but is analogous to a photograph (*R v Cook* [1987] QB 417, [1987] 1 All ER 1049, CA); yet in truth it appears to be a compendious summary of numerous statements by the witness to the police officer.

Res gestae statements

At common law previous consistent statements were sometimes admissible as part of the res gestae. Now, so far as these statements are tendered as evidence of their truth, the exception has been swallowed up by the Civil Evidence Act 1995. But so far as they are tendered as evidence of the fact that they were made, they will continue to be admissible; s 1 of the Act which abolishes common law hearsay exceptions will not apply to evidence which is original rather than hearsay in character (eg *Milne v Leisler* (1862) 7 H & N 786).

Rebutting afterthought

At common law, if in cross-examination it was suggested to a witness that he had fabricated his story, his previous consistent statements could be admitted, not as evidence of the truth of what they asserted, but to show consistency. See now Civil Evidence Act 1995, s 6(2)(*b*): p 363, ante. It is not necessary that *recent* fabrication or invention be alleged (see *Wentworth v Rogers (No 10)* (1987) 8 NSWLR 398 at 401; *R v Sekhon* (1986) 85 Cr App Rep 19, CA; and see *Fox v General Medical Council* [1960] 3 All ER 225, [1960] 1 WLR 1017, PC; *Nominal Defendant v Clements* (1960) 104 CLR 476; *R v Oyesiku* (1971) 56 Cr App Rep 240, CA).

Miscellaneous

Writers have noted that in practice there are other exceptions to the old rule. One example is the accused's statements favourable to himself which are part of admissions tendered against him (*R v Duncan* (1981) 73 Cr App Rep 359, CA; *R v Sharp* [1988] 1 All ER 65, [1988] 1 WLR 7, HL). There is no discretion to exclude these statements despite their prejudicial effect on a co-accused (*Lobban v R* [1995] 2 All ER 602, [1995] 1 WLR 877, PC). Another example is pre-trial identifications by identity witnesses (Gooderson, [1968] CLJ 64; see p 99 and pp 337–8, ante). A statement which is not inculpatory made to the police on being taxed with incriminating facts has been held admissible because of showing the reaction of the accused (*R v Storey* (1968) 52 Cr App Rep 334, CA), but it is not evidence of the facts stated, and since it need not be drawn to the attention of the jury if the accused fails to testify (*R v Barbery* (1975) 62 Cr App Rep 248, CA) it must only be admissible to show some consistency; it is highly questionable whether the cases supporting admissibility on this basis are correct.

(iv) Unfavourable and hostile witnesses

A party may be disappointed by the evidence a witness called by him gives. The witness may not 'come up to proof' – he may tell a different story to the court from that told outside it. If he merely fails to testify to certain facts or testifies to the opposite of what was expected, he is an 'unfavourable' witness. A hostile witness is one who is 'unwilling, if called by a party who cannot ask him leading questions, to tell the truth and the whole truth in answer to non-leading questions – to tell the truth for the advancement of justice' (*R v Hayden* [1959] VLR 102 at 103, per Sholl J). A witness is hostile not merely if he contradicts a previous statement, but also if he refuses to answer: *R v Thompson* (1976) 64 Cr App Rep 96, CA. The decision as to a witness's hostility is one in the discretion of the judge, and on this issue his decision will only rarely be reversed, depending as it does on observation of demeanour and detailed knowledge of the course of the trial. However, it is probably too much to say it will never be reversed (*Wentworth v Rogers (No 10)* (1987) 8 NSWLR 398 at 407; cf *Rice v Howard* (1886) 16 QBD 681). Hostility can be inferred from previous inconsistent statements, including those made orally: *R v Prefas* (1986) 86 Cr App Rep 111, CA.

The normal rule is that a party may not impeach his own witness, ie may not treat him as if he is under cross-examination. At common law, an unfavourable witness could be contradicted by calling other evidence (*Ewer v Ambrose* (1825) 3 B & C 746); and a hostile witness could also be asked leading questions and challenged regarding his means of knowledge and powers of observation; but no evidence of lack of veracity could be adduced (eg proof of convictions). At common law it was doubtful whether previous inconsistent statements could be proved. In 1854 legislation which is now the Criminal Procedure Act 1865, s 3, was enacted. It applies to both civil and criminal cases. It provides: 'A party producing a witness shall not be allowed to impeach his credit by general evidence of bad character, but he may, in case the witness shall, in the opinion of the judge, prove adverse, contradict him by other evidence, or, by leave of the judge, prove that he has made at other times a statement inconsistent with his present testimony; but before such last-mentioned proof can be given the circumstances of the supposed statement, sufficient to designate the particular occasion, must be mentioned to the witness, and he must be asked whether or not he has made such statement.'

'Adverse' means 'hostile'. Does it follow that the common law power to introduce evidence contradicting an unfavourable witness is lost? This disastrous result is avoided by one of two means. Cockburn CJ preferred to ignore this conclusion as being based on 'a great blunder' (*Greenough v Eccles* (1859) 5 CBNS 786 at 806). Williams and Willes JJ said 'we think the preferable construction is that in case the witness shall, in the opinion of the judge, prove "hostile" the party producing him may not only contradict him by other witnesses, as he might heretofore have done, and may still do, if the witness is unfavourable, but may also, by leave of the judge, prove that he has made inconsistent statements' (28 LJCP 160 at 163).

The judge at common law had a discretion as to the mode in which an examination of the hostile witness should be conducted, and that discretion has not been destroyed by s 3 of the Criminal Procedure Act 1865: *R v Thompson* (1976) 64 Cr App Rep 96, CA. While s 3 of the Act applies to hostile witnesses, ss 4 and 5, to be considered shortly, do not; it follows that evidence cannot be called as of right to show that a hostile witness has made a previous inconsistent statement, and that the judge has a discretion to refuse leave for evidence to be called to prove such a statement: *R v Booth* (1981) 74 Cr App Rep 123, CA. The court has a discretion to permit a witness to be cross-examined by his own counsel to elicit the facts asserted in a prior written statement of the witness, and to reserve to counsel the right to cross-examine generally if the witness can be shown to be hostile: *R v Thynne* [1977] VR 98, following an unreported decision of Sir Owen Dixon in *R v Neal* (17 April 1947, unreported).

(v)   Previous inconsistent statements

Similar rules apply to previous inconsistent statements put, not to a hostile witness, but to an opponent's witness while he is being cross-examined.

Criminal Procedure Act 1865

4 If a witness, upon cross-examination as to a former statement made by him relative to the subject matter of the indictment or proceeding, and inconsistent with his present testimony, does not distinctly admit that he has made such statement, proof may be given that he did in fact make it; but before such proof can be given the circumstances of the supposed statement sufficient to designate the particular occasion, must be mentioned to the witness, and he must be asked whether or not he has made such statement.

5 A witness may be cross-examined as to previous statements made by him in writing or reduced into writing relative to the subject matter of the indictment or proceeding, without such writing being shown to him; but if it is intended to contradict such witness by the writing, his attention must, before such contradictory proof can be given, be called to those parts of the writing which are to be used for the purpose of so contradicting him: provided always, that it shall be competent for the judge, at any time during the trial, to require the production of the writing for his inspection, and he may thereupon make such use of it for the purpose of the trial as he may think fit.

NOTES

These sections apply in both civil and criminal cases: s 4 concerns oral statements and s 5 written ones.

In certain circumstances only parts of a document containing inconsistent statements should be admitted; further, the tender of an inconsistent statement under the sections does not authorise the tender of other out-of-court statements of the witness which are consistent with his testimony in order to sustain his credit: *R v Oyesiku* (1971) 56 Cr App Rep 240 at 244–5, CA; *R v Beattie* (1989) 89 Cr App Rep 302, CA. Nothing in these sections prevents the previous statement of a witness inconsistent with his testimony from being put to him to challenge his credibility, even if non-compliance with them does not allow the evidence of the making of the inconsistent statement to be given: *R v Funderburk* [1990] 2 All ER 482, [1990] 1 WLR 587, CA.

The Civil Evidence Act 1995 (see p 363, ante) makes all previous statements admissible evidence of the truth of what they assert, but in the case of previous inconsistent statements requires (see s 6(3)) compliance with ss 4 and 5 of the Criminal Procedure Act 1865. In criminal cases the former rule that they go only to show inconsistency applies. There is no inflexible rule that the jury must be directed that the evidence is unreliable: *R v Governor of Pentonville Prison, ex p Alves* [1993] AC 284 at 291-2, [1992] 4 All ER 787 at 792-3, HL; *R v Goodway* [1993] 4 All ER 894 at 899, CA; *Driscoll v R* (1977) 137 CLR 517 at 536–7 per Gibbs J, disapproving *R v Golder* (1960) 45 Cr App Rep 5 at 11, CCA, and *R v Oliva* [1965] 3 All ER 116 at 123, [1965] 1 WLR 1028 at 1036–7, CA.

(vi)   Cross-examination on documents

At common law a witness could not be asked questions about the contents of the document unless it was first shown to the witness and tendered: *Queen's Case* (1820) 2 Brod & Bing 284. That rule is modified, so far as a witness's own documents are concerned, by s 5 of the Criminal Procedure Act 1865 (above). A witness who is a party can be asked to make admissions about the contents of documents not in evidence, whether he is the author or not, if the contents are within his personal knowledge. There is a dispute about whether he can be compelled to answer, but the better view is that he can; if he could not, a hitherto unrecognised privilege would exist. A witness may be shown a document (whether or not he is the author and whether or not it is admissible) and asked whether, having read the document, he still adheres to his former testimony: sometimes he will change that testimony at that point. But that does not make the document admissible, and it is impermissible for the cross-examiner to go further by describing the document: if he does so he can be compelled to tender it.

(vii)   Collateral questions

The answers given by a witness to questions put in cross-examination about collateral facts are final. The jury may not believe the answers, but this process cannot be encouraged by the cross-examiner introducing contradictory evidence. The rule is intended to prevent side issues arising; see *A-G v Hitchcock* (1847) 1 Exch 91 at 103–4:

> 'The reason why a party is obliged to take the answer of a witness is, that if he were permitted to go into it, it is only justice to allow the witness to call other evidence in support of the testimony he has given, and as these witnesses might be cross-examined as to their conduct, such a course would be productive of endless collateral issues. Suppose, for instance, witness A is accused of having committed some offence; witness B is called to prove it when, on witness B's cross-examination, he is asked whether he has not made some statement, to prove which witness C is called, so that it would be necessary to try all these issues, before one step could be obtained towards the adjudication of the particular case before the Court.'

At 105 Rolfe B said:

> 'If we lived for a thousand years instead of about 60 or 70, and every case were of sufficient importance, it might be possible, and perhaps proper, to throw a light on matters in which every possible question might be suggested, for the purpose of seeing by such means whether the whole was unfounded, or what portion of it was not, and to raise every possible inquiry as to the truth of the statements made. But I do not see how that could be; in fact, mankind finds it to be impossible.'

Further, false statements on collateral matters may be insignificant, for '[n]o witness can be prepared to support his character as to particular facts': *Harris v Tippett* (1811) 2 Camp 637 at 638, per Lawrence J. Further, in *A-G v Hitchcock* at 103 Alderson B referred to 'the inconvenience that would arise from the witness being called upon to answer to particular acts of his life, which he might have been able to explain, if he had reasonable notice to do so, and to have shown that all the acts of his life had been perfectly correct and pure, although other witnesses were called to prove the contrary.'

The usual test for what a collateral fact is was stated by Pollock CB in *A-G v Hitchcock* (1847) 1 Exch 91 at 99:

> '[I]f the answer of a witness is a matter which you would be allowed on your own part to prove in evidence . . . then it is a matter on which you may contradict him.'

Thus collateral facts are those relevant to credibility rather than to the main issues. *Piddington v Bennett and Wood Pty Ltd* (1940) 63 CLR 533 and *R v Burke* (1858) 8 Cox CC 44 hold that evidence that a particular witness was not present at some event he claimed to be at, or that he cannot understand a language he claimed to, is evidence of collateral facts. Though the evidence mentioned may be very important, it is still evidence going to credibility and hence collateral to the issues in the case. It is for this reason that exceptions to the rule exist, and that those exceptions should not be completely closed; the possibility of the standard exceptions being added to has recently been left open: *R v Funderburk* [1990] 2 All ER 482, [1990] 1 WLR 587, CA.

There are several exceptions, apart from previous inconsistent statements, discussed p 478, ante. In the case of all these exceptions to the collateral answers rule, apart from previous inconsistent statements, the evidence may be introduced without there first being a denial of the fact proved; but it is convenient to treat them together in this way. If the witness denies that he has been convicted, his convictions may be proved to show his lack of credibility; the conviction need not be of a kind relevant to truth-telling (Criminal Procedure Act 1865, s 6, which applies to both civil and criminal cases). Questions about spent convictions are prohibited in civil proceedings by s 4(1) of the Rehabilitation of Offenders Act 1974. Such questions are permitted in criminal proceedings by s 7(2), but, pursuant to a Practice Direction, questions about them are to be avoided as far as possible: see p 275, ante.

Do all convictions tend to show that a witness is not credible? Holmes J in *Gertz v Fitchberg RR* 137 Mass 77 at 78 (1884) said: 'When it is proved that a witness has been convicted of a crime, the only ground for disbelieving him which such proof affords is the general readiness to do evil which the conviction may be supposed to show. It is from that general disposition alone that the jury is asked to infer a readiness to lie in the particular case, and thence that he has lied in fact. The evidence has no tendency to prove that he was mistaken, but only that he has perjured himself, and it reaches that conclusion solely through the general proposition that he is of bad character and unworthy of credit.' If this kind of reasoning is to be adopted safely, the evidence offered to prove a mendacious disposition must be substantially relevant to such a disposition. There is difficulty in determining in a particular case what that evidence is. The Criminal Law Revision Committee in its Eleventh Report (1972), para 160 said:

'We do not think it necessary or appropriate to attempt to define what should be the test for deciding whether a question to a witness other than the accused should be admissible on the ground that the fact to which it relates is relevant to his credibility as a witness. The view has been expressed to and in the Committee that the only kinds of misconduct which are relevant for this purpose are those involving dishonesty or perjury. Others think that a serious offence of violence, for example, may be relevant on the ground that the fact that the witness has been guilty of an outrageous disregard of the standards of good behaviour is something which it is right to take into account when considering whether to believe him or a well-behaved witness on a matter in issue.'

Bentham, in *A Rationale of Judicial Evidence* (1827) Bk V, ch 13, s 4, suggested that the only convictions admissible to impeach a witness's credibility should be of two kinds. The first comprised 'crimes of mendacity'. The second comprised:

'such other offences of the predatory cast (such as theft, highway robbery, and house-breaking), as suppose what may be called a general prostration of character; though here, too, the inference from such an act will be very inconclusive, unless it appear connected with a habit of the same kind. But, in the case of all offences in the description of which mendacity is not involved, the inference will stand lower in the scale of strength by a very determinate and perceptible degree.'

Bentham also said that other offences such as those produced by 'the irascible passions, and offences produced by the sexual appetite', did not support an inference of non-credibility. On the other hand, one argument for the general admissibility of bad behaviour to show want of credit is that:

'if a witness has, for his own purposes, chosen to do things which he must have been aware were serious breaches of accepted codes of proper behaviour in the community, then the court or a jury may reasonably feel a doubt as to how far it can rely on his having refrained, in his evidence, from committing, for his own purposes, breaches of the accepted code against giving false evidence' (Victorian Law Reform Commission Report on *Rape Prosecution (Court Procedures and Rules of Evidence)* No 5 (1976), para 60).

The rule that while extensive questioning on collateral matters is permitted, the answers are generally final, produces difficulty. It may encourage perjury: a witness may know that his false answer to a question on a collateral matter will be final: a different rule might make him strive to tell the truth for fear of being exposed when evidence rebutting his story is called. In a sense the law encourages the asking of questions to set up innuendoes, for the disappointed cross-examiner can appeal to nothing more. On one view, it would be better to restrict substantially the number of collateral questions which can be asked but expand the number of exceptions where the answers are not final. If a question is meritorious enough to be asked, why cannot a false answer to it be exposed?

Bias

The witness's denials of taking bribes, or of being on very good or bad terms with a party may be contradicted.

Incapacity to tell the truth

The rules here may be illustrated by two criminal cases, the principles of which apply equally to civil cases.

R v Richardson   [1969] 1 QB 299, [1968] 2 All ER 761, CA

Edmund Davies LJ: 1. A witness may be asked whether he has knowledge of the impugned witness's general reputation for veracity and whether (from such knowledge) he would believe the impugned witness's sworn testimony.

2. The witness called to impeach the credibility of a previous witness may also express his individual opinion (based upon his personal knowledge) as to whether the latter is to be believed upon his oath and is *not* confined to giving evidence merely of general reputation.

3. But whether his opinion as to the impugned witness's credibility be based simply upon the latter's general reputation for veracity or upon his personal knowledge, the witness cannot be permitted to indicate during his examination-in-chief the particular facts, circumstances or incidents which formed the basis of his opinion, although he may be cross-examined as to them.

NOTE

How satisfactory are the *Richardson* rules? Opinion evidence as to character for truth-telling seems an unsatisfactory form of evidence. 'A personal opinion that a defendant is a person of good character is so subjective as not to be subject to meaningful cross-examination; cross-examination would degenerate into an argument with the witness, and rebuttal witnesses who happened to hold contrary opinions would have to be permitted to testify': *United States v White* 225 F Supp 514 at 522 (1963). If an opinion is based on specific incidents, it may be sound; if it is not based on specific incidents, it will rest on rumour, reputation or prejudice. As to prejudice, opinion evidence is peculiarly liable to be impaired by emotions of hatred or motives of revenge. Turning to reputation evidence, so far as it rests on a collection of rumours, it is flimsy material. Is 'the court to receive the gossip of some idler in a club? Rumour is a lying jade, begotten by gossip out of hearsay, and is not fit to be admitted to audience in a court of law': *Plato Films Ltd v Speidel* [1961] AC 1090 at 1136, [1961] 1 All ER 876 at 888 per Lord Denning, citing *Scott v Sampson* (1882) 8 QBD 491 at 507, per Cave J. The admission of rumours 'at its best [would open] a lucky line of inquiry as to a shapeless and obscure subject matter. At its worst it opens a veritable Pandora's box of irresponsible gossip, innuendo and smear': *Michelson v United States* 335 US 469 at 480 (1948) per Jackson J. In *The Nature of the Judicial Process* (New Haven, 1921) pp 156–7, Cardozo J commented on 'an exaggerated reliance upon general reputation as a test for the ascertainment of the character of litigants or witnesses. Such a faith is a survival of more simple times. It was justified in days when men lived in small communities. Perhaps it has some justification even now in rural districts. In the life of great cities, it has made evidence of character a farce.' In short, it is said that a settled reputation may be impossible to acquire in modern urban conditions, where people are frequently unknown to their neighbours and tend to move suddenly and often. This objection could probably be met by investigating a person's reputation, not in his geographical neighbourhood, but among his circle at work, among friends, among tradespeople with whom he deals, and within any religious, political or other organisation to which he belongs. Further, the merits of reputation evidence over opinion evidence have been justified in the following way:

'An opinion as to reputation . . . (although composed of numerous individual subjective opinions) is essentially an objective fact about a defendant, thus subject to reasonably limited cross-examination. A witness can be accurate or inaccurate as to reputation, but his opinion as to character is essentially his own personal estimate' (*United States v White* 255 F Supp 514 at 522 (1963)).

The arguments against reputation evidence are as follows. One reason was classically explained by Stephen, *A Digest of the Law of Evidence* (4th edn, London, 1893) p 179:

'A witness may with perfect truth swear that a man, who to his knowledge has been a receiver of stolen goods for years, has an excellent character for honesty, if he has had the good luck to conceal his crimes from his neighbours. It is the essence of successful hypocrisy to combine a good reputation with a bad disposition.'

In the words of Holt CJ:

'A man is not born a knave; there must be time to make him so, nor is he presently discovered after he becomes one. A man may be reputed an able man this year, and yet be a beggar the next' (*R v Swensden* (1702) 14 State Tr 559 at 596).

Further, a witness as to reputation is only

'allowed to summarise what he has heard in the community, although much of it may have been said by persons less qualified to judge than himself. The evidence which the law permits is not as to the personality of the defendant but only as to the shadow his daily life has cast in his neighbourhood' (*Michelson v United States* 335 US 469 at 477 (1948), per Jackson J).

Thirdly, reputation can be composed of matter which may be misleading as to a person's disposition.

'Arrest without more does not, in law any more than in reason, impeach the integrity or impair the credibility of a witness. It happens to the innocent as well as to the guilty . . . Arrest without more may nevertheless impair or cloud one's reputation. False arrest may do that. Even to be acquitted may damage one's good name if the community receives the verdict with a wink and chooses to remember the defendant as one who ought to have been convicted' (*Michelson v United States* 335 US 469 at 482 (1948) per Jackson J).

Fourthly, a person's reputation may vary sharply depending on the group selected to establish it.

'Clannish witnesses, whose intercourse and business are always limited to a particular class of kindred spirits, who may constitute a majority of the neighbourhood, often entertain peculiar and contracted views of general character, when applied to those who may not agree with them on social, religious, or political tenets. And thus, by a majority of one neighbourhood, a man might be represented as possessing an excellent general character; while in an adjoining neighbourhood, where he is equally well known, he might be described as a man of great moral turpitude' (*Carter v Cavenaugh* 1 Greene 171 at 173 (1848), per Greene J, quoted by Wigmore, para 922).

Fifthly, the sharp common law distinction between permitting proof of reputation but not specific instances in chief leads to technical difficulties.

'[T]he result is often rather artificial, because an impeaching witness may be cross-examined on the reasons for his opinion, and this can leave the party whose witness has been impeached in an awkward dilemma. If he wishes to challenge the impeaching witness's opinion he will have to allow him to state the facts on which it is based, and will not be able to contradict them by other evidence. On the other hand, if he does not cross-examine the court is likely to think the worst of his witness': Hoffmann (1970) p 332.

See also *R v Adamstein* 1937 CPD 331 at 334. The objections to reputation evidence were summarised thus by Wigmore, para 1986:

'Put any one of us on trial for a false charge, and ask him whether he would not rather invoke in his vindication . . . [the testimony] of those few whose long intimacy and trust has made them ready to demonstrate their faith to the jury, than any amount of colourful assertions about reputation. Take the place of a juryman, and speculate whether he is helped more by the witnesses whose personal intimacy gives to their belief a first and highest value, or by those who merely repeat a form of words in which the term "reputation" occurs . . . The Anglo-American rules of evidence have occasionally taken some curious twistings in the course of their development; but they have never done anything so curious in the way of shutting out evidential light as when they decided to exclude the person who knows as much as can humanly be known about the character of another, and have still admitted the secondhand, irresponsible produce of multiplied guesses and gossip which we term "reputation".'

Similarly in *R v Rowton* (1865) Le & Ca 520 at 534, Erle CJ (dissenting) said:

'Suppose a witness to character were to say, "this man has been in my employ for 20 years. I have had experience of his conduct; but I have never heard a human being express an opinion of him in my life. For my own part, I have always regarded him in the highest esteem and respect, and have had abundant experience that he is one of the worthiest men in the world . . ." To my mind personal experience gives cogency to the evidence; whereas such a statement as "I have heard some persons speak well of him", or "I have heard general report in favour of the prisoner," has a very slight effect in comparison.'

However, there is one fundamental justification for the present law. Evidence of reputation avoids:

'innumerable collateral issues which, if it were attempted to prove character by direct testimony, would complicate and confuse the trial, distract the minds of jurymen and befog the chief issues in the litigation' (*Michelson v United States* 335 US 469 at 478 (1948), per Jackson J).

The present law is obscure as to how far the party calling a witness who is alleged to have an untruthful disposition is able to explain the circumstances of convictions and specific incidents (so far as they have been referred to) which on their face reveal such a disposition so as to show that in fact they do not. There seems to be no relevant Commonwealth authority. Wigmore followed the majority American view that a witness should be capable of being rehabilitated in this way.

'It is true that no issue could be allowed to be formed on the witness's explanations, and thus there would be no security against false statements by him. Nevertheless, having a regard to the publicity of one's discredit on the stand and the necessity of guarding against the abuses of the impeachment-process and of preventing the witness-box from becoming a place of dread and loathing, it would seem a harmless charity to allow the witness to make such protestations on his own behalf as he may feel able to make with a due regard to the penalties of perjury' (para 1117).

But the Supreme Judicial Court of Massachusetts took a different view in *Lamoureux v New York, New Haven Hartford Rly Co* 169 Mass 338 at 340 (1897) per Holmes J:

'Logically, there is no doubt that evidence tending to diminish the wickedness of the act, like evidence of good character, which is admissible, does meet, as far as it goes, the evidence afforded by the conviction, since that discredits only by tending to show either general bad character, or bad character of a kind more or less likely to be associated with untruthfulness. Nevertheless, the conviction must be left unexplained. Obviously, the guilt of the witness cannot be retried . . . It is no less impossible to go behind the sentence to determine the degree of guilt. Apart from any technical objection, it is impracticable to introduce what may be a long investigation of a wholly collateral matter into a case to which it is foreign, and it is not to be expected or allowed that the party producing the record should also put in testimony to meet the explanation ready in the mouth of the convicted person. Yet if one side goes into the matter, the other must be allowed to also.'

Toohey v Metropolitan Police Commissioner   [1965] AC 595, [1965] 1 All ER 506, HL

The appellant and two other men were charged with assault with intent to rob Madden, a sixteen-year-old boy. The police found the accused in an alley with Madden, the latter being dishevelled and hysterical. The defence was that the accused had found Madden in a drunken condition and were trying to help him home when he became hysterical. A police surgeon said in evidence at the first trial that Madden smelt of alcohol, that his hysteria would have been exacerbated by alcohol and that he might be more prone to hysteria than ordinary people. The jury disagreed. At a second trial the doctor's evidence was excluded. The House of Lords held this to be wrong.

Lord Pearce: It is common knowledge that hysteria can be produced by fear. The hysteria of the victim of an alleged assault may, if he is a person of normal stability, confirm a jury in the belief that he has been assaulted. When, however, the victim is unstable and hysterical by nature, the hysteria can raise a doubt whether in truth an assault ever occurred or whether it was the figment of an hysterical imagination. Here the real question to be determined was whether, as the prosecution alleged, the episode created the hysteria, or whether, on the other hand, as the defence alleged, the hysteria created the episode. To that issue medical evidence as to the hysteric and unstable nature of the alleged victim was relevant. It might be that, on a careful examination of the medical evidence, the predisposition to hysteria and instability was not enough to create a real doubt whether there was any assault at all and might have inclined the jury to believe the account given by the accused. On that ground the defence was entitled to have the evidence considered by the jury.

The second question, whether it was permissible to impeach the credibility of Madden, qua witness, by medical evidence of his hysterical and unstable nature, raises a wider and more important problem which applies to evidence in criminal and civil cases alike.

The Court of Criminal Appeal held that such evidence was not admissible since they were bound by the case of *R v Gunewardene*. Undoubtedly they were right in thinking that on this point the present case is not distinguishable from it. In *Gunewardene's Case* [1951] 2 KB 600 at 609, [1951] 2 All ER 290 at 294, CCA, the appellant (to quote the words of Lord Goddard CJ) 'wished to call [Doctor Leigh] to say that he . . . had examined the witness and had come to the conclusion that the man was suffering from a disease of the mind and that therefore he regarded his testimony as unreliable. In our opinion that is exactly what the cases show cannot be done.' It was there held that the most that the doctor could have been asked on oath was: 'From your knowledge of the witness, would you believe him on his oath?' And although it was open to the other side in cross-examination to probe the particular reasons for the belief, the doctor could not give them in examination in chief. Thus, the only evidence which a doctor could give in chief would seem mysterious or meaningless to the jury; and if it was not amplified by questions in cross-examination (from which opposing counsel might well refrain) it would be liable to be robbed of its proper effect. Moreover, the principle in *Gunewardene's Case* would exclude altogether the evidence of a doctor who cannot go so far as to say that he would not believe the witness on oath. It would not allow a doctor to testify (as is desired in the present case) to the abnormality and unreliability of the witness, or (as may happen in some other case) to the fact that the witness, by reason of some delusion, would on some matters not be credible, whereas on others he might be quite reliable.

Throughout *Gunewardene's Case* the court dealt with the problem created by the mental disease and mental abnormality of the witness as if it were identical with the problem of moral discredit and unveracity. They referred to many cases dealing with bad character and reputation, but to none which dealt with mental disturbance.

From olden times it has been the practice to allow evidence of bad reputation to discredit a witness's testimony. It is perhaps not very logical and not very useful to allow such evidence founded on hearsay. None of your Lordships and none of the counsel before you could remember being concerned in a case where such evidence was called. But the rule has been sanctified through the centuries in legal examinations and text-books and in some rare cases, and it does not create injustice. Its scope is conveniently summarised by Professor Cross (Evidence, 2nd edn (1963), p 225):

'In *Mawson v Hartsink* (1802) 4 Esp 102 it was held that the witness must be asked whether he is aware of the impugned witness's reputation for veracity and whether, from such knowledge, he would believe the impugned witness on oath. In *R v Watson* (1817) 2 Stark 116 at 152, however, it was held that the witness might simply state whether he would believe the oath of the person about whom he was asked, and although *R v Rowton* (1865) Le & Ca 520 decides that, when asked about a prisoner's character, the witness must speak to the accused's general reputation and not give his personal opinion of the accused's disposition, *R v Brown* (1867) LR 1 CCR 70 sanctions the form of question approved in *R v Watson*.'

Where a witness's general reputation, so far as concerns veracity, has been thus demolished, it seems that it may be reinstated by other witnesses who give evidence that he is worthy of credit or who discredit the discrediting witness (Taylor on Evidence, 12th edn, vol II, para 1473; Stephen on Evidence, 12th edn, Art 146). Thus far, and no further, it appears, may the process of recrimination go (Taylor, para 1473, citing *R v Lord Stafford* (1680) 7 State Tr 1293 at

1484). How far the evidence is confined to veracity alone or may extend to moral turpitude generally seems a matter of some doubt (see Taylor, para 1471).

There seems little point, however, for present purposes in exploring these archaic niceties. The old cases are concerned with lying as an aspect of bad character and are of little help in establishing any principle that will deal with modern scientific knowledge of mental disease and its effect on the reliability of a witness. I accept all of the judgment in *Gunewardene's Case* in so far as it deals with the older cases and the topic with which they were concerned. But, in my opinion, the court erred in using it as a guide to the admissibility of medical evidence concerning illness or abnormality affecting the mind of a witness and reducing his capacity to give reliable evidence. This unreliability may have two aspects either separate from one another or acting jointly to create confusion. The witness may, through his mental trouble, derive a fanciful or untrue picture from events while they are actually occurring, or he may have a fanciful or untrue recollection of them which distorts his evidence at the time when he is giving it.

The only general principles which can be derived from the older cases are these. On the one hand, the courts have sought to prevent juries from being beguiled by the evidence of witnesses who could be shown to be, through defect or character, wholly unworthy of belief. On the other hand, however, they have sought to prevent the trial of a case becoming clogged with a number of side issues, such as might arise if there could be an investigation of matters which had no relevance to the issue save in so far as they tended to show the veracity or falsity of the witness who was giving evidence which *was* relevant to the issue. Many controversies which might thus obliquely throw some light on the issues must in practice be discarded because there is not an infinity of time, money and mental comprehension available to make use of them.

There is one older case (*R v Hill*) in which the Court for Crown Cases Reserved considered how it should deal with the evidence of a lunatic who was rational on some points. Evidence was given by doctors as to his credibility. Alderson B in argument made the sensible observation (1851) (20 LJMC 222 at 224–5):

'It seems to me almost approaching to an absurdity to say that a jury may, by hearing the statement of doctors, be able to say whether a man was insane when he made his will, and yet that they should not be competent to say whether a man be in a state of mind to enable him to give credible evidence when they see him before them.'

Lord Campbell CJ in giving judgment said (ibid, at 225):

'The true rule seems to me to be that it was for the judge to see whether the witness understands the nature of an oath and, if he does, to admit his testimony. No doubt, before he is sworn, the lunatic may be cross-examined, and evidence may be called to show that he labours under such a diseased mind as to be inadmissible; but, in the absence of such evidence he is prima facie admissible, and the jury may give such credit as they please to his testimony.'

The point was not quite the same as that which is before your Lordships, since the question was whether the lunatic should be allowed to give evidence at all. But there is inherent, I think, in the judgments an intention that the jury should have the best opportunity of arriving at the truth and that the medical evidence with regard to the witness's credibility should be before them.

Human evidence shares the frailties of those who give it. It is subject to many cross-currents such as partiality, prejudice, self-interest and, above all, imagination and inaccuracy. Those are matters with which the jury, helped by cross-examination and common sense, must do their best. But when a witness through physical (in which I include mental) disease or abnormality is not capable of giving a true or reliable account to the jury, it must surely be allowable for medical science to reveal this vital hidden fact to them. If a witness purported to give evidence of something which he believed that he had seen at a distance of 50 yards, it must surely be possible to call the evidence of an oculist to the effect that the witness could not possibly see anything at a greater distance than 20 yards, or the evidence of a surgeon who had removed a cataract from which the witness was suffering at the material time and which would have prevented him from seeing what he thought he saw. So, too, must it be allowable to call medical evidence of mental illness which makes a witness incapable of giving reliable evidence, whether through the existence of delusions or otherwise.

It is obviously in the interest of justice that such evidence should be available. The only argument that I can see against its admission is that there might be a conflict between the doctors and that there would then be a trial within a trial. But such cases would be rare and, if they arose, they would not create any insuperable difficulty, since there are many cases in practice where a trial within a trial is achieved without difficulty. And in such a case (unlike the issues relating to confessions) there would not be the inconvenience of having to exclude the jury since the dispute would be for their use and their instruction.

Mr Buzzard very fairly expressed himself as unable to support the judgment in the case of *Gunewardene* since, in the Crown's view, the important thing was that the jury should be enabled to arrive at the truth and do justice.

In *R v Pedrini* [[1964] Crim LR 719], *Times*, July 28, 29, 1964, before the Court of Criminal Appeal no reliance was placed on *Gunewardene's Case*. Without opposition from the Crown, since justice seemed to demand it, the court considered the evidence of three doctors as to the mental condition at the relevant time of a witness who had subsequently become insane. Lord Parker CJ said of that evidence:

'That it is fresh evidence this court is prepared to accept: that it is relevant evidence there is no doubt; that it is credible evidence in the sense that it is capable of belief and of carrying some weight is also clear.'

In my view, the court was right in not excluding the medical evidence in that case.

Gunewardene's Case was, in my opinion, wrongly decided. Medical evidence is admissible to show that a witness suffers from some disease or defect or abnormality of mind that affects the reliability of his evidence. Such evidence is not confined to a general opinion of the unreliability of the witness but may give all the matters necessary to show, not only the foundation of and reasons for the diagnosis, but also the extent to which the credibility of the witness is affected.

[Lords Reid, Morris of Borth-y-Gest, Hodson and Donovan agreed.]

NOTE

See *Lowery v R* [1974] AC 85, [1973] 3 All ER 662, PC. It follows from *Toohey's* Case that evidence of any physical or mental trait which reveals a defective capacity to observe, remember or communicate is admissible, including mental disease, drunkenness, drug addiction, short-sightedness, colour blindness, deafness, old age, speech defects and extreme youth.

(viii)   Evidence in rebuttal

All evidence which one side intends to call should be called before the end of that side's case in chief. One major exception to this is where the exceptions to the rule that answers to collateral questions are final apply. Another is where the occasion for calling further evidence could not reasonably have been foreseen. There are few others: new evidence can only be called if the judge gives leave, and he will only do so if it relates to an issue which could not have been foreseen.

2   Criminal cases

A   ORDER

If the accused pleads not guilty, the Crown has the right to begin because it must bear the evidential burden of proof on some issue unless the accused has made a formal admission on that point. The Crown will make an opening speech, call witnesses, and make a closing speech after the evidence of the accused's witnesses (if any); the accused will then reply. If the accused submits that there is no case to answer, a ruling is given at once without the accused being put to his election whether to call evidence or not. The judge should stop the case if there is no evidence, taking the prosecution case at its highest, on which a properly directed jury could convict: *R v Galbraith* [1981] 2 All ER 1060, [1981] 1 WLR 1039, CA, and see ch 3, ante. An appeal may be dismissed even though it is the accused's own witnesses who incriminate him so that the submission of no case was wrongfully rejected (*R v Power* [1919] 1 KB 572, CCA). The position is different if the submission is wrongfully rejected and the incriminating evidence comes from a co-accused (*R v Abbott* [1955] 2 QB 497, [1955] 2 All ER 899). Where the only witness to the facts of the case called by the defence is the accused, he must be called as a witness immediately after the close of the prosecution case: Criminal Evidence Act 1898, s 2. Even where there are other witnesses for the defence, it is the usual practice for the accused to be called before them (*R v Smith* [1968] 2 All ER 115, [1968] 1 WLR 636, CA); this prevents him trimming his evidence. In exceptional cases the order may change, eg because a witness wishes to leave shortly, or in the interests of comprehension it is desirable to establish some matter as background to the accused's evidence, and the court has a discretion to allow this under s 79 of the Police and Criminal Evidence Act 1984. It has been suggested that the general rule may operate unfairly, eg where the accused desires to call witnesses first who may make a much more favourable impression than he will: Griew [1969] Crim LR 347 at 354–5.

B   KINDS OF EXAMINATION

No special comment need be made for criminal cases on the general problems of examination-in-chief, cross-examination and re-examination.

C   SPECIAL PROBLEMS

No special comment need be made for criminal cases on leading questions, the refreshing of memory, unfavourable and hostile witnesses, or previous inconsistent statements.

(i)   Previous consistent statements: complaints

There is one special kind of previous consistent statement relevant in criminal cases: the complaint of the victim in a sex case.

Kilby v R   (1973) 129 **CLR 460**

The accused was convicted of rape. The victim had made no immediate complaint. The High Court of Australia refused the accused's application for special leave to appeal.

Barwick CJ: [T]he applicant does not raise or rely on the failure of the judge to instruct the jury as to the effect upon the credibility of the prosecutrix of a failure to complain. His counsel submits that as a matter of law a judge on a trial of an accused for rape is bound in every case to instruct the jury, no matter what the circumstances, that the failure to make such a complaint is evidence of consent by the woman to the intercourse. The submission is founded on the proposition that because evidence of proximate complaint is evidence, as it was said, that the woman had not consented, the lack of complaint must be evidence of consent. But, in my opinion, even granting the premises, the conclusion does not follow. Further, evidence of a complaint at the earliest reasonable opportunity is exceptionally admitted only as evidence of consistency in the account given by the woman claiming to have been raped: that is to say, it is admitted as matter going to her credit (see *R v Lillyman* [1896] 2 QB 167, per Hawkins J at 170, [1895–9] All ER Rep 586; *Sparks v R* [1964] AC 964 at 979, [1964] 1 All ER 727). Because the account with which the complaint is said to show consistency is an account of intercourse without consent, it has often been said that the evidence of the complaint is evidence negating consent. In my opinion, this manner of expressing the function of the evidence of proximate complaint is not correct: though, as it shows consistency in her account of rape, the fact of the complaint buttresses her evidence of no consent or, as it was said in *R v Lillyman*, supra, is inconsistent with consent. At times also it is said with technical inaccuracy that the evidence of such a complaint is corroborative of the woman's evidence of the rape. It is quite clearly not so corroborative (see *R v Christie* [1914] AC 545; *Eade v R* (1924) 34 CLR 154), though it is so spoken of in American literature (see *Wigmore on Evidence*, 3rd edn, vol IV, p 219, para 1134 and p 227, para 1137; vol VI, p 173, para 1761).

However, having regard to the importance of the matter and the need to have uniformity of practice and the avoidance of laxity in the use of evidence or lack of evidence of proximate complaint, it is proper that I should examine the course of decision in the courts.

Wigmore, in para 1134 in vol IV of the 3rd edition, says as to the admission of evidence of proximate complaint by a prosecutrix in rape:

'Down to the beginning of the 1800s, evidence of this sort was received by the courts as a matter of old tradition and practice, with little or no thought of any principles to support it. The tradition went back by a continuous thread to the primitive rule of hue-and-cry: and the precise nature of the survival is more fully explained in dealing with the hearsay exception of res gestae. But as more and more attention began to be given, in the early 1800s, to the principles underlying every sort of evidence, there came to be felt a need of explaining on principle this inherited and hitherto unquestioned practice; and thus the various aspects of its significance began to be thought of' [p 219].

Wigmore gives the American experience in some detail: but, though this is instructive, we are here concerned with the experience of the common law of England which we have inherited and which in this field we still apply without modification.

A review of the subject begins, in my opinion, with *R v Lillyman*, supra. The trial judge at the time of an indictment for rape had admitted, over the objection of counsel for the accused, all that the prosecutrix had said to her mistress very shortly after the commission of the acts of the accused of which the prosecutrix complained. The Court of Crown Cases Reserved (Lord Russell of Killowen CJ, Pollock B, Hawkins, Cave and Wills JJ) decided that the details of the complaints were admissible and took occasion to state the basis of admissibility and the function of the evidence of a proximate complaint. Prior to that decision there had developed in England a practice of excluding the details of a complaint by a prosecutrix, whilst admitting the fact that she had complained at a time proximate to the occurrence forming the basis of the charge against the accused.

It is worth mentioning in passing that Sir Robert Finlay the Solicitor-General in arguing for the Crown in *Lillyman's Case* submitted that 'the principle upon which the fact of the complaint having been made is allowed to be given in evidence is that it is the natural expression of the woman's feelings that as soon as possible after the occurrence she should tell her mother, or her mistress, or some person in a confidential relation, what has happened; it is *further* admissible as evidence of non-consent' ([1896] 2 QB at 169). But quite clearly the court did not accept the whole of that submission. Passages in the judgment delivered for the court by Hawkins J to my mind make this quite plain:

'It is necessary, in the first place, to have a clear understanding as to the principles upon which evidence of such a complaint, not on oath, nor made in the presence of the prisoner, nor forming part of the res gestae, can be admitted. It clearly is not admissible as evidence of the

facts complained of: those facts must therefore be established, if at all, upon oath by the prosecutrix or other credible witness, and, strictly speaking, evidence of them ought to be given
before evidence of the complaint is admitted. The complaint can only be used as evidence of
the consistency of the conduct of the prosecutrix with the story told by her in the witness-box,
and as being inconsistent with her consent to that of which she complains' (at 170).

Here the emphasis is that the complaint is not probative but only an aid to the credibility of the
prosecutrix. When it is said that the complaint can be used 'as being inconsistent with her consent to that of which she complains' the Court, in my opinion, is but stating the obverse of the
statement that the complaint tends to show consistency in the evidence of the prosecutrix which,
whether consent be an issue in the trial or not, must in the nature of things be an account of an
occurrence taking place without her consent.

The passage cited by Hawkins J from *Blackstone* shows that the admission of evidence of the
complaint is based solely on the effect it has on the credit of a prosecutrix

'. . . but the credibility of her testimony, and how far forth she is to be believed, must be left to
the jury upon the circumstances of fact that concur in that testimony. For instance: if the witness be of good fame; if she presently discovered the offence, and made search for the
offender . . . these and the like are concurring circumstances, which give greater probability to
her evidence. But, on the other side, if she be of evil fame, and stand unsupported by others;
if she concealed the injury for any considerable time after she had opportunity to complain; if
the place, where the fact was alleged to be committed, was where it was possible she might
have been heard, and she made no outcry; these and the like circumstances carry a strong, but
not conclusive, presumption that her testimony is false or feigned' (*Lillyman's Case* [1896] 2
QB 167 at 171).

Having dealt with the submission that the particulars of the complaint ought not to be admitted
and having examined in that connexion a course of decision between 1779 and 1877, the judgment proceeded to express the court's definitive opinion:

'After very careful consideration we have arrived at the conclusion that we are bound by no
authority to support the existing usage of limiting evidence of the complaint to the bare fact
that a complaint was made, and that reason and good sense are against our doing so. The evidence is admissible only upon the ground that it was a complaint of that which is charged
against the prisoner, and can be legitimately used only for the purpose of enabling the jury to
judge for themselves whether the conduct of the woman was consistent with her testimony on
oath given in the witness-box negativing her consent, and affirming that the acts complained
of were against her will, and in accordance with the conduct they would expect in a truthful
woman under the circumstances detailed by her' (see the report at 177).

In my opinion, nothing in this judgment lends any support to the proposition that evidence of
the making of the complaint is evidence of any fact other than the fact of the making of the complaint itself and of the terms in which it is claimed to have been made. When Hawkins J in the
first of the two passages which I have quoted from *Lillyman's Case* spoke of the evidence of a
complaint as being inconsistent with consent he was not, in my opinion, intending to place its
admissibility upon a second and different ground from that of its tendency to show consistency
in the conduct of the prosecutrix. He was merely indicating the extent of its effect on the credit
of the prosecutrix.

In my opinion, the error which has been made by text writers and in subsequent decisions is
in treating this remark of Hawkins J as if it did set up a second and independent ground of
admissibility. In my respectful opinion, it did not.

In *R v Lillyman*, reference was made to the passage in *Hawkins' Pleas of the Crown* where it is
said: 'It is a strong, but not a conclusive, presumption against a woman that she made no complaint in a reasonable time after the fact' (at 170–1 of the report). But just as the fact of a
proximate complaint tends to support credibility of the complainant so its absence may be a
considerable factor where a tribunal of fact is deciding on the credibility of the complainant.
The word 'presumption', in this connexion, is not, of course, a reference to a presumption of
law but is no more, in my opinion, than a statement that a tribunal of fact might well consider
that a woman who made no complaint was not to be believed when she gave an account of
events to which she gave no consent. This use of the word 'presumption' has assisted to give

rise to misconception as to the basis of admissibility of a proximate complaint and as to the effect of the absence of such a complaint.

In any case, to say that *Lillyman's Case* recognises that the evidence of a proximate complaint may be used to negative consent is to make an ambiguous statement. If it means that in so far as a complaint tends to buttress the evidence of the prosecutrix that what occurred did occur without her consent and in so far as belief in the truth of her statement would negative consent, it may be an acceptable statement, though, I think, prone to be, as it has proved to be, misleading. If, of course, it means that the evidence of a complaint is direct evidence negativing consent, I am of opinion that the statement is completely unwarranted, both in point of precedent so far as *Lillyman's Case* is concerned and in point of logic. It is true that Ridley J in *R v Osborne* [1905] 1 KB 551, [1904–7] All ER Rep 54, treated the evidence of proximate complaint as admissible on two grounds, founding himself on *Lillyman's Case*. He did not intend to depart from the decision or to enlarge its reasoning. But as I have indicated, *Lillyman's Case* does not really warrant the conclusion that there are two distinct grounds of admissibility of evidence of proximate complaint. Always the basic authority for the contrary proposition in the texts and in the decision has been *Lillyman's Case*.

Phipson in all its editions has stated the rule thus:

'In cases of rape, indecent assault, and similar offences, the fact that the prosecutrix or prosecutor made a complaint, shortly after the outrage, of the matters charged against the prisoner, together with the particulars of the complaint, are admissible as evidence in chief for the prosecution, not to prove the truth of the matters stated, but (1) to confirm her or his testimony, and (2) where consent is in issue, to disprove consent' (para 355, 11th edn).

See also *Archbold's Criminal Pleading Evidence and Practice*, 36th edn, p 392, para 1077:

'In *R v Lillyman*, supra, it was held after consideration of the earlier authorities, that upon the trial of an indictment for rape or other kindred offences against women or girls (including indecent assault and sexual intercourse with girls under thirteen and between thirteen and sixteen) the fact that a complaint was made by the prosecutrix shortly after the alleged occurrence, and the particulars of such complaint, may so far as they relate to the charge against the prisoner, be given in evidence by the prosecution, not as being evidence of the facts complained of but as evidence of the consistency of the conduct of the prosecutrix with the story told by her in the witness-box, and as negativing consent on her part. The mere complaint is no evidence of the facts complained of, and its admissibility depends on proof of the facts by sworn or other legalised testimony: *R v Brasier* (1779) 1 Leach 199; *R v Wood* (1877) 14 Cox CC 46.

In *R v Osborne* [1905] 1 KB 551, the indictment was for an indecent assault on a girl under thirteen, and consent was therefore immaterial. It was held that in the case of charge of sexual offences against females, evidence of fresh complaint is admissible 'whether non-consent is legally a necessary part of the issue or whether on the other hand it is what may be called a collateral issue of fact' in consequence of the story told by the complainant in the witness-box, and the complaint is not admissible merely as negativing consent, but as being consistent with the sworn evidence of the complainant.'

Though Ridley J in *R v Osborne*, supra, said that evidence was admitted because, if believed, it was consistent with a complainant's story in evidence and also that it was inconsistent with consent, he did not say at any time that it was evidence of the absence of consent. Indeed on neither of the bases of the admissibility which his Lordship expressed is the complaint probative of any fact, nor even of the facts made in the complaint.

Jordan CJ in *Smith v Commonwealth Life Assurance Society Ltd* (1935) 35 SRNSW 552 said at 556:

'Such evidence is admissible, not because what was said by way of complaint can be treated as corroborating the evidence of the facts of the alleged happening given by the witness in the witness-box, but, firstly, because absence of complaint is strong evidence of consent in any case in which consent is material, and secondly because the fact that a complaint was made at the time in terms similar to the evidence afterwards given, goes to negative the possibility that what is now said in evidence is an afterthought – an invented story prepared after the event – a possibility which is regarded as existing in a special degree in this class of case.'

In support of these propositions the learned Chief Justice cited *R v Osborne* and *R v Christie*, supra. In my respectful submission neither of these cases lends support for either of these propositions. *Halsbury*, 3rd edn, vol 10, para 859 at 468, in my opinion, puts the matter in proper perspective when it is there said:

'The admissibility of the particulars of a complaint made soon after the commission of an alleged offence in the absence of the defendant by the person in respect of whom a crime is alleged to have been committed is peculiar to rape, indecent assault and similar offences upon females, and also offences of indecency between male persons. This evidence is not to be taken in proof of the facts complained of, but only as matter to be borne in mind by the jury in considering the consistency, and, therefore, the credibility, of the complainant's story, including the consideration of the question of consent if the prisoner raises that as a defence.'

The admission of a recent complaint in cases of sexual offences is exceptional in the law of evidence. Whatever the historical reason for an exception, the admissibility of that evidence in modern times can only be placed, in my opinion, upon the consistency of statement or conduct which it tends to show, the evidence having itself no probative value as to any fact in contest but, merely and exceptionally constituting a buttress to the credit of the woman who has given evidence of having been subject to the sexual offence.

To understand the reasons for the admissibility and the use which can properly be made of the evidence of recent complaint is to deny the validity of the applicant's proposition that lack of complaint is probative of consent. I can see no ground in logic for saying that because evidence of complaint is admitted to show consistency in the story told by the woman, evidence of non-complaint is evidence of her consent to the intercourse. In my opinion, quite apart from the fact that there may be many reasons why a complaint is not made, the want of a complaint does not found an inference of consent. It does tell against the consistency of the woman's account and accordingly is clearly relevant to her credibility in that respect.

I am clearly of opinion, therefore, that a trial judge is not only [scil not] bound as a matter of law but not entitled to instruct a jury in the trial of an accused on a charge of rape that the failure of the woman claiming to have been raped to complain at the earliest possible opportunity is evidence of her consent to the intercourse. Statements to the contrary in *R v Hinton* [1961] Qd R 17 and in *R v Mayberry* (unreported) in the Court of Criminal Appeal of Queensland are not, in my opinion, supportable.

[McTiernan, Menzies, Stephen and Mason JJ agreed.]

NOTES

1. The complaint may be made by male victims as well as female: 'probably little attention would or should be paid to a complaint by an abandoned male person of mature years, but perhaps that observation goes rather to the weight, than to the admissibility, of the complaint' (*R v Camelleri* [1922] 2 KB 122 at 125, CCA).
2. The law on complaints applies whether or not consent is in issue (*R v Osborne* [1905] 1 KB 551).
3. The complaint must be made at the first opportunity after the offence which reasonably offers itself. There is little of general value to be said about this difficult question of degree.
4. The complaint must be made voluntarily in the sense that leading or intimidating questions must not be used (eg *R v Adams* [1965] Qd R 255).
5. The details of the complaint may be given, not merely the fact of the complaint (*R v Lillyman* [1896] 2 QB 167).
6. Since complaints only prove consistency and are not evidence of the truth of what they assert, they are not, when proved by someone other than the

maker, exceptions to the hearsay rule. For the same reason they do not corroborate the maker, and this conclusion is also supported by the fact that they are not independent of the witness to be corroborated (*Eade v R* (1924) 34 CLR 154).

7. Since the only relevance of complaints is to show consistency in testimony, a complaint is admissible if the complainant does not testify (*Sparks v R* [1964] AC 964 at 979, [1964] 1 All ER 727 at 734, PC). Not even the fact of complaint may be admitted in these circumstances (cf *R v Wallwork* (1958) 122 JP 299, CCA). However, a complaint may be admitted if the complainant gives evidence, though not of the complaint: *Breen v R* (1976) 180 CLR 536.

8. It is not clear whether the complaint rules apply to sexual allegations in civil cases, or to all allegations of violence in both criminal and civil cases. There is some authority for these extensions (*R v Wink* (1834) 6 C & P 397; *Berry v Berry* (1898) 78 LT 688; *Jones v South Eastern and Chatham Rly Co's Managing Committee* (1918) 87 LJKB 775 at 778; *Fromhold v Fromhold* [1952] 1 TLR 1522 at 1526, 1528 per Denning and Hodson LJJ). But in *De B v De B* [1950] VLR 242 a wife's complaint of her husband's sodomy was held inadmissible in a divorce case because the intimate nature of marriage made it very unlikely that there could be said to be any lack of consistency on the part of a wife who did not make immediate complaint of her husband's unwanted behaviour but later sued for divorce.

(ii) Collateral questions

At common law, rape cases provided the ۱sual examples of collateral questions. A complainant of rape who deniea intercourse with other men could not be contradicted. In *R v Holmes* (1871) LR 1 CCR 334 at 336, Kelly CB said:

> 'if such evidence as that here proposed were admitted, the whole history of the prosecutrix's life might be gone into; if a charge might be made as to one man, it might be made as to fifty, and that without notice to the prosecutrix. It would not only involve a multitude of collateral cases, but an inquiry into matters as to which the prosecutrix might be wholly unprepared, and so work great injustice.'

Indeed, it is difficult to see how the question could ever be relevant even to credibility, though extreme promiscuity might be relevant to consent. But if she denies previous or subsequent voluntary intercourse with the accused she may be contradicted, for the evidence is relevant to the issue of consent (*R v Riley* (1887) 18 QBD 481; *R v Aloisio* (1969) 90 WN (Pt 1) NSW 111). Similarly, her denials of being a prostitute may be contradicted (*R v Bashir* [1969] 3 All ER 692, [1969] 1 WLR 1303). That body of law has been substantially qualified by s 2 of the Sexual Offences (Amendment) Act 1976, which provides that where there is a plea of not guilty to rape, no evidence is to be adduced and no question in cross-examination asked by or on behalf of any defendant about sexual experience of the complainant with a person other than that defendant without the judge's leave; that leave is only to be applied for in the jury's absence, and is to be given if and only if the judge is satisfied that it would be unfair to the defendant to refuse leave. See *R v Lawrence* [1977] Crim LR 492; *R v Mills* (1978) 68 Cr App Rep 327, CA; *R v Fenlon*

(1980) 71 Cr App Rep 307, CA. The principles embodied in the Act have been applied to a trial on a charge of unlawful sexual intercourse: *R v Funderburk* [1990] 2 All ER 482, [1990] 1 WLR 587, CA.

(iii) Evidence in rebuttal

A party may not 'split his case': save in special circumstances he must call his evidence together and is not permitted to re-open his case after his opponent has closed his. This rule is applied with particular strictness against the prosecution in a criminal case: *Shaw v R* (1952) 85 CLR 365. The exceptions to the rule fall into four groups. The first concerns evidence admitted as an exception to the rule prohibiting the rebuttal of answers to questions on collateral matters. The second relates to evidence on purely formal matters, eg that a particular official whose consent is necessary for a prosecution has given it. The third relates to evidence which the party adducing it was unable to foresee as relevant. There is old authority for the view that the matter must be one which 'no human ingenuity' could have foreseen: *R v Frost* (1839) 4 State Tr NS 85 at 386, per Tindal CJ. The rule is probably stricter in criminal than civil cases, but even in criminal cases the modern law is probably less extreme. In *Shaw v R* (1952) 85 CLR 365, at 379–80 Dixon, McTiernan, Webb and Kitto JJ said:

'The formula . . . has little to recommend it. The words "which no human ingenuity can foresee" hardly express a legal principle. They are rhetorical, but if literally understood they lay down a test which could almost never be satisfied . . . It seems to us unsafe to adopt a rigid formula in view of the almost infinite variety of difficulties that may arise at a criminal trial. It is probably enough to say that the occasion must be very special or exceptional to warrant a departure from the principle that the prosecution must offer all its proofs during the progress of the Crown case and before the prisoner is called upon for his defence . . . [G]enerally speaking an occasion will not suffice for allowing an exceptional course if it ought reasonably to have been foreseen. Again, it may be pointed out that even an unexpected occasion may be of such a nature that it would have been covered, had the Crown case been fully and strictly proved.'

In the same case Fullagar J said at 383–4:

'The words "*ex improviso*" and the words "which no human ingenuity can foresee" convey radically different meanings, the latter being in no sense a translation of the former. The latter words do not occur in the report in Carrington and Payne [9 C & P 129 at 159] and they have, to my mind, the almost unmistakable character of a "gloss" in the correct sense of that much abused word – a note by a misguided commentator, which has by some mischance become incorporated in the text. Moreover, the rule is stated as applying equally to criminal and civil cases, and I should not imagine that anybody would suppose that the question should be approached from the same point of view in both classes of case. In the second place, the rule so stated is on its face fundamentally unsound and calculated not to aid but impede the administration of justice. After all, the aim of legal proceedings, including criminal proceedings, is supposed to be to elicit the truth so far as human imperfection permits . . .'

The fourth exception is that the evidence is fresh in the sense of being unavailable to be adduced at the usual time (see *R v Kane* (1977) 65 Cr App Rep 270, CA).

Examples of the judge giving leave for the admission of evidence in rebuttal after the close of a party's case occur most commonly when the accused raises some unexpected last minute defence. One example is a late alibi (*R v Flynn*

(1957) 42 Cr App Rep 15, CCA); but now advance notice of an alibi must be given (Criminal Justice Act 1967, s 11). Evidence in rebuttal is more likely to be admitted where the evidence which is now clearly relevant to credibility could only have been marginally relevant to guilt in chief (*R v Levy* (1966) 50 Cr App Rep 198, CCA; *R v Halford* (1978) 67 Cr App Rep 318, CA), or is only made relevant by the accused's attack on the prosecution witnesses' characters (*R v Milliken* (1969) 53 Cr App Rep 330, CA). The mere failure to call a witness in chief through overlooking the importance of her evidence in a long and complicated trial is not sufficient to entitle the witness to be called in reply: *R v Pilcher* (1974) 60 Cr App Rep 1, CA. See generally *R v Chin* (1985) 157 CLR 671.

QUESTIONS

To what extent can and ought the judge
(a)   ask questions of witnesses;
(b)   call witnesses whom the parties have not called?

See Phipson, paras 11–30; Sheppard (1982) 56 ALJ 234.

FURTHER READING

Gooderson [1968] CLJ 64; Newark and Samuels [1978] Crim LR 408; Simpson (1976) 50 ALJ 410; Zuckerman, ch 7.

PART SEVEN

Matters which need not be Proved by Evidence

CHAPTER 21

Judicial Notice

1 Introduction

In general, all material facts – whether facts in issue or subordinate facts – must be proved by evidence. In consequence the court cannot act on material which the parties have not had the opportunity of rebutting or qualifying, whether or not that material is obtained privately (see *Reynolds v Llanelly Associated Tinplate Co Ltd* [1948] 1 All ER 140; *Cavenett v Chambers* [1968] SASR 97) or from other cases: *Roper v Taylor's Central Garages (Exeter) Ltd* [1951] 2 TLR 284. To do so is in effect an infringement of the rules of natural justice. A juror, as will be seen, may take into account certain matters of general knowledge, but if he reveals special knowledge, he should be warned against communicating it to his fellow jurors and he should be warned to decide the case only on the evidence: *Mangano v Farleigh Nettheim Pty Ltd* (1965) 65 SRNSW 228.

But the world of trials is not a Cartesian one. The mind of the trier of fact is not a complete blank waiting only for the parties to write. Hence there are exceptions to the main rule.

First, the trier of fact may take for granted the English language so far as the ordinary meaning of generally used words is concerned (*Chapman v Kirke* [1948] 2 KB 450 at 454, [1948] 2 All ER 556) but not technical ones. Thus when a witness uses the word 'car' in a case about a car accident, his hearers, at least until corrected by evidence, think about an automobile, not any other vehicle: they assume it to have an engine, probably an internal combustion engine, and four wheels with rubber tyres.

Secondly, the trier of fact may take into account the ordinary data of day-to-day living and his own experience of the ordinary progress of affairs and the habits of mankind. He cannot and ought not to ignore it. He cannot begin to reason without drawing on some store of accepted knowledge. This is particularly so in relation to estimating the relevance and weight of evidence. A multitude of facts are thus relied on without being proved, for example that it is common for the possessor of housebreaking implements to use them for criminal purposes. If a witness talks of a 'car', his hearers apply their basic knowledge of how cars work and how their drivers normally behave: *Burns v Lipman* (1974) 132 CLR 157 at 161. A jury can infer substantial intoxication from the accused's having two and a half times the legal blood alcohol limit: *R v Hunt* [1980] RTR 29, CA. This type of knowledge can be difficult to distinguish from those facts, discussed below, which are judicially noticed without inquiry.

Thirdly, the trier of fact may assume the ordinary processes of simple mathematical and syllogistic reasoning and may draw inferences as to the causes and effects of established facts. If a witness says 'it was wet and dark, we had no lights, and our car was doing 100 miles per hour', his hearers will, subject to evidence, draw some conclusions as to the cause of an accident.

Fourthly, evidence becomes unnecessary where the basic facts of presumptions are proved: see ch 4, ante.

Fifthly, evidence is not necessary to prove matters of fact of which judicial notice is taken: see pp 502–7, post.

Sixthly, evidence is not necessary to prove matters of fact which have been formally admitted: see ch 1, ante.

It must also be borne in mind that the operation of estoppels may render evidence unnecessary; and there is a seventh 'exception' which is in truth not really an exception. What has just been said relates to matters in issue between the parties – 'adjudicative facts' in the terminology of KC Davis, 55 Harv LR 364 at 404–7. It does not relate to 'legislative facts' – those which judges take into account in deciding whether to create or extend a common law rule or how to construe a statute (particularly a constitutional statute), and those which administrative tribunals take into account in exercising discretions. They are facts about economic or social background, business organisation or human behaviour; they are inherently controversial. Recent examples include the factors considered by the High Court of Australia in determining the scope of legal professional privilege in *Grant v Downs* (1976) 135 CLR 674 at 685–8; and the assertion of the United States Supreme Court in *Hawkins v United States* 358 US 74 at 78 (1958), in deciding not to depart from the common law rule that one spouse cannot testify against another, that 'adverse testimony given in criminal proceedings would, we think, be likely to destroy almost any marriage'. An example of the much laxer practice relating to legislative facts is reliance on the 'Brandeis brief' relating to the ill effects of long hours of work on females by the United States Supreme Court in *Miller v Oregon* 208 US 412 (1907). Holmes J said, and it appears to be the common law generally, that 'the court may ascertain as it sees fit any fact that is merely a ground for laying down a rule of law': *Chastleton Corpn v Sinclair* 264 US 543 at 548 (1924). A particular exception to the normal rules of proof concerns facts relevant to whether legislation is within power in federal systems (*Gerhardy v Brown* (1985) 159 CLR 70 at 141–2); if this is not sui generis, it is an extension of the legislative fact doctrine.

Finally, the specialist knowledge of judges may sometimes be taken into account by them.

Wetherall v Harrison   [1976] QB 773, [1976] 1 All ER 241, Divisional Court

An issue arose in criminal proceedings heard before magistrates as to whether a defendant from whom a blood sample was about to be taken had suffered an actual fit or whether he was simulating a fit.

Lord Widgery CJ: On the bench was a practising registered medical practitioner, Dr Robertson, and the bench:

'had regard to his professional opinion of the [defendant's] reactions and behaviour according to the evidence, and Dr Robertson's own reasons are separately attached.'

Now I take that to mean that in the retiring room Dr Robertson, possibly at the invitation of the other members of the bench, gave his views on the matter traversed by Dr Price, in other words, gave his view as to whether it was a simulated fit or a genuine fit. The justices said not only did they listen to Dr Robertson's reasons but they also had a layman's experience and viewpoint of war-time inoculations and the fear that they could create in certain individuals.

The matter comes before us really in this form, that we are invited to say whether the justices acted with propriety in having regard to information given to them by Dr Robertson and drawing on their own war-time experiences so far as they did. In the event, they acquitted the defendant, obviously not being satisfied that his fit was simulated and therefore not being satisfied that he acted without reasonable excuse.

Mr Barker, in putting the matter before us, is really inviting us to say, for the advantage of justices hereafter, what should happen when a justice has specialised knowledge of this kind; should he use it or should he not.

In argument we were referred to three authorities. The only one I need refer to, and the most recent, is *Reynolds v Llanelly Associated Tinplate Co Ltd* [1948] 1 All ER 140. That was concerned with arbitrators and judges and the extent to which they could have regard to their own personal knowledge. I do not think that the position of a justice of the peace is the same, in this regard, as the position of a trained judge. If you have a judge sitting alone, trying a civil case, it is perfectly feasible and sensible that he should be instructed and trained to exclude certain factors from his consideration of the problem. Justices are not so trained. They are much more like jurymen in this respect. I think it would be wrong to start with the proposition that justices' use of their own local or personal knowledge is governed by exactly the same rule as is laid down in the case of trained judges. I do not believe that a serious restriction on a justice's use of his own knowledge or the knowledge of his colleagues can really be enforced. Laymen (by which I mean non-lawyers) sitting as justices considering a case which has just been heard before them lack the ability to put out of their minds certain features of the case. In particular, if the justice is a specialist, be he a doctor, or an engineer or an accountant, or what you will, it is not possible for him to approach the decision in the case as though he had not got that training, and indeed I think it would be a very bad thing if he had to. In a sense, the bench of justices are like a jury, they are a cross-section of people, and one of the advantages which they have is that they bring a lot of varied experience into the court room and use it.

So I start with the proposition that it is not improper for a justice who has special knowledge of the circumstances forming the background to a particular case to draw on that special knowledge in interpretation of the evidence which he has heard. I stress that last sentence, because it would be quite wrong if the justice went on, as it were, to give evidence to himself in contradiction of that which has been heard in court. He is not there to give evidence to himself, still more is he not there to give evidence to other justices; but that he can employ his basic knowledge in considering, weighing up and assessing the evidence given before the court is I think beyond doubt.

Furthermore, I do not see why he should not, certainly if requested to by his fellow justices, tell his fellow justices the way in which his specialised knowledge has caused him to look at the evidence. In no bench of justices should there be a leader, so aggressive that he tries to assume responsibility for the decision and excludes the others, whether he is proceeding on the basis of a specialised subject or not, and that certainly goes for justices with a specialised knowledge, because it would be quite wrong for the doctor in the present case to have gone into the justices' retiring room and immediately proceeded to persuade all the justices because of his specialised knowledge. He ought really to have waited until asked to make a contribution on his specialist subject. Whether he is asked or not, he should not press his views unduly on the rest of the bench. He should tell them in a temperate and orderly way what he thinks about the case, if they want to know, and then leave them to form their own conclusion if they wish so to do. Here again it is most important that the justice with specialised knowledge should not proceed to give evidence himself to his fellow justices contradictory to that which they have heard in the court. He can explain the evidence they have heard: he can give his own view as to how the case should go and how it should be decided; but he should not be giving evidence himself behind closed doors which is not available to the parties.

Applying those principles to the instant case, there was certainly no reason why Dr Robertson should not, when forming his own conclusion about this case, have referred to his own knowledge, and his own knowledge and experience was that this kind of fit was genuine, and knowing that it would be right that in reviewing and considering the evidence in this case he should have that knowledge in the background and use it if he thought fit. Since his fellow justices obviously knew he was a doctor and I think asked him for the benefit of his views, I see no reason at all why he should not tell them what his views were. That does not seem to me to be contrary to any principle to be applied here, and I do not believe in this case either that the doctor went beyond the scope of the authority which I am trying to apply.

For my part therefore I would say that this is a case in which there is no reason to suppose that the procedure employed was wrong and therefore there is no error of law disclosed in the papers, and therefore the appeal under these circumstances has to be dismissed.

O'Connor J: I agree. I would only add a few words on the topic of the way in which justices with specialised knowledge should approach their duties in using it. I endorse fully what Lord Widgery CJ has said, but they must not, so to speak, start giving evidence in the case because it offends a number of our rules; above all, it is not in the presence of the parties and is not open to cross-examination. But if that is borne in mind, that the person with specialised knowledge must not give evidence, then it seems to me that it is entirely legitimate for him to express his views that he himself has been helped to form on the evidence in the case and on the issues in the case as a result of his own specialised knowledge and to communicate that to his fellow justices, if he so wishes, always bearing in mind that he must not start substituting what he might have said in evidence, as opposed to using his knowledge to assess the evidence which is available.

Lawson J: I agree with both judgments that have been delivered.

NOTE

Local justices may take into account their knowledge of local conditions: *Ingram v Percival* [1969] 1 QB 548, [1968] 3 All ER 657 (though that decision is questionable, the fact there not being notorious: cf *Reynolds v Llanelly Associated Tinplate Co Ltd* [1948] 1 All ER 140); *Borthwick v Vickers* [1973] RTR 390.

Further, the modern state has created many specialist tribunals which value property, assess workers' compensation, determine industrial disputes, administer town planning legislation and the like. The judges who sit in those tribunals may have been appointed by reason of special expertise, or they may acquire it by experience on the tribunal. A judge may within limits take into account his own special expertise, when sitting in a special tribunal: *Stauffner v Hanley* [1978] ACLD 384. See also *Dugdale v Kraft Foods Ltd* [1977] 1 All ER 454, [1976] 1 WLR 1288, stating that the expertise in question should be made public so that the witnesses can deal with it.

2   Judicial notice at common law

The common law doctrine is that

'whenever a fact is so generally known that every ordinary person may be reasonably presumed to be aware of it, the court "notices" it, either simpliciter *or* if it is at once satisfied of the fact without more, or after such information and investigation as it considers reliable and necessary in order to eliminate any reasonable doubt' (*Holland v Jones* (1917) 23 CLR 149 at 153 per Isaacs J).

See also *Commonwealth Shipping Representative v Peninsular and Oriental Branch Service* [1923] AC 191 at 211–2 per Lord Sumner.

There are also, by force of statute, numerous facts of which judicial notice is taken. The main purpose of the doctrine is to save time in the hearing of cases and to save costs in the proof of facts which would often be very difficult without it.

'To require that a Judge should affect a cloistered aloofness from facts that every other man in court is fully aware of, and should insist on having proof on oath of what, as a man of the world, he knows already better than any witness can tell him, is a rule that may easily become pedantic and futile' (*Commonwealth Shipping Representative v Peninsular and Oriental Branch Service* [1923] AC 191 at 211 per Lord Sumner).

It also avoids a diversity of judicial findings of fact. And it facilitates judicial control over the jury in that it precludes ludicrous jury findings.

The first of Isaacs J's categories requires the matter to be so notorious as not to be capable of reasonable dispute.

'Judicial notice is a judicial shortcut, a doing away . . . with the formal necessity for evidence, because there is no real necessity for it. So far as matters of common knowledge are concerned, it is saying there is no need of formally offering evidence of those things, because practically everyone knows them in advance, and there can be no question about them' (*Varcoe v Lee* 181 P 233 (1919)).

In *Varcoe* judicial notice was taken that a well-known San Francisco street was in a business district. Examples of this type of fact are that the period of human gestation exceeds a fortnight (*R v Luffe* (1807) 8 East 193) and is about nine months but necessarily less than 360 days (*Preston-Jones v Preston-Jones* [1951] AC 391, [1951] 1 All ER 124), that a boy riding a bicycle in London runs a risk of injury from traffic (*Dennis v A J White & Co* [1917] AC 479 at 492), and that the value of money has fallen since 1189: *Bryant v Foot* (1868) LR 3 QB 497. The notoriety may exist only among a small number of people – the residents of a particular area, practitioners of a particular profession or trade, for example. The courts are more willing to notice general facts than specific ones, and more willing to notice subsidiary facts rather than those which by themselves are determinative of a case.

The second of Isaacs J's categories is exemplified in diverse ways, and in respect of some of them there is dispute as to whether in truth judicial notice is strictly speaking taken.

(a) Such 'political' facts as the recognition of the sovereignty of a foreign state (*Duff Development Co v Government of Kelantan* [1924] AC 797), the membership of a particular diplomatic mission (*Engelke v Musmann* [1928] AC 433), the extent of territorial waters (*The Fagernes* [1927] P 311, CA) and the existence of a state of war (*R v Bottrill, ex p Kuechenmeister* [1947] KB 41, [1946] 2 All ER 434). In case of uncertainty the court acts on a certificate from the appropriate Minister of State. However, whether a certain ship is engaged in warlike operations (*Shaw Savill and Albion Co Ltd v Commonwealth* (1940) 66 CLR 344 at 364) and who is in de facto control of the foreign country (*Anglo Czechoslovak and Prague Credit Bank v Janssen* [1943] VLR 185 at 197–9) are matters of fact, not executive opinion, and judicial notice may not be taken of them.

On one view, these 'political' facts are not really judicially noticed: their handling by the courts merely reflects the subordination, in this respect, of the courts to the executive. A justification for the rule additional to the usual justification for taking judicial notice arises: the undesirability of the courts reaching different conclusions on matters of national policy from those reached by an executive responsible to elected popular representatives. On the other hand, some judges seek to limit the doctrine so as to prevent any undue erosion of judicial independence: *Corporate Affairs Commission v Bradley* [1974] 1 NSWLR 391 at 404 per Hutley JA; see also *Kawasaki Kisen Kabushiki Kaisha of Kobe v Bantham SS Co Ltd (No 2)* [1939] 2 KB 544 at 552, [1939] 1 All ER 819, CA.

(b) The court may examine appropriate works of learning – histories, treatises, almanacs, tables – to answer questions as to historical facts and past rituals (*Read v Bishop of Lincoln* [1892] AC 644), present political creeds (*Australian Communist Party v Commonwealth* (1950) 83 CLR 1 at 196), scientific matters such as the position of seeds on a plant (*Horman v Bingham* [1972] VR 29) or the effects of chronic alcoholism (*Re Coffee, Timbury v Coffee* (1941) 66 CLR 277 at 283–4 and 293), facts of nature such as when the tide is high or when the sun sets, mathematical tables of life expectancy or interest calculations, geographical matters and aesthetic matters. In some jurisdictions statute has perhaps widened the law slightly by permitting reference to authoritative works. At this point the taking of judicial notice approaches its common boundary with the reception of expert evidence: a fact judicially noticed may not be contradicted, but the facts discovered in the course of the inquiry leading to the taking of the notice may be. A question also arises as to whether or not the evidence is received subject to a concealed hearsay exception or on some other basis.

(c) Judicial notice may be taken of general customs which have been proved with some frequency in other cases: *George v Davies* [1911] 2 KB 445 at 448; *Brandao v Barnett* (1846) 12 Cl & Fin 787.

(d) Judicial notice is taken of the practice of professions: *Re Rosher, Rosher v Rosher* (1884) 26 Ch D 801 (conveyancer); *Davey v Harrow Corpn* [1958] 1 QB 60 at 69, [1957] 2 All ER 305 at 307 (surveyors).

(e) Judicial notice is taken of the nature, functions and workings of scientific or technical instruments such as clocks, speedometers, radar speed meters, thermometers, scales and electronic weapons detectors. Evidence may be adduced, however, to show that the particular instrument in question is defective: see *State v Graham* 322 SW 2d 188 (1959) (radar trap); *United States v Lopez* 328 F Supp 1077 (1971) (flux-gate magnetometer to detect aircraft highjackers). In relation to some devices, judicial acceptance is swift. In relation to others, the courts divide, and a long time elapses before judicial notice is taken, eg voice prints (*People v King* 266 Cal App 2d 437 (1968)). Some will probably never be generally accepted, eg lie detectors (see Elliott in Campbell and Waller, pp 100–39; *Frye v United States* 293 F 1013 (1923); cf *Commonwealth v A Juvenile* 313 NE 2d 120 (1974); indeed their use is sometimes made unlawful: Lie Detectors Act 1983 (NSW)). The reluctance is there perhaps only partly a matter of scientific unreliability; since a lie detector purports to determine credibility, which will often be the heart of the matter in a trial, there is judicial reluctance to abandon the ultimate jury function to a machine or an expert.

Some general points may be noted.

Where reference to extraneous works of authority is made, the parties must be given the opportunity to contradict or comment on the work.

What was once a fact requiring inquiry before it could be judicially noticed may become a notorious one, eg the uniqueness of the corrugations on the skin of the fingers: *Parker v R* (1912) 14 CLR 681; the fact that a certain device was an approved device for the purposes of breath testing legislation: *R v Jones* [1969] 3 All ER 1559, [1970] 1 WLR 16, CA. A current issue is the reliability of the statistical probabilities prepared on the basis of DNA profiling: see Young [1991] Crim LR 264. And facts notorious at one time may cease to be so.

If judicial notice is taken after inquiry it may not be necessary to call witnesses, and often they are not called. But if they are called, the rules of evidence apply, and the evidence of the witnesses may, it seems, be rebutted: cf Carter, p 124.

3 Judicial notice: statutes

There are many statutes permitting or compelling judicial notice to be taken, eg of public Acts of Parliament (Interpretation Act 1978, s 3) and of signatures of judges of the superior courts appended to any judicial or official document (Evidence Act 1845, s 2). See generally, Phipson, ch 2.

4 General

It appears to be the law (contrary to Wigmore's view at para 2567) that if a judge decides to take judicial notice of a fact after inquiry, even if the inquiry involved hearing witnesses (as in *McQuaker v Goddard* [1940] 1 KB 687 at 700–1) he must withdraw it from the jury even if the witnesses disagree. The doctrine of judicial notice thus only facilitates proof in a special sense: it narrows the scope of proof, and usurps the role of the trier of fact. It is for that reason that the doctrine ought not to be applied loosely: it closes for one party a possible avenue to victory. The American Federal Rules of Evidence, r 201(g), follow that approach in civil cases, but provide that in criminal cases 'the court shall instruct the jury that it may, but is not required to, accept as conclusive any fact judicially noticed'. This is presumably on the theory that the right to jury trial includes a right to an irrational verdict in favour of the accused. A related question is whether juries, magistrates and judges sitting without a jury should be more ready to take notice of locally notorious facts than judges sitting with juries, for where the former are concerned there is no possibility of usurping the jury's role: see Carter in Campbell and Waller, p 108.

There is obscurity about the consequence of taking judicial notice of a fact in one respect. On one view, the judge's decision is a precedent, so that sometimes later courts are bound by wrong facts (eg *McQuaker v Goddard* [1940] 1

KB 687, [1940] 1 All ER 471, which appears to be an erroneous decision as to the capacity of camels to procreate without human assistance). On another view (see Carter in Campbell and Waller, p 94), it is only the taking of judicial notice of legislative facts which creates binding precedents:

> 'Taking judicial notice of an adjudicative fact is a substitute for proof, and it should no more create a binding precedent than does a finding based on proof – although there is, of course, often an intrinsic likelihood of repetition. On the other hand, legislative fact finding may well be instrumental in the formulation of a rule of law to which the doctrine of stare decisis will be applicable: following the decision of the Court of Appeal in *McQuaker v Goddard* it could not be contended in an inferior court that a camel is to be classified as a wild animal for the purposes of tort liability.'

A difficulty in the first view is that what was judicially noticed in *McQuaker's* Case was a fact from which non-wildness was inferred so as in effect to create a rule of law. Would a later court really be bound to find that fact as opposed to following the rule of law laid down? The difficulty in the second is that it would be surprising if earlier judicial findings as to customs or the workings of machines were not followed by later courts. It would no doubt be even more surprising if courts kept perpetuating factual error, and on any view it must be possible to persuade a court to depart from a fact judicially noticed earlier on production of something in the nature of fresh or better evidence.

Evidence is not admissible in rebuttal of facts judicially noticed. But those facts are usually, on analysis, found to be of extreme generality. That judicial notice is taken of a signature merely means that the signature is recognised as being similar to that of the person whose signature it purports to be: that fact cannot be contradicted by evidence, but a different fact, that the particular signature *is* that of the person whose signature it purports to be, is capable of rebuttal by proof of forgery: *Holland v Jones* (1917) 23 CLR 149 at 154. And while the court may judicially notice a practice, a party is at liberty to prove that in a particular instance the practice was departed from.

Distinct from the doctrine of judicial notice is the doctrine that the judge knows the law of the forum, which he can investigate in any way he sees fit. It is not a matter capable of disproof before him, but merely of argument by reference to the sources of the law. On the other hand, foreign law is a matter of fact, usually to be proved by expert testimony.

FURTHER READING

Thyer, ch 7; Morgan, *Some Problems of Proof under the Anglo-American System of Litigation*, p 36; Nokes (1958) 74 LQR 59; Morgan, 57 Harv LR 269 (1944); Davis 55 Col LR 945 (1955); Wigmore, paras 2565–83; McCormick, 2nd edn, ch 35; Schiff (1963) 41 Can Bar Rev 335 at 338–55; Manchester (1979) 42 Mod LR 22.

QUESTIONS

1. A judge is a keen mountaineer. Can he take account of his experience as such in a case involving the strength of an alpine rope? What should he say to

the parties on the subject? See *R v Field* (1895) 64 LJMC 158.

2. Can a court take account of

(a) the difficulty in 1983 of obtaining a job?

(b) the occurrence of inflation since 1945? (*National Trustees Executors and Agency Co of Australasia Ltd v A-G for the State of Victoria* [1973] VR 610.)

(c) the rate of inflation in 1983 and the rate of interest in 1983?

(See *Rendell v Paul* (1979) 22 SASR 459 at 465–6; *Saul v Menon* [1980] 2 NSWLR 314 at 324–6.)

3. Should evidence be admitted in disproof of facts which are judicially noticed? See Thayer, p 308, Wigmore, para 2567; McCormick, 2nd edn, pp 769–71; Morgan 57 Harv LR 269 at 279.

4. It seems that if the judge is invited to take judicial notice of a fact and the necessary preconditions are made out, he must do so: see *R v Aspinall* (1876) 2 QBD 48 at 61–2. But must he do so if not so invited? For example, if the prosecution fails to prove a fact which is of common knowledge, may the judge take judicial notice of it and remove that issue from the jury? If the judge does not, may the jury do so on its own?

5. Juries can act on their general experience of human nature and the world. To the extent that their generalisations rest on tradition, folklore, myth and prejudice, and to the extent that they are thus unsure, should expert evidence of normal behaviour be admissible?

6. A judge should use any expert knowledge he has 'to enable him to understand the witnesses, not as a substitute for witnesses'. How real is that distinction? See Eggleston, p 142; Young (1989) 5 Aust Bar Rev 199.

Index

Accomplice
  evidence of, 104–106
Accused
  character. *See* CHARACTER, EVIDENCE OF
  protection of, 5
  witness, as. *See* WITNESS
Acquittal
  no appeal from, 4
Admissibility
  conditional, 7
  facts antecedent to, standard of proof, 41
  one purpose, for, 7
  rules of law, 6, 7
Admissions
  corroboration, as, 107
  formal, 6
  informal, 6
Affirmation
  option of, 413
  witness, of, 411–415
Agent provocateur
  evidence obtained by, 219, 235–240
  incitement by, 235–240
Appointment
  omnia praesumuntur rite esse acta, presumption of, 74
Asylum
  well-founded fear of persecution, standard of proof, 49
Attorney-General's reference
  evidence as subject of, 4
Automatism
  burden of proving, 22–24

Best evidence
  rule, 9
Blood tests
  evidence of, 10
Burden of proof
  absence of reasonable and probable cause, proving, 20
  accident, of, 21
  automatism defence, 22–24
  care or supervision order, for, 45

Burden of proof – *continued*
  competence of witness, of, 405
  confession, admissibility of, 165
  Criminal Law Revision Committee, recommendations of, 19, 20
  defence, as to, 17, 18
  duty to produce evidence, 15
  evidential –
    accused, on, 17, 18
    discharging, standard of proof, 56, 57
    incidence of, 16
    meaning, 15
    need to know, 16
    reason for, 16, 17
    shifting, 34, 35
  exception, exemption, proviso, excuse or qualification, as to, 19, 26, 27
  facts peculiarly within one party's knowledge, of, 18
  frustration, cause of, 19, 24–26
  game, qualification to unlawful possession of, 26, 27
  incidence, determining, 16–33
  insanity, of, 33, 35, 36
  legal –
    failure to make out, 16
    incidence of, 16
    insanity, proof of, 18
    meaning, 15
    shifting, 35
  legitimacy, of, 35
  licence in force, as to, 27, 28
  meaning, 15
  mechanical defect, proving, 27
  negative averment, 26
  negative, proving, 17
  persuasive, meaning, 15
  probative, meaning, 15
  proportion of morphine in controlled drug, proving, 28–32
  provocation, as to, 33
  rules, 3
  shifting, 34–36
  statutory defence, of, 29

509

Burden of proof – *continued*
terminology, 16
uncommon fact, of, 19
unconsciousness as result of sudden illness,
as to, 21, 22

Character, evidence of
character, meaning, 284–286
Criminal Evidence Act provisions, 277
Criminal Law revision Committee,
recommendations of, 298
cross-examination as to –
acquittal, of, 291
admissible evidence, concerning, 290, 291
admission of being in trouble, after,
279–286
approval of judge, requiring, 304
co-accused, of, 299–301, 308–311
credibility, impugning, 278
credit, as to, 283, 284
attacking, 303
defence –
evidence of bad character put by, 290
rebutting, 279–286, 289
denial of charge, effect of, 292, 296
discretion of judge, 298, 304–311
evidence in chief, matter in, 279–286
explanation of offence, in relation to, 287
fabrication of charge, after allegation
of, 293
generally, 276
good character, accused seeking to
establish, 291
imputation, nature of defence involving,
306
imputations on character of accused or
witnesses, where, 292–299
lying, allegation of, 294, 295
necessary, attack on prosecution alleged
to be, 296, 307
one count, imputations against witness
on, 307
other offence, as to, 281, 282
admission of, 286–289
pre-existing law, 288
prohibition –
absolute character of, 280
application of, 278–290
consequences of lifting, 301–311
lifting, 290–301
proportionality, test of, 297
purpose, 302–304
questions tending to show bad character,
on, 278–286
rape, allegation of consent in, 292, 294
rationale, 277
record, in relation to, 278
refusal of permission for, 305, 310
relevance, 301, 302
remarks incidental to defence, 295

Character, evidence of – *continued*
cross-examination as to – *continued*
rules governing, 280
shield, 277
similar fact evidence, as to, 278, 290
statutory provisions, 277
tending to incriminate, 279–286
veracity, testing, 302
warning as to loss of shield, 298
defence witnesses, prosecution attacking,
298
good, introduction of, 275, 276
indivisibility of, 304
moral disposition, including, 285, 289, 293
prosecution, character of, 297
reputation, character as, 284–286, 296
similar fact evidence. *See* SIMILAR FACT
EVIDENCE
Charterparty
frustration, proving cause of, 24–26
Child
civil cases, hearsay evidence in, 367–369
likely to suffer significant harm, standard of
proof, 43–49
meaning, 410
witness, as –
competence, presumption of, 409
duty to speak the truth, understanding,
411
oath, taking, 411, 412
television link, through, 410, 411
unsworn evidence of, 408–412
video recording of interview with, 349,
411
Circumstantial evidence
meaning, 6
presumptions based on, 7, 60
Civil cases
evidence in, 4
trial. *See* TRIAL
Collateral facts
meaning, 5
Collusion
meaning, 262
more than one complainant, evidence of,
261–264
probative value of similar fact evidence,
affecting, 263
Commorientes
presumption, 61, 62
Computer
statements produced by, admissibility, 348,
349
Confession
admissibility –
American system, 169, 170
burden of proof, 165
code, 153
committal proceedings, examination
in, 155

Confession – *continued*
admissibility – *continued*
historical background, 169–175
judge and jury, roles of, 162–164
justification of rule, 173–175
maker, against, 155
objection to, 162
privilege against self-incrimination, claim of, 164
purposes of rule, 169–175
requirement to prove, 155
scope of rule, 165–168
standard of proof, 165
test, time of, 162, 163
trial within a trial, 155, 162–164
voluntary character, 182–184
American law –
due process, breach of, 197
Escobedo-Miranda doctrine, 198–200, 204, 205
groups of, 197
illegal detention, 197
interrogation manuals, 200–202
judge-made, 205
prosecution, importance of confession to, 205
untrue confession, producing, 202–204
co-ordination tests, rules not extending to, 168
common law, 153
conduct as, 168
conduct of investigations. *See* INVESTIGATIONS, CONDUCT OF
discretion to exclude, 212
excluded, 4
exclusionary rule –
mandatory, 155
statutory provision, 153–155
fairness, 211
illegal or improper means, obtained by, 235
inadmissible, evidence obtained from –
other jurisdictions, in, 178–180
property, recovery of, 175, 176
relevance, 175
statutory provision, 178
subsequently discovered facts, 175–177
inculpatory and exculpatory statements, 167
jury acting on, 164
meaning, 153, 165
mentally unsound person, by, 209, 210
misconduct, obtained by, inadmissibility, 154
oppression, obtained by –
anything said or done, in relation to, 161, 162
causal link, 161
dictionary meaning, given, 158
information given by police as, 155–158
schizophrenic terror or delusion, questioning bringing about, 159

Confession – *continued*
oppression, obtained by – *continued*
term of art, as, 158
vitiating factor, as, 154
other jurisdictions, in, 206
partly adverse statement, covering, 165, 166
person under arrest, by, 210, 211
police violence, extracted by, 163
psychological problem of, 173
reasons for, 172, 173
Scotland, in, 206
tape-recording of, 174
uncorroborated, 103
unreliability –
circumstances of, 157
objective, 160
potential, 161
prejudicial and probative value, 159–161
unsigned written, 211
voluntary –
maker, admissible against, 153
meaning, 153
weak-minded persons, by, 171, 172
whole, putting in evidence, 165, 166
witches, of, 171
Contempt of court
standard of proof, 41
Controlled drug
possession, proof of proportion of, 28–32
Convictions
credibility, and, 481, 482
later proceedings, evidence in –
appeal, subject to, 396
conclusive presumption, 400
defamation actions, 400
innocence, burden of proving, 396–399
issues, 400
persuasive presumptions, 394–400
proof, requiring, 395
standard of proof, 399
statutory provisions, 399, 400
weight given to, 397, 398
wrong, defendant arguing, 395, 396
spent. *See* SPENT CONVICTIONS
Corroboration
accomplices, evidence of, 104–106
admissions, 107
collusion, 261–264
common law, at, 80, 81
confession, of, 103
evidence amounting to, 80
evidence to be supported, adding to, 104–106
examples of, 106–113
general requirement, points in favour of, 81, 82
identification evidence, of, 79, 83–99. *See also* IDENTIFICATION EVIDENCE

Corroboration – *continued*
jury, warning to –
duty as to, 101–103
full corroboration warning, 79, 80
statutory provisions, 103, 104
lies, 107–110
mandatory requirements, 99, 100
meaning, 79
mere opportunity not being, 113
more than one complainant, by, 261–264
perjury, of, 100
person to be corroborated supplying, 107
previous occasions, conduct on, 112, 113
prudential reasons for, 83
requirements, origins of, 80, 81
samples, failure to give, 112
silence in court, 111, 112
silence out of court, 110, 111
situation of witness, by reason of, 82
subject-matter of case requiring, 82
Court of Appeal
law of evidence, development of, 5
Crown privilege
ambit of, 458
Bank of England documents, for, 446–450
claim to, 440
claiming, method of, 440
class ground, on, 443
communications from outsiders, attaching
to, 451
confidentiality, on grounds of, 456–466
criminal cases, claim in, 450
extension of, 461, 466
foreign state, 451
imports, in relation to, 453–455
income tax assessment, in relation to, 455,
456
industrial action, based on risk of, 451
NSPCC, complaint to, 456–466
police probationary reports, for, 441–446
private society, claim by, 456–466
public service, construction of, 452
scope of, 118
State interest, exclusion on grounds of,
440–467. *See also* PUBLIC INTEREST
IMMUNITY
use of phrase, 453

Dangerous driving
mechanical defect, burden of proving, 27
unconsciousness as result of sudden illness,
proof of, 21, 22
Death
presumptions, 59, 63–67
Deceased persons, declarations of
accused, on behalf of, 342
course of duty, in, 340
dying declarations, 341
interest, against, 339
pedigree, 340

Deceased persons, declarations of
– *continued*
public or general rights, as to, 340
religious beliefs, inquiry into, 341, 342
settled hopeless expectation of death, 341,
342
veracity, 342
wills, concerning, 341
Defence
burden of proof, 17, 18
Divorce
adultery, standard of proof, 54, 55
cruelty, standard of proof, 50, 51
Documents
authenticity, challenging, 382
contents, proof of, 375–379
copies, statutory provisions as to use of, 379
cross-examination on, 479, 480
execution, presumed date of, 382
existence, reference made to establish, 378
failure to stamp, effect of, 382
memory, refreshing, 474, 475
original, meaning, 378, 379
parol evidence, 383
precise words, reliance on, 378
primary evidence of, 375, 376, 378
private –
due execution, 379
opposing party, in possession of, 380
proof of execution of, 379–383
proper custody of, 380
secondary evidence of, 5, 6, 375–379
signature or handwriting, proof of, 380–382
statements in as evidence –
civil cases, in, 366
computer, produced by, 348, 349
criminal investigation, document
prepared for, 347
discretion to admit, 346, 347
exclusionary hearsay rule, application of,
346
intelligibility, 348
person making, knowledge of, 346, 347
proof of admissibility, 348
statutory provisions, 343–346
words used in, reliance on, 375

Eavesdropping
evidence obtained by, 244
legal professional privilege, effect on, 433,
434
Entrapment
evidence obtained by, 240, 241
Estoppel
evidence unnecessary, where, 500
Evidence
American Law Institute Model, 4
criminal evidence, as law of, 4
excluded, 3
modern form of law, 3

Evidence – *continued*
not objected to, status of, 11
proof of facts by, 499
rules of, 3
supporting. *See* CORROBORATION
Expert evidence
area of, 387–389
common law, at, 385–393
conflict of, 391
expertise, matter calling for, 386
foreign law, proof of, 386, 387, 393
hearsay, 391
independence, 385
legal professional privilege, 426
nature of substance, as to, 387–389
new fields of expertise, recognition of,
389, 390
notice of intention to adduce, 393
ordinary human nature, as to, 390, 391
orthodoxy and admissibility, tension
between, 393
psychiatrists, of, 390
psychologists, of, 390
purpose of, 384
rejection of, 387
ultimate issue, as to, 392
where required, 386
Expert witness
case, selection to prove, 384
evidence of. *See* EXPERT EVIDENCE
general view of, 384
no connection with facts of history of
matter, having, 391
qualifications, 385
scientific criteria for testing accuracy of
conclusions, furnishing, 391
valuer, 391

Facts
legislative, 500
proof, not requiring, 499, 500
Facts in issue
meaning, 5
proof of, 5
Film
evidence, as, 10
Fingerprints
evidence of, 10
lies as to, 215
Foreign law
proof of, 386, 387, 393
Formal admissions
proof not required, 6
Fraudulent misrepresentation
proceedings, standard of proof in, 52–54
Frustration
cause, burden of proof, 19, 24–26

Game
lawful possession, proof of, 26, 27

Handling stolen goods
similar fact evidence 275
Hearsay, rule against
accused, application against, 315
assertive statements, admission of, 318, 319
best evidence, desirability of, 316
civil cases, in –
abolition, trend towards, 365
business records, proof of, 366, 367
child, evidence of, 367–369
common law exceptions, preservation
of, 366
documents, statements contained in, 366
generally, 361–367
other jurisdictions, in, 369–373
out-of-court statements, admissibility
of, 366
prior findings, evidence of, 394–396
restrictive, being, 361
statutory provisions, 362–365
US rules, 369–373
value of hearsay evidence, 373, 374
civil rule, 315
code, enactment of, 361
common law exceptions, 339
common law rule, 315
criticism of, 317
cross-examination, statements by persons
not subject to, 315, 316
evidence of truth of statements, hearsay
admitted as, 319, 320, 324
exceptions –
absent deponent, depositions of, 349
agreed statements, 349
child, video recording of interview
with, 349
civil cases, in. *See* civil cases, in, *above*
complication of, 317
computer, statements produced by, 348,
349
deceased persons, statements of, 339–342.
See also DECEASED PERSONS, DECLAR-
ATIONS OF
documents, statements in, 343–348
further reform of, 359
previous cases, witnesses in, 359
public documents, statements in, 342
res gestae. *See* RES GESTAE
statutory, 343–349
express assertions, extending to, 321
formulations of, 315
general, 5
hearsay, meaning, 5
implied assertions –
cross-examination on, 334
declaration against interest, 330
drug dealing, telephone calls inferring,
324–330
evidence of fact of conversation, as, 325
exception, within, 332

Hearsay, rule against – *continued*
implied assertions – *continued*
gaming, telephone calls inferring, 328, 329
groups of cases, 321, 322
hearsay, whether, 332–334
identification, 331, 332
inferences, drawing, 326, 334
manufacture, freedom from risk of, 333
meaning, 321
mental incapacity, as to, 322, 323
negative hearsay, 335
non-assertive conduct, as, 333
probative value of, 334
running away as, 332, 334, 335
side issues, not raising, 323
telephone calls, inference drawn from, 324–330
inaccuracy, danger of, 316
juries, undue weight attached by, 317
limits of –
implied assertions, 321–335
original evidence, 317–319
reliable evidence, exclusion of, 319–321
negative hearsay, 335
not applying, where, 336
opinion. *See* OPINION EVIDENCE
prior findings, evidence of –
appeal, convictions subject to, 396
arbitration, not applying to findings in, 396
civil provisions, 394–396
conclusive presumption, 400
defamation actions, 400
innocence, burden of proving, 396–399
issues, 400
persuasive presumptions, 394–400
proof, requiring, 395
standard of proof, 399
statutory provisions, 399, 400
weight given to, 397, 398
wrong, defendant arguing, 395, 396
proliferation of evidence, preventing, 316
rationale, 315–317
reform, possibilities for, 361
res gestae exception, 331, 332
scope of hearsay, decisions on, 321
statutory modification of, 326
value of hearsay, 350
House of Lords
appeal to, 4, 5
Hypnotism
evidence induced by, 10

Identification evidence
accuracy of observation, 83, 84
admissibility, 94
admission and reception, rules for, 96, 97
circumstances of, 87
Code of Practice, 97, 98
cross-examination as to, 86

Identification evidence – *continued*
defective memory, 85
dock, in, 92
evidence supporting, 88
exclusion of, 98
fragility, 84
gathering, 92–99
guidelines for, 87–89, 91
miscarriages of justice, 87, 89
mistakes, reasons for, 84–86
opinion, as, 385
parade –
failure to hold, 99
pitfalls, 85, 86
precautions, 93
preference for, 96, 98
suspect asking for, 97
value of, 85
photograph, by, 93–98
police methods, 85
poor quality, of, 88, 90, 92, 99
previous identification, admissibility of acts of, 99
problems with, 95
several witnesses, of, 84
special care with, 79
special problem of, 84
trial, evaluation at, 87–92
uncertainty of, 95
weight of, 93
Improperly obtained evidence. *See* UNFAIR AND IMPROPERLY OBTAINED EVIDENCE
Informers
statements by, 443, 451, 457, 466
Insanity
burden of proof, 18, 33, 35, 36
standard of proof, 54
Investigations, conduct of
American law –
due process, breach of, 197
Escobedo-Miranda doctrine, 198–200, 204, 205
groups of, 197
illegal detention, 197
interrogation manuals, 200–202
judge-made, 205
prosecution, importance of confession to, 205
untrue confession, producing, 202–204
breaches of code, 195
cautions, 190, 191, 196, 197
codes of practice, 184, 185
custody records, 187
detained persons –
charging, 194, 197
delay in notifying arrest or allowing access to legal advice, 194, 195
incommunicado, not to be held, 189
legal advice, right to, 189, 190, 195, 196
property of, 188

Investigations, conduct of – *continued*
detention, treatment and questioning by
police officers, Code of Conduct for,
185–195
development of rules, 181
exclusion of evidence obtained in breach of
rules, 180, 181
impropriety, 183
initial action, 187, 188
interviews, 191–193, 196
investigators other than police, by, 197
Judges' Rules, 181, 182
other jurisdictions, in, 206
Scotland, in, 206
statutory provisions, 184

Judge
admission of confession, function in
relation to, 162–164
discretion to exclude evidence, 7
functions of, 8
jury, control over, 8
specialist knowledge of, 500–502
Judgment
later proceedings, evidence in –
conclusive presumption, 400
defamation actions, 400
persuasive presumptions, 394–400
wrong, defendant arguing, 395, 396
Judicial notice
common law doctrine, 502–505
customs, of, 504
historical facts, 504
inquiry, after, 505
meaning, 4
notorious facts, of, 503, 505
political facts, 503, 504
professional practice, of, 504
proof not required, 6
purpose of, 503
rebuttal, evidence in, 506
scientific facts, 504
statutory provisions, 505
wrong facts, of, 505, 506
Jury
admission of confession, function in
relation to, 162–164
corroboration, warning as to –
duty as to, 101–103
full corroboration warning, 79, 80
statutory provisions, 103, 104
functions of, 8
judicial control over, 8
standard of proof, explaining, 37
Justices' licence
burden of proof as to, 27, 28

Legal professional privilege
administration of justice, interests of, 422
bad faith, disclosure by lawyer in, 435
claim of, inferences drawn from, 425

Legal professional privilege – *continued*
common interest, parties with, 428
communications, confidentiality of, 416
confidential, communication to be, 426
copies of documents, position of, 429
counsel, destruction by, 425
crime or fraud, communications in
furtherance of, 428
criminal design, letter preparing for,
419–421
defendant's hands, documents falling into,
429–437
discovery, protection of communications
from, 423
dominant purpose of documents, 423
eavesdropping, information obtained by,
433, 434
excluded information, 427
existing or contemplated litigation, communications for purposes of, 418, 419
expert, in relation to, 426
foreign legal adviser, in respect of, 425, 426
government, applying to, 426
improperly obtained evidence, admission
of, 435
inquiry report, status of, 421–425
judicial and quasi-judicial proceedings,
in, 427
lawyer, person being, 426, 434
lawyer-client relationship, requirement
of, 426
loss of, 429–437
rationale, 417
scope of, 418–429
searches for material covered by, 428
statutory provisions, effect of, 429
successors in title, extending to, 425
third party, restraining production by, 433
trick, documents obtained by, 436
waiver of, 427, 436
Legitimacy
burden of proof, 35
presumptions, 59, 61, 67, 68
Lie detector
evidence under, 10
Lies
corroboration, as, 107–110

Magistrate
person in custody brought before, 212
Malicious prosecution
absence of reasonable and probable cause,
proving, 20
Marriage
cohabitation and repute, presumption
of, 69
conflicting presumptions as to, 76–78
validity, presumption of, 68
Murder
accident, burden of proof, 21
provocation, burden of proof, 33

Oath
reform of law, 413–415
witness, of, 411–415
Opinion evidence
common law, at, 385
expert. *See* EXPERT EVIDENCE; EXPERT
WITNESS
fitness to drive, as to, 385
identity, of, 385
meaning, 384
opinion, meaning, 384
orthodox doctrine, 384
statutory reform, 393
ultimate issue, on, 385

Pedigree
deceased persons, declarations of, 340
Perjury
corroboration, 100
privilege against self-incrimination, effect
of, 128
Photograph
evidence, as, 10
identification by, 93–98
Police
conduct of investigations. *See* INVESTI-
GATIONS, CONDUCT OF
Presumptions
basic fact, proof of, 58
categories of, 58
circumstantial evidence, based on, 60
commorientes, 61, 62
conclusive, meaning, 58, 59
conduct and general practice, as to, 76
conflicting, 76–78
continuance, of, 75
convenience, promoting, 61
death, of, 59, 63–67
disproving, burden of, 58, 59
evidential, 58–60, 75, 76
habits, evidence of, 75
irrebuttable, 59
law, of, 59
legitimacy, of, 59, 61, 67, 68
mechanical devices, working of, 76
motive, as to, 75
natural consequences of acts, intending, 75
persuasive –
cohabitation and repute, of, 69
commorientes, 61, 62
death, of, 59, 63–67
legitimacy, of, 59, 61, 67, 68
marriage, validity of, 68
meaning, 58, 59
omnia praesumuntur rite esse acta, 74
possession, 74
provisional presumption having effect
of, 73
res ipsa loquitur, 69–74
shifting, not, 73

Presumptions – *continued*
preponderance of probability, according
with, 60
procedural purposes, 61
provisional, 58, 60, 75, 76
persuasive presumption, having effect
of, 73
reasons for, 60–62
satisfactory explanation, failure to give, 76
social policy, reasons of, 61
spoliation doctrine, 76
time, saving, 61
types of, 58
Privilege
abolished, 438
Crown. *See* CROWN PRIVILEGE
excluded material, for, 439
foreign state, 451
journalists, of, 438, 439
legal professional. *See* LEGAL PROFESSIONAL
PRIVILEGE
new, creation of, 438, 439
patent agent, communications with, 438,
439
previous litigation, in relation to, 467
private, 416
public policy. *See* CROWN PRIVILEGE; PUBLIC
INTEREST IMMUNITY
restriction of, 416
self-incrimination, against. *See* SELF-
INCRIMINATION, PRIVILEGE AGAINST
special procedure material, for, 439
trade mark agent, communications with,
438, 439
types of, 416
without prejudice statements, 437
Property
possession, presumption as to, 74
Public documents
statements in as evidence, 342
Public interest immunity
analysis of objection, 447
Bank of England documents, for, 446–450
claim to, 440
claiming, method of, 440
clash of interests, approach to, 447, 448
communications from outsiders, attaching
to, 451
confidentiality, on grounds of, 456–466
criminal cases, claim in, 450
edited documents, 450
exclusion on grounds of, 440
extension of, 461, 466
government papers, attaching to, 445, 448
imports, in relation to, 453–455
income tax assessment, in relation to, 455,
456
industrial action, based on risk of, 451
informers, statements by, 443, 451, 457,
466

Public interest immunity – *continued*
inspection of documents by court, 449,
451
Minister's certificate –
appeal, right of, 446
class cases, in, 448
conclusive, whether, 444
grounds for, 444
judicial review, 447
overruling, 445
questioning, 443
NSPCC, complaint to, 456–466
police probationary reports, for, 441–446
private society, claim by, 456–466
proper functioning of public service, for,
443
public bodies, attaching to, 442
public service, construction of, 452
refusal of consent to gaming licence, letter
relating to, 451–453
State interest, exclusion on grounds of,
440–467
types of interest, 442

Radar reception
evidence, as, 10
Rape
recent complaint of, 489–494
Real evidence
blood tests, 10
meaning, 6
tape recordings, 9, 10
Res gestae
assertion of truth, words used as, 352, 353
basis of admissibility, 351, 352
collection of rules, as, 350, 351
concoction, possibility of, 353, 355
doctrine of, 350
event in issue, statements concerning, 357
examples of, 357–359
formulation of rules, difficulty of, 351
hearsay exception, as, 331, 332, 351, 352
illustrations of, 353
involvement of speaker, proof establishing,
354
making of statement, circumstances of,
355, 356
meaning, 350
mental or emotional state of maker, statements about, 358
original evidence, as, 359
physical sensation, statements of, 358, 359
previous consistent statements, 476
reliability of, 352
spontaneity, 354, 355
statements accompanying and explaining
relevant acts, 357
traditional rule, narrow interpretation
of, 352
use of, 352, 353, 356

Res ipsa loquitur
adducing evidence as to cause of accident,
effect of, 73
allegation of negligence, supporting, 69, 70
debate as to, 72
effect of, 72
jury, leaving case to, 69
presumption, as, 69–74
process of logic, as, 70–72
rule, types of, 74
Right to silence. *See also* SILENCE
immunities, group of, 136
preservation of, 140
reasons for, 136, 137
statutory provisions not abolishing,
136–142

Samples
failure to give as corroboration, 112
Search warrant
evidence obtained without, 221, 222,
226–228
Self-incrimination, privilege against
administrative tribunals, before, 124
admission, after, 121
American Constitution, provisions of, 125
bad laws and procedures, frustrating, 128,
129
civil action, not extending to exposure
to, 117
drawbacks of, 126
examination before Court of Bankruptcy,
admission of, 130, 131
failure to claim, 123
historical background of, 124, 125
importance of, 124–129
impossibility of enforcing answers to
questions, recognising, 128
indirect answers, extending to, 118
interpretation of statutes abrogating, 134
judge, role of, 118–124
opposition to, 125, 126
pardon, witness having, 119
penalty, exposing deponent to, 117, 118
perjury, reducing risk of, 128
personal nature of, 118
production of incriminating documents,
extension to, 117
proof of guilt by prosecution, as rule for,
126, 127
purposes served by, 126
restriction of, 416
risk of prosecution, 122
spouses, in favour of, 117
statement of, 117
statutory removal of, 127, 129
statutory restrictions on, 129–134
tax cases, in, 131–133
tendency to incriminate, ascertaining,
119–122

Self-incrimination, privilege against
– continued
trustee, invoked by, 119, 120
voir dire, claimed on, 164
waiver of, 117, 118
warning as to, 123
witness, invoked by, 123
witnesses coming forward, removing
obstacles to, 127, 128
wrongful rejection of claim to, 122
Sexual abuse
standard of proof, 43–49, 51, 52
Sexual offences
recent complaint in, 489–494
Silence
corroboration, as, 110–112
defence, making harder to believe, 143,
144, 150
guilt or liability, as sign of, 143, 148–150,
151
implied admission, as, 143, 147, 148, 151
inferences drawn from –
consciousness of guilt, 143, 148–150,
151
consent, 143, 147, 148, 151
direction as to, 140–142
inferences from opposing case, strengthening, 150, 151, 152
justification, 145
out-of-court silence, from, 145–150
preconditions, 136
prima facie case, following making out
of, 142
silence in court, from, 150–152
statutory provisions, 137–140
part of statement approved by, 144
reasons for, 144
right to. *See* RIGHT TO SILENCE
statement, not, 166
Similar fact evidence
accused, introduced by, 257
acquittal, relating to, 257
actus reus, proof of, 258, 259
bad disposition, tending to show, 253–256,
272
basis of admission, 258–260
characteristics of guilty man, unlikelihood
of innocent man having, 266
circumstances of deaths, of, 270, 271
co-accused, attacking, 274, 275
coincidence, appeal to, 258, 264
collusion, 261–264
common law rule –
basis of admission, 258–260
formulation of, 271, 272
generally, 253–271
limits, 257, 258
rationale, 257
continuing nature, offences of, 273
corroboration, 261–264
cross-examination as to, 278, 290

Similar fact evidence *– continued*
defence, rebutting, 258, 274
evidence as a whole, bearing in mind, 259
examples of, 273–275
formulation of rule, 271, 272
high degree of similarity, showing, 272
homosexuality, of, 267
identity, as to, 265–267
incest, of, 268–270
issues, identification of, 258
limits of principle, 257, 258
logical fallacy, 259
narrow view, 267
number of similar facts, 265
prejudicial effect, 253
previous misconduct, of, 269, 270
principle, where operating, 254
prior good conduct, of, 257
probative force, 260
prosecution, introduced by, 257
proximity in time, 264, 265
rationale, 257
relevance to alleged act, 253, 254
rules of law, disputes about, 265
same transaction, facts part of, 273, 274
statutory rules, 275
striking similarity, 259–261
system or technique, showing, 264
Spent convictions
civil cases, no questions to be put in, 481
reference to, 275
Standard of proof
balance of probabilities, 37, 40
beyond reasonable doubt, 37–39
civil cases, in, 37
civil proceedings, crime alleged in, 52–54
comfortable satisfaction, use of term, 39
confession, admissibility of, 165
contempt of court, of, 41
criminal cases, in, 37
divorce –
adultery, proof of, 54, 55
cruelty, proof of, 50, 51
each item of evidence, considering, 41
each juror, satisfying, 42
evidence needed to meet, 52
evidential burden, discharge of, 56, 57
facts antecedent to admissibility, of, 41
formulation of, 37–42
fraudulent misrepresentation, action for,
52–54
insanity, plea of, 54
intermediate, 50, 52
jury, explaining to, 37
justification of, 42, 43
morally certain, use of term, 38
past events and future events, as to, 43–50
satisfied, use of term, 38
sentence, facts relevant to, 41
sexual abuse, of, 43–49, 51, 52
well-founded fear of persecution, as to, 49

Tape recordings
  admission of, 9, 10
  confession, of, 174
  written translations of, 10
Tracker dogs
  behaviour, evidence of, 10
Transcript
  foreign language, of, 10
Trial
  civil cases –
    collateral questions to, 480–488
    cross-examination, 472, 473
    examination-in-chief, 472
    no case to answer, submission of, 471,
      472
    order in, 471, 472
    rebuttal, evidence in, 488
    re-examination, 473
  criminal cases –
    collateral questions to, 494
    examination in, 489
    order in, 488, 489
    previous consistent statements, 489–494
    rebuttal, evidence in, 495, 495
    sex cases, complaints in, 489–494
Tribunals
  specialist knowledge of, 502
Truth drug
  evidence under, 10

Unfair and improperly obtained evidence
  accused, unfairness to, 208–212
  adverse effect, having, 214
  agent provocateur, obtained by, 219,
    235–240
  America, in, 243–248
  breach of confidence, obtained by, 219
  breach of contract, obtained by, 219
  burden of proof as to exclusion, 214, 215
  Canada, in, 228–235
  civil actions relating to, 250
  cogency of evidence, 234
  common law discretion, 208–212
  Commonwealth, in, 219–243
  conflict of interests, 220
  crime, obtained by, 219
  disrepute, administration of justice brought
    into, 228–235
  doctor, examination by, 224–226
  eavesdropping and wiretapping, obtained
    by, 244–246
  Eire, in, 225, 226
  England and America, differences between,
    248–251
  entrapment, obtained by, 240, 241
  exclusion of, 4
  exclusionary rule –
    collateral inquiry, involving, 250
    deterrent effect, 250, 251
    England and America, differences
      between, 248–251

Unfair and improperly obtained evidence
  – *continued*
  exclusionary rule – *continued*
    guilty, protecting, 249
    police, burden on, 251
  extent of exclusion, 209
  fingerprint, lie concerning, 215
  general discretion to exclude, 241–243
  illegal removal of documents, 223, 224
  improper treatment of accused, obtained
    by, 213, 214
  interviews not recorded, where, 215–218
  invasion of privacy, obtained by, 219
  judicial discretions, evolution of, 208
  liberties, infringement of, 243, 244
  magistrate, bringing person in custody
    before, 212
  probative value, 209
  proceedings, unfairness of, 212–219
  prosecution, proposed to be relied on
    by, 214
  real evidence, 232
  relevance, 222, 223
  relevant circumstances, 228–235
  relevant factors, 240
  rule of general inclusion, merits of,
    248–252
  samples, obtaining illegally, 221
  Scotland, in, 219–222, 226
  search and seizure, security against, 246,
    247
  search warrant, lack of, 221, 222, 226–228
  statutory discretion, 212–219
  tort, obtained by, 219
  trespass, obtained by, 225, 226
  trick, obtained by, 219
  unconscious trick, reference to, 233
  unfairness jurisdiction, 208

Video recording
  child witness, of interview with, 349, 411

Weight
  notion of, 7
  question of fact, as, 7
Will
  attestation, proof of, 382
  deceased testator, declarations of, 341
Wiretapping
  evidence obtained by, 244–246
Without prejudice statements
  privilege attaching to, 437
Witness
  accomplice as, 406
  accused as –
    defence, for, 406, 407
    prosecution, not competent for, 406
  afterthought, rebuttal of, 477
  bias, 482
  character, evidence as to, 482, 483
  child. *See* CHILD

Witness – *continued*
  civil cases –
    collateral questions to, 480–488
    compellability, 406
    competence, 406
    cross-examination, 472, 473
    examination-in-chief, 472
    previous consistent statements, 476,
      477
    rebuttal, evidence in, 488
    re-examination, 473
  compellable –
    civil cases, in, 406
    criminal cases, in, 406–408
    meaning, 405
  competent –
    civil cases, in, 406
    criminal cases, in, 406–408
    evidence, reliance on, 405
    meaning, 405
    proving, onus of, 405
  credibility, evidence going to, 480, 481
  criminal cases –
    collateral questions to, 494
    compellability, 406–408
    competence, 406–408
    examination in, 489

Witness – *continued*
  criminal cases – *continued*
    previous consistent statements, 489–494
    rebuttal, evidence in, 495, 495
    sex cases, complaints in, 489–494
  direct testimony, meaning, 5
  documents, cross-examination on, 479, 480
  expert. *See* EXPERT WITNESS
  hostile, 477, 478
  hysterical and unstable state, in, 486
  incapacity to tell the truth, showing, 482
  indirect testimony. *See* HEARSAY, RULE
    AGAINST
  leading questions, 473, 474
  memory, refreshing, 474, 475
  oath and affirmation, 411–415
  previous cases, in, evidence of, 359
  previous inconsistent statements, 478, 479
  questions unduly embarrassing, exclusion
    of, 439
  reputation evidence, 483–488
  rights and duties of, 4
  single, evidence of, 83
  spouse of accused as, 406–408
  unfavourable, 477, 478
Words
  ordinary meaning of, 499